the
AMERICANA
ANNUAL

1984

GROLIER

AN ENCYCLOPEDIA OF THE EVENTS OF 1983

YEARBOOK OF THE ENCYCLOPEDIA AMERICANA

This annual has been prepared as a yearbook for general encyclopedias. It is also published as *Encyclopedia Year Book*.

Contents

Feature Articles of the Year

THE YEAR IN REVIEW   Page 6

Peter Jennings, anchor and senior editor of ABC's *World News Tonight,* comments on 1983's major world developments. A staff-prepared, month-by-month chronology of the year's news follows, beginning on page 10.

GRENADA — FLASH POINT IN THE CARIBBEAN   Page 28

The October U.S. action against Grenada's Communist government surprised the world. Syndicated newspaper writer Richard C. Schroeder reports on the major military events and the postwar rehabilitation process; pertinent historical background of Grenada, the tiniest country in the Western Hemisphere, also is provided.

THE BICENTENNIAL OF AIR AND SPACE FLIGHT   Page 35

Prepared under the guidance of aviation authority Lawrence F. Mihlon, this feature records highlights of 200 years of manned flight as well as the various ceremonies in honor of the anniversary.

PUBLIC EDUCATION IN AMERICA — CALLS FOR REFORMS   Page 39

American education was taken to task during 1983, as a series of reports were released emphasizing various educational deficiencies and the need for reform. Longtime education specialist Fred M. Hechinger clarifies these issues.

ESPIONAGE   Page 47

Lyman B. Kirkpatrick, Jr., an authority on U.S. intelligence and a one-time member of the U.S. Central Intelligence Agency, reports on burgeoning world espionage, whether military information gathering or the amassing of high-tech industrial secrets. A synopsis of recent spy cases is included.

THE NEW HOME VIDEO   Page 55

In the late 1970s new electronic media began to revolutionize audio-visual entertaining and information delivery. Author and editor Jeffrey H. Hacker discusses the remarkable changes now taking place.

THE NEW TALL BUILDINGS   Page 64

As new skyscrapers sprout up in cities across the United States, Charles K. Hoyt of the *Architectural Record* takes a look at some of the design innovations that have been unveiled.

ETHICS AND MODERN MEDICINE   Page 68

Morris B. Abram, chairman of the President's Commission for the Study of Ethical Problems in Medicine and Biomedical and Behavioral Research, considers the ethical questions raised by advances in modern medicine, as presented in the commission's report.

PEOPLE, PLACES, AND THINGS   Page 74

The Alphabetical Section

Separate entries on the continents, major nations of the world, U.S. states, Canadian provinces, and chief cities will be found under their own alphabetically arranged headings.

ECONOMICS AND INDUSTRY

Advertising	81	Food	228	Retailing	445
Agriculture	92	Housing	257	Stocks and Bonds	491
Automobiles	126	Industrial Review	268	Taxation	499
Banking	129	Interior Design	274	Transportation	515
Business and		International Trade		Travel	520
Corporate Affairs	152	and Finance	276	United States:	
Canada: The Economy	161	Labor	304	The Economy	543
Consumer Affairs	187	Publishing	429	Wine	559
Fashion	223				

GOVERNMENT, HUMAN WELFARE, LAW, AND POLITICS

Arms Control	109	Environment	213	Refugees and	
Children	173	Ethnic Groups	219	Immigration	437
Cities and Urban		Law	312	Religion	438
Affairs	179	Military Affairs	356	Social Welfare	452
Crime	188	Philanthropy	411	Third World	514
Drugs and Drug		Postal Service	422	United Nations	531
Abuse	199	Prisons	423	Women	561

HUMANITIES, ARTS, AND HOBBIES

Architecture	103	Gardening and		Photography	413
Art	112	Horticulture	234	Recordings	434
Canada:		Great Britain:		Sports	463
The Arts	161	The Arts	253	Stamps and Stamp	
Coins and Coin		Libraries	320	Collecting	490
Collecting	180	Literature	323	Television and	
Dance	195	Motion Pictures	363	Radio	502
Education	201	Music	368	Theater	509

SCIENCE AND TECHNOLOGY

Anthropology	100	Computers	185	Microbiology	351
Archaeology	101	Energy	205	Oceanography	402
Astronomy	120	Engineering, Civil	210	Physics	415
Biochemistry	132	Genetics	235	Polar Research	420
Chemistry	171	Geology	236	Space Exploration	459
Communication		Medicine and Health	340	Zoos and Zoology	569
Technology	183	Meteorology	345		

MISCELLANEOUS

Accidents and		Biography	133	Prizes and Awards	425
Disasters	80	Obituaries	389		

SPECIAL REPORTS

Communication Technology:		Labor: Job Search and Retraining	305
The Changing Telecommunications		Law: The Overburdened U.S.	
Industry	184	Supreme Court	313
Crime: The Crackdown on Drunk		Meteorology: The Weather Year	346
Driving	191	Sports: The New USFL	473
Energy: OPEC — A New Appraisal	208	Transportation: The Highways —	
Geology: Earthquake Prediction	237	An Update	519
Great Britain: The Falkland Islands		United States: The New Deal	
— One Year After War	251	Through 50 Years	542
Industrial Review: The Stagnant U.S.		United States: The War Powers	
Steel Industry	271	Resolution	549
Industrial Review: High-Tech Industry	272		
International Trade and Finance:			
The World Debt	277		

STATISTICS AND TABULAR DATA   571

CONTRIBUTORS   589

INDEX   593

American Broadcasting Companies, Inc.

The Year in Review

By Peter Jennings, ABC News

About the Author: Peter Jennings was named sole anchor and senior editor of ABC's *World News Tonight* in August 1983. Until then he had been London correspondent in the show's three-anchor format, as well as chief of ABC's foreign news operations.

Americans in 1983 cheered a long-awaited economic recovery and military success on a tiny Caribbean island called Grenada. The centennials of two American institutions also were celebrated: more than two million people gathered for the 100th birthday party for the Brooklyn Bridge, and the New York Metropolitan Opera marked its 100th anniversary with a gala concert. In Poland the awarding of the Nobel Peace Prize to Lech Walesa and a visit by native son Pope John Paul II brought joy and solidarity. Argentines looked to the future with optimism, as they voted overwhelmingly for a return to civilian government. And Australians popped champagne corks for a victory in the America's Cup yachting competition.

All in all, however, the world had little to celebrate, as 1983 became another year for the international terrorist. Car bombs, truck bombs, and package bombs took a deadly toll around the globe. Many were concentrated in the Middle East. In April dozens of people were killed when a car bomb demolished most of the U.S. embassy in Beirut. In October an incredibly powerful truck bomb destroyed U.S. Marine barracks in Lebanon, killing 241 American servicemen; a simultaneous attack on a nearby French installation killed 58. The Israeli headquarters in Tyre was truck-bombed in November, leaving 60 dead, and the U.S. embassy in Kuwait was rocked in December. But the carnage certainly was not limited to the Middle East: 18 died in the bombing of South African Air Force headquarters in Pretoria, and 19 people, including five South Korean government officials, died in an explosion in Rangoon, Burma. There was little evidence, but strong suspicion, that these bombings were the work of terrorist groups getting secret support from radical governments. Other acts were not. A week before Christmas, Harrods department store in London was struck by a bomb blast, killing 5. But not all victims were even human: gunmen suspected of being from the Irish Republican Army kidnapped Sherger, a prize thoroughbred race horse.

Lebanon proved to be the worst trouble spot in the Middle East. Israel and Lebanon reached an agreement on the withdrawal of foreign troops from Lebanon, but the agreement never reached fruition because neither Israel nor Syria would be the first to move out. In Israel, Prime Minister Menahem Begin resigned from office, marking the end of an era.

A rebellion in the ranks of the Palestine Liberation Organization (PLO), sponsored by Syria, led to the emasculation of the PLO as a major political force. Yasir Arafat and his supporters were driven to a last stand in the northern Lebanese port city of Tripoli and then were forced to escape to Tunisia. It was not clear at year's end if Arafat could ever regain his former influence.

Despite protest demonstrations by millions of Europeans, NATO allies proceeded with the deployment of new, U.S.-built nuclear missiles, a step that had been planned since 1979. The Soviet Union promptly canceled further arms-control talks with the United States. The whereabouts of Soviet President Yuri Andropoy became a mystery. He made no public appearances after August, leading to speculation that he was seriously ill. The Kremlin said that Andropov was merely suffering from a bad cold. No one was convinced.

A Soviet fighter plane on September 1 shot down an unarmed Korean passenger jetliner which had overflown a Soviet military base on Sakhalin Island in the Pacific Ocean. All 269 persons aboard, including U.S. Rep. Lawrence McDonald, a Democrat from Georgia, were killed in the crash.

In another major trouble spot, Central America, Lt. Cmdr. Albert Schaufelberger became the first U.S. military adviser to be killed in El Salvador; he was assassinated by leftist rebels. Opposition at home grew over apparent U.S. efforts to topple the Sandinista regime in Nicaragua.

A prominent leader of the political opposition in the Philippines, Benigno Aquino, was assassinated in August as he returned home to Manila after three years of self-imposed exile.

In Africa, Libyan-backed rebels tried to overthrow the government of Chad, and both the United States and France came to the aid of Chad's government. With demand for world oil remaining weak, Nigeria, whose economy depends on oil sales, ordered all aliens out of the country; a flood of refugees poured into neighboring states. In a showcase of the democratic process, Nigeria's President Shehu Shagari was returned to office in August national elections, but he was ousted in a military coup on the last day of the year. Meanwhile, South Africa's exclusively white voters changed their constitution to permit very limited voting rights to the so-called "colored" population, those of Indian descent or mixed blood, but continued to deny those rights to the large black majority.

U.S. Marines remained part of the multinational peacekeeping force in Lebanon throughout 1983. Following the deaths of some 250 Marines in Lebanon and no apparent solution to the trouble in sight, the question at year's end was: "Is it time to bring the soldiers home?"

© James Nachtwey/Black Star

Sir Paul Scoon, right, *the governor-general of the tiny Caribbean island of Grenada, was a major newsmaker in 1983. Following the October overthrow of the Marxist government on Grenada, the 48-year-old former schoolteacher was the only constitutional authority on the island and had the responsibility of establishing an interim government. In late May, Colonial Williamsburg (VA) was the setting for the ninth summit of the leaders of the seven major industrialized nations. Together with Gaston Thorn of the European Community, the leaders issued the Williamsburg Declaration on Economic Recovery, which noted clear signs of improvement but also renewed the "commitment to reduce structural budget deficits."*

UPI

The U.S. economy showed a healthy recovery, with most indicators improving. Unemployment, which began the year near 11%, was down to 8% by year's end. Many developing and underdeveloped nations, however, were floundering in debt. American Telephone & Telegraph, the giant Bell System, was split by court order into smaller regional companies, changing the way most Americans do business with the phone company.

Although the presidential elections would not be held until 1984, American politicians, as usual, began running early. President Reagan refused to announce his candidacy for reelection, but eight Democratic hopefuls were in the race, including the Rev. Jesse Jackson, the first major black candidate for the office. Blacks enjoyed a good year at the polls, as Harold Washington was elected mayor of Chicago and W. Wilson Goode won in Philadelphia. Vanessa Williams of New York became the first black Miss America.

In European politics, Italy and Portugal joined the ranks of a growing Socialist belt on the Mediterranean. Farther north, in Britain, Conservative Margaret Thatcher easily won reelection. In Japan, Prime Minister Yasuhiro Nakasone lost his absolute majority in parliament but stayed in office with the support of smaller parties.

Architect and philosopher Buckminster Fuller died at age 87. It was a sad year for the arts: 1983 saw the passing of such greats as Eubie Blake, Tennessee Williams, George Balanchine, Harry James, and Ira Gershwin. Television journalists Frank Reynolds and Jessica Savitch died. Barney Clark, the first person to receive a permanent artificial heart, died after being kept alive for 112 days.

It was a good year for the U.S. space program. Sally Ride became the first American woman to travel in space, aboard the space shuttle *Challenger,* and Guion Bluford became the first American black to do so. The unmanned space probe Pioneer 10, launched 11 years earlier, passed out of the solar system in 1983, headed into the unknown.

U.S. Interior Secretary James Watt, known equally for his controversial environmental policies and his outrageous statements, resigned under pressure. In Bolivia, Klaus Barbie, a convicted Nazi war criminal known as the "Butcher of Lyons" for his activities during World War II, was extradited to France to stand trial for war crimes.

On television, millions watched the fictional portrayal of the aftermath of nuclear war in *The Day After*. A real conflict, World War II, drew millions of viewers to the miniseries *The Winds of War*. And the final installment of the series *M*A*S*H* drew the largest audience of any prime-time television show.

The Baltimore Orioles won the World Series. The Washington Redskins won the Super Bowl. *Gandhi* won the Oscar as the year's best film. *A Chorus Line* became the longest-running show in Broadway history. And Cabbage Patch Kids were the craze of the Christmas season.

A theater milestone was reached in September 1983 when "A Chorus Line" succeeded "Grease" as the longest-running show in the history of Broadway. Dancers from the present and past casts celebrated the record-breaking 3,389th performance. The prize-winning musical has toured the United States, Canada, and Europe.

January

3 The first session of the 98th Congress convenes, with economic recovery and Social Security reform as top priorities.

The Polish government establishes officially sanctioned trade unions to replace the outlawed Solidarity federation.

5 At the close of a two-day Warsaw Pact meeting in Prague, the Soviet Union and its allies offer a nonaggression pact with members of the North Atlantic Treaty Organization (NATO). Among the proposals is a mutual commitment "not to be the first to use either nuclear or conventional weapons." The West responds cautiously.

6 Britain's Prime Minister Margaret Thatcher shuffles her Cabinet. Among the new members is Michael Heseltine, who replaces John Nott as minister of defense.

7 The Reagan administration lifts a five-year U.S. embargo on arms sales to Guatemala. A U.S. State Department spokesman declares that Guatemala has made progress in the area of human rights, making the action possible.

8 As a "gesture of support," Britain's Prime Minister Thatcher arrives in the Falkland Islands on a surprise visit. In spring 1982, Britain and Argentina fought a war over jurisdiction over the South Atlantic islands.

10 The Nonaligned Nations Movement opens a special six-day conference in Managua, Nicaragua, to discuss current problems in Latin America and the Caribbean.

12 Japan's Prime Minister Yasuhiro Nakasone and South Korea's President Chun Doo Hwan conclude two days of talks in Seoul. Japan agrees to lend South Korea $4 billion (U.S.) over a five-year period.

The White House announces that Eugene V. Rostow has been dismissed as director of the Arms Control and Disarmament Agency and that Kenneth L. Adelman, deputy representative at the UN, will be named to the post.

Early in the new year, a series of severe Pacific rainstorms cause 11 deaths and an estimated $70 million in damage in California. For beachfront property owners in Malibu, below, the loss was substantial.

13 Following three weeks of negotiations, Israel and Lebanon agree on an agenda for peace talks.

17 China's Prime Minister Zhao Ziyang concludes a ten-nation tour of Africa.

Dana Fineman/Sygma

Citing economic difficulties and an increase in civil unrest, the Nigerian government orders all illegal aliens to leave the country by February 1. Most of the aliens, about two million from Ghana alone, had come to Nigeria looking for jobs during the country's oil boom. The expulsion sets off a mass exodus to neighboring countries.

Two women, Margaret Heckler and Elizabeth Dole (right), are named to the Reagan cabinet as 1983 begins. They are to succeed Richard S. Schweiker (left) and Drew Lewis as secretary of health and human services and secretary of transportation, respectively.

18 South Africa announces that it is dissolving the four-year-old National Assembly in South-West Africa (Namibia) and resuming direct control over the territory.

In Britain a bipartisan committee of inquiry clears the Thatcher government of blame for failing to anticipate or prevent actions by Argentina that led to the 1982 Falklands War.

In Washington, President Reagan and Japan's Prime Minister Nakasone hold a "very fruitful" review of trade and defense issues.

Soviet Foreign Minister Andrei Gromyko concludes a two-day visit to Bonn, West Germany, where he urges his hosts not to go through with deployment of new U.S. intermediate-range nuclear missiles, scheduled for the fall.

19 China announces that it is banning additional 1983 purchases of cotton, soybeans, and chemical fibers from the United States. On January 15 the Reagan administration imposed a ban on the import of Chinese textiles after talks on such trade had broken down.

Canada's Prime Minister Pierre Elliott Trudeau concludes a 16-day tour of Asia for the purpose of promoting trade.

23 The nuclear-powered Soviet satellite Cosmos 1402 plunges through the earth's atmosphere and breaks into burning pieces as it falls harmlessly into the Indian Ocean.

25 In the annual State of the Union Message, President Reagan calls for a freeze in the growth of federal spending and a "standby" tax increase of up to $50 billion for fiscal 1986–88.

Pope John Paul II signs a new code of canon law.

30 The Washington Redskins defeat the Miami Dolphins, 27–17, in pro football's Super Bowl XVII.

31 President Reagan formally presents Congress his budget for fiscal 1984; a deficit of $188.8 billion is projected.

February

2 On a 12-day, four-nation tour of Asia, U.S. Secretary of State George Shultz holds talks with Chinese leaders in Peking on a broad range of topics, including Taiwan, the world economy, and Sino-U.S. trade relations.

The 1984 U.S. presidential campaign gets under way, as California Sen. Alan Cranston (D) becomes the first candidate formally to announce his bid.

At the Vatican, Pope John Paul II formally installs 18 new cardinals, including Archbishop Jozef Glemp, the primate of Poland, and Joseph I. Bernardin, the archbishop of Chicago.

4 The U.S. Labor Department announces that in January, for the first time in 17 months, the unemployment rate fell—from 10.8% in December to 10.4%.

5 After being arrested in Bolivia on January 25, Klaus Barbie, the head of the Gestapo in Lyons from 1942 to 1944, is returned to France and charged with "crimes against humanity, murder, torture, arbitrary arrests, and jailings."

6 Gen. Alfredo Stroessner is elected to his seventh term as president of Paraguay.

7 Elizabeth H. Dole is sworn in as U.S. secretary of transportation.

8 The $13.5-million thoroughbred race horse Shergar is kidnapped by gunmen from a stud farm at Newbridge, Ireland. The five-year-old bay, former winner of the Irish Sweeps Derby and English Derby, is owned by Aga Khan.

10 Leaders of the Independent Truckers Association (ITA) call off an 11-day strike. The truckers had been protesting new federal legislation increasing the excise tax on gasoline and diesel fuel and raising the registration fee for large trucks.

Canada and the United States sign an agreement permitting the United States to test unarmed cruise missiles in northern Alberta.

Moshe Arens, Israel's ambassador to the United States, inspects an honor guard after being named to succeed Ariel Sharon as defense minister.

11 Ariel Sharon resigns as Israel's defense minister in the wake of a state investigating commission report that the nation's top civilian and military leaders bore "indirect responsibility" for the massacre of Palestinians by Lebanese Christian Phalangist militia in September 1982. Sharon is asked to stay in the cabinet as minister without portfolio, and Moshe Arens is chosen as his successor in the defense ministry.

Sven Nackstrand/Gamma-Liaison

The International Monetary Fund (IMF) increases its basic lending pool by 47.4%, from $66 billion (U.S.) to $98.5 billion, so as to meet the growing demand of developing nations for emergency funds to help lower their foreign debts.

13   Spyros Kyprianou is reelected to a five-year term as president of Cyprus.

16   President Reagan reveals that the United States has sent Air Force AWACS reconnaissance planes to Egypt for "training exercises" in light of reported tensions along the Libyan-Sudanese border.

22   At a joint news conference with President Hosni Mubarak of Egypt, Sudan's President Mohammed al-Nemery confirms U.S. reports of a plot by Libya to overthrow his government.

Capping a nine-day meeting in Algiers, the Palestinian National Council refuses to consider U.S. President Reagan's plan as a "sound basis" for peace in the Middle East.

The U.S. government offers to purchase all homes and businesses in Times Beach, a Missouri town recently afflicted by flooding and dioxin contamination.

24   The government of India reports that at least 1,300 persons have died in the three weeks prior to and during elections in the north-eastern state of Assam. The Congress (I) Party of Prime Minister Indira Gandhi claims to have won the majority of seats. Early in January, however, the party had suffered defeat in three other states, forcing Gandhi to overhaul her cabinet.

The U.S. Commission on Wartime Relocation and Internment of Civilians releases a 467-page report concluding that the relocation and internment of 120,000 Japanese-American citizens and resident aliens during World War II was a "grave injustice."

25   American playwright Tennessee Williams, 71, dies in New York.

26   Britain's Queen Elizabeth and Prince Philip begin a ten-day visit to the West Coast of the United States.

© Regis Bossu/Sygma

In West Germany in February, politicians went on the campaign trail, and the electorate prepared to vote. Helmut Kohl's ruling coalition was returned to power on March 6.

March

2   Pope John Paul II arrives in Costa Rica, beginning an eight-day, eight-nation tour of Central America and the Caribbean.

6   The ruling center-right coalition of West Germany's Chancellor Helmut Kohl, a Christian Democrat, wins a strong majority in national elections for the Bundestag (lower house of parliament). The Greens, a leftist antinuclear and environmentalist movement, earns its first 27 seats in the 498-seat body.

9   Margaret Heckler is sworn in as U.S. secretary of health and human services.

10   President Reagan calls for an additional $110 million in military aid to El Salvador during fiscal 1983, up from the $60 million he had requested ten days earlier; Congress had authorized $26 million for the year.

India and Pakistan sign an agreement to form a joint commission to improve economic and cultural relations; talks continue on a nonaggression treaty.

The People's Consultative Assembly of Indonesia unanimously re-elects President Suharto to a fourth five-year term.

Breese/Gamma-Liaison

President Reagan asks William Ruckelshaus to return as administrator of the Environmental Protection Agency.

11 Robert Hawke, leader of the Australian Labor Party (ALP), and a new 27-member cabinet are sworn into office. The ALP won a solid victory in parliamentary elections March 5, ousting the Liberal-National Party coalition of Prime Minister Malcolm Fraser.

12 The seventh summit of the Nonaligned Nations Movement concludes in New Delhi, India. The six-day conference focused on the world economy and disarmament. Four new members—Bahamas, Barbados, Colombia, and Vanuatu—were admitted, bringing the total membership to 101.

14 For the first time in its 23-year history, the Organization of Petroleum Exporting Countries (OPEC) agrees to cut its price for crude oil—from $34 to $29—and set national output quotas.

21 After two days of negotiations, the eight countries belonging to the European Monetary System agree on a realignment of currency values; the West German mark is increased 5.5%, and the French franc is devalued 2.5%.

President Reagan names William Ruckelshaus as administrator of the Environmental Protection Agency, replacing Anne McGill Burford, who resigned March 9 in the face of mounting public pressure and congressional investigations into possible mismanagement and conflict of interest in the agency.

23 In a nationally televised address, President Reagan calls for a long-term research and development program to create an antiballistic missile (ABM) system capable of destroying Soviet nuclear missiles before they reach their targets.

Addressing the UN Security Council, Nicaragua's deputy foreign minister, Victor Hugo Trinoco, charges that at least 2,000 U.S.-supported rebels based in Honduras have invaded his country.

Barney Clark, 62, the first human patient to receive a permanent artificial heart, dies at the University of Utah Medical Center, where the device had been implanted 112 days before.

30 Roy L. Williams, president of the International Brotherhood of Teamsters, is sentenced to 55 years in prison for his December 1982 conviction of having attempted to bribe a U.S. senator.

April

1 Tens of thousands of antinuclear protestors turn out for Easter weekend protests in West Germany and Great Britain. Peaceful demonstrations against NATO plans to deploy nuclear missiles in Europe are staged at military bases, research centers, and several major cities.

4 In São Paulo, Brazil, a "March Against Unemployment" by some 2,500 demonstrators erupts into three days of rioting.

North Carolina State University upsets the University of Houston, 54–52, to win the NCAA Division I basketball championship.

5 The French government expels 47 Soviet diplomats, journalists, and trade officials on charges of espionage.

7 The Chinese government cancels all remaining sports and cultural exchanges with the United States during 1983, three days after the U.S. government granted asylum to China's top female tennis player, Hu Na.

The Socialist government of France wins a vote of confidence on a sweeping austerity program to reverse the country's trade deficit and strengthen the franc.

9 After a successful five-day mission, the U.S. space shuttle *Challenger* is landed safely at Edwards Air Force base in California. The mission, *Challenger*'s first, featured the first American space walk in nine years.

11 The President's Commission on Strategic Forces submits its formal report, calling for the MX missile to be based in existing silos, recommending development of a single-warhead intercontinental ballistic missile, and disputing the "window of vulnerability" theory advanced by President Reagan.

The annual "Days of Remembrance of Victims of the Holocaust" opens in Washington, DC, with more than 15,000 holocaust survivors and their relatives in attendance; it is the largest such reunion ever held.

12 U.S. Rep. Harold Washington (D) defeats Bernard Epton to become the first black mayor of the city of Chicago.

Following a week of heavy rains and flooding in Louisiana, Mississippi, Tennessee, and Alabama, at least 15 persons are reported dead and 50,000 left homeless, with damage estimated at $600 million.

14 Kenneth L. Adelman is confirmed by the U.S. Senate as director of the Arms Control and Disarmament Agency, despite a negative recommendation by the Foreign Relations Committee.

In response to a flurry of congressional criticism, President Reagan denies that providing covert aid to Nicaraguan rebel forces is a violation of U.S. law.

18 The U.S. embassy in Beirut is leveled by a car-bomb explosion, leaving several dozen persons dead and more than 100 injured; a pro-Iranian group claims responsibility.

20 President Reagan signs into law a bill to ensure the long-term solvency of the Social Security system.

21 Jackie Presser, 56, is sworn in as president of the International Brotherhood of Teamsters. He replaces Roy L. Williams, who resigned after being sentenced to 55 years in prison for his December 1982 conviction of having attempted to bribe a U.S. senator.

Jacques Chenet/"Newsweek"

Rep. Harold Washington, 61, uses his oratorical skills to stage a successful bid for Chicago's city hall.

© Bill Pierce/Sygma

The entire central façade of the U.S. embassy in Beirut, Lebanon, collapses following a massive car-bomb explosion.

25 Austria's Socialist Party selects Fred Sinowatz to succeed Bruno Kreisky as the nation's chancellor. Parliamentary elections the day before left the Socialists as the country's largest party but without an absolute majority, prompting Kreisky to resign.

26 In a continuing "bull market" atmosphere, the Dow Jones Industrial Average of trading on the New York Stock Exchange breaks the 1,200 barrier, closing at 1,209.46 on 97.25 million shares.

The National Commission on Excellence in Education, created in 1981, issues a 36-page report which warns that "a rising tide of mediocrity" in U.S. schools "threatens our very future as a nation and a people."

27 Addressing a special joint session of Congress, President Reagan warns that events in Central America pose a real threat to U.S. security and urges approval for increased military and economic aid; Sen. Christopher Dodd (CT) responds on behalf of Democrats by opposing any increases and calling for negotiated settlements.

29 Mexico and Brazil end three days of talks during which a series of agreements on trade, industry, and reciprocal credit were made.

30 Gen. Prem Tinsulanonda is reappointed prime minister of Thailand.

May

1 Violent antigovernment protests mark the May Day holiday in cities throughout Poland.

3 At a welcoming dinner in Moscow for East German head of state Erich Honecker, Soviet leader Yuri Andropov offers the West a proposal for limiting nuclear weapons in Europe; the plan calls for a cut in the number of warheads rather than missiles.

The National Conference of Catholic Bishops, meeting in Chicago, approves an amended third draft of a pastoral letter that denounces the nuclear arms race and calls for a "halt" to the development and deployment of new weapon systems.

4 Chairman Lee Iacocca of the Chrysler Corporation announces that the company will pay off $400 million in federally guaranteed loans by the end of June. The total $1.2 billion (U.S.) in federal bailout money, which saved Chrysler from bankruptcy in 1980, was not scheduled for repayment until 1990.

6 The government of West Germany announces that the so-called "Hitler Diaries" discovered by *Stern* magazine had been proven by chemical tests to be forgeries.

7 In the first official contact between the two countries since 1949, a delegation from China arrives in Seoul, South Korea, to negotiate the return of a plane hijacked there two days before.

9 Representatives of the 24-member Organization for Economic Cooperation and Development (OECD) open two days of talks in Paris on common trade and political problems.

11 In response to a call by the copper workers' union and other labor groups, thousands of Chileans take to the streets for three days of protest against the economic policies of President Augusto Pinochet Ugarte.

The West German magazine "Stern" ceased publishing the alleged diaries of Adolf Hitler after chemical tests proved the documents to be forgeries. The magazine's chief editors then resigned.

13   The U.S. Federal Reserve Board announces that industrial production had increased 2.1% in April, the largest one-month gain in nearly eight years.

17   Israel and Lebanon sign a U.S.-mediated agreement on the withdrawal of all foreign troops from Lebanese soil. Prospects for the actual withdrawal in the near future, however, are cast in doubt by Syria's rejection of the plan.

The New York Islanders win their fourth consecutive Stanley Cup, symbolic of the National Hockey League championship, with a 4–2 victory over the Edmonton Oilers.

18   Owen F. Bieber, 53, is elected president of the United Auto Workers (UAW), replacing Douglas Fraser, who is retiring.

20   In one of the most severe terrorist attacks ever in South Africa, a car bomb explodes outside the Pretoria headquarters of the national air force, killing 18 persons and injuring 200 others. The African National Congress (ANC), an outlawed black nationalist group, claims responsibility.

President Reagan announces that a 1982 ban on the sale of 75 F-16 fighter planes to Israel is being lifted.

24   The U.S. Supreme Court rules, 8–1, that the Internal Revenue Service can legally deny tax exemptions to racially biased public schools.

25   Navy Lt. Cmdr. Albert Schaufelberger, deputy commander of the U.S. Military Group in El Salvador, is assassinated by leftist rebels. He is the first American military adviser to be killed in that country.

In a controversial move, President Reagan dismisses three of the six members of the U.S. Civil Rights Commission, all three Democrats who oppose his civil-rights policies; Reagan's nominations, subject to Senate confirmation, are all Republicans.

29   Tom Sneva wins the 67th Indianapolis 500 automobile race.

30   The leaders of the seven major industrial democracies—the United States, Canada, Japan, West Germany, France, Great Britain, and Italy—conclude the ninth in a series of annual summit conferences, this year held in Williamsburg, VA. In a final joint statement, the participants declare that "we now clearly see signs of recovery" from the worldwide economic recession.

31   The Philadelphia 76ers win the National Basketball Association (NBA) championship by defeating the Los Angeles Lakers, 115–108, in the fourth game of their best-of-seven play-off series.

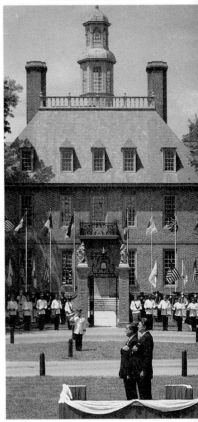

President Reagan welcomes Japan's Prime Minister Yasuhiro Nakasone to colonial Williamsburg, the site of the 1983 summit conference of the leaders of the major industrial democracies.

Pierre Perrin/Gamma Liaison

June

2   Richard B. Stone, the new U.S. special envoy to Central America, begins a 12-day fact-finding tour.

At the close of a two-day meeting in Brussels, defense ministers from the NATO countries reaffirm their commitment to deploy U.S. medium-range nuclear missiles in Europe by December unless an agreement is reached in the U.S.-Soviet arms control talks in Geneva.

8   A new three-party, center-right coalition government, headed by Prime Minister Kaare Willoch, takes office in Norway.

The 19th summit conference of the Organization of African Unity (OAU) convenes in Addis Ababa, Ethiopia.

Margaret Thatcher persuades voters in Britain that under Conservative Party rule the nation "has recovered its confidence and self-respect."

9 The Conservative Party of Britain's Prime Minister Margaret Thatcher increases its parliamentary majority in national elections, winning 397 of 650 seats in the House of Commons; the opposition Labour Party takes only 209 seats in its weakest showing since World War II.

Ending a political stalemate that began with parliamentary elections April 25, Portugal's Mario Soares is sworn in as prime minister of a coalition government made up of the Social Democratic Party and his own Socialist Party.

10 Delegates from the northern and southern branches of American Presbyterians vote to reunite as the Presbyterian Church (U.S.A.), the nation's fourth largest Protestant denomination.

11 In the wake of her election victory, Britain's Prime Minister Thatcher revamps her cabinet; among the changes is the removal of Francis Pym as foreign secretary and the naming of Sir Geoffrey Howe as his replacement.

Brian Mulroney, a 44-year-old lawyer and businessman, is elected leader of Canada's Progressive Conservative Party.

15 In a series of three cases, the U.S. Supreme Court limits the power of state and local governments to restrict access to legal abortion; the rulings bolster the landmark holding in *Roe v. Wade* (1973), which gave women the unrestricted right to have an abortion in the first trimester of pregnancy.

16 Yuri Andropov, secretary-general of the Soviet Communist Party, is elected chairman of the Presidium of the Supreme Soviet, or president.

17 Leaders of the ten European Community (EC) nations open three days of talks in Stuttgart, West Germany; budget matters head the agenda.

18 Paul A. Volcker is appointed by President Reagan to a second term as chairman of the Federal Reserve Board.

During a 17-day session that began June 6, the National People's Congress of China appoints Li Xiannian president, a largely ceremonial position not occupied since 1968.

23 At the conclusion of a highly charged, eight-day visit to his native Poland, Pope John Paul II is allowed a private meeting with former Solidarity leader Lech Walesa. Throughout his tour, which also highlighted a meeting with Gen. Wojciech Jaruzelski, the pontiff stressed Polish nationalism and human rights.

Large crowds, pro-Solidarity banners, and V-for-victory signs are featured as Pope John Paul II returns to his homeland.

In a decision that significantly shifts the balance of power in U.S. government, the Supreme Court rules, 5–4, that the "legislative veto" exercised by Congress to limit the powers of the president and regulatory agencies is unconstitutional (*Immigration and Naturalization Service v. Chadha*).

18 The space shuttle *Challenger* is launched from Cape Canaveral, FL, carrying the first U.S. woman astronaut, Sally K. Ride, and four other crew members.

24 Growing disaffection between the Palestine Liberation Organization (PLO) and the Syrian government, as well as dissension within the PLO itself, are brought into the open as Damascus expels organization leader Yasir Arafat; the move comes amid increasing evidence of Syrian support for a rebel PLO faction.

27 National parliamentary elections in Italy leave the Christian Democrats with a reduced majority; the Communist Party also suffers a loss, while a number of smaller parties make advances.

28 In a growing political controversy, President Reagan is barraged with questions at a news conference about a 1980 Carter campaign briefing book that had come into the possession of the Reagan camp and had been used in preparation for the televised debate between the two candidates.

UPI

Dr. Sally K. Ride, 32-year-old astrophysicist, is the first American woman astronaut.

July

1 A 10% cut in U.S. federal income tax, the third phase of the Reagan administration's tax reduction plan, goes into effect.

3 The UN Conference on Trade and Development (UNCTAD) concludes a month-long session in Belgrade, Yugoslavia, having resolved none of the major differences between industrialized and Third World nations.

4 The 12 member-nations of the Caribbean Community (Caricom) open a five-day summit conference at Port of Spain, Trinidad, with the U.S. Caribbean Basin Initiative high on the agenda.

6 Ending an 11-year losing streak, the American League defeats the National League, 13–3, in baseball's All-Star Game.

7 West German Chancellor Helmut Kohl concludes a four-day visit to the Soviet Union; talks focused on arms control.

U.S. Vice-President George Bush winds up an eight-nation tour of Europe, while Secretary of State George Shultz concludes a trip to four Asian capitals, with stopovers in the Middle East.

8 Turkish terrorist Mehmet Ali Agca, convicted of shooting Pope John Paul II in May 1981, tells reporters that he was aided by the Soviet secret police (KGB) and "Bulgarian services."

According to the U.S. Commerce Department, the nation's Gross National Product grew at a seasonally adjusted annual rate of 8.7% in the second quarter, far outstripping government forecasts.

9 The National Women's Political Caucus opens in San Antonio, TX, with strong criticism of the Reagan administration.

13 The British House of Commons rejects a motion to restore the death penalty, abolished in 1965.

18 President Reagan announces the formation of a 12-member, bipartisan commission to make recommendations on U.S. policy in Central America; the body will be headed by former Secretary of State Henry Kissinger.

19 Israeli Prime Minister Menahem Begin postpones a visit to Washington scheduled for the following week, citing "personal reasons."

20 The U.S. House of Representatives votes to censure two of its members, Rep. Daniel Crane (R-IL) and Rep. Gerry Studds (D-MA), for sexual misconduct involving congressional pages.

21 Polish leaders declare an end to martial law, imposed in December 1981, and partial amnesty for political prisoners. At the same time, however, they enact a series of special restrictions that ensure tight control over political, social, and economic life in the country.

22 President Reagan announces that Philip Habib is stepping down as chief U.S. negotiator in the Middle East and will be replaced by Robert C. McFarlane, deputy national security adviser.

25 The Washington Public Power Supply System (WPPSS) files documents stating that it cannot repay $2.25 billion in bonds. It is the largest default in municipal bond history.

26 As part of its action on the defense authorization bill for 1984, the U.S. Senate approves $2.6 billion for the production and deployment of the controversial MX missile; the House approved the same amount July 21, only to reduce it to $2.2 billion the next day. Both bodies released $625 million for research and development in late May.

28 The United States and Soviet Union reach a five-year grain agreement, by which the USSR must increase its annual purchases by at least 50%.

After three days of heated debate, the U.S. House of Representatives votes, 228–195, to bar covert aid to Nicaraguan rebel forces. In a televised news conference July 26, President Reagan denied that his administration is seeking a larger role in Central America and said that upcoming joint maneuvers with Honduras would provide a "shield for democracy and development."

Both houses of U.S. Congress repeal a 1982 law requiring financial institutions to withhold for taxes 10% of interest and dividend income.

© James Nachtwey/Black Star

In July a U.S. military advance team arrived in Honduras to prepare for joint U.S.-Honduran military maneuvers. The exercises, involving as many as 5,000 U.S. military personnel, were to deter "Nicaragua from aggression."

August

1 After a week of violence, the worst in Sri Lanka since it became independent in 1948, more than 200 persons are reported killed and 50,000 homeless in clashes between the Buddhist Sinhalese majority and Hindu Tamil minority.

3 The House of Representatives narrowly approves a Senate-authorized, administration-supported increase of $8.4 billion in the U.S. contribution to the International Monetary Fund (IMF).

4 Bettino Craxi, 49, is sworn in as the first Socialist prime minister of Italy. He heads a five-party coalition government.

5 In a coup led by former Premier Thomas Sankara, the government of Upper Volta's President Jean-Baptiste Ouedraogo is overthrown; a national revolutionary council takes over.

The plan by which American Telephone and Telegraph Co. (AT&T) would divest 22 of its local telephone companies is given final approval by U.S. District Judge Harold Greene. The company is ordered to stop using the name and logo of Bell Telephone.

The U.S. Labor Department reports that the nation's seasonally adjusted unemployment rate fell from 9.8% in June to 9.3% in July, the largest one-month decline since 1959.

8 President Efrain Rios Montt of Guatemala is ousted by the military. His defense minister, Brig. Gen. Oscar Humberto Mejia Victores, is installed as head of state.

Television news anchorwoman Christine Craft is awarded $500,000 in a sex discrimination suit against station KMBC-TV of Kansas City, MO. Craft contended that she had been demoted because she was "too old, unattractive and not deferential enough to men."

11 Over protests by the opposition, President Shehu Shagari is declared the winner of Nigeria's first civilian-supervised elections since the end of military rule in 1979.

12 Pakistan's President Zia ul-Haq promises national elections and a return to constitutional democracy by 1985.

In his third cabinet shuffle in one year, Canada's Prime Minister Pierre Elliott Trudeau names five new ministers and reassigns eight others.

14 With the support of French troops, Chadian government forces establish an east-west defense line that virtually halts the advance of Libyan-backed rebels, led by former Chad President Goukouni Oueddei. The success of Libyan and insurgent forces in northern Chad earlier in the month prompted France and the United States to step up military aid to the government of President Hissène Habré.

16 A report issued by the U.S. Justice Department confirms that Klaus Barbie, head of the German Gestapo in Lyons, France, from 1942 to 1944 and presently awaiting trial there for "crimes against humanity," had been employed as a spy by the U.S. Army in the years following World War II.

17 Joshua Nkomo, leader of the political opposition in Zimbabwe, reclaims his seat in parliament after ending a five-month, self-imposed exile in London.

18 Hurricane Alicia whips through southern Texas, leaving 17 persons dead and property damage valued at up to $1.3 billion.

American Telephone and Telegraph's new logo is a blue and white globe design. It replaces the circled bell, a familiar symbol since 1889.

In Washington, DC, August 28, some 250,000 persons marked the 20th anniversary of the 1963 March on Washington and Martin Luther King's famous "I have a dream" speech.

21 Philippine opposition leader Benigno S. Aquino, Jr., is assassinated at Manila Airport only minutes after returning from the United States, where he had been in self-imposed exile for three years. Opposition groups blame the Marcos government.

26 Chile's President Augusto Pinochet Ugarte declares that the state of emergency in effect since 1978 will be lifted the next day. The move comes after a newly formed opposition alliance called for his resignation August 6 and a fourth national day of antigovernment protest August 11.

27 With the official theme of "Jobs, Peace, and Freedom," an estimated 250,000 Americans converge on Washington, DC, to commemorate the August 1963 civil-rights march.

28 A new wave of full-scale fighting breaks out between Lebanese army units and Druse Muslim militia in and around Beirut. U.S. Marines, part of the multinational peacekeeping force, are drawn into their first combat.

September

1 A Korean Air Lines Boeing 747, flight 007 from New York to Seoul, is downed by a Soviet heat-seeking missile after crossing into Soviet airspace. All 240 passengers, including U.S. Rep. Larry McDonald (D-GA), and 29 crew members are killed.

President Reagan orders 2,000 Marines into position off the coast of Lebanon to "assure the safety" of the 1,370 already in Beirut.

2 Israel's Foreign Minister Yitzhak Shamir is elected successor to Prime Minister Menahem Begin as leader of the governing Herut Party, likely making him the country's next premier. Begin announced August 28 that he would be resigning for personal reasons.

After two months of inordinately dry, hot weather, U.S. Secretary of Agriculture John Block begins declaring drought disaster areas throughout the nation.

WANTED: FOR THE MURDER OF FLIGHT 007

YURI ANDROPOV

THE MASSACRE OF FLIGHT 007

LARRY McDONALD

THIS TIME WE WILL NOT FORGET!

Tryggvi McDonald, 23-year-old son of the late U.S. Rep. Lawrence P. McDonald (D-GA), the archconservative killed aboard Korean Air Lines Flight 007, knew what his father would have said about the incident: "The Soviet Union should be expelled from the community of civilized nations."

5   The space shuttle *Challenger* completes a trouble-free six-day mission with a night landing at Edwards Air Force Base in California. Among the five astronauts aboard is Lt. Col. Guion S. Bluford, Jr., the first U.S. black to travel in space.

10   The government of Peru lifts its state of emergency in most parts of the country.

11   Jimmy Connors defeats Ivan Lendl to capture his fifth men's singles title at the U.S. Open tennis championships in Queens, NY. In the women's final the day before, Martina Navratilova took her first singles championship by beating Chris Evert Lloyd.

12   Former Gov. Daniel J. Evans, a Republican, is sworn in as U.S. senator from Washington. He takes the seat left vacant by Democratic Sen. Henry Jackson, who died September 1.

13   Zimbabwe's Prime Minister Robert Mugabe ends a four-day U.S. visit with his first personal meeting with President Reagan.

19   The islands of St. Kitts-Nevis celebrate independence from Great Britain. The world's 168th nation is officially named St. Christopher and Nevis.

26   The result of negotiations sponsored by Saudi Arabia, a cease-fire among the various political and religious groups at war in Lebanon takes effect at 6:00 A.M. The agreement also includes a commitment to convene national reconciliation talks.

   On the first trip to Canada by a British prime minister in more than a quarter of a century, Margaret Thatcher addresses a joint session of Parliament in Ottawa.

   Chairman Frank Borman of Eastern Airlines, the fourth largest U.S. carrier, asks employees to take a 15% pay cut to help the company avert bankruptcy. Two days earlier, Continental Airlines, the nation's eighth largest carrier, filed for protection under Chapter 11 of the bankruptcy law and laid off all employees.

   In the seventh and deciding race of the America's Cup yachting competition, *Australia II* defeats the U.S. defender, *Liberty*.

The Dow Jones Industrial Average of trading on the New York Stock Exchange closes at 1260.77, a new record high.

28   During a five-day trip to China for talks on strategic cooperation, U.S. Secretary of Defense Caspar Weinberger announces that Premier Zhao Ziyang and President Reagan will exchange state visits in 1984.

29   Amid concern for his personal safety, President Reagan announces the cancellation of his planned visit to the Philippines during a trip to Asia in early November. In addition to the Philippines, site of domestic unrest since the August 21 assassination of political opposition leader Benigno Aquino, Thailand and Indonesia are dropped from the itinerary. Congressional business in Washington is given as the reason.

October

2   Neil Kinnock, a 41-year-old Welshman, is elected leader of Great Britain's Labour Party, succeeding Michael Foot.

4   A 24-hour national strike to protest low wages and high inflation shuts down business, industry, and public transportation in Argentina.

5   Lech Walesa, the founder of Poland's outlawed trade union Solidarity, is named the winner of the 1983 Nobel Peace Prize.

6   Brazil announces an agreement with 66 major world banks for a five-year grace period for repayment of $12 billion in loans.

9   Five South Korean cabinet ministers, two advisers to President Chun Doo Hwan, ten other South Koreans, and three Burmese journalists are killed in a bomb explosion at a wreath-laying ceremony in Rangoon, Burma. President Chun, delayed in traffic, was the apparent target of the blast, for which North Korea was blamed.

The U.S. National Bipartisan Commission on Central America, appointed by President Reagan and led by former Secretary of State Henry Kissinger, sets out on a six-day, six-nation fact-finding tour.

11   One day after being sworn in, Israeli Prime Minister Yitzhak Shamir and his cabinet announce an emergency economic austerity plan that includes a 23% devaluation of the shekel and an average 50% cut in government subsidies for basic goods and services.

© J. Hoagland/Gamma-Liaison

On the third leg of a six-nation fact-finding tour, the U.S. National Bipartisan Commission on Central America met with government and political opposition leaders in San Salvador. The head of the commission, former Secretary of State Henry Kissinger (second from left), said it was "absolutely imperative" that democracy and human rights be "preserved and extended."

The United States sends several assault ships and a frigate to the Arabian Sea after five French fighter planes are reported to have arrived in Iraq and after Iran renews threats to shut off the Persian Gulf from oil traffic if the West continues to supply arms to Iraq.

12 Former Japanese Prime Minister Kakuei Tanaka is found guilty of taking bribes from Lockheed Corp. in exchange for arranging the sale of the U.S. company's TriStar jets to All Nippon Airways.

13 U.S. National Security Adviser William Clark is the surprise choice of President Reagan to succeed James Watt as secretary of the interior. Watt resigned October 9 in the face of growing pressure.

16 In what was regarded as a last-ditch effort to promote a settlement in U.S.-Soviet arms reduction talks in Geneva, the foreign ministers of West Germany and the USSR, Hans-Dietrich Genscher and Andrei Gromyko, end two days of negotiations, with no progress reported.

The Baltimore Orioles shut out the Philadelphia Phillies, 5–0, in Game 5 to win baseball's 80th World Series.

17 President Reagan formally notifies the U.S. Federal Election Commission that he is forming a reelection campaign committee, but he puts off a final decision on his candidacy.

Special Middle East envoy Robert McFarlane is named President Reagan's national security adviser, replacing William Clark.

22 A gunman takes six persons hostage at the Augusta (GA) National Golf Club and demands to speak with President Reagan, who is on another part of the course. Reagan talks on the telephone with the intruder, who surrenders several hours later.

President Ferdinand Marcos of the Philippines swears in a new, civilian panel to investigate the assassination of Benigno Aquino. The original commission resigned in mid-October.

New York's Metropolitan Opera celebrates its 100th anniversary.

23 A truck loaded with explosives barrels into a U.S. Marine headquarters building at Lebanon's Beirut International Airport, killing 239 members of the American peacekeeping contingent. A simultaneous attack takes place at the nearby French compound.

Two days of demonstrations by some 2 million people against the planned deployment of 572 additional U.S. nuclear missiles in Western Europe winds down in major cities across the continent.

25 U.S. Marines and Army Rangers, along with troops from six Caribbean nations, invade the island of Grenada in what President Reagan describes as "a joint effort to restore order and democracy." Grenadian Prime Minister Maurice Bishop had been put under house arrest on October 13 and killed by army soldiers six days later. On October 20 a military council headed by Gen. Hudson Austin had assumed power.

28 An earthquake measuring 6.9 on the Richter Scale, the strongest in the contiguous 48 states since 1959, hits Idaho and seven other northwestern states.

30 A massive earthquake in the mountainous region of eastern Turkey leaves thousands of people dead or homeless in freezing temperatures.

31 Raúl Alfonsin, a center-leftist of the Radical Party, emerges as the surprise winner of Argentina's presidential election the day before.

A federal judge in Kansas City, MO, overrules an August jury decision that TV newscaster Christine Craft had been the victim of sex discrimination; he throws out the $500,000 award and orders a new trial.

UPI

President Reagan's choice of William P. Clark, above, to succeed James Watt as secretary of the interior came under fire. Various environmental groups claimed that Clark lacked experience in the field.

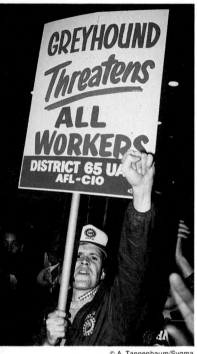

© A. Tannenbaum/Sygma

Drivers and terminal employees of Greyhound Lines, Inc., which operates 60% of U.S. intercity bus mileage, went on nationwide strike November 3. At issue was a proposed 9.5% pay cut. Using newly hired workers and supervisory staff, the company resumed service two weeks later, resulting in sometimes violent demonstrations. A settlement finally was reached in December.

2 The U.S. Defense Department declares that "hostilities have ceased" on Grenada and that troop withdrawal will begin shortly.

South African whites vote overwhelmingly in favor of a new constitution giving a limited political role to "coloreds," those of Asian or mixed-race descent; blacks are excluded.

3 The Rev. Jesse Jackson, 42-year-old civil-rights leader, announces his candidacy for the 1984 Democratic presidential nomination.

4 A suicide truck bombing of Israeli headquarters in Tyre, southern Lebanon, leaves 60 dead and 30 wounded; a pro-Iranian group claims responsibility. Israeli planes attack Palestinian positions.

5 Soviet party leader Yuri Andropov fails to attend the annual parade in Moscow commemorating the 1917 Bolshevik revolution; it is the first time a Soviet head of state misses the event.

6 Turkey's conservative Motherland Party, led by Turgut Ozal, wins 211 of 400 seats in national parliamentary elections.

8 Off-year elections are held across the United States.

11 Representatives of the warring factions in Lebanon end their first round of national reconciliation talks in Geneva; some progress is reported.

13 During a trip to Japan and South Korea, President Reagan visits U.S. soldiers in the demilitarized zone between South and North Korea.

15 Turkish Cypriots declare their part of the island an independent state, the Turkish Republic of Northern Cyprus.

18 The first session of the 98th U.S. Congress adjourns.

22 President John F. Kennedy is remembered on the 20th anniversary of his assassination.

23 The Soviet Union pulls out of talks in Geneva on intermediate-range nuclear forces (INF) to protest the planned deployment of new U.S. missiles in Western Europe. On November 22 the West German parliament voted to proceed with deployment.

Rebel forces of the Palestine Liberation Organization (PLO) accept a cease-fire plan promoted by Saudi Arabia to halt shelling of Tripoli, Lebanon. One week earlier the PLO rebels, supported by Syria, had driven Chairman Yasir Arafat from his last military stronghold and into downtown Tripoli.

24 Israel releases some 4,500 Palestinian and Lebanese prisoners in exchange for the return of six of its captured soldiers.

28 The U.S. space shuttle *Columbia* lifts off from Cape Canaveral carrying a research lab built by the European Space Agency.

29 Winding up two days of talks in Washington with Israel's Prime Minister Yitzhak Shamir, President Reagan announces that they "have agreed to establish a joint political-military group to examine ways in which we can enhance Israeli-U.S. cooperation."

30 Dutch brewery chairman Alfred H. Heineken and his chauffeur are freed by police from an unguarded warehouse in Amsterdam, where they had been held by kidnappers for three weeks.

December

1 Rita Lavelle, dismissed February 7 as head of the U.S. Environmental Protection Agency's toxic-waste cleanup program, is found guilty of perjury and obstructing a Congressional inquiry.

4 During a series of air strikes against Syrian antiaircraft batteries east of Beirut, Lebanon, two U.S. warplanes are shot down. One flier is killed, and another, Navy Lt. Robert O. Goodman, is captured by the Syrians.

Jaime Lusinchi of the Democratic Action Party wins a landslide victory in Venezuelan presidential elections.

6 Leaders of the ten European Community (EC) nations end a three-day summit in Athens, Greece, without an agreement on key financial issues. The body is said to be on the brink of bankruptcy.

8 Strategic Arms Reduction Talks (START) between the United States and the USSR adjourn in Geneva with the Soviets refusing to set a date for the next round.

9 The annual winter meeting of the Organization of Petroleum Exporting Countries (OPEC) concludes in Geneva with no changes made in its benchmark price ($29 per barrel) or production quotas.

10 Danuta Walesa, wife of Polish Solidarity leader Lech Walesa, accepts the 1983 Nobel Peace Prize, on behalf of her husband, in Oslo, Norway.

12 In a series of six car bombings in Kuwait, the U.S. embassy is left in rubble, with six persons killed.

15 The last U.S. troops leave Grenada; 300 noncombat personnel remain.

In order to advance a peace settlement in Namibia, South Africa announces at the United Nations that it will begin withdrawing its troops from southern Angola on Jan. 31, 1984.

17 A car-bomb explosion outside Harrods, the famous London department store, kills five persons and injures 77.

20 Yasir Arafat, leader of the Palestine Liberation Organization (PLO), and 4,000 of his loyalists are evacuated by a Greek ferry from Tripoli, Lebanon, where they had been under siege by Syrian-backed PLO dissidents.

22 A special Pentagon commission on the October 23 truck bombing of the U.S. Marine headquarters in Beirut concludes that there were serious failures in the military chain of command. A House of Representatives subcommittee report made public December 19 came to a similar conclusion.

26 Japan's Prime Minister Yasuhiro Nakasone is formally elected to a second term. His Liberal Democratic Party lost its parliamentary majority in elections December 18, but it clung to power with the support of independents.

28 The United States gives formal notice to the United Nations Educational, Scientific and Cultural Organization (UNESCO) that it will withdraw from the agency Jan. 1, 1985, unless substantial policy changes are made.

31 President Shehu Shagari of Nigeria is overthrown in a military coup. Maj. Gen. Mohammed Buhari assumes power.

"Time" Magazine

Although Syria's President Hafez al-Assad, who had been away from the public scene for some time, was photographed inspecting a new Damascus bridge, above, rumors of illness and debate regarding his successor persisted.

GRENADA

© M. Naythons/Gamma-Liaison

Flash Point in the Caribbean

By Richard C. Schroeder

The smallest country in the Western Hemisphere (133 sq mi; 346 km²)—and one of the most beautiful—Grenada provided an unlikely setting for armed conflict. Located in the Windward Islands off the coast of Venezuela, the former British colony began to be viewed as a strategic threat by the Reagan administration when its Socialist government allowed Cuba and the Soviet Union to introduce military equipment and help build an airfield at Point Salines, the southern tip.

U.S. President Ronald Reagan startled the nation and most of the world on the morning of Oct. 25, 1983, when he announced that American troops, accompanied by a small contingent of forces from several Caribbean nations, had invaded the tiny island of Grenada in the southeastern Caribbean.

The reason for the invasion, the president declared, was a state of growing chaos in Grenada, a spice-exporting country of only 133 sq mi (346 km²) and 110,000 people. In the days preceding the invasion, the island's prime minister, Maurice Bishop, had been deposed by a rebel group led by Deputy Prime Minister Bernard Coard and placed under house arrest. Freed by a band of his supporters on October 19, Bishop was recaptured and executed by units of the Grenadian army the same day. In the meantime, control of the island was seized by a "Revolutionary Military Council," headed by army commander Gen. Hudson Austin. Following Bishop's death, General Austin imposed a 24-hour curfew, declaring that violators would be "shot on sight."

President Reagan said in his press conference that the United States was acting out of concern for the safety of an estimated 1,000 Americans on Grenada, the majority of them students at St. George's Medical College in the island's capital. In addition, the president stated, the United States had

On October 25, a week after an even more hard-line Marxist regime seized power, U.S. Marines and Army Rangers were helicoptered onto the island. It was the first major U.S. military intervention in the hemisphere since 1965 in the Dominican Republic.

Eddie Adams/Gamma-Liaison

been asked to participate in the intervention by the governments of Antigua, Barbados, Dominica, Jamaica, St. Lucia, and St. Vincent, all of whom had supplied constabulary units for the action. Prime Minister Eugenia Charles of Dominica stood at the president's side as he made the announcement.

Unexpected Resistance. The invasion began at dawn, shortly after 5:30 A.M. Grenada time, on October 25. Marines stormed ashore at Pearls Airport in the northeastern part of the island and quickly secured control of the small civilian facility. A short time later the main part of the invasion force, airborne Army Rangers, parachuted onto the runway of a new international airport under construction at Point Salines at the southwestern tip of the island. The Rangers came under unexpectedly heavy fire from elements of the Grenadian army and especially from organized units of Cuban construction workers at the site. The airport itself was secured within two hours, but fighting continued sporadically in other parts of the island for the next four days. Because of the unexpected intensity of some of the fighting, White House officials at one point told reporters that there were 1,200 Cubans on Grenada, nearly twice the pre-invasion estimate. The figure was later scaled down to 750.

According to the Pentagon, the initial invasion force consisted of 1,900 Marines, Paratroopers, and Rangers and 300 men from other Caribbean islands. Over the next few days the number of U.S. combat troops on the island grew to 6,000.

About the Author: A syndicated writer on Latin America for U.S. newspapers, Richard C. Schroeder is chief of the Washington Bureau of *Vision* magazine. As an Eisenhower Exchange Fellow in 1972, he did extensive research on the Caribbean. Mr. Schroeder also has been the director of public information for the Inter American University in San German, Puerto Rico, and coordinator of information programs for the Alliance for Progress. He is the coauthor of *Dateline Latin America*.

Addressing the Organization of American States on June 1, Prime Minister Maurice Bishop assured the United States that the new airport under construction on Grenada would not be available to Cuban or Soviet military planes. The softening of his anti-U.S. position apparently led to the October coup by hard-line Marxists on the island.

Casualty reports were imprecise. The Pentagon reported that 18 U.S. soldiers were killed and 86 wounded; some of the casualties came from battlefield accidents rather than hostile fire. A Defense Department spokesman said that 59 opposing soldiers were killed and 57 wounded; the deputy U.S. military commander on Grenada estimated that 71 Cubans and 160 Grenadians had been killed. Twenty Grenadian civilians died when U.S. planes accidentally bombed the mental-ward wing of Grenada's hospital, which stood next to army headquarters at Fort Rupert on a hill overlooking St. George's.

At the time of the invasion, Defense Department officials said that U.S. troops would leave the island "within a week," turning peacekeeping operations over to a multilateral force from the other Caribbean islands. Some 2,300 U.S. troops were withdrawn during the first week of November, and 1,500 more left before Thanksgiving. Under the 60-day limit of the War Powers Act (*see* special report, page 549), all combat units were to be recalled by December 23 unless Congress specifically authorized an extended presence. Early in November, the House of Representatives adopted a resolution declaring that the president was legally bound to withdraw U.S. forces by the deadline. Similar language passed the Senate but later was killed. Congress adjourned for the year on November 18, leaving the question up in the air.

On December 9, President Reagan told congressional leaders that U.S. troops in Grenada had been reduced to 2,700, but he said, "it is not possible to predict" when all U.S. military forces would be withdrawn. The following day, however, the White House announced that the remaining combat forces and most of the support units would depart Grenada by December 15, leaving behind a contingent of 300 military police, technicians, and other backup troops.

Rehabilitation Process. The immediate post-invasion task was to restore order and to repair damaged roads, buildings, and other facilities. During the first day of fighting, U.S. troops managed to locate the island's governor-general, Sir Paul Scoon, the representative of the queen of England who is head of the Grenadian state under the island's constitution. Scoon, the only constitutional authority left on the island, was given the job of setting up an interim government, enlisting nonpolitical Grenadians overseas and some on the island who had no connection with the Bishop government or with the group that overthrew him.

The interim government got off to a shaky start when Alister McIntyre, a ranking Grenadian official of the United Nations who had been tapped as interim prime minister, was unable to take the post for health reasons. In early December, a British legal expert, seconded by the British Commonwealth nations to act as adviser to Scoon and the interim government, suddenly resigned, saying, "There is no adequate and effective civil government in Grenada."

Meanwhile, the U.S. and Caribbean occupying forces were trying to identify and detain surviving members of the former government, officers of the 2,000-man Grenadian army, mem-

After separate landings by air and sea, U.S. troops fanned out, above, in search of Grenadian resisters and a Cuban force of as many as 1,200 military advisers and armed construction workers. With the help of air strikes and artillery fire, below, the advancing Americans took control of St. George's, the capital, and key outlying positions. As the fighting dwindled, the last "pockets of resistance" took hold in the mountainous central region of the island.

By October 28, according to U.S. military sources, 638 Cubans and 17 Grenadians, as above, had been taken prisoner. Another 36 of the opposition force were reported killed; 56 were wounded.

A major objective of ''Operation Urgent Fury,'' as the U.S. military action was dubbed, was to ensure the safety of some 500 American students at the St. George's University School of Medicine. The evacuation, above, was made from Point Salínes on the second and third days of the operation. For the students, return to home soil, below, was cause for giving thanks. Meanwhile, whole warehouses of Soviet-made weapons, ammunition, and other equipment were being found on Grenada.

bers of Bishop's political party (the New Jewel Movement), and others who might pose a security threat. Among those who were taken into custody were Coard, leader of the coup against Bishop, and General Austin, chief of the army. Most of the Soviet, Cuban, and other communist-country nationals were evacuated from Grenada in the first two weeks of occupation, but the chargé d'affaires at the Cuban embassy stayed on until early December.

World Response. Initial reaction to the intervention from other countries was highly critical. After the United States vetoed a UN Security Council resolution condemning the invasion, the General Assembly voted 108 to 9, with 27 abstentions, for a resolution that "deeply deplored" the invasion and called it a "flagrant violation of international law." In a move that took Washington by surprise, British Prime Minister Margaret Thatcher publicly criticized the U.S. action.

Within the United States, however, there was substantial support for the initiative. Public opinion polls showed that a majority of Americans approved of the intervention and that President Reagan's popularity may actually have been bolstered by it. Congressional response was mild.

In the weeks that followed, international reaction appeared to soften, especially as it became evident that the Soviet Union and Cuba had been building a formidable military presence in Grenada and that the people of Grenada, in general, seemed to welcome the arrival of U.S. troops. (At the same time, few Grenadians were in favor of a permanent or long-term foreign presence.)

U.S. troops discovered large caches of weapons, ammunition, and other military supplies seemingly out of proportion to the requirements of Grenada's small army. Captured documents showed that secret agreements between Grenada and Cuba, the Soviet Union, and North Korea covered the delivery of arms and supplies through the end of 1985. They included the supply of 3,000 AK47 assault rifles from the USSR; 1,000 AK47s from North Korea; 2,500 used Soviet carbines; 7,000 mines; 15,000 grenades; 1,000 pistols; 30 sniper rifles; and 74 rocket-propelled grenade launchers.

The invasion drove a deep rift between the English-speaking members of the Organization of American States (OAS), most of whom had participated in the action, and the Latin American members, to whom the principle of nonintervention is the foundation of the OAS Charter. At the OAS' General Assembly in November, numerous speeches condemned the invasion, but no move was made to bring a formal resolution of censure against the United States or the Caribbean countries who had initiated the action.

News Blackout. There was, however, major controversy over the U.S. administration's handling of reporting of the intervention. The White House turned most of the news management over to the Pentagon. U.S. reporters and cameramen were not permitted to accompany troops when they landed on Grenada. A group of newsmen who tried to slip ashore in a

Sygma

Gen. Hudson Austin, commander of the Grenadian army, headed the Revolutionary Military Council that seized power from Prime Minister Bishop. Austin was captured October 30 in southeastern Grenada. He was to be held in U.S. custody until the naming of a new government.

rented fishing boat was picked up and held overnight on a nearby U.S. warship, while aircraft carrying newsmen were warned away by U.S. fighter planes. For three days the only news of the action came from Pentagon briefers in Washington and on the nearby island of Barbados. Finally, on October 28, arrangements were made for a limited press pool from Barbados to visit the island, under close military supervision. The pool arrangements remained in effect for several days.

Background to the Crisis. Grenada, a British colony for more than two centuries, has been a thorn in the side of the United States virtually since it achieved independence in 1974. Its first post-independence prime minister was Sir Eric Gairy. Gairy's rule was harsh, and opposition leaders were intimidated, beaten, and sometimes killed by a band of thugs known as the "Mongoose Gang."

Gairy was ousted in March 1979 by Maurice Bishop, the head of a group of 40 members of the New Jewel Movement. ("Jewel" is an acronym that stands for Joint Effort for Welfare, Education, and Liberty.) Bishop, a moderate socialist, quickly developed close ties to Cuba and the Soviet Union, to the distress of the U.S. government.

Washington's concern focused on a new international airport, with a 9,000-ft (2 743-m) runway, being constructed at Point Salines with Cuban technical and financial assistance. U.S. officials, including President Reagan, repeatedly charged that the airport was intended for use as a forward base by Cuban MiG fighter planes and as a refueling stop for cargo aircraft ferrying war materiel from the Soviet bloc to Central America. Bishop steadfastly insisted that the airport was necessary for the development of tourism, potentially an important source of foreign exchange for the poor island.

In a May 1983 visit to the United States, Bishop met with William Clark, then President Reagan's national security adviser, and Kenneth Dam, undersecretary of state, to assure them that Grenada wanted improved relations. After the visit Bishop seemed to soften his anti-U.S. rhetoric, and it was apparently his moderate stance that led to his downfall.

U.S. Presence in Grenada. Even as the United States began to phase out its combat units in Grenada, it became apparent that the Reagan administration intended to build a long-term U.S. presence on the island. During the first month of occupation, Washington earmarked $18.4 million for emergency assistance to the island, an amount nearly equal to all Cuban and Soviet aid during 1982. By late November, plans had been formulated for an additional allotment of $30 million.

The Peace Corps sent doctors and teachers to replace the Cubans who had staffed Grenada's schools and its sole hospital since 1979. The American Newspaper Publishers Association sent equipment to help restart the island's newspaper, suppressed during the Bishop regime. And, with White House assurances that Grenada would be included in duty-free privileges under the Caribbean Basin Initiative, U.S. businessmen flocked to the island seeking investment opportunities.

200 Years of Air & Space Flight

On Nov. 21, 1783, a massive hot-air balloon built by the French brothers Joseph and Jacques-Étienne Montgolfier rose slowly from the Bois de Boulogne outside Paris. Made of blue cotton cloth with gold embroidery, the *montgolfière* carried a basket. Inside the basket were scientist Pilâtre de Rozier and his friend, the Marquis d'Arlandes. For 25 minutes the two passengers enjoyed a view of the French capital from 300 ft (91 m) up. It was the first free manned flight in history.

On Jan. 3, 1983, U.S. President Ronald Reagan signed a proclamation designating 1983 as the Bicentennial of Air and Space Flight. The document began with an account of that first Paris balloon adventure and continued with the following:

> This epochal flight fulfilled mankind's desire, as old as the myth of Icarus, to become airborne. But it was also something more than the fulfillment of a dream. Montgolfier's achievement was a concrete demonstration of the power of technological know-how when coupled with the yearnings of the human spirit. For the first time, man had freed not only his imagination but his physical self from the forces of gravity. With every advance, our imagination and knowledge have leaped forward—from Montgolfier to the Wright brothers, through the moon walks and the space shuttle.

> In the 200 years since that first flight, man's quest to understand the unknown has resulted in our ability to fly higher, faster, safer, and farther. We race the sun as we move from continent to continent in a matter of hours. We have vastly multiplied commerce and communication among far-flung

A replica of the first Montgolfier hot-air balloon was inflated on the Washington Mall as part of the Smithsonian Air and Space Museum's celebration of the bicentennial of flight.

Editor's Note: This report on the Bicentennial of Air and Space Flight was prepared under the guidance of Lawrence F. Mihlon. An internationally recognized authority on aviation, Mr. Mihlon is serving as the managing director of the U.S. Organizing Committee of the Bicentennial. He also is the producer of the film *Night Flight,* based on the popular book by Antoine de St. Exupery; the film is on permanent exhibition at the French Air Museum at Le Bourget.

On the back of its carrier, a Boeing 747, the U.S. space shuttle Enterprise *was on display at the Paris Air Show. The maiden flight of its sister ship,* Challenger, *was an official bicentennial event.*

peoples. We have flown 250 thousand miles to explore the surface of the moon, and, with this unprecedented triumph of spirit and technology, changed forever our view of the earth. She is a delicate blue jewel in the darkness of space.

President Reagan called on the government and the people to observe the occasion with "appropriate ceremonies and activities," adding "nothing displays the great deeds of which man is capable better than the history of flight." The United States joined with other countries in marking the event with air races, balloon rallies, exhibits, and seminars. The National Air and Space Museum at the Smithsonian Institution in Washington, DC, sponsored a series of commemorative exhibitions, multimedia shows, lectures, and demonstrations throughout 1983. President Reagan announced a new aviation education program. And the inaugural flight of the space shuttle *Challenger,* launched April 4, was officially designated a bicentennial event. On November 18, Congress earmarked funds for the climax of the U.S. celebrations, beginning June 24, 1984, the anniversary of the first U.S. manned flight, and ending on July 4, 1984, with the theme "Air and Space USA."

In France, meanwhile, the anniversary was observed at the 35th Paris Air Show, held in the spring at Le Bourget airport with flyovers of Paris, Bonn, Rome, and London by the U.S. space shuttle *Enterprise,* astride its 747 transporter; in reenactments of early Montgolfier balloon flights; in a special exhibit at the Grand Palais in Paris, "La part du rêve—de la montgolfière au satellite" (The Place of Dreams—from the balloon to the satellite); and with a variety of France's own balloon races and rallies.

According to French Prime Minister Pierre Mauroy, the history of flight has unified the peoples of the world in a spirit of common endeavor and shared adventure: "It was the whole of Paris that went to Le Bourget to welcome Lindbergh. It was all the countries of Latin America who wept over the five-day disappearance of Guillaumet over the Andes. It was the whole world which mourned the disappearance of Mermoz in the South Atlantic. And it was millions of TV viewers who watched...Armstrong and Aldrin on the moon."

Air and Space Chronology

Nov. 21, 1783. Pilâtre de Rozier and the Marquis d'Arlandes sail over Paris for 25 minutes in a Montgolfier balloon, beginning the age of manned flight.

June 24, 1784. At Baltimore, MD, 13-year-old Edward Warren soars aloft in a hot-air balloon built by Peter Carnes. "It was the first time a citizen of the United States had left the ground in a flying machine."

Jan. 9, 1793. Jean Blanchard makes the first free-flight U.S. balloon voyage, a 45-minute jaunt from Philadelphia to Gloucester county, NJ.

Sept. 20, 1898. In the first controlled flight of a motorized, lighter-than-air craft (balloon), Alberto Santos-Dumont of Brazil rudders over Paris rooftops and ascends to 1,500 ft (457 m).

July 2, 1900. Count Ferdinand von Zeppelin soars across the German-Swiss border in a 420-ft (128-m) aluminum-framed dirigible.

Dec. 17, 1903. Orville Wright completes the first successful trial of a heavier-than-air, engine-driven flyer at Kitty Hawk, NC. The plane travels 120 ft (37 m); Wilbur runs alongside.

Oct. 23, 1906. Alberto Santos-Dumont introduces powered airflight in Europe with a 197-ft (60-m) hop in a box-kite "aeromobile."

July 25, 1909. Louis Blériot of France makes an airborne crossing of the English Channel, from Calais to Dover, in a monoplane with a three-cylinder engine.

Jan. 26, 1911. Glenn H. Curtiss introduces the first practical seaplane, flown over San Diego Bay. A designer and flyer, Curtiss was a

Flight firsts: A plane awaits takeoff from Philadelphia on the first regular airmail run, May 1918. Igor Sikorsky gets the helicopter industry off the ground in his VS-300, September 1939. Amelia Earhart became the first woman to fly the Atlantic alone, May 20–21, 1932. The Boeing 707 jetliner revolutionized commercial air transport, beginning in 1959.

pioneer in airplane manufacturing and the "father of naval aviation."

Sept. 17–Dec. 10, 1911. Calbreath P. Rodgers survives 15 crashes to achieve the first U.S. transcontinental flight, from New York to Pasadena.

Jan. 1, 1914. Regularly scheduled air passenger service begins with a connection between St. Petersburg and Tampa, FL, in a Benoist flying boat. There was room for only one passenger.

May 15, 1918. The U.S. Post Office Department initiates regular air mail service between Washington, New York, and Philadelphia.

May 15–31, 1919. In a U.S. Navy Curtiss NC-4 seaplane, Lt. Cdr. A.C. Read makes the first transatlantic air crossing, from New York to Plymouth, England, with stops in Newfoundland, the Azores, and Portugal.

June 14–15, 1919. Capt. John Alcock and Lt. Arthur Whitten-Brown of the Royal Air Force complete the first nonstop transatlantic flight in a Vickers-Vimy biplane bomber.

May 2–3, 1923. U.S. army lieutenants John A. Macready and Oakley G. Kelly fly nonstop from New York to San Diego in a Fokker T-2 monoplane.

Sept. 28, 1924. Two of four Douglas World Cruiser biplanes land in Seattle, WA, completing the first around-the-world airplane trip. Flying time is 15 days, 11 hours, 7 minutes.

May 9, 1926. Lt. Cmdr. Richard E. Byrd flies over the North Pole in a Fokker trimotor plane.

May 20–21, 1927. Charles A. Lindbergh becomes the first person to cross the Atlantic alone, piloting the single-engine *Spirit of St. Louis* from New York to Paris in 33½ hours.

Nov. 28, 1929. Byrd crosses the South Pole.

June 23–July 1, 1933. Wiley Post makes the first solo flight around the world in a Lockheed Vega monoplane, the *Winnie Mae.* The trip takes 7 days, 18 hours, 49 minutes.

May 6, 1937. The German dirigible airship *Hindenburg* explodes and burns on landing at Lakehurst, NJ, effectively eliminating lighter-than-air ships from commercial aviation.

Aug. 27, 1939. The first gas turbine engine (jet) plane, the German Heinkel He-178, makes its maiden flight.

Oct. 14, 1947. Flying the rocket-powered Bell *XS-1,* U.S. Air Force Capt. Chuck Yeager becomes the first pilot to break the sound barrier, exceeding 762 mph (1 226 km/h).

May 2, 1952. British Overseas Airways inaugurates scheduled jetliner passenger service with the de Havilland *Comet.*

Oct. 4, 1957. The Soviet Union launches the earth satellite *Sputnik 1.*

Jan. 31, 1958. The United States sends its first earth satellite, *Explorer 1,* into orbit.

April 12, 1961. Soviet Cosmonaut Yuri A. Gagarin, in *Vostok 1,* becomes the first human space traveler, completing one earth orbit.

May 5, 1961. In the Mercury capsule *Freedom 1,* U.S. astronaut Alan B. Shepard, Jr., is rocketed into a suborbital trajectory over the Atlantic.

Feb. 20, 1962. Astronaut John H. Glenn, Jr., circles the earth three times in *Friendship 7.*

July 20, 1969. Astronauts Neil A. Armstrong and Edwin E. Aldrin, Jr., accomplish the first manned moon landing in the Apollo II lunar module *Eagle.* They walk on the surface for two hours.

April 19, 1971. The USSR launches the first orbiting space station, called *Salyut.*

July 17, 1975. U.S. and Soviet spacecraft are linked over the Atlantic in a joint Apollo-Soyuz earth orbital mission.

Jan. 21, 1976. The Anglo-French supersonic transport *Concorde* begins commercial flights.

Aug. 11–17, 1978. U.S. businessmen Ben Abruzzo, Maxie Anderson, and Larry Newman make the first transatlantic balloon flight.

April 12–14, 1981. The U.S. space shuttle *Colombia,* a reusable plane-like craft, is successfully launched and, 54 hours later, landed by astronauts John Young and Robert Crippen.

The age of manned space flight begins: Soviet cosmonaut Yuri Gagarin awaits lift-off in Vostok 1, *April 12, 1961.*

Novosti from Sovfoto

Education in America— Calls for Reform

Langley/"The Christian Science Monitor"

By Fred M. Hechinger

About the Author: Fred M. Hechinger, president of The New York Times Foundation, Inc. writes a weekly "About Education" column for the *Times*. A former education editor for the *Times* and other publications, as well as a past president of the Education Writers Association, he is the author/ coauthor of several books, including *Higher Learning in the Nation's Service* (1981). The recipient of numerous honors, Mr. Hechinger has taught at the City University of New York and at the New School for Social Research.

Suddenly, in the spring of 1983, the state of the schools in the United States appeared to be viewed as almost synonymous with the state of the nation. Within weeks, high-level commissions, President Ronald Reagan, and the contenders for the 1984 Democratic nomination for the presidency issued extensive reports on the deficiencies of public education and recommendations for reform. After years of general public apathy, the schools aroused concern and rose near the top of the national agenda.

What Had Gone Wrong? The National Commission on Excellence in Education, an 18-member panel appointed by Secretary of Education T. H. Bell and chaired by David P. Gardner, president of the University of Utah and president-elect of the University of California, charged that "the educational foundations of our society are presently being eroded by a rising tide of mediocrity that threatens our very future as a nation and a people." Entitled "A Nation at Risk: The Imperative for Educational Reform," the report charged that American students showed poorly in comparison with those of other industrial countries; that 23 million Americans are functionally illiterate; that achievements by high-school students on standardized tests today are lower than they were when Sputnik was launched by the Soviet Union in 1957; and that a high proportion of 17-year-olds are unable to draw intelligent conclusions from written material.

On June 30, 1983, President Ronald Reagan and Secretary of Education Terrel H. Bell (right, holding banner) addressed a forum at Pioneer High School in Whittier, CA. The recommendations of the National Commission on Excellence in Education were the topic of discussion.

The commission found that secondary school course contents have been "homogenized, diluted, and diffused to the point that they no longer have a central purpose." In such a "cafeteria-style" system, "the appetizers and desserts can easily be mistaken for the main courses." For instance, while calculus is available in schools enrolling about 60% of all students, only 6% complete it. Given excessive options to take elective courses, many students avoid the hard subjects, such as mathematics, science, and foreign languages.

In answer to widespread public dissatisfaction over students' accomplishments, minimum competency tests are now required by 37 states. But the commission considered many of the tests too easy. Perhaps most serious, the quality of teaching has declined, as many teachers are drawn from the bottom quarter of their college class. Since the average teacher's salary after 12 years in the classroom is only $17,000, it is difficult to attract able and ambitious young people to the profession.

Another important report, entitled "Making the Grade," by a task force of the Twentieth Century Fund, diagnosed some of the same shortcomings but, unlike the Commission on Excellence which spoke mainly to the states, localities, parents, and students, addressed itself to the political leadership in Washington. If the threat to the nation is to be averted, it warned, federal leadership must play a key role. In calling for larger federal subsidies, the task force said that "good teachers are as valuable to the nation as new tanks or fighter planes or a new highway."

Joining in both the criticism of the schools' performance and in the call for reform, a National Task Force on Education for Economic Growth, established by the Education Commission of the States and headed by Gov. James B. Hunt of North Carolina, said the cause of the problem is that "we have expected too little of our schools over the past two decades—and we have gotten too little. The result is that our schools are not doing an adequate job for today's requirements in the workplace, much less tomorrow's.'' The Carnegie Foundation for the Advancement of Teaching, directed by its president, Ernest L. Boyer, took a hard look at the high schools. It recommended improved teaching of English, adoption of a ''core curriculum'' for all students, reform of teacher-training programs, greater salaries and autonomy for teachers, and mandatory community service for students.

In large part, the schools are the victims of their own success. The past three decades have seen unprecedented growth in enrollments (until a decline in the number of children began in the early 1970s) and in the commitment to equality of opportunity. The post-World War II baby boom led to a phenomenal increase in the number of school-age youngsters. The end of school segregation in the wake of the historic 1954 ruling by the U.S. Supreme Court and the victories of the civil-rights movement opened up educational opportunities to large numbers of minority youngsters who previously had been neglected and shunted aside. Amid all the criticisms of the schools, it should be noted that nearly 80% of the nation's school-age population now graduates from high school, far more than in most other countries.

Such all-inclusiveness creates problems. In order for the schools to accommodate all, educational quality has suffered. Great numbers of youngsters from severely deprived home backgrounds needed much remedial attention. Substantial efforts were made, particularly through federal subsidies provided under the terms of the Elementary and Secondary Education Act of 1965 and Project Head Start. Nevertheless, when so great a mass, with such widely divergent abilities, suddenly arrives in school, averages suffer. Numbers, however, are not alone to blame. The schools were also the victims of forces beyond their control which undermined quality controls in every sector of society, and undermined them in education at the very moment when substantial improvement seemed on the way.

© Fredrik D. Bodin/Picture Group

Strikes by teachers—with wages a main issue—have become a common occurrence in school districts across the United States. There is current widespread agreement that teachers' salaries should be increased.

H. Armstrong Roberts

Language labs seek to familiarize students with pronunciation techniques. For a high-school student planning to attend college, the National Commission on Excellence in Education encourages two years of foreign-language study.

The 1950s had, in fact, seen the beginnings of a strong education-reform movement. The launching of Sputnik led President Dwight D. Eisenhower to sponsor federal legislation to improve education. The National Defense Education Act of 1958 underwrote a drive for excellence in science, mathematics, and foreign-language teaching. At the same time, reform proposals by the late James Bryant Conant, a former president of Harvard University, in his book, *The American High School Today,* swept the country. His recommendations for tougher requirements in the traditional academic subjects were adopted throughout the nation. Noted university scientists descended from their ivory towers to help improve the high-school curriculum.

The movement, unfortunately, proved short-lived. The youth rebellion, aided by radical adults, which began with a 1964 uprising at Berkeley, led to an ideological counterrevolution against academic requirements, scuttled many quality controls, such as grading of students' work, and generally subscribed to an extreme egalitarianism that considered quality incompatible with equality. What counted was what students considered relevant; as they chose what they wanted to study, every subject came to be considered equal to every other. It hardly was surprising that individual achievements, as well as Scholastic Aptitude Test (SAT) scores, went into steep decline.

During the same period, dramatically higher enrollments caused a serious teacher shortage. Schools had to hire many teachers who were ill-prepared in general and to use them to teach subjects in which they were not qualified at all. Although educators were to blame for some of the decline in quality, it is misleading to diagnose what has gone wrong in the schools without taking a close look at dominant trends in the society at large. The schools, contrary to popular wishful thinking, do not shape the country's ways; they reflect them. The period of low scholastic efforts and achievements coincides with a similar downhill slide in every other sector—in domestic industrial output, international competition, productivity, and overall quality controls. Deficient performance in the nation's classrooms often was equaled by similar laxity in executive suites and on assembly lines. The growing need for remedial instruction in the schools, to make up for what should have been mastered at an earlier age, seemed part of the same phenomenon as the recall of defective manufactured products.

Change and Reform. More important than criticism of past errors, however, is the renewed drive to bring about change and reform. It began in early 1983 with a meeting called jointly by Dr. David Hamburg, the new president of the Carnegie Corporation of New York, and Governor Hunt. As some 50 high-level persons in politics, business, labor, education, and science met to consider the need for action, Sen. Paul Tsongas (D-MA) said: ''There is no reason why 1983 can't be the breakthrough year to make the United States competitive again.'' By May, the task force that grew out of the meeting called on schools and business leaders to develop partnerships to bring about education reform, urged governors and state education leaders to develop action plans to boost the quality

Although "no homework" has long been a favorite cry at the end of the school day, recent calls for reform include more away–from–school study.

H. Armstrong Roberts

© Fredrik D. Bodin/Picture Group

In seeking to cut down leisure time, some experts even urge longer school hours and a school year of 20–40 more days.

of education from kindergarten through high school, and recommended a hard look at the quality of the teaching staffs.

Both Governor Hunt's task force and the Commission on Excellence urged a return to firm, explicit, and demanding requirements in discipline, attendance, and homework. Most of the current reform proposals denounce past policies of promoting pupils from grade to grade merely on the basis of age, instead of requiring proof of satisfactory achievements. The Commission on Excellence calls for a minimum in the Five New Basics—four years of English, three years of mathematics, three years of science, three years of social studies, and half a year of computer science. It also recommends two years in a foreign language in high school for those intending to go to college. At the same time, it urges colleges to raise their admissions requirements as a way of putting continuing pressure on the schools. Perhaps most radical, the commission would like to see the school day lengthened to seven hours from its present five; and the school year to between 200 and 220 days from its present average of 180.

The issue that has caught the attention of the public and the policy-makers more than any other is the question of how to get better teachers. This is, of course, as it should be since education reform depends on the quality of the teaching staff. If it is a natural issue, it is, however, also most controversial. While there is virtually universal agreement that the roadblock to attracting and keeping better teachers is the low pay scale and the rigidly confining ceiling, there is far less agreement on ways of removing that obstacle. Merit pay for outstanding teachers is the proposal that has been given most public attention, and has become one of President Reagan's favorite topics. Yet, it is also the proposal most suspect among teachers themselves. Who, they ask, determines what constitutes special merit? What is to prevent abuse by administrators who either might play favorites or would be tempted to reward, not the ablest, but the most docile teachers? One strategy to get around those objections is the creation of a new career slot, usually dubbed "master teachers." This new position would not be based on seniority or particularly meritorious service, but rather as remuneration for different functions, such as training other teachers or organizing teaching teams. Although a master teaching proposal, allowing incentive payments for certain teachers and put forward by Gov. Lamar Alexander of Tennessee, was defeated narrowly in the state senate, the concept remains alive and is likely to become part of the total plan to improve teaching conditions. Other parts of the package probably will have to include an upgrading of the salary scale for all teachers in many communities. In addition, several states now require new teachers to take competency examinations before they can enter the classroom.

Since mathematics and science are hardest hit by the teacher shortage, the U.S. House of Representatives passed and the Senate considered in 1983 a bill authorizing emergency funding for math, science, and foreign-language programs in the schools. In terms of math and science, some proposals, including that by the Commission on Excellence, urge differential pay in these fields. The argument is that, because science and mathematics teaching faces direct competition from high-paying industrial jobs, special considerations are essential and justifiable, as the commission put it, on the theory that professional pay must be "market-sensitive." Others disagree. They say that to single out teachers in some subjects would disturb personal relationships among colleagues in the same school. Even many science teachers, who would stand to benefit, are opposed, saying that it matters to them how their fellow-teachers in the humanities and arts would feel. Or, as Albert Shanker, the president of the American Federation of Teachers and himself a former mathematics teacher, has put it: "Mathematics and science is not enough. . . . If you get better mathematics and science and everything else is sloppy, it won't work."

Whatever the solution, and it probably will turn out to be a stitching together of parts from a variety of proposals, it appears certain that improvement of the condition of teaching —better salaries, more flexible careers, better school discipline, greater public recognition, and new opportunities for teachers to work part-time with business, industry, and university laboratories—will be part of the foundation for the coming school reforms.

But about the nature of that reform there remains much uncertainty and disagreement. Harder work and more clearly defined requirements are sure to be part of the new trend; but many voices are being raised in warning against what appears to some a simplistic "get tough" flavor. If there is to be a seven-hour school day and an increased load of homework, too, some observers ask, when will youngsters have any time to pursue important nonschool interests?; when will they be able to let their imagination roam? "You have to motivate, you have to attract, you can't bludgeon" says Anthony J. Alvarado who as the new chancellor of the New York City schools heads the country's biggest school system.

The Twentieth Century Fund's report, expressing similar concern, suggests that some youngsters who are failing in their

Mathematics and science are areas of prime concern. Three years of high-school courses in each is being recommended; higher pay for teachers of these subjects is being debated.

Dr. John I. Goodlad, an educator for 40 years, believes in a restructuring of the school systems. His report, "A Place Called School," based on a $4 million study, was issued in 1983.

present school environment might not need more toughness but a more congenial setting, possibly through the creation of small public academies where they will get personal attention. In addition, the report stressed the importance of "the primacy of English"—the need for all non-English speaking children and youths to be inducted into the common language as rapidly as possible.

While many of the prescriptions for better schools have a traditional flavor, there are those who believe that the proposed changes are not drastic enough. John I. Goodlad, former dean of the Graduate School of Education at the University of California, Los Angeles, who has studied the schools for eight years and probably has visited more classrooms than any other observer, warns that a little tinkering will not be enough. He wants the power for change to move from the bureaucracy to the schoolhouse and classroom, while also giving greater responsibility, including some teaching, to the abler students. And Theodore R. Sizer, former dean of the Graduate School of Education at Harvard, who also heads a major study of the nation's high schools, believes that, despite current rhetoric about school improvement, no serious change will take place unless the structure of the schools is revamped. Schools, he says, must set themselves simpler, better-defined goals; students entering high schools with deficiencies in reading, writing, and math should concentrate on those subjects exclusively until they master them; skills of reasoning, imagining, analyzing, and synthesizing must become the core of high-school work. The goal ought to be for students to teach themselves, Mr. Sizer believes, instead of "being delivered a service." Today, "the torrent of facts poured over them is overwhelming," he charges. Like Mr. Goodlad, he believes that, if schools are to respond properly to the different ways students learn, teachers must have control over schedules and programs. Good teachers, he says, value their autonomy.

What emerges from all the ferment is that change is sure to come, even if the form of that change is far from certain. Somewhat ironically, just as the outcry about the schools' failure is loudest, the schools have, in fact, begun to improve their performance in the past three to five years. Test scores in virtually every area, from reading to college aptitude, have started to improve. Discipline in many schools is tighter. Young people are working harder and are more career conscious. The computer is playing an increasingly important part in teaching and learning.

Yet, the public perception, including that expressed by commissions, task forces, and politicians, is lagging behind the encouraging reality. Many experts say that this is the normal way of things and that the perception is bound to catch up with favorable changes already taking place; but most experts also warn that the new public awareness should not be allowed to pass; that the opportunity for far-reaching school reform must not be wasted; and that failure to act now could mean that the moment will pass and disillusionment will replace today's great hopes and expectations.

Photo Trends

Soviet diplomats expelled from France for spying leave the Paris embassy April 5.

By Lyman B. Kirkpatrick, Jr.

On Sept. 4, 1983, three days after a South Korean commercial airliner had been shot down over strategic Soviet territory, Soviet Col. Gen. Semyon Romanov suggested that the Korean jet had been mistaken for a U.S. spy plane. Later that day, the U.S. government revealed that an RC-135 reconnaissance plane indeed had been in the general vicinity (but over international waters) monitoring Soviet transmissions.

Earlier in the year, on April 5, the government of France announced that it was expelling 47 Soviet diplomats, journalists, and trade officials for having "engaged in a systematic search on French territory for technical and scientific information, particularly in the military area"—in other words, for spying.

In U.S. district court in San Francisco, employees of Hitachi, Japan's third largest computer manufacturer, pleaded guilty February 8 to having conspired to steal confidential information from International Business Machines Corp. (IBM). Three other men had been indicted on similar charges in June 1982, and a third case was pending against Mitsubishi Electric Corp., also for stealing trade secrets from IBM.

About the Author: Lyman B. Kirkpatrick, Jr., is professor emeritus of political science at Brown University. He served in the U.S. Central Intelligence Agency from 1945 to 1965, rising to executive director in 1962. He has written several books on U.S. intelligence and security, including *The Real CIA* (1968), *Captains Without Eyes: Major Intelligence Failures in World War II* (1969), and *The U.S. Intelligence Community: Foreign Policy and Domestic Activities* (1973).

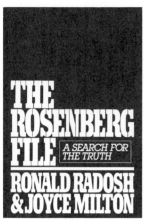

Based on interviews and government files obtained under the Freedom of Information Act, a new book concluded that Julius Rosenberg had indeed given U.S. atomic secrets to the Soviet Union in the 1940s. Wife Ethel, however, was found not to be deeply involved.

Espionage, be it for strategic military information or high-tech industrial secrets, has become a topic of media coverage as perhaps never before—newspaper accounts of diplomatic expulsions appear regularly; in an October cover story, *Newsweek* reported that "the cloaks and daggers have been brought out of cold storage" at the CIA; and a major motion picture (*Daniel*) and controversial new book (*The Rosenberg File*) renewed interest in the famous 1950s spy case. While spying of course has a long history, global intelligence-gathering has entered a new era of greatly expanded and highly sophisticated activity. For every case that is uncovered and reported in the media, untold numbers carry on undetected.

Espionage, Intelligence, and Politics. The 1980s have seen no surcease of international wars, as flare points throughout the world have erupted into combat. Some are prolonged wars, such as that between Iran and Iraq, while others are sharp, quick engagements which the warring parties are anxious to end out of fear of heavy economic and combat losses.

As the first third of the 1980s passes into history, espionage provides an accurate barometer of the flare points between peoples and blocs of nations, and of the deteriorating relations between the United States and the Soviet Union and their respective allies. It is a time in which the superpowers have expanded all phases of their intelligence operations, while other nations have increased their more moderate regional coverage. It is an era in which the electronic revolution has had a major impact on intelligence collection and production, but the human factor remains far from obsolete; human beings still have to put listening devices in place and interpret the findings. More and more scholars hold key posts in intelligence services, as do scientists, engineers, and technicians.

'SUCH A FALSE, VILE, BASE, MALICIOUS, DEFAMATORY SLANDER, MONSIEUR! WHAT COOKIES?'

But the spy is far from extinct, as the more sophisticated services recognize that the most secret information can be obtained only by one person from another.

Very little information is made public by the United States or any other country about its intelligence operations; the most taboo area is espionage per se. While it is very rare for any nation to admit that it engages in espionage, the number of arrests, diplomatic expulsions, trials, imprisonments, and even executions throughout the world indicates that it is very much a part of 20th-century international affairs. In 1982 some 49 Soviet diplomats (intelligence operatives) were expelled from foreign countries, compared with 17 in 1981. European nations expelled 23, followed by the Western Hemisphere with 19, and Asia and the Pacific with 7. The group of 47 expelled by France in April 1983 was said to include the "resident," or chief of the Committee Soviet State Security Activities in France. This was the third large group of Russians to be expelled by a foreign government in 12 years. In 1971 the British asked 105 to leave; in 1980 Pakistan sent home 100.

Mass expulsions are less frequent than individual or "case" expulsions, when a single agent or team of operatives is declared *persona non grata*. In 1978 three Soviet agents working out of the United Nations in New York tried to "buy" a U.S. Navy officer; they were expelled to focus world attention on a blatant misuse of the institution of the UN. In 1982, Maj. Gen. Vasily I. Chitov, the senior military officer at the Soviet embassy in Washington, was taken into custody by the FBI after a high-speed car chase; he was carrying U.S. government classified documents. The official had been observed removing a package from a "dead drop"—a prearranged spot in Rock Creek Park (a recreation area in a residential neighborhood) where his source had left the package of papers in the crotch of a tree. Chitov was promptly expelled from the country.

Many governments choose not to publicize the expulsion of Soviet officials, perhaps on the assumption that it is best not to embarrass the Kremlin in the international arena. Evidence strongly suggests, however, that the Soviets do not concern themselves with world opinion as much as with the actual material their agents retrieve. Thus, they seem to look upon espionage as a valid means for collecting desired information and correctly assume that many other nations see things the same way rather than follow any moral principles or standards of conduct.

The size and activities of U.S. intelligence services remain a well-kept secret. Like all other federal government activities, they are funded by appropriation bills passed by Congress. However, only the benign activities of these services—such as training, research, and travel—are included in the budget made public. The more sensitive activities are included in classified budgets and buried under other categories. These appropriations are reviewed in hearings held in secret and are known only to members of the intelligence committees of the Congress. If legislation is needed, it is handled by both houses in a manner appropriate to the degree of sensitivity.

"San Francisco Examiner"

James Durward Harper, Jr., a California computer engineer, was arrested by the FBI on October 15 for selling U.S. missile secrets to Poland. Harper allegedly received $250,000 for taking classified documents to Warsaw in 1980. According to the FBI, Soviet KGB agents then were flown in to review the material.

CIA

Tass from Sovfoto

U.S. and Soviet spy chiefs: William J. Casey, left, was named director of the Central Intelligence Agency (CIA) in 1980, after managing Ronald Reagan's presidential campaign. Viktor M. Cherbikov, right, was made head of the State Security Committee (KGB) in late 1982; he had risen through the ranks during Yuri Andropov's tenure as KGB chief (1967–82).

Espionage is of course only one form of intelligence-gathering. Both the United States and Soviet Union use reconnaissance satellites to observe key installations in each other's territory. U.S. photographic reconnaissance satellites constitute a primary source of military intelligence. From altitudes of 150 mi (241 km), photographs can be produced in sufficient detail to reveal the faces of people and the numbers on motor vehicle license plates. The U.S. K-11 satellite produces such precise maps that photos of Iran enable the identification of individual mullahs (Muslim clerics). Landsat 4, a U.S. earth-resources satellite, photographs wildlife habitats from 438 mi (705 km) in space. The increased intelligence capacity of satellites has resulted from the replacement of photographic film with more sensitive electronic devices, the development of new optical instruments, and the extension of camera focal length by a system of mirrors.

In August 1981, the United States asked China and the Soviet Union to convey the deep concern of the U.S. government to North Korea over the firing of a surface-to-air missile at a U.S. SR-71 reconnaissance aircraft south of the demilitarized zone separating North and South Korea. The mission of the aircraft was to photograph military installations from altitudes of up to 90,000 ft (27 432 m), while still remaining in international airspace. The plane can fly more than 2,000 mi (3 219 km) and photograph 100,000 sq mi (260 000 km^2) in one hour. The photographs are of sufficient quality to enable the precise description of any military equipment on the ground.

(*Continued on page 54*)

AN INTERNATIONAL SYNOPSIS

Afghanistan. The Soviet invasion of Afghanistan in December 1979 established Peshawar, a headquarters for many Afghan rebel groups, as the espionage center of the area. The city today teems with Russian agents; one person who was apprehended reported 50 Soviet spy cells in the refugee camps.

Bangladesh. Two Soviet embassy attachés were expelled after being arrested while attempting to burn 588 roles of film on a roadside.

Canada. In May 1983, the Canadian government introduced legislation to set up a clandestine intelligence service, subject to judicial review; it would take over certain functions from the Royal Canadian Mounted Police. In September, two Soviet trade officials were sent home after the Security Service of the Royal Canadian Mounted Police discovered their efforts to purchase high-technology secrets.

Costa Rica. On Nov. 11, 1982, Costa Rican authorities ordered 17 Soviet diplomats to leave the country and canceled the visas of two Soviet couriers who regularly traveled between Costa Rica and Nicaragua.

France. One of the highest-ranking military officers ever to be indicted on espionage charges was Gen. Heinz Bernhart Zorn, chief of staff of the East German Air Force until 1977; he was arrested in Lille, France, while carrying papers on French tanks and antitank weapons.

Germany. The federal prosecutor's office in Karlsrühe, West Germany, reported the arrest on Nov. 10, 1980, of three individuals who had been charged with spying for East Germany. Those apprehended were Walter Erb, 38, an engineer and trade-union official; Eberhard Lippold, 49, a musicologist; and Jürgen Kreisser, 36, who was suspected of passing information on the West Berlin Working Group For Human Rights, which investigates alleged violations of human rights in East Germany. In August 1980, Henryk Dimski, 48, confessed to West German police in Bonn that he had sent to the Polish intelligence service in Warsaw reports on secret documents and on high-ranking visitors to the U.S. embassy in Bonn.

A mid-1982 report issued by the Federal Office for the Protection of the Constitution (BFV) of the Bonn government stated that in 1981 about 109 Soviets in West Germany and Berlin were considered active intelligence officers and 77 more were suspect. In addition, at the Soviet embassy in Bonn, intelligence operatives were said to number 31, including the staff of the military attaché. There also were six in the trade office in Cologne, 13 in the Hamburg Consulate General, and 50 in the Soviet military missions in Baden-Baden, Buende, and Frankfurt. Other intelligence operatives were said to include a Soviet press correspondent and a SOVEXPORTFILM employee.

Great Britain. With the death of Anthony Blount in London in 1983, one of the most notorious Soviet espionage networks in modern British history was left with only one survivor, H. A. R. Philby, who had defected to the Soviet Union in 1963.

In December 1982, Hugh Hambleton, a former professor at the London School of Economics and at Laval University in Quebec, was sentenced to ten years in prison by a London court for giving NATO secrets to a Soviet agent. At one point he claimed to have been a double-agent working for Canada and France as well as the USSR. At trial, however, he admitted only to selecting documents to give to the Soviets.

In summer 1982, Geoffrey A. Prime, a British linguistics expert who had worked for the Government Communications Headquarters at Cheltenham, was arrested and charged with passing classified information to the Soviet Union. He was turned in by his wife, to whom he had confessed working for the Russians for 14 years. When arrested, Prime revealed that he had identified to the Soviets the targets of British and U.S. surveillance and had revealed which of their codes had been broken. His sentence was 35 years in prison for espionage, plus three years for sexual offenses against small girls.

Britain's Geoffrey Prime turned over secrets to the Soviets.

Lea/Spooner/Gamma-Liaison

A radar station at Wakkanai, northern Japan, tracked the Korean Airlines 747 shot down by a Soviet fighter September 1.

On Feb. 27, 1982, V. F. Zadneprovsky, an officer in the Soviet trade delegation in London, was apprehended while attempting to obtain classified information and was expelled. The Soviet naval attaché, Captain Anatoly Zotov, was charged with attempting to establish an agent network to obtain military secrets, and was expelled Dec. 5, 1982.

Indonesia. In February 1982, Indonesia expelled Lt. Col. Serge Y. Yegorov, assistant military attaché in Jakarta, for espionage. Yegorov was arrested with a camera and film he had received from an Indonesian military officer. Also expelled in February was a GRU (main Soviet military intelligence organization) officer, Aleksandr Firenko, who operated under the cover of an AEROFLOT representative. An embassy attaché charged with trying to prevent Firenko's arrest also was expelled.

Israel. A 30-year-old Arab doctor, a resident of Ramallah in the Israeli-occupied West Bank, was arrested in October 1980 as a Soviet spy. The Israeli report said that he had been recruited by Palestinians while studying medicine in the Soviet Union. On returning to Ramallah, he was instructed by Soviet intelligence to carry out missions in Israel and the occupied areas, transmitting information through the Soviet embassy in Amman, Jordan.

Italy. An advanced radar system slated for use by NATO countries and the United States was the object of a plot in November 1980 by nine men in Rome who hoped to sell the blueprints to the Soviet Union; an Italian navy captain who was asked to act as a middleman revealed the plot to the police, who arrested the conspirators. Press reports on Dec. 7, 1982, said an unidentified Soviet diplomat had been expelled for espionage. On Dec. 17, 1982, Lt. Col. Ivan Khellag, assistant Soviet military attaché in Rome, was expelled for attempting to obtain NATO defense plans.

Japan. In what Japanese newspapers called the worst spy scandal since World War II, the Soviet military attaché, Col. Yuri N. Kozlov, refused to appear before police and left for Moscow in January 1980. His departure followed that of Maj. Gen. Pyotr I. Rybalkin, who vacated his post in November 1978. Both were involved in obtaining top-secret information on the military situation in China from Maj. Gen. Yukihisa Mayanaga of Japan's Self-Defense Force.

Stanislav A. Levchenko, who worked under the cover of the foreign affairs magazine *Novoye Vremye* (New Times) in Tokyo in the 1970s, labeled Japan "a paradise for spies." Among the agents he claimed as contacts in the Japanese security services were Socialist politicians and the head of the Japan-Soviet friendship association.

Norway. Norway expelled Oleg Dokudovskiy and Yevgeniy Vopilovskiy of the Soviet trade mission after they tried to bribe employees of companies working on an F-16 aircraft project and tried to set up front companies to export high-tech U.S. products to the USSR.

Portugal. On Jan. 22, 1982, Press Counselor Yuri Babyants and Attaché Mikhail Morosov were asked to leave Lisbon, presumably for attempted espionage. This was followed by a request from the government that the Soviet, Polish, and East German embassies reduce their staffs by 30%; the Portuguese specifically named the 12 officials who were to leave.

Singapore. Two Soviets were expelled from Singapore on Feb. 22, 1982: Anatoly Larkin, second secretary and press attaché at the Soviet embassy, was accused of representing himself as a Swedish journalist and trying to obtain sensitive military information from an army officer; and the marine superintendent overseeing repairs of Soviet merchant vessels at a local shipyard was charged with running an intelligence network since 1979.

Spain. On April 28, 1982, Director Vasiliy Fedorin and engineer Vladimir Tirtishnikov were expelled on espionage charges; both were GRU officers. Fedorin tried to infiltrate the Spanish air force and was attempting to obtain details from journalists and military personnel on U.S. weapons sold to Spain. Tirtishnikov was trying to recruit individuals in electronic companies working on industrial-security matters and military communications.

Sweden. In April 1982, Albert Liepa, Soviet vice-consul in Stockholm, left after being charged with trying to influence the Latvian exile community. On December 23, Yuriy Averine, the Soviet consul in Gothenburg, and Lt. Col. Piotr Skirokiy, assistant military attaché in the Soviet embassy in Stockholm, were declared *persona non grata* for espionage. Anatoly Kolyev, an official at the Soviet shipping registry in Gothenburg, also was charged. Together they allegedly made about 15 recruitment attempts on individuals working in advanced electronics and defense industries. In reporting on the case, the Swedish newspaper *Expressen* said that nearly 80 accredited Soviet diplomats in Sweden work for either the KGB or GRU.

Switzerland. In June 1983, Switzerland announced the arrest of Dieter Felix, 49, a former South African naval officer, and his wife, Ruth Gerhard. Felix confessed to spying for the Soviets since 1964, and Gerhard confessed to acting as a courier since 1970; they operated out of Zurich, collecting military intelligence on South Africa. On Aug. 4, 1982, the Swiss Justice Ministry announced that an assistant to the Soviet military attaché in Bern had been detained by police after meeting with an informant; he was found to possess incriminating documents. The same day, an employee of the Soviet consulate in Geneva was arrested after trying to persuade a Swiss citizen to seek a job in the foreign ministry. Both Soviet diplomats left the country. On Aug. 21, 1982, Leonid Barabonov, the AEROFLOT director in Geneva, left Switzerland "under suspicion of espionage." The Swiss police have reported 240 cases of espionage since 1948, most of them involving Soviet and Eastern-bloc citizens.

United States. Lt. Christopher M. Cooke, deputy commander of a Titan-2 missile-launch crew in Kansas in 1982, was court-martialed by the Air Force and charged with "passing vital national security information" to the Soviet Union. In return for an offer of immunity, Cooke acknowledged visiting the Soviet embassy in Washington and described the information he provided them. On Feb. 22, 1982, he was given an "other than honorable" discharge and released.

David H. Barnett, a former U.S. intelligence agency employee, was sentenced in January 1983 to 18 years in prison for selling sensitive information to the USSR.

In mid-October 1983, a 49-year-old computer engineer in California's "Silicon Valley," James Durward Harper, Jr., was arrested and charged with selling military secrets to Poland. In exchange for more than $250,000, Harper allegedly provided valuable data on ballistic missile research, which Warsaw then passed on to Soviet agents. The documents were described by the U.S. Defense Department as "extremely sensitive."

Soviet Ambassador Boris Pankin leaves an April 26 meeting with Sweden's Prime Minister Olof Palme after receiving an official protest for submarine violations of Swedish waters in 1982. An investigation panel cited at least 40 cases.

Svenskt/Pictorial Parade

Industrial Espionage. Despite the advent of space satellites and long-range sensors, industrial espionage as practiced by mere mortals became the most intense area of intelligence competition throughout the industrial world. Acquisition of scientific and technical information became a top priority not only for intelligence services but also for business organizations anxious to improve their competitive positions.

The advent of the computer opened a new arena for espionage. Perhaps nothing illustrates the vulnerability of the computer more graphically than FBI raids on the homes of young computer experts in 11 U.S. cities who had obtained unauthorized access into computer systems. One youngster admitted that he had managed to intercept and read a Defense Department computer, but had retained no information.

With computer courses now commonplace in most high schools in the United States and a requirement in many universities, expertise in the technology is becoming ordinary. This, in turn, is accelerating the need for greater security. The FBI and Defense Department have taken extensive measures to protect classified information: the FBI is spending $40.6 million to protect computers and cryptographic systems.

In private industry as well, extensive and expensive measures are being taken to prevent industrial espionage. Computers are placed in shielded rooms to prevent outside interception. Employees are subject to security investigations and warned against discussing company business except when explicitly authorized. Company property is placed under guard and watched by private investigators. Knowledge of corporate success or failure is carefully protected until made public.

Industrial espionage is not confined to information stored in computers. There is a constant effort to acquire controlled technology. This is well demonstrated by the quest for nuclear technology. Four nations which refuse to open their atomic facilities to international inspection are Argentina, India, Israel, and South Africa. Despite their unwillingness, the United States made 57 sales of nuclear material to them in a one-year period. More than 1,000 licenses have been approved for export of nuclear material to China.

In France industrial espionage apparently was a factor in the mysterious death of Lt. Col. Bernard Nut. In February 1983, Nut was reportedly killed by a double agent after he had advised the Italian police of the activities of Viktor Pronin, a KGB officer who worked under the cover of the Rome office of AEROFLOT. Nut had also exposed the activities of Patrick Gurrier, who was engaged in industrial espionage while posing as an archivist.

As the world's industrialized powers move into the high-tech age of supercomputers, elaborate satellite communications and defense systems, and nuclear energy—for peaceful purposes or otherwise—espionage seems destined to be affected in terms of both purpose and conduct. It will be used by governments and private concerns to obtain high-tech secrets, and it will make use of those secrets to become more efficient.

THE NEW HOME VIDEO

RCA

The videodisc player is one of several new electronic media that have revolutionized the use of the television.

By Jeffrey H. Hacker

"Hey, we just got a *television set*. Philco. Ten-inch screen! Come over and watch Uncle Miltie with us."

The year was 1949, or thereabout, and a remarkable new device was finding its way into the American home. By the end of that year, more than one million living rooms around the country were equipped with a TV. While there were still skeptics who called television "a passing fancy," there were millions of others who were "just waiting for the prices to come down." Those families lucky enough to own a set—with its hulking mahogany console and a screen the size of this page—were the envy of their neighborhoods. Friends, relatives, and passing acquaintances would visit in the evening to watch Milton Berle's *Texaco Star Theatre,* Ed Sullivan's *Toast of the Town,* or *Arthur Godfrey's Talent Scouts.*

In the ten years following World War II, watching television replaced going to the movies and listening to radio shows as the dominant leisure-time activity in the United States. By 1955 more than 30 million American households—nearly 65% —owned at least one set. Meanwhile, movie-theater attendance plummeted from 4.2 billion (U.S.) in 1945 to 2.5 billion in 1955; radio lost its big-name stars—and much of its audience—to the small screen.

About the Author: Jeffrey H. Hacker is not only editor of this annual but also serves as a free-lance writer and editor for other publications. In the latter capacity, he undertook an extensive study of the home-video market in 1983. Mr. Hacker has written three books for young adults—*Government Subsidy to Industry* (1982), *Franklin D. Roosevelt* (1983), and *Carl Sandburg* (1984).

During the first three decades of television in America, commercial broadcasting provided nearly all of the programming fare available on the home screen. From the start the medium was dominated by the three broadcast networks—ABC, CBS, and NBC. Primitive live broadcasts gave way to high-budget videotaped productions; TV sales and average viewing time climbed steadily; and advertiser spending grew by the billions. The dominance of the three networks went virtually unchallenged.

Then, in the latter part of the 1970s, things began to change. The emergence of a handful of new electronic media —cable and pay TV, videocassette recorders, videodisc players, and others—opened a new era in audiovisual entertainment and information delivery. Each of these systems requires the use of a conventional television screen, but each brings to it some new capability, kind of programming, or expanded viewing option. Those with foresight recognized early that the new "home video" * eventually would challenge broadcast television in the same way that TV had posed a threat to movies. Indeed, as the popularity of these new systems has proliferated, the conventional TV networks *and* Hollywood have been forced to rethink the future—and seriously.

* Editor's Note: The term "home video" is sometimes used to refer only to videocassettes and videodiscs. Here, as in many other sources, it refers to the entire range of new electronic media.

RCA

RCA

Courtesy of Warner Amex/QUBE

Home video hardware: RCA's top-of-the-line stereo videocassette recorder (above, left) is the VJT700, with 8-event/3-week programming, 133-channel capability, and electronic program indexing. The company's first consumer video camera, the CC030 (above), allows the user to make color movies for immediate playback on a VCR. The home console (left) for the QUBE III interactive cable system (see pages 61–62) can carry eight-digit commands, allowing such home services as financial management, tele-shopping, security, and pay-per-view programming.

Cable News Network

Among the attractions of the new electronic media are specialized or "narrowcast" programming, available for some families on as many as 60 different channels; the opportunity to see first-run feature movies in the comforts of home, without commercial interruption; the ability to record shows off the air (without even being there) and to view them at a more convenient time; a way to make home movies that can be seen on the TV screen within minutes; immediate access to information stored by a centralized computer; and even, for some, a way to shop, bank, or buy plane tickets by use of a typewriter-like keyboard in the living room. Add to these live satellite transmissions from around the globe and screens the size of a wall or wrist watch, and one paints a scenario that would have looked like science fiction when the first Philcos were taken home less than 40 years ago.

In 1980, Atlanta entrepreneur Ted Turner raised eyebrows in the established news media by launching Cable News Network (CNN), a 24-hour all-news cable service. By early 1983, CNN had reached well over 15 million U.S. households.

Basic Cable. Unlike conventional broadcasting, cable television transmits signals via cable rather than through the air. A home must be "wired" for cable before it can receive the signal. System operators bid for the exclusive right to wire certain areas; in the United States, the top 20 multiple system operators (MSOs) are responsible for some 60% of the nation's basic subscribers. In exchange for a monthly subscription fee ($10–$12), the viewer gets access to the variety of program networks (up to several dozen channels) carried by that cable system. Among the top U.S. basic cable networks and superstations (regular TV stations bounced off satellites to cable antennas) are the WTBS-TV Superstation (Turner Broadcasting); the Entertainment and Sports Programming Network (ESPN); CBN (Christian Broadcast Network); Satellite Cable Network; USA Cable Network; and C-Span (Cable Satellite Public Affairs Network). Narrowcasting, the foundation of basic cable programming, is exemplified by such other specialized networks as MTV: Music Television, The Weather Channel, and the Cable Health Network (CHN).

Cable television actually dates back to the late 1940s. Its original use was to bring television to remote areas in which over-the-air signals were blocked by mountains or trees. These systems became known as community antenna television (CATV). The problem with CATV, however, was that it could carry only a very limited number of VHF (Very High Frequency) channels. Cable television as we know it today emerged in the mid-1970s with the advent of satellite distribution capability and increased system channel-capacity. By mid-1983 there were some 30 million basic cable subscribers in the United States, a "penetration" rate of about 35% of all TV households. By 1990, some predict, up to two thirds of American TV homes will have cable service.

Pay TV. In addition to receiving basic service, the cable subscriber can pay an extra monthly premium to receive one or more special pay-TV channels. The top pay-cable services currently feature movies, but live music performances, sports, comedies, serials, and a variety of made-for-pay (analogous to made-for-TV) programming formats are finding slots in the schedule. The four leading services—Home Box Office (HBO), Showtime, The Movie Channel, and Cinemax—accounted for more than 90% of the approximately 25 million pay-cable subscribers in the United States in 1983. HBO (owned by Time Inc.) has been the leader since the beginning. In 1975 it became the first pay-cable station with nationwide reach, and today it is at the center of a furious battle with Hollywood for control of movie licensing and distribution. In 1983, HBO was to spend some $250 million on special movie deals that would guarantee it exclusive pay-cable rights.

Another option for the cable subscriber, although still on a limited basis, is pay-per-view television. By this system, the subscriber pays on a program-by-program basis rather than a monthly basis. Championship-boxing matches, concerts, and movies have had promising results on pay-per-view. Motion-picture history was made in February 1983 when Universal Studios released *The Pirates of Penzance* simultaneously in theaters and on pay-per-view. Though the results were not spectacular, the event itself underscored the sweeping revolution taking place in the video-entertainment industry. Many expect pay-per-view to be a multibillion-dollar business once addressable converters—by which cable operators can activate or deactivate a system from their own end—become widespread, perhaps in 1984 or 1985.

Pay services are not exclusive to cable television. Over-the-air subscription television (STV) is a broadcast system that transmits one channel of pay programming using a scrambled signal. The subscriber pays a monthly fee for a decoder, which unscrambles the signal. STV also has been used on a pay-per-view basis. In recent years, STV has proven to be successful in areas not wired for cable. Thus, as cable has extended its reach, STV has been experiencing a sharp decline in subscribers.

Multipoint distribution service (MDS) is another form of pay TV. MDS transmits the TV signal via a microwave sys-

In February 1983, Universal Studios released "The Pirates of Penzance" simultaneously in movie theaters and on pay-per-view TV. Movie "windows," the intervals between release to various distribution outlets, have been shortened steadily.

tem, and it is limited to line-of-sight transmission of one channel over a short distance. It has found success in urban areas not yet wired for cable. Although operators have petitioned the Federal Communications Commission (FCC) for multi-channel licenses, MDS will continue to take a back seat to cable.

Yet another pay-TV system, expected to have greater success than STV or MDS, is direct broadcast satellite (DBS) service. By this system, pay programming will be transmitted by a high-powered communications satellite directly to the viewer's house. The signal will be received on a small dish antenna (3 ft—.92 m—in diameter) on the viewer's roof. The subscriber would lease the antenna, as well as special decoding equipment. The first DBS service was expected to be in operation by late 1983. Inter-American Satellite Television, owned by Australian publisher Rupert Murdoch, leased five transponders on the Satellite Business Systems-3 satellite, launched by the space shuttle *Columbia* in November 1982. Seven other companies have gained FCC approval to offer DBS service.

Videocassettes. While cable TV is the leading contender in the new home-video market, videocassettes represent the fastest growing segment. The videocassette recorder (VCR) performs three basic functions: it can tape-record television programs and play them back at a more convenient time

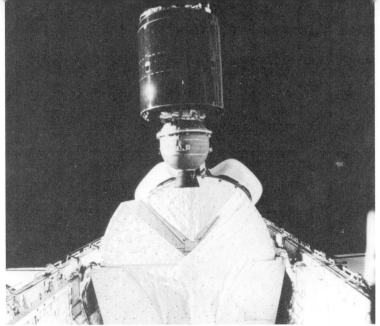

Satellite Business Systems-3, a high-power communications satellite, is poised for release from the space shuttle Columbia in late 1982. SBS-3 will be used for direct-to-home broadcast TV service (DBS).

Satellite Business Systems

(called "time shifting"); it can play pre-recorded programs purchased or rented by the viewer; and, with the addition of a special camera, it can be used to make color home movies for immediate TV viewing.

While the first video tape recorders began to be used in television studios as early as the 1950s, they were too bulky and too expensive for home use. The first successful consumer VCR was the Sony Betamax, introduced in 1975. Priced at $1,300, it had a one-hour recording capability using ½-inch (1.3-cm) tape cassettes. Another Japanese manufacturer, JVC, developed a competing format, the Video Home System (VHS), introduced in the United States in 1977. The VHS system had a two-hour recording capability and sold for $1,000. Since 1977 both the Beta and VHS cassette formats have been improved substantially. In addition to lower prices, higher resolution, and longer recording time (up to eight hours per cassette), they now include such features as stereo sound, push-button tuning, fast forward and reverse scanning, slow motion, audio-dubbing capability, and programmable timing devices. Virtually all VCRs on the market in the United States today are made in Japan. By mid-1983 nearly seven million U.S. consumers (8% of TV households) had bought a VCR, and sales were running at a quarter million units per month.

Time shifting (using blank tapes) remains the most common use of the VCR, but more and more owners are turning to prerecorded tapes. Movies dominate the list of offerings, but such special-interest, nonfilm programming as the best-selling "Jane Fonda's Workout" is finding a growing market. Rentals ($2 to $6 per night) vastly outstrip prerecorded cassette sales, but this too is changing as retail prices decline; many cassettes that would have sold for $80 or more in 1982 dropped as low as $30 in 1983.

Videodiscs. Among the newest of the audiovisual media is the videodisc player, used for playing flat discs that resemble conventional records. Priced as low as $250, the disc player is more affordable than the VCR (the discs themselves are also cheaper), but it has the distinct disadvantage of being a play-back-only system, with no recording capability. RCA's capacitance electronic disc (CED) system, introduced in March 1981, uses a diamond stylus that converts the material recorded in microscopic grooves on the disc. Another kind of player, the laser optical disc (LD) system, uses a low-power laser to scan the disc. Although the LD player has been on the market slightly longer than the CED, it lags far behind in sales. In truth, neither disc system has sold so well as originally predicted. Nevertheless, the cumulative population of disc players in the United States surpassed a half million in 1983, and sales were picking up steam. Promoters of disc technology remain optimistic because of the device's interactive (two-way) capability and high sound quality. The year 1983 saw introduction of laser disc jukeboxes and arcade games with live-action or cartoon film. Work also continued on the development of a videodisc system with recording capability, though this is still several years off.

Interactive Cable and Videotext. The age of consumer service television and home access to data base information is rapidly being brought out of the science-fiction pages and into the American living room. While still in the stages of technological experimentation and market testing, interactive cable and videotext systems can—and do—provide these capabilities.

Interactive cable is a system by which the subscriber can both receive and send back information through a television set. The user is given a keypad to transmit single- or multiple-digit codes that are processed and stored by a computer at the system operator's end. The technology allows for a variety of convenient consumer services, several of which are already available in certain areas.

QUBE III is Warner Amex's new-generation interactive cable system. In addition to sending back information, the viewer can receive up to 110 channels.

Courtesy of Warner Amex/QUBE

Interactive cable was actually introduced in 1977, when Warner Amex Cable Communications launched its Qube system in Columbus, OH. Now available in several Midwestern cities, Qube has had particular success as a 24-hour home security surveillance system. Opinion polling—of political issues, topics discussed on talk shows, and program criticism— is another primary use; Qube also has had success as a pay-per-view service. Warner's chief rival in interactive cable is Cox Cable, whose Indax system is being tested in San Diego and Omaha. While the commercial viability of two-way cable is yet uncertain, the prospect of at-home shopping and banking holds long-term promise.

Yet another new technology with interactive capability is videotext. The term is actually used to denote two distinct systems—teletext and viewdata. The former is a one-way system in which textual information is transmitted ''piggyback'' on the normal broadcast TV signal. The text is prepared in video frames, or ''pages,'' which the user calls up by pressing the appropriate number on a keypad. Viewdata, by contrast, is a two-way system in which the user can communicate with a central computer data bank. The signal is carried back and forth by phone lines, cable, or microwave, as opposed to broadcast. Another important difference between viewdata and teletext is the kind and amount of information that can be carried. While the former offers general, broad-appeal information, viewdata can provide such specific, detailed data as restaurant listings, transportation schedules, and encyclopedia entries. With its interactive capability, therefore, viewdata would allow the user to call up a plane schedule and order tickets. The problem with videotext generally, at least for the time being, is high cost. While the majority of users are still in business and industry, the home market is beginning to grow.

© 1983 Viewdata Corporation of America, Inc.

Linked to a central computer data bank, videotext systems bring useful information to the home television screen. Interactive formats allow the user not only to call up plane schedules, for example, but also to order tickets.

Problems and Opportunities. The video revolution that began in the late 1970s has been unprecedented in the history of the entertainment/information media. Never before have so many new and promising technologies come on the scene virtually all at once. The traditional audiovisual media—motion pictures and broadcast television—have been seriously challenged. By the same token, the new electronic media have also begun to face competition from each other. The videodisc player, for example, initially slated for grand success, has suffered at the hands of the VCR, whose recording capability makes it the device of choice for the uncertain consumer.

The competitive arena during the first five years of the video revolution has been surrounded by an atmosphere of unfettered, free-market wheeling and dealing. The scramble for consumer dollars has given rise to joint ventures, mergers, acquisitions, novel financial arrangements, and enormous capital investment, some of it rash. Only in 1983 did the first boundaries really begin to be set up by the government. A proposed deal by which several movie studios would jointly operate Showtime and The Movie Channel—the second and third largest pay-TV services—was opposed by the U.S. Justice Department on grounds of antitrust. The parties went back to the drawing board and in September announced a new plan acceptable to Washington.

A variety of other issues within and between the various media point up some of the problems in the home-video marketplace. In the so-called Sony Betamax Case, expected to be resolved by the U.S. Supreme Court in 1984, program producers are claiming that VCR manufacturers and retailers are liable when consumers record copyrighted material off the air. Meanwhile, the studios also have a beef with videocassette retailers. Under the "first-sale doctrine" of copyright law, retailers are able to pocket all the money from prerecorded cassette rentals once they buy the tape; the widespread availability of cheap rentals has discouraged consumer purchases, thereby costing the studios millions of dollars every year. Finally, a movement is under way in both the United States and other countries to combat one of the most serious problems facing video—piracy. The illegal duplication and sale of movies on cassette and the unscrambling of cable signals by non-subscribers are two areas in which legislation and/or counteractive technology are needed.

When and however such issues are resolved will go a long way in determining the success or failure of the audiovisual media, both old and new. All in all, however, it is already clear that the emergent electronic media together have opened a new chapter in the history of the media. For just as the new home video compete with each other, they also promote and feed each other. As cable TV offers more and better programming, for example, the time-shifting capability of the VCR will make the device even more appealing. Just as for television itself in the 1940s, home video—in one or several forms—will become a household fixture once the public becomes more aware of what it has to offer and, of course, "when the prices come down."

THE NEW TALL BUILDINGS

By Charles K. Hoyt

A major building boom has been occurring currently in cities across the United States. Despite an economic recession, construction of almost 800 million square feet (74.3 million m²) of new urban office space has begun since 1980. This building boom is not only altering the skylines of many cities, including Chicago, Houston, Louisville, Boston, New York, and Miami, but is keeping the architectural offices extremely busy. With these new tall buildings, significant changes in architectural design have resulted. Corporations today are no longer satisfied with the often boxy, ungainly, and forbidding buildings of yesterday and are seeking a more memorable urban presence. The urban real-estate market has become extremely competitive, and the building landlords are looking for more imaginative architectural results to lure tenants. According to Cesar Pelli, dean of Yale's School of Architecture, architects "are now free to create a new generation of skyscrapers—optimistic, celebratory, joyful, public, accepting their roles as icons."

As typified by the shimmering new office building at One South Wacker in downtown Chicago, the boxy buildings of yesterday have given way to irregularly shaped structures that create a startling effect.

About the Author: Charles K. Hoyt, a member of The American Institute of Architects (AIA), is associate editor of *Architectural Record*. As is evident from the titles of the books that he has written, including *Building for Commerce and Industry* (1978); *Public, Municipal, and Community Buildings* (1980); and *Interior Spaces Designed by Architects* (1983), Mr. Hoyt has a special interest in the city skyscraper. He currently is chairman of the AIA Historic Buildings Committee in New York City.

The new architectural design can be seen in the many irregular shapes that mark the new tall buildings. It is not uncommon to find the old box style approach at the very least fractured by several indentations and irregularities of the roofline. Other new styles are so different from the previous rectilinearity that they are hardly recognizable as the product of the same technology. And there are a number of reasons for this design transformation besides the desire to create a startling effect. Primarily there is the ability to better relate the outlook from interior spaces to views, to better orient the walls to sun angles and the consequent thermal advantages derived, and to increase the number of corner offices. (If the irregular plan produces ten corners, there is an increase of six highly desirable interior spaces over those in the old box.)

Keith Palmer/James R. Steinkamp
Greg Hursley

Two elements characteristic of the new architectural style are more creative use of interior space and classically inspired ornamentation. A new addition to the Chicago Board of Trade, left, is highlighted by a vast central atrium with glass-enclosed elevators. The Portland Building, above, stands as a monument to post-modernist decoration; inside, the entrance lobby is surrounded by public information and security areas, with an art gallery on the second floor.

Allen Freeman

A second change in the new breed of high rise is to create a memorable public space inside. Since builders and landlords do not want this to be dead space with no income value, the idea is to invite the public in to liven the space and to patronize shops and restaurants that give out onto it. Often taking the form of tall skylit atriums through which rise escalators and glass-enclosed elevators for a further sense of movement and activity, these new lobbies—handled properly—can be true public amenities that benefit every level of the cities' population.

A third new element that characterizes the current tall buildings is ornament, and this often takes the classically inspired form of the Post Modernists' loose interpretations that began at a much smaller scale in the applied columns and pediments that were attached to cabinet work in residences and apartment renovations. Now these same columns and pediments can be seen at colossal scale on 50-story buildings—although not all of the current decorative movement follows this school. There are also variations in which, for instance, the exterior walls will be of two or more materials (for example, granite and aluminum panels) that are applied in a decorative pattern.

It seems almost undeniable that the new generation of high-rise buildings offers an increased amenity and grace to the skylines and street experiences. But, like all architecture, its success depends on the skill of the specific designer. At least, there is now the incentive for more memorable new skyscrapers.

In New York, three new giants etch the skyline: (center, right to left) the neoclassical, pediment-capped AT&T Building; the granite-and-glass IBM Center; and the futuristic Trump Tower.

ETHICS AND MODERN MEDICINE

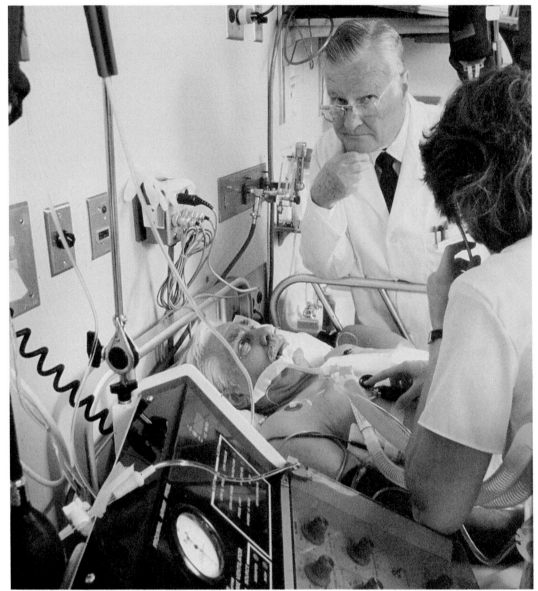

By Morris B. Abram

In December 1982, when Barney Clark's surgeons completed the first implantation of a totally mechanical heart in a human patient, the phones rang off the hook in Suite 555 of a standard government rental at 2000 K Street, Washington, DC. Suddenly, issues with which the President's Commission on Biomedical Ethics had been grappling for three years were the subject of intense public concern. One caller asked: "Is it ethical for surgeons to perform such acrobatics?" Another worried: "What kind of permission was required?" Still another wondered whether it was fair to devote so many medical resources to one man. A cluster of callers pointed out that widespread use of such artificial devices eventually would force decisions as to whether and when the machines should be shut off. "Who decides, and how?" they inquired.

The landmark procedure performed on Barney Clark was the latest in a series of medical breakthroughs that have posed perplexing ethical questions regarding illness and death, access to medical care, and research on human subjects. In the last quarter-century, the development of advanced life-sustaining treatments and technologies has raised a host of thorny issues for legal, medical, and religious institutions, as well as for the general public. In response, Congress in 1978 set up the President's Commission for the Study of Ethical Problems in Medicine and Biomedical and Behavioral Research. Beginning its work in January 1980, the body addressed itself to the difficult ethical questions that loom ever larger with each advance by modern medicine—such questions as:

About the Author: Morris B. Abram served as chairman of the President's Commission for the Study of Ethical Problems in Medicine and Biomedical and Behavioral Research (1979–83). A partner in the law firm of Paul, Weiss, Rifkind, Wharton & Garrison, Mr. Abram has also been president of the American Jewish Committee (1963–68); representative to the UN Commission on Human Rights (1965–68); and president of Brandeis University (1968–70). He has lectured at Oxford University on medical ethics and human rights.

• When is a person dead? Is it when brain function stops? Or is a person without brain function whose breathing and heartbeat are sustained only by a machine still alive?
• How should decisions be made as to who gets scarce and costly new treatment, such as interferon or an artificial heart?
• Does a civilized society have a responsibility to see that each citizen has access to medical care, and if so at what level?
• Should a patient be allowed to refuse treatment? What if it means that he or she will die?
• May a child refuse treatment? May parents or doctors withhold life-saving treatment from a newborn with a birth defect? Does this constitute murder?
• Should people with a genetic disease reproduce?
• Should there be limits to research into genetic engineering?
• How much should a doctor tell a patient? Is there ever a time—as in cases where the news is dismal—when a doctor should deliberately withhold information from a patient?

Intervention and Experimentation. The greatest strides in life-sustaining medical intervention have been made since the mid- to late 1940s. Antibiotics, chemotherapies, respirators, renal dialysis, sophisticated incubators, advances in anesthesia, and organ transplants are just some of the important breakthroughs that give truth to the statement by Dr. Arnold Relman, editor of *The New England Journal of Medicine,* that "for almost any life-threatening condition there is some intervention capable of delaying the moment of death."

Hand in glove with the exponential progress of modern medicine has been a developing sensitivity to the ethical issues involved. Some ugly cases of human experimentation have shaken us into awareness. In 1947, 15 prominent German doctors were convicted at Nuremberg for the "medical experiments" they performed on concentration camp inmates during World War II; one result of the judgment was a set of standards for research on human subjects, known as the Nuremberg Code. Also in the 1940s, the U.S. Public Health Service deliberately withheld standard treatments (and diagnoses) from scores of Alabama blacks suffering from syphilis in order to observe the untreated progress of the disease; the program was continued until 1972. And in 1963, doctors injected live cancer cells into patients at the Jewish Chronic Disease Hospital in Brooklyn, NY, as part of an experiment with no therapeutic benefit to the patients.

Disclosure of such inexcusable horrors led to public outcry and the creation in 1974 of the National Commission for the Protection of Human Subjects of Biomedical and Behavioral Research. When that body's charter expired, Congress passed a bill in 1978 to create the President's Commission to study a wider range of bioethical and health care issues.

Defining Death. The use of respirators and other modern equipment has forced serious reconsideration of the fundamental question of death. What is it, and when precisely does it occur? By 1978 the use of life-support systems had rendered the whole question so murky that Congress posed as one of its first questions to the President's Commission "the matter of defining death, including the advisability of developing a uniform definition. . . ."

The traditional legal and medical definition of death is irreversible cessation of circulatory and respiratory functions. After much deliberation, the Commission concluded that this definition is no longer adequate and that there should be an alternative basis for the determination. The Commission drafted a statute now approved by the American Medical Association, American Bar Association, and National Conference of Commissioners of Uniform State Laws. That statute, already enacted in 13 states and the District of Columbia, adds "or an irreversible cessation of all functions of the entire brain" to the established definition.

The Uniform Definition of Death Act was the sole legislative recommendation made by the President's Commission. The body was not created to make legal prescriptions, and it recognized that most medical/ethical decisions could not be reduced to legal norms. It did feel, however, that its uniform definition of death was appropriate to modern conditions. By its criterion, Karen Ann Quinlan, though probably irreversibly comatose, is not dead because the continued functioning of her brain stem allows her to breathe without a respirator. Korean boxer Duk Koo Kim, meanwhile, rendered comatose in a November 1982 bout, was declared dead on the basis of the brain criterion. That he subsequently was made an organ donor illustrates the usefulness of the uniform statute. Moreover, the Commission felt, the new definition can put an end to the sometimes cruel charade of treating a dead body as a living person and can allow family and friends to begin a normal grieving process.

Fred Conrad/Sygma

The parents of Karen Ann Quinlan won court permission in 1976 to have their daughter taken off a respirator, but her lower brain has kept her alive.

Access to Health Care. Despite government health programs and private insurance coverage, there are 20 to 25 million Americans, many of them hard-working and self-supporting, who do not have access to adequate medical care even in the best of times. For extraordinary "catastrophic" treatment, the problems of affordability and equitability of access are even more acute.

A key question faced by the President's Commission was whether there are ethical responsibilities attached to health care different from those arising from other public needs. While there is no constitutional right to medical care, the Commission did conclude that there is a special ethical claim. According to its report, health care is unique because of its role in "relieving suffering, preventing premature death, restoring functioning, . . . and giving evidence of mutual empathy and compassion." Furthermore, it stated, "differences in the need for health care are for the most part undeserved and not within the individual's control."

Bearing significantly on the issue of access has been a drastic inflation in medical costs and a sharp increase in national expenditures on health care. With nearly 10% of U.S. national income spent on health—proportionately more even than in Western European countries with socialized medicine—eliminating waste and containing costs become imperative. This, however, will raise new questions of equitable access. The cost of free renal dialysis, for example, was originally budgeted at $200 million annually, but it is now running at an estimated $2,000,000,000 per year. Who should be declared ineligible?

Foregoing Treatment. No ethical question engages the public interest more than a decision—by or on behalf of a patient —to forego life-preserving medical treatment. Several highly publicized cases have dramatized the issue:

• The administration of antibiotics to Karen Ann Quinlan for pneumonia. Should such a patient continue to be treated and fed artificially even though a decision has been made to withdraw artificial respiration?
• The "Bloomington baby," a child with Down's Syndrome whose parents rejected a simple operation that would have allowed it to survive. The Indiana Supreme Court concurred with the parent's decision, but was it right in doing so? Is the child's "quality of life" a justifiable consideration?
• The "Perlmutter Case," in which a retired taxi driver living on a respirator asked to be relieved of the device when his wife of 45 years died unexpectedly. His doctor refused to order the device removed; the Florida Supreme Court agreed with Perlmutter's family that the machine could be detached, and Perlmutter died. Who was right?

As these cases demonstrated, around the gravely ill hover not only the angel of death but also the devils of human uncertainty, a miasma of ambiguity. According to Dr. Willard Gaylin, president of the Institute of Society, Ethics, and the Life Sciences, the uncertainty is not all bad. "I think that it's truly important that [such] things be ambiguous and anguished. I think that ambiguity is good for you—it serves the complexity of the issues very well. To make these issues pain-free when you are talking about death and life trivializes the problem."

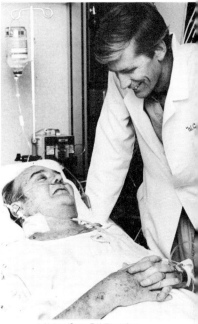

© Nelson/Owen T.K./Black Star

Barney Clark, the first human patient to receive a permanent artificial heart, smiles for his surgeon, Dr. William DeVries, after the procedure in December 1982. Clark lived for 112 days on the artificial heart, until March 23, 1983.

On the general question of foregoing treatment, the President's Commission endorsed the right of a responsible and responsive patient to make his or her own decision, where that decision is informed, uncoerced, and made in consultation with a physician, family, friends, and, if desired, clergy. Adults unable to make a choice should be represented by a surrogate who so far as possible should voice the expressed wish or evident desire of the patient. Children should be represented by their parents. Medical personnel must be sensitive to the possibility of a confused decision by a competent patient and to a less than disinterested opinion by a surrogate. In the face of uncertainty, there should be a presumption in favor of extending rather than terminating life.

The Commission emphatically rejected any additional legislation or routine judicial interaction, favoring the current *ad hoc* practice. The ultimate decision should be made with great circumspection at bedside amid the ambiguity and tensions generated by "fear and trembling"—fear of the criminal and civil law and trembling because of the awesome finality of death. Decisions made in this crucible, the Committee felt, will be as ethically correct as can be expected.

Informed Consent. Traditional medical practice, based on the ethical precepts of the ancient Greek physician Hippocrates, invested doctors with a protective paternalism over the patient. Informed consent had no place in those precepts:

Perform [these duties] calmly and adroitly, concealing most things from the patient while you are attending to him. Give necessary orders with cheerfulness and sincerity, turning his attention away from what is being done to him; sometimes reprove sharply and emphatically, and sometimes comfort with solicitude and attention, revealing nothing of the patient's future or present condition.

In the context of ancient Greece, Hippocrates' views may have been defensible: scientific knowledge was so meager that whatever he told a patient would probably have been untrue. Today, however, doctors know a great deal, and it is an ethical imperative that every patient be informed of all the facts needed to make an autonomous decision regarding treatment. The patient dealing with risk should be told of all probable and possible consequences of a particular therapy, as well as the consequences of no therapy. Full dialogue between doctor and patient should be encouraged.

In a national survey contracted by the President's Commission on Biomedical Ethics and conducted by Lou Harris and Associates, 79% of the public polled and 55% of the physicians polled said that the primary purpose of the consent form is to protect the doctor from lawsuits. This was very much at variance with the Commission's own view that informed consent is a therapeutic advantage, as well as an ethical imperative. According to its report, the informed patient gets better faster, frequently is less anxious, and is better able to monitor his condition, report untoward side effects, and cooperate generally with the medical team.

Genetics. Progress in the field of genetics has generated another slew of sticky bioethical questions. Prenatal and carrier screening tests for Tay-Sachs disease, sickle-cell anemia, phenylketonuria, and neural tube defects already exist. Recent research suggests that a test for cystic fibrosis may be on the horizon. Genetic screening to identify carriers of a dreadful disease or to detect a defective child in the womb raises the questions of whether carrier parents should risk conception and whether fetuses with a detected disease should be burdened with a life of physical, social, and psychological disadvantage. Lurking in the background, of course, is the issue of abortion.

The President's Commission supported genetic screening and counseling under certain conditions. Mandatory programs should be confined to cases in which voluntary testing proves inadequate to prevent serious harm to the defenseless, including children. The Commission opposed the turning over of genetic information to unrelated third parties and discouraged the use of amniocentesis to choose the sex of children.

Even more profound are the potential ethical implications of genetic engineering. Although the public's first expressed fears were about the "escape" of dangerous microorganisms from the laboratory, a deeper anxiety has emerged—that work in this field will be used for eugenics, remaking the human race by controlling the hereditary qualities passed on from parents to children.

Although genetic engineering techniques are advancing rapidly—and have helped develop some important new pharmaceuticals—there is no present potential for remaking human kind. While they can be used to correct certain human genetic defects, this is still a purely medical application. When such corrections can affect not only a person's life but also the germ cell inheritance, closer scrutiny will be appropriate.

The Commission felt that it would be useless and irresponsible to legislate against genetic engineering. If it does not occur in one country it will in another. On the other hand, prudence and the public interest clearly call for the establishment of a nongovernmental body to keep a watchful eye on work in this field and to report on any new developments.

Neither the President's Commission on Biomedical Ethics nor this article has exhausted the list of important ethical issues raised by modern medicine. Artificial insemination, in vitro fertilization, and embryo implantation are just a few of the other new procedures that have given rise to sometimes heated debate. While it has not been possible in this text to represent the many strong arguments on all sides of the various issues, variant positions are acknowledged and many are respected. In the final analysis, one can observe in America a basic inclination to deal ethically in such matters. Once personhood is established—the definition of personhood is itself at the center of some vital issues, including abortion—there is a fundamental urge to apply ethical standards in deciding how a person should be treated. As new developments continue to be made in medicine, new questions will be raised as to what standards should be applied.

"The regimen I adopt shall be for the benefit of the patients according to my ability and judgment, and not for their hurt or for any wrong. I will give no deadly drug to any, though it be asked of me, nor will I counsel such. . . . Whatsoever house I enter, there I will go for the benefit of the sick, refraining from all wrongdoing or corruption. . . ."

—from The Hippocratic Oath

People, Places and Things

J. P. Laffont/Sygma

© Gianfranco Gorgoni/Contact

New York City celebrated the 100th birthday of the Brooklyn Bridge on May 24; the party was capped by a brilliant fireworks display over the mile-long architectural wonder. In Miami's Biscayne Bay, the artist Christo skirted 11 islands with sheets of flamingo-pink plastic; "Surrounded Islands," as he called his oeuvre, drew mixed reviews.

Twenty-year-old Vanessa Williams, left, of New York became the first black to be crowned Miss America. Henry Dekker, below, of Danbury, CT, became the first blind person to sail alone from San Francisco to Hawaii; Dekker and his 25-ft (7.6-m) sloop, "Dark Star," made the 2,376-mi (3 824-km) voyage in 23 days. Britain's Queen Elizabeth and Prince Philip, bottom, toured the west coast of the United States and British Columbia in late February and early March. Despite severe rains, which prevented them from sailing up the California coast as planned, the royal couple was kept busy by banquets, receptions, and visits to tourist attractions.

UPI

Tad I. Tamura/Gamma-Liaison

© Roger Sandler/Picture Group

Michael Evans/The White House

The ever-popular Beach Boys were welcomed at the White House for a charity concert. The group was the center of attention when Interior Secretary James Watt banned them from July 4 celebrations on the Washington Mall because they had, in the past, attracted "the wrong element." When Watt found out who their fans were, he dropped the ban. Also in Washington, at the Kennedy Center, stars turned out for a gala celebration of Bob Hope's 80th birthday.

Jack Buxbaum

Willy Loman Goes to China—24 years after it opened on Broadway, "Death of a Salesman" was staged in Peking. The production was directed by playwright Arthur Miller.

© Inge Morath/Magnum

Mickey Mouse goes to Japan—Within a month of its April 1983 opening, Tokyo Disneyland had attracted 1 million visitors; at that rate it would receive 1 of every 12 Japanese annually. September 3 marked the bicentennial of the Treaty of Paris, which officially ended the American Revolution. Volunteers dressed as 18th century American soldiers paraded in Paris as part of the observances.

Kaku Kurita/Gamma-Liaison

Olivier Vedrine/Gamma-Liaison

The Alphabetical Section

Oslo, Norway, Dec. 10, 1983.

The electrician from Gdansk, the carpenter's son from the Vistula valley, has managed to lift the banner of freedom and humanity so high that the whole world can once again see it. The power of his belief and vision is unweakened. He stands as an inspiration and a shining example to all those who, under different conditions, fight for freedom and humanity.

—Egil Aarvik, chairman of the Norwegian Nobel Committee, upon awarding the 1983 Nobel Peace Prize to Lech Walesa

For the first time a Pole has been awarded a prize which Alfred Nobel founded for activities toward bringing the nations of the world close together.

The most ardent hopes of my compatriots are linked with this idea; in spite of the violence, cruelty and brutality which characterize the conflicts splitting the present-day world.

We desire peace, and that is why we have never resorted to physical force.

We crave for justice, and that is why we are so persistent in the struggle for our rights.

We seek freedom of convictions, and that is why we have never attempted to enslave man's conscience nor shall we ever attempt to do so.

We are fighting for the right of the working people to organize and for the dignity of human labor. We respect the dignity and the rights of every man and every nation. The road to a brighter future for the world leads through honest reconciliation of conflicting interests and not through hatred and bloodshed. To follow that road means to enhance the moral power of the all-embracing idea of human solidarity.

—Lech Walesa in Nobel speech delivered (in Polish) by his wife, Danuta.

After being named winner of the 1983 Nobel Peace Prize on October 5, 40-year-old Lech Walesa, leader of the banned Polish trade union Solidarity, took time for some quiet reflection and his favorite hobby at a pond near Gdansk.
Michel Philippot/Sygma

ACCIDENTS AND DISASTERS

AVIATION

Jan. 16—At the Ankara airport, a Turkish jetliner crashes while landing, killing 46 persons.

June 2—An Air Canada jet emergency lands in Cincinnati, OH, after catching fire in flight; 23 are killed.

July 11—An Ecuadoran jetliner attempting to land in Cuenca, Ecuador, crashes, killing 119 persons.

Sept. 23—In the mountains of Abu Dhabi a jetliner crashes, killing all 112 persons aboard.

Nov. 8—In southern Angola an Angolan jetliner crashes just after takeoff, killing 126 persons.

Nov. 27—A crash of a 747 jetliner near Madrid, Spain's Barajas airport kills 183 persons.

Nov. 28—A Nigerian airliner crashes 300 mi (483 km) east of Lagos, Nigeria, killing 53 persons.

Dec. 7—In Madrid, two Spanish jetliners collide on a takeoff runway, killing about 90 people.

EARTHQUAKES AND VOLCANOES

March 31—An earthquake centered in Popayán, Colombia, kills at least 250 people.

May 26—Earthquake-induced sea waves hit the western coast of Japan's Honshu Island, killing at least 81 people; 21 others are missing.

Oct. 30—A major earthquake in eastern Turkey leaves more than 1,300 people dead.

Dec. 22—An earthquake in Guinea kills 300.

FIRES AND EXPLOSIONS

Feb. 13—Fire in a movie theater in Turin, Italy, kills 64.

Feb. 16–19—In parts of two southern Australian states, brush fires kill 71 persons.

March 7—Near Eregli, Turkey, at least 98 miners are killed in a coal-mine explosion.

April 18—In Taegu, South Korea, fire in a disco kills 25.

May 8—Gunpowder and fireworks explode at a Roman Catholic church in Tlapacoya, Mexico, killing 19.

June 7—A coal mine explosion in southern Serbia in Yugoslavia kills 21 persons.

June 22—In Oroszlany, Hungary, a coal mine explosion kills 36 miners.

Sept. 12—In South Africa's Natal Province at the Hlobane coal mine, a gas explosion kills 64.

Dec. 17—Fire in a Madrid discotheque kills 81.

LAND AND SEA TRANSPORTATION

Feb. 12—A coal ship capsizes off Chincoteague Island, VA, killing 33 persons.

Feb. 19—Freight and passenger trains collide near Guaymas, Mexico, killing at least 64 people.

March 1—A ferry capsizes in the Sanshui River in China's Guangdong province, killing 147 persons.

May 25—A Nile River steamboat and two towed barges catch fire and sink in Lake Nasser; at least 196 people are dead; many others are missing.

May 27—In the Indian state of Madhya Pradesh, a bus plunges into a gorge, killing about 60.

June 5—A Soviet passenger ship rams a railway bridge across the Volga River at the city of Ulyanovsk, killing more than 100 people.

Aug. 4—An overloaded passenger boat sinks in the Java Sea north of Masalembo Island; 104 are missing.

Aug. 10 (reported)—A Soviet nuclear-powered submarine sinks in the northern Pacific; about 90 crewmen are believed killed.

Aug. 31—In Pojuca, Brazil, a derailed train carrying fuel catches fire and explodes, killing 42.

Sept. 12—A bus plunges down a ravine in the Andes Mountains 85 mi (137 km) south of Quito, Ecuador, killing 50 persons.

Sept. 28—Near the town of Gospic, Yugoslavia, a commuter train collides with a bus, killing 25.

Nov. 1 (reported)—A U.S. oil drilling ship sinks in the South China Sea; 81 persons are missing.

Nov. 23 (reported)—A ferry sinks in a typhoon off the Philippines Mindanao Island; more than 200 people are missing.

Nov. 26 (reported)—An overloaded ferryboat on Lake Victoria in Tanzania capsizes, killing at least 55.

Dec. 24—Near Hwange, Zimbabwe, a train derails, killing 31.

STORMS AND FLOODS

Jan. 23–30—Heavy flooding from four storms along the California coast kills 11 persons. In Utah and Arizona, storm-related accidents (Jan. 27) take the lives of ten in two separate plane crashes.

Feb. 11–12—A U.S. East Coast blizzard kills 11.

Feb. 18—A blizzard in Lebanon kills as many as 47.

Feb. 27–March 5—Pacific storms hit the California coast; 13 persons are killed.

March 20–22—Floods and mudslides in northern Peru and Bolivia kill at least 260; hundreds are missing.

April 6–12—Rains and floods kill 15 persons in four southern states. A tornado touched off by the storms hits Inverness, FL, killing 3.

April 11—A tornado in Fujian Province of southern China kills 54 persons.

April 30 (reported)—Storms in several Bangladesh towns in the last week kill 63 persons.

April 30—Near Chepén, Peru, a flash flood sweeps over a bridge spanning the Chaman River, more than 50 people are feared dead.

May 12 (reported)—Tornadoes, hail, and rainstorms in late April and early May kill 275 people and injure 11,000 in China's Hunan province.

May 15–18—Storms in the Indian states of Punjab, Haryana, and Uttar Pradesh kill at least 31.

May 18–22—Floods, tornadoes, and hail hit the Gulf coast and Mid Atlantic area, killing 32.

July 7–14—In the Brazilian states of Rio Grande do Sol, Paraná, and Santa Caterina, severe flooding has caused more than 100 deaths.

July 15—A storm bringing strong tidal waves hits the Philippine Islands, killing 45 persons.

July 22 (reported)—Flood waters from China's Yangtze River have killed at least 100 people.

July 23—Flooding and mudslides in southwestern Honshu in Japan kill 75 persons; at least 43 others are missing.

Aug. 5–7—In Bangladesh three boats carrying victims from weeklong floods sink, raising to 41 the number of deaths. Sixty people are missing after their boat sank during a storm on Aug. 5.

Aug. 18—Hurricane Alicia hits the Texas coast, killing 17.

Aug. 22 (reported)—Monsoon rains in India claim 982 lives over the last two months.

Aug. 26–27—In Spain's Basque region, floods kill at least 37 along the French-Spanish border.

Sept. 1–18—Monsoon flooding in five Indian states, particularly in Uttar Pradesh, Assam, Sikkim, and Bihar, have killed nearly 400 people.

Sept. 18–24—Flooding in northern and northwestern Bangladesh kills at least 61 people.

Oct. 17 (reported)—Two typhoons strike northern and central Vietnam, killing 40 persons.

Nov. 29 (reported)—A blizzard closes major highways and airports in Wyoming, Kansas, Colorado, Nebraska, South Dakota, Minnesota, and Iowa and has been blamed for the death of 56 persons.

Dec. 17–29—U.S. winter storms contribute to the deaths of more than 370 people.

Dec. 23—Heavy rain in the Indian state of Tamil Nadu kills at least 26 people.

MISCELLANEOUS

March 7—A landslide engulfs a village in China's Gansu province, killing more than 270 people.

April 27—A landslide in Chimborazo province in Ecuador kills more than 100 people.

June 8 (reported)—A two-week heat wave in parts of India causes 101 deaths.

July 23—Over more than a two-week period, 87 heat-related deaths have occurred in Missouri, Illinois, Kentucky, Georgia, North Carolina, Indiana, Ohio, Arkansas, New York, Tennessee, and Maryland.

July 28—A mudslide at the Guavio Dam site 87 mi (140 km) east of Bogotá, Colombia, kills about 160.

Aug. 14 (reported)—In northern India at least 53 were trampled to death while visiting a religious shrine.

ADVERTISING

During the summer of 1983, with the arrival of economic recovery, advertising budgets that had been cut in 1981–82 started to recover. If not producing rosy optimism, the turnaround did brighten advertising agencies' outlook for the year. Advertising expenditures were expected to grow by 12%, 2% more than in 1982. The only thing standing in the way of greater enthusiasm at ad agencies was continued slim profit margins, due to operating costs. In 1983 more agencies began to charge for previously free services and to add fees on top of their commissions from clients.

Laws and Regulations. The Reagan administration's efforts to reduce bureaucratic control continued to affect federal regulatory agencies in 1983. The dismantling of the self-regulatory National Association of Broadcasters (NAB) in 1982 resulted in greater network self-regulation and the strengthening of the National Advertising Division of the Council of Better Business Bureaus. In 1983 the Federal Trade Commission (FTC) was stripped of its power to make rules banning advertisements that it considers to be "unfair" (as opposed to "deceptive"), although it can still bring an action for unfairness after the fact. As expected, the FTC also was banned from policing the business practice of doctors, lawyers, and other professionals. A U.S. Court of Appeals, however, upheld the FTC's power to take action regarding advertising that fails to disclose material facts. In a decision against a subsidiary of American Home Products, the court said that the Federal Trade Commission was on firm ground when it took action against the firm for its Anacin commercials because they did not disclose that Anacin contains aspirin.

Two important legal developments relating to advertising occurred during the year: 1) There was an increase in the use of Section 43a of the Lanham Act as a tactical marketing weapon. This statute from the 1940s prevents a company from saying anything deceptive about its own products in advertising. Burger King's "Battle of the Burgers" comparative ad campaign, for example, resulted in a lawsuit by the

Symbols of changing times: To keep up in the Age of Physical Fitness, some of advertising's most familiar figures have slimmed down noticeably. After 79 years, the Campbell's Soup kids finally shed some weight (but kept their rosy cheeks). At age 89, the White Rock goddess appears to have discovered the fountain of youth. Originally, said the company, she was 5'4" (1.63 m) and 140 lbs (64 kg). Today she is 5'8" (1.73 m) and 118 lbs (54 kg).

Courtesy, Campbell Soup Company

Courtesy, White Rock

two competitors named in the advertisements, Wendys and McDonalds, both citing the Lanham Act. 2) The Ninth Circuit Court of Appeals decided against General Mills Fun Group Inc. (owner of Parker Brothers) in its suit to prevent another company from marketing a game called "Anti-Monopoly." General Mills charged trademark violation of its well-known game "Monopoly." The court ruled that the word "monopoly" had become generic, thereby allowing others to use it. The U.S. Supreme Court refused to review the case.

Media. In the wake of the recession, advertiser demand for the media was uneven, with some areas of the industry brightening early in 1983 and others gaining slowly throughout the summer. Demand for daytime network TV increased dramatically after being practically stagnant for more than three years. Barter syndication received a shot in the arm from advertiser reaction to 1982 network price increases and highly valued new syndicated program offerings. Spot TV, spurred on by an increase in local retail activity, began to show life. Magazines, which had a poor year in 1982, were up 6% in advertising pages and 11% in revenues in the first half of 1983, according to the Publishers Index Bureau. Cable TV continued to experience growth pains, but programming got a needed boost from the first really successful and inventive cable format, MTV (Music Television). Radio, while nowhere near as successful as newspapers or TV, stemmed its 1982 growth decline. A major effort to improve the image of radio as a cost-efficient, effective advertising medium had a positive impact on sales.

Without the NAB to protect the TV networks, the industry witnessed pressure from some advertisers to accept shorter commercials—two 15-second spots for unrelated products in a 30-second time frame.

Volume. Advertisers were expected to increase total outlays by 12% to $74.36 billion (U.S.) in 1983. During the previous two recession-ridden years, volume growth was only 10%. Once again newspaper buys represented nearly one third of the overall outlays, with $20.18 billion, a 14% increase over 1982. Magazine advertising was up 10% to $4.08 billion. Television buys were up 13% (no change) to $16.15 billion, reflecting increases in local gains (up 15% to $4.32 billion), spot (up 12% to $4.88 billion), and network (up 12% to $6.95 billion). The weakest gains included radio, up 9% to $5.08 billion; business publications, up only 2% to $1.92 billion; and direct mail, up 13% to $11.92 billion. Growth in outdoor advertising and miscellaneous (everything from bus-shelter ads to skywriting) were about the same as in 1982, with outdoor up 10% to $790 million and miscellaneous up 11% to $14.5 billion.

Canada. Gross advertising revenues rose by 9.5% over 1982, to $5.2 billion. Daily newspapers still accounted for the largest share (26%) at $1.352 billion. Weekly newspapers showed a gain of 12.5% over 1982 to $260 million. Broadcast outlays expanded in both media: radio was up 14% to $520 million, and television was up 17% to $936 million. Catalogs and direct mail rose to $1.04 billion and outdoor advertising to $312 million. Magazines showed the least positive results: general magazines showed some growth, to $266 million, largely as a result of the demise of the major weekend supplements, but business magazines experienced only 1% growth, to $156 million.

EDWARD H. MEYER, *Grey Advertising Inc.*

AFGHANISTAN

By the end of 1983 the USSR had been fighting in Afghanistan longer than it fought against the Germans in World War II, but neither a political nor a military solution was in sight. The Soviets and the Afghan resistance forces escalated the level of violence to a stalemate at a higher plateau. Their tactics became more sophisticated and adaptable without either side achieving a clear-cut victory.

Military Operations. Soviet ground forces adopted largely defensive positions in 1983, relying on air strikes in an effort to destroy the civilian base of support for the guerrillas. Villages and entire areas were carpet bombed, producing massive civilian casualties.

Reliable Western sources agreed that there were 110,000 Soviet troops in Afghanistan in 1983, with 30,000 in reserve across the Soviet border; 15,000 Soviet soldiers, 40,000 freedom fighters, and 200,000 civilians had been killed since 1979; 200,000 freedom fighters were mobilized, with about 20,000 engaged at any one time; and 20,000 unreliable soldiers were left in the decimated Afghan army. In addition the number of Afghan refugees totaled four million, with about three million in Pakistan and one million in Iran.

Major Soviet operations in 1983 were concentrated in the Shomali region north of Kabul and around the cities of Ghazni, Herat, and Kandahar. Pakistan officially protested in July to both the USSR and Afghanistan over 22 violations of its airspace and 11 ground intrusions during the first half of 1983.

Both sides improved their military operations during 1983. The Soviets adapted their weaponry and command structures to the special weather, terrain, and guerrilla conditions of Afghanistan. The resistance was better armed and operated in a more unified and professional manner. There was a small increase in the number of Soviet troops, probably the result of bringing in new security troops to release combat soldiers from guard duty.

In a detailed report to Congress and the United Nations, U.S. Secretary of State

George P. Shultz presented laboratory evidence of Soviet use of chemical warfare in Afghanistan. In another report, the Pentagon concluded that the Soviets could not win with present troop levels, that they were experimenting widely with new tactics and weapons, and that Soviet troop morale was very low. Afghan army desertions continued at a high rate, and at least three large-scale mutinies occurred in Kabul, Khost, and Ghazni, in which Afghan soldiers killed their officers and Soviet advisers and went over to the resistance forces with their weapons.

International Diplomacy. While military operations escalated, diplomatic efforts to reach a political solution continued. A UN initiative was led by special representative Diego Cordovez, who served as intermediary at indirect talks in Geneva between Afghanistan and Pakistan in April and again in June. Late in 1982, Pakistani President Mohammed Zia ul-Haq spoke with Soviet Communist Party leader Yuri Andropov during the funeral of Leonid Brezhnev and reported that the Soviet position seemed "flexible." Andropov promptly denied this, stating bluntly that the USSR would remain in Afghanistan "until foreign armed intervention ceases." He reaffirmed the "legitimacy" of the Soviet-sponsored Babrak Karmal government in Afghanistan and asserted that Western hopes for a change in Soviet positions were "illusory."

Communist China declared that the presence of Soviet troops in Afghanistan was a "threat to the security of China," and the Afghan resistance leaders in Pakistan said that they would not accept any settlement made at Geneva unless they were included in the negotiations—a condition rejected by Kabul.

In March the conference of nonaligned nations in New Delhi compromised on a statement calling for a political settlement and "an end to all foreign intervention" in Afghanistan. UN Secretary General Pérez de Cuéllar met with Andropov in March and was "encouraged" by the Soviet attitude, but two weeks later at Geneva the Soviet-backed Afghans remained as inflexible as ever. A second round of talks in Geneva in June was strongly backed by the United States, but it proved equally fruitless, stalled by Soviet refusal to set a withdrawal time and Afghanistan's refusal to permit the Afghan resistance to participate in the negotiations.

The United States, while officially supporting a political solution as proposed by the United Nations, leaked to the press in June that it had increased the covert supply of arms to the *mujahidin* (freedom fighters). Secretary of State Shultz, visiting Pakistan in July, stood at the Khyber Pass and assured the Afghans: "Fellow freedom-fighters, we are with you!" In response the Afghan government began to harass the American embassy in Kabul, arresting most of its Afghan employees and expelling an American diplomat in May, allegedly for selling pornography to buy rugs.

In July the former Afghan king, Mohammed Zahir Shah, who was deposed in 1973, broke his long silence and announced from exile in Rome that he was prepared to act as a unifying leader for the various resistance groups. His offer was accepted by several moderate groups, but the fundamentalist factions led by the Jamiat-i-Islam refused his suggestion.

Political Developments. Despite four years of Soviet occupation and support, the Babrak Karmal government made no progress in con-

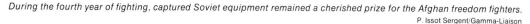

During the fourth year of fighting, captured Soviet equipment remained a cherished prize for the Afghan freedom fighters.
P. Issot Sergent/Gamma-Liaison

solidating its power. In the countryside it had no popular support. In the capital and larger provincial towns its authority rested on Soviet bayonets and on small numbers of sycophantic Communist Party members.

Three simultaneous wars were going on in Afghanistan in 1983: between the Soviets and the freedom fighters; between the Khalq and Parcham Communist factions; and between the various resistance political groups headquartered in Pakistan. Political assassinations between Parcham and Khalq have become common occurrences, and the Khalqis are widely believed to be cooperating with the resistance, giving advance warnings of government operations to the freedom fighters.

Resistance groups also are divided and hostile toward each other. Several fundamentalist groups are accused of attacking the more moderate organizations, and they also battle among themselves, maneuvering for primacy in the resistance. In the Andarab Valley, a key area north of Kabul, two fundamentalist groups, the Jamiat-i-Islam and the Hezb-i-Islam, have engaged in open warfare. A similar situation hampers the success of one of the most effective guerrilla operations in the Panjshir Valley led by Ahmad Shah Massood. In the Hazarajat Highlands the radical Shiite supporters of the Ayatollah Khomeini battle with their more moderate Shiite co-religionists.

Political turmoil in the government and in the resistance has produced at least two important results: the government is unable to enlist fresh recruits into its army, and guerrilla leaders are growing more independent of the Peshawar-based political organizations. The government has resorted to using gangs to round up young men in the streets and even to invade homes in search of draft-age men.

Resistance Operations. Despite the political turmoil, individual groups of *mujahidin* were better organized and armed in 1983 than in previous years. Guerrilla attacks in urban areas increased, and this ability of the freedom fighters to carry the offensive from the countryside to the urban areas was the most characteristic escalation during 1983.

Mujahidin delegations also traveled abroad and met with world leaders, including President Reagan. They testified before the U.S. Congress and before the so-called People's Tribunals in Paris and Oslo concerning Soviet atrocities—the most notorious being the burning of 105 villagers of Padkhawab-e-Shana by Soviet soldiers who poured gasoline into an underground shelter and set it afire.

A new development for the resistance was the truce negotiated in the Panjshir by Ahmad Shah Massood with the Soviets, bypassing the Babrak government. The truce started in the spring and lasted for six months. Although criticized by some resistance leaders, Massood was able to rearm and regroup and to organize the Panjshir area into a ministate, establishing an efficient military organization and a political administration.

Aside from the Panjshir, resistance operations were most active in Paktia province bordering on Pakistan, where *mujahidin* besieged the important towns of Matun, Urgun, Khost, and Jaji, forcing the Soviets to supply the towns by air. Other areas of intense resistance activity were Herat and Ghazni.

Another important resistance activity during 1983 was the operation of ten mobile transmitters of Radio Free Kabul. Especially galling to the Soviets were the broadcasts in Russian to Soviet troops by prominent Soviet dissidents.

The Economy. During 1983 the Afghan economy was almost totally dependent on the USSR. Afghanistan received a large share of total Soviet foreign economic aid—about $800 million worth, mostly in food and commodities. The USSR also made Indian rupees (repayment for arms sales) available to purchase commodities in India for the Afghan market. The USSR recouped some of its aid by increasing the extraction of Afghan minerals. It monopolized the supplies of natural gas at 40% below world prices. Soviet experts, in total control of economic planning, allocated only 10% of domestic investment to agriculture, although Afghanistan is primarily an agricultural country.

Inflation rose to an annual rate of 39%, marking a total rise of 250% in the cost of living since the Soviet invasion. Food shortages have caused food prices to skyrocket. Famine conditions were reported in the countryside, causing a flood of refugees, mostly women and children, into Kabul, which has grown from a population of 900,000 in 1979 to 1.3 million. At the same time, the exodus of skilled and intellectual workers, as well as the flight of draft-age young men, have created acute labor shortages only partly alleviated by the estimated 4,000 Soviet technicians now in the country. In every sector of the economy the process of converting Afghanistan into an economic colony of the USSR continued apace.

LEON B. POULLADA
University of Nebraska

AFGHANISTAN • Information Highlights

Official Name: Democratic Republic of Afghanistan.
Location: Central Asia.
Area: 250,000 sq mi (647 500 km²).
Population (July 1983 est.): 14,177,000.
Chief Cities (1979 census): Kabul, the capital, 913,164; Kandahar, 178,409; Herat, 140,323.
Government: *Head of state,* Babrak Karmal, president (took power Dec. 1979). *Head of government,* Soltan Ali Keshtmand, prime minister (named June 1981). *Policymaking body*—57-member Revolutionary Council.
Monetary Unit: Afghani (50.6 afghanis equal U.S.$1, July 1983).
Gross National Product (1981–82 U.S.$): $2,400,000,000.

AFRICA

Africa in 1983 suffered its most calamitous drought in more than a century. Critical water shortages drastically lowered yields of all commercial and food crops, reducing export earnings and triggering mass starvation on a scale exceeding the drought-induced famine of 1973, which claimed more than one million lives. Severely malnourished bovine and human populations led to increases in disease. This coincided with foreign exchange shortages, which limited imports of essential grains, vaccines, and medicines.

The drought most devastatingly affected 22 countries embracing 140 million people. Crops failed in a vast belt stretching from Lesotho through East Africa to Ethiopia and around the Sahara's southern rim through West Africa's Sahel. Under normal conditions, this broad arc is a major source of food. According to the UN Food and Agricultural Organization (FAO), 1982–83 food production fell dramatically in nearly every country. Cereal production dropped in sub-Saharan Africa by 7% and by 10% on a per capita basis. FAO officials contended that the prospects for 1983–84 were even more alarming.

The 1983 drought represented an acceleration of a steadily worsening continent-wide crisis in food production. From 1960 the amount of food produced in Africa increased less than 2% annually, and now it has begun to drop even lower. In the same period, population increased by more than 3% per year, and it now is rising steadily. Africa now grows less food per person than it did 20 years ago.

Africa's food problems are not simply the result of persistent drought. Shortsighted and politically motivated economic policies over the last two decades also are to blame. Many governments sought to ensure cheap food for highly politicized and socially volatile urban consumers by manipulating market forces. Prices paid to local farmers were kept artificially low, often below production costs, and many staples that could be grown locally were imported at a loss of precious currency exchange. Of 41 sub-Saharan countries, only five in 1983 could meet their own food needs from domestic production. Fiscal resources have been diverted from development projects to drought and famine relief. More than two million people in the poorer and most deeply affected countries—such as Ethiopia, Somalia, Chad, and Ghana—have fled to neighboring states, straining their meager resources and creating domestic social and political turmoil. An increasing number of countries have become dependent on Western donors for food assistance—even Zimbabwe and South Africa, which historically have been net food exporters to the rest of the continent.

Wide World

Famine victims in Ethiopia receive emergency treatment. Drought had serious effects in 22 African countries.

The great drought, clearly the biggest and most intractable issue of 1983, was compounded by a severe fiscal crisis. Never since the commencement of the independence era a quarter of a century ago has Africa's economic situation been more precarious. Recession in the Western industrialized countries, as well as falling demand, reduced African export earnings. This led to a deterioration in public revenue, declines in real growth rates, and an explosion in public debt. Governments had to increase their foreign borrowing at a time when interest rates reached historic highs in overseas financial markets. Consequently, debt service obligations rose to the extent that even critical elements of local infrastructures could not be maintained. Domestically, salaries in the public and private employment sectors were reduced or delayed. This contributed to work stoppages, productivity declines, and an escalation in corruption and extortion. Externally, many countries—notably Zaire, with its $4 billion (U.S.) debt—fell deeper into arrears on debt payments of interest and principal to private banks, despite previous debt reschedulings. Consequently, 1983 was the year that African

Spotlight on Nigeria: Africa's most populous nation and the world's fourth largest democracy, Nigeria elected President Shehu Shagari (above left) to a second four-year term on August 6. Shagari's second term was short-lived, however, as he was overthrown in a military coup on December 31. During Shagari's tenure much attention focused on the nation's oil industry (below), which was affected adversely by a world glut and OPEC quotas. The oil problems led to economic difficulties for Nigeria. Another issue was the expenditure of millions of foreign exchange dollars to move the capital from the overcrowded city of Lagos (above right) to Abuja, a new city in central Nigeria.

governments of all ideological persuasions flocked to the International Monetary Fund (IMF) for emergency funds to cover their politically and economically destabilizing balance-of-payments deficits. In 1983 alone, the IMF approved financial arrangements for nearly one third of Africa's countries. Pressure from the IMF and creditor countries was forcing governments to institute economic austerity programs that included painfully sharp and politically dangerous cuts in urban food subsidies, currency devaluations, tax increases and wage freezes, and drastic cutbacks in national development plans. Debates over whether or not to take the bitter IMF pill contributed to deep ideological splits and cabinet shake-ups. In 1983 more than half of Africa's governments experienced a major cabinet reshuffle.

The world press has been quick to catalog Africa's agonies and to criticize its miscalculations. Not surprisingly the press came under greater attack from governments which, because of economic uncertainty, were more insecure and less tolerant of criticism and negative reportage. Foreign correspondents were an especially vulnerable target. Never before has the issue of press freedom in Africa been so passionately debated and under such intense and sustained attack. Zimbabwe and Morocco were only two of nearly a score of countries that launched formal campaigns against foreign correspondents and expelled them. South Africa and Zimbabwe, which had enjoyed a reputation for a relatively free and independent press, tightened their control over news gathering and dissemination. In July, six southern African nations signed the Kadoma Declaration, agreeing to ban foreign journalists who report to bureaus based in South Africa. By contrast, in confident Nigeria the foreign and domestic press flourished and remained robustly free and unbridled in their criticism of local events. Nigeria was an exception to the accelerating trend toward greater government control and censorship; its press remained one of the freest in the Third World.

In 1983, Africa took a major step away from dependence on the Western press by launching the Pan-African News Agency (PANA). In May, PANA broadcast its first news release from headquarters in Dakar, Senegal. Twenty-two African nations joined PANA, and it was expected to take its place among Reuters, UPI, Associated Press, and Agence France Press as a major world news agency.

In another renewed effort toward pan-African unity, the 19th annual summit of the Organization of African Unity (OAU) commanded the best attendance in its 20-year history. Ethiopian head of state Col. Mengistu Haile Mariam was unanimously elected chairman for 1983–84, and resolutions were passed with little rancor. The summit's cooperative spirit stood in sharp contrast to the previous year's failure, after two tries, to obtain the requisite quorum. In June the last-minute voluntary withdrawal of the Saharan Arab Democratic Republic (SADR) saved the summit from a third collapse. Morocco and its allies refused to recognize the legitimacy of the SADR and in 1982 opposed its admission as the organization's 51st member. Since 1967 the SADR and its Polisario affiliate have been locked in a war with Morocco for control over Western Sahara, the disputed former Spanish colony.

The OAU's condition remained critical despite half-hearted gestures of unity. It was in deep deficit, with only two countries up-to-date on their annual dues. And the organization's credibility has been weakened by its inability to resolve conflicts among its own members and its unwillingness to act against members whose policies run counter to the charter's principles.

West Africa

In Nigeria the year opened with the abrupt expulsion of nearly two million foreign workers. It was the largest forced migration in West African history. The bulk of those expelled were from Ghana, a country already near bankruptcy and with severe food and employment problems. Nigeria's expulsion order came in response to serious domestic unemployment and economic decline, brought on in part by the world oil glut. More than 90% of the country's foreign exchange earnings are derived from its petroleum exports. The deportations created extreme personal hardship and further exacerbated Nigeria's already tense relations with its fellow members of the Economic Community of West African States (ECOWAS).

Nigeria's image was somewhat restored in August and September, after a series of free national elections reaffirmed the country's commitment to a multiparty representative democracy. President Alhaji Shehu Shagari was returned to power after securing an impressive 47% of the popular vote in a hotly contested, six-party race. He drew widely from across religious, ethnic, and regional boundaries in a nation of nearly 90 million citizens and more than 200 distinct cultures. The ruling National Party of Nigeria (NPN) secured more than half the state governorships and clear legislative majorities in the Senate, House, and state assemblies, in spite of sporadic violence at the polls and massive ballot rigging by all parties.

Charging that Nigeria had become "enslaved by a handful of people who had been sharing the wealth . . . and were determined to remain in office at any cost," military men removed Shagari from the presidency on December 31.

Senegal's President Abdou Diouf was reelected by an overwhelming majority, and his Socialist Party won a strong legislative major-

Citing economic difficulties caused by the world oil glut, Nigeria expelled nearly 2 million illegal aliens in January. Most were from Ghana, which opened its border with neighboring Togo to allow its nationals to return home.

ity in the February general elections. So sweeping were the victories that 11 of the country's opposition parties accused the government of electoral improprieties and for several months boycotted parliamentary sessions.

Events went less well in landlocked Upper Volta, one of the poorest countries in the world. The moderate military regime of President Jean-Baptiste Ouedraogo was overthrown in an August coup by his recently purged prime minister, Cap. Thomas Sankara. Ouedraogo had only held power for ten months, having ousted a two-year-old civilian-military junta. Sankara's accession to power greatly strained relations with neighboring Ivory Coast, which feared the new regime's pro-Libyan sentiments.

In Cameroon serious tension developed over a bitter power struggle between President Paul Biya and his predecessor, Ahmadou Ahidjo. In November 1982, Ahidjo voluntarily retired from office but continued to involve himself in government affairs. By early 1983 it had boiled down to a struggle over control of the leadership of the ruling Union Nationale Camerounaise. Ahidjo lost, but in the process party splits severely damaged Cameroon's international reputation for political stability and contributed to considerable social unrest in the Fulani-dominated north, where the former president still enjoyed support.

On the regional front, ECOWAS succeeded in stimulating greater cooperation among the various member Anglophone and Francophone countries. By midyear Ghana had reopened its border with Togo and Ivory Coast and prepared to sell electricity to the Ivoirians. At the ECOWAS summit in Conakry, Guinea, Mali became the first of seven West African states to receive loans from the new ECOWAS Fund. The European Community (EC) will cofinance a regional telecommunications network.

Northeast Africa

In Sudan, President Jaafar al-Nemery was reelected, having run unopposed in an election that attracted few voters. Deteriorating economic conditions led to broader opposition and more intense political turmoil. Early in the year, the United States increased its military support and dispatched AWACS surveillance planes in response to an alleged Libyan-led coup attempt.

Most of Nemery's opposition came from the non-Arab south, where he hoped to consolidate his power by redividing the area into three regions. Considerable popular sentiment against this was expressed by the antigovernment Anya Nya II guerrilla movement. Sudan is Egypt's major breadbasket, and the Nemery government is dependent on Egyptian and U.S. economic and military aid for its own survival. In a risky effort to regain popular support at home, Nemery freed all 13,000 prison inmates, including political detainees.

Neighboring Marxist Ethiopia was in the grip of its worst drought and famine in a decade. This was compounded by a protracted and financially ruinous struggle against secessionist movements in the northern provinces of Tigre and Eritrea. Offensives against both movements failed, but the warfare and drought drove thousands of starving families into neighboring Sudan, which itself was straining to feed its population. In both countries, food relief efforts have been seriously hampered by harassment from guerrilla groups seeking supplies.

In Somalia, on the Horn of Africa, the 14-year-old government of President Mohammed Siad Barre fought to survive against almost insuperable odds. Large sections of the country were in a state of anarchy, brought on by an intensification of historically rooted clan warfare and antigovernment guerrillas. In the northern region, talk of secession grew as Barre's grip on the situation weakened.

East Africa

Kenya's President Daniel arap Moi ran unopposed in the September general elections and won in an atmosphere of widespread voter apathy. Prospective candidates for legislative seats had to be cleared by the country's only legal political party, the Kenya African National Union (KANU). Consequently, government opponents were unable to run, perhaps accounting for the uncomfortable fact that less than 50% of registered voters went to the polls. Afterward observers argued whether Moi and his allies had received a clear mandate.

Throughout 1983, President Moi consolidated his authority by weakening the historically preeminent position of the Kikuyu ethnic group. Charles Njonjo, a Kikuyu and for two decades one of Kenya's most politically powerful citizens, was suspended from the party and his cabinet post for allegedly traitorous activities. A power behind the throne since the days of Jomo Kenyatta, Njonjo was one of the most conservative, pro-Western members of the government and was partly responsible for Kenya's withdrawal from the East African Community more than a decade ago.

Neighboring Uganda, struggling to recover from the Idi Amin era, continued to be buffeted by mass killings and banditry in the northern region and the suburbs of Kampala, the capital. President Milton Obote failed to bring the Uganda National Liberation Army under control. Though nominally a government force, the army often acted independently and was responsible for much of the violence, kidnappings, and systematic looting of villages. Moreover, some veterans impersonated soldiers and police and extorted money and property from civilians.

In Tanzania the economic situation worsened, and the country which in the 1960s and 1970s had made ''self-reliance'' its development goal was forced to approach the IMF and other donors for emergency food and loans. Most of the experimental Ujamaa communal farming villages faltered for lack of funds and material. Shortages of food staples and industrial spare parts brought the economy to a standstill. Zanzibar island, which by contrast had prospered in recent years, chafed under mainland rule and threatened to secede. Despite cabinet reshuffles, President Julius Nyerere's control over internal developments appeared weaker and less certain than at any time since the abortive 1964 army mutiny and rebellion on Zanzibar.

Central Africa

In the Republic of Chad, the longest civil war in the history of independent Africa took a more violent turn, provoking the most serious foreign military intervention on African soil since the Congo crisis of the early 1960s. In late June, rebel forces supported by the Libyan military attacked a vital outpost in northern Chad. This rebellion against the government of President Hissène Habré was led by Goukouni Oueddei, the former head of Chad who in June 1982 had been ousted by Habré with covert U.S. support. Chad, with a population of approximately 4.7 million, is about four fifths the size of Alaska. Though poor in natural resources, it commands an enviable geographical position. It is bounded by six countries and is comparable to a keystone, linking northern, eastern, and equatorial Africa and the Arab Muslim north with the Christian and animist south. Sudan, Nigeria, and Zaire feared that the fall of Habré would transform strategic Chad into a launchpad for Libyan expansionism and Islamic fundamentalism south of the Sahara. In response to the June rebel invasion, the United States rushed $25 million in military aid and airlifted more than 2,000 Israeli-trained Zaire paratroopers. France, sensitive to U.S. initiatives in Africa and bound by a defense treaty with its former colony, dispatched an additional 2,000 French paratroopers and eight fighter jets. By September, Libya had withdrawn most of its troops and aircraft, and the 18-year-old civil war had returned to an inconclusive stalemate. A month later, Habré had to contend with an escalation of guerrilla activity in the vital cotton- and food-producing region south of Chad's war-torn capital, Ndjamena.

Southward, in Angola, another long civil war began to escalate. South African-supported guerrilla forces of the National Union for the Total Independence of Angola (UNITA) made impressive territorial gains and claimed nearly one third of the country. Under its charismatic leader, Dr. Jonas Savimbi, it infiltrated far north of the Benguela railway, the vital east-west artery that geographically divides the country in half. The legitimate Marxist government of José Eduardo dos Santos weakened under the strain of internal struggles between the ideologues and pragmatists. By late 1983 the protracted war had disrupted Angola's principal transportation and communications infrastructures and plunged the economy into deep depression. UNITA's gains coincided with greater U.S. and South African pressure on the Angolans to remove the Cuban troops and relinquish their support for South West Africa People's Organization (SWAPO), which, from bases in Angola, was fighting for the independence of neighboring Namibia.

Southern Africa

East, central, and southern Africa have begun to cooperate more closely on technical, trade, transport, and communications matters through two new organizations: the Southern African Development Coordination Conference (SADCC) and the larger Eastern and Southern African Preferential Trade Area (PTA). The former, in particular, aims at reducing southern Africa's economic dependence on South Africa. SADCC, underfinanced and factionalized, has had little success in reducing its vulnerability to South Africa's destabilizing strategies. In 1983 political cohesion among member states in both organizations was severely tested by border disputes, ideological differences, and sabotage of key installations by guerrillas operating in neighboring countries. Moreover, South Africa saw the organizations as threats to its own spheres of influence and sought to hold Botswana, Swaziland, and Lesotho within its own Southern African Customs Union (SACU).

In South Africa the Botha administration mounted a public relations campaign among the nation's 4.5 million whites in support of a referendum on constitutional changes that would give a limited role in government to the 2.5 million mixed-ancestry Coloureds and one million Indians. The changes called for a tricameral parliament, with separate houses for each group. The 18 million Africans, or 73% of the population, would be totally excluded. The changes would also endow the state president with vastly increased powers, effectively transforming South Africa into an executive presidential system. Those proposals divided Afrikaner- and English-speaking voters, as well as Coloureds and Indians, but the Blacks united against them. Thirty-two organizations from all quarters formed the multiracial United Democratic Front to fight the proposals. Nearly 12,000 opponents gathered in August at a mass meeting outside Cape Town. It was the largest antigovernment rally in some 20 years.

Meanwhile, black unions became more powerful and united. In June the 25,000-member, all-black National Union of Mineworkers was recognized by the Chamber of Mines and negotiated a wage agreement with them, a first in South Africa's century-old mining industry. But as the government allowed blacks to expand their union activities, they also imprisoned their most militant and outspoken leaders. Undaunted, black unions, representing more than 300,000 workers, took major steps in forming a unified Trade Union Federation.

In late May, an African National Congress (ANC) car-bomb explosion in downtown Pretoria took 18 lives and wounded 217 in the bloodiest guerrilla attack in the nation's history. The government retaliated with an air raid on a suspected ANC base in Mozambique.

Economic depression and Mozambique National Resistance (MNR) guerrilla attacks on rural villages have forced Mozambique peasants into the congested urban areas. In response, the Marxist government instituted an influx-control similar to South Africa's, though not racially motivated. In 1983 tens of thousands of unemployed urban dwellers were rusticated to labor-short state farms.

In Zimbabwe, Prime Minister Robert Mugabe and his ruling Zimbabwe African National Union (ZANU) were locked in bitter power struggles with the courts and the opposition party, the Zimbabwe African Peoples Union (ZAPU). Defendants in treason trials who were acquitted by High Court judges were immediately rearrested under an Emergency Powers Act dating from white Rhodesian days. In his quest for a one-party state, Mugabe launched a major offensive in western Zimbabwe, the power base of Joshua Nkomo and his ZAPU party. The security situation in Matabeleland deteriorated dramatically in early 1983, as bands of Ndebele dissidents, many of them former soldiers, increased their attacks on white farmers, government installations, and alleged ZANU sympathizers. Mugabe dispatched a North Korean-trained, all-Shona brigade, which resorted to terrorist tactics. By mid-March more than one thousand Ndebele civilians had been killed or wounded. Nkomo and his staff fled into voluntary exile, and his party was thrown into disarray. Major religious organizations and the world press accused the brigade of atrocities. By May the violence on both sides had subsided, and the brigade was soon withdrawn. Nkomo returned in August to resume his parliamentary seat in an atmosphere of government intimidation. But the dissidents' violence and the brutal government retaliation generated feelings of insecurity and ethnic bitterness.

In Namibia hopes dimmed for an international settlement following the collapse in early 1983 of the interim government and South Africa's reimposition of direct rule. Throughout 1983 high-level negotiations on independence remained at an impasse, despite a mission to southern Africa by UN Secretary-General Javier Pérez de Cuellar.

RICHARD W. HULL, *New York University*

Pierre Perrin/Gamma-Liaison

Spotlight on Chad: An 18-year-long civil war in the north-central African state of Chad took on new dimensions in 1983. Government forces of President Hissène Habré (left) were overrun at strategic northern outposts by Libyan-backed insurgents in midsummer. Former President Goukouni Oueddei (bottom, center), whom Habré had overthrown in 1982, led the rebels. As Libyan troops, planes, and artillery steadily forced Habré's army into retreat, France and the United States stepped up military and economic aid. French troops (center) halted the rebel advance and stayed on to help keep the peace.

Pierre Perrin/Gamma Liaison

Brandily/Gamma-Liaison

Danek/Gamma-Liaison

A Midwest farmer inspects his unusually poor corn crop, which was caused by the worst drought in 47 years.

AGRICULTURE

U.S. and world crop yields were generally down in 1983, largely because of adverse weather conditions. New government programs, trade arrangements, price levels, and management systems were instituted.

United States. The crop year in the United States started with favorable weather. By midsummer, however, the weather turned hot and dry over major farming areas in the Midwest and the South. Persisting through August, the drought—the worst since 1936—reduced yields of major crops far below their record levels of recent years. Total grain production also was down, both because of reduced yields and a government program called PIK (payment-in-kind) to reduce crop acreage. The PIK program was put into effect at planting time, before the bad weather began. Yields per acre were 2.16 metric tons for corn, .68 tons for soybeans, and 1.08 tons for wheat.* Total 1983 production

* 1 metric ton equals 1.102 short tons. All tonnages given in this article are metric.

was 116 million tons of corn, 41 million tons of soybeans, 42 million tons of wheat, and 8 million bales (1.7 million tons) of cotton. These levels compared with 1982 figures of 213 million, 62 million, 76 million, and 12 million (2.6 million tons), respectively. Corn, the nation's major crop, had the smallest yield since 1970.

The smaller crops caused prices to rise quite sharply. By late August, corn was $3.69 per bushel, compared with $2.12 at the same time in 1982. Soybean was $8.81, compared with $5.34; wheat was $3.86, compared with $3.62; and cotton was 73 cents per pound, compared with 60 cents in 1982. Hog prices were high at the start of the year but declined 25% by midyear, as pork supplies increased. In mid-July, hogs were $46.00 per cwt (hundredweight), compared with $59.50 a year earlier. Fed beef was down slightly because of large supplies. The mid-July price of finished beef was $61.12 per cwt, compared with $66.40 in 1982. Egg and broiler prices were up somewhat over the previous year. Farmland prices again declined in 1983, and the speculative bubble of 1970–80s had burst. Production costs were up again. Some farmers went bankrupt during the year, but PIK saved the majority that faced financial risk.

U.S. grain exports remained depressed after having increased continuously from 1960 through 1981. Agricultural exports in the first six months of 1983 were down 13% from 1982 and remained low throughout the year. On July 28, the United States and Soviet Union finally came to a long-term agreement on grain trade. President Reagan had agreed in April to discuss a new accord, and the Soviets in May accepted the offer to begin negotiations. The 1975 five-year agreement required them to buy 6 million metric tons annually but no more than 8 million without approval by the U.S. government. Although that agreement ran out in 1981, it had been extended annually ever since. (President Jimmy Carter declared a partial embargo in 1980.) The new agreement also runs for five years; it requires the Soviets to buy at least 9 million tons of grain per year and allows them to buy up to 12 million tons without seeking the permission of the U.S. government.

Because of large grain crops in recent years, depressed exports, and low prices, the U.S. government returned to the PIK subsidy program, which it had used 22 years earlier. Under PIK, the government gives farmers surplus feed grains, wheat, and cotton for removing land from cultivation—80% of the normal yield for feed grains, 90% for wheat, and 80% for cotton. Under the program, farmers left idle more than 80 million acres (32 million ha), or about 20% of all U.S. cropland, in 1983.

The PIK program was put into effect because the vast grain crop of 1982 left a large carryover as the nation went into 1983. Grain prices were low at the beginning of the year, and President Reagan announced the subsidy program on January 11. In 1982 the government had asked farmers to leave some of their land idle, but few did so because there were no direct payments and because the only benefits to farmers was eligibility for nonrecourse loans. The 1983 PIK program came at the urging of Budget Director David Stockman. He considered that since the government already owned the commodities or had loans on them to the farmers, the payments really would not cost anything (although treasury payments were involved when the government made loans to the farmers for the commodities and then dismissed those loans).

The PIK program, however, did not entirely solve the surplus problem. Even with reduced crop production in 1983, the mammoth carryover from 1982 caused the nation to go into 1984 with large commodity stocks. Corn and rice stocks at the end of 1983 were 50% of normal utilization, while wheat and cotton stocks were 70% of utilization.

The cost of U.S. farm programs in 1983 was staggering. The total cost of all programs to bolster farm prices and incomes was more than $21 billion. This amount was more than the total 1982 farm income of $19 billion. (By the time the costs of the PIK program extending in 1984 are included, it is estimated that the total cost of 1983 programs might be as high as $31 billion.) These tremendous costs gave rise to concern by the executive branch, Congress, and the public at large. Secretary Block said that lower-cost programs must be found. Congress began hearings on a new farm bill to be enacted in 1984. As long as U.S. and world crops are large and prices remain depressed, some form of supply control may be continued.

The government continued to give away some of the surplus cheese and butter which it had acquired under its dairy subsidy program. Prices for dairy commodities were held so high that farmers continued to produce surplus quantities of milk, which then passed into the government's hands in the form of butter and cheese. By April 1983, the stocks of butter, cheese, and dried milk stored by the government were up 17%, 21%, and 24%, respectively, from the same time in 1982. Congressional action provided for a reduction in the number of dairy cows and in milk production through a program to buy dairy cows by an assessment per hundredweight of milk sold by farmers.

Many U.S. farmers continued to be under high financial risk, and a fairly large number declared bankruptcy. The financial stress grew mainly out of the extremely high prices farmers had paid for land in recent years, the large indebtedness on it, and high interest rates.

U.S. agriculture remained the most efficient in the world. Each farm worker produced enough food for 78 other persons. Only 2.7% of the nation's population was in agriculture, and U.S. consumers spent only 15% of their disposable income for food. In the Soviet Union, by comparison, agriculture requires 26% of the nation's work force and consumers spend 40% of their income for food. Parallel figures run up to 80% in some of the poor developing countries.

USSR and Eastern Europe. The Soviet Union produced an estimated 200 million metric tons of grain in 1983. This was about 10% more than in each of the previous two years and the most produced since 1978. However, production was still 38 million tons less than planned. The crop shortfall required the USSR to continue large grain imports in its attempt to increase livestock production and the general quality of diets. Good fodder crops in 1982 allowed the nation to increase milk and red meat production by about 5% in 1983. The Soviets entered 1983 with noticeably better feed supplies as a result of continued grain imports and good fodder crops; cattle, hogs, and poultry had

American farmers and their supporters attended a rally in Des Moines, IA, in March to support minimum prices for corn and soybeans and a moratorium on farm foreclosures.

UPI

reached record levels by early in the year. The Soviet Union therefore reduced grain import volumes from the United States by about half in 1983—to the lowest since 1977—but it still was one of the United States' top ten export markets, and the new grain deal will increase the volume substantially in 1984. Two important policy changes were made in pricing and farm management. In early 1983, price increases were announced for a wide range of farm commodities. The purpose was to increase production profitability and provide incentives for greater output. On the management side, farm brigades were given tracts of land to operate. The brigades were given a share of production so as to establish a better link between labor remuneration and productivity.

Other Eastern European countries also changed prices and management systems. Food prices were increased by 4% in Hungary and considerably more in Poland. Some agricultural decision-making was shifted from the national to the local level in Rumania and Bulgaria; the shift was even more pronounced in Hungary and Yugoslavia. While weather was more favorable than in 1982, all Eastern European countries had trouble acquiring such farm inputs as fertilizer and pesticides. All countries also were restrained in the purchase of farm machinery and other equipment because of their strained borrowing conditions with Western nations. Most stressed was Poland, where 40% of broiler-producing capacity remained unused because of the inability to borrow funds to purchase feed grains. Poland's agriculture was handicapped also by a lack of funds to buy spare parts for tractors, harvesters, and other machinery. After his June visit, Pope John Paul II announced a $5 billion aid program to bolster the production of Poland's medium-size and larger private farms. Funds were to be obtained from Western governments, private foundations, and the Catholic Church. The Polish government and the Peasant Party of Poland agreed on a constitutional amendment to legalize private farming and land ownership.

Western Europe. Grain production again was high in Western Europe, and imports from the United States declined because of the large crop. Farm income continued to improve because of disinflation and economy recovery. The Economic Community (EC) further increased its expenditures to support agriculture. The subsidization of exports absorbed a large share of this increase. Through these subsidies, the EC kept its farm products highly competitive in world markets. The EC also raised support payments on agricultural commodities by 13.6%.

Other Major Exporters. Canada increased its grain acreage even though the Canadian Wheat Board reduced support prices for small grains; wheat exports were at record levels in 1982–83. Favorable weather returned to Australia, and the nation again became a sizable exporter with a large 1983 grain crop; meat production in 1983 was down following the 1982 drought. In New Zealand, the government initiated programs to increase livestock production substantially; lamb and sheep exports to the Middle East and the Soviet Union were not as large as expected. New Zealand and Australia put into effect the Closer Economic Relationship (CER), drafted in 1982. The CER called for a reduction in protectionism and allowed for more trade between the two countries.

Virtually every nation in southern Africa suffered a drought in 1983. Such countries as Zambia, Zaire, and Lesotho, which normally import corn from South Africa and Zimbabwe, will need to import from the United States in 1984. With unfavorable weather also in northern Africa, Morocco, Algeria, and Tunisia will import about 7 million tons of grain from the United States. Wheat production was up in other Middle East countries.

Asia. Wheat and coarse grain production increased in China, but rice production was below the 1982 record crop. With growing domestic production, imports of all farm products except grain have declined. While traditionally a large importer of cotton, China's imports dropped to less than 500,000 bales (.11 million metric tons) in 1983. Southern Asia had record 1983 wheat crops, while early estimates indicated a normal rice crop, and oilseed production was high in most countries of the region. Prolonged rains dampened Pakistan's wheat crop, and it had to import about 400,000 tons. Japan increased its corn imports from the United States, as livestock production was expanded, but it shifted most of its sorghum imports to Argentina.

Latin America. National monetary crises forced Mexico and Brazil to reduce food imports. With normal weather, crop output rose in Latin America but did not get back to trend levels. With internal political uncertainty, agriculture was the only sector which expanded in Argentina during 1983. Total grain output was at a record level of 31 million tons.

Agricultural Policies and Trade. A panel examining U.S. allegations that the EC had violated rules of the General Agreement on Tariffs and Trade (GATT) through subsidization of wheat exports ruled only that the EC limit the use of subsidies in flour exports. The United States expressed dissatisfaction with the panel's findings. Pakistan made a three-year agreement to deliver rice to Guinea-Bissau, while Thailand signed a similar agreement with Senegal. Cuba signed barter agreements with several Eastern European countries, while Costa Rica bartered coffee to Israel for agrochemicals.

EARL O. HEADY
Iowa State University

ALABAMA

The health of the governor, problems related to the election of a reapportioned legislature, and the possible adoption of a new constitution were big news in Alabama in 1983. Economically, there were signs of recovery. Severe flooding and a tornado struck sections of the state in early December.

The Governor. Gov. George C. Wallace (D), 64, was inaugurated for his fourth term on January 17. During the first three months of his new administration, Wallace was hospitalized for a total of five weeks because of a colon infection and reactions to medication. The governor has been paralyzed since an assassination attempt during the 1972 presidential campaign.

Legislative Elections. Following earlier Justice Department approval, a three-judge federal court on April 11 gave its endorsement to a state legislative reapportionment plan enacted in a February special session. This was the first state-adopted plan ever to be accepted by federal authorities as fair to black voters.

Republican legislative candidates were nominated in September 6 primaries, and Democratic selections were made by the party's state committee on October 1. Twelve incumbent Democratic legislators were denied renomination. Several attributed their defeat to the influence of the Alabama Education Association, the Alabama Labor Council, and the Alabama Democratic Conference, a black affiliate of the state party. Sixteen candidates who failed to receive Democratic nominations subsequently ran as independents. In the November 8 balloting, 8 independents and 16 Republicans were elected. In what was interpreted as moderate voter reaction to the method by which its nominees had been selected, Democratic seats dropped from 129 to 115.

New Constitution Proposed. The Alabama state legislature met in regular session from April to August. The most important result of the body's deliberations was a new constitu-

UPI

Some 1,200 blacks marched from Eufaula to Montgomery to protest police violence and promote voter registration.

tion, offered as a replacement for the much-amended Constitution of 1901. On September 30 a state circuit judge ruled that the proposed constitution could not go on the ballot as a single amendment. The Alabama Supreme Court initially set aside that decision. However, on November 2 the court ruled 6–3 that the present Constitution requires a convention if a new charter is to be written. Therefore no referendum was held on election day.

The legislature passed few other bills of major significance, except for ones providing educational and general fund appropriations. However, several minor measures proposed by Governor Wallace to augment general state revenues were enacted.

Economic Improvement. Alabama's unemployment rate was above 15% early in the year, but by August it had declined to some 12%. When state revenue collections exceeded original expectations, proration of state funds for education was decreased from 10 to 5%.

Capital Punishment. On April 22, convicted murderer John Louis Evans III, 33, was electrocuted at the Holman state penitentiary.

WILLIAM H. STEWART
The University of Alabama

ALABAMA · Information Highlights

Area: 51,705 sq mi (133 916 km²).

Population (1982 est.): 3,943,000.

Chief Cities (1980 census): Montgomery, the capital, 178,157; Birmingham, 284,413; Mobile, 200,452.

Government (1983): *Chief Officers*—governor, George C. Wallace (D); lt. gov., Bill Baxley (D). *Legislature*—Senate, 35 members; House of Representatives, 105 members.

State Finances (fiscal year 1981): *Revenues,* $5,105,000,000; *expenditures,* $4,374,000,000.

Personal Income (1982): $34,101,000,000; per capita, $8,649.

Labor Force (July 1983): *Nonagricultural wage and salary earners,* 1,319,300; *unemployed,* 228,300 (13.0% of total force).

Education (fall 1981): *Enrollment*—public elementary schools, 518,534; public secondary, 224,914; colleges and universities (1981–1982), 166,375 students. *Public school expenditures* (1980–81), $1,086,372,000 ($1,384 per pupil).

ALASKA

Items of concern and interest in Alaska during 1983 included the problem of alcoholism, a change in the state's time zones, the oil industry, and the final report of the Alaska Statehood Commission. The year also marked the first full year of a new Democratic gubernatorial administration.

Politics. In winning the November 1982 election, William Sheffield apparently had benefited from his opposition to two major initiative measures on the ballot—attempts to relocate the state capital from Juneau to a point north of Anchorage and to eliminate the regulations which give preference in hunting and fishing to individuals dependent on fish and game for subsistence. Richard Randolph, the Libertarian standard-bearer, had campaigned for the governor's office instead of seeking re-election to his seat in the state House of Representatives in an attempt to gain the party a place on the state election ballot in future contests. He was successful in that effort, but the defeat of his fellow Libertarian in the House by a Democratic challenger left the party without legislative representation for the first time in five years.

The governor's plans for reassertion of executive authority in budgetary matters and for reorganization of the executive branch were met by intense opposition from the ideologically divided legislature. The first session of the 13th Legislature ended with the House adjourning repeatedly in an attempt to force Senate adjournment and thus preclude the joint session required to confirm gubernatorial appointments to cabinet-level positions. Sheffield, with the concurrence of Senate leadership, called a special session to consider his nominees and forced recalcitrant House members to attend the session by providing them with an escort of state troopers. The confirmation process went smoothly once a quorum was achieved, but the House leadership later filed a legal action challenging the constitutionality of the governor's action.

The legislature enacted laws to raise the legal age for consumption of alcoholic beverages from 19 to 21 years and substantially increased the penalties for operating motor vehicles while under the influence of alcohol—including a provision for state confiscation of automobiles of third-time offenders.

Beginning in late October, the state's four time zones became two. Most of Alaska now operates within the Yukon time zone, which is one hour earlier than Pacific standard time. State officials had requested the change since the previous four time zones had caused problems.

The Alaska Statehood Commission, a body created specifically to examine the relationship between the state and the federal government,

ALASKA • Information Highlights

Area: 591,004 sq mi (1 530 700 km²).
Population (1982 est.): 438,000.
Chief Cities (1980 census): Juneau, the capital, 19,528; Anchorage, 173,017; Fairbanks, 22,645; Sitka, 7,803.
Government (1983): *Chief Officers*—governor, William Sheffield (D); lt. gov., Stephen McAlpine (D). *Legislature*—Senate, 20 members; House of Representatives, 40 members.
State Finances (fiscal year 1982): *Revenues,* $5,889,000,000; *expenditures,* $3,281,000,000.
Personal Income (1982): $7,118,000,000; per capita, $16,257.
Labor Force (July 1983): *Nonagricultural wage and salary earners,* 227,100; *unemployed* (July 1983), 19,900 (8.5% of total force).
Education: *Enrollment* (fall 1981)—public elementary schools, 63,756; public secondary, 27,102; colleges and universities (fall 1982), 24,556 students. *Public school expenditures* (1981–82), $478,589,000.

issued its final report in 1983. Among other things, the report calls for lifting the export ban on oil produced in Prudhoe Bay, abolition of the Jones Act, and the creation of a legal action fund for state and local governments. The commission also suggested amendments to the U.S. Constitution in order to strengthen the role of the states, but stopped short of calling for Alaska's secession.

A statewide association of Alaska Native villages with Indian Reorganization Act (IRA) councils was formed to address more effectively the potential impacts of state actions on Alaska Native lands once they become alienable (and subject to taxation) under the provisions of the Alaska Native Claims Settlement Act (ANCSA).

Economics. Lowered oil production and falling prices caused a decline in the amount of revenues taken in by the states from oil produced from the Prudhoe Bay fields, resulting in a lower level of state financial assistance available to local governments, both in the form of capital construction projects and in the amount of state revenue sharing. Some cutbacks in state agencies already had taken place. Combined with the recent failure of the consortium attempting to construct an Alaskan Natural Gas Transportation System (ANGTS) to obtain funding for the project, this substantially dampened the economic forecast for the state. Employment was at a higher level in 1983 than in any year since the oil pipeline was completed, but unemployment also approached record levels.

Other. The state and federal governments were negotiating an agreement to transfer the Alaska Railroad to the state. As of 1983 the railway was the only such facility operated by the federal government.

The U.S. government ended its control over the Pribilof Islands late in the year.

CARL E. SHEPRO
University of Alaska, Fairbanks

ALBANIA

Enver Hoxha, founder and first secretary of the Albanian Party of Labor (APL), turned 75 in 1983. Despite his age and rumored poor health, Secretary Hoxha maintained an active schedule and continued to play the dominant role in national affairs, as he has for nearly four decades.

Politics. While news from his isolated, radically Communist state is strictly censored, the leading candidate to succeed Hoxha appeared to be Ramiz Alia, president of the Presidium and a member of the APL Politburo. During 1983 he traveled throughout the country extolling the achievements of the regíme. His extensive coverage in the Albanian media reinforced the perception that he was the successor-designate.

Lenka Cuko, another member of the Politburo, was elected to the party Secretariat in January; she became the first woman to serve on that body since 1960. Her appointment was intended to recognize the increasingly important role of women in Albanian life. According to official data, women held 32% of administrative positions in the country.

At the June session of the People's Assembly, it was announced that the Office of State Investigations had been detached from the Ministry of the Interior and placed under the direct jurisdiction of the Assembly. The move apparently was intended to strengthen the position of the APL leadership in dealing with opponents.

In April elections for district and local legislators and judges, only 175 of 1,653,838 voters cast their ballots against regime-endorsed candidates. The results were termed "another manifestation of the steel-like unity of the [APL] and the people." In June, however, a national seminar was held to deal with the "apathy," "inertia," and "inactivity" in local political and judicial bodies.

Foreign Relations. Albania and China signed a trade and payments protocol October 4, suggesting a move toward warmer relations. Commercial ties between the two countries had been suspended in 1978 over political and eco-

Camera Press/Photo Trends

Enver Hoxha, who continued to play a dominant role in Albanian affairs, cast his vote in local April elections.

nomic differences between Tiranë and the post-Mao leadership in Peking.

Publication of Hoxha's critical account of Albanian-Yugoslav relations, *The Titoists,* in December 1982 launched a new round of polemics between the two countries. Tiranë accused the Yugoslavian government of continuing to mistreat ethnic Albanians in Kosovo and Macedonia and reiterated its demand that Kosovo be granted republic status within the Yugoslav federation.

Albania in May rejected an invitation by the Greek government to attend a conference aimed at establishing a nuclear-free zone in the Balkans. Albanian-Greek relations were strained further by a June bomb explosion at the Albanian Embassy in Athens. Tiranë blamed "right-wing Greek extremists" and demanded that the Papandreou government take appropriate measures to curb their activities. By year's end, however, tensions appeared to have subsided.

Albania's hostility toward the United States and Soviet Union, meanwhile, showed no signs of diminishing. According to Tiranë, the "imperialist and reactionary" superpowers were intent only on maintaining their superiority in nuclear weaponry and on dominating the Third World. The Albanian press also devoted considerable attention to the domestic and social problems confronting the Soviet Union and the United States.

NICHOLAS C. PANO
Professor of History
Western Illinois University

ALBANIA • Information Highlights

Official Name: People's Socialist Republic of Albania.
Location: Southern Europe, Balkan peninsula.
Area: 11,100 sq mi (28 749 km²).
Population (July 1983 est.): 2,846,000.
Government: *Head of state,* Ramiz Alia, president of the Presidium (took office November 1982). First secretary of the Albanian Party of Labor, Enver Hoxha (took office 1941). *Head of government,* Adil Carcani (took office January 1982). *Legislature* (unicameral)—People's Assembly, 250 members.
Monetary Unit: Lek (7 Lekë equal U.S.$1, July 1983).
Gross National Product (1981 est. U.S.$): $2,380,000,000.

ALBERTA

Because of its natural resources, Alberta had been largely shielded from recent economic problems. But in 1983 it experienced difficulties as oil and gas prices stabilized and even declined. By fall, however, an economic upturn was becoming evident.

The Economy. Unemployment rates remained in the 10–11% range in 1983, while residential vacancies increased from 0.1% to 5%. The tourist industry declined, and emigration to other provinces exceeded immigration. The provincial deficit exceeded C$1 billion. In October the provincial government announced a 13% increase in the income tax.

Increasing vacancy rates inhibited new starts on commercial and apartment buildings, but starts on single-family dwellings exceeded those of 1982. Large institutional projects that were completed included Edmonton's Convention Center, Calgary's Saddledome Arena, and the University of Alberta's new fieldhouse.

It was generally a good year for agriculture. Very high yields of cereal crops were common, except in the southern part of the province, where precipitation was low. After three years of near-drought conditions, the Peace River area reaped abundant harvests.

Education. All postsecondary educational institutions reached record enrollments in 1983. This influx and the limited availability of government aid resulted in restricted registrations and discontinuance of some programs, decreased academic staffs, fewer library acquisitions, and other problems. At other levels, decreasing enrollments, shifting school populations, and financial stringencies led to school board confrontations with both parents and teachers. By October, some school staffs had taken or planned to take strike action.

Also controversial was the minister of education's move to restore provincial examinations at the grade-12 level, and to abolish the Board of Teacher Education and Certification in Alberta.

ALBERTA · Information Highlights

Area: 255,285 sq mi (661 189 km²).
Population (July 1983): 2,350,100.
Chief Cities (1981 census): Edmonton, the capital, 532,246; Calgary, 592,743; Lethbridge, 54,072; Red Deer, 46,393; St. Albert, 31,996.
Government (1983): *Chief Officers*—lt. gov., Frank Lynch-Staunton; premier, Peter Lougheed (Progressive-Conservative); atty. gen., Neil S. Crawford. Legislative Assembly, 79 members.
Education (1982–83): *Enrollment*—elementary and secondary schools, 455,700 pupils; postsecondary, 50,240 students.
Public Finance (1983 fiscal year, est.): *Revenues*, $13,225,500,000; *expenditures*, $10,287,600,000.
Personal Income (average weekly salary, March 1983): $459.07.
Unemployment Rate (August 1983, seasonally adjusted): 11.1%.
(All monetary figures are in Canadian dollars.)

Health Services. Universality of medical and hospital care (medicare) was threatened as provincial insurance rates were increased, benefits were discontinued for persons in default on payments for three months, hospitals were encouraged to charge user fees, and many physicians were overbilling patients. One result was a threat by the federal government to discontinue subsidization of the program.

Environment. A two-month-long blowout from a wild gas well in central Alberta, which also caught fire, caused widespread discomfort and illness, and resulted in two deaths. Other problems included industrial contamination of the Athabasca and sewage contamination of the Saskatchewan rivers. Backed-up sewers resulted in extensive damage in Sherwood Park. June rains kept forest fire loss at the lowest level in several years.

Elections. With no federal or provincial elections scheduled for 1983, attention turned to elections at the municipal level. Edmonton voters elected Lawrence Decore their mayor, and Calgary reelected Mayor Ralph Klein. Across the province, incumbents or former incumbents generally were reelected.

Sports. Edmonton's World University Games, opened by Queen Elizabeth on July 1, attracted about 4,000 athletes from some 75 countries, and Calgary continued to prepare for the 1988 Winter Olympics. At the professional level, both cities had very viable, well-supported football and hockey teams.

J. W. CHALMERS
Concordia College, Edmonton

ALGERIA

After spending his first four years in office consolidating his position at home, Algeria's President Chadli Benjedid in 1983 moved further away from the economic and foreign policies of his predecessor, Houari Boumedienne. Chadli's leadership, combined with sound and successful economic policies, propelled Algeria to a position of regional dominance.

Foreign Relations. In early 1983, Chadli made conciliatory moves toward his North African neighbors, renewing the 25-year-old dream of Maghreb unity. His new approach culminated in a summit with Morocco's King Hassan II in February and resulted in the opening of borders and the exchange of ambassadors with Tunisia and Morocco.

The meeting with Hassan was the first Algeria-Morocco summit in the seven years since the two countries split over Algeria's support for the Polisario guerrillas, who are fighting with Morocco for control of western Sahara. Morocco has charged that the Polisario are Algerian-backed mercenaries, while Algeria supports them as representatives of the Sahrawi people. Though neither country has softened its position, the Algeria-Morocco rapprochement raised hopes that a settlement is possible.

Algeria's relations with the United States had been improving since Algeria negotiated the release of the Americans held hostage in Iran in 1980. In December 1982, U.S. Secretary of Commerce Malcolm Baldrige led a delegation of representatives of 30 American firms on a trip to Algeria to discuss U.S. private investment in that country. The trip produced a report describing the climate for U.S. investment in Algeria as very favorable. In September, U.S. Vice-President George Bush became the highest-ranking American official to visit Algeria. Algeria also began to lessen its dependence on the Soviet Union. One step in that direction was a series of arms deals that were negotiated with France, Italy, and the United Kingdom.

Economy. Observers in Algeria have noted that life for the average Algerian has improved during the four years of Chadli's presidency. This trend continued in 1983, with increased amounts of money being invested in hospitals, schools, housing, and agriculture.

The government began encouraging private-sector expansion by loosening currency regulations and allowing Algerians to maintain foreign-currency bank accounts, while banks began lending money to private investors. This strengthening of the private sector has led to the creation of more jobs. It was estimated in 1983 that private industry provided more than one third of all the jobs in Algeria.

The key to Algeria's economic success was the reduction of the country's dependence on oil exports. In 1983, oil exports accounted for only about 20% of Algeria's foreign-exchange earnings. While other countries exporting oil were feeling the effects of 1983's lower oil prices, Algeria was exporting natural gas, liquefied gas, and refined petroleum products. Sonatrach, the state oil and gas corporation,

---

> **ALGERIA • Information Highlights**
>
> **Official Name:** Democratic and Popular Republic of Algeria.
> **Location:** North Africa.
> **Area:** 950,000 sq mi (2 460 500 km²).
> **Population** (July 1983): 20,695,000.
> **Chief Cities** (1980 est.): Algiers, the capital, 2,200,000; Oran, 633,000; Constantine, 384,000.
> **Government:** *Head of state,* Chadli Benjedid, president (took office Feb. 1979). *Head of government,* Mohammed Ben Ahmed Abdelghani, prime minister (took office March 1979).
> **Monetary Unit:** Dinar (4.85 dinars equal U.S.$1, July 1983).
> **Gross Domestic Product** (1982 U.S.$): $42,900,000,000.
> **Economic Index** (June 1982): *Consumer Prices* (1970 = 100), all items, 273.9; food, 353.3.
> **Foreign Trade** (1981 U.S.$): *Imports,* $10,891,000,000; *exports,* $14,486,000,000.

was able to tailor its mix of exports to respond to world demand, making Algeria's economy resilient even in the face of unstable petroleum prices.

The gas pipeline linking Italy and Algeria, which was completed in 1981, went into service in the middle of 1983; Italy agreed to purchase Algerian gas for 20 years. Gas agreements were also concluded with Belgian, French, and American companies. The early success of the pipeline led to proposals for another pipeline linking Algeria with Spain.

The world's lending institutions showed confidence in Sonatrach by granting it a $700 million loan on easy terms. It was the first time in three years that an Algerian borrower needed to raise money in the foreign market.

A serious drought cut Algeria's food production to 70% of the normal harvest, and food imports cost $2 billion (U.S.) in 1983. Price increases for essential commodities were announced in the middle of the year in order to curtail the country's $2.5 billion trade deficit.

MICHAEL MAREN, *"Africa Report"*

President Chadli (right) and a large crowd welcomed Tunisia's President Habib Bourguiba to Algeria in late May.
T. Hierry
Campion/Gamma-Liaison

ANTHROPOLOGY

The major event of the year in anthropology was the publication of a book, *Margaret Mead and Samoa: The Making and Unmaking of an Anthropological Myth*, by Derek Freeman (Harvard University Press, 1983). Freeman, emeritus professor of anthropology at the Australian National University, wrote this critique of Mead's research in Samoa ostensibly to criticize American cultural anthropology for ignoring biological hereditary factors, which he believes are at least as important as cultural factors in shaping human behavior. Mead's first book, *Coming of Age in Samoa*, made an argument for the primacy of culture (nurture) over nature.

Although Freeman denies any bias, his book has been seen as a personal attack on Mead, since he waited until after her death to finish it. Lowell Holmes, an anthropologist at Wichita State University who knew Mead and spent several years in Samoa restudying her work, said that although he faulted her for certain errors in research, Freeman's work is quite at variance with his own observations and that Mead's research was "remarkably reliable." A number of prominent anthropologists—among them David Schneider, Ward Goodenough, and Marvin Harris—have pointed out that if Freeman's book was an attempt to demonstrate that the doctrine of cultural determinism is false, then this was not the way to do it since Mead was only one of a host of cultural determinists. It was, in their view, an unscientific, personal attack on Margaret Mead.

Piltdown Fossil Hoax. John Hathaway Winslow, a U.S. scientist and scholar formerly of the University of California and Trinity College, Dublin, suggested a new candidate for the perpetrator of the Piltdown Fossil Hoax. In a September 1983 magazine article, Winslow claimed that Sir Arthur Conan Doyle, creator of the Sherlock Holmes stories, had the "knowledge, skill, imagination, access, tools, and motivation" to carry out the prank. Not only did Doyle know the Sussex area where the fossils were found, but he was also knowledgeable in the fields of chemistry and anatomy and had a reputation for being a jokester.

The Debate Over Lucy. Lucy, the fossil regarded as the oldest human ancestor since its discovery by Donald C. Johanson, director of the Institute of Human Origins in Berkeley, CA, and dubbed *Australopithecus afarensis*, may be younger than at first thought. In a report published in a British science journal, Noel T. Boaz of New York University suggested that Lucy may be 2.9 to 3.2 million years old rather than the 3.6 million years originally estimated. The change in dating is based on a revision of the age of the rock just above the stratum in which Lucy was found. The rock had altered geologically and was difficult to

date. Johanson conceded the possibility of the new dating but believes that the morphology of *afarensis* indicates a "distinct and more primitive species than *africanus*."

At a meeting at the Institute of Human Origins, the debate continued over whether Lucy actually walked. Johanson and Owen Lovejoy, of Kent State University, describe Lucy as a fully erect bipedal form. Randall Susman and Jack Stern of SUNY-Stony Brook depict Lucy as a tree-dweller. They point to anatomical characteristics of finger, toe, shoulder, hip, and pelvis bones, which, they say, suggest that our human ancestors, after divergence from the ape, continued to live in trees for a few million years. Russell Tuttle of the University of Chicago sees *afarensis* as having had an essentially modern bipedal gait while retaining significant anatomical adaptations to arboreality.

Other. A previously unknown group of people is reported to have been contacted by the Punan, an aboriginal population of the Malaysian jungle on the island of Borneo. The newly discovered group, numbering 43, speak a dialect of Punan, have no knowledge of agriculture, and maintain their population by incest after the death of their original mates.

The American Anthropological Association (AAA) proposed a merger of all anthropological societies for tax purposes. Each group would keep its own identity and elect its own officers but would be represented on the executive board of the AAA.

HERMAN J. JAFFE
Brooklyn College, CUNY

ARCHAEOLOGY

Amid a variety of significant developments in archaeology in late 1982 and 1983, the most important clarifications came from water-logged muddy sites and spotless laboratories where techniques of chemistry were applied.

Eastern Hemisphere

Palaeolithic Humans. Palaeomagnetic dating at Ulalkina in the Altai Mountains of Soviet Asia indicated an age of some 700,000 years, making it by far the oldest site in central Asia. A crude tool set found there consists of choppers, cornered choppers, cores, and retouched flakes.

Pipeline trenching in Italy came upon the remains of a man and an elephant, in well-preserved side-by-side skeletons. The man appears to be of the Pre-Neanderthal type intermediate between Neanderthal and *Homo erectus* and should date to nearly 300,000 years ago. The dual interment appears to have been caused by a hunting accident in which the man tried to dispatch an elephant bogged down in quick-mud.

An amazing array of rich sites (18,000–13,000 B.C.) were found at a hydroelectric dam project in the Franklin and Gordon River valleys of Tasmania. Fraser Cave produced evidence of some of the oldest inhabitants of Australia, who made core-tools and scrapers from "Darwin glass," a stone retrieved from a meteorite crater 30 mi (48 km) away. Red ochre was brought to the site for decoration, and bone awls seem to have been used to manufacture skin clothing. The significance of the sites caused the Australian government to abandon the hydroelectric project.

Dietary Data. Chemical analyses based on the greater content of strontium in plant foods than in meat have shown scientists that at about 8,000 B.C. there was an abrupt increase in the vegetal diet of people in Israel and Iran. This coincides with other evidence that farming had started just at this time, indicating that the first agriculturists were more dependent on plants than hitherto had been realized.

Similar studies relied on the fact that the metabolism of corn fixes an unusual ratio of carbon 12 to carbon 13 isotopes. These show that in Peru a commitment was made to a corn diet 3,000 years earlier than previously thought. Nitrogen isotope ratios can also be used to determine the role of marine vs. terrestrial food resources in diets of coastal peoples.

Rice Paddy Archaeology. Bronze-Age Yayoi farmers in Japan about 2,000 years ago could not grow much rice because of the unreliability of their methods, but the swampy paddies around eight dwelling houses at Kainakanoko preserve otherwise-unknown wooden agricultural tools. Along with the tools are wooden carvings of human-like figures, thought to have been used in the thanksgiving ceremonies connected with the harvest.

Iron Age Surprises. From a collapsed family burial vault on a hill near Mt. Zion, Jerusalem, Israeli archaeologists have recovered more than 1,000 artifacts, including silver jewelry and other items of the 7th century B.C. One such ornament is an unusual silver scroll bearing an inscribed prayer containing the name *Yahweh,* the ancient Hebrew spelling of Jehovah. It is the oldest known usage of the name by nearly 700 years.

At the bottom of a deep well at Fellbach-Schmiden, West Germany, archaeologists found many wooden objects made by Celtic barbarians in the last decades before the Roman conquest. Along with easily dated pottery and fibulae of the late Iron Age, came wooden statues of two goats and a stag. These are the first purely Celtic wooden sculptures ever recovered, and they closely resemble the wooden sculptures of contemporary horse nomads of eastern Europe and central Asia.

On a farm near Hammelev, Denmark, one spot had been used for a manure pile as far back as any records show. However, when an ancient gold finger ring found at the bottom of the manure spurred excavation, archaeologists found a 2,000-year-old, T-shaped bunker formed by chalk blocks. The cellar held many ceramic jars and much stored food, especially pork and fish. The cellar conforms to Tacitus' description of Germanic hiding places in times of trouble, suggesting that the spot had been used as a manure pile for two millennia!

Illerup Moor in Jutland, Denmark, was the scene of great battles from about A.D. 200 to 500. From the earlier period, archaeologists have recovered a sword some 32 inches (81 cm) long, splendidly equipped with a hilt of gold, silver, and ivory. Described as "the most splendid sword" of the Iron Age in Europe, it is a fitting companion to a shield garnished with eight golden discs bearing the embossed faces of bemused-looking warriors.

At Heslerton Parish, Yorkshire, English archaeologists have found an Anglo-Saxon cemetery covered over with wet sediments that preserved the most extensive series of Anglo-Saxon (ca. A.D. 500–700) textiles known. Also uncovered at the site was a cruciform brooch with the inscription of a person's name in early runic.

Preservative Lead. One of the best-preserved medieval bodies ever found was retrieved from a lead coffin in a monastic cemetery in Wales. The body of the knight Sir Robert de Harrington still had pink skin. Examination revealed dental caries, a last breakfast of grapes and porridge, and fatal injuries (crushing of the chest and neck) suffered in jousting or combat in the year 1297.

Raising the *Mary Rose*. The excellently preserved battle carrack *Mary Rose,* flagship of Henry VIII's war fleet, was recovered from the muddy waters of Portsmouth, England, 437 years after it sank while en route to engage French naval forces. More than 17,000 Renaissance artifacts were recovered by the archaeological team, which included Prince Charles as both a patron and undersea diver.

Toxic Lead. The largest group of bodies yet found from the disastrous A.D. 79 eruption of Mount Vesuvius came to light at the seaside baths of Herculaneum, sister city to ill-fated Pompeii. The 26 people had almost reached safety when they were knocked down by a 56 mph (90 km/hr) air blast preceding the mudflow. One man died with sword and scabbard; a wooden boat, flipped keel-up by the turbulent sea, was preserved almost intact.

The 26 skeletons, as well as others from the area, were examined for traces of lead poisoning from the water pipes and glazed vessels so widely used in the Roman world. They showed lead levels twice as high as among modern Americans, who have nine times more lead in their bones than prehistoric Greeks. Romano-British bones, analyzed in another study, did not show these high lead levels.

Raised from the English Channel near Portsmouth in late 1982, Henry VIII's warship the "Mary Rose" (on platform) has provided archaeologists with a treasure trove of Tudor artifacts.

Western Hemisphere

Chemical analyses of the bones of both whites and blacks from antebellum graves at a tobacco plantation in Stratford, VA, showed much higher levels of lead in the well-to-do whites, who had lead plumbing and dined from glazed pottery. The slaves, lacking such amenities, had lower lead levels, as did poor whites.

Early American West. The first positive association of humans and mammoths west of the Rockies was made by the Nevada State Museum at Black Rock Desert, where tusks and a stone scraper and graver were found in an ancient lake bed, in deposits dated 10,000 to 30,000 years ago. The first frozen mammoth to be systematically excavated in the New World was recovered in central Alaska.

Prehistoric Butchering. Blood residues from the surfaces of flint and obsidian tools were recovered by a British Columbian archaeologist. Hemoglobin crystallized from the residues showed that flake knives from the boreal forest of Canada had been used to process reindeer, grizzly, moose, and other meats from 1,000 to 6,000 years ago.

Prehistoric Indian Art. In the Desert Southwest, from Death Valley to the Arizona-Nevada border, archaeologists are making an effort to record and preserve hundreds of recently recognized *geoglyphs*, huge figural designs made by the removal of surface soil or the building up of rock alignments on the desert floor. Their sizes range from a few feet to several hundred yards. Designs include loops, deer, serpents, humans, and horses.

From eastern Tennessee came the first reported Indian cave art. The many drawings were made with fingertips in soft mud between A.D. 900 and 1400. Some designs are merely squiggles, but snakes, turtles, possums, turkeys, and warriors are recognizable.

Mississippian Towns. The most recent fully reported Mississippian-period town is Cemohechobee, which also doubled as a ceremonial center on the Chattahoochee River in Florida. Besides temple mounds, houses, and much evidence of pottery and food remains, the deity statuette, usually found in such sites, was made of ceramic. One burial, doubtlessly a chief, wore a copper headband fitted with copper representations of spear heads. Feathers seem to have been stuffed in the top of the headband to produce the customary Indian headdress.

In another northern Florida temple mound, at Lake Jackson, archaeologists recovered not only copper axes but also several individuals buried with copper breastplates decorated by repoussé designs showing eagle warriors, one wielding a war club and holding the severed head of an enemy.

Viking Pastoralists. In the high end of fjords 1,312 ft (400 m) above sea level in Greenland have been found the summer pasture stations of the transhumant Norse settlers of medieval Greenland. These sites have been left as if the herdsmen had just departed for the winter at lower elevations and may shed some light on the disappearance of the Norse Greenlanders.

RALPH M. ROWLETT
Department of Anthropology
University of Missouri-Columbia

ARCHITECTURE

Notable new buildings continued, as in prior years, to be produced in a broad spectrum of styles. At one extreme was what was dubbed in the architectural press as "Romantic Hi-tech" which, while using such severe materials and forms as sharp-edged aluminum panels and the rigid geometry of the International Style so popular for modern buildings during the last four decades, produced playful and imaginative results. The new style used the design language in colorful and unexpected ways, such as checkerboard-wall patterns and spaces cut out of buildings in ways that seemed to defy the structural grid and rational organization. New examples of this style include the U.S. Department of Energy's new facility at Argonne National Laboratories outside Chicago, designed by architects Murphy/Jahn, and the Herman Miller Rosewell Facility in Rosewell GA, by Heery & Heery.

In the stylistic middle of design were such notable architects as Ulrich Franzen with his Champion Plaza Building in Stamford, CT, designed in the International Syle. But even here there were new elements, including the different window treatments on walls facing in different directions to reduce thermal-gain.

At the opposite extreme from "Romantic Hi-Tech" was Post-Modernism, with its usually crisp, sometimes playful adaptation of historic and especially classic styles. Examples completed in 1983 included the Alumni Center for the University of Michigan by architect Hugh Newell Jacobsen, a brick building with horizontal bands of light colored stone and massing that echo the nearby collegiate tradi-

tional structures from the 1920s but is clearly new in its fresh appearance. One of the highest honor awards by the American Institute of Architects (AIA) for 1983 went to a quintessential example of Post-Modern design completed in the previous year, The Portland Building in Oregon designed by Michael Graves. The large rectangular block of public offices had aroused considerable controversy during its design and construction for the highly decorative treatment of the façades which, rather than borrowing strictly from classic styles, involves a wide range of styles including Art Deco. Design work proceeded on a 27-story office building in Louisville, KY, for which Graves in 1982 had won a national competition sponsored by Humana, Inc.

Architect Charles Moore was the winner of a national competition to design additions to the government complex in Beverly Hills, CA, that would unite the various buildings, including the Spanish-Baroque-style city hall of 1932, in functional and esthetic ways. The winning scheme brought automobiles into a giant circular central space in recognition of their dominant influence on local life-styles, while using a series of grand spaces that enhanced especially the city hall by their formality.

Some new buildings went so far in the Post-Modernist direction that they appeared in fact to be the older buildings from which the new elements were copied. Examples of this meticulous recreative process include the Beneficial Center in Peapack-Gladstone, NJ, by the Hillier Group, a campus-like arrangement of low office buildings of both early 19th-century and Palladian inspiration. The general trend in house design continued back toward premod-

Evelyn Hofer

I(eoh) M(ing) Pei, left, 66-year-old Chinese-American architect, was awarded the 1983 Pritzker Architecture Prize for giving "this century some of its most beautiful interior spaces and exterior forms." Pei's most recent works include the Fragrant Hill Hotel, below, near Peking (Beijing), China. The hotel's southern façade overlooks a reflecting pool. The prize was established in 1979 "to reward a creative endeavor not honored by the Nobel Prizes."

C. C. Pei

ern forms, including smaller traditionally placed windows and doors, clapboard siding, and gabled roofs.

Preservation. The battle to save authentic old buildings continued. Lever House, a relatively new building completed in 1952 by architects Skidmore Owings & Merrill and a history-book landmark in its influence on the deluge of International-Style square glass boxes that would follow with usually less finesse, was designated a New York City landmark in the face of developers' plans to demolish it.

Promising less fortuitous results for preservation, a bill with obvious national implications was introduced in the New York State legislature that would remove landmark designation from church properties. While proposing to free religious groups to carry on their sites, the proposal also would free them to demolish many notable buildings that opponents pointed out add to communities and the public good.

Some significant losses for preservation included the conversion of the Biltmore Hotel in New York City by Environetics Architects and owners Builtland Partners into an office building by stripping the structure (oversized for current local zoning and hence new construction of that size) of its memorable Beaux Arts façades and interior spaces. These spaces included the world-famous Palm Court with its clock under which many generations of debutantes had met their dates. The owners had promised to keep at least this space in exchange for not having the entire building designated an official landmark, and they further enraged preservationists by their unauthorized demolition of that space even while preservation negotiations were in progress.

Still, the overall trend was greatly in favor of preservation—partially for economic reasons. In fact, the rehabilitation of existing structures of all kinds topped some $100 billion (U.S.) in 1983, almost twice the value of new construction. The reasons were seen as decreased financial risk by developers, reduced costs, speed of construction, and appreciation of older buildings' character by everyone. Officially designated buildings of recognized historic value were the subject of some $1 billion of expenditure under the provisions of 1977 federal legislation as amended in 1981. Under the act, a building must be of certified historic character to qualify for substantial tax savings in its rehabilitation. Applications for the benefits showed some eight-fold increase compared with the number in the act's first year. However, modifications to the application process, including user fees, could temper this tide.

Economic Recovery and General Trends. Architects were buoyed greatly by the general economic recovery, which, in construction, was felt mostly in housing. The inordinately large number of office buildings, planned in the last upturn and coming to completion in 1983 and the immediately preceding years, meant that there was little new design work. Because of supply exceeding demand, not much design work was anticipated for the near future either. (*See* feature article pages 64–67.)

For American architects working outside the United States, there was much talk about new markets for professional services in the Far East, although by far the largest proportion of foreign work continued to be in the Middle East, where oil dollars, although somewhat constricted, continued to flow. Architects, like all business people, were encouraged to work abroad by new domestic-tax exclusions of 75% on salaries.

Surveys showed that many architects, held back by the previous economic dip, were buying computers, but mostly for such clerical functions as billing and word processing, with only some drafting functions. The consensus was that the available software was not ready for full-scale design efforts. Spurred on by such organizations as the Society for Marketing Professional Services, a group of promotion specialists in the design field, architects joined fellow professionals in entering new fields.

Awards. There were four recipients in the annual Owens-Corning Fiberglas Energy-Conservation Awards. They were the Norstar Building in Buffalo, NY, by Cannon Design Inc., Architects; the Government Services Insurance System Headquarters in Manila, the Philippines, by The Architects Collaborative, Inc.; the Albany County Airport Passenger Terminal in Colonie, NY, by Einhorn Yaffee Prescott Krouner, P.C., Architects; and the Civil/Mineral Engineering Building in Minneapolis, MN, by BRW Architects. As was the recent tendency, the new designs relied mainly on nonmechanical means, such as passive solar heating and natural daylight, to replace electrical sources.

The AIA presented its gold medal for 1983 to Nathaniel Owings, founding partner of Skidmore Owings & Merrill, the largest architectural and engineering practice in the United States with some 1,500 employees in nine offices. Owings was cited for his work with his firm, for his "seminal contribution to the revitalization of Washington's Pennsylvania Avenue and the Capitol Mall, and for his role in the resurgence of national concern for conservation and preservation of the natural and built environment." Holabird & Root was the winner of the 1983 AIA firm award. The firm was started more than a century ago in Chicago as Holabird & Roche; today it employs some 175 people. The AIA's design award for enduring design (known as the 25-year award) went to the Price Tower in Bartlesville, OK, designed by Frank Lloyd Wright and completed in 1956. The 1983 Edward C. Kemper award went to Jules Gregory.

CHARLES HOYT, *"Architectural Record"*

ARGENTINA

In the midst of an unprecedented fiscal crisis, which persisted throughout 1983, Argentina's military junta scheduled popular elections to provide the transition from nearly eight years of army rule to democratic government.

The Elections. Elections for the presidency, congress, and state governorships were held on October 30. Eighty percent of those eligible to vote did so. In a major upset, Raúl Alfonsín, of the minority Radical Civic Union, won 52% of the popular vote, decisively defeating the Peronist presidential candidate, Italo Luder, who received only 40%. In accumulating a 1.75-million-vote advantage, Alfonsín was able to retain Radical middle-class backing and also to pick up substantial working-class support.

The new administration took the oath of office at the Congress building on December 10. More than 100,000 people poured into the streets as the new chief executive traveled in a convertible from the swearing in to the presidential palace. Addressing the crowd from city hall, Alfonsín said: "We know that these are hard and difficult moments, but we do not have a single doubt. We Argentines are going to pull out. . . . We will become the country that we deserve."

Several heads of state attended the ceremonies. George Bush represented the United States. The U.S. vice-president later reportedly discussed Argentina's nuclear-development program, its debt, and other issues with the new president.

The Radicals also won a majority of the seats in the lower chamber of the congress. The senators were chosen on November 27 by the states, in which Peronists won more of the governorships than the Radicals.

Peronists attributed their resounding defeat to Luder's lackluster campaign style and to discord within the labor movement. Calls for the resignation of party leaders left the majority party in disarray. Former Senator Luder and former Peronist Foreign Minister Angel Robledo attempted to form a loyal opposition, while factions supporting former President María Estela ("Isabel") Martínez de Perón called for her return to active politics. (On September 9 the military government had lifted a curb on her holding a public office. She had been in self-imposed exile in Spain for two years following her release from a five-year house arrest related to a conviction for inappropriate use of public funds.) With Lorenzo Miguel, the militant head of a group of 62 unions, as vice-president and effective head of the Peronist party, the union wing of the party appeared to be dominating the political wing.

The Transition. A lawyer and former congressman, Alfonsín was expected to incorporate Western European social democratic ideas into his administration. He promised to restore human rights, which had been denied during the nearly eight years of military rule. He would force all of the ranking army generals and half of the brigadier generals into retirement. Similar purges were anticipated by the air force, but reductions among naval officers would be less severe. Labor unions also awaited presidential reforms; during his campaign, Alfonsín attacked a labor "bureaucracy" and promised union elections that would diminish the power of their leaders.

As for the economy, the president-elect called for price, wage, and interest controls. He agreed to repay a $39 billion (U.S.) foreign debt after his government had negotiated more generous terms. Increased expenditures on education and welfare would come from reductions in defense outlays. Alfonsín appointed Dante Caputo as foreign minister, while the defense portfolio went to Radical strategist Raúl Borrás, and neo-Keynesian Bernardo Grinspun was named to head the economic ministry.

Among the more controversial acts of the military regime of Gen. Reynaldo Bignone in its final months were the decreeing of an amnesty law and tough new antiterrorist legislation. The amnesty relieved the military and civilian death squads of any responsibility for abuses and excesses against civilians in the "dirty war" between 1976 and 1982, in which up to 15,000 persons disappeared.

With inflation projected at nearly 1,000% for the year, calls for wage increases had a special sense of urgency.

T. La Penna/Gamma-Liaison

© D. Goldberg/Sygma

The election of Raúl Alfonsin of the center-left Radical Civic Union party ended eight years of military rule.

In August, 45,000 people participated in an antiamnesty march, and in September two judges declared the amnesty law "absolutely null and void." It was expected that the incoming civilian regime would repeal the amnesty law. Reaction to the antiterrorist decree was vociferous. The measure allowed police to enter homes without search warrants, hold suspects without informing the courts, open mail, and tap telephones.

A military inquiry into the conduct of the Falklands (Malvinas) War was turned over to the presidency in September and referred to the armed forces. However, it was leaked that the military commission had called for the court-martialing of the then president and also the military junta in office at that time.

Labor Unrest. With the inflation rate for 1983 projected up to 1,000% and living standards plummeting, pressure grew during the latter half of 1983 for wage hikes. In August, 100,000 railroad workers seeking an increase in the minimum monthly wage staged a 24-hour nationwide strike, halting service.

Attempting to head off a third general strike in recent months, the Bignone government raised the basic legal wage to 1,600 pesos monthly and authorized an 800-peso, onetime bonus. A 24-hour general strike occurred on October 24 after workers claimed that negotiations with the Bignone government had been

fruitless and urged the incorporation of the 800-peso bonus into monthly paychecks. Following the November elections, union leader Saúl Ubaldini threatened the president-elect with whatever strikes might be needed for labor to obtain what it deserved.

Debt Negotiations. At the beginning of the year, $2 billion in interest on the 1982 private-sector debt remained unpaid. Argentina sought an additional $11.75 billion on the international market to cover payments due in 1983, more than half of which represented existing obligations that Argentine authorities helped to rearrange. With a standby credit of $2.1 billion from the International Monetary Fund (IMF) being worked out, Argentina was able to obtain a $1.1 billion "bridge" loan on Dec. 31, 1982. The IMF aid package was approved in January, after Argentina had agreed to cut costs, reduce inflation, expand exports while curbing imports, and institute a sincere austerity program.

Later in January the Swiss-based Bank of International Settlements authorized a short-term loan of $500 million to Argentina. In August a much-delayed medium-term loan of $1.5 billion was extended to Argentina. Further financing was needed but had to await the change in government in December. To receive payments under the aforementioned arrangements, Argentina had to undergo quarterly full-dress reviews of its economic performance by the IMF. The most difficult target proved to be holding inflation to an annual rate of 160%.

The protracted negotiations conducted by central bank president Julio González del Solar and economy minister Jorge Wehbe attempted to head off a default on loan payments that could trigger a world banking crisis. President Bignone reiterated on October 4 that his administration had no intention of defaulting on the loans, but a moratorium on payment of $830 million due in October was forced by an "ultranationalist" federal judge in Santa Cruz Province. The judge objected to a provision in the renegotiation agreement concerning the

---

ARGENTINA • Information Highlights

Official Name: Republic of Argentina.
Location: Southern South America.
Area: 1,070,000 sq mi (2 771 300 km²).
Population (July 1983 est.): 29,627,000.
Chief Cities: (1980 census): Buenos Aires, the capital, 2,908,001; Córdoba, 990,007; Rosario, 935,471.
Government: *Head of state and government,* Raúl Alfonsín, president (took office Dec. 10, 1983). *Legislature*—Senate and Chamber of Deputies.
Monetary Unit: Peso (19.5 pesos equal U.S.$1, Dec. 7, 1983, financial rate).
Gross National Product (1981 U.S.$): $124,600,000,000.
Economic Indexes (1982): *Consumer Prices,* all items (1974 = 100), 315,807; food, 344,639. *Industrial Production* (1975 = 100), 79.
Foreign Trade (1982 U.S.$): *Imports,* $5,230,000,000; *exports,* $7,518,000,000.

$230 million debt of the national airline, Aerolíneas Argentinas, placing court jurisdiction in New York, where the headquarters of the lead bank in the rescheduling was located.

Because the airline contract was supposed to be a model in the debt renegotiation of some 31 state-owned corporations, representing 30% of the country's external indebtedness, the judge's decision created turmoil in world financial circles. If upheld, the impact of the decision on debt renegotiations in other countries could be calamitous. The case was removed to an appeals court, but its decision awaited installation of the new government.

Foreign Relations. The battle for the Falkland Islands shifted to the United Nations, where Secretary-General Javier Pérez de Cuéllar, mediator of the dispute, received notes in August on provocations from both Argentina and Great Britain. At the General Assembly in September, Sir Geoffrey Howe, the British foreign minister, reiterated Britain's resolve to defend the islanders from any new attack and reaffirmed his government's disposition to normalize relations with Argentina.

On November 16 the General Assembly again approved a Latin American resolution calling on the Falklands sovereignty issue to be settled through negotiation. Only eight nations joined Britain in opposing the initiative, while 54 abstained and 87 voted in favor.

Larry L. Pippin, *University of the Pacific*

ARIZONA

Water remained the dominant issue in this desert state. Late snowfalls and record runoff from the Rocky Mountains caused the worst flooding in this century on the Colorado River. Dams were filled to capacity in June and July. The Bureau of Reclamation, in a controversial decision, released the water, which surged downstream and caused some $10.6 million in damage in Yuma, LaPaz, and Mohave counties on the California border. President Ronald Reagan declared these counties federal disaster areas.

In October, unseasonable rains—approximately 6 inches (15 cm) in less than a week—fell on southeastern Arizona. Normally dry stream beds became rampaging rivers that swept over highways, bridges, homes, and crop lands, causing ten deaths. The preliminary damage estimate exceeded $400 million. For the second time in six months, President Reagan declared Arizona counties federal disaster areas. Controversy again followed in the wake of the floodwaters as critics condemned state and local authorities who have continued to approve floodplain construction.

Central Arizona Project. Paradoxically, given the floods of 1983, the completion of the Central Arizona Project was a continuing major

---

ARIZONA • Information Highlights

Area: 114,000 sq mi (295 260 km²).
Population (1982 est.): 2,860,000.
Chief Cities (1980 census): Phoenix, the capital, 764,911; Tucson, 330,537; Mesa, 152,453; Tempe, 106,743.
Government (1983): *Chief Officers*—governor, Bruce E. Babbitt (D). *Legislature*—Senate, 30 members; House of Representatives, 60 members.
State Finances (fiscal year 1982): *Revenues,* $3,501,000,000; *expenditures,* $3,245,000,000.
Personal Income (1982): $29,100,000,000; per capita, $10,173.
Labor Force (July 1983): *Nonagricultural wage and salary earners,* 1,019,000; *unemployed,* 135,000 (10.2% of total force).
Education: *Enrollment* (fall 1981)—public elementary schools, 355,275; public secondary, 151,924; colleges and universities (1981–82), 205,169. *Public school expenditures* (1980–81), $1,103,550,000 ($1,914 per pupil).

---

concern in southern Arizona. The project will carry scarce water from the Colorado River east to the sun-parched agricultural areas and cities of Phoenix and Tucson. The once-controversial project, which is now an article of faith with the state's politicians, is scheduled for completion in 1992—if future funding is shared. This means that, assuming annual federal appropriations continue, the state must decide how to provide its estimated $1 billion share of the additional $2.3 billion needed to complete the project.

Copper Strike. Some 1,400 copper workers at the state's largest copper producer, Phelps Dodge, walked off their jobs when their contract expired on June 30. The threat of violence increased in this already tense situation when Phelps Dodge followed through on its decision to resume operations by replacing strikers with nonunion workers at its installations in Morenci, Ajo, and Douglas. In August, Gov. Bruce Babbitt ordered the National Guard and state police to these locations in support of the company's decision. Some 2,200 copper workers remained on strike, bringing the total of unemployed miners in the state to 10,200.

Economy. Apart from the continuing problems of the copper industry, which was hit hard by the recession and then by labor problems, other areas of the state's economy seemed to be following the national recovery. Arizona's warm winters and spectacular scenery appeared to be once more drawing visitors to its cities and resorts. With the drop in interest rates, residential construction approached near-record rates in Tucson and Phoenix.

Prisons. Arizona prisons are now 1,000 to 1,200 over capacity, and the dangers posed by this overflowing prison population can no longer be ignored. Governor Babbitt called the legislature into special session in October to address the problem.

James W. Clarke
University of Arizona

ARKANSAS

Contention over changes in state policies, politicking for the 1984 gubernatorial election, and urban electoral and appointment victories for blacks dominated government affairs in 1983. Business waited for an elusive economic recovery.

Legislature. In a 68-day regular session torn by dissension within and between chambers, the General Assembly passed several controversial measures. Included were those increasing the maximum weight for trucks using public highways from 73,280 to 80,000 pounds (33 269–36 320 kg) and imposing a weight-mileage fee on these trucks; mandating jail sentences and other stiff penalties for driving while intoxicated; legalizing bank-holding companies; increasing the beer and alcohol tax; permitting teacher retirement after 30 years of service; and exempting church child-care centers from state licensing requirements. In response, Oklahoma levied a retaliatory tax on Arkansas trucks; secular interests instituted a federal establishment-of-a-religion suit; and the Commercial National and First National banks of Little Rock merged to form the First Commercial Bank, the state's largest.

In October, Gov. Bill Clinton called a special legislative session to pass a state court-ordered revision of the public school aid formula, to raise state educational standards, and to increase taxes to finance the changes.

Appointments. Governor Clinton fulfilled a campaign promise by appointing blacks to top administrative jobs. His appointments included Tommy L. Sproles of Little Rock as the first black on the Game and Fish Commission; Mahlon Martin, former Little Rock city manager, as director of the Department of Finance and Administration; and Curtis Ivery of Fort Smith as commissioner of social services. The governor, unsuccessful in getting an elected Public Service Commission, appointed to the regulatory body three consumer-oriented persons unexperienced in utility regulation: a banker, James W. Daniel of Marshall; a woman mayor of Lake City and former music teacher, Pat Qualls; and, as chairman, a university professor and former legislator, Robert E. Johnston of Little Rock.

Education. The governor selected his wife, Hillary Rodham Clinton, to chair a special Education Standards Committee, which proposed changes in public school standards, such as mandatory kindergarten, student and teacher competency tests, and completion of 20 rather than 16 units for high school graduation. To implement this program, the governor campaigned vigorously for public support of legislation for strict educational standards, additional revenue from increases in the three-cent sales tax, natural gas severance tax, and corporate income tax; and school district consolidation (111 of the 371 school districts have fewer than 360 students). The legislature refused to increase the severance and income taxes.

As an increase in black enrollment frustrated integration efforts, the Little Rock school district petitioned the federal court to consolidate the Little Rock (70% black), North Little Rock (35% black), and Pulaski County (23% black) school districts.

Politics. Leo Chitman became the first elected black mayor of a large Arkansas city, West Memphis. After the U.S. Supreme Court required ward (rather than at-large) city council elections in West Helena, blacks won 4 of the 7 contested seats on the previously all-white eight-member council.

WILLIAM C. NOLAN
Southern Arkansas University

Bill Clinton (D), who took the oath as governor of Arkansas for a second time in 1983, sought to "lead by listening."

Wide World

ARMS CONTROL

Barling in "The Christian Science Monitor" © 1983 TCSPS

In early November 1983, a conference was held in Washington, DC, to address the subject "The World After Nuclear War." The conference report, to which some 100 atmospheric scientists contributed, pointed to more catastrophic consequences of worldwide nuclear war than generally had been indicated by previous studies. On November 20, ABC Television aired *The Day After,* a movie-length representation of the possible consequences of a nuclear attack on Kansas City, MO, and the nearby university town of Lawrence, KS. These national events, plus numerous more localized activities, helped to keep many in the United States and the rest of the world working for the elusive goal of arms control.

Nuclear Freeze Movement. The nuclear freeze movement did not achieve its basic objective in 1983—a mutual, verifiable U.S.-Soviet freeze on the development, production, and deployment of nuclear weapons. Specifically the freeze movement was not able to prevent the initial deployment in December of what was programmed to be 576 new U.S. Pershing II and Cruise missiles in West Germany, Britain, Italy, Belgium, and the Netherlands. Nor were supporters of the freeze proposal on Capitol Hill able to stop the Reagan administration from obtaining $2.1 billion from the Congress to produce the first 21 of an eventual 100 MX intercontinental ballistic mis-

siles (ICBMs). The closest freeze proponents came to halting the MX program was in the House of Representatives in November, when the Reagan funding bill was passed by only 13 votes. Passage in the Senate was easier.

The president's success in the Congress was attributed to negotiations between moderate Democrats and White House staffers, which resulted in President Reagan agreeing to move more forcefully with arms control initiatives if the Congress would fund the beginning MX production. Reflecting this point of view during the MX debate was Rep. Albert Gore (D-TN), who said to the House of Representatives, "The president so far has lived up to his end of this unprecedented bargain, and the Congress must live up to its end." In response, those attempting to delete the MX funding from the $247 billion defense spending bill asserted that the administration was not sincerely interested in arms control.

In another loss, freeze supporters were not able to prevent the Congress from approving $6 billion for production of ten B-1 jet bombers. These will be added to the single plane bought in 1981 and the seven purchased in 1982. The B-1 is intended to replace the B-52 as the primary strategic nuclear bomber operated by the Strategic Air Command.

Some in the freeze movement believed their reduced effectiveness was due to a general

Yuri A. Kvitsinsky and Paul H. Nitze (right) represented the USSR and the United States, respectively, at Intermediate-range Nuclear Forces talks in Geneva. In November the USSR announced a "discontinuation of the present round of talks." Nitze called the action "unjustified" and "unfortunate."

hardening of the public's attitude toward the Soviet Union in the wake of several events in the fall that were seized upon by President Reagan to support his thesis that the Soviet Union was an "evil empire." Foremost among these events were the September downing by a Soviet interceptor plane of a Korean Air Lines jet carrying 269 people; the terrorist attack on U.S. Marine barracks in Beirut, Lebanon, killing 239; and charges by the administration that the Soviets and Cubans were planning to export additional terrorism to Central and South America from the island of Grenada.

In the NATO countries, the peace movement was able to generate large demonstrations. The genesis for an amalgamation of various peace groups from across Western Europe was the U.S. decision to deploy the Pershing II and Cruise missiles. In Britain the Labour Party endorsed unilateral nuclear disarmament; in West Germany the Social Democratic Party mounted moderate opposition to the missile deployments, while the most forceful opponents were in the small but vocal Green Party. The demonstrators and antimissile marchers frequently were associated with one or several Christian churches.

The peace movement in Western Europe, like the freeze movement in the United States, failed to change the position of the five governments involved in the missile deployment, and the weapons began arriving in November. Government officials maintained that the new U.S. missiles were required to balance the buildup of Soviet SS-20s and to demonstrate resolve against Soviet intimidation tactics. Some officials warned that the West European peace movement was receiving money and organizational assistance from indigenous Communists, the governments of East European nations, and the Soviet Union.

INF and START Negotiations. U.S. and Soviet arms-control negotiators were busy but unsuccessful in separate bargaining sessions held in Geneva, Switzerland. The Americans in the INF talks (Intermediate-range Nuclear Forces) pushed for adoption of President Reagan's zero-zero optional proposal. This plan called for the United States to refrain from deploying any of the new missiles in Western Europe provided the Soviets dismantle their SS-20s, which threaten the NATO countries. A problem for the negotiators was the Soviet insistence that 162 British and French missiles should be included in any arms accord and the U.S. rejection of such a proposal on the grounds that the allied missiles were independent of NATO. The INF negotiations ended on a sour note in late November when the Soviet delegates did what they had threatened to do should the U.S. missiles be deployed—they walked out of the meetings for an indefinite period of time. Similarly, the fifth round of the START negotiations ended December 8 with the Soviets refusing to set a date for resumption.

Under pressure from the freeze advocates in Congress, the Reagan administration advanced a new proposal at the START negotiations (Strategic Arms Reduction Talks). The new concept was called "build down." The central feature of the build-down idea was that for every new ICBM or SLBM warhead added to either nation's arsenal, older warheads would have to be destroyed. For every new ICBM warhead deployed, two old warheads would be eliminated; for every two new submarine-launched ballistic missile (SLBM) warheads deployed, three would be removed. As for bombers, the formula called for a straight one-for-one substitution of a new plane for every old one. Over a ten-year period the U.S. proposal would result in the warhead arsenals being reduced to 5,000 for each superpower. The initial Soviet response to the U.S. build-down proposal was negative, although Moscow did not flatly reject the basic concept.

The Soviet proposal at the START negotiations was substantially different from that of the United States. Moscow suggested that reductions in ballistic-missile warheads should proceed downward from the SALT II (Strategic Arms Limitation Talks) ceilings of 14,600 to a much higher limit than that proposed by Washington, 11,400.

During 1983, U.S. hardliners raised questions about Soviet cheating on SALT II provisions, which had not been ratified by the Senate but which the Reagan administration had pledged to respect. The charges were made in reference to possible Soviet testing of more than the one new ICBM permitted under SALT II; to the development of ABM radar, which was prohibited; and to the encoding of missile test telemetry, which also was banned.

New Concerns. The Reagan administration's support for a new ICBM (Small ICBM, SICBM, or Midgetman), which would be deployed in a mobile launcher, and the development of a similar weapon by the Soviet Union created a particular worry for those interested in arms control. It was feared that the mobile ICBMs would be difficult to locate by satellite cameras, thus making verification of their numbers nearly impossible. There seemed to be no solution to this problem except for an old idea that the Soviets had repeatedly rejected—on-site inspection of factories.

Another concern was the possibility that the United States and USSR were moving toward the adoption of antisatellite weapon systems. Termed ASAT, the new weapons would be capable of destroying satellites as they orbit the earth. Members of the Union of Concerned Scientists, a prominent group in the arms-control movement, were so worried about this matter that their representatives presented a draft ASAT treaty to the Senate Foreign Relations Committee in May. The proposed treaty would prohibit signatories from attacking or changing the flight trajectories of any space objects. Nations that signed would also be prevented fom testing ASAT weapons or placing such weapons in earth orbit, on celestial bodies, or anywhere else in outer space.

The Reagan administration took another perspective on the ASAT problem. This was to counter Soviet ASAT development with what Washington believes is a superior program. The projected U.S. ASAT system is composed of F-15 jet fighters that carry a two-stage rocket, called a Miniature Homing Vehicle (MHV), to the edge of the earth's atmosphere. From that vantage point the MHVs are guided to high-velocity intercept by means of a laser gyroscope and a set of small jet engines. In contrast, the Soviet ASAT is launched by a SS-9 rocket into an orbit close to the satellite against which it is to be used. A nonnuclear detonation destroys the satellite with the shrapnel from the explosion.

Two concerns prompted the Union of Concerned Scientists to suggest the ban on ASAT weapons. One was the belief that the arms race should not be extended into space. The other was the worry that a destabilizing situation would result should either of the superpowers face the prospect of their satellites being destroyed. The fear was based on the contention that satellite reconnaissance provides timely intelligence of the other superpower's activities, which reduces uncertainties and misunderstandings about the other side's actions.

Of greater concern to many in the arms-control community was the president's call for development of directed-energy defense systems, including lasers. These so-called "Star Wars" weapons would be used to defend against Soviet warheads following a ballistic trajectory into space and then to their targets. The major fears expressed over such technology (admittedly decades away) were that the Soviets will be goaded into developing their own comparable defense system and devise means to counter the U.S. defenses. The latter response could include terrain-hugging cruise missiles, low-flying bombers, and depressed-trajectory ballistic missiles. All of these counter-systems would take advantage of the fact that the directed-energy weapons are less effective in the densest portions of the atmosphere than in the near-vacuum of space. Many in the U.S. arms-control movement contended that entering a "Star Wars" competition with the Soviets would cost a great deal of money, would increase instability as each nation tried to match the other, and in the long run would provide no greater security for either party. Moreover, they argued, development and deployment of directed-energy weapons would violate the 1972 treaty signed by the two superpowers limiting antiballistic-missile systems. The Reagan administration maintained that it had to start ASAT development immediately so that any Soviet violation from ABM treaty restrictions could be quickly countered.

The U.S. Team. In January 1983, President Reagan announced that he was accepting the resignation of Eugene V. Rostow as director of the Arms Control and Disarmament Agency (ACDA). Reagan's nominee to replace Rostow was Kenneth L. Adelman, then the number-two official in the U.S. mission to the United Nations. Adelman was confirmed by the Senate on April 14 despite formal opposition by the Foreign Relations Committee. Edward Rowny and Paul Nitze continued to represent the Reagan administration at the START and INF negotiations in Geneva—as long as they lasted.

ROBERT M. LAWRENCE
Colorado State University

ART

A takeover battle for the London-based auction house of Sotheby Parke Bernet, an improved sales picture, a traveling collection of Vatican treasures, several major retrospectives, and a number of new museums and galleries highlighted a big year in art.

The Battle for Sotheby. At venerable Sotheby Parke Bernet, there was more drama behind the scenes than in the auction rooms. A loss of $3.6 million in fiscal 1982, compared with a profit of $7.5 million in 1981, led two of the company's major stockholders, American financiers Marshall Cogan and Stephen Swid, who together held 29.9% of Sotheby stock, to cite mismanagement and to express their intention of acquiring a majority and replacing the directors; they offered some $96 million at $8.20 per share. The case became a tangled political issue, however, with the British unwilling to lose a firm that had been based in London for 240 years and claiming that the Americans were unfit to run it. Sotheby's board of directors was supported by many of the principal employees who threatened to resign if the Americans won, and by the English government which referred the case to the British Monopolies and Mergers Commission, which traditionally takes six months to render a decision. In the face of such determined opposition and to avoid harming the company with a long delay, Cogan and Swid withdrew. Ironically, the new buyer, who did have the approval of the Sotheby board, is also an American. Alfred Taubman, a Detroit real-estate dealer and art collector, offered to buy out the first group at $10.70 a share. The $125-million deal was approved by the British government in mid-September.

Auctions. Meanwhile, Sotheby tried to regain its position in the art auction business. From September through December 1982, worldwide sales at Sotheby's fell by 40%, with its main competitor, Christie Manson & Woods International, surpassing it for the first time. In May 1983, Sotheby took a big step toward regaining its reputation for spectacular sales with $37.4 million worth of art sold in a single night; this broke the previous record of $32 million, set in 1978 for the Hirsch Collection. The principal paintings came from the H. O. Havemeyer collection, those remaining in the family after the donation of more than 2,000 works to the Metropolitan Museum in 1929. *Waiting,* a pastel on paper by Degas, went to the Norton Simon Museum of Pasadena and the J. Paul Getty Museum of Malibu for $3.7 million, the highest price ever paid for an Impressionist painting; another Degas, *The Café Concert,* sold for $3.74 million. Before the auction these two works had been estimated at $1.75 and $2 million, respectively. New auction records were also set for paintings by Corot and Manet. From another collection sold the same night, *Nude Bather* by Renoir brought $2.75 million, a record for this artist.

The same week, Christie's sold $15.5 million worth of Impressionist and modern paintings, with almost half going to American collectors. On the whole, contemporary paintings did not do so well, but there were exceptions. Willem de Kooning's *Two Women,* painted in oil and charcoal in the mid-1950s, was bought by a dealer for $1.2 million, the highest price ever paid at auction for a living American artist. Records were also set for Sam Francis, Richard Lindner, and Jasper Johns. In June three dealers paid $1.8 million for Charles Sheeler's 1931 *Classic Landscape.* Sold at Sotheby's, it was the second highest price ever

Detail © Sotheby Parke Bernet/Art Resource

During an active year for the art auction business, "Waiting," a pastel on paper by Edgar Degas, was sold to the Norton Simon Museum of Pasadena, CA, and the J. Paul Getty Museum of Malibu for $3.7 million.

Courtesy, Christie Manson & Woods International, Inc.

paid for an American painting. Works by Bierstadt and Remington also set records. At Christie's, sales of American art rose from $8.8 to $15 million, an increase of 70%. Among the works sold was a watercolor by Thomas Eakins at $550,000, a record for the artist. Hiram Powers' statue from the late 1860s, *The Greek Slave*, the first nude female figure ever publicly exhibited in the United States, sold for $198,000, a record for an American marble; it was the only one of eight versions of this piece to have come up for auction in 70 years. In November, Christie's auctioned Manet and Cézanne paintings for about $3.9 million each, a record for the Manet.

The biggest surprises were in furniture sales. One of the most popular auctions of the year was in January when Christie's sold the contents of the Linden's, the former Washington, DC, home of Miriam and George Morris. At Sotheby's, a pair of Duncan Phyfe card tables, one of only two known pairs by the famous New York furniture maker of the early 19th century, was sold for $275,000, more than twice the previous high for furniture of the period. The tables were heirlooms belonging to two brothers; in 1976 when the owner of one of them inquired about selling, he was told his table might bring a purchase price of between $7,000 and $10,000.

New York far outstripped London in art sales, though some records were also set there. *Composition with Red, Blue and Yellow*, painted by Mondrian in 1942, was bought by a Japanese private collector for $2,156,000, while a Miró set a record at $1,480,000. The reasons for the improvement in sales were attributed in part to the high quality of the works offered and in part to lower interest rates.

The Vatican Show. Three years of planning and hard work—as well as diplomacy—finally culminated in the opening of the much heralded "The Vatican Collections: The Papacy and Art" at the Metropolitan Museum in February. It moved to the Art Institute in Chicago from July through October and to the Fine Arts Museum of San Francisco from November through February 1984. The Vatican has never before permitted such a large part of its treasures, 237 works, to travel. A cross-section of the rich Vatican museums, the show includes such world-famous pieces as the 1st-century B.C. marble fragment known as the Belvedere Torso, which profoundly influenced Michelangelo; the so-called Apollo Belvedere, a Roman copy of a Greek bronze, for centuries considered the epitome of classical art; the Early Christian statue of Christ as the Good Shepherd; one of the tapestries designed by Raphael for the Sistine Chapel; Leonardo's painting of Saint Jerome; Caravaggio's *Deposition of Christ;* ivories and metal and enamel work from the treasury of St. Peter's; and pieces from its ethnographic and modern art collections.

The arrangement was not chronological, but designed to illustrate the collecting habits of the popes through the ages. This intellectual approach was criticized by some as robbing the show of a coherent character and making it difficult to appreciate, in spite of the quality and beauty of individual works in it. In fact, attendance was not as high as that of the Tutankhamen show in 1978 and, according to a survey conducted for the museum, 20% of the audience was disappointed. The same survey, however, drew very satisfactory conclusions to help the Met justify its position as a recipient of public funds. The out-of-town visitors attracted to New York City by the show, 19% of whom had never before visited the Met, spent about $101 million during their stay, an average of $304 per person. The most expensive traveling art show ever mounted—$8 million for transportation and more than $1 million for installation—"The Vatican Collections" was underwritten by several U.S. corporations and foundations.

Museum News. The Metropolitan Museum opened the last of its 32 modernized galleries named for their donor, Lila Acheson Wallace, displaying in chronological sequence virtually its complete Egyptian collection. Comprising some 40,000 objects—including a complete temple, wall reliefs, statues, mummies, furniture, ceramics, jewelry, and thousands of sherds—it is now recognized as one of the most important Egyptian collections in the world. Brought together since the beginning of the century, with almost 80% of the pieces coming from excavations sponsored by the museum itself, the collection had never before been adequately exhibited. Plans for a reorganization started about 25 years ago, when it was realized that the growth of the collection would be limited by Egyptian government restrictions on the removal of excavated material from that country. The new plan includes all objects in the Met's own permanent exhibition. Long, narrow study halls supplement the main galleries, so that both specialists and the general public can be served. Over the past decade, the museum staff worked in close cooperation with the official architects, Kevin Roche John Dinkeloo Associates, to modernize the Egyptian wing and install the objects. The first phase, completed in 1976, was of the earliest material —from 300,000 B.C. to 1991 B.C.—and of the latest—from 380 B.C. to A.D. 641. The second phase installed objects from 1379 to 380 B.C. and included the Temple of Dendur. The part now finished installs the rich treasures from the Middle Kingdom, from 1991 to 1379 B.C. This collection is extremely extensive and valuable because the material comes from two sites excavated by the museum, Thebes and Lisht, important during this period. Among the monuments are larger-than-life-size seated figures of Queen Hatshepsut, monumental public sculptures in which she sometimes appears as a pharaoh and sometimes as a sphinx.

The Metropolitan also inaugurated its permanent exhibit of interiors by Frank Lloyd Wright, from his Francis W. Little House in Wayzata, MN. The living room, with its 14-ft- (4.3-m-) high ceiling and 30 by 45-ft (9.1 by 13.7-m) ground area, is considered one of Wright's finest interiors of the so-called Prairie Houses. A temporary exhibit of drawings, furniture, and stained glass complemented the room. Also shown were Japanese prints collected by Wright and sold to the museum.

On the West Coast, the J. Paul Getty Museum in Malibu, CA, with its $1 billion endowment, commands attention. Ambitious plans call for a center for advanced studies in art history and a conservation institute, as well as a new museum building. The existing building, modeled after the Villa of the Papyri at Herculaneum, will remain for the classical art section, while the new museum will house the later art still being acquired. The most spectacular acquisition of the year was the purchase of the entire manuscript collection of Dr. and Mrs. Paul Ludwig of Aachen, West Germany. The last great collection of its kind still in private hands, it numbers 144 manuscripts from the 7th to the 16th centuries, all collected piece by piece over the past 30 years. Another recent acquisition was a painting by Dosso Dossi, sold by the Marquess of Northampton for almost $3 million.

Also in the Los Angeles area, a number of new galleries opened by the Los Angeles County Museum permit the exhibition of many works formerly in storage. The newest museum in the city is the Museum of Contemporary Art which does not yet have its own building but already put on, in temporary quarters, its first show of works from four major international collections.

Another new museum was inaugurated on the East Coast, the Portland (ME) Museum of Art, in a $11.6 million building given by Charles Shipman Payson and bearing his name. Designed by Henry Nichols Cobb of I. M. Pei, it is a four-story, red brick structure with a façade in classical architectural style.

A new museum opened in Lisbon by the Calouste Gulbenkian Foundation is the first in Portugal to be dedicated to modern art and emphasizing local work. It is next door to the building that houses the late Armenian millionaire's own collection of older art works.

Exhibitions. The most spectacular European exhibition of the year was held in Lugano, Switzerland, at the villa of Baron Thyssen-Bornemisza: "Masterpieces of Impressionism and Post-Impressionism from Soviet Museums." On loan were 40 late-19th and early-20th century paintings collected by two Russians, Ivan Morozow and Sergei Shuchkin, in western Europe before World War I. Most of them have not been seen outside the Soviet Union since that time. Included were eight paintings each by Picasso and Cezanne, nine by Gauguin, six by Matisse, and three each by Monet, Renoir, and Van Gogh. In exchange, 40 Thyssen Old Masters were on view at the two museums that now own the modern paintings, the Hermitage in Leningrad and the Pushkin in Moscow.

Other European exhibitions also featured modern art. At the Grand Palais in Paris, the centenary of the death of Edouard Manet (1832–1883) was marked by a show which brought together virtually all of his works avail-

THE VATICAN COLLECTIONS

Photos, Scala/Art Resource

"The Vatican Collections: The Papacy and Art" brought together 237 paintings, sculptures, tapestries, and other works from classical antiquity to the 20th century. The Belvedere Torso, upper left, was sculpted in Athens in the 1st century B.C. and was an inspiration to Michelangelo. Among the most important works in the show was Caravaggio's newly restored "The Deposition," above, painted in 1604. Also from the 17th century was Carlo Maratta's "The Portrait of Clement IX," detail left, considered a masterpiece of psychological portraiture.

The Metropolitan Museum of Art, Museé d'Orsay

The Solomon R. Guggenheim Museum

able for lending—paintings, watercolors, drawings, and prints. Much of the show was on display at the Metropolitan in New York from September through November, but some of the most famous paintings, including *Dejeuner sur l'Herbe* and *Olympia*, were not permitted to cross the Atlantic. At the Tate Gallery in London, 232 paintings, collages, drawings, sculptures, and prints under the title "The Essential Cubism: Braque, Picasso & Their Friends, 1907–20" were assembled from private collections and the not-yet-opened Picasso Museum in Paris. Many of the works had not been seen by the general public.

Several notable exhibitions during 1983 were devoted to Surrealist artists. Salvador Dali, now 80, was honored by a major retrospective at the Museum of Contemporary Art in Madrid. The show was opened officially by the king and queen of Spain, with the heir to the throne standing in for the artist, who was unable to attend. (Though not in good health, Dali continues to produce new paintings.) At the exhibition were many less well-known works from Dali's early years, before he became famous as a Surrealist. It thereby allows the visitor to follow Dali's progression from Impressionism through Pointillism, Futurism, Cubism, and Neo-Cubism to Surrealism. There were also more recent works in yet another Surrealist style. In Paris, René Magritte (1898–1967) was the subject of a show at the Musée de la Publicité, "Magritte et les Publicitaires," which documented his influence on contemporary advertising art. His paintings and motifs,

like the cloud coming through an open window, have been copied and imitated for ads, posters, and book jackets. At the Guggenheim Museum in New York, two other Surrealists, Yves Tanguy (1900–55) and Joan Miró (b. 1893), were exhibited.

Two modern sculptors had important shows during the year. Julio Gonzalez (1876–1942) is not well known to the general public, but his fellow artists consider him one of the most important innovators of our time. He has been called the father of 20th-century iron sculpture. Born in Spain, Gonzalez went to Paris and met and collaborated with Picasso from 1929 to 1931. In 1983 the Guggenheim gave him his first comprehensive show—some 250 objects, including metal sculptures, paintings, and drawings. It was interesting to note that some of the sculptures were tiny in size, influenced by the jewelry tradition of his family and oddly at variance with the usual monumental size of iron sculpture. The other sculptor, Henry Moore (b. 1898), is world famous. His large abstract sculptures stand in public places all over the world. His first American retrospective, "Henry Moore: 60 Years of his Art," was held at New York's Metropolitan from May through September. Paradoxically, mostly small objects were exhibited—drawings, prints, and sculpture in wood, stone, and bronze. At the same time, Columbia University, which has owned Moore's *Three Way Piece: Points* since 1957, announced the creation of a Henry Moore Sculpture Reserve on its 450-acre (180-ha) Harriman, NY, campus. Moore himself approved the wooded area as an ideal place for the outdoor display of his sculpture and loaned two of his works to join the recently acquired 16-ft (4.9-m) bronze *Large Interior Form*. It is hoped that more pieces will join them in this beautiful outdoor museum.

Members of two American families noted for their patronage of the arts continued the tradition with major donations. Paul Mellon, whose father was responsible for building the National Gallery in Washington and for the nucleus of its collection, presented 93 works, mainly Impressionist and Post-Impressionist paintings, to that institution; he also donated 16 French paintings to the Art Gallery at Yale University, whose Yale Center for British Art he founded a few years earlier. From the estate of John Hay Whitney, the Museum of Modern Art in New York received eight important but almost unknown paintings which will reinforce and complete given areas. Since the main part of the museum is still under construction, the paintings were first viewed at the National Gallery together with about 100 other Whitney paintings, some recently donated to the Na-

tional Gallery and the Yale Art Gallery, and others still belonging to the family.

The year 1983 marked the 500th anniversary of the birth of the great Italian Renaissance artist, Raphael (1483–1520). It was the occasion for special exhibitions and numerous scholarly meetings and books assessing the accomplishments of the artist. At the National Gallery, "Raphael and America" included many of his paintings and drawings, but focused primarily on his influence in the United States. In Rome a significant event was the return for one week of the tapestries Raphael had designed for the Sistine Chapel walls. The tapestries had been dispersed after the sack of Rome in 1527. Reacquired by the Vatican before the end of that century, they were not returned to the chapel but displayed in the museum. Recently restored to their original glowing colors, they were hung briefly in their original place beneath the frescoed ceiling by Michelangelo, also recently restored, providing a memorable experience.

ISA RAGUSA
Princeton University

Raphael's "The Miraculous Draught of Fishes," a tapestry in silk and wool, was seen at "The Vatican Collections."

Detail, Courtesy, The Vatican Museum

Matsumoto/Sygma

South Korea mourned the loss of 17 government officials killed in a terrorist bombing in Burma.

Death stalked the continent in a series of bizarre incidents that threatened to escalate tension among the world's great powers. The absence of major retaliatory actions reflected the inability of governments to agree on appropriate responses as much as restraint on the part of the powers.

Jetliner Crisis. Worldwide protest followed the death of 269 persons September 1 when a Korean Airlines (KAL) 747 civilian passenger plane was shot down by a Soviet fighter in the Sea of Japan off the northeastern coast of the Soviet Union. The Korean aircraft was unquestionably off course, and the USSR claimed that it was on a spy mission. An American RC-135 reconnaissance plane had earlier been in the area of the incident—which may have accounted for Soviet sensitivity to the intrusion into its airspace—but the 747 could hardly have been mistaken for the U.S. plane.

U.S. President Ronald Reagan charged that the "murder of innocent civilians is a serious international issue between the Soviet Union and civilized people everywhere. . . ." Despite the absence of a truly strong U.S. or other national response, the impact of the incident was great. It heightened Japan's perception of the potential Soviet threat to its national security, and it strengthened U.S.-Japanese military ties. But it also emphasized the lack of means available to a medium-size nation, such as South Korea, when involved in a major incident with a superpower like the Soviet Union.

Burma Bombing. No less hopelessly, South Korea figured in another bizarre incident: an

explosion October 9 in a mausoleum in Rangoon, Burma, in which 17 visiting Korean officials and four Burmese were killed. The blast occurred only minutes before the arrival of South Korea's President Chun Doo Hwan on the first stop of an 18-day multinational Asian tour (which was subsequently canceled).

There had been recurrent rumors in Seoul that rival Communist North Korea would do something to disrupt President Chun's diplomatic tour. Three "Korean terrorists" were identified by the Burmese as responsible for the bombing; two were found guilty and one was killed, trying to escape. The United States, which had 39,000 troops in South Korea, urged restraint, especially with President Reagan scheduled to visit the country in November.

Manila Murder. The murder in Manila on August 21 of Philippine opposition leader Benigno Aquino, Jr., returning from self-imposed exile in the United States, also occurred with unexpected suddenness. The charismatic Aquino, regarded as the only civilian politician with sufficient mass appeal to succeed President Ferdinand Marcos, was shot as he left the plane that brought him back to his homeland. A long series of protests followed his death. Eleven persons died in a violent demonstration September 21; by mid-October the count had risen to more than 50. For reasons of security, President Reagan canceled a November visit.

Ethnic Violence. Several countries in Asia—including India, Pakistan, Indonesia, Burma, and Sri Lanka—witnessed outbreaks of ethnic violence during 1983. The sudden midyear flareup in Sri Lanka was particularly destructive of human lives, as well as property and businesses. Tamil Indian separatists were accused of murdering 13 soldiers (of majority Sinhalese ethnicity) in an ambush July 23 near the northern town of Jaffna. In the week of widespread rioting and violence that followed, more than 200 persons were killed and 50,000 left homeless. According to President Junius Jayewardene, a foreign power (the Soviet Union) was behind the violence. Severe friction between Sinhalese and Tamils has existed in Sri Lanka since it gained independence in 1948.

None of these incidents—the shooting down of the KAL 747, the Rangoon bombing, the Aquino murder, or the Sri Lanka rioting—led to expanded violence or foreign intervention. Tensions, however, clearly were raised.

Continuing Wars. Asia's two wars—in Afghanistan and Cambodia—sputtered on, as adjacent Communist powers fought local resistance elements, who were aided (albeit clandestinely and modestly) by neighboring non-Communist governments.

The next-door Communist state fighting in Afghanistan was of course the Soviet Union, which sought to maintain the unpopular puppet regime of President Babrak Karmal. Soviet participation in the Afghan war was in its fourth year, and neither victory nor withdrawal was in sight.

In the Indochinese state of Cambodia (Kampuchea), it was Vietnam that was the adjoining Communist country battling indigenous insurgent forces—a coalition of anti-Communist and anti-Vietnamese (and anti-Soviet) Communist elements—on behalf of the Hanoi-established regime of Heng Samrin. Vietnam promised early in the year to withdraw some of its troops, which numbered 200,000; although some were removed, how many and whether or not they were replaced were not clear.

Indochina Peacemaking. The withdrawal of Vietnamese troops from Cambodia has been a major goal of the member states of the Association of Southeast Asian Nations (ASEAN)—the Philippines, Thailand, Indonesia, Malaysia, and Singapore—since Hanoi's soldiers first invaded the country in 1978. At a meeting of their foreign ministers in June, the ASEAN states abandoned their insistence on an international conference as a framework for a solution, calling on Vietnam to withdraw its troops from the Thai-Cambodian border as a first step toward a complete pullout. Hanoi countered that the ASEAN governments were ignoring "the threat to peace and security in Southeast Asia" posed by China, which supplied and otherwise supported the anti-Vietnamese Cambodian resistance elements. Indonesia, among the ASEAN states, also saw China as more of a threat to the area than the USSR.

The Powers Negotiate. Three major U.S. leaders—Secretary of State George Shultz, Defense Secretary Caspar Weinberger, and Commerce Secretary Malcolm Baldridge—visited China during the year. In addition, President Reagan agreed to visit China in April 1984; Chinese Premier Zhao Ziyang would travel to the United States in January 1984. Weinberger's September 1983 visit resulted in an agreement on the sale of defensive weapons and on high-technology transfer, signaling a new phase in the continuing improvement of Sino-U.S. relations.

Representatives of China and the Soviet Union met in March for the first time since Yuri Andropov assumed leadership of the USSR in November 1982. There was little progress, however, not least of all because of Chinese efforts to put pressure on Vietnam to quit Cambodia as a precondition for normalization of relations.

Relations thawed somewhat between the Chinese and non-Communist South Koreans, as Peking for the first time granted a visa to a Seoul official, to attend a UN Food and Agricultural Organization meeting. Japan and South Korea, while still on strained terms, moved significantly closer when Japan's Prime Minister Yasuhiro Nakasone traveled to Seoul in January, the first visit by a Japanese premier since normalization of relations in 1965.

Nakasone also visited Washington in January, siding with U.S. plans to station new missiles in Europe and the U.S. position on nuclear weapons in the Geneva talks with the Soviet Union. Japan, which had expressed concern over the proposed Soviet transfer of SS20 missiles from Europe to Siberia, did not abandon its support of U.S. arms policy when Soviet leader Andropov offered new assurances. Arms as well as trade issues dominated President Reagan's talks with Nakasone in Tokyo in November.

Prime Minister Nakasone, whose government increased defense spending 6.88% for the 1984 fiscal year, toured the ASEAN countries in May to explain his country's new military emphasis.

No Progress. In March, India hosted the summit of nonaligned nations, which discussed economic issues but achieved no major results. U.S. Secretary of State Shultz traveled to India and Pakistan in June and July, respectively, but no important breakthroughs developed between the two feuding nations. Stalemate developed in talks between China and Great Britain over Hong Kong and the colony's future when the British lease expires in 1997; the Hong Kong dollar dropped to an all-time low as a consequence. Rumanian efforts to mediate differences between Peking and Hanoi made no visible progress.

RICHARD BUTWELL
The University of South Dakota

ASTRONOMY

Searching for extraterrestrial intelligence again gained the approval of the U.S. government in 1983. A bill, sponsored by Sen. William Proxmire (D-WI) in 1981, prohibited the National Aeronautics and Space Administration (NASA) from funding such work. But promptings by many scientists caused Proxmire to change his mind, and NASA's 1983 budget contained $1.5 million for continuing the quest.

Threatened Telescopes. Astronomers were surprised to learn that two major telescopes may be shut down or their work severely compromised. Since 1956 Ohio State and Ohio Wesleyan universities have operated jointly the "Big Ear" radio telescope, one of the world's largest. But in 1983 Ohio Wesleyan sold the land on which the instrument sits, and Big Ear's future became uncertain. Then, in June, the city council in San Diego, CA, voted to use high-pressure sodium streetlighting. This illumination scatters into the night sky and cannot be effectively filtered out. Thus, it may severely curtail work with the famous 200-inch (508-cm) reflector, which is located only 40 mi (64 km) from the city on Palomar mountain.

Meteorites and Satellites. Among the smallest bodies of the solar system are the meteorites, which occasionally land on the earth's surface. One ounce-sized fragment, discovered in Antarctica in 1982, was identified by several American scientists, from its appearance and chemical composition, as having come from the moon. Thus, for the first time a meteorite's place of origin has been determined. In a similar development, evidence is mounting that a group of rare meteorites called SNCs originated on Mars.

Triton. The largest satellite of Neptune, Triton, was found to have a probable sea of liquid nitrogen a few feet deep near its south pole. Such a feature would be unique among planetary satellites, though Saturn's largest satellite, Titan, recently has been suspected of harboring an ocean of liquid ethane and methane.

An eclipse of the sun was photographed June 11 in Yogyakarta, Indonesia; totality lasted 5 minutes.

William P. Sterne, Jr.

Comets. On Oct. 16, 1982, Halley's Comet was detected on the inbound leg of its scheduled 1986 passage by the sun. The Palomar 200-inch telescope, equipped with a state-of-the-art electronic detector, was used by David Jewitt and G. Edward Danielson for the long-awaited recovery. Halley's Comet was then 1 billion mi (1.6 billion km) from the earth, outside the orbit of Saturn.

Astronomers were taken by surprise when Comet IRAS-Araki-Alcock sped past earth on May 11, only eight days after its true nature became known. At its closest, the comet's distance was only 3 million mi or 4.8 million km (12 times farther away than the moon). Observers with clear, dark skies then saw an amazing sight—Comet IRAS-Araki-Alcock appeared as a fuzzy glow six or more times larger than the full moon.

Another Solar System? One of the most intriguing discoveries by the Infrared Astronomy Satellite, launched in January 1983, is that a cloud of solid bodies circles Vega, the fifth brightest star in the sky. The cloud has a diameter of some 7 billion mi (11 billion km), twice as large as that spanned by the planets of the solar system. Early speculation suggested that this cloud is a young planetary system in the process of formation. The size of the objects contained in the cloud was not known by late 1983.

Stars. During 1983 the importance of our galaxy's so-called millisecond pulsar became evident, due to investigations by astronomers worldwide. Discovered in late 1982, this highly magnetized neutron star, with a diameter of only one or two miles, spins around 642 times per second. The millisecond pulsar, made of matter crushed to 10^{14} (1 followed by 14 zeros) times the density of water, may turn out to be the most accurate clock in the universe. Already the pulsar's rotation period has been measured to one part in 10^{14}, equaling the precision with which our atomic-clock time standards are known.

An object in the Large Magellanic Cloud (a companion galaxy to our Milky Way), designated R136a, was proposed as the most massive star known. With a bulk some 2,000 times greater than the sun's, it is losing its starstuff very rapidly by astronomical standards—a solar mass every one or two thousand years. R136a shines as bright as 10 million suns.

Our Galaxy. Four years of observation by the European Space Agency's COS B satellite were studied by H. Mayer-Hasselwander of West Germany. His work revealed that our Milky Way galaxy emits gamma rays. This radiation, occurring at the highest energies known, is concentrated in the plane of the Milky Way. Astronomers interpret the gamma rays as resulting from the interaction of high-energy cosmic rays and the atomic and molecular hydrogen that exists between the stars.

Other Galaxies. On July 3, R. Evans, an Australian amateur astronomer, discovered a supernova in Messier 83, a relatively nearby galaxy in the constellation of Hydra. Supernovae are exploding stars, and this one was of the most brilliant and least known type—at its peak it shone with the light of 10 billion suns. For many months, astronomers examined this "new" star with detectors that scanned the spectrum from X rays to radio waves, searching for clues to the origin of these spectacular events.

Quasars. These starlike galaxies are widely believed to be the ultimate celestial powerhouses, being a trillion or so times more luminous than the sun. The source of their energy is still unknown, though they may be powered by a black hole—a gravitational sink so powerful that nothing can escape it. Because quasars are so luminous, they can be seen at immense distances. Recently, the optical quasar counterpart of the radio source PKS 2000-330 was found by a team of European astronomers to be some 10 to 20 billion light-years from earth, making it the most distant object known. In fact, if the universe is the size we believe it to be, PKS 2000-330 lies quite close to its edge.

Black Holes. Evidence continues to mount that black holes are real features of the universe. Because black holes cannot be seen, they can be detected only by their gravitational effects on other bodies. One search technique is to find a visible star in a binary system that has a very massive but unseen companion. (Any star with a mass greater than about twice the sun's must either shed the excess or become a black hole.) In 1983 a team of American and Canadian astronomers found the best black-hole candidate yet; it is located in the Large Magellanic Cloud. They concluded that the visible component of the X-ray source LMC X-3 has an unseen companion with a mass greater than 9 suns.

Cosmology. The objective of cosmology is to describe the observed universe and to explain how it got that way. In 1983 theoretical investigations by Alan Guth of Harvard University suggested that the volume of the universe may be 10^{60} times larger than scientists had supposed. To him the universe seemed too homogeneous and its parts expanded too regularly. Incredible luck would have been needed in the context of the 50-year-old Big Bang theory, which postulates that at the creation an expansion of space-time began out of which everything was made later.

There also may be an infinity of universes out there, each completely isolated from all the others. This concept of a plurality of worlds is very old, but scientists now are beginning to see ways to transpose the issue from metaphysics to science.

LEIF J. ROBINSON, *Sky & Telescope*

AUSTRALIA

© David Austen/Black Star

As the new prime minister, Robert Hawke undertook "the task of national reconciliation."

Economic problems and political redirection dominated the Australian scene in 1983. In his eighth year as Liberal prime minister, Malcolm Fraser was defeated in a general election in March which swept the Australian Labor Party (ALP) to power under its new leader Robert J. Hawke (*see* BIOGRAPHY). The 5% swing to the ALP from the 1980 poll reflected disillusionment with Fraser.

The year opened with clear signs of a sagging economy and unemployment levels not seen since the 1930s. The severe setback stemmed from widespread and searing drought and price declines in export commodities, especially metals and coal, which severely slowed mining and resources expansion. In spite of a wage freeze which Fraser had introduced, Australia was caught at a disadvantage in terms of international competitiveness, and unemployment rose above 10%. Hawke took office with a federal deficit running at A$100 million a week, and an adverse balance of payments. His first major move as prime minister was to devalue the Australian dollar by 10%; strong capital inflow and improved trading results soon reduced the depreciation to below 5%. Businessmen, at first apprehensive about ALP intentions, became persuaded that Hawke's pragmatism would prevail over ALP ideology, and by midyear some signs of revived business confidence were evident. However, profitability remained at unsatisfactory levels. The wages pause ended in September with an announced 4.3% general rise.

One of the emotive issues of the election involved the Tasmanian government's plan to dam the Franklin River in the island's southwest for hydroelectric development. Hawke undertook to invoke federal powers to restrain the state government. After demonstrators protested the plan, the struggle to "Save the Franklin" moved from the banks of the river to the High Court and resulted in a majority decision favoring the federal government.

For much of the year headlines told of crime and corruption. One report found that "the seepage of corruption has left an ever-darkening and ever-widening taint" and considered crime "institutionalized in New South Wales, the nerve center for operations in the rest of Australia." In October, questions in federal parliament pointed to involvement of a New South Wales minister in bribery, and the fallout from the corruption issue was destabilizing the state's ALP government.

Political Realignment. The election campaign developed around promises and personalities rather than policies. The campaign opened with the ALP caucus dropping Bill Hayden in favor of Hawke, a consistent contender for power. Hawke espoused populist causes, including environmental issues, and was seen as a pragmatist on economic matters. Hawke dominated the ALP image and enjoyed admiring media coverage. Commentators saw the new party leader pursuing a "presidential" style in his independence of attitude toward ALP policy priorities, in the strength of expertise surrounding his regime, and in his courting of personal popularity to back his views.

After taking office, Hawke moved toward a radical change of public-service organization to allow the top echelon to be recruited by ministers—a departure from the independent, nonpartisan approach that has traditionally permeated the public service.

The parliamentary and trade union wings of the ALP worked in harmony. The major strains showed up in diverging lines of policy followed by Hawke and minority factions within the ALP, especially the Socialist Left. Uranium mining, which a vocal faction sought to have phased out, remained in contention, with Hawke supporting expanded production.

Expulsion of a Soviet official believed to be a KGB agent, and the subsequent revelation that he had developed a close personal though "innocent" friendship with a former ALP official seeking business ties with the USSR, led Hawke to order a major inquiry into national security matters. A welter of heated dialogue on personal issues and possible ministerial involvement in "political martyrdom" dominated the inquiry.

A Royal Commission inquiring into the affairs of the Ship Painters and Dockers Union revealed fraud networks relating to taxation, foreign-currency transactions, and corporation and banking infringements on a large scale. As a result of these findings, criminal charges were filed against more than 12 men.

The Liberal Party underwent change following the election and Fraser's subsequent resignation from parliament. The leadership went to Andrew Peacock, a lawyer and former foreign affairs minister. As party leader, Peacock stressed the restructuring of the tax system and a need to roll back the spending habits of "a gigantically inflated administrative system."

Domestic Policy. In the excitement of Labor's return to office, much of the thrust of the Fraser years slipped away. Prime Minister Hawke replaced direct pressure on the unions with reliance on his powers of persuasion as a former union leader. Generally backed by an admiring press, Hawke made "consensus" in moderating rises in income and prices the watchword; at the same time the public was conditioned to accept an A$8.4 billion federal deficit as "reasonable" under current economic circumstances in the nation and throughout the world. This rate of deficit was soon greatly exceeded, however.

In September, 300 of the country's influential businessmen met for the launching of the Business Council of Australia by Hawke. The

© Tim Graham/Sygma

Prince Charles and Princess Diana were received warmly during their six-week tour of Australia and New Zealand.

council's aims would be pursued in what council president Sir Arvi Parbo described as "broad national interest" rather than lobbying on a narrow front.

Meanwhile some media exposure was given to a call for major reform of national wage fixing to link wage movements with productivity rather than with price rises. Other voices were being heard seeking an end to penalty rates applied to all work outside daylight hours of a five-day workweek. A third reform being urged would end the Arbitration Commission's inability to enforce its awards against recalcitrant unions.

Late in September, together with a "catch-up" general wage rise of 4.3%, the Arbitration Commission promised a return to a central wage-fixing system indexed by the Consumer Price Index (CPI), provided unions agreed to forgo any additional claims.

The year's legislative activity covered 150 new measures embodying various phases of ALP policy, including a health scheme funded by a general income surtax (to operate from 1984). Among the many official bodies created were the Economic Planning Advisory Council and the Car Industry Council, both including nominees of government, unions, and industry.

The Economic Thrust. In May a series of measures gave the first legislative thrust to ALP policy by placing curbs on pension out-

---

AUSTRALIA • Information Highlights

Official Name: Commonwealth of Australia.
Location: Southwestern Pacific Ocean.
Area: 2,969,997 sq mi (7 692 300 km²).
Population (July 1983 est.): 15,265,000.
Chief Cities (June 30, 1981): Canberra, the capital, 246,100; Sydney, 3,280,900; Melbourne, 2,803,600.
Government: *Head of state,* Elizabeth II, queen; represented by Sir Ninian Martin Stephens, governor-general (took office July 1982). *Head of government,* Robert Hawke, prime minister (took office March 11, 1983). *Legislature*—Parliament: Senate and House of Representatives.
Monetary Unit: Australian dollar (1.0961 A$ equals U.S.$1, Nov. 4, 1983).
Gross National Product (1981 U.S.$): $140,300,000,000.
Economic Indexes (1982): *Consumer Prices* (1970 = 100), all items, 328.1; food, 319.1. *Industrial Production* (1975 = 100), 107.
Foreign Trade (1982 U.S.$): *Imports,* $24,187,000,000; *exports,* $22,002,000,000.

lays for the nonindigent. The budget presented in August offered fiscal expansion to boost the level of economic activity, which has shown a 2% decline in preceding months, as a relief measure until private sector demand was shown to be on the rise. Special emphasis was placed on "moderation" and "the responsible approach."

The budget was a compound of Treasury caution and traditional ALP largess. Outlays were projected on a 16% increase over the previous year (when they rose 18%). The expected increase in revenue was set at 9%, leading to a projected deficit of almost 5% of gross domestic product compared with less than 3% in the previous year. Budget initiatives included substantially increased spending on public housing and capital works, increases in unemployment benefits and retraining programs, and provision for universal medical and hospital payments. Personal and corporate tax rates remained unchanged, and tax incentives for industrial investment were continued. High-technology undertakings were promised tax write-offs.

Foreign Policy and Defense. Prime Minister Hawke gave no solace to ALP factions seeking to loosen treaty ties with the United States and to oppose Indonesia over its absorption of East Timor. He made it clear that he intended to continue the firm commitment to the Western alliance and the broad principles of U.S. foreign policy. The ANZUS treaty with the United States and New Zealand remained basic to foreign relationships and defense. This was affirmed by Hawke during June visits to Djakarta and Washington and by Foreign Affairs Minister Bill Hayden at the ANZUS Council in Washington in July. Nevertheless, in the government's view, Hayden indicated, "regional security arrangements" had an "equal if not a higher priority." By advocating a policy favoring a "political settlement in Cambodia," Hayden was at odds with the Association of Southeast Asian Nations (ASEAN)—an organization with which he had earlier endeavored to have Australia identify more closely.

Other News. Bounteous midyear rains and a record acreage sown by Australia's 50,000 wheat farmers brought the promise of an excellent year-end harvest and the hope that rural towns would revive after the debilitation of long and severe drought.

The most felicitous extravaganza emanated from Newport, RI, in concert with *Australia II*'s successful bid to win the America's Cup in September. The unprecedented media saturation accorded the historic challenge included live television coverage and publication of special editions of major newspapers.

Hope for redirection of Aboriginal cultural activity was voiced by the newly appointed chairman of the Aboriginal Arts Board, who foreshadowed changes from the organization's support of a "museum-style preservation of culture" in favor of support for all contemporary and traditional artists. At the same time, Aboriginal spokesmen intensified their call for state governments to hand over large areas of land—a campaign that had only limited success.

For the fourth successive year the national birthrate showed a rising trend. Statistics revealed that the distribution of income had become more uneven, with the top 10% of income earners receiving an average of A$28,011, while 1981–82 average income was A$13,020 for males and A$6,230 for females. Surveys showed that by mid-1983, 1 in 4 of all Australians depended on a federal pension.

R. M. YOUNGER, *Australian Author*

A national celebration erupts after the 12-meter yacht "Australia II" captured the America's Cup in September.

Barry Baker

AUSTRIA

Parliamentary elections, the resignation of longtime Chancellor Bruno Kreisky, and a visit by Pope John Paul II highlighted events in Austria during 1983.

Politics. Elections to the 183-seat National Council were held April 24, with 90.6% of the electorate turning out to vote. The campaign had been a desultory one, with economic issues dominant. Unemployment was on a slight increase (1.9% in 1980, 2.4% in 1981, and 3.7% in 1982), and ways to deal with the problem evoked the most discussion. The majority Social Democrats advocated more government work programs, while the Christian Democrats spoke of supporting private industry. The latter also attacked the rising budget deficit and Socialist proposals of tax reform.

When the votes were counted, the Socialists had lost the absolute majority of seats which they held since 1971. Their representation dropped from 95 to 90, while the Christian Democrats' climbed from 77 to 81 and the Freedom Party's rose from 11 to 12. Five other parties entered slates but won no seats—the Communist Party, which has not been represented in parliament since 1959; the United Green Party, which focuses on environmental issues; the Austrian Alternative List, which appeals to women, the jobless, homosexuals, and ethnic minorities; the Austrian Party, which contested the election in Vienna, Styria, and Tyrol; and the Stop Foreigners Party, which took part in the Vienna balloting.

True to an election-eve promise to "take my hat and go" if the Socialists did not win a clear majority, Chancellor Kreisky announced that he would in fact be stepping down after 13 years in office. His resignation became official May 11. Fred Sinowatz, meanwhile, vice-chancellor and minister of education and the arts, had been chosen as his successor April 25; Kreisky for the time being retained his chairmanship of the party. On May 18, Sinowatz announced a 15-member coalition cabinet consisting of 12 Social Democrats and 3 Freedom Party members, as well as eight secretaries of state, five of them Social Democrats and three from the Freedom Party. Norbert Steger, head of the Freedom Party, became vice-chancellor and minister of trade; and Socialist Erwin Lanc, former minister of interior, became minister of foreign affairs. Sinowatz and his new government were sworn in May 24.

In Vienna municipal elections, also held on April 24, the Social Democrats saw their representation decline from 62 to 61, while the Christian Democrats' increased from 35 to 37 and the Freedom Party's dropped from 3 to 2.

Foreign Affairs. Then Chancellor Kreisky, accompanied by other high-ranking Austrian officials, made a visit to the United States, February 2–8. President Ronald Reagan took the occasion to announce the appointment of Helene von Damm as the new U.S. ambassador to Austria; the post had been vacant since the death of Ambassador Theodore Cummings in March 1982. During their talks, Kreisky and Reagan clarified differences over Austria's trade with Eastern bloc countries, and both leaders stressed the close and cooperative bilateral relations that exist between their countries. On his September tour of Europe, U.S. Vice-President George Bush visited Vienna for two days and met with Chancellor Sinowatz.

With Franz Cardinal König acting as host, jubilant crowds welcomed Pope John Paul II to Austria on September 10. The three-day visit coincided with the 300th anniversary of the lifting of the Turkish second siege of Vienna by Christian armies under the leadership of King John III Sobieski of Poland. On the last day of his visit, the pope made a pilgrimage to Mariazell, Austria's most revered religious shrine.

In March, Austria joined with eight other European countries, the United States, and Canada in signing a pact which would permit individuals sentenced for crimes abroad to serve their terms in their home countries, the effect of which might be to reduce the sentences or even grant a pardon.

Economy. Overall the Austrian economy continued to stagnate in 1983, though there were signs of revival. Car sales were up 23% during the first half of the year. A real growth of between 1.0% and 1.5% was forecast for 1983. Inflation declined from a rate of 6.8% in 1981 and 5.5% in 1982 to a projected 4.7% in 1983. Unemployment, averaging 3.7% in 1982, was expected to rise to 4.2% in 1983. The budget deficit, 27.5 billion schillings in 1981 and 45.4 billion in 1982, was projected to hold steady for 1983. The trade deficit was expected to rise moderately, to approximately 69.2 billion schillings.

ERNST C. HELMREICH, *Professor of History, emeritus, Bowdoin College*

AUSTRIA • Information Highlights

Official Name: Republic of Austria.
Location: Central Europe.
Area: 32,400 sq mi (83 916 km²).
Population (July 1983 est.): 7,584,000.
Chief Cities (1981 census): Vienna, the capital, 1,515,666; Graz, 243,405; Linz, 197,962; Salzburg, 138,213; Innsbruck, 116,100.
Government: *Head of state,* Rudolf Kirchschläger, president (took office July 1974). *Head of government,* Fred Sinowatz, chancellor (took office May 24, 1983). *Legislature*—Federal Assembly: Federal Council and National Council.
Monetary Unit: Schilling (18.26 schillings equal U.S. $1, Oct. 5, 1983).
Gross National Product (1981 U.S. $): $66,600,000,-000.
Economic Indexes (1982): *Consumer Prices* (1970 = 100), all items, 207.1; food, 188.3. *Industrial production* (1975 = 100), 122.
Foreign Trade (1981 U.S. $): *Imports,* $19,557,000,-000; *exports,* $15,568,000,000.

AUTOMOBILES

Chrysler Corporation

Lee Iacocca (left) repays the last two thirds of Chrysler's federally guaranteed loans.

One of the most protracted slumps in the history of the U.S. automobile industry came to an end during the 1983 model run. Car production rebounded 10.2% from the 25-year low of the 1982 model run, as consumer demand for new vehicles climbed back toward the brisk levels of the late 1970s.

Although production of 5,683,194 cars in the 1983 model run still ran nearly 4 million units below 1979, the second highest of all time, industry executives and analysts were in agreement that a full-fledged recovery was under way as the 1984-model season opened. Domestic truck output climbed to 1,764,845 in the first nine months of 1983, an increase of 16.1% compared with the same period in 1982, adding to forecasts of continued production and sales growth in the following year.

With cars back in demand, especially the higher-priced full-size and intermediate models, U.S. producers were reopening plants long closed to save costs. The number of autoworkers indefinitely laid off, which had peaked at more than 200,000 in 1982, was reduced to about 110,000 at the outset of 1984-model production.

The upsurge in sales of higher-priced cars, those delivering for $10,000 or more with a full list of optional equipment, proved especially beneficial for General Motors. GM's output of 1982 models had plunged 24%, or about one million cars, from the 1981 total, but 1983 brought the No. 1 automaker a 4.4% snapback to 3,365,448 units, thanks to substantial gains by Oldsmobile, Buick, and Cadillac.

Oldsmobile, paced by its Cutlass Supreme and Ciera intermediate series, posted a 30.5% jump in 1983-model output to 916,576 cars.

Buick, reaching a model-year sales record, built 808,415 cars, up 9.3%. Cadillac advanced 31.8% to 292,714 cars.

By contrast, the two GM divisions most associated with lower-priced cars again suffered declines in the 1983 cycle. Chevrolet, still the leader over Ford in industry sales, nevertheless fell 3.4% to 1,040,874 cars. Pontiac plummeted 36.6% to 306,869.

Long second to Chevrolet in industry sales, the Ford division of Ford Motor Co. was closely pursued by Oldsmobile in 1983. The GM division actually outproduced Ford-named cars in the 1983 run, 916,576 to 829,867, although Ford remained slightly ahead in overall retail sales. Ford Motor Co. production, however, benefited from stepped-up sales of higher-priced cars and climbed 11.9% during the 1983 run to 1,304,280 cars. Ford division gained 10.5% to 829,867, and Lincoln-Mercury climbed 14.4% to 474,413. Midyear introductions of redesigned Thunderbird, Cougar, Tempo, and Topaz models gave Ford a lift which offset declines in its Escort subcompact, still the industry's top-selling nameplate.

A banner year was registered by Chrysler Corp., near bankruptcy in 1981. The No. 3 automaker not only paid off all of its federally guaranteed loans of $1.2 billion, but also brought its workers up to parity with GM and Ford employees on wages and fringe benefits. Chrysler production spurted 24.5% in the 1983 run to 737,835 cars.

Another success was achieved by American Motors, whose parent company is the French state-owned automaker Renault. The Renault Alliance, built by AMC in Kenosha, WI, surpassed its first-year target of 100,000 and reached 142,805 in unit volume. AMC discontinued production of its Concord and Spirit cars in 1983 to concentrate on the Renault-based cars and the four-wheel-drive Eagle.

Rounding out the domestic production group was the Volkswagen Rabbit, which dropped 29.4% to 73,400, and the Honda Accord, of which 33,508 units were assembled in its new plant at Marysville, OH.

The 1984 Models. Rising demand for new cars, as reflected in the sales upturn for 1983 models, spurred the domestic automakers to emphasize higher-priced performance and convenience features on the 1984 models. The trend toward the "upscale" segments of the market reflected the industry's optimism for continued sales gains and the desire to maximize profits in the higher-priced lines after an economic downturn which had lasted almost four years.

The Big Three automakers underscored their high expectations for new models by raising suggested retail list prices an average of $191 to $254, or between 2% and 3%. But dealer inventories of unsold new models were lean as the 1984-model season opened, and minimal resistance was expected by dealers to the increases, which were only about half the average annual advances made in the boom years of the late 1970s.

With each automaker and importer required to meet a Corporate Average Fuel Economy (CAFE) of 26.5 miles per gallon for 1984 models, fuel-miserly engines and vehicles were not completely neglected for 1984. In fact, Ford offered a diesel-engine option for its lowest-priced Escort and Lynx subcompacts. But Ford and GM failed to meet the previous 1983-model CAFE average of 26 mpg because of excess sales of full-size and intermediate cars

WORLD MOTOR VEHICLE DATA, 1982

Country	Passenger Car Production	Truck and Bus Production	Motor Vehicle Registrations
Argentina	106,880	25,236	4,464,238
Australia	371,422	37,148	7,564,700
Austria	7,051	8,129	2,512,735
Belgium	243,289	34,725	3,546,123
Brazil	718,843	140,452	10,290,744
Canada	807,645	468,807	13,932,000
Czechoslovakia	173,517	50,420	2,802,164
France	2,777,125	371,682	22,350,000
East Germany	179,500	38,000	3,152,100
West Germany	3,761,436*	301,229	25,266,717
Hungary	-	13,600	1,144,302
India	42,673	109,576	1,425,057
Italy	1,297,351	155,692	20,423,829
Japan	6,881,586	3,850,208	39,620,957
Korea	94,460	73,024	561,666
Mexico	300,579	172,058	6,544,987
The Netherlands	86,000	10,050	4,981,000
Poland	229,111	47,240	3,342,709
Portugal	-	100	1,288,000
Rumania	75,000	50,000	380,000
Spain	927,500	142,007	9,409,576
Sweden	294,792	54,799	3,083,567
Switzerland	-	768	2,569,257
United Kingdom	887,679	268,798	17,522,294
United States	5,073,496	1,912,660	158,456,511†
USSR	1,320,000	890,000	17,157,800
Yugoslavia	211,372	29,944	2,978,008
Total	26,868,307	9,257,352	427,373,835‡

* Includes 273,846 micro-buses. † U.S. total includes 123,461,507 cars and 34,995,004 trucks and buses. ‡ World total includes 331,161,771 cars and 96,212,064 trucks and buses, of which 398,371,041 vehicles are from countries shown above. *Source:* Motor Vehicle Manufacturers Association of the United States, Inc.

with larger engines. Though the "noncompliant" pair made up for the shortfall through application of credits from past-year CAFE showings, GM proposed that the final CAFE requirement of 27.5 mpg on 1985 models be rolled back by the Department of Transportation to disencumber the market for bigger cars.

Restyled 1984 models included the Chevrolet Corvette two-seater; three GM full-size cars with front-wheel drive—the Buick Electra, Cadillac deVille, and Oldsmobile 98; and Ford's Lincoln Mark VII with "aerodynamic

Chrysler Corporation

An innovative seven-passenger "minivan," the 1984 Plymouth Voyager was part of the trend toward front-wheel drive.

In the subcompact market, American Motors looked for success with the Renault Encore hatchback.

lines," resembling the 1983 Thunderbird and early-arriving 1984 Tempo. Chrysler Corp. introduced a new seven-passenger "minivan" in the Dodge Caravan and Plymouth Voyager, a domestic industry first with front-wheel drive, as well as two turbo-charged sports coupes called the Chrysler Laser and Dodge Daytona. Station wagon models were added to GM's midsize front-wheel-drive series—the Chevrolet Celebrity, Pontiac 6000, Buick Century, and Oldsmobile Cutlass Ciera. Pontiac's Fiero joined the growing ranks of two-seater coupes.

For 1984, American Motors introduced Renault Encore hatchback editions of the successful year-old Renault Alliance notchbacks. Volkswagen of America made the diesel engine standard on its U.S.-built Rabbit line and chalked up brisk sales of a new Rabbit GTI sports coupe with a peppier 1.8-liter gasoline engine. American Honda expanded production of the Honda Accord car at its Ohio assembly plant by phasing in the Accord hatchback body style in the fall of 1983.

The Imports. Despite a third year of voluntary limitations on U.S. shipments decreed by the Japanese government, sales of all imports in the first nine months of 1983 actually rose by 7.2% to 1,803,613 cars. The Japanese car "quota" for exports to the United States remained at 1,680,000 units for the 1983–84 year (ending March 31, 1984), but a prospective new "importer"—GM—was pressing for an increase for the 1984–85 year.

Underlying GM's request for relaxation of the quota was the No. 1 automaker's plans to import close to 300,000 small cars from Japan in the 1985 year—200,000 compacts from its partner Isuzu and close to 100,000 minicom-pacts from Suzuki. The one-liter "minicar" would be a precedent-setting size for the U.S. market, although Suzuki, Nissan, and several other Japanese automakers have produced such small cars for many years.

GM also hoped to break ground on the 1985 U.S. market with another Japanese producer—Toyota. A proposal to reopen the closed GM assembly plant at Fremont, CA, for assembly of a new Toyota Corolla subcompact, to be sold by Chevrolet dealers, was submitted to the Federal Trade Commission (FTC) for review.

Nissan (Datsun) replaced Toyota as the leading seller of imported cars in the United States during the first nine months of 1983. Honda, whose Accord assembly plant in Ohio was gaining production speed, continued in third place, followed by Mazda and Subaru. Led by the Swedish Volvo in sixth place, the higher-priced European sedans and coupes all improved their volumes from 1982.

Among foreign entries, performance and economy shared the 1984-model spotlight. Honda's new Civic CRX two-seater won the EPA fuel-ratings derby with a highway average of 51-miles-per-gallon, outstripping imported diesel-engine cars with a 1.3-liter gasoline engine. Toyota offered a front-wheel-drive Corolla subcompact series with a diesel option, as well as a turbocharged diesel for its Camry compact. Nissan's 300ZX, latest edition of the top-selling U.S. sports coupe, was wholly revamped for 1984. The entire Subaru line was turbocharged. Mercedes-Benz introduced the 190 series, an all-new compact priced from $24,000.

MAYNARD M. GORDON
Editor, "Motor News Analysis"

BANGLADESH

Bangladesh remained under martial law throughout 1983. On December 11, military ruler Lt. Gen. Hossein Mohammed Ershad proclaimed himself president and dissolved the cabinet. The next day he declared that martial law would remain in effect until after presidential and parliamentary elections, scheduled for May 1984. Ershad, who took power in a March 1982 coup and suspended the constitution, assumed the presidency in an apparent effort to consolidate power before the 1984 balloting.

Political parties continued to be plagued by factionalism, but several formed alliances. A leftist 15-party group included the Awami League, led by Hasina Wajid, the daughter of Sheikh Mujibur Rahman. A more rightist seven-party alliance included the Bangladesh National Party, headed by former President Abdus Sattar. Both groups agreed on a five-point program that called for an early end to martial law and for early elections.

The urgency of resolving the country's political uncertainties was underlined by violence at Dhaka University in February, by an unsuccessful military coup attempt in August, and by sporadic incidents of tribal unrest in the Chittagong Hills.

In March, Ershad announced an 18-point development program, calling for agricultural self-sufficiency and full employment. The regime took further steps to implement its key program of administrative decentralization.

Economic Conditions. The Bangladesh economy improved only slightly in 1983. Gross domestic product grew 3.8% in fiscal 1983, up from virtually no growth in the previous year but short of the anticipated 6%. Inflation was held to 12%, and balance-of-payments stability nearly tripled foreign exchange reserves.

Overseas employment continued to increase, but the value of foreign-exchange remittances suffered a slight decline. Several public-sector industries were returned to private ownership to increase productivity.

BANGLADESH • Information Highlights

Official Name: People's Republic of Bangladesh.
Location: South Asia.
Area: 55,019 sq mi (142 500 km²).
Population (July 1983 est.): 96,539,000.
Chief Cities (1981 census): Dhaka, the capital, 3,458,602; Chittagong, 1,388,476; Khulna, 623,184.
Government: *Head of state and government,* Hossein Mohammed Ershad, chief executive (assumed power March 24, 1982) and president (Dec. 1983).
Monetary Unit: Taka (24.500 taka equal U.S.$1, June 1983).
Gross National Product (1982 U.S.$): $9,300,-000,000.
Economic Index (1981): *Consumer Prices* (1972 = 100), *all items,* 454.7; food, 435.4.
Foreign Trade (1982 U.S.$): *Imports,* $2,300,000,000; *exports,* $769,000,000.

On the negative side, unemployment remained high, the value of the taka continued to deteriorate, the year's food production was hurt by severe flooding, and the second five-year plan had to be revised downward in the face of reduced resources. Bangladesh remained dependent on external assistance.

Foreign Relations. Tensions with India increased. Little progress was made on the persistent river waters issue, now under study by a binational Joint Rivers Commission. Bangladeshis were angered by India's decision to seal the border with barbed wire to halt the flow of "illegal immigrants" into riot-torn Assam State. Conversely, Indians were upset by Bangladesh's failure to consult India before agreeing to supply transit and port facilities to the nearby landlocked kingdom of Bhutan.

Bangladesh was host for the Islamic Foreign Ministers Conference in late 1983. General Ershad attended the nonaligned summit in New Delhi in March, visited Yugoslavia in June, and Washington, DC, in October.

WILLIAM L. RICHTER
Kansas State University

BANKING

American commercial banking in 1983 continued to reflect the gradual deregulation of the industry. Little by little the three basic legal restraints that have determined banking's structure have been breaking down.

Deregulation. The McFadden Act of 1927 limited banks to their home state, unless invited in by another state or already operating across state lines. In 1983 more and more banks were joined across state lines as state legislatures invited out-of-state banks in, and as banks then opened up new offices and merged out-of-state banks. These moves were made to obtain geographical growth and to take advantage of other states' easier banking laws on such issues as usury ceilings. Thrift institutions (thrifts) also moved interstate to a considerable degree. But here the moves were made largely because regulators allowed an out-of-state institution to buy an ailing thrift in a different state if the offer was markedly above what an in-state bidder would pay for the troubled thrift.

The Glass Steagall Act of 1933—a law that separated commercial banking from investment banking (the sale and distribution of securities) —experienced further breakdown in 1983. More banks entered the discount brokerage business, ruled to be legal for banks even under the Glass Steagall Act, while investment bankers bought banks and made the acquisition legal by turning them into "nonbanks" by eliminating a function, such as commercial lending.

As thrifts also started to offer commercial loans—a power granted to them under the 1982 deregulation act—more and more the differences among banks, thrifts, and investment banks began to atrophy, with observers feeling that soon all financial institutions would be allowed to offer all types of financial service.

Interest Rates. It was in interest rate ceilings that 1983 witnessed the greatest change in banking. Until Dec. 14, 1982, commercial banks were not allowed to compete with money funds for high-interest, liquid savings. Yet in the first nine months after legalization of this service, such deposits in banks grew from zero to more than $350 billion (U.S.). At the same time the older money funds were reduced to less than $160 billion from more than $250 billion in mid-December.

Banks also were freed to pay whatever rate they wanted on certificates of deposit that mature in more than a month. The era of strict governmental control over what banks could pay depositors was fast becoming history, except for the small savings account and the corporate depositor.

With the freedom to pay top dollar for deposits, however, banking began to move away from service competition to price competition, just as cut-rate stores offer lower prices but do not provide the service that department stores provide. In banking this should mean fewer branches, more reliance on automated banking without tellers, and higher charges for such "exception items" as overdrawn accounts.

Loans. Banks showed an improvement in soundness in 1983. Because of lower interest rates, fewer banks were left with the classic squeeze of financing long-term, fixed-rate loans with high-cost, short-term deposits because they were paying less for these deposit balances than they had to pay in 1982. Banks also have been making more variable-rate loans, in which rates move up and down as general interest rates move. This flexibility has also helped banks get away from the earnings squeeze that they faced in 1982 and earlier.

Where banks have had problems, however, has been in the legacy of foreign loans. Major banks have lent very large amounts to Brazil, Argentina, Mexico, and other nations that cannot afford to service their debts, with the result that either the banks must refinance the loans and offer more lenient terms or accept a real prospect of serious default. This fear has been a shadow in the minds of bank investors, keeping bank stocks from doing as well as might be expected from 1983 bank earnings.

Federal Reserve. While bank interest rates seemed unusually high, this was the legacy of a federal budget deficit of almost $200 billion. The Federal Reserve Board found it necessary again to rely on modest monetary restraint as its basic weapon for preventing the resurgence of inflation.

The Federal Reserve faced opposition to its tight money policy from those wanting more

UPI

Paul Volcker testifies before the Senate Banking Committee after being renamed Federal Reserve Board chairman.

rapid economic growth, but it appeared to hold firm in making anti-inflation policy the key to its operations. It did, however, find growing support for the idea of separating the Federal Reserve's monetary-control policies from its regulatory authority over banking. This was a natural development: as banks and nonbanks become more alike, more and more lawmakers are wondering why there should be different regulators for banks, for thrifts, and for other financial institutions. As financial institutions become more homogeneous, their regulators also are likely to become more homogeneous.

Canada. In Canada, conditions in banking reflected a similar trend toward growing competition. Because the banks are fewer, however, the emphasis in 1983 was on pressure to enable the foreign banks to play a greater role in domestic banking operations. Until now foreign banks have been limited to controlling 8% of the Canadian banking market, and pressures are building to expand the limit.

Canadian banks also face difficulties with regard to problem loans on their books. But in Canada much of the problem stems from the decline in the fortunes of the oil industry.

See also UNITED STATES—The Economy.

PAUL S. NADLER, *Professor of Finance*
Rutgers—The State University of New Jersey

BELGIUM

Throughout 1983 this small democracy suffered from economic and political difficulties.

The Economy. Despite the births of two sets of sextuplets, two major spy/espionage cases, a killer earthquake, and the deaths of former King Leopold III and the Prince Regent Charles (who bridged the rule of Leopold and the present King Baudouin), economic troubles controlled the 1983 headlines in Belgium. The austerity program of the coalition government of Prime Minister Wilfried Martens called for giant sacrifices in a nation racked with the Common Market's highest unemployment rate and public deficit. Martens gained some modest successes in cutting back public spending, but there was widespread criticism of the government's wage and benefits reductions. Once-docile unions responded against the Martens measures with strikes in September that paralyzed transport, mail, and other public services. It was the worst labor unrest since the early 1960s.

However, many persons questioned whether the wage cuts and reductions in social benefits were distributed equitably. Certainly the public employees' strikes were based on the notion that the budget cuts not only were antiunion but also favored business with various tax breaks and liberalized stock-trading procedures.

The depressed southern region of Wallonia experienced unprecedented stresses from the declining steel industry, which was forced to fire many additional steelworkers in order to abide by a Common Market order to cut back their production capacity.

Politics and Security. Belgium, a land of two divergent cultural and linguistic groups—the Dutch-speaking Flemish and the French-speaking Walloons—continued to suffer through the process of partial separation after 153 years fully united. The Egmont Plan to establish two individually governed regions of Flanders and Wallonia did not move forward rapidly during 1983, primarily due to the country's economic and financial crises. Increasingly the role of the

BELGIUM • Information Highlights
Official Name: Kingdom of Belgium.
Location: Northwestern Europe.
Area: 11,799 sq mi (30 562 km²).
Population (July 1983 est.): 9,865,000.
Chief Cities (Dec. 31, 1981): Brussels, the capital, 994,774; Ghent, 237,687; Liège, 211,528; Antwerp, 183,025; Bruges, 118,048.
Government: *Head of state,* Baudouin I, king (acceded 1951). *Head of government,* Wilfried Martens, prime minister (formed new government Dec. 1981). *Legislature*—Parliament: Senate and Chamber of Representatives.
Monetary Unit: Franc (55.48 francs equal U.S.$1, Dec. 8, 1983).
Gross Domestic Product (1982 U.S.$): $84,262,000,000.
Economic Indexes (1982): *Consumer Prices* (1970 = 100), all items, 238.1; food, 207.7. *Industrial Production* (1975 = 100), 112.
Foreign Trade (1982 with Luxembourg U.S.$): *Imports,* $58,007,000,000; *exports,* $52,392,000,000.

capital, Brussels, in this decentralization of power has become the focal point of conflict and antagonisms. Many people, including the *Bruxellois,* seek a semiautonomous third region for the giant metropolitan area in this project to leave the central government with only foreign, defense, and some fiscal responsibilities.

A major security issue plagued Belgium and interjected itself into political party struggles. Belgium was scheduled to deploy 48 cruise missiles early in 1984. The government avoided a parliamentary debate on the matter, and the Socialist Party, which led the opposition to the Martens government, disassociated itself from the 1979 NATO agreement to deploy medium-range missiles by the end of 1983 if U.S.-Soviet discussions in Geneva did not yield specific arms-limitation plans. The missiles controversy produced substantial ripple effects on several domestic issues.

Leopold III. King Leopold III died on September 25. The fourth king of the Belgians and father of the ruling monarch, Leopold was forced to abdicate in 1951. His conduct during World War II, especially his surrender to the Nazis in 1940, further divided Flemings and Walloons, and Conservatives and Socialists.

PIERRE-HENRI LAURENT, *Tufts University*

Van Parys/Photo Trends

In Brussels in February, King Baudouin (second from right) and other members of the Belgian royal family were hosts to Jordan's King Hussein and Queen Noor (third and fourth from right).

BIOCHEMISTRY

In 1982–1983, sensational discoveries were made toward understanding the mechanism of cancer development and how genes can be manipulated in animals.

Cancer. Oncogenes are active cancer-causing genes first found in certain tumor viruses. Scientists discovered that normal animal cells (including human) contain genes chemically related to the viral oncogenes. These latent cellular oncogenes—proto-oncogenes—are thought to participate in normal growth control and differentiation but, when activated, they are expressed inappropriately perhaps because they have been modified to produce an abnormal product, or because the product is made in excessive amounts or at the wrong time. In any event, the result is the transformation of the cell into the cancerous state.

Recent research has established at least two ways by which proto-oncogenes can become activated. In human bladder cancer, a single mutation involving the replacement of one nucleotide by another in a gene called *ras* makes the cells malignant. (Nucleotides are subunits of DNA, the genetic material.) On the other hand, some human cancers, including Burkitt's lymphoma, are caused when a gene called *myc* moves from one chromosome to another chromosome in proximity to specific regions active in antibody production. The cells with this rearrangement come to predominate in a tumor. Thus, both mutations and chromosomal aberrations can activate proto-oncogenes. Since chemically related proto-oncogenes occur in many animals, they are thought to serve important functions in normal cells. But what their normal function is and how they transform cells after activation are unknown.

The answer became known for one of the oncogenes called *sis*. Research from several laboratories indicates that this gene codes for a protein similar or identical to the platelet-derived growth factor (PDGF). In all probability, *sis* gene is the gene for PDGF. In the body, PDGF is released from platelets at a wound site to help repair damage. As the wound heals, the amount of PDGF decreases, and the cell growth stops. It appears that in some cancers, *sis* is expressed inappropriately so that excessive amounts of PDGF are produced leading to the uncontrolled growth typical of cancer.

More recently, three groups of researchers have demonstrated that at least two separate genetic changes are needed to make normal cells malignant. One group, led by Robert Weinberg at the Massachusetts Institute of Technology, has discovered that two kinds of oncogenes (*ras* and *myc*) administered together, but neither alone, will transform normal rat embryo cells growing in a laboratory into a cancerous state. The gene *myc* makes the cells grow indefinitely (become "immortalized"), whereas *ras* makes them grow rapidly and endows them with surface properties characteristic of a malignant cell. (Chemical carcinogens also can substitute for *myc* in "immortalizing" cells.) Studies were underway in 1983 to group the 20 or so known oncogenes into categories depending upon whether they fill the role of *ras* or *myc*. Since activation of *ras* involves a mutation and that of *myc* rearrangement of chromosomes, both events may be required for cancer development.

Genetic Engineering. Scientists at the National Heart, Lung, and Blood Institute, the University of Illinois College of Medicine, and The Johns Hopkins University used a drug to manipulate a hemoglobin gene and succeeded in partially correcting severe anemia in patients with β-thalassemia and sickle-cell anemia. In the human fetus, two genes—α and γ—direct the production of hemoglobin, the reddish protein in red blood cells that carries oxygen to body tissues. Toward the end of gestation, the γ gene is switched off as a result of the addition of chemical entities called methyl groups, and a new gene—β—becomes active in manufacturing adult hemoglobin. Both β-thalassemia and sickle-cell anemia are due to a defective β gene. The researchers reasoned that a drug that removed the methyl groups might reactivate the γ hemoglobin gene. When the cancer drug 5-azacytidine—known to remove methyl groups—was given to patients, they began to produce fetal hemoglobin and showed alleviation of symptoms.

Another exciting development was reported by a group of biochemists from the University of Washington, the University of Pennsylvania, and the Salk Institute, who succeeded in transplanting a gene for a growth hormone from rats into mice. The rat gene was first fused to a segment of DNA—called MT promoter—previously isolated from mice. The MT promoter serves two functions: It enables the mice cells to accept the foreign gene message, and it can be switched on by certain metals including zinc so that the adjoining genes are activated. Next, the fused rat gene was injected into 170 fertilized mouse eggs, which were then implanted in the reproductive tracts of foster mouse mothers. These females gave birth to 21 mice, 7 of which carried the intact transferred gene with its MT promoter. After weaning, the mice were given a diet containing zinc to activate the MT promoter. Six of the 7 mice grew significantly faster than their littermates who did not acquire the rat gene. In fact, some mice contained 800 times the normal amount of the growth hormone and were twice the normal size. It may now be possible to develop rapidly growing strains of domestic animals, including cows, pigs, and sheep. This research appears to bring the day closer for genetic manipulation in humans, raising sticky ethical questions.

PREM P. BATRA, *Wright State University*

BIOGRAPHY

A selection of profiles of persons prominent in the news during 1983 appears on pages 133–46. The affiliation of the contributor is listed on pages 589–92; biographies that do not include a contributor's name were prepared by the staff. Included are sketches of:

Attenborough, Sir Richard
Bernardin, Joseph Louis Cardinal
Bieber, Owen Frederick
Bluford, Guion Stewart, Jr.
Carlton, Steven Norman
Craxi, Benedetto (Bettino)
Cuomo, Mario Matthew
Deukmejian, George
Dole, Elizabeth Hanford
Hawke, Robert James Lee

Heckler, Margaret Mary
Iacocca, Lee Anthony
Jackson, The Rev. Jesse Louis
King, Stephen Edwin
Lange, Jessica
Lucas, George
McClintock, Barbara
McFarlane, Robert Carl
Malone, Moses
Moore, Dudley Stuart

Mulroney, M. Brian
Nakasone, Yasuhiro
Ride, Sally Kristen
Shagari, Alhaji Shehu
Shamir, Yitzhak
Stone, Richard B.
Tandy, Jessica
Ueberroth, Peter V.
Washington, Harold

ATTENBOROUGH, Sir Richard

For British film director Sir Richard Attenborough, the release of *Gandhi* in late 1982 was the culmination of a 20-year effort. That effort was recognized in April 1983, when the film won no less than eight Academy Awards, including best picture and best director.

Attenborough, whose career spans acting and producing as well as directing, had the idea for his film after reading a biography of India's political and religious leader, Mohandas K. Gandhi (1869–1948). For Attenborough, the idea became something of an obsession. Four different writers attempted the screenplay, and several studios considered but then rejected the filming. To keep his project alive, Attenborough took well-paying roles in some low-quality films and turned down the post of associate director of Britain's National Theatre. Eventually the $22 million film was backed by two independent motion picture companies and India's National Film Development Corporation, with Attenborough as both director and producer. In the former capacity, he opted for a traditional and understated style. "Content is

Sir Richard Attenborough

all-important to me," he said in an interview. "I want people to be moved by the story."

Background. Richard Attenborough was born Aug. 29, 1923, in Cambridge, England. The son of a college administrator, he was drawn to acting and studied at the Royal Academy of Dramatic Art. In 1942 he made his London stage debut in *Ah! Wilderness* and his screen debut in *In Which We Serve.* His portrayal of a coward in that film led him to be typecast in similar roles for several years, but he did go on to play a variety of leading parts.

In 1959, Attenborough formed Beaver Films, in partnership with Bryan Forbes, to coproduce *Whistle Down the Wind* (1961). From then on he turned increasingly to producing, although he continued to appear in both U.S. and British films. His first directorial effort was *Oh What a Lovely War!* (1969), followed by *Young Winston* (1972), *A Bridge Too Far* (1977), and others. Attenborough was knighted in 1976 for his contributions to British film, and he acts as chairman of the British Film Institute and the Royal Academy of Dramatic Art.

Attenborough's reputation in the film industry is one of integrity and modesty. He has been married to actress Sheila Sim since 1944 and is the brother of British television producer David Attenborough.

ELAINE P. SEDITO

BERNARDIN, Joseph Louis Cardinal

After being named to head the largest Roman Catholic archdiocese in the United States, the archdiocese of Chicago (July 1982), elevated to the rank of cardinal (February 1983), and given the task of shepherding the bishops' pastoral letter on war and peace (spring 1983), Joseph Cardinal Bernardin has emerged as the leading U.S. Catholic churchman.

Characterized by many church leaders as one of the most respected and admired Catholic prelates in the world, he was first general secretary of the twin national agencies of the U.S. bishops, the National Conference of Catholic Bishops and the U.S. Catholic Conference, from 1968 to 1972. After being chosen archbishop of Cincinnati in 1972, he was elected third president of the two conferences in 1974.

Among the indications of esteem shown Cardinal Bernardin by his fellow bishops are: his consistent representations of the American Church at the world Synod of Bishops in Rome, and his many interventions with the pope and the Vatican on behalf of American Catholic interests, ranging from canon law to the arms race. Cardinal Bernardin is described by his associates and friends as pastoral, open-minded, intellectual, a listener, a man of prayer, effective, compassionate and, most of all, a reconciler of views and people.

Prior to his appointment to the Chicago See, he accepted the immense task of heading a bishops' committee that would develop the historic pastoral, "The

UPI

Joseph Louis Cardinal Bernardin

Challenge of Peace: God's Promise and Our Response,'' which, in effect, condemns the worldwide arms race and the use of nuclear weapons. Cardinal Bernardin demonstrated his leadership and ability to reconcile divergent views and factions by getting the pastoral ''hammered out'' with a consensus of the committee and the body of bishops as well.

Background. Born in Columbia, SC, on April 2, 1928, to Italian immigrant parents, Joseph Louis Bernardin studied for the priesthood at St. Mary Seminary in Baltimore, received a master's degree in education from Catholic University in Washington, and was ordained a priest of the Charleston, SC, diocese in 1952. Before being named auxiliary bishop of Atlanta in 1966, he served as chancellor and vicar general for the Charleston diocese.

ROBERT L. JOHNSTON

BIEBER, Owen Frederick

Succeeding Douglas Fraser, who retired in 1982 after 47 years in the union, Owen F. Bieber opened a new era for the United Auto Workers (UAW) when he was elected president May 18, 1983. Bieber, 53, became the first UAW leader who was not in the generation of organizers that had worked with the late Walter Reuther to found the union. Despite a careful, low-key approach, the 6'5" (1.96-m), 250-lb (113-kg) native of Michigan quickly made clear that he would pursue the traditional goals of the union with stepped-up ''activism.'' Addressing the UAW convention in Dallas the day after his election, Bieber declared: ''I was not on the battlefield during the great struggles of the 1930s but, by God, I am a product, heart and soul, of what was created in those difficult struggles.''

In his first major challenge as union president, Bieber reached agreement with Chrysler Corp. on a new, 26-month contract on Sept. 5 (Labor Day), 1983. The settlement called for a $2.42 per hour wage increase, giving Chrysler workers ''parity'' with UAW members at General Motors and Ford. Chrysler employees overwhelmingly ratified the contract one week later.

Background. Owen Frederick Bieber was born Dec. 28, 1929, in North Dorr, MI, and he remained in the Grand Rapids area until well into his adulthood. The son of an automobile worker, Owen followed in his father's footsteps. After attending Visitation Elementary School and Catholic Central High, he got his first job at age 18 in a factory—bending heavy-gauge wire and fitting it

into a die to make car-seat frames for Cadillacs and Hudsons.

By the age of 20, Bieber had been elected shop steward and begun his climb up the union ladder. In 1956 he became president of Local 687, and in 1962 he was hired by the union's national leadership, which had recognized his organizational talents and political savvy during the presidential campaign of John F. Kennedy. Building his reputation on patient, methodical planning, Bieber was nominated as UAW vice-president in 1980 and assigned to the General Motors department. When then-President Douglas Fraser reached mandatory retirement age for UAW officers, the union's 26-member Executive Board settled on the self-effacing Bieber to be his successor. He was nominated by the board in November 1982 and officially elected six months later.

Now living in the Detroit area, Bieber and his wife, Shirley, have three sons and two daughters.

BLUFORD, Guion Stewart, Jr.

A married father of two who describes himself as ''a quietish person who loves airplanes,'' 40-year-old Air Force Lt. Col. Guion (''Guy'') Bluford launched into the public eye in August 1983, when he became the first black American to travel in space. As a ''mission specialist'' on the six-day, STS 8 mission of the U.S. space shuttle *Challenger,* Bluford deployed the Insat-1B communications-weather satellite for India, helped test the shuttle's 50-ft (15-m) mechanical retrieval arm, and conducted experiments with electrophoresis, the separation of biological materials by passing them through an electrical field. The former fighter pilot, who has a Ph.D. in aerospace engineering, underplays the racial breakthrough, finding greater excitement in just being able to fly in the orbiter. He does not, however, shy away from being a role model for blacks. ''I hope,'' he told reporters, ''that other blacks can look upon me and say, 'Hey! He had the opportunity to and he succeeded in his profession, so maybe I can do it in mine.' ''

Background. The son of a mechanical engineer and a special-education teacher, Guy Bluford was born and reared in west Philadelphia. Always fascinated by airplanes, Guy decided in junior high school that he would become an aerospace engineer. After being graduated from Overbrook High School in 1960, he was accepted into the aerospace engineering program at Pennsylvania State University. For his senior thesis he studied the aerodynamics of the boomerang.

Joining the U.S. Air Force after college, Bluford attended pilot training at Williams Air Force Base in Arizona and earned his wings in 1965. After flying 144 combat missions—65 of them over North Vietnam—in an F-4 fighter squadron, he was assigned to Sheppard Air Force Base in Texas as an instructor pilot. In 1972, Bluford entered the Air Force Institute of Technology (AFIT) and was awarded his master's degree in aerospace engineering two years later. His next assignment was the Air Force Flight Dynamics Laboratory, where he worked his way up to chief of the aerodynamics and airframe branch. At the same time, he was completing his doctorate at AFIT.

Colonel Bluford was selected by NASA as an astronaut candidate in January 1978. After a one-year training program and evaluation period, he was made eligible for assignment as a space shuttle mission specialist.

Bluford lives with his wife Linda, an accountant, in Houston. His hobby ''is going to work.''

CARLTON, Steven Norman

Known to his teammates and Philadelphia baseball fans simply as ''Lefty,'' 38-year-old Steve Carlton has proven to be one of the most successful and durable pitchers in major league history. While his record for the 1983 season, 15–16, was mediocre by Carlton's standards, the Phillies ace reached two important milestones. By the end of the regular season, his 277 strikeouts (most in the major leagues) had moved him into first place on the all-time list, with a career total of 3,709. (The old record of 3,508 by Walter Johnson had actually been broken by another active player, Nolan Ryan of Houston, but Carlton far outpaced Ryan over the rest of the season.) Also by the end of the 1983 campaign, Lefty had earned his 300th career victory, becoming only the 16th pitcher in history to do so. His record stood at an even 300–200, for an impressive winning percentage of .600.

For the 6'4" (1.93 m) future Hall of Famer, win number 300 was doubly sweet because it came in the heat of a pennant race. Two weeks later, in the National League Championship Series against the LA Dodgers, Carlton won two games and led his team to the World Series. He had only one start in the October Classic, losing a close (3–2) decision to the Baltimore Orioles in Game 3.

Background. Steven Norman Carlton was born in Miami, FL, on Dec. 22, 1944. He attended Miami Dade Junior College, but by the age of 20 was already pitching for the St. Louis Cardinals. Carlton had his first 20-win season in 1971, only to be traded to Philadelphia that winter. The following year he compiled a 27–10 record and earned his first Cy Young Award, given to the best pitcher in each league. Carlton was accorded that honor again in 1977, 1980, and 1982; he is the only pitcher ever to win the Cy Young four times.

Despite all his success, Steve Carlton remains one of the most enigmatic figures in baseball. A private person in a public game, he has long refused to grant media interviews. After his 300th career win, for example, he took refuge in the Phillies' clubhouse, leaving his wife Beverly to confront reporters. Asked if there was anything the public might want to know about him, she said, "Well, he likes Ukrainian food." Other preferences known outside his home pertain mostly to his training methods. He works out regularly with a martial arts instructor and after games rests his pitching arm in a barrel of rice. "Steve would like to play another ten years," said Beverly. Combining the competitiveness and fastball of a rookie with the experience of a veteran, he seems to stand a pretty good chance.

Steve Carlton

UPI

CRAXI, Benedetto (Bettino)

Bettino Craxi, secretary of Italy's Socialist Party, became premier of Italy on Aug. 4, 1983. It was only the third time since 1945 that a non-Christian Democrat has held the post. Craxi's appointment by Socialist President Sandro Pertini gave southern Europe's "olive belt" another Socialist government to supplement those in Portugal, Spain, France, and Greece.

Craxi, who in recent years had become Italy's "power broker," forced parliamentary elections ahead of time on June 26–27, 1983. The Christian Democrats suffered a big loss from 38.3% to 32.9%, while the Socialists rose from 9.8% to 11.4%, placing third after the Communist Party (30%). Craxi's new government is a five-party coalition of the center-left (Socialists, Christian Democrats, Republicans, Social Democrats, and Liberals). His own party holds only 5 of 29 portfolios, while the Christian Democrats retain 16, including the deputy premiership and the foreign, treasury, and interior ministries.

Premier Craxi has called for financial austerity and a firm commitment to the European Community and to NATO. His program also includes a determination to cut the nation's inflation rate from 16% to 10% by 1984, but not at the expense of the unemployed, who numbered 9.9% in mid-1983. He also announced plans to cut public spending in health care and social security and to raise the retirement age. In this way he hopes to freeze the huge deficit in the public spending sector. He also promised to strengthen the police and to combat the Mafia.

Background. Son of a Socialist lawyer who had moved from Sicily to Milan, Benedetto (his formal name) Craxi was born in that city on Feb. 24, 1934. He studied law briefly at the University of Milan, where he met and married Anna Mancini, daughter of a Socialist rail worker. They have a son and a daughter.

Joining the Socialist Party at 18, the ambitious Craxi became its provincial secretary in Lombardy in 1965. In 1968 he was elected to Parliament as head of the Socialist bloc and has been reelected regularly since then. In 1976 he was elected national secretary of the party. Strongly opposed to Soviet-style Communism, Craxi persuaded his Socialist Party to adopt the red carnation as its new emblem, symbolizing moderation.

The 49-year-old premier is tall, balding, and informal in his dress. Cartoonists emphasize his physical resemblance to Mussolini. In Rome he has lived in a hotel while his family remain in a rented apartment in Milan. Craxi likes art and the cinema and enjoys reading history. He has published three volumes of political essays.

CHARLES F. DELZELL

CUOMO, Mario Matthew

His tale is a political Cinderella story. A year after he was written off by skeptics as a long-shot candidate for New York State's governorship, Mario M. Cuomo became the state's 52nd chief executive, widely acclaimed as one of the most articulate new figures in the Democratic Party.

Inaugurated on New Year's Day 1983, Cuomo attracted national attention with a speech that displayed his peculiar mix of economic liberalism and traditional social values. The state must think of itself as a "family," he said, "feeling one another's pain, sharing one another's blessings. . . ."

Just days later he passed his first major test as governor, when inmates at the Ossining Correctional Facility in Westchester took 19 guards hostage in a riot largely caused by conditions resulting from record prison overcrowding. The siege was ended in 53 hours with no lost lives and no major concessions by the administration.

By the end of his first 100 days in office, Governor Cuomo had scored another coup: He and the Legislature reached agreement on a new state budget. For New York, it was an unusual display of harmony and timeliness.

Several other events also propelled the 51-year-old governor into the national spotlight. Like his predeces-

UPI

Gov. Mario Cuomo

sor, Hugh Carey, he vetoed a death-penalty bill. He also became a pointman on nuclear-power safety when Suffolk County's refusal to participate in emergency planning threatened to keep shut the nearly completed Shoreham nuclear-power plant. The federal government almost simultaneously said it would close two nuclear reactors at Indian Point unless an adequate emergency response plan was put into place there. Cuomo first argued that nuclear safety was a federal responsibility but ultimately agreed to assign state workers to help with safety exercises at Indian Point. Under less time pressure at Shoreham, he appointed a task force to study the matter.

Background. Born to Italian immigrants in south Jamaica, Queens, NY, June 15, 1932, Cuomo now lives just a short distance away in a more affluent section of the borough. He was graduated summa cum laude from St. John's University in Queens in 1953 and cum laude from St. John's Law School in 1956. He then practiced law, and later joined the law faculty at St. John's.

While Cuomo is hailed as a new face nationally, he has been a public figure in New York since the late 1960s and early 1970s when he mediated two housing disputes in Queens. He made his first bid for public office in 1974 as the official party choice for lieutenant governor, and lost. Nevertheless, Gov. Hugh L. Carey, who had defeated Cuomo's running mate, Howard Samuels, in the Democratic primary, appointed Cuomo as secretary of state in 1975.

Cuomo's most devastating defeat came in 1977 when he ran for mayor of New York City at Carey's urging and lost a primary runoff to Edward Koch. Running as a Liberal, Cuomo was defeated by Koch again in the general election. Before he scored an upset win over Koch in the 1982 Democratic gubernatorial primary, Cuomo had won only one campaign—as lieutenant governor as part of a team with Carey in 1978.

He is married to the former Matilda Raffa and has five children.

ALISON MITCHELL

DEUKMEJIAN, George, Jr.

George Deukmejian, Jr., was inaugurated as California's 35th governor on Jan. 3, 1983, on the west steps of the recently remodeled state capitol. After a conventional inaugural ball, which his predecessor, Edmund Brown, Jr., had shunned, the new governor quickly found that there would be no traditional "honeymoon" period. From a $4 billion surplus in 1978, the state had gone to a projected $1.5 billion deficit in fiscal 1983. The Republican governor's conservative views and determination to avoid a tax increase by making heavy spending cuts put him into immediate conflict with the moderate-to-liberal Democratic legislative leaders. The legislature eventually conceded more in compromises than did Deukmejian, who surprised opponents by his unbending commitment to his campaign promises. The California budget finally agreed upon reflected more than $1 billion in spending cuts. The cuts affected especially health and welfare programs, state salaries, higher education, and regulatory agencies. Deukmejian did agree, however, to a standby 1% sales tax increase. He was defeated only on a reapportionment plan, and in that by the California courts.

Background. Courken George Deukmejian, Jr., was born June 6, 1928, near Albany, NY, into a lower-middle-class family of Armenian descent. He was graduated from nearby Siena College in 1949, received a law degree in 1952 from St. John's University in New York City, and was admitted to the New York bar. He served two years in the United States Army as an enlisted man.

The future governor moved to California in 1955. The next year he passed the state bar examination and soon settled in Long Beach to practice law. He married Gloria M. Saatjian in 1957. They have three children. He established connections and a community identification by joining the local Episcopal church and becoming active in the Boy Scouts, the YMCA, the Chamber of Commerce, the Elks, and the Lions.

In 1962, Deukmejian was elected to the state assembly, serving until 1967, when he became a state senator and eventually Republican leader. In 1979, he became attorney general of California, a position of legal and administrative power, as well as of political opportunity. Deukmejian used the position to gain public recognition as well as credibility with conservative Republican leaders.

The 1982 race for governor was very close. Deukmejian managed his victory (by a margin of 52,000 votes)

Gov. George Deukmejian

Wide World

over Tom Bradley, the black mayor of Los Angeles, through his edge with absentee votes, for which the rules of use had recently been simplified.

George Deukmejian in ideology and to some degree in style is in the mode of President Ronald Reagan, a former California governor.

See also CALIFORNIA.

CHARLES R. ADRIAN

DOLE, Elizabeth Hanford

Although President Reagan began a Jan. 5, 1983, news conference by announcing that he had selected Elizabeth Dole to succeed Drew Lewis as secretary of transportation, the nominee needed no introduction to the White House press corps. At the time, Mrs. Dole was serving as an assistant for public liaison in the White House—a position that involves bringing "together various nongovernment organizations to meet with the president to develop" agreement regarding administration policies and programs. In addition, she is part of the "second most powerful couple" in the capital, being married to Sen. Robert J. Dole (R-KS), the chairman of the Senate Finance Committee.

Mrs. Dole's nomination was sent formally to the Senate on January 25 and was confirmed by a 97-0 vote on February 1. Immediately after being sworn in by Associate Justice Sandra Day O'Connor on February 7, the new cabinet officer faced a national crisis—a strike by independent truckers. The strikers were protesting recently enacted federal taxes and fees on gasoline, diesel fuel, and truck usage. The strike, which was marked by periodic acts of violence, was canceled on February 10. Secretary Dole welcomed its end, stating that her department was "ready and willing" to discuss the issues involved and would "work with the industry and the states to achieve uniformity in state regulations and registration fees."

Background. Elizabeth Hanford Dole was born on July 29, 1936, in Salisbury, NC. After receiving a political science degree with honors from Duke University, she did postgraduate work at Oxford University and then took a master's in education and a law degree from Harvard. With Washington acting as a "magnet," she was admitted to the DC bar in 1966 and worked as a staff assistant in the Department of Health, Education, and Welfare (1966–67). Following a brief period of law practice, Miss Hanford was associate director and later executive director of the President's Commission for Consumer Interests. In 1971–73 she served as a deputy director of the Office of Consumer Affairs at the White House, working under Virginia Knauer. In 1973, President Nixon appointed her to a seven-year term on the Federal Trade Commission (FTC), where her speciality became consumer interests.

The future cabinet officer took a leave of absence from the FTC to work on the campaign of her new husband, who was running with President Ford on the 1976 GOP ticket. Following the unsuccessful campaign, she returned to the FTC but resigned three years later to help her husband in his own short-lived bid for the White House. After Senator Dole withdrew as presidential candidate, she joined the Reagan team.

A registered Democrat during her early Washington years, she became an independent in the early 1970s and a registered Republican in the mid-1970s. Of her marriage and career, Mrs. Dole has said: "There's a lot of interest, but no conflict."

Elizabeth Hanford Dole

UPI

HAWKE, Robert James Lee

After a 28-month career in the Australian House of Representatives, Robert Hawke moved to the leadership of the Australian Labor Party (ALP) caucus in February 1983 and gained office as prime minister with a landslide victory in the general election of March 5. Hawke's mastery of the electronic media and his campaign theme of national reconciliation and reconstruction through "consensus" contributed to the ALP election success.

In his first months in office, Hawke showed a forceful, presidential style that quickly kindled factional criticism within his party. Ignoring the ALP's broadly egalitarian values and traditional preoccupation with economic and social reform, Hawke has been viewed widely as a hybrid conservative. In domestic affairs he stresses the need to limit budget deficits, even though this puts a brake on social welfare outlays, and to restrain wages. In international affairs his thrust is to scale down Australia's ambitions from the global to the regional. During his first months at the helm, the persuasive but sometimes abrasive prime minister dropped elements of formally-approved ALP policies that conflicted with the realities of power as he saw them. According to one newspaper, at least, "in his fashion he is truer to Labor traditions than are the left-wing dogmatists snapping at his heels."

Background. Robert James Lee Hawke was born on Dec. 9, 1929, in a small town in South Australia. Religion was a dominant factor in his upbringing: his father was a clergyman, and his mother was an active religionist. The family moved to Perth, Western Australia, where Robert attended a parochial school and later the University of Western Australia. Chosen the state's Rhodes Scholar in 1952, he was at Oxford until 1955, returning to a research role at the Australian National University in Canberra. In 1958 he became a research economist at the Australian Council of Trade Unions (ACTU) in Melbourne and, as a prime force behind escalating wage demands, started his rise through the nation's labor movement.

Hawke quickly enhanced his reputation as an ACTU legal advocate and a persuasive spokesman for the unions. In 1970 he was chosen ACTU president and four years later added the presidency of the ALP. When a "safe" seat in the House of Representatives (with a strong Labor constituency) became available in 1980, Hawke ran and won easily. The ambitious and always popular unionist was immediately seen as a potential parliamentary leader. He narrowly lost a challenge for the party-caucus leadership in mid-1982 but was victorious in February 1983.

Robert Hawke and his wife, Hazel, have a son and two daughters. In April 1983 they welcomed their first grandchild.

R. M. YOUNGER

Wide World

Margaret Mary Heckler

HECKLER, Margaret Mary

On March 9, 1983, Margaret Heckler, a former eight-term Republican congresswoman from Massachusetts, was sworn in by Associate Justice Sandra Day O'Connor as secretary of health and human services. The new member of the Reagan cabinet took over a department with more than 140,000 employees and a budget exceeding $270 billion. (Only the total federal budget and the budget of the Soviet Union are larger.)

In nominating her to the post on January 12, the president called Mrs. Heckler "a practical and compassionate public servant." The Senate confirmed the appointment by a vote of 82–3 on March 3.

Matters of policy concerned Mrs. Heckler during her first months in office. The medical and nutritional needs of handicapped infants, the Social Security program (especially disability cases), and federal research to combat acquired immune deficiency syndrome (AIDS) were areas of special concern.

Although Mrs. Heckler had spent a large amount ($966,621) in her 1982 campaign for reelection to the House of Representatives, she was defeated by Barney Frank, a liberal Democrat. The future cabinet officer had first won election to the House in 1966, after defeating Rep. Joseph W. Martin, Jr., a party leader and former House speaker, in the GOP primary. During her 16 years in the House, she frequently changed committee assignments, serving on the agriculture, banking, government operations', science, and veterans' affairs' panels. She also was a member of the Joint Economics Committee.

The second woman to be named to the cabinet within a week, Mrs. Heckler was a strong supporter of the Equal Rights Amendment and cochairwoman of the Congressional Women's Caucus. In 1975 she was a delegate to the national commission observing International Women's Year.

Background. Margaret Mary O'Shaughnessy Heckler was born to Irish-Catholic immigrants, John and Bridget O'Shaughnessy, in Flushing, NY, on June 21, 1931. After attending Albertus Magnus College in New Haven, CT, on a scholarship, she earned a law degree at Boston College. She then was admitted to the Massachusetts bar and practiced law in Boston for ten years.

The future legislator and cabinet officer was married to John M. Heckler, now a prominent Boston investment banker, on Aug. 29, 1953. They are the parents of two daughters and a son. The Hecklers maintain homes in Wellesley, MA, and a Washington suburb.

IACOCCA, Lee Anthony

For Lee Iacocca, the irrepressible 58-year-old chairman of the Chrysler Corporation, 1983 was a year of sweet success. The first news came in February, when it was announced that the company had made a profit of $170 million in 1982; it was the first time since 1977 that the third largest U.S. automobile manufacturer had posted a year-end gain. The black ink continued to flow in 1983, as profits for the first quarter alone hit $172 million and by midyear had reached a total of $310 million. On May 4, meanwhile, Chairman Iacocca announced that the company would begin to repay the $1.2 billion (U.S.) in federally guaranteed loans that had saved it from bankruptcy in 1980. Although repayment was not scheduled to begin until 1990, a check for $409.9 million was presented to the U.S. Trust Co. on June 15; the remaining $800 million (plus interest) would be paid by September.

According to Chairman Iacocca, the debt repayment marked "a great day for everyone associated with Chrysler." To company employees as well as to industry analysts, however, credit for the turnaround goes largely to Iacocca himself. A demanding, no-nonsense manager, he kept the company alive by cutting away the fat and guiding a leaner corporate machine through a treacherous market, largely on the strength of the fuel-efficient K-cars. Raised in the industry as a salesman and marketing strategist, Iacocca also boosted the corporate image with his personal charm and air of confidence in a highly successful series of television advertisements. The well-tailored, slightly balding, cigar-smoking executive is perhaps the best known and most respected figure in American industry today.

Background. The son of Italian immigrants, Lido Anthony Iacocca was born in Allentown, PA, on Oct. 15, 1924. Among his father's several businesses was a car rental company that used Model-A Fords. Lee, as he preferred to be called, decided early on that he wanted to become a Ford executive. After receiving a B.S. in industrial engineering from Lehigh University in 1945 and an M.A. in mechanical engineering from Princeton in 1946, Iacocca completed an executive training program for Ford in Dearborn, MI.

Starting out in sales and marketing at the Eastern district office, Iacocca rose quickly through the Ford ranks and was called back to Dearborn in 1956. At age 36 he was named corporate vice-president and general manager of the Ford division. Stressing the importance of the youth market and the need for a moderately priced, sporty car, he was responsible for the development of the Mustang, one of the most successful car

Lee Anthony Iacocca

Andrew Sacks/Black Star

models ever. On Dec. 10, 1970, Henry Ford II officially named Iacocca president of the company. Despite his success in that post, Iacocca was let go in July 1978; personal differences with Mr. Ford was the most commonly cited explanation. In any case, just four months later, ailing Chrysler named Iacocca as its new head.

Lee Iacocca lives in the Detroit suburb of Bloomfield Hills. His wife of 27 years, the former Mary McCleary, died May 16, 1983. Together they had two daughters.

JACKSON, The Rev. Jesse Louis

"There's a freedom train a-comin', but you've got to register to ride." That was the message the Rev. Jesse Jackson carried across the United States in 1983, as he sought to add more black voters to the election rolls. Voter registration was nothing new for Jackson, a veteran civil-rights activist and self-styled "country preacher." But this time the stakes were considerably higher because by late in the year Jackson was actively seeking the Democratic presidential nomination.

It was partly due to Jackson's voter registration efforts in Chicago that black congressman Harold Washington won the rancorous election for mayor in April 1983. Washington's victory, boosted by a heavy black turnout, inspired talk of a black presidential candidate who could rally black voters and prevent the Democratic Party from taking its sizable black constituency for granted. By late spring, Jackson appeared to be off and running. He visited Iowa and New Hampshire, two key states in the early presidential nominating process, and early polls showed him running ahead of four of the party's six announced candidates. At the summer convention of Jackson's own organization, Operation PUSH (People United to Save Humanity), three of those candidates came courting as Jackson loyalists chanted enthusiastically, "Run, Jesse, run!" "If you run you may lose," proclaimed the would-be candidate, "but if you don't run you're guaranteed to lose."

Background. Jesse Louis Jackson was born Oct. 8, 1941, in Greenville, NC. As an undergraduate at North Carolina A&T University, he participated in the 1963 Greensboro sit-ins to protest segregation. Later, while studying at Chicago Theological Seminary, he joined the Rev. Martin Luther King, Jr.'s march from Selma to Birmingham (AL) for black voting rights. King chose Jackson to organize the Chicago branch of Operation Breadbasket, a program that helped integrate several companies through the threat of a black boycott. After King's assassination in 1968—with Jackson at his side—the newly ordained Baptist minister struck out on his own. In 1971 he formed Operation PUSH and won acclaim for his "I am somebody" campaign to exhort youngsters to excellence.

Always controversial, Jackson traveled to the Middle East in 1979, at a time of strained relations between U.S. blacks and Jews; there he met with Yasir Arafat, head of the PLO and a steadfast enemy of Israel. Jackson also continued to lobby for black economic equality by monitoring major corporations and seeking to persuade them to hire more blacks. In 1982 he organized a boycott of Anheuser-Busch, the largest U.S. brewery, in order to pressure the company into using more black employees and wholesale distributors.

The Rev. Jackson lives in Chicago with his wife, Jacqueline, and their five children.

DENNIS A. WILLIAMS

KING, Stephen Edwin

Stephen King, the dean of contemporary popular horror writers, tingled his readers' spines anew in 1983 with two new novels, *Christine* and *Pet Sematary*. The year also saw the release of the films, *Cujo* and *The Dead Zone*, based on two of the chilling tales that have brought his name repeatedly to the top of the best-seller lists.

King's novels have been termed heavy-handed and inelegant, but most critics agree that he is a master sto-

Jerry Bauer/Doubleday

Stephen Edwin King

ryteller who keeps readers riveted through pages of heart-stopping terror. Typically, he jolts his fans by inserting elements of horror into situations that are mundane. Thus his first success, *Carrie* (1974), tells of a teenage girl who uses telekinetic powers to take ghastly revenge on her schoolmates and her town. *Salem's Lot* (1975) places vampires in a small Maine town. *Cujo* (1981) is the tale of a friendly St. Bernard who embarks on a bloody rampage after being bitten by a bat. In *Christine* the agent of destruction is a 1958 Plymouth with a mind of its own, while in *Pet Sematary* an Indian burial ground provides the means for a mysterious return to life.

In a nonfiction overview of the horror genre (*Danse Macabre,* 1981), King accounted for the appeal of thrillers by saying, "We make up horrors to help us cope with the real ones." For whatever reason, his books demonstrably have appeal: During 1983, more than 30 million King books were in print.

Background. Stephen Edwin King was born on Sept. 21, 1947, in Portland, ME. An introverted child, he became fascinated with radio horror tales and science-fiction films and stories. He began writing short stories in high school; by the time he was graduated from the University of Maine in 1970 with a B.S. in English, he had sold two of his tales.

Several lean years followed, during which King continued to write short fiction and taught English at a Maine private school. He also tried his hand at longer works, producing two novels that were rejected by a series of publishers. Discouraged, he nearly threw the manuscript of *Carrie* in the trash.

Carrie's publication brought King a measure of success, but it was the 1976 film version of the story that boosted sales of the book to more than 4 million and truly brought his name to prominence. He followed up with *Salem's Lot,* which was later turned into a television miniseries; *The Shining* (1976), which Stanley Kubrick filmed and promoted as the "ultimate horror movie;" and *Night Shift* (1978), a collection of short stories. In 1980, he became the first U.S. writer to have three books on the best-seller lists at once—*The Shining, The Dead Zone* (1979), and *Firestarter* (1980). Later projects included collaboration on the 1982 film *Creepshow.*

A tall, easygoing man who sports tortoiseshell eyeglasses and (usually) a beard, King lives in Bangor, ME. He has been married since 1971 to Tabitha Jane Spruce, herself the author of two novels—*Small World* (1981) and *Caretakers* (1983). They have three children.

ELAINE P. SEDITO

LANGE, Jessica

Once typecast as an empty-headed starlet, Jessica Lange took film audiences by storm in 1982–83 with critically acclaimed performances in two films, *Frances* and *Tootsie*. In the first, her searing portrayal of the doomed 1930s star Frances Farmer brought her an Academy Award nomination as best actress. In the second, she played opposite Dustin Hoffman in the comedy hit of the year, winning the Academy Award, the New York Film Critics Award, and National Film Critics Award as best supporting actress. She was the first actress since Theresa Wright in 1943 to be nominated in both major Academy Award categories.

A dedicated actress with a delicate, wholesome beauty, Lange had been virtually on the shelf for six years. Her first film part, the dumb but winsome blond kidnapped by King Kong in producer Dino De Laurentiis' 1976 remake of that classic, led critics to confuse the actress with the role. She did not get another part for two years. When she returned to the screen in Bob Fosse's *All That Jazz* (1979), it was in a minor role. Her next films, the comedy *How to Beat the High Cost of Living* (1980) and a controversial remake of *The Postman Always Rings Twice* (1981), were box-office flops, although her performances were generally praised. It was not until *Frances* and *Tootsie* were released in late 1982 that her talent and versatility won wide recognition.

Background. Jessica Lange was born on April 20, 1949, in rural Minnesota. After graduating from high school at Cloquet, MN, she enrolled in the University of Minnesota to study art. There she met Paco Grande, a photographer whom she later married, and then left school to travel with him around the country. In 1971, divorced and unhappy with the political climate in the United States, she moved to Paris, where for more than two years she studied mime and danced with the Opéra Comique.

On her return to the United States, Lange supported herself by modeling and waitressing in New York City. When De Laurentiis announced a search for an un-

Jessica Lange

UPI

known to play the heroine's part in *King Kong,* a friend submitted her picture. She was flown to Hollywood for a screen test and won the part. In the lean years that followed *King Kong,* Lange returned to New York to study acting. It was at this time that she became fascinated with the tragic life of Frances Farmer.

Jessica Lange's friends and associates describe her as an intensely private person. She divides her time among Hollywood, a retreat in Minnesota, and New York. With ballet dancer and choreographer Mikhail Baryshnikov, Lange has one son.

ELAINE P. SEDITO

LUCAS, George

Set "a long time ago in a galaxy far, far away," filmmaker George Lucas' *Star Wars* began the phenomenally successful trilogy that culminated in 1983 with the release of its third part *Return of the Jedi.* Lucas, creating a combination science-fiction, fairy-tale saga which proved irresistible to movie audiences, has earned the nomenclature "Mr. Blockbuster." In just six days after its opening, *Return of the Jedi* smashed box-office records, earning a remarkable $41 million (nearly $10 million more than its cost). Lucas' *Star Wars* (1977) and *The Empire Strikes Back* (1980), parts one and two of the trilogy, ranked numbers two and three, respectively, in box-office receipts in 1983. In addition Lucas produced the fifth-ranked *Raiders of the Lost Ark* (1981), which was directed by his good friend Steven Spielberg. A young introverted filmmaker whose first major hit was *American Graffiti* (1973), he has been hailed by some as the Walt Disney of this generation. Despite the glory, Lucas indicates that the sacrifices he made for the *Star Wars* series were considerable and "may have been greater than [he] wanted."

Background. A native Californian, George Lucas, Jr., was born on May 14, 1944, in Modesto. Academically he was a poor student who, by his own admission, "barely squeaked through high school." Lucas' father, the owner of a stationery store in Modesto, has described his son as "hard to understand" and "always dreaming up things." Lucas' early interest in racing cars was alleviated after a near-fatal auto accident just days before his high-school graduation. As a social science major at Modesto Junior College he became interested in cinematography and from there enrolled in the film school of the University of Southern California in Los Angeles (B.A., 1966). His first full-length feature *THX-1138* (1971) was expanded from a prize-winning film he had made while a university student. With his second feature, *American Graffiti,* based somewhat on his own adolescence in Modesto, Lucas' penchant for profit-making pictures began. The film cost $780,000 to produce but had returned $145 million worldwide by 1983.

Mr. Lucas is separated from his wife, film editor Marcia Griffin, whom he married in 1969. They have an adopted daughter, Amanda. He talks of the possibility of producing other films in the *Star Wars* series—films that record what led to the downfall of the Republic (occurrences before *Star Wars* began) and then sequels to *Jedi.* He plans first, however, to take a two-year sabbatical.

McCLINTOCK, Barbara

When the 1983 Nobel Prize in Physiology or Medicine was awarded to Barbara McClintock, 81, it mainly honored work done more than 30 years before—work that was neither appreciated nor accepted until quite recently. In 1951, McClintock reported that genes can "jump." That is, they can move from one spot to another on a chromosome, or even from one chromosome to another. The theory was unorthodox, contradicting the widely held belief that genes are arranged on chromosomes in fixed patterns. "No one much believed her or cared," said a colleague. "It didn't help that she was a woman."

Barton Silverman/NYT Pictures

Barbara McClintock

McClintock's theory was based on her observations of maize plants. She saw that as some parts of corn seedlings lost color, other parts were gaining color. She also concluded that mobile genes were responsible for the color of the kernels. Depending on if and when the genes jumped, the kernels would be dark, pale, or speckled.

It wasn't until the 1970s that other scientists confirmed McClintock's theories or, as Nobelist James D. Watson said, "caught up with Barbara." Yet her work has great practical significance. It has helped explain how resistance to antibiotics can be passed from one bacterium to another. There also are indications that jumping genes may be involved in the transformation of normal genes into cancerous ones.

McClintock, who works and publishes by herself, was the first woman to win an unshared Nobel Prize in Physiology or Medicine and the third woman to receive an unshared Nobel in Science. The honor followed many others bestowed on her in recent years. Among them were the National Medal of Science and the Lasker Award. In 1981 the MacArthur Foundation chose her as its first Prize Fellow Laureate, guaranteeing her an annual, tax-free income of $60,000 for life.

McClintock has always been a loner. In the laboratory her colleagues have been her subjects—the maize plants with which she has long worked. "It might seem unfair," she said about the Nobel Prize, "to reward a person for having so much pleasure over the years, asking the maize plant to solve specific problems and then watching its responses."

Background. Barbara McClintock was born in 1902 in Hartford, CT. She entered Cornell University in 1919, planning to major in plant breeding. When that department refused to accept a woman as a major, she turned to botany. She did her graduate work, also at Cornell, in plant genetics, earning a doctorate in 1927. After teaching at various universities, she moved in 1942 to Cold Spring Harbor Laboratory on Long Island, NY, where she has remained ever since. She lives in an apartment on the grounds of the laboratory, a short walk from the building where she works and which bears her name. Usually she is in her lab seven days a week, from early morning until nighttime.

JENNY TESAR

McFARLANE, Robert Carl

For retired Marine Corps lieutenant colonel and longtime government official Robert C. McFarlane, 1983 was a year of hat changing. In January, as deputy director of the National Security Council (NSC), he was named chairman of the international broadcasting sub-committee of a cabinet-level body to promote U.S. foreign policy abroad. Then on July 22, President Ronald Reagan announced that the 46-year-old McFarlane would replace Philip Habib as chief U.S. negotiator in the Middle East, with the personal rank of ambassador. Over the next three months, he conducted nonstop "shuttle diplomacy" in search of an elusive Middle East peace, finally calling for deployment of U.S. Marines in Lebanon. Then on October 17, President Reagan elevated him to the post of national security adviser, replacing William P. Clark, who was taking over as secretary of the interior.

Making the announcement in the White House press room, President Reagan said that McFarlane had earned "my utmost confidence and respect" and would bring "more than experience" to the job. With his reputation as a middle-of-the-road Republican who can work smoothly with members of both parties, the appointment of "Bud" McFarlane was seen as an effort by the administration to bring a more flexible approach to arms control, Soviet relations, and other foreign policy issues. Hard-line conservatives expressed disappointment at his naming.

Background. Robert Carl McFarlane was born July 12, 1937. His father, William Doddridge McFarlane, was a New Deal Democratic congressman from Texas (1933–39). Robert attended the U.S. Naval Academy and served in the Marines until 1979, winning a Distinguished Service Medal.

From 1973 to 1975, McFarlane was military assistant to then National Security Adviser Henry Kissinger. From 1976 to the end of the Ford administration in January 1977, he worked under another former military man who became national security adviser, Brent Scowcroft. After retiring from the Marine Corps in 1979, McFarlane became a member of the professional staff of the Senate Committee on Armed Services. And during the Reagan administration, he was a close counselor and troubleshooter for Secretary of State Alexander Haig, Jr., before being made deputy director of NSC in January 1982.

All business in public, the graying father of three is said to have a wry sense of humor. He resides with his family in Bethesda, MD.

MALONE, Moses

In September 1982, when the Philadelphia 76ers signed 6'11" (2.11-m), 250-lb (113-kg) center Moses Malone to a six-year contract, basketball fans in the City of Brotherly Love began looking forward to their first National Basketball Association (NBA) championship since the Wilt Chamberlain era a decade-and-a-half before. Led by Julius "Dr. J" Erving and a host of other stars, the Sixers had accumulated the league's best record over the previous six seasons but had fallen short of "the big one" each time. With the lowly Houston Rockets, meanwhile, Malone had twice won the league's most valuable player (MVP) award and three times led the league in rebounding. When he inked the $13.2 million deal with Philadelphia, making him the highest-paid athlete in the world, Moses was expected to do nothing less than lead the 76ers to pro basketball's "promised land."

He did not let them down. With a blue-collar effort that betrayed his chairman-of-the-board salary, Malone hustled, muscled, rebounded, and shot his team to a remarkable 65–17 regular-season record and an awesome 12–1 mark in post-season play. The final play-off series, against the defending champion Los Angeles Lakers, was a four-games-to-none whitewash in which Philadelphia's powerful center simply wore down his opponents. "We're just like a train," said Malone. "Once we get our motor going, we just get more aggressive." Dominating the game as had Chamberlain himself, the 29-year-old Malone was unanimously selected MVP of the play-offs. His league-leading 15.3 rebounds per game (for a fourth title) and 24.5 points average earned him the league's regular-season MVP award for the third time.

Background. Moses Malone was born March 23, 1954, into abject poverty in Petersburg, VA. He was the only child of parents who were 5'2" (1.57-m) and 5'6" (1.68-m) tall. Always taciturn and shy, Moses found an outlet in basketball, often shooting by himself until 1 or 2 A.M. By the time he was graduated from Petersburg High School, the 19-year-old phenom was being recruited by 300 colleges. Instead, Moses decided to become the first player ever to go directly to the professional ranks, signing a reported $3 million, ten-year contract with the Utah Stars of the now-defunct American Basketball Association. Gaining experience and adding weight to his frame, Malone gave notice that he would be a force to reckon with when he joined the Houston Rockets of the NBA in 1977.

Having added a league championship to all of his personal achievements, Malone's next goal is to bring a second straight title to Philadelphia in 1983–84. He lives with his wife, Alfreda, and their three-year-old son, Moses, Jr., in Philadelphia.

MOORE, Dudley Stuart John

British actor Dudley Moore broke new ground in 1983, when he appeared at New York's Carnegie Hall as a concert pianist, playing Beethoven's Triple Concerto. The year also saw the release of *Lovesick* and *Romantic Comedy*, the latest in a string of box-office hits that have established the 5'2½" (1.59-m) Moore as a popular, if unlikely, romantic film lead.

The role of concert pianist is not surprising for Dudley Moore. Best known as a film and cabaret comedian, he is also an accomplished jazz pianist and composer. He studied music at Oxford and has written the scores for several films. But while Moore said that he planned to pursue his concert career, it seems unlikely that he will give up acting. Virtually unknown to American film audiences five years earlier, he reportedly drew a salary

Dudley Moore

Courtesy, Orion Pictures

of $2.5 million for *Unfaithfully Yours*, a remake of the Preston Sturges comedy, being filmed in 1983.

Background. Dudley Stuart John Moore was born on April 19, 1935, in the London suburb of Dagenham. The son of a railway electrician and a shorthand typist, he grew up in a working class neighborhood. A club foot and his small size made Dudley the butt of many a schoolroom joke and, in defense, he became the "class clown." At the same time, however, he was developing his talents as a pianist—work that paid off when he won a scholarship to Magdalen College, Oxford. There he appeared in student stage productions and earned two degrees, bachelor of arts and bachelor of music.

Moore made his professional debut two years after leaving Oxford in 1958, teaming up with Alan Bennett, Jonathan Miller, and Peter Cook in the satiric revue *Beyond the Fringe*. First produced in Edinburgh in 1960, the revue was widely acclaimed and later staged in London, New York, and other cities. During the 1960s and 1970s, Moore collaborated with Cook on a second revue, a BBC television series, and five films. Among the movies were the farcical *The Wrong Box* (1966) and a comic version of the Faust legend, *Bedazzled* (1967), for which he also wrote the music.

In 1977, Moore split with Cook and moved to Hollywood. His first U.S. film role was that of a sex-crazed swinger in *Foul Play* (1978). The following year he scored his first major box-office success, playing a man in the throes of a midlife crisis in Blake Edwards' *10*; his portrayal of a drunken but engaging playboy in *Arthur* (1981) cemented that success.

Twice married (to actresses Suzy Kendall and Tuesday Weld) and divorced, Moore has one son. He lives in Marina del Rey, CA, where, besides music and films, he enjoys the Hollywood social scene.

ELAINE P. SEDITO

MULRONEY, M. Brian

In Canada, no major political party has ever chosen so politically inexperienced a leader as the Progressive Conservative (PC) Party did on June 11, 1983. At that time, the PC's new leader, Brian Mulroney, had never even run in a local election. Since his party was virtually shut out in his native Quebec, the former Toronto lawyer preferred not to blight his political ambitions by defeat. However, his background as arbitrator and negotiator may be excellent preparation for the leadership post of a divided party and a fractious country. Image-makers and cartoonists have emphasized Mulroney's superabundance of chin; others note his close contact with leading media figures, his ceaseless telephone contact, and his conviviality. Mulroney's Irish background and his wife's Croatian ancestry can be an asset in the labyrinth of Canadian ethnic politics, while the image of stable family life may be reassuring in conservative times. *See also* CANADA.

Background. The son of an industrial electrician, the third of six children, M. Brian Mulroney was born on March 20, 1939, in Baie Comeau, Quebec. He grew up in a comfortable Catholic, Liberal working-class home. He spoke English at home, French at school, and emerged with an easy colloquial bilingual eloquence that, with his charm, later proved to be great political assets. At 13 he went to St. Thomas College in New Brunswick and in 1955 to St. Francis Xavier University in Antigonish, N.S. It was then that he became a Conservative, swept up in the emotion that made John Diefenbaker the Tory leader in 1956 and prime minister in 1957. At 19, Mulroney went to Dalhousie University to study law, switched promptly to Laval University in Quebec, and completed his professional training in French.

As a young lawyer in Montreal, Mulroney specialized in labor law, spent his spare time in the Conservatives' backrooms, and cultivated a political circle he had begun at Laval with such party members as Michel Cogger, a major force in his leadership ambitions, and Michael Meighen, later a party president. At 34 he married Mila Pivnicki, 19-year-old daughter of a Croatian emigré

M. Brian Mulroney

and head of psychiatry at Royal Victoria Hospital in Montreal. An engineering student close to graduation, Mila Mulroney abandoned her career to play a traditional role as wife and mother of three.

Fresh from a high-profile role as management representative on Quebec's Cliche Commission investigating union corruption, Mulroney threw himself into the Tories' 1976 leadership convention. By a mixture of freshness, eloquence, and skillful organization, he placed third. He next became president of the Iron Ore Company of Canada, a subsidiary of Cleveland's Hanna Corporation. While his own finances recovered, the company remained in the red but Mulroney's special skills as conciliator were evident when peace followed years of labor turmoil. Even Mulroney's decision to close down Iron Ore's Schefferville operation on the eve of the 1983 leadership campaign, devastating the small mining town, was turned to his advantage after workers accepted generous settlement terms without audible demur.

DESMOND MORTON

NAKASONE, Yasuhiro

Yasuhiro Nakasone, who held his first cabinet portfolio at the unusually young age of 41, waited in the wings a long time before becoming prime minister of Japan. For more than two decades he was a man that many Japanese assumed someday would lead the nation. He headed a small faction in the majority Liberal-Democratic Party (LDP), however, and regularly fell just short of the premiership. Then, in the LDP primary election on Nov. 23, 1982, Nakasone overwhelmed three opponents by winning 58% of the votes cast by party members. In the 57th extraordinary session of the Diet on November 26, he was designated Japan's 45th prime minister and immediately formed the country's 71st cabinet.

During his early days in office, Nakasone displayed two characteristics uncommon in Japanese leadership: eloquence and administrative style. Before the Japan Society in New York, he spoke of the need to build for the "information society" for the 21st century.

However in late 1983 elections, the LDP lost its majority in the lower house and Nakasone remained prime minister only with the support of some independents. He called the elections "a severe result for me" and said that he would "have to take cautious steps."

Background. Born on May 27, 1918, in Takasaki, Gunma Prefecture, Nakasone was graduated from middle school at the head of his class, attended Shizuoka Higher School, and enrolled in the University of Tokyo, where he studied political science. After graduation he went directly into the higher civil service, but was drafted into the navy and became a lieutenant commander by the end of World War II.

In 1946, Nakasone left government service to begin political campaigning in the third electoral district (Gunma), relying—as he has ever since—on his support organization, the *Seiun Juku* (Lofty Aspirations Society). Nakasone was first elected to the House of Representatives in April 1947, at the age of 28, and has since been reelected 13 successive times.

Nakasone won his first cabinet post, minister of science and technology, in June 1959. After the death of his mentor, Ichiro Kono, Nakasone launched his own faction within the LDP. During his long career in Japanese government, Nakasone has served as transportation minister (1967–68), director of defense (1970–71), minister of international trade and industry (1972–74), and director of the Administrative Management Agency (1980–82). He also has served as secretary-general of the LDP and chairman of the LDP executive council.

The affable new leader of Japan enjoys outdoor sports, haiku, classical music, and growing orchids. His favorite hobby, however, is painting; his work has been shown in several exhibitions. With his wife, the former Tsutako Kobayashi, Nakasone has a son, two daughters, and five grandchildren.

ARDATH W. BURKS

RIDE, Sally Kristen

It began with the chance spotting of an announcement in a Stanford University campus newspaper. The year was 1977, and the National Aeronautics and Space Administration (NASA) was looking for scientists who wanted to be astronauts; women were encouraged to apply. Among those who did was Sally K. Ride, then working on her doctorate in astrophysics. The following year, NASA accepted Dr. Ride and five other women as "mission specialists." On June 18, 1983, Ride was rocketed into orbit along with four men aboard the space shuttle *Challenger* on a six-day mission. After 36 manned flights over 22 years, the United States had put a woman in space. Despite the uniqueness of her role, the 32-year-old Californian, described by a crewmate as "a very cool operator," emphasized that she is an astronaut and a scientist who *happens* to be a woman.

Background. Sally Kristen Ride was born May 26, 1951, to a college professor, Dale, and his wife, Joyce. Growing up in the Los Angeles suburb of Encino, Sally showed early promise as a tennis player; at one point, Billie Jean King urged her to turn professional. During her junior year in high school, however, a physiology teacher sparked a fascination with the scientific method. Ride pursued her interest in science at Swarthmore College in Philadelphia, and then at Stanford, where she earned bachelor degrees in physics and English. Regarding the latter, she said, "I needed a break from equations." Ride went on to receive her Ph.D. in 1978, specializing in X-ray astronomy and free-electron lasers.

A year after being selected as an astronaut, Ride was assigned to the team designing the shuttle's remote manipulator arm. In the course of the training, she also received her pilot's license. Later, on the shuttle's second and third missions (STS 2 and STS 3), she was the capsule communicator, relaying the flight director's instructions to the astronauts. In July 1982, Dr. Ride and Steven A. Hawley became the first members of the astronaut corps to marry.

As mission specialist on the flight of June 1983, officially referred to as STS 7, Dr. Ride operated the 50-ft (15-m) mechanical arm designed to release and then retrieve satellites. A key objective of the mission, the delicate exercise was considered a complete success. The retrieval capability will prove important in the shuttle program, allowing it to refuel and repair satellites while in orbit. Upon landing June 24 at Edwards Air Force Base (CA), Dr. Ride said, coolly, "I'm sure it's the most fun I'll ever have in my life."

SHAGARI, Alhaji Shehu

Alhaji Shehu Usman Aliu Shagari was reelected president of the Republic of Nigeria in August 1983, receiving 48% of the 25.5 million votes cast. The election showed that the president's popularity and that of his party, the National Party of Nigeria (NPN), had not been affected by a two-year downturn in the economy. A group of Nigeria's military leaders, however, concerned about the economy and the "corruption" of the nation's leaders, did not feel that Nigeria was experiencing "real democracy" and overthrew Shagari on December 31. The president was arrested.

Shehu Shagari had been first elected president in 1979, reintroducing civilian control to Nigeria after a 13-year period of military rule. That election culminated a life of public service for the northerner.

Background. The president was born in April 1925 in Shagari, a village in Sokoto State. Young Shagari entered Koranic school at age four, and two years later began school at Yabo. Unlike most of his Muslim contemporaries he did not end his education after elementary school, but continued at Kaduna College, Zaria; The Teachers Training College, Zaria; and finally the Sokoto Middle School, where he received his university degree in science in 1951. Shagari already had begun a 14-year teaching career in which he attained by 1953 the position of senior visiting teacher for Sokoto Province.

Shagari's first political association was with Aminu Kano, who persuaded him to join the Northern Teachers Association and later the Northern Peoples Congress (NPC). As one of the better-educated northerners, he was elected to the Federal House of Representatives in 1954. Four years later Prime Minister Alhaji Abubakar Tafawa Balewa chose him as his parliamentary secretary. After Nigeria's independence, Shagari became a member of Balewa's government, as minister for economic development (1959–60), establishments (1960–62), internal affairs (1962–65), and works (1965–66). In each position he performed quietly and efficiently.

The military takeover in 1966 never threatened him. During the first years of the military regimes he was content to stay in the North, becoming secretary-general of the Sokoto Educational Development Fund in 1966 and state commissioner for education in 1968. He was brought back to the central government by Gen. Yakubu Gowon as federal commissioner for economic development and reconstruction in 1970 and the following year became the commissioner of finance. After Gen. Olusegun Obasanjo announced the return of government to civilian control in 1978, Shagari helped form the NPN and was chosen president in 1979 in preference to other better-known candidates.

A devout Muslim, President Shagari has 2 wives and 15 children.

HARRY A. GAILEY

SHAMIR, Yitzhak

Yitzhak Shamir, the prime minister of Israel, is a stocky man who combines great strength of will with a modest and unostentatious demeanor. Shamir became prime minister on October 10, in succession to Menahem Begin, after 43 days in which the country was without a normally functioning government. His early life has similarities to Begin's. He, too, was born in eastern Poland, then part of the Russian Empire; but he left Poland earlier, and the two men never met until both were in Palestine.

Background. Most authorities give Shamir's birth date as Nov. 3, 1914, though his own entry in *Who's Who in Israel* says 1915. He was born in Kuzinoy, the son of Shlomo and Penina Jazernicki. He adopted the name Shamir, meaning "thorn," after coming to Palestine.

He was educated in a Jewish elementary school, and then in a Jewish high school in the nearby town of Bialystok. As a student, Shamir was, like Begin, a member of Betar, an activist branch of the Zionist movement. He began to study law at the University of Warsaw but after

Atlan/Sygma

Yitzhak Shamir

some two years immigrated to Palestine, where for a time he continued his law studies at the Hebrew University of Jerusalem and worked as a bookkeeper and in construction. In 1937, Shamir joined the radical Irgun Zvai Leumi (National Military Organization).

With the outbreak of World War II in 1939, Irgun suspended actions against Britain, the mandatory power, in favor of cooperation in the war. A small number of dissidents, Shamir being one, viewing Britain as still the primary enemy, seceded to found Lohamei Herut Yisrael (Fighters for the Freedom of Israel), more generally known as the Stern gang, after its leader Abraham Stern. After Stern was killed by the British in 1942, Shamir became one of the triumvirate who ran LHY, both of his associates also being from Poland. In these years of underground struggle Shamir was twice arrested by the British, escaping both times.

After the founding of Israel in 1948, Shamir shunned the public limelight for seven years. Between 1955 and 1965 he was head of the Paris station of Mossad, the formidable Israeli intelligence service. After leaving Mossad, he was in business in Israel. In 1970 he joined Begin's Herut Party. Elected to the Knesset in 1973, he rapidly became one of the leading members of the opposition. On his party's coming to power in 1977 as part of the Likud bloc with Begin as prime minister, Shamir became speaker of the Knesset, an office he discharged effectively until he became minister of foreign affairs under Begin on March 11, 1980.

A firm but pragmatic foreign minister, he met privately with his Soviet counterpart Andrei Gromyko at the United Nations in 1981, visited Latin America in 1981 and 1982, and with some success began to restore African contacts ruptured since 1973. He accepted as irreversible the agreements with Egypt.

Shamir and his wife have two children.

ARTHUR CAMPBELL TURNER

STONE, Richard B.

In April 1983, President Ronald Reagan selected former U.S. Sen. Richard B. Stone as ambassador at large, to serve as special representative of the president to Central America. Stone was sworn in June 1, and departed the next day for a fact-finding trip to Central

America, Mexico, Colombia, and Venezuela, in most cases talking with the president or chief executive of the nation visited.

He was empowered to try to persuade the Salvadorean government to commence talks with rebel groups for the purpose of getting their participation in the next elections for mayors and delegates to the constituent assembly (probably postponed to 1984), and perhaps bring an end to the four-year civil war. He also consulted with representatives of leftist organizations in El Salvador and found that they were more concerned with taking part in a provisional government to supervise the elections than voting in an election that they alleged would be rigged against them. Stone's bringing the factions together for the first time in three years must be considered a success, but he had much less impact in Nicaragua. Officials of that government had clashed with him in the past over his lobbying efforts in behalf of Guatemala's former government of Romeo Lucas García, and they accused him of "lacking moral values." His own evaluation of the Nicaraguan talks was that they were "useful."

By late 1983, Stone had had moderate success, keeping a low profile, while working behind the scenes to promote dialogue among the many Central American factions. His former relationship as lobbyist to Guatemala no longer seemed to be a major obstacle, and it appeared that most parties were willing to talk with him. Not the least of his problems was that his appointment was greeted originally with criticism at home by members of his own Democratic Party in the Senate as well as Assistant Secretary of State for Inter-American Affairs Thomas Enders. Enders was reassigned about the time of Stone's nomination.

Background. Richard B. Stone was born in New York City on Sept. 22, 1928. He received a bachelor's degree from Harvard in 1949 and a law degree from Columbia University in 1954, then engaged in private law practice briefly before becoming city attorney of Miami, FL (1966–67). He served four years in the Florida Senate and four years as secretary of state of Florida. In 1974 he was elected to the U.S. Senate, serving one term.

He is married to the former Marlene Lois Singer and has three children.

THOMAS L. KARNES

Richard B. Stone

UPI

Jessica Tandy

UPI

TANDY, Jessica

Jessica Tandy maintained her position as one of Broadway's most honored stars in 1983, winning the Tony Award as best actress in a play for her work in *Foxfire.* The play also continued a tradition of acclaimed performances with her husband, actor Hume Cronyn.

Tandy first took Broadway by storm in 1947, as Blanche DuBois in Tennessee Williams' *A Streetcar Named Desire.* Her protrayal earned her a Tony the following year and led one critic to remark that she played her part with "insight as vibrant and pitiless as Mr. Williams' writing." Tandem appearances with Cronyn began with the comedy hit *The Fourposter* in 1951; more recently, the couple won acclaim for *The Gin Game* (1977).

Foxfire, a depiction of Appalachian rural life that opened in 1982, was the couple's eleventh stage appearance. Tandy played a mountain widow; Cronyn portrayed her late husband—still very much alive in memory. While the play received mixed reviews, both performances were praised. During 1983, Tandy also was seen in supporting roles in two late 1982 films, *Still of the Night* and *Best Friends,* and recreated her role of Blanche DuBois in a stage tribute to Tennessee Williams, who died during the year. In December she returned to Broadway in *The Glass Menagerie.*

Background. Jessica Tandy was born on June 7, 1909, in London. Her father, a salesman, died when she was 12, and she grew up in poor circumstances. At 15 she enrolled in London's Ben Greet Academy of Acting. She made her London stage debut in 1929 in *The Rumour,* but it was her portrayal of the impetuous schoolgirl Manuela in *Children in Uniform* (1932) that established her as one of London's leading actresses. A wide range of roles, including repertory appearances with the Old Vic Company, followed.

Tandy appeared in several New York plays during the 1930s with varying success. In 1940, while in New York for a production called *Jupiter Laughs,* she met Cronyn.

They were married in 1942, after her divorce from British actor Jack Hawkins. Cronyn was in demand as a character actor in films, and the couple moved to Hollywood. But during the next few years Tandy was unable to land major film roles. She appeared with Cronyn in *The Seventh Cross* (1944) and then, in 1946, took the lead in a Los Angeles theater in *Portrait of a Madonna,* a one-act play by Tennessee Williams directed by her husband. It was this role that led to her selection for the part of Blanche DuBois.

Following her success in *Streetcar,* Tandy and Cronyn moved back to New York, where they remained dedicated to the stage. Both were elected to the Theater Hall of Fame in 1979. Their close relationship on and off stage has brought them the title First Couple of the American Theater.

ELAINE P. SEDITO

UEBERROTH, Peter V.

As president of the Los Angeles Olympic Organizing Committee (LAOOC), 46-year-old Peter Ueberroth has responsibility for organizing and staging the biggest, most elaborate sporting event ever held. The Games of the XXIII Modern Olympiad in the summer of 1984 will attract more athletes (12,000) from more countries (140) than any previous Olympics. More events (217 in 22 sports) will be seen by more people (some 2.5 billion on worldwide television) than ever before. Thanks to Ueberroth, the only thing smaller about the 1984 Games is the operating budget.

For the first time in Olympic history, responsibility for organizing and financing the Games rests with an independent, nonprofit organization and not with the city itself. As head of that body, Ueberroth, a self-made millionaire in the travel industry, devised a novel financial arrangement by which LA taxpayers will not be charged one cent for the Games. Funding for the 16-day extravaganza will come entirely from television revenues, commercial sponsorships, and ticket sales. By reusing competition venues built for the 1932 Olympics and by taking advantage of the varied athletic facilities of southern California, Ueberroth and the LAOOC hope to keep their outlay to $500 million—about one third that of the 1976 Montreal Games. Having successfully wooed commercial sponsors and with preparations proceeding within budget, Ueberroth has dared to predict that the LA Games will generate a fiscal surplus, unheard of in this era of Olympian-size overruns.

Peter V. Ueberroth

UPI

Background. The son of a building-supply salesman, Ueberroth was born in Chicago in 1938 and grew up in several California communities. A four-letter man at Fremont (CA) High School, Ueberroth won a partial scholarship to San Jose State in a sport that was totally new to him—water polo. In 1956 he tried out for the U.S. Olympic team and only narrowly missed.

After earning a business degree in 1959, Ueberroth took an office job in Honolulu with a small airline, and one year later, at age 22, was named a vice-president and 3% stockholder. In 1963 he sold his stock to form his own company, Transportation Consultants International (TCI). Business boomed, and within ten years Ueberroth had acquired a major travel agency chain and resort-management firm. The holding company, First Travel Corp., was established in 1974 and became the second largest travel corporation in North America with more than 1,500 employees. On April 1, 1979, Ueberroth took a "70% pay cut" to run the LA Olympics.

Ueberroth is described by his friends and business associates as outwardly charming and "laid back," but fundamentally decisive and forceful. He enjoys scuba diving, golf, and tennis, and is "a student of the Olympic Games." With his wife and two daughters, Ueberroth has lived in Los Angeles since 1961.

WASHINGTON, Harold

Harold Washington, 61, was sworn in as the first black mayor of Chicago, the second largest U.S. city, on April 30, 1983. Eighteen days earlier, Washington had won a narrow victory over Republican Bernard Epton, a former state legislator. Earlier, on February 22, he had toppled incumbent Mayor Jane M. Byrne and Cook County State Attorney Richard M. Daley, son of the late Mayor Richard J. Daley, in the Democratic primary.

His election, which made him one of the more prominent and powerful black men in the United States, came as somewhat of a surprise. A history of legal problems, and the fact he was not well known to most Chicagoans prior to 1983 made him an early underdog. A heavy black-voter registration and Washington's oratorical skills in mayoral debates soon changed the picture.

Background. The future mayor was born April 15, 1922, in Cook County Hospital in Chicago. He grew up in a middle-class family on the city's South Side and attended public school. During World War II, Harold Washington served in the U.S. Army Air Corps, but never saw combat because of his race.

After the war, Washington studied at Roosevelt University in Chicago, a mostly white school where he won his first election as senior-class president. Washington, who was a gifted orator even as a college student, obtained his law degree from Northwestern University and in 1955 took over the law practice of his late father, Roy. As a young lawyer he became active in the Democratic political machine in the city and an assistant corporation counsel for Chicago.

Washington was elected a state representative in 1964. Twelve years later he moved to the state Senate. In 1980 he was elected to Congress.

Washington's successful political career has been marked with personal legal problems. He was convicted in 1972 of failing to file federal income taxes for four years and was sentenced to 40 days in jail, fined $1,036.68, and placed on probation for three years. In 1969 the Illinois Supreme Court had suspended Washington's law license for accepting fees from clients and not performing any legal services. That suspension was extended to 1975 because of the tax conviction. Commenting during the mayoral campaign on his legal trouble, Washington said: "I'm not proud of it. I don't go around with a neon sign announcing it. Nor do I sneak around like a thief in the night. I've paid my dues."

Mayor Washington, a chain-smoking workaholic, was divorced in 1955, following ten years of marriage. In 1983 he and Mary E. Smith, a teacher, announced their engagement.

ROBERT ENSTAD

BOLIVIA

Problems of stabilizing the democratic government of President Hernan Siles Zuazo, which had taken office in November 1982, were the center of political attention during the year. A major step had been taken in December 1982 with the dismissal of former President Luis Garcia Meza and about a dozen other top officers from the armed forces. In May the government ordered the arrest of Garcia Meza and 29 others for "corruption and economic crimes," specifically involving illegal use of $50 million of government funds.

Government Problems. Problems for the regime came from within the civilian political forces. In January, President Siles faced his first political crisis when six ministers of the Revolutionary Left Movement (MIR) of Vice-President Jaime Paz Zamorra withdrew from the cabinet. Negotiations during the year to bring them back into the government were not successful. A second cabinet crisis in May resulted in replacement of three members of Siles' National Revolutionary Movement of the Left (MNRI) by other members of the same party.

More critical challenges came from the worker and peasant organizations. In April the Miners Federation seized control of the government-owned mines and of the Bolivian Mining Corporation (COMIBOL). They demanded "co-government" of the state mining industry. This was conceded two months later.

In June, at the Second National Peasant Congress, peasant leader Generao Flores demanded co-government in the political sphere. He wanted half the ministers to be named by the Bolivian Workers' Central, to which the peasants belong. However, President Siles was not willing to concede this arrangement.

Economy. The economic situation was difficult. Problems arising from the world recession, inflation, and a large foreign debt were intensified by severe floods in some parts of

Bolivia and a drought in much of the highlands. The drought was particularly severe, threatening a shortage of potatoes, the principal foodstuff of the Indian peasant. Early in June the U.S. Agency for International Development (AID) announced an emergency food aid program for Bolivia, Ecuador, and Peru.

Inflation remained severe. It was estimated that from March to May prices of basic household items rose by an average of 53%. In August the government decreed a general 40% wage increase, to partly offset the inflation.

In March the Siles government announced a general economic program. It stressed government aid to industry, private mining, and the agricultural sector. The program met a positive response from business elements but substantial criticism from the labor movement.

Foreign Relations. The most notable foreign-relations event was the arrest and deportation to France of Klaus Barbie early in February. Barbie had been head of the Gestapo in Lyons during World War II and had lived in Bolivia since the mid-1950s. President Siles honored a French request for his arrest and extradition. At the end of March, President Siles made a three-day trip to France, where he received official thanks for his action in the Barbie case. In April the U.S. Department of Justice sent a special investigator to Bolivia to look into charges that U.S. intelligence officials had spirited Barbie out of Europe and into Bolivia.

ROBERT J. ALEXANDER, *Rutgers University*

BOSTON

A history-making election dominated events in Boston in 1983. Kevin H. White, the mayor since 1968, announced he would not run again. White had been under heavy criticism for alleged corruption in his administration.

A large and varied field of candidates responded to White's announcement. They included David Finnegan, a former Boston School Committee member and radio talk show host; city councilmen Raymond Flynn and Frederick Langone and former councilman Lawrence DiCara; Robert Kiley, who had headed the Massachusetts Bay Transportation Authority; Suffolk County Sheriff Dennis Kearney; and former State Rep. Melvin King.

The election was the first to be held under a new city charter provision approved in 1982. Under the new plan, both the school committee and the city council will be made up of one representative from each of nine neighborhood districts plus four "at large" members on each body. Dispute over the drawing of the district lines had led to intervention by the courts, which ordered revisions in the districts and delayed the primary and final elections until October 11 and November 15, respectively.

BOLIVIA • Information Highlights

Official Name: Republic of Bolivia.
Location: West-central South America.
Area: 424,000 sq mi (1 098 160 km²).
Population (July 1983 est.): 5,883,000.
Chief Cities (1982 est.): Sucre, the legal capital, 79,941; LaPaz, the actual capital, 881,404; Santa Cruz de la Sierra, 376,912; Cochabamba, 281,962.
Government: *Head of state and government,* Gen. Hernan Siles Zuazo, president, inaugurated Oct. 10, 1982. *Legislature*—Congress: Senate and Chamber of Deputies.
Monetary Unit: Peso (500 pesos equal U.S.$1, Dec. 1, 1983, financial rate).
Gross National Product (1981 U.S.$): $7,400,-000,000.
Economic Index (May 1983): *Consumer Prices* (1970 = 100), all items, 4,511.7; food, 5,210.2.
Foreign Trade (1982 U.S.$): *Imports,* $496,000,-000,000; *exports,* $832,000,000,000.

The son of an Irish immigrant longshoreman and a native of South Boston, Raymond Flynn, 44, was elected mayor.

In the primary, the mayoral finalists were Flynn and King, the only black candidate. Both had emphasized the need to concentrate on neighborhood development as opposed to continuing the rapid buildup of the city's downtown area. The big surprise in the primary was the defeat of Finnegan.

In November, Flynn easily defeated King, receiving 65% of the vote. Incumbents won the "at large" spots on the city council and school committee, but many new faces emerged in the district contests. For Flynn, his victory promised a change in both style and substance in City Hall as he promised to reach out to the neighborhoods with his self-styled "populism." For King, the election marked the emergence of black voters, who supported him overwhelmingly, as a powerful force in Boston politics.

See also MASSACHUSETTS.

HARVEY BOULAY, *Rogerson House*

BRAZIL

Debt-ridden Brazil continued its transition from military to civilian rule even as civil disturbances erupted in response to economic belt-tightening proposed to placate international creditors.

Government and Politics. Brazil has lived under military rule since 1964, when the army capsized a mercurial civilian chief executive. But soon after Gen. João Baptista Figueiredo became president in 1979, he announced his commitment to an *abertura,* or democratization.

In accord with this objective, new governors took office on March 15, 1983, following the first direct election for state leaders in 18 years. The ruling, military-backed Social Democratic Party (PDS) won 13 state houses. However, opposition parties captured 62% of the vote to win ten states responsible for generating three quarters of Brazil's gross national product. The leading opposition group, the Brazilian Democratic Movement Party (PMDB), emerged victorious in 9 of these 10, including the key industrial centers of São Paulo and Minas Gerais.

The upset victory in Rio de Janeiro of socialist Leonel Brizola, nominee of the Democratic Labor Party (PDT), demonstrated the fairness of the contests. Brizola was one of three successful candidates formerly banned and subsequently granted amnesty by his country's military rulers. As governor of Rio Grande do Sul in 1964, Brizola had urged noncommissioned officers to imprison their superiors in order to thwart a coup d'etat against his brother-in-law, President João Goulart.

Opposition gains at the state level were complemented by stunning advances in the House of Representatives, where the PDS was forced to ally with the 13-member Brazilian Workers Party (PTB) to achieve a 248-to-232-seat governing majority. In return for PTB support, the government reportedly agreed to increase compensation to workers fired from their jobs, diminish official control over unions, and reduce the workweek to 45 hours.

Still, the PDS held a firm grip on the Senate and the electoral college. The latter will accomplish the indirect election of a president in 1985 unless rules are changed that give the vote of one citizen in remote northeastern and Amazonian states, hotbeds of PDS strength, as much weight as 22 votes cast in industrialized cities such as São Paulo. Vice-President Aureliano Chaves, a civilian and PDS member, became a leading presidential prospect when he deftly discharged executive functions following Figueiredo's July 15 double bypass heart surgery in a U.S. hospital.

Opposition leaders know that widespread economic and social distress could derail the comeback of democracy. Thus, Gov. André Franco Montoro of São Paulo assumed a strong law-and-order stance in the face of strikes and protest marches. Meanwhile, Governor Brizola denounced a general strike as divisive and deplored supermarket looting as a scheme by right-wingers to keep the armed forces in power.

Economy. Brazil's economic malaise dominated all other aspects of national life. Fiscal cutbacks combined with the worldwide recession to induce a 15% drop in industrial output and a 40% fall in investment in 1983. The inflation rate exceeded 200%, and unemployment afflicted 1 of every 5 members of the work force. Massive flooding in the south and a protracted drought in the northeast, known as "Brazil's India" because of its profound poverty, exacerbated economic problems.

Amid these conditions, Brazil tried to come to terms with a $90 billion (U.S.) external debt, swollen by a decade of foreign borrowing to spur industrialization and fund oil imports. Creditors emphasized that additional loans depended on Brazil's implementing an austerity plan negotiated with the International Monetary Fund (IMF) in February, shortly after Figueiredo had devalued the cruzeiro by 23% against the dollar. The IMF package, designed to enlarge government revenues and cut expenditures, included reduced subsidies for petroleum products, foodstuffs, small businesses, and exports; an average hike of 45% on oil and gas prices; curbs on official borrowing, deemed responsible for high interest charges and a huge government deficit; and higher capital gains and personal income taxes on the affluent.

The IMF approved a $4.9 billion standby credit for Brazil in February, but withheld a second payment of $411 million until November because the government dragged its feet on cost cutting. In a further effort to bring the economy into line with IMF targets, Brazil took steps to limit outlays by highly inefficient state-owned enterprises. On July 13, the government announced that future cost-of-living increases for workers, formerly 100%, would be held to 80% of inflation—with adjustments made twice annually rather than quarterly. The new measures sparked a wave of strikes.

The labor activism preceded mounting political opposition, spearheaded by the PMDB, against Brazil's being "dictated to" by the International Monetary Fund. So virulent and persistent was the anti-IMF campaign that in September opposition congressmen, joined by PTB members who had broken ranks with the PDS, turned thumbs down on the proposed wage-compression scheme. The government introduced a milder version of the bill.

Foreign commercial banks reacted to the uproar in Brazil by agreeing, in order to avoid a default that might tumble the international financial system, to soften the terms on $5.5 billion worth of loans falling due in 1984. Shantytown dwellers responded to the debt impasse by looting hundreds of supermarkets in Rio and other cities.

A trade surplus of nearly $6 billion proved one bright spot in a bleak economic picture. Also encouraging was a $400 million World Bank loan to support agriculture and industry. Brazil is the world's largest recipient of funds from the Bank, which also granted the giant Latin American nation a $302.3 million credit for water projects.

Foreign Affairs. In mid-April, Brazilian authorities seized East European- and U.S.-made arms, described as "medicine" on the manifest, aboard four Libyan planes destined for Managua, Nicaragua, that landed to refuel in Manaus and Recife. Two months later, each aircraft was permitted to return to Tripoli only after Brazil's ambassador to Tripoli confirmed that the previous flight had arrived with its cargo intact. Reportedly, this action came after Libya, its second-largest customer, threatened to stop buying munitions from Brazil. In addition, Libyan President Muammar el-Qaddafi, who had been negotiating a $250 million purchase of Brazilian planes, suggested a severing of relations with Brazil if the dispute were not resolved to his satisfaction.

The arms affair aside, President Figueiredo, during a visit to Mexico, claimed that Washington had driven Nicaragua to align itself with the Soviet bloc. "If Nicaragua had received economic aid from rich countries, especially the United States," he said, "then it would not be in the current situation." He also charged that U.S. policy undermined the right of self-determination by Central American states.

Figueiredo signed a barter agreement with Mexico under which Brazil would exchange manufactured goods for Mexican oil. The accord embraced a "reciprocal credit system" to be regulated by the two countries' central banks, thus permitting importers to pay for products from the other nation in their own currency. Brazil has become Mexico's largest Latin American trading partner and sixth largest overall, and Mexico has become Brazil's most important foreign oil supplier; daily shipments increased from 60,000 to 80,000 barrels.

On May 10, China signed a contract with five Western oil companies, including Petrobras of Brazil, to drill for offshore oil.

GEORGE W. GRAYSON
College of William and Mary

BRAZIL • Information Highlights

Official Name: Federative Republic of Brazil.
Location: Eastern South America.
Area: 3,290,000 sq mi (8 521 000 km²).
Population (July 1983 est.): 131,305,000.
Chief Cities (1980 census): Brasilia, the capital, 1,202,683; São Paulo, 8,584,896; Rio de Janeiro, 5,184,292; Belo Horizonte, 1,814,990.
Government: *Head of state and government,* João Baptista Figueiredo. president (took office March 1979). *Legislature*—National Congress: Federal Senate and Chamber of Deputies.
Monetary Unit: Cruzeiro (914 cruzeiros equal US.$1, Dec. 1, 1983).
Gross Domestic Product (1981 U.S.$): $288,124,-000,000.
Economic Indexes (1982): *Consumer Prices* (1972 = 100), all items, 4,900.9; food, 5,336.9. *Industrial Production* (1975 = 100), 130.
Foreign Trade (1982 U.S.$): *Imports,* $22,637,-000,000; *exports,* $20,190,000,000.

BRITISH COLUMBIA

It was a year of political turmoil in British Columbia.

Politics and Government. A provincial general election was held on May 5, before any sitting of the legislature or presentation of a budget for 1983–84. The Social Credit government increased its seats by 4 to 35, and the New Democratic Party dropped from 26 to 22 seats. The NDP leader, Dave Barrett, announced his intention to step down in the wake of this third election defeat by Bill Bennett. The Social Credit share of the total vote rose from 48.2 to 49.8%.

A July budget announced a new program for leaner and more efficient government. In the face of the continuing economic recession and declining personal income tax and natural gas revenues, expenditures were forecast at C$8,445,000,000, with a projected deficit of $1,603,000,000. A total of $415 million was allocated to an Employment Development account. Tax increases included a rise in sales tax from 6 to 7% and the removal of exemptions from long-distance telephone calls and prepared meals costing more than $7 per person. Hospital coinsurance charges also were increased. The new restraint package proposed extending the public sector Compensation Stabilization Program and holding salary levels to adjustments of plus or minus 5%. In addition there was to be a 25% reduction in the direct staffing of the public service by September 1984. A number of regulatory bodies were to be dismantled. Certain other government activities were to be turned over to the private sector. School boards and colleges and the medical profession were to come under tighter centralized controls. The legislative details of these measures were contained in 26 bills which accompanied the budget. Proposed revisions to public service labor law also permitted employees to be fired without cause, and by August 1,600 public employees had been terminated.

BRITISH COLUMBIA • Information Highlights

Area: 366,255 sq mi (948 600 km²).
Population (July 1983): 2,826,800.
Chief Cities (1981 census): Victoria, the capital, 64,379; Vancouver, 414,281; Prince George, 67,559; Kamloops, 64,048; Kelowna, 59,196; Nanaimo, 47,069.
Government (1983): *Chief Officers*—lt. gov., Henry Bell-Irving; premier, William R. Bennett (Social Credit Party); atty. gen., L. Allan Willaims. *Legislature*—Legislative Assembly, 57 members.
Education (1982–83): *Enrollment*—elementary and secondary schools, 537,100 pupils; postsecondary, 50,620 students.
Public Finance (1984 fiscal year budget): *Revenues* $6,800,000,000; *expenditures* $8,400,000,000.
Personal Income (average weekly salary, March 1983): $471.35
Employment Rate (August 1983, seasonally adjusted): 14.1%.
(All monetary figures are in Canadian dollars.)

The legislature was adjourned on October 21. Several major items, including the proposals affecting human rights, the rentalsman, and restrictions on the scope of bargaining for government employees, had not been passed.

On November 1, 35,000 provincial government employees took strike action in a dispute that centered on layoff procedures and seniority rights. A week later they were joined by public-school teachers and support staff. The prospect of a province-wide general strike against the restraint program was averted on November 13 by a collective agreement.

The Economy. During 1982 the gross provincial product fell by an estimated 7%, and in the first half of 1983 nearly 200,000 workers remained unemployed. Fluctuations in lumber and pulp prices blunted any optimism for any rapid recovery in the forest industry. Low demand and falling prices led to the suspension or cutback of mining operations. Coal has replaced copper as the most valuable mineral resource within British Columbia, and the two new major northeastern coal mines at Tumbler Ridge were to begin their shipments to Japan by the end of 1983. In the natural gas industry, hearings were opened on proposals to build a pipeline to Vancouver Island.

NORMAN J. RUFF, *University of Victoria*

BULGARIA

In 1983, Bulgaria remained unswervingly "socialist" and under the firm, doctrinaire guidance of the president and first secretary of the Bulgarian Communist Party, Todor Zhivkov. At the same time its image abroad suffered setbacks.

Domestic Affairs. In April, the Bulgarian media and party organizations debated a contemplated labor law that would penalize industrial managers who submitted false estimates of their future needs for skilled personnel in order to help favored students gain coveted admission to universities and technical colleges. Enterprises that failed to provide suitable positions for such students on their graduation would be required to reimburse the state for the cost of the "wasted" education.

Foreign Protests. In February, the U.S. State Department identified Bulgaria as one of the countries employing Vietnamese workers who had volunteered to work as "indentured labor" to help pay Vietnam's debt to the Soviet Union and its East European allies. It charged that a large part of their wages was withheld and that their working conditions were in violation of international labor standards.

In late 1982 and early 1983, a major, unresolved controversy raged over Italian allegations that the Bulgarian security services, collaborating with their Soviet counterparts, had been involved in the attempted assassination of Pope John Paul II in the Vatican on May 13, 1981. Bulgaria protested the arrest in November 1982 of Sergei Antonov, a senior executive of the Bulgarian national airline in Rome, who had been implicated by Mehmet Ali Agca, the convicted would-be assassin. Italian authorities were also investigating the possibility that Bulgarian agents working in Rome had planned to assassinate Lech Walesa, leader of the now defunct Polish independent labor movement Solidarity, during his visit to Italy in January 1981. Both Bulgaria and the Soviet Union denied all of the allegations, and relations between Italy and Bulgaria remained severely strained. In April, Bulgaria convicted two Italian citizens on charges of military espionage.

Foreign Alliances and Assistance. The traditionally close ties between Bulgaria and the Soviet Union remained secure. Zhivkov led a delegation consisting of Grisha Filipov, chairman of the Council of Ministers, Gen. Dobri Dzhurov, minister of people's defense, and Foreign Minister Petar Mladenov to the Warsaw Pact summit meeting in Prague in January.

In March, Bulgaria signed a three-year, $165 million trade and assistance agreement with Nicaragua, including the construction of a deep-water port on the Atlantic.

JOSEPH F. ZACEK
State University of New York at Albany

BURMA

Brig. Gen. Tin Oo (55), third-ranking leader of the Burma Socialist Program Party (BSPP), sought early in 1983 to oust Defense Minister Kyaw Htin. He also tried to reduce the inflexibility of former Gen. Ne Win's "Burmese Way to Socialism" and was able to place key subordinates in important military, administrative, and diplomatic posts. For a while his support rivaled that commanded by Ne Win (72), who had stepped down as president in 1981 but remained chairman of the BSPP.

Tin Oo was charged in August with misuse of state funds and sentenced to five life-terms.

President San Yu and Kyaw Htin were the chief beneficiaries of Tin Oo's reversal as the struggle to succeed Ne Win intensified.

Insurrections. In June the army attacked the insurgent Karens deep in that ethnic minority's highland territory—and for the first time ever during the rainy season. This offensive followed the heaviest action in years against the Karens, in February and March.

Earlier in February the Karens had sought to reestablish a presence in central Burma, where both they and the country's Communists once possessed strongholds. Some of the Communists also reportedly returned to this area. The two groups made efforts to draw closer together and to strengthen their cooperation with other rebels in Burma. But the moves of both Communists and Karens out of their mountain strongholds may have had more to do with declining external aid and the need to move nearer to Burma's population centers.

The Economy. Burma's gross national product grew 7.1% during the fiscal year ending in March 1983, but the black market continued to be the source of one third of the GNP. The cost of imports rose as export prices declined. The government emphasized capital development to the neglect of consumer needs.

Foreign Relations. Japan and West Germany remained Burma's chief sources of aid. Burma sought observer status at the nonaligned nations' meeting in India. Rangoon had quit the group in 1979 because of its perceived pro-Communist bias.

On October 9 North Korean agents in Rangoon bombed a monument about to be visited by South Korean leaders. Seventeen Korean and four Burmese officials were killed in the incident. Two North Korean military officers were found guilty by a Burmese court in December; a third was killed earlier, trying to escape. Burma broke diplomatic relations with North Korea as a result of the attack.

RICHARD BUTWELL
University of South Dakota

BUSINESS AND CORPORATE AFFAIRS

To the U.S. business community in general, 1983 turned out to be a better year than anticipated, as the economy came out of the 1981–82 recession with a stronger upward thrust than had been predicted, and optimism prevailed in many areas of business. Toward the end of 1983 inflation was running at approximately 5%. Unemployment, which had peaked early in 1983 at 11.4%, dropped to below 9% by the end of the year.

Consumers' confidence in the recovery was reflected in a sharp increase in retail sales and a surge in automobile sales. The gross national product rose from a $3,110 billion rate in the fourth quarter of 1982 to $3,363 billion for the third quarter of 1983. The economy was definitely on the rebound, and the business community was benefiting from the turnaround.

Profits and Losses. As reflected in quarterly profit reports, the benefits from the recovery were definitely being felt by many U.S. corporations. A survey of 506 corporations showed that third-quarter earnings for 1983 surged by 29% over the same period in 1982. The Big Three auto manufacturers (Ford, General Motors, and Chrysler) reported combined earnings of $1.17 billion, a third-quarter record, as against a combined loss of $186.6 million in the year-earlier period. The airlines also showed a large aggregate gain—profits rose 93%—but the prosperity certainly was not shared by everyone in the industry. Profits for building-materials producers were up 113%; drug and variety stores were up 181%; department stores, 55%; rubber companies, 58%; and textile concerns, 66%. In addition, the huge oil industry posted a moderate gain.

Not all industries, though, shared in the good times brought by the economic recovery. It was not a profitable year for the steel industry and the farm-equipment manufacturers, though they were able to cut heavy losses. The housing industry had flurries indicating the possibility of a fairly strong recovery, but high interest rates for mortgages continued to plague the industry.

Bankruptcies and Near Bankruptcies. Changes in the bankruptcy law enacted by Congress in 1978 continued to have some startling effects. Prior to 1978 the law allowed a company to file for Chapter 11 bankruptcy only if it was insolvent—that is, if its liabilities exceeded the market value of its assets or if it could not meet maturing debt. After Congress deleted those tests, solvent companies that foresaw possible financial difficulties began to file for bankruptcy. In 1982, Manville Corp. sought protection under the bankruptcy law in the face of 16,000 suits filed against it by victims of asbestos-related diseases; the potential liabilities, totaling $2 billion, could have left the company insolvent. Solvent companies that filed for bankruptcy in 1983 because of possible financial difficulties in the future included Continental Airlines and Wilson Foods. Unions accused the companies of filing for bankruptcy in order to break their union contracts; under bankruptcy proceedings union-negotiated contracts become null and void.

Don Phelan Inc.

Executive change at Lehman Brothers Kuhn Loeb: Lewis Glucksman (center) *took over from Peter Peterson as chairman and Peter Dawkins* (left), *former Army Heisman Trophy winner and recently retired brigadier general, became director of the public finance department.*

A number of airlines were in trouble. Following Braniff Airlines in 1982, Continental filed for bankruptcy in September 1983 and Eastern threatened to do the same. The situation at Trans World Airlines (TWA) was such that the parent company, Trans World Corporation, considered divesting itself of the airline division because of its lack of profitability. (*See also* TRANSPORTATION.)

One bankruptcy filing that was particularly shocking was that of Baldwin-United Corp. The Cincinnati piano company had borrowed heavily to move into the insurance business, and its collapse in September 1983 was one of the largest financial failures in U.S. history. The company was a casualty of overexpansion, built on complex financial maneuverings.

Mergers and Divestitures. The big news in terms of mergers and divestitures during 1983 was the breakup of American Telephone & Telegraph (AT&T), better known as the Bell System. The divestiture was part of a court-approved agreement between the U.S. Department of Justice and AT&T. On Jan. 1, 1984, AT&T was broken up into seven companies, plus AT&T itself. Seven separate telephone companies were set up across the country, each one giving service to a particular region. The companies are: NYNEX, Bell Atlantic, BellSouth, Ameritech, Southwestern Bell, U.S. West, and Pacific Telesis. As a result of the divestiture, AT&T is out of the local telephone business and has more competition in the long-distance and telephone-equipment businesses. It continues to own Western Electric and Bell Laboratories and is now able to compete in other areas of the telecommunications field that formerly were prohibited to it. (*See also* COMMUNICATION TECHNOLOGY.)

Like Trans World Corp. hoping to divest itself of TWA, DuPont Co. made plans to sell most of the assets of its Conoco Chemicals subsidiary for $600 million in cash.

Merger activity slowed down during 1983, but some significant moves still were being made. LTV Corp., which owns the third-largest steel company in the United States, Jones & Laughlin Steel Corp., agreed to acquire the fourth-ranked Republic Steel Corp. for $770 million, subject to approval by shareholders of both concerns and the Department of Justice.

Santa Fe Industries and the Southern Pacific Co. announced an agreement late in 1983 to merge all their operations, a deal valued at $5.2 billion that would create the nation's third-largest railroad system. The Interstate Commerce Commission, whose approval of the deal was necessary, indicated that it was receptive to the merger.

The Computer Business. Probably in no area of business during 1983 was there more activity than in the computer field. The year ushered in the beginning of the shakeout process in a severely competitive industry. Many competitors who envisioned a continuation of the spectacular profits of previous years began to have second thoughts. The sale of home computers had soared from about two million in 1982 to more than five million in 1983, but spectacular profits were turning into disastrous losses for some companies. Warner's Atari operation had losses of about $300 million in the first half alone, while Texas Instruments and Mattel each had losses of about $100 million. The computer industry was shaken with the news in October that Texas Instruments was withdrawing from the home computer business.

Osborne Computer Corp., which considered itself to be the pioneer in the personal computer business, filed for bankruptcy in September. Digital Equipment Corp. announced a drop of 76% in its third-quarter profits, while Coleco's third-quarter profits dipped low enough to send its stock from $65 in 1982 to $26 in late 1983. National Data Communications Inc. filed for bankruptcy, as did Computer Devices Inc.

Toward the end of 1983, International Business Machines (IBM) introduced its PCjr personal computer, which was expected to reshape the $2 billion market for home computers by raising the complexity and price of popular hardware. Commodore International remained the leader in home computer sales.

The computer industry was convinced that its greatest challenge was marketing: convincing most households that they need to have a home computer. Despite all the publicity, only about 5% of 84 million U.S. households owned a home computer by the end of 1983. (*See also* COMPUTERS.)

Management Personnel. Mary Cunningham resigned as a vice-president at Joseph E. Seagram & Sons to join with her husband, William M. Agee, who had been chief executive officer of Bendix Corp., to form the consulting firm of Semper Enterprises Inc. In the financial world, a significant realignment in management took place at the investment firm of Lehman Brothers Kuhn Loeb; the chairman and co-chief executive, Peter G. Peterson, reluctantly resigned in favor of Lewis L. Glucksman. The world's largest maker of photographic equipment, Eastman Kodak, named Colby H. Chandler, a 21-year company veteran, as its new chief executive officer. Thomas C. Graham took over the reins of U.S. Steel Corp. in May, and made it clear in short order that no tradition would be held sacred in the battle to turn the company around. This was shown in his willingness to buy steel from Great Britain and to shut down U.S. plants if the price were right. Meanwhile at IBM, John R. Opel was named to succeed Frank T. Cary as chairman and John F. Akers replaced Opel as president. And at CBS Inc., Thomas H. Wyman officially succeeded William S. Paley as chairman.

STEWART M. LEE, *Geneva College*

CALIFORNIA

George Deukmejian, a conservative Republican in the style of President Reagan, was inaugurated 35th governor of California on Jan. 3, 1983. He entered office paired with Democratic majorities in both houses of the legislature and was immediately plunged into conflict as the state faced a $1.5 billion deficit in the 1983 fiscal year and he was pledged to no tax increases. (*See also* BIOGRAPHY.)

Financial Problems. In his budget message, Governor Deukmejian proposed an immediate spending cut of $750 million, with an equal amount in debt to be carried forward into the next fiscal year—the first time the state had ever considered deliberate deficit spending.

Democratic leaders pushed hard for a tax increase, pointing to local government and higher education demands, together with future state deficit prospects, but the governor remained adamant. After great controversy, a compromise was reached in mid-February that would sharply cut the budget, accelerate some tax collections, authorize short-term borrowing, and provide for a 1-cent sales-tax increase (to 7 cents) if general-fund revenues did not rise enough to assure that the state could meet its obligations in fiscal 1984. Four days later, Standard and Poor's Corporation reduced California's traditionally high credit rating to AA while criticizing the state's slowness to respond to Proposition 13 of 1979, which greatly reduced property-tax revenues.

The Budget. The 1984 fiscal budget created a second money crisis within the same legislative session. Leaders sought to increase the budget with support from educators and local officials, but the governor held fast. The central issue became the state's community colleges. The governor called upon them to levy tuition for the first time. Their leaders and the Democrats refused, leaving them $108.5 million below their budgets of the previous year and forcing them to lay off faculty and reduce course offerings. Adding to the conflict was a bitter battle over a Republican proposal for an initiative to reapportion the legislature, which had been severely gerrymandered by the Democrats after the 1980 census. The state supreme court held the move to be unconstitutional.

The legislature finally sent the governor a budget of $27.3 billion, 21 days later than the state constitution required and the tardiest in state history. Deukmejian reduced items totaling $1.1 billion by veto. None of these was overridden. The budget cut hard into higher education, local government aid, state employee salaries, and health and environmental programs, but it would retire the short-term debt and increase funds for education through high school. The budget did, in fact, increase state taxes and receipts through many minor changes, but the economy recovered enough to prevent triggering the sales-tax increase. The residual partisan bitterness, unusual in California, was reflected in the governor's 24 vetoes of non-finance bills, sponsored by Democrats.

The fiscal conflict left little room for important bills to be passed. A new way of financing the state schools was adopted, state standards for high school graduation were imposed, and changes were made in rules for merit pay and for dismissal of teachers. But legislators failed to rewrite legislation on welfare, grants-in-aid, or campaign expenditures.

Prisons. California prisons are 30% overcrowded. In 1983, state courts ordered the renovation or closing of Folsom and San Quentin —old, grim, maximum-security facilities. The legislature passed three bills that will provide new space for more than 11,000 inmates.

Earthquakes and Weather. A powerful earthquake measuring Richter 6.5, the state's most severe jolt since 1971, struck the San Joaquin Valley farming village of Coalinga on May 2. It was followed by dozens of aftershocks and secondary tremors and caused more than $31 million in damage, although no one was killed or seriously injured. During a severe, wet winter, four major storms did enormous damage to the state's coastline and beaches. They caused 11 deaths and the evacuation of 2,000 persons. Four counties were declared disaster areas.

Other Developments. In May, Roger Hedgecock (R), a county supervisor, was elected mayor of San Diego to succeed U.S. Sen. Pete Wilson. And in June, Sala Burton (D) was elected to the congressional seat left vacant by the death of her husband, Philip, on April 10.

In April the *Oakland Tribune* was sold by the Gannett newspapers to a group of investors including Robert C. Maynard, who became the first black to head a major metropolitan newspaper in the United States.

CHARLES R. ADRIAN
University of California, Riverside

CALIFORNIA • Information Highlights

Area: 158,706 sq mi (411 049 km²).
Population (1982 est.): 24,724,000.
Chief Cities (1980 census): Sacramento, the capital, 275,741; Los Angeles, 2,966,763; San Diego, 875,504; San Francisco, 678,974; San Jose, 629,546.
Government (1983): *Chief Officers*—governor, George Deukmejian (R); lt. gov., Leo McCarthy (D). *Legislature*—Senate, 40 members; Assembly, 80 members.
State Finances (fiscal year 1982): *Revenues,* $42,247,000,000; *expenditures,* $40,444,000,000.
Personal Income (1982): $310,704,000,000; per capita, $12,567.
Labor Force (July 1982): *Nonagricultural wage and salary earners,* 9,846,900; *unemployed,* 1,181,900 (9.5% of total force).
Education: *Enrollment* (fall 1981)—public elementary schools, 2,769,788; public secondary, 1,276,368; colleges and universities (1982), 1,842,963. *Public school expenditures* (1981–82), $12,009,959,000.

CAMBODIA

Tom Fawthrop/Photo Trends

Vietnamese forces continued to occupy Cambodia, and a pro-Hanoi regime stayed in power.

Cambodia remained occupied by Vietnamese forces, which were harassed by Cambodian resistance groups. No change in the situation seemed likely unless or until the Sino-Soviet struggle abated.

Cambodia has been at war since 1970. Since 1979 a Vietnamese army of about 160,000 troops has occupied the main towns and highways and propped up a pro-Vietnamese regime in Phnom Penh. The Soviet Union is the main supporter of Vietnam and provides military aid to the Phnom Penh regime.

China backs the Cambodian resistance groups and ties down another large Vietnamese army on the Sino-Vietnamese border. What mainly holds Hanoi and Moscow together is their deep distrust of Peking. As long as this distrust remains—and it shows no signs of ending—Vietnam is likely to keep its forces in Cambodia.

Politically, the year 1983 was almost a replay of the four previous years for Cambodia. Military activity was regulated by the seasons. Diplomatic activity was governed by the calendar of international meetings.

Military Activity. The Vietnamese forces are favored by the dry season—December to May. They can move their tanks over the rough terrain of western Cambodia and engage the resistance groups near the Thai border. Occasionally they cross the border and engage the Thai army. In the spring of 1983, Vietnamese attacks caused greater casualties than in previous years but failed to destroy the limited capability of the resistance.

During the summer rainy season the resistance can move its small, lightly equipped forces over muddy trails and harass the Vietnamese in many provinces of Cambodia. The Communist and non-Communist resistance groups mounted these attacks in the summer of 1983 but failed to dislodge the Vietnamese.

Diplomacy. Meanwhile the two sides carried on a diplomatic struggle at the nonaligned-nations meeting in New Delhi in March and at rival summit meetings with their sponsors in June and July. The main political duel was at the UN General Assembly in the fall.

The nonaligned summit refused to seat either the pro-Vietnamese Cambodians or the resistance groups. This was a victory of sorts for Vietnam, because the resistance groups have more friends abroad. They had hoped to have their leader, Prince Norodom Sihanouk, address the meeting.

In June the foreign ministers of the five neighboring countries that support the resistance groups met in Bangkok. These countries—Thailand, Malaysia, Singapore, Indonesia, and the Philippines—compose the Association of Southeast Asian Nations (ASEAN). They renewed their demand that Vietnam withdraw from Cambodia and allow free elections.

In July the foreign minister of Vietnam met with the pro-Vietnam ministers of Laos and Cambodia. They claimed Vietnam was withdrawing troops as a gesture of good will, but press reports indicated otherwise.

At the UN General Assembly in October, the ASEAN countries won more than 100 votes for a resolution to seat the resistance as the government of Cambodia—and for a second resolution that condemned "foreign" (meaning Vietnamese) aggression in Cambodia.

The Economy. Cambodia's gradual recovery from the intense fighting of the 1970s was reported by foreign visitors. One result was that many Western governments reduced their humanitarian aid. But they continued to help refugees at the Thai-Cambodian border.

PETER A. POOLE

CAMBODIA · Information Highlights

Official Name: The People's Republic of Kampuchea.
Location: Southeast Asia.
Area: 69,898 sq mi (181 036 km²).
Population (July 1983 est.): 5,996,000.
Chief City (1981 est.): Phnom Penh, the capital, 200,000.
Government: *Head of state and government,* Heng Samrin (took office 1981).
Monetary Unit: Riel (4 riels equal U.S.$, Dec. 1982).

CANADA

Canadians in 1983 were assured that economic recovery was in progress. Their dollar was stable; inflation dropped from double digits to 6%; consumer spending and the stock market revived. Few Canadians seemed convinced or grateful. A majority promised to vote for the opposition Progressive Conservative (PC) Party despite PC divisions and a change of leadership. Pierre Elliott Trudeau's Liberal government courted business and Washington, struggled with such old issues as bilingualism and the Crowsnest Pass freight rate, and continued to control public sector wages. People wondered whether the prime minister would run again. While Trudeau kept Canadians guessing, he was no less an enigma on the world scene. The friend of peace, détente, and the North-South dialogue lectured Third World countries on their greed, responded sharply to Soviet destruction of a Korean airliner, but also traveled widely to foster his plan for global disarmament.

In late December it was announced that Jeanne Sauve, 61, would become the 23rd governor-general of Canada in January 1984.

Politics. Many Canadians noted the 15th anniversary of Trudeau's Liberal leadership. Some wondered whether he would keep his 1980 promise to resign or whether his government's unpopularity would persuade him to struggle against adversity. Polls showed the Conservatives with more than 50% public support,

On a January tour of Asia to promote trade, Prime Minister Trudeau and his son, Sacha, 9, met the sultan of Brunei.

Canapress Photo Service

largely because inroads in the Liberal base in French Canada reinforced Conservative dominance in the four Western provinces and parts of Ontario. The New Democrats, Canada's social democratic party, languished with between one sixth and one fifth of the electorate, a victim of widespread "Trudeauphobia" and an infusion of the conservatism fashionable in both Britain and the United States.

In Parliament, it was a year of unfinished business, conducted in the face of a confident and often obstructionist opposition. The government finally passed its access to information bill, though wide protection for personal privacy and federal cabinet documents ensured that Canadians were far from "freedom of information." The government also worked to establish a civilian security agency, recommended by a royal commission that investigated handling of espionage and domestic subversion by the Royal Canadian Mounted Police (RCMP) in the 1970s. The proposal creating a civilian Security Intelligence Service was savaged by civil libertarians and conservatives, who upheld the prestige of the RCMP.

In return for subsidizing a railway line through the Crowsnest Pass into mineral-rich southern British Columbia, Ottawa in 1897 had extracted a promise from railway companies to freeze freight rates on prairie wheat and other farm products. With a brief interval during and after World War I, the "Crow rate" has governed the economics of prairie agriculture ever since, encouraging export of the favored products but giving railways no reason to improve their lines or service. Attempts to modernize the Crow rate after almost a century pitted grain farmers, for whom realistic freight rates would be ruinous, against cattle ranchers who complained that cheap freight rates funnel away feed grains to their competitors in eastern Canada. In 1983 the Liberals set out to tackle the Crow rate, offering a massive subsidy in return for rapid progress to market-based freight rates. Even those who accepted the need to scrap a sacred regional benefit fought furiously over how the subsidy would be distributed—to farmers, to the railways to hasten capital improvements, or some combination. The New Democrats, strong among Western wheat producers, steadfastedly opposed any change; Conservatives managed to conceal deep party splits on the issue.

The Tories. The Progressive Conservatives had other problems that might have been fatal had the government party not been so profoundly unpopular. In late January, PC leader Joe Clark mustered only 66.9% of the 2,406 votes against a leadership review, only a fraction of a point more backing than he had in 1981. It seemed a poor reward for two years of shrewd opposition tactics and a massive lead in the opinion polls, and Clark decided to give his party the leadership convention so many Con-

Canapress Photo Service

Brian Mulroney, who had never held elective office, was voted leader of the Progressive Conservative Party in June.

servatives seemed to want. The alternative was renewed sniping from his enemies in the parliamentary caucus and beyond. Brian Mulroney, third-place finisher in the 1976 leadership convention, had never ceased organizing for a comeback. In February he officially supported Clark, but his organizers discreetly encouraged Clark's enemies. The result was a head start in a race that eventually mustered seven serious candidates for the leadership post, ranging from a millionaire Edmonton hockey club owner to a progressive-minded former mayor of Toronto. Besides Clark and Mulroney, the only other candidate with a chance was a former minister of finance, John Crosbie, a Newfoundland politician whose budget in 1979 had helped bring down the Clark government.

When Conservative delegates finally voted at the Ottawa Civic Centre on June 11, it took nine hours to reach a decision. Polls had predicted that a majority of those present wanted anyone but Clark, and the polls were right. Blamed for a poor image, the downfall of his short-lived government, and the failure to reward the power-starved party faithful, Clark and his loyalists made few converts. When Brian Mulroney emerged in second place on the first ballot, his victory was certain. John Crosbie, however popular with delegates for his toughness and wit, suffered for his cutting wit and his utter lack of French. Quebec was the decisive issue. Urged by backers to save the party from Mulroney by going to Crosbie, Joe Clark refused. His strong French-Canadian contingent could not stomach Crosbie.

CANADA · Information Highlights

Official Name: Canada.
Location: Northern North America.
Area: 3,851,809 sq mi (9 976 185 km²).
Population (July 1983): 24,907,100.
Chief Cities: (1981 census): Ottawa, the capital, 295,163; Montreal, 980,354; Toronto, 599,217.
Government: *Head of state*, Elizabeth II, queen; represented by Edward Schreyer, governor-general (took office Jan. 22, 1979). *Head of government*, Pierre Elliott Trudeau, prime minister (took office March 1980). *Legislature*—Parliament: Senate and House of Commons.
Monetary Unit: Canadian dollar (1.231 dollars equal U.S. $1, Oct. 19, 1983).
Gross National Product (second quarter 1983 C$): $384,400,000,000.
Economic Indexes: *Consumer Prices* (July 1983, 1981 = 100), all items, 117.9; food, 112.7; *industrial production* (March 1983, 1975 = 100) 114.
Foreign Trade (1982 C$): *Imports*, $66,239,000,000; *exports*, $84,577,000,000.

Candidate				Ballot
	1st	*2nd*	*3rd*	*4th*
Brian Mulroney	874	1021	1036	1584
Joe Clark	1091	1085	1058	1325
John Crosbie	639	781	858	
David Crombie	116	67		
Michael Wilson	144			
Peter Pocklington	102			
John Gamble	17			
Neil Fraser	5			

Canapress Photo Service

Controversial Finance Minister Marc Lalonde moved to the right in his April 1983 budget, courting big business.

With a safe seat vacated by a supporter, Brian Mulroney won easy entry to the House of Commons in August from the Nova Scotia riding of Central Nova. Continued Conservative strength was better illustrated in British Columbia where a Tory candidate, Gerry St. Germain, regained Mission-Port Moody from the NDP. Conservatives began to feel confident that victory would be theirs in a 1984 federal general election.

Such confidence might be premature. Marc Lalonde, who took over the federal finance ministry in 1982, moved sharply to the right in his April 1983 budget, courting business by abolishing or modifying many of the reforms of his predecessor and charming critics by a smooth attentiveness to their wishes. On the other flank, Monique Bégin, minister of national health and welfare, made herself the defender of Canada's popular Medicare scheme, increasingly eroded by provincially imposed user-fees and widespread overbilling by medical practitioners. Since Conservative or sympathetic governments were in power in 8 of the 10 provinces, Brian Mulroney and his parliamentary caucus could only blame the Liberals for not providing enough money. The new Conservative leader also had to find a compromise between his own support, as a Quebecer, for bilingualism in Manitoba, and passionate hostility to French language rights among many of his Western backers.

Smaller parties also posed a challenge. New Democrats survived their own regional splits at a biennial federal convention at Regina, Saskatchewan, defied much media speculation by confirming their own leader, Ed Broadbent, and hoped for fresh labor support as unemployment and falling real wages hurt their working-class constituency. In Quebec, where Joe Clark had hoped to make real gains through his opposition to Canada's new constitution, Brian Mulroney faced not only Liberals but a new federal version of the separatist Parti Québécois, the Parti Nationaliste, launched in October.

In late 1983, Mulroney appeared determined to win power because of the government's unpopularity, not by asserting his own ideas. Beyond a ritual insistence that cooperation between labor and management, Ottawa and the provinces, East and West, is preferable to confrontation, he said little. Only in external affairs did the new Tory leader take a distinct stand, preaching closer U.S. links, major defense spending, and blunt rejection of Trudeau moderation on Cold War issues.

The Economy. As usual, the economy shaped both news and politics in 1983. In the headlines, continuing high unemployment, reaching 12.8% in December 1982 and falling only to 11.8% in August, overshadowed news about declining inflation and reviving business confidence. A group of Catholic bishops began the year with a blunt attack on both business and government for deliberately favoring "the wants of the rich over the needs of the poor." There was little practical echo of their militant sentiments, although a short-lived riot in Campbellton, N.B., pitted unemployed local workers against Quebecers who crossed the provincial border to take jobs. Unions lost members and influence except in the reviving auto industry, where ground lost in givebacks was partially recovered.

In Ottawa, the Trudeau government looked to business and the United States to bring recovery. The 1982 "6 & 5" restraint program, limiting as many workers as Ottawa could control to 6% and 5% wage increases, continued. Most Canadians told pollsters that they doubted the program had worked; they also insisted that it continue. Although public employees' wages had been behind private sector wage settlements since 1977, the public continued to believe that its employees were overpaid. Restraint was popular. In July, British Columbia's Social Credit government sought to capitalize on opinion when it unveiled a radical program abolishing rent controls, the human-rights commission, and 25% of all civil-service jobs. Protected, Ottawa and the other provinces pursued more restrained restraint programs. Only Manitoba, with an NDP government, bucked the trend, inviting its employees instead to contribute to a $200 million jobs fund.

A new Royal Commission on the Economic Union and Development Prospects for Canada began its work of seeking consensus and charting a national course into an age of high technology and fierce international competition. Cynics argued that it was only a vehicle for its chairman, Donald Macdonald, a potential successor to Pierre Elliott Trudeau as Liberal leader. Others argued that Canada needed new ideas. In response to obvious government failure to meet its goal of "high and stable levels of employment," Lloyd Axworthy, another leadership hopeful, warned Canadians that job-sharing might be the only way to produce employment for millions of Canadians. Axworthy, who at the time was head of the employment and immigration ministry, found himself shifted to the department of transport in the prime minister's late-summer cabinet shuffle.

Tough economic times took the bloom off high-tech firms in computers, mass transit, and aerospace. Hardest hit was the state-owned Canadair of Montreal, whose new Challenger executive jet left it a record C$1.4 billion in the red for 1982. The alternative, Ottawa warned, was to forget any Canadian role in high technology.

Resources. Key sectors of the Canadian economy which remained hard hit in the worldwide recession included the resource industries. British Columbia's radical assault on its public sector owed much to continued weakness in the market for its forest products. Mining was hard hit by a continued slump in base metal prices; workers, unions, and entire communities felt the impact. On both coasts, the fishing industry faced disaster, though for different reasons. On the Pacific, over-fishing threatened salmon stocks with extinction. Proposals to cut the fishing fleet were complicated by stubborn opposition by fishermen themselves and by the U.S. Senate's refusal to ratify a badly needed U.S.-Canadian fishing agreement. On the Atlantic coast, the latest of many inquiries and commissions, headed by Michael Kirby, recommended drastic restructuring of an overexpanded, debt-ridden industry. Provincial governments, notably that of Newfoundland's Premier Brian Peckford, echoed the protests of fish companies, ports, and fishermen whose future would be affected by the Kirby recommendations. Only the arrival of receivers from an impatient Bank of Nova Scotia forced a compromise. In the outcome, Nova Scotia and Newfoundland each emerged with a single large company controlling the provincial fishing industry, with capital and management furnished by Ottawa, the provinces, and the banks.

While the 15-year struggle between Newfoundland sealers and their critics ended in defeat for the industry, other environmental causes did not fare well in 1983. Nova Scotia landowners, fighting aerial spraying of chemicals banned in the United States, lost their case and expected to lose their property to pay

THE CANADIAN MINISTRY

Pierre Elliott Trudeau, prime minister
Allan Joseph MacEachen, minister of external affairs
Jean-Luc Pepin, minister of external relations
Jean Chrétien, minister of energy
John Munro, minister of indian affairs and northern development
H. A. (Bud) Olson, government leader in the Senate
Herb Gray, president of the treasury board
Eugene Whelan, minister of agriculture
André Ouellet, minister of labor
Marc Lalonde, minister of finance
Romeo LeBlanc, minister of public works and housing
John Roberts, minister of employment and immigration
Monique Bégin, minister of national health and welfare
Jean-Jacques Blais, minister of national defence
Francis Fox, minister of communications
Pierre De Bane, minister of fisheries and oceans
Hazen Argue, minister of state for the wheat board
Gerald Regan, minister of state for international trade
Mark MacGuigan, minister of justice
Robert Kaplan, solicitor general
Pierre Bussieres, minister of national revenue
Charles Lapointe, minister of supply and services
Yvon Pinard, president of the Privy Council
Ed Lumley, minister of industry
Donald Johnston, minister of state for economic development, science, and technology
Lloyd Axworthy, minister of transport
Judy Erola, minister of consumer affairs and minister responsible for the status of women
Jack Austin, minister of state for social development
Charles Caccia, minister of environment
Serge Joyal, secretary of state
Bennett Campbell, minister of veterans affairs
Roy MacLaren, minister of state (finance)
Roger Simmons, minister of state for mines
Celine Hervieux-Payette, minister responsible for fitness and amateur sport
David Collenette, minister of state for multiculturalism
David Smith, minister of state for small business and tourism

heavy costs and damages. The cross-border campaign to curb emissions that produce acid rain had a promising start and then faltered when U.S. industrial lobbyists countered the acid rain coalition in Washington, and Ontario Hydro, a major acid rain contributor, turned to coal-fired generation when some of its CANDU nuclear reactors had to be shut down for repairs. The United States and Canada did sign an acid rain study agreement in August and a pact to further reduce phosphorous pollutants in the Great Lakes in October.

External Affairs. Environment and resource issues helped bring Canadian external policies closer to home. While Trudeau paid an extensive visit to Southeast Asia early in the year, his most important and friendly contacts were with Washington. The sharp philosophical differences on economics and the Cold War which had once sharply separated the Liberal government and the Reagan administration eased to the vanishing point as bemused Canadians heard their prime minister insist to the U.S. president that there were no differences between the two nations.

There were certainly differences among Canadians as the disarmament movement focused on preventing testing of the U.S. Cruise missile at the Primrose Weapons Testing Range in northern Alberta and Saskatchewan. By the time the government chose a quiet summer weekend to announce that testing would proceed, months of anti-Cruise campaigning had had the paradoxical result of increasing support for Cruise testing. When the Korean Airlines Flight 007 was destroyed by Soviet fighters in early September, Ottawa cancelled Soviet flying rights, delivered reprimands, and demanded compensation for its own ten dead citizens.

Ottawa's policies, were predicated on public mood and Canada's hosts of economic hostages to Washington's goodwill, from potato exports to trucking licenses. Lumber exports from British Columbia were not barred from the United States, and Canada's share of the auto-trade agreement, after years of massive deficits, moved into the black when American consumers again began buying the big car models which Canadian factories were still making. In tough times, it paid to be realisitc, a message Prime Minister Trudeau delivered to Third World leaders in October. By demanding the whole loaf in their North-South negotiations, he told them, they had received no bread. There was no sign in 1983 that his new obsequiousness to Washington had offended most Canadians. On the contrary, as usual in tough times, their customary nationalism had faded. They were bemused when, in late 1983, Ottawa suddenly talked of Canada's role of peacemaker.

People. In 1983, amid the preoccupations of economics and political leadership, some old issues and a few new ones surfaced. By opening abortion clinics in Winnipeg and Toronto, Dr. Henry Morgenthaler challenged the law and provoked rival mass demonstrations by pro-Life and pro-Choice supporters. Manitobans were also torn by an even older issue, bilingualism. Aware that the courts could throw out every provincial law since 1890, when Manitobans had unconstitutionally abolished French as an official language, the Pawley government worked out a compromise with Manitoba's tiny French-speaking minority and attempted to sell it to the majority. The NDP government's Conservative opponents took up the challenge and probed the depths of anti-French feeling in the province. Other ethnic minorities, in effect a majority in Manitoba's multiracial society, largely supported the NDP government. A provincial dispute became national when Prime Minister Trudeau sought to involve the new Tory leader in the issue. A compromise allowed all three federal parties to back the Manitoba initiatives, while Brian Mulroney's antibilingual caucus members sat silently. A potential embarrassment for the new Tory leader was sidestepped.

DESMOND MORTON
Erindale College, University of Toronto

In early March, Britain's Queen Elizabeth was in Vancouver, B.C., to mark the beginning of construction on EXPO 86.

UPC

The Economy

The year 1983 marked the beginning of a cyclical upturn in the Canadian economy, which, having gone through the most serious recession since the 1930s, was on the mend. The real gross national product (GNP), after a sharp decline by 6.5% during the six consecutive quarters of 1982–83, took an upturn at an annual rate of 7.6% during the first two quarters of the year. This was spurred by a growth in consumer spending, a healthy increase in housing starts, rising inventories, and improvements in manufacturing capacity utilization. At year's end it was almost certain that the economy was poised for a stronger-than-expected recovery.

The tide of inflation was stemmed. During the second quarter of the year, annual wage increases, which constitute a potential source of inflation, were settled at 5.9%, way down from the 14% of the fourth quarter of 1981. The overall Consumer Price Index (CPI) for September remained at 5% above a year earlier. In the regulated sector, however, prices of goods and services—which constitute 23% of CPI and include items such as alcohol, cable vision, and dairy products—were still increasing by 9.2% in August.

The Canadian fight against inflation, however, has inflicted enormous social costs in the form of double-digit unemployment rates. With 1.2 million people officially out of work, elements of fear and passive acceptance have emerged among the unemployed. Though in part current unemployment is due to technological displacement, higher labor force participation rate, and increased foreign competition from such Pacific countries as Japan, its major cause lies in government experimentation with monetarism. The experiment has brought high interest rates and precipitated a dramatic decline in investment spending by firms and households. Some relief in the unemployment situation was in sight by late 1983. The first two quarters of the year witnessed a significant upsurge in the level of economic activity. Consumer spending, for example, grew rapidly in the second quarter with an annual growth rate of 5.9% as compared with 3.5% in the first quarter mainly because of a strong sales performance for durable goods, autos, furniture, and appliances. Similar strength was recorded by spending on residential construction, which soared as housing starts grew when home buyers took advantage of the federal government's $3,000 new home grants.

The external sector showed a sharp buoyancy as the strengthening U.S. economy induced higher Canadian exports. In money terms, the merchandise surplus reached a record high annual rate of C$20.7 billion, up from $16.7 billion in the first quarter. Capital spending during the year was expected to reach C$73.8 billion, up about 1.4% from an early 1983 projection. The third quarter profit margin after tax of 100 companies surveyed by the *Financial Post* was up 3.2% from 1.4% a year earlier, and investors' confidence in the economy showed somewhat of an improvement.

R. P. SETH, *Mount Saint Vincent University*

The Arts

Canadian art groups began the year wondering what effect the report of the Federal Cultural Policy Review Committee would have. The committee spent two years investigating Canadian culture, at a cost of C$3.5 million. Its report, released in November 1982, was called the Applebaum-Hébert report (and nicknamed "Applebert") after the committee's cochairmen, composer Louis Applebaum and author Jacques Hébert. The report recommended increased government aid for a wide variety of groups. It also recommended drastic action for two major elements of the arts, the Canadian Broadcasting Corporation (CBC) and the National Film Board (NFB). The report criticized the CBC and said it should return to its role as encourager of Canadian culture. To that end, it recommended that CBC television retain its news programs but give up all commercials and sell most of its studios to private producers, who could then sell their products to CBC. As for the NFB, Applebert recommended it cease almost all production and instead become a school for filmmakers and a center for film research.

Effects of the report, however, have been minimal. A Canadian government beset with economic woes had no extra money to encourage artistic endeavors. The drastic actions proposed for CBC and NFB did not come to pass. Furthermore, at the annual Academy Awards in Hollywood, CBC television won an Oscar in the feature-length documentary category for *Just Another Missing Kid*. NFB won an Oscar

CONSUMER PRICE INDEX

September 1983 vs Year Earlier

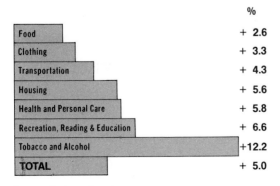

	%
Food	+ 2.6
Clothing	+ 3.3
Transportation	+ 4.3
Housing	+ 5.6
Health and Personal Care	+ 5.8
Recreation, Reading & Education	+ 6.6
Tobacco and Alcohol	+12.2
TOTAL	+ 5.0

Source: Statistics Canada

in the short documentary category for *If You Love This Planet,* a film that gained publicity when the U.S. Justice Department decreed that it be labeled political propaganda.

As the year waned, most Canadian art groups decided that, like so many other government reports, Applebert did not appear destined to move from recommendations to actions.

Visual Arts. A bright spot on the arts landscape was the October 15 opening by Governor-General Edward Schreyer of the new Vancouver, B.C., Art Gallery at Robson Square. The gallery's new home is the 72-year-old former courthouse building, magnificently remodeled at a cost of $20 million. Two shows opened the new gallery: *Vancouver: Art and Artists,* a retrospective of 50 years of art in Vancouver, and a collection of masterpieces from the National Gallery of Canada.

The gallery's old home at 1145 West Georgia Street, built in 1931 for $100,000, had become seriously inadequate. The new gallery is world class, with four times the exhibition space of the old one. The soaring, glass-domed rotunda of the old courthouse was retained and beautified in the new gallery, which has a large basement level and four stories above.

The gallery's pride is its collection of 188 works by Canadian artist Emily Carr, including 147 drawings and paintings, together with ceramics and sketchbooks. These will be permanently displayed on a rotating basis.

Architect of the classical old courthouse was Francis Rattenbury, who designed the legislative buildings in Victoria, B.C. Architect of the remodeling was Arthur Erickson, whose modern courthouse, with an enormous sloping glass roof, is next to the gallery.

The new gallery has two other enviable attributes: its remodeling costs were within budget and, thanks to a profitable sale of the old gallery, it has an $8 million endowment. Half the interest on the endowment will go toward running expenses, and half toward buying works of art.

In Cobourg, Ont., a much older building, the 123-year-old Victoria Hall, the city's original town hall, was reopened after an 11-year campaign by the Society for the Preservation of Victoria Hall. The society raised $6 million to have the Victorian structure completely restored. The building now houses the Art Gallery of Northumberland. The rebuilt concert hall was opened with production of a musical, *Tracks,* a lively look at Cobourg's history in the 1850s, written by bp nichol and Mary Burton.

Forty magnificent paintings by Dutch masters were shown at the Art Gallery of Ontario in Toronto. On tour from the Royal Picture Gallery at The Hague, they included works by Vermeer and Rembrandt. They had already been shown in four U.S. cities. Alex Colville's retrospective exhibition also appeared at the Art Gallery of Ontario, before moving to Montreal, Halifax, and Vancouver and to Berlin and Cologne, Germany.

The year's biggest art work was undoubtedly *Ranch,* Allan Wood's creation on a 320-acre (130 ha) ranch in a valley south of Calgary, Alta. The buildings were constructed of brightly painted canvas on wooden supports. Nonpoisonous paint was used in case cattle and wild animals developed a taste for Wood's art. *Ranch,* which cost an estimated $500,000, required 60,000 yd (54 600 m) of canvas and 1,200 gal (4 550L) of paint. The beautiful surroundings with their natural colors contrasted effectively with Wood's vivid canvas structures.

Highly successful artist Toni Onley scheduled a public burning of 1,000 of his prints, worth about $1 million, to protest tax regulations that categorized him as a manufacturer whose unsold works had to be assessed for taxation. However, he canceled the burning when federal Communications Minister Francis Fox promised him tax regulations for artists would be reviewed.

Performing Arts. The 31st season of the Stratford Festival saw a splendid *As You Like It,* directed by John Hirsch and designed by Desmond Heeley, with Roberta Maxwell and Nicholas Pennell outstanding as Rosalind and Jaques. Other hits were Brian Macdonald's production of *The Gondoliers* and *Tartuffe,* directed by John Hirsch.

The Shaw Festival at Niagra-on-the-Lake included this trio by Shaw: *O'Flaherty, V.C.,* directed by Paul Reynolds, with Dan Lett in the title role; *The Simpleton of the Unexpected Isles,* directed by Denise Coffey, with Tom Wood and Douglas Rain in leading roles; and *Candida,* directed by Bill Glassco, with Goldie Semple as Candida and striking sets by Astric Janson. The Ben Travers farce, *Rookery Nook,* directed by Derek Goldby, was well received, as was a repeat of the previous year's success, *Cyrano de Bergerac,* directed by Goldby.

The renovated St. Lawrence Centre in Toronto reopened with Tom Stoppard's *On the Razzle,* directed by Edward Gilbert. Alan Lund, artistic director of the Charlottetown Festival, took *Singin' and Dancin' Tonight,* a revue comprising 45 Canadian songs, on a countrywide tour.

Television. Pay TV came to Canada in February with World View Television, a multilingual channel; First Choice, a movie and sports channel whose presentations included Playboy Enterprises films; and C Channel, the only pay TV channel in the world devoted to cultural events, such as opera and ballet. Four months later C Channel went into receivership, having only 25,000 subscribers and debts of $11 million. In April, Canadian Satellite Communications in Whitehorse, Yukon Territory, began broadcasting television to the Canadian north.

DAVID SAVAGE, *Simon Fraser University*

CARIBBEAN

The two major events of 1983 in the Caribbean stood in marked contrast. The first was the passage by the U.S. Congress of President Ronald Reagan's Caribbean Basin Initiative (CBI), giving the Caribbean islands and Central American countries a 12-year period of duty-free entry into the United States for a variety of their exports. The second was the "invasion" of Grenada by U.S. troops, accompanied by a small contingent from six eastern Caribbean states (*see* feature article, page 28). If the invasion was, as many believed, an assertion of American power in a critical region close to the United States, the passage of the CBI seemingly signified the willingness of the United States to assume responsibility for the economic well-being of the same area.

CBI. The CBI was approved by Congress in late July, nearly one and a half years after the legislation first had been introduced. In President Reagan's original proposal, the CBI had three principal sections: 1) an emergency supplemental foreign-aid appropriation of $355 million for currency support; 2) duty-free entry into the United States for exports, except textiles and apparel, from Caribbean basin countries; and 3) tax incentives for U.S. firms investing in manufacturing plants in the region. The 97th Congress passed the first part but failed to act on the others.

When the legislation was reintroduced in the 98th Congress in early 1983, the provision for investment tax incentives had been eliminated. In its place was a clause permitting U.S. businessmen to claim income-tax deductions for expenses incurred at conventions in CBI-eligible countries. In the final version approved by Congress, the list of products denied duty-free entry was expanded to include, in addition to textiles and apparel, footwear, handbags, luggage, flat goods, work gloves, leather apparel, canned tuna, petroleum and petroleum products, and certain watches and parts. The legislation excluded "Communist-ruled" countries from duty-free benefits, a provision that appeared to affect Nicaragua and probably would have excluded Grenada had the U.S. incursion not taken place. Cuba was specifically excluded.

Independence. The dual-island federation of St. Christopher (St. Kitts) and Nevis achieved independence from Great Britain on September 19, bringing to 12 the number of independent former British colonies in the region. The new nation quickly became a member of the United Nations but withdrew its application for membership in the Organization of American States (OAS) when it became apparent that Latin American countries in the OAS would block the application in retaliation for St. Christopher's support of the Grenada action.

Anniversary. The Caribbean Common Market (CARICOM), the regional economic integration organization of the former British Caribbean colonies, marked its tenth anniversary by convoking a meeting of heads of government in Port-of-Spain, Trinidad, beginning July 4. The government leaders noted that considerable progress had been made in the past decade in promoting intraregional trade and in addressing common problems in such fields as transportation and education. But it was also recognized that many problems remain. The economic recession had led many CARICOM governments to introduce restrictions on imports and to manipulate currency exchange rates. The leaders also took note of the dangers of a festering border dispute between one of its members, Guyana, and neighboring Venezuela.

Earlier in the year, heads of 16 Caribbean governments met with Canadian Prime Minister Pierre Trudeau to discuss Canada's development assistance to the region. Trudeau reaffirmed Canada's commitment to double its aid to $350 million over the next four years. U.S. aid, meanwhile, also continued to rise. Jamaica became the third-highest per capita recipient of U.S. aid (after Israel and El Salvador). In fiscal 1982, Jamaica received $143.5 million in U.S. funds. In fiscal 1983 the United States committed $125 million in direct aid, $102.3 million in Export-Import Bank credits, and $68 million in commodity credits.

Haiti. Rumors circulated in Haiti that President-for-Life Jean Claude Duvalier was seriously ill and planned to leave the country for medical treatment. The rumors were fueled by changes in the Haitian constitution establishing provisions for presidential succession and procedures for the temporary replacement of the president in case of absence or illness. Officials denied the rumors.

In April the Haitian government, working with the Inter-American Institute for Cooperation in Agriculture (IICA), began a campaign to kill 200,000 of the nation's pigs in an effort to check an outbreak of African Swine Fever. A reforestation program, designed to restore tree cover to Haiti's denuded mountain slopes, planted its 2 millionth tree at midyear. The program is funded by the U.S. Agency for International Development and managed by the Pan American Development Foundation.

Dominican Republic. Economic activity began to pick up in the Dominican Republic, which shares the island of Hispaniola with Haiti. President Salvador Jorge Blanco announced that the economy had grown 4% in the first half of 1983, compared with a rate of 0.6% in the same period of 1982. The government successfully renegotiated $800 million in payments due on its foreign debt and obtained a $450 million, three-year loan from the International Monetary Fund. Imports were restricted.

RICHARD C. SCHROEDER, *"Visión" Magazine*

The Contadora Group, including (l–r) the presidents of Colombia, Honduras, and Panama, offered various peace plans.

CENTRAL AMERICA

Pope John Paul II made an eight-nation visit to Central America in March 1983, preaching reconciliation and the integrity of the family but making little progress in soothing the bitterness that grips so much of the region. In the United States, both public opinion and the Congress were divided on questions of intervention and increased military aid to Central American governments and rebel forces fighting a Marxist regime.

In May, President Ronald Reagan replaced Assistant Secretary of State for Latin American Affairs Thomas O. Enders, apparently for not being tough enough with the Sandinista government in power in Nicaragua and the rebels in Guatemala and El Salvador. But at about the same time, President Reagan appointed former Florida Sen. Richard B. Stone (*see* BIOGRAPHY) to be his special envoy to Central America for the purpose of holding discussions with all political factions in the hope of finding some grounds for peace talks.

A new element appeared during the year—the so-called Contadora Group, consisting of Mexico, Venezuela, Colombia, and Panama, allied with five Central American states (El Salvador, Nicaragua, Honduras, Guatemala, and Costa Rica). Their delegates met several times with peace proposals and hoped to agree on treaties that might disarm the tensions of the region.

President Reagan created a 12-member National Bipartisan Commission on Central America in May, headed by former Secretary of State Henry Kissinger, to conduct a fact-finding study and to advise the president on long-range solutions to Central American problems. The president also signed into law his Caribbean Basin Initiative, proposed in 1982. The measure included 12 years of free trade for many products entering the United States from Caribbean states, fiscal incentives for investment, increased economic aid, technical assistance, and coordination of development programs with other aid-granting states. The trade benefits were effective in January 1984.

At the end of the year the major new developments appeared to be a growing disenchantment on the part of the Reagan administration with the failure of the Salvadoran government to end assassinations there, and with the inability of the Nicaraguan rebels to occupy and hold any Sandinista territory. At the same time the show of force in Grenada in October seemed to have convinced the Nicaraguan junta that a U.S. invasion was just a matter of time, perhaps explaining the junta's sudden discussion of an election in 1985, as well as the departure from Nicaragua of thousands of Cubans.

Belize. As the people of Belize celebrated the second anniversary of its independence, the government announced the availability of a $10 million loan from the United States under the Caribbean Basin Initiative program. The aid was especially welcome because little else in the way of assistance was forthcoming, and the market for sugar, a major export, was weak.

In the face of a strong United Democratic Party, which polled 47% of the votes in the 1979 elections, Prime Minister George Price had to hold together growing factionalism in his People's United Party. In spite of disorders in neighboring states and the presence of several thousand refugees from El Salvador and Guatemala, Belize was free from guerrilla movements as it prepared for elections in 1984.

President Efraín Ríos Montt of Guatemala reiterated that since his country claimed Belize and did not recognize its independence, he would negotiate only with Great Britain over the matter of a boundary revision. Prime Minister Price reportedly favored giving Guatemala access to the sea through Belize but would not yield "one square centimeter of territory." In October, Belize was invited to attend sessions of the Organization of American States (OAS) in Washington as an observer, but Guatemala opposed the entrance of Belize into the OAS until the territorial "dispute is settled in Guatemala's favor."

The United States never had much interest in Belize while it was a British colony, but the relationship of the two countries has become much closer since Belize became independent. In April, President Reagan appointed Malcolm R. Barnebey as the first U.S. ambassador to Belize, and the ambassador has encouraged the new nation's participation in the Caribbean Basin Initiative.

Costa Rica. While most Central Americans continued their preoccupation with military struggles, Costa Ricans seemed more concerned with the state of their nation's economy, just as they were in 1982. Some economic progress has been made, but old and new financial problems have bedeviled the country. The per capita foreign debt was one of the highest in the world, and the nation remained about $500 million in arrears in interest payments. The social-security system had trouble meeting its obligations, unemployment hovered at 10%, and inflation occasionally reached triple digits.

Coffee and banana prices were lower, and one multinational corporation complained that Costa Rican production costs were among the world's highest. The three major banana producers threatened to pull out unless export taxes were reduced. Livestock and beef prices also were down, and tourism declined greatly. The rising cost of living provoked many strikes in August and September, with workers asking for raises up to 2,500 colones a month and receiving about 450 as a maximum.

Costa Rica is an obvious candidate for aid under the Caribbean Basin Initiative program, but by late 1983 little effect was visible. The International Monetary Fund (IMF) advanced $100.6 million in standby credit in December 1982, and the United States promised $160 million for 1983 and nearly as much for 1984, the largest amount granted to any country in Central America except El Salvador. In September the IMF granted Costa Rica a loan of $19.5 million to help offset reduced export earnings.

The U.S. Army's Southern Command in Panama offered to build a 200-mi (321-km) network of roads and bridges, with Costa Rican assistance, along the Nicaraguan border. Details had not been worked out by late 1983, but President Luis Alberto Monge was reported studying the consequences of this help, which would obviously aid Costa Rica's economy as well as its defense. President Monge received

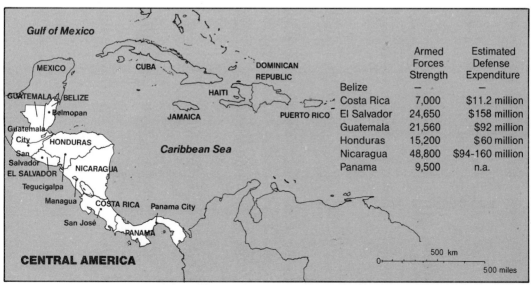

	Armed Forces Strength	Estimated Defense Expenditure
Belize	—	—
Costa Rica	7,000	$11.2 million
El Salvador	24,650	$158 million
Guatemala	21,560	$92 million
Honduras	15,200	$60 million
Nicaragua	48,800	$94-160 million
Panama	9,500	n.a.

Map designed by Blackbirch Graphics; source of defense information, the International Institute for Strategic Studies

CENTRAL AMERICA · Information Highlights

Nation	Population (in millions)	Area (sq mi)	(km²)	Capital	Head of State and Government
Belize	.154	8,870	22 973	Belmopan	Elmira Minita Gordon, governor-general George Price, prime minister
Costa Rica	2.6	19,691	51 000	San José	Luis Alberto Monge, president
El Salvador	4.7	8,265	21 400	San Salvador	Alvaro Magaña, president
Guatemala	7.7	42,039	108 880	Guatemala City	Oscar Humberto Mejía Victores, president
Honduras	4.3	43,301	112 150	Tegucigalpa	Roberto Suazo Córdova, president
Nicaragua	2.8	57,104	147 900	Managua	Daniel Ortega Saavedra, junta coordinator
Panama	2.0	29,204	75 650	Panama City	Ricardo de la Espriella, president

criticism from the Left that he was too pro-American, and his foreign minister, Fernando Volio Jiménez, resigned in November over Monge's alleged lack of neutrality. In May, Costa Rica had asked the OAS for a contingent of troops from Venezuela, Mexico, Panama, and Colombia to guard the northern frontier because Costa Rica had disbanded its army in 1949.

Nicaragua regularly protested that Costa Rica had become a haven for anti-Sandinista refugees plotting the overthrow of the Nicaraguan government. Costa Rica deplored the presence within its borders of an estimated 150,000 exiles from all over Central America—a situation that produced a great burden on the nation's resources and caused often bitter animosity at the personal level, even when official relations remained amicable. Nicaraguan exiles, especially, were described as in "lamentable health," the most serious medical problem being malaria. In September, Nicaragua pro-

tested that planes from Costa Rica had bombed Nicaraguan airbases, but Foreign Minister Volio denied the charges. In November, President Monge officially proclaimed Costa Rica's policy of "permanent" neutrality.

El Salvador. The civilian government of Alvaro Magaña did little to change conditions in El Salvador in 1983 as that nation entered its fourth year of civil war. The administration could keep the rebels from holding towns and cities but could not eliminate their successful attacks when the army turned its attention elsewhere. Nor could the president put an end to the assassinations being carried out by right-wing death squads. In one week in November the army admitted killing 100 civilians, including women and children classified by the government as subversives. In four years politically motivated murders may have reached 45,000. The United States was considering sanctions to bring significant improvement in the country's human-rights record, but it did not force an immediate change.

Except for Egypt and Israel, no nation received more economic aid from the United States, yet the rebellion showed no sign of being brought under control. Changes were made in the general staff without consequence, and on at least one occasion 1,200 soldiers mutinied against the government. On May 25, U.S. Navy Commander Albert A. Schaufelberger, deputy chief of the 55 American military advisers in El Salvador, was murdered in his car. The case was not settled by late 1983, nor was that of the three American nuns and a lay worker who had been murdered in 1980.

The Reagan administration seemed to feel that the only practical solution was more American funds, weapons, and training for the Salvadoran troops, and it battled with Congress over these matters. One consequence was to begin training some 2,400 Salvadoran troops in Honduras, meeting most congressional objections but increasing tensions between Honduras and El Salvador.

During his visit in March, Pope John Paul II was told by President Magaña that elections for president and other offices would be held in December 1983, but in November, Magaña said they would be held in March 1984.

In El Salvador soldiers continued to protect themselves from sniper fire as the civil war was in its fourth year.

UPI

UPI

Brig. Gen. Oscar Humberto Mejia Victores became president of Guatemala after a coup and promised elections in 1984.

The land-reform program, begun in 1980 at American insistence, made little progress in 1983. One union claimed that 10,000 peasants had been evicted from land once given to them. Other farmers were able to make a start on new plots, but prices were low, interest rates were high, and markets were weak as the economy continued to suffer from the civil war.

Guatemala. After less than 18 months in office, beleaguered President Efraín Ríos Montt was driven from power on August 8 in a nearly bloodless coup. He was replaced as chief of state by Gen. Oscar Humberto Mejía Victores, the minister of defense. Ríos Montt had been president since March 1982, when he acquired that position also by a bloodless coup.

Ríos Montt had promised improvements for his country. A strongly religious man, he had declared war on immorality in office and probably did bring some favorable changes. On March 23 he lifted the state of siege imposed in June 1982, giving some evidence that human-rights conditions were improving, but he remained vague about the date of elections and continued to permit the functioning of secret courts with power to issue the death sentence.

In June he faced a barracks revolt but suppressed it by transferring some military units and granting concessions to a number of high-ranking officers. He also was forced to disband a group of junior officers who had been his personal advisers. Ríos Montt weathered another coup in July by removing several dozen officers from their high-level government jobs and announcing plans for an election in July 1984. In all he faced down seven rebellions of some sort until he was ousted in August.

As president, Ríos Montt had been an anomaly in Central American annals. A member of a Protestant church headquartered in Eureka, CA, he held very strict fundamentalist beliefs. His successor, Gen. Mejía Victores, a career officer with 35 years of service, probably is more conservative than Ríos Montt. He once served on the staff of President Romeo Lucas García, whose administration was charged with the murder of thousands of Guatemalans. The usual juggling and chair-switching occurred in the new government, but the direction of these changes remained unclear in 1983. The press seemed to be somewhat freer than under Ríos Montt, but Mejía Victores gave evidence that he would be very critical of the Catholic church for "cooperating with subversives." His major problem, however, would be whether he could control the military.

Human-rights conditions scarcely improved during the year. In 1982 the rector of the University of San Carlos had been murdered, and in 1983 some 34 persons connected with the school were missing. In July, Ríos Montt's sister was kidnapped, and in September the sister of the new president also was taken captive. Neither president would negotiate, and at the end of October both women reportedly were released by the leftists who had taken them. In March six political enemies were executed by the Ríos Montt government, despite the pope's plea for mercy.

The government's ruthless campaigns had nearly rid Guatemala of opposition, but it had also driven thousands of Indians from their villages into southern Mexico. The Indians—whose numbers have been variously estimated from 10,000 to 100,000—were living poorly in 30 camps across the northern border of Guate-

Nicaraguan troops were on the lookout for Honduran-based rebels who launched attacks against the Sandinista regime.

Atlan/Sygma

mala, straining relations with Mexico. Guatemala has urged the Indians to accept the government's offer to return home safely, but the Indians have remained unconvinced.

In 1977, President Jimmy Carter had criticized the Guatemalan government for its human-rights record, and in retaliation Guatemala refused to accept further military aid. Since that date almost all U.S. military aid has been suspended. President Reagan has wanted to resume the assistance ever since Ríos Montt took office, but the necessary conditions required by Congress have not been met. In late November 1983, the United States told the new Guatemalan regime that continued abuses of human rights had also reduced economic aid.

Honduras. One of the Central American peace treaties signed at the Washington Peace Conference of 1907 provided that Honduras would remain neutral in the many Central American conflicts and prohibited military action within its boundaries. That treaty has long since been dissolved, but many Hondurans would favor its revival. On one border is the enemy of the 1969 Soccer War, El Salvador, plus left-wing Salvadoran rebels who would like to see the Honduran government overthrown. On another border is Marxist Nicaragua, using all its propaganda to spread communism to Honduras.

In 1983, Honduras became a major target of Cuban subversion as that nation allegedly was training some 300 rebels to overthrow the government of President Roberto Suazo Córdova. Also in 1983 the army bypassed the administration and made an agreement with the U.S. government to have Americans train Salvadoran troops on Honduras soil. This plan came about because the U.S. Congress would not approve training Salvadoran troops in El Salvador, and felt that bringing them to the United States would be too expensive.

Tensions increased in the summer when the number of Salvadorans training on Honduras' north coast was increased to about 2,400 just as President Reagan announced plans for "Big Pine II," the largest of a number of joint military exercises staged in Central America since 1965. The combination of Salvadoran troops and the vast American operation frightened many Hondurans. Nevertheless, Hondurans and Green Beret troops rapidly began the modernization of facilities at Trujillo and Puerto Castilla on the north coast and at San Lorenzo overlooking the Bay of Fonseca. The number of Americans involved and the precise nature of their equipment remained classified, but it appeared that about 5,000 men were engaged in war games and that they were participating in amphibious training in cooperation with elements of the U.S. fleet, including battleships, on both the Atlantic and Pacific coasts of Central America.

By Central American standards, Honduras has fairly strong unions and a free press, but next to Haiti it is the poorest nation in Latin America. In addition to the many international problems, President Suazo Córdova faces perhaps 20% unemployment and per capita incomes that average about $500 annually. World prices of bananas and coffee sagged again in 1983, the external public debt has risen steadily since 1978, investment is weak, and the gross domestic product has declined for the first time in many years. Before it could receive increased credits from international lending agencies, Honduras was directed by the IMF to reduce its spending. Many Hondurans hoped that "Big Pine II" would at least improve some of the backward infrastructure, if not the overall economy.

In Nicaragua, Sandinistas accused Honduras of harboring exiles who plotted to overthrow the Nicaraguan regime while remaining secure behind the protective shield of U.S. troops. In August, when Nicaragua declared itself unable to meet payments on a trade deficit, Honduras suspended grain shipments. On the north coast, new roads helped local farmers and merchants, but in the wake of the Ameri-

Nicaragua's Daniel Ortega told visiting Pope John Paul II that one can be "both a believer and a revolutionary."

UPI

can maneuvers came inflation, and many opponents of the Suazo Córdova administration sought the end of the American presence.

Nicaragua. In March, during Pope John Paul II's trip to Central America, the pope said Mass in Nicaragua for an estimated 500,000 people. The Sandinista government treated him very coolly; in turn, he attacked the so-called "people's church" and admonished the faithful to strict obedience to the bishops.

The pageantry of the pope's tour and the continuing military struggles on the Nicaraguan borders could not conceal the critical changes in the nation's economy during 1982 and 1983. For the first time since the Sandinistas took office in 1979, the gross domestic product not only failed to grow significantly, but it actually declined by about 1.5%. Construction and mining were the worst-affected sectors. The contraction came from a sharp decline in investments and exports. High unemployment, price controls, and large increases in government spending contributed to this malaise. Some of the few remaining private businesses, such as sugar producers, were hurt by U.S. sanctions. The government could boast that it had reduced illiteracy and infant mortality meaningfully, and that some 60,000 peasants had been given allotments of land.

During the year the Sandinistas exhibited growing concern for their nation's security. Declaring the need to "counter CIA efforts" to destabilize the administration, the military junta in July extended the state of national emergency for another year, effectively limiting freedom of expression, speech, and travel.

On the Costa Rican border, Edén Pastora Gómez, leader of the Democratic Revolutionary Alliance and a former member of the junta, disdained help from the United States but spoke of how the Marxists had betrayed the revolution and caused him to withdraw from that government. The rebels refused to cooperate with the larger Nicaraguan Democratic Forces on the Honduran border, which received substantial amounts of U.S. military assistance but bore the stigma of support from the former Somocistas. Between the two groups they claimed the deaths of some 500 government troops in 1983 and pushed the nation into plans for universal military service. Neither faction yet proved able to hold conquered territory for any period of time.

Although the United States and Nicaragua expelled members of each other's diplomatic corps, relations were not broken. Richard Stone, President Reagan's envoy to Central America, continued to meet Nicaraguan officials in search of some means to ease tensions.

By October it appeared that U.S. pressure on the Sandinista regime was increasing. President Reagan admitted Central Intelligence Agency (CIA) complicity in rebel attacks on government oil storage tanks near Corinto, threatening the nation's oil supply. Nicaragua then proposed treaties to curtail Central American arms traffic, but the United States exhibited little interest in bilateral talks. In December the government announced an amnesty program for most Nicaraguans who had fled the country after the Sandinistas came into power in July 1979.

The U.S. actions in Grenada in October clearly distressed the Nicaraguan junta. Perhaps in a move to forestall similar action in Nicaragua, thousands of Cuban advisers, including teachers, left for home in November. When operation "Big Pine II" expanded into massive war games in nearby Honduras and along the Nicaraguan coast, the Sandinistas became even more nervous about the future.

Panama. As he had announced in the spring, Gen. Rubén Darío Paredes del Rio resigned his position as commanding general of the Panama National Guard—traditionally the strongest post in the nation—and declared his intention to run for president in the elections scheduled for the summer of 1984. A new constitution provides for the first direct election since 1972. A conservative, Gen. Darío Paredes has the support of the ruling party in Panama. By late 1983 no other candidate had announced. Gen. Manuel Antonio Noriega took command of the National Guard.

In March, Pope John Paul II visited Panama during his Central American tour. His well-attended Mass was devoid of political comment.

The 1978 treaty with the United States is gradually changing the Canal Zone as Americans leave and are replaced by Panamanians. The canal continues to function smoothly, and it is regularly utilized to capacity. The Canal Zone treaty also calls for the closing of the military school at Ft. Gulick, called the School of the Americas, unless the two nations agree to extend its life after October 1984. The school greatly aids the Panama economy.

A member of the so-called Contadora group, Panama played an active role in attempting to resolve the disputes between the Nicaraguan government and the Reagan administration. In October, Panama officials met with the Kissinger fact-finding commission to brief it on some of the regional problems. A more sensitive issue, resulting in the firing of the vice-president, is the degree of Panama's participation in the Central American Defense Council (CONDECA). The council is opposed by some Panamanians because of its early ties with the Somocistas and the U.S. Army.

Panama's major exports of petroleum derivatives, bananas, shrimp, and sugar all declined in 1982–83, while the government protested that the sales of smuggled Taiwanese goods at very low prices were cutting into legitimate trade and creating unemployment.

THOMAS L. KARNES
Arizona State University

CHAD

The civil war that appeared to end with the occupation of Ndjamena, the capital city, by Hissène Habré's Forces Armées du Nord the previous year escalated in early 1983. Deposed President Goukouni Oueddei, who had fled to Libya, managed to reconcile his differences with other dissidents and raised a substantial army. Backed by Libyan ground and air units, his new force attacked southward and in May took the oasis town of Ounianga. Security in Ndjamena was maintained by a 200-man Zairois contingent, which allowed Habré's main force to defend the north; reinforcements were rushed to the regional capital of Faya-Largeau, Habré's birthplace. Nevertheless, the rebels and Libyans captured Faya-Largeau in late June, and Oueddei's army pressed on toward Abeche near the border with Sudan.

Libyan intervention and the loss of Faya-Largeau focused world attention on the war, and Chad became an arena for international power politics. Although vigorously denied by Libya's President Muammar el-Qaddafi, Libyan troops with Soviet-built tanks and planes played a key role in Oueddei's victories. The U.S. government in early May warned of Libyan participation and took the lead in mobilizing outside support for Habré. President Ronald Reagan denounced Qaddafi's imperialism and dispatched AWAC aircraft, supported by fighters, to Sudan. Made available to Habré was $25 million in U.S. aid, including 30 Redeye antiaircraft missiles for Chad's forward troops. President Mobutu Sese Seko of Zaire sent more troops to police the rear echelons. Skirmishes between Nigerian army units and Habré's forces in the Lake Chad area were ended in June, and Nigeria lent its support to the United States, the Organization of African Unity (OAU), and the United Nations, who were trying to arrange a cease-fire.

The major unknown factor in the equation in early July was the attitude of France. President François Mitterrand, a Socialist who had been critical of his predecessor's Chad policy, was at first reluctant to make any specific commitments. U.S. officials were critical of Mitterrand's neutral stance at a time of potential disaster for Habré. This pressure and the worsening military situation prompted Mitterrand in August to commit French ground and air units to defend central and southern Chad. By September more than 1,000 French troops had been airlifted to Chad, with an expected main force of 3,000. Equally important was the dispatch of Gazelle attack helicopters and fast, heavily armed Jaguar fighter-bombers. Many of the French troops were sent immediately north to reinforce the defense line. The aircraft were used also in minor attacks warning the Libyan and rebel forces not to pass further south. The French reinforcements and U.S. pressure caused the Libyan government to be more tractable, and the rebel advance was halted. On August 26, President Mitterrand explained that his objective was to stop the rebel occupation of heavily populated southern Chad; French troops would not be used to retake the north. He joined with leaders of most African states, who wanted a negotiated settlement. By October it had become apparent that Oueddei and Qaddafi were not eager to challenge the French and seemed amenable to reconciliation if negotiations were supervised by the OAU. Unofficial reports from Paris that a division of Chad between contending forces might be the solution were denied by all concerned parties.

See also AFRICA.

HARRY A. GAILEY
San Jose State University

Zaire's President Mobutu (left) toured Ndjamena with President Habré "to show that Chad does not stand alone."

UPI

CHAD · Information Highlights

Official Name: Republic of Chad.
Location: North-central Africa.
Area: 496,000 sq mi (1 284 640 km²).
Population (July 1983): 4,990,000.
Chief Cities (1979 est.): Ndjamena, the capital, 303,000.
Government: *Head of state and government,* Hissène Habré, president (seized control June 7, 1982).
Monetary Unit: CFA franc (381.88 CFA francs equal U.S.$1, June 1983).
Gross National Product Per Capita (1981): $328.

CHEMISTRY

Chemical events in 1983 included the re-emergence of an old controversy over an ion's structure, the extension of measurements to ultrafast times and greater sensitivities, and a new process for producing polymers.

Norbornyl Cation. At a symposium of the American Chemical Society held in Seattle in late March, a controversy that had simmered for more than two decades boiled over again. The controversy had its genesis in experiments reported by the late Saul Winstein of the University of California at Los Angeles 34 years earlier. Winstein studied reactions of derivatives of norbornane, a compound of 7 carbon atoms and 12 hydrogens with an unusual, bridged structure. In examining reactions of two structurally similar starting norbornanes, he found that one reacted roughly 400 times faster than the other, yet both reactions produced the same end products—an expected compound and its unexpected mirror image. To explain his peculiar results, Winstein focused on the nature of a short-lived intermediate in the reaction, the norbornyl cation. (A cation is a chemical species with a positive charge.) He proposed that the positive charge of this intermediate was "smeared out" over a three-carbon ring in its structure, rather than localized on one carbon atom. Because Winstein's picture was at variance with then-popular views of bonding, it was termed "nonclassical."

The question of the cation's structure was important both from a theoretical viewpoint and because similar species occur in commercially important processes. In 1962, Herbert C. Brown of Purdue University proposed an alternative explanation of Winstein's results. Brown asserted that the experiments also could be explained by supposing a coexistence of two classical forms of the cation with the positive charge located first on one carbon atom and then another, and rapidly hopping back and forth. This proposed quick interconversion came to be called the "windshield-wiper rearrangement," because a bond would simultaneously flip from one carbon to the other. Brown argued that the nonclassical cation picture had been too readily accepted, and steric factors might cause the different rates.

George A. Olah at the University of Southern California has become the main protagonist of nonclassical viewpoint. Concurrent with Brown's original proposal, Olah began to develop methods for capturing the cation intermediates as stable forms. Subsequent spectroscopic examinations of the cations by Olah and others appear to have convinced most chemists that the nonclassical picture is correct. At the Seattle symposium, Olah termed evidence for the nonclassical structure to be "unequivocal" and declared the topic a closed issue. Brown argued that attention should be focused on the solution reaction rates and that measurements of the cation under other conditions (needed to keep it stable) are irrelevant to the rate question.

Measurements. Scientists use the prefix "femto" to refer to a millionth of a billionth, or ten to the negative 15th power. Advances in instrumentation now permit chemical phenomena to be examined on a time scale of femtoseconds. C. V. Shank and colleagues at Bell Laboratories in New Jersey reported the creation of light pulses as short as 30 femtoseconds. Initial applications were to examine ultrafast changes of the semiconductor gallium arsenide and the polymer polyacetylene after exposure to the short light flashes. An even more exotic prefix is "atto," meaning a billionth of a billionth, or ten to the negative 18th power. Workers at Los Alamos Scientific Laboratory reported that they had pushed detection limits of the already sensitive laser-induced fluorescence technique into the attogram region. Using a modified flow system, they achieved a detection limit of just 28 attograms for the dye rhodamine 6G in water. This corresponds to 35,000 molecules.

Polymers. Polymers are large molecules, usually chains, formed by chemically linking smaller molecules, monomers, together. Examples include plastics, synthetic rubber, and synthetic fibers. In late August 1983, duPont Company chemists announced a new polymer production method that promises to give chemists more control of the product, reduce expenses, and cut pollution. The process is called "group transfer polymerization," and involves migration of an activating trimethylsilyl group to the growing chain end during each monomer addition step. Chains continue to grow so long as monomer is fed in. By varying the added monomer, considerable flexibility and control appear possible, with mild reaction conditions. Furthermore, since more concentrated monomer solutions are used and all monomer is consumed, there is less wastage than presently.

The "Octet Rule." The "octet rule" states that in forming compounds, atoms such as carbon and oxygen tend to surround themselves with eight valence electrons. However, when such atoms combine with lithium the octet rule is not necessarily followed, according to theoretical calculations by Paul Schleyer and co-workers at Erlangen, West Germany, and John Pople of Carnegie-Mellon University, Pittsburgh. The octet rule explains the combination of carbon with four lithium atoms, but the calculations predict that stable compounds also should form with either five or six lithium atoms about the central carbon. Earlier these researchers had made similar predictions of "hypervalent" compounds of oxygen and lithium. Experimental evidence supporting the predictions is available for some species.

PAUL G. SEYBOLD, *Wright State University*

Wide World

Mayor Washington and the candidates defeated in the primary, Byrne and Daley, right, attend a unity luncheon.

CHICAGO

Chicago's big story in 1983 was named Harold Washington (*see* BIOGRAPHY). In becoming the city's first black mayor, the former congressman ousted incumbent mayor Jane M. Byrne in the February 22 Democratic primary and narrowly squeezed out former State Rep. Bernard Epton in the April 12 general election. The Washington-Epton battle attracted nationwide attention for its emphasis on the race issue. Another victim of Washington's success was Cook County State's Attorney Richard M. Daley, who hoped to follow in the footsteps of his late father; Daley finished third in the Democratic primary.

Conflict in the City Council. Washington's dramatic election ended the cozy, rubber-stamp relationship that had existed for years between the mayor's office and the City Council. The new mayor vowed to do away with "politics-as-usual," but the white majority bloc in the council did not give in even though all of the aldermen were fellow Democrats.

The fireworks started at the first council meeting May 2. Mayor Washington, sensing opposition to his efforts to give black aldermen more power, abruptly adjourned the meeting and walked off the floor. Twenty-nine white aldermen, led by Cook County Democratic chairman Edward R. Vrdolyak, quickly reconvened the meeting and pushed through new rules and committee assignments. The 21-member minority bloc of liberal black and white aldermen cried foul and joined with Washington in challenging the new council organization in the courts.

For weeks legislation was at a stalemate. Ultimately the Illinois Supreme Court held for the majority bloc, and the new mayor said he would abide by the ruling and respect the "loyal opposition" within his own party. Nonetheless, the feud between Washington and the "Vrdolyak 29" continued. The majority bloc voted down most of the legislation the mayor wanted; the minority faction supported the mayor all the way. For weeks the two sides squabbled over efforts by Washington to fire hundreds of city employees to balance the corporate budget.

Washington moved slowly in naming his own people to important city positions, but the predominantly white political machine that had long ruled Chicago gradually began to crumble. The city got its first black police superintendent and an Hispanic as fire commissioner.

Education. For the sixth time since 1969, the Chicago Teacher's Union went on strike October 3. Unlike previous disputes, the mayor would not intervene in salary negotiations with the city board of education, and the job action went on until October 25, when the 27,000-member union agreed to a 5% wage increase.

In August, President Ronald Reagan vetoed a $20 million congressional appropriation to help Chicago implement a federally mandated school-desegregation plan. Civil-rights groups criticized the action. The administration also appealed a federal-court order that the government pay $14.6 million to desegregate Chicago schools.

Fairs and Festivals. The city's continuing budget crunch forced the mayor to cancel city sponsorship of ChicagoFest, a summertime festival of food and entertainment at Navy Pier. A private group took over sponsorship but lost money as attendance plummeted.

Chicago was chosen in 1983 by the Bureau of International Expositions to host one of two world's fairs in 1992 celebrating the 500th anniversary of Columbus' discovery of America; the other will be held in Seville, Spain. It was the first time the world body sanctioned two world expositions to be held at one time. Plans call for the Chicago fair to be at Meigs Field.

ROBERT ENSTAD, *"Chicago Tribune"*

CHILDREN

The number of children in the United States, which declined from 1970 to 1980, is on the rise. The U.S. Census Bureau projects that by 1990 the under-18 population will reach 64,300,000, up nearly one million from the 1980 census figure. And with the increase has come growing concern about issues that directly affect children. Four such issues were in the fore in 1983—poverty, day care, abduction, and the persistent problem of child abuse.

Poverty. The number of children living at poverty and near-poverty levels rose dramatically from 1980 to 1983. According to the Congressional Budget Office, poverty rates for children fell from 27% to 16% through the 1960s and 1970s but then jumped to almost 20%. In April 1983, Congressional Budget Office Director Alice M. Rivlin told the House Select Committee on Children, Youth, and Families that more than a fourth of U.S. children lived in households with incomes below 125% of the poverty level.

According to Rivlin and other experts, two factors—high unemployment and an increase in the number of single-parent families—were to blame for the rising poverty rate. The proportion of children in single-parent families roughly paralleled the poverty rate, rising from 13% in 1970 to 21% from 1970 to 1983.

Nonpayment of child support was cited as a major burden for these families. Census figures released during the year showed that fewer than half of women awarded child-support payments were receiving the full amount. Actions to enforce payment—mediation, jailing fathers, and the use of IRS computers to track them down—met with limited success. During 1983, the federal government and some states were working on plans to deduct late payments from tax refunds.

The outlook for poor children was not bright. Noting that welfare benefits have "declined significantly," Rivlin told the congressional committee, "The number of children living in poverty will probably remain high in the near future and may continue to increase."

Day Care. For many families, finding someone to watch the children while the parents are at work has emerged as a major concern. Half of U.S. mothers now work outside the home, census figures show, and about 7 million children aged 6 or under are in some kind of day-care arrangement.

Arrangements range from care at relatives' or neighbors' homes to live-in housekeepers. Increasingly, however, parents are turning to the nation's more than 22,000 child-care centers. Many centers are run by churches or nonprofit groups. But, sensing a growing market, a number of large, for-profit day-care chains have entered the field. One of the largest is Kinder Care, which in 1983 operated nearly 800 centers in 38 states and Canada. And about 500 employers provide day care for their workers.

Day-care costs, meanwhile, averaging $60 to $70 a week, have become a major item in family budgets. Federal budget cuts have forced many centers that serve poor families to restrict their programs. Another concern is the quality of care offered. In most states, there are few restrictions on day care. And the question of how day care affects young children remains unanswered. Some experts say children in day care develop more quickly; others contend that there's no place like home.

Missing Children. Roughly 50,000 children are abducted by strangers each year in the United States, according to government and private estimates. Between 20,000 and 40,000 of these cases go unsolved.

The federal Missing Children's Act, signed into law in October 1982, set up procedures for parents of missing children to file information with the Federal Bureau of Investigation, for use in the FBI's computers. As an outgrowth of the new law, voluntary fingerprinting programs were started for children in more than a dozen states in 1983. The prints, which would provide police with a method of identifying missing children, were to be turned over to parents or filed with the police.

New Jersey alone fingerprinted 45,000 children in the first three months of its program, reflecting wide acceptance by parents of fingerprinting. But the fingerprinting programs also were criticized for creating an atmosphere of fear. And some critics charged that prints on file with the police could be misused, involving children in criminal investigations.

Child Abuse. The number of reported cases of child abuse topped 950,000 in 1982 and threatened to hit the 1 million mark in 1983. In the mid-1970s, by contrast, less than half that many cases were reported. Officials credited much of the alarming increase to greater public awareness of child abuse and greater willingness—on the part of schools, hospitals, social agencies, and police—to report it. Still, they estimated that 75% to 90% of child-abuse cases were unreported.

Two kinds of child-abuse services gained favor in many communities during the year— crisis centers and hot lines. The centers provide temporary housing for abused children. Hot lines offer counseling for parents, who can call anonymously.

But the problem remains both pernicious and difficult to solve. Children who are abused often grow up to repeat the pattern with their own children. Law enforcement agencies are often at a loss because the line between a spanking and an illegal beating is blurry. Further, police and social agencies often disagree on whether a family should be broken up, to prevent further abuse, or counseled together.

ELAINE P. SEDITO, *Free-Lance Writer*

CHILE

Surprise concessions to civilians opposed to continued military rule followed renegotiation of the $17 billion (U.S.) foreign debt and numerous business failures brought about by a recession said to be the worst since 1930.

Government and Politics. In response to a series of monthly protests, the government of Gen. Augusto Pinochet Ugarte had agreed to lift the state of emergency and curfew on Aug. 29, 1983, which had been in effect since 1973. The government allowed citizens to organize meetings without police approval, and amnesty was granted to 1,160 exiles living abroad. Among several hundred returning out of an estimated 10,000 exiles were Christian Democratic leaders Renán Fuentealba, Andrés Zaldívar Larraín, and Jaime Castillo Velasco; Carlos Podlech, chairman of the National Wheat Producers Association; and Cesar Godoy Urrutia, an 81-year-old former Communist Party deputy. On August 10, Pinochet named a majority of civilians to the cabinet for only the second time since the military assumed government control in September 1973. It was the fifth shuffle in a year.

Beginning May 11, party leaders, businessmen, labor, and farm leaders united to stage one-day-a-month protests. Thousands of Chileans protested in the streets of Chile's largest cities despite curfews and the arrests of organizers such as Gabriel Valdés Subercaseaux, president of the outlawed Christian Democratic Party, and Rodolfo Seguel, the 29-year-old head of Chile's copper workers. (Later charges against Valdés were dropped.) Other citizens showed their anger by setting street bonfires, honking car horns, and beating pots and pans in a fashion similar to that of the protests staged by Chileans against the regime of Salvador Allende Gossens in 1973.

Several senior military officers were known to be disturbed by the high unemployment that had idled between 20% and 30% of the labor force and by charges of corruption involving the president's daughter and son-in-law. Air Force Gen. Fernando Matthei Aubel, also a member of the ruling junta, said it was time for Chile to "open a political debate" and said his troops would not participate in further repression of peaceful protesters. Naval commanders also refused to use force to quell demonstrations in Valparaíso, Chile's principal port city. However, on August 11–12, at least 27 persons were killed, scores wounded, and more than 1,000 arrested by 18,000 army troops, quelling that month's demonstration. In early September the government extended the emergency powers for six months.

Newly appointed Interior Minister Sergio Onofre Jarpa Reyes also held meetings with representatives of the Democratic Alliance, an informal coalition of leaders of the Republican Right, Social Democrats, Christian Democrats, Radicals, and Socialists. In September he said that parliamentary elections could take place by the end of 1984.

The Economy. The International Monetary Fund (IMF) and the Bank for International Settlements (BIS) agreed to several short-term loans to help ease Chile's financial difficulties in January and March after the government had allowed foreign-exchange reserves to decline to $1.74 billion. In September, the IMF and 20 consortia of about 600 banks agreed to a new repayment schedule for $3.6 billion in principal and $2 billion in interest due in 1983.

The Chilean government agreed to increase import tariffs from 10% to 20%, to refinance 30% of the debt of small businesses up to a maximum of about $350,000, and tightened foreign-exchange controls in "parallel markets."

Copper exports increased to $905.3 million between January and July 1983, or 5% more than in the same 1982 period. Shellfish and seafood exports were also expected to increase in 1983 beyond the $410 million exported in 1982. The Central Bank reported exports totaling $2.24 billion for the first seven months of 1983 compared with imports of $1.53 billion.

Foreign Relations. France recalled its ambassador on May 18 "for consultations" following the arrest of more than 1,500 persons in the May 11 demonstrations. French Foreign Minister Claude Cheysson accused the Chilean regime of many violations of human rights. Spanish Ambassador Mariano Fontecilla expressed his government's concern over the May 11 demonstrations to Chile's Foreign Minister Miguel Schweitzer. The Swedish chargé d'affaires was summoned to the foreign ministry after the Swedish government publicly criticized the Pinochet government regarding the August protests.

While Foreign Minister Schweitzer delivered an "energetic note of protest" over the August 17 landing of Argentine marines on one of the Hermanos Islands in the disputed Beagle Channel, Interior Minister Jarpa downplayed the incident prior to talks in Buenos Aires.

NEALE J. PEARSON, *Texas Tech University*

CHILE • Information Highlights

Official Name: Republic of Chile.
Location: Southwestern coast of South America.
Area: 292,133 sq mi (756 624 km²).
Population (July 1983 est.): 11,486,000.
Chief Cities (June 1982 est.): Santiago, the capital, 4,039,287; Viña del Mar, 290,014.
Government: *Head of state and government,* Gen. Augusto Pinochet Ugarte, president (took power Sept. 1973). *Legislature*—Congress (dissolved Sept. 1973).
Monetary Unit: Peso (83.85 pesos equal U.S.$1, floating rate, Nov. 4, 1983).
Gross Domestic Product (1982 U.S.$): $26,032,-000,000.
Economic Index (1982): *Consumer Prices* (1970= 100), all items, 552,122; food, 592,957.

CHINA, PEOPLE'S REPUBLIC OF

Chairman Deng Xiaoping remained China's paramount leader with a firm hold on military power, but the election of a new head of state (president) represented a further effort to shift from the Maoist type of cultist personal rule to formal institutionalism.

Industrial modernization continued to be the chief objective of China's economic policy. But budget deficits caused by industrial renovation made it necessary to limit the spending of individual enterprises on capital construction. To spur agricultural production, China allowed peasants to retain more profits.

China had serious disputes with the United States but stopped short of irremediable crises. It held talks with the Soviet Union but was reluctant to make any major agreements. Though determined that Cambodia was not to be suppressed, it avoided large-scale war with Vietnam. Peking stressed nonalignment and supported the Third World in its struggles against foreign domination.

Domestic Affairs

People's Congress. The sixth session of the National People's Congress, China's nominal parliament, was convened June 6 in Peking (Beijing). A major item on the agenda was the election of China's new president, an office that had been vacant for 15 years. The last president, Liu Shaoqi, was purged by Mao Zedong during the Cultural Revolution. The post was then abolished but reinstated in the constitution in 1982, in which it was given largely ceremonial functions.

Li Xiannian, 78-year-old former finance minister and deputy premier, was elected president by the People's Congress on June 18; he was the only candidate for the post. A veteran revolutionary, Li had played an important role in China's economic planning during the early years of the Communist regime. He was skeptical of Deng Xiaoping's economic policy, especially its emphasis on light industry over heavy industry. In giving him the largely ceremonial office, Deng was in fact easing him out of the inner circle of power. Ulanhu, 77, an ethnic Mongolian and a member of the Politburo, was designated vice-president; the original candidate had been Liao Chengzhi, who died eight days before the pro forma balloting. Peng Zhen, 81, was named chairman of the Standing Committee of the People's Congress, to succeed Ye Jianying, who, at 85, finally retired for reasons of "age and failing health." Marshal Ye had resisted Deng's call in 1982 that "old comrades" step down to make way for younger men. Somewhat influential in the army, he had been considered an obstacle to Deng's policies. As expected, Zhao Ziyang was reappointed premier.

Deng Xiaoping was elected chairman of a new State Military Commission to handle day-

The sixth session of the National People's Congress, right, China's nominal parliament, met for 17 days in June 1983. A report on the work of the government during the previous five years and readjustments to the current five-year plan were features of the session. In addition, Li Xiannian, below, former finance minister and deputy premier, was appointed president, a mostly ceremonial post last occupied in 1968.

Photos UPI

to-day military affairs. Already chairman of the Communist Party's Military Commission, Deng's appointment further consolidated his military power.

Deng and Rectification. The publication of the *Selected Works of Deng Xiaoping* in July was hailed by the Chinese press as a "major event in the political life of the Chinese people." The book received the kind of lavish praise once reserved for Mao Zedong. But the publication was not intended to herald a personality cult; rather, it was a statement of Deng's thoughts that should serve as guidelines for the Chinese Communists.

In October the Communist Central Committee called for a "rectification" campaign to weed out corrupt, incompetent, and radical cadres. The campaign would include the screening of the party's 40 million members and the reregistering of only those who met the party's new standards of ideology. It would eliminate leftist Maoist remnants and recruit more scientists, technicians, and other educated men and women who could effectively carry out Deng's pragmatic policies and ideological objectives.

The Military. China's military program centered on modernization of equipment and training. Outdated weapons and poor command and control systems required extensive renovation if China were to face a modern war. Peking directed its attention to such crucial areas as development of strategic guided missiles and production of nuclear fuel and bombs.

To ensure central control and remove leftists hostile to its policies, Peking had begun a military reorganization in 1982. By January 1983, Deng's trusted generals had been placed in the commands of five key military areas: the Wuhan region in central China, the Canton region in the south, the Chengtu region in the southwest, the Nanjing region in the east, and the Lanzhou region in the northwest.

Crime and Punishment. As crime became more widespread, China took stern measures against persons committing embezzlement, bribery, fraud, and smuggling. Severe punishments for rather light offenses were given wide publicity to warn other culprits. Those condemned to death for murder, rape, robbery, and arson were paraded through crowded streets before execution. Especially troublesome was rapidly growing youth crime in several provinces. Thousands of young men and women who had been dispatched to the remote countryside to "learn" from peasants sneaked back to the cities, where they were unable to get employment because of lack of status as legal residents. Many became hoodlums and took to stealing, mugging, and robbing. In June 1983 more than 15,000 young persons were rounded up and returned to rural areas. Ruffianism spread even to youths aged 14–18, especially from labor and peasant families.

Economy. China remained committed to industrial modernization, but it found that the growth of revenue could not keep up with the demands of renovation. The state budget for 1983 was expected to run a deficit of about $1.765 billion (U.S.), with expenditures amounting to about $74.235 billion and revenues about $72.470 billion.

China's economic growth target for 1983 was set at 4%. Light industry was emphasized over heavy industry, whose production had risen sharply in 1982, upsetting the government's plan of restraint. The 1983 plan cut back steel production but called for increases in coal and oil output, considered essential to industrial growth.

The budget deficit in 1982 was in part caused by the failure to control production of heavy industrial goods and investment in capital construction. This in turn was due to freedom given to localities and factories to plan their own developments. To rectify the situation, Peking urged close adherence to guidelines issued by the central government and stricter approval requirements for individual projects. But many enterprises ignored the government's instructions, and, to the chagrin of Peking, heavy industrial production in the first quarter of 1983 rose 11.7%, while light industry registered only a 6.9% growth.

Incentive. To increase state revenues, China decided to spur productivity through an incentive program. The government was to tax the produce of state-owned enterprises and then divide the profits with them. Previously, the state had taken all the profits; now industrial managements were expected to exploit their own resources to make profits of which they would keep a share. The new system was a success in both industrial and agricultural sectors. It helped cut costs and provide better benefits for workers.

The new agricultural policies introduced by the Deng administration began to pay off in China's farmlands. Simply by encouraging the nation's peasants to work harder and earn more, the regime was able to increase crop yields. The government had raised farm prices and allowed producers to keep whatever they grew above the portion allotted to the state. Farmers also were permitted to take part in sideline enterprises that produced such basic goods as bricks, bottles, shoes, and clothing. Meanwhile the government phased out the commune system and emphasized the family as the basic unit of farm production.

Culture and Control. China's opening to the outside world and its absorption of Western technology and industrial methods brought in powerful capitalist influences. The displacement of rigid Maoist control by a more flexible system further encouraged independence and deviation. The result was confusion not only at the ideological level but also in practical life. In

Guangdong province, which borders the British colony of Hong Kong, the urge for money-making and hedonism brought so much smuggling and corruption that the government had to launch a campaign against "capitalist vices."

Under the Deng leadership, Chinese writers and artists were allowed more independence than before. Satires soon appeared that mocked contemporary Chinese society by the use of ancient stories. On July 20 the official *People's Daily* issued stern warnings against the "impure" tendencies of the literary community, which "indulged in bourgeois liberalism and individualism, in total disregard of the people's interests."

Seeing the importance of technical experts to China's program of modernization, Deng Xiaoping called for special recognition of science and technology professionals. On March 28, 1983, Communist China for the first time conferred doctoral degrees on 18 scientists. Peking had sent 16,000 students abroad, including 10,000 to the United States, for technical studies. Nevertheless, hostility toward intellectuals as a remnant of Maoist tradition still prevailed in rural areas and the army.

Foreign Affairs

United States. The Taiwan question remained an obstacle to further improvement of Sino-U.S. relations. U.S. President Ronald Reagan affirmed that the United States would not turn its back on Taiwan and that it would continue to sell arms to Taipei until the People's Republic peacefully resolved the dispute over the island. Peking, however, continued to oppose the arms sales and demanded that the United States cut off official and semiofficial relations with Taiwan.

In an attempt to ease the tension, U.S. Secretary of State George Shultz arrived in Peking on February 2. After four days of discussions, however, important differences between the two sides remained unresolved. Besides the Taiwan issue, the Chinese also complained about U.S. restrictions on Chinese textile imports and the difficulty of buying certain advanced technology that required special licenses.

In July 1982, 19-year-old Chinese tennis player Hu Na defected during a tournament in Santa Clara, CA. She applied for political asylum on the grounds that Chinese officials had been trying to coerce her into joining the Communist Party and that she feared being caught up in political struggles in China. When the U.S. Justice Department granted her asylum in April 1983, China issued a strong protest, declaring that the American action was "a grave incident harming the relations between the two countries." It proceeded to cancel 19 cultural and sports exchange programs sponsored by the U.S. government for 1983. The cancellation did not affect Chinese students studying in America, nor did it hold up agreements signed on May 11 for scientific cooperation in the areas of high-energy physics, transportation, aeronautics, and biomedical science.

In late May, U.S. Commerce Secretary Malcolm Baldrige led a delegation to Peking for the first session of the Sino-U.S. Joint Commission on Commerce and Trade. In talks concerning technology with potential military uses, the secretary told his Chinese counterpart, Chen Muhua, that the United States would ease export restrictions through more efficient application of existing regulations. The U.S. pledge did not satisfy the Chinese, however, who called for the removal of all strictures. In June, Washington decided that China could purchase sensitive technology on the same basis as other friendly nations.

On Jan. 15, 1983, after four months of unsuccessful negotiations for a new agreement, the United States unilaterally imposed quotas limiting Chinese textile imports to the 1982 level. Peking immediately retaliated by banning purchases of cotton, soybeans, and synthetic fibers from the United States; it then stopped signing contracts for U.S. wheat. In March the two countries resumed negotiations in Peking, but it was not until August 19 that they came to an agreement under which the growth of Chinese textile imports to the United States would be limited to about 3% a year. Thereupon China lifted its ban on imports of U.S. agricultural and fiber products.

U.S. Secretary of Defense Caspar Weinberger visited Peking in September to seek closer strategic cooperation. China said that it would not attach itself to any power but was willing to cooperate to speed up its military modernization. Peking showed no interest in any exchange of military training programs and was reluctant to buy U.S. arms. It was more inter-

National Defense Minister Zhang Aiping welcomed U.S. Defense Secretary Caspar Weinberger to Peking in September.

UPI

ested in acquiring technology to build weapons systems itself; that would be more economical and at the same time would avoid the humiliation of depending on foreign countries for military equipment. On September 28, at the end of the talks, Weinberger announced that President Reagan and Premier Zhao Ziyang would exchange official visits in 1984.

Western Europe. Squabbles with the United States turned Peking's attention to West European countries. In February, during her trip to Great Britain, France, Austria, and Belgium, China's Foreign Trade Minister Chen Muhua spoke of broad opportunities for foreign investment in China. It came as no surprise when Peking in May awarded a contract for offshore oil exploration to a group of Western firms headed by British Petroleum Co. But the major problem in Sino-British relations was Hong Kong, over which China had repeatedly announced that it would regain sovereignty when the British lease on most of the territory expires in 1997. Several rounds of talks ended without results.

In the first high-level contact between the two nations since 1949, France's President François Mitterrand visited China in May. The meetings had mixed results. Peking had hoped that France would put pressure on Vietnam to remove its troops from Cambodia, but Mitterrand was not prepared to sever ties with Hanoi or back the Cambodian regime in exile. The French were willing to sell Mirage 2000 fighter planes to China, but the Chinese backed out on the ground that they could not afford the high price. Peking did agree in principle to let the French install four nuclear reactors in China for more than $2 billion.

Soviet Union. China resumed talks with the USSR in March 1983, at a time when its relations with the United States became strained over Taiwan. It demanded that Moscow remove three obstacles to the normalization of relations: Soviet support for the Vietnamese occupation of Cambodia, Soviet occupation forces in Afghanistan, and the buildup of Soviet forces along the Chinese border and in Mongolia. Moscow refused to discuss the first

two conditions but indicated some flexibility on troop pullbacks. No breakthrough was expected from the talks, though both sides agreed to treble their trade to about $1 billion. Sports and academic contacts increased, and some steps were taken to reopen two trading posts along the Central Asian border in the Xinjiang region. Peking also agreed to restore border trade between Heilongjiang province and the Soviet Far East.

Japan. China maintained friendly relations with Japan in 1983 and was particularly keen to receive Japanese assistance for its economic programs. During her visit to Tokyo in February, Foreign Trade Minister Chen Muhua requested Japanese loans of about $5.36 billion for industrial construction. In June, Japan agreed to lend China the equivalent of $287 million for the construction of a railway from Yanzhou to Shijiusuo in Shandong province, for the expansion of the Peking-Qinhuangdao railway, and for a petrochemical project in northeast China. The loan, at an interest rate of 3%, was to be repaid over 30 years.

Both China and Japan were strongly opposed to Soviet deployment of SS-20 medium-range nuclear missiles to eastern Asia.

Southeast Asia. Sino-Vietnamese relations became highly tense in March as the two countries accused each other of incursions and provocations. On April 16, China's frontier guards in the Guangxi region shelled Vietnamese barracks "in retaliation for their bombardments." The shelling soon spread to the Yunnan border area. The Chinese attack was obviously aimed at disrupting Vietnam's powerful offensive launched against the Chinese-backed insurgents in Cambodia at that time. In May, Hanoi withdrew part of its force from Cambodia, but Peking demanded withdrawal of all Vietnamese troops.

Africa. Premier Zhao Ziyang began a month-long tour of Africa on Dec. 20, 1982. The journey covered 11 nations—Egypt, Algeria, Morocco, Gabon, Guinea, Zaire, Congo, Zambia, Zimbabwe, Tanzania, and Kenya. Zhao was the first high-ranking Chinese official to visit Africa since Premier Zhou Enlai toured the continent in 1963–64. China wanted to show the African peoples that it was independent of the foreign policy of the superpowers—the Soviet Union and the United States—which were following a course of "hegemony and expansionism." Peking emphasized that it belonged to the Third World and desired to strengthen solidarity with the developing nations. While stressing economic cooperation, Premier Zhao had no major plans to propose and seemed more interested in moderate, practical projects. In Kinshasa, however, the Chinese leader announced that Zaire would not have to repay $100 million lent by China in 1973.

See also TAIWAN (Republic of China).

CHESTER C. TAN, *New York University*

CHINA · Information Highlights

Official Name: People's Republic of China.
Location: Central-eastern Asia.
Area: 3,706,560 sq mi (9 600 000 km²).
Population (July 1983): 1,059,802,000.
Chief Cities (1982 census): Peking, the capital, 9,230,687; Shanghai, 11,859,748; Tianjin, 7,764,141.
Government: *Head of state,* Li Xiannian, president (took office June 1983). *Heads of government,* Zhao Ziyang, premier (took office Sept. 1980); Deng Xiaoping, chairman, Central Advisory Commission. *Legislature* (unicameral)—National People's Congress.
Monetary Unit: Yuan (1.984 yuan equal U.S.$1, June 1983).
Foreign Trade: (1982 U.S.$): *Imports,* $19,529,000,000; *exports,* $21,474,000,000.

CITIES AND URBAN AFFAIRS

Even though the national economy showed strong signs of recovery, 1983 for U.S. cities was a year marked by continued accommodation to economic stress. Politically the year was highlighted by a dramatic increase in black electoral consciousness and the election of a number of black mayors. There were also important policy initiatives in housing, planning, and transportation.

Elections. Perhaps the single most significant event of the year was the rancorous Chicago mayoral election in April. The February Democratic primary pitted incumbent Jane Byrne against Richard M. Daley, the son of the late mayor, and black Rep. Harold Washington. Even though Chicago is only 40% black, the split white vote, combined with an effective black registration drive, gave Washington a primary victory. Though Chicago has not had a Republican mayor since 1927, the 1983 candidate, the relatively unknown white state legislator Bernard Epton, came within 40,000 votes (of 1.6 million cast) of defeating Washington. The election of the Windy City's first black mayor signaled the demise of the once-vaunted Chicago political machine.

In part encouraged by Washington's success, voters in Philadelphia and Boston nominated black candidates for the first time. In Philadelphia, former City Administrator W. Wilson Goode was elected in a campaign that avoided the blatant racism that had characterized the Chicago contest. In Boston, the two candidates who survived the nonpartisan primary to succeed retiring Mayor Kevin White were white Irish Councilman Ray Flynn and black activist Melvin King. Flynn won easily even though King received an impressive 20% of the white vote. Ironically, Baltimore, with a majority black population, overwhelmingly reelected white Mayor Don Schaefer, who has been closely identified with that city's renaissance.

Black mayoral candidates also were successful in Gary, IN, where Richard Hatcher was elected to his fifth term; Charlotte, NC, where Harvey Gantt took an impressive 39% of the white vote; Hartford, CT; and Flint, MI. In Miami, incumbent Maurice Ferre, a Puerto Rican, was reelected to a sixth term in a heated contest with Xavier Suarze, a Cuban. Women incumbents were reelected in San Francisco and Houston, and Donna Owens' election in Toledo was one of the few bright spots for Republicans. Another was the reelection of William Hudnut in Indianapolis.

The registration of black urban voters in record numbers, increasing numbers of white voters willing to vote for black candidates, and the growing number of black, Hispanic, and women mayors all were likely to have a profound impact on urban America. Consequences

© Brad Power/Picture Group
W. Wilson Goode, 45, won Philadelphia's mayoral race.

also were expected nationally as reflected by the presidential candidacy of Jesse Jackson.

Economics and Intergovernmental Relations. Elections were an important but temporary diversion from the ongoing economic and fiscal problems facing U.S. cities. Despite the national economic recovery, two thirds of the cities expected budget deficits by the end of 1983, up from 43% in 1982. Larger cities coped more effectively than smaller cities, which had less budgetary flexibility. The rising deficits were caused by declining federal aid (down to 7% of total revenue from 8.3% in 1982), a loss of tax revenue due to the recession, and an 8% increase in local expenditures. Aid to cities from the states, however, rose 7.4% in 1983. Local communities also helped themselves by raising local taxes, primarily on income and sales rather than property.

Efforts by the cities to become more self-sufficient through imaginative policies, new revenue sources, and service adjustments faced several new challenges in 1983. The most immediate of these was an attempt by the federal government to restrict so-called "back door" subsidies—the indirect aid cities receive as a result of federal tax exemptions and deductions. The major target in 1983 was the tax-exempt municipal bond for private purposes (as opposed to general obligation bonds) and especially the industrial revenue bond (IRB). The federal concern was real, since private-purpose municipal bonds had grown dramatically (600% since 1975). Local governments have relied on the IRB as a major instrument for economic development, providing below-market interest rates for new industrial and commercial enterprises.

Cities also witnessed new problems related to the authority of local governments to raise

179

revenue and make effective policy. One was proposed legislation to deregulate the cable-television industry, restricting the controls local government could exercise. A more pervasive challenge came from a 1982 Supreme Court ruling that threatened the immunity from antitrust suits that local governments have enjoyed in the regulation of taxi fares, ambulance service, waste controls, zoning, and land use, as well as the provision of such services as garbage collection and airport management.

Policy Issues. Baltimore and Miami opened the nation's first new rail transit systems in several years. Voters in Dallas approved a referendum to establish a Dallas Area Rapid Transit (DART) system.

Several cities made important decisions concerning planning, zoning, and development incentives. San Francisco issued a bold new downtown plan that includes height limitations, transfer rights, and developer charges to support low- and moderate-income housing. New York City moved to sell development rights in an effort to save the Manhattan theater district and spur development in targeted areas. Other cities, including Chicago, adopted tax increment financing schemes, permitting public interest projects to be paid for out of dedicated additional property-tax income.

The recovery of the housing market was encouraged by federal legislation emphasizing rehabilitation of existing housing in low-income neighborhoods and new construction for areas in greatest need. The legislation includes an experimental rent-supplement voucher program designed to replace the expensive Section 8 subsidy program terminated in 1982.

Louis H. Masotti, *Northwestern University*

COINS AND COIN COLLECTING

After a decline caused by the economic recession, activity among coin collectors turned upward in 1983.

Heated debate arose over Congressional approval of the Olympic Coin Act. The act authorized striking a $10 gold piece—the first legal-tender gold coin issued in the United States in more than 50 years—and two silver dollars. The legislation stipulates that a surcharge on the coins will be earmarked for the Olympic program. Several numismatic authorities, testifying before the House Banking Subcommittee on Consumer Affairs and Coinage, stressed the importance of attractive designs and efficient marketing for the Olympic issues.

Numismatic authorities also appeared before the Senate Committee on Banking, Finance, and Urban Affairs to comment on the American Gold Eagle Coin Act, which calls for striking a coin similar in design to the $20 gold piece of 1908. In addition, they testified with regard to Senate Bill 269, which provides for

U.S. Department of the Treasury

issuing two legal-tender silver coins. The first, targeted as a collector coin, will resemble the Morgan dollar of the early 1900s; the second, a trade coin, will feature a Liberty design.

Collector interest in the 1982 George Washington commemorative half dollar and in the American Arts gold medallions climbed in 1983. The medallion program, authorized by Congress in 1978, provides for issuing ten medals honoring outstanding Americans in the arts. Those selected for 1983 were the poet Robert Frost and the sculptor Alexander Calder.

National Coin Week, sponsored each April by the American Numismatic Association, received widespread recognition when President Reagan proclaimed that the event should be observed nationally. Created to introduce the public to the pleasures of coin collecting, National Coin Week captures the attention of thousands of collectors.

An outstanding collection of books about Chinese history and coinage, most of them written in Chinese, was acquired by the American Numismatic Association. Assembled by the late Rev. Arthur Braddan Coole, a respected authority on Chinese numismatics, the collection is the world's largest of its kind.

New York City's historic Assay Office, where millions of dollars worth of gold and silver were refined, was auctioned publicly on July 20. The granite-covered structure was closed in 1982, after 50 years of operation, because of cutbacks in federal spending.

In September, to commemorate its 125th anniversary, the American Numismatic Society (as distinct from the Association) held a two-day celebration at its headquarters in New York City. A specially commissioned anniversary medal was struck for the occasion, and a permanent exhibition concerning the history of coinage was officially dedicated.

Barbara J. Gregory, *"The Numismatist"*

COLOMBIA

The first full year in office for Conservative President Belisario Betancur Cuartas saw the almost complete failure of his amnesty plan for Colombia's various guerrilla groups. In fact, guerrilla activity was stepped up. President Betancur's popularity among the masses remained high, however. In foreign affairs, Colombia put increasing distance between itself and the United States, particularly on the issue of U.S. actions in Central America. The drug trade with the United States continued unabated, with a resultant state of near-anarchy in Medellín, Colombia's second-largest city. The Colombian economy showed increasing signs of strain in 1983, as growth slowed from previous years and the nation's debt increased.

Politics. President Betancur's proposal to grant political and legal amnesty to any guerrillas who would voluntarily turn themselves in to government forces was declared a failure by Defense Minister Fernando Landazabal in May. Landazabal blamed the guerrillas for rejecting the government's "fair" offer, but other sources indicated that the harsh treatment meted out to some 200 guerrillas who accepted the government's offer was instrumental in the plan's failure. At the end of May, Otto Morales Benitez, the highly respected president of the Amnesty Commission, resigned, stating his disillusionment with the process. Subsequently, the Colombian army instituted large-scale operations against the guerrillas on several fronts. By the end of the year, the army offensive seemed to have isolated the once-powerful M-19 movement in the eastern plains region of the country. The M-19 suffered a major blow in April when its leader, Jaime Bateman Cayon, was killed in a plane crash near the Panamanian border. A new development was the emergence of a right-wing terrorist group called *Muerte A Secuestradores* (Death to the Kidnappers), or MAS. In February, 163 MAS members, including 11 army officers, were arrested by the government.

In spite of some policy reverses, President Betancur's popularity remained high. In August the president changed his cabinet in an attempt to strengthen his position among both Liberals and Conservatives. Six of the 13 ministers were replaced. The military high command also was shuffled in an attempt to dispel rumors of an impending coup by disaffected military officers.

The deleterious effects of the drug trade continued to be felt in Colombian society. Medellín, the reputed center for much of the trade, experienced more than 1,000 deaths a month, many related to gang wars between different factions in the drug business.

The Economy. Inflation remained a major problem in 1983. The cost of living rose by 10.49% in the first five months of the year, and an annual increase of more than 25% was esti-

An earthquake March 31 destroyed about half the city of Popayán, including the cathedral, and killed 250 people.

UPI

COLOMBIA • Information Highlights

Official Name: Republic of Colombia.
Location: Northwest South America.
Area: 440,000 sq mi (1 139 600 km²).
Population (July 1983): 27,663,000,000.
Chief Cities (1979 est.): Bogotá, the capital, 4,055,909; Medellín, 1,506,661; Cali, 1,316,137.
Government: *Head of state and government,* Belisario Betancur Cuartas, president (took office Aug. 1982). *Legislature*—Congress: Senate and Chamber of Representatives.
Monetary Unit: Peso (78.5 pesos equal U.S.$1, June 1983).
Gross National Product (1981 U.S.$): $34,000,-000,000.
Economic Index (1982): *Consumer Prices* (1970 = 100), all items, 1,092.5; food, 1,333.5.
Foreign Trade (1982 U.S.$): *Imports,* $4,937,000,000; *exports,* $3,235,000,000.

mated. Interest rates dropped slightly, from 28% to 26%. The gross national product (GNP) increased by less than 4%, while foreign debt increased from $9 billion (U.S.) to close to $11 billion. The ratio of debt to GNP increased from 25.4 to 28.4%, but was still well below that of other Latin American nations. In spite of the continuing recession, the Colombian government announced a massive new program of public investment, which called for foreign loans of $7 billion over the next three years.

Foreign Affairs. Colombia continued to be in the forefront of efforts by the Contadora group to mediate hostilities in Central America. In March, Colombia became a member of the conference of nonaligned nations. President Betancur's message to the Williamsburg summit in May called for substantial modification of the world economic order to benefit the poor nations.

Disasters. On March 31, an earthquake killed 250 persons and injured 3,000 in Popayán, in southern Colombia. On July 28, a mudslide killed 160 workers at a dam site 100 mi (161 km) east of Bogotá.

ERNEST A. DUFF
Randolph-Macon Women's College

COLORADO

Colorado workers and taxpayers, who enjoyed high employment and tax relief during the energy boom of the 1970s, encountered some economic problems in 1983 as the recession tapered off.

The Economy. The state registered a civilian unemployment rate of 6.5% in August, as compared with a seasonally adjusted rate of 9.5% for the entire country. While that indicated that Colorado was better off than most states, the rate—which had been 7.2% a year earlier and 5.0% in August 1981—remained disturbing.

While drying up tax revenues, the recession had also increased demands on state services. More than 12,000 people were added to the Medicaid rolls in the first six months of 1983, prompting Gov. Richard D. Lamm to suggest sharp curtailments in the program.

Instead, the Republican-controlled legislature adopted a fiscal rescue package that included a temporary increase in the state sales tax from 3% to 3.5%. The legislature also borrowed from several trust funds and dictated across-the-board budget cuts to meet the shortfall. Confident they had turned a projected deficit of $120 million into a $60 million surplus, the lawmakers adjourned on May 22. However, they had anticipated paying out only $190 million in state income tax refunds through May, whereas laid-off workers, battered businesses, and other recession victims actually increased the refund total to $257 million by the end of that month. Faced with that problem and other

---

COLORADO · Information Highlights

Area: 104,091 sq mi (269 596 km²).
Population (1982 est.): 3,045,000.
Chief Cities (1980 census): Denver, the capital, 491,396; Colorado Springs, 214,821; Aurora, 158,588.
Government (1983): *Chief Officers—governor*, Richard D. Lamm (D); lt. gov., Nancy Dick (D). *General Assembly—Senate*, 35 members; House of Representatives, 65 members.
State Finances (fiscal year 1982): *Revenues*, $3,805,000,000; *expenditures*, $3,635,000,000.
Personal Income (1982): $37,453,000,000; per capita, $12,302.
Labor Force (July 1983): *Nonagricultural wage and salary earners*, 1,345,100; *unemployed*, 111,500 (6.7% of total force).
Education: *Enrollment* (fall 1981)—public elementary schools, 376,043; public secondary, 168,131; colleges and universities (fall 1982), 171,821. *Public school expenditures* (1981–82), $1,731,841,-000.

---

revenue shortfalls, Governor Lamm called a special session of the legislature in September to deal anew with the budget.

The special session passed another tax-increase package of $88 million and trimmed another $60 million from state programs, about half of it by cutting aid to education. The new tax package extended further the half-cent sales-tax increase, doubled the cigarette tax from 5 to 10 cents a package, and eliminated an income-tax credit. Although Colorado was the first state to "index" its income tax to avoid automatic tax increases due to inflation, that feature was temporarily suspended in order to raise more revenue.

Denver Election. In Denver, Federico Peña became the first Hispanic to win the office of mayor when he defeated former District Attorney Dale Tooley in the June 21 runoff election. William H. McNichols, Jr., who had served as mayor for 14 years, finished third in the May primary. Peña immediately began a sweeping reorganization of the city government.

Other Events. Union Oil Company of California continued work on its Parachute Creek plant, hoping for a 1984 opening. The only large oil-shale project still alive in Colorado, the operation enjoys a federal guarantee to purchase $400 million worth of fuel extracted from the shale.

The Air Force won congressional approval to build a $1.2 billion Space Operations Center at Colorado Springs to monitor and control all U.S. military-related satellites.

Sports. Denver fielded a franchise, the Denver Gold, in the fledgling U.S. Football League. In the USFL championship game, held in Denver on June 17, the Michigan Panthers defeated the Philadelphia Stars, 24–22.

"Elwaymania" engulfed the state's sports fans when the Denver Broncos traded with Baltimore for the right to sign star Stanford quarterback John Elway to a five-year, $5 million contract. (*See also* SPORTS—Football.)

BOB EWEGEN, *"The Denver Post"*

COMMUNICATION TECHNOLOGY

An event of great significance in the world of telecommunications occurred in 1983, the initial stage of the restructuring of the Bell System in accordance with a consent decree between AT&T and the U.S. Department of Justice. (*See* special report, page 184.) In technology, the major forces were the growth of digital systems; the extension of photonics in lightwave communication systems for long-distance, transoceanic, and local applications; and progress in the utilization of microprocessors in all elements of the communication network.

Transmission and Switching Systems. AT&T put into operation the largest lightwave communication system in the world, connecting New York and Washington, DC. This initial 372-mi (599-km) link will be extended in 1984 to Boston and Virginia for a total length of 776 mi (1 249 km).

A lightwave communication system uses strands of ultra-pure glass to carry rapid pulses of light from a tiny semiconductor laser or light-emitting diode. The pulses, transmitted at a rate of roughly 90 million times per second, form a digital code which represents the original voice signal in a telephone conversation or the 0-1 (off-on) language of computer, data, and video communications. The AT&T lightwave system can carry up to 80,000 simultaneous conversations in a small 1-cm cable.

Other long-distance lightwave projects are under construction in the United States, Canada, Japan, West Germany, and France. An undersea digital lightwave system linking North America and Europe is being planned by an international consortium of 28 communication carriers and administrations for service in 1988.

Lightguide cable systems for use in the local loop also were developed. Such systems, which extend from the central office to a terminal near the customer's premises, bring such wide-band services as high-speed data, facsimile, and video into the home or office. More than 300 such carrier systems have been installed by the Bell System.

The use of the NASA space shuttle *Challenger* to launch TDRS-1 (Tracking and Data Relay Satellite) and other communication satellites attracted worldwide attention. Additional satellites for domestic communications were launched in 1983 by AT&T with its Telstar 3 and by MCI, which acquired 24 satellite channels from Hughes Communications, Inc. in its Galaxy series. Telstar 3 is equipped with a new single sideband modulation system which quadruples the capacity of the satellite transponders for voice communication.

Digital electronic switching systems are rapidly replacing older switching equipment in central offices. The digital format and computerized call-handling represent significant advances toward a nationwide digital network that will be able to deliver new services—voice and video, electronic messages, and broadband access to all kinds of information.

Microelectronics and Microprocessors. In 1983 advances in microelectronics and microprocessors continued to provide the technologies for new transmission and switching systems, for new telephone and PBX instrumentation, and for new data and video services.

A 256-kilobit random access memory (RAM) chip for use in telecommunication equipment began to appear during 1983.

An experimental semiconductor laser capable of being tuned electronically to more than ten discrete single frequencies was developed by Bell Laboratories. It utilizes an unusual two-cavity construction smaller than a grain of salt, obtained by cleaving a wafer of indium-gallium-arsenide phosphide. The new device is called a cleaved-coupled-cavity, or C^3, laser and is characterized by a high degree of spectral purity. In one experiment, a lightwave system utilizing the new laser transmitted information at a rate of 420 million bits per second (Mb/s) over a distance of 100 mi (160 km) without amplifying repeaters.

M. D. FAGEN, *Formerly, Bell Laboratories*

Ann Logan/SNET

The Changing Telecommunications Industry

On Jan. 1, 1984, a major transformation of the telecommunications industry in the United States occurred. The Bell System, with its parent organization, the American Telephone and Telegraph Company which was established in 1885, was radically changed in its structure, its operations, and in the degree of control by government regulation. These changes were brought about by a U.S. District Court approval of the procedure for implementing a consent decree between the Department of Justice and AT&T, following dismissal of an antitrust suit filed by the Department of Justice in 1974. In addition, regulatory actions by the Federal Communications Commission (FCC) to increase competition and decrease regulation in the telecommunications business were important factors in the changing scene.

Changes in Structure and Function. As a consequence of the decree, AT&T was required to divest its 22 wholly owned Operating Telephone Companies, which henceforth will operate independently to provide local telephone services and offer access to local telephone customers to all long-distance communications companies. The Operating Companies are grouped into seven regional entities in the same geographical area.

With the divestiture of the local telephone companies, the decree removes restrictions from AT&T, freeing it to engage in competition with other companies in most aspects of the telecommunications business, including manufacture and sales, national and international. It continues to own Bell Laboratories and the Western Electric Company which have long been leaders in research, development, and manufacture of complex communications systems. Subsidiaries are in the unregulated, competitive lines, providing equipment and systems for residential and business use.

AT&T, under regulation, will continue to be one provider of long-distance service in competition with other vendors. In 1982, the Long Lines division of AT&T handled about 90% of the nation's telephone, data, and video-telecommunications traffic.

Effects of Change. The Bell System, as it was previously constituted, grew during a period of almost 100 years. One of its guiding principles was that of "universal service," that is, operating under regulation in such a way as to make telephone service as widely available as possible. With restructuring, universal service remains a goal, but gives way to competition and deregulation as the controlling factors. Economic forces in the marketplace will determine pricing.

Deregulation undoubtedly will provide more choices for consumers and greater control over the price of telephone service and equipment. However, with the cessation of the "averaging" that could be performed with a fully regulated industry, the customers ultimately will pay the real costs of the service provided. This will be evident in flat-rate charges for linking the customer's home to the network, in local rates based on measured usage of telephone service, and other means to bring charges in line with costs for specific services.

Competition in the long-distance service is very much in evidence. Most of the companies lease lines from the Bell System but some use their own networks. From selected cities to selected terminals, at particular calling times, these "specialized common carriers" are able to provide service at rates below those charged by AT&T which is committed to worldwide service on a nonrestricted basis. The main non-Bell companies engaged in long-distance communications are Microwave Communications, Inc. (MCI), General Telephone and Electronics (GTE) which acquired Southern Pacific's Sprint system, International Telephone and Telegraph (ITT), and Western Union.

Freedom of choice in customer equipment is also very much in evidence. Telephones in a bewildering array of shapes, sizes, and functions can be bought at prices from $15 to $300. For most people it will be cheaper to buy a telephone than to pay a monthly rental charge. The less expensive telephones pay for themselves in about one year.

For the business office, there is a great variety of PBXs (Private Branch Exchanges). Combining switching functions with computer technology, PBXs control intracompany communications, data processing, routing of external calls, conferencing arrangements, and a host of other functions. Bell faces competition from such other manufacturers as Northern Telecom, ITT, Rolm, and L. M. Ericsson.

The Future. Telecommunications today includes much more than "plain old telephone service" (POTS). Computers and video screens are routinely becoming part of the user's terminal equipment. He or she will be an active participant in "The Information Age."

Lightwave fibers and coaxial cable will become important communication links in this new age. Digital techniques, the microprocessor and software, or programs, are some of the other technological bricks with which the telecommunications edifice is being built.

M. D. FAGEN

COMPUTERS

It was a confusing year for the computer industry. As prices dropped and more and more people found chores for the versatile machines, computers swept into corporate offices and homes across the United States. Businesses bought nearly two million personal computers in 1983, and another five million were sold for home use. Sales of large office and mainframe computers picked up as well, thanks to the economic recovery. Future prospects looked even brighter as new models were introduced that were easier to use.

Despite the growing popularity of computers, however, it was a roller-coaster year for the manufacturers. A price war among the leading makers of small home computers—Atari, Commodore, and Texas Instruments—brought the price of those machines down to less than $100 from as high as $1,000 a year earlier. But the price cutting backfired, since it all but eliminated the profit on the machines. Together, the leading makers lost a total of some $500 million in 1983.

Similarly, while more personal computers than ever were being sold, many makers of more elaborate machines—which sell for $1,500 to $5,000—also were experiencing financial difficulty. The problem for many of the smaller companies was simply three letters: IBM. International Business Machines Corp., the world's largest computer manufacturer, was so successful with its Personal Computer that it grabbed 26% of the market, squeezing out many players. Osborne Computer Corp., the industry's first fatality, filed for protection under the Bankruptcy Act. Later in the year, Texas Instruments got out of the small computer business.

Although the business proved tricky for the manufacturers, they did introduce many exciting new products that make computers easier to use. Most notable was the Lisa computer from Apple Computer Inc. Instead of requiring the user to type arcane commands into the computer on a keyboard, Lisa has a small, hand-held box—called a "mouse"—that controls an arrow on the computer's television screen. The user simply points the arrow to the desired function and then activates it. Because the computer is so easy to use, Apple expects people to learn to operate Lisa in 20 minutes instead of the usual 20 hours.

But making computers easier to use is expensive: Lisa sells for $7,000. Now, however, computer companies are rushing to bring the same easy-to-use features to less expensive models. One such machine is the model 150 from Hewlett-Packard Co. This personal computer, which sells for approximately $4,000 has a touch-sensitive screen. The user just touches the screen at a particular spot to tell the computer what to do.

Consumers interested in buying a computer for their home are especially interested in how easy the machine is to use. Therefore, instead of selling each part of a computer system by itself, as most had been doing, manufacturers in 1983 began introducing models that are complete and ready to run when they come out of the box. Leading the way was Coleco Industries Inc.'s Adam computer, a $600, self-contained system that is ready to operate as an electronic word processor and typewriter. And other models are on the way.

At the same time that they are becoming easier to use, computers are becoming more portable, too. Several small, light-weight models—about the size of a looseleaf binder—that operate on batteries were introduced during 1983. For example, the Radio Shack division of Tandy Corp. unveiled the TRS-80 model 100 computer, which can be used on the go for writing letters and performing calculations. The $800 device can also be hooked up to a telephone line to retrieve information, such as stock prices and plane schedules, from electronic database libraries.

Ultimately, computer designers hope to make the machines so smart that they will understand English or any other human language and be able to solve problems entirely on their own. Their first efforts in this area, called artificial intelligence (AI), moved out of the laboratories and into the marketplace in 1983. IBM, for instance, began selling rudimentary AI products for its own computers that let the business executive ask the computer for information with English-language sentences. And General Electric Co. developed a computerized trouble-shooting system that can diagnose problems with train locomotives as well as any expert mechanic.

As computers proliferate and become smarter and easier to use, they are radically transforming people's lives—especially in the workplace. In 1983 only about 3% of all white collar workers in the United States used computers; by 1990, according to estimates by International Data Corp., that figure should climb to some 65%. The new office systems are allowing managers to analyze more information before making critical business decisions, enabling them to cut down on mistakes and increase efficiency. Electronic mail systems route reports and memos around a company at the speed of light. And teleconferencing cuts down on expensive travel time by letting people at different branch offices talk face-to-face via television linkups.

Because computers are performing so many of the tedious, menial tasks in an office today, workers can do more interesting jobs more quickly. But unless workers become comfortable in the world of computers, they may have a difficult time in the job market.

ANTHONY DURNIAK, *"Business Week"*

Part of the Mianus River Bridge collapsed; repairs totaled some $37 million.

CONNECTICUT

The second-largest robbery in U.S. history, the torching of two synagogues and the homes of a rabbi and Jewish state legislator, highway tragedies, and corruption charges against public officials made news in Connecticut during 1983.

Crime. Victor M. Gerena, a guard for Wells Fargo Armored Services Corp., was the chief suspect in the theft of $7 million in cash from the Wells Fargo terminal in West Hartford on September 12. Police said Gerena, 25, tied up two fellow employees and fled with the money. At year's end he was still at large. The only larger robbery in the United States occurred in 1982, when $11 million was stolen from an armored car company in New York.

West Hartford police were also looking for the arsonist or arsonists who set fires at the Young Israel Synagogue on August 11, the Emanuel Synagogue on August 15, the home of Rabbi Solomon Krupka of Young Israel Synagogue on August 16, and the home of State Rep. Joan R. Kemler on September 17.

Highway Tragedies. On June 28, at about 1:30 A.M., a 100-ft (30-m) section of the heavily traveled Connecticut Turnpike (I-95) in Greenwich fell into the Mianus River, plunging four vehicles into the shallow waters 70 ft (21 m) below and taking three lives. Three others were seriously injured.

Earlier, on January 19, a tractor-trailer truck rammed into a row of cars stopped at the Stratford toll station, killing seven persons. The truck driver was charged with seven counts of misconduct with a motor vehicle.

Corruption. On April 4, former state Transportation Commissioner Arthur B. Powers pleaded guilty to two counts of hindering the prosecution and was fined $1,500 and ordered to perform certain community services. Powers, who had been arrested in April 1982 after a grand jury investigation, was originally charged with several felonies, including perjury, related to allegations over the selection of architects and engineers for state contracts.

After nearly six years, an investigation into job selling in New Britain ended September 29, when Alfred S. Pettinelli, the city's former personnel director, was sentenced to six months in jail. Others convicted in the cases included a police chief, two fire chiefs, and the third-ranking officer in the state police.

Business. Shareholders of CBT Corp., holding company of Connecticut Bank & Trust, the state's largest commercial bank, and shareholders of the Bank of New England in Boston approved a merger of the two institutions; the merger was expected to be completed in early 1984. The state legislature in June approved a measure permitting Connecticut banks to merge with other New England banks. Colonial Bancrop of Waterbury and the Bank of Boston were other institutions to declare their merger.

Robert Carlson was appointed president and chief operating officer of United Technologies Corp.

Other. As of Oct. 1, 1983, the state drinking age was raised from 19 to 20. The legislature voted the USS *Nautilus,* the first nuclear-powered submarine, built in Groton, the official state ship.

ROBERT F. MURPHY, *"The Hartford Courant"*

CONNECTICUT • Information Highlights

Area: 5,018 sq mi (12 997 km²).
Population: (1982 est.): 3,153,000.
Chief Cities (1980 census): Hartford, the capital, 136,392; Bridgeport, 142,546; New Haven, 126,109.
Government (1983): *Chief Officers*—governor, William A. O'Neill (D); lt. gov., Joseph J. Fauliso (D). *General Assembly*—Senate, 36 members; House of Representatives, 151 members.
State Finances (fiscal year 1982): *Revenues,* $4,300,000,000; *expenditures,* $3,994,000,000.
Personal Income (1982): $43,351,000,000; per capita, $13,748.
Labor Force (June 1983): *Nonagricultural wage and salary earners,* 1,440,100; *unemployed,* 104,600 (6.4% of total force).
Education: *Enrollment* (fall 1981)—public elementary schools, 347,490; public secondary, 157,896; colleges and universities (1982), 162,194. *Public school expenditures* (1982), $1,580,877,000.

CONSUMER AFFAIRS

One of the very significant developments that had a favorable impact on U.S. consumers in 1983 was the continued moderation of the rate of inflation. After increases of 13.3% in 1979, 12.4% in 1980, and 8.9% in 1981, the drop in inflation to 3.9% in 1982 was a welcome relief. By mid-1983, prices were increasing at an annual rate of only 2.4%. The severe drought during the summer was expected to push food prices up during 1984. Many economists forecast a rate of inflation of 5–5½% in 1984.

Consumer Spending and the Recession. The worst recession since the Great Depression of the 1930s bottomed out in November 1982. Much of the stimulus for the turnaround was due to a sharp upturn in consumer spending. Personal consumption spending was at an annual rate of $1.94 trillion during the first quarter of 1982, but it increased in each of the following quarters and by mid-1983 was at an annual rate of $2.15 trillion. A feeling of optimism was emerging, as inflation moderated and the unemployment rate started to go down.

U.S. Office of Consumer Affairs. Virginia Knauer, who had been special assistant to the president, was named special adviser to the president for consumer affairs. Knauer also continued as director of the U.S. Office of Consumer Affairs and as chairperson of the Consumer Affairs Council, a government organization of agency consumer representatives.

The "Legislative Veto." Because enough members of the U.S. business community let their congressional representatives know just how overburdened they felt by federal agency regulations, Congress had passed a series of laws over several decades giving itself the right to veto agency regulations. In 1983, Congress vetoed the Federal Trade Commission (FTC) regulation that would have required automobile dealers to post on used cars a list of the defects of which they were aware. But Congress chose not to veto an FTC rule that requires funeral homes to give prices over the telephone, to itemize funeral expenses on bills, and to inform customers of such things as state requirements on embalming and the use of burial vaults.

The action of Congress giving itself the right to veto agency regulations was challenged in the courts. In June the U.S. Supreme Court ruled that the "legislative veto" was an unconstitutional violation of the principle of separation of powers. (*See also* LAW.)

Regulation versus Deregulation. The Reagan administration's goal of reducing federal government regulation continued with mixed results. The U.S. Office of Consumers' Education was eliminated. Budgets were reduced for the Federal Trade Commission and the Consumer Products Safety Commission. The National Highway Traffic Safety Administration (NHTSA) reduced the bumper standard to 2½ mph (4 km/h); the previous standard required that cars have no damage from a 5-mph (8-km/h) impact. But NHTSA's attempt to revoke a ruling made during the Carter administration requiring that passive restraint systems be installed in all new cars was overturned by the U.S. Supreme Court; a passive restraint system is either a harness attached to the car door which is automatically in place when the door is closed, or an airbag. It was the responsibility of Secretary of Transportation Elizabeth Dole to decide what the department regulation will be in order to be in compliance with the court's ruling.

The business community expressed concern over state regulations moving in to fill the void caused by federal deregulation. Many in the business community began to realize that it might be better to have one federal regulation than 50 different state regulations.

State Action. State legislators were busy during the year, with significant consumer action taken in a number of states. More and more states passed laws requiring child restraint seats in cars. More than a dozen states passed a "lemon law," and others considered such legislation; while there are variations in the "lemon laws" from state to state, all basically stipulate that if a serious problem with a new car is not corrected properly within a specified period of time, the car buyer is to have his or her money refunded or receive another new car. All states except Indiana have passed legislation to facilitate the dispensing of generic drugs for their more expensive brand-name equivalents. A number of states passed "plain language" laws, requiring that contracts be written in understandable English.

Product Safety. A severe blow to the Consumer Product Safety Commission was a U.S. Court of Appeals ruling that reversed the commission's ban on the sale of urea formaldehyde insulation and a decision by the U.S. Department of Justice not to appeal the decision. In spite of the court ruling, a curtailment in funds, and pressure from the administration to "go easy" on regulations, the commission remained active in 1983. It established a toll-free hotline (800-638-CPSC) to facilitate communication from citizens and businesses.

Consumerism: Where does it stand? Despite the antiregulatory mood of much of the general public when Ronald Reagan was elected president, a Louis Harris survey in 1983 confirmed that consumerism was still a popular cause. According to the survey results, the U.S. public was even more concerned about a number of consumer problems than it had been in 1976, when an earlier survey was made. More than 80% of the respondents believed that the activities of the consumer movement have done some or a great deal of good.

STEWART M. LEE, *Geneva College*

CRIME

According to 1983 statistics, the crime rate for serious offenses in the United States decreased by 4% in 1982. Most experts presumed that the decline, the first since 1977, reflected the smaller percentage of young persons in the population, a consequence of the drop in birth rate a generation ago. Young people are particularly crime-prone because more of them are unemployed than their elders, they are generally more willing to take risks, and they possess the strength and agility needed to carry out criminal offenses.

A sharp drop in household burglaries contributed particularly to the crime rate decrease. The U.S. national victimization survey, involving door-to-door interviews by Census Bureau workers with 132,000 persons in 58,000 housing units, showed a 10% reduction in household burglaries, to a total of 6,663,000. Residential larcenies—differentiated from burglaries in that they do not involve illegal entry—dropped 5%. This represented their third consecutive year of decline and the lowest rate since 1973. The reduction largely reflected larcenies of money or goods of less than $50 value; it may be that inflation has reduced the incentive to commit such petty thefts or has made them less often worth the victims' trouble to report.

Violent crimes, however, such as homicide, rape, and aggravated assault, remained at about the same level in 1982 as in 1981, according to the victimization survey. The rate of violent crime showed 34.3 victimizations per 1,000 persons aged 12 and over. The rape rate for the year equaled 1.4 victimizations for each 1,000 women in the United Sates.

Preliminary figures released by the Federal Bureau of Investigation (FBI), based on crimes which become known to the police, corroborated the 4% decline found from the household census. The FBI tabulated 12.6 million serious violations for the year, the lowest total since the 12.2 million-level of 1979. "Serious violations" are defined as murder, rape, robbery, aggravated assault, burglary, motor-vehicle theft, larceny, and arson. In the FBI statistics, each category showed a decline except aggravated assault, which rose by 1%.

Despite the encouraging numerical news, authorities remained wary of drawing sweeping conclusions. U.S. Attorney General William French Smith said that the decline noted in the federal surveys was "very encouraging," but that "it's too early to say whether it's a trend." Similarly, Paul Zolbe, chief of the FBI's statistical unit, said: "The trouble with data like this is that it takes a long time to tell if there's been a real turnaround."

Murder Rates. Examination of the FBI report for the year showed that Odessa, TX, was the most dangerous U.S. city for homicides. With 29.8 slayings per 100,000 residents, the Texas oil center narrowly exceeded Miami's rate of 29.7, which was a drop for the Florida metropolis from the previous year's rate of 34.5 per 100,000. Odessa city officials attributed the high homicide rate to economic fluctuations in the oil industry. Oil booms had attracted transients seeking employment, and busts left them angry. Bar fights and street brawls with lethal outcomes were said to be the consequence of economic frustrations.

Following Odessa and Miami in homicide rates were Houston (28.2); New Orleans (25.3); Longview-Marshall, TX (21.6); Jackson, MS (20.3); Las Vegas (19.5); Stockton, CA (19.5); New York (19.1); and San Antonio (18.5).

Alaska, with 18.5 homicides per 100,000 persons, was the most lethal state. The National Coalition to Ban Handguns maintained that the Alaska rate reflected the fact that it was a "gun-loving" place. Others insisted that the figure was primarily a function of a disproportionate number of males in the state's population and the byproduct of a lingering frontier spirit.

Death Penalty. The attempt to control murder by the use of capital punishment remained virtually stalemated in the United States through the year. The number of persons under sentences of death stood at about 1,200, but legal maneuvers kept them alive, averting what critics of the death penalty insist would be a "national bloodbath of vengeance," and what proponents of capital punishment would label "effective deterrence" or "deserved punishment."

Five persons suffered the death penalty during the year. On April 23, John Louis Evans III, 33, died in the electric chair at Hollman prison in Ardmore, AL. Evans had been convicted of the murder in 1977 of a pawnbroker in Mobile, carried out while the man's two daughters looked on. It required three separate jolts of the electric current to execute Evans. The second was administered three minutes following the first, and the third seven minutes after that. When the first bolt failed to kill Evans, his lawyers insisted that the governor immediately be petitioned for a stay, on the grounds that another such act would represent "cruel and unusual punishment." The governor refused, and Evans' attorney later charged that his client had been "tortured in the name of vengeance and the disguise of justice." Prison officials maintained that a loose electrode had necessitated the successive electric charges, but that Evans "never knew what hit him" after the first charge, and that "for all practical purposes" he was dead following the second.

On September 13, Jimmy Lee Gray, 34, was executed in the gas chamber at Parchman State Prison in Mississippi. Gray had been convicted of killing a three-year-old girl whom he had kidnapped, raped, and then drowned in 1976. At that time, Gray was on parole after having served seven years for the slaying of his 18-year-old girlfriend.

Gray was the eighth person to be executed in the United States since 1976. Describing Gray's execution, a reporter noted that after the lethal cyanide gas was let into the death chamber, Gray's body jerked violently at the leather straps binding his legs, chest, and arms. His head slumped forward and pitched backward a number of times over eight minutes following the gas release. Doctors, however, said that he was dead within two minutes after the gas was released.

New controversy over the death penalty and "cruel and unusual punishment" came up in October, when James Autry, a 29-year-old deathrow inmate at the Texas penitentiary in Austin, was granted a reprieve by U.S. Supreme Court Justice Byron White even as the convicted murderer lay strapped down awaiting the lethal injection. A stay of execution had been voted down by the Court two days earlier, but White changed his position over a new constitutional issue raised by Autry's lawyers.

Late in the year, convicted murderers Robert Austin Sullivan, Robert Wayne Williams, and John Eldon Smith were executed in Florida, Louisiana, and Georgia, respectively.

In July, the British House of Commons reaffirmed, by a vote of 368 to 223, its opposition to capital punishment for murderers. It had been expected that the national election earlier in the year, which saw a resounding victory for the Conservatives, would have provided strong parliamentary support for the death penalty. Debate on the subject was revived because the 572 murders in England and Wales in 1982 represented an increase of 25 for the year and was the most ever. However, the 145 votes by which the death penalty measure was defeated was only a marginally smaller total than the 162 by which a similar measure had lost the year before with a more liberal parliament. Capital punishment remains in force in England for treason, but many persons believe that the negative vote in 1983 permanently put to rest any question of extending its use. Others, however, noted that the issue had been clouded by the matter of the Irish Republican Army, and the judgment that use of the death penalty against terrorists from Northern Ireland might further inflame the situation there.

In the Soviet Union, meanwhile, capital punishment continued to be employed extensively. It is inflicted by shooting. Vladimir Lenin, the founder of the Soviet state, repeatedly advocated capital punishment, and recent Soviet reports have said that "humanism" means being lenient with minor offenders but unyielding with those who cause "irresponsible suffering in the lives of individual Soviet citizens." No official execution figures are provided, but in 1983 the Soviet press carried about 40 stories of death sentences; some Western observers believe that there are as many as 600 executions annually. Typical of newspaper coverage of such events is the following: "Grechukhin, A. N., previously convicted of serious crimes, on finishing his term did not take the path of reform and misused alcoholic beverages. While in a drunken state, and without any reason, he killed a woman, and in this connection was sentenced to the extreme measure of punishment—the death penalty. The sentence has been carried out." Capital punishment in the Soviet Union is also used frequently against persons convicted of economic offences, such as embezzlement and bribery.

Presidential Policies. In his State of the Union Message to Congress in January 1983, President Ronald Reagan singled out organized crime and drug trafficking for particular federal

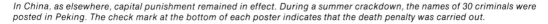

In China, as elsewhere, capital punishment remained in effect. During a summer crackdown, the names of 30 criminals were posted in Peking. The check mark at the bottom of each poster indicates that the death penalty was carried out.

UPI

The cause of victim's rights picked up steam in 1983. Gov. Christopher Bond of Missouri, left, chats with Frank L. Brown and his mother after Brown became the first person to be paid under the state's Crime Victim's Compensation Fund, created in 1981.

UPI

law enforcement attention. "It is high time we make our cities safe again," the president proclaimed. "This administration hereby declares war on those who are poisoning our young people." Later in the year, President Reagan appointed the Task Force on Organized Crime, but internal squabbling led to the resignation of its executive director in September and a delay in the group's efforts.

In February, the President's Task Force on Victims of Crime offered suggestions to alleviate the plight of those who suffer from illegal acts. Among the proposals were a system of payments from criminals to their victims; tightening the laws on bail, evidence, and parole; and training programs to increase the sensitivity of legislators and law enforcement officers to the possible traumas experienced by victims of crime. The task force also suggested the following addition to the Constitution's Sixth Amendment: "Likewise, the victim, in every criminal prosecution, shall have the right to be present and to be heard at all critical stages of the judicial proceedings." Lois Haight Herrington, chair of the task force, noting the wide use of case studies in the group's report, stressed the emotional impact of such material, pointing out: "So many victims have said, 'He attacked me. Why did I have to sell my car to pay my medical bills while he still has his car?'"

Drug use, another of the president's targets, was said to have declined during 1983 to figures well below the peaks of the 1960s and 1970s. A February report by the federal Department of Health and Human Services noted, nonetheless, that the United States probably has the highest level of illicit drug use of any country in the industrialized world. (*See also* DRUGS and DRUG ABUSE.)

At year's end, the president was pushing Congress to enact crime control legislation that included the following:

- Uniform sentencing and elimination of parole.
- Making a defendant's potential danger to society a factor in setting bail.
- Putting the burden of proof on defendants using the insanity defense.
- Allowing surplus federal buildings to be used for state and local prisons.

President Reagan was also supporting measures to tighten drug and labor racketeering laws, facilitate the seizure of assets from narcotic traffickers, and provide federal aid to successful state and local law enforcement programs.

Good Samaritans. On the basis of an August legislative act, being a "Good Samaritan" became a legal duty in Minnesota, not a personal option. Only Vermont has a similar statute, enacted in 1976, though most U.S. jurisdictions have laws that relieve persons from possible liability when they render emergency aid to distressed individuals. Most European countries (but not England) require citizens to provide assistance to those in need, when they can.

Employee Theft. According to a study by sociologists at the University of Minnesota, one third of 9,175 randomly-selected workers in 47 corporations admitted stealing company property. Nearly two thirds said that they did such things as take extra-long lunch hours and breaks, misuse sick leave, and use drugs or alcohol while on the job. The highest levels of theft were reported by unmarried male employees between the ages of 16 and 25. Less theft was carried out against employers who were believed to be genuinely concerned with the workers. A particularly spectacular example of employee theft came in mid-September when a security guard for the Wells Fargo company was suspected of stealing $7 million in cash from the company garage in West Hartford, CT. It was the second-largest robbery in U.S. history, exceeded only by the $11 million that had been taken from the Sentry Armored Car Courier Company in the Bronx in 1982.

GILBERT GEIS
University of California, Irvine

CRIME / SPECIAL REPORT

The Crackdown on Drunk Driving

"If you are going to drink, don't drive! If you are going to drive, don't drink!" That is the message that U.S. law enforcement officials have been trying to impress upon the public with increasing urgency.

Unlike many other criminal offenses that produce injury and death, drunk driving is susceptible to control. Sober persons can take over driving chores; bartenders or party hosts can refuse to provide additional drinks to an inebriated person; and police patrols and roadblocks may be able to capture a drunk driver before someone is hurt or killed.

It is against this background that an intensified campaign to control drunk driving has been launched in the United States. The crusade was triggered in particular by fatalities involving young children whose parents thereafter dedicated themselves to bringing about changes in the laws, and law enforcement, pertaining to drunk driving.

An initial force in the campaign was Candy Lightner, a southern Californian whose daughter was killed in 1980 by a drunk driver; Lightner formed Mothers Against Drunken Drivers (MADD). Similar organizations soon sprang up across the country. A Shreveport, LA, truck driver enrolled colleagues in a group devoted to reporting all vehicles seen weaving on the highways. In mid-1982, the Mississippi Medical Association formed Physicians Against Drunk Driving; that group sought to move beyond repairing the wounds to trying to head off drunk-driving accidents before they occur.

The intensified campaign, which also included new or stricter laws in many states, appears to have had striking results. Highway fatalities dropped from 49,301 in 1981 (about half of which involved drivers who were intoxicated) to 43,990 in 1982. It was the largest one-year decrease since 1974, the year of the gasoline shortage. Figures from the National Safety Council showed that from January to May 1983, traffic deaths in the United States had reached the lowest rate since 1913. Two reasons were said to account for the sharp decline: fewer drunk drivers and increased use of seat belts.

Enforcement. Efforts to curb drunk driving have followed a number of routes. Among them are the raising of the age at which persons can legally operate motor vehicles. Young drivers are involved in more serious traffic accidents than older persons; their inexperience with driving, combined with the loss of control through intoxication (also generally a new experience for them) are a particularly dangerous combination. Among others, the State of New York raised the permissible age for consumption of alcoholic beverages from 18 to 19 in 1982; the following year Connecticut raised its drinking age from 19 to 20. The 32-member President's Commission on Drunk Driving, headed by former Secretary of Transportation John Volpe, recommended in December 1983 a minimum drinking age of 21 in all states in its final report. The proposal was backed by "evidence of a direct correlation between the minimum drinking age and alcohol-related crashes. . . ." Other recommendations suggested enactment of victim-assistance programs, that all health-insurance policies provide coverage for alcoholic and other drug-related medical treatment, prohibition of possession of open alcoholic containers or alcoholic consumption in automobiles, and that repeat offenders be screened for alcoholism.

Tougher and mandatory penalties, also a recommendation of the President's Commission, represent another method for curbing drunk driving. Under close scrutiny are the Scandinavian countries, where drunk driving carries an automatic prison term. Penalty structures in the United States continue to be milder than those in Scandinavia, but much tougher than in former years. The Highway Users Federation in Washington, DC, reported that more than 27 states had imposed harsher penalties on drunk drivers in 1983. For first offenses, these penalties typically involve heavy fines and/or short jail terms, as well as mandatory counseling for persons deemed to have alcoholism problems. Prison terms and license loss are apt to be imposed for a second or subsequent conviction. States also have been reducing the level of blood alcohol necessary to sustain a conviction for drunk driving. At present that level typically is 0.1%.

Not everyone, however, unconditionally endorses the stepped-up campaign against drunk drivers. Joseph Gusfield of the University of California at San Diego, for example, argues in his book, *The Culture of Public Problems: Drinking-Driving and the Symbolic Order,* that current perceptions of the problem represent just one of many ways it might reasonably be viewed. He notes, for instance, that "the absence of alternative modes of transportation is logically as much a cause of drinking-driving as is the use of alcohol." Gusfield also maintains that "the effectiveness of legal sanctions as a method for deterring drinking-driving and for preventing accidents is more limited than the legislative and judicial acts that fill libraries will lead one to think."

GILBERT GEIS

CUBA

Cuba in 1983 entered a new period of austerity because of continuing economic difficulties. As a result of external pressures, principally from the United States, the government of President Fidel Castro at first appeared to adopt a less strident posture in foreign affairs. That it was continuing to play a key role in Central American revolutionary strife, however, was made clear by the events in Grenada during the fall (*see* feature article, page 28). Meanwhile, the number of Cuban troops in Africa remained the same as in 1982—about 13,000 in Ethiopia and 20,000 in Angola.

Economy. The country's life was adversely affected by the persistent low world-market price of sugar, Cuba's main product and export. Not only was the price of about 10 cents per pound actually below the island's production cost, but, according to Western estimates, Cuba produced slightly less than 7 million metric tons (7.7 million short tons) in 1983, some 1.2 million (1.32 million) less than in 1982. Its sugar reserves nearly exhausted by export commitments, Havana in the fall had to purchase 100 000 metric tons (110,000 T) of Brazilian crude for domestic consumption. Heavy spring and summer rains flooded large areas of the country, damaging several crops, among them tobacco, another cash export.

Havana was forced to seek, and did obtain, deferment of interest payments on its $3.5 billion (U.S.) debt to its Western lenders, principally in Europe. Cubans had to tighten their belts as the price of gasoline and many consumer goods were increased. With fewer imports of Western raw materials, the output of many industries declined. In 1983, according to the Central Planning Board, the national treasury had hard currency to pay for only 63% of the essential Western imports.

The Soviet Union continued to bear the burden of keeping the Cuban economy afloat. The 1983 cost of Soviet aid was estimated at more than $3 billion, with no indications that it would decline in coming years. Moreover, under the existing treaty with Moscow, Cuba in 1986 would have to begin repaying a debt of $9 billion accumulated through 1976. The total Cuban indebtedness to the Soviet Union has been estimated at more than $20 billion.

Foreign Affairs. Conceding its economic dependence on the USSR, Cuba portrayed itself as independent in the conduct of foreign affairs. "Not in the past, not now or ever have we made decisions at the cost of others or expected others to fight for us," declared Castro July 26. The Cuban leader was commenting on the deployment of U.S. troops in Central America, which he interpreted as a direct threat to Nicaragua, his ally, and to his own regime. In June, Vice-President Carlos Rafael Rodriguez described Cuban-U.S. relations as

CUBA · Information Highlights

Official Name: Republic of Cuba.
Location: Caribbean Sea.
Area: 44,200 sq mi (114 478 km²).
Population (July 1983 est.): 9,852,000.
Chief Cities (1981 census): Havana, the capital, 1,924,886; Santiago de Cuba, 345,289; Camagüey, 245,235.
Government: *Head of state and government,* Fidel Castro Ruz, president (took office under a new constitution, Dec. 1976). *Legislature* (unicameral) —National Assembly of People's Power.
Monetary Unit: Peso (0.8351 peso equals U.S.$1, February 1983—noncommercial rate).
Gross National Product (1981 U.S.$): $16,000,-000,000.

being at the "lowest point" since 1959, when the Castro regime came to power. Noting that since 1981, Cuba had added 500,000 men and women to the Territorial Militias, the civil defense force, Rodriguez said that the possibility of a U.S. attack was "much nearer than at any other time." Presenting itself as a small independent country threatened by a neighboring superpower, and to deflect U.S. policy in Central America, Cuba sought to improve relations with key Western European and Latin American states. Without admitting any role in the conflict, Castro expressed support for a negotiated settlement of the Central American crisis and endorsed the efforts of the five-nation Contadora Group.

France's Foreign Minister Claude Cheysson visited Cuba in August (as did other West European officials during the year); talks centered on the problems in the Caribbean. Cuba and Bolivia reestablished diplomatic relations. And ties with Argentina, following Havana's strong backing of the Buenos Aires government in the 1982 Falklands war, improved significantly. The two countries signed a broad range of commercial agreements. Cuba reportedly assured Argentina that it would no longer have anything to do with leftist guerrillas there; Argentina told Cuba that it had withdrawn its military advisers from Honduras, where they had been training anti-Nicaraguan guerrillas.

The Cuban government reacted strongly to the overthrow and assassination of Grenada's Prime Minister Maurice Bishop, a good friend of Castro. Havana called for an investigation of the death of Bishop and several of his ministers. "If they were executed in cold blood," said an official communiqué declaring three days of mourning, "those responsible deserve exemplary punishment."

Cuban-U.S. Relations. Three thorny issues arose between Washington and Havana during 1983. Two of them—pertaining to refugees and hijacking—went unresolved. The third had to do with Cuban presence on Grenada.

On May 24 the United States asked Cuba to take back several thousand of the 125,000 Cubans who had arrived during the 1980 Mariel boatlift and some of whom were common criminals placed on refugee boats by the Havana regime. The Reagan administration, concerned principally with the repatriation of some 800 Cubans at the Atlanta (GA) Federal Prison, told Cuba that until it agreed to take back the "criminals," the U.S. Interests Section in Havana would not issue U.S. visas to any Cubans except immediate relatives of American citizens. On June 17 the Cuban government replied that it was willing to discuss the return of some of the Mariel refugees but only as part of overall conversations on "normalization of migration" between the two countries. On July 7 a spokesman for the U.S. State Department, in what appeared to be a rejection of the Cuban note, stated that the United States did not want to broaden the refugee talks, which, he said, should be "limited to the subject at hand."

A rash of plane hijackings to Cuba in midyear also resulted in an exchange of diplomatic notes. In early June the State Department issued a statement accusing Havana of failing to punish the hijackers. On June 15 a Cuban note was delivered to the head of the U.S. Interests Section in Havana detailing punishments given to hijackers since 1980. It maintained that prior to 1981 hijackers received prison sentences of two to five years and that since then the sentences had averaged 15 years. Later in the year, Havana permitted U.S. journalists to interview some of the American hijackers in a prison outside the capital.

GEORGE VOLSKY, *University of Miami*

UPI

Rauf Denktaş, Turkish Cypriot leader, called the UN Security Council vote denouncing the establishment of an independent Turkish Cypriot republic "unacceptable."

CYPRUS

A presidential election was held in Cyprus during 1983, and the political situation became more complicated when the Turkish Cypriots unilaterally declared independence in the northern parts of the island.

Presidential Election. With the help of Cyprus' powerful Communist party, AKEL, President Spyros Kyprianou, a Greek Cypriot and leader of the small Democratic Party, was reelected on February 13 to a second five-year term. The official proclamation of his victory was made the next day. The Turkish Cypriots did not participate in the election.

Background of the Independence Proclamation. During 1983 the problem of how to reconcile the Greek Cypriots and the Turkish Cypriots became even more intractable. The actual division of the island between Greek and Turkish Cypriots dates from 1974 when Turkey invaded Cyprus. The invasion was in response to a coup against the Cypriot government led by a Greek Cypriot faction backed by Greece's military government of the day. Turkey proceeded to occupy important territories in the north from which about 200,000 Greek Cypriots fled. The Turkish Cypriots then congre-

gated in the north. In 1975 their territories, accounting for about 37% of the land area of Cyprus, were proclaimed to be the Turkish Federated State of Cyprus. Except for Turkey, which continued its occupation, this political entity was not recognized by any other state, and through the years after the Turkish occupation, efforts by the UN to find a solution were unproductive, as were intercommunal talks held intermittently under UN auspices.

Declaration of Independence. In May 1983 the UN General Assembly by a vote of 103 to 5 with 20 abstentions passed a strongly pro-Greek Cypriot resolution calling for an immediate withdrawal of the Turkish forces of occupation from Cyprus. Rauf Denktaş, president of the Turkish Federated State of Cy-

---

CYPRUS • Information Highlights

Official Name: Republic of Cyprus.
Location: Eastern Mediterranean.
Area: 3,572 sq mi (9 251 km²).
Population (July 1983): 653,000.
Chief Cities (1980 est.): Nicosia, the capital, 125,100; Limassol, 105,200; Famagusta, 39,500.
Government: *Head of state and government,* Spyros Kyprianou, president (took office Aug. 1977). *Legislature*—House of Representatives.
Monetary Unit: Pound (0.537 pound equals U.S.$1, July 1983).
Gross National Product (1981 U.S.$): $2,075,-000,000.
Economic Index (1982): *Consumer Prices* (1977 = 100), all items, 157.3; food, 155.7.
Foreign Trade (1982 U.S.$): Imports, $1,249,000,000; *exports,* $569,000,000.

prus, threatened to proclaim his part of the island independent. That unilateral declaration of independence did come in a unanimous vote of the Turkish Cypriot Assembly on Nov. 15, 1983, when the occupied territories were renamed the Turkish Republic of Northern Cyprus. There was an indication, however, in the independence proclamation that the Turkish Cypriots still hoped to find an accommodation with the Greek Cypriots if the latter would accept a bizonal federation.

Turkey immediately recognized the declaration of independence. But it was strongly denounced by Greece and Britain, the two countries that in 1960 had formally guaranteed the treaty arrangement by which Cyprus had gained its independence. Joining in the denunciation were the United States and all the members of the European Community (EC). On November 18, 13 members of the UN Security Council passed a British-sponsored resolution calling on the Turkish Cypriots to withdraw their declaration. Pakistan, Turkey's friend, supported the resolution, and Jordan abstained.

In the wake of the independence proclamation, Kyprianou visited the United States, saw President Reagan, and issued complimentary statements about the U.S. stance.

GEORGE J. MARCOPOULOS, *Tufts University*

CZECHOSLOVAKIA

As in previous years, the government of Czechoslovakia sought to improve the performance of the economy and continued to repress dissidents and expand antireligious measures.

Economy. Operating under the "Set of Measures to Improve the System of Planned National Economic Management" introduced in 1981, the economy did perform somewhat better than in earlier years. An official announcement was made that the following percentile increases above the same period of 1982 had been achieved in the first half of 1983: industrial production, 3.2%; labor productivity in industry, 2.4%; construction, 4%; labor productivity in construction, 3.9%; engineering goods, 4.85%; electronics, 7.5%; food industry, 4.9%; milk output, 11.6%; freight transportation, 2.3%; retail trade, 3.8%; wages, 2.9%; exports, 7.4%; and imports, 8.8%. Production costs were lowered by 0.9%.

On the other hand, meat output decreased by 0.7%, poultry production by 1.7%, and only 31.6% of residential housing planned for 1983 was completed by midyear. Nor were planned targets attained in the quality and technical level of a number of products. The regime's strenuous efforts to earn more hard currency by substantially increasing exports to nonsocialist countries brought about only a meager 1.3% increase. Preliminary reports about the harvest indicated that grain production would reach some 10.2 million metric tons (11.2 million T), which was said to be 170,000 metric tons (187,390 T) more than planned, but was actually well below the hoped-for 11 million metric tons (12.1 million T). The production of corn and potatoes remained below the planned targets. Increases of up to 25% were decreed in February for a number of consumer goods.

Antireligion Campaign. Concerned that the leaders of Czechoslovakia's Roman Catholics might be encouraged by the pope's June visit to Poland and worried by the Polish Roman Catholic Church's continued strong support for the Solidarity movement, the regime stepped up its antichurch campaign. Detentions, searches of homes, and other forms of harassment of priests, monks, and nuns became more frequent. The pope's elevation of two exiled Czechoslovak prelates to bishops who were to provide pastoral care for Czechoslovaks in exile was attacked in the Czechoslovak media.

Government Reshuffle. In June a minor reorganization of the federal cabinet took place. The former minister of the interior, Jan Obžina, became vice-premier and was put in charge of the federal ministry for technical development and investments. New ministers were appointed to head the federal ministries of labor and social affairs, agriculture, and the interior.

World Peace Rally. In June, Prague hosted a massive "World Assembly for Peace and Life and Against Nuclear War." It was sponsored by the Communist-controlled World Peace Council and the Czechoslovak Peace Committee and was attended by some 3,500 delegates from 132 countries. The assembly condemned "the plans to deploy first-strike nuclear missiles in Western Europe." A separate meeting of the Czechoslovak Charter 77 of the human-rights movement was broken up by police.

EDWARD TABORSKY
University of Texas at Austin

CZECHOSLOVAKIA • Information Highlights

Official Name: Czechoslovak Socialist Republic.
Location: East-central Europe.
Area: 49,399 sq mi (127 946 km²).
Population (July 1983): 15,420,000.
Chief Cities (Dec. 31, 1981 est.): Prague, the capital, 1,182,445; Bratislava, 388,260; Brno, 371,668.
Government: *Head of state,* Gustav Husák, president (took office 1975). *Head of government,* Lubomir Strougal, premier (took office 1970). *Communist party, secretary-general,* Gustav Husák (took office 1969). *Legislature*—Federal Assembly: Chamber of House of Nations and Chamber of House of the People.
Monetary Unit: Koruna (12.34 koruny equal U.S.$1, July 1983).
Gross National Product (1981 U.S.$): $137,200,-000,000.
Economic Indexes (1981): *Consumer Prices* (1970 = 100), all items, 112.7; food, 105.8. *Industrial Production* (1975 = 100), 130.
Foreign Trade (1982 U.S.$): *Imports,* $15,499,-000,000; *exports,* $15,734,000,000.

The acclaimed "Glass Pieces," performed by the New York City Ballet, blended minimalist technique with classical ballet.

DANCE

Although a series of crises threatened to affect the dance world profoundly in the first half of 1983, the year as a whole encompassed a large number of new talents, major premieres, and unexpected revivals. The resiliency of dance organizations and the creativity in the field came to the forefront by the year's end.

An important if sad news event was the death on April 30 of George Balanchine, the Russian-born choreographer who was the New York City Ballet's artistic director and cofounder. The company appointed Jerome Robbins, another celebrated choreographer long associated with the troupe, and Peter Martins, a principal dancer and a relatively new choreographer, to direct the City Ballet. Each was given the new title of balletmaster-in-chief. Lincoln Kirstein, the company's cofounder, remained as general director. Mr. Martins announced he would stop dancing by January 1984. In December he gave a farewell performance in *The Nutcracker* with the City Ballet. Mr. Robbins made his debut as Drosselmeier in the same production.

American Ballet Theatre encountered difficulties of another sort. A financially disappointing and unusually long (11-week) season at the Metropolitan Opera House and the aftermath of labor problems left the group criticized on artistic grounds and in a severe financial situation. When some on its board of trustees made demands that Mikhail Baryshnikov considered an infringement upon his authority as artistic director, he sent a letter of resignation. The resignation was rejected, and Baryshnikov promised to remain with the company through the end of its New York season in June 1984, but his future with the company was in doubt.

Martha Graham rocked the world of the arts by publicly protesting the National Endowment for the Arts' rejection of her company's application for a challenge grant. The 89-year-old modern-dance pioneer, whose statement sparked a letter-writing campaign in her favor to the federal agency, declared she had been discriminated against because of her age and a bias on the selection panel. The Endowment for the Arts representatives denied these charges, but entered into talks with the Graham company.

The Ballet Season. In ballet, the major companies seemed to surmount their difficulties. After a financial crisis and a move to a second home at the Los Angeles Music Center, the Joffrey Ballet produced its best New York season in many years. Two of its most successful and controversial premieres came from William Forsythe, a Joffrey-trained American who has emerged as a major choreographer in Europe. *Love Songs*, to recordings by Aretha Franklin and Dionne Warwick, treated the battle of the sexes with rough partnering and an emotional truth that startled some in the audience. The same blend of pop culture and formal sophistication was used in *Square Deal,* where the dancers discussed the nature of ballet in fragmentary phrases spliced with fragments of movement.

The Joffrey dancers were in superb form in the other world premieres—Gerald Arpino's *Round of Angels, Italian Suite, Quarter-Tones for Mr. B*, and in the company's first performances of Jiri Kylian's *Dream Dances*, Paul Taylor's *Cloven Kingdom*, and Frederick Ashton's *Five Brahms Waltzes in the Manner of Isadora*.

The New York City Ballet's big success was Jerome Robbins' *Glass Pieces*. Closely in

195

tune with the repetitive music of the experimental composer, Philip Glass, Robbins retained the avant-garde trappings of "minimalist" dance. Even so the women were on toe and the ballet's core was a classical duet for Bart Cook and Maria Calegari. *I'm Old Fashioned,* also by Robbins, did not work as well but was acclaimed for its conception—the use of a film duet by Fred Astaire and Rita Hayworth as a theme for balletic variations. Morton Gould composed the musical variations based on the title song.

A new choreographer to emerge from the City Ballet's ranks was Helgi Tomasson, a principal dancer whose own pure classical style was reflected in his ballet, *Ballet d'Isoline,* to music by André Messager. Peter Martins' *Rossini Quartets* and Jacques d'Amboise's *Celebration* made up the City Ballet's other premieres. Valentina and Leonid Kozlov, who defected in 1979 from Moscow's Bolshoi Ballet, joined the company.

American Ballet Theatre rescued a "lost" Balanchine ballet from oblivion with its unexpected staging, from dance notation, of the choreographer's 1947 *Symphonie Concertante.* Set to Mozart, the ballet remains a showpiece of neoclassical style.

Unlike such revivals or company premieres —which included Robbins' *New York Export: Opus Jazz* and Erik Bruhn's production of *La Sylphide*—most of the new works were insubstantial. These were John McFall's *Interludes* and *Follow the Feet,* Lynne Taylor-Corbett's *Estuary* and Jiri Kylian's *Torso.* The picture brightened with *Bach Partita,* Twyla Tharp's first large-scale ballet in a totally classical style. Other Tharp works for the company were *Once Upon a Time* and *Sinatra Suite,* both for Baryshnikov. *Cinderella* was scheduled for year's end.

Dance Theater of Harlem also staged a rarely seen ballet—*Les Biches,* Bronislava Nijinska's famed 1924 comedy of manners.

James Kudelka, a Canadian choreographer, received strong praise for powerful ballets in several companies. *Passages* was danced by the American Ballet Theatre II company; *Hedda* by the National Ballet of Canada; and *Genesis* and *In Paradisum* by Les Grands Ballets Canadiens.

Foreign Influences. Among visiting foreign companies, Britain's Royal Ballet, with a new star in Alessandra Ferri, and Roland Petit's National Ballet of Marseille from France had the most impact.

Other foreign troupes included Maurice Béjart's Ballet of the 20th Century from Brussels and, as part of the Brooklyn Academy of Music's "Ballet International" series, the Hamburg Ballet, the Basel Ballet, and London Contemporary Dance Theatre. Nureyev appeared with the Zurich Ballet in his *Manfred* and *Don Quixote.* The Ballet Nuevo Mundo de Caracas, England's Imperial Ballet, and several Israeli companies—Batsheva, Bat-Dor, Mirali Sharon, and the Kibbutz Dance Company—also came to the United States.

A striking debut by five French experimental modern-dance companies took place at the American Dance Festival in Durham, NC. All focused on theatricality and themes of alienation, testifying to the burgeoning dance activity in France.

Modern Dance. A similarly outstanding group of events took place in the Brooklyn Academy's "Next Wave" series which emphasized a collaboration among experimental

The *"Anniversary Waltz"* was choreographed especially for the San Francisco Ballet's 50th anniversary gala of January 1983.

choreographers, painters, and composers. The dance works in this stimulating series included *Set and Reset* by Trisha Brown, Robert Rauschenberg, and Laurie Anderson; *Available Light* by Lucinda Childs, Frank O. Gehry, and John Adams; *Hemispheres* by Molissa Fenley, Francesco Clemente, and Anthony Davis; and *Wind Devil* by Nina Wiener, Judy Pfaff, and Sergio Cervetti. Rina Schenfeld and Carolyn Carlson also took part in the series.

Modern dance's major choreographers created important works. Merce Cunningham offered *Quartet* along with *Coast Zone*. Paul Taylor presented *Sunset* as well as *Snow White*. Martha Graham presented *Phaedra's Dream* on tour. The highlights of Alvin Ailey's 25th anniversary year included Bill T. Jones' *Fever Swamp*, Talley Beatty's *Blueshift*, Ailey's *Isba*, and a revival of Lester Horton's *To José Clemente Orozco*. Erick Hawkins' company presented his new *Summer-Clouds People*.

The third annual Samuel H. Scripps-American Dance Festival Award, a $25,000 prize in modern dance, went to Paul Taylor.

ANNA KISSELGOFF, *"The New York Times"*

DELAWARE

Delaware's attention in 1983 was focused largely on economic recovery, fiscal restraint, environmental cleanup, and the improvement of public education.

Legislation. The major effort of the 132d General Assembly was to pass a budget under the restraint of a projected drop in revenue. Expenditures in the 1983 fiscal budget had to be cut in midyear as a result of a drop in revenues, while the 1984 budget provided for no tax increases and no pay increases for state employees.

The legislature passed and the governor signed a bill creating a Department of Services of Children, Youth, and Their Families, based on the need to strengthen services for young people as a result of an increase in the number of child neglect and abuse cases. The legislature also acted to reform the method of granting financial aid to outside agencies. It considered but did not pass a proposal to allow banks in Delaware to sell insurance.

The Economy. Delaware's economy showed signs of improvement in 1983. Unemployment dropped to 7.7% in July 1983, as compared with 10% in August 1982. The number of new banks moving to Delaware as a result of the 1981 Financial Center Development Act increased to 15.

The hot, dry summer produced a boom year for Delaware's beach communities, but the agriculture sector, with its heavy reliance on the poultry industry, suffered great losses due to

---

DELAWARE • Information Highlights

Area: 2,044 sq mi (5 294 km²).
Population (1982 est.): 602,000.
Chief Cities (1980 census): Dover, the capital, 23,512; Wilmington, 70,195; Newark, 25,247; Elsmere, 6,493.
Government (1983): *Chief Officers*—governor, Pierre S. duPont IV (R); lt. gov., Michael N. Castle (R). *General Assembly*—Senate, 21 members; House of Representatives, 41 members.
State Finances (fiscal year 1982): *Revenues,* $1,190,000,000; *expenditures,* $1,084,000,000.
Personal Income (1982): $7,065,000,000, per capita, $11,731.
Labor Force (July 1983): *Nonagricultural wage and salary earners,* 265,100; *Unemployed,* 23,100 (7.6% of total force).
Education: *Enrollment* (fall 1981)—public elementary schools, 60,287; public secondary, 34,785; colleges and universities (1982), 32,454. *Public school expenditures* (1981–82), $316,318,000.

---

the severe heat. Most other sectors of the economy showed improvement in late 1983.

Construction of office buildings continued at a brisk pace in downtown Wilmington; Hercules, Inc. opened its new corporate headquarters there. The ultramodern design of this major new addition to the downtown skyline became a focal point for local debate on architectural style.

In a further move to improve Delaware's recovery, the state applied to the federal government for the designation of two areas as foreign trade zones. If approved, the zones would be eligible for tax exemptions on goods handled within their borders.

The Environment. A moratorium on rezoning approvals was placed on the inland bays and the Atlantic coastal region by the Sussex County Council. Gov. Pierre duPont also appointed a blue-ribbon task force to propose new solutions for coping with major threats to recreational and natural resources as a result of rapid, uncontrolled growth in the coastal region. In northern Delaware, the most appropriate method for cleaning up hazardous waste dumpsites was under consideration.

Education. Public-school enrollment showed a slight decrease in 1982–83, while private-school enrollments continued to increase slightly. A major study of public attitudes toward schools in northern New Castle County showed increased public confidence in the schools that had been the subject of court-ordered desegregation in 1978. The court order had resulted in consolidation of 11 school districts and the inauguration of busing on a wide scale.

The University of Delaware observed a year-long celebration of the 150th anniversary of its founding with symposia, convocations, and visits by notable guests to the campus in Newark. An honorary doctorate was awarded to Vice-President George Bush in November.

JEROME R. LEWIS, *University of Delaware*

DENMARK

The four-party, center-right coalition government of the Conservative Poul Schlüter (consisting of members of the Conservative, Liberal, Center Democrat, and the Christian People's parties), which took office in September 1982, rode out a number of crises and faced threats of nationwide strikes early in the year. A new contract between employers and labor served to postpone such a possibility until 1985, but a harbor strike during the first six weeks of the year proved to be harmful.

Both the Danish people and government seemed lukewarm toward the planned deployment of Pershing missiles in Europe. In February the Folketing (parliament), after a heated debate, agreed to help forestall the deployment of Soviet SS-20 missiles in Soviet-bloc European countries, while "taking note of" the Western position at the Geneva arms talks and confirming its support for efforts to establish a nuclear-free zone. Subsequently, the four government parties, with the Social Democrats, agreed to cut defense expenditures by sizable amounts in 1983 as well as 1984.

An "oil war" erupted between Denmark and Sweden in late summer when the Danes started to drill for oil in the Kattegat, the body of water separating the two countries. The actual maritime boundary had never been definitely established east of three small Danish islands. However, at a September conference the Danes won the right to continue exploring for oil, and the question of a final delimitation in the waters of the Kattegat was left for decision at year's end.

Greenland. The April elections for the Landsting (parliament) of Greenland, which since 1979 has enjoyed home rule, resulted in the opposition party, Atassut, obtaining 46.6% of the vote, with the governing party, Siumut, receiving 42.3%. The parties, however, were deadlocked in the Landsting, with 12 seats each. A small left-wing party, Inuit Araqagiit,

Oskar Lund/Gamma-Liaison

Kent Kirk (pipe) was captain of the Danish trawler that deliberately violated Britain's new 12-mi (19-km) restricted fishing zone. A British court fined Kirk $51,200.

won 2 seats with 10.6% of the vote, enabling it to turn the scales on controversial matters. It was agreed that Jonathan Motzfeldt of the Siumut would continue as chairman of the body.

In June, Greenland, Faeroe Islands, and the Åland Islands were granted representation in the Nordic Council with two members each. They were not, however, full-fledged sovereign members of the council.

The Greenlanders in July welcomed the establishment of their first university, Inuit University at Nuuk (Godthaab). The initial enrollment of students was 14.

Fishery Settlements. Conflicts over fisheries in the seas around Greenland as well as the North Sea were tentatively settled. The Greenlanders had objected to the great volume of cod caught by the West German fishing fleet, this being one reason that the Greenland government was determined to secede from the European Community (EC) in 1985. Denmark proper had also been involved in a fisheries conflict with both West Germany and Britain. A settlement was announced in December 1982 that slightly increased Denmark's mackerel quota and set the total Danish annual catch in the North Sea at 24% of the EC haul.

General. In June, Mogens Glistrup, a longtime member of the Folketing and the founder of the Progressive Party, was found guilty of tax fraud and sentenced to three years in jail and fined one million kroner. He was soon after ousted from the Folketing.

ERIK J. FRIIS
"The Scandinavian-American Bulletin"

DRUGS AND DRUG ABUSE

Although the problem of drug abuse seemed to have leveled off in the United States by 1983, many other nations were experiencing a surprising upsurge of heroin and cocaine dependence among their populations. Some of these nations have been traditional suppliers of drugs. As their populations become over-involved in drug-abuse problems, their attitudes about elimination of drug supplies hardens.

U.S. Trends. A 1983 survey of high-school seniors showed declines in nearly all classes of illicit drug use. Marijuana use, for example, dropped from 37% in 1979 to 29% in 1982. Daily use of marijuana by seniors decreased from 11% in 1979 to 6% in 1982. Young people's attitudes toward marijuana use also were changing, with about 60% attributing great risk to regular marijuana, up from 35% in 1978. Other classes of drugs also have been used at a diminishing rate or have leveled off. One exception is the increased consumption of over-the-counter diet pills, which 14% of girls in senior year of high school currently use. Another exception is the adult use of cocaine, still increasing at a rate of about 10% per year. Particularly pernicious is the use of cocaine intravenously and of "freebasing" (smoking) of alkaloidal cocaine, believed to be practiced by about 15% of cocaine users. These rapid delivery systems produce such extreme "highs" and, eventually, extreme "lows" that the user is compelled to continue the practice.

The generally favorable trend hardly means that the drug-abuse problem has been solved. Substances with a potential for harm are still being consumed widely. At the same time Americans continue to become more tolerant of illegal drug use. The availability of drugs at an affordable price, increasing consumer affluence, or a national resurgence of discontent as during the Vietnam or Watergate eras could reverse the current pattern.

International Trends. The West European countries, with their large middle classes and open borders, are very concerned about the sharp rise in heroin and, more recently, cocaine usage. Traditionally, these countries have had only small numbers of drug-dependent people. Now international drug-smuggling networks have been established, and high quality heroin—high in comparison to the heroin in the United States—is readily available in the metropolitan areas of Common Market countries. For example, Great Britain, which counted only 3,000 to 4,000 heroin dependent people in the past, had an estimated 30,000 in 1983. Similar increases have occurred in other European nations.

Southeast Asia also is burdened with a growing heroin problem. Such countries as Thailand, Burma, and Malaysia are being flooded with low-cost, high-grade heroin from the opium in the Golden Triangle (the border hill country of Burma, Thailand, and Laos). Traditionally, these nations were rural opium-smoking cultures. Now, part of that population has turned to heroin, but it is in the large cities where an explosive increase of intravenous and inhaled heroin use has occurred. By mid-1983, Bangkok may have had more narcotic addicts than New York City.

Cocaine is a growing problem in Western Europe, and in other lands whose populations can afford the drug. New plantings of the coca bush in Colombia, Peru, and adjacent nations have increased the coca-leaf crop substantially. Cocaine abuse could become a worldwide problem during the mid/late 1980s.

As an example of how much coca is available for conversion to cocaine, the indigenous populations of Peru, Bolivia, and other South American countries are becoming exposed to large quantities of coca paste. Coca paste is the first extraction product of coca leaves and contains about 80% cocaine sulfate. This material is sold in Lima, Peru, and other cities, where tens of thousands are dependent on smoking coca paste. It is inexpensive and produces a profound "high," but also fair numbers of paranoid psychotic reactions.

The cocaine economy is such that violence and corruption become a part of the business transactions. Entire nations can be destabilized with the proceeds of the cocaine industry. Law enforcement and government officials, attorneys and physicians, all have been bought as needed with income from the cocaine trade.

Supply Reduction. The importance of a program balanced in reduction of demand and supplies for effectively dealing with substance abuse cannot be denied. Along with vigorous attempts to treat the user and to prevent the development of new users, interdiction of illegal drugs also must be carried out. This is best done at the source, the point at which the plant is grown or the drug is manufactured.

As an example, Colombia has become the source of 80% of the imported marijuana, 75% of the cocaine (about 30 metric tons), and 85% of the illicit Quaaludes that arrive in the United States. The spraying of the well dispersed coca and marijuana plantations is an enormous project, but talks and plans with the government of Colombia were progressing in 1983. Herbicide spraying of marijuana and opium fields in Mexico has demonstrated the feasibility of such efforts. Not one case of paraquat poisoning has been found in marijuana users or in workers on the ground following a marijuana eradication program. Although large seizures of cocaine and marijuana have been made while these drugs were in transit, they do not constitute more than about 10% of the amount that crosses the U.S. boundary.

SIDNEY COHEN, *Neuropsychiatric Institute UCLA School of Medicine*

ECUADOR

Politics in 1983 was focused to a considerable extent on preparations for the January 1984 general elections. In July, 5 of the 17 officially recognized political parties, principally of the right, had formed a coalition, Frente de Reconstruccion Nacional. The coalition included Social Christians, Liberals, Conservatives, Revolutionary Nationalists, and Conciliacion Institucionalistas. By September, there were eight presidential candidates.

Strikes. One of the most significant political crises of the year came in March, when the Workers Front (FUT), consisting of the principal trade union groups, called a general strike. It lasted two days, and it had the support of students and various employer groups, as well as unions. Organized to protest against economic policies of President Osvaldo Hurtado Larrea, the strike ended without a resolution of the issues between the labor movement and the administration.

In June there was a strike of teachers demanding a 60% salary increase. Early in the month 20,000 people in Quito demonstrated in support of the teachers. Some of the teachers went on a hunger strike.

Economy. Ecuador was adversely affected in 1983 by its sizable foreign debt and by the worldwide inflation and recession.

In May an announcement was made that consumer prices had risen 4.8% in the previous month. During the first six months, prices increased by approximately 30%. By October, the annual inflation rate was above 60%.

In January, Ecuador and its creditors agreed on the handling of part of its foreign debt of $4.68 billion (U.S.). It was decided that payment on 26% of the debt that was soon to fall due would be deferred for seven years, with a two-year grace period. In April, President Hurtado visited the United States for further negotiations on the refinancing of the overall Ecuadorean debt.

In February, Ecuador joined two other Latin American countries in stabilizing prices of their major export, petroleum. Ecuador, Mexico, and Venezuela agreed not to engage in competitive price cuts for this product.

A few months later the government's petroleum corporation announced an important discovery of oil. It was estimated that the new find might yield 300 million barrels.

In March, the government devalued the sucre from 33 to 42 to the U.S. dollar. It also took measures to raise interest rates and the price of fuels and to regulate imports and exports. These measures brought considerable political protest.

In June, the International Monetary Fund agreed to provide Ecuador with the equivalent of $170 million so that it could deal with its balance-of-payments problem.

UPI

President Osvaldo Hurtado Larrea discussed the world's economy in an address before the UN Trusteeship Council.

Floods. Ecuador suffered from climatic conditions that affected all the Pacific countries of South America. A change in ocean currents caused massive rainfall that created flooding in Ecuador. An avalanche on the Pan American Highway at Cunchi buried four cars and three buses and brought death to more than 100 people. Flooding resulted in extensive damage to the country's agriculture, particularly along the coast. The government requested that its political opponents agree to a political truce while it dealt with results of the flooding, but the request was largely ignored. In May the Inter-American Development Bank granted Ecuador a loan of $40 million to repair flood damage, and the Andean Development Corporation granted an additional $5 million.

See also LATIN AMERICA.

ROBERT J. ALEXANDER
Rutgers University

ECUADOR • Information Highlights

Official Name: Republic of Ecuador.
Location: Northwest South America.
Area: 106,000 sq mi (274 540 km²).
Population (July 1983 est.): 8,811,000.
Government: *Head of state and government,* Osvaldo Hurtado Larrea, president (took office May 1981). *Legislature* (unicameral)—Congress.
Monetary Unit: Sucre (51.56 sucres equal U.S.$1, floating rate, Nov. 9, 1983).
Gross National Product (1982 U.S.$): $12,334,-000,000.
Economic Index (1982): *Consumer Prices* (1970 = 100), all items, 116.3; food, 117.1.
Foreign Trade (1982 U.S.$): *Imports,* $2,130,000,000; *exports,* $2,286,000,000.

EDUCATION

The year 1983 saw a blitz of national reports critical of U.S. schools, led by the administration-appointed National Commission on Excellence in Education's (NCEE's) *A Nation at Risk.* A June poll by *Newsweek* showed education reform as second to unemployment as a 1984 election issue. Educators, previously defensive about criticism, welcomed the new concern by leaders and the public that raised school reform to a national priority. (*See* feature article, page 39.)

Politics and Education. As the political spotlight focused on education. President Reagan urged prayer in public schools, tuition tax-credit for parents of children in private schools (both defeated by the 1982 Congress), vouchers for parents to pay for private or public schools of their choice, and a smaller federal role in education.

Critics charged Reagan with being misleading in attacking federal "intrusion" in elementary and secondary education. Most federal school funds ($4.5 billion of the $6.5 billion for elementary, secondary, and vocational education in fiscal 1983) were part of a drive to equalize educational opportunity for disadvantaged minorities, the handicapped, and women.

Control has always been local, not federal, analysts said. The tax revolts of the 1970s had denied public schools funds needed in the 1980s, and Reagan's cuts aggravated their plight even further. Observers noted that Congress had partially restored Reagan's cuts in 1982 and, as school reform became a national issue, that the president reduced 1983 proposed education cuts from $14 billion to $8.3 billion. Reagan was faulted for attributing to the NCEE recommendations he favors but ones it never made: school prayer, tuition tax-credit, and a reduced federal role. In a June 8 letter, four former U.S. commissioners of education called for more federal aid to implement recommended reforms. A poll of the 18-member NCEE found wide disapproval of Reagan's cuts in federal aid to education; eight of the ten members who responded called for more aid.

Democratic presidential hopefuls also seized on the national concern to improve education. On February 22, Sen. Gary Hart (D-CO) introduced into the senate a National Education Association (NEA)-favored American Defense Education Act to upgrade science, math, and languages. In May former Vice-President Walter F. Mondale proposed an $11 billion program for education excellence. In June, Sen. Ernest F. Hollings (D-SC) proposed a $14 billion federal program which included a $5,000 pay-raise for every teacher. On June 29, Sen. John Glenn (D-OH) proposed an extra $4 billion in federal aid to improve schools.

Merit Pay. Pressure for merit pay emerged as a way to attract and keep the ablest teach-

ers. The most publicized merit-pay plans were in Tennessee (praised by President Reagan but narrowly defeated by the state senate because of teacher opposition); Florida (also not passed); and California (which would pay the ablest 5% of teachers much more to help beginning and less effective teachers). The U.S. House Education and Labor Committee on June 16 appointed a task force to study merit pay.

NEA and American Federation of Teachers (AFT) critics said that merit pay has been tried and has failed because it fosters administrative favoritism and teacher jealousy and dissension, and that the present average national teacher salary-range ($12,000–$17,000 for nine months) is too low to attract and hold high-quality people. As the merit-pay idea gained momentum, however, teacher-union leaders gave it qualified support as an adjunct to raising basic pay.

Prayer. On July 14, two U.S. constitutional amendment proposals went to the Senate for debate. A Reagan-backed plan for voluntary prayer or scripture reading by teachers or students specifically prohibited state or federal officials from drafting a prayer. The other plan was Sen. Orrin Hatch's (R-UT) silent prayer or meditation amendment. Opponents foresaw a major debate and perhaps a filibuster against both amendments, with little chance of passage.

Florida High School Literacy Test. In May a federal court upheld Florida's minimum-competency literacy test for a high-school diploma. The law was challenged as discriminating against black students. Written on an eighth-grade level, the test can be taken from the tenth grade and repeated up to five times, with remedial classes available. Of Florida's 86,000 high-school seniors in 1983, 1,200—two thirds of them black—failed the exam and received

© Stayskal 1983/"Chicago Tribune"

" BOY, DID I GET INTO TROUBLE. I FELL ASLEEP AND HE THOUGHT I WAS PRAYING! "

certificates of completion instead of diplomas. The legal precedent was important because of criticism of automatic promotion and because Florida was the first of 37 states that now require passing a literacy test to receive a high-school diploma.

Bob Jones University. On May 24 the U.S. Supreme Court upheld, 8–1, the Internal Revenue Service's (IRS's) right to deny tax exemption to Bob Jones University (Greenville, SC) because it discriminates against blacks. The Christian school admits black students but forbids interracial dating and marriage. The decision was seen as a civil-rights victory and an administration defeat. (Reagan had accused the IRS of exceeding its authority).

Tuition Tax-Credit. On May 24 the Senate Finance Committee approved for debate a Reagan-backed tuition tax-credit bill allowing parents an income-tax credit of half the cost per child in private elementary and secondary schools—up to $100 in 1983, $200 in 1984, and $300 thereafter. The bill applies to families with a yearly income of less than $40,000; it provides smaller credits for incomes between $40,000 and $50,000; and it is not applicable for incomes above $50,000. A similar Reagan-backed bill failed in the 1982 Congress.

Opponents said the bill removes bright students and middle-class support from public schools, helps private schools that discriminate against blacks and the poor, and in the next three years would cost $1.6 billion in lost federal taxes. The bill was said to appeal politically to rich conservatives, fundamentalists who favor and run religious schools, Catholics with children in parochial schools, and anti-black blue-collar workers.

Many who believed the bill would not pass a constitutional test were disturbed by a July ruling from the U.S. Supreme Court, which upheld, 5–4, a Minnesota law permitting state income-tax deductions for tuition and other costs paid by parents with children in both private and public schools. While some thought the Minnesota ruling would help the tuition tax-credit bill, AFT President Albert Shanker predicted that any more pro-tuition tax-credit votes in Congress would be offset by the new national concern for public-school reform.

Chicago Desegregation. Contending that Chicago needed federal funds to finance school desegregation, a federal district judge on June 30 ordered $14.6 million in federal funds for this purpose, with another $250 million over the next five years. President Reagan claimed that the judge had no right to determine federal spending priorities. To resolve the dilemma Congress voted $20 million, but Reagan vetoed the bill on August 13, saying that desegregation funds could come from Chicago's $90 million in federal education aid. The Chicago school board replied that these funds were earmarked already for its poverty program.

College Loans and the Draft. Federal law denies federally guaranteed student loans to college men who fail to register for a possible draft. After a challenge by six Minnesota students, U.S. District Judge Donald D. Alsop issued an injunction against the law. On June 29 the U.S. Supreme Court unanimously suspended Judge Alsop's order, thus reaffirming that colleges and universities from September 1 could not make such loans to men who have not registered. Higher-education officials, who first balked at tying student loans to the draft law, have generally agreed to implement the draft-registration requirement.

Teacher Strikes. Teacher strikes, fewer than in previous years, affected more than 13,200 teachers and 225,000 pupils in eight states. Job actions were called in 21 districts in Michigan; five in Washington; three each in Rhode Island and Illinois (including Chicago); two each in Pennsylvania and New Jersey; and one each in Missouri and Massachusetts.

Enrollment Down, Costs Up. Elementary- and secondary-school enrollment declined for the eighth consecutive year; higher-education enrollment also began to decline. Estimated school statistics for 1983–84 (1982–83 in parentheses) were: Enrollments, kindergarten through grade 8—30.8 million (30.9 million), with the decline expected to reverse in mid-1980s; high school—13.5 million (13.8 million), with a decline projected through the 1980s; higher—12.4 million (same), with a decrease projected to 1990; and total—56.7 million (57.1 million).

In 1983 education directly involved 60.2 million persons (61 million), or 25.7% (26%) of the total U.S. population of 234 million. Expenditures were: public elementary and secondary school—$124.7 billion ($120.3 billion) and nonpublic elementary and secondary—$16.3 billion ($15.3 billion), for a total of $141 billion ($135.6 billion); public higher education—$59 billion ($53.2 billion) and nonpublic higher education—$30 billion ($26.5 billion), for a total of $89 billion ($79.7 billion). The grand total cost was $230 billion ($215.3 billion), of which 9% came from the federal government (same), 39% from state governments (same), 24% from local governments (25%), and 28% from other sources, including tuition, fees, endowment earnings, and private gifts and grants (27%).

Number of teachers: elementary and secondary—2.4 million (2.45 million); higher—870,000 (same); and total—3.27 million (3.32 million), plus 300,000 administrators and other staff.

Graduates: high school—2.8 million (3 million), with more than 2.7 million expected in 1984; bachelor's degrees—980,000 (965,000); first professional degrees—75,000 (74,000); master's—300,000 (307,000); and doctorates—33,000 (same).

FRANKLIN PARKER, *West Virginia University*

Egypt's President Hosni Mubarak (left) sought to end his isolation from Jordan's King Hussein and other Arab leaders.

EGYPT

There were relatively few major developments of international importance and no significant outbreaks of violence in Egypt during 1983. The lack of turmoil must itself count as a considerable achievement: in the contemporary Middle East, stability is a triumph. President Hosni Mubarak proved himself adept at keeping the machinery of the government and economy turning. His style was consistently described as "cautious," "low-key," and "sensible."

Economy. Mubarak's caution was especially evident in economic matters, as he was reluctant to make changes in the policies of his predecessor, the late Anwar el-Sadat. No real advances were made in streamlining the ponderous government bureaucracy, which employs some 2 million of the work force. Only the most peripheral attacks were made on Egypt's "price phobia"—the policy of setting prices by government fiat for reasons of political expedience rather than economic reality. Food and other basics, for example, are subsidized at about $2.7 billion (U.S.) annually; removing the subsidies would run the risk of riots similar to those in 1977, when the price of bread was raised. Artificially low prices for farm products discourage food production, and so Egypt has to import nearly half its food. The situation is exacerbated by an annual population increase of more than 1 million.

The paradox of U.S. economic assistance—which (apart from military aid) exceeds $1 billion per year, more than to any other developing country—is that it makes it easier for Egypt to resist making necessary, beneficial changes in its system.

The government's five-year plan for 1983–87 was approved by the People's Assembly in January. The program includes several goals, such as increasing investment and annual growth and reducing the balance-of-payments deficit; the government will try to increase exports 8.5% and hold import growth to 4%. Little progress in these directions was shown in 1983.

Domestic Affairs. In an action that clearly was intended to have symbolic importance, Esmat Sadat, half brother of the late president, and three of his sons were brought to trial in December 1982 on 24 charges, including corruption, tax evasion, fraud, and illegal property deals. They were found guilty on all charges Feb. 12, 1983, and sentenced to one year in prison. On March 13, two of the three cabinet members whom the trial had shown to be involved in the Sadat's dealings were dismissed from office.

Although the year was notably devoid of public disturbances, the government maintained its vigilance against such possibilities. The state of emergency first proclaimed after President Sadat's assassination continued in force, "as a precautionary measure to fight extremism.'' Mass trials of Muslim extremists also continued, and there were some allegations of mistreatment of prisoners.

On July 20 a new election law was passed by the National Assembly (in which the government National Democratic Party controls more than 90% of the seats). The clear effect of the law, which denies parliamentary representation to parties gaining less than 8% of the vote, will be to eliminate small parties from the Assembly. President Mubarak has been increasingly critical of the opposition parties, calling them irresponsible and destructive of national unity. Representatives of the minority parties opposed the new electoral law and threatened to boycott the 1984 election.

The presidential decree of 1981 that had deposed Shenouda III, spiritual leader of Egypt's Coptic Christians, was upheld by an administrative court in Cairo on April 12. The court found fault, however, with the interim arrangements under which Shenouda had been replaced by a five-man panel to oversee the church's finances and administration.

The massive task of repairing the hydro-electric equipment on the Aswan Dam got under way. Defects in the Soviet-built turbines had been increasingly troublesome since 1967. In 1981 the United States undertook to finance the $85 million, five-year repair project.

Egyptian-Sudanese Integration. The first steps to implement the Egyptian-Sudanese Charter of Integration, signed in October 1982, took place in 1983. The first meeting of the Higher Council for Integration, under the joint chairmanship of presidents Mubarak and Jaafar al-Nemery, was held in Khartoum in February. The Nile Valley Parliament, with 30 members from each country, met for the first time, also in the Sudanese capital, May 25–31; the mainly procedural meeting set up committees to discuss the inauguration of a common currency, the exchange of agricultural experts, and the removal of trade barriers.

U.S. Relations. President Mubarak visited Washington and met with President Ronald Reagan at the end of January and again at the end of September. There were, however, some strains in the relationship. Mubarak was anxious not to appear too close to the United States, presumably to placate internal critics. The U.S. response in February to the resurgence of an apparent Libyan threat to the Sudan (four AWACS planes were sent to Egypt and the carrier *Nimitz* was stationed off the Libyan coast) was described by some Egyptian officials as an overreaction, and there was some controversy as to whether or not the steps had been taken in response to Egyptian requests.

Events in Chad during June and July—when rebel forces supported by Libya took over the northern third of the country—led to AWACS planes again being sent to Egypt. Joint U.S.-Egyptian military maneuvers began August 10 and lasted a month, but the Egyptian government imposed a total blackout on reports. Talks about the building of a U.S.-financed naval base at Ras Bannas on the Red Sea were suspended in mid-May. Sadat in 1981 had promised that the base would be available for U.S. use in an emergency, but Mubarak's attitude was much more qualified.

President Mubarak was also moving in various ways toward a rapprochement with the Soviet Union. Some Soviet advisers had been readmitted in 1982, and on Feb. 15, 1983, Foreign Minister Kamal Hassan Ali said that Egypt was ready to resume full diplomatic relations. Nevertheless, U.S. financial support is still essential to Egypt, and when Kamal Hassan visited Washington in December it was primarily in the hope of raising the level of U.S. military grants in fiscal 1985 to $1.4 billion from the proposed $1.1 billion.

Mideast Relations. If Mubarak was cautiously approaching the Soviet Union, he was edging in the other direction in relations with Israel. The Egyptian ambassador (withdrawn in 1982) did not return to his post in 1983. Mubarak criticized Israel in speeches to the non-aligned summit in New Delhi (March 12) and the UN General Assembly (September 28). PLO leader Yasir Arafat, who passed through Egypt on December 23 after his debacle in Lebanon, was met cordially by Mubarak, to the annoyance of Israel. All this was no doubt part of a calculated campaign—partly successful— to end Egypt's isolation in the Arab world. The foreign minister of Iraq, to which Egypt has given substantial assistance in its war with Iran, visited Egypt on July 3 for the first time since the Camp David accords. A trade agreement in December ended a five-year trade boycott by Jordan and looked toward a total removal of tariffs and other barriers between the two countries. Trade agreements with Iraq and Lebanon also were signed during the course of the year.

ARTHUR CAMPBELL TURNER
University of California, Riverside

EGYPT • Information Highlights

Official Name: Arab Republic of Egypt.
Location: Northeastern Africa.
Area: 386,200 sq mi (1 000 258 km^2).
Population (July 1983 est.): 45,851,000.
Government: *Head of state*, Hosni Mubarak, president (took office Oct. 1981). *Head of government*, Ahmed Fuad Mohieddin, prime minister (took office Jan. 1982). *Legislature* (unicameral)—People's Assembly.
Monetary Unit: Pound (0.699 pound equals U.S.$1, Dec. 30, 1983).
Gross National Product (1981–82 U.S.$): $30,800,000,000.
Economic Index (1982): *Consumer Prices* (1970 = 100), all items, 310.1; food, 387.8.
Foreign Trade (1982 U.S.$): *Imports*, $7,755,000,000; *exports*, $3,120,000,000.

ENERGY

The supply of energy was not a major issue in the United States during 1983. Scarcity was only a memory as an oil glut and a gas bubble dominated the energy picture.

Three factors explained the continuation of the oil glut that had developed in 1982: a weak worldwide economy, continuing efforts aimed at oil conservation, and the development of additional oil-production capacity, particularly in Mexico and the North Sea. The gas bubble resulted from reduced demand caused by a less-than-robust economy, abnormally warm weather in the winter of 1982–83, energy conservation efforts, and rapidly rising prices for natural gas.

These two surplus-supply situations had differing effects on consumer prices. As a result of weak world demand for oil, the Organization of Petroleum Exporting Countries (OPEC) formally reduced the benchmark price from $34 to $29 per barrel. This resulted in lower gasoline and fuel-oil prices for Americans. By comparison, some consumers saw the price they paid for natural gas increase by as much as 25%. The anomaly of surplus supply and rising prices made natural gas the predominant energy concern in 1983.

The Natural Gas Anomaly

To understand the natural gas issue, one must recall the perceptions of supply immediately following the shortage in the cold winter of 1976–77. At that time, it was widely believed that the United States faced a declining supply of gas. Based on this perception, Congress passed the Natural Gas Policy Act (NGPA) of 1978. That legislation established two broad categories of regulated prices for conventional gas but eliminated price regulation for hard-to-produce gas—for example, that produced from wells deeper than 15,000 ft (4 570 m).

"Take-or-Pay" Contracts. Responding to a combination of the NGPA pricing system and a belief that gas would be in short supply, a number of gas pipeline companies signed what were known as "take-or-pay" contracts with producers of high-cost, unregulated gas. These contracts legally obligated pipeline companies to pay producers in some cases as much as $9 per thousand cubic feet, even if they did not take the gas.

To understand the actions of the pipeline companies, it is important to know that at any point in time they have large numbers of purchase contracts. Some of the contracts may be as much as 20 years old with purchase prices of less than $1 per thousand cubic feet. Pipeline companies expected to charge consumers an average of purchase prices, which in some cases ranged from less than a dollar to as much

© G. Mathieson/Gamma-Liaison
Secretary Donald Hodel presents the National Energy Policy Plan, calling for minimal federal control of markets.

as $9 per thousand cubic feet. Most of the old, low-cost contracts, however, did not have "take-or-pay" provisions.

Given the "take-or-pay" contracts, when demand for gas dropped, the pipeline companies found themselves forced to buy high-priced gas while refusing low-priced gas. These prices were passed on to consumers. Thus the anomaly existed of a plentiful gas supply occurring at the same time as a rapid increase in price.

Deregulation. Consumers reacted by demanding governmental action to reduce prices. Partly in response to this pressure, President Reagan proposed controversial legislation that would have totally deregulated prices. Supporters of deregulation advanced two arguments. First, since the partial deregulation in 1978, discoveries of new gas reserves had been enough to replace the gas produced and used each year. Second, proponents contended, conservation efforts by Americans had already, and would in the future, put a ceiling on gas demand. Thus, deregulation would result in abundant reserves and conservation-limited demand—and, therefore, cheap gas.

Opponents of deregulation called for continued and increased regulation, arguing three points. First, they questioned the abundance of yet-to-be-discovered gas, noting that there was no scientific basis for believing that large, new gas reserves could be discovered. Second, they maintained, the reduction in gas demand, which during the first six months of 1983 was down by 10% from the comparable 1982 period, was more the result of a poor economy and a very warm winter than of energy conservation. Third, opponents said, the result would be excessive windfall profits for the large oil companies, which own 50% of low-cost, regulated gas.

By the end of the year, no resolution of these conflicting views had been found.

Other Sources and Issues

Without the pressure of rapidly rising prices to focus public attention, most debate on the nongas portion of the nation's energy system occurred within the professional energy community. The boundaries of that debate were set by the fact that during the first half of 1983 overall energy consumption was roughly 6% lower than in the similar period of 1982. Overall domestic energy production was lower by roughly 7%, with the difference made up by imports. This situation, in the context of a world oil surplus, caused most observers of the nation's energy system to be optimistic about the future.

Some energy analysts predicted years of abundant, low-cost energy with the likelihood of further reductions in OPEC prices. Most optimists, however, put some qualifiers on their optimism. Those qualifications resulted because there were areas of substantial uncertainty concerning energy supply and demand. First, as was true of natural gas, there were very real differences in opinion as to the cause of declining demand for energy. The optimists

believe that energy conservation is the primary cause of declining demand. The pessimists believe the cause to be a depressed worldwide economy, and that as the economy rebounds, so will energy demand.

Oil. The most unpredictable and difficult-to-assess source of energy continued to be oil. Discoveries of new domestic reserves during the year were not sufficient to replace production. Most experts believe U.S. oil reserves will continue to decline. Even if the United States continues to reduce oil consumption, the best that can be hoped for is that the nation will remain dependent on imports for over a third of its oil through the rest of the century.

Any significant increase in oil consumption, either in the United States or in the rest of the world, that reduces the surplus could make the nation susceptible to another oil shock. An exchange reported in the Sept. 26, 1983, issue of *Time* magazine most accurately characterized the situation with regard to a third oil shock. In response to a comment by Walter Heller, chairman of the Council of Economic Advisers under President Kennedy, that "There is no third oil shock anywhere in sight," James McKie, professor of economics at the University of Texas, agreed but added a caveat: "There was no second oil shock in sight before 1978 and no first oil shock in sight prior to 1973. The history of energy prices is a history of surprises."

The Washington Public Power Supply System (WPPSS) defaulted on $2.25 billion in bonds for two nuclear power plants.
Washington Public Power Supply System

The concern expressed by McKie was underlined by a study carried out by the International Energy Agency (IEA), reported in September. The IEA indicated that a third oil shock could drive the price of oil, over a very short period of time, from its present $29 per barrel to as much as $98 per barrel. Simply stated, although optimism characterized the general view of the nation's energy system during 1983, experts disagreed on how long that would last.

Municipal Default. Numerous other events during the year pointed up why many energy experts expressed only cautious optimism about the future. One widely reported development was the default in July by the Washington Public Power Supply System (WPPSS) on $2.25 billion worth of bonds that had been sold to pay for the construction of two nuclear-power plants. WPPSS is a consortium of electricity producers established in the northwestern United States. It had committed itself to the construction of five nuclear-power plants. The electricity-generating organizations in the Northwest created WPPSS, based on projections of heavy future demand for electricity. Since the creation of WPPSS, projections of electricity demand have been significantly reduced and, in parallel, the costs of the nuclear-power plants have significantly increased. These factors led to the largest municipal bond default in U.S. history.

Nuclear Energy. The WPPSS default was only the most graphic example of what has occurred in the electric-power industry since the 1973 oil embargo. That industry, once the cardinal example of a secure, predictable industry, continued during 1983 to make adjustments to declining demand and the skyrocketing costs of nuclear plants. A number of utilities that found themselves with excess generating capacity canceled plans to build nuclear plants.

Similarly, the nation's effort to build a second-generation nuclear-power plant remained unresolved. Construction on that plant, a liquid-metal, fast-breeder reactor that was to be located on the Clinch River in Tennessee, was authorized by Congress in 1970 with an expected cost of $700 million. More than $1 billion has been spent on the design and purchase of equipment for the plant, but no construction has begun. Estimates of the completion costs range between $3 and $8 billion. The Reagan administration remained committed to the Clinch River plant and pushed hard in 1983 for new legislation that would allow construction to proceed. By the end of the year, however, it had not been possible to achieve congressional approval, and the Clinch River facility remained stalemated.

Industrial Recession. A recession in the oil industry that had begun during 1982 continued through 1983. In the latter half of the year, the number of operating drilling rigs began to increase, but the number was still less than half of what it had been at the peak of the oil boom in 1981. Oil industry profits were down, and bankruptcies continued. Those sections of the country, particularly Texas and Oklahoma, that had escaped the initial economic recession because of a booming oil industry were, in 1983, lagging behind in economic recovery.

Federal Leasing. As secretary of the interior, James Watt continued to press for accelerated leasing of energy resources on federal lands. Under the secretary's expanded five-year offshore lease schedule for the Outer Continental Shelf (OCS), the Interior Department posted the largest single sale in history—$3.5 billion was bid for 3.2 million acres (1.3 million ha) in the Gulf of Mexico. However, environmental interest groups were vigorously opposing accelerated offshore leasing in Alaska, California, and New England. The number of court challenges to federal leasing increased markedly during 1983. It appeared likely that, except for the Gulf of Mexico, there would be a slowdown in OCS leasing until a number of the issues were resolved in the courts.

Similarly, Secretary Watt's accelerated leasing of federal coal lands became a point of major controversy. In an effort to increase the amount of coal acreage leased, Secretary Watt had modified leasing procedures. Many of his critics believed those modifications resulted in the sale of coal lands for less than they were worth, and Congress acted to block any additional leasing until an independent commission had reviewed the leasing procedures. In discussing that commission, Secretary Watt characterized the members as "a black, a woman, two Jews, and a cripple." These comments created a major furor and led, for the first time, to calls by influential Republican senators for his resignation. Secretary Watt resigned on Oct. 9, 1983. The administration, however, was quick to emphasize that there would be no change in Watt's policies under the new secretary, William P. Clark.

Department of Energy. The Reagan administration had come into office with the goal of abolishing the Department of Energy, established in 1977. By the end of 1983, in the face of substantial congressional opposition, the administration appeared to have given up its efforts to eliminate the department. Its 1983 budget proposals for the department, however, continued the administration's push to withdraw substantial support for energy research and development with two exceptions: long-range research devoted primarily to high-energy physics, and support for nuclear breeder and fusion work. As in 1981 and 1982, however, Congress modified the administration's proposals and maintained support for fossil fuels, solar energy, and conservation.

DON E. KASH
The University of Oklahoma

OPEC—A New Appraisal

Suomen Kuvapalvelu Oy/Gamma-Liaison

OPEC conferences have been the focus of international attention since the 1970s.

The Organization of Petroleum Exporting Countries—most commonly referred to as OPEC—managed to weather major problems in 1983, problems that threatened the very survival of the oil cartel. And while the future of OPEC no longer seemed as bright as it once had, the experiences of the year indicated that OPEC might very well be on the international economic scene for a long time to come.

Background. OPEC was established in 1960 as an instrument of its member countries to control their own oil-producing destinies rather than leave the future to the big Western oil companies, which until then had called most of the shots on the world oil market. (OPEC has 13 members—Algeria, Ecuador, Gabon, Indonesia, Iran, Iraq, Kuwait, Libya, Nigeria, Qatar, Saudi Arabia, United Arab Emirates, and Venezuela.) Despite the presence of non-Arab members in OPEC, it is the Arab states of the Persian Gulf that have the most influence over the organization because the Persian Gulf area contains enormous oil reserves.

In the 1960s, OPEC was hardly noticed. This changed in the wake of the 1973 Arab-Israeli war and the Arab oil boycott against countries friendly to Israel. Suddenly OPEC was perceived in the international arena as an all-powerful giant that could determine oil prices at will. Even some OPEC members—the so-called "hawks" that constantly wanted to increase oil prices—suffered from this hubris. From 1974 through 1981 the world's oil-con-

suming countries quivered in fear as OPEC announced one price rise after another. During this period the base price of a barrel of OPEC oil soared from about $3 per barrel to $34 per barrel. The temporary halt of Iranian oil production caused by the 1979 revolution that ousted the shah only spurred the upward price spiral.

But in 1982 and 1983 the roof fell in on OPEC. The cartel had to answer to the simple law of supply and demand. The world had an oil glut. The glut came about for a number of reasons. A worldwide recession in both rich and poor countries led to a decline in the demand for oil. Inflationary pressures—caused partially by rising oil prices—eventually resulted in an economic downturn. Perhaps more important was that soaring OPEC oil prices stimulated the production of energy from non-OPEC sources. High oil prices meant that the United States and other countries could once again profitably develop their domestic energy resources. Low OPEC prices in the 1960s had made much U.S. oil production unprofitable—it was cheaper to import OPEC oil. Also, high OPEC prices in the 1970s gave Mexico, the Soviet Union, and Britain (with its North Sea oil) a chance to carve out large hunks from the international oil market at the expense of OPEC.

In addition, nonfossil energy, ranging from nuclear power to wind and solar sources, seemed to be the wave of the future. Energy sources that were too expensive when OPEC oil was cheap seemed economical as OPEC oil became more and more expensive.

Ironically, OPEC forced the world to practice energy conservation. It is estimated that high oil prices led to a 32% improvement in energy efficiency in the United States. Other industrialized countries posted similar results, reducing even more oil demand.

At the height of its power, OPEC accounted for two thirds of the non-Communist world's oil production. By 1983 this OPEC share was down to about 40%. In 1979, OPEC could pump 31 million barrels per day and still find plenty of buyers. In 1983, OPEC production ranged from 17 million to 19 million barrels per day—and even this amount was considered too much for the oil market.

OPEC states that had accumulated large balance-of-payments surpluses now were running huge deficits. Such OPEC members as Nigeria and Venezuela, which had embarked on development programs, found themselves in heavy debt because of falling oil revenues.

1983 Developments. OPEC's effort to deal with the oil glut by reducing production was only partially successful. Some OPEC countries cheated, producing more oil than the agreed quotas. But even without cheating, there was still too much oil on the market.

In March 1983, OPEC ministers meeting in Geneva took what was for the cartel a revolutionary step. For the first time in the 23-year history of OPEC, the organization lowered its base price. The new price was $29 per barrel, $5 lower than the previous $34 base price. Production was set at 17.5 million barrels per day.

During the year, OPEC managed to keep the price from sinking further. At times, production did exceed quotas, but not enough to destroy OPEC's price-production structure.

Most OPEC members were unhappy with the situation. Libya had been the leader of the "hawks" in demanding constantly increasing prices. Nigeria and Venezuela needed more funds to pay their debts. Iran and Iraq wanted more revenues to finance the war they had been waging since 1980. But despite complaints and grumbling, the March agreement was reaffirmed in December when OPEC officials again met in Geneva. Even the most disgruntled members—Iran and Libya in particular—had to accept that there was no other solution to OPEC's problems.

The Outlook. A further decline in the OPEC base price could not be ruled out. The cartel can no longer block price decreases. But 1983 showed that OPEC had enough power to slow these decreases. Without concerted action by OPEC members in 1983, world oil prices might have fallen much more than was the case.

A key element in OPEC's success is the power wielded by Saudi Arabia—the cartel's

UPI

The oil ministers from Saudi Arabia, Venezuela, and Algeria discuss prices-quotas at an emergency OPEC summit.

largest producer—in keeping OPEC oil prices and production in line with international economic reality. At the height of the oil boom, Saudi Arabia increased its daily production to 11 million barrels per day in order to put enough oil on the market to keep the price from going even higher. The Saudis had long warned that high prices would contribute to an oil glut. On the other hand, in 1983, Saudi Arabia was producing less than 5 million barrels per day to prevent the glut from becoming worse. Saudi Arabia played a major role in working out the March agreement on the price cut and production controls. In the final analysis, if the "hawks" in OPEC proved too stubborn, Saudi Arabia could out-produce, undersell them, and go it alone.

Although OPEC has often been portrayed as a villain, the fact of the matter is that more often than not the cartel has reacted to international economic factors over which it had little control. In the raging international inflation of the 1970s, oil prices soared. When recession set in during the early 1980s, OPEC's price had to fall.

While OPEC is not as powerful as it was in the 1970s, its huge oil reserves make the cartel vitally important to the non-Communist world. Oil is still the number one world energy source. In a crisis the countries of the free world would have to turn to OPEC for simple strategic reasons. OPEC oil is readily accessible and such OPEC members as Saudi Arabia have been traditionally pro-Western. The Western countries are in a better position in dealing with Saudi Arabia—OPEC's de facto leader—than in having to rely on the Soviet Union, the world's largest oil producer, for its energy.

AARON R. EINFRANK

A six-lane bridge spanning Seattle's Harbor Island features precast girders and a concrete cast-in-place deck.

ENGINEERING, CIVIL

Despite high construction costs, many diverse engineering projects were under way in the United States and other nations during 1983.

Bridges

United States. At Seattle, WA, work continued on the high-level Duwamish Waterway Crossing on the West Seattle Freeway, a $150 million, 5,700-ft (1 737-m) bridge. The six-lane highway structure consists of twin, posttensioned, concrete box girders—a 590-ft (180-m) center span, flanked by 375-ft (114-m) side spans, with 140-ft (43-m) vertical clearance at the center. The rest of the crossing consists of precast girders with cast-in-place concrete deck. The new bridge, scheduled for completion in 1984, will replace two low-level lift spans.

Northern Ireland. The country's longest bridge is scheduled for completion in 1984 across the River Foyle, connecting Londonderry on the left bank with planned area development on the right bank. The four-lane, $30 million, steel box-girder structure, 1,716 ft (523 m) long, includes a 536-ft (163-m) center span flanked by 590-ft (180-m) side spans. Spans consist of two separate steel boxes made up of 60-ft (18-m) flat plate, welded segments. The segments were placed on barges, towed to the site, and lifted into position by jacks.

Switzerland. North of the Italian border, Switzerland is building Biaschina Viaduct, a four-lane bridge spanning the Ticino River gorge. Posttensioned segmental box girders, with span lengths up to 525 ft (160 m), are supported on piers with a maximum height of 291 ft (89 m). The highest point on the dual, 46-ft- (14-m-) wide structure is 328 ft (100 m) above the river; viaduct length is 2,116 ft (645 m). The project is part of Switzerland's 164-mi (264-km) Highway 2 from West Germany to Italy, scheduled for completion in 1986. Cost of the viaduct alone is estimated at $14.4 million.

South Africa. A 12-mi (19-km) stretch of new highway, including three arch bridges, neared completion east of Cape Town along the Indian Ocean. One 541-ft (165-m) arch crosses the Bobbejaans River; a 620-ft (189-m) arch spans Groot River; and the third and largest span, the Bloukrans Gorge bridge, measures 892 ft (272 m) between spring points, with its deck 689 ft (210 m) above the Bloukrans River. All bridges are concrete arches with decks of prestressed concrete to provide 52.5-ft (16-m), four-lane roadways. Construction started in 1980 and is scheduled for completion by 1984 at a cost of $26 million for the bridges alone.

Canals

United States. In 1983 the U.S. Bureau of Reclamation finished a $9 million, 9-mi (14-km) canal section as part of its Central Arizona Project. Excavation totaled 1.7 million yd³ (1.3 million m³) from the 20 to 30-ft- (6 to 9-m-) deep channel with a bottom width of 24 ft (7 m). The contractor on the irrigation waterway employed a custom-built, 240-ft- (73-m-) long traveling conveyor working with a continuous belt loader. Excavated spoil was wasted along the 500-ft (152-m) right of way.

Another large BuRec project is under way on a 14-mi (23-km) section of the New Rockford Canal in North Dakota. The $6.4 million waterway involves more than 2 million yd³ (1.5 million m³) of material in obtaining a 44-ft (13-m) bottom width. Completion is scheduled for 1986.

India. A water pact between India and Bangladesh is expected to be revived in order to provide a 200-mi (322-km) by 650-ft- (198-m-) wide irrigation canal. The proposed channel would divert water from the Brahmaputra River in northeast India through Bangladesh to replenish the diminishing flow of the Ganges River. The diverted water would irrigate 10 million acres (4 million ha) of Bangladesh territory, as well as increase the flow of water along the southern branch of the Ganges.

Dams

United States. In Oklahoma the U.S. Bureau of Reclamation is building the McGee Creek Dam to supply water to Oklahoma City. The earthfill barrier, with rock slope protection, is 1,969 ft (600 m) by 154 ft (47 m) high. The project also includes a 4,592-ft (1 400-m) earthfill dam with a maximum height of 59 ft (18 m). Nearly 2.6 million yd³ (2 million m³) of earthfill make up the embankments. Begun in 1982, the $28 million job is scheduled to be finished in 1985.

Venezuela. Guri Dam on the Caroni River, which was started in 1965 and is being built in three stages, eventually will supply 10,300 Mw of electric power to the Guayana industrial complex at the confluence of the Orinoco and Caroni rivers. The project ran into difficulties, but the $4.6 billion (U.S.) hydroelectric expansion is due for completion by 1986. The 1,579-ft (481-m) concrete gravity structure is being raised from 348 ft (106 m) to 532 ft (162 m), and lengthened by 1,900 ft (579 m) to 3,479 ft (1 060 m), increasing the power pool from 14.3 million acre-ft to 110 million acre-ft. It would then be one of the world's largest hydroelectric projects, supplying 60% of the country's electricity. Included are earth and rockfill embankments totaling 5.5 mi (8.9 km), involving 93 million yd³ (71 million m³) of fill.

Norway. The Norwegian State Power Authority is building the Ulla-Foerre hydroelectric project, about 140 mi (225 km) west of Oslo, to develop 2,020 Mw of electric power. The $1.25 billion scheme includes four major dams and 78 mi (126 km) of connecting tunnels. The barriers will form Blasjo Reservoir, elevation 3,300 ft (1 006 m), from which water will flow through tunnels to three power plants. The four dams are: Oddutjorn, a rockfill embankment 460 ft (140 m) high by 1,600 ft (488 m); Forreskard, another rockfill dam, 260 ft (79 m) high by 1,600 ft (488 m); Storvatn, an asphaltic-concrete core earthfill, 300 ft (91 m) high by 4,600 ft (1 402 m); and Forrevatn, to be the tallest concrete arch dam in Scandinavia with a height of 260 ft (79 m) by 4,300 ft (1 311 m).

Work continued on Oklahoma's McGee Creek Water Project, which includes a massive earthfill barrier and dam.

M. Trevino/U.S. Dept. of Interior, Bureau of Reclamation

Blasjo Reservoir will hold 790 billion gal (2 990 billion l), but will take three years to fill after the dams are completed in 1987.

South Korea. Multipurpose Chungju Dam is a concrete gravity structure 62 mi (100 km) southeast of Seoul on the Han River. The $655 million project will store water for municipal use, flood control, and irrigation, as well as to generate 400 Mw of power for Seoul and Inchon. The dam is 320 ft (98 m) high by 1,522 ft (464 m) and impounds 1.6 million acre-ft of water. During construction the river was diverted through two tunnels 39 ft (12 m) in diameter and 2,050 ft and 2,297 ft (625 m and 700 m) long. An underground powerhouse is equipped with four 100-Mw turbines and is scheduled for completion in 1985.

Tunnels

United States. Work was again under way on a 3.4-mi (5.5-km) section of New York City's Water Tunnel No. 3. Tunneling on the 24-ft- (7-m-) diameter bore, 13.3 mi (21 km) long, started in 1970 but had been delayed by labor and fiscal problems. Eventually, the third water tunnel will extend 20.3 mi (33 km) to carry water from a reservoir in Westchester County through The Bronx and Manhattan, then under the East River to Queens. The present work lies 460 to 500 ft (140 to 152 m) under

Manhattan and will cost about $120 million. The rock tunnel, excavated by drilling and blasting, will be concrete-lined. Tunnel No. 3, due for completion by the end of the century, will supplement two existing tunnels.

Colombia. A 24-mi (39-km), 12-ft- (4-m-) diameter bore is being driven under the Andes Mountains to supply water to Bogotá. The $250 million tunnel is stage 1 of a hydroelectric project to bring water from Chingaza Reservoir, fed by the Bogotá River, to Colombia's capital. Work on the tunnel, at various depths under the mountains, is due for completion in 1984. Water will drop from an elevation of 10,611 ft (3 234 m) at the reservoir to 8,374 ft (2 552 m) where it connects to the existing distribution system for Bogotá.

Japan. Japan completed the pilot bore for the 34-mi (55-km) Seikan Tunnel, 800 ft (244 m) under Tsugaru Strait to join the main island of Honshu with the northern island of Hokkaido. The 20-year project was driven by boring machines and conventional mining. The oval-shaped pilot tunnel, 16.5 ft (5 m) wide by 10 ft (3 m) high, lies below the service tunnel and the main, two-track 38-ft- (12-m-) wide by 15-ft- (5-m-) high oval-shaped tunnel. The world's longest railroad tunnel, due for completion in 1984, will cost more than $2 billion.

WILLIAM H. QUIRK
Construction Consultant

New York City's Tunnel No. 3, to be completed by the end of the century, will be 20.3 mi (33 km) long.

City of New York/Bureau of Water Supply

ENVIRONMENT

Backed by the International Union for the Conservation of Nature and Natural Resources (IUCN), several nations, both developed and developing, took steps to initiate programs under the World Conservation Strategy, a global blueprint for conservation launched by IUCN in 1980. A number of major international meetings on conservation and the environment also took place during 1983.

In the United States, environmental groups and the Reagan administration remained at odds over the policies of Secretary of the Interior James Watt, who in October resigned because his "usefulness" to the administration had "come to an end." Earlier in the year, Environmental Protection Agency (EPA) Administrator Anne Gorsuch Burford resigned in the face of a congressional investigation and mounting public opposition. Still, the Reagan administration took some steps that many, if not all, conservation groups viewed favorably.

World Developments

Hailing the agreement as a "milestone," the IUCN established a formal collaboration with the International Planned Parenthood Federation (IPPF) to protect the "global environment and to reduce the pressure of population growth." The agreement between the two organizations was signed during January in London. Underlying the pact, according to the IUCN, was the provision in the World Conservation Strategy that recognizes "the importance of integrating action on the issues of environment, resources, and population."

The World Conservation Strategy, a guideline for IUCN activities, was developed with the help of the United Nations Environment Programme and the World Wildlife Fund, in collaboration with the UN Food and Agriculture Organization (FAO) and the UN Educational, Scientific, and Cultural Organization (UNESCO).

Under the terms of the agreement between the IUCN and Planned Parenthood, the two groups would work together through meetings, workshops, and field projects, and would consult each other on policy matters. They also would create joint strategies for public education on the relationship between population and environmental problems.

CITES. More than 300 participants from 62 nations and conservation organizations met during April in Botswana for the fourth session of the Conference of Parties to the Convention on International Trade in Endangered Species of Fauna and Flora (CITES).

Discussions at the meeting demonstrated that CITES is a flexible arrangement, recognizing the need for legitimate use of natural re-

© Bill Nation/Sygma

On September 1, EPA added 133 hazardous waste sites to its "national priority list," bringing the total to 546.

sources while protecting those in danger. Attempts by some delegates to eliminate restrictions on trade in products from wolves and otters, as well as various items of ivory, were withdrawn. Participants also decided to ban all international trade in several species of whales —minke, Bryde's, pigmy right, and four types of bottlenose.

At the same time, heeding a request by several African countries, the delegates also removed some protection for the leopard in parts of southern and eastern Africa where the species is not considered in any danger. Leopards can be hunted, and products from the animals, such as pelts, can be traded as personal effects. This arrangement allows for control of leopards where they endanger people and livestock, while preventing a rebirth of illegal trade in furs.

The number of nations to join CITES continued to increase during the year. St. Lucia became a member of the pact in March, Thailand joined in April, and the Congo became the 81st member in May.

National Conservation Strategies. Several countries worked on preparing their national conservation strategies under the guidelines of the World Conservation Strategy. Prepared by the World Wildlife Fund-Italy and financed by the federal ministry of agriculture, the Italian conservation strategy headed toward implementation on a national level. A mission from the IUCN and World Wildlife Fund visited

Madagascar in April to draw up a framework under which that country's government could develop its version of the strategy. And meetings were held by the IUCN and the government of Senegal for a similar purpose. The Netherlands began a study to investigate possible review of the government's national and international policies as they affect the World Conservation Strategy.

Park Protection Plans. An action plan evolving out of the 1982 World National Parks Congress in Bali was presented through the IUCN. Its aim is to help agencies of various countries in protecting parks and other nature preserves. Ten objectives were announced as part of the plan, which calls for the establishment by 1992 of a worldwide network of national parks and protected areas covering all terrestrial ecological regions. Marine, coastal, and freshwater protected areas were to be incorporated into the network, while the ecological and managerial quality of already-protected areas were to be upgraded. Other objectives included economic support for countries trying to manage protected areas, creation of an effective international monitoring and inventory service, and promoting international cooperation in behalf of national parks and preserves.

Caribbean Marine Protection. Meeting at Cartagena, Colombia, in March 1983, several Caribbean governments and the European Community (EC) agreed on a convention that would protect and develop the Caribbean marine environment as well as combat oil spills.

All attending governments from the area except Costa Rica, Cuba, Guatemala, and Trinidad and Tobago signed the agreement. The ones that did not said that they agreed with the provisions but could not formally accept because of domestic technical, juridical, or constitutional reasons. The countries that did sign were Colombia, Grenada, Honduras, Jamaica,

Mexico, Nicaragua, Panama, St. Lucia, and Venezuela, as well as the United States, France, the Netherlands, and the United Kingdom. The signatories declared their willingness to recognize the Caribbean's special environmental characteristics, its vulnerability to pollution, and the need to consider environmental problems in plans for development.

Rhino Horn. A decrease in commercial demand for rhinoceros horn was reported in April by the IUCN. Rhino horn is used in Asia for various products, ranging from folk medicines to dagger handles. Prices as high as $1,000 per kilo had fueled poaching and led to a drastic decline in the population of black African rhinos. Among the reasons cited for the drop in demand was that Japan and Hong Kong, two major consumers, stopped importing. The horn of the saiga antelope, a species extremely abundant in northern Asia, has become an acceptable substitute for that of the rhino as a source of medicinal preparations. North Yemen, which had imported large amounts of rhino horn for dagger handles, has banned the importation of the product.

Environment/Development Seminar. A five-day seminar on environmental planning for sustainable development was held in spring 1983 at the Tufts University European Center on Lake Annency, France. Representatives from international conservation and development organizations attended the session, aimed at promoting development based on the use of renewable natural resources.

U.S. Developments

James Watt and Administration Policy. The resignation of Interior Secretary James Watt in October culminated an ongoing feud with most of the country's environmental groups. Ironically, it was Watt's outspoken comments on

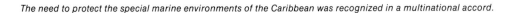

The need to protect the special marine environments of the Caribbean was recognized in a multinational accord.

Bradley Smith/Photo Researchers

Secretary of the Interior James Watt, left, shares a laugh with the groom at the February wedding of EPA Administrator Anne Gorsuch Burford, right. Secretary Watt and Mrs. Burford both resigned later in the year amid controversy.

nonenvironmental matters that precipitated his departure. The resignation came soon after he was quoted in the media for what many considered inappropriate ethnic remarks about appointees to an advisory commission. Behind the resignation, however, was a great swell of public opposition to Watt's attitudes and policies on the environment.

One of the critical areas of contention was the use of federally owned lands. Watt and the administration opened a vast amount of federal land for energy exploration—more than during the tenure of any previous secretary of the interior. Watt pushed for increased private enterprise on public lands, alarming such environmental groups as the National Audubon Society and the Sierra Club. And the secretary also advocated increased multiple use of such public lands as wilderness areas and national parks, an approach opposed by some conservation groups.

Perhaps the most heated debate of the year was over the Alaska National Hunting Bill, which would reopen millions of acres of Alaskan wilderness to sportsmen, as well as subsistence hunters who had already been allowed to hunt there. The Sierra Club and National Audubon Society, while not opposed to sport hunting, fought intensely against the bill, which was backed by the Interior Department, the National Rifle Association, and several hunting groups. Congress was largely split on party lines, with Republicans for and Democrats against the bill.

Another area of disagreement was Watt's policy of improving facilities in national parks

and other public holdings before acquiring new lands. Watt initiated a $1 billion, five-year rehabilitation program that many environmental organizations felt was at the expense of land acquisition, particularly of areas that might serve as buffers for existing parks and wild areas.

Reagan's nominee for successor to Watt, National Security Adviser William P. Clark, was opposed by environmental groups on grounds of inexperience. With Watt having represented the basic administration philosophy, and with other Interior officials still in place, little change was expected in policy.

New Refuges. Amid all the criticism of its land programs, however, the Interior Department did acquire some important new lands. One was the ecologically important Currituck National Wildlife Refuge on North Carolina's Outer Banks. Officially added to the National Wildlife Refuge System on August 2, the 5,175-acre (2 070-ha) tract is in an area that supports 150,000 wintering waterfowl. The Carter administration, urged on by environmentalists, had proposed establishing a 15,880-acre (6 352-ha) refuge in the region at a cost of $94 million, but it never received Congressional approval. The area obtained by the Reagan administration had been held by the Nature Conservancy and was thus already a preserve, though not under federal protection. Part of the land was donated to the government by the Conservancy. The remainder was purchased at a cost of $500,000.

Another significant land acquisition was of 14,175 acres (5 736 ha) added to the Yukon

© O. Franken/Sygma

After soil testing in Times Beach, MO, showed severe dioxin contamination, EPA offered to buy up town property.

Delta National Wildlife Refuge and the Kenai National Wildlife Refuge. The areas were obtained from a coalition of Alaskan corporations. In exchange, the corporations were granted temporary use of a portion of St. Matthew Island in the Alaska Maritime National Wildlife Refuge as a base for oil and gas exploration in the Bering Sea. The rights to use of the island eventually will return to the federal government.

EPA. William D. Ruckelshaus, a timber company executive who had been head of the federal Environmental Protection Agency from 1970 to 1973, returned to the post in May 1983. His appointment by President Reagan followed a long controversy over the management of EPA's "Superfund," intended to pay for the cleanup of toxic waste dumps. That controversy resulted in the dismissal of Superfund chief Rita Lavelle in February, and the resignation of EPA head Anne Gorsuch Burford a few weeks later.

Established in 1980 to help pay the price of cleaning up toxic wastes in such places as Times Beach, MO, a community found to be contaminated by the chemical dioxin from industrial wastes, the Superfund came under increasing Congressional criticism. The EPA was accused of misusing money in the fund, of holding back on cleanup, and of favoring industries involved in the nation's toxic waste problem.

Lavelle was dismissed after charges that she had harassed an EPA staff member who was criticizing the handling of the fund. Anne Gorsuch, who became Anne Burford by marriage to Interior Department aide Robert Burford during the controversy, was a casualty of the issue after it threatened to reach "Watergate" proportions.

Times Beach. One of Burford's last acts as EPA chief was to fly to Times Beach in February to inform residents that the EPA would buy their property for a total of $33 million. The community of 2,000 people 25 mi (40 km) southwest of St. Louis had been contaminated by dioxin in landfills and by oil sprayed on its streets to control dust in the 1970s.

Eagle Killings. An undercover investigation by agents of the United States Fish and Wildlife Service revealed that up to 300 bald eagles, protected under law, had been killed over the previous three years to supply feathers, beaks, talons, and bones for a black market in Native American artifacts. The items were used to make reproductions of headdresses, rattles, jewelry, lances, whistles, and various ornaments sold to hobbyists and collectors. Many of the items made from eagle parts, and of several other species of birds as well, were shipped to Europe, where interest in American Indians "is strong," according to the Fish and Wildlife Service. The illicit market in eagle parts is highly lucrative. War bonnets made of eagle feathers can sell for $5,000. Ceremonial fans often bring a price of up to $800.

Most of the eagles were killed near the Karl E. Mundt National Wildlife Refuge in South Dakota and Nebraska, established in 1974 as a sanctuary for wintering and migrating eagles. The birds were killed with baited traps or shot while roosting in trees at night. Under federal regulations, the Fish and Wildlife Service provides Native Americans with eagle feathers, for legitimate religious uses only, from a feather repository in Pocatello, ID. The feathers are obtained from birds found dead from accidents or other causes. Feathers may not be traded, bartered, or sold.

Acid Rain. Acidity in rainfall continued to be a problem during the year, with environmentalists calling for a 50% reduction in the amount of sulfur dioxide emitted from coal-fired power plants, one of the precursors of acid rain and snow. Industry and the Reagan administration took the stand that more needs to be understood about acid precipitation and its impact before expensive controls are put into effect.

Acid rain has caused some lakes, notably in northern New York State, to lose their fish. Mostly, however, these lakes have poor buffer zones or bottoms that retain acidity. The extent of the acid rain problem is not entirely clear. The Sport Fishing Institute, for example, maintained that acid rain is a threat to aquatic life in certain parts of the country but perhaps not a major danger to freshwater fish over a large area. A 1983 report from the National Academy of Sciences, on the other hand, said that the problem of acid rain is of such magnitude that acid deposition in the environment should be cut by half. This means that sulfur dioxide pollution would have to be reduced by at least 12 million tons in the eastern United States.

In August the United States and Canada signed an agreement to conduct a joint project to monitor the flow of pollutants that cause acid rain. The accord calls for the two nations to release and then trace an inert (and harmless) gas from plants in Ohio and Ontario, regarded as two primary sources of pollution. (*See also* CANADA.)

Greenhouse Effect. In mid-October, EPA issued an alarming new report, indicating that the "greenhouse effect"—a warming trend caused by buildup of carbon dioxide in the atmosphere—will begin to be felt as early as the 1990s. The rise in average temperatures would have far-reaching consequences on world climates, coastlines, and agricultural production. Calling for immediate measures to deal with the threat, the report called for "a soberness and sense of urgency" and "innovative thinking and strategy-building."

EDWARD R. RICCIUTI
Environment, Science, and Outdoor Writer

As flora and fauna continue to suffer, acid rain has become a highly charged political and economic issue.
© Michael Melford/Wheeler Pictures

ETHIOPIA

Michel Philippot/Sygma

In June, Addis Ababa, Ethiopia's capital, welcomed delegates to the 19th OAU summit conference.

In 1983 famine once again struck Ethiopia; the United States maintained its military pressure, while Ethiopia intensified its military attacks against Somalia; and head of state Mengistu Haile Mariam was named chairman of the Organization of African Unity (OAU).

Famine. Hundreds of thousands of Ethiopians were afflicted by the worst drought and famine to hit northern Ethiopia in a decade. Distribution of food was hampered by the low-keyed but continuing guerrilla war taking place in Eritrea and Tigre, two of the worst afflicted regions. Begemdir and Wallo regions also were affected. The United States, despite its poor diplomatic relations with Ethiopia, shipped $6.7 million in food aid during 1983 and was planning to send an additional $3 million in aid. M. Peter McPherson, director of the Agency for International Development, maintained that although Ethiopia is a "Soviet ally . . . a hungry child knows no politics and you cannot blame a child for what the government does."

The Horn of Africa. In July the United States announced that 5,500 of its troops would take part in military exercises in Egypt, while 1,350 additional troops would engage in war games in Oman and the Sudan. One month later the Pentagon dispatched 2,800 U.S. troops to Somalia for joint military exercises. These maneuvers were seen as part of the U.S. policy to isolate and bring pressure upon the Soviet-dominated states in the region—Ethiopia, Libya, South Yemen. In response to the increasing U.S.-Somali pressure, Ethiopia, in July, launched ground and air attacks against Somalia, invading the central part of the country. While the Ethiopian forces were driven back, the attack was seen as a warning that Ethiopia would not continue to tolerate Somalia's growing dependency upon the United States.

It was revealed in August that Israel, despite the nonexistence of diplomatic relations, has maintained close but secret ties with Ethiopia since 1977, and has been secretly selling arms to Ethiopia. Israeli Prime Minister Mena-

hem Begin was reported to have pressed the United States to reestablish relations with Ethiopia.

Secessionist Troubles. The Eritrea and Tigre regions continued their struggle to secede from Ethiopia. Although their respective movements have been unsuccessful, they continue to tie down more than 100,000 Ethiopian troops. In early June ten Western relief workers, who were held for a month by Tigre guerrillas, were released unharmed. In the same month two teenage boys from northern Ethiopia maintained that they had been persecuted and fled the country on a U.S. freighter.

OAU. Twenty years after the founding of the OAU in Addis Ababa under the auspices of former Ethiopian Emperor Haile Selassie I, Mengistu Halie Mariam was named its new chairman. In his first speech as chairman, Mengistu declared that U.S. involvement in the Horn of Africa was evidence of "the effort of the U.S. administration to work against the forces of democracy and socialism."

Domestic Politics. It was announced by the Ethiopian domestic news service that in 1984 a vanguard political party would be established.

PETER SCHWAB
State University of New York at Purchase

ETHIOPIA · Information Highlights

Official Name: Socialist Ethiopia.
Location: Eastern Africa.
Area: 455,000 sq mi (1 178 450 km²).
Population (July 1983 est.): 31,265,000.
Chief Cities (July 1980): Addis Ababa, the capital, 1,277,159; Asmara, 424,532; Dire Dawa, 82,024.
Government: *Head of state and government,* Mengistu Haile Mariam, chairman of the Provisional Military Administrative Committee (took office Feb. 1977).
Monetary Unit: Birr (2.07 birr equal U.S. $1, June 1983).
Gross Domestic Product (1981 U.S. $): $4,500,000,-000.
Economic Index (March 1982): *Consumer Prices* (1970 = 100), all items, 267.9; food, 291.2.
Foreign Trade (1981 U.S. $): *Imports,* $738,000,000; *exports,* $374,000,000.

Rev. Jesse Jackson predicted that there would be 4 million new black voters registered before November 1984.

ETHNIC GROUPS

"Our time has come!" So declared Rev. Jesse L. Jackson to an enthusiastic audience in the Washington Convention Center in November 1983, as he announced his candidacy for president of the United States. Jackson's declaration, which had been anticipated for months, climaxed the political maneuvering that was a dominant concern of U.S. minority groups throughout the year. Chicago and Philadelphia, the country's second- and fourth-largest cities, elected their first black mayors, and Denver chose its first Hispanic mayor. These political breakthroughs and their ramifications set the stage for unprecedented minority-group involvement in the national elections of 1984.

Black Politics. The least conclusive but most fascinating political movement was the transformation of Jackson from civil-rights activist to presidential contender. Several leading black politicians and activists, Jackson among them, began openly discussing the possibility of a black presidential candidate in the spring of 1983 as part of a strategy to increase black clout at the polls. The primary purpose of such a candidacy would be to increase black voter registration. The Joint Center for Political Studies, a Washington-based research organization, determined that the number of unregistered black voters in several states was greater than President Ronald Reagan's victory margin in those states in 1980. Presumably, if those people registered and voted Democratic, as blacks usually do, the Democratic Party would

have a better chance to reclaim the White House. Black politicians, however, did not want simply to deliver black votes to the Democrats; they sought a greater voice in shaping party policy.

Still, several prominent black politicians did not endorse Jackson. They considered that he was unlikely to win the nomination and that his failure might leave new black voters disenchanted or leave white candidates feeling they owed nothing to black voters. Some also feared that Jackson's candidacy might hurt former Vice-President Walter Mondale, the Democratic front-runner who was considered most sympathetic to blacks.

Jackson, however, maintained that the time was right for a black candidacy that could directly affect the outcome of the presidential nominating process. (Former Rep. Shirley Chisholm of New York made a token run in 1972.) Even those who disagreed with Jackson conceded that he was easily the most articulate and charismatic of the eight Democratic candidates, and that he would inspire thousands of unregistered voters to participate in the electoral process.

The possible results of such participation were demonstrated dramatically in Chicago, where Rep. Harold Washington won the election for mayor. Washington's victory was prefaced with a black-voter registration drive that was aided considerably by the Chicago-based Jackson. A record 82% of all Chicago's voters went to the polls in what was the closest and most bitter election the city had seen in decades. Washington had scored an upset victory in the city's Democratic primary when incumbent Mayor Jane Byrne and state's attorney Richard Daley, son of the late long-time mayor, split the vote of whites and party regulars. In the general election, little-known Republican candidate Bernard Epton mounted a strong challenge in a racially polarized climate that attracted national media attention. In the end black voters overwhelmingly supported Washington along with enough whites to carry him to victory. But the mayor's stated goal of reforming the city's political "machine" continued to be blocked by the city council.

In contrast, the Philadelphia election of W. Wilson Goode was free of controversy. Goode ran a traditional campaign, seeking endorsements from Democratic Party leaders, visiting white precincts, and winning the support of labor unions. He also studiously avoided contact with Jackson, hoping not to make race an issue. As a result, Goode won 25% of the white vote, 98% of the large black turnout, and an overall 55% majority.

In Boston, Melvin H. King, a former state legislator and civil-rights activist, became the first black finalist in that city's mayoral election. Although King lost, his achievement in gaining a runoff was significant.

Hispanics. Even more low-keyed than Goode's triumph in Philadelphia was the election of Federico Peña as mayor of Denver. The city is only 18% Hispanic, but Peña, a former state legislator, built a winning coalition of Hispanics, Asians, blacks, women, young whites, and labor. With his victory, he joined Mayors Henry Cisneros of San Antonio and Maurice Ferre of Miami as Hispanic leaders of major U.S. cities.

Toney Anaya, the country's only current Hispanic governor, took office in Santa Fe, NM, in 1983 and proceeded to spend a good deal of time out of the state. As chairman of a group called Hispanic Force '84, Anaya traveled across America to increase the registration of Hispanic voters. According to the 1980 census, Hispanics made up only 6.4% of the population. But they were the fastest-growing minority group, with a median age of just 23. In addition, millions of Hispanics were resident aliens who could become eligible to vote if they attained citizenship. The Southwest Voter Registration Education Project, a nonpartisan group based in San Antonio, also launched a drive to add one million Hispanics to the voter rolls by the 1984 election.

The untapped potential of Hispanic voters was not lost on either major political party. President Reagan, who won 30% of the Hispanic vote in 1980, traveled to Miami's Little Havana, spoke at an observance of the Mexican holiday Cinco de Mayo in San Antonio, and met with Hispanic representatives in Washington during National Hispanic Heritage week in September.

The political significance of Hispanics to the Democratic Party was made clear in Congress. The House of Representatives was considering a bill that would change the nation's immigration laws. The bill would have imposed civil and criminal penalties on employers who knowingly hired illegal aliens. But some Hispanic activists feared that that provision might prompt employers to discriminate against all Hispanics. Members of the Congressional Hispanic Caucus who opposed the bill passed word to House Speaker Thomas P. (Tip) O'Neill that President Reagan planned to veto the bill. By doing so, they said, Reagan would win favor with Hispanic voters and the Democratic House would be blamed for passing the measure. O'Neill tabled the bill.

Civil Rights. The U.S. Supreme Court ruled 8 to 1 that the Internal Revenue Service had a right to deny tax-exempt status to private schools that practice racial discrimination. Bob Jones University of Greenville, SC, and the Goldsboro Christian Schools of North Carolina had sued the government when their tax-exempt status was denied. Bob Jones prohibits interracial dating; the Goldsboro schools deny admission to blacks. Both schools claimed that their policies were religiously based and that the denial was a breach of their freedom of religion. A year before the decision, President Reagan had provoked a controversy by seeking to grant tax-exempt status to those schools and others that practiced discrimination. Instead, the case was allowed to run its course. Ironically, even though the court's ruling upheld the original government position, it was seen as a setback for the president.

The president had greater success in his effort to tame the U.S. Civil Rights Commission, a body charged with investigating and assessing enforcement of federal civil-rights legislation. The panel had been critical of that enforcement under the Reagan administration. In May the president appointed three new members of the commission who, like himself, were opposed to school busing for racial integration and to racial quotas in hiring. But the Senate made no move to confirm the new members. In October, Reagan simply fired the three liberal commissioners he sought to replace, Mary Frances Berry, Blandina Cardenas Ramirez, and Rabbi Murray Saltzman. Congressional Democrats and Republicans criticized the move as an attempt by the president to stifle dissent. Berry and Cardenas Ramirez sued, claiming that the president did not have authority to dismiss them. At the same time, the entire commission was faced with extinction as its legal authority had expired on September 30th. In November, however, Congress passed legislation that would give the panel new life and preserve a measure of its independence. Congress and the president would each appoint four members.

DENNIS A. WILLIAMS, *"Newsweek"*

EUROPE

James Colburn/Photoreporters
The prospect of new nuclear missiles in Western Europe raised political and diplomatic tensions.

The year 1983 saw an intensification in Europe of the disquiet that began in 1973 when the sudden raising of oil prices plunged the continent into recession.

The emergence of Yuri Andropov as secretary–general of the Soviet Communist Party in late 1982 did not bring any revival of East-West détente. The West European powers, which had linked their agreement to station new U.S.missiles on their territory to evidence of serious efforts by Washington to reach agreement with the Soviet Union on arms reduction, watched with concern the continual disagreements between U.S. and Soviet negotiators in the parallel Geneva negotiations on intermediate-range nuclear forces (INF) and on strategic weapons (Strategic Arms Reduction Talks, or START). Protests against the arms race were voiced in many West European countries; in West Germany, a new party, the Greens, won representation in parliament on a platform of nuclear disarmament.

Economic conditions remained troubled. In spite of a decrease in oil prices, an increase in the value of the U.S. dollar caused balance-of-payments problems for many countries. Unemployment remained high, and several countries showed no growth in national product. Elections showed a continuation of the trend established in recent years toward Socialist governments in southern Europe and conservative governments in northern Europe. Although less dramatic than in previous years, terrorism by discontented national and religious minorities furthered the sense of insecurity.

East-West Negotiations. Détente was not restored largely because of Soviet attempts to repress rebellious forces in Afghanistan and the maintenance until July of martial law in Poland. Although the 35 countries participating in the Madrid Conference on Security and Coopera-

tion in Europe were able to reach a compromise in July after almost three years of negotiation, the document merely promised future meetings on disarmament and vaguely defined progress on human rights. The final sessions in September were used by Western governments to excoriate the Soviet Union for shooting down a South Korean civilian airliner in Soviet airspace.

The arms talks in Geneva were mainly concerned with the agreement made by the North Atlantic Treaty Organization (NATO) powers in 1979 to install 572 U.S. nuclear missiles in Western Europe beginning in 1983 unless progress had been made in arms reduction talks with the Soviet Union. West Germany, which was to accept 108 Pershing-II missiles, and Italy, which had agreed to 112 cruise missiles, made determined efforts to foster compromise. But by year's end the START and INF talks broke down, and protests continued, especially in West Germany, where they took the form of parliamentary opposition by the Greens, massive public demonstrations, and attacks on U.S. military installations. Most Europeans, however, seemed to agree with Britain's Prime Minister Margaret Thatcher that the Warsaw Pact's superiority in conventional forces, backed by Soviet intermediate-range missiles targeted at Western Europe, could only be countered by the acceptance of additional U.S.missiles. Suspicion of Soviet intentions was evidenced by the expulsion of large numbers of Soviet diplomatic and commercial personnel on grounds of spying.

The Stumbling European Economy. U.S. economic progress in 1983 was not matched in Western Europe. Many Europeans even blamed the low U.S. inflation rate for attracting capital funds needed in Europe and thereby further strengthening the dollar in relation to European currencies. Although U.S. purchases

221

of European goods were encouraged by the strong dollar, European countries saw the dollar's strength as a danger to their recovery. Not only were they compelled to keep interest rates high, but their imports of oil had to be paid for in dollars. Thus, although the Organization of Petroleum Exporting Countries (OPEC) dropped the price of oil from $34 to $29 per barrel, most countries did not reap any benefits because of high dollar exchange rates. European banks were also shaken by the threat of large loan defaults by such countries as Mexico, Brazil, and Poland. Protectionism, already practiced by the European Community (EC) for its agricultural products, threatened to spread worldwide. The United States, for example, severely restricted steel imports.

The southern European countries were again worst off. Portugal, with an inflation rate of 20% and a government deficit of $2 billion (U.S.), was compelled to introduce a harsh austerity program. Italy, with almost 10% of its workforce unemployed, seemed likely to experience a real decline in GNP.

Even the stronger economies showed little vitality. The West German economy, the strongest in Europe, was unlikely to grow more than 1–2% or to reduce its 9% unemployment rate. In the long run, EC economists saw little prospect of reversing the structural unemployment that was producing deep tension among the working class of countries like France. Perhaps most disheartening of all was the growing public sentiment that the EC was exacerbating the situation by such measures as the common agricultural policy. French farmers went so far as to attack trucks bringing imports from competing regions of the EC.

A December summit meeting of Common Market leaders failed to resolve a deadlock over proposed cuts in farm subsidies and a British demand for a $1 billion budget refund. The impasse was said to leave the ten-nation body on the brink of bankruptcy.

The most unpopular austerity measures were taken by France's Socialist president, François Mitterrand. After his election in 1981, Mitterrand had increased government social spending and attempted to reduce unemployment by reducing the workweek. With a record trade deficit, high inflation, and the loss of half of the franc's value in relation to the U.S. dollar, Mitterrand in March 1983 imposed large spending cuts, a surtax on income, a forced loan from every taxpayer, and tight limits on currency exports. These measures, combined with proposed university reforms that infuriated students, led to widespread rioting.

In Eastern Europe, discontent was greatest in Poland, where martial law since 1981 had failed to alleviate the country's economic difficulties. In July 1983 the government of Gen. Wojciech Jaruzelski lifted martial law but at the same time reimposed a six-day workweek and threatened sanctions against those quitting their jobs. The deadlock between the government and the population as a whole, which paralyzed prospects for economic recovery, was worsened by continued demonstrations in favor of the banned trade union Solidarity.

Political Repercussions. In the years of recession since 1973, European electorates had frequently reacted to economic hardship by ousting established governments, whether of the right or left. Socialist parties had made great progress in southern Europe. One of the most startling examples was the October 1982 election victory of the Spanish Socialist Party, which made Felipe González the country's first Socialist premier since 1936. This trend continued in 1983. In June, Socialist Mario Soares was returned to power in Portugal after his party had won 36% of the vote. Both González and Soares, however, rather than pressing for the socialization of their respective economies, found it necessary to demand sacrifices through increased taxes, decreased subsidies, and currency devaluations. Disillusionment with the Christian Democrats, who had dominated every postwar government in Italy, was evidenced by a sharp decline in popular support in June elections. The Christian Democrats then supported Socialist Bettino Craxi as premier.

In northern Europe, the trend toward more conservative government had been highlighted by the parliamentary defeat of the Socialists in Denmark in September 1982 and the nomination of Helmut Kohl the following month to succeed Socialist Helmut Schmidt as chancellor of West Germany. In March 1983, Kohl led a coalition of Christian Democrats and Free Democrats to an impressive election victory, endorsing his austerity program and his support of private industry and new U.S. missiles.

In Britain, Conservative Prime Minister Thatcher was returned to power in June with an absolute majority of 144 members in parliament. Although her victory was due in part to the strong challenge mounted by the Social Democrats against the Labourites for the moderate working-class vote, Thatcher's victory was also an endorsement of her tough line.

Terrorism. Thatcher's firmness helped reduce by half the number of terrorist attacks in Northern Ireland by the Irish Republican Army, which was severely weakened by the arrest of several of its leaders. However, terrorism still remained a constant danger on the continent. Armenian terrorist attacks against Turkish diplomatic and commercial personnel were carried out in Portugal, Belgium, and France. Catalans and Basques in southern France declared their intention to join the autonomy movements being conducted by their compatriots in Spain. Corsican attacks on property of the French government and of mainland residents increased.

F. ROY WILLIS, *University of California, Davis*

FASHION

The focus of fashion in 1983 remained more on the bottom line, less on the hem line. Despite the economic upturn evident during the year, the consumer remained somewhat conservative with regard to spending. Even the affluent were careful, and couture lines felt the pinch as well as did the more moderately priced lines.

Of particular significance was the fact that increasing numbers of consumers were discovering discount or off-price stores that featured branded merchandise at from 20% to 60% less than the traditional department or specialty stores. In an effort to offset declining sales, many retail chains opened their own off-price outlets or acquired existing ones. Those who did not began developing and promoting special merchandise branded with their own private labels.

Top designers such as Anne Klein, John Anthony, and Calvin Klein fought consumer price resistance and foreign competition by opening new divisions that offered their signa-

Gideon Lewin/Bill Blass

Tailored three-quarter-length coats, oversized jackets, pants suits, and hats suggested a polished elegance.

Avant-garde Japanese designs influenced fashion in 1983.

Courtesy, Issey Miyake

ture looks at substantially lower prices. Halston, whose clients include Liza Minnelli, Elizabeth Taylor, and other celebrities and socialites, staged a coup of sorts by signing a multimillion dollar contract with one of middle America's largest retailers, J.C. Penney, to design clothing that would retail from $22 to $200. Introduced in the fall of 1983, the line was deemed an incredible success.

The Japanese Influence. This was also the year of what was called the "Japan-ing" of fashion. In Paris at the fall showing, three Japanese designers—Issey Miyake, Rei Kawakubo, and Yohji Yamamoto—startled press and buyers alike with their avant-garde designs. Called exciting by some and outrageous by others, these collections featured clothes seemingly inspired by derelicts, street waifs, and bag ladies. To the accompaniment of deafening atonal music, models in macabre makeup and ragged hair barged down the runway wrapped in layers of oversized dull colored clothing, tied or knotted in place, which featured such bizarre details as tears, holes, slashes, paint splatters, and jagged or uneven hems. The accessories included oversized men's galoshes, wide strips of rubber or cloth wrapping the feet, battered top hats, or tattered head ties. As a total look it was overwhelming, but isolated elements became fashion influences. A trend to rougher, more primitive textures and patterns, softer and more drapable fabrics, and a return to layering began to emerge at year's end, as well as a new feeling for proportion and a more somber color palette.

The Apparel. In womenswear, details more than design marked this year's fashion. In suits, the styling was classic and ranged from boxy short jackets over full skirts to lightly fitted blazers—single and double breasted—over slim skirts. The style focus of suits was on the lapels, which might be peaked and wide, narrow and rounded, or ruffled, rippled, squared, asymmetric or trompe l'oeil. There were often single lapels done in a contrasting color or fabric, and Bill Blass featured a dinner suit with a single lapel sequined to simulate a slice of watermelon.

In dresses, too, details made the difference. While the prevailing shape was the lightly fitted

The chemise returned as a favored silhouette.

chemise, buttons and back interest marked them as current. When styled as a coat dress, buttons in single or double rows were down the front, sides, or back of the chemise. The dolman-sleeved, T-shirt-styled chemise focused attention on the back via low cut V necklines, cowling, lace insets, bow treatments, and even a hint of a bustle.

The sweater became haute couture and was an important part of every fashion collection in Europe and the United States. Imaginatively designed, they were show stoppers, whether classic, sophisticated, sportive, or glamorous. There were rugged tweedy turtlenecks and cardigans, soft mohair and angora jackets, intarsia, argyle, or fair-isle patterned vests and pullovers, as well as unique creations such as Mariuccia Mandelli's graphic pullovers with polar bear or bird motifs. Ralph Lauren brought back the 1930s with his "Sun Valley" ski sweaters with reindeer and snowflake patterns. For late day, there was an array of dazzling sweaters, beaded, bejeweled, or knit of metallic yarns, with many trimmed with fur.

The pantsuit made a fashion comeback. A creation of the 1950s, it was a popular alternative to hemline confusion in the 1960s but was banished to pastel polyester oblivion in the 1970s. In 1983 it took on new chic in a polished executive way, trimly tailored in sharp gabardines and flannels and femininely accessorized with fedora, sleek handbag, and delicate pump. While not for every boardroom, it was a fashion alternative to the business suit for female executives.

Color and Accessories. Black and white were the dominant colors for the year combined as in fall-winter tweeds or plaids or monochromatically in spring-summer linen dressing. Occasionally the severity was relieved by a shock of color, including magenta, chrome yellow, cobalt, or emerald used as an accent in pieces such as camisoles, blouses, or sweaters. In collections such as those of Bill Blass, Calvin Klein, and Oscar de la Renta, an item such as a jacket or coat would be shown in a range of hot colors amid the basic black and white core of the line.

Color was the key to the newness in accessories, however. Brilliant hues alone or combined in blocks or patterns were seen in shoes, bags, belts, and even gloves. Often textures were also mixed, with the popular combination being snake, suede, and kidskin, each in a different color.

Another element common to accessories was the look of quality and elegance. In shoes, the ubiquitous pump in a mid to high heel was delicately shaped and tastefully detailed on the vamp or at the back with stitching, piping, bows, buttons, insets, cutouts, or appliqué. For evening, they were decorated with rhinestones or other jeweled accents. Bags, both the popular sportive pouches or the more rigid

Sweaters were an important part of the fashionable wardrobe in 1983. For men, women, and children alike, the season's outdoor wear included the popular ski sweater, patterned with skiers, reindeer, and snowflakes.

Courtesy, Ralph Lauren

framed bags, were crafted of the finest and softest leathers and featured trapunto stitching, artistic closures, pleats, and tucks. Belts, wide and narrow and worn low at the hip line, were colorful strips of snake or suede with large, ornate buckles. Gloves, the finishing touch to this year's fashion, were color spliced or cuffed in contrasting brights or raffishly layered in two colors with a long jersey glove topped by a fingerless style worn over it.

Animal prints and patterns were everywhere, and zebras, tigers, leopards, and other fauna lent their spots and stripes to scarves, shoes, belts, bags, and hats. In addition, clingy evening sweaters and gowns were beaded in wildlife pelt patterns. Perry Ellis with his zebra pullover and Anne Klein's bronze and black tiger knits made fashion news. Smooth leathers were stenciled or embossed to reproduce the look of animal and reptile skins for bags and belts; elephant, ostrich, and eelskin were novelties.

Menswear. Menswear, always evolutionary rather than revolutionary, retained the quality look of past seasons but, influenced by the popularity of sportswear, became more relaxed. There was a "separates" approach to dressing that allowed for a less formal mix of fabric, color, and texture—even in business dressing.

The traditional suit with matching jacket and trousers was still seen but, increasingly, nonmatching, coordinated combinations were shown, mixing genteel country tweeds with flannel or gabardine. The jackets to these "suits" were roomier, with less padding, lower button placement, and were designed in a new peaked-lapel, double-breasted style. However, even the traditional single-breasted, notched-collared type was less fitted so as to comfortably accommodate the sweaters and vests that had become an essential part of suit dressing.

Trousers were fully cut but had a narrower leg, and many featured waistband buttons to anchor the braces or suspenders that were the newest fashion accessory. Carrying through with this more casual approach, shirts were cut of softer, more lightweight fabrics; knit or bow ties completed the look of ease.

Coats were burly and oversized. The steamer, raglan-sleeved balmacaan, or great coat were generously cut and long—to within two inches above the ankle. Done in thick tweeds in patterns such as chevron, diamonds, or pheasant's eye, they were made to wear over the newer, full-cut jackets and sweaters.

Shoes were tasseled loafers or tied wing-tipped oxfords in elegant suedes, leathers, or novelties such as lizard or crocodile. Boots were the short English riding style in leather.

For nonbusiness hours, sportswear shown in 1983 had authentic styling with action-ease details, including underarm grommets, gussets, raglan sleeves, big pockets with storm flaps to cover zipper or Velcro closures, and elasticized or adjustable waistbands.

Survival gear was the inspiration for much of the outdoor wear. There were Arctic parkas and thick ski sweaters. Rough and tumble cords, covers, and twills were fabrics for trousers cut like ski or riding pants of hiker's knickers. Mufflers, heavy leather or knit gloves, and work boots with lug soles were essential.

ANN ELKINS
"Good Housekeeping Magazine"

At the Great Kremlin Palace in June, the Finnish-Soviet friendship and cooperation treaty was extended for 20 years.

FINLAND

The last day of 1982 saw a dramatic restructuring of the Kalevi Sorsa cabinet. When three government ministers representing the People's Democratic League (Communists) voted against the government on a parliamentary bill to increase defense spending, the three and a nonpolitical minister were replaced by three members of the Social Democratic Party and one from the Liberal Party.

In the parliamentary elections held on March 20–21, 1983, the Social Democrats strengthened their position as the largest party in Finland, corralling 28.5% of the vote for the 200-seat parliament. The People's Democratic League lost eight seats, the Conservatives were on the retreat, and the Center Party held its own. It came as a surprise that the Rural Party increased its seats from 6 to 17, and the "Greens" (the environmental party) won a foothold in parliament with two seats. Among those who lost their seats was Johannes Virolainen, a presidential candidate in 1982.

The parliament opened its first session on April 8. The new speaker of parliament was Erkki Pystynen of the Conservative Party, the first member of that party to hold this office in 50 years.

In keeping with tradition, the Sorsa cabinet on April 11 submitted its resignation to the president. After hectic and long-drawn-out negotiations, the new cabinet was announced on May 6 and, as expected, was once again headed by Kalevi Sorsa, a Social Democrat. Four parties were included in a new coalition: the Social Democratic Party, the Center Party, the Rural Party, and the Swedish People's Party. Paavo Väyrynen of the Center Party was appointed minister of foreign affairs. It was also announced that a new government department had been created, namely the ministry of the environment. Among some of the challenges facing the new cabinet and parliament were needed changes in the Constitution, reforms in the field of education, and the ever-present unemployment.

In early June, President Koivisto led a large Finnish delegation to Moscow, at which time the 35th anniversary of the signing of the Finnish-Russian Treaty of Friendship, Cooperation and Mutual Assistance was observed. Foreign ministers Paavo Väyrynen and Andrei Gromyko signed a protocol that after ratification will renew the treaty until 2003.

In September the president traveled to the United States, where he spoke at the United Nations and conferred with President Reagan.

Economics. A new governor of the Bank of Finland was appointed on May 27, this all-important post going to Rolf Kullberg, a banker of long experience who belonged to no political party. He succeeded the 60-year-old Ahti Karjalainen, a former prime minister, who was asked to resign "for the public good."

In one week in October the currency was twice devalued, first by 4% then by 6%. The action was partly in response to a 16% devaluation by Sweden, a major international competitor in the sale of forestry products.

Culture. The main Finnish cultural event abroad was the U.S. debut of the Finnish National Opera in the spring.

ERIK J. FRIIS
"The Scandinavian-American Bulletin"

FINLAND • Information Highlights

Official Name: Republic of Finland.
Location: Northern Europe.
Area: 130,000 sq mi (336 700 km²).
Population (July 1983): 4,850,000.
Chief City (Dec. 31, 1981): Helskinski, the capital, 484,014.
Government: *Head of state,* Mauno Koivisto, president (took office Jan. 27, 1982). *Head of government,* Kalevi Sorsa, prime minister (took office May 6, 1983). *Legislature* (unicameral)—Eduskunta.
Monetary Unit: Markka (5.6630 markkaa equal U.S. $1, Oct. 20, 1983.)
Gross Domestic Product: (1982 U.S.$): $47,573,000,000.
Economic Indexes (1982): *Consumer Prices* (1970 = 100), all items, 358.2; food, 380.5. *Industrial Production* (1975 = 100), 129.
Foreign Trade (1982 U.S.$): *Imports,* $13,382,-000,000; *exports,* $13,127,000,000.

FLORIDA

In 1983, Florida leaders strengthened consumer protection and devised a strategy to improve the state's economy, public-school system, and highways.

Consumer Protection. The legislature enacted a tough Motor Vehicle Warranty Enforcement Act to require auto dealers to refund the purchase price or replace new motor vehicles that require chronic repairs; extended to ten days the period during which a consumer may back out of a contract; and required hospitals to notify all other hospitals in the state of any disciplinary actions against a physician. A stronger housing discrimination code also passed.

Economy. While Florida's economy remained strong during 1983, with an unemployment rate that ranged from 1 to 2½ percentage points below the national average, Gov. Bob Graham and other leaders sought new industry more actively than ever. Touting Florida as having the nation's best business climate, state industrial development leaders traversed the nation seeking "high-tech" industry. The governor personally concentrated on attracting more film-makers and also led a trade delegation to Japan. The goal was not to deemphasize agriculture and tourism, which have been the foundation of the state economy. In fact tourism soared to record levels following the 1982 opening of Epcot Center.

Economists believe Florida must attract clean industry in order to provide adequate stable employment for a population that is growing at a faster rate than jobs are being created in agriculture and tourism. Awareness of this rapid growth led the governor and legislature to assemble a group of 150 leaders to begin drafting a growth management strategy.

Education. Improving the quality of public education has been a high priority since the late 1970s as Florida led the nation in developing

Gandy Photographers/Courtesy, Tampa-DDA

There has been extensive redevelopment in Tampa as city leaders seek new financial, high-tech, and other industries.

minimum standards for high-school graduates and more demanding teacher-training programs. However, interest in attracting high-tech industry has contributed to a new effort to raise the achievement level of students, especially in math and science. The legislature adopted the RAISE program (Raise Achievement in Secondary Education). The law requires students to have an additional class in both math and science and two years of foreign language in order to enter a Florida university. A longer school day also is required. This will be coupled with a merit-pay plan for teachers. Business leaders supported the program but mounted a battle to repeal the increase in the state corporate-income tax that was enacted to finance it.

Highway Construction. State and local governments have not been able to maintain existing roads nor construct new ones to serve a growing population. A special session of the legislature provided new highway funds by increasing the state motor-fuel tax. County governments also were granted authority to levy up to four cents per gallon for five years for local road construction.

Tax Revolt. A coalition of Florida retirees, out-of-state developers, and antigovernment conservatives successfully circulated a petition that will enable Florida voters to vote in November 1984 on a constitutional amendment that would force state and local governments to roll back *all* taxes and revenues to the 1980 level.

J. LARRY DURRENCE
Florida Southern College

FLORIDA • Information Highlights

Area: 58,664 sq mi (151 940 km²).
Population (1982 est.): 10,416,000.
Chief Cities (1980 census): Tallahassee, the capital, 81,548; Jacksonville, 540,898; Miami, 346,931; Tampa, 271,523; St. Petersburg, 236,893.
Government (1983): *Chief Officers*—governor, Bob Graham (D); lt. gov., Wayne Mixson (D). *Legislature*—Senate, 40 members; House of Representatives, 120 members.
State Finances (Fiscal year 1982): *Revenues,* $9,364,000,000; *expenditures,* $9,322,000,000.
Personal Income (1982): $114,387,000,000; *per capita,* $10,987.
Labor Force (July 1983): *Nonagricultural wage and salary earners,* 3,801,000; *unemployed,* 409,100 (8.2% of total force).
Education: *Enrollment* (fall 1981)—public elementary schools, 1,035,323; public secondary, 452,398; colleges and universities (1982), 436,606. *Public school expenditures* (1981–82), $4,221,319,000.

FOOD

The year 1983 started out as a promising one for the world's population. Food supplies as well as crop forecasts appeared to be on the upswing, and the effort to improve human nutrition and feed the world's hungry seemed to be gaining momentum. As the year progressed, however, weather and world tensions began to cloud the picture. In the United States, forecasts of bumper crops of corn, wheat, and other staple crops were scaled down because of heavy spring rains and floods, and then revised downward again because of drought. In addition, turmoil in the Middle East and elsewhere, as well as the worldwide economic recession, had an immediate negative effect on food supplies and costs.

World Food Supply and Population. As reported by the U.S. Census Bureau, the world had its biggest 12-month population increase in history in 1982–83. The one-year increase of 82,077,000 people brought the total world population to 4,721,887,000 in mid-June. While the growth rate has leveled off at about 1.8% yearly, the percentage applies to larger numbers each year; hence the increase. As the numbers rise, so does the need for more food and better feeding programs.

Throughout the world, weather conditions affected crops and yields. Chinese and Korean farm harvests recovered from previous poor crops, and there were signs that the drought in Australia was easing, lending optimism that the wheat crop would partially recover. It had been estimated that nearly 60% of the farms in Australia were hit by drought. Other countries that expected lower wheat harvests were South Africa, Turkey, the USSR, and Argentina. In coarse grains (primarily corn), early growing conditions outside the United States were generally favorable, and harvests were expected to be above normal. Production in Western Europe was expected to be lower because of fewer planted acres, while Eastern Europe and Canada would be 5–10% less.

World production of milled rice was expected to rise 2% to 281 million metric tons*, primarily because of a significant increase in Chinese output. World trade in wheat and rice was expected to be lower in 1983 than in the previous several years, with coarse grains totaling slightly higher. Geographical areas expected to increase imports in coarse grains were Africa, the Middle East, South Korea, Taiwan, and Mexico, and possibly China, Eastern Europe, and the Soviet Union.

In oilseeds (soybeans, sunflower seeds, rapeseeds, tree-crop oils, and peanuts), the production/consumption situation was difficult to assess, depending largely on the extent of economic recovery. While 1982–83 world oilseed production was estimated to be 6–7% above the previous year, forecasts indicated a 2% decline in 1983–84, to 178 million tons. Significantly, much of the increase in usage was predicted to be in such selected products as tree-oils and soybean meals, or products that have specific uses such as animal feeds.

U.S.-Soviet Grain Negotiations. Although the USSR increased grain production to an estimated 200 million tons, the harvest was still 38 million tons below the desired projection. While the 1983 total represented an increase of 20 million tons, the Soviets agreed to a new five-year, $10 billion U.S. grain sales agreement, which became effective October 1. The agreement requires the Soviets to purchase at least 9 million tons of U.S. wheat and corn each year until 1988, an increase of 50% annually; up to 12 million tons per year can be purchased without additional negotiations. It is expected to bring $2 billion to the U.S. farm economy in the first year.

* 1 metric ton equals 1.102 short tons. All tonnages given in this article are metric.

UPI

At a Washington, DC, supermarket, Secretary of Agriculture John Block and his wife, Sue, picked out a week's supply of groceries to test the maximum food-stamp allowance of $58. Their bill came to $54.14.

U.S. Food Supply. The U.S. food supply as measured by wheat, corn, and soybean production was affected initially by spring rains and floods, then by summertime drought. The lack of rainfall in the central and eastern portions of the country resulted in the worst drought in a half-century. A September 1 survey by the U.S. Department of Agriculture indicated a decline of 48% from the previous year's record corn crop, to about 4.39 billion bushels, the smallest amount since 1970. Some of the drop could be attributed to the payment-in-kind (PIK) subsidy program. In soybeans (not included in PIK), the harvest was estimated to be down 33%, to 1.53 billion bushels, the smallest amount since 1976. A similar but less drastic effect was expected in wheat-growing areas.

Wholesale food prices rose only 1.4%, the smallest increase in 15 years. In August, because of the prolonged heat wave and drought, farm prices rose 4.6%. Most food prices had declined in July, but in August vegetables rose 16.5%. Other foods, such as eggs, poultry, and pork, also were higher. Beef and veal prices dropped and were expected to decline even further because producers were sending their animals to slaughter rather than paying higher prices for feed. Meat prices were expected to rise during late 1983 and early 1984. Overall, the U.S. food supply was predicted to be ample over the next year, with prices increasing.

Although weather played a stronger than usual role on crop yields and costs, a new government program also had a significant effect on farm production figures. The federal program, called payment-in-kind (PIK), was instituted under the guidance of the U.S. Department of Agriculture. Basically, the program subsidizes farmers for taking land out of production. Designed to reduce surpluses, raise prices, cut government costs for grain storage, and save production expenses, it removed from cultivation a total of 82.3 million acres (32.9 million ha).

The U.S. Food Industry. Although the recession lowered the ability of Americans to spend extravagantly on food, the food industry appeared to meet the challenge of selective consumer buying through introduction of new and/or improved items, the appeal of health-related foods, and expanded marketing techniques.

In the field of food packaging, a revolution of sorts swept the country. The new technique is called "aseptic packaging." Closely related to the retort pouch, aseptic packaging utilizes a sterilized container made of thin layers of paper, foil, and polyethylene into which sterilized liquids are sealed in an airtight manner. The technique was approved in 1981 by the U.S. Food and Drug Administration (FDA). The approval was expected to result in 750 million aseptic packages of food being marketed in 1983 and some 4 billion units in 1987. Products currently being packaged aseptically are liquids or semi-liquids, such as fruit juices, milk and milk drinks, yogurt, and alcoholic beverages. The primary advantages of aseptic packaging are convenience, easy opening, lower energy costs, no need for refrigerated storage, better flavor retention, and lower consumer costs.

Along with record heat in many parts of the United States came a deluge of new soft drinks. In a market that sold some $25 billion worth of soft drinks in 1982, nine new cola drinks were introduced in a period of 18 months. Led by giants Coca-Cola and PepsiCo, the trend has been mainly toward diet or low-calorie drinks, and decaffeinated regular and diet colas. Coincidentally, soft-drink advertising expanded to appeal to male users of diet drinks. There are an estimated 235 soft-drink brands, a 50% increase in seven years. Perhaps adding to the glut, the FDA on July 1 approved the use of Aspartame, a synthetic sweetener, for use in soft drinks. Shortly after the approval, both Coca-Cola and Royal Crown announced that they would be supplied the sweetener by its manufacturer.

Nutrition and Health. Food programs and hunger made headlines in the United States during 1983. President Reagan continued to call for cuts in certain programs, while the Democrats opposed such actions. To prove that a family of four could live on a food budget, Agriculture Secretary Block and other officials held public shopping trips in local supermarkets. The program, "Making Food Dollars Count," utilized the maximum allowable food-stamp allowance of $58 per week to demonstrate that enough nutritious food is provided. USDA also worked on revising the Thrifty Food Plan, upon which the Food Stamp Act is based. The changes were in the types of food that make up the nutritional elements, not in the total cost or allowance.

As the U.S. public has become more conscious of health and fitness, food trends and consumption have been significantly affected. Aside from regional or ethnic tastes, the trend toward fresh, lower-calorie, increased-fiber, and low-sodium foods is increasing. At the same time, nutritionists remain concerned about the consumption of "fast foods," "imitations," and "substitutes."

On the international front, a unique approach to an old problem earned the 1983 Food Technology Industrial Achievement Award. Presented by the Institute of Food Technologists to the Food and Nutrition Studies Foundation and Delicias Food Products (PADSA) of Mexico, the award was given for the development of commercialization of Soyaven, a nutritious, low-cost infant formula. The process employs inexpensive, locally grown raw materials and a drying process that is both energy efficient and low in cost.

KIRBY M. HAYES
University of Massachusetts

FRANCE

With the Socialist government of President François Mitterrand in power for its second full year, 1983 in France was marked by economic belt-tightening and a sharp slowdown in social reforms. Facing the reality of difficult economic times, the government instituted austerity measures which, according to by-election results and opinion polls, were met with declining popularity. The year also saw widespread public demonstrations. With legislative elections not before 1986 and those for the president not before 1988, however, the Left could hope that an improvement in the economic situation would help it to gain some of the lost confidence.

Domestic Affairs

For President Mitterrand the year began badly: a television appearance scheduled for January 1 from his home in Latché had to be postponed because a truck carrying technical equipment necessary for the transmission failed to arrive. The program took place the next day, but much of the solemnity of the president's declarations was lost. The incident set the tone for Mitterrand's plight in 1983.

As the year got underway, campaigning was in full swing for March municipal elections. On January 20 the two main opposition parties—Rassemblement pour la République (RPR) and Union pour la Démocratie Française (UDF)—announced a common election policy. Some days before, former President Valery Giscard d'Estaing (UDF) had alerted the public of the seriousness of France's external debt. On January 23, Jacques Chirac, leader of the RPR, presented a "recovery program" for the country to get out of the "disastrous" situation which, according to him, the left-wing government had put it in. In the first round of voting on March 6, the left suffered a pronounced setback, obtaining only 39.74% of the votes cast (against 50.89% for the opposition) and losing 16 towns with populations of more than 30,000. In the second round of voting the following week, the left lost another 15 towns; the opposition registered sweeping victories in Lyons and Paris, where Chirac was triumphantly re-elected mayor.

The election results had major consequences in the cabinet. On March 20, Foreign Trade Minister Michel Jobert resigned, and two days later the government of Prime Minister Pierre Mauroy was reshuffled. Several ministers changed portfolio, and another left because he was not completely in agreement with the policies being followed: Jean-Pierre Chevènement, representing the left wing of the Socialist Party. The new government, while comprising 14 Socialist and 2 Communist ministers, was seen as a significant shift toward the center.

Economic austerity measures announced March 25, four days after a 2.5% devaluation of the franc, brought vehement protests from the opposition and disquiet even within the majority. The Communist Party, although part of the new cabinet, found that this policy closely resembled the remedies advocated by former Prime Minister Raymond Barre, who had always spoken of the need for "austerity."

Another disquieting subject for the government was student demonstrations—medical students in particular—which developed in the spring. The protests were directed against educational reforms proposed by the cabinet. At one stage it was feared that a crisis like that of 1968 would occur. By the end of May, however, student agitation had calmed. Then it was the turn of the police. On June 3, 2,500 policemen demonstrated in Paris after two of their

President Mitterrand (bottom left) poses with Prime Minister Mauroy and his new, more centrist government in March.

In the spring, French medical students protested educational reform proposed by the cabinet.

colleagues had been killed. Encouraged by the political opposition, they reproached Justice Minister Robert Badinter for his "laxity" in the fight against crime. Home Secretary Gaston Defferre, who was booed by the demonstrators, dealt with them severely: the leaders of the protest and certain high-ranking police officers were dismissed.

The hostility between the Left and the Right was once again made evident by the controversy between President Mitterrand and Mayor Chirac over the organization of a World Exhibition in Paris in 1989. Chirac asserted that the project would cost the city too much and that it would be better to hold the exhibition in a Paris suburb. In view of these objections and reservations, the president gave in and announced on July 5 that France would not hold the exhibition. The need for economic restraint had, in the end, decided the issue.

During the summer, after political passions had quieted some, the highbrow Paris daily *Le Monde*, politically close to the Socialists, opened its columns to "left-wing intellectuals," who generally expressed their disillusionment with government policy; it seemed to them to be lacking in dash, liberality, and high ideals. For most of the French, however, the problems of daily living appeared to be of greater concern. They manifested their lack of confidence in their leaders by voting consistently for the opposition in local and senatorial elections during the fall. Similarly, in October balloting for the leaders of the Social Security Service, the left-wing trade unions—the CGT and the CFDT—suffered heavy losses. Though somewhat prematurely, the leaders of the opposition took advantage of these setbacks to pose the question of Mitterrand's ability to govern should the Right win the legislative elections in 1986. Meanwhile, the Socialist

Party held its annual congress at the end of October, demonstrating (at least on the surface) unanimous approval of government policy. It was not a time to be quarreling.

Economy. The publication of 1982 economic-performance statistics had the government worried about the state of the nation. Unemployment rose only 5.6% for the entire year, but inflation remained high (9.7%), and the balance of payments deficit reached 92.7 billion francs (about U.S. $13 billion), an increase of 83.2%. Production was stagnant, and factory owners complained of being overburdened by taxes. Nor were they particularly allayed by the few measures in their favor announced by Economic and Finance Minister Jacques Delors at the beginning of January.

The situation seemed to get worse during the first months of 1983, and in March came the devaluation (the third since the Left came to power), the reshuffling of the cabinet, and the announcement of the austerity plan. The one belt-tightening measure that caused the most fuss, because it was regarded as a threat to liberty, was a reduction in the amount of cash allowed to a tourist for traveling abroad. There was also, among other things, an additional levy of 1% on taxable income for 1982 and a compulsory loan to the government of 10% for a good number of taxpayers.

Delors' plan obviously could not produce results at once, especially with the dollar continuing to rise (in December it reached a record trading value of 8.46 francs), thus increasing the cost of imports. After declining slightly for some months, the number of unemployed went up in May; consequently, the contributions for unemployment insurance had to be increased for both employers and employees. In July and August, however, the situation was a little better: inflation had fallen somewhat, as had the foreign-trade deficit. This did not prevent the government from planning to tax high- and medium-level incomes more heavily in the 1984 budget, which was adopted in September. When the consumer price index for September became known, it was obvious that Delors could not win his battle to keep the cost of living to a rise of 8% for 1983; after nine months the increase was already 7.6%. Only the foreign-trade deficit continued to drop, thanks to the positive effects of the devaluation of the franc.

In its struggle for economic improvement, the cabinet was aided by a relative lack of social demands. Certain groups felt wronged by the austerity measures and let the government know with strikes and demonstrations: travel agents in March, pig farmers in April, artisans and small shopkeepers in May, chemists in July, and postal workers in September and October. But there were no great waves of industrial strikes, as the left-wing trade unions did not stir up the discontent they might have if a right-wing government had been in power.

Immigrants. Of the approximately 4.5 million foreigners living in France, the majority are well assimilated and accepted by the French population. Yet there are some—those from Africa and especially those from North Africa—whose presence provokes controversy. In 1982 the Socialist government endeavored to regularize the situation of immigrants working in France without permits (usually for absurdly low wages). Still, there are many who cannot find work, many of them young people who wander the streets and are blamed—often unfairly—for committing crimes. Several incidents during 1983 drew new attention to this social problem.

In February, Muslim workers at a Citroën factory in a Parisian suburb went on strike to ask for better working conditions and a place to worship. Blows were exchanged between strikers and nonstrikers, and the labor minister accused the CGT trade union of inciting the unrest. Then, during the March municipal elections, violence broke out in Marseilles, where an 11-year-old gypsy child was killed by a bomb explosion. Both left-wing and right-wing parties reproached themselves for stirring up hatred during the election campaign. In July, incidents multiplied between Muslims and native Frenchmen in the Parisian suburbs. The worst occurred on July 9, when a young Algerian was shot while playing with fireworks. President Mitterrand personally visited several suburbs to get an idea of the conditions in which people lived. On August 2 a member of the cabinet, Georgina Dufoix, declared that it was impossible to accept new immigrants into France. On August 31 a series of measures to deter illegal immigration was announced. Right-wing groups went so far as to call for the return of certain foreigners, even those legally installed, to their original countries. The municipal election at Dreux on September 11, won by the opposition, was dominated by this thorny question.

Terrorism. Although less bloody than in 1982, terrorism continued to be a serious preoccupation for those in power. Acts of violence by Armenian groups were especially frequent and bloody. A bomb explosion February 28 at a travel agency specializing in trips in Turkey killed 1 person and injured 4 others; the Secret Armenian Army claimed responsibility. On July 15 an explosion in front of the Turkish Airlines counter at Orly Airport left 7 persons dead and 55 others injured. Three days after this attack, for which the Secret Armenian Army also claimed responsibility, the police arrested an Armenian of Syrian nationality who at first admitted to having placed the bomb but later denied it. On September 30, at the International Fair of Marseilles, another bombing, this one claimed by several organizations, two of them Armenian, killed 1 person and injured 26 others.

Corsican Nationalists also carried out acts of terrorism, though perhaps less blind and damaging to human life. On January 5 the cabinet announced a campaign against violence in Corsica: the National Front for the Liberation of Corsica (FLNC) was outlawed and a well-known policeman, Superintendent Robert Broussard, was appointed chief commissioner of police on the island. On March 25 several members of the FLNC were arrested, suspected of having killed a soldier of the French Legion in 1982. On April 29 there were 15 attacks committed on the French mainland, all of them claimed by the FLNC. The same day the police arrested several members of the organization, but on May 23, the FLNC perpetrated 43 bomb explosions on Corsica. On June 13 and 14, President Mitterrand visited the island and condemned ''violence and revolution.'' The disappearance a month later of a Corsican independence fighter, Guy Orsoni, marked the reappearance of hostility with the French gov-

---

FRANCE • Information Highlights

Official Name: French Republic.
Location: Western Europe.
Area: 213,000 sq mi (551 670 km²).
Population (July 1983): 54,604,000.
Government: *Head of state,* François Mitterrand, president (took office May 1981). *Chief minister,* Pierre Mauroy, prime minister (took office May 1981). *Legislature*—Parliament: Senate and National Assembly.
Monetary Unit: Franc (8.4525 francs equal U.S.$1, Dec. 21, 1983).
Gross Domestic Product (1982 U.S.$): $537,353,-000,000.
Economic Index (1982): *Consumer Prices* (1970 = 100), all items, 318.7; food, 326.2. *Industrial Production* (1975 = 100), 112.
Foreign Trade (1982 U.S.$): *Imports,* $115,405,000,000; *Exports,* $92,268,000,000.

ernment, held responsible by the nationalists for his death. A leading civil servant, Pierre-Jean Massimi, was killed in the north of the island on September 13. Out of the Corsican problem, a controversy developed over the role of certain members of the Gendarmerie, given special missions by the president or his circle and found to be involved in affairs that some newspapers labeled "ambiguous."

Foreign Affairs

The good relations that France maintained with some Latin American countries were evidenced at the beginning of 1983 when Bolivia agreed to turn over the German war criminal Klaus Barbie, former chief of the Gestapo in Lyons, who had been arrested for fraud in La Paz. Sent to France on February 4, he was immediately imprisoned to await trial for war crimes. The gratitude of the French government became evident when the Bolivian President Hernán Siles Zuazo came to Paris on March 29 and 30; it was learned that France had granted a large credit and tripled its technical aid to Bolivia. In August the United States admitted to having recruited Klaus Barbie after the war as an informant, allowing him to escape French justice. Washington expressed its "regrets" to Paris.

But the problem of the dollar was more preoccupying for the French government, which accused the Americans of doing nothing to control its currency and thereby upsetting the European monetary system. "It is not normal," declared President Mitterrand in May, "that the American budget deficit should be paid by us." The French leader had an opportunity to express his views at the Williamsburg (VA) Economic Summit Conference in late May, but he received little satisfaction; the joint "declaration on economic recovery" outlined only vague and limited objectives. On the other hand, on the question of new U.S. missiles in Europe, the French government repeatedly manifested its support for American policy during 1983, despite the disagreement of French Communists.

A brief crisis with the Soviet Union arose in April, when 47 Soviet diplomats, accused of espionage, were suddenly expelled from France; Moscow reacted with moderation. After the downing of the South Korean Boeing-747 by the Soviet Union on September 1, France joined in the censure pronounced by other Western countries. President Mitterrand had an opportunity to reemphasize his objections when Soviet Foreign Minister Andrei Gromyko visited Paris September 9–10.

The year 1983 also saw France become directly involved in the civil war in Chad. On July 31, Chadian President Hissène Habré asked France and the United States to intervene with air support. After some hesitation, the French government on August 6 dispatched four military aircraft. A few days later it sent 3,000 soldiers, and on August 21 it dispatched eight more planes. President Mitterrand maintained that the French forces were defensive and not offensive. Many Socialists and even more Communists in France expressed their opposition to a "colonialist intervention" in Chad.

In the Iran-Iraq war, meanwhile, France came to the support of Baghdad, delivering equipment despite Iraq's very heavy debt. In September it was learned that the French were about to send five Super-Etendard fighter planes to their ally, which caused Iran to threaten to close the Straits of Hormuz. The aircraft left France discreetly some time in October. During a visit to Tunisia October 27–29, President Mitterrand maintained that France did not consider itself an enemy of Iran.

In Lebanon, French troops were included in the multinational peacekeeping force introduced in September 1982. After several soldiers were killed in combat, Paris on September 22 sent out Super-Etendard planes to bombard the artillery batteries that were firing upon the French contingent. On October 23, at virtually the same time that the U.S. headquarters at Beirut airport was leveled by a terrorist bombing, French barracks in west Beirut also were attacked by a truck loaded with TNT; 58 Frenchmen were killed. President Mitterrand went at once to Beirut to observe the wreckage and pay respect to his troops. He announced that the French force would stay in Lebanon on its "mission of peace." The Communists, who had called for the return of the troops in late September, said that France should not have involved itself in what was really a civil war.

On November 16, in a television appearance to talk about his foreign policy, President Mitterrand spoke of the attack: "Those who have done it know that they will suffer a well deserved punishment." The day after, eight Super-Etendard planes were sent to bomb a camp held by Iranian and pro-Syrian soldiers near Beirut. It was first announced in France that the raid had caused great damage and many deaths, but a few days later, Defense Minister Charles Hernu said that it was above all a "warning" intended to prevent other attacks against French soldiers.

However on December 21, a pickup truck loaded with explosives blew up outside a French military command post in East Beirut. At least 19 persons, including a French soldier, were killed and more than 40 were injured by the blast. The attack was considered part of the continuing campaign against the multinational force stationed in Lebanon.

See also LEBANON; MIDDLE EAST.

MONIQUE MADIER
French Writer and Editor

GARDENING AND HORTICULTURE

The 1982–83 Gardens For All/Gallup National Gardening Survey reported that gardening was the number one outdoor activity in the United States, surpassing jogging, swimming, and golf. More than 38 million households (46%) were participating in gardening. An additional 6 million households were involved in container, rooftop, and patio gardening. The survey reported that 94% of all vegetable gardens contained tomatoes, 68% peppers, and 66% green beans. For the first time, oriental vegetables were listed on the survey (5%). The largest gain was reported in herb culture, increasing from 10% to 16%.

The Gross National Home Gardening Product (GNHGP), the total production value of all home gardens, produced on 1.7 million acres (687 966 ha), exceeded $18,000,000,000.

Seeds In Space. The George W. Park Seed Company of Greenwood, SC, sponsored the first U.S. seed experiment in space. The National Aeronautics and Space Administration's shuttle, *Challenger,* carried 44 varieties of seeds into space in April 1983. One half of the seeds was packed in Dacron bags, and the other half was in polyethylene, laminated, aluminum foil pouches. Flower, herb, and vegetable seeds were selected relative to their economic importance. The purpose of the Park experiment was to study the impact of temperature fluctuation, vacuum, gravity forces, and radiation on germination rate, seed vigor, induced dormancy, the seed-coat integrity, and varietal purity.

New Plant Varieties. Two new varieties of plants, "SweetHeart" strawberry and the "Explorer" potato, were introduced by the Pan-American Seed Co., West Chicago, IL, beginning a revolution in horticulture. These plants are unique in that they are produced from seed. They have been accepted widely by the home gardener. Strawberries have been propagated from vegetative parts since the Middle Ages, and potatoes have grown from pieces of tuber with one or two "eyes" for more than 400 years.

Literary Contributions. Two horticultural reference books were completed and released in 1982–83. The final volume of *The New York Botanical Garden Illustrated Encyclopedia of Horticulture* was published in 1982 by Garland Publishing, Inc., New York, completing the ten-volume set. Thomas H. Everett, senior horticulture specialist with the New York Botanical Gardens, authored the 3-million word, 3,600-page work. The ten volumes contain 7,000 entries, more than 10,000 photos, and references on more than 20,000 species. This horticultural masterwork received international acclaim from Britain's Royal Horticultural

Pan-American Seed Co.

The new "SweetHeart" strawberry is grown from seed.

Society and The Royal Botanical Gardens members' association newsletter, Hamilton, Ontario, Canada.

The Ortho Problem Solver, published by Ortho Information Services, Chevron Chemical Co., San Francisco, CA, has become known as "the reference book of the 1980s." It was developed to help professional and amateur gardeners alike diagnose 1,969 garden problems, understand their causes, and find solutions. This 1,124-page reference includes more than 2,500 color photos for identification.

Honors and Expositions. The International Horticultural Exhibition, "IGA '83," was held near Munich, West Germany, from April 28 through Oct. 9, 1983. The exhibition, held every ten years, was a horticultural spectacular, spread over 176 acres (71 ha). It included exemplary gardens, landscapes, and floral displays, and introduced new gardening techniques as well as the latest scientific methods. Plants from all over the world were on exhibit. More than 8 million visitors attended IGA '83.

The 100th anniversary meeting of the American Seed Trade Association was held in San Francisco in June 1983. Theodore C. Torrey, a vegetable breeder of international renown, was presented with the 1983 All-American Selections Medallion "for outstanding achievement in horticulture." Mr. Torrey's hybrids include such well known varieties as Burpee's Big Girl tomato, Ambrosia cantaloupe, Burpee Hybrid and Richgreen zucchini squash, and such space-saving vegetables as the Pixie Hybrid tomato, Sugar Bush watermelon, and Butterbush squash.

R. L. SNODSMITH, *Ornamental Horticulturist*

GENETICS

The year 1983 brought continuing advances in the understanding of genetic processes. Research in behavior genetics yielded new information on the importance of the uterine environment in determining adult behavior. In cancer research, the protein product of a cancer-causing animal viral gene was found to be virtually identical to a normal human growth-promoting protein. Also of interest was the discovery that herbicide resistance in crop-destroying weeds is caused by a mutation in the chloroplasts of the weed plants. Finally, the year saw new efforts to restrict recombinant-DNA research.

Behavior Genetics. In an inbred line of any organism, all individuals of the same sex arc genetically identical. This is the result of brother-sister matings over many generations. One consequence of inbreeding is that any differences among the males or females are caused by differences in environment during either prenatal or postnatal life. For inbred strains that produce litters, such as mice, the uterine environment will include the siblings located on both sides of the developing animal. The siblings may be of the same or opposite sex. The intrauterine positions of all individuals can be established by delivering the litter through a cesarean section.

In a recent set of experiments, Dr. Ronald Gandelman and his associates at Rutgers University examined the behavior of adult females whose location *in utero* was between two males (mFm), and that of females whose prenatal position was between two other females (fFf). The specific behavior under study was learning to avoid an electric shock by pressing a lever immediately after a pre-shock warning light was flashed. It was found that fFf mice were more successful than mFm mice in learning to avoid the shock. It was hypothesized that, during development, mFm mice are exposed to a higher concentration of the male hormone testosterone than their fFf siblings, and that this difference in prenatal environment results in the poorer learning performance of mFm mice.

Cancer and Growth Factor Gene. The abnormal cell division that results in a cancerous growth is believed to be brought about by the production of an excess amount of one or more growth-promoting proteins. It is assumed that these proteins are produced by genes that are either in the organism or introduced into it by viruses. Cancer-causing viral genes, called *onc* genes, appear to have normal gene-equivalents in all organisms, including humans.

It was recently discovered, by Dr. Russell F. Doolittle of the University of California and his colleagues at other institutions, that the protein product of the onc gene carried by a cancer-causing virus (simian sarcoma virus), isolated from a tumor in a monkey, is almost identical in its amino acid composition to the protein PDGF (platelet-derived growth factor), which is produced by a normal human growth-promoting gene. In human beings, PDGF is stored in the blood platelets and released into the serum during blood clotting. PDGF stimulates the growth of the underlying connective tissue, thereby aiding wound-healing. PDGF also stimulates the growth of smooth muscle cells and nervous system glial cells. It is not yet known, however, whether there is any association between a human cancer and excess production of PDGF.

Herbicide Resistance. Among the many problems that confront farmers is the growth of weeds that reduce crop yields. The problem can be combated by herbicides, providing that the crop plant is resistant to the specific herbicide. In the case of corn, the herbicide atrazine has had great success. This chemical compound kills the weeds by binding to a protein in the electron transport system of their leaf-cells' chloroplasts. This causes a block in the system, depriving the leaf cells of the energy needed for photosynthesis. Corn plants are atrazine-resistant because they, unlike weeds, contain enzymes that destroy the herbicide. Unfortunately, weed plants that are resistant to atrazine periodically are found.

Dr. Charles Arntzen of Michigan State University and others in various laboratories have investigated atrazine resistance in weeds. They have discovered that resistance depends on a mutation in the cells' chloroplasts. The mutation results in the amino acid replacement of a glycine for a serine in the chloroplast protein to which atrazine normally binds. The herbicide cannot bind to the altered form of the protein.

Genetic Engineering. The potential ability to alter the hereditary constitution of a human being through recombinant-DNA techniques has raised the fear in some people that genetic engineering could result in an alteration of the human species itself. A resolution signed in 1983 by leaders of virtually every major church group in the United States declares that "efforts to engineer specific traits into the germline of the human species should not be attempted." While implementation of such a resolution would prevent any abuse for political, racial, or social purposes, it would also guarantee the continued suffering of persons afflicted with diseases for which gene splicing may provide a cure (sickle cell anemia, cystic fibrosis, muscular dystrophy, and others).

In its 1983 published report, the President's Commission for the Study of Ethical Problems in Medicine and Biomedical and Behavioral Research held that recombinant-DNA has enormous potential for good and that research should be continued. At the same time, it recommended that the government establish an "appropriate oversight body."

LOUIS LEVINE, *City College of New York*

GEOLOGY

Geology continued in a healthy state in its technological, academic, and professional aspects in 1983. There were many noteworthy events that impinged directly on human lifestyles almost everywhere, often in adverse ways. There was a trend toward better rapport between scientists and the public. Careful writing and splendid illustrations on geologic topics appeared in all the semipopular science-oriented magazines. Even the most esoteric aspects of earth science, such as plate tectonics, were explained to laymen on a sophisticated level.

Disasters and Near Disasters. Floods, earthquakes, volcanic eruptions, and fierce coastal storms struck on an almost regular basis in 1983, but loss of life was relatively low. Erratic weather from El Niño (abnormally high water temperatures in the equatorial Pacific) and perhaps from the eruption of the Mexican volcano El Chichón in 1982 gave rise to damaging waves and floods on Pacific shores. Storms that struck the California coast in March completely destroyed 60 homes and caused more than $200 million in damage. Inland, in Utah, it was the "year of the slide." A mass of saturated rock and mud moved down a canyon to block a river and cover a major highway and railroad tracks. During the year, all major U.S. rivers ran far above average levels, and devastating floods occurred in southern Brazil, India, and Pakistan.

A hydrologic event of major proportions threatens Louisiana, as nature works to alter the course of the lower Mississippi River. It is well known that the river not only builds its delta forward but also frequently changes course as it abandons higher ground to fill in adjacent lower tracts. The present "crowfoot" delta has been in existence for about 600 years, and the time has come for diversion into the Atchafalaya distributary. The diversion is prevented by an artificial structure that has been seriously weakened by floods. How long the dam will hold is not certain, but geologic opinion, based on decades of study, is that the Mississippi River cannot be denied its normal geologic proclivities very long.

Notable earthquakes in 1983 included the world's strongest in more than 1½ years, 7.9 on the Richter Scale, in the South Pacific near New Britain Island on March 18; no lives were lost. Less intense but far more damaging was a quake October 30 in the mountainous region of eastern Turkey; measuring 7.1, it left at least 1,200 persons dead and thousands more homeless in the bitter cold. Also in late October, Idaho and seven other Northwest states were hit by the strongest earthquake, 6.9, on the U.S. mainland since 1959; loss of life was minimal, but property damage was extensive. On May 2, Coalinga, CA, was shaken by a quake that measured 6.5; 48 persons were injured and 300 buildings destroyed, with total damage estimated at $31 million. The Coalinga temblor was followed by thousands of after shocks, including two large ones on May 8 (magnitudes of 5.1 and 4.5) and another on May 24 (4.8). Geologists were surprised to find no surface breaks and attributed the quake, with an epi-

Lava flows from Sicily's erupting volcano, Mt. Etna, causing extensive damage to property.

© Giansanti/Sygma

GEOLOGY / SPECIAL REPORT

Earthquake Prediction

In May 1983, Fresno county, CA, was hit by the most destructive earthquake in the United States in more than ten years. Immediately after such a disaster a public outcry for greater attention to the field of earthquake prediction follows. However the science of earthquake prediction is quite young. In fact by mid-1983, only two earthquakes—one in China in 1975 and one in the USSR in 1978—had been predicted with a degree of accuracy.

Japan, China, the Soviet Union, and United States have commissioned agencies to pursue appropriate seismological studies. In the United States, the National Science Foundation (NSF) and the U.S. Geological Survey (USGS) share responsibility for such research. In addition, the National Earthquake Prediction Council, a standing committee of scientists headed by Caltech's Clarence R. Allen, reports to the USGS.

Although the advantages of successful earthquake prediction are obvious, the science is also a source of danger in itself. Consequences of urgent but erroneous alerts, of repeated unnecessary evacuations, and of conflicting warnings from competing agencies are not difficult to imagine. And who is to issue such forecasts and dictate suggested or mandatory actions? Political, economic, and social stakes are high and consequences fearful. Currently those who are taking responsible unemotional action in the public realm are faced with evaluating a multitude of possible clues, including physical changes in the environment, reactions of animals, and psychic signals from human brains.

An ideal earthquake prediction would announce well in advance the time, locality, and intensity of an impending destructive quake. Although this ideal probably will never be realized, there have been positive steps toward it. Thousands of epicenters have been charted, and the existence of zones, belts, or clusters of intense activity is well documented. It is apparent also that most such zones are associated with fault systems and that there is a cause and effect relationship between movement on faults and shaking of associated material. Significant progress has been made in identifying active or "earthquake" faults, and faults of all kinds are included on all geological maps after they have been located. There are many kinds of faults—active and inactive, shallow and deep-seated, steeply dipping and inclined. Movements range from vertical to horizontal.

The best earthquake predictor is a good geologic map with faults and historic earthquake epicenters superimposed. Concerned citizens can obtain such a map from their state geological survey and judge for themselves the earthquake risk of almost any area. Movements do not take place instantaneously along the entire length of a system. The San Andreas system, the best known and potentially the most deadly one in the United States, is divided into four segments that have reacted more or less independently. Some portions "creep" slowly producing "silent" quakes; others move in jerky fashion; and still others are apparently "locked" in position. Fault segments that have not moved, even though they might be expected to do so, create so-called "seismic gaps." The potential for future movement allowing such segments to catch up as it were is considered to be relatively great.

To be able to predict when an active fault will move is the first step in predicting an earthquake. Many precursors, including swelling of the surface, emission of radon gas, changes in gravity or magnetism, build up of strain, acceleration of movements across known faults, unusual rise or fall of groundwater levels, and speeding up of foreshocks, are known. The technology and instruments for detecting these clues are in existence. Laser beams, for example, can detect movements on a submillimeter scale. California will continue to be a vital test area with a concentration of technical studies.

All possible means of prediction, no matter how far fetched or improbable, must be considered. Practically every animal known to man has been hailed as a quake predictor. Thus, according to animal watchers, when an earthquake is approaching, worms and snakes emerge from their burrows, dogs howl, cats become nervous, birds flee their nests, pigs climb fences, horses bolt, and goldfish jump out of their bowls. No seismologist is willing to discount entirely such behavior. The ability to detect delicate vibrations, subsonic signals, electrical charges, and faint traces of unusual gases is not beyond the known capability of animals. Such abilities may be intensified in certain species, and it may be possible that careful selection will produce breeds capable of detecting earthquakes.

People who knowingly choose to settle or remain in an area prone to earthquakes should think and plan ahead for the inevitable. No truer statement has been made than that attributed to a veteran geologist: The longer it has been since the last earthquake, the sooner the next one will come.

W. Lee Stokes

center 6 mi (9.7 km) beneath the surface, to movement on a buried, previously unsuspected thrust fault much older than the San Andreas, which passes 20 mi (32 km) west of Coalinga. Other major earthquakes took place May 26 in the Sea of Japan off the coast of Honshu, measuring 7.8 and leaving 60 dead and 55 missing; June 24 on the east coast of Taiwan, 6.5, no damage; July 5 in southern Alaska, 6.3, no damage; August 17 in northern Philippines, 6.2, with 14 killed and 80 injured.

Volcanic action included eruptions of Etna on Sicily, March 28 and again in late June and early July. Artificial channels opened by explosives temporarily diverted lava flows, but tourist installations and many vacation cottages were destroyed on the upper slopes. Hawaii's Kilauea, the world's most active volcano, was unusually restless. Activity began in early January, with eruptions from the East Rift Zone. Fire fountains 500 ft (152 m) high were produced, and flows threatened a number of homes. There were additional outbursts in February, late March, late June, and July. During the June–July phase, flows destroyed 16 homes in the Royal Gardens subdivision. In mid-August another strong eruption took place, producing two new flows and lava fountains 120 ft (36 m) high. Through long study, volcanologists are able to predict Kilauea's eruptions 24 hours in advance. Also, looking far into the future, they confidently predict that a small volcano, Loihi, now in the process of building a cone about 19 mi (31 km) south of Kilauea, eventually will become the dominant member of the chain of mostly submarine extinct volcanoes that stretches 2,600 mi (4 184 km) to the Aleutian trench. The most destructive eruptions of 1983 were that of Una Una, Sulawesi, Indonesia, July 18–21, which destroyed most homes, vegetation, and animal life on Una Una island; and that of Mount Oyama on the Japanese island of Miyakejima, October 3; one village was buried and another destroyed by fire.

By studying the deposits of past volcanic events, geologists have reason to believe that as many as a dozen volcanoes of the western United States are likely to resume activity in the not-too-distant future. Mount St. Helens may be only the harbinger of renewed volcanism. The Mono-Inyo Craters, a string of eruptive centers stretching from Mono Lake into the western end of Long Valley, CA, are, after St. Helens, the most frequently active volcanoes in the western United States. Long Valley is a huge sunken crater, or caldera, produced 700,000 years ago. The great number of earthquakes, some of 6.0 or greater, and a swelling up of up to 16 inches (40 cm) at Mammoth Lakes are taken by most seismologists as evidence of upward movement of magma from several miles below the surface.

Maps. An event of international importance was the appearance late in the year of the final five sheets of the Geological World Atlas, a project 72 years in the making. Previously published sheets included those of North America, Africa, Europe, Asia, Antarctica, the Pacific Ocean, and the Indian Ocean. The maps include lithologic, metamorphic, tectonic, stratigraphic, geophysical, and bathymetric data.

Ocean Drilling. Exploratory drilling of the ocean basins and bordering areas and shelves will continue but with considerable reorganization. Faced with having to upgrade the aging and inadequate research vessel *Glomar Challenger* or of spending $90 million on conversion of the oversized *Explorer,* the National Science Foundation was heartened by a third option when the petroleum industry offered for lease one of its idle ships, the *Sedco 472.* A change in administration also is in progress, as scientific ocean drilling is moved from within the National Science Foundation's Directorate for Astronomical, Atmospheric, Earth, and Ocean Sciences (AAEO) into the agency's Division of Ocean Sciences. The Office of Scientific Ocean Drilling (OSOD) probably will become a section within the Division of Ocean Sciences.

Another projected change will come with the transferral of operation management from Scripps Institute of Oceanography to Texas A&M University. Scripps has been running the program since 1968. Texas A&M is taking over by virtue of its engineering expertise and large commitment to funding. The university promises a new building to house the deep-sea cores, to give an "extremely favorable overhead rate," and to fill managerial positions with senior faculty members whose salaries come in part from state funds.

Specimens. An unusually significant meteorite turned up in collections from the Allan Hills field on the Antarctic ice cap. Catalogued as ALPA81005, it is considered by almost all authorities to have originated on the moon. In physical and chemical properties it resembles rock types obtained by the Apollo space missions. More important than its intrinsic properties, however, are the questions it raises about how such a fragment could have been expelled from the moon and traveled to earth.

Grains of the mineral zircon ($ZrSiO_4$) were extracted from sedimentary rock in western Australia and are currently the oldest known indigenous earthly material. Dated at 4.2 billion years old, they indicate that undiscovered parent rocks of that age may exist in the area.

Finally, a specimen that should appeal to anyone: a 137-lb (62-kg) gold nugget brought in by a miner from the state of Para in northern Brazil. Sold to the government for $996,924, it is the largest nugget ever found in that country and compares well with the world's largest nugget, found in Australia and weighing 149.6 lbs (67.9 kg).

WILLIAM LEE STOKES
University of Utah

GEORGIA

Crime and fiscal matters were major concerns in Georgia during 1983.

Legislature. In his first term as governor, former State Rep. Joe Frank Harris pushed through his record $4 billion budget and won approval for several proposals in his anticrime package. Harris engineered the passage of tough drunk-driving legislation, providing for stiffer penalties—increased fines and license-suspension periods—for those caught driving with a blood-alcohol level of .12%. A bill to raise Georgia's legal drinking age from 19 to 21, failed to pass, however, as did legislation which would allow bar owners to be sued if they served alcohol to intoxicated customers who either killed or injured someone while driving. Harris' bill requiring that drivers under 18 take alcohol and drug education courses was approved by both houses. Harris-backed "life without parole" legislation was passed in amended version to provide that convicted murderers serve 28 years before becoming eligible for parole.

The legislature gave farmers and timberland owners a 25% reduction on their property-tax assessment but refused to allow utility companies to institute temporary rate hikes.

In other action, the General Assembly approved legislation that requires that children under the age of four be placed in child restraint devices while riding in an automobile; that gives local governments the right to fine developers who threaten the quality of the state's water resources; and that repeals Georgia's "head of household law" whereby "a wife's legal and civil existence is merged in the husband."

Economy. Metro Atlanta's persistently strong economy was expected to generate 30,000 new jobs by year's end.

Because of Atlanta's growth, the economy statewide was recovering more rapidly than that of the nation. Georgia's job growth in the first quarter was at a 2.7% annual rate, compared with 0.7% nationally. In fact, figures showed that because of the diversified economic base in Atlanta, the state was able to withstand the recession with relative ease.

Developer John Portman announced the planned construction of another downtown Atlanta office tower. Its completion was to coincide with the opening of the downtown Marriott hotel complex, expansion of the Georgia World Congress Center, completion of the rapid rail transit system, and reconstruction of the interstate highway network.

Other News. Publicity surrounded former governor George Busbee when the state's involuntary separation rule was invoked to enable him to qualify for an immediate pension of $57,000. Busbee declined to accept the pension until he reaches age 60. Former President Jimmy Carter was also a source of controversy because of his apparent support of a four-lane parkway to provide access to the proposed Carter library.

Georgia's college desegregation plan won federal approval despite a negative review by the plaintiff, the NAACP, in the original suit.

Turner Broadcasting System announced that it would buy Satellite News for $25 million.

In December convicted murderer John Eldon Smith was executed in Jackson.

KAY BECK, *Georgia State University*

GEORGIA • Information Highlights

Area: 58,910 sq mi (152 577 km²).
Population (1982 est.): 5,639,000.
Chief Cities (1980 census): Atlanta, the capital, 425,022; Columbus, 169,441; Savannah, 141,634.
Government (1983): *Chief Officers*—governor, Joe Frank Harris (D); lt. gov., Zell Miller (D). *General Assembly*—Senate, 56 members; House of Representatives, 180 members.
State Finances (fiscal year 1982): *Revenues,* $6,144,000,000; *expenditures,* $6,007,000,000.
Personal Income (1982): $54,035,000,000; per capita, $9,583.
Labor Force (July 1983): *Nonagricultural wage and salary earners,* 2,236,200; *unemployed,* 196,000 (7.3% of total force).
Education: *Enrollment* (fall 1981)—public elementary schools, 736,565; public secondary, 319,552; colleges and universities (fall 1982), 198,367. *Public school expenditures* (1981–82), $2,188,759,-000.

Atlanta's $20 million High Museum, built by Richard Meier and Partners, was dedicated in October 1983. The white porcelain, granite, and glass museum houses an auditorium, galleries, and a spacious four-story skylit atrium.

© Esto

GERMANY

West German Chancellor Helmut Kohl staged a successful election campaign early in 1983.

In spite of growing East-West tensions in Europe over the planned North Atlantic Treaty Organization (NATO) deployment of new intermediate-range missiles, relations between the Federal Republic of Germany (West Germany) and the German Democratic Republic (East Germany or DDR) generally improved during 1983. While the West German Christian Democrats, including current Chancellor Helmut Kohl, had been very critical of the Socialist-Liberal *Ostpolitik* (policy of normalizing West Germany's relations with Eastern Europe and the Soviet Union) from 1969 to 1982, they essentially continued that policy after being returned to power in 1982–83. This was dramatically demonstrated in June 1983 by an announcement that the Kohl government would guarantee a $400 million loan, organized by a West German banking syndicate, to the DDR. The loan guarantee enabled East Germany to obtain badly needed hard currency credit at normal interest rates. Negotiated in strict secrecy, the loan became a political sensation when it was revealed that the Bavarian minister-president and staunch *Ostpolitik* opponent Franz Josef Strauss had helped to initiate the entire project. To the dismay of his conservative supporters, Strauss also went to East Germany and met with party leader Erich Honecker. Later in the year, the Honecker regime reciprocated for the loan by easing foreign-exchange requirements for West Germans visiting the DDR. By the fall of 1983, negotiations for new cultural and scientific agreements also were underway. Trade between the two German states reached record levels. East Germany was expected to lower the age limit (currently at 60 for women and 63 for men) for visits to West Germany. Although the DDR's

initiatives in these areas almost certainly were taken with the approval of the Soviet Union, both German states apparently were trying to insulate their own bilateral relations from the larger East-West struggle.

Federal Republic of Germany (West Germany)

The most significant political development of 1983 was the stunning election victory of Chancellor Helmut Kohl on March 6. His Christian Democratic Party (CDU) won 48.8% of the popular vote and increased its representation from 226 to 244 seats in the 498-member Bundestag (lower house). Its coalition partner, the Free Democrats (FDP), led by Foreign Minister Hans-Dietrich Genscher, received 7.0% of the vote and 34 seats. The ruling CDU-FDP coalition thereby held a solid majority of 50+ seats in the parliament. The CDU triumph was even greater if one considers that more than half of the Free Democrats' support came from CDU voters, who split their ballots. There was no doubt that a large majority of Germans on March 6 wanted Helmut Kohl and his coalition to stay in power.

The clear losers in the election were the Social Democrats (SPD), who dropped to their lowest level, 38.2% and 193 seats, since 1965. For the first time since 1965, the SPD campaigned as an opposition party, and it was led by a chancellor candidate, Hans-Jochen Vogel, who had less than six months to prepare for the role. The party leadership responsible for the campaign, former Chancellor Willy Brandt and General Secretary Peter Glotz, held to the belief that there was a majority "to the left of the CDU." By emphasizing the "new politics" issues—the environment, nuclear power, and Germany's relationship with the United States —they believed that sufficient support could be attracted from the Green constituency and new voters to make an SPD-Green alignment numerically if not politically possible. But by moving to the left to attract Green support, the SPD lost important segments of its traditional core electorate: skilled workers, lower- and middle-level white collar and technical employees.

For the first time in 30 years, a new party, the Greens, entered parliament; they took 5.6% of the vote and 27 seats. The Greens owed their success to widespread and growing concern about the environment, especially the effects of nuclear power, and the NATO decision to station new intermediate-range nuclear missiles on German soil. The latter issue had sparked the emergence in 1981 of a "Peace Movement," from which the Greens drew much support.

While the media, the Greens, and the SPD emphasized the importance of the missile issue, the majority of the electorate was more concerned about such economic issues as unemployment, government spending, and the viability of the social security system. The Christian Democrats were seen by most voters as more competent to deal with these problems than the Social Democrats or the Greens. Almost two million SPD voters switched to the Christian Democrats largely because of these economic factors.

The government's major problem remained economic recovery. Cuts in spending for social programs, tax incentives for investors, and increases in consumer taxes were the major features of its program. The 1984 budget, adopted in late 1983, was the first to reflect fully these priorities of the Kohl government. The budget also bore the imprint of Finance Minister Gerhard Stoltenberg, generally regarded as the most important and powerful Christian Democratic member of the government after Chancellor Kohl. The budget called for only a 1.8% increase in spending, the smallest in more than 20 years. That modest increase was also below the 3% real growth rate projected for 1984. Many social programs were reduced: unemployment benefits for single workers, health insurance, student aid, and family support. The anticipated budget deficit of $14.4 billion was the lowest since 1980.

Economic Performance. After two years of decline, the West German economy in 1983

Leaders of the opposition in West Germany included (left to right): Hans Jochen Vogel and Willy Brandt, both Social Democrats, and Petra Kelly and Marie Beck-Oberdorf, both members of the antinuclear party, the Greens.

Photo Trends

Photo Trends

To the West German parliament, French President Mitterrand (right front) called for a united Western alliance.

began a modest recovery. Unemployment, which reached a 30-year high of 10.4% in February, dropped to 8.6% by late in the year. Industrial output increased rapidly in the second half, and for the first time since 1980 the gross domestic product showed a real gain of about 1%. Exports were generally stable, although the balance-of-payments surplus was not so high as in 1982. Inflation also dropped, to about 3%. In comparison with its neighbors, especially Great Britain and France, the German economy was relatively healthy in 1983.

Significant problems did remain. Structural unemployment caused by the loss of such major markets as textiles, shipping, and consumer electronics to cheaper foreign competition accounted for about half of the total unemployment level. West Germany was also weak in several high-technology areas: microelectronics, robotics, and genetic engineering. Whether its traditional "smokestack" economy (machinery, automobiles, and chemicals) can prosper in the decades ahead is an open question.

Social Conditions. Popular pressure to reduce the number of foreign residents increased throughout the year. Between 1980 and 1983 the proportion of the population that favored "sending the foreigners home" increased from 35% to 69%. This was due in part to the poor economy, but it also reflected a fear in many Germans that their lifestyle would be fundamentally altered if the influx of foreigners, especially those from non-European countries, continued.

The Kohl government remained strongly committed to reducing West Germany's 4.6 million foreign residents. Emigration to the Federal Republic by the dependents of foreign workers was made more difficult. Those workers unemployed or on a reduced workweek who leave voluntarily were offered grants of about $4,000, with $700 for each dependent.

Civil Liberties. The national census and the planned introduction of a computerized identification system for all citizens became major issues during the year. In April the Federal Constitutional Court issued an injunction halt-

---

WEST GERMANY • Information Highlights

Official Name: Federal Republic of Germany.
Location: North-central Europe.
Area: 96,000 sq mi (248 640 km²).
Population (July 1983): 61,543,000.
Chief Cities (June 30, 1981): Bonn, the capital, 289,400; West Berlin, 1,890,300; Hamburg, 1,640,000; Munich, 1,294,000.
Government: *Head of state,* Karl Carstens, president (took office July 1979). *Head of government,* Helmut Kohl, federal chancellor (took office Oct. 1982). *Legislature*—Parliament: Bundesrat and Bundestag.
Monetary Unit: Deutsche mark (2.6715 D. marks equal U.S.$1, Nov. 4, 1983).
Gross National Product (1982 U.S.$): $659,153,-000,000.
Economic Indexes (1982): *Consumer Prices* (1970 = 100), all items, 183.3; food, 170.7. *Industrial Production* (1975 = 100), 114.
Foreign Trade (1982 U.S.$): *Imports,* $155,856,000,000; *exports,* $176,428,000,000.

ing the national census, which had been scheduled to begin later that month. The court was critical of a provision in the law, passed unanimously by the parliament in 1982, that allowed authorities to compare the new census data with domicile registration information already collected by state authorities and available to the police and other public agencies. The campaign against the census was led by the Greens and libertarian groups, who were concerned about possible abuse of the data by the police and security officials. In an interview following the injunction, the president of the court declared that the political parties ''were out of touch with the opinions, emotions, and fears of the people.''

Civil libertarians felt that the new identification system also could be easily abused by police and security forces. Under the plan, each adult would receive a coded plastic card containing a variety of personal data that could be read by any authority with the appropriate computer terminal. Strong opposition forced the government to reconsider the plan.

Environment. In addition to continued public concern over nuclear-power plants, environmentalists in 1983 drew attention to the increasing damage done to Germany's forests by acid rain. West Germany is more affected by acid rain than any other country in Europe. About 1.4 million acres (560 000 ha) of woodland—or about 1 tree in 12—have been damaged already. As a partial solution, the government proposed the introduction of lead-free gasoline to reduce the emission of damaging exhaust fumes.

Foreign Policy. The missile issue and its implications for Germany's relationship with the United States, the Soviet Union, and its Western European neighbors dominated German foreign policy during the year. In the event that negotiations between the United States and the Soviet Union were not successful, the NATO countries, according to a 1979 decision, planned to deploy 572 intermediate-range missiles in five countries between December 1983 and the end of 1986. West Germany would be the only country where U.S. Pershing II ballistic missiles, which could reach Soviet territory within ten minutes, were to be stationed.

At a special convention in November 1983, the Social Democratic Party rejected the deployment of the Pershing missiles. Shortly thereafter, Chancellor Kohl recommended deployment to the parliament, and after two days of intense debate, the stationing of the missiles was approved by a solid majority.

The Kohl government, which supported the NATO decision from the beginning, considered its March election victory a confirmation of its position. The massive nationwide protests held in October and November were dismissed as unrepresentative of the attitudes of the majority of Germans. However, the government did urge the Reagan administration to be flexible in the Geneva negotiations and to consider the widespread public concern about an escalation of the arms race. The U.S. invasion of Grenada in October did not help the Kohl government's effort for the missiles. Foreign Minister Genscher rebuked the United States for the invasion.

In early July, Chancellor Kohl traveled to Moscow for his first meeting with Soviet President Yuri Andropov. Regardless of the outcome at Geneva, both Moscow and Bonn

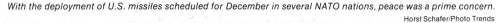

With the deployment of U.S. missiles scheduled for December in several NATO nations, peace was a prime concern.

Horst Schafer/Photo Trends

would like to continue the pattern of normal, if not friendly, relations, which has existed since the late 1960s. During 1983, Bonn was very careful in its responses to Soviet pressure against the missile deployment plan.

The growing opposition to the missiles was also a concern to France, Germany's most important neighbor. Some French officials viewed Germany's reaction to the NATO decision as part of a growing trend toward neutralism in foreign policy and a corresponding increase in sentiment for reunification. The French government was most alarmed at the opposition of the Social Democrats. For the time being, at least, public opinion polls showed that about 4 out of every 5 Germans supported NATO and rejected any neutralist course in foreign policy.

German Democratic Republic (East Germany)

During 1983 the ruling Socialist Unity Party and its leader, Erich Honecker, continued to struggle with the problems of economic decline, a growing foreign debt, the DDR's own peace movement, and increased pressures from Moscow to produce more and better products for the Socialist bloc. The celebrations of the 500th anniversary of Martin Luther's birth and the centennial of Karl Marx's death gave the regime an opportunity to present its best side to visitors, but they did little to resolve its long-term problems.

Economy. At the COMECON (Council for Mutual Economic Assistance, the Communist counterpart to the Common Market) meeting of trade ministers in October, the East Germans did not escape the general Soviet criticism toward its Eastern European allies: Soviet shipments of raw materials, especially oil, were not matched by adequate exports of finished industrial goods to the Socialist "motherland." The East Germans were also once again reminded that they have the highest standard of living of

Photo Trends

Meeting in Moscow with East Germany's Erich Honecker (left), Yuri Andropov offered a new arms limitation plan.

any Communist country, including the Soviet Union. But while obligated to pay the increasing costs of raw materials with high-quality exports to the Soviet Union, East Germany was also dependent on exports to the West to pay its debt service costs. Thus, the stagnant economic situation in Western Europe had a definite impact on the East German economy. At present East Germany must deliver about 40% of its exports to the Soviet Union to pay for fuel and raw materials; by 1985 oil alone will consume about one third of East Germany's total exports. The foreign debt problem was so severe that West German bankers estimated that the DDR would need an additional $1 billion (U.S.) by early 1984.

Social Conditions. In spite of strong official opposition, an East German peace movement continued to flourish during 1983. The movement, which urged disarmament by both East and West, was the only significant dissident force in the DDR. It was closely connected with certain elements within the Protestant Church. In July, authorities deported a large group of activists centered in Jena.

The problems of acid rain and air pollution were also the focus of several small protest demonstrations in various cities. Five urban areas already showed extensive environmental damage: Halle, Leipzig, Dresden, Karl-Marx Stadt, and Berlin.

Foreign Policy. Unwavering support for the Soviet Union continued to be the cornerstone

---

EAST GERMANY • Information Highlights

Official Name: German Democratic Republic.
Location: North-central Europe.
Area: 41,800 sq mi (108 262 km²).
Population (July 1983 est.): 16,724,000.
Chief Cities (1980): East Berlin, the capital, 1,145,743; Leipzig, 563,388; Dresden, 516,284.
Government: *Head of state,* Erich Honecker, chairman of the Council of State. *Head of government,* Willi Stoph, chairman of the Council of Ministers Presidium. General secretary of the Socialist Unity (Communist) Party, Erich Honecker (took office 1971). *Legislature* (unicameral)—Volkskammer (People's Chamber).
Monetary Unit: DDR mark (2.65 DDR marks equal U.S.$1, June 1983).
Gross National Product (1981 U.S.$): $162,000,000,000.
Economic Index (1982): *Industrial Production* (1975 = 100), 138.
Foreign Trade (1982 U.S.$): *Imports,* $21,743,000,000; *exports,* $20,196,000,000.

of East German foreign policy. In 1983, however, Honecker attempted to demonstrate both to the hard-liners in his own regime and to Moscow that a moderate approach to the West can bring concrete economic benefits.

In Asia and Africa, East Germany was an important surrogate for the Soviet Union. Economic, technical, and military assistance missions were now widespread throughout the Third World. These activities were thought to strengthen the DDR's bargaining position within the Communist bloc. The regime also was able to insulate itself from the events in Poland.

West Berlin

The general improvement in intra-German relations during 1983 and the modest economic recovery in West Germany also had a positive impact on West Berlin. Unemployment in the city began to decline in midyear, and the number of foreign residents, both legal and illegal, dropped slightly.

The new Christian Democratic-Free Democratic government, led by Lord Mayor Richard von Weizsäcker, was another stabilizing factor. The CDU, after almost three decades in opposition, replaced the scandal-ridden SPD government in 1981. The new government pursued a moderate course in dealing with the city's chronic economic and social problems—an aging population, a radical youth subculture, and a severe housing shortage.

Lord Mayor von Weizsäcker was also a strong supporter of continuity and a pragmatic approach to East Germany and the Soviet Union. He met with Honecker in September and attended the convention of the East German Protestant Church in Wittenberg. His unquestioned integrity and prestige (he belongs to one of Germany's most famous families) also enhanced West Berlin's image in 1983. But it was rumored that von Weizsäcker will leave Berlin in 1984 to assume the presidency of the Federal Republic in Bonn.

DAVID P. CONRADT, *University of Florida*

GHANA

Ghana's economic problems continued to mount in 1983, increased by the necessity of absorbing more than a million refugees who were expelled from Nigeria in January. Production of cocoa, the major export crop, was down for the fourth year. Interest on foreign debts took the bulk of the government's earnings. The "hungry season," which formerly affected only the Northern Territories, had spread throughout the country, and the government's food-distribution system was a shambles. Official prices established for basic foodstuffs were ignored, and inflation was in double-digit fig-

---

GHANA · Information Highlights
Official Name: Republic of Ghana.
Location: West Africa.
Area: 92,000 sq mi (238 280 km²).
Population (July 1983): 13,367,000.
Chief Cities (1977 est.): Accra, the capital, 840,000; Kumasi, 353,000; Tema, 169,500.
Government: *Head of state and government,* Flight-Lt. Jerry Rawlings (assumed power Dec. 1981). *Legislature*—Constituent Assembly (dissolved Dec. 1981).
Monetary Unit: Cedi (2.750 cedis equal U.S. $1, June 1983).
Gross National Product (1981 U.S. $): $9,400,-000,000.
Economic Index (Dec. 1982): *Consumer Prices* (1970 = 100), all items, 9,294.8; food, 13,407.6.
Foreign Trade (1981 U.S.$): *Imports,* $1,106,000,000; *exports,* $1,063,000,000.

---

ures. A 110-pound (50-kg) bag of corn sold for 4,000 new cedis in Accra, although the official price was 280 new cedis. Unemployment continued high, especially in Accra and Kumasi.

Flight Lt. Jerry Rawlings, chairman of the ruling Provisional National Defense Council (PNDC), met these problems with more government controls, backed by threats of police action against law violators. The PNDC also improved relations with Libya, the USSR, and Communist-bloc countries, and announced the goal of converting to a socialist state.

The state of the economy and the government's growing radicalism caused a series of conflicts between police and demonstrators. The most serious of these occurred in early June in Accra and Kumasi, where students, workers, and police clashed over demands for a total alteration of the government. Unemployed workers were arrested in the major cities over their demands for better wages.

The general unrest culminated in June in the second attempt in less than a year by disgruntled soldiers to overthrow the PNDC and unseat Rawlings. A previous coup had been crushed on Nov. 23, 1982, and some of the revolutionaries had escaped to Togo. Early in the morning of June 19 these soldiers crossed the border, attacked three prisons in Accra and Nswam, and released 52 military prisoners. At first successful, the rebels seized the Ghana Broadcasting Company buildings and announced to the nation the overthrow of the PNDC. Within hours, troops loyal to the regime had retaken the radio and television station, captured some of the rebels, closed the borders, and set up road blocks throughout the country. Casualties were few, and Rawlings' hold on the government was assured. Trials of those accused of complicity in the coup were held in conjunction with those accused of participating in the previous uprising. A special tribunal sentenced 20 persons to death, 15 in absentia; 4 were executed on August 13.

HARRY A. GAILEY
San Jose State University

GREAT BRITAIN

The most important event of the year in Great Britain was the general election in June. Prime Minister Margaret Thatcher was returned to power with a greatly increased majority and consolidated the triumph of the British version of right-wing, supply-side economics.

Otherwise it proved another difficult year. In spite of ministers' repeated promises that the long-awaited economic upturn was about to appear, there were few real signs of increased production. Unemployment remained intolerably high at more than 3 million, or 13% of the work force, and the pound sterling—like most other European currencies—fell sharply against the dollar. In Britain this was made worse by the world oil glut, and by the end of the year the pound was slithering to a record low $1.40. A year-end terrorist bombing of London's most famous department store outraged Britons.

The "Falklands Factor." Mrs. Thatcher's popularity, which had been low at the beginning of 1982, was enormously increased by the success of the Falklands campaign against Argentina. The so-called "Falklands factor" remained with her through the first part of 1983. It brought her a reputation for courage and determination. It was implied, none too subtly, that just as she had pursued the course she believed right in wartime and had finally triumphed, so her economic policies would, in spite of all difficulties, be proved correct.

The prime minister herself brought home the message with an unannounced visit to the islands in January, arriving there after an arduous 24-hour flight, much of the time in a highly uncomfortable Hercules troop transport. Television pictures back in Britain showed the warm and grateful reception she had won from the islanders and undoubtedly helped to link her own personality to the country's military success.

She was helped, too, by the official report on the background of and reasons for the war. Though this report, prepared by public figures and politicians from all parties, contained criticisms of Britain's military and diplomatic intelligence, it did not blame the government for failing to grasp Argentine intentions.

All these elements no doubt helped the government to deflect domestic criticism of the huge cost of maintaining the military base on the Falklands. At a time when ministers at home were predicting large cuts in public expenditure, it was announced that about one billion pounds was to be spent on building a new airport on the islands. This would enable jets to fly all the way from Britain to the South Atlantic and would cost a sum roughly equivalent to $1 million for every inhabitant of the islands. (*See also* page 251.)

The Election Campaign. Under the British system, Mrs. Thatcher could have waited until the spring of 1984 before announcing the next general election. Instead, she scheduled elections for June 9. Many of her senior ministers were becoming worried about the economy's failure to improve, and they feared that in a year's time their popularity might be much lower. Mrs. Thatcher herself wanted to stay on but was finally persuaded by her colleagues to seek a renewal of her mandate.

She need not have worried. Though the election was fought with unprecedented efficiency by her party, the effort was scarcely worthwhile: at no time did the opinion polls suggest the remotest chance that she might fail. The main interest for many commentators lay in which party would come in second—either the Labour Party, which had been in existence for almost the whole century and had formed the government for almost half the period since World War II, or the new alliance of the Lib-

In August, Margaret and Denis Thatcher took leave of 10 Downing Street for a Switzerland vacation. June elections gave Mrs. Thatcher a new lease at the official residence.

erals and the Social Democrats, a party that had been in existence for less than two years. A number of opinion polls near voting day suggested that the latter would do better.

The Labour Party could hardly have been in worse shape. Its defeat in the election of 1979 had left it battered and bewildered. Its left wing had conducted a remorseless campaign to make sure that it did not return to the traditional center ground of British politics. Activists at grass-roots level made sure that candidates approved the leftist line and moved to expel some of those members of Parliament (MPs) who did not. Parliament was the scene of constant struggles between the left and the more right-wing centrists, and the party's governing body was more noted for the acrimony with which it conducted its meetings than for any political skill or expertise.

On top of this, it had in Michael Foot an elderly leader who, while immensely popular among his colleagues, was regarded as old and inadequate by the electorate. A product of the age before television, Foot was a fine platform speaker who could rouse a loyal crowd with a few words. On TV he appeared hesitant, evasive, and sometimes incomprehensible. Labour MPs' fear that he would lead them to defeat was blended with their great affection for the old man, and nobody proved willing to get him replaced. Some labor union leaders, the Labour Party's moneybags, made a half-hearted effort to ditch Foot, but this failed because of his stubbornness and the unwillingness of their chosen replacement, Peter Shore, to wield the knife.

The greatest shock for the party, and one of the most seismic moments in post-World War II British politics, came with the Bermondsey by-election in February. Bermondsey was a classic example of a Labour parliamentary seat; located in the London inner city, its inhabitants were poor and had suffered badly from the Conservatives' economic policies. It was a fight Labour had to win.

As it was, the left-dominated local party chose as its candidate Peter Tatchell, a young man who was himself left-wing; an Australian by birth standing in an area not noted for its tolerance of any outsiders, still less foreigners; and an admitted homosexual. Tatchell was subjected to a desperate campaign of vilification by the press, not least by Rupert Murdoch's *Sun,* which lost few opportunities to attack him or inquire into his private life. Tatchell went down to a disastrous defeat, being beaten by the Liberal candidate, Simon Hughes.

All this created the image of a party hardly capable of managing itself, let alone the country. The Social Democratic Party (SDP), firmly in alliance with the middle-of-the-road Liberal Party, took heart, and though Labour later held onto another working-class constituency, Darlington, it became clear that the battle was on

Michael Foot, 70, who resigned as Labour leader after the party's defeat at the polls, had time for contemplation.

to discover who would be the primary opposition to the Conservatives.

The election campaign itself was extremely lackluster, mainly because Mrs. Thatcher's return appeared to be predestined. She herself embarked on a series of carefully planned "mini-tours" to different parts of the country. These were brief and had the principal purpose of providing vivid images for the TV cameras. Most days she would make a single speech designed to hammer home a single point.

By contrast, Michael Foot found himself launched into an arduous and inefficiently organized "grand tour" that often took him through regions where his party could have no chance whatever of success. The Labour Party displayed hopeless incompetence throughout the campaign in almost every department: speakers were not available for TV and radio; candidates turned up for meetings that had not been organized; and the advertising campaign was poorly funded and negative.

In the midst of this chaos, the issues tended to be lost. The Conservatives painted Labour as the party of weakness regarding national defense and were greatly assisted by a clash between Labour leaders on the question of nuclear weapons. The party's stance was officially in favour of unilateral nuclear disarmament. This would have meant a refusal to buy the U.S. Trident missile system, the revocation of permission to station Tomahawk cruise missiles in Britain, and the scrapping of the existing Polaris missiles. More right-wing Labour spokesmen, such as the "shadow" Foreign Secretary (secretary of state) Denis Healey and former Prime Minister James Callaghan, made it clear that they felt the British people would not accept such complete disarmament in the face of the Soviet Union. The Conservatives found it easy to exploit both this split and what they understood to be the public fears of being left defenseless.

Labour made some mileage in accusing the Conservatives of wanting to break up the National Health Service, the system of socialized medicine that guarantees free treatment for all citizens and that, in spite of its failings, remains a source of great comfort and reassurance to most British people. Mrs. Thatcher, however, made it clear that, while she wanted to see private medicine used to a greater extent, she would defend the NHS itself.

Meanwhile, the SDP/Liberal alliance was showing well in the opinion polls. They had a different problem: while the Liberal leader David Steel was highly regarded by the public, his equivalent in the SDP, Roy Jenkins, was not coming across. At a meeting of party bigwigs midway through the campaign, it was decided that Steel should effectively take over the leadership of the alliance for the moment, even though the two parties were jointly offering Jenkins as their choice for prime minister. Aided by Steel's greater impact—he is young and energetic and conveys an impression of sincerity—the alliance made slow but dogged strides, pitching their appeal on the failings of the other two main parties.

Election Results. In the end, polling was a disastrous day for Labour. In the south of England, apart from a few seats in London, it was virtually obliterated. In hundreds of seats, alliance candidates even swept them out of second place.

Only in the north, in Scotland, and in the decaying inner cities did Labour hold on. The final tally on the day after polling showed that it crashed to only 209 seats in the new enlarged 650-seat House of Commons, compared with 397 held by the Conservatives. Its share of the vote had fallen to 27.6%, the lowest it had scored since becoming one of the country's two main parties. It was a crushing and humiliating defeat.

The Liberal/SDP alliance was, in a sense, even more unfortunate. With 25.4% of the popular vote, it was close behind Labour. Yet the inequities of the British voting system, which give an unfairly large proportion of parliamentary seats to the biggest parties, meant that between them the two moderate groupings scored only 23 MPs. The Liberals, established and well dug into particular areas, managed 17 seats—mainly if not exclusively in Scotland, Wales, and the Southwest. The SDP, with its vote evenly and ineffectively spread across the country, took only six seats. Dozens of their former MPs who had quit Labour for the new party found themselves swept from power. Two out of the so-called "Gang of Four," the SDP's founding fathers, also lost. One who succeeded was Roy Jenkins, but since it was generally agreed that his unimpressive campaigning had contributed to the defeats, he lost little time in resigning the party leadership. He was replaced immediately and without opposition by David Owen, a former foreign secretary whose evident skills and experience had impressed many people at the time of the Falklands War. Owen had a reputation for arrogance and made it clear that he saw himself as a future alliance prime minister rather than Steel, but with an election many years distant, this seemed unimportant.

The anguish of the Labour Party was much greater. Both wings immediately began to blame each other for the appalling defeat. The right argued that the electorate had been frightened by the left. The left riposted that their policies would have been endorsed by the electorate if the right had not reneged.

Both sides privately blamed Michael Foot for many of their misfortunes. Two days after the defeat Foot announced his resignation and a lengthy battle began for his succession. This, for the first time, was to be decided by an electoral college, including the labor unions, party grass-roots activists, and members of Parliament.

The battle was less acrimonious than it might have been, since the winner emerged early. He was Neil Kinnock, a 41-year-old teacher from Wales, who had never held public office. However, he had a youthful and attractive manner, an instinctive understanding of how to use television, and a supple rhetorical

---

GREAT BRITAIN • Information Highlights

Official Name: United Kingdom of Great Britain and Northern Ireland.
Location: Island, western Europe.
Area: 94,200 sq mi (243 978 km²).
Population (July 1983): 56,078,000.
Chief Cities (1981 census): London, the capital, 6,696,008; Birmingham, 1,006,908; Glasgow, 763,162; Leeds, 704,974; Sheffield, 536,770; Liverpool, 510,306.
Government: *Head of state,* Elizabeth II, queen (acceded Feb. 1952). *Head of government,* Margaret Thatcher, prime minister (took office May 1979). *Legislature*—Parliament: House of Lords and House of Commons.
Monetary Unit: Pound (0.704 pound equals U.S.$1, Dec. 20, 1983).
Gross Domestic Product (1982 U.S.$): $473,424,000,000.
Economic Indexes (1982): *Consumer Prices* (1970 = 100), all items, 438.3; food, 462.9. *Industrial Production* (1975 = 100), 104.
Foreign Trade (1982 U.S.$): *Imports,* $99,656,000,000; *exports,* $96,994,000,000.

S. Franklin/Sygma

UPI

style. Though an expert in very few subjects, he could speak engagingly and even convincingly on many. He was nominally on the left of the party, but that wing's adherents swiftly noticed that he was moving toward the center. For example, he began to hedge his party's antinuclear policy. He also let it be known that, as his deputy, he would prefer Roy Hattersley, a former cabinet minister unashamedly on the right of the party.

Kinnock easily won on the first ballot, as did Hattersley as deputy an hour later. The Labour Party immediately began to project its new leader as a symbol of their new, reformed, youthful image, and as the Conservative government's problems mounted, so did Labour's standing in the opinion polls. Kinnock revealed a tendency to talk for far too long, but since his excesses could easily be edited out of TV performances, it was only his colleagues in Parliament who suffered.

The Thatcher Government. Mrs. Thatcher immediately stamped her increased authority upon her government. Most surprisingly, she sacked Foreign Secretary Francis Pym, a landowner of distinctly liberal views who had, at one time, been seen as a future premier. She also promoted one of her most ardent supporters, Energy Secretary Nigel Lawson, to the post of chancellor of the exchequer (financial secretary).

Oddly enough, however, her views on foreign affairs appeared to be softening. In November she said for the first time that the West should open a dialogue with the Soviet Union, and in December she took the extraordinary step of welcoming the new, democratically elected President Raúl Alfonsín of Argentina to office. This was seen as an exceptional gesture of goodwill since the two countries were still nominally at war.

The government's difficulties centered in large part on its relationship with the United States. Mrs. Thatcher had long been proud of her friendship with President Ronald Reagan and had made it one of her electoral assets.

SS-20 DEPLOYMENT

NUMBER OF MISSILES DEPLOYED BY DECEMBER 1979

NUMBER OF MISSILES DEPLOYED BY NOVEMBER 1981 (COMMENCEMENT OF GENEVA INF NEGOTIATIONS)

NUMBER OF MISSILES DEPLOYED BY OCTOBER 1983

RANGE OF MISSILE

Informing the House of Commons on November 14 that the first American-made cruise missiles had arrived in Britain, Defense Secretary Michael Heseltine, right, used a chart to illustrate the increased deployment of Soviet SS-20 missiles. Cecil Parkinson, below, resigned as secretary for industry and trade after acknowledging an extra-marital affair. He decided to remain with his wife Ann, also below.

However, she opposed the U.S. invasion of Grenada, which is a part of the British Commonwealth and nominally ruled by Queen Elizabeth. The actual invasion caught her and her ministers entirely by surprise. The U.S. administration's decision to resume arms sales to Argentina also was opposed strongly by her, and it consequently did further damage to her standing at home.

Peace Movement. The peace movement was increasingly vocal in Britain, if not necessarily any better supported. Public opinion ranged from those who backed the U.S. position to supporters of the Campaign for Nuclear Disarmament (CND), which wants all nuclear weapons of all kinds cleared out of the country. Their best-known supporters were the "Greenham Common Women," a group of women who had pitched camp outside the gates of the U.S. base near London where the first cruise missiles were to be installed.

Though mocked and derided in the Conservative press as malcontent deviants, the women received a growing measure of support as the year went by. Fears that U.S. policy was directed more to the defense of the continental United States rather than to any notion of general Western security helped to fuel support for CND, as did the British government's refusal to insist on a dual key to the missiles. This would have made it impossible for cruise missiles to be fired without the agreement of both governments. Among some people, including many who supported the West's possession of nuclear weapons, the fear grew that cruise might defend only the United States while making Europe the first target in a nuclear exchange.

Northern Ireland. Sinn Fein, the political arm of the Irish Republican Army (IRA), gained ground in the general election, winning a seat in Parliament. However, the victor, Gerry Adams, already had declared that he would boycott Parliament if elected. Ulster's other nationalist party, the more moderate Social Democratic and Labor Party, also won a seat in Parliament.

Violence in Northern Ireland continued in 1983 and included a murderous attack by gunmen on a Protestant church in November and the assassination of a prominent Protestant Unionist in December. Terrorist violence culminated in London on December 17, when a car bomb exploded outside Harrods department store, killing 5 persons and injuring 91.

The Falkland Islands—One Year After War

A year after Britain recovered the Falklands from an Argentine invasion force on June 14, 1982, the British had been unable to obtain a declaration from Argentina that hostilities in the South Atlantic were over. Britain refused to resume negotiations with Argentina regarding the islands' future, as called for in a United Nations resolution of Nov. 4, 1982, until that precondition had been met. Both Great Britain and Argentina began significant arms buildups in the region in 1983.

Britain's Prime Minister Margaret Thatcher made an unannounced journey to the Falklands, held by Britain for 150 years, in January 1983. For five days she visited with about half of the 1,800 inhabitants and some 4,000 troops stationed there, and paused at the graves of British military men killed while fighting for "freedom and justice." Thatcher assured the appreciative islanders of Britain's commitment to their defense. The Thatcher junket was criticized by Argentine President Reynaldo Bignone and his foreign minister, Juan Ramón Aguirre Lanari. Thatcher's opponents in the British Parliament saw the prime minister as fulfilling a role of "colonial conqueror."

It was inevitable that the short-lived war in the South Atlantic would be investigated thoroughly. A defense ministry inquiry was released in December 1982. It concluded that Britain should retain a strike capacity in addition to its role in the North Atlantic Treaty Organization (NATO). Press censorship during the conflict was criticized, as was the navy's lack of a credible early-warning system against low-flying warplanes.

As Mrs. Thatcher returned from her "pilgrimage" to the Falklands, a 90-page report on the government's role in the South Atlantic, prepared by a six-member multiparty committee presided over by Lord Franks and appointed by Mrs. Thatcher, was made public. The committee's findings rejected the allegation that Mrs. Thatcher's government could have prevented the 74-day Falklands war. The handling of intelligence by officials from several government departments was criticized, as was the Foreign Office, for "underestimating certain signals" from Buenos Aires.

An elated Mrs. Thatcher proceeded with her policy of "Fortress Falklands." A $3.3 billion (U.S.), three-year package called for expenditures amounting to $7 million per Falklands family. A 4,000-man garrison would remain on the islands and the construction of an airport suitable for military aircraft was planned. More than $30 million would be allocated for developing the colony. Argentina's rearmament included the replacement of $800 million in lost equipment and purchase of weapons systems deemed indispensable to modern warfare.

A week after Thatcher's Conservative landslide victory on June 9, the defense committee of the House of Commons released its inquiry. While defending the "Fortress Falklands" concept, it found that the sovereignty question would not be resolved quickly and that a rearmed Argentina could launch "sporadic attacks" against the islands. Specifically, the committee called for construction of an airport on the islands. Concern was expressed over the effect that the buildup in the South Atlantic would have on Britain's obligations under NATO.

The inquiry most critical of Mrs. Thatcher's handling of the Falklands affair was the one prepared by a special committee on foreign affairs of the House of Commons, headed by Sir Anthony Kershaw. Kershaw's findings had not been considered by the full committee prior to its dissolution at the time of the June 9 election. The report was not made public until July 12. It concluded that the political and material costs of Mrs. Thatcher's "Fortress Falklands" policy were a "burden" and that it would have a negative effect on British policy, now and in the future.

Even if London's queries into the Falklands episode failed to produce a scapegoat, that was not the case in Argentina. The military government's inquiry into the Falklands defeat and the arrest of former President Leopoldo Galtieri appeared to be integral parts of a campaign to make Galtieri responsible for the failure of the Falklands operation. Lt. Gen. Galtieri (ret.), mastermind of the islands' invasion by Argentine forces, served a 45-day jail sentence. The severe action resulted from the publication in a leading Buenos Aires daily of a long and damaging interview on the Falklands war. Galtieri had not obtained the prior permission that military regulations require before discussing political matters with the press. While justifying his acts regarding the Falklands on a miscalculation of the responses of the U.S. and British governments to an Argentine invasion of the islands, Galtieri placed the blame for the Falklands debacle on his field commanders.

As of March 1983, the Thatcher government no longer regarded the wishes of the Falklanders as paramount, insisting instead that they must be "taken into account." Then Foreign Secretary Francis Pym reiterated the principle of self-determination for the Falkland islanders on May 24.

LARRY L. PIPPIN

The IRA acknowledged responsibility for the bombing but claimed that the attack was unauthorized.

Newsmakers. In the fall Mrs. Thatcher faced a relatively minor problem but one that commanded extensive space in the newspapers. Her minister for industry—and, many felt, her chosen successor—was Cecil Parkinson. As chairman of the Conservative Party, Parkinson had been in command of the monumentally successful election campaign, and he was already being tapped as a future prime minister. Then, in a joint lawyers' statement, he and his former secretary, a young woman named Sara Keays, admitted that she was pregnant by him. He had, however, decided to stay with his wife and family.

Faced with a real-life soap opera in high places, the nation split in two between those who supported him against a vengeful woman and those who backed her against a faithless man. Mrs. Thatcher immediately made it clear that she had no intention of sacking Parkinson, and he made a successful speech at the Conservatives' annual conference a week after his admission. Miss Keays then made a lengthy statement to the *Times* newspaper making further charges of misconduct against him. Parkinson promptly resigned office.

Queen Elizabeth toured the United States and India, and Prince Charles and Princess Diana made long visits to Australia and Canada. It soon became clear that public interest was far greater in her than in him.

Crime. Britain's largest mass murder was revealed in February when police, searching the blocked drains of a house in north London, discovered pieces of human remains. They arrested Denis Nilsen, a quiet clerk who worked in an unemployment pay office. He was convicted of murdering six young men, but it was certain that the true figure was nearer to 20. All his victims had been rootless drifters who had come to London seeking a better life.

In January, police searching for an armed criminal, David Martin, followed a car in which Martin's girlfriend was a passenger. Without warning they opened fire on the driver who, like Martin, was blond, but who in fact was a completely innocent friend of the girl's. The driver, Stephen Waldorf, survived by a medical miracle, but the case caused immense shock in Britain where the police are traditionally unarmed and where shooting in the streets is almost unheard of. The two detectives involved were later acquitted of various charges, including attempted murder.

One important vote in Parliament came in early July when MPs voted by large majorities against the return of capital punishment for any crime at all. Since the composition of the House was more right-wing and more populist than at any time since World War II, it was concluded that the matter would not be raised again for many years.

The Press. It was a bad year for the press. Two of the country's leading newspapers, *The Times* and *The Sunday Times,* were taken in by the forged Hitler diaries, an affair that also did woeful damage to the reputation of Lord Dacre (formerly Professor Hugh Trevor-Roper), a leading historian who at first declared the diaries genuine.

Damaging industrial disputes occurred with the labor unions, who were resisting the arrival of computer technology, and the proprietors of the various papers found themselves as incapable of agreeing with each other as they were in defeating the unions. In late November, Britain's national newspapers were closed for two days because of the dispute. Competition for circulation led to the introduction of ever more fanciful prize competitions, some offering a million pounds, though it was notable that much more money than that was spent on publicizing the gimmicks.

SIMON HOGGART
"The Observer"

Still popular with the public, Princess Diana visited a West Indian community center in Brixton, London, in October.

The Arts

Under the continuing stress of the economic recession, the arts and politics became enmeshed in conflicts and reassessments during 1983. After announcing a boost in the arts budget in January (with the Arts Council granted £93.5 million, about $140 million), the new Minister for the Arts, Lord Gowrie, demanded 1% back by midyear. The chairman of the Arts Council, Sir William Rees-Mogg, forced to spread the cuts across the board, reacted by suggesting that overspending in other areas of government created the situation. Arts Council subsidy is still the lifeblood of artistic enterprise in Britain, with help from business running at £12.5 million (about $19 million) yearly.

Also in 1983, John Drummond, artistic director of the Edinburgh Festival, ended his five-year tenure spectacularly. Among the hundreds of festival events of theater, music, and art packed into three weeks, the major events were clustered around the theme of "Vienna 1900." A notable exhibition of paintings featured works by Egon Schiele and Gustav Klimt and also surprising paintings by Arnold Schönberg. The Glasgow Citizens Theatre, one of Britain's leading young companies, contributed a giant production of Karl Kraus's *The Last Days of Mankind* in its first performance in Britain. Among Edinburgh dance events, Ballet Rambert's *Colour Moves*, with sets and costumes by painter Bridget Riley, opened to wide approval.

Theater. Altogether it was a year when the British could be less accused of chauvinism. Yuri Lyubimov of Moscow's Taganka Theatre directed Michael Pennington in *Crime and Punishment* at the Lyric, Hammersmith, and Glenda Jackson faced a hostile provincial tour before bringing Bothto Strauss' *Great and Small* to London's West End.

The commercial theater, fighting both a value-added tax (VAT) on seat prices and the big subsidized companies, struggled to retain its sparkle. Most successful were John Dexter's revival of *Heartbreak House*, in which Diana Rigg and Rex Harrison shone; and *Man and Superman*, with Peter O'Toole.

At the Royal Shakespeare Company (RSC), actor Derek Jacobi added a dashing *Cyrano de Bergerac* to his already successful season, and Helen Mirren won praise in *The Roaring Girl* and for a definitive Cleopatra. In October the company took a risk with a new revolutionary play by David Edgar, *Maydays*.

The National Theatre through much of 1983 seemed to excel in revivals, with Peter Wood's production of *The Rivals* playing alongside a new translation of Alfred de Musset's *Lorenzaccio*, both boasting bravura sets by designer John Gunter. At year's end, Peter Hall directed a new Marvin Hamlisch musical *Jean Seberg*, based on the life of the Hollywood starlet.

Royal Haymarket Theatre

Rex Harrison starred with Diana Rigg in the big hit of London's theater season, a revival of "Heartbreak House."

Music. At the Barbican Arts Centre the commercial success of impresario Raymond Gubbay, whose concerts of familiar favorites averaged a 90% audience, caused embarrassment to the resident subsidized orchestra, the London Symphony, which barely achieved a 65% house in its first year there. On the South Bank, poor attendances at the concert halls were also evident.

Although the Royal Opera House, trying to buy international stars with an inadequate budget, was attacked in 1983 for artistic staleness, the English National Opera staged five excellent new productions and the revivals *Rigoletto* and *Toussaint*. Opera at the Glyndebourne Festival (a new production of *Idomeneo*, the first operatic venture by RSC director Trevor Nunn), Buxton Festival (Antonio Vivaldi's *Griselda*, staged for the first time in Britain), and Aldeburgh (a new version of Benjamin Britten's *Turn of the Screw*) won praise.

South Bank Summer Music, under artistic director Simon Rattle, opened with the first-ever performance in Britain of Leoš Janáček's *Osud*. Contemporary music provided a highlight later in the year, with "The Great British Music Festival," six concerts of British music from 1925 to 1975, and a further eight programs in the "Music of Eight Decades" series given by the BBC Symphony Orchestra and the London Sinfonietta. A high point of the musical year for many was Alfred Brendel's performances of the complete Beethoven piano sonatas at the Queen Elizabeth Hall.

Anchorman Frank Bough (top row, center) and crew debuted in British TV's early morning "Breakfast Time."

Dance. Home companies and visitors provided a wide choice, with new works from Kenneth MacMillan at the Royal Ballet and Siobhan Davies at the London Contemporary Dance Theatre. Jonathan Burrows' new ballet, *The Winter Play* at Sadlers Wells, was perhaps the best received. Among visitors, the New York City Ballet at Covent Garden won the most intense appreciation.

Visual Arts. The Tate Gallery mounted one of the biggest draws of the year with Douglas Cooper's "The Essential Cubism." Later in the year an exhibition of the "New Art" of Britain at the Tate was surrounded by critical argument. At year's end, the Hayward mounted a retrospective of French Artist Raoul Dufy. At the Royal Academy, the year opened with a first-ever visit from Spain of the paintings of Bartolomé Murillo and closed with "The Genius of Venice 1500 to 1600."

Television and Films. The bright, if perhaps fragile, return to life of British films continued, with the many Oscars won by *Ghandi* putting confidence, if not funds, into further production. Noted theater director Richard Eyre's first film *The Ploughman's Lunch*, Michael Radford's first feature *Another Time, Another Place*, as well as *Ascendancy*, were well received. The arrival of Channel Four, a new commercial television channel, also gave some continuity to film patronage.

MAUREEN GREEN
Author and Journalist, London

GREECE

Events in Greece during 1983 were greatly affected by the personal leadership of the Socialist prime minister, Andreas Papandreou.

The Socialist Government and its Critics. On Oct. 18, 1983, Prime Minister Papandreou celebrated two years of rule by his political party, the Panhellenic Socialist Movement (PASOK), with a gigantic, orchestrated rally in Athens attended by hundreds of thousands of his supporters. The event and the governmental program it extolled were both sharply criticized by Papandreou's main parliamentary opposition, the New Democracy Party, founded in 1974 by the current Greek president, Constantine Caramanlis, who throughout 1983 maintained a dignified position above the fray.

Critics of Papandreou pointed out that as prime minister he had not acted consistently with promises he had made in his 1981 electoral campaign. At that time he had called for a reappraisal of Greece's membership in the European Community (EC), the removal of U.S. bases from Greece, and the disassociation of Greece from NATO. Yet in his two-year rule he had made accommodations in all three areas.

Papandreou and the EC. Far from reconsidering Greece's role in the EC, Papandreou's government took over the rotating presidency of the EC Council for a six-month period beginning July 1, 1983.

The U.S. Bases. After months of negotiations, Greece and the United States came to an understanding in July 1983 and signed an agreement in September concerning the retention of U.S. bases in Greece. This was ratified by the Greek Parliament in early November with the support of the New Democracy Party, which had always espoused the need for the bases.

Greece, NATO, and Turkey. While remaining in NATO, the Papandreou government did not allow Greek forces to participate in NATO maneuvers in the Aegean Sea, there being con-

---

GREECE • Information Highlights

Official Name: Hellenic Republic.
Location: Southwestern Europe.
Area: 51,199 sq mi (132 608 km²).
Population (July 1983): 9,898,000.
Chief Cities (1981 census): Athens, the capital, 885,136; Salonika, 402,443; Piraeus, 187,458 (1971).
Government: *Head of state,* Constantine Caramanlis, president (took office May 1980). *Head of government,* Andreas Papandreou, prime minister (took office Oct. 1981). *Legislature*—Parliament.
Monetary Unit: Drachma (96.9 drachmas equal U.S.$1, Dec. 1, 1983).
Gross National Product (1982 U.S.$): $38,359,-000,000.
Economic Index (1982): *Consumer Prices* (1970 = 100), all items, 571.5; food, 669.9. *Industrial Production* (1975 = 100), 123.
Foreign Trade (1982 U.S.$): *Imports,* $10,023,-000,000; *exports,* $4,297,000,000.

tinued disagreement about including the Greek island of Lemnos in the operation. No doubt the Greek government realized that Greek withdrawal from NATO would only benefit Turkey, with whom Greece had a number of disagreements, including Cyprus. The unilateral declaration of independence by the Turkish Cypriots on Nov. 15, 1983, was condemned by Papandreou and raised tensions between Greece and Turkey.

Greco-Soviet Relations. Seeking to retain the support of the extreme left-wing of PASOK, Papandreou adopted a conciliatory attitude toward the Soviet Union. Soviet Prime Minister Nikolai A. Tikhonov visited Athens in February, and later in the year Greece refused to join in any condemnation of the Soviets for downing the Korean airliner.

Greece and the United States. Friction developed in 1983 with the United States over some of Papandreou's policies. His government complained of U.S. military aircraft overflights on Greek territory; it called for a postponement of the deployment of new U.S. missiles in Europe; it criticized the U.S. intervention in Grenada; and it would not allow U.S. military planes to refuel in Greece on the way to their duties in Lebanon. But the signing of the accord on U.S. bases in Greece seemed to indicate a more conciliatory feeling in both countries.

Economy. In 1983, Greece faced high inflation, unemployment, and an unfavorable balance of payments. A wage freeze was instituted that Papandreou promised would end in 1984.

Royal Birth. Queen Anne-Marie, wife of the deposed King Constantine II, gave birth in London on June 9, 1983, to the couple's fourth child, a daughter named Theodora. Princess Theodora was baptized on October 21 at London's St. Sophia Greek Orthodox Cathedral with Queen Elizabeth II as a godparent.

See also CYPRUS; TURKEY.

GEORGE J. MARCOPOULOS, *Tufts University*

GUYANA

The authoritarian regime of President Forbes Burnham remained in power in Guyana throughout 1983. In February the government organized the celebration of Burnham's 60th birthday. School children paraded in his honor, and the government-owned *Sunday Chronicle* eulogized him.

Strikes and Political Opposition. During the year the most serious opposition to the Burnham government came from organized workers, particularly the bauxite employees, once supporters of the regime. In May they carried out two one-day general strikes at the mining center of Linden to protest shortages of food and other items. They were joined by teachers and other workers of the area.

GUYANA · Information Highlights

Official Name: Cooperative Republic of Guyana.
Location: Northeast coast of South America.
Area: 83,000 sq mi (214 970 km²).
Population (July 1983 est.): 834,000.
Government: *Head of state,* Forbes Burnham, president (took office Jan. 1981). *Head of government,* Ptolemy Reid, prime minister (took office Oct. 1980). *Legislature* (unicameral)—National Assembly.
Monetary Unit: Guyana dollar (3.00 G. dollars equal U.S.$1, July 1983).
Gross National Product (1981 U.S.$): $490,000,000.
Economic Index (1982): *Consumer Prices,* (1970 = 100), all items, 390.2; food, 527.2.
Foreign Trade (1982 U.S.$): *Imports,* $283,000,000; *exports,* $256,000,000.

There was a reported realignment among the opposition parties. The formerly far-left Working People's Alliance (WPA) was said to be gaining support at the expense of Cheddi Jagan's People's Progressive Party, the country's Communist party and traditional opponent of Burnham's People's National Congress. At the same time, the WPA seemed to be adopting a more moderate stance. It supported a series of meetings called by the Guyana Council of Churches to protest government actions.

Economy. The economy continued in a state of crisis throughout the year. Production of the three major exports—bauxite, sugar, and rice —all declined significantly. The consequent lack of foreign exchange resulted in recurring shortages of foodstuffs and other goods.

In May, President Burnham announced that he had rejected conditions set by the International Monetary Fund (IMF) for providing economic help to Guyana. The IMF had demanded 50% depreciation of the Guyanese currency, price increases, a wage freeze, and other things.

Foreign Affairs. Relations with Venezuela and the United States were in the forefront of Guyana's foreign concerns in 1983.

In March, Guyana accepted a Venezuelan suggestion that UN Secretary-General Javier Pérez de Cuellar be asked to mediate the border dispute between the two countries.

Relations with the United States deteriorated during the year. In May, Guyana declared two U.S. embassy officials persona non grata, charging them with interfering in Guyanese domestic affairs because of conversations they had had with bauxite strikers. In August the United States vetoed a loan that the World Bank was proposing to extend to Guyana.

In October, Guyana refused to join other Caribbean countries and the United States in intervening in Grenada. When that intervention took place anyway, Guyana cosponsored a motion in the UN Security Council condemning the action.

ROBERT J. ALEXANDER
Rutgers University

HAWAII

Hawaii's financial climate, unlike its much-heralded sea breeze and sunny skies, began to look bleak in 1983. The fiscal surpluses which the state government had enjoyed in previous years began to vanish as the mainland recession moved into the local economy. Sugar and pineapple, the island's main agricultural products, ran into hard times. Only tourism held its own. Volcanic eruptions and a strong mid-November earthquake also struck the state.

Finance and Labor. The state government, normally receptive to demands for higher pay, unexpectedly balked when contracts for some 44,000 public employees came up for renewal. Under Hawaii's unique collective bargaining law for government workers, the state is the lead negotiator for both state and county governments. Instead of the 18% average pay raise of the previous biennium, the state proposed a moratorium on wage increases in fiscal 1983–84 and a 2.88% raise in fiscal 1984–85. Gov. George Ariyoshi's financial experts, the state Council of Revenues, urged fiscal restraint for the biennium that began July 1, 1983. The unions, aware of a $120 million surplus in the fiscal 1982–83 budget, rejected the "hold-the-line" contract offer and began preparations for individual strikes, permissible under state law.

Environment. Troubles with pesticides, which caused multiple recalls of fresh milk from grocery store shelves in 1982, resurfaced again in 1983. This time the problem was drinking water contaminated with ethylene dibromide (EDB), used to control insects in pineapple fields. Unacceptable levels of EDB were found in city-controlled wells on the island of Oahu. Several wells in the central plain were closed while authorities tried to purge them of the chemical. Further tests showed traces of another outlawed chemical, trichloropropane (TCP).

When the Environmental Protection Agency moved to ban EDB's use in pineapple fields, Governor Ariyoshi protested, claiming that the chemical was getting into civilian water supplies from underground military fuel tanks adjoining the plantations. There was no confirmation from the Defense Department, and the EPA imposed its ban in September.

Prisons and Politics. The governor's problems with the U.S. Justice Department over the state's prisons continued in 1983. The Justice Department, concerned about alleged civil-rights violations, filed suit in federal district court in March to inspect Hawaii's prisons. A three-member panel of federal judges dismissed the suit on grounds that the Justice Department had failed to give specifics. The federal authorities complied in July, however, and government attorneys indicated that they would refile the suit. Before that happened, state and federal counsel got together and the inspections began.

Governor Ariyoshi, who was reelected to a third term in 1982, will be in office until 1986 but cannot seek a fourth term. His troubles with the federal government over the prisons came after a frustrating legislative session in which his long-range planning program was stonewalled by opposition from members of his own Democratic Party.

CHARLES H. TURNER
"The Honolulu Advertiser"

HAWAII • Information Highlights

Area: 6,471 sq mi (16 760 km²).
Population (1982 est.): 994,000.
Chief Cities (1980 census): Honolulu, the capital, 365,048; Pearl City, 42,575; Kailua, 35,812; Hilo, 35,269.
Government (1983): *Chief Officers*—governor, George R. Ariyoshi (D); lt. gov., John Waihee III (D). *Legislature*—Senate, 25 members; House of Representatives, 51 members.
State Finances (fiscal year 1982): *Revenues*, $2,146,000,000; *expenditures,* $1,994,000,000.
Personal Income (1982): $11,579,000,000; per capita $11,652.
Labor Force (Sept. 1983): *Nonagricultural wage and salary earners,* 425,850; *unemployed,* 28,300 (6.2% of total force).
Education: *Enrollment* (fall 1981)—public elementary schools, 109,272; public secondary, 53,533; colleges and universities (1982), 51,788. *Public school expenditures* (1982), $373,652,000.

During a long series of eruptions in 1983, lava spurts 300 ft (91 m) into the air at Hawaii Volcanoes National Park.

UPI

HONG KONG

Concern over Hong Kong's political future continued to grow in 1983 as China insisted on the entire colony's return to Chinese sovereignty after the lease on the New Territories expires in 1997. The colony could not survive without the New Territories in any case.

Future Prospects. Throughout the year, the government remained tight-lipped over the progress of the talks between Britain and China over the Hong Kong lease issue. Residents of Hong Kong have now accepted the inevitability of its future as a part of China. Although China has been stating repeatedly that "nothing will change in the socioeconomic system of Hong Kong, and its continued stability and prosperity will be maintained," the dismal view of its future was revealed by the increasing outflow of capital, diminishing new investment, sluggish property market, and weakening Hong Kong dollar. In September 1983, for example, the local currency dropped to a record low exchange rate of HK\$9.45 to U.S.\$1.00. In the first half year, Hong Kong entrepreneurs had invested millions of dollars in Canadian manufacturing industries. A Hong Kong financial group bought the 191-room Pickwick Hotel in San Francisco for more than \$50 million and planned to build a new 320-room tower behind it. Another group spent more than \$80 million to build a hotel, condominium, and office complex in downtown Toronto. Some big government projects were delayed, and the proposed replacement airport on Lan Tau Island was shelved because of lack of funds. Most Hong Kong residents preferred the status quo under British rule to China's plan of making the colony a "special administrative region."

The Economy. In the first four months of 1983, Hong Kong's exports increased by 9%, imports by 4%, and re-exports by 8%, compared with the same period in 1982. The gross domestic product, which rose only 2.4% in 1982 was forecast to rise by 4% in 1983.

In 1983 the Transpotech Co., a British firm, was engaged to conduct a \$5.8 million test on the Electronic Road Pricing System. The first system of its kind, it is designed to discourage motor traffic on congested roads by electronically imposing tolls on motorists. If the test proves successful, the ERPS will go into operation in Hong Kong by 1987. In May, Lazard Freres & Co. was engaged to conduct an economic study of the purchase of electricity from China's proposed nuclear power plant at Daya Bay, about 45 miles (70 km) northeast of Hong Kong.

Refugees. Since the fall of Saigon, Hong Kong has absorbed 14,000 Vietnamese boat people. In December 1982, Hong Kong still had 12,631 unsettled Vietnamese refugees.

CHUEN-YAN DAVID LAI
University of Victoria

HOUSING

Swiftly and even more powerfully than had been anticipated, the U.S. housing market, ignited by lower interest rates and fueled by eager young families who had postponed buying, surged strongly in 1983. It was a dramatic illustration of the old axiom that as housing goes so goes the economy, a truth demonstrated in seven recession-recovery cycles since the end of World War II. It was an axiom recognized by President Ronald Reagan, who told home builders that they were "the heroes of today's economy."

After having fallen to a 36-year low of just 1.06 million starts in 1982, the pace of homebuilding in late 1983 indicated a final figure of at least 1.6 million units, the highest since 1979.

The impact was huge. The National Association of Home Builders (NAHB) estimated that the additional units added \$15.5 billion (U.S.) in wages and \$7 billion in federal, state, and local taxes. The housing recovery, it said, pumped a total of \$70 billion "into an economy desperate for an infusion of fresh blood."

Nobody doubted that interest rates provided the spark. In October 1981 the Federal Housing Administration (FHA) mortgage rate was 17.5%, and NAHB estimated that fewer than 8% of U.S. households could afford to buy a new home. By May 1983 the mortgage rate was 11.5%, and 19% of the nation's families could afford a purchase.

Only months before, millions of Americans had felt they might never afford a house, and so they seized the opportunity. Demographics added pressure: in no other decade had so many people—at least 40 million—been scheduled to pass through the 25-to-34 age bracket, the prime home-buying population segment. Affordability was achieved also by the building of smaller houses with fewer amenities, a trend that had begun in 1978. Government statistics showed that the median-sized home in 1983 enclosed about 1,500 sq ft (130 m²), or about 50 sq ft (4.5 m²) less than five years earlier. The little luxuries that people had come to expect also grew scarcer. There were fewer new houses with four or more bedrooms, with basements, with fireplaces, or with garages. Moreover, houses were built on smaller lots, often in clusters or attached in townhouse style. Builders claimed that the high cost of land had made it necessary to do so; in 1983 about 25 cents of every construction dollar went for land, compared with only 11 cents in 1949.

Recognizing that price increases would have to be contained if people were to be well-housed, the Department of Housing and Urban Development (HUD) sought to encourage simpler building codes and innovative construction methods. Those alone, HUD maintained, might reduce the cost of new homes by as

Cary Wolinsky/Stock, Boston

Economic reasons as well as an interest in architectural preservation have led Americans, especially young couples, to rebuild older structures instead of buying new homes.

much as 20%. Most builders did not need to be told, and nearly every so-called "stick" or on-site builder employed methods that differed radically from those used a decade before. One of the biggest changes was in the use of factory-built parts, ranging up to entire apartment units. And the modular home, 95% finished at the factory, was increasingly the choice of larger builders.

There were indications, in fact, that large, publicly owned builders, able to raise huge amounts of money, to operate in many sections of the country, and to protect themselves by diversifying, were the wave of the future. Led by U.S. Homes, a billion-dollar company, at least ten U.S. home builders reported sales of $200 million or more. Such firms were taking an increasingly larger percentage of markets in many areas.

The most active area for U.S. home building remained the Sunbelt. According to the Harvard-MIT Joint Center For Urban Studies,

it was likely that three fourths of all housing starts in the decade of the 1980s would be in the South and West, due in part to the steady migration to those areas. But throughout the country, the center said, another migration was also under way, the movement of families from metropolitan cities to smaller towns and outlying areas.

Among the attractions of smaller towns, of course, were lower prices. But various surveys showed that many Americans were also interested in obtaining instant roots through the purchase of older, more commodious homes, and the opportunity to participate in community affairs that sometimes were too formidable in large cities. That opportunity was becoming available to more and more people as employers freed from central cities by electronic communications, often found business easier to conduct in the country.

Whatever the causative factors, housing prices continued along a familiar upward course. The NAHB estimated that the median price of new single-family houses rose to about $76,000 in 1983, from $69,300 in 1982 and $32,500 in 1973. The National Association of Realtors said that the median price of existing houses exceeded $70,000, compared with $67,800 a year earlier and $28,900 in 1973.

The realtors remained upset. Price increases over a three-year period fell below the rate of inflation, they said, and they blamed high interest rates for the affordability problems that were created. Sales of existing homes rose sharply to an annual rate of 2.74 million late in the year, but the realtors maintained that the total was "well below the 3.5 million to 4 million transactions needed annually to meet normal mobility and changing housing requirements of the population."

As the year ended, housing groups were warning with increasing stridency that the big federal budget deficit could end whatever improvements there had been in the market. David Smith, NAHB vice-president, said ominously: "Our chief economist has warned us not to make any commitments beyond the summer of 1984." That, said Smith, was when "the promise of a sustained, housing-led economic recovery could end."

All in all, the U.S. housing industry was worried about shadows from the past being projected into the future. From the past was the ogre of housing depressions, seven of which had occurred since 1950—the worst of them in 1973–1975 and 1978–1981. With a record like that, the industry feared more of the same. Making the fears more real, it said, was the prospect of a collision between the borrowing needs of the federal government and those of individuals and industry. That would almost inevitably mean higher interest rates, forcing millions of potential buyers from the market.

JOHN CUNNIFF, *The Associated Press*

HUNGARY

Hungary's successful experiment with "market socialism," the New Economic Mechanism adopted after 1968, continued to make the country the showcase of the Communist world, with a high standard of living and a steadily rising growth rate.

Economic Affairs. Facing a liquidity crisis, Hungary was able to secure Western loans despite the drying up of Western bank financing for the East European countries following the Polish crisis. In April, Hungary received a $100 million bridge loan from the Bank for International Settlement and a $200 million Euromarket commercial bank loan. In June, the World Bank approved two 15-year loans totaling $239.4 million for grain storage and industrial energy conservation projects in Hungary.

On July 19–20, a delegation headed by Hungary's Communist party chief, János Kádár, met in Moscow with Soviet President Yuri Andropov to discuss trade and economic matters. At that time the Soviets hinted at their own interest in Hungary's economic reforms.

It was announced in May that the country's already flourishing agricultural sector was to be improved further by a radical modernization of the curriculum at the state's agricultural colleges and universities.

Political Affairs. Domestic politics were marked by increasingly belligerent popular dissidence. In March, Hungarian writers openly criticized censorship and party control of the press. In May, for the first time, an unofficial peace group marched through Budapest bearing banners and messages critical of both Moscow and Washington. The regime retaliated with police raids on underground publishing centers in Budapest and on the homes of noted dissidents Ferenc Kőszeg and László Rajk. In July it announced that the bodies of 250 "freedom fighters" killed in the revolution of 1956

Photo Trends

An apartment complex nears completion in Kaposvár. New housing is an objective of the current five-year plan.

would be removed from the national cemetery and reburied elsewhere in a mass grave.

Despite these frictions, the government decided to pursue its plan for modest political liberalization. In July it announced its decision to permit contested candidacies for the 1985 parliamentary elections.

Foreign Relations. A top level delegation consisting of Kádár, György Lázár, chairman of the Council of Ministers, Minister of Defense Gen. Lajos Czinege, and Foreign Minister Frigyes Puja attended the Warsaw Pact summit meeting in Prague, Jaunary 4–5. In July it was announced that Péter Várkonyi, a close associate of Kádár, would replace Puja, but no changes were indicated in Hungary's Soviet-aligned foreign policy.

Official foreign visitors to Hungary in 1983 included Soviet Defense Minister Dmitri Ustinov, China's Deputy Foreign Minister Qian Qichen, and Robert Mugabe, prime minister of Zimbabwe.

JOSEPH F. ZACEK
Professor of History
State University of New York at Albany

HUNGARY • Information Highlights

Official Name: Hungarian People's Republic.
Location: East-central Europe.
Area: 35,900 sq mi (92 981 km²).
Population (July 1983): 10,691,000.
Chief Cities: (Jan. 1, 1982): Budapest, the capital, 2,063,745; Miskolc, 210,368; Debrecen, 196,095.
Government: *Head of state,* Pál Losonczi, chairman of the presidential council (took office April 1967). *Head of government,* György Lázár, premier (took office 1975). First secretary of the Hungarian Socialist Workers' Party, János Kádár (took office 1956). *Legislature* (unicameral)—National Assembly.
Monetary Unit: Forint (35.58 forints equal U.S.$1, June 1983).
Gross National Product (1981 U.S.$): $63,700,-000,000.
Economic Indexes (1982): *Consumer Prices* (1970 = 100), all items, 173.7; food, 178.9. *Industrial Production* (1975 = 100), 124.
Foreign Trade (1982 U.S.$): Imports, $8,825,000,000; exports, $8,795,000,000.

ICELAND

National parliamentary elections held in April gave no clear mandates but illustrated weakening voter loyalty to the traditional partisan causes. Two new political entities—the Social Democratic Federation and the Women's Slate—made notable headway, winning 7 of 60 seats, mainly at the expense of the Social Democrats and Progressives. By late May the Progressives and the larger Independence Party (IP), respectively centrist and conservative, formed a government coalition headed by Steingrímur Hermannsson (Progressive) and backed by 37 members of Althing (parliament). Named to serve as foreign minister was Geir Hallgrímsson, chairman of the IP, who lost in a cliff-hanger bid for reelection to Althing after faring dismally in the IP Reykjavík primary. The premier of the outgoing cabinet, Gunnar Thoroddsen, 72, did not enter the race. Thoroddsen, who won his first Althing seat when he was just 23, died in late September.

Economy. The new government promptly took drastic steps to curb Iceland's galloping inflation, which seemed headed for 130% or higher. Central to the new economic policies were a sharp currency devaluation and a suspension of the wage-indexation system. Signs of great progress toward a key goal of the government—lowering the inflation rate to about 30% by year's end—were in evidence by fall.

But the belt-tightening policies were exacting heavy sacrifices. The National Economic Institute forecast that general purchasing power would plunge by more than 25% from 1982, though disposable incomes presumably would drop far less thanks to the fast rollback of inflation. How organized labor, surprisingly docile in recent years, ultimately would react to the wage freeze remained an open question. Payments on external debts were a growing burden, accounting for roughly one quarter of foreign-exchange earnings. Farm subsidies also remained a problem.

Fisheries. It appeared that Iceland's all-important groundfish take would be close to the disappointing level of 1982. It was hoped that the ban on capelin fishing could be eased, as the once-teeming pelagic stock seemed to be recovering satisfactorily from near-collapse. Exporters of herring, stockfish, and salted groundfish faced worrisome marketing prospects. The controversy over the excessive size of the fishing fleet intensified.

Energy. In September the government approved a controversial provisional accord with Alusuisse, the owner of a big aluminum smelter in southwestern Iceland which buys a huge portion of all electricity generated in the country. The deal substantially boosted the kilowatt rate payable by the plant.

HAUKUR BÖDVARSSON
Free-lance journalist, Reykjavík

IDAHO

Though lagging behind the pace of recovery nationwide, Idaho's economy showed signs of increased vigor by fall of 1983. Income rose in both logging and construction, the two industries most responsible for a drop in the unemployment rate from 11% to nearly 7%. Tourism was similarly on the rebound. On the negative side, activity and employment in mining were as depressed as in the previous year. A cooler-than-normal summer decreased yields for most crops, but higher prices seemed likely to keep agricultural revenues near the 1982 level.

Tax Increases. Struggling to balance a $69 million deficit from fiscal 1983, the Idaho legislature passed tax increases totaling $148 million. This sum represented the greatest total tax hike in state history.

The gasoline and sales taxes were the main focus of legislative action. Two cents were added to the gasoline tax as a means of improving the decaying highway system. The sales-tax increase came in two stages. Effective March 1, the 20-year-old sales tax rate of 3% was raised to 4%. Revenues from this increase were dedicated to repaying the 1983 deficit, and the hike thus did nothing to solve 1984 budgetary woes. Another .5% was tacked on in April, leaving the state with a sales tax of 4.5 cents on the dollar. Both additions to the sales tax were due to expire on June 30, 1984.

Legislature. Disagreement over the proper funding level for public schools and higher education kept the 47th Idaho legislature in session for a record 95 days. Republican House Speaker Tom Stivers stoutly adhered to a revenue projection of $394 million for the fiscal 1984 general fund. Democratic Gov. John Evans insisted upon a figure nearer $470 million. The impasse was finally broken when the House defeated a $208 million public schools appropriation that had won narrow approval in the Senate. This defeat set the stage for the second sales tax increase and for adjournment.

ICELAND • Information Highlights

Official Name: Republic of Iceland.
Location: North Atlantic Ocean.
Area: 39,749 sq mi (102 952 km²).
Population (July 1983): 236,000.
Chief Cities (Oct. 1982): Reykjavík, the capital, 84,593; Kópavogur, 13,996; Akureyrí, 13,605.
Government: *Head of state,* Vigdís Finnbogadóttir, president (took office Aug. 1980). *Head of government,* Steingrímur Hermannsson, prime minister (took office May 1983). *Legislature*—Althing: Upper House and Lower House.
Monetary Unit: Króna (27.43 krónur equal U.S. $1, June 1983).
Gross National Product (1981 U.S.$): $2,833,-000,000.
Foreign Trade (1982 U.S.$): *Imports,* $942,000,000; *exports,* $685,000,000.

IDAHO · Information Highlights

Area: 83,564 sq mi (216 431 km²).
Population (1982 est.): 958,000.
Chief Cities (1980 census): Boise, the capital, 102,160; Pocatello, 46,340; Idaho Falls, 39,590.
Government (1983): *Chief Officers—governor,* John V. Evans (D); lt. gov., David H. Leroy (R). *Legislature—*Senate, 35 members; House of Representatives, 70 members.
State Finances (fiscal year 1982): *Revenues,* $1,237,000,000; *expenditures,* $1,209,000,000.
Personal Income (1982): $8,716,000,000; per capita, $9,029.
Labor Force (July 1983): *Nonagricultural wage and salary earners,* 315,300; *unemployed,* 42,800 (9.3% of total force).
Education: *Enrollment* (fall 1981)—public elementary schools, 145,547; public secondary, 58,977; colleges and universities (1981–82), 42,758 students. *Public school expenditures* (1980–81), $392,165,000 ($1,780 per pupil).

The legislature ended its regular session on April 14, agreeing on a 1984 general fund budget of $451.6 million. Governor Evans promptly vetoed appropriations of $215 million for public schools and $70 million for higher education, calling both inadequate. He also called the legislators back into special session, but the call proved anticlimactic. The Republican-dominated legislature met for one day (May 9) and passed education bills identical to those vetoed by the governor.

Hansen Indictment. On April 7, second district Republican Rep. George Hansen became the first public official in the United States to be indicted under the 1978 Ethics in Public Government Act. A Washington, DC, grand jury charged Hansen with four counts of failure to make full disclosure of personal finances. Hansen pled innocent to all charges.

M. C. HENBERG, *University of Idaho*

ILLINOIS

Illinois taxpayers were hit with sharp tax increases in 1983, as the state's treasury almost ran dry.

For most Illinois residents, the state's fiscal problems came as a surprise. During his 1982 reelection campaign, Gov. James R. Thompson (R) had stated his strong opposition to any tax increases. Shortly after his reelection, however, the governor announced what he said was an "unexpected" dip in state revenues. Weeks later he asked the General Assembly for a record $1.6 billion hike in state income, sales, gasoline, and other taxes. Critics charged that Thompson had known the situation and had hidden the facts to assure his victory.

Months of political bickering and compromise between Thompson and the Democratic-controlled legislature produced a $1 billion tax increase. State income taxes were raised temporarily to 3%, until July 1, 1984; the state sales tax was increased from 2.5% to 3.5%; gasoline taxes went up 3.5 cents per gallon; and vehicle license fees also were increased. All told, it was the state's biggest tax hike in 14 years, coming only hours after Illinois ended its 1983 fiscal year with a balance of $110 million, the lowest level in five years.

Labor. Governor Thompson paid off a campaign debt to organized labor by signing legislation giving all public employees except police and firemen collective bargaining rights and the right to strike. Almost 430,000 public employees were affected by the law. Thompson said that public employees deserved the same rights that workers in the private sector have enjoyed for 50 years. Labor leaders applauded the action. The Illinois Municipal League and Illinois State Chamber of Commerce, however, warned that it would lead to higher taxes and more fiscal problems for local governments.

Economy. Recovery from the 1981–82 recession was slow in Illinois. Unemployment remained at the double-digit level for most of the year. Among the ten largest industrial states, Illinois was fourth in joblessness.

Illinois farmers suffered a cold, wet spring and a hot, dry summer. July and August brought the worst drought in 50 years and one of the hottest summers on record. The National Weather Service estimated that the drought caused $7 billion in crop damage, with the Corn Belt in Illinois and Iowa particularly hard hit. Forecasters said that corn production would be down 600,000 to 800,000 bushels.

Tragedy. Air Illinois, a small commuter airline serving smaller cities in the state, had its first air crash in October. Eleven persons died in the accident near downstate Pickneyville during a thunderstorm. Ironically, Air Illinois had paid off the mortgage on the aircraft the same day.

Politics. Four Democrats entered the campaign for the U.S. Senate seat of Charles H. Percy, a Republican, who comes up for reelection in 1984.

See also CHICAGO.

ROBERT ENSTAD, *"Chicago Tribune"*

ILLINOIS · Information Highlights

Area: 56,345 sq mi (145 934 km²).
Population (1982): 11,448,000.
Chief Cities (1980 census): Springfield, the capital, 99,637; Chicago, 3,005,072; Rockford, 139,712.
Government (1983): *Chief Officers—governor,* James R. Thompson (R). *General Assembly—*Senate, 59 members; House of Representatives, 177 members.
State Finances (fiscal year 1981): *Revenues,* $14,250,000,000; *expenditures,* $13,934,000,000.
Personal Income (1982): $138,519,000,000; per capita, $12,100.
Labor Force (June 1983): *Nonagricultural wage and salary earners,* 4,529,900; *unemployed,* 718,500 (12.7% of total force).
Education: *Enrollment* (fall 1981)—public elementary schools, 1,304,192; public secondary, 619,892; colleges and universities (1981–82), 659,623 students. *Public school expenditures* (1980–81), $4,652,477,000 ($2,441 per pupil).

INDIA

© Baldev/Sygma

Amid pleas for unity, violence persisted between Hindus and Bengali Muslims in the state of Assam.

The position of Prime Minister Indira Gandhi and her Congress (I) party remained unchallenged at the national level throughout 1983, but they suffered unexpected reverses in elections to legislative assemblies in some key states. Two states—Assam and the Punjab—experienced the worst waves of violence since the immediate aftermath of independence and partition in 1947. The economy showed some signs of resilience, in spite of declines in both the agricultural and industrial sectors. In foreign affairs the highlight was India's hosting of the seventh nonaligned summit conference.

Politics. Important elections to state assemblies were held in Andhra Pradesh, Karnataka, and Tripura in January; in Assam, Meghalaya, and the Union Territory of Delhi in February; and in Jammu and Kashmir in June. The two southern states of Andhra Pradesh and Karnataka had long been Congress (I) party strongholds, and Prime Minister Gandhi was confident they would continue to be so. She and other top leaders of her party and government campaigned assiduously in both states. In Andhra Pradesh an entirely new state party, called the Telegu Desam, led by one of India's leading film stars, N. T. Rama Rao, won more than three times as many seats as the Congress (I). It immediately formed a government, with Rama Rao as chief minister, replacing a Congress (I) ministry. The results in the neighboring state of Karnataka were closer but even more unexpected. The coalition of a national party, the Janata, and a hastily formed state party, known as the Kranti Ranga, won 20 more seats than the Congress (I), and with the aid of smaller anti-Congress groups it was able to form a government, with Ramakrishna Hegde as chief minister. In the eastern border

tribal state of Tripura, the ruling Communist Party of India (Marxist) was easily able to overcome a Congress (I) challenge, even though Prime Minister Gandhi had visited the state to solicit support for her party.

In Assam, widespread ethnic violence, arising mainly from opposition of native Assamese to "foreign"—mostly Bengali—residents, had marked the political and social scene for some time. The state had been under president's rule —direct control by the central government— since March 1982. Prime Minister Gandhi was strongly advised not to go ahead with the assembly elections scheduled for February, but she felt that they should be held as scheduled in spite of the danger of increased violence and bloodshed. She visited the state several times during the election campaign. The violence before, during, and after the voting was even worse than anticipated. In a period of about six weeks in February and early March, several thousand people (estimates ranged from 1,000 to 5,000), mostly Bengalis, were killed, and more than 200,000 were left homeless. Because of the large-scale violence and the boycott of the elections by almost all of the opposition parties and groups, only about 10% of eligible voters cast ballots. In several constituencies the voting could not be held or was declared invalid. Congress (I) won most of the seats in the constituencies where the voting did take place, and it formed a new government. On February 27 president's rule was ended.

The Congress (I) became the largest single party in Meghalaya without obtaining a majority of the seats in the state assembly. In the Union Territory of Delhi it scored a major triumph, which partially offset its losses in Andhra Pradesh and Karnataka. It won decisive majorities in both the Delhi Metropolitan Council and the Delhi Municipal Corporation, both of which had been controlled by the Janata party. In Jammu and Kashmir in June, the Congress (I)—with Gandhi playing an active role—made a special effort to oust the ruling National Conference, but it won only 26 seats in the state assembly; the National Conference took 45.

After the wave of state assembly elections, the Congress (I) was in power or shared power in 15 of the 22 Indian states, but the entire south was lost to it, and substantial parts of the northeast and northwest were governed by opposition parties. Two important political trends emerged more clearly after the elections: 1) a growth in the power of regional state parties, which had not yet emerged as significant forces on the national stage (although the formation of a Southern Council by the chief ministers of four southern states was a development that attracted nationwide attention), accompanied by at least a relative decline in strength of the so-called national parties, including even the Congress (I); and 2) the revival of the perennial issue of the proper balance between the central government and the states, with proponents of an increasing role for the states becoming so effective that Prime Minister Gandhi, with obvious reluctance, appointed a commission to look into the whole question of center-state relations.

Early in 1983 the prime minister made some significant changes in the organization of both her party and her government. in an obvious effort to avert the deterioration in both. The party changes included the appointment of a veteran political leader, Kamlapati Tripathi, as copresident, and of Gandhi's son, Rajiv, who was showing little promise as his mother's possible heir, and a southern political leader, C. M. Stephen, as general secretaries. Prime Minister Gandhi shocked the top officials in her administration by calling for their resignations, but she reappointed all but seven of them, with some changes in portfolio, and made about a dozen new appointments to top posts. Opposition parties were so weak on the national level that they could do little to take advantage of the internal difficulties and relative decline of the Congress (I).

In 1983 two so-called political fronts were formed, one in which the Lok Dal and the Bharatiya Janata party were the main groupings, and the other dominated by the Janata party; but both were hardly more than paper

In the ethnic turbulence surrounding state elections in late February, native Assamese called for the deportation of immigrant Bengalis. Raids against Muslim villages left thousands of Bengalis dead and countless others homeless.

fronts, and together they had less than one seventh of the seats in the Lok Sabha (House of the People).

On April 3, Mrs. Maneka Gandhi, the estranged daughter-in-law of the prime minister, announced the formation of a new political party, the Rashtriya Sanjay Manch (National Sanjay Organization). Although the new party had little real strength, its formation attracted considerable attention because of the feud between Indira Gandhi and the widow of her son, Sanjay.

Next to Assam, the strategic northwestern state of the Punjab, India's wealthiest agricultural region, was the scene of the most serious unrest and violence during the year, mainly between Sikhs (the Punjab is their homeland) and Hindus. Sikh demands for greater autonomy ranged all the way from modest concessions to an independent Sikh state of "Khalistan." Following the outbreak of major violence in 1982, which continued throughout 1983, more than 150 people were killed and some 150,000 Sikhs were arrested. In October, after a fresh wave of violence, president's rule was reimposed.

Economy. In 1982–83 the gross domestic product (GDP) rose by only about 2.0%, mainly because of a slowing of the growth rate in both agriculture and industry. Because of severe drought in ten of the richest grain-producing states, the output of food grains was well below expected levels. Exports increased substantially and imports to a lesser extent, but India was still faced with large balance-of-trade and balance-of-payments deficits.

Members of a World Bank team and the Aid-to-India Consortium both commended India's economic performance under very adverse circumstances. The Bank team reported that "the drought and world recession accounted for a difficult year" and that a growth rate of 2.0% was "a commendable achievement when compared with the drought years of the past." It pointed out that in 1982–83 the Indian government's policies "succeeded largely in protecting not only the high level of investment, but also the poorer consumer by sharply reducing the rate of inflation, and through judicious procurement (domestic and external) and distribution of food." The Aid-to-India Consortium, meeting in Paris in June, pledged $3.6 billion (U.S.) in development assistance to India in 1983–84 (slightly less than the amount pledged in 1982–83). It was impressed with India's "relatively commendable performance despite depressed world markets and a severe drought." It also commended India's "more open trade regime" and the "improved management and capacity in areas of power, oil, coal, and transport." At the Consortium meeting, David Hopper, chairman of the World Bank, said that India's recent economic policies had been "wise, prudent, and correct."

INDIA • Information Highlights

Official Name: Republic of India.
Location: South Asia.
Area: 1,269,338 sq mi (3 287 590 km²).
Population (July 1983 est.): 740,009,000.
Chief Cities (1981 census): New Delhi, the capital, 4,865,077; Bombay, 8,227,332; Calcutta, 3,291,655.
Government: Head of state, Zail Singh, president (took office July 1982). Head of government, Indira Gandhi, prime minister (took office January 1980). Legislature—Parliament: Rajya Sabha (Council of States) and Lok Sabha (House of the People).
Monetary Unit: Rupee (10.44 rupees equal U.S.$1, Dec. 1, 1983).
Gross National Product (1982 U.S.$): $156,600,-000,000.
Economic Indexes: Consumer Prices (1982), all items, 249.5; food, 241.5 (1970 = 100). Industrial production, 144 (1975 = 100).
Foreign Trade (1982 U.S.$): Imports, $14,088,-000,000; exports, $8,111,000,000.

The budget for 1983–84, presented to the parliament on February 28 by Finance Minister Pranab Mukherjee, revealed some of the strains upon the country's economy and resources. It provided for a substantial increase in taxes, external loans of about $1.6 billion, an increase of 21% in allocations for the Sixth Five-Year Plan (1980–85), and a 12% increase in defense expenditures, much higher than in any other major item of non-plan spending. The deficit was estimated at more than $1.5 billion.

Foreign Affairs. From March 7 to 12, representatives of 101 member states and organizations, including 60 heads of state or government, participated in the seventh summit conference of nonaligned nations, held in India's capital city, New Delhi. When the conference could not be held in Baghdad, as originally scheduled, because of the Iran-Iraq war, India agreed to act as host. It was a major feat of planning and logistics to prepare for such a large gathering on such short notice. The conference was a landmark in the nonaligned movement because it put at least a temporary end to the pro-Soviet trends that had been so noticeable at the sixth summit in Havana in 1979, under the influence of Fidel Castro. The more moderate and balanced position of the movement was symbolized by the transfer of the chairmanship from Cuba to India.

Gandhi was able to prevent major disagreements among the delegates from disrupting the meeting and to persuade the delegates to adopt more moderate resolutions than those that emerged from the Havana meeting. An economic declaration called for greater economic and financial assistance to developing countries, greater access to world markets, and a UN conference to consider the reconstruction of the world monetary system. In a statement on disarmament the delegates appealed to the great powers to halt the arms race, especially the production and deployment of nuclear weapons. A political declaration contained sweeping criticisms of the great powers, including eleven specific references to the United States and only one to the Soviet Union. This declaration called for a withdrawal of "foreign troops" from Afghanistan and for a halt to "imperialist interference" in Central America. It also criticized both superpowers for their naval presence and rivalries in the Indian Ocean. For the first time the nonaligned movement endorsed the claim of the Indian Ocean ministate of Mauritius to the Chagos Archipelago, where the U.S. naval base on Diego Garcia is located.

In addition to the large number of heads of state or government who came to New Delhi for the nonaligned summit meeting, several other leaders, including Britain's Queen Elizabeth II, the president of Nigeria, the prime ministers of Canada and Yugoslavia, and the Agha Khan, made official visits to India during the year. In April an 11-member Chinese delegation came to India, nominally at the invitation of the Indo-China Society. In November representatives of the Commonwealth gathered in New Delhi for their biennial meeting.

In June, Prime Minister Gandhi made an 11-day tour of five European nations—Finland, Denmark, Norway, Austria, and Yugoslavia. In Yugoslavia she delivered the Raul Prebisch Lecture to the delegates of the sixth meeting of the United Nations Conference on Trade and Development (UNCTAD-VI), on the topic "Peace and Development." In September she came to New York to address the UN General Assembly.

Considerable publicity accompanied U.S. Secretary of State George Shultz's four-day visit in late June and early July. While in India he joined his counterpart, P.V. Narasimha Rao, in presiding over a meeting of the Indo-U.S. Joint Commission. Indians were particularly gratified by his assurance that the United States would supply spare parts for the nuclear-power plant at Tarapur if they could not be obtained from anywhere else.

An agreement reached by Gandhi and President Ronald Reagan during her visit to the United States in the summer of 1982—to resolve the dispute over the supply of nuclear fuel for the Tarapur plant by arranging for France to provide the fuel—led, after prolonged negotiations, to the signing of a commercial implementation between India and France on March 24, 1983.

An agreement to set up an Indo-Pakistan Joint Commission, signed in New Delhi on March 10, was an important step in improving the still-strained relations between India and Pakistan.

Census. Final results of the 1981 census, announced in January 1983, indicated that the population of India in the spring of 1981 was 685,200,000, an increase of 25% during the preceding decade.

NORMAN D. PALMER, *Professor Emeritus*
University of Pennsylvania

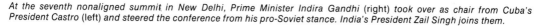

At the seventh nonaligned summit in New Delhi, Prime Minister Indira Gandhi (right) took over as chair from Cuba's President Castro (left) and steered the conference from his pro-Soviet stance. India's President Zail Singh joins them.

© A. Nogues/Sygma

INDIANA

Utility regulation was the dominant issue in the regular 61-day session of the 1983 Indiana General Assembly. Drought and the resulting decline in agricultural production affected all segments of Hoosier society.

Legislature. Driven by constituents' anger over rising utility rates, lawmakers spent 3 of the 4 months of the legislative session discussing reform. Debate focused on utility companies' requests to pass on to customers the cost of construction work in progress (CWIP). Faced with Gov. Robert D. Orr's threat of a special legislative session, legislators enacted a compromise measure prohibiting more than one rate-increase application every 15 months and requiring utilities to obtain approval from the Public Service Commission before building plants but avoiding the issue of CWIP.

Lawmakers also enacted an open-records bill permitting Hoosiers to inspect and copy records of most public agencies. Exempted were the politically controlled vehicle-license branches. Critics secured a second measure requiring branches to file annual income and expenditure reports. Litigation questioning the secrecy and constitutionality of the entire system was pending late in the year. Phase III of an administration-backed economic-development program aimed at creating a better business climate in the state included institutes for new business ventures, grants and loans to local communities, tax abatement, and tax breaks for businesses locating in downtrodden "enterprise zones." Criticism erupted over certain public-safety measures tightening drunk-driving laws. Legislation extended the minimum period of license suspension for first-time offenders, mandated a one-year suspension for refusing a Breathalyzer test, and provided for an automatic ten-year suspension of habitual offenders' licenses.

Defeated once again were "beer baron" measures that would have permitted exclusive sales territories for beer distributors, a proposed constitutional amendment to legalize a lottery and pari-mutuel gambling, local-option income taxes for counties, and daylight saving time. Legislators also rejected pay raises for themselves, the governor, and state officers and voted down lethal injections as a replacement for the electric chair.

Budget. Faced with a large budget deficit, the legislature met in special session in December 1982 to boost state sales and income taxes $1.8 billion by 1985. Although painful, the tax increases enabled the 1983 legislature to pass the state's two-year budget package with ease. Budget bills, including federal funding, totaled $13.8 billion. State employees, previously hurt by economic retrenchment, received a 10.2% pay-increase package for each year of the biennium; to initiate Orr's "decade of excellence" for education, lawmakers granted public schools a total 13% increase in state and local funding for the two years; general operating funds for state universities totaled 13.3%, with construction budgets almost ignored; and the Department of Mental Health received a 12% budget increase, huge by current standards.

Agriculture. Indiana's agriculture was hard hit by the worst drought in approximately 50 years. Corn and soybean production was drastically reduced, and predictions indicated that at least 70% of Hoosier farmers would show a financial loss equal to or exceeding 30%. As a result, all 92 Indiana counties were declared disaster areas.

LORNA LUTES SYLVESTER
"Indiana Magazine of History"

INDIANA • Information Highlights

Area: 36,185 sq mi (93 719 km²).
Population (1982 est.): 5,471,000.
Chief Cities (1980 census): Indianapolis, the capital, 700,807; Fort Wayne, 172,028; Gary, 151,953.
Government (1983): *Chief Officers*—governor, Robert D. Orr (R); lt. gov., John Mutz (R). *General Assembly*—Senate, 50 members; House of Representatives, 100 members.
State Finances (fiscal year 1982): *Revenues,* $5,657,000,000; *expenditures,* $5,694,000,000.
Personal Income (1982): $54,819,000,000; per capita, $10,021.
Labor Force (July 1983): *Nonagricultural wage and salary earners,* 1,991,700; *unemployed,* 233,900 (9.2% of total force).
Education: *Enrollment* (fall 1981)—public elementary schools, 690,810; public secondary, 334,362; colleges and universities (fall 1982), 253,529 students. *Public school expenditures* (1981–82), $2,294,161,000.

INDONESIA

In March, President Suharto was unanimously elected to a fourth term by the People's Consultative Assembly, a super-parliament which meets every five years to choose the president and vice-president and set the general goals of state policy.

President Suharto's cabinet choices did offer some surprises, however. Adam Malik was replaced as vice-president by Gen. Umar Wirahadikusumah. Gen. Benny Murdani, an intelligence officer who is a Roman Catholic in a Muslim country, was named commander of the armed forces and the powerful Operational Command to Restore Security and Order. Since Suharto came to power in 1966, no subordinate has simultaneously held so many key positions. Admiral Sudomo, longtime internal security chief, was given the ministry of manpower. Finally, the principal architect of Indonesia's economic development during the previous 18 years, Widjojo Nitisastro, was replaced as coordinating minister for the economy by Ali Wardhana and as head of the development planning board (BAPPENAS) by

Roland Neveu/Gamma-Liaison

President Suharto attended the opening of the restored 1,200-year-old Buddhist temple of Borobudur, on Java.

J. B. Sumarlin. Suharto increased his cabinet from 24 to 32 members.

During the rest of the year, political debate centered on two issues: the execution without trial of recidivists and Suharto's apparent determination to impose a "single ideological basis" (*asas tunggal*) on all social organizations. The executions, which received considerable support from a public angered by a rising crime rate, began in the central Javanese city of Yogyakarta. They then spread to other provinces and Jakarta.

The Suharto government attempted to require all organizations to adopt the state ideology of Pancasila (five principles of: belief in God, humanitarianism, nationalism, democracy, and social justice) as their sole governing principle.

Economy. The combined effects of the world recession and the stagnant international oil market hit Indonesia hard in 1983. GNP growth declined to 2%, lower than at any time since the mid-1960s. In January the government introduced an austerity budget, denying pay raises to civil servants for the second year in a row and slashing subsidies on petroleum products and foodstuffs. To encourage nonoil exports, the rupiah was devalued 27.5% against the U.S. dollar in March. Most surprising was the cancellation in May of more than $10 billion (U.S.) worth of foreign exchange development projects in order to deal with an increasingly serious balance of payments problem. All of these moves were applauded by the foreign business and banking communities as indications that the new economic leadership would continue Widjojo's pragmatic, market-oriented policies.

Foreign Affairs. Timor, the former Portuguese colony that is now Indonesia's 27th province, continued to trouble Jakarta's foreign and domestic policymakers. An Australian parliamentary delegation visited the island in late June and reported that the Timorese nationalist *Fretilin* forces appeared no longer to control any significant territory or population.

Official visitors to Jakarta included Canada's Prime Minister Pierre Elliott Trudeau in January and Japan's Prime Minister Yasuhiro Nakasone in May.

See also ASIA.

R. WILLIAM LIDDLE
The Ohio State University

INDONESIA • Information Highlights

Official Name: Republic of Indonesia.
Location: Southeast Asia.
Area: 736,000 sq mi (1 906 240 km²).
Population (July 1983): 160,932,000.
Chief Cities (1980 census): Jakarta, the capital, 6,480,000; Surabaya, 2,017,000; Bandung, 1,461,000; Medan, 1,373,000.
Government: *Head of state and government,* Suharto, president (took office for fourth five-year term March 1983). *Legislature* (unicameral)—People's Consultative Assembly.
Monetary Unit: Rupiah (978.75 rupiahs equal U.S.$1, Nov. 4, 1983).
Gross National Product (1982 U.S.$): $93,500,-000,000.
Economic Index (1982): *Consumer Prices* (1970 = 100), all items, 192.1; food, 185.8.
Foreign Trade (1982 U.S.$): *Imports,* $16,858,-000,000; *exports,* 22,293,000,000.

Signaling economic recovery, a Pittsburgh steel mill runs at night. While still low, steel plant utilization crept up.

INDUSTRIAL REVIEW

Industrial production rebounded strongly in the United States and Canada in 1983. The recovery in Europe was sluggish, reflecting a rather slow comeback of the general economy from the severe recession of 1982.

The United States. Industrial production in the United States gained about 6.5% in 1983, putting the annual average of the index of the Federal Reserve Board (FRB) close to 148 (1967 = 100). The gain followed a sharp drop of 8.2% in 1982. According to preliminary estimates, the gain was spurred by an 8% increase in manufacturing, following an 8.5% drop in 1982. Utilities increased production by 1.5%, after a 0.2% decline. The mining sector registered a decline of about 8% that came on the heels of an 11.3% drop in 1982. The 1983 drop was due largely to a sharp drop in oil and gas extraction, which just about repeated the 10.7% decline posted for 1982. Coal production reflected a reduction in export demand, and dropped about 9% to 751 million tons in 1983.

Durable-goods producers showed an overall gain of more than 8%. Spurred by lower interest rates, home construction and auto sales took off in 1983. The effect was to boost the output of lumber and wood products by more than 23%, after a 5.4% loss in 1982. Household furniture output also recovered strongly, up more than 17% after dropping 5.9%. Fixtures and office-furniture production increased only 2.6%, following a meager 0.7% gain. Cement

and structural clay products output rose more than 16%, after a 14.9% drop. Concrete and miscellaneous clay products increased some 18%, compared with a 15.2% slide. Glass and glass products gained 1.9%, following a 9.5% drop.

Output of primary metals was up 14%, compared with a 30.2% decline. Basic steel mill products showed a 17% gain, a sharp turnaround from the 39.2% falloff in 1982. The industry poured 92 million tons of raw steel, compared with 75 million tons in 1982. Steel mill product shipments also increased 14%, reaching 70 million tons. Most of the increase came from flat-rolled products used in the auto and appliance industries (*see* special report, page 271). Production of nonferrous metals gained by more than 9%.

Transportation equipment rebounded with a 25% gain, a welcome development after three years of decline that ended in a 9.4% drop in 1982. Automobile production jumped nearly 40% on the FRB index, after dropping 15.4%. Passenger-car production climbed to 6.9 million, compared with 5.1 million in 1982. Truck output increased 26%, to 2.4 million. Most of the increase in truck production was accounted for by light trucks; trucks with a gross vehicle weight of more than 10,000 lbs (4 536 kg) showed an output decline of about 19%.

Production of aircraft and parts dropped about 2%, following a 6.5% decline in 1982. Ship and boat builders registered a gain of 0.4%, after an 11.4% loss. Railroad equipment output fell by close to 60% on top of a 49.2%

loss in 1982. Production of mobile homes was up more than 20% after moving up 0.6% in 1982.

The manufacturers of nonelectrical machinery raised production a little under 2%, compared with a 12.9% drop in 1982. Helping the gain was office-equipment production, boosted by the demand for computers, which increased more than 8% after declining 3.9%.

Reflecting low farm income and heavy inventories, farm equipment output fell 13%, following a 28.3% falloff. Construction machinery, too, was a heavy loser, down about 16% after plummeting 23.4%. Metalworking-machinery production was down a little more than 3%, after declining 14.7%. General-industrial-machinery production was up by about 3%, after dropping 18.9% in 1982. Electrical-machinery production advanced above 9%, after dropping 5%. Television and radio production raced ahead by nearly 17%, after declining by 14.9%. Output of household appliances increased by more than 14%, after a 12.6% loss. Communication-equipment production was up about 7%, following a 3.6% gain. Electronic components registered a nearly 13% gain, after edging up 0.2%. Production of instruments was down about 1%, following a 5% drop. While consumer instruments products continued to decline, equipment instruments output rose 4%.

Nondurable-goods production rose 8% during 1983, after dropping 5.2% in 1982. Rubber and plastics products bounced back with a gain of almost 15%, following a 7% drop. Tire production, spurred by the revival in passenger-car output, rolled up a 14% gain, after a 3.1% decline. Plastics products gained 17%, reversing a 6.8% loss. Rubber output, excluding tires, was up nearly 6%, after an 11.8% drop.

Chemicals production rose nearly 10%, following a 9% loss in 1982. The weakest sector was agricultural chemicals where output continued to decline: almost 8% in 1983 on top of a 13.6% fall in 1982. Synthetic materials output rose nearly 19%, following an 11.5% drop. Drugs and medicines posted an 8% gain, after no change in the preceding year. Soaps and toiletries showed a nearly 5% increase, after declining 3.1%. Basic chemicals advanced about 11%, following a 15.9% slide. Paint production was up 6%, compared with a 9.2% drop.

Petroleum products continued weak, with a 0.2% decline that followed a drop of 6.1%. Food products gained nearly 5%, after declining 0.6%. Tobacco products showed a 2% loss, following a 3.5% drop. Textile mill products increased 15%, after an 8.3% decline. Apparel production advanced almost 9%, recouping a 9.9% loss. Leather products output was up 0.8%, after plunging 12%. Printing and publishing output rose 4.5%, after no change in 1982. Paper and paper-products production was up 9%, reversing a 2.8% decline.

Ordnance output continued to advance strongly with an increase of 10% on top of a 7.2% gain. Fabricated-metal products registered an output gain of 5%, after dropping 15.9% in 1982.

Output gains in manufacturing helped boost productivity. An advance at an annual rate of 12.1% in the third quarter was the best performance since the fourth quarter of 1980. Manufacturing output per hour of all persons rose at an annual rate of 9.6% for the first nine months of the year. That helped reduce unit

New carbonated soft drinks, including low-calorie and decaffeinated versions of standard brands, continued to flood the market. The estimated 235 varieties on store shelves in 1983 represented a 50% increase over seven years.

© Len Speier

UPI   Courtesy, Seiko

Toys and Gifts: The latest rage was the flat-nosed Cabbage Patch Doll; Coleco Industries shipped 2.5 million, but supply fell well short of demand. Seiko came out with the first-ever TV wristwatch, available from authorized dealers in the fall.

labor costs at an annual rate of 4.1% during the same span.

Expanding manufacturing activity showed up in higher job totals. Manufacturing employment in November stood well above 19 million, about 5% higher than at year-end 1982. Producers of durable goods added about 6.9% more jobs, for a total of 11.3 million. The biggest increase was 17% by the lumber and wood-products industry, raising the count to about 710,000. Makers of furniture and fixtures added 9% to their employment, increasing the total to above 470,000. Transportation-equipment makers added nearly 11.5%, for a job count of 1.9 million. Electric- and electronic-equipment industry added almost 8% to their payrolls, to reach 2.1 million. Stone, clay, and glass products job count increased by 6%, to about 600,000. Fabricated-metals producers added 5.6%, for a total of 1.4 million. Primary-metal industries saw their employment increase by more than 5%, to 857,000. Nonelectrical-machinery industry employment increased 3.5%, to 2.2 million. Instrument producers shaved their job total by 0.1%, to 700,000. Jobs in the mining industry dropped almost 3%, to about one million.

Other Countries. Economic recovery was rather sluggish in Europe, depressing industrial production in West Germany, France, and Italy. The worst performance was in Italy, where industrial production dropped almost 5% in 1983, after a 2.3% decline in 1982. France, after registering a 2.8% drop in 1982, showed a further decline of 3%. West Germany posted a 0.1% decline, following a 3.2% drop in 1982. Belgium's output slipped 0.1%, after declining 0.9%. The bright spot was the United King-

dom, where output rose 2.6%, after rising 1.5% in 1982. Industrial production in the Netherlands eked out a 0.7% increase, following a decline of 3.3% in 1982.

Among major trading partners of the United States, Japan saw its industrial output rise by about 3%, after a 0.3% increase in 1982. Production in Canada, after plummeting 12.1% in 1982, advanced 4.5%, thanks to strength in wood, transportation, and furniture industries.

Industrial production in the Soviet Union recently has been growing more slowly. The increase was 2.2% in 1982, following a 2.5% growth in 1981. That is about half the rate called for in the 1981–85 plan, and substantially slower than the average annual growth rates of 5.9% during the 1971–75 period and 3.2% during 1976–80. Practically every industrial branch slowed down in the most recent period, and the trend in the productivity of labor and capital employed in industry was down.

The growth of energy production in the USSR also slowed down. After boosting oil production from 7.1 million barrels per day in 1971 to 11 million in 1978, output edged from a rate of 12.0 million b/d in 1980 to 12.2 million in 1981 and to 12.3 million b/d in 1983. Natural gas production was the exception: it almost doubled between 1970 and 1978, and went from 15.4 trillion cubic feet in 1980 to 17.4 trillion cubic feet in 1982.

A major reason for the slowdown in Soviet production growth in 1982 was a widespread shortage of raw materials. For example, slow growth in coal production and its deteriorating quality hurt electric power and ferrous metallurgy industries.

AGO AMBRE, *U.S. Department of Commerce*

INDUSTRIAL REVIEW / SPECIAL REPORT

The Stagnant U.S. Steel Industry

Because of a prolonged slump in steel demand, 1983 was a pivotal year of far-reaching changes in the operations and structure of the American steel industry. Indeed, 1983 may mark the end of the industry's high-volume production era. In order to understand what happened in 1983, we should first review why these changes were necessary.

At the start of the year, the domestic steel industry reported a net loss for 1982 of $3.2 billion (U.S.). Production was at its lowest level in 36 years. Imports were at a record high. More than 165,000 employees were on layoff, and another 14,000 were working short workweeks. Not since the Great Depression had times been so tough for the industry.

The steel industry responded to this crisis by closing many of its older mills and moving production to its modern facilities. In such traditional steelmaking cities as Lackawanna, NY, and Pittsburgh, PA, steelworkers witnessed the metamorphosis of once-busy mills into empty hulks. This drastic action improved the profitability of the industry by reducing the amount of business needed to break even. And the resulting higher work load for the remaining mills helped to improve their productivity.

Because of the steps taken, the amount of steelmaking capability used in 1983 improved to more than 55% despite no increase in the number of orders received. In 1982, 48% of steelmaking capability had been used. Normal utilization rates are 80%.

The closed plants had become obsolete because of past industry cutbacks in modernization funds. It is estimated that the industry now will have to spend $6 billion a year to modernize itself. Unfortunately, depressed market conditions and widespread discounting have prevented steelmakers from raising prices to generate this money. This is the industry's biggest problem.

Pennsylvania's drop from its position as the number one steel-producing state to third place behind Indiana and Ohio illustrates where the orders of the closed mills were sent. Steel production was moving from the Ohio Valley to the shores of the Great Lakes. There are two reasons why these mills were saved while others were closed: their location and the number of continuous casters being used in these mills. A mill on the Great Lakes has an advantage because it has an inexpensive route for shipping and receiving very large quantities of materials. The continuous casters, machines which convert liquid steel directly into finished products, offer savings in energy and manpower.

In 1983 more than 30% of the raw steel poured in the United States went through casters. This compares with 28% in 1982 and 22% in 1981. However, 1983's level was far below the 79% and 53% casting levels of the Japanese and European steel industries, respectively.

To catch up, the U.S. steel industry scheduled the installation of 16 new casters between the beginning of 1982 and the end of 1984. By the end of the 1980s, it is estimated that half of the raw steel made in the United States will be continuously cast.

The installation of vital cost-reducing and productivity-improving casters by the steel industry during 1983 was accompanied by an increase in the installation of high-technology items. Computers for process control, lasers for measuring wear and distance, and processes for fine-tuning the refining of steel in the ladle instead of the furnace, were implemented throughout the industry.

Despite these improvements, however, the industry believes that it will not be able to survive without new investment incentives, enforceable trade laws, and changes in antitrust legislation that would allow more mergers. To bring about these changes the industry began a lobbying effort in 1983.

THOMAS MCALOON

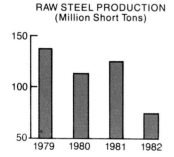

RAW STEEL PRODUCTION
(Million Short Tons)

U.S. STEEL INDUSTRY
PROFITS AND LOSS
(Billions of Dollars)

NUMBER OF
U.S. STEELWORKERS
(Thousands)

Source of Information: Iron and Steel Society

High-Tech Industry

Texas Instruments

Advances in the computer/electronic field have revolutionized industry. Computers now are mass-produced.

The phrase "high technology" has achieved considerable prominence throughout the world over the past few years. In essence it refers to new commercial/industrial developments based on advances in scientific research. Its significance has been heightened by a worldwide recession which has encouraged companies, countries, and research institutions to seek new ways to increase productivity and enhance overall economic growth.

Since the 1950s, computer/electronic technology application has been recognized widely as an area of dramatic growth directly related to advances in basic scientific knowledge. The "Route 128" (Boston), "Silicon Valley" (California), and "Research Triangle" (North Carolina) areas have been regarded as dynamic centers of activity for new firms based on the exploitation of these new technologies. In recent years, new "high-tech highways" and planned research parks have blossomed throughout the United States.

The Joint Economic Committee of the U.S. Congress has defined high-tech industries as heterogeneous collections of firms which 1) are more labor- than capital-intensive; 2) employ a high percentage of technicians, scientists, and engineers; 3) thrive on the application of scientific advances to the marketplace, in the form of new products and systems; and 4) require more research and development (R&D) than do other manufacturing industries.

The industries usually identified as measuring the rate of economic growth in high technology are: chemical products; electronic and electrical devices; machinery; transportation equipment; medical, optical, and photographic goods; and measuring, timing, controlling, and analyzing instruments. The newer high-tech markets include: robotics/automation; computer-aided design engineering; manufacturing and management; office automation; bio-engineered medicine; polymers/plastics; agri-genetics; telecommunications; and personal computers/electronic games.

Two areas of activity in 1982–83 added to the growing recognition of high technology as a significant force in society. The phenomenal growth of the personal computer industry, led by Apple and IBM, enhanced public acceptance of high technology in ways never achieved by video games and digital watches. A second event of consequence was the recovery of the stock market, led by companies specializing in the new technologies.

Research and Development. A less visible but in many ways more important development in recent years has been the growing symbiotic relationship between university scientists and industry in the United States. In the area of bio-technology alone, more than $260 million has been invested by a small group of high-tech firms in scientific research programs at leading universities.

The qualitative research capacity of institutions of higher education is a major attraction for high-tech firms. Scientific and technical faculties increasingly take advantage of this interest in their expertise to apply knowledge to commercially useful purposes. Technological innovation and scientific discovery, together with venture capital, are the two essential ingredients for the successful development and growth of new companies. Universities provide the first and attract the second. New and expanded high-tech development is the result.

High-tech R&D partnerships also are being formed, following the lead of the Japanese. A number of firms in the same industry have pooled their resources to mount large-scale research efforts to accelerate the rate of scientific innovation. A major event in 1983 was the formation of a 12-firm joint R&D venture known as Microelectronics and Computer Technology Corporation (MCC). With an initial budget of $75 million and a ten-year research program, MCC has the potential to become a significant national technology resource. Because of its size, scope, and anticipated economic impact, 57 cities competed for MCC before it chose to locate in Austin, TX.

A second major R&D joint venture, the Semiconductor Research Corporation (SRC), comprising 15 of the largest U.S. computer chip firms, including Hewlett Packard, IBM, and Motorola, has located in the North Carolina Research Triangle.

Large-scale research ventures are considered vital for the success of high-tech businesses because of their capital needs and the rapidity of technological change. They are, however, challenging traditional corporate practices and raising important issues in antitrust law which are being addressed by the Congress and Department of Justice.

Potential, Productivity, and a "New Economy." Because of its high visibility and spectacular growth, high technology is perceived to have the potential to replace or revitalize dying smokestack industries, to create jobs for the unemployed, and to defend the U.S. economy from foreign competition. Unfortunately, this potential is often overestimated. While high technology clearly must play a role in the industrial transformation of America as it moves toward the 21st century, it is not a panacea for the economic ills of the nation.

In 1983 the U.S. Bureau of Labor Statistics estimated that over the next ten years high technology would account for less than half of the two million jobs lost in manufacturing in the previous three years. Even though high-tech industries will generate ten times the number of jobs anticipated from other industries, the absolute number of jobs created is likely to be less than one million. Fewer than one third of these will be in technical occupations. The explanation for this lies in the fact that the high-tech base is small, while productivity is high and improving because of, ironically, automation.

The entire output of the high-tech sector is less than twice that of the automobile industry. The three million workers in high tech currently represent only 3% of the U.S. nonagricultural work force, and it is estimated that it will grow to only 4% by 1993. Productivity from high-tech employees is expected to increase by 46%, almost double the 24% projected for manufacturing and services.

Despite these sobering statistics, public agencies have become increasingly conscious of high technology's potential. Legislative packages, administrative initiatives, and commission reports that focus on the removal of restrictions on innovations, bold investments in R&D, and the stimulation of scientific education are indicative of the rising tide of interest and concern with America's "new economy." By late 1983 there were more than 200 high-tech bills pending in Congress. More than 150 state programs have been established. And innovative local efforts are being made with increasing frequency.

The United States is indisputably on the move from a "bang and clunk" era to one in which things whir quietly. Because of high technology, the U.S. economy is undergoing a transformation more dramatic and traumatic than anything since the Industrial Revolution.

LOUIS H. MASOTTI and JAMES R. MURRAY

Robots, given credit for improved industrial efficiency, are themselves manufactured in assembly-line fashion.

Unimation Inc.

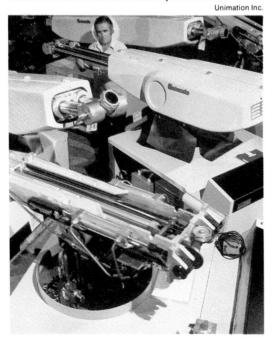

The post-modernist style is evidenced by the classical ornamentation in this New Jersey living room—sculpted marble fireplace, arched doorways, artifacts in museum-like display, and wall lights reminiscent of the Olympic torch.

INTERIOR DESIGN

Post-modernism, Ornamentalism, Neo-classicism, and a return to decoration all are terms that have been used to describe an important new movement in interior design. While modernists stripped structures bare of ornament, post-modernists *apply* ornament because, in the words of architect Robert Venturi, "less is a bore."

Ornamentalism is not just a fashion but a serious effort by a coterie of contemporary interior designers to bring classical decoration. Pilasters, moldings, columns, and arches in the Greek or Roman style head the list of ornamental features. The design logic behind this new decorative permissiveness is that space can be defined to give the viewer a greater sense of "rooms." This can be achieved by framing windows and doors with classically symmetrical facades or by using columns to define specific activity areas in large, unstructured spaces. The decorations, however, need not be structural. Most, in fact, are merely cut out of sheet rock or fashioned out of gypsum board.

The background often used in this design style is like a canvas painted in light, pale colors. The palette was established in 1979 by avant-gardist Michael Graves, whose use of peach, mauve, pink, and melon marked an abrupt change from the safe neutrals of the modernists. Graves, who uses the term "Neo-classicism" to describe his design vocabulary, startled architects that year with his rendering of the Sunar Showroom (the first of three) in New York. His use of traditional architectural elements provides a visual encyclopedia of Neo-classicism. In 1982 Graves completed the Portland (OR) Building, an urban monument of lively arcades and rich polychrome facades with classic ornamentation. The public interiors, mainly a visual arts gallery, bear Pompeiian-style walls of mauve or pink, with blue tiling.

Another Post-modernist architect, Robert Stern, took a page from architectural history—mainly Egyptian—for the design of a poolhouse in New Jersey. Ovoid pediments on tall columns and clustered or singly spaced metal palm trees could evoke thoughts of Brighton Pavilion. False walls, pilasters, columns, and a mantle supported by caryatids were decorations that had been used in the living room of the same house. In a New York City duplex apartment, Stern blends classical architectural elements with flowing space to create a vision of luxury.

JEANNE WEEKS

Norman McGrath

A more subdued classicism is reflected in a Montreal law office (above), highlighted by pilasters and minimal pediments framing the doorways. As seen in the Sunar Showrooms (below), designed by avant-gardist Michael Graves, light colors—especially peach, mauve, pink, and melon—are typical of the neo-classical design background.

Idaha

INTERNATIONAL TRADE AND FINANCE

After a protracted global recession, economic recovery got underway in 1983, led by a solid recovery in the United States.

"Today there are welcome signs that the shadows are beginning to recede," World Bank President A.W. Clausen told the joint annual meeting of that multilateral institution and the International Monetary Fund (IMF) on September 27 in Washington, DC. IMF Managing Director Jacques de Larosière told the same gathering that gross national product (GNP, output of goods and services) in the industrial countries as a group was expanding at an annual rate of 3–4%.

Economic Progress. The recovery actually got underway in November 1982 in the United States, which accounts for some 20% of world production. Many economists were forecasting a slow expansion. Instead it turned out to be a normal if not vigorous recovery. Indeed, Martin S. Feldstein, chairman of President Ronald Reagan's Council of Economic Advisers, had to increase his forecast a few times from the extremely conservative 3.1% real growth in GNP that he had predicted early in the year.

Canada's economy picked up at about the same time and expanded at a good pace, helped along by exports to its southern neighbor. The economies of most other industrial nations also were moving up, though more slowly. They were enjoying the first solid growth in three years. France and Italy were exceptions. Faced with high inflation and international payments problems, they imposed austerity programs and faced the prospect of what economists term "negative growth." The developing countries also were beginning to feel the warmth of economic vitality as the year wore on, pleased with a rise by midsummer of 14% in the price of commodities they export.

There were other signs of progress in 1983:

• World trade, which actually contracted in volume by 2.5% in 1982, was starting to move up again.

• Inflation was under much better control. In the United States, consumer prices in October were only 2.9% above their level of a year earlier. In the industrial world as a whole, prices were up only about 5% from the year before. Wage increases were moderated, and solid gains in productivity meant that manufacturers were better able to manage their costs. Further, the tendency of the last two decades for inflation to get worse from business cycle to business cycle was stopped. The aggregate inflation rate in the industrial world in the 1974–75 slump never dropped below 8%.

• Interest rates in most nations were well below their peaks. In the United States, interest charges were running at approximately half their highest rate in early 1981. Although real interest rates (after deducting inflation) remained extraordinarily high, consumers and businessmen almost ignored the cost and continued borrowing and spending the nation into recovery.

• To their chagrin, the OPEC nations discovered that they had pushed oil prices too high. New production from the Alaskan North Slope, Mexico, the British North Sea, and elsewhere began competing keenly with OPEC oil. Moreover, the higher prices and recession had prompted greater energy conservation among their customers than nearly anyone had anticipated. In the United States, the 6.1 million barrels per day of OPEC oil that had been imported during 1977 was cut to 1.1 million barrels per day in early 1983. OPEC's 60% share of the non-Communist world's oil exports in 1979 slipped to about 35%. Faced with a surplus in world oil markets and dropping spot-market prices, the OPEC nations scrambled to reach an agreement on prices and production levels. After months of bickering, a deal was made in early spring providing for a new market price of $29 per barrel, down from $32, and a production ceiling of 17.5 million barrels per day.

• U.S. stock prices, which began to rise in August 1982, continued their bull market well into 1983 before leveling off somewhat during the summer. In the first nine months of the year, the Wilshire 5000 stock index—which measures 5,000 New York Stock Exchange, American Stock Exchange, and popularly traded over-the-counter securities—was up just over 21%. Americans were some $500 billion (U.S.) richer on paper than the year before. Stocks in several other industrial nations also moved up in price.

• A fast recovery was trimming the size of the huge U.S. budget deficit, a deficit which seemed to trouble leaders of other industrial nations almost as much as it did President Reagan and Congress. European leaders held that the U.S. deficit was keeping world interest rates too high and slowing their own recoveries. For the fiscal year ended Sept. 30, 1983, the deficit ran about $195 billion, less than earlier forecast. The Reagan administration, Congress, and the two major parties were divided on how to remedy the "structural" deficit, i.e., the deficit that will continue even after the economy has reached close to full employment in the years ahead.

• The international debt problem appeared to be under somewhat better control. Commented the IMF's de Larosière: "Considerable progress has been made in dealing with this threat." He also warned, however, of "a long process of convalescence" before the economies of many heavily indebted countries are

(Continued on page 279)

The World Debt

Langley in "The Christian Science Monitor" © 1983 TCSPS

The international debt crisis—a vicious circle of lending, threatened default, and more lending—has been attended by a certain Alfred Hitchcock suspense. In the 1980s many economists and financial analysts have built up tension with dire warnings of impending doom. Financial leaders have had to mount several emergency rescues, adding to the nervous strain. Still, as of late 1983, none of the major actors in this world-scale drama had been fatally wounded.

Although the people of several developing countries were struck hard by economic austerity as their leaders sought to bring international loan payments into closer balance, no major debtor nation repudiated its debts, announced a default, or even declared a prolonged moratorium. Nor did any major commercial bank or other creditor suffer disastrous losses on their international loans. Of course, many such banks were not comfortable with some of these loans because of delayed payments, the rescheduling of past loans, and the necessity of lending even more money to the troubled debtors. Indeed, many bankers and financial leaders spent much time on airplanes, flying to gatherings to sort out the latest debtor crisis—be it in Brazil, Argentina, or some other nation—attending long sessions to work out packages restructuring the loans. It was a tense time for many.

By autumn 1983, however, there was more cause for optimism. Commented Martin Feldstein, the top economic adviser to President Ronald Reagan, in a talk to the Los Angeles World Affairs Council on October 27: "A year ago there were many who feared that the international debt situation would precipitate a collapse of the world financial system, plunging the world economy into deep recession. But international cooperation and the statesmanlike behavior of the debtor countries and commercial banks have permitted the crisis to be averted."

Causes. Perhaps, Feldstein speculated, everyone had acted so responsibly because no one was wholly to blame for the situation. The commercial banks did take excessive risks in some of their credit extensions in the 1970s. Some of the debtor countries borrowed too much and spent some of it unwisely on unprofitable investments or on expanding government programs.

The basic cause, however, was a sudden and unexpected change in world economic conditions. In the period since 1979, the price of oil tripled. For the developing, nonoil-producing countries, the value of oil imports rose from 6% of total merchandise imports in 1973 to 20% in 1980–82; the additional cost amounted to $260 billion (U.S.) over the decade, according to economist William R. Cline. The real exchange value of the dollar rose 55%, meaning that the developing countries had to export even more goods to buy imports or to service their dollar debts. Nominal interest rates, including inflation, averaged 15.8% on the debts of developing nations in 1981–82, compared with an average of 10.2% prior to that. The rise in interest added perhaps $41 billion to the debt burden in 1981–82 beyond what the nations might have anticipated from previous real interest rates (after subtracting inflation). Real interest rates themselves rose to unprecedented heights. Perhaps worst of all, the industrial nations sank into a deep and prolonged recession. Commodity prices, important to many developing countries, plunged. Exports paid for fewer imports, a factor that cost the developing, nonoil-producing countries an estimated $79 billion in 1981–82. World trade actually dropped in 1982 and only started to recover in 1983. The debtor countries were hit again—to the tune of perhaps $21 billion. In all, the developing nations had a hard time earning the foreign exchange needed to pay the interest or principal payments due on their massive loans. Economist

Cline estimated that these external shocks—the higher cost of oil, higher interest charges, worse terms-of-trade, and reduced export volume—added some $401 billion to their debts in the decade after 1973.

Martin Feldstein noted that while no single one of these factors could have precipitated such a serious financial problem, the combination certainly could—and did. Poland's declaration in May 1981 that it did not have the $2.5 billion due its creditors that year created considerable nervousness. The announcement by Mexico in August 1982 that it could not make interest payments on its debt of more than $80 billion prompted a near panic. The psychology of financial institutions changed drastically: whereas bankers had been jetting about the capitals of the developing nations to offer money, now they were highly reluctant to make new loans, especially in Latin America and Eastern Europe.

Size and Scope. The severity of the world debt crisis is evidenced by some statistics. For nonoil developing countries (which actually include some new oil exporters, such as Mexico and Egypt) the total debt multiplied nearly fivefold from 1973 to 1982, reaching approximately $612 billion. The estimated debt of the five Organization of Petroleum Exporting Countries (OPEC) not flush with surplus petrodollars—Algeria, Ecuador, Indonesia, Nigeria, and Venezuela—added another $80 billion. Net East European debt in hard currency, excluding the USSR, accounted for another $53 billion. Together, the three groups owed about $745 billion at the end of 1982. The International Monetary Fund (IMF) estimated at mid-1983 that commercial banks alone would increase their loans to nonoil developing countries by $15–20 billion in 1983.

The debt had been growing an average of 19% per year from 1973 to 1982. After deducting for inflation, the real growth was 8.7% annually, still a rapid rate. Moreover, the debt-service burden had worsened. Primarily because of higher interest rates, the interest on short- and long-term debts, plus amortization on long-term debts, rose from an average of 15.4% of exports of goods and services in 1973–77 to 22.2% in 1981–82.

For the three largest debtors—Brazil, Mexico, and Argentina—debt growth between 1973 and 1982 was considerably higher than the overall average. Brazil's debt rose by a factor of 6.4, to $88 billion; Mexico's went up a multiple of 9.5, to $82 billion; and Argentina's was up 5.9 times, to $38 billion. Other countries, however, such as South Korea, Indonesia, and Venezuela, kept their debt growth below the average.

Economist Cline, writing in a study published by the Institute for International Eco-

nomics, pointed out that higher inflation (which depreciates the value of the outstanding principal of the loans) and higher interest rates meant, in effect, that the developing countries were paying back their debts faster in real terms. Many countries suffered what economists call a "liquidity" crisis. They were not bankrupt, but they did not have access to necessary funds. When economic recovery in the industrial nations and lower interest rates came along, they would have enough resources and exports to service their debts. In the meantime, however, these nations were having difficulty meeting their obligations. Lenders were nervous about making more loans, and credit availability dropped dramatically in the last half of 1982 and in 1983.

Compounding the financial blows from worsening world economic conditions, some developing nations made domestic policy mistakes. Mexico allowed the peso to become seriously overvalued and permitted budget deficits to soar to 16.5% of the nation's gross national product (GNP, the output of goods and services) in 1982. Both Mexico and Brazil followed an economic strategy of high growth in their domestic economies, based in part on the use of foreign money. Argentina suffered from severe inflation, a greatly overvalued peso, and the shock of the Falklands War.

By mid-1983, the debt-servicing problems of Mexico and Argentina had spread to Brazil, Chile, Peru, and Venezuela. Previous problems persisted in Costa Rica, Nicaragua, Bolivia, and Ecuador. Only Colombia, which had carefully avoided heavy debts, was managing handily.

Possible Consequences. Banks by this time had enormous "exposure" in loans to sovereign debtors. For U.S. banks, the ratio of exposure to capital base on loans to nonoil developing countries and East European nations had risen from 131.6% in 1977 to 155% in 1982. Including the five previously mentioned OPEC countries, the total 1982 exposure stood at 182.3% of capital. For the nine largest U.S. banks, that ratio was even higher—282.8% for loans to all three of the nation groups.

Said Cline: ". . . exposure to developing countries poses a substantial potential vulnerability" for U.S. banks. Indeed, about two thirds of the debt has been in some sense at risk, as evidenced by interruptions in loan servicing in 1982–83. "Accordingly, potential vulnerability of the financial system must be taken seriously." he added.

Even under the worst of circumstances, however, it is unlikely that this body of debt would become worthless overnight. Although in the vast majority of rescheduling cases the debt is carried at full value on the banks' books, the U.S. Federal Reserve System has promised to come to the rescue if the financial system were ever in serious danger. Still, says Cline, "there would be enormous risks from a large-scale banking crisis." Most bankers would agree. Some major banks could become insolvent, causing considerable alarm.

Remedies. By the fall of 1983, at least, nothing of that sort had happened. Debtors, government officials, and commercial bankers had learned a great deal about how to handle each individual debt crisis. In 1982 there were four successful major rescue operations—of Mexico, Brazil, Argentina, and Yugoslavia. In each case, the International Monetary Fund (IMF) played a key role; the IMF explicitly told the private banks that if they did not provide new funds themselves, there would be no new IMF money whatsoever. The banks, contrary to some political charges, were not being bailed out by the IMF. In return for its own provision of financing, the IMF insisted on austerity programs designed to bring each nation's international payments into better balance. These frequently required a reduction in the nation's budget deficit, a slowing of the supply of new money to the economy, a devaluation of the currency, the trimming of subsidies, and other measures. The austerity programs were unpopular in many cases, vehemently opposed in others. In Brazil, for example, strikes and demonstrations were held through much of the year.

Austerity packages mean a reduction in the domestic standard of living so as to reduce imports and make room for more exports. In some cases, the industrial countries and the Bank for International Settlements would provide short-term "bridge loans" to get a country by until the IMF could work out a complete rescue package with the commercial banks and the national governments involved. That package normally involved the rescheduling of old debt and the addition of new money. The industrial countries, the international agencies, the borrowers, and the banks all showed in 1983 that they could cooperate effectively to deal with the international debt problem. They did, for example, manage to handle second-round debt negotiations with both Brazil and Argentina.

Moreover, by the fall of 1983, a new organization, the Institute of International Finance, had been established by some 180 commercial banks from 39 nations to make its members "better international lenders" by, among other things, gathering more information about the economies and debt structures of developing countries.

Most important, however, the world economic recovery was in full swing. Cline calculated that the debt problems of the developing countries "should be manageable and should show considerable improvement" if the economies of the industrial countries grow by at least a 3% annual rate in 1984–86—thereby taking in more imports from the poorer nations. The latest data in the United States and abroad offered some hope for such growth. It just could be that as the months go by the debt problem will prove less scary than most Hitchcock movies.

DAVID R. FRANCIS

---

restored to health. (*See* special report, page 277.)

Funding Bodies. For much of the year, the IMF managing director was busy with austerity and rescheduling packages for debtor countries or finding adequate finances to make IMF loans. In January 1983, for instance, the finance ministers of the ten leading industrial nations agreed to expand substantially, roughly from $6.9 billion to $18 billion, the so-called General Arrangements to Borrow. This money, which as a rule had been used for balance-of-payments help for industrial countries, was opened up for use by all of the nearly 150 members of the IMF. Saudi Arabia joined in the effort by providing some $1.7 billion.

In addition, the finance ministers making up the IMF's Interim Committee agreed a month later on a 47.5% hike in quotas, thereby lifting the Fund's basic resources to some $96 billion. Implementation of the quota boost, however, awaited action by the U.S. Congress, which approved an $8.4 billion U.S. contribution just before adjourning. The quota increase needed ratification by countries with 70% of quotas before it would take effect. President Reagan, in his speech to the Fund's annual meeting, warned that the legislation was "not only crucial to the recovery of America's trading partners abroad, and to the stability of the entire financial system . . . [but] also necessary to a sustained recovery in the United States."

The United States was also causing concern at the World Bank and its affiliate, the International Development Association (IDA). Congress was a year behind in approving a U.S. contribution to IDA, which makes easy-term loans to the world's poorest countries. The Reagan administration, moreover, was insisting on a relatively small contribution to the next replenishment of IDA funds. The World Bank hoped for $16 billion spread over the next three years; other industrial nations spoke of $12 billion; the United States was saying $9 billion, which was less than the previous replenishment. Beryl Sprinkel, U.S. undersecretary

© Lynn Johnson/Black Star

With the U.S. trade deficit mounting, "Buy America" and protectionism in general were the prevailing trade trends.

of the treasury for monetary affairs, argued that Congress would provide no more than $750 million per year in light of the needs of domestic social programs. André de Iattre, special representative for IDA negotiations, told the press that a U.S. contribution of only $9 billion "would severely impair the ability of the association to play an effective role. . . ."

Currencies and Trade. The U.S. dollar remained strong against other currencies during 1983. In the 12 months prior to September, it was up 14% against the British pound, about 7% against the West German mark, and 14% against the French franc; it slipped 7% against the Japanese yen. Many experts figured the dollar to be overvalued by 12–20% against most of its major trading partners. Whether so or not, the U.S. trade deficit was growing rapidly, as American firms found it harder to sell abroad and imported goods became more competitive with domestic products. The merchandise trade deficit, it was estimated, would reach some $60 billion in 1983 and even more in 1984.

Both in the United States and abroad, political pressures for various protectionist measures were strong. The director-general of the General Agreement on Tariffs and Trade (GATT) warned at the opening of the sixth session of the United Nations Conference on Trade and Development at Belgrade in early June that "if the world economy is to gather strength, we need open trade policies now." Speaking of the developing countries, he said ". . . if their debt burden is not to become insupportable, they must have the possibility of achieving a rate of increase in their export earnings that keeps pace with the growth in their debt-servicing requirements." At the same session, IMF Managing Director de Larosière called for a rollback of trade restrictions and a dismantling of trade-distorting domestic measures, but 1983 showed no dramatic trend toward the closing of borders to trade.

The Euromarket. The lengthy slump in the world economy, though lifting, still took its toll in the Euromarket. Total funds raised in this international market by businesses and government declined 17% between 1981 and the first half of 1983. However, Citicorp and other participants anticipated a turnaround in international borrowing as the recovery picked up steam. Actually, two segments of the market were moving in opposite directions during that period: syndicated Eurocredits extended by commercial banks for the medium-term were down 45%, while external bond issues were up 66%. U.S. borrowers drew heavily on the Eurobond market since it offered somewhat cheaper credit than at home.

The Industrial Powers. Heads of state of the seven major industrial countries again held an economic summit meeting, the ninth such assembly, this time in Williamsburg, VA, during the last five days of May. The leaders talked of trying for "convergent" national economic policies. For the first time at such a gathering they looked at defense, agreeing on a statement balancing a broad commitment to arms control with a warning to Moscow that deployment of a new generation of U.S. missiles in Europe was certain unless negotiations with the Soviets produce mutual reductions.

The arrival of economic recovery did not bring the industrial nations into any sort of economic Valhalla. Unemployment remained high. The Paris-based Organization for Economic Cooperation and Development (OECD) figured that it would take 20,000 extra jobs every day during the last five years of this decade to slash the number of jobless in the non-Communist industrial nations to the 18 million level of 1979. Surprisingly, the grim unemployment levels prompted relatively little political turmoil. Nonetheless, political leaders were relieved at the prospect of a recovery that would improve the lot of their people and their chances for reelection.

DAVID R. FRANCIS
"The Christian Science Monitor"

IOWA

On Jan. 14, 1983, Terry Branstad, a 36-year-old Republican, was sworn in as Iowa's new governor, becoming the youngest chief executive in the nation as well as the youngest in state history. With a Democrat, Bob Anderson, taking over as lieutenant governor, it was the first time in Iowa's history that the state's two top executives were from opposing parties.

Also during 1983, the U.S. Census Bureau reported that between 80,000 and 100,000 more people moved out of Iowa than into the state in the recession years of 1979–82; unemployment continued to be higher than normal but below the national average; and a new state department of corrections was established.

Agriculture. In 1983 more federal farm-program dollars poured into Iowa than ever in history, with Iowans receiving $1.6 billion. This was more than was received by farmers in any other state. Approximately 40% of the normal corn acres were in the payment-in-kind (PIK) program and brought to the state's farmers about $1.3 billion. Because of the PIK program and a severe drought, measured to be the worst in nearly 50 years, soybean production fell off by 18% and the corn harvest was the smallest in 20 years, only 756 million bushels. Adding to the farm problems was extensive summer heat.

The Legislature. The 70th Iowa General Assembly, meeting in its first session in 1983, was controlled by the Democratic Party. The Democratic margin in the House was 60–40 and in the state Senate 28–22.

The 1983 General Assembly lasted 125 days and sent 217 bills to the governor's desk. Forty-six of the governor's 54 proposals were enacted. The executive veto was asserted a total of 16 times.

Final appropriations were nearly $12.5 million higher than the $2.048 billion recommended by the chief executive. However, in an item veto exercised following the adjournment

Wide World

An Iowa banking official removes cash from the Exchange Bank of Bloomfield, a privately owned bank that failed.

of the legislature, Branstad cut the "jobs bill" by the same amount. The governor also vetoed a bill calling for a state lottery. Gubernatorial proposals for a dramatic change in the way utility rates are set, for the establishment of a Consumer Appellate Advocate to appear before the Iowa Commerce Commission in rate regulation cases, and an Iowa Fund to encourage investment in the state were approved.

Governor Branstad broke with his fiscal conservative image and asked for an increase in the sales tax from three to four cents per dollar. Because of the state's financial crisis, the recommended budget called for a wage freeze for all state employees, with a 6.6% increase in the second year of the biennium. Both the sales tax increase and the wage proposal were enacted. The governor asked for no major cuts in state programs but did not recommend any new projects. In order to increase jobs in Iowa, the governor favored several building programs, particularly at the state universities. Some degree of property-tax relief was approved through increases in state aid to secondary and elementary school districts. Likewise, the enacted budget had the state assume a greater share of the costs of the state court system. Legalized pari-mutuel betting and funding for a racing commission also passed.

The state's financial problems continued into late summer. In order to avoid a deficit, the governor cut all appropriations by 2.8%.

RUSSELL M. ROSS, *University of Iowa*

IOWA • Information Highlights

Area: 56,275 sq mi (145 752 km²).

Population (1982 est.): 2,905,000.

Chief Cities (1980 census): Des Moines, the capital, 191,003; Cedar Rapids, 110,243; Davenport, 103,264; Sioux City, 82,003.

Government (1983): *Chief Officers*—governor, Terry E. Branstad (R); lt. gov., Bob Anderson (D). *General Assembly*—Senate, 50 members; House of Representatives, 100 members.

State Finances (fiscal year 1982): *Revenues,* $3,885,000,000; *expenditures,* $3,903,000,000.

Personal Income (1982): $31,347,000,000; per capita, $10,791.

Labor Force (July 1983): *Nonagricultural wage and salary earners,* 999,300; *unemployed,* 105,300 (7.4% of total force).

Education: *Enrollment* (fall 1981)—public elementary schools, 341,218; public secondary, 174,998; colleges and universities (fall 1982), 147,862 students. *Public school expenditures* (1981–82), $1,435,964,000.

IRAN

Iran under the rule of the Ayatollah Ruhollah Khomeini again assumed the role of international villain in 1983. But this time the policies of Khomeini's Islamic regime threatened a crisis that could have worldwide ramifications. Iran's threat to block oil shipments from the Persian Gulf raised the possibility that the United States and its allies would have to intervene militarily to keep the vitally needed oil flowing to the Western world. Reported links between Iran and international terrorist actions—particularly the murderous assaults on U.S. and French peacekeeping forces in Beirut—also forced Western governments to consider retaliatory actions against Iran if indeed it were proved that the Khomeini regime was directly behind the terror. Added to this was the continuation of the Iran-Iraq war, which neither the West nor the Soviet Union wanted an intransigent Iran to win. And making Iran's international image even worse was the domestic repression that has marked the Khomeini regime since it came to power in 1979.

War. Iran was determined to overthrow the Iraqi regime of President Saddam Hussein. To this end, Tehran continued to sacrifice thousands of Iranian troops in a grinding war of attrition. Iranian civilians also suffered when Iraq hit Iranian population centers near the border with missile, artillery, and air attacks. Neither side could truthfully claim any significant territorial advancement.

For the Shiite Islamic clergymen running Iran, the death toll was not too high. This was a holy war which had the backing of the majority of Iran's mostly illiterate population. More importantly, the reputation of the regime was based to a large extent on the promise to win the war at any cost. Concessions or conciliation might call into question the wisdom of the policies that resulted in such heavy casualties since the war started in September 1980. Thus, the Tehran government turned down all peace overtures, including a mediation effort by the United Nations Security Council.

Threat. Part of Iran's war strategy was a threat to blockade the Strait of Hormuz at the mouth of the Persian Gulf. Such a blockade would cut off Persian Gulf oil to the West, including Saudi Arabian oil. But the main aim of the threat was to prevent Iraq from attempting to knock out major Iranian oil export facilities, particularly the large oil export terminal on Kharg Island. Iran was financing the war with its own oil exports, which were as high as two million barrels per day.

By threatening the blockade, Iran was also protesting Western support for Iraq, especially military aid from France. Indeed, French-supplied Super Etendard jets equipped with Exocet missiles were capable of causing havoc to Iranian oil export. Tehran in addition was threatening such oil-exporting Gulf states as Saudi Arabia and Kuwait that had given financial and other aid to Iraq. In effect, Iran was saying that if Iranian oil export facilities were knocked out, then no other Persian Gulf state would be allowed to export oil.

U.S. President Ronald Reagan was quick to warn that any attempt to blockade the Strait of Hormuz would not be tolerated by Washington. American naval ships intensified their patrols around the strait, and Iran retaliated by increasing air surveillance of American ships. A conflict could not be ruled out.

The United States could easily clear the strait of Iranian mines or sunken ships, and the Iranian air force was no threat to U.S. air power. However, there was a danger that a U.S.-Iranian clash could tempt the Soviet Union to send its troops into Iran. Since the days of the czars, Iran has been a target of Russian imperialism just as Afghanistan was before Moscow launched an invasion of that country in 1979.

Caution. Perhaps it was the threat of unforeseen consequences that led to a measure of caution on the part of the Khomeini regime. Iran did not try to knock out the Kirkuk oil fields in northern Iraq or the pipeline that carries oil from these fields to Turkey and the outside world. An attack on the Kirkuk fields most probably would have caused Iraq's President Hussein to order an all-out attack on Kharg Island. Hussein needed the Kirkuk fields and the pipeline just as Iran needed Kharg Island—to carry on the war.

Terror. The Khomeini regime denied that it was involved in the attacks on U.S. and French peacekeepers in Beirut, or in any other terrorist acts. Western governments found it hard to prove direct links between the Tehran government and the terrorist activity, but it was also true that Iran had "volunteers" in Lebanon fighting on the side of Syria. More importantly, Lebanon's Shiite Muslim community maintained strong ties with the Shiite regime in Teh-

---

IRAN · Information Highlights

Official Name: Islamic Republic of Iran.
Location: Southwest Asia.
Area: 63,600 sq mi (1 647 240 km²).
Population (July 1983 est.): 42,490,000.
Chief Cities: (1980 est.): Tehran, the capital, 6,000,000.
Government: Supreme faqih, Ayatollah Ruhollah Khomeini. *Head of state,* Mohammed Ali Khamenei, president (took office Oct. 1981). *Head of government,* Mir Hussein Moussavi-Khamenei, premier (took office Oct. 1981). *Legislature* (unicameral)—Parliament.
Monetary Unit: Rial (87.311 rials equal U.S.$1, September 1983).
Gross National Product (1982 U.S.$1): $66,500,000,000.
Economic Index (1982): *Consumer Prices* (1970 = 100), all items, 488.3; food (1981), 495.9.

As the Ayatollah Ruhollah Khomeini, top, believed to be about 84
years old, still held the allegiance
of the masses, the war with Iraq
raged on. An already-leaking offshore oil installation at Nowruz,
left, was bombed March 2, causing
the worst oil spill ever in the Persian Gulf; with thousands of barrels pouring out each day, the well
was not capped until late September. Below: At a training camp
near Persepolis, 15-year-old volunteers are led in prayer.

Foreign Ministers Ali Akbar Velyati, left, of Iran and Tariq Aziz of Iraq traded barbs at the United Nations.

ran, and Lebanese Shiite militia fired often on the peacekeeping troops in Beirut. Shiite Muslims were also involved in attacks on the U.S. and French embassies in Kuwait. In short, while Khomeini may not have given the direct order for these terrorist acts, his brand of fanatic Shiite Islam did at least provide an ideological impulse to "holy war" terrorism throughout the Middle East.

USSR. Iran's relations with the Soviet Union, meanwhile, worsened even more after the Khomeini government outlawed the Iranian Communist (Tudeh) Party in May and arrested many party members. During the trials in Tehran, many Iranian Communists admitted to spying for Moscow. In addition, Iran was furious that Moscow was stepping up its arms supplies to hated Iraq.

Domestic Affairs. With the war becoming an end in itself, domestic politics took a back seat during 1983. There was undoubtedly political maneuvering in preparation for the time when 84-year-old Khomeini would depart the scene. On the surface, at least, there was the appearance of total unity.

The regime managed to fuse religious fanaticism and patriotism to offset discontent over food shortages and other hardships on the people.

Domestic repression was particularly brutal in the case of the Bahai religious sect. In May, President Reagan personally appealed to Iran to stop the executions of members of the Bahai faith. Tehran derisively rejected the Reagan appeal and continued the killings.

The once-powerful Mujahedeen-e-Khalq (People's Fighters or Holy Warriors), a Marxist Islamic group that had staged an intensive terrorist campaign against the regime, virtually ceased to exist in 1983. And rebel Kurds in the northwestern part of the country came under heavy pressure from the Iranian armed forces, causing some Kurds to side with Iraq in the war.

See also ENERGY—OPEC: A New Appraisal; MIDDLE EAST.

AARON R. EINFRANK
Free-lance Foreign Correspondent

IRAQ

Iraq appeared to reach the limits of its resources in its war with Iran. At the same time, fears were expressed in the international community that the regime of President Saddam Hussein in desperation might take action that would have serious implications for countries not involved directly in the conflict.

The war hit Iraq harder than Iran in both human and material terms. The smaller Iraqi population was simply not able to absorb heavy casualties in the way the much larger Iranian population did. And Iraqis were not imbued with the holy-war fanaticism that characterized their opponents.

Iraq was able to export far less oil than Iran because the Iranian navy controlled the Persian Gulf. It was estimated that Iraq at most was able to export 700,000 barrels of oil per day, primarily through the pipeline leading to Turkey. Prior to the war, Iraq exported more than four million barrels of oil daily.

Iraq's once-vast foreign currency and gold reserves had disappeared because of the cost of the war. Iraq's Arab allies were no longer able to give Baghdad large sums to finance the struggle. Instead of cash, Saudi Arabia and Kuwait donated oil to Iraq in 1983. This oil had to be sold on a world market already suffering from an oil glut.

Foreign Minister Tariq Aziz traveled to Egypt in July, becoming the first high-ranking Iraqi to visit Cairo since the two nations broke diplomatic relations following the Camp David accords. Meanwhile, Egypt has been supplying Iraq with arms and ammunitions, and an estimated 1.3 million Egyptians were working in Iraq.

Austerity measures had to be imposed on the Iraqi population. Ambitious development projects, including bridges, factories, and housing, were abandoned. Iraq was deeply in debt.

Plots. President Hussein bore the responsibility for leading Iraq into war. And one of the prime conditions for peace laid down by Iran was the ouster of Hussein. Such an action would most likely come as a result of dissidence within Hussein's own ruling Baath (Arab Socialist) Party.

During the year, there were rumors of plots against Hussein. Western newsmen reported from Baghdad that Iraqi Interior Minister Barzan Tikriti, a half brother of Hussein, had been ousted. There also were reports of other changes in the government structure, including the September dismissal of Finance Minister Thamin Razzuqi Shaykhli. In spite of these reported rumored changes, President Hussein managed to hold on to power.

Iraq's Shiite Muslim community, many of whom owe loyalty to Iran's Shiite leader Ayatollah Khomeini, remained restive. There were reports of Shiite terrorist acts against the Hussein government, which is dominated by Sunni-sect Muslims like Hussein.

Hussein tried to make peace with the Kurdish rebels who were fighting Iraqi troops in the northern part of the country. In fact, Iraq permitted elections for a regional legislative council in Kurdistan in an attempt to reduce Kurdish nationalism. Some Kurds in both Iraq and Iran sided with Iraq in the war. But this peace policy toward the Kurds was only partially successful.

Assistance. The United States, France, and other Western nations tilted toward Iraq in the conflict. The United States offered financial credits to Iraq to buy American food. France supplied arms, including jets and surface-to-air missiles, in return for Iraqi oil. France also

Krpan-Sipa/Black Star
Iraq permitted the Kurds to vote in elections for a regional council, which was to have limited legislative power.

agreed in 1983 to lend Iraq five Super Etendard bombers, capable of firing Exocets missiles.

The Western countries did not want an Iraqi collapse, but they also did not want an Iraqi victory over Iran. More importantly, the United States and other Western countries wanted to prevent any action by Iraq that might lead to Iran following through on its threat to blockade oil supplies from the Persian Gulf.

During 1983, Iraq threatened to knock out Iran's major oil-export terminal at Kharg Island. Iran responded that if this were to happen, no oil would leave the Persian Gulf because the outlet to the sea—the Strait of Hormuz—would be blockaded by the Iranian armed forces.

Thanks in part to Western pressure, Iraq did nothing to precipitate an Iranian blockade of the Gulf. Some Iranian oil installations were hit and some ships were sunk by the Iraqis, but these were only token attacks. Such attacks did result in the worst oil spill in Persian Gulf history. The spill began in the Nowruz offshore oil field in early February and was enlargened by Iraqi air attacks on March 2. The wells were not reported capped until September.

Iraq did announce that it was planning to resume oil shipments through the Gulf despite the Iranian navy. Iraqi oil-export facilities on the coast, which had been damaged badly in the war, were being rebuilt. The problem for the West was that if Iran interfered with tankers carrying Iraqi oil, this almost certainly would force Hussein to hit Kharg Island. Then the West would again be faced with the Iranian threat to blockade the Strait of Hormuz through which much of the West's oil passes.

See also MIDDLE EAST.

AARON R. EINFRANK
Free-lance Foreign Correspondent

IRAQ • Information Highlights

Official Name: Republic of Iraq.
Location: Southwest Asia.
Area: 172,000 sq mi (445 480 km²).
Population (July 1983 est.): 14,509,000.
Government: Head of state and government, Saddam Hussein Takriti, president (took office July 1979).
Monetary Unit: Dinar (0.311 dinar equals U.S.$1, September 1983).
Gross National Product (1981 U.S.$): $31,300,-000,000.

IRELAND

The coalition government of Fine Gael and Labour, formed by Garret FitzGerald on Dec. 14, 1982, struggled to deal with the country's economic problems during 1983. A huge national debt contributed to high interest rates, while rising prices and declining productivity forced the administration to prescribe painful remedies. Having raised the excise duty on tobacco, drink, and gasoline in a minibudget on January 7, Financial Minister Alan Dukes introduced an austerity budget on February 9 in an effort to raise £350,000,000 (Irish pounds) in additional revenue. Dukes increased the income tax as well as the value-added tax. The new budget raised the income tax of those in the highest bracket to 65% and imposed a heavier burden of indirect taxation on working-class families. Social welfare benefits were increased.

Elections. Elections to the Irish Senate (Seanad Eireann) in January resulted in the return of 25 Fine Gael, 18 Fianna Fail, and 7 Labour candidates. Voters also elected six independents standing for university seats along with three senators from Northern Ireland.

Government Scandal. On January 20 two top police officers resigned after the *Irish Times* accused the police of tapping the phones of several Dublin journalists. A few days later, two prominent members of the Fianna Fail shadow cabinet, Ray McSharry, former Tanaiste or deputy prime minister, and Sean Doherty, former minister of justice, gave up their posts after allegations that they had approved a wiretap on the telephone of a colleague in the previous government of Charles Haughey. Denying any knowledge of these illegal taps, Haughey refused to heed calls to resign the leadership of the Fianna Fail Party.

Prime Ministers FitzGerald and Mrs. Thatcher of Britain reviewed the situation in Northern Ireland in November.
UPI

Abortion Issue. During the spring and summer a well-organized pressure group launched a campaign to insert an amendment into the Irish constitution that would forbid abortion. Although abortion already was illegal in the republic, the antiabortion lobby insisted on holding a national referendum to decide the issue. On April 27, antiabortion forces in the Dail (the Irish Lower House) rejected the government's more moderate position and approved a stronger, if ambiguous, statement that committed the state to defend the right to life of the unborn child. With only 52% of the electorate turning out on September 7, voters approved the pro-life amendment by a 2–1 margin. This outcome represented a serious defeat for the forces of secularism, liberalism, and reconciliation with the Protestant majority in Northern Ireland.

Relations with England and Northern Ireland. Representatives of the leading political parties of the republic met with leaders of the Social Democratic and Labour Party of Northern Ireland in Dublin Castle on May 30 to exchange views about reunification of the country. During June the forum served as a clearinghouse for ideas about ways of resolving the lethal conflict over partition. On July 27, Irish and British officials worked out a plan for conferring on matters of mutual interest. On November 7, Prime Minister FitzGerald flew to London to discuss the Northern Ireland problem with British Prime Minister Margaret Thatcher.

Horse Theft. The Irish horse-racing world suffered a severe shock on February 8, when armed men invaded the stud farm of the Agha Khan at Newbridge, County Kildare, and stole Shergar, the thoroughbred winner of the English Derby and Irish Sweeps Derby. After demanding a ransom of $2,700,000, the thieves disappeared, and in spite of a massive search the police failed to find the celebrated horse.

L. PERRY CURTIS, JR., *Brown University*

ISRAEL

Israel's military presence in Lebanon and crises in the economy led to a series of important diplomatic and domestic policy decisions during 1983. The nation also got a new prime minister and a new president.

Lebanon. Less than two weeks after an agenda was agreed upon, peace talks between Israel and Lebanon stalled in late January 1983. Lebanon demanded the immediate withdrawal of Israeli forces and rejected Israel's demand for normalization of relations, including an end to hostile propaganda, the movement of people and products between the two countries, and the maintenance of security along the Israeli border.

Finally, on May 17, Israel and Lebanon signed an accord, providing for Israeli withdrawal from Lebanon simultaneously with Syrian and PLO forces, and for negotiations for normalization of relations between the two countries within six months.

By July, Prime Minister Menahem Begin's cabinet, responding to pressure at home and abroad, decided to redeploy the Israeli forces to a new defense line along the Awali River north of Sidon and to hand over the evacuated areas to the Lebanese army and the multinational force, without reciprocal moves on the part of Syria and the PLO; the withdrawal was completed on September 4.

On November 4 the Israeli headquarters in Tyre, southern Lebanon, was leveled by a suicide truck-bombing, like that perpetrated against U.S. and French installations less than two weeks before, killing 28 Israeli soldiers and 32 Lebanese civilians. Retaliatory air attacks were launched against Palestinian positions within hours.

Politics and Domestic Affairs. On the domestic political scene, crisis was precipitated early in the year by the findings of the commission investigating the Beirut massacre of September 1982. Prime Minister Begin weathered three no-confidence motions initiated by opposition parties in the Knesset. Defense Minister Ariel Sharon, charged with "indirect responsibility" for the massacre, was removed from his post, and Moshe Arens, ambassador to the United States, was appointed to replace him.

In May, Chaim Herzog, former ambassador to the UN, was inaugurated as Israel's sixth president. A new political party, Mitzad, the Zionist Religious Camp, was formed by prominent Orthodox nationalists. Mapam, the United Workers Party, voted by a narrow margin to continue its 15-year alliance with the Labor Party. The vote constituted a defeat for members advocating the formation of a new left-wing Zionist party.

In declining health, Prime Minister Begin announced August 28 that he intended to resign. Party leaders and cabinet members pleaded with him to reconsider his decision, but he reaffirmed his decision two days later. Uncertainty reigned while the Herut Party elected as its leader Foreign Minister Yitzhak

On May 17 negotiators Antoine Fattal of Lebanon (left) and David Kimche of Israel (center) signed an agreement on the withdrawal of Israeli troops. U.S. envoy Morris Draper (right), who participated in the talks, signed as a witness.

Sven Nackstrand/Gamma-Liaison

© Milner/Sygma

Yitzhak Shamir (right) could not win the support of Labor Party leaders but was able to form a new Likud-led government.

Shamir (*see* BIOGRAPHY), who immediately entered into talks with the leader of the opposition Labor Party, Shimon Peres, to form a national unity government. When those talks failed, Shamir sought and won the backing of a Likud coalition like Begin's. A 64-member government was approved October 10.

No new national trends emerged in October municipal elections. Incumbent mayors Teddy Kollek of Jerusalem and Shlomo Lahat of Tel Aviv were reelected by landslides. In Arab population centers, however, election results showed a significant deterioration of Communist strength.

Economy. High defense expenditures, an increase in imports, and a decline in export sales plunged Israel deeply into foreign debt. Early in the year, share prices fell drastically on an overinflated Tel Aviv Stock Market, prompting wage earners to buy shares in commercial banks as a security against galloping inflation, expected to reach 200% by year's end. In October, as rumors spread of imminent devaluation of the shekel, a panicky public sold $450 million in bank shares in one day and converted the cash to dollars, causing a bank crisis. The stock market closed for one week, and the cabinet met in an emergency session to consider measures for saving the economy from total collapse. The shekel was devalued 23% on October 11; two days later, Finance Minister Yoram Aridor resigned after the government rejected his plan to link—perhaps even replace —the shekel with the U.S. dollar.

Four days later, a new finance minister was appointed, Yigal Cohen-Orgad, who took drastic measures to stabilize the economy. Government subsidies were removed from basic commodities, raising their prices by 50%; lev-

ies were imposed on education and travel; and the current value of bank shares was guaranteed if redeemed within five years. The most dramatic move was the reversal of Begin's bold policy of economic freedom and the abolition of foreign-exchange controls instituted six years earlier. As of November 1, Israelis could no longer purchase foreign currency freely; dollar purchases were limited to $3,000 for those traveling abroad. Prime Minister Shamir declared that the austerity program would continue "until economic health is restored."

The Israeli public received this news with the same stoicism it displayed during a four-month doctor strike which crippled the nation's public health services during the spring. The work stoppage, by some 8,500 physicians demanding higher wages and shorter working hours, began in March and climaxed in a two-week hunger strike in June involving 3,000 hospital doctors. Most of the major hospitals had

On the eve of strict austerity measures, which caused prices to soar, Israeli shoppers cleared supermarket shelves.

to turn away all but the most critical cases. The action ended with the promise of a 60% pay increase distributed over two years. The subsequent currency devaluation, however, canceled out the gains.

As thousands of home buyers were unable to meet payments because of stock losses, many contractors were on the verge of financial ruin, presaging a major decline in home construction.

An economic boost came from the U.S. Congress, which allocated up to $300 million in credits for Israel to spend on the U.S. Lavi warplane, and $250 million in foreign military sales credits for arms and military equipment purchased from domestic manufacturers.

Foreign Relations. In August an accord was reached with Liberia, the second African nation to resume diplomatic relations broken off under Arab pressure following the 1973 Yom Kippur War. By the terms of the agreement Israel was to provide medical and agricultural expertise and to help in the establishment of a shipping company in Liberia. Despite a renewal of dialogue in November, progress in normalization of relations with Egypt continued to be stalled by the latter's refusal to return its ambassador to Israel, contingent on Israeli withdrawal from Lebanon.

In the Soviet Union, the government-sponsored Anti-Zionist Committee of the Soviet Republic, established in spring 1982 as a weapon against Israel, grew into a mass movement. The 12-year sentence given in October to Jewish activist Yosef Begun by a Soviet court for teaching Hebrew was the culmination of what the U.S. State Department called an "increase in officially sanctioned anti-Semitism." The Is-

raeli government issued an official statement denouncing Soviet discrimination against Jews and appealed to all lovers of freedom to help secure Begun's release. In sharp departure from the policies of the Labor Alignment, the Likud government assumed the role of world Jewry's official representative. In that capacity, a special Knesset committee was formed in July to take up the question of 1,500 Jews that disappeared in Argentina, and a group of Israeli leaders visited Ethiopia to investigate the conditions of the country's 28,000 Falasha Jews.

Settlements in Judea and Samaria continued to raise controversy. Amid protests from the Peace Now group and the U.S. State Department, several new settlements were established during the year. Incidents of terror escalated in the area, with Hebron as focal point of violence. The murder of a yeshiva student in the Hebron market touched off an angry rampage by the Jewish residents of the city. The restoration of the Jewish quarter destroyed in 1929 remained the center of Arab bitterness and the cause of several bomb-throwing incidents. Since the Israeli withdrawal from Sinai in 1981–82, terrorist acts also increased in the Gaza strip and on the roads traversing those areas. A UN commission studying the living conditions among Palestinians living in the West Bank and Gaza found that economic conditions and medical services had improved.

During a two-day visit to Washington in late November, Prime Minister Shamir reached a major agreement with the United States on increased military and trade cooperation.

LIVIA E. BITTON-JACKSON
Herbert H. Lehman College, CUNY

© Sygma

President Sandro Pertini (left) presided as Bettino Craxi was sworn in as premier.

In 1983, Italy chose, for the first time, a Socialist to head its government as the economy continued in the doldrums. Italy played an active role during the year as peacekeeper in the Mediterranean region.

Politics and Domestic Affairs.

The Fanfani Government. Italy began the year with a four-party coalition government that had been formed on Nov. 30, 1982, by Amintore Fanfani, a Christian Democrat. It included Socialists, Social Democrats, and Liberals. Premier Fanfani's austerity program called for a more flexible *scala mobile* (wage indexing), sharp tax increases, and a $10 billion (U.S.) spending cut. By mid-January 1983 this monetarist-type program caused hundreds of thousands of Italian workers to demonstrate in sometimes violent protests. Within the government the Social Democrats and Liberals bitterly attacked the tax increases that had been adopted some days earlier at the cabinet level.

By April the political situation was in crisis. Bettino Craxi, secretary of Italy's Socialist Party and the country's current "kingmaker" (*see* BIOGRAPHY), demanded early general elections, thus setting the stage for the collapse of Fanfani's coalition government. On April 29 the Fanfani government resigned.

Elections. President Sandro Pertini, although a Socialist himself, delayed his decision to dissolve Parliament, because this would be the fourth time in a row that a parliament had been dissolved before the end of its regular term. Finally, on May 5, Pertini announced that general elections would be held on June 26–27 (one year ahead of normal scheduling) and that Fanfani would stay on meanwhile as

caretaker premier. The crisis was further complicated by the sudden death of the president of the Senate, Tommaso Morlino, whom Pertini had begged to work out a solution that would avoid new elections.

The electorate viewed the ensuing campaign with considerable apathy. The stagnant economy was the main issue, along with the question raised by the Communist Party about the proposed deployment by NATO of cruise missiles in Sicily. During the campaign, Craxi made it clear that he ruled out the possibility of forming a coalition government with the Communist Party, which was advocating this as a "democratic alternative."

In the voting the ruling Christian Democrats suffered a sharp decline from 38.3% to 32.9% —their biggest setback in more than three decades. Craxi's Socialists climbed modestly from 9.8% to 11.4%, placing third after Enrico Berlinguer's Communist Party (29.9%). Political experts observed that the results offered little hope that the next coalition government would be better able than its predecessors to embark upon a drastic new economic course.

The Craxi Government. On August 4, after a month of tortuous negotiations among the centrist parties, 49-year-old Bettino Craxi became Italy's first Socialist premier. He had never before held a ministerial portfolio—a most unusual thing in Italian politics. Craxi joined the ranks of Socialists who were heading governments in the "sunbelt" of France, Spain, Portugal, and Greece—to say nothing of Sweden. This was only the third time since 1945 that a non-Christian Democrat held the Italian premiership. Craxi's new government was a broader five-party coalition of the center-left (Socialists, Christian Democrats, Republicans, Social Democrats, and Liberals). Craxi's own party garnered only 5 of the 29 portfolios, whereas the Christian Democrats retained 16, including the deputy premiership and the foreign ministry (Giulio Andreotti). The ministry of defense was reassigned from the Socialist, Lelio Lagorio, to the former Republican premier, Giovanni Spadolini.

Premier Craxi reaffirmed Italy's staunch partnership in the European Community and NATO. Although his economic program was a bit less rigorous than Fanfani's, he called for financial stringency and promised to whittle the nation's inflation rate from 16% in mid-1983 to 10% by 1984. He declared that this would not be done at the expense of the unemployed, who numbered 9.9% in mid-1983, yet he also indicated that he was determined to eliminate tens of thousands of unproductive jobs in the state sector of the economy. Craxi also revealed plans to raise the retirement age and to reduce public spending in health care and social security. (More than 5 million Italians receive disability pensions.)

Craxi hoped in this way to freeze the immense deficit in the public-spending category that is now estimated at more than $56 billion, or 15% of Italy's total output of goods and services. Finally, Craxi vowed to strengthen the police, to continue the fight against terrorism, and to crack down on the Mafia.

The new government won solid votes of confidence in Parliament on August 12–13. In September, after the "Ferragosto" holidays, the government got down to work in trying to implement its ambitious program. Officials announced that they expected a 15% increase in tax revenues in 1984.

Scandals. Corruption continues to pervade the Italian political scene at almost every level. Even the Communist Party, which had long prided itself on its "honesty" in running local governments, suffered a blow on March 17 when its mayor of Turin, Diego Novelli, had to resign in the wake of a bribery scandal. The Socialist government in Piedmont also resigned two days earlier in the face of similar bribery charges.

Repercussions of the 1981 scandal involving the conspiratorial "P-2" Masonic Lodge organized by Licio Gelli for anti-Communist purposes continued to make headlines. Gelli, who had fled to South America, was later arrested in Geneva when he tried to withdraw $50 million from Banco Ambrosiano-connected funds. Italy was seeking Gelli's extradition when suddenly on August 9 he escaped from jail in Geneva, causing an uproar in both countries.

Meanwhile, the Banco Ambrosiano scandal of 1982 that involved the banker Roberto Calvi, who was also a member of the "P-2" Lodge, continued to simmer. Calvi had fled to London, where he was found hanged under Blackfriars Bridge in June 1982. A preliminary inquest in London had ruled his death to be a suicide, but many Italians suspected foul play. In June 1983 a British jury unanimously returned an open verdict, meaning they could not decide whether Calvi had killed himself or was murdered.

Terrorism. Throughout 1983 the government continued its vigorous crackdown on terrorists and other criminals. On January 24 a jury sentenced 32 members of the Red Brigades to life imprisonment for the kidnapping and murder of former Premier Aldo Moro in 1978.

One week later, U.S. Brig. Gen. James L. Dozier, who had been rescued in Padua from terrorists in January 1982, made a surprise visit to Rome, where he awarded U.S. Defense Department medals to 14 Italian policemen who had liberated him. The Italian government declared that many of the terrorists and kidnappers, as well as drug pushers, were linked to the Mafia in Sicily and Calabria, to the Camorra in Naples, and to other underworld organizations in Sardinia and elsewhere. On June 17, police in Naples arrested 900 Camorra suspects.

Terrorists retaliated one week later (on national election day) by killing in a street ambush Bruno Caccia, the chief public prosecutor in Turin. On July 31 a magistrate in Palermo also was killed. Despite these murders, it seemed clear that the government was gaining the upper hand in its war against terrorism.

Umberto II. On March 18 former King Umberto II, who had served briefly as Italy's "May King" in 1946, died in Switzerland at the age of 78. He had been banished from Italy in June 1946 after a referendum established the republic. Umberto nourished dreams of coming back to his homeland to die, but officials of the republic turned down this request. The former king bequeathed to the Holy See the famous Shroud of Turin, venerated by many as the burial cloth of Christ.

Centenary of Mussolini's Birth. On July 29 thousands of neo-Fascists wearing black shirts

---

ITALY • Information Highlights

Official Name: Italian Republic.
Location: Southern Europe.
Area: 116,300 sq mi (301 217 km²).
Population (July 1983): 56,345,000.
Chief Cities (Dec. 1980): Rome, the capital, 2,916,414; Milan, 1,655,599; Naples, 1,219,362; Turin, 1,143,263.
Government: Head of state, Alessandro (Sandro) Pertini, president (took office July 1978). Head of government, Bettino Craxi, prime minister (sworn in Aug. 4, 1983). Legislature—Parliament: Senate and Chamber of Deputies.
Monetary Unit: Lira (1618.5 lire equal U.S.$1, Nov. 16, 1983).
Gross Domestic Product (1981 U.S.$): $350,154,-000,000.
Economic Indexes (1982): Consumer Prices (1970 = 100), all items, 513.7; food, 489.0. Industrial Production (1975 = 100), 125.
Foreign Trade (1982 U.S.$): Imports, $86,211,-000,000; exports, $73,481,000,000.

© Sygma

Under heavy guard, Mehmet Ali Agca, who was convicted of attempting to assassinate Pope John Paul II in 1981, was taken to St. Peter's Square for a reenactment of the crime.

gathered in Predappio (Romagna) to commemorate the 100th anniversary of Benito Mussolini's birth. The anniversary sparked a spate of books on the Fascist dictator who headed Italy's government from 1922 until 1943.

Foreign Relations

NATO. Italy remained strongly committed to NATO and provided the headquarters for its naval and air forces in the Mediterranean. Italy played an increasingly active role in peacekeeping in this region, with a defense treaty with Malta (1981) and the construction of new super-radar installations on Pantelleria, a strategically located island between Sicily and Africa. Moreover, Italy joined the United States, France, and Britain in dispatching peacekeeping forces into war-torn Lebanon. The Italian contingent numbered 1,400 soldiers, as compared with 1,200 U.S. Marines, 2,100 French paratroopers, and 100 British soldiers. The Italians sought to maintain a strictly neutral stance toward the warring Lebanese factions.

Italy supported the U.S. position with regard to deploying new medium-range NATO missiles in Europe to counteract the USSR's SS-20 missiles. When the U.S.-Soviet arms talks in Geneva broke down in mid-November, the Italian parliament approved Craxi's plans to station 112 Cruise missiles in Sicily.

In his tour of seven NATO countries in February 1983, U.S. Vice-President George Bush hailed Italy as "one of the strongest members of our alliance and one of America's closest friends, perhaps the best."

Communist Party Policy. At the national congress of the Italian Communist Party (PCI) in March, Secretary Enrico Berlinguer, who is usually at odds with the Kremlin, denounced the imposition of martial law in Poland and declared flatly that Italian Communists do not want Italy to leave NATO. Unlike other Communist parties in Europe, the Italian one called for reduction of missiles by both East and West. It sought to persuade the Italian government to put off the scheduled installation of missiles in Sicily.

This Communist policy was accelerated after the meeting in May at Williamsburg, VA, of the heads of government of the "Big 7" industrial powers, among whom was Italy's Premier Fanfani. It became one of the major themes of the PCI during the ensuing election campaign. On October 22 the PCI cosponsored with other left-wing, nongovernmental parties and groups a gigantic but peaceful demonstration in Rome against missile deployment.

Craxi's Foreign Policy Debut. On October 16, Premier Craxi attended a conference in Athens of fellow Socialist premiers from Western Europe. He then flew to Washington for talks with President Reagan. Craxi agreed to closer cooperation in the fight against the international drug traffic. He was supportive of U.S. policies regarding missile deployment and the multinational peacekeeping force in Lebanon. But he made it clear that he was not happy with President Reagan's Central American policy. He also expressed concern over the overvalued dollar, which causes Italy to pay dearly for its imports. Italy has an unfavorable balance of trade estimated at almost $6 billion.

Following the October 23 car-bombing attack in Beirut on American and French barracks, Foreign Minister Andreotti flew to Paris for conferences with his French, American, and British counterparts over the crisis in Lebanon. Numerous Italian soldiers have been wounded there. Italy reaffirmed its determination to keep its forces in Lebanon.

When the Reagan administration ordered an invasion of Grenada on October 25, Italy's criticism was muffled, but Italy sided with other NATO countries in backing the UN resolution that "deplored" the American intervention.

The Bulgarian "Connection." Relations with Bulgaria and the USSR worsened in December 1982 when Italian police alleged that Sergei I. Antonov, a Bulgarian airlines official in Rome, assisted the Turkish gunman, Mehmet Ali Agca, in the attempted assassination of Pope John Paul II in St. Peter's Square on May 13, 1981. These allegations were based on Agca's testimony. By October 1983, further investigations seemed to cast some doubt on the veracity of Agca's allegations.

CHARLES F. DELZELL, *Vanderbilt University*

JAPAN

As those of most advanced industrial democracies, Japan's economy during 1983 was slowly emerging from the worldwide recession. On September 16 the Japanese Economic Planning Agency (EPA) announced that inflation-adjusted gross national product (GNP) registered a 0.9% growth in the first quarter (April–June) of the 1983 fiscal year. The rise translated into a real annual growth rate of 3.6%, with estimated GNP at a total of 273,189 billion yen (about $1.2 trillion). Real growth continued to rely heavily on overseas demand, however, and Japan's trade surpluses were a cause of friction with the West.

On the internal political front, the majority Liberal-Democratic Party (LDP) nervously awaited legal resolution of the so-called Lockheed affair. The case, dating from 1976, concerned procurement of aircraft for All Nippon Airways and involved LDP leader and former Prime Minister Kakuei Tanaka. By year's end the long-range effects of his guilty verdict were still not entirely clear.

At the Williamsburg economic summit meeting in May, Prime Minister Yasuhiro Nakasone affirmed efforts to achieve sustained growth without inflation, to maintain free trade, and to nurture North-South cooperation. In his visits to the United States, Nakasone referred to Japanese-American relations as "the cornerstone" of Japan's foreign policy.

Domestic Affairs

Despite Tanaka's legal difficulties, the LDP strengthened its majority in both Diet houses. After the election for the (upper) House of Councillors in June, the LDP held 137 of 252 seats, along with 286 of 511 seats in the (lower) House of Representatives. The Japan Socialist Party (JSP), with 44 seats in the upper and 100 in the lower house, led the opposition, followed by representatives of the Clean Government Party (Komeito), the Democratic Socialist Party (DSP), and the Japan Communist Party (JCP). The June national election was marked by the smallest voter turnout (57%) since World War II and by the appearance of many small, single-issue groups, including the Salaried Workers, the Welfare (for physically handicapped), the Movement for Peace & Democracy (MPD), the Non-Partisan, and the Sex Liberation parties.

Party Politics. In November 1982, Yashuhiro Nakasone became Japan's 17th postwar prime minister, after having won a primary in the LDP and having been selected by the Diet. His cabinet, announced immediately, reflected a delicate equilibrium among LDP factions and support by the powerful Tanaka faction. Shintaro Abe (Fukuda faction) became foreign minister; Noboru Takeshita (Tanaka faction)

UPI

Wearing a formal Japanese kimono, Prime Minister Yasuhiro Nakasone strolls in the garden of his official residence.

became finance minister; Masaharu Gotoda (Tanaka faction) was made chief cabinet secretary; and Susumu Nikaido (Tanaka faction) remained secretary-general of the party. Takeo Fukuda, former prime minister, announced that he would continue to try to eliminate "the Tanaka influence" from government.

The anti-Tanaka movement received a boost on October 11, when the Tokyo District Court found the former prime minister guilty of having accepted $2.1 million in bribes to arrange purchases of Lockheed aircraft. Tanaka was sentenced to four years in prison and to pay $2.1 million in fines, exactly the amount of the reported bribe. He was the first Japanese to be indicted for bribery alleged to have occurred while serving as head of government. Although the decision caused a furor in the public and press, most Japanese had already discounted the guilty verdict. In any case, Tanaka remained free as he appealed to the Tokyo High Court and promised to carry the case to the Supreme Court.

Emperor Hirohito (fourth from left) is joined by his family for a New Year's photograph at Tokyo's Imperial Palace.

In March, support for the Nakasone regime in public opinion polls was down to 29%, the disapproval rate as high as 43%. As the prime minister steadily disassociated himself from Tanaka, however, Nakasone's support rate by late August had risen to 43%, and his nonsupport rate had fallen to 37%. Moreover, in unified local elections held on April 10, LDP-endorsed candidates won 11 of 13 contests for governorships at the prefectural level. The victories included that of incumbent Tokyo Gov. Shunichi Suzuki, who was supported directly by the prime minister.

Of greater significance was the LDP victory in the House of Councillors election. Campaigning began on June 3, with a speech delivered by the prime minister at Shibuya in Tokyo. Nakasone promised to carry out an income tax cut by the end of the year. The 13th upper house poll was held June 26, with half (126) of the seats contested; of these, half (50) of the national constituency seats were decided for the first time with a proportional representation formula. In the poll, the LDP won an additional three seats which, with its 69 seats not up for election, gave the party more than half (137) of the total. The JSP, which had 26 seats up for election, won only 22, so that its total fell to 44. Assuming responsibility for the party's weak showing, Chairman Ichio Asukata became the second successive Socialist leader to resign. Masashi Ishibashi, 58, was elected as his successor.

Ultimately, however, Prime Minister Nakasone faced a deadlock in the Diet, as opposition parties used the Tanaka verdict to attack the LDP. Nakasone was forced to dissolve the Diet and set lower house elections for December 18. In this poll the LDP failed to reach the 270-seat level required to control all committees. Although Nakasone remained prime minister with the support of independents, he now had the difficult task of managing Japan by means of coalition rather than majority politics.

Economy. On March 7 the lower house in plenary session gave its approval to the budget for fiscal 1983 (April 1983 through March 1984). It was an austerity budget with an increase in expenditures of only 1.4%, to a total of 50.4 trillion yen (about $201.5 billion). Defense expenditures were excepted from zero-based budgeting and increased 6.5% over the previous year. Prime Minister Nakasone told a press conference that the decision to raise defense spending was at his own initiative, in view of the importance he attached to Japanese-American relations. Washington had regularly urged Tokyo to increase the quality of its Self-Defense Forces (SDF).

At the end of August, the Finance Ministry received agency requests for fiscal 1984, the first budget drafted under the Nakasone regime. The total came to 52.3 trillion yen, an increase of 3.8% over fiscal 1983. Total revenue for 1984 was projected at only 49.5 trillion yen, which would leave a shortfall of 2.8 trillion yen unless requests were cut. In 1983, Japan carried a debt load (covered by bond issues) which exceeded 100 trillion yen for the first time. The budget, which was being finalized by the Nakasone cabinet, reflected more the stringent line urged by the Finance Ministry than growth-oriented policies advocated by the EPA. A cut of 10% was planned for most sectors, except defense and foreign aid.

In fiscal 1982, the unemployment rate, after seasonal adjustment, averaged 2.5% (a total of 1,430,000 out of work), the highest since records have been kept. Inflation, however, was easing up. The consumer price index for all Japan (seasonally adjusted) stood at 109.7 in May (1980 = 100; May 1982 = 106.9).

Social Issues. During the year Japanese became increasingly alarmed over the incidence of violence in the educational community. In February, Education Ministry officials held a conference with experts to consider the problem of coping with juvenile delinquency, especially among middle-school students. On September 19 the National Police Agency (NPA) reported more than 1,200 cases of school violence in 51 higher and 760 middle

Japanese farmers voice their opposition to a U.S. request to remove import quotas on beef and citrus products.

schools during the first half of 1983, a 26% increase over the corresponding period in 1982.

According to a private report released in September, Japan's population was expected to peak in the year 2010 at about 128,321,000. Those aged 65 or older (9.1% of the total in 1980) would constitute 18.6% of the population in 2010. Projections were based on figures which showed that in 1980, the per-woman birth rate had declined to 1.75, while average life spans were expected to rise to 75 for men and 80 for women by the year 2000.

Natural Disasters. During 1983, Japanese were constantly reminded that they live in a turbulent region of the earth. On May 26 a severe earthquake, which registered 7.7 on the Richter scale, ravaged northern Japan. The NPA reported that, as of May 31, 47 deaths were recorded in Akita, 3 in Hokkaido, and 8 in Aomori prefectures. Many of the casualties occurred when tidal waves swept in from the sea. On August 27 a strong but less damaging quake rumbled across the area from central Japan to southern Kyushu.

Major storms added to Japanese woes. In late July, torrential rains swept over central Japan and claimed the lives of at least 100 persons. On August 17, Typhoon No. 5 battered the Kanto (around Tokyo), Tokai, and Chubu areas, causing widespread damage. On September 28, Typhoon No. 10 swept across northern Kyushu and, according to the NPA, left 8 persons dead, 10 missing, and 47 others injured.

Foreign Affairs

In a policy speech delivered to the 100th session of the Diet on September 10, Prime Minister Nakasone described Japan's efforts toward the "internationalization" of its economy. It is still necessary, he added, to avert trade friction, especially in a climate of rising protectionism abroad. The prime minister also stated that Japan has an international responsibility to enhance economic and technical cooperation with developing countries.

United States. Numerous high-level meetings held in Tokyo and Washington demonstrated how closely linked were the foreign policies of Japan and the United States. Prime Minister Nakasone was in the United States on two occasions (January and May); President Ronald Reagan visited Tokyo in November; Secretary of State George Shultz consulted with Japanese leaders in Tokyo in late January; and Secretary of Defense Weinberger met with Japanese defense agency officials in Washington in August.

On his first visit, shortly after he assumed the premiership, Nakasone reaffirmed to President Reagan the "close alliance" between Japan and the United States. The president praised Japan's recent market-opening steps and defense efforts. The two leaders remained divided, however, as to the matter of Japanese agricultural imports.

Upon his return to Tokyo, Nakasone told the Diet that Japan and the United States might plan joint operations to blockade strategic straits in Northeast Asia. Japanese forces should serve as a "shield," U.S. forces as the "lance," in the "concentric" defense strategies of the two nations. Meanwhile the press interpreted a remark by the prime minister, made in Washington, as suggesting that Japan could become "an unsinkable aircraft carrier" in Asia. Immediately the press and public opinion judged that the outspoken Nakasone had gone too far.

Nonetheless, on August 22, U.S. Defense Secretary Weinberger urged his Japanese counterpart, Kazuo Tanikawa, to consider increases in defense spending for fiscal 1984 in order to undertake defense of sea lanes extending some 1,000 nautical miles into the Pacific.

When Prime Minister Nakasone was again in the United States in May, to attend the seven-nation summit at Williamsburg, he reaffirmed his support for the deployment of nuclear missiles in NATO nations. At the same time he urged President Reagan to continue arms talks with the Soviet Union and called on the USSR to cooperate toward successful conclusion of an agreement.

The other major theme in negotiations between Japan and the United States, as well as European Community (EC) nations, was Japan's continuing and towering trade surplus. In the fiscal year ending March 1983, Japanese exports to the United States were off almost 9%. Imports from Japan's biggest trading partner, however, were also down, by 5%, with a resulting trade imbalance of $12.3 billion.

The Japanese business press claimed that Americans were "obsessed" with threats in the high-technology sector. "Industrial targeting"—publicly sponsored research and development—had been identified as the root-cause of trade problems, exacerbated by the depressed yen as against the dollar. In February, U.S. Trade Representative William Brock had signed an agreement on high technology in Tokyo, but controversy continued as Japan's trade surplus remained high.

JAPAN • Information Highlights

Official Name: Japan.
Location: East Asia.
Area: 14,300 sq mi (370 370 km²).
Population (July 1983): 119,205,000.
Chief Cities (1980 est.): Tokyo, the capital, 11,468,516; Yokohama, 2,773,822; Osaka, 2,648,158; Nagoya, 2,087,884.
Government: Head of state, Hirohito, emperor (acceded Dec. 1926). Head of government, Yasuhiro Nakasone, prime minister (took office Nov. 1982). Legislature—Diet: House of Councillors and House of Representatives.
Monetary Unit: Yen (231.90 yen equal U.S.$1, Dec. 29, 1983).
Economic Index (1982): Industrial Production (1975 = 100), 139.
Foreign Trade (1982 U.S.$): Imports, $131,932,-000,000; exports, $138,911,000,000.

On April 1, President Reagan ordered a tenfold increase in import duties on large motorcycles in a move to curb Japanese sales in the United States. On the automobile front, Japan continued to maintain exports to the United States at the same level as in previous years (1,680,000 units).

Meanwhile, Japanese were exploring a different path. With several companies, including Honda, having already invested in plants in the United States, Toyota Motors on February 17 signed an agreement with General Motors to produce up to 200,000 Toyota-designed passenger cars in an idle GM assembly plant in Fremont, CA.

USSR. Relations with the Soviet Union came to revolve around the death of 28 Japanese passengers aboard Korean Air Lines (KAL) Flight 007, which was shot down September 1 by a Soviet fighter between Hokkaido and Kamchatka. On September 14 in Tokyo, the Foreign Ministry presented to Soviet Ambassador Vladimir Y. Pavlov a demand for a formal apology and compensation. The note was rejected outright. Although Japan did join other nations in suspending flights to and from the USSR until the end of September, Tokyo proceeded cautiously with its protests.

The KAL incident highlighted the major issue in Japanese-Soviet relations—Japan's claims to the "northern territories." The southern Kurile islands, claimed by Japan but occupied by Soviet forces since World War II, were near the site of search operations conducted by joint U.S. Navy and Japanese maritime defense forces to find the missing "black box" recording device from the downed 747.

China, Korea, and Southeast Asia. Beginning February 18, LDP Secretary-General Nikaido made a four-day trip to China in order to offset Chinese concern over Japanese military cooperation with the United States and South Korea. In Peking, Nikaido and Chinese Foreign Minister Wu Xueqian expressed apprehension about possible Soviet transfer of SS-20 missiles to East Asia after a potential agreement with the United States on arms control in Europe. A bilateral ministerial conference, also held in Peking, September 4–6, brought together six cabinet ministers each from Japan and China. An agreement to prevent double taxation was signed, and delegates discussed China's request for Japanese yen loans in fiscal 1984.

In Seoul, January 11–12, Prime Minister Nakasone became the first Japanese head of government to visit South Korea in almost four decades. He signed with President Chun Doo Hwan a long-delayed $4 billion economic aid package. On August 30 in Tokyo, Japan and South Korea wound up a two-day ministerial conference with a promise to extend personnel, intellectual, and cultural exchanges.

ARDATH W. BURKS, *Rutgers University*

JORDAN

Jordan's King Hussein, spurred by American diplomatic pledges, in 1983 again made a major but unsuccessful attempt to define a key role for himself in determining the future status of the Israeli-occupied West Bank. Arab rivalries and the United States' inability to see its proposals enacted were the key reasons for the failure.

West Bank Negotiations. Hussein based his efforts on a September 1982 U.S. proposal calling for Jordan-Israel talks aimed at creating a Palestinian self-government on the West Bank and Gaza in "association" with Jordan. He sought to negotiate a formula by which he could represent West Bank Palestinians. Hussein had applauded the plan when it was announced, but because of a 1974 Arab summit decision to name the Palestine Liberation Organization (PLO) as the Palestinians' sole representative, he could not enter the negotiations without PLO-Arab authorization.

Hussein was motivated by his conviction that unless talks began in 1983, Israel's accelerated settlement activity on the West Bank would end in outright annexation. Moreover, U.S. President Ronald Reagan had pledged that in return for Hussein's participation, Israel would be pressured to "freeze" its settlement activity and the administration would support Jordan's 1983 arms requests before the U.S. Congress.

PLO Talks. Preliminary bargaining with PLO chairman Yasir Arafat actually began shortly after the U.S. plan was unveiled. However, the skepticism surrounding an announcement following mid-December 1982 meetings that pledged "joint political moves at all levels" and a special relationship proved to be well-founded.

Hussein's face-to-face talks with Arafat in January seemed to yield success despite Syrian intervention. Syria opposed the U.S. plan because it did not address the Golan Heights, which Israel had annexed from Syria. How-

A. de Wildenberg/Sygma

Jordan's King Hussein (right) met several times with PLO chairman Yasir Arafat over the future of the West Bank.

ever, Syrian pressure on radical elements in the PLO led to the rejection of the U.S. proposal by the PLO's government-in-exile, the Palestine National Congress, in a late February vote in Algiers.

Arafat's actions also complicated Hussein's attempt. During a March 3 meeting with Saudi Arabia's Prince Bandar ibn Sultan, Hussein learned that Arafat had authorized the Saudis to negotiate a better bargain for the PLO on the West Bank than that envisioned by the U.S. plan.

Attempts to clarify matters during March 7 meetings with Arafat did not produce substantive results. However, April 2–4 discussions produced a preliminary agreement on a formula for a joint Jordanian-Palestinian delegation to

---

JORDAN • Information Highlights

Official Name: Hashemite Kingdom of Jordan.
Location: Southwest Asia.
Area: 37,100 sq mi (96 089 km²).
Population (July 1983 est.): 3,436,000.
Chief Cities (Dec. 1980): Amman, the capital, 694,400; Zarqa, 238,200; Irbid, 121,600.
Government: *Head of state,* Hussein ibn Talal, king (acceded Aug. 1952). *Head of government,* Mudar Badran, prime minister (took office Aug. 1980). *Legislature*—National Consultative Assembly.
Monetary Unit: Dinar (.3715 dinar equals U.S.$1, Dec. 1, 1983).
Gross National Product (1982 est. U.S.$): $3,878,000,000.
Economic Index (1982): *Consumer Prices* (1970 = 100), all items, 206.7; food, 177.2.
Foreign Trade (1982 U.S.$): *Imports, $3,241,000,000; exports, $737,000,000.*

negotiate with Israel. Arafat delayed final agreement for 48 hours, leaving Amman to consult with other PLO leaders. Consensus could not be reached, Arafat did not return to Amman, and, on April 10, Hussein declared he would not take part in any negotiations based on President Reagan's 1982 proposal.

The Reagan administration's failure to deliver either a slowdown in Israeli settlement activity or Congressional support for Jordanian arms requests also contributed to Hussein's decision. Indeed, following the April 10 announcement, Congress made aid conditional on Jordan's diplomatic recognition of Israel. Further, the rejection of a Reagan request for funding a covert, joint U.S.-Jordanian rapid deployment force on November 1 confirmed Hussein's suspicions of U.S. policy.

Economics. Jordan's economic situation continued to improve in 1983. Although defense spending ($560 million) accounts for 25% of the annual budget, export revenues increased by 37% during the year, and foreign aid exceeded $1 billion (U.S.). Trade relations were improved by a month-long, six-nation Asian tour that King Hussein and Queen Noor completed on September 29.

F. NICHOLAS WILLARD

KANSAS

A hot and dry summer that affected late summer and fall crops also influenced the Kansas economy during 1983. With some of the major industries rehiring workers that had been laid off during the recent recession, the small harvests of these crops tended to cancel out the gains.

Agriculture. In the spring of 1983, Kansas farmers agreed to reduce acreage in production by signing up for the U.S. Department of Agriculture's "payment-in-kind" (PIK) subsidy program. Wheat acreage was reduced by more than 12 million acres (1 acre equals 0.40469 hectares), and another 2.3 million acres previously used for corn and grain sorghum also were idled.

The 1983 wheat crop, however, was the second largest recorded in the state, and Kansas led the nation in wheat production. The state Crop and Livestock Reporting Service put the total at 453.6 million bushels (1 bushel equals 35.239 liters) for a record-setting 42 bushels per acre yield. In spite of signups for the PIK program, total production from the 10.8 million acres harvested was down only 2% from the 1982 record crop of 462 million bushels from 13.2 million acres.

Drought conditions, which made July, August, and September the driest third quarter since record keeping began in 1887, adversely affected the production of dry land corn and sorghum. The state's corn crop yield was esti-

KANSAS • Information Highlights
Area: 82,277 sq mi (213 097 km^2).
Population (1982 est.): 2,408,000.
Chief Cities (1980 census): Topeka, the capital, 115,266; Wichita, 279,835; Kansas City, 161,148.
Government (1983): *Chief Officers*—governor, John Carlin (D); lt. gov., Tom Docking (D). *Legislature* —Senate, 40 members; House of Representatives, 125 members.
State Finances (fiscal year 1982): *Revenues,* $2,751,000,000; *expenditures,* $2,634,000,000.
Personal Income (1982): $28,325,000,000; per capita, $11,765.
Labor Force (July 1983): *Nonagricultural wage and salary earners,* 902,100; *unemployed,* 68,000 (5.7% of total force).
Education: *Enrollment* (fall 1981)—public elementary schools, 282,014; public secondary, 127,895; colleges and universities (1982), 141,661. *Public school expenditures* (1981–82), $1,192,482,000.

mated at 75.6 million bushels, as compared with 140 million harvested in 1982. Irrigated crops survived the drought, while unirrigated ones were largely destroyed.

Legislation. Meeting in the midst of the fiscal year in which Gov. John Carlin (D) ordered state agencies to cut their allocated budgets by 4%, the major concern of the 1983 legislative session was finances. A severence tax on oil, gas, coal, and salt was passed after unsuccessful attempts in previous years. The new tax was expected to raise more than $98 million in revenue in its first year.

After a five-year impasse between Governor Carlin and the legislature, the 1983 session dealt with the problem of a deteriorating highway system. An accelerated program of road repair and improvement was approved, with funding to come from an increase in the motor-fuels tax and transfers from other funds.

Other legislation provided for increases in the income tax on higher incomes and in liquor and cigarette taxes and for the creation of a commission that will help develop educational and economic development programs through advanced technology.

Environment. Chemical leaks in a nearby spring at the state's only hazardous waste dump, the Furley site near Wichita, were of concern to Kansans in 1983. Congressman Dan Glickman, a Wichita Democrat, requested the U.S. Environmental Protection Agency (EPA) to conduct a thorough test of the groundwater in the area. This request, made when the owners of the site were attempting to reopen it after it had been closed since 1981, resulted in tests that showed evidence of dioxin contamination. Congressman Glickman advocated that the site be closed permanently.

Governor Docking. Robert B. Docking (D), the only Kansas governor elected to serve four two-year terms (1967–74), died at his home in Arkansas City on October 8.

PATRICIA A. MICHAELIS
Kansas State Historical Society

KENTUCKY

Kentucky in 1983 struggled to recover from the effects of the economic recession and to improve its educational system. It also elected its first woman governor.

Economic Conditions. Kentucky's economy is heavily dependent on agriculture, and a prolonged drought in the summer of 1983 was damaging not only to the farmers but also to the economic health of the state. It was estimated that the tobacco crop would be only half, and the corn crop only two thirds, of the totals produced in 1982.

Kentucky lagged behind many other states in its recovery from the recession. The major manufacturing plants in Louisville and other large cities recalled workers at a slow pace. Coal production and prices continued to lag, in part because of the problems facing the national steel industry. Efforts being taken by the federal government to reduce the effects of acid rain also threatened the coal industry.

As a consequence of these problems, state revenue continued to lag behind projections, and the administration of Gov. John Y. Brown was forced to impose cutbacks on spending already budgeted for the 1983–84 fiscal year.

Education. As Kentuckians began to realize that the state faced major long-term economic problems and needed to attract more industry, attention was increasingly devoted to weaknesses in the educational system. A number of national studies in 1983 had emphasized the state's weaknesses in education. Kentucky ranked low in levels of funding for education, teachers salaries, and student rankings on test scores; and it ranked near the bottom in the proportions of students graduating from high school and of those going to college.

During the year a number of steps were taken to raise educational standards. The state increased the high school curriculum requirements; the public universities raised admission

UPI

Lt. Gov. Martha Layne Collins (D), a 46-year-old former teacher, was elected Kentucky's first woman governor.

requirements; and a number of proposals were developed for testing the competence of both students and teachers. The Council on Higher Education grappled with the questions involving the high costs and possible duplication of professional programs such as medicine, dentistry, and law in the state universities.

Politics. Educational issues played a major role in election campaigns, with a number of programs being proposed to improve standards, although candidates were cautious in their statements about higher levels of spending for education.

The Democratic gubernatorial primary on May 24 was an extremely close three-way contest. Lt. Gov. Martha Layne Collins defeated Louisville Mayor Harvey Sloane by only 4,500 votes. Governor Brown launched a belated campaign on behalf of a member of his cabinet, Grady Stumbo, but Stumbo finished a close third. The Republican Party, after a prolonged search, found a major candidate to run for governor: Jim Bunning, a state senator and former major league pitcher.

In the general election on November 8, Martha Layne Collins won by a margin of about 55%, becoming the first woman governor in the state's history and only the third woman in the country's history to be elected governor without succeeding her husband to the office. Democratic candidates easily won all other statewide offices. For the second year in a row, voters in Louisville and Jefferson County narrowly voted against a plan to merge those two units of government.

Malcolm E. Jewell, *University of Kentucky*

KENTUCKY · Information Highlights

Area: 40,409 sq mi (104 659 km²).
Population (1982 est.): 3,667,000.
Chief Cities (1980 census): Frankfort, the capital, 25,973; Louisville, 298,840; Lexington-Fayette, 204,165.
Government (1983): *Chief Officers*—governor, Martha Layne Collins (D); lt. gov., Steven Beshear. *General Assembly*—Senate, 38 members; House of Representatives, 100 members.
State Finances (fiscal year 1982): *Revenues,* $4,885,000,000; *expenditures,* $4,726,000,000.
Personal Income (1981): $32,762,000,000; per capita, $8,934.
Labor Force (July 1983): *Nonagricultural wage and salary earners,* 1,149,800; *unemployed,* 186,200 (11.4% of total force).
Education: *Enrollment* (fall 1981)—public elementary schools, 458,781; public secondary, 199,569; colleges and universities (1981–82), 144,154. *Public school expenditures* (1981–82), $1,083,878,000.

KENYA

A surprise national election and continued political and economic repercussions from the attempted coup d'etat in 1982 dominated events in Kenya in 1983.

Elections. Hoping to consolidate his power and purge "disloyal elements," President Daniel arap Moi dissolved parliament and ordered national elections for September 1983. With Moi's Kenya African National Union (KANU) the only legal party, and he the only presidential candidate, the outcome was foregone. However, there were many contests between KANU members in most districts, and final returns showed that three cabinet ministers had been defeated. With KANU's monopoly on national power assured from the start, elections centered on local concerns and individual personalities. Only 50% of the eligible voters went to the polls.

Moi's Consolidation of Power. Even before the election, President Moi moved to assure his control of KANU and of Kenya. Feeling insecure because of the attempted coup and still unpopular among the dominant Kikuyu tribe, Moi removed the powerful minister of constitutional affairs and his chief rival, Charles Njonjo, in July 1983. The nominal charge was a plausible accusation of irregularities in Njonjo's handling of foreign-aid money, and a possible link to a South African company. In reality, Moi was displacing a popular and powerful rival, who might have been involved in the coup attempt as well. As a result of Njonjo's fall, Vice-President Mwai Kibaki, a leader of the Kikuyu and a close ally of Moi, became the second most powerful figure in the country

and Moi's possible successor. In a further consolidation of power following the elections, Moi appointed a new cabinet, with even less power to the Kikuyus.

Coup Aftermath. President Moi began freeing many Air Force officers and men charged with complicity in the 1982 coup attempt. However, nine mutineers were sentenced to death and more than 900 were imprisoned for up to 25 years for their role in the uprising. Many later were amnestied on condition of being confined to their rural home villages. The alleged leader of the coup, Pvt. Hezekiah Ochuka, was granted political asylum in Tanzania, further straining relations between the two countries.

Moi also suspended classes at Nairobi University, charging that many students took part in pro-coup riots and that lecturers had abetted the revolt by criticism of the new one-party state and government corruption. KANU also began publishing its own party newspaper, *The Kenya Times,* as an alternative to the two main papers, the *Nation* and the *Standard,* which were both accused of "negitavism" and "sensationalism" in reporting on the coup attempt. Though the university was reopened, Moi continued his crackdown by confining longtime opposition leader Oginga Odinga to his rural hometown and by arresting Odinga's son, Raila, for treason. The president also went so far as to accuse a foreign power (most likely meaning Britain) with being behind the revolt. Though totally without foundation, the charge indicated the depth to which the Air Force mutiny had shaken the stability of Kenya.

Economic Affairs. Kenya's economy continued to decline in 1983. The shilling was devalued by 15% in late 1982, and the country was forced to ask the International Monetary Fund (IMF) for a $190 million loan as well as a standby credit of $175.95 million in special drawing rights for 18 months. Despite a budget deficit of $550 million, pay for army officers was raised 30% and an eighth year of free primary education was announced.

ROBERT GARFIELD, *DePaul University*

President Daniel arap Moi called parliamentary elections to purge his one-party nation of forces disloyal to him.
Wide World

KOREA

Wide World

In November, President Reagan inspected the U.S. Army outpost at the demilitarized zone separating North and South Korea. The president called U.S. soldiers at the zone "the front line of freedom."

The year 1983 saw continued tensions between the two Koreas and a series of jarring shocks. In September, Soviet fighter planes attacked a Korean Air Lines passenger jet that had strayed over Soviet territory. All 269 people aboard were killed. On October 9, three North Korean agents killed 17 South Korean officials who were accompanying President Chun Doo Hwan on a state visit to Burma.

The year ended on a more tranquil note, however, as President Ronald Reagan visited Seoul in mid-November and renewed pledges of U.S. political, economic, and military support. He sought to reduce regional tensions by saying that the United States was prepared to take part in discussions with North Korea in any forum in which the South was equally represented. He also called attention to human-rights violations in the South.

South Korea

The shooting down of the Korean Air Lines jet and the massacre of Korean officials in Rangoon, Burma, were the most dramatic shocks suffered by the Republic of Korea in 1983, but there were other disturbing events as well.

Politics. Major banking scandals focused attention on corruption in high places. Student demonstrations in Seoul and other cities challenged President Chun's authoritarian regime. Tension remained high between North and South Korean forces facing each other along the demilitarized zone. The South Korean economy was recovering from the recent recession, with export industries leading the way. But some of Korea's major customers, including the United States, were becoming more protective of their own industries. Korean economists feared that this could threaten the nation's recovery.

President Chun Doo Hwan came to power in South Korea in 1980 following the assassi-

nation of President Park Chung Hee. Chun, also a former general, has ruled South Korea in the authoritarian tradition of Park. Although he released some political prisoners early in 1983, many dissidents were jailed or placed under house arrest before President Reagan's November visit. Only one dissident was permitted to meet President Reagan.

Economy. The year was a good one for the Korean economy. High growth and low inflation rates seemed to mark a full recovery from the severe recession. In 1980, the growth rate was negative, and inflation soared to more than 28%. In 1983, inflation was down to 2%, and the growth rate was 9.6% for the first half of the year and was expected to exceed 7% for the full year.

Most sectors of the economy did reasonably well, but there was considerable nervousness because Koreans knew they were entering a period of tighter government budgets. The 1970s had been a period of rapid industrial expansion with an ever-broadening range of products from textiles to super tankers being produced by Koreans for export. During most of the decade, South Korea found it easy to borrow funds abroad. South Korea entered the decade of the 1980s with a huge foreign debt that totaled $38 billion (U.S.) late in 1983.

In the recent worldwide recession, foreign markets and sources of foreign capital disappeared. During 1981 and 1982, South Korea, like its northern neighbor, was forced to resort to huge public works projects to keep its people employed and to prevent a serious depression. In 1983, South Korea's export industries benefited from a revival of overseas demand. Through October 1983, merchandise exports were 8.7% ahead of the same period of 1982. However, one formerly lucrative source of income failed to rebound. South Korean construction firms have come to rely heavily on major contracts in the oil-rich countries of the

SOUTH KOREA · Information Highlights

Official Name: Republic of Korea.
Location: Northeastern Asia.
Area: 38,190 sq mi (98 913 km²).
Population (July 1983 est.): 41,287,000.
Chief City (1982 est.): Seoul, the capital, 9,074,127.
Government: *Head of state,* Chun Doo Hwan, president (formally inaugurated March 1981). *Head of government,* Kim Sang Hyup, prime minister (appointed June 24, 1982). *Legislature*—National Assembly.
Monetary Unit: Won (783.1 won equal U.S.$1, July 1983).
Gross Domestic Product (1982): $68,419,000,000.
Economic Indexes (1982): *Consumer Prices* (1970 = 100), all items, 586.4; food, 672.0. *Industrial Production* (1975 = 100), 248.
Foreign Trade (1982 U.S.$): *Imports,* $24,251,000,000; *exports,* $21,853,000,000.

Middle East. As these countries have fallen on somewhat leaner times in the 1980s, the remittances of Korean firms and Korean workers from this region have declined.

South Korea now has the dubious honor of having the fourth-largest foreign debt of any nation. However, bankers consider South Korea creditworthy because it has maintained a satisfactory ratio of reserves. Yet while South Korea has continued to obtain foreign loans when it needs them, it has had to pay higher interest rates because competition for scarce capital has become more intense. The fact that Korea's neighbor, the Philippines, had to reschedule its foreign debt in 1983 produced a negative impact on bankers who also hold Korea's debt.

The South Korean government began in 1983 to institute a policy of freezing most government expenditures in an effort to hold down price inflation. South Korea spends a third of its budget on defense and another 22% on education. These items will be allowed to increase by only 2 or 3% in 1984. Government officials will receive no pay raises, and social services will be funded at a very low level. The government will spend its economic development funds on projects that encourage growth in related areas of the economy. Such projects include the sports complex for the 1988 Summer Olympics, which will be held in South Korea, and the expansion of Kimpo Airport to encourage tourism.

Foreign Relations. The South Korean government continued to broaden its range of international contacts in 1983. This policy was aimed at gaining the widest possible recognition of South Korea as a legitimate state and reducing international support for North Korea. Foreign Minister Lee Bum Suk was the main architect of this policy and South Korea's most effective diplomat. He was one of the persons killed in the Rangoon massacre. His successor, Lee Won Kyung, was believed to be unlikely to press for better ties with the Communist nations until the recent traumas have passed. But he and Chun would continue to court the Western and nonaligned nations.

Ironically, the massacre also brought much sympathy and support to South Korea at the expense of North Korea. The Burmese government announced that its investigation proved that North Korea carried out the massacre. Burma, which had been closer to Pyongyang than Seoul, severed diplomatic relations and withdrew diplomatic recognition from North Korea—an unusually drastic step.

A number of other nations, including Japan, reduced their contacts with North Korea. President Reagan's policy, announced during his visit to Seoul, was to support South Korea but to try to prevent tensions in the region from getting worse. He thus expressed willingness to allow contact between U.S. and North Korean officials, but this in no way implied an interest in establishing diplomatic relations with the North.

Japan has been virtually allied with South Korea for the past two decades, despite the residue of bad feeling between the two peoples that remains from the 1910–1945 period when Japan ruled Korea as a colony. Japan and South Korea are both allied militarily with the United States, but Japanese military officials are still viewed with suspicion by the Koreans. Japan and South Korea depend heavily on one

UPI

Lee Kil Woo, 4, (left) and Ahn Ji Sook, 7, traveled to the United States with President and Mrs. Reagan. After undergoing open heart surgery and receiving a visit from the first lady, the children were to return to South Korea in time for Christmas.

another as trading partners. Japan's Prime Minister Yasuhiro Nakasone visited Seoul in January. At year's end, Japan was in the process of approving a new multibillion yen loan to aid South Korea's development.

North Korea

The Democratic People's Republic of Korea (North Korea) faced a narrowing range of choices in 1983. This was partly due to external forces and partly the result of actions by the North Korean leaders themselves. The unsettled state of relations between the Soviet Union, China, and the United States and the worldwide shortage of development capital added to North Korea's difficulty in gaining international support.

Politics. In the category of self-created problems, President Kim Il Sung's decision to name his son, Kim Jong Il, as his successor was a form of nepotism that was impossible to justify in terms of Marxist ideology. There was undoubtedly some hesitancy on the part of the other Communist states to give the arrangement their stamp of approval. The Chinese, however, apparently decided it was more important to enhance their influence with Kim Il Sung than to express disapproval of his effort to create a family dynasty. According to press reports, Kim Jong Il was invited to China for an unannounced visit in June 1983.

Foreign Relations. The North Korean government continued to pursue its major aim of gaining the widest possible recognition of its legitimacy at the expense of its rival, South Korea. But in 1983, this quest encountered a series of stumbling blocks. South Korea was chosen as the site of the 1988 Summer Olympics, despite the most intensive lobbying efforts by North Korea to block or reverse the decision. The Inter-Parliamentary Union (IPU) also chose to hold its next meeting in Seoul. Since the speaker of the Finnish parliament was also president of the IPU, the North Korean ambassador to Finland did everything he could to reverse the decision. Finally, he presented a bouquet of flowers to the Finnish leader's wife with $5,000 concealed among the roses. The bribe was refused. North Korean diplomats have also been expelled from Finland, Sweden, and Denmark for trying to sell luxury items and narcotics on the black market to earn foreign exchange for their government.

Following the September 1983 bombing incident in Rangoon by three North Korean officers, other Asian nations—including Thailand, Japan, and the Philippines—followed Burma's lead and denounced North Korea and reduced their commercial or political ties with the country. President Chun of South Korea charged that North Korean agents had previously tried to kill him when he visited the Philippines and Canada. Japanese press reports suggested that the bombing would have had to be authorized at the highest level in North Korea.

Tension between the two Koreas had been high before the Rangoon incident. In August 1983, South Korea claimed that it had sunk what they described as a North Korean spy boat and killed four North Korean frogmen in South Korean waters. The North accused the South of "armed provocation." After the Rangoon bombing incident, the forces of both Koreas were placed on alert, and officers on both sides reportedly wanted to attack each other. The influence of the United States and Japan and quite possibly China helped to dissuade the two Koreas from military action. Japan has neither diplomatic ties nor civil aviation links with North Korea, but after the Rangoon bombing it announced that meetings between Japanese and North Korean officials would cease and charter flights to Pyongyang might be halted. According to press reports, Japan and China also established a formal channel to coordinate their responses to increased tensions on the Korean peninsula.

Economy. The sanctions imposed on North Korea by other nations after the Rangoon bombing had a limited impact on North Korea's economy since Pyongyang's economic and political ties abroad were already minimal. Burma was one country with which North Korea had been increasing its trade. This ended following the terrorist attack, and South Korea may take over some projects begun by North Korea in Burma.

Japan was potentially North Korea's most valuable non-Communist economic partner, but Japan has been generally unwilling to provide new investment capital to North Korea since the latter began to have serious difficulties paying its debts in 1975. North Korea's total foreign debt stood at about $2 billion at year's end.

North Korea continued to tinker with the organization of its economic system. The most recent reorganizations have been described as improving efficiency by putting party leaders over economic technocrats.

PETER A. POOLE

NORTH KOREA · Information Highlights

Official Name: Democratic People's Republic of Korea.
Location: Northeastern Asia.
Area: 47,000 sq mi (121 730 km²).
Population (July 1983 est.): 18,802,000.
Chief Cities (July 1980 est.): Pyongyang, the capital, 1,445,000; Hamhung, 780,000.
Government: *Head of state,* Kim Il Sung, president (nominally since Dec. 1972; actually in power since May 1948). *Head of government,* Li Jong Ok, premier (took office Dec. 1977). *Legislature* (unicameral)—Supreme People's Assembly. The Korea Workers' (Communist) Party: General Secretary, Kim Il Sung.
Gross National Product (1982 U.S.$): $18,766,-000,000.

LABOR

In 1983 there just were not enough jobs to go around. All over the free world, unemployment took its toll, leaving millions of workers and their families with physical and emotional wounds as well as economic losses. Many others lived the year in fear of possible layoffs.

In many countries, governments were forced to cut social-welfare programs and raise taxes. In countries where labor-management relations are handled through collective bargaining, the ever-present reservoir of hungry job seekers undermined union strength.

United States

The beginning of an economic recovery in the United States raised full-time employment to 75,047,000. By October, 3,684,000 more workers were gainfully employed than a year earlier. Another 18,226,000 were working part-time, but for about one third of them the cutback was involuntary.

Business conditions, an uncontrolled flood of imports, the ever-widening use of automated equipment, and continued high interest rates left 9,896,000 U.S. workers jobless. Another 1,457,000 were reported by the Bureau of Labor Statistics to be so discouraged that they had dropped out of the job market.

Faced with problems that could never be handled through collective bargaining, American union leaders turned more attention to alternate solutions.

Political Action. Breaking with a century-old tradition, the AFL-CIO voted for the first time at its October convention to endorse a candidate for the U.S. presidency before the primary elections. The near-unanimous choice was former Vice-President Walter Mondale (D), a former senator from Minnesota, a protégé of the late Sen. Hubert H. Humphrey, and a lifelong champion of labor. The endorsement followed a recommendation by the AFL-CIO General Board, the result of extensive discussions, soundings at union meetings, some mail balloting, straw votes, and polling of union members. The endorsement brought to the Mondale candidacy financial resources and a pool of campaign workers in every one of the nation's 50 states.

The convention also committed the AFL-CIO to undertake in 1984 the "greatest registration and get-out-the-vote campaign." Effective political action, the resolution stated, is necessary for the achievement of AFL-CIO economic and social goals that no longer can be achieved through collective bargaining.

For 1984 and 1985 the convention voted two-cent increases in the monthly per capita payments to the AFL-CIO by affiliated unions to finance voter-registration activities, urban affairs, grass-roots lobbying, and internal communications. By July 1985 the federation's 98 unions will be paying 35 cents per month per member, on a total membership of 14 million.

Other policies voted at the biennial convention covered a national commitment to full employment, expanded job training and retraining programs, labor-law reform, women's rights

Hot weather did not prevent communication workers from picketing during their nationwide strike, August 7–28.

LABOR / SPECIAL REPORT

Job Search and Retraining

With unemployment in the United States unusually high in 1982 and 1983, public and private institutions have developed various programs to help the unemployed find jobs. These efforts include dissemination of information about job vacancies, techniques to find employment, and job retraining. General concern that a significant portion of the laid off workers would have to change occupations and industries generated particular interest in job retraining. In fact, most forecasters indicated that many of the workers who lost their jobs in durable manufacturing industries would never return to their workplace.

The first step to help unemployed workers is to provide them with information about job vacancies. The U.S. government, in cooperation with the states, has maintained job-service agencies that attempt to match idle workers with employers seeking to fill job vacancies. Most employers, however, do not register their job vacancies with the public job-service agencies. Private organizations complement the work of the public agencies, but unemployed workers frequently cannot afford to avail themselves of the services because of the fees charged by the private organizations.

Knowledge about job vacancies is only one step toward finding a job. Many displaced workers do not have salable skills to acquire a job. Some may lack a basic education, including proficiency in reading, writing, and arithmetic. Very few have experience in job search. They may lack the skills to develop a résumé and be unaware of the best way to sell themselves to a prospective employer. These unemployed may be offered job counseling, including information about skill requirements for job openings and advice regarding the interview process. Many others need occupational skill training.

Finally, some unemployed workers who have skills may find themselves stranded in labor surplus areas where there is no demand for their skills, even though other areas experience shortages of such skilled workers. The best solution to the problems of these workers is relocation. Such migration may prove costly not only to the displaced workers who experience difficulties in uprooting themselves and their families, but also wasteful of social capital—schools, churches, and other public facilities—which may go underutilized in older communities at the same time that growing regions are forced to invest resources in such facilities.

A number of institutions have been established to provide for the needs of dislocated workers. Preventive measures are clearly the most desirable, and many employers provide retraining for their employees as products are abandoned or technology improved. Training or retraining ranges from a few hours devoted to orientation to special instruction that may last as long as a year or more. Information on the extent of retraining offered by private employers is scarce. The American Society for Training and Development estimated in 1983 that private company outlays for training amounted to roughly $7 billion (U.S.), but no separate accounting of retraining expenditures is available. Other surveys by the Bureau of National Affairs found that one of every seven companies contacted had retraining programs. Most large companies with 10,000 or more employees provide some retraining for management or white-collar personnel. Training or retraining programs for manual workers are much rarer.

In 1983 a great deal of occupational training was provided by 9,000 noncollegiate postsecondary schools. About three fourths of the 2 million students enrolled in these schools attended proprietary institutions, and the balance were enrolled in nonprofit and publicly supported schools. Public state and local junior colleges also were offering occupational training. The proportion of enrollees in these schools who were age 25 years or older has been rising. According to the latest figures, the older students accounted for more than a third of the 4 million students enrolled in these schools. No doubt, a great many were undergoing retraining or preparing themselves for new occupations. In addition several states have established programs for dislocated workers. The California Economic Adjustment Team is the best publicized of these programs.

The federal Job Training Partnership Act of 1982 made specific provision for assisting displaced workers. Workers terminated from their jobs or notified of pending layoffs and who are unlikely to return to the industry or occupation, and long-term unemployed with limited employment potential, are eligible for assistance. States that wish to participate in the program must match the federal government's contributions, but the matching requirements for states with above average unemployment are reduced by 10% for each percentage point that the state unemployment rate is above the national average. Federal appropriations for fiscal 1983 reached $110 million and have been used for establishing job-search clubs at a cost of some $700 per participant and for retraining.

SAR A. LEVITAN

(including enactment of the Equal Rights Amendment), civil rights, and increased federal aid to education.

The convention renewed its call for a National Industrial Policy and the creation of a tripartite board of government, management, and labor representatives to revive sick industries and support promising new industries.

The delegates asked government support of $9 and $11 billion a year to repair and maintain the nation's highways, bridges, water supply systems, and waste-water treatment facilities. This proposal originated with a panel of leaders from management and labor headed by Exxon Chairman C. C. Garvin, Jr., and AFL-CIO President Lane Kirkland. Professor John T. Dunlop of Harvard University coordinated the panel's deliberations.

Collective Bargaining. Negotiated wage settlements during the first ten months of 1983 were the lowest in the 15 years for which the U.S. Department of Labor has collected statistics.

Major collective-bargaining agreements provided for an average pay raise of 1.7% for the first contract year, compared with 9.1% the last time the same parties bargained. About one fifth of those affected took wage cuts, and another fifth got no specific wage increases. For most workers that meant an actual decline in real wages after price increases were taken into account. The Consumer Price Index for October was 2.9% above a year earlier, the smallest rise in years. Weekly earnings for nonsupervisory employees averaged $286.18 in October, up $16.91 from a year earlier.

Overall, the process of wage reductions slowed during 1983, being limited mostly to industries hurt by imports or by low-wage competition from deregulated industries.

The year began with auto workers at Chrysler regaining some of the wage concessions made two years earlier to keep that corporation afloat. On Labor Day the company and the UAW reached agreement on a new, 26-month contract.

At the Ford River Rouge steel plant in Dearborn, MI, workers agreed to a 20% cut in wages and benefits over three years to avoid closing mills that were losing $12 million a month. In return, Ford management was obligated to spend $200 million over several years on new equipment to become more competitive in world markets.

The year's largest work stoppage saw some 400,000 members of the Communications Workers and International Brotherhood of Electrical Workers strike American Telephone & Telegraph Co. (AT&T) for three weeks in August. The settlement raised wages 16.4% over three years and committed AT&T to retrain workers whose jobs are threatened by technological change. Those close to retirement will get extra pay to ease the transition.

One of the year's longest strikes—206 days—ended when workers at Caterpillar Tractor Corp. in Illinois accepted a three-year contract freezing wages but continuing a quarterly cost-of-living adjustment. The contract provided for profit sharing.

J. P. Stevens & Co., a bitter foe of organized labor before signing a union contract three years earlier, agreed in October to pay the Amalgamated Clothing & Textile Workers $1.2 million to resolve all unfair labor charges under federal law. Another $200,000 will go to workers hurt by company violations.

A nationwide strike by drivers and terminal employees of Greyhound Lines Inc., which operates 60% of U.S. intercity bus mileage, shut down operations November 3. The company, which had asked employees to accept a nearly 10% pay cut, replaced the strikers and resumed service two weeks later—to sometimes violent resistance. On December 20 the 12,000 striking employees voted overwhelmingly in favor of a three-year, compromise pact.

Organizing. The move toward fewer, stronger unions continued in 1983. The 160-year-old Hat, Cap & Millinery Workers affiliated with the Amalgamated Clothing & Textile Workers. The National Association of Government Employees merged with the Service Employees International Union. The Granite Cutters Association merged with the Tile, Marble, Terrazo Finishers & Shopmen. And the Graphic Arts International Union merged with the International Printing & Graphic Communications Workers Union to become the Graphics Communications International Union.

Some key industrial unions reported big losses in membership. The United Auto Workers (UAW) showed a decline from 1.5 million members in the mid-1970s to 1.1 million in 1983. The Steelworkers Union reported a 43% loss from 1.3 million in the late 1970s to 750,000. And the Machinists & Aerospace Workers were down to 600,000, almost 30% below its peak.

Unions active in the public sector, however, were still growing. Among them were the State, County & Municipal Employees, the Communications Workers, the Service Employees, the Teachers and the Postal Unions.

Leadership. Four of the largest U.S. unions picked new presidents in 1983. The National Education Association (NEA) elected an Alexandria, VA, high school teacher, Mary Hatwood Futrell, 43, to replace Willard McGuire, who was barred from succeeding himself after two 2-year terms. The International Brotherhood of Teamsters chose Jackie Presser, 57, its Cleveland, OH, vice-president, to replace Roy L. Williams, who resigned after being convicted in a criminal case involving an attempt to bribe a U.S. senator.

The United Auto Workers elected Owen Bieber, 53, a vice-president (General Motors

In May, Owen Bieber (left) *was elected to succeed Douglas Fraser* (right) *as president of the United Auto Workers. Bieber, 53, had been UAW vice-president.*

UPI

Department), to succeed Douglas A. Fraser, who retired. (*See* BIOGRAPHY.)

The United Steelworkers named its secretary, Lynn Williams, 59, a Canadian, as acting temporary president to succeed Lloyd McBride, who died in November. A referendum election was called for March 29, 1984.

Bankruptcies. Of serious concern to U.S. union leaders was management's increasing use of the Federal Bankruptcy Act to nullify union contracts. Corporations that lacked neither cash reserves nor positive net worth used Chapter 11 of the act to abrogate collective agreements, cut wages and staff, and cancel other commitments. Twenty-two employers—including Continental Airlines and Wilson Meat Packing—were known to have filed for bankruptcy for this purpose.

A bipartisan bill to deal with such use of the bankruptcy act was passed by the Senate but failed to come to a vote in the House of Representatives.

Solidarity Day. On September 5, Labor Day was observed with parades and rallies in 151 communities. An estimated 1.3 million participated.

International

After an absence of nearly 15 years, AFL-CIO delegates, led by President Lane Kirkland, attended the 1983 World Congress of the International Confederation of Free Trade Unions (ICFTU) at Oslo, Norway, in June. The organization has 136 affiliates in 96 countries, representing 85 million workers.

The 1983 World Congress adopted resolutions dealing with unemployment, poverty, women's work, technological change, trade-union rights in the private and public sectors, and multinational corporations.

Noting that there had been 130 armed conflicts in the world since the end of World War II, the Congress adopted a statement on Peace, Security and Disarmament calling for:

• immediate steps toward balanced disarmament under effective international control but rejecting unilateral disarmament and a nuclear freeze;

• rejection of the use of force to resolve political and economic problems;

• support for détente between East and West;

• immediate cessation of nuclear weapon production and testing;

• bilateral agreements between the United States and Soviet Union for reduction, withdrawal, and production of missiles of all kinds.

Canada. The Canadian Labour Congress (CLC) blamed record unemployment, bankruptcies, and home and farm foreclosures on the government's "blind insistence to fight inflation by deliberately causing a depression."

In March the CLC adopted its own Economic Recovery Act, calling for increased investment in low-cost housing, transportation, and reforestation; tax cuts for low and modest income earners; and extension of unemployment benefits by 26 weeks for those who have exhausted their benefits.

Wage settlements during the first half of 1983 were generally lower than in 1982.

Legislation hostile to union organization and activities was introduced in several provincial legislatures and was fought by the CLC.

The new Canadian Federation of Labour (CFL), representing ten building-trades unions with 215,000 members, moved its Ottawa headquarters to Sparks Street across from Parliament Hill. In its first full year, the CFL established provincial councils in Prince Edward Island and Alberta and developed a Canada-wide education program for union leaders. Unlike the CLC, which is wedded to the New Democratic Party, the CFL is nonpartisan in its politics.

Great Britain. Despite staggering unemployment, which usually swings voters to its side, the Labour Party took a drubbing in the June parliamentary elections. Despite strong union support, the Labour Party got 20% fewer votes than in 1979. Its platform of more nationalization, larger social programs, and unilateral disarmament proved unpopular. By contrast, the new Liberal-Social Democratic Alliance—the latter former members of the Labour Party—scored heavily in total votes but not in parliamentary seats. It ran second to the Conservatives and ahead of Labour in 312 constituencies out of 630.

The lost election notwithstanding, both the Labour Party and the Trades Union Congress at their annual September convention reaffirmed their opposition to the government's defense policies and to U.S nuclear bases in Great Britain.

Unemployment cut union membership. The total number of members dropped nearly 500,000 to 10.5 million, still more than 50% of the labor force. Wage settlements were modest despite improvements in productivity and absenteeism. Strikes were fewer, occurring mostly in public services.

The Trade Union Reform Act, sponsored by the Conservatives, led to a national confrontation with the printing trades union. All national newspapers were shut down for two days, after which a court ordered that assets of the National Graphical Association be seized to pay a fine of $225,000 for illegal picketing.

The reform act, among other things, requires a secret ballot vote before a strike can be called, a secret ballot to elect union officers at least every five years, and a secret ballot to renew authorization for political funds at least every ten years.

France. Unemployment moved back to the double-digit level during 1983. After a sweeping program of nationalization, expansion of social services, and protective labor legislation, trade and budget deficits forced the Socialist-led government into austerity measures. In 1982, nationalized industries had lost $1.4 billion (U.S.); 1983 promised still higher losses. The new program included the third devaluation of the franc since the Socialists came to power, restrictions on government spending, and increases in prices and taxes. The social security program was cut, a 10% surcharge tax was levied on personal income, and all individuals were required to lend the government 10% of the previous year's income tax as compulsory savings. Wage increases during the first nine months barely exceeded the rise in consumer prices.

Italy. Ending 38 years of rule by right and center parties, a Socialist, Bettino Craxi, became head of a five-party coalition government. Economic conditions forced the new government to introduce an austerity budget including higher taxes and cuts in expenditures for health, pensions, disability, and other welfare programs. The cuts were opposed by the trade unions and the left-wing parties.

Earlier, after long and difficult negotiations, labor and management agreed on the *scala mobile*, an automatic cost-of-living formula. Future adjustments would be 18% less than actual increases in the index. Negotiated wage increases above the *scala mobile* are limited to 100,000 lire a year. Working hours are to be reduced in two steps from 40 to 39 hours by 1985.

Federal Republic of Germany. The year 1983 was a difficult one for labor in West Germany. Unemployment ranged from 8.6% to 10.4%. Wage settlements were modest, slightly below the increases in living costs. The government continued to cut social programs. Relations between government and unions were tense, limited to occasional informal meetings. The unions were preparing to press for a cut in working hours to provide employment.

Sweden. To deal with rising unemployment, a budget deficit, and inflation, the government raised taxes—including payroll taxes—froze prices, and persuaded Swedish unions to accept what amounted to nearly a 5% cut in real wages.

Japan. The year's "spring offensive" (*Shunto*) brought workers in major industries an average wage increase of 4.4%, less than in any previous year. It barely exceeded the rise in consumer prices. Because of increases in taxes and social security contributions, the higher wages represented an actual decrease in real wages for most workers.

A remarkable agreement on robots was signed in March by the giant Nissan auto company. The pact guaranteed workers against layoffs due to the introduction of robots or other microelectronic equipment.

For the first time, more than half of the women in Japan are part of the work force.

An All-Japan Council of private-sector unions was formed, consisting of 41 unions with a membership of 4,230,000 and including affiliates of both Domei and Sohyo, the two largest Japanese labor federations.

GORDON H. COLE and JOSEPH MIRE

LAOS

The Laotian economy continued to revive from the Indochinese wars that ended in 1975.

Politics. In 1983 no changes took place in leadership roles or in the nature of the Communist political process. But the refugee outflow—which had averaged 1,000 persons a month—virtually stopped. Moreover, 2,300 Laotian refugees officially returned to their homeland, and five times as many clandestinely crossed back into the country. Some 75,000 of the 300,000 Lao and minority Hmong who had fled after 1975 were still in refugee camps in neighboring non-Communist Thailand.

Occasional violence by remnant anti-Communist elements—such as the April murder of two Czech mining experts—posed no threat to the regime of Premier Kaysone Phomvihane. The March arrest of many officials, charged with misuse of foreign aid funds, revealed fairly extensive corruption but no plotting against the regime.

The Economy. Goods from many countries were available in the shops of Viangchan (Vientiane), the Laotian capital. Smuggling of timber, coffee, and opium—through Thailand—earned hard currencies to buy bicycles, radios, and other items from Japan and the West. Thai exports to Laos, which totaled $42.1 million in 1982, were valued at $23.6 million for the first half of 1983. Smuggled goods probably accounted for one third more. Because illegal trade took place at the black market rate of 105 kips to the U.S. dollar (three times the official rate), the government in June effectively devalued the kip, creating a special rate of 108 to the dollar for private commerce.

The late monsoon caused the government to lower its expectation of a rice harvest of 1.2 million tons, which would have made Laos nearly self-sufficient in that staple. Three years of good monsoons had raised output to 1.1 million tons by 1982, but lack of incentives for peasant producers had required an annual import of 30,000 tons from Thailand. Fruits and vegetables were plentiful, ending dependence on Thailand.

Foreign Affairs. Relations with the United States improved after a temporary setback in 1982. A U.S. official visiting Viangchan in October 1982 had said that Washington would consider upgrading diplomatic relations to the ambassadorial level if progress was made in accounting for servicemen missing in Laos since the Indochinese wars. This statement was not made public at the time. Subsequently, former Special Forces officer ''Bo'' Gritz attempted to rescue allegedly detained U.S. airmen. The U.S. Defense Department officially classified only two servicemen as still missing in action, and the Reagan administration denied any connection with Gritz' action.

The Gritz incident confused the Laotian government and delayed, but did not reverse, improvement of relations. In February 1983 representatives of the official, Hawaii-based Joint Casualty Resolution Center met for the first time with Laotian leaders in Viangchan. President Reagan's special emissary, former Sen. S. I. Hayakawa, traveled to Laos in May.

Vietnam, which still had 50,000 troops in Laos, encouraged its weaker neighbor to expand ties with non-Communist lands to lessen the two Indochinese governments' dependence on the USSR. Nonetheless, the Soviets continued to be a major presence: 5,000 Soviet nationals were believed to be in Laos training air force and ground troops, building roads and other facilities, and advising government ministries.

RICHARD BUTWELL
University of South Dakota

LATIN AMERICA

Latin American economic problems and political and military crises drove the United States into deeper involvement in 1983. While a majority of Americans believed that the countries of Latin America and the Caribbean merited greater U.S. attention, debate grew over the proper role of the United States in the affairs of its neighbors.

Military. The most startling event of 1983 was the U.S. military action in Grenada, a tiny island in the southeastern Caribbean (*see* feature article, page 28). But throughout the year, the United States was also embroiled in a clandestine surrogate war in Nicaragua, supporting rebels trying to topple Nicaragua's leftist Sandinista government. The United States also supplied arms and training to help the army of El Salvador combat ongoing leftist insurgency. And it equipped, trained, and participated in joint military maneuvers with the armed forces of Honduras.

In October the commanding general of the U.S. Army's Southern Command, based in Panama, participated in a meeting in Guatemala City at which the defense ministers of Guatemala, El Salvador, Honduras, and Panama agreed to reactivate the Central American

---

LAOS • Information Highlights

Official Name: Lao People's Democratic Republic.
Location: Southeast Asia.
Area: 91,430 sq mi (236 804 km^2).
Population (July 1983): 3,647,000.
Government: *Head of state,* Prince Souphanouvong, president. *Head of government,* Kaysone Phomvihane, prime minister. *Legislature* (unicameral) —National Congress of People's Representatives.
Gross National Product (1982 U.S.$): $320,000,000.
Foreign Trade (1981 U.S.$1): *Imports,* $85,000,000; *exports,* $9,000,000.

Chilean opposition groups held mass protests throughout 1983. Above, the women's movement calls for "democracy now."

Defense Council (CONDECA) to combat subversion in the area.

U.S. Commission. In August, President Ronald Reagan appointed a special commission, headed by former Secretary of State Henry Kissinger, to help frame a new long-term U.S. policy toward Central America. The group went on extensive fact-finding tours and was scheduled to submit its recommendations in January 1984.

The president also reshuffled some officials responsible for implementing U.S. policy in Latin America. In June, Thomas O. Enders was replaced as Assistant Secretary for Inter-American Affairs by Langhorne A. Motley, the U.S. ambassador to Brazil. Simultaneously, Deane R. Hinton was relieved as U.S. ambassador to El Salvador. In an unrelated development, but one with important implications for Latin American policy, William Clark, the president's national security adviser, was nominated as secretary of the interior. His place was taken by Robert C. McFarlane.

Contadora. Meanwhile, a group of Latin American nations spent most of the year seeking negotiated solutions to Central American problems. Colombia, Mexico, Panama, and Venezuela made up the "Contadora Group," so named for the Panamanian island where the foreign ministers of the four countries first met to consider collective diplomatic initiatives in the Central American crisis. In October the group produced a 21-point document outlining conditions for the peaceful settlement of Central American disputes. In general, the United States seemed supportive of the Contadora initiatives, but it was reluctant to agree to specific measures to implement the group's recommendations.

Economic. Latin America's economic crisis persisted throughout the year, with continuing high inflation and unemployment rates and severe debt repayment problems. There were signs, however, that some countries of the region had weathered the worst of the storm.

In a report issued in August, the Inter-American Development Bank (IDB) said that, "After 15 years (1964–1980) of impressive expansion, during which the regional economy never failed to grow by at least 4% annually, Latin America has entered the third year of a severe recession. . . . There are no expectations that significant recovery will take place in 1983, given economic conditions in the industrialized countries, to which the region is so closely linked commercially and financially."

The IDB economists also found some positive portents. "A major adjustment of the Latin American economies was under way in 1982 and is continuing this year," the report observed. "The external sector imbalances that had become evident in 1980–81 were being corrected everywhere in Latin America. . . . There are strong reasons for expecting that the region will resume its dynamic growth."

In September the Organization of American States (OAS) convoked a special conference in Caracas, Venezuela, on Latin American debt and trade problems. A document called "Bases for Understanding" won unanimous support from all delegations, including that of the United States. Latin American countries are making "extraordinary efforts to cope with the present crisis," the document said, emphasizing that "efforts to make adjustments must necessarily be equitable and coordinated for all who are involved . . . namely creditor and debtor countries, multilateral financial institutions and international private banks. . . ." A companion resolution urged that Latin America's debt repayment schedule "be brought into line with the region's payment capacity and its economic development needs."

During the year, the two largest debtor countries in the hemisphere responded quite differently to the crisis. Brazil's foreign debt rose to $92 billion (U.S.), the highest in the developing world, and the nation fell into arrears on its repayments. Not until late November did the Brazilian government reach an agreement with the International Monetary Fund (IMF) that would permit it to resume drawing IMF funds, cut off since early in the year. On the other hand, Mexico, the region's second-biggest debtor with foreign obligations of $87 billion, kept up-to-date with its payments and experienced modest recovery.

Because of Latin America's weakened purchasing power, the United States suffered a rare deficit of some $3.5 billion in its trade with Latin America in 1982. Prices for Latin commodity exports rose slightly during 1983, but not enough to produce a significant change in the region's shortage of foreign exchange.

At midyear, the U.S. Congress approved the Caribbean Basin Initiative (CBI), a program that will provide duty-free entry into the United States over a 12-year period for a variety of goods from Central America and the Caribbean islands (*see* page 163).

Political. In May the Latin American news magazine *Visión* published a cover story analyzing what it called a "military retreat" from Latin American politics. The magazine noted that in "at least nine Latin American nations" there were movements to restore, to one degree or another, civilian control of the political process. In October, Argentina elected a new civilian government, which was installed in December. The process of "abertura," or opening to democracy, continued in Brazil. The government of El Salvador scheduled presidential elections for March 25, 1984. There was a military coup in Guatemala in August, but the new regime said it would hold 1984 elections.

Inter-American System. The "invasion" of Grenada split the OAS just as the Falkland Islands crisis had done a year before. The Caribbean member states supported the action, while the Latin American countries condemned it. OAS Secretary-General Alejandro Orfila unexpectedly resigned during the organization's annual General Assembly in November. The Caribbean states immediately proposed as his successor Val. T. McComie, a Barbadian diplomat serving as OAS assistant secretary-general. Latin American support coalesced around Brazil's deputy foreign minister, João Clemente Baena Soares. A special election was set for March 1984.

Church. Pope John Paul II visited Central America in February, issuing a fervent plea for

UPI
Cubans taken prisoner on Grenada are escorted by U.S. Marines to a transport plane for their return to Havana.

peace in the area. But in most of the hemisphere, the Church remained embattled, under political attack from the left and the right, and facing an increasing challenge from a nascent fundamentalist Protestant movement, which claimed tens of thousands of new converts during the year. The growing importance of Protestantism was evident in the 17-month rule of Gen. Efrain Rios Montt in Guatemala, who was deposed in August. Rios Montt, a born-again Christian, openly proclaimed his faith, and it was said to be a factor in his downfall.

Human Rights. Various reports issued during the year by Amnesty International, the OAS Human Rights Commission, the U.S. State Department, and others indicated that respect for human rights remained at a low level in Latin America during the year. Countries singled out for criticism included Argentina, Chile, Cuba, Guatemala, El Salvador, Nicaragua, Paraguay, Surinam, and Uruguay.

Weather. Freakish weather added to Latin America's problems during the year. A report issued by the North American Office of the UN Food and Agriculture Organization (FAO) noted that, "In the first six months of the year, an almost incredible patchwork of alternate drought and flood destroyed crops in Ecuador, Peru, Bolivia, and parts of northern Argentina. Slightly less severe but still very damaging effects . . . were felt in Brazil, Colombia, Central America, Mexico, and Cuba."

RICHARD C. SCHROEDER, *"Visión" Magazine*

LAW

United States

Though several notable legal disputes and policy questions were resolved in the U.S. federal and state court systems, 1983 was, for the most part, a year of struggling for a consensus on many social and criminal justice issues. The U.S. Supreme Court handed down many badly splintered rulings while failing to resolve several important cases. The Congress and the Executive Branch witnessed sporadic but largely unsuccessful efforts by conservatives to push their agenda of moral causes. At the state level, too, there was no clear sign of any particular direction.

Supreme Court. Some legal questions were decided unequivocally. By an 8-to-1 vote the Supreme Court prohibited tax exemptions for racially discriminating schools (*Bob Jones University v. U.S.*). Ten years after declaring that women had the right to choose abortion, the highest court reaffirmed and expanded its *Roe v. Wade* decision. By a 6–3 majority, the court ruled unconstitutional a variety of restrictions on abortion, including a 24-hour waiting period, elaborate "informed consent" requirements decided by individual states, parental or judicial consent for all abortions performed on minors, and a requirement that second-trimester abortions be performed in a hospital (*Akron v. Akron Center for Reproductive Health; Planned Parenthood of Kansas City, Missouri v. Ashcroft*). And in a 7–2 vote, the court said that the Pregnancy Discrimination Act of 1978, requiring disability benefits to pregnant employees, applies not only to female employees but also to dependent spouses of male employees (*Newport News Shipbuilding v. Equal Employment Opportunity Commission*).

Of the 180 cases decided during the 1982–83 Supreme Court term, 40 related to criminal law and procedure, more than in any other area. The tribunal tended to limit earlier, more liberal criminal law decisions, but there were some noteworthy exceptions. In *Kolender v. Lawson,* for example, the judges held that a police officer could not arrest a person who merely failed to identify himself to the satisfaction of the officer; the California vagrancy law was struck down for vagueness. In *U.S. v. Place* the judges upheld the right of police to expose a traveler's luggage to a narcotics-sniffing dog; the justices did assert, however, that the luggage may be detained only for a brief period of time. The court was not yet ready or able to declare that there should be a "good-faith" exception to the exclusionary rule (requiring judges to disallow criminal evidence obtained in violation of the Fourth Amendment). It sidestepped the issue in *Illinois v. Gates* but accepted for its 1983–84 term three cases in which the matter could be clarified.

The court also avoided ruling on a challenge to a lower court decision in a reverse discrimination case, whereby layoffs of senior nonminority workers were permitted to preserve the jobs of minorities hired in response to a consent decree under Title VII of the Civil Rights Act. After hearing oral arguments in *Boston Firefighters Union v. Boston Chapter, NAACP,* the judges dismissed the case as moot.

By the narrowest of margins, 5–4, the court ruled that it was illegal under Title VII of the Civil Rights Act for employees to provide retirement benefits that discriminate on the basis of sex (*Arizona Governing Committee v. Norris*). However, the four dissenters were joined by Justice Sandra O'Connor in limiting the financial effect of the decision. Only future benefits based on annuity contributions need be equalized. It remains up to Congress, which was lobbied extensively by both camps, to decide the extent to which the insurance and pension industries could distinguish between the sexes in setting premiums and benefits.

In a decision that featured six separate opinions, the high court tried to resolve whether Title VI, which prohibits racial discrimination in federally funded programs, requires proof of discriminatory intent or simply discriminatory effect (*Guardians v. Civil Service Commission of New York*). The narrowly divided court held that proof of discriminatory effect was sufficient for prospective injunctive relief but that discriminatory intent must be proved to justify back pay and damage awards.

Four death-penalty cases were decided during the 1982–83 term. In each instance the penalty was upheld, and in *Barefoot v. Estelle* the justices permitted federal appeals to be expedited in death-penalty cases, making it harder for death-row inmates to stretch out the legal process.

By another 5–4 vote, the Supreme Court invalidated a life sentence without parole given to a repeat offender convicted of passing a bad check (*Solem v. Helm*). Helm was a six-time felon whose thefts totaled only $230. (In a 1980 case from Texas the court had approved a life sentence for another individual whose crimes also totaled about $230.)

Again 5–4, the court ruled that a Minnesota law granting a $700.00 state-tax reduction for expenses at public or private schools was not unconstitutional even though the benefits would go mainly to religious schools. This did not, however, affect the legality of tuition tax credits, which the court had struck down in a New York case a decade earlier.

In a landmark case regarding the separation of powers, the Supreme Court convincingly struck down the so-called "legislative veto" (*Immigration and Naturalization Service v. Chadha*). The decision jeopardized provisions in some 200 laws pertaining to the environ-

The Overburdened U.S. Supreme Court

American Bar Association

In his annual State of the Judiciary address at the American Bar Association convention in February 1983, Chief Justice Warren E. Burger proposed a temporary new federal appeals court to help ease the "grave" caseload burden of the U.S. Supreme Court. His proposal culminated a period in which the high-court justices had focused attention on what Burger called "perhaps the most important single, immediate problem facing the judiciary." While the various members had proposed different solutions, Burger asserted that the justices who had spoken out were "essentially of one mind: that there is indeed a very grave problem and something must be done."

The Problem. The workload of the U.S. Supreme Court has grown considerably in recent years. The 1961 term was the first in which the court received more than 2,000 requests to hear cases. By 1967 that figure had reached 3,000, and in each of the last three terms (1980–82) it has been more than 4,000.

The number of cases that the court agrees to give full consideration also has grown. During the 1950s and 1960s, the court each term reached about 100 "full" decisions, in which it issued signed majority opinions. The figures in the 1970s and 1980s have been somewhat higher, rising to 151 in the 1982 term.

There is a growing consensus that these numbers constitute a serious problem. One aspect of the problem is delay. The length of time between the court's acceptance of a case and the hearing date has increased steadily. More broadly, many people feel that the quality of the court's work suffers as a result of case-load pressure. In recent years, most members of the court have spoken publicly about this burden, indicating that they are troubled by their current situation. According to Burger, the justices work at least 60 hours per week just to keep up.

Solutions. There is less of a consensus as to how exactly the Supreme Court's workload should be lightened. The justices generally agree that Congress should aid the court by repealing provisions that require it to hear certain categories of cases. Because such repeal would have only a moderate effect, however, consideration has been given to more sweeping proposals, including the creation of a new national court of appeals.

The idea of such a court is not new. In 1972 a study group established by Chief Justice Burger proposed a national court of appeals to screen requests for Supreme Court hearings. The proposed court would eliminate those requests that its members deemed unworthy and pass along the rest for the Supreme Court's consideration. In 1975 a commission created by Congress proposed a different body with the same name. By this proposal, the Supreme Court would send to the new court any cases that the justices think require a national decision but not a decision by the Supreme Court itself.

Neither proposal came close to obtaining the necessary Congressional approval. Some justices and legal scholars objected that either version of a national court of appeals would detract from the Supreme Court's essential functions. In part because of these objections, the idea of a new court lay dormant for several years.

Chief Justice Burger in 1983 sought to revive interest in the new court by making it temporary. He would attach a panel to the Court of Appeals for the Federal Circuit in Washington, DC, itself a fairly new court with specialized functions. The panel would be composed of a rotating group of judges from the federal courts of appeal. For five years the panel would decide cases involving conflicts between courts of appeal on legal issues that otherwise the Supreme Court might feel obliged to hear. Congress, meanwhile, could consider permanent measures to relieve the burden.

A similar proposal already had been introduced in Congress, and Burger's proposal has gained considerable support. Justices Lewis Powell and Sandra Day O'Connor have endorsed it, while Justice John Paul Stevens has expressed opposition. Several justices have offered their views on other proposals to reduce the court's burden. As in the past, the court and the legal community are divided between those who think that fundamental changes are necessary to protect the court from growing caseloads and those who fear the effect of such changes on the court's role. The second group is typified by Justice William Brennan, who opposes a national court of appeals and thinks the Supreme Court can help itself simply by deciding fewer cases.

Prospects for the Future. This division makes the adoption of the Burger proposal or any other sweeping change less likely. Congress will be reluctant to alter the basic structure of the federal judicial system without broad support for a specific proposal. Any further increases in the court's workload, however, will bring more pressure for action, and some sweeping change may become inevitable as a means to protect the court.

LAWRENCE BAUM

---

ment, consumer affairs, federal pay, executive organization, and national security.

In a unanimous opinion, the justices ruled that the National Highway Traffic Safety Administration could not arbitrarily revoke the rule that new cars must be equipped with airbags or automatic seat belts. The Supreme Court ordered the Transportation Department to implement the regulation or come up with a better explanation for not doing so.

Other Supreme Court decisions declared unconstitutional a federal law that made it a crime to send unsolicited contraceptive advertisements through the mail and struck down a New Jersey redistricting of congressional seats for departing from "precise mathematical equality" without citing compelling reasons. (A federal district judge in Boston ruled that the city's election districts violated the constitutional principle of one man, one vote.)

The ideological balance on the court suggested that any additional appointment by President Reagan could cause a conservative realignment. The administration could take comfort that Justice O'Connor's stand on her first abortion decision refuted fears expressed by right-to-life critics of her appointment.

Congress, the Judiciary, and Constitutional Amendments. Congress in 1983 considered several proposals to expand the federal judiciary. Most of the proposals dealt with the role of bankruptcy judges. In 1982 the Supreme Court had ruled that it was unconstitutional to assign bankruptcy cases grounded on state law to bankruptcy judges who do not have life tenure and guarantees against salary reductions.

Several efforts to amend the U.S. Constitution marked time before Congress. A states' rights constitutional amendment to overturn the 1973 Supreme Court decision to legalize abortion (*Roe v. Wade*) could not even muster majority support. Divisions among supporters of legalized prayer kept their issue from advancing, and a lower court decided that Alabama's school prayer law was unconstitutional. While a new Equal Rights Amendment could get the necessary two-thirds vote in the House, the votes were not there in the Senate and the proponents bided their time.

Lower Federal and State Courts. A federal court of appeals overturned the Reagan administration's so-called "squeal rule", whereby health-care providers receiving federal funds must notify parents when contraceptives are given to minors, regardless of the family situation. The court ruled that this rule went beyond the intent of Congress.

Several cases were decided regarding nonregistration for the military draft. In a test of the Solomon Amendment, a federal district court judge in Minnesota barred the government from denying federal education loans to students who had not registered for the draft. In California, though, a court of appeals panel in a 2–1 decision overturned a district court acquittal of a nonregistrant who claimed he was a victim of selective prosecution.

Public attention in 1983 also turned to several cases involving political asylum. The Walter Polavchak case dealt with a minor who wished to remain in the United States after his parents returned to the USSR. His older sister, who was on her own passport, was not challenged in her request for asylum. The American Civil Liberties Union represented the parents in contending that Walter was a runaway who was treated differently from most because his parents were Soviet citizens and were not charged with child abuse. The Illinois Supreme Court ruled in favor of the parents.

When Chinese tennis star Hu Na asked for political asylum in July 1982, she was supported by the State Department's Bureau of Human Rights and Humanitarian Affairs but opposed by the China desk. The Immigration and Naturalization Service delayed a decision but finally granted her asylum in April 1983. China accused the United States of infringing on its sovereignty.

China was displeased by another decision in 1983. A federal court ruled that China was liable for $41 million in payments on railway bonds issued by the imperial government in 1911. China had not even contested the case in U.S. court, expecting the U.S. government to intervene to kill the claim. It said that as a sovereign government it was immune from prosecution in a foreign court and that, in any case, the bonds represented an "odious debt" incurred by a corrupt government. Though sovereign immunity does not extend to a commercial activity, most courts would have agreed that the plaintiff's case was stale since it was not put forward until 40 years after the previous government had stopped paying interest and 18 years after the bonds had matured.

Several civil-rights cases were newsworthy in 1983. Two involved Gary Thomas Rowe, an FBI undercover agent who had participated in Ku Klux Klan activities in the 1960s. In one case the children of Viola Liuzzo, a civil-rights worker murdered in Alabama in 1965, were unsuccessful in their negligence suit against the FBI for failure to prevent the violent act; Rowe was in the car from which the fatal gunshot was fired. In the other case, a freedom bus rider who had been beaten up won an award after it was disclosed at trial that Rowe had admitted helping beat up black bus riders and that the FBI had been told the incident was going to take place.

Seven New Orleans police officers stood trial in Dallas for denying several individuals their civil rights during the course of a criminal investigation into the killing of a policeman. The case had been moved to Dallas because of extensive press coverage. (State and federal grand juries had refused to indict any of the police officers for the killing of four blacks, including two suspects in the police slaying.) The jury convicted three of the officers of violating the civil rights of a black man who charged that he was brutally interrogated. The other four officers were acquitted of all charges.

In another Louisiana matter, the state repealed a 1970 law that had designated anyone with $1/32$ "negro blood" as black. A state court judge had earlier upheld the classification.

A Tennessee statute allowing police officers to use deadly force to capture unarmed suspects fleeing nonviolent felonies was declared unconstitutional by a federal appeals court as an unreasonable method of seizure.

Two sex discrimination cases attracted media attention in 1983. A U.S. Court of Appeals struck down as vague a Minnesota law forbidding discrimination on the basis of sex in places of public accommodation. The suit was brought by the U.S. Jaycees, who sought injunctive relief after the Minnesota Department of Human Rights ordered the organization to cease banning female members. The court concluded that the all-male membership requirement was shielded by the constitutional right of association. TV anchorwoman Christine Craft was awarded $500,000 in a suit against a Kansas City station for demoting her because she was "too old, unattractive, and not deferential enough to men"; in October, however, the judgment was thrown out and a new trial ordered.

The nuclear-power industry continued to take its lumps. First the Supreme Court unani-

Wide World

A federal jury awarded newscaster Christine Craft $500,000 in a sex discrimination suit, but the judge overruled.

mously upheld California's nuclear power moratorium. The state legislature had voted to block new nuclear-power plants pending a natural solution to the problem of nuclear-waste disposal. The court said that Congress had left sufficient authority to the states to regulate the pace of nuclear power for economic reasons. Then the Washington State Supreme Court upheld a lower court ruling that 88 utilities were not obligated to meet payments on the bonds of the Washington Public Power Supply System (WPPSS). The latter ruling precipitated the largest municipal default in history, $2.25 billion (U.S.), and lawsuits from debt holders.

A tug-of-war between rival factions of the Chicago Democratic Party organization reached the courts. After the election of Mayor Harold Washington in April, his political foes on the City Council, headed by the Cook County Democratic chairman, proceeded to use their voting majority to organize the legislative body. Washington declared their actions illegal, but the State Supreme Court sustained the majority's control. In another case, however, a federal judge gave the mayor authority to replace 900 high-level municipal employees.

Ethics. After six years of debate, the American Bar Association (ABA) adopted a new model code of ethics (Rules of Professional Conduct). The new code reaffirmed the primacy of the client's interests but acknowledged duties of the attorney to his profession and society in the event of client fraud, perjured testimony, or impending substantial bodily harm. The code is not binding on the states, some of which are expected to adopt less restrictive rules on client-attorney confidentiality.

International Law

On Sept. 1, 1983, the world learned that a missing South Korean passenger plane had been downed by a Soviet SU-15 fighter and that all 269 persons aboard had been killed. Only that bare fact was uncontested. Everything else about the incident was the subject of heated dispute, raising highly charged legal questions in the international community. Flight 007 was more than 300 mi (483 km) off course, over Soviet airspace. Was this the result of innocent human or navigational equipment error, of attempted espionage, or of entrapment? Were the Soviets guilty of criminal negligence or only of military confusion and rigidity? Was the decision to down the plane made by a field commander or in Moscow? Could the government be held liable?

The first class-action lawsuit was filed in a U.S. District Court one day after the air disaster. The plaintiffs, relatives of those aboard the plane, sought $99 billion (U.S.) in compensation and punitive damages, mostly from the Soviet government. This approach did not seem likely to succeed. Once the intitial outcry and calls for sanctions subsided, a more promising course appeared to be through bilateral diplomatic procedures, a coordination of claims filed by nations in behalf of their deceased nationals.

There had been five previous cases of commercial airliners being shot at by foreign governments. In neither of the two cases involving the USSR was any compensation forthcoming; Bulgaria, Israel, and China did make restitution. In both cases, the Soviets insisted that they had fired only warning shots, justified by the fact that the plane had strayed from the agreed-upon air traffic corridor.

Maritime Disputes. Although 177 nations had signed the Law of the Sea Treaty (LOST) in December 1982, there was a plethora of disputes regarding maritime rights in 1983.

The United States was the most prominent holdout from the new accord. The Reagan administration, concerned about provisions regarding ocean mining, argued that almost everything in the treaty was already law and that the United States could profit from the provisions without signing the treaty. It also contended that since it would not sign the treaty, it was not bound by it. Though the USSR and 15 other major industrial countries did not sign the convention in 1982, the United States failed to convince its Western partners to go it alone with a minitreaty. Japan, which was going through a change of government in late 1982, subsequently signed the document, as did France.

A total of 143 states signed the Final Act of the Conference on the Law of the Sea, which entitled them to attend meetings of the Preparatory Commission. That is an interim body charged with preparing the rules and regulations for the International Seabed Authority and a provisional agenda for the first session of its governing bodies. The Preparatory Commission began meeting in March 1983.

Acting unilaterally, the United States declared a 200-mi Exclusive Economic Zone (EEZ) for commercial development of living and nonliving natural resources. This was an attempt to show that a nation could control seabed and other resources without LOST. The United States hoped to attract 52 other countries with EEZ possibilities into joint ventures. The USSR and Japan, with the largest far-seas fishing fleets, strongly opposed 200-mi fishing zones. Though Canada joined with the United States in establishing a 200-mi zone, allowing the two countries to control cod and salmon fishing, there was bitter conflict between U.S. and Canadian fishermen where their 200-mi zones overlap.

The United States was not alone in fishing disputes. When provisional European Community fishing accords expired Jan. 1, 1983, Britain imposed a ban on commercial fishing by Denmark in coastal North Sea waters. Denmark had felt that it was entitled by tradition to larger mackerel and herring catches in British waters than the draft agreement allowed. A Danish skipper broke U.K. laws to protest the new restrictions. He was arrested and fined $48,000 for trespassing but promised to appeal. By January 25 a compromise was hammered out.

The 40-nation International Whaling Commission (IWC) received more than usual attention for its 1983 meeting. It coincided with a "spy" mission by antiwhaling activists who claimed to have evidence of Soviet whaling violations in Siberia. Japan, the USSR, and Norway still resisted the 1982 IWC decision to phase out all commercial whaling by 1986; Peru withdrew its objection.

Third World countries, buoyed by the passage of LOST, asked the UN to intervene to give them a role in the future status of Antarctica. With environmentalists protesting outside, delegates from 14 signatories of the Antarctica Treaty met in Bonn to establish guidelines for the development of minerals beneath the frozen continent. Half of the signatories claimed slices of land, while other nations rejected those claims. A fishing agreement for surrounding waters was reached.

Outer Space. In early 1983, for the second time in four years, a uranium-powered Soviet satellite fell into the earth's atmosphere. Moscow insisted that the risk of damage was miniscule. Whereas the Carter administration had urged a ban on nuclear reactors in space, the Reagan administration, with its concept of space as the "high ground" in future wars, did not renew that suggestion.

See also GRENADA, page 28.

MARTIN GRUBERG
University of Wisconsin-Oshkosh

LEBANON

Alain Nogues/Sygma

President Amin Gemayel: "Our country is dying. It moans under the weight of ruins and fears."

The incapacity of Lebanon's warring political factions to end not only eight years of open warfare but also centuries of sectarian strife was increased in 1983 by the continued presence and interference of foreign forces. President Amin Gemayel's efforts to reach a national consensus and rid the nation of occupying armies were thus undermined, as each competing faction, with outside help, sought either to extend its gains or protect its advantages.

Gemayel's task was exceedingly complex, perhaps impossible. Although symbolic progress was achieved by convening a November meeting with Lebanon's principal sectarian leaders, developments during the course of the year convinced many that partition rather than reunification lay in the future. Israel still occupied the southern third of the country; Syria firmly held more than half; factional militias were firmly entrenched in their fiefdoms; the multi-national peacekeeping forces (MNF) had been drawn tangibly into the nation's tragedy; and Gemayel, whose army controlled only the capital, was publicly derided as the "mayor of Beirut."

Withdrawal Negotiations. Since the end of overt hostilities between Israel, the PLO, and Syria in September 1982, Gemayel had maintained that uniting Lebanon was impossible without the withdrawal of foreign troops. Ironically, he had requested that the MNF contingent be increased from 3,200 to 60,000 troops to afford him both the time and the stability in which to rebuild the Lebanese Army and to reassert the central government's authority.

Arranging that departure, however, was beyond Gemayel's grasp. Israel refused to withdraw until the PLO was gone and then only if Syria simultaneously withdrew its 50,000 men. In the face of Syria's refusal either to withdraw or to negotiate directly with Israel, then Israeli Prime Minister Menahem Begin offered Gemayel withdrawal in exchange for an Israeli security presence in southern Lebanon and normalization of political, diplomatic, and economic relations. Although President Gemayel entered negotiations with Israel, he recognized that "normalization" would threaten his ties to the Arab world and intensify his internal problems. More importantly, removing Syrian troops could not be achieved unless Syria's President Hafez al-Assad agreed to what was negotiated with Israel.

Begun late in December 1982, the Lebanese-Israeli talks showed little progress until U.S. Secretary of State George Shultz intervened in late April. Shuttling between Beirut and Jerusalem for 17 days, Secretary Shultz's mediation enabled the negotiating teams to clear the final hurdles. A compromise was reached on the supervision of security arrangements in southern Lebanon, while future relations between the two governments and the fate of renegade Lebanese Army Officer Saad Haddad, an Israeli proxy since 1978, were addressed in secret side letters.

Ratified on May 17, the pact's primary significance was that Gemayel actually agreed to it. During a May 12 meeting in Damascus, Lebanon's Foreign Minister Elie Salem had been warned by his Syrian counterpart, Abdel Halim al-Khaddam, not to sign. Because the agreement could not be implemented without Syrian acquiescence, it served no purpose. Indeed, because of Syria's opposition and concomitant

317

arming of Lebanon's Muslim dissidents, the pact became the major obstacle to addressing the basic political questions standing between the government and national unity.

National Salvation Front. When Israel announced on July 20 that it would withdraw its troops from the Beirut suburbs and the Chouf Mountains to more defensible positions south of the capital, permanent partition was threatened by the formation of a new, Syrian-backed opposition coalition. Headed by Druze leader Walid Jumblatt, Sunni Muslim Rashid Karami, and former President Sulieman Franjieh, a longtime Maronite Christian rival to Gemayel's Phalangist Party, the National Salvation Front declared that it would not participate in any national reconciliation talks while the May 17 agreement was in effect. Further, the leaders announced their intention to provide civil administration in Syrian-controlled areas.

Throughout August, artillery duels between government troops and the rival militias added to the tension, as all sides got ready to take over the strategic positions the Israelis were planning to vacate. The withdrawal, beginning September 3, precipitated a chain of events that further polarized the country, drew the United States and France into the hostilities, and sparked international criticism.

Warfare in the Chouf. The strategic heights dominating Beirut and the international airport were the scene of three weeks of fierce fighting that broke out September 4. Syrian-armed Druze militia forces successfully drove Phalangist troops from most of the Chouf, but bitter fighting between Jumblatt's men and army-backed Christians at the key village of Suq al-Gharb prolonged the hostilities and involved U.S. and French forces. On September 8, U.S. warships and Marine artillery batteries opened fire on Druze positions to retaliate for indiscriminate shelling of American peacekeeping troops. By September 19 it had become clear that U.S. forces were directly supporting a co-ordinated, government-Phalangist drive to clear Druze forces from the Suq al-Gharb area. While U.S. guns pounded Druze positions in the foothills, French aircraft were retaliating against Shiite Muslim militia positions east of Beirut.

As the fighting escalated, President Gemayel employed Saudi Arabia's Prince Bandar ibn Sultan, ambassador-designate to the United States, to mediate proposals for a cease-fire. The negotiations revolved around two conditions imposed by Jumblatt and Syria's Assad: that a cease-fire could be achieved only if reconciliation talks were to follow immediately and that Jumblatt and Assad would determine the composition of the government's delegation to those talks. Surprisingly, Gemayel agreed to the conditions.

Cease-fire and Beirut Tragedy. On September 26, the cease-fire—by some counts the 179th since 1976—was formally announced. Arrangements for consolidating and supervising the accord were made, and an "urgent and comprehensive" conference was scheduled to begin the national reconciliation process. The conference was delayed for more than a month because of the principals' disagreement over the site and conditions for the meeting. Jumblatt, the target of an assassination attempt in Beirut the previous December, refused to meet in Lebanon. Christian leader Camille Chamoun refused to negotiate until the Israelis and the Syrians withdrew, and Phalangist leaders insisted on forming a new national unity government before reconciliation could begin. Most of the factions did participate in an October 13 meeting to discuss the agenda, but only one opposition leader appeared at the scheduled opening of the talks October 20.

Rescheduling the talks was delayed again on October 23, when the U.S. Marine and French compounds were hit by terrorist truck-bomb attacks; the bombings left 241 Americans and 58 Frenchmen dead. Although neither France nor the United States struck back, calls for the pullout of MNF troops, particularly by the U.S. Congress, placed Gemayel under intense pressure to make early concessions to the Muslims to speed a political settlement.

Reconciliation Talks. On October 31 in Geneva, Switzerland, the leaders of Lebanon's principal factions met for the first time in eight years. Amin Gemayel represented the government, and his father, Pierre, represented the Phalangists. The Druze, the Sunnis of northern Lebanon, and the Shiite Amal militia were represented by Jumblatt, Karami, and Nabih Berri, respectively. Chamoun and Franjieh spoke for anti-Gemayel Christians, Saeb Salam represented Beirut's Muslims, and Adel Osseirane spoke for non-Amal Shiites. Syria's Khaddam and Saudi Deputy Foreign Minister Muhammad Massoud were official observers.

The negotiations adjourned after four days (and then resumed until November 11) to provide Gemayel a chance to fashion a response to the Syrian demand that the conferees immediately address the question of renouncing the May 17 agreement with Israel. However important Syria's intervention, reconciliation would

---

LEBANON • Information Highlights

Official Name: Republic of Lebanon.
Location: Southwest Asia.
Area: 4,000 sq mi (10 360 km^2).
Population (July 1983 est.): 2,598,000.
Government: *Head of state,* Amin Gemayel, president (took office Sept. 1982). *Head of government,* Chafiq al-Wazan, prime minister (took office Oct. 1980). *Legislature* (unicameral)—National Assembly.
Monetary Unit: Lebanese pound (5.46 pounds equal U.S.$1, Dec. 16, 1983.)
Gross National Product (1981 U.S.$): $4,190,-000,000.

Leaders of the principal warring factions convened reconciliation talks October 31 in Geneva, adjourning November 11.

be based on revising the unwritten 1943 National Pact, the agreement by which official political power had been distributed since independence. Under this accord, Maronites were awarded the presidency, command of the army, and the directorship of the central bank; the prime minister was always a Sunni, the foreign minister a Greek Orthodox, and the speaker of parliament a Shiite.

In November the Muslims, the majority of the population since the late 1950s, were willing to concede the presidency to the Maronites. However, the Shiites, the largest single Muslim population group, and the Druze, effectively shut out in 1943 but now eclipsing the larger Sunni population in political power, wanted major changes. Jumblatt had called for popular rather than parliamentary elections for the presidency, a lower house based on proportional representation (rather than the current 6–5 Christian majority), and an upper house headed by a Druze and based on equal confessional representation. Because the talks adjourned before the Shiite position had been elaborated, there was speculation that the rival Muslim factions would contribute more to the talks' eventual failure than would Christian intransigence.

Continuing Upheaval. The final two months of the year saw no surcease in the violence. On November 4 another truck-bombing, this time of an Israeli installation in Tyre, killed 60; Israel launched a new series of air strikes against Palestinian positions and against a training base belonging to the pro-Iranian group suspected of the bombings. Around Beirut, the cease-fire was crumbling as heavy fighting broke out again between the Lebanese Army and Druze militia. In the north, meanwhile, Yasir Arafat and his loyalists were being driven by Syrian-backed PLO rebels from their last military stronghold and into downtown Tripoli; only a Saudi cease-fire formula, accepted by the PLO groups on November 23, averted destruction of that port city. On December 20, Arafat and 4,000 PLO supporters were evacuated from Tripoli in Greek ships flying the UN flag.

December also saw more U.S. military involvement—and casualties. In response to Syrian attacks from the hills above Beirut, the United States launched air strikes December 4; two of its planes were shot down, and eight Marines were killed in heavy artillery fire. U.S. warships stationed offshore stepped up shelling of hill positions.

A new intra-Lebanese cease-fire—the 180th—went into effect December 16. It lasted eight days.

Economy. Even had national reconciliation been achieved in 1983, Lebanon's financial and reconstruction needs would have remained overwhelming. In June the Council of Development and Reconstruction proposed a ten-year, $15 billion (U.S.) plan to rebuild roads, schools, housing, and electrical generating capacity; a World Bank study estimated that $6 billion would be needed by 1985 as part of an overall $17 billion program by 1990. Economic rebirth, however, was predicated on attaining a reasonable degree of internal security.

Nevertheless, there were signs of progress. In the six months following the February redeployment of government troops in East Beirut, customs revenues from the previously militia-held port facility increased to $169 million, up from only $46 million a year earlier. Although gross domestic product was half its 1974 level, deposits in commercial banks had increased fivefold since 1975.

F. NICHOLAS WILLARD

LIBRARIES

Librarians in the United States spent 1983 defending the gains made since the end of World War II in funding and freedom of communication. Much of the defense occurred in Washington where the Library Services and Construction Act was amended and reauthorized, the flow of federal information confronted new barriers, there was a proposal to modify the educational qualifications required of federal librarians, and there was controversy over a report on copyright law.

Federal Funding. In December 1982 the federal government decided to fund the Library Services and Construction Act (LSCA) at the same rate, save a small increase in the research library program, during fiscal year 1983 as it had during 1982. Taking into account the effect of inflation, this meant less funding than in the preceding fiscal year. The situation left librarians pessimistic about the survival of the act, which was due to expire in fiscal 1984. On March 24, 1983, the construction title of the LSCA was funded for the first time in a decade when $50 million was provided for the construction and renovation of public library facilities. A House subcommittee also began hearings on extension and revision of LSCA.

The Education and Labor Committee of the House approved a five-year (1983–88) reauthorization and revision of the LSCA on May 16. On November 1, President Reagan signed the bill funding LSCA for fiscal 1984. Public library services ($65 million) and interlibrary cooperation ($15 million) were funded at their highest levels ever. However, no monies at all were appropriated for public library construction and renovation.

Other National Developments. Beginning in late 1982 and continuing into 1983, the Reagan administration acted on several fronts to limit public access to government information. Citing as authority the Paperwork Reduction Act of 1980, the president terminated some federal publications, restricted the free distribution of

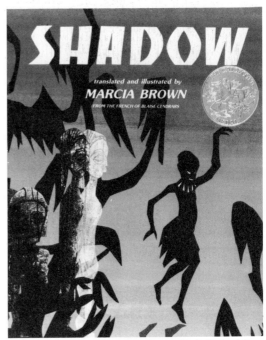

© 1982 Marcia Brown/Courtesy, Charles Scribner's Sons
Shadow, *by Marcia Brown, won the ALA's Caldecott Medal.*

others, and cut back the data gathering of the federal government's two largest collectors of statistics—the Census Bureau and the Bureau of Labor Statistics. In addition, President Reagan signed a special order increasing the amount of government information that could be classified for security reasons, thereby limiting the applications of the Freedom of Information Act. Finally, the administration sought to close a number of government bookstores and federal information centers as well as to put government publications on a break-even basis. In response, the Council of the American Library Association (ALA) approved a Resolution to Government Agencies on Access to Information.

Proposed salary grade-level reductions by the Office of Personnel Management for government librarians with graduate education led librarians to protest that the changes downgraded the profession and discriminated against women, since most of those affected are women. The librarians also contended that such changes at the federal level would quickly affect the states and localities.

The Office of Management and Budget decided that some of the services now provided by federal libraries should be privately contracted.

In January 1983 the Register of Copyright sent to Congress a five-year review of the Copyright Act of 1976. The report observed that "substantial quantities of photocopies prepared by and for library patrons are made for job-related reasons, rather than for the type of

LIBRARY AWARDS OF 1983

Beta Phi Mu Award for distinguished service to education for librarianship: J. Periam Danton, professor emeritus, School of Library and Information Studies, University of California, Berkeley

Randolph J. Caldecott Medal for the most distinguished picture book for children: Marcia Brown, *Shadow*

Melvil Dewey Award for creative professional achievement of a high order: Edward G. Holley, dean, School of Library Science, University of North Carolina

Grolier Foundation Award for unusual contribution to the stimulation and guidance of reading by children and young people: Zena Sutherland, editor, *Bulletin of the Center for Children's Books*, University of Chicago

John Phillip Imroth Memorial Award presented to an intellectual freedom fighter . . . who has demonstrated remarkable personal courage: Nat Hentoff, staff writer, *The Village Voice* and *The New Yorker*

Joseph W. Lippincott Award for distinguished service to the profession of librarianship: Russell Bidlack, dean, School of Library Science, University of Michigan

John Newbery Medal for the most distinguished contribution to literature for children: Cynthia Voight, *Dicey's Song*

private scholarship, study, or research most favored by the law.'' Some librarians held that the report favored publishers and denied, as the report contends, that librarians are confused about the copyright law and their role in its enforcement. In a related development, to the dismay of librarians, OCLC, Inc., the largest on-line depository of cataloging records, sought to copyright those records.

Settled out of court on April 24 was a copyright infringement suit against New York University brought by the Association of American Publishers. The settlement requires the university to instruct its faculty in what is allowed and forbidden under the Copyright Act.

The task force created to implement the resolutions of the 1979 White House Conference on Library and Information Services urged that a second conference be held in 1989, to be preceded by state and territorial conferences.

Other News. It was announced in April that the Richard M. Nixon Presidential Library and Museum would be located in San Clemente, CA. On the Twin Cities campus of the University of Minnesota, 37 women librarians were awarded $905,000 in the settlement of a sex discrimination complaint. Richard W. McCoy, formerly director of the Wisconsin State Office of Information Systems Management, became president of the Research Libraries Group.

American Library Association. Again during 1983, questions of money and organization dominated the association's January midwinter conference in San Antonio and its 102d Annual Conference in Los Angeles in June. At San Antonio, the ALA was told that its committees and offices were dominated by a self-perpetuating elite and that its revenue problems ultimately would require an increase in membership dues. In Los Angeles, Brooke E. Sheldon, dean of the school of library science, Texas Woman's University, became president of the association. The Public Library Association and the Library and Information Technology Association, both constituents of ALA, held their first national conferences in 1983. The association announced that its 104th Annual Conference would be held in its headquarters city, Chicago, July 5–12, 1985.

The association once again sponsored National Library Week, April 17–23, using as its theme, "Go For It! Use Your Library."

The association's Committee on Accreditation and its Standing Committee on Library Education expressed interest in "New Directions for Library and Information Science Education," a study conducted by King Research for the U.S. Department of Education.

International Events. The 49th Council Meeting of the International Federation of Library Associations and Institutions convened in Munich, August 21–27. Nairobi, Kenya, will be the host city for the 1984 council meeting.

DAN BERGEN, *University of Rhode Island*

LIBYA

Despite declining oil revenues, Libyan support for revolutionary movements in Africa and the Middle East continued during 1983, and evidence surfaced of Libya's assistance to Latin American radicals as well.

African Policy. Sudan, Chad, and, to a lesser extent, Egypt felt most threatened by Libya during the year. In February, Libya was reportedly massing troops and aircraft along its short frontier with Sudan as part of a plot to overthrow the regime of Sudanese President Jaafar al-Nemery. At the same time, Sudanese authorities arrested a number of suspected Libyan agents in the country. In response to requests from Egypt, which claimed that Libyan planes had violated its airspace, the United States sent several AWACS planes to Cairo and positioned naval vessels, including the American aircraft carrier *Nimitz*, off the Libyan coast.

Libya denied any involvement in the alleged Sudan coup attempt, accusing the United States of fabricating the story to strengthen its own hand in the region. Libya took its accusations to the UN Security Council, which debated the charges of U.S. aggression but declined to act.

The isolation of Libya in the region, coupled with the quick response of the United States in these events, prompted Libya to sign a treaty of friendship and cooperation with the Soviet Union. Although largely symbolic, the treaty was intended to serve as a warning to Libya's enemies.

At the time of the Libyan-Sudanese incident in February, Chadian rebels controlled by Goukouni Oueddei and aided by Libyan troops and mercenaries held large portions of northern Chad. In midsummer the insurgents began a major campaign, backed by units of the Libyan army and air force, against the government of Hissène Habré. Libyan soldiers in Chad numbered 3,000 to 4,000. Again the United States sent AWACS to the area, this time basing them in Sudan, and dispatched navy ships to the central Mediterranean.

LIBYA • Information Highlights

Official Name: Socialist People's Libyan Arab Jamahiriya ("state of the masses").
Location: North Africa.
Area: 679,000 sq mi (1 758 610 km²).
Population (July 1983 est.): 3,498,000.
Government: *Head of state,* Muammar el-Qaddafi, secretary-general of the General People's Congress (took office 1969). *Legislature*—General People's Congress (met initially Nov. 1976).
Monetary Unit: Dinar (0.296 dinar equals U.S.$1, July 1983).
Gross Domestic Product (1982 U.S.$): $25,000,-000,000.
Foreign Trade (1981 U.S.$): *Imports,* $8,382,000,000; *exports,* $15,576,000,000.

Col. Muammar el-Qaddafi denounces French and U.S. intervention in the Chad war. The Libyan leader was in Tunisia in August for talks on bilateral and regional cooperation. At right is Tunisian Prime Minister Mohamed Mzali.

© A. Nogues/Sygma

Several important towns fell to the rebels before the Libyan-assisted assault was halted when French military forces were brought in to aid Habré's hard-pressed troops. No progress was made in reaching a political settlement, however, and Libyan units remained in Chad.

Such adventures have long persuaded many African states that Colonel Qaddafi wants to create a Libyan-dominated confederation in the Saharan region. Libya's support for the new government of Upper Volta, which came to power in a coup in August, reinforced this conviction, as did the long-standing Libyan support for Polisario, the Western Saharan movement that has fought to keep Morocco from annexing the former Spanish Sahara. When Polisario abandoned in June, at least for the moment, its campaign for representation in the Organization of African Unity (OAU), Qaddafi was dealt a serious setback. This rebuff may have prompted him to focus more sharply on Chad and to initiate the summer offensive there. Soon after the June meeting of the OAU, Qaddafi met for the first time in many years with Morocco's King Hassan II and pledged his neutrality in the ongoing Moroccan conflict with Polisario.

Middle Eastern Policy. Libya continued to maintain a hard line toward Israel and any Arab groups perceived to be wavering in their anti-Zionism. Palestine Liberation Organization (PLO) leader Yasir Arafat accused Libya of supporting rebellious factions within the PLO that had expressed dissatisfaction with the organization's declining militancy against Israel and had challenged Arafat's leadership. Although a truce between Arafat and Qaddafi was eventually patched together by Arab third parties, Libya's support for the rebels reduced the effectiveness of moderate PLO elements.

Latin American Policy. Of greater concern to the United States was Libya's sending arms and materiel to Nicaragua. This was learned in April when a Libyan transport plane, refueling in Brazil, was found to contain not medical supplies, as had been asserted, but armaments. Brazil came under heavy pressure to prevent the passage of the weapons to Nicaragua but sought to preserve its economic ties with Libya, which had become the second most important purchaser of Brazilian military equipment.

Although the cargo was eventually returned to Libya, the existence of a supply link between Latin America and Libya disturbed American officials, who suspected that Libyan supplies might also be reaching Salvadoran and Colombian rebels. Argentina's former President Leopoldo Galtieri confirmed that Libya had supplied arms to his country as well.

Oil Industry. Libya was one of the member nations of the Organization of Petroleum Exporting Countries (OPEC) that resisted efforts led by Saudi Arabia early in 1983 to curb oil production by instituting quotas as a response to the glut caused by economic recession in the West, overproduction, and the coming on line of additional non-OPEC sources of oil. Saudi attempts to raise the premium, or differential, charged for Libyan oil especially angered the Libyans. A general agreement arrived at in March cut production in Libya to 1.1 million barrels a day, lowering oil revenues considerably. The government suspended development projects and allowed the import only of essential items.

The oil industry in the country was further hurt by the complete withdrawal of Mobil Oil from Libya after a year of fruitless negotiations with the government. Mobil claimed that Libya had unilaterally violated its 1955 concession agreement by manipulating oil prices, taxes, and royalties and threatened to attempt to recover from Libya compensation for lost profits, future profits, and the value of its abandoned assets.

King Idris. Although the event was little noticed in Libya, the death on May 25 of the nation's first and only monarch, King Idris, in exile in Cairo, at the age of 93, removed the most prominent Libyan political figure of the 20th century prior to the 1969 revolution.

KENNETH J. PERKINS
University of South Carolina

LITERATURE

In a lively year for book publishing, outlets for first novels, short stories, and poetry appeared to be on the rise. Biography, essay, and history were flourishing. British novelist William Golding won the Nobel Prize (see page 331); Canada's Governor General Awards for English and French fiction went to Guy Vanderhaeghe (Man Descending) and Roger Fournier (Le cercle de arenes); France's Prix Goncourt was awarded to Frederick Tristan (Les Egarés); and the John Newbery Medal for children's fiction went to Cynthia Vogt for Dicey's Song. In U.S. letters, three giants of the previous generation were back on the scene. A previously unpublished autobiographical novel by Theodore Dreiser, An Amateur Laborer, came out in November. An important short story by William Faulkner, "Father Abraham," appeared in print for the first time. And Ernest Hemingway was back in vogue, with sales of his books higher than ever.

American Literature

As large trade publishers have found themselves committed more and more to high volume and quick turnover, small independent publishers have again become important to American literature. There are now estimated to be more than 1,000 small presses in the United States, many devoted to publishing talented writers, often in beautifully designed, carefully produced editions. These presses not only contribute to the literature of the future by letting young voices be heard, but they also preserve the literature of the past with reprints of important works that have gone out of print. R. R. Bowker's new magazine Small Presses: The Magazine of Independent Book Publishing recognizes the importance of the movement.

Novels. The literary event of 1983 was to have been the publication of a novel that Norman Mailer had been working on for more than ten years. But Ancient Evenings, an epic covering 1,000 years under the Egyptian pharaohs, did not live up to expectations. Despite massive research and some brilliant scenes, Mailer's attempt to recreate a civilization and capture its attitudes on sex, death, and immortality did not, many felt, have a life of its own.

That life was found in Mark Helprin's Winter's Tale. Richly imagined, the book blends the real and the fantastic in an odyssey that begins in a magical version of 19th-century Manhattan and ends in an apocalyptic future.

Russell Hoban came out with Pilgermann, a lyrical inquiry into the vagaries of human behavior as seen through the eyes of a wandering Jewish pilgrim in the 11th century.

With Ironweed, William Kennedy completed his trilogy—begun with Legs (1975) and Billy Phelan's Greatest Game (1978)—on life in Albany, NY, in the 1930s. Kennedy blends the lyricism of James Joyce and the naturalism of James T. Farrell into a distinctive narrative style. He is both mythopoeic and realistic in his depiction of politicians and bootleggers, the big fish and the small fry in a squalid city that becomes a moral arena for men who try to affirm themselves in circumstances over which they have no real control.

In Oral History, Lee Smith uses a college student doing a research paper to recreate the marvelous, astringent voice of southern Appalachia. Her interviews uncover a complicated history of killings, incest, and betrayal in a family whose land by the 1960s seems destined to be the site of a theme park. Paule Marshall produced another finely crafted work, Praisesong for the Widow, the story of a middle-aged black woman whose trip to the Caribbean is a pilgrimage to her historic past, her youth, and her buried self. The burden of the past and the inadequacies of the present are deeply felt by the protagonist in Cynthia Ozick's The Cannibal Galaxy. A Jewish refugee who starts a successful school in America, he is trapped by both his hopes and fears, his idealism and his pessimism. Ozick's critique of contemporary life is akin to Isaac Bashevis Singer's in The Penitent, a vivid monologue by a once-worldly man who now finds peace only in the most old-fashioned orthodoxy.

A serious social commentary underlies the 20th work by comic novelist Peter De Vries, Slouching Towards Kalamazoo; a story of "coming of age" in the midwest of the 1950s, it seems to foreshadow the social crises of contemporary America. Toby Olson's celebrated first novel, Seaview, has a dying woman and her husband traveling across the United States toward a golf course for a strange confrontation of cultures. Thomas Berger's The Feud suggests the fragility of the social fabric by showing trivial incidents growing uncontrollably into major disasters.

In August, Judith Rossner combines fine social observation on middle-class life in New York with penetrating psychological insight into her characters as she alternates point of view between a troubled middle-aged psychoanalyst and her patient, a young woman with a difficult childhood. Philip Roth's The Anatomy Lesson completes his trilogy—begun with The Ghost Writer (1979) and Zuckerman Unbound (1981)—about his talented, afflicted, seriocomic creation, the writer Nathan Zuckerman. In this work Zuckerman is now ailing, balding, and unable to write.

First novels showed great diversity. James Wilcox's Modern Baptists is tumultuously comic. Joan Chase's During the Reign of the Queen of Persia conveys the dark side of farm life. And Gordon Lish's *Dear Mr. Capote* is about a murderer looking for a biographer.

Short Stories. While regional short stories of the 19th century tended to emphasize the richness and vitality of local customs, many contemporary short-story writers focus on regions to dramatize the loss of a sense of place and the discontinuity with the past. In *Moon Deluxe*, Frederick Barthelme's Sunbelt South is a brilliantly delineated vacuum in which directionless men drift passively in and out of apartment complex rentals and barely felt relationships. In John Rolfe Gardiner's *Going On Like This*, Virginia has become a world of bedroom communities and interstate highways. Professional and domestic pressures dominate New England in Nicholas Delbanco's *About My Table*. The characters in *The Stories of Breece D'J Pancake* are hardly enriched by the hills of West Virginia, a poor, dying land of coal mines and subsistence farms. (The oddly named author committed suicide in 1979.)

Nor is city life celebrated. The vigor of Pittsburgh does not inspire the characters of David Walton's *Evening Out*. New York is a scene of dislocation and isolation in Laura Furman's *Watch Time Fly*. And Stephen Dixon satirizes that city's intellectual community in *Movies*. On the other hand, the Americans in Paul Theroux's *The London Embassy* have a lively environment in which to act our variations on their roles as innocents abroad.

While all of these writers are acute observers of manners and customs, they raise issues deeper than local color, or the lack of it. Nowhere is this seen more clearly than in Raymond Carver's third major collection, *Cathedral*. His landscape is Midwestern, but his interests are universal: the peculiar nature of life, its incomprehensible losses, people's failures to understand each other, and the unpredictable moments of stillness and epiphany.

Donald Barthelme's *Overnight to Many Distant Cities* again shows his impeccable ear and his ability to fracture story forms. Andre Dubus' *The Times are Never So Bad* runs counter to most contemporary serious fiction in its high incidence of real violence. M. F. K. Fisher is overtly autobiographical in her movingly affirmative stories of elderly people, *Sister Age*. *The Short Stories of Bernard Malamud*, his 25 most endearing and enduring contributions to the short-story form, show the continued viability of the conventional narrative.

Poetry. Serious, ambitious poetry in America continues to find only a small, specialized audience. So, despite their energy and their delights, such books as Frank Bidart's *The Sacrifice* or Nicholas Christopher's *On Tour With Rita* are likely to become known to only a few. A book of verse is likely to get more attention if the writer is famous for something other than poetry. Ntozake Shange's vivid *A Daughter's Geography* and Erica Jong's direct and highly personal *Ordinary Miracles* are therefore likely to be widely read. It is not that the American public has completely lost interest in poetry; it is perhaps that few poets today have the mixture of bravura and subtlety, directness and complexity that creates a strong following.

Sometimes a poet's achievement is appreciated only retrospectively. Louis Martz's edition of H. D.'s *Collected Poems 1912–1944* makes clear that the handful of imagist poems reprinted in most anthologies do not fully demonstrate the richness of her work or her importance in American literature. Alvin H. Rosenfeld's *Collected Poems of John Wheelwright* brings to light the neglected New England poet whose blend of modernism and Marxism would have been more influential had he not been killed in an accident at age 43.

Collections that allow the reader to weigh the poet's work over a decade or more tend to get more attention than slim volumes of new poems. James Schevill's *The American Fantasies: Collected Poems 1945–81*, for example, brings together his renderings of the voices of America from all walks of life. Norman Dubie similarly enhances his reputation with *Selected and New Poems*.

Putting out a collection and a new volume in the same year attracts notice to both. Albert Goldbarth, a relatively young poet, produced *Faith* as well as *Original Light: New and Selected Poems 1973–83*; Charles Simic put out *Austerities* and *Weather Forecast for Utopia and Vicinity: Poems 1967–1982*; and the accomplished Louis Simpson's *The Best Hour of the Night* and *People Live Here: Selected Poems 1949–1983* evidence his quiet eloquence.

The long wait since his previous book contributed to the appropriate attention paid to Gary Snyder's *Axe Handles*. But works by established poets who publish regularly—such as Robert Creeley's *Mirrors*, W. S. Merwin's *Opening the Hand*, or A. R. Ammons' *Lake Effect Country*—often do not get the attention they deserve.

The persistence of younger poets in the face of such lack of reward testifies to their sincerity. The books themselves—such as David Bottoms' *In a U-Haul North of Damascus*, Amy Clampitt's *The Kingfisher*, or Dave Smith's *In the House of the Judge*—testify to their talent.

Criticism. Several novelists produced notable works of social and literary criticism. Walker Percy's *Lost in the Cosmos* is a satirical self-help book and philosophical primer. Cynthia Ozick is both penetrating and controversial in *Art & Ardor*. John Updike's *Hugging the Shore* collects his graceful essays. And the late John Gardner left some useful and inspiring advice in *On Becoming a Novelist*.

JEROME H. STERN, *Florida State University*

AMERICAN LITERATURE: MAJOR WORKS | 1983

NOVELS

Adler, Renata, *Pitch Dark*
Algren, Nelson, *The Devil's Stocking*
Batchelor, John Calvin, *The Birth of the People's Republic of Antarctica*
Berger, Thomas, *The Feud*
Brown, Rita Mae, *Sudden Death*
Calisher, Hortense, *Mysteries of Motion*
Caputo, Philip, *DelCorso's Gallery*
Charyn, Jerome, *Pinocchio's Nose*
Chase, Joan, *During the Reign of the Queen of Persia*
De Vries, Peter, *Slouching Towards Kalamazoo*
Ephron, Nora, *Heartburn*
Farrell, James T., *Sam Holman*
Goyen, William, *Arcadio*
Hannah, Barry, *The Tennis Handsome*
Helprin, Mark, *Winter's Tale*
Hoban, Russell, *Pilgermann*
Johnson, Denis, *Angels*
Kennedy, William, *Ironweed*
Lish, Gordon, *Dear Mr. Capote*
Loewinsohn, Ron, *Magnetic Field(s)*
Mailer, Norman, *Ancient Evenings*
Marshall, Paule, *Praisesong for the Widow*
Michener, James A., *Poland*
Olson, Toby, *Seaview*
Ozick, Cynthia, *The Cannibal Galaxy*

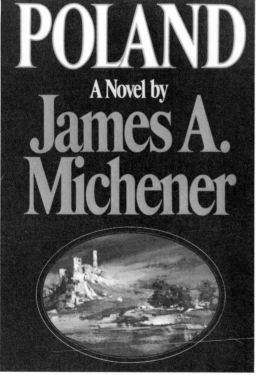

Richard Adelson/Peter Cox/Courtesy, © Random House 1983

Pesetsky, Bette, *Author From a Savage People*
Rechy, John, *Bodies and Souls*
Rossner, Judith, *August*
Roth, Philip, *The Anatomy Lesson*
Schwartz, Lynne Sharon, *Disturbances in the Field*
Singer, Isaac Bashevis, *The Penitent*
Smith, Lee, *Oral History*
Solenstein, John, *Good Thunder*
Sorrentino, Gilbert, *Blue Pastoral*
Towers, Robert, *The Summoning*

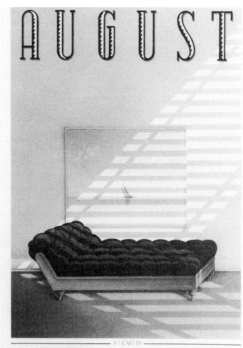

© Fred Marcellino 1983/Courtesy, Houghton Mifflin Company

Vidal, Gore, *Duluth*
Wambaugh, Joseph, *The Delta Star*
Wilcox, James, *Modern Baptists*
Wolitzer, Hilma, *In the Palomar Arms*

SHORT STORIES

Auchincloss, Louis, *Narcissa and Other Fables*
Barthelme, Donald, *Overnight to Many Distant Cities*
Barthelme, Frederick, *Moon Deluxe*
Carver, Raymond, *Cathedral*
Delbanco, Nicholas, *About My Table*
Dixon, Stephen, *Movies*
Dubus, Andre, *The Times are Never So Bad*
Fisher, M. F. K., *Sister Age*
Furman, Laura, *Watch Time Fly*
Gardiner, John Rolfe, *Going On Like This*
Godwin, Gail, *Mr. Bedford and the Muses*
Goodman, Ivy, *Heart Failure*
Malamud, Bernard, *The Short Stories of Bernard Malamud*
Nye, Robert, *The Facts of Life and Other Fiction*
Pancake, Breece D'J, *The Stories of Breece D'J Pancake*
Penner, Jonathan, *Private Parties*
Robison, Mary, *An Amateur's Guide to the Night*
Tallent, Elizabeth, *In Constant Flight*
Theroux, Paul, *The London Embassy*
Walton, David, *Evening Out*

POETRY

Ammons, A. R., *Lake Effect Country*
Anderson, Jack, *Selected Poems*
Bidart, Frank, *The Sacrifice*
Bottoms, David, *In a U-Haul North of Damascus*
Clampitt, Amy, *The Kingfisher*
Christopher, Nicholas, *On Tour with Rita*
Creeley, Robert, *Mirrors*
H. D., *Collected Poems 1912–1944,* ed. Louis Martz
Dubie, Norman, *Selected and New Poems*
Goldbarth, Albert, *Faith; Original Light: New and Selected Poems 1973–1983*
Halpern, Daniel, *Seasonal Heights*
Jong, Erica, *Ordinary Miracles*
Knox, Caroline, *The House Party*

Louthan, Robert, *Living in Code*
Merwin, W. S., *Opening the Hand*
Morris, Herbert, *Peru*
Sandy, Stephen, *Riding to Greylock*
Schevill, James, *The American Fantasies: Collected Poems 1945–1981*
Shange, Ntozake, *A Daughter's Geography*
Simic, Charles, *Austerities; Weather Forecast for Utopia and Vicinity: Poems 1967–1982*
Simpson, Louis, *The Best Hour of the Night; People Live Here: Selected Poems 1949–1983*
Smith, Dave, *In the House of the Judge*
Snyder, Gary, *Axe Handles*
Stafford, William, and Bell, Marvin, *Segues: A Correspondence in Poetry*
Tichy, Susan, *The Hands in Exile*
Van Duyn, Mona, *Letters From a Father*
Wagoner, David, *First Light*
Collected Poems of John Wheelwright, ed. Alvin H. Rosenfeld

HISTORY AND BIOGRAPHY

Berry, Faith, *Langston Hughes Before and Beyond Harlem*
Bruccoli, Matthew J., *James Gould Cozzens: A Life Apart*
Didion, Joan, *Salvador*
Donaldson, Scott, *Fool for Love: F. Scott Fitzgerald*
Ferrell, Robert H. (ed.), *Dear Bess: The Letters from Harry to Bess Truman, 1910–1959*
Field, Andrew, *Djuna: The Life and Times of Djuna Barnes*
Hahn, Steven, *The Roots of Southern Populism*
Harrison, Gilbert, *The Enthusiast: A Life of Thornton Wilder*

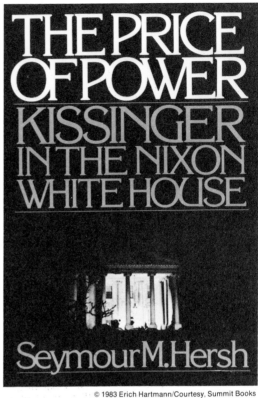

© 1983 Erich Hartmann/Courtesy, Summit Books

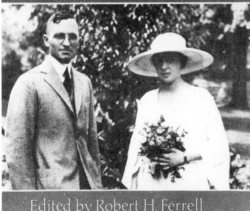

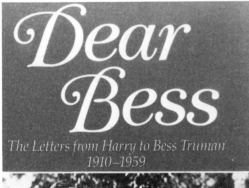

Edward P. Diehl/Harry S. Truman Library/Courtesy, W. W. Norton & Company

Hersh, Seymour M., *The Price of Power: Kissinger in the Nixon White House*
Horowitz, Irving Louis, *C. Wright Mills An American Utopian*
Johnson, Diane, *Dashiel Hammett: A Life*

Johnson, Joyce, *Minor Characters*
Landes, David S., *Revolution in Time: Clocks and the Making of the Modern World*
Lorenz, Clarissa, *Lorelei Two: My Life with Conrad Aiken*
Matthiessen, Peter, *In the Spirit of Crazy Horse*
Nagel, Paul C., *Descent From Glory: Four Generations of the John Adams Family*
Nicosia, Gerald, *Memory Babe: A Critical Biography of Jack Kerouac*
Radosh, Ronald, and Milton, Joyce, *The Rosenberg File: A Search For the Truth*
Robinson, Phyllis C., *Willa: The Life of Willa Cather*
Sears, Stephen W., *Landscape Turned Red: The Battle of Antietam*
Shivers, Alfred S., *The Life of Maxwell Anderson*
Thomas, John L., *Alternative America: Henry George, Edward Bellamy, Henry Demarest Lloyd and the Adversary Tradition*
Torrey, E. Fuller, *The Roots of Treason: Ezra Pound and the Secret of St. Elizabeth's*
Wyatt-Brown, Bertram, *Southern Honor: Ethics and Behavior in the Old South*

CRITICISM AND CULTURE

Bettelheim, Bruno, *Freud and Man's Soul*
Bok, Sissela, *Secrets: On the Ethics of Concealment and Revelation*
Gardner, John, *On Becoming a Novelist*
Hardwick, Elizabeth, *Bartleby in Manhattan*
McPhee, John, *In Suspect Terrain*
Moon, William Least Heat, *Blue Highways: A Journey into America*
Ozick, Cynthia, *Art & Ardor*
Percy, Walker, *Lost in the Cosmos: The Last Self-Help Book*
Updike, John, *Hugging the Shore*
Wilson, Edmund, *The Forties: From Notebooks and Diaries of the Period,* ed. Leon Edel; *The Portable Edmund Wilson,* ed. Lewis M. Dabney

Children's Literature

A noticeable trend among the some 2,000 children's book titles published in 1983 was the emphasis on education-oriented material in response to parental concern for children's academic progress. Numerous books were devoted to computer literacy and to helping the very young in vocabulary building, reading, and elementary mathematics. Figures from books and movies—Smurfs, E.T., Luke Skywalker, and R2-D2—were employed in inexpensive series books to aid in mastery of spelling, the alphabet, multiplication, and scientific concepts. Pop-up books were used to explain the human body, rocketry, and outer space.

Two of the more enthusiastically received books of the year were Alice and Martin Provensen's *The Glorious Flight*, a sumptuously illustrated account of Louis Blériot's pioneering efforts in aviation that culminated in a 1909 flight across the English Channel, and Chris Van Allsburg's *The Wreck of the Zephyr*, a handsomely illustrated picture book with full-color pastel paintings, about a boy out to prove he is the world's greatest sailor.

The American Library Association's (ALA's) John Newbery Medal went to Cynthia Voigt for *Dicey's Song*, a novel about four abandoned children adjusting to a new life with their grandmother. The ALA's Randolph Caldecott Medal was awarded to Marcia Brown for her illustrations in *Shadow*, French poet Blaise Cendrars' version of an African folk tale. Miss Brown, who also translated *Shadow*, won the medal in 1955 for *Cinderella* and in 1962 for *Once a Mouse . . .* as well. The American Book Awards in various categories of children's literature were awarded to cowinners Barbara Cooney for *Miss Rumphius*, the story of a woman who sowed the Maine coastline with lupine seeds, and William Steig for *Doctor De Soto*, in which a dentist mouse outwits a fox patient; to Mary Ann Hoberman and illustrator Betty Fraser for *A House Is a House for Me*, a rhymed tour of dwellings for various animals, people, and things; to Jean Fritz for *Homesick: My Own Story*, an account of the author's growing up as the daughter of missionaries in China in the late 1920s; to cowinners Paula Fox for *A Place Apart*, the story of a 13-year-old girl's search for order and security in her changing world, and to Joyce Carol Thomas for *Marked by Fire*, a novel about the joys and sorrows of a black girl growing up in a small Oklahoma community; and to James Giblin for *Chimney Sweeps*, a history of the trade from the 12th century to the present.

For the picture-book audience (ages 3 to 6), the most noteworthy books were *Peter Spier's Christmas*, a wordless book showing a family's preparation, celebration, and clean up of the holiday; Molly Bang's retelling of a Japanese tale, *The Crane Wife*, in *Dawn*, which is set in New England whaling days; Vera B. Williams' *Something Special for Me*, about a young Hispanic girl's search for a birthday present to buy; three books by *The New Yorker* magazine cartoonist James Stevenson: *Grandpa's Great City Tour*, an alphabet book, *What's Under My Bed?*, nighttime reassurance, and *Barbara's Birthday*, an extravagant celebration in a pop-up book. Another pop-up deserving of mention was John S. Goodall's scenes of pastoral Edwardian life in *Lavinia's Cottage*.

For children between 7 and 10, the best new books were *Arnold of the Ducks* by Mordicai Gerstein, in which a human boy is adopted by a flock of ducks; Nonny Hogrogian's retelling of a Grimm tale in *The Devil with Three Golden Hairs;* Mitsumasa Anno's pictorial journey across America in *Anno's U.S.A.;* Arnold Lobel's *The Book of Pigericks*, colorfully illustrated limericks about pigs; and *The Month-Brothers*, a Slavic tale about an orphan girl's quest in a wintry magical forest, illustrated by Diane Stanley.

In the ages 9 to 12 category the books most outstanding were Roald Dahl's *The Witches*, a tale about a seven-year-old schoolboy—transformed into a mouse—and his grandmother against the Grand High Witch of All the World and her sister conspirators; Elizabeth George Speare's *The Sign of the Beaver*, a story about a boy's survival in the Maine wilderness of the late 1760s; Beverly Cleary's 27th book, *Dear Mr. Henshaw*, cast in the form of letters and a diary in which a ten-year-old boy reveals his longing for an absent father; Patricia Wrightson's *A Little Fear*, about an elderly woman battling an aged gnome for possession of an isolated Australian cottage; and Betsy Byars' *The Glory Girl*, about a young girl in a family of gospel singers discovering her self-worth.

Among the year's best novels for young teenagers were Kathryn Lasky's *Beyond the Divide*, the adventures of a 14-year-old Amish girl traveling westward by wagon train; Suzanne Newton's *I Will Call It Georgie's Blues*, set in a small southern town, and in which some dark secrets of a minister's family are revealed; Robert Cormier's *The Bumblebee Flies Anyway*, a grim story about three boys in a hospital for the incurably ill; and Virginia Hamilton's *The Magical Adventures of Pretty Pearl*, a fantasy using the black idiom, combining myth, folklore, and history and about a god child coming down from Mount Kenya to help her people being sold into slavery.

In poetry the most noteworthy volume was *The Random House Book of Poetry for Children*, a treasury of 572 poems, edited by Jack Prelustsky and illustrated by Arnold Lobel. Jean Fritz's *The Double Life of Pocahontas* and M. E. Kerr's *Me Me Me Me Me* were outstanding in biography and autobiography.

GEORGE A. WOODS, *"The New York Times"*

Canadian Literature: English

In English-language Canadian fiction, collections of short stories were numerous. In nonfiction, some writers focused on Canada's history, politics, and economy, while others looked at its people.

Nonfiction. Celebrated Canadian kidnappings are the subject of Toronto writer Derrick Murdoch's aptly titled *Disappearances.* In *Bacchanalia Revisited,* James H. Gray details Canada's growing number of alcoholics and urges temperance.

The province of Quebec drew the attention of several writers. *The Dream of a Nation,* by Susan Mann Trofimenkoff, is a well-documented history of Quebec. The fortifications of Quebec City through history are described in *Quebec, the Fortified City: From the 17th to the 19th Century,* by André Charbonneau, Yvon Desloges, and Marc Lafrance. The history of one of the province's oldest and wealthiest families is given in *The Molson Saga,* by Shirley E. Woods.

Across the country, in British Columbia, five professors researched for five years to produce *The Reins of Power—Governing British Columbia,* by Terence Morley, Norman J. Ruff, Neil A. Swainson, R. Jeremy Wilson, and Walter D. Young. In *The Ghost Walker,* R. D. Lawrence tells how he was able to gain the friendship of a wild cougar in BC's Selkirk Mountains. Glen Williams' *Not for Export* concerns the imbalance between Canada's export of finished goods and raw materials. Ed Shafer's *Canada's Oil and the American Empire* is about the oil problems of Canada and the United States. *The Nuclear Arms Race,* edited by Ernie Regehr and Simon Rosenblum, is a collection of writings that spell out the horrors of a nuclear war and urge Canada to disarm.

Best-selling Pierre Berton's *The Klondike Quest* is a collection of photographs of the Klondike gold rush, 1897–99, linked by the author's comments. Biology professor M. Brock Fenton's *Just Bats* is a lively and learned look at the creatures he finds fascinating.

Dangerous Patriots: Canada's Unknown Prisoners of War, by William and Kathleen Repka, relates how in 1940 the Canadian government put more than 100 leftists and radicals in its prisoner of war camps without their being charged or tried. Daniel G. Dancock's *In Enemy Hands: Canadian Prisoners of War, 1939–45,* records the suffering, and in some cases death, of Canadians captured at the hands of Germans and Japanese during World War II.

The 70th birthday of Canada's leading literary critic was commemorated by the publication of *Centre and Labyrinth—Essays in Honor of Northrop Frye,* edited by Eleanor Cook, Chaviva Hosek, Jay MacPherson, Patricia Parker, and Julian Patrick. *Storm Signals: More*

Undiplomatic Diaries, 1962–71 is the fourth volume of diplomat Charles Ritchie's diaries. Historian C. P. Stacey's *A Date with History* is his autobiography. *The de Haviland Story,* by Fred Hotson, tells of de Haviland planes in peace and war.

Poetry. *Writing Right—Poetry by Canadian Women,* edited by Douglas Barbour and Marni L. Stanley, is a collection of poetry by 16 Canadian poetesses, with drawings by eight Canadian women. *Split/Levels* is Judith Fitzgerald's sixth volume of poetry. Weldon Hanbury's *A Surfeit of Love* is a promising first volume. Milton Acorn's *Dig Up My Heart* is subtitled *Selected Poems 1952–83.* His *Captain Neal MacDougal & the Naked Goddess* is a collection of 38 sonnets which he pretends are from the log of a 19th-century Prince Edward Island sea captain. Erin Moure's *Wanted Alive,* her second volume, shows emotion and humor. David Helwig's *The Rain Falls Like Rain* presents previously published poems along with some new ones.

Fiction. Among the year's notable collections of short stories was Margaret Atwood's *Murder in the Dark,* which she subtitled *Short Fictions and Prose Poems,* and George Bowering's *A Place to Die,* a group of experimental stories. Other volumes included *Rainshadow: Stories from Vancouver Island,* edited by Ron Smith and Stephen Guppy; Sandra Bursell's *Night Travellers,* stories set in rural Manitoba; D. M. Fraser's highly original tales, *The Voice of Emma Sachs;* Kevin Roberts' *Flash Harry and the Daughters of Divine Light;* and *Maddened by Mystery,* a collection of Canadian detective stories, edited by Michael Richardson.

Among the year's novels was Morley Callaghan's *A Time for Judas,* an unusual retelling of the Christ story. His life, according to the theory, needed a betrayer to be dramatically complete; Judas, out of loyalty rather than treachery, obliged. Brian Moore's *Cold Heaven* is about a doctor's adulterous wife who has a vision of the Virgin Mary in California but says nothing about it and suffers strange consequences. In Leon Rooke's *Shakespeare's Dog*, William Shakespeare has a dog named Hooker that can talk, and well enough to narrate this engaging novel. Equally unusual is Anne Rosenberg's *The Bee Book*, which relates the life of a bee to that of the novel's leading character, a woman searching for the perfect mate. Robert Harlow's *Paul Nolan* traces the falling apart of a man dedicated to sex. Bruce Allen's *The Aberhart Summer* is set in Alberta during the summer of 1935, when evangelist William Aberhart becomes Social Credit premier. Rudy Wiebe's *My Lovely Enemy* concerns a professor who falls in love with a colleague's wife. Stephen Vizinczey's *An Innocent Millionaire* is about a young man who recovers a great treasure from a sunken Spanish galleon but finds that his new wealth is the target for others' greed.

DAVID SAVAGE, *Simon Fraser University*

Canadian Literature: French

French Québécois publishers turned out a great many titles during 1983, with more nonfiction and essays than in previous years. French presses in Ontario, Manitoba, and Acadia were particularly productive. Two classic novels of Quebec, *Maria Chapdelaine* and *Bonheur d'occasion*, were adapted to the screen, and a third, *Les Fous de Bassan* by Anne Hébert, is in the process of being filmed. In addition, three well-known Quebec authors died during the year: novelists Gabrielle Roy and Yves Thériault, who had dominated the Quebec literary scene for 30 years, and the self-effacing poet Gatien Lapointe, founder of the Editions des Forges.

Essays and Criticism. In the essay, major works included two studies of the Parti Pris movement so important in the 1960s—Paul Chamberland's *Un parti pris anthropologique* and Pierre Maheu's *Un parti pris révolutionnaire*—and Naïm Kattan's cogent analysis of feeling and desire in *Le désir et le pouvoir*. Three historical studies deal respectively with French immigration to New France, Franco-Ontarian immigration, and the establishment of francophones in the United States: Marcel Trudel's *Catalogue des immigrants;* Germain Lemieux's *La vie paysanne 1860–1900,* and the collective study *Du continent perdu à l'archipel retrouvé: le Québec et l'Amérique française*. As for literary studies, noteworthy new works were Patrick Imbert's *Roman québécois contemporain et clichés*, Roger Motut's *M.*

Constantin-Meyer, and Donald Smith's interviews with Quebec authors, *L'ecrevain et son ombre*. Two books describe the contribution to Quebec letters of literary institutions: Claude Janelle's *Les Editions du Jour* traces the growth of that publishing house in the 1960s, while the memoirs of editor-publisher Pierre Tisseyre are narrated in Jean-Pierre Guay's *Lorsque notre littérature était jeune*.

Other Nonfiction. Political memoirs were popular in 1983. Claude Charron's *Désobéir* was a best-seller, as Gérard Pelletier's first volume, *Les Années impatientes 1950–1960*, was expected to be. Among "coffee table" books, the striking photos by Mia and Klaus in *Montréal* complement their previous volume, *Québec*. The exquisite scrigraphs by Japanese artist Miyaki Tanobe help make Alain Stanké's reedition of *Bonheur d'occasion*, selling for $3,000, a collector's item and a striking memorial to its author, the late Gabrielle Roy.

Fiction. It was fortuitous that both Roy and Thériault published works of fiction prior to their passing. Roy's *De quoi t'ennuies-tu, Eveline?* had been written some 20 years earlier but never published, while Thériault's collection of short stories, *L'Herbe de tendresse,* brings together the major themes of his many works of fiction. In the field of the novel, many lesser-known writers appeared in print. Roger Fournier's *Le Cercle des arènes* won the Governor-General's Award for fiction (1982), and Alice Parizeau produced her second novel, *La Charge des sangliers*. Francophone writers outside Quebec were unusually active. Hélène Brodeur's *Entre l'aube et le jour* chronicles the history of Franco-Ontarians; Jeanine Landry-Thériault's *Un soleil mauve sur la baie* offers an Acadian perspective on interracial marriage; and the young heroine of Annette Saint-Pierre's *La Fille bègue* reflects Franco-Manitoban concerns. A well-received first novel was Marguérite Anderson's semiautobiographical *De mémoire de femme*. The whimsical tone of Pierre Châtillon's volume of short stories, *La Fille arc-en-ciel*, contrasts sharply with the tragic violence of Madeleine Ferron's *Sur le chemin Craig*, about the settling of Irish immigrants in the Beauce region near Quebec City in 1858.

Poetry. Small presses in Quebec continued to encourage the writing of poetry. Les Editions du Noroît published several volumes, as did Les Herbes rouges. Les Editions des Forges produced readings of Gatien Lapointe's poetry (*Anthologie sonore 1956–1982*) prior to his death in October. Another retrospective appeared, Pierre Chatillon's *Poèmes* (1956–1982), as did Rina Lasnier's latest work, *Chant perdu*. The poet-editor Gaston Miron, founder of the Hexagone movement, received the prestigious Prix David for his contribution to Quebec poetry.

RAMON HATHORN, *University of Guelph*

English Literature

Biography, which has gained new freedom and assurance since World War II, was an especially notable element of British letters in 1983, although fiction and poetry also thrived. British award-winning authors included William Golding, who won the Nobel Prize for literature, and J. M. Coetzee, who won the Booker Prize for fiction for a Kafkaesque novel set in South Africa, *Life and Times of Michael K.*

Nonfiction. Frances Spalding's *Vanessa Bell* is the first, and perhaps the definitive, biography of the painter who was a sister of Virginia Woolf and a central figure in the Bloomsbury Group. Victoria Glendinning's *Vita* is the first biography to be devoted singly to Victoria Sackville-West, although, like Vanessa Bell, Sackville-West, a friend of Virginia Woolf, has frequently appeared in other books. Robert Skidelsky's *John Maynard Keynes: Hopes Betrayed, 1883–1920* is the first volume of a new study of the life of the economist who was a friend and neighbor of the Woolfs and Bells.

Various diaries and autobiographies were published. Philip M. Williams' edition of *The Diary of Hugh Gaitskell, 1945–1956* covers the crucial years when Gaitskell was a cabinet minister and then leader of the opposition during the Suez crisis. John Goodwin's selection from Peter Hall's diaries gives a day-to-day account of Hall's experiences as director of Britain's National Theatre. Michael Redgrave's autobiography, *In My Mind's Eye*, tells of an actor's life. Richard Cobb, a historian, wrote in *Still Life* of his childhood in Tunbridge Wells; and Rosemary Sutcliffe, author of tales for young people, of her early life in *Blue Remembered Hills*. Danny Abse, a poet and a doctor, produced *A Strong Dose of Himself;* A. J. P. Taylor, a historian, *A Personal History;* and G. S. Fraser, poet and teacher, *A Stranger and Afraid: Autobiography of an Intellectual.*

Collected essays by a novelist and a poet, respectively, were Angus Wilson's *Diversity and Depth in Fiction* and D. J. Enright's *A Mania for Sentences.*

Fiction. Several major writers published novels in 1983. Anthony Powell's *O, How the Wheel Becomes It!* is an ironic study of the career of a minor writer; Stanley Middleton's *Entry into Jerusalem*, a perceptive examination of the life of a painter. In *The Philosopher's Pupil*, Iris Murdoch, with the help of a skeptical philosopher and a priest who has lost his faith, among other denizens of the spa town that she creates, continues her exposition of problems in philosophy, life, and literature. In Alan Sillitoe's *The Lost Flying Boat*, a former Royal Air Force crew, in quest of treasure in Antarctica, are driven to reconsider their lives and to ask some ultimate questions. John le Carré's *The Little Drummer Girl* also combines adventure with weightier considerations: suffering in the Middle East and relationships among spying, terrorism, and acting. Doris Lessing continued her "Canopus in Argus" series with *The Sentimental Agents in the Volyen Empire*, and Lawrence Durrell his series about a Gnostic sect with *Sebastian.*

Four novels gained archetypal significance as they portrayed aspects of life in Ireland. William Trevor's *Fools of Fortune* describes the experiences of a prosperous country family from the time of the potato blight of 1846 to a Black and Tan raid in 1920, which destroyed most of their home, killed the father, and adversely affected his descendants to the present day. Clare Boylan depicts in *Holy Pictures* the growth to womanhood of girls in a Catholic family and a convent school in Dublin. In M. S. Powers' *Hunt for the Autumn Clowns*, tragedy overtakes a mentally retarded teenager, his teacher, and his priest on an island off the western Irish coast. Terrorist links blight a love affair in Bernard Mac Laverty's *Cal*, set in Ulster.

Other notable novels were David Wheldon's *The Viaduct*, J. P. McDonach's *The Channering Worm*, Penelope Mortimer's *The Handyman*, Graham Swift's *Waterland*, Malcolm Bradbury's *Rates of Exchange*, and John Fuller's *Flying to Nowhere.*

Among collections of short stories were John M. Harrison's *The Ice Monkey*, George Mackay Brown's *Andrina*, Robert Nye's *The Facts of Life and Other Fictions*, Margaret Barrington's *David's Daughter Tamar*, and Clare Boylan's *A Nail on the Head.*

Poetry. Ted Hughes' *River* was perhaps the outstanding book of English poetry of 1983. A sensual, sharp-eyed examination of a river at various times of day and year, it may be as important as his earlier *Crow.*

There were also distinguished books from poets in Northern Ireland. In *Loose Ends*, John Hewitt defines his Protestant "planter" heritage and his allegiances in lithe, austere verse. In *Quoof*, Paul Muldoon describes personal experiences with elegant detachment and the effects of bombs in Belfast with surrealistic clarity. Violence colors with despair some of Derek Mahon's poems in *The Hunt by Night*. Tom Paulin's poems in *Liberty Tree* also reflect the troubles, past and present, in Northern Ireland, but he looks forward optimistically to the possibility of a "risen République/a new song for a new constitution."

Among other collections were George Barker's *Anno Domini*, Norman MacCaig's *A World of Difference*, Elizabeth Jennings' *Celebrations and Elegies*, Anne Stevenson's *Minute by Glass Minute*, Patricia Beer's *The Lie of the Land*, and Carol Rumens' *Scenes from the Gingerbread House.*

J. K. JOHNSTONE, *University of Saskatchewan*

William Golding   UPI

On October 6, the 1983 Nobel Prize in Literature was awarded to 72-year-old British novelist William Golding, author of *Lord of the Flies*. In making the announcement, the Swedish Academy cited Golding "for his novels which, with the perspicuity of realistic narrative art and the diversity and universality of myth, illuminate the human condition in the world of today." The elfin literary cult figure, who lives and writes in a farmhouse in Wiltshire, England, became the seventh British author to win the prize.

The son of a schoolmaster and suffragette, William Gerald Golding was born Sept. 9, 1911. He studied at Oxford and served in the Royal Navy during World War II. In addition to *Lord of the Flies* (1954), an allegory about English schoolboys marooned on a desert island, his novels include *Pincher Martin* (1956), *Free Fall* (1959), *The Spire* (1964), *Darkness Visible* (1979), and *Rites of Passage* (1980). The essay collection *A Moving Target* was published in 1982, and a new novel, *The Paper Man*, was to appear in 1984.

World Literature*

It was something of an oddity that the year 1983, despite the crowning of Colombia's Gabriel García Márquez in December 1982 as the 79th Nobel Prize laureate, did not bring forth a new Spanish-American masterpiece. Emigré authors Luisa Valenzuela and Heberto Padilla weighed in with important, politically charged novels set during recent turbulent eras in their respective homelands of Argentina (*The Lizard's Tail*) and Cuba (*Heroes Are Grazing in My Garden*). Of the major figures from "the Boom" of the last 25 years, however, only Peru's Mario Vargas Llosa and Mexico's Octavio Paz were heard from: the former with a short play, *Kathie and the Hippopotamus*, which

* Titles translated.

vacillates uneasily between farce and profound musings on "the relations between life and fiction"; the latter with a hefty critical-philosophical study of poetry and faith based on the lifework of the 17th-century Mexican author Sor Juana Inés de la Cruz.

What 1983 did bring was a banner harvest of new writing and new releases from Central and Eastern Europe, from Asia, the Near East, and Africa, from France and Italy, and from the Germanic world. Even Spain and Portugal, usually overshadowed by the more dynamic Latin Americans, produced two novels which could justifiably stand alongside the most innovative works of the 1960s and 1970s in the New World: Juan Goytisolo's *Landscape After the Battle*, a phantasmagoria of worldwide rebellion among the downtrodden and suppressed in Paris and Southern Europe; and Antônio Lobo Antunes' *South of Nowhere*, a remarkable account of colonial ambition and depravity in Angola, based on the author's own experiences there as a military surgeon and told in a gripping monologue form reminiscent of Camus' *The Fall*.

East European. The East European year in literature was marked by important new works from several of the region's most prominent figures. The flamboyant Russian poet Yevgeny Yevtushenko, whose public readings in the late 1950s and 1960s drew thousands of frenzied, idolatrous listeners but whose verse has often been maligned by serious critics as facile and sentimental, stunned his readers with a richly modulated and daringly frank novel, *Where Berries Grow*; touching on such near-taboo topics as poverty versus privilege in Soviet life, the novel presents a mosaic of incidents loosely tied together in reverse chronological sequence by the musings and recollections of a famous cosmonaut. Abroad, new verse collections by Joseph Brodsky in the United States (*New Verses for August* and *Urania*) and Natalia Gorbanevskaya in France (*The Wooden Angel*) confirmed both poets' preeminent positions in the Russian literary diaspora, while émigré novelist Vasily Aksyonov brought out a collection of five provocatively absurdist plays, only one of which had been granted permission for staging while the writer was still residing in Moscow. Ilya Suslov, like Brodsky and Aksyonov a "third wave" Soviet exile in the United States (though less well known than they), added to his reputation as one of the finest contemporary Russian humorists and short-story writers with the prose collection *Exit to the Sea*.

Polish author and 1980 Nobel recipient Czesław Miłosz issued his six 1981 Norton Lectures from Harvard University in book form as *The Witness of Poetry*, casting his eye toward both the destructive past and the millennial future in an effort to underscore the importance of poetry as a mediator of human destiny. A particularly significant point in Hungarian national history, October 1956, was evoked by Budapest native Ferenc Karinthy in his new work, *Autumn Comes to Budapest*, one of the few Hungarian novels of the ensuing quarter-century even to treat that traumatic period, much less to draw on firsthand personal experiences; the novel has been uniformly praised as one of the finest in postwar Hungary, and Karinthy has been hailed as an example of the morally responsible writer par excellence. Death-camp survivor Elie Wiesel, a native of Transylvania who now teaches in Boston but writes in French, continued his own themes of moral responsibility and learning from the past; his harrowing new book, *Words of a Stranger*, evokes not only the Holocaust but also the horrors of Cambodia and the Gulag, forcing us again to see, to remember, to question, to learn, to hope for change and betterment. And 1978 Nobel winner Isaac Bashevis Singer released the English version of *The Penitent*, a confessional novel immediately recognized by his Yiddish readers only a few years earlier as a contemplative examination of Jewish identity in the modern world.

Oriental. In the Far East, the year produced new works of dependable quality from such prominent Japanese novelists as Jun Ishikawa (*The Sixfold Journey*), Shusaku Endo (*A Woman's Life*), Noma Prize-winner Nobuo Kojima

Nobelist Isaac Bashevis Singer released ''The Penitent,'' the English version of a Yiddish novel published in 1974.
© Nancy Crampton/Farrar, Straus and Giroux

(*Reasons for Parting*), and Kenzaburo Oe, whose intimate first-person work *Raintree* continues his deeply personal obsession with the twin themes of nuclear war and his own deformed child. For Western readers, selections from two starkly divergent but immensely respected writers were made available in English for the first time: the popular poet Shuntaro Tanikawa (*Selected Poems*) and the octogenarian Buddhist short-story writer Kikuo Itaya (*Tengu Child*).

Recent Chinese literature reached the West via two excellent anthologies, one titled *20th-Century Chinese Drama* (Indiana University Press) and the other a remarkable collection of fiction, poetry, and essays produced during the brief liberalization of 1979–81 by the so-called ''Mao Generation,'' *Mao's Harvest* (Oxford University Press). Just as important perhaps was the first appearance of the late Lao She's largely autobiographical novel *Beneath the Red Banner*, left unfinished when Red Guards drove the famous humorist to suicide in 1966 during the early days of the Cultural Revolution; although the title conveys ironic parallels to life under the red flag of the People's Republic, the actual reference is to the Manchu political organization to which Lao's poverty-stricken family belonged at the time of the Boxer Rebellion.

Other Asian. From elsewhere in Asia came other notable contributions, including the fable-like new novel *A Tiger for Malgudi* by India's grand old man of fiction, R. K. Narayan, the latest in his continuing series of gently ironic works set in the mythical South India town of Malgudi. The short stories of South Korea's Ty Pak in *Guilt Payment* offer moving portraits of the Korean War and of subsequent emigration, expatriation, and regeneration. And in one of the year's most unusual developments, the chief ombudsman of Papua New Guinea, Ignatius Kilage, published a deeply sensitive and well-written novella, *My Mother Calls Me Yaltep*, detailing the island nation's evolution from a 1930's subsistence economy based on stone tools to a modern democracy in the 1970s.

Near Eastern. Two of Israel's finest Hebrew novelists brought out works of enormously contrasting natures: Aharon Appelfeld's *Tzili* traces the atrocity-filled odyssey of its virtually autistic young heroine across war-torn Europe to Palestine, while Benjamin Tammuz's *Requiem for Na'aman* invests a tale of modern Israel's resettlement with mythic import through biblical parallels with the story of Abraham. The masterwork of Turkey's late poet Nazim Hikmet, the verse novel *Human Landscapes*, was finally translated into English, offering Western readers its epic account of ''an encyclopedia of famous people,'' including lonely workers, peasants, and craftsmen. Egyptian author Ahdaf Soueif's short-story collection *Aisha*, though written in English, retains a strong Arabic flavor in idiom and outlook through the ritual nature by which it expresses emotions and through the distinctly "foreign" hue of its accounts of such matters as weddings, virginity, and the role of servility in marital relations.

African and West Indian. The year in Africa and the West Indies belonged principally to Francophone authors, although the single most outstanding event was publication of Nigerian writer Amos Tutuola's 1948 novel *Wild Hunter in the Bush of the Ghosts* in its original form, complete with manuscript facsimile and photographs of the "ghosts" that figure in the narrative. Congolese poet Tchicaya U Tam'si produced in *The Medusas* a superb récit involving sorcery and intrigue in wartime Africa and drawing on oral story-telling traditions to augment the work's poetic force. Mongo Beti's novel *The Two Mothers of Guillaume Ismael Dzwatama* marked the Cameroonian author's move toward the new popular literature in Africa, using a more realistic mode than in his earlier fiction and blending a concern with the evolving roles of African women into a dramatization of the plight of a corrupt, dictatorial country. And the preeminent Antillean poet, Aimé Césaire of Martinique, brought out a new verse collection, obliquely titled *I, Laminaria*, which draws on his 40 years of travel and political and literary activity and which shows no diminution whatsoever in the poet's creative power. In addition, much of Césaire's poetic oeuvre was made available in English in *The Collected Poetry* (University of California Press).

French. In France proper, 1983 brought the usual large number of prizewinning novels set in medieval times and spanning several generations of romantic figures, as well as the customary spate of hybrid works that engage much of the nation's critical debate. But four new books by three French "classics" and one gifted maverick stand out as perhaps the year's most remarkable achievements. The most challenging and controversial of the four is *Women*, a 570-page "postmodernist picaresque roman à clef" by Philippe Sollers, best known as the editor of the renowned quarterly *Tel Quel* (now called *L'Infini*); the work leaps mirthfully from barely disguised scandalous accounts involving members of the *Tel Quel* circle, to amorous peregrinations through Europe and America, to debates on blasphemy and Catholicism, to the establishment of a new regime controlled by women and based on Marxist-Freudian tenets. Of the three classic writers, two are octogenarians: Nathalie Sarraute, in *Infancy*, gives an autobiography in dialogue form, using her "second presence" to support, probe, and even occasionally undermine the first as she recounts the memories of her early years; and the prolific, multitalented Julien Green brought

out the 12th and next-to-last volume of his *Journal*, the most important series of works in this genre since those of André Gide more than 40 years ago—conscious, highly crafted literary works filled with acute observation, exemplary intelligence, and almost inordinate human decency. The third classic was the late Jean-Paul Sartre, whose posthumous *Notebooks of the Phony War* provide a record of the brief period of military service at age 34 that forced him for the first time to "shed his old skin," to live among others and subject himself to unflinching scrutiny in quest of true existential "authenticity"; the publication of these *Notebooks* adds an enormously significant text to the corpus of Sartre's work.

Italian. The year in Italian literature was highlighted by the work of that country's two most famous women authors. Elsa Morante's *Aracoeli* recounts the story of a fortyish psychopathic narrator's weekend search for his long-dead Andalusian peasant mother, tracing in the process a powerfully shattering portrait of increasing emotional deprivation from infancy to adulthood. Natalia Ginzburg, meanwhile, turned her fiction-writing talents to the creation of an exhaustive, fact-based novelistic account of the celebrated 19th-century writer Alessandro Manzoni's forebears in the well-received work *The Manzoni Family*.

Germanic. Last but in no way least, the year 1983 brought several fine books by authors from the Germanic areas, including successful works by Swedish Academy members Per Olov Sundman (*The Polar Voyage of the Icebreaker "Ymer," Summer 1980*, using fictional techniques to report on the actual voyage) and Kerstin Ekman (*A City of Light*), a new work of fiction by the prolific and versatile Norwegian writer Ole Sarvig (*I Sing for Myself*), and new publications by such leading German-language literati as Austrian novelist Peter Handke (*The Chinaman of Pain*), émigré East German poet Günter Kunert (*Still Life*), West German novelists Hermann Lenz (*The Stranger*) and Gabriele Wohmann (*The Shortest Day of the Year*), and East German prose writers Christa Wolf (*Cassandra*) and Irmtraud Morgner (*Amanda*). If any single book stands out, however, it must be West German author Uwe Johnson's *Anniversaries 4*, the final installment of a masterful and richly nuanced sociopsychological tetralogy centered on the life of the transplanted German bank employee Gesine Cresspahl and her young daughter Marie in New York during the late 1960s; moving freely between the 1930s, the war years, and the more recent past and between two continents, the novel ends with the Soviet occupation of Czechoslovakia on Aug. 20, 1968. By general critical consensus, the tetralogy is the closest the Germans have come to producing a true epic since the glory days of Thomas Mann.

William Riggan, *"World Literature Today"*

LONDON

The Greater London Council (GLC), the government of London, faced abolishment in 1983. For some time, Britain's Conservative government, led by Margaret Thatcher, has been irritated because many of its financial directives have been ignored by the main metropolitan governing bodies. Many of them, including the London council, are controlled by Labour majorities.

The Greater London Council—whose offices at County Hall, just across the river from the House of Commons, have displayed neon signs indicating London's total number of unemployed for all the world, but especially members of Parliament, to see—has been a source of special annoyance for Mrs. Thatcher. According to the Conservative manifesto, which Mrs. Thatcher presented to the nation during her 1983 reelection campaign, the GLC and other major metropolitan councils would be disbanded. The powers of such councils would go to local boroughs, more amenable to central directives. Numerous protests—especially from arts bodies who appreciate the role of the GLC in underwriting London's main orchestras, as well as contributing to major theaters and galleries with annual grants totalling £2.1 million ($3.2 million)—did not make the Conservative Party think again. The GLC's attempt to cut bus and subway fares and subsidize them, which was defeated in court in 1982, added to the mutual hostility.

After Mrs. Thatcher's landslide reelection, it was obvious that something would be done. The timetable for the demise of the council was to depend on a government proposal, expected in late 1983. In July the newly elected government introduced a White Paper, stating that "the organization of London's public transport services needs major change" and outlining its plan to take the running of the London Transport away from the GLC within a year. Two separate operating companies, responsive to London Regional Transport, a holding company in control of the transport minister, would operate the system.

MAUREEN GREEN
Free-lance Writer

LOS ANGELES

Except for the weather and chronic municipal government financial problems, 1983 was a quiet year in Los Angeles. But as a sign of change in the state administration, action was begun to build the long-delayed Century Freeway, designed to relieve a traffic bottleneck outside the city's principal airport.

Finance. The first approximation made for an austere city budget fell far short of the balance required by law. Mayor Thomas Bradley then proposed a property-tax increase that he believed would be legal under the existing Proposition 13 restrictions. The city council rejected this plan and countered with a payroll tax, which was obviously unpopular. A temporary increase in various taxes then was agreed upon. Part of the financial problem stemmed from cutbacks in state aid. The county also cut its budget sharply, especially for juvenile offenders, probation, and the public defender. The county's largest employees' union, the Service Employees' Local 660, launched a large but apparently unsuccessful media campaign to try to prevent pay and benefits reductions. (*See* CALIFORNIA.)

Police. The civilian Los Angeles Police Commission voted to abolish the Public Disorder Intelligence Division, which had been criticized for gathering information on public officials and on nonviolent radical groups as well as others. Supporters of the group, established in 1970, said it would be needed especially during the forthcoming 1984 Summer Olympics, when terrorism would be a threat. The division was allowed to continue only until a satisfactory approach to antiterrorism could be devised.

Schools. Teachers were granted a 7.8% pay increase from a last-minute state-aid grant. But differences between the school board and the teachers' union remained, centered on establishment of agency shop fees, suspension procedures, and involuntary assignment to ghetto schools.

Weather. An unusually rainy winter was followed by record-breaking summer heat and high humidity. High tides and rains caused heavy coastal flooding and beach erosion from four great storms in January. The pattern was repeated in August, a most unusual time for storms. It was the hottest August in the 106 years of record-keeping, but no water or electrical-power crises resulted.

Sports. The city's preparations for the 1984 Olympics, including a major remodeling of Los Angeles International Airport, went forward. A minimal involvement of local governments and public funds and an austere budget were features of the planning for the Games. The adequacy of housing and transportation remained a question, and critics complained that sports events will be held in locations too widely scattered. Security considerations also remained controversial and the cause of interagency police disputes.

The Lakers played for the NBA title once again but were defeated in four games by the Philadelphia 76ers. The football Rams sought to rebuild by hiring John Robinson of USC as head coach. The former Oakland Raiders won several court battles while seeking to stay in Los Angeles. The Dodgers captured their division's title.

CHARLES R. ADRIAN
University of California, Riverside

LOUISIANA

A gubernatorial election, fiscal matters, and reapportionment were major news stories in Louisiana during 1983.

Election. In what is believed to be the most expensive gubernatorial race in U.S. history, Louisianans voted overwhelmingly on Oct. 22, 1983, to return former Gov. Edwin W. Edwards to office. Edwards, a Democrat, was governor from 1972 to 1980 but was constitutionally prohibited from succeeding himself after two successive terms.

Edwards won a landslide 1983 victory over Republican Gov. David C. Treen, who was seeking his second term. Edwards won 1,006,561 votes, or 62.3% of the total, while Treen captured 588,508 votes or 36.4%. Minor candidates captured the other 2.3%.

Edwards spent $12.6 million in winning back the governorship, while Treen spent $6.4 million. During the hard-hitting campaign, Edwards hammered at Treen's leadership ability and the state's huge fiscal deficit. Treen countered that falling petroleum revenues, which account for a large share of the state budget, caused the financial problems. His own campaign attacked Edwards' honesty and integrity. The day after the election, the victorious candidate commented that he had sought to regain the governorship to prove his honesty.

In a separate action, voters in New Orleans rejected an amendment that would have permitted the city's mayors to serve more than two terms in office.

The Legislature. After the election, at an end-of-the-year special session, the legislature took actions that would affect the pocketbooks, the environment, and political power in the state.

By December, the state budget was short $240 million in revenues. To partially remedy the shortfall, the legislature raised state personal income taxes $136.5 million, canceling a $100 million cut that had been enacted three years earlier, when oil revenues were high. The rest of the 1983 deficit will be made up through cuts in spending averaging 1.6% in state agencies. Governor Treen said that without the tax hike, state services would have to be curtailed and some employees laid off.

In a federal court-ordered reapportionment of the state's congressional districts, the legislature created the first district with a black majority in the state's history. The new 2nd District, which includes almost all of the city of New Orleans, is 58.6% black in population and 54% in voter registration. The district is now represented by Lindy Boggs, a liberal Democrat. The 1st District, represented by Republican Robert Livingston, Jr., was shifted from part of New Orleans to predominantly conservative suburban areas. The 3rd District, represented by Democrat Billy Tauzin, was altered slightly, and the other five districts were untouched.

A new state Department of Environmental Quality, which had been created earlier in the year, was put in limbo during the special session. Governor-elect Edwards asked the legislature to suspend the department until he could propose a governmental reorganization after taking office in March 1984. Over the objections of conservative and black legislators alike, the legislators canceled a presidential primary set for April 1984. Opponents said organized labor would dominate a party caucus to choose delegates to the Democratic National Convention, giving former Vice-President Walter Mondale the edge.

During its regular session, the legislature passed a hazardous waste site law, established an endowment to supplement academic programs at Louisiana State University, and set up a program for salary increases for teachers.

Other. As in recent years, Louisiana had its share of criminal trials involving well-known persons. The state was shocked when former LSU football All-American Billy Cannon was accused of counterfeiting. He was convicted in federal court and sentenced to five years. Nationally known feminist Ginny Foat of California was acquitted by a jury of a murder that her former husband said she had committed in Jefferson Parish outside of New Orleans 18 years before.

The state saw its first execution in 22 years, when Robert Wayne Williams was electrocuted in December for the shotgun murder of a Baton Rouge security guard.

Ten parishes were ravaged by major floods early in April. More than 3,000 families were displaced from their homes, 289 persons were injured and 2 died. Tornadoes caused heavy property damage in the state one month later.

JOSEPH W. DARBY III, *"The Times-Picayune/ States-Item," New Orleans*

LOUISIANA • Information Highlights

Area: 47,752 sq mi (123 678 km²).
Population (1982): 4,362,000.
Chief Cities (1980 census): Baton Rouge, the capital, 219,486; New Orleans, 557,927; Shreveport, 205,815; Lafayette, 81,961; Lake Charles, 75,051.
Government (1983): *Chief Officers*—governor, David C. Treen (R); lt. gov., Robert L. Freeman (D). *Legislature*—Senate, 39 members; House of Representatives, 105 members.
State Finances (fiscal year 1982): *Revenues,* $6,453,000,000; *expenditures,* $6,463,000,000.
Personal Income (1982): $44,633,000,000; per capita, $10,231.
Labor Force (July 1983): *Nonagricultural wage and salary earners,* 1,583,500; *unemployed,* 233,900 (12.4% of total force).
Education: *Enrollment* (fall 1981)—public elementary schools, 543,275; public secondary, 238,778; colleges and universities (1981–82), 174,656. *Public school expenditures* (1981–82): $1,627,000,000.

MAINE

As many of the 3.3 million visitors to (and 1.1 million residents of) Maine in the summer of 1983 may have suspected, the state entertained a record number of vacationers. With June-through-August turnpike traffic up 7.4% over the same period in 1982 (compared with average increases of 2.5% in the previous three summers), many travelers may have wondered if their favorite vacation spot had reached its limits.

Economy and Finance. Several indicators underscored the positive impact on the state economy. Maine's personal income continued to grow at a rate exceeding the national average, while unemployment percentages stayed consistently below the national average. "Maine came through the recession with less pain than many other states," explained state statistician Galen Rose, "because the state's manufacturing mix is diverse and not centered on durable goods."

Fiscal indicators supported the evidence of economic vitality. According to some projections there would be a $10 million surplus in state coffers by the end of fiscal 1984. That, however, depended in large measure on whether the legislature would choose to step up spending. "A much more reliable signal that this state's fiscal health continues to improve," said Deputy State Treasurer Maurice F. Stickney, "is the credit-rating upgrading recently assigned Maine by Moody's. During 1983 that rating went from AA to AA-plus, and Maine was one of just three states to earn that sort of recognition. It's a solid affirmation of the state's financial stability."

While slow but steady increases continued in the state's population—7,000 Maine residents were added to the 1,125,027 counted in the 1980 census—financial and real estate development grew dramatically. In Portland, the state's largest city, plans were being made for new luxury condominiums and one of the largest metropolitan shopping malls in New England. Pulp and paper harvesters and processors, the state's largest industry and land owners, began to recover from the recession of the previous year. As the national economy recovered, so too did Maine's paper-products manufacturers.

Politics and Government. In contrast to the quickening pace of recreational and industrial activity in Maine during 1983, the political arena remained unusually quiet. There were repeated rumors that Gov. Joseph Brennan, a Democrat whose term expires in January 1987, might challenge the popular U.S. Sen. William Cohen, a Republican whose term ends in 1985. Brennan, however, denied such plans.

In late March the Democratic-controlled state legislature passed a simple congressional redistricting plan that affected only 18,000 people. The body earlier abandoned a plan that would have thrown the state's two members of the House of Representatives, both Republicans, into the same district.

With no candidates and several bond issues and constitutional amendments on the November ballot in 1983, the off-year election was dominated by a referendum question on the status of the moose, Maine's official state animal. In the first election in U.S. history to decide the status of a game animal, Maine voters had to decide whether to limit the number of moose that could be shot during a special hunting season or whether the moose should be restored to the protected status it had enjoyed since 1930. Voters decided to keep the hunt.

JOHN N. COLE, *"Maine Times"*

MALAYSIA

The murder conviction of a cabinet minister and the retirement of others prompted a cabinet reorganization at midyear. The Malaysian economy showed signs of recovery as steps were taken to increase private sector participation. And occupation of a disputed island threatened confrontation with Vietnam.

Politics and Government. In March, Minister of Culture, Youth, and Sports Mokhtar bin Haji Hashim was sentenced to death for the murder of a rival for state party leadership during the 1982 election campaign. A June 2 cabinet reorganization brought the elevation of former Muslim Youth Movement leader Anwar Ibrahim, who replaced Mokhtar in the cabinet.

The retirement of Lee San Choon as president of the Malaysian Chinese Association (MCA) and minister of transportation led to the naming of Chong Hon Nyan to succeed him as minister, assuring continued MCA control of the transportation post. On May 1, Neo Yee Pan was chosen as acting MCA president, and Mak Hon Kam replaced Neo as acting deputy president.

MAINE • Information Highlights

Area: 33,265 sq mi (86 156 km²).
Population (1982 est.): 1,131,000.
Chief Cities (1980 census): Augusta, the capital, 21,819; Portland, 61,572; Lewiston, 40,481; Bangor, 31,643.
Government (1983): *Chief Officer*—governor, Joseph E. Brennan (D). *Legislature*—Senate, 33 members; House of Representatives, 151 members.
State Finances (fiscal year 1982): *Revenues,* $1,572,000,000; *expenditures,* $1,527,000,000.
Personal Income (1982): $10,249,000,000; per capita, $9,042.
Labor Force (July 1983): *Nonagricultural wage and salary earners,* 418,000; *unemployed,* 56,500 (10.0% of total force).
Education: *Enrollment* (fall 1981)—public elementary schools, 148,769; public secondary, 67,524; colleges and universities (fall 1982), 47,719. *Public school expenditures* (1981–82), $515,744,000.

MALAYSIA • Information Highlights

Official Name: Malaysia.
Location: Southeast Asia.
Area: 128,400 sq mi (332 556 km²).
Population (July 1983): 14,995,000.
Government: *Head of state*, Sultan Ahmad Shah (took office April 1979). *Head of government*, Mahathir Mohammad, prime minister (took office July 1981). *Legislature*—Parliament: Dewan Negara (Senate) and Dewan Ra'ayat (House of Representatives).
Monetary Unit: Ringgit (Malaysian dollar) (2.332 ringgits equal U.S.$1, June 1983).
Gross Domestic Product (1982 U.S.$): $25,936,-000,000.
Economic Indexes (1981): *Consumer Prices* (1970 = 100), all items, 194.4; food, 209. *Industrial Production* (1975 = 100), 165.
Foreign Trade (1981 U.S.$): *Imports*, $13,132,-000,000; *exports*, $12,884,000,000.

The Hisbul Muslimin (Hamim) party was formed in March by longtime Parti Islam (PAS) president Asri Haji Muda. Asri had been ousted from the party presidency in October 1982 and left the PAS in January 1983.

Iban dissatisfaction with the National Front-member Sarawak National Party (SNAP) led to mass resignations and the formation of the Sarawak Dayak Party. SNAP, although dependent on Dayak support, was headed by a Chinese, James Wong.

Economy. Strengthening international markets and domestic demand, as well as increased agricultural, forestry, and oil production, induced Malaysia to raise its economic growth forecasts for 1983 from an original 5% to 5.5–6%. Cuts were announced in government spending, but foreign borrowing, which had doubled the public debt since 1980, was more than $2 billion.

Heavy losses by many public agencies prompted a "privatization" policy which sought corporate participation in providing public services. Possible target areas announced by the government included transportation, electricity, and hospitals. The first manifestation, however, was the approval of a private television station. The government-backed Bank Bumiputra's Honk Kong subsidiary, Bumiputra Finance, was revealed as a major backer of the bankrupt Hong Kong Carrian group.

Foreign Affairs. In September the government announced that, during joint exercises in June with fellow members of the Five-Power Defence Arrangement (Australia, Great Britain, New Zealand, and Singapore), Malaysian commandos occupied the atoll of Terumbu Layang Layang in the internationally disputed Spratly Islands off the coast of Sabah. Vietnam occupies most of the atolls in the Spratly group, including Amboyna Cay, claimed by Malaysia. The Malaysia claim is based on its declaration of a 200-mi (321-km) exclusive economic zone off its continental shelf. Oil and gas reserves have been reported in the area.

In April, following talks in London, Prime Minister Mahathir Mohammad announced the end of a government program to boycott British goods. In 1982, Mahathir had ordered government buyers to avoid purchasing British goods as a protest against soaring educational fees levied against foreign students.

K. MULLINER, *Ohio University*

MANITOBA

Manitobans will remember 1983 for its record high summer temperatures, as well as for the unusually hot, acrimonious debate in the legislature, where the longest sitting on record was marked by bitter debate.

The New Democratic government of Premier Howard Pawley battled the continuing recession with the creation of a $200 million government jobs fund to alleviate the plight of the 54,000 Manitobans unemployed in January. By June it claimed it had created work for 6,700 people. The government also projected a record budget deficit of $579 million and raised the sales tax from 5 to 6%. Gasoline, liquor, and tobacco taxes also were raised, and a 1.5% surtax on employer payrolls was continued for another year.

The government passed controversial legislation making the use of seat belts and motorcycle helmets compulsory, despite massive opposition from motorcyclists. It also pushed through a farmland protection act, preventing non-Manitobans from owning more than 10 acres (4 ha) of farmland. It introduced sweeping private pension plan reforms and measures to increase protection for people investing their savings in mortgages. Other reforms included changes in the Workplace Safety Act, which strengthened the rights of employees to refuse dangerous work and increased fines for employers who violate the act.

The most bitter political debate surrounded the government's plans to declare Manitoba an officially bilingual province and entrench the language rights of French Manitobans in the Canadian Constitution. Critics claimed the se-

MANITOBA • Information Highlights

Area: 251,000 sq mi (650 090 km²).
Population (July 1983 est.): 1,048,300.
Chief Cities (1981 census): Winnipeg, the capital, 564,473; Brandon, 36,242; Thompson, 14,288.
Government (1983): *Chief Officers*—lt. gov., Pearl McGonigal; premier, Howard Pawley (New Democratic Party); atty. gen., Roland Penner. *Legislature*—Legislative Assembly, 57 members.
Education (1982–83): *Enrollment*—elementary and secondary schools, 213,000; postsecondary, 20,320 students.
Public Finance (1983 fiscal year) *Revenues*, $2,859,-800,000; *expenditures*, $3,067,400,000.
Personal Income (average weekly salary, March 1983): $365.65.
Unemployment Rate (August 1983, seasonally adjusted): 8.8%.
(All monetary figures are in Canadian dollars.)

cretly negotiated plan actually expanded the French rights laid down in the 1870 Manitoba Act and would be expensive to implement. After an Opposition filibuster and massive public opposition, the government was forced to hold lengthy public hearings in September and to dilute its original plan.

In other political news, Conservative Opposition leader Sterling Lyon announced he would resign in December, while his deputy, Bud Sherman, said he would seek to win the federal seat of Winnipeg-Fort Garry, held by federal Transport Minister Lloyd Axworthy.

The discomfort of record summer temperatures was aggravated by a massive hatching of mosquitoes, and in July a provincial health emergency was declared because of the high risk of western equine encephalitis (sleeping sickness)—a disease carried by the mosquito. Winnipeg and other cities were aerially sprayed twice with the chemical Malathion.

Despite hot, dry conditions, United Grain Growers reported farmers were expected to harvest the second-largest crop in history, and the Canadian Wheat Board announced new sales to East Germany.

PETER CARLYLE-GORDGE
Free-lance Writer and Broadcaster, Winnipeg

MARYLAND

A mayoral race in Baltimore, crop-damaging weather, and the environmental health of the Chesapeake Bay were at the forefront of Maryland affairs in 1983.

Baltimore. Democrat William Donald Schaefer was elected to a fourth term as mayor of Baltimore, defeating Republican Samuel Culotta. Registered Democrats outnumbered Republicans in Baltimore by about 10 to 1, and Schaefer's greatest challenge came in the primary campaign from former Circuit Court Judge William Murphy, Jr., a black. Murphy had received the endorsements of a number of national black leaders and toured the country in a series of fund-raisers, but Schaefer defeated him soundly, 165,986 to 60,353. The population of Baltimore is 50% black, and Schaefer's victory ran counter to the national trend of blacks winning major posts in cities with a black majority.

Schaefer's running mate, Hyman Pressman, held off the challenge of a black legislator to remain city comptroller, a position he has held for 20 years. At the same time, City Council President Clarence Burns, a black who had been appointed to the office, won election over white candidates.

Agriculture. Maryland agriculture suffered from extremely bad weather during 1983. A cool, wet spring delayed planting, and an exceptionally hot, dry summer devastated important crops. Losses were estimated at $175 million, mostly in corn, soybeans, and tobacco; in some areas, crop losses hit 50%. Preliminary action by the federal government granted disaster status to half the state.

Chesapeake Bay. Considerable attention was focused on the health of the Chesapeake Bay, which, as a shipping route and producer of finfish and shellfish, is a major factor in the state's economy. Three studies of the bay and its problems were released during the second half of the year. A preliminary staff report to the Maryland General Assembly's Environmental Matters Committee called for "strong medicine" for deteriorating water quality, with particular emphasis on reducing phosphorus. A seven-year, $27 million study by the U.S. Environmental Protection Agency came to similar conclusions, depicting the bay as an ecosystem in decline because of harmful sewage plant discharges, farm chemical runoff, and industrial toxic waste. And a study by the Virginia Institute of Marine Science showed a marked decline in submerged grasses, beginning in 1972 when tropical storm Agnes dumped large amounts of fresh water and contaminated runoff into the bay. Pollutants damage the vegetation, and excessive nutrients in runoff cause algae to grow out of control, choking off oxygen from bay grasses. Without grasses, populations of shad, striped bass, oysters, clams, and crabs decline rapidly.

The governors of Maryland, Pennsylvania, and Virginia agreed on efforts to reverse the decline of the Chesapeake.

Economy. Unemployment in Maryland remained well below the national average, but economic difficulties troubled the western quarter of the state. Of several major businesses that closed or curtailed operations there, the greatest impact was experienced when Fairchild Republic announced the closing of its main aircraft plant in Hagerstown, putting 1,000 people out of work.

PEGGY CUNNINGHAM
"Baltimore News American"

MARYLAND • Information Highlights

Area: 10,460 sq mi (27 091 km²).
Population (1982 est.): 4,265,000.
Chief Cities (1980 census): Annapolis, the capital, 31,740; Baltimore, 786,775; Rockville, 43,811.
Government (1983): *Chief Officers*—governor, Harry R. Hughes (D); lt. gov., J. Joseph Curran, Jr. (D). *General Assembly*—Senate, 47 members; House of Delegates, 141 members.
State Finances (fiscal year 1982): *Revenues,* $6,281,-000,000; *expenditures,* $6,260,000,000.
Personal Income (1982): $52,195,000,000; per capita, $12,238.
Labor Force (July 1983): *Nonagricultural wage and salary earners,* 1,685,700; *unemployed,* 139,600 (6.3% of total force).
Education: *Enrollment* (fall 1981)—public elementary schools, 472,288; public secondary, 249,553; colleges and universities (fall 1982), 234,585. *Public school expenditures* (1981–82), $1,961,142,-000.

MASSACHUSETTS

The Bay State began 1983 with a new gubernatorial administration, as Michael S. Dukakis, a Democrat, took office in January. Dukakis had defeated incumbent Democrat Edward J. King in the September 1982 party primary; King had beaten Dukakis in 1978. Dukakis' first term as governor, 1975–79, was marked by persistent controversy involving what many perceived to be the governor's inflexible operating style. The year 1983 revealed a quite different approach, as Dukakis repeatedly worked for compromise solutions on a number of difficult issues. The annual budget, which in previous years had been hammered out in an atmosphere of confrontation, was approved in relative calm. Among other knotty problems were a "right to know" law regarding hazardous substances in the workplace, pitting labor and management interests against each other; the construction of a third tunnel under Boston harbor to carry traffic to Logan International Airport and the reconstruction of a major highway around Boston; and the establishment of statewide minimum standards for the conversion of existing residences into condominiums, over which landlord and tenant groups clashed. In each case negotiations were arranged by the governor's staff.

In late March state blue laws banning retail sales on Sundays were lifted. Religious groups opposed the repeal; proponents estimated that it would bring the state more than $1 billion in additional sales and create 15,000 new jobs.

Jobs and Industry. In economic affairs, Massachusetts' relatively low unemployment rate continued to hold. At midyear the state had 6.2% unemployed, compared with the national average of 9.3%. Some economists predicted, however, that the long period of expansion for high-technology industry, which had helped keep the state in good economic health through recent recessions, might be on the wane.

UPI

By a 420–3 vote, U.S. Rep. Gerry Studds (D-MA, tenth district) was censured by the House for sexual misconduct.

Education. Massachusetts' higher education institutions, a key ingredient in the high-tech economy and a major industry in the state, were experiencing a number of changes during the year. Private colleges, which enroll more students than the public system, were coping with the effects of a national decline in college-age population, reduced federal aid, and higher operating costs. The state's public college system had the added pressure of demands for lowered taxes and appropriations. In an autumn meeting in Worcester, the presidents of more than 70 public and independent schools called for joint efforts to shore up higher education in the state.

Other. Massachusetts citizens of all faiths were saddened by the death of Humberto Cardinal Medeiros, archbishop of the Boston diocese, on September 17. Cardinal Medeiros, who was 67, had been appointed to the Massachusetts post, the second-largest diocese in the country, in 1970. His tenure was marked by difficult decisions over the role of the Catholic school system in Boston when court-ordered desegregation, beginning in 1974, led many white students to seek admission to parochial schools.

The 1983 baseball season marked the end of an era for a generation of fans throughout New England, as Carl Yastrzemski retired after 23 years with the Boston Red Sox. There also was a bitter dispute among the team's owners, which was settled in favor of Mrs. Tom Yawkey, widow of the longtime club owner.

HARVEY BOULAY, *Rogerson House*

MASSACHUSETTS • Information Highlights

Area: 8,284 sq mi (21 456 km²).
Population (1982): 5,781,000.
Chief Cities (1980 census): Boston, the capital, 562,994; Worcester, 161,799; Springfield, 152,-319.
Government (1983): *Chief Officers*—governor, Michael S. Dukakis (D); lt. gov., John F. Kerry (D). *General Court*—Senate, 40 members; House of Representatives, 160 members.
State Finances (fiscal year 1982): *Revenues,* $8,752,-000,000; *expenditures,* $8,631,000,000.
Personal Income (1982): $69,882,000,000; per capita, $12,088.
Labor Force (July 1983): *Nonagricultural wage and salary earners,* 2,591,000; *unemployed,* 189,900 (6.2% of total force).
Education: *Enrollment* (fall 1981)—public elementary schools, 645,218; public secondary, 351,337; colleges and universities (fall 1982), 407,557. *Public school expenditures* (1981–82), $2,681,224,-000.

MEDICINE
AND HEALTH

In 1983 much attention, both by the medical community and by the general public, was given to two diseases whose names were unfamiliar just a few years ago: AIDS and Alzheimer's disease. Both are frightening illnesses for which there are no known cures.

Victims of other diseases are more fortunate. New drugs, improved technologies, and an increased understanding of the diseases offer asthmatics, heart-disease patients, and kidney-stone sufferers the possibility of improved health and shorter hospital stays.

AIDS. Acquired Immune Deficiency Syndrome (AIDS) suppresses the body's immune system, leaving victims vulnerable to a variety of fatal illnesses. The major risk groups are male homosexuals and intravenous drug users. The disease is spread almost exclusively through sexual contact and infected blood products.

As of Nov. 7, 1983, the national Center for Disease Control reported that there had been 2,678 cases and 1,102 deaths in the United States since the first documented cases in 1978. The 41% mortality rate is deceptive; statistics show that within two years after diagnosis, 80% of the victims have died. On the other hand, it is conceivable that thousands of mild cases also are occurring but are not diagnosed as AIDS and are not life-threatening. U.S. federal and state governments have allocated millions of dollars for AIDS research, which is proceeding along three main lines: discovering the cause, finding a cure, and developing a test to identify potential carriers.

By late in the year, AIDS was being recognized as a worldwide problem. Cases had been reported in 33 countries, especially in Europe.

Diseases of Pregnancy. Researchers at Loyola University discovered a microorganism that they believe is associated with toxemia of pregnancy. This disease is second only to hemorrhaging as a cause of maternal and fetal death. It may cause up to 5 million deaths worldwide annually and is a common cause of premature births. The newly discovered organism (*Hydatoxi lualba*) is similar to hookworms and filarial worms. Pregnant laboratory animals injected with organisms taken from the placenta of infected mothers developed toxemia syndrome. Nonpregnant animals and animals injected with human placenta from nontoxemic mothers did not.

The incidence of ectopic pregnancy has increased dramatically in the United States since 1970. In this disorder, the fetus develops in an ovary or other extrauterine location rather than in the uterus. This is potentially fatal for the mother, since the fetus grows in a place too small to contain it. If not removed in the first ten weeks of pregnancy, the fetus will burst the tube. Some 400 women and more than 250,000 unborn children died as a result of ectopic pregnancy between 1970 and 1978.

The causes of the increase in ectopic pregnancy are unclear. Scientists believe that an important factor is the trend toward becoming pregnant at older ages than in the past. Inadequate gynecological care and such sexually related diseases as gonorrhea also are believed to be important factors.

Contraceptives. Studies in the United States and Great Britain support evidence that the use of birth control pills increases the risk of contracting cancer. One study showed that young women who use birth control pills containing high levels of progestogen for at least five years are four times more likely to develop breast cancer than are other women. A second study indicated that women who use the pills have a 75% greater risk of developing cancer of the cervix than women who use intrauterine devices. And a third study found a link between prolonged use of birth control pills and the risk of contracting superficial spreading melanoma, a malignant skin cancer.

In April the U.S. Food and Drug Administration (FDA) approved a new method of birth control, the vaginal contraceptive sponge. It was invented by Bruce W. Vorhauer, a biomedical engineer in California. The sponge is made of polyurethane and is permeated with nonoxynol-9, a widely used spermicide. No prescriptions are needed to purchase the sponge, and it does not have to be fitted by a physician. FDA tests showed the sponge is 85% effective in preventing pregnancies, about the same rate as for diaphragms. (Birth control pills have an effectiveness rate of almost 100% when used properly.)

Heart Disease. Barney B. Clark, the first human recipient of an artificial heart, died on March 23, 1983. He had survived 112 days on the plastic implant, which was connected by hoses to an external power supply. Clark's death was due to disease in various parts of his body. The University of Utah, where the operation took place, imposed a moratorium on further implants while the procedure was reviewed.

A three-year study of people who survived a heart attack indicated that four symptoms can be used to predict which victims are most likely to suffer a second, fatal attack. The symptoms are: 1) an accumulation of fluid in the lungs, 2) a reduction in the pumping action of the heart's left ventricle, 3) shortness of breath or chest pain that began at least a month before the first heart attack, and 4) irregular heartbeats (arrhythmia). Patients in the study who had none of these symptoms had only a 2% chance of dying from a second heart attack within two years after the first attack. Patients with all four symptoms faced a 60% risk. As a result of the study, many hospitals have instituted procedures to profile and treat heart-attack patients who are at risk.

Many patients who undergo coronary bypass surgery could safely postpone the operation and perhaps avoid it entirely. A study of 780 patients from around the United States found that 92% of the patients who had surgery were still alive after six years; so were 90% of those who were treated only with medications —a difference that is statistically meaningless. The study did not contradict earlier studies that showed the value of surgery for patients with severe angina or major blockage of the left main coronary artery. Rather, it indicated that patients with mild to moderate chest pains could wait until symptoms worsen. So could patients without pain who already had one heart attack, even though they have significant blockages in one or more coronary arteries. These groups represent about 13% of the patients who have been undergoing the operation. Dr. Eugene Passamani of the National Heart, Lung and Blood Institute pointed out that bypass surgery is most successful and safest the first time it is done. This suggests that it may be best to wait to operate until absolutely necessary.

Alzheimer's Disease. This degenerative mental disorder is characterized by memory loss, shrinking social and work activities, episodes of confusion, and poor judgment. It is the leading cause of dementia in middle-aged and elderly people, afflicting an estimated 2.5 million Americans. The cause of the disease is unclear, and there is no specific treatment, but several promising drugs are currently being tested. People with Alzheimer's generally have a low level of the chemical acetylcholine (ACH); that deficiency is believed to cause some of the disease's symptoms. Researchers at Albert Einstein College of Medicine in New York enhanced the ACH levels of eight Alzheimer's disease victims with daily doses of physostigmine supplemented with lecithin. Six of the eight patients improved significantly with respect to memory, both in total recall and in the length of time during which memorized items could be retained.

Two Massachusetts physicians who examined differences in clinical symptoms between early- and late-onset victims of Alzheimer's disease noted significant differences in survival rates between the two groups. None of the early-onset patients (those developing symptoms before age 65) reached their life expectancy. In contrast, those who developed symptoms at 65 or later generally survived to their statistical longevity. Left-handedness and language problems were a disproportionately common feature of the early-onset patients. The researchers speculated that these people may have an inherited abnormality in which the

Mark Glickman/Photo Trends

Demonstrations publicizing the horrors of the disease AIDS occurred frequently in cities across the United States.

left hemisphere matures more slowly than usual. The possible genetic link appears to be supported by another study that indicated that senile patients with language disorders are more likely to have a family history of dementia.

Asthma. French researchers have found that the effectiveness of corticosteroids in treating asthma is improved if the drugs are taken upon waking. Taking the major dosage after the sleep cycle reduces the suppression of the adrenal gland and minimizes other undesirable side effects. It also maximizes the beneficial effects of the drug, such as improving airway function. Tests with several other asthma medications indicate that they too are most effective when taken early in the morning.

According to Dr. Sheldon L. Spector of UCLA, one out of three female asthmatics who become pregnant experiences a significant worsening of her asthmatic symptoms. These can create serious problems since some asthma medications may adversely affect the fetus. "Pregnant asthmatic patients should avoid all medications if possible, including alcohol, cigarettes, and excessive caffeine," said Spector. He added that caution also must be used during breast-feeding, since many asthma drugs have been found in breast milk.

Studies currently in progress indicate that injections can be used to protect some patients against asthma attacks. For example, a three-month series of injections utilizing cat allergen significantly decreased the intensity of symptoms normally experienced by patients with a history of asthma upon exposure to cats.

Medical Technology. West German doctors have developed two new techniques for treating kidney stones. One method involves inserting a tube into the kidney. The tube contains instruments and fiber-optic devices that enable surgeons to see the kidney. Depending on the specific case, the surgeons either remove the stone under direct vision or pulverize it with ultrasound, then remove the small pieces with a suction device. The procedure is less risky and less painful than traditional operations and shortens by several weeks the patient's recovery period.

The second method does not involve surgery at all. After a local anesthetic is injected, the patient is seated in a tank filled with water. A shock wave generator is focused on the kidney stone. Hundreds of high-energy electric shock waves—each sounding like a pistol shot —are used to pulverize the stone. Within two days following the treatment, the pieces of the stone are passed in the patient's urine.

Diagnosis of upper-airway obstructions, such as those caused by infections, injury, or the swallowing of foreign objects, can be improved dramatically with the use of a flexible fiber-optic tube. According to Dr. Pierre A. Vauthy of The Toledo Hospital and Medical College of Ohio at Toledo, the tube, which has a diameter of about 3.3 mm (.13 inch) is especially useful in infants. It is superior to older forms of diagnosis, such as the radiograph, and causes less discomfort than rigid probes.

Scientists at General Electric have developed a nuclear magnetic resonance (NMR) system that can chemically analyze any part of a living human—without biopsies or other invasive procedures. The patient is simply placed in a powerful magnetic field and "probed" with high-frequency radio signals. If desired, the data can be computer-reconstructed to form cross-sectional images of the body's tissues and organs. NMR may someday help doctors detect tumors and other medical problems long before they could be detected by conventional techniques.

Smoking. Several studies provided new evidence of the adverse effects of passive smoking (inhalation of smoke by nonsmokers who live or work with smokers). A study of the Amish people of Pennsylvania, who are nonsmokers, showed that those who are exposed to smokers and breathe smoke-filled air have a higher rate of lung cancer than those who have little contact.

Researchers at Cleveland Metropolitan General Hospital and Case Western Reserve University showed that when a nonsmoking pregnant woman is exposed to the cigarette smoke of other people, the fetal blood contains significant amounts of smoke by-products. The researchers said that this "is consistent with the possibility that passive smoking might adversely affect the fetus."

Edward A. Martell, a radiochemist with the National Center for Atmospheric Research, reported that cigarette smoke concentrates radioactive radon gas in the lungs of both smokers and passive smokers. Radon gas and its decay products are found in almost all structures. They are common in building materials, soils, and water from artesian wells. According to Martell, concentrations of radon gas are about ten times higher indoors than outdoors in summer and are much higher inside energy-efficient homes in winter. In smoke-filled rooms, the decay products build up on smoke particles. When inhaled, some of these particles are concentrated in the lungs, exposing the tissues to large doses of alpha radiation. Martell's research indicates that people who haved smoked one pack per day over a 40-year period have received a cumulative dose of about 100 rads of alpha radiation at tissue sites in the lung. Such dosages are considered strong enough to produce cancer.

A study conducted at the University of California at San Francisco concluded that people who switch to low-nicotine cigarettes inhale as much nicotine as they did when smoking regular cigarettes. The researchers found that when people switch to low-nicotine cigarettes they smoke more, inhale more deeply, or puff more frequently, thereby absorbing as much nicotine as before.

Alcohol Use. According to a report commissioned by a U.S. Senate subcommittee, the economic cost of alcohol abuse in the United States may reach $120 billion per year. This translates to an average of about $10,000 for each problem drinker. About half of the costs are for health care and half for indirect outlays (on-the-job problems, automobile accidents, etc.). The study, designed to determine the value of Medicare payments for alcohol-abuse treatment programs, questioned "whether current reimbursement policy supports the provision of the most cost-effective treatment." It said that "reimbursement systems—particularly Medicare and Medicaid—have generally encouraged the use of inpatient, medically based treatment of alcoholism." Yet, though this is significantly more expensive than community-based programs, little difference in effectiveness was found.

Scientists have found a chemical abnormality in the way that alcoholics metabolize alcohol. Unlike nonalcoholics, severe alcoholics produce a compound called 2,3-butanediol during alcohol metabolism. According to Dr. David D. Rutstein of Harvard, one of the researchers, the finding strengthens evidence that alcoholism is a disease rather than a social phenomenon. It also may lead to a test for predisposition to alcoholism, which would warn people who might be afflicted.

Recommended Weight. The Metropolitan Life Insurance Company in March released new tables, based on mortality research of millions of policyholders, indicating the "ideal weight" an adult person should maintain to live a long life. As against figures released in 1959, recommended weights are generally higher. Ranges are given below.

1983 Metropolitan Height and Weight Tables
(Men and Women, According to Frame, Ages 25–59)

Height (In Shoes)[1]	Weight in Pounds (In Indoor Clothing)[2]		
	Small Frame	Medium Frame	Large Frame
Men			
5'2"	128–134	131–141	138–150
5'3"	130–136	133–143	140–153
5'4"	132–138	135–145	142–156
5'5"	134–140	137–148	144–160
5'6"	136–142	139–151	146–164
5'7"	138–145	142–154	149–168
5'8"	140–148	145–157	152–172
5'9"	142–151	148–160	155–176
5'10"	144–154	151–163	158–180
5'11"	146–157	154–166	161–184
6'0"	149–160	157–170	164–188
6'1"	152–164	160–174	168–192
6'2"	155–168	164–178	172–197
6'3"	158–172	167–182	176–202
6'4"	162–176	171–187	181–207
Women			
4'10"	102–111	109–121	118–131
4'11"	103–113	111–123	120–134
5'0"	104–115	113–126	122–137
5'1"	106–118	115–129	125–140
5'2"	108–121	118–132	128–143
5'3"	111–124	121–135	131–147
5'4"	114–127	124–138	134–151
5'5"	117–130	127–141	137–155
5'6"	120–133	130–144	140–159
5'7"	123–136	133–147	143–163
5'8"	126–139	136–150	146–167
5'9"	129–142	139–153	149–170
5'10"	132–145	142–156	152–173
5'11"	135–148	145–159	155–176
6'0"	138–151	148–162	158–179

[1] Shoes with 1-inch heels. [2] Indoor clothing 5 lbs for men, 3 lbs for women. Courtesy, Metropolitan Life Insurance Company.

JENNY TESAR
Medicine and Science Writer

Dentistry

While the upturn in the U.S. economy prompted many Americans to resume seeking regular dental care in 1983, the recession-induced slump in dental visits continued in certain economically depressed areas. Traditional health care delivery has been altered by fluctuating economic conditions, and the practice of dentistry, responding to a new competitive climate, will experience fundamental changes over the next two decades. According to the Institute for Marketing Professional Services, 75% of U.S. dentists will be in group practice by 1998. Because the dental market is now "saturated" in some areas, the American Dental Association (ADA) recommended that dentists form individual practice associations (IPAs) to increase patient loads. Under the ADA definition, an IPA contracts with pur-

chasers—such as unions, corporations, insurance firms, or HMOs (Health Maintenance Organizations)—to provide dental care to enrolled individuals for a fixed monthly premium. Helping fuel this trend toward group practice will be a growing number of Americans covered by dental insurance plans.

Osteoarthritis. The girl who is captain of the cheerleading squad, class vice-president, prom queen, and an "A" student could be a prime candidate for a degenerative jaw disorder known as osteoarthritis (OA), according to Dr. Charles Stewart of Emory University School of Dentistry. Patients with OA of the jaw joint have been observed to have higher than average levels of anxiety and stress. "The subjects examined in our study—all female adolescents —exhibited a distinctive personality pattern," said Dr. Stewart. "We could characterize them as overachievers." Stewart indicated that OA in these teenagers may be the result of repeated tightening of the jaw muscles, induced by psychological stress. Signs of the disorder include jaw popping and clicking, headaches, pain, and muscle tenderness around the temporomandibular joint or jaw hinge joint. Treatments include analgesics, muscle relaxants, mouth splints, exercise, heat applications, physical therapy, and in some cases surgery.

Periodontal Disease. A microscopic technique for observing oral bacteria is helping dentists identify persons highly susceptible to periodontal (gum) disease, reported investigators at the National Institute of Dental Research (NIDR). The procedure, which allows researchers to examine bacterial samples immediately after they have been taken from the patient's mouth, could greatly increase the speed and effectiveness with which periodontal disease is diagnosed. Periodontal disease, the number one cause of tooth loss in adults, results when large amounts of certain kinds of bacteria establish themselves between the gums and the roots of teeth. Diagnostic techniques have depended on clinical and anatomical evaluation of the oral tissues; routine bacteriologic evaluations were hampered by a lack of techniques suitable for use in the dental office. "In time," the NIDR researchers said, "direct examinations of bacterial plaque specimens during regular dental check-ups could enable dentists to spot the presence of disease-causing microorganisms before the disease takes hold."

A new study has established a clear relationship between smoking and periodontal disease. A comparison of the smoking and dental histories of a representative population sample indicated that the gums of people who smoke are in poorer condition than those of persons who have never smoked or people who have quit. "This study doesn't prove that smoking causes gum disease," said Dr. Amid Ismail of the University of Michigan School of Dentistry, "but the evidence leans strongly in that direction. Even smokers with good dental hygiene habits have significantly poorer periodontal health than nonsmokers and former smokers." Though the smokers surveyed were generally younger than the nonsmokers and former smokers, the smokers still had higher rates of gum disease. In addition, past smokers have better periodontal health than smokers, but poorer periodontal health than nonsmokers. According to the study, the incidence of gum disease does not increase with the number of years a person has smoked; the number of cigarettes smoked per day does not seem to matter; and there is no significant difference in periodontal health among cigarette, cigar, and pipe smokers.

Xylitol. Could a between-meal snack be beneficial to a child's dental health? It could be if the snack contains xylitol rather than sugar, suggest University of Michigan researchers. Speaking at the annual meeting of the American Association for Dental Research, they reported that frequent chewing of xylitol gum leads to a reduction in the cavity-causing *streptococci mutans*. Xylitol is a sugar substitute that is as sweet as sucrose (natural sugar) but devoid of its tooth-decay action.

LOU JOSEPH, *Hill and Knowlton*

Mental Health

An estimated 1.7 million older Americans who suffer Alzheimer's disease, a progressively incapacitating central nervous system disorder, were heartened by news in 1983 that brain conditions believed to underlie the disorder appear to be modifiable. Alzheimer's disease affects approximately 6% of persons aged 65 and older, causing severe intellectual impairment and memory loss. The illness is the major factor responsible for placement of the elderly in nursing homes, at a national cost of more than $10 billion annually.

In March investigators at The John Hopkins University announced the results of a study of patients with Alzheimer's disease, showing a selective loss of neurons in the brain's *nucleus basalis* region. The affected cells constitute a pathway for the neurotransmitter acetylcholine, a substance associated with cognitive functions. The implications of this finding were underscored by simultaneous reports of slight improvement for short periods of time among patients administered drugs, such as naloxone and physostigmine, that act indirectly on acetylcholine-bearing neurons. Though the drug findings were preliminary, they suggested that the brain may be receptive to medications designed to act specifically on the affected neurotransmitter system.

In recognition of the increasing public health toll that Alzheimer's disease will levy as the U.S. population grows older, Secretary of Health and Human Services Margaret Heckler in March established a special task force to coordinate the research efforts of several U.S. Public Health Service agencies.

Brain and Behavior. The year also brought continued progress in long-term research designed to elucidate the biological bases of behavior. Among the most exciting of such research is that of Eric Kandel, at Columbia University, who focused on the learning process at the cellular level in *Aplysia*, a marine snail. Kandel identified specific cells in the snail's nervous system and delineated the neural circuitry. His studies demonstrated that even simple learning tasks modify chemical functioning at the synapse—the point at which adjoining cells communicate—and that these changes may be responsible for the animal's learning and memory capabilities.

Kandel's findings suggest that genetic expression is not set permanently at birth but can be modulated through environmental events. Extrapolating his findings to human behavior, he speculates that psychotic disorders may reflect "hardwired" defects, or alterations in the structure of specific genes, while neurotic disorders may result from environmental or learned modifications of genetic impact on neuronal function.

Kandel's research suggests a direct link between biology and behavior. Future studies may determine that the development and treatment of psychiatric disorders reflect degrees of physiologic changes in brain function.

Schizophrenia. University of Maryland scientists reported in *The New England Journal of Medicine* in March that hemodialysis showed no general therapeutic efficacy in treating schizophrenia, a severe mental disorder of unkown cause which affects 1–2% of the U.S. population. The treatment was first proposed in 1977, when researchers noticed dramatic improvement in a schizophrenic patient who also received hemodialysis for renal disease; the process involves filtration of the blood through an artificial membrane for purification. In the recent study, 17 patients received both real and sham dialysis treatments, and no improvement resulted in either instance. The researchers, while reporting negative findings, did not rule out the possibility that a small subset of patients may be responsive to the treatment.

AIDS. Growing recognition of the mental health risks of Acquired Immune Deficiency Syndrome (AIDS) stimulated research as well as educational efforts to sensitize health-care personnel to the special needs of patients. Of particular interest to mental-health investigators are behavioral—for example, psycho-immunological—factors that may play a role in the course and progress of the illness.

HERBERT PARDES
Director, National Institute of Mental Health

METEOROLOGY

Innovative observation systems, supercomputers, and new research techniques continued to broaden scientific understanding of atmospheric physics and chemistry, weather behavior, and climate change during 1983.

Observation Systems. The U.S. National Oceanic and Atmospheric Administration (NOAA) demonstrated a system of radars for measuring winds in clear air. Also developed by NOAA was a laser device which can detect the difference between rain and snow. Helium-filled balloons the size of a football field were launched to measure stratospheric water-vapor concentrations at altitudes of up to 25 mi (40 km). Closer to the ground, meteorologists experimented with weather measurements using instruments attached to "ultralight aircraft"—motorized hang-gliders.

Satellite Meteorology. NOAA during the year also launched the meteorological polar orbiter NOAA 8, which, besides sophisticated weather detection devices, also carries equipment for detection of aircraft and ship distress signals. GOES 6, a U.S. geostationary meteorological satellite parked over the equator, became operational, offering broad views of the west every 30 minutes. The U.S. Air Force launched a new weather satellite to detect and observe developing weather patterns over remote areas. And scientists announced a detailed proposal to launch lightning sensors on a geostationary meteorological satellite later this decade. Amid all the progress of the U.S. meteorological satellite program, however, the Reagan administration proposed to sell the nation's four weather satellite systems, and LANDSAT, to private interests; the LANDSAT system is used to identify flood-sensitive areas.

Weather Forecasting. NOAA continued to develop its Prototype Regional Observing and Forecasting Service (PROFS), which involves a dense network of automated ground stations, radars, satellite display systems, and other high technology. Researchers in 1983 studied the possibility of detecting killer tornadoes from larger cloud-void regions observable from meteorological satellites. The European Centre for Medium-Range Weather Forecasting, using a high-powered super-computer, has extended the useful range of large-scale numerical weather forecasts to 5–6 days. The British Meteorological Office also uses a new super-computer in its forecasting operations. The U.S. Weather Service is installing its own super-computer, capable of up to 80 million instructions per second, for operational forecasting. Citing the Florida Keys, where the escape route for some 70,000 residents is a two-lane road with 50 bridges, the U.S. National Hurricane Center estimated that evacuation would require more than 20 hours advance notice, whereas current hurricane landfall prediction models can give only 12 hours advance notice.

Climate and Weather. Under intensive research, the El Niño phenomenon—a major ocean warming in the equatorial Pacific—is believed to have contributed to unusually heavy rains in southern California, Ecuador, and Peru, drought conditions in Australia and Indonesia, and an unusually mild winter in much of the United States.

Lightning. In 1983 scientists discovered a method for detecting electrical currents inside clouds from ground-based equipment, a task that previously required instrumented aircraft. On a mountaintop in New Mexico, researchers stimulated lightning discharges from storm clouds using a tethered rocket device only 165 ft (50 m) from a research radar site. Astronauts aboard the space shuttle observed a spectacular Y-shaped lightning discharge in a thunderstorm in Brazil. Measuring tens of miles long, the observation was part of a new research program to correlate lightning measures in space and ground-based observation sites. A series of eight antennae deployed along the eastern seaboard of the United States can now record every cloud-to-ground lightning discharge from Maine to North Carolina, and westward to Ohio. Records show that only about 1% as many discharges occur in winter storms as compared with summer storms.

Atmospheric Chemistry. Effluent from the eruption of Mexico's El Chichon volcano in 1982 was estimated to contain as much as 10 million tons (9 million metric tons) of sulfuric acid, formed from the emitted sulfur dioxide; this was more than ten times the amount spewed from Mount St. Helens in 1980. Scientists studying aerosol samples taken during a cruise from Germany to South America showed that biomass burning in tropical regions is an important source of soot carbon and potassium in the atmosphere. New research suggests that ozone changes caused by aircraft emissions could be positive or negative depending on the altitude at which the emission takes place. A pollutant-laden haze over the Arctic was measured to contain mostly carbon soot and hydrocarbons normally found in dry cleaning fluids and in fossil fuel combustion.

Acid Rain. Precipitation ten times more acidic than "normal" occurs in every state and province of eastern North America. Research has provided evidence of consequent damage to crops, forests, and aquatic life in acidified lakes, and chemical erosion of limestone monuments, bridges, and buildings. The U.S. Office of Technology Assessment estimated that electric utilities spew more than 16 million tons (14.4 million metric tons) of sulfur dioxide into the atmosphere east of the Mississippi each year, more than 70% of the total in the east.

OWEN E. THOMPSON
University of Maryland

The Weather Year

December 1982–February 1983. Most of the United States experienced warmer-than-average winter temperatures. The northern Plains were 10 to 12°F (5–7°C) above average, while the Texas panhandle and the Gulf Coast were slightly cooler than average. The Eastern seaboard had a widespread record-breaking warm spell in early December, and balmy conditions again prevailed at Christmas.

Holiday travelers in Colorado, Nebraska, and Wyoming were stranded by a Christmas Eve blizzard. Denver received 24 inches (61 cm) of snow in 24 hours, setting a new one-day snowfall record. Winds gusting to 80 mph (128 km/hr) piled drifts to 8 ft (2.4 m), and at one point every major Colorado highway east of the Continental Divide was closed. Several days later a similar storm buried the Minneapolis area with up to 17 inches (43 cm) of snow, stopping the postal service and halting all travel between the Twin Cities. On the southeastern side of this storm system, heavy rains and tornadoes broke out across Arkansas, Mississippi, Missouri, and Oklahoma.

In late December, more than 15 inches (38 cm) of rain sent rivers over their banks in Louisiana, Mississippi, and Texas. The deluge over the lower Mississippi Valley continued in January. A succession of rainstorms pounded the West Coast during the month, with torrential rains and hurricane-force winds. Parts of San Diego's Crystal Pier toppled into the sea.

February brought no respite for the beleaguered West Coast, as a large low-pressure center in the Gulf of Alaska coninued to spawn storms that brought gale-force winds, heavy rains, thunderstorms, and even tornadoes to southern California. A paralyzing snowstorm hit the East Coast in midmonth, dumping 17 to 24 inches (43–60 cm) of snow from central Virginia through southern New England.

The 1982–83 winter season was the third warmest on record for the entire Northern Hemisphere since records began in 1882. A major feature of this season was the warm sea-surface temperatures in the tropical Pacific Ocean off the South American coast—the phenomenon called El Niño. Positive departures of 7 to 9°F (4–5°C) were recorded over the central and eastern Pacific. Major changes occurred in the precipitation patterns from Indonesia to South America. Severe flooding from persistent heavy rains affected Ecuador and northern Peru, while record dryness occurred in Indonesia, the Philippines, and Australia.

Most of Europe had a warm and dry winter, but storms over southern France in late December caused severe flooding. A cold spell in early January left 300 people dead in India. Severe to extreme drought continued in southern Africa, especially in Mozambique, South Africa, Zambia, and Zimbabwe.

March–May. Spring was cool and wet over a large portion of the continental United States. Temperatures were near average along the West Coast and the northern Plains, and above average in New England and the Pacific Northwest. Storms continued to move ashore along the Pacific Coast in early March, and the snowpack in the Sierra Nevada mountains was two to three times average. Monthly temperatures in the northern Plains and Great Lakes areas averaged 4 to 6°F (2–3°C) above normal.

April was cool and wet throughout most of the country. Monthly negative departures of 4 to 6°F (2–3°C) were common. By contrast, Alaskan cities were from 4 to 8°F (2–4°C) warmer than normal. Torrential rains triggered massive flooding through the lower Mississippi Valley and Gulf Coast states.

May was a month of extremes for the central and western Rocky Mountains. In mid-month a spring blizzard dumped nearly a foot of snow on parts of Colorado and Wyoming. The cold air produced record low temperatures in 17 major cities from Delaware to New Mexico. Mississippi, Louisiana, and Texas continued to battle raging floodwaters resulting from more than 15 inches (38 cm) of rainfall on May 23–24. A heat wave late in the month caused rapid melting of the snowpack in the Rockies. The main street of Salt Lake City was turned into a canal to divert the snowmelt runoff and prevent additional flooding.

Western Europe experienced an excessively wet and cool spring. The Rhine River in Germany overflowed twice during the season, flooding city streets in Bonn and Cologne. Heavy rains continued to plague regions of Argentina, Brazil, Ecuador, and Peru, while rains in March and April brought relief to drought-stricken southeastern Australia.

June–August. Summer began with a continuation of the cool, wet weather of spring. However, in mid-June a warming trend developed in the Northeast and spread throughout the eastern half of the United States to become a record-breaking heat wave. Precipitation was below average in the Corn Belt, the Ohio and Tennessee valleys, and on the southern Atlantic Coast. Portions of the West Coast and central Rockies received over two and one-half times their normal rainfall.

July was warmer than average east of the Rocky Mountains and cooler in the West. Monthly rainfall was below average throughout

The United States generally experienced a wet spring. The early April snowpack in the Sierra Nevada Mountains in California, below, was two to three times above normal, buried homes, and damaged power lines. More than 2 inches (5 cm) of rain fell in Louisville, KY, in a 24-hour period May 1, causing heavy flooding.

most of the country, and parts of South Carolina were especially dry. The heat wave in the central and northern Plains persisted through August. The corn crop experienced severe moisture stress as a result of the high temperatures and scarce rainfall.

Hurricane Alicia swept ashore along the Texas Gulf Coast near Galveston on August 18, bringing high winds and tides, tornadoes, and heavy rains to surrounding communities. As the storm weakened, it brought welcome rains to the parched central Plains.

Agricultural crops in East and West Germany and Poland suffered from a summer of above-average temperatures and below-average precipitation. In western Europe, it was a cool and dry season. Wet weather in southern France, Italy, and Spain during the month of August hampered crop growth. Southern Japan was struck by Typhoon Abby during the third week of August. Heavy rains and high winds produced severe localized flooding in Japan and central China.

September–November. Autumn was mild over most of the continental United States. The heat wave that had begun in early summer continued through mid-September in the central Plains and Northeast. Precipitation was above average in the mid-Atlantic region and the desert Southwest. An outbreak of cold Canadian air in mid-September produced record low temperatures as far east as Indiana and as far south as Alabama. Late in the month an influx of tropical moisture over southern Arizona and New Mexico resulted in flooding.

The northern Plains were exceedingly mild in October. The remnants of Hurricane Tico dumped more than 10 inches (25 cm) of rain in parts of Missouri, Oklahoma, and Texas, with the most serious flooding occurring in central Oklahoma. In early November, heavy rains throughout the lower Missouri Valley produced some local flooding. During the latter third of the month, two major snowstorms blanketed the central Rockies and Plains. Blizzard conditions were reported in Colorado, Kansas, Nebraska, and Wyoming.

Seasonal temperatures were near normal throughout much of Europe, but precipitation was below average over most of the region. In contrast, southern Brazil and China experienced much above-average seasonal precipitation. Hurricane Tico slammed into the western coast of Mexico on October 18, forcing the evacuation of 25,000 persons.

See also ACCIDENTS AND DISASTERS.

IDA HAKKARINEN

MEXICO

Inheriting a scandal-ridden government that had brought the nation close to bankruptcy, President Miguel de la Madrid Hurtado, who took office Dec. 1, 1982, moved quickly to restore domestic and international confidence in Mexico. In foreign policy, the president continued Mexican opposition to foreign intervention in the affairs of its Central American neighbors.

Politics. Emphasizing the necessity of a moral renovation, de la Madrid launched a major anticorruption campaign in January. A Comptroller-General ministry was created to enforce more tightly defined rules on corruption by public officials and to monitor public accounts. The secret police force was abolished, and 60 chiefs of other police forces were fired.

The de la Madrid administration surprised many observers by taking action against corrupt officials of the previous administration, since anticorruption campaigns rarely have been more than promises. The most spectacular case was the July indictment and imprisonment of Sen. Jorge Díaz Serrano, director-general of the government oil company (PEMEX) from 1976 to 1981 and the "architect" of Mexico's oil boom. Díaz Serrano was accused of defrauding PEMEX of $34 million

On March 3, Mexico's Secretary of the Treasury Jesus Silva Herzog (right) prepares to sign a $5 billion loan agreement between the Mexican government and U.S. banks.

UPI

(U.S.) in the 1980 purchase of two natural gas tankers from a Belgian firm; in late July 1983 he was expelled from the Senate and jailed. Earlier in the year the government had brought indictments against two other PEMEX officials for defrauding $22 million from the company. Both fled the country. In August the government asked Swiss authorities to freeze the $5 million bank account of one of the officials.

New revelations of fraud, embezzlement, and violence within the Oil Workers' Union of the Mexican Republic further shocked the nation in August. Union head Salvador Barragán Camacho accused fellow union official Héctor García Hernández of having stolen $6.6 million in union funds. García fled to the United States, where he accused Barragán and Joaquín Hernández Galicia of having stolen more than $130 million from the union. In September, García was kidnapped at gunpoint and taken to Mexico City, where he was turned over to government authorities and jailed. Union officers began accusing each other of murder and murder plots. Government officials began investigating the union, one of the nation's most powerful political forces.

President de la Madrid's Institutional Revolutionary Party (PRI) faced antigovernment outbursts and electoral defeats in numerous municipalities during 1983. In January eight persons died when police used force to dislodge government opponents from the town hall of Villa Flores, Chiapas. The takeover was one of 40 in various states since municipal elections in December 1982. The protesters accused the government of electoral fraud. In March a mob burned the city hall of Pánuco, Veracruz, to protest the police killing of a worker. In April two persons died in a fight between PRI forces and those of the United Mexican Socialist Party, which controlled a Guerrero town. The same month, the National Action Party mayor of a town in Chiapas was murdered by his defeated PRI opponent.

State and local elections during the summer produced further losses for the government. In Durango and Chihuahua states, the National Action Party won the mayoralties of the state capitals as well as those of other large towns. In Oaxaca state, the PRI maintained control of the state capital but had been forced to recognize victories of opposition parties and civic groups or join coalition governments in every other important city. Similar losses occurred in state legislative races. The possibility of a sweep of state elections in Baja California North by the National Action Party in September prompted President de la Madrid to make a two-day campaign trip to the state. He exhorted the citizens to support his party and give him time to end corruption and abuse. He also announced new public works programs.

Economic Policy. Severe austerity measures required by the International Monetary Fund were implemented to slash Mexico's large budget deficit, hold down government spending, and slow inflation. Deficit financing was sliced in half to 8.5% of the gross domestic product and was to be reduced further to 4% in 1988. Increases in the prices of government and parastatal services, taxes on high incomes, and the value-added tax, as well as a decreased rate of money-supply growth, moderated inflation.

The National Development Plan promised monetary stability, decentralization of the production system, promotion of exports, the stimulation of agriculture, and income redistribution by 1988. Specific targets included a 10%-per-year growth in nonpetroleum exports, the creation of a strong capital goods industry, and the development of an efficient industrial arm in the public sector.

Public Finance. Negotiations between international banks and the government achieved the rescheduling of payments on most of Mexico's $85 billion foreign debt, on which only interest payments had been made since August 1982. New economic development loans were obtained from foreign banks. The almost $1.9 billion loan from the Bank of International Settlements was repaid. *See also* page 277.

Stockholders of the private banks nationalized in September 1982 learned in August 1983 that they would be repaid with ten-year government bonds worth some $5 billion, a figure many considered insufficient. The banks were to be consolidated into fewer institutions and converted to national credit societies.

Economic Performance. The economy was expected to decline 2–5% in 1983, with greater drop-offs in the mining, automotive, and construction industries. In spite of some large harvests, the nation imported 8.5 million tons of grains. A decline in imports produced a $6.6 billion trade surplus by midyear. Net income from tourism and border transactions rose because of a decline in Mexican tourism abroad. The inflation rate dropped from 100% in 1982 to about 70% in 1983. Oil exports again rose and produced more than $15 billion in income.

In spite of the high inflation rate and major strikes by public- and private-sector unions in May and June, the government increased wages by only 15.6% instead of the 50% demanded by workers. In a major departure, President de la Madrid publicly rebuked Fidel Velásquez, leader of the nation's largest union. In August representatives of labor, private business, and government signed the Pact of Solidarity, a promise to keep wages and prices under control.

Social Conditions. The government of Mexico took a variety of steps to ameliorate the adverse effects of the national depression on low-income groups. In January of 1983 an emergency program to create 750,000 new jobs was started. Public health and social security services were expanded, while health care was made a constitutional right. New low-income housing was begun. Family planning was given renewed impetus. Major efforts were made to combat a crime wave.

Proposals to decentralize education, legalize abortion, and decriminalize adultery stirred controversy. The left wanted a continuation of centralized control of education, while social conservatives and the Catholic Church strongly opposed the abortion and adultery proposals.

In September, Attorney General Sergio García Ramirez proposed a major revision of the penal code. Among the changes would be the elimination of the standard presumption of intent for any person committing a crime.

Foreign Policy. Unlike his immediate predecessors, President de la Madrid kept a low profile in foreign affairs. Several times during the year he issued pointed criticisms of the show of force by the United States in Central America and Grenada. As a member of the Contadora Group (which also included Panama, Colombia, and Venezuela), Mexico called for negotiated settlements to conflicts in Central America, the end of foreign involvement in the internal affairs of other nations, and respect of the right of nations to determine their own destiny. In his August meeting with U.S. President Ronald Reagan, President de la Madrid reiterated Mexico's foreign policy position. He also sought the lowering of U.S. tariff barriers to Mexican goods and better protection of Mexican nationals in the United States. Reagan confirmed a further $2 billion credit for the Mexican purchase of U.S. agricultural products and offered to increase U.S. purchases of Mexican oil.

Much of the government's efforts were concentrated on negotiating loans and trade agreements in an effort to pull the nation out of its economic depression. De la Madrid did host visits by the presidents of Brazil and Colombia, as well as the prime minister of Belize.

DONALD J. MABRY
Mississippi State University

MEXICO • Information Highlights

Official Name: The United Mexican States.
Location: Southern North America.
Area: 764,014 sq mi (1 978 800 km²).
Population (July 1983 est.): 75,702,000.
Chief Cities (1980 census): Mexico City, the capital, 9,377,300; (1979 est.): Guadalajara, 1,906,145; Monterrey, 1,064,629.
Government: *Head of state and government,* Miguel de la Madrid Hurtado, president (took office Dec. 1982). *Legislature*—Congress: Senate and Chamber of Deputies.
Monetary Unit: Peso (158.95 pesos equal U.S.$1, floating rate, Nov. 4, 1983).
Gross National Product (1981 U.S.$): $229,040,-000,000.
Economic Indexes (1982): *Consumer Prices* (1972 = 100), all items, 850.4; food, 819.1. *Industrial Production,* (1981, 1975 = 100), 156.
Foreign Trade (1982 U.S.$): *Imports,* $15,042,-000,000; *exports,* $2,101,000,000.

MICHIGAN

After 20 years of Republican administration, Michigan got a Democratic governor in 1983. The state also began to recover from several years of economic recession.

Government. Gov. James J. Blanchard, a former U.S. congressman, assumed office in January 1983, succeeding Republican William G. Milliken. The new governor's first effort was to push an economic program designed to avoid an anticipated $900 million budget deficit. The program included a 38% increase in the state income tax to 6.35%, the highest in the nation; budget cuts of $225 million; and proposals to reduce unemployment by encouraging private industry. The tax increase led to the ouster of two Democratic legislators in voter-initiated special elections.

The governor touched off a major controversy by appointing Sister Agnes Mary Mansour, a Roman Catholic nun, as director of the state Department of Social Services; part of the job is administering state funds for abortions for the poor. After weeks of public debate, during which she refused an order by Detroit Archbishop Edmund Szoka to condemn abortion funding, she bowed to pressure from the Vatican and resigned from her Sisters of Mercy order.

Moody's Investors Service, which in 1982 gave the state the nation's lowest credit rating, raised it to the highest.

Economy and Business. The state's long-stagnant economy showed signs of recovery. The auto industry reported increased profits—a combined $1.82 billion in the second quarter, twice the earnings in the same period of 1982—and called back many laid-off employees.

Once-tottering Chrysler Corp. repaid its $1.2 billion in federally guaranteed loans seven years before they were due and in September bought and retired 14.4 million stock warrants held by the federal government. The actions

UPI
Sister Agnes Mary Mansour, a Catholic nun, left her order and stayed on as director of the Michigan welfare system.

ended Washington's bailout program to save Chrysler from bankruptcy in 1980.

Chrysler reported profits of $582.6 million in the first three quarters of 1983. Ford Motor Co., which lost $657.8 million in 1982, reported earnings of $1.094 billion in the first nine months; on July 14, Ford declared its first dividend in four years. General Motors Corp. reported earnings of $2.4 billion in the first half. The auto companies reported in October that 130,050 workers were on indefinite layoff, compared with 237,150 one year earlier.

In June, Governor Blanchard proposed a public-private investment fund and asked for $54 million in state "seed money" to help it finance business growth and create jobs. On October 6, the governor proposed a 20-point plan to rebuild Michigan's crippled economy. The package included help for auto suppliers, food processors, and forestry firms. Blanchard said he was also committed to business-tax relief and other commercial incentives.

Jobs. Unemployment in Michigan dropped from 17.3% in December 1982 to 13.6% in September 1983. To ease unemployment the state instituted a Youth Corps, which provided 25,000 public-service summer jobs.

Detroit. The first municipal corruption trial in Detroit in four decades opened September 26 in Federal District Court. Defendants included Charles M. Beckham, 35, former director of the Detroit Water and Sewerage Department, accused of soliciting bribes from disposal firms. The jury could not reach a verdict, and a mistrial was declared December 13.

CHARLES THEISEN, *"The Detroit News"*

MICHIGAN • Information Highlights

Area: 58,527 sq mi (151 585 km²).

Population (1982 est.): 9,109,000.

Chief Cities (1980 census): Lansing, the capital, 130,414; Detroit, 1,203,339; Grand Rapids, 181,843; Warren, 161,134; Flint, 159,611; Sterling Heights, 108,999.

Government (1983): *Chief Officers*—governor, James Blanchard (D); lt. gov., Martha Griffiths (D). *Legislature*—Senate, 38 members; House of Representatives, 110 members.

State Finances (fiscal year 1982): *Revenues,* $14,587,000,000; *expenditures,* $13,997,000,000.

Personal Income (1982): $99,802,000,000; per capita $10,956.

Labor Force (July 1983): *Nonagricultural wage and salary earners,* 3,178,500; *unemployed,* 574,800 (13.1% of total force).

Education: *Enrollment* (fall 1981)—public elementary schools, 1,182,083; public secondary, 620,951; colleges and universities (fall 1982), 508,240 students. *Public school expenditures* (1981–82): $4,908,037,000.

MICROBIOLOGY

The year 1983 was an eventful one for microbiologists. It saw a dramatic increase in the success rate of human organ-transplant operations because of the use of the protein Cyclosporin-A; the promising use of bacteria in mosquito-control programs; and the use of recombinant-DNA techniques to obtain bacteria that produce rennin for cheese processing. Also of interest was the discovery that a disease formerly thought to be bacterial in origin is actually caused by a virus living within the bacteria. Finally, there was one answer to the question of how ocean-drifting flora and fauna obtain nitrogen-containing compounds.

Organ Transplants and Cyclosporin-A. Organs transplanted surgically often are rejected because of the action of the recipient's T-type lymphocytes. Until recently the drugs used to deactivate the T-type lymphocytes also neutralized the patient's other white blood cells, increasing the susceptibility to infection. This situation has changed dramatically as a result of research by Dr. Jean Borel, who isolated the protein Cyclosporin-A from the soil fungus *Trichoderma polysporum.* This compound has the unique ability to deactivate T-type lymphocytes without affecting other white blood cells. The use of Cyclosporin-A in organ transplants has increased success rates by up to 35%.

Mosquito Control. Mosquitoes transmit the causative agents of various diseases (malaria, yellow fever, encephalitis, and others) to humans and other animals. A recent approach to the control of mosquito populations has been the use of microorganisms that attack and destroy mosquito larvae. In one such program, Dr. John Spizizen of the University of Arizona experimented with the soil bacterium *Bacillus sphaericus.* This bacterium produces spores that can be sprayed on the surface of mosquito-breeding pools. The spores are eaten by the mosquito larvae and germinate in their intestinal tracts. The bacteria that develop from the spores produce a poisonous chemical compound (toxin) that kills the larvae. Unfortunately, this species of bacteria does not reproduce rapidly enough to make the obtaining of large numbers of spores commercially feasible. It was discovered, however, that the gene that controls toxin production is located in the bacterium's small ring of DNA (plasmid). Using recombinant-DNA techniques, the gene for toxin production has been transferred to the plasmid of the species *Bacillus subtilis,* which also forms spores and which does reproduce rapidly enough to permit commercial use. Another advantage of the genetically engineered *B. subtilis* is that it is harmless to people.

Cheese Processing. A critical step in cheese production is the coagulation of the milk protein casein by the enzyme rennin. For at least 4,000 years rennin has been obtained from the tissue of the fourth stomach of an unweaned calf when it is slaughtered for veal. Recently, through recombinant-DNA techniques, Drs. J. S. Emtage and P. A. Lowe of Celltech in Great Britain placed the gene from rennin production into bacterial cells. Rennin produced by the bacteria was found to be just as effective as the rennin obtained from calf stomachs.

Bacteria-Associated, Viral-Caused Disease. Toxic-shock syndrome—a disease characterized by fever, low blood pressure, vomiting, and diarrhea—has been found mainly among menstruating women who use high-absorbency tampons. The use of these tampons apparently provides conditions favorable to the growth of bacteria—probably *Staphylococcus aureus*—and the subsequent release of toxins.

In studying the disease, Dr. John Zabriskie at Rockefeller University investigated 12 strains of *S. aureus* obtained from toxic-shock patients and 18 strains from individuals who did not have the disease. It was found that 11 of the 12 toxic-shock-associated bacterial strains contained a particular type of virus, while only one of the 18 control strains did. In order to prove that the virus actually causes the disease, it must be shown that only those *S. aureus* containing the particular virus can produce the toxin that elicits toxic-shock symptoms. It is important to note that scarlet fever and diphtheria are produced only by those strains of their respective bacterial species that carry particular viruses.

Nitrogen in the Ocean. All organisms require a continuing supply of nitrogen-containing compounds in order to form protoplasm. For those plants and animals, collectively called plankton, that live in the oceans and drift with the currents, the source of these compounds was unknown until only recently. Research by Drs. M. W. Silver and A. L. Alldredge at the University of California revealed that microscopic green algae of the species *Rizosolenia castracanei* and *R. imbricata* var. *shrubsolei* contain large numbers of bacteria within their cells. These bacteria live, grow, and divide within the algal cells. Moreover, when the algal cells divide, the bacteria are distributed to daughter cells.

Further investigation found that these bacteria contain the enzyme nitrogenase, which permits them to "fix" atmospheric nitrogen—i.e., to form chemical compounds containing this essential element. The fixed nitrogen is then available to both the bacteria and their algal hosts for the production of protein. When the algae are eaten or die, and their cellular contents are broken down, the fixed nitrogen becomes available to other organisms in the various ocean food chains. It has been estimated that this particular association of algae and bacteria accounts for about 14% of the nitrogen required to support ocean organisms.

LOUIS LEVINE, *City College of New York*

MIDDLE EAST

The year 1983 was an unhappy, indecisive, and confusing one in the Middle East. No doubt there have been other years in which the actual number of deaths by violence was higher, but there hardly ever was a time when the problems of the region—or at least certain areas within it—appeared so intractable and the prospects for solution so slender. Indeed, the Middle East has become such an arena of imbroglios that the very use of the word "problems" may be inappropriate, for the word itself implies at least the possibility of solution. The region today displays so much factionalism, so many old and conflicting claims to the same pieces of territory, and so much in the way of religious fanaticism (this last ominously increasing now) that these are perhaps more precisely termed chronic conditions, intractable situations which no magic wand of conversion to rationality and no foreign intervention will in any foreseeable future "solve."

Few Winners. Policymakers concerned with the region, whether belonging to states within it or to countries outside, had little in 1983 on which to congratulate themselves. Many policies seemed to be based on past inertia rather than fresh thinking. U.S. policy in Lebanon was regarded by many good critics as highly dubious, well meaning but fumbling; harsher critics contended that it led to the completely pointless deaths of a total of 257 U.S. Marines by year's end. Iran and Iraq continued to be locked in a wasteful and purposeless struggle. Menaham Begin, the formerly ebullient prime minister of Israel, was now tired and dispirited, and he resigned in September. President Hosni Mubarak of Egypt, meanwhile, was engaged in a cautious holding operation.

One apparent "winner" in Mideast affairs was President Hafez al-Assad of Syria. Assad, whose own position even two years before looked precarious as he ruthlessly fought internal opposition, seemed in 1983, by a policy of brinkmanship and spoiling, to be in a fair position to achieve his major objectives: to weaken the power of the Gemayel government in Lebanon and enhance that of the Muslim opposition, turning Lebanon (or at least much of it) into a client state; to frustrate and embarrass the United States and discourage its friends and allies in the region, while at the same time raising the prestige of the radical states and of Syria's backer, the Soviet Union; and, in general, to establish a kind of *pax Syriaca* in the Arab Middle East.

Lebanon. As had been the case for several years, there were two areas in the Middle East on which world attention focused in 1983—Lebanon and the war between Iran and Iraq. Indeed, there was a curious tendency to focus largely on the former, though it certainly could be argued that the latter was at least equally significant and had greater potentialities for disastrous ramifications.

The tangled skein of Lebanese politics never looked more tangled than in 1983. There were so many political factions and religious sects, so many minorities and minorities within minorities, and so many crosscurrents that situations verged at times on the totally incomprehensible. Yet the year had begun with a certain promise.

In Israel an independent judicial commission had been appointed to inquire into the circumstances of the massacres at the Shatila and Sabra refugee camps near Beirut in September 1982. This was an extraordinarily open and self-critical procedure, totally unthinkable in any other Middle East country. The report of the commission, published on February 8, held that, although the actual massacre had been carried out by Phalangist Lebanese Christian militia, various Israeli political and military leaders bore some degree of indirect responsibility. Criticism was directed particularly at Defense Minister Ariel Sharon, who resigned February 11 (though he remained in the cabinet as minister without portfolio).

The opening months of the year saw prolonged negotiations between Lebanon and Israel, with the United States also participating, on the withdrawal of all foreign troops from Lebanon. The negotiations, which had actually begun Dec. 28, 1982, were the first direct talks between officials of the two countries since March 1949. The negotiations followed a tortuous and difficult course from the beginning, often threatening to deadlock. Israel had hoped that they would result in a complete normalization of relations with Lebanon, as the 1979 peace treaty had done with Egypt (at least in theory). It soon became apparent, however, that some concession was necessary to the Lebanese fear that such an explicit move would damage Lebanon's relations with other Arab states. Other difficulties then arose in regard to Israel's concern about creating security arrangements in southern Lebanon.

Finally, more than four months after the talks had begun, and after nine days of shuttle diplomacy by U.S. Secretary of State George Shultz, the Lebanese government on May 4 accepted a U.S. proposal on the withdrawal of Israeli troops from Lebanon. The compromise met Israeli needs by providing that, after the withdrawal of its forces, there would be a continuing if limited Israeli role in the security arrangements in southern Lebanon. The agreement was something of a triumph, especially for the chief U.S. negotiators, Morris Draper and Philip Habib, but it was immediately rendered nugatory. Withdrawal of Israeli forces was conditional on withdrawal of Syrian forces as well, and the Syrians, who had not been party to the negotiations, rejected the agreement with unexpected vehemence; indeed

The October 23 truck bombing of U.S. Marine headquarters at Beirut airport cast new doubts on the peacekeeping mission.

Damascus impugned the legitimacy of the Gemayel government which had concluded it. U.S. efforts to enlist Jordan and Saudi Arabia in support of the plan were unavailing.

There thus remained some 30,000 to 40,000 Israeli troops in southern Lebanon, about 40,000 Syrian troops in the Bekaa Valley and northern Lebanon, and 8,000 or more PLO troops in Syrian-occupied areas, these having trickled back after their expulsion by sea from Beirut the year before. In addition there were the mixed, UN-sponsored UNIFIL forces of some 7,000 in southern Lebanon, and, of course, the multinational "peacekeeping" force in the Beirut area, which had first been placed there in September 1982. The latter consisted of some 1,600 U.S. Marines, 2,000 French, and more than 2,100 Italians; a small contingent of 100 British troops was added in February.

By late summer the situation in Lebanon had deteriorated sharply and the level of violence had risen markedly. It was a trend that continued for the rest of the year. West Beirut was racked by factional violence toward the end of August, at which time also two U.S. Marines and four French soldiers were killed. The Lebanese army regained control of West Beirut, but a new situation arose September 3–4, when Israeli forces completed a swift redeployment out of the mountains south of the capital (a move opposed by the United States) into a new fortified defense zone in southern Lebanon. Since the Lebanese army was unable

to fill the void, Druze militia in the hills moved swiftly to take up the vacated Israeli positions. Heavy fighting broke out between Druze and Christian forces. The former won, overrunning the key Christian town of Bhamdun on September 6. There was no obstacle to a linkup between the Syrian forces in eastern Lebanon and the Muslim militias surrounding the capital. From this time forward the U.S. Marines became increasingly subject to attack by the Syrian-backed Muslim forces on the higher ground a few miles to the east of them. Their situation was exposed and vulnerable.

More significant than this tactical vulnerability was a fundamental change for the worse in the role of the international contingents. The point was put very clearly at year's end in the report of a special U.S. Defense Department investigation. The report observed that what originally was envisaged as a peacekeeping mission operating in a neutral way in a more or less benign environment had now become little more than a partisan military mission operating in a hostile environment in support of one of the participants in a bitter civil war. It was hardly surprising that U.S. Secretary of Defense Caspar Weinberger reported toward the end of the year that all 15 nations that had been invited to send contingents to join the multinational force had declined; indeed, the Italians were about to halve the size of their peacekeeping contingent, and the French were about to withdraw theirs from the Beirut area and move them farther south.

Saudi Prince Bandar ibn Sultan (center) acted as mediator in Lebanese cease-fire negotiations. A truce was called September 26, but it lasted only a week.

Terrorist Attacks. The subject of the Pentagon inquiry was responsibility for the appalling event of October 23, when a suicide truck bombing of a U.S. Marine headquarters building at the Beirut airport resulted in the death of 241 Americans; a similar attack at the nearby French compound killed 58. Though the most lethal, the bombing of the U.S. facility was all of a piece with a number of other attacks during the year. It was very similar in modus operandi to the destruction of the U.S. embassy in Beirut on April 18, which resulted in 46 deaths; to the truck explosion at the Israeli headquarters in Tyre on November 4, which killed 60; and to the attacks on the U.S. and French embassies in Kuwait on December 12, which sent a chill of apprehension through the conservative states of the Gulf.

A disquieting pattern was seen in these various acts of terrorism. It was widely believed that the attacks were so efficiently and professionally executed that they must have been the work of state organizations rather than independent terrorist groups. If true, this constituted a new and dreadful phenomenon—state-sponsored terrorism. The states most often alleged to be implicated were Iran and Syria. The latter, certainly, had no interest in establishing a stable and democratic Lebanon. It simply regards that country as a lost piece of its own territory.

The Palestinian Problem. The question of the future of the West Bank and Gaza—largely Arab in population but occupied by Israel since the Six-Day War of 1967—was somewhat lost to sight in the violent chaos of Lebanon. The issue remained unsettled, however, and progress toward the "autonomy" envisaged at Camp David was nonexistent. The Israeli settlement policy on the West Bank continued to be implemented. The Reagan plan of Sept. 1, 1982—which looked toward the creation of a Palestinian political entity associated with the kingdom of Jordan—was perhaps the most constructive and auspicious approach ever made to this problem, but unfortunately it remained without support from any of the principal parties involved—Israel, Jordan, or the PLO.

There was a crucial moment, in April, when PLO leader Yasir Arafat and King Hussein held talks in Amman to find some mutually beneficial course of action. There was some hope that Arafat would authorize the king to enter negotiations with Israel on behalf of the Palestinians to pursue the Reagan plan. The talks broke down April 10. Arafat had perhaps lost his one great opportunity not merely to represent his people flamboyantly but to achieve something concrete for them. Nor did he save his position as leader of the PLO; by late in the year he had been expelled ignominiously from Tripoli, Lebanon, by more extremist, dissident PLO factions backed by Syria. This was only the latest in a series of expulsions for Arafat, who the year before had been driven out of Beirut, then later out of Syria. Shortly after his evacuation from Tripoli on December 20, the embattled PLO chief was warmly received by President Mubarak in Egypt. The gesture was somewhat mysteriously applauded by the United States, which had announced November 29 that it had taken steps to increase strategic cooperation with Israel.

Iran-Iraq War. In September the Iranian-Iraqi war passed from its third into its fourth year, with no conclusion in sight. All hope of victory for Iraq (which started the war) had now passed, but neither did there seem to be much likelihood that Iran could achieve such success as actually to destroy the hated regime in Baghdad. Iraq continued to be under heavy strain, especially financial, and has had to bear the war casualties with only one third the population of its opponent. Still, it held on successfully and blunted several Iranian offensives during the course of the year. There were several efforts by third parties to bring the conflict to a compromise end, but none of these initiatives had any success or showed any real promise of bringing the parties together.

A rift within the Palestine Liberation Organization (PLO) widened during the first half of the year and exploded in violence in subsequent months. Supporters of PLO leader Yasir Arafat, below, were driven back by a rebel faction supported by Syria. Arafat's last military stronghold was the Beddawi refugee camp outside Tripoli, Lebanon, right. His loyalists then were forced into downtown Tripoli and evacuated from that port city in December.

Azar/Gamma-Liaison

© A. Yaghodzadeh/Sygma

Iran launched a major attack on the central front in April, another one in July in rugged and lightly defended terrain of Kurdistan where hitherto there had been little fighting, followed by another major offensive on the central front. The common pattern of all the fighting was of initial Iranian successes, pushed ruthlessly in the face of considerable casualties, but in the end the capturing of only a few miles of territory—a pattern curiously reminiscent of the Western Front in 1914–18.

A major concern was ecological damage. In early March, Iraqi damage to Iranian oil wells at the northern end of the Persian Gulf resulted in spillage that caused extensive pollution and threatened wildlife over an enormous area. The wells were not capped until late September, according to Iranian sources, but later reports indicated that damage was less extensive than had at first been feared.

At the end of June it was reported that France—perhaps Iraq's most consistent supporter—had agreed to "lend" Baghdad five Super Etendard jets armed with Exocet missiles. The planes did not actually arrive until October, and then they apparently remained unused. It was thought that the only conceivable use that Iraq could find for such weapons was some desperate attempt to force Iran to the bargaining table. Almost from the beginning, the Iranian-Iraqi war has been characterized by a curious (and welcome) restraint in attacking the many vulnerable cities and oil installations on both sides. However, Iraq during 1983 did attack some ships on their way to or from Iranian ports.

Brighter Spots. Not quite all the developments in the Middle East during 1983 were negative. Turkey, after three years of military rule (which had in fact succeeded in stamping out the terrorism that had been rampant before 1980), returned to civilian rule following elections in November.

Among other positive developments were the restoration of normal relations between Oman and South Yemen, as the latter abandoned its efforts to take over the Dhofar province; the reestablishment of diplomatic links between Israel and Zaire and some other African states; and the gradual lessening of Egypt's isolation in the Arab world.

See also articles on individual countries; NATIONS OF THE WORLD.

ARTHUR CAMPBELL TURNER
University of California, Riverside

MILITARY AFFAIRS

The military relationship between the United States and the Soviet Union, which rests upon the mutual possession of strategic nuclear weapons, was sufficiently stable during 1983 that an unusual number of jolts and shocks did not trigger major war. The series of disturbances included the Soviet downing of a civilian Korean jetliner with Americans, including a member of Congress, on board; the first U.S. military death in Central America; the killing of

The Pershing II, an intermediate-range missile, underwent testing before being deployed in West Germany.

Greg Mathieson/Gamma-Liaison

239 Marines in a terrorist bombing in Beirut Lebanon; and the U.S. action in Grenada.

Whether the stability based on nuclear balance would continue into the future was the subject of sharp debate within the United States and between Washington and Moscow, as both superpowers moved further toward the development of major new weapons and correlative concepts that, if adopted, would dominate strategic nuclear relations into the next century. The U.S. part of the new strategic analysis was set forth in a study ordered by President Ronald Reagan.

President's Commission on Strategic Forces. Following substantial but inconclusive debate by Congress in 1982 over the appropriate deployment mode for the new MX missile, President Reagan impaneled a special group to advise him on ". . . the purpose, character, size, and composition of the strategic forces of the United States." Officially titled the President's Commission on Strategic Forces, the group came to be known as the Scowcroft Commission after the name of its chairman, Brent Scowcroft, a former Air Force general. The impact of the Scowcroft Report, issued in April, was strengthened by the participation (either as actual members or counselors) of two former secretaries of state—Alexander Haig, Jr., and Henry Kissinger—and four former secretaries of defense—Harold Brown, Melvin R. Laird, Donald H. Rumsfeld, and James R. Schlesinger.

Much of the analysis in the commission's report dealt with the problems of structuring U.S. strategic nuclear forces in the 1980s and 1990s in a way that would reduce the risk of nuclear war by utilizing effective arms control, while simultaneously containing the threat of aggressive totalitarianism on the part of the Soviet Union and its agents. One of the central thrusts of the Scowcroft Report was support of continued maintenance of the "triad" concept, featuring deployment by the United States of three separate and independent delivery systems for nuclear weapons against the Soviet Union or other target areas. The three delivery systems are intercontinental ballistic missiles (ICBMs), submarine-launched ballistic missiles (SLBMs), and bombers, some of which are being equipped with Cruise missiles.

The Scowcroft Commission called attention to trends in the development of advanced weapons that may require innovative responses by the United States to preserve the viability of the triad. Of primary concern was the increasing accuracy of strategic weapons, particularly ICBMs. According to the Scowcroft Report, "These accuracy developments and the ability of an attacker to use more than one warhead to attack each fixed target on the other side increasingly put at risk targets of high value such as fixed launchers for MIRVed (multiple individually targeted reentry vehicles) ICBMs."

Commission members wrestled with the problems posed for U.S. ICBMs by the increasing accuracy of Soviet counterparts, which could be used in a first strike to eliminate a significant component of the American triad. While noting advancements in protecting ICBM silos against the effects of nuclear explosions, called ''superhardening,'' the Scowcroft Commission suggested that more dramatic means be adopted to protect U.S. ICBMs from attack. Specifically, the report recommended that new techniques in guidance, the miniaturization of electronic components protecting against nuclear effects, and the use of solid fuels together offer the possibility of an entirely new ICBM, one that would derive its ability to survive a Soviet first strike from the fact that it is mobile.

The new ICBM is officially called the Small ICBM (or SICBM). The Midgetman, as it is more commonly known, would be a single-warhead missile and would weigh approximately 15 tons (13.5 metric tons), in contrast to the nearly 100-ton (90-mt) weight of the MX. The Scowcroft Commission recommended that design and engineering of the SICBM begin at once, leading to full-scale development in 1987 and initial operating capability in the early 1990s.

According to the Scowcroft Commission, the SICBM offers a special advantage over the MX and such existing ICBMs as the Minuteman II and III. Because of its small size, the SICBM would be carried in hardened, mobile launchers that could be dispersed among military installations in the western United States during peacetime. During a period of actual or potential hostility, the SICBM launchers could then be moved from the military areas to complicate the Soviet task of locating and firing at them. In addition to being difficult to find and destroy, the SICBM would provide a less attractive target to the Soviets because it carries only one warhead, compared with the ten warheads carried by the MX and the three carried by the Minuteman III. Deployment of the SICBM, the commission pointed out, would be compatible with arms-control efforts to reduce the number of ICBM warheads currently in service.

For its part, the Soviet Union appeared to be developing missiles generally comparable to the U.S. SICBM. Whether this development is a result of the suggestion in the Scowcroft Report that both nations would enter a more stable relationship if each deployed single-warhead missiles in a mobile mode, or because the Soviet planners had engaged in analysis similar to that of the United States, was not known.

To the dismay of those who opposed the MX on grounds that it was unduly threatening to the Soviet Union and that it was vulnerable in its fixed launcher-silo to a Soviet first strike, the Scowcroft Report recommended deploying a limited number of the new ICBMs. The justification was that the MX is essential to compensate for the current Soviet advantage in large ICBMs, and to encourage the Soviets to adopt a SICBM by putting their large ICBMs at risk.

"Star Wars" Weapons. For a decade or more, reports had been circulating that the Soviet Union was engaged in the development of various laser and particle-beam weapons that might knock U.S. satellites and warheads from the skies. In 1983 the American response to such a possibility was put into high gear by the Reagan administration. It began with a March speech by the president in which he called for the study of a space-based defense concept.

By fall the president had received the recommendation of an interagency study group that the United States commence a five-year, $18–$27 billion program to prove the feasibility of a space-based defense system against ballistic missile attack. The study suggested the possibility of a layered defense with the capability to intercept Soviet missiles during the boost phase of their flight, intercept the warheads after they have separated from the missiles during the post-boost phase, and even destroy the warheads near the terminus of their ballistic trajectory. The administration was careful to note the technical difficulties in the new concept and cautioned that success might not come until after the year 2000. Taking a more optimistic view was a political action committee formed to raise $1 million dollars for distribution to political candidates who would endorse the space-based missile defense idea. Called the American Space Frontiers Committee, the group was led by a former Air Force general, Danny Graham, and Rep. Ken Kramer (CO).

On several occasions White House spokesmen hinted that if both the United States and Soviet Union cooperated in the mutual deployment of space-based defenses the danger of missile attack might be substantially reduced.

Warsaw Pact-NATO: A Comparison

	Defense Expenditure		
	1982 U.S.$ million	1982 % of GNP	Number in Armed Forces 1983
NATO			
Belgium	2,799	3.3	94,700
Britain	24,200	5.1	320,600
Canada	5,989	2.0	82,900
Denmark	1,122	2.0	30,700
France	21,969	4.1	492,300
W. Germany	28,453	4.3	495,000
Greece	2,574	6.7	185,000
Italy	8,924	2.6	373,100
Luxembourg	41	1.2	700
Netherlands	4,468	3.3	103,000
WARSAW PACT			
Bulgaria	1,287	2.2–2.9	162,300
Czechoslovakia	3,774	2.8–5.2	204,500
E. Germany	6,163	3.7–6.5	167,000
Hungary	1,318	2.4	105,000
Poland	6,254	n.a	340,000
Rumania	1,297	1.6	189,500
Soviet Union	23,000	n.a	5,050,000

Source: International Institute for Strategic Studies

© R Neveu/Gamma-Liaison

After modernization, the battleship USS "New Jersey" joined the Pacific fleet, took part in summer maneuvers in Central America, and later saw action in Lebanon.

Critics of the space-based defense plan suggested that such a system would merely serve to militarize space at great cost; little additional security would be provided because both nations would strive to develop means to penetrate the other's defenses. Furthermore, some argued, early success on the part of the United States in obtaining a space-based defense system would tend to destabilize the current nuclear relationship; it might appear to Moscow that the United States could strike with impunity, no longer concerned about a Soviet retaliatory attack. Others felt that a space-based defense would be in contravention of the 1972 ABM treaty, which restricts such arms.

War Powers. In 1983, U.S. military lives were lost in El Salvador, Lebanon, and Grenada. These casualties led to a confrontation between the president and Congress. According to the War Powers Resolution, passed in 1973, the president must notify Congress within 48 hours of the "circumstances necessitating" the use of force, indicating the constitutional basis for the use of force and estimating the "scope and duration" of U.S. involvement. Participation in hostilities must end within 60 days if the Congress does not approve its continuation or if Congress mandates an end of the fighting by a concurrent resolution. In October 1983, President Reagan worked out a compromise with Congress regarding the continued presence of U.S. Ma-

rines in Lebanon. Later, Congress also voted to declare the War Powers Resolution in effect in Grenada. (*See* special report, page 549.)

The Euromissile Problem. The most hotly debated weapons deployment of 1983 was the U.S. plan to base 572 new nuclear missiles in Western Europe and the Soviet counterthreat to place new missiles in East Germany and Czechoslovakia.

Despite substantial opposition in Europe and the United States, the Reagan administration began the initial deployment of 108 Pershing II missiles in West Germany and 464 cruise missiles in Great Britain, West Germany, Italy, the Netherlands, and Belgium in December. The planned deployment will require three years to complete. President Reagan gave as justification for the action the previous Soviet deployment in Eastern Europe of some 250 new SS-20 missiles, which carry three warheads and have an estimated range of 3,000 mi (4 828 km), thus threatening all of Western Europe. Moscow described the quick-firing Pershing II, a single-warhead missile with a range of 1,000 mi (1 609 km), as a first-strike weapon that could be fired against USSR and Eastern Europe.

A month before the U.S. deployment began, Soviet President Yuri Andropov made two proposals. One was to freeze the number of SS-20s in the Asian section of the USSR as long as the nuclear threat from the West does not increase in that region; Washington answered that the proposal "held promise." Secondly, Andropov offered to reduce the number of SS-20s in Eastern Europe to approximately 140, roughly equal to the number of analogous weapons possessed by Britain and France, if the United States would refrain from deploying any of its new missiles. The Soviets maintained that a balance would then exist in Europe between Soviet and Western missiles. Washington rejected this logic, claiming that the British and French missiles were not under NATO authority and should not be balanced against Soviet weaponry.

Sino-U.S. Military Cooperation. After months of negotiation, U.S. Secretary of Defense Caspar Weinberger announced during a trip to China in September that the United States was "fully prepared" to sell weapons, including air defense and tank defense systems, to Peking. High technology, some with military applications, also would be shared, according to Weinberger. Although the talks between the U.S. defense secretary and Chinese Vice-Premier Deng Xiaoping did not result in any formal strategic relationship between the two nations, Secretary Weinberger was quoted as saying that the exchange "on the global situation enhanced our mutual trust and confidence."

See also ARMS CONTROL.

ROBERT M. LAWRENCE
Colorado State University

MINNESOTA

The year 1983 in Minnesota saw substantial economic recovery as well as improvement in the state's troubled fiscal condition. At the same time there was continuing concern about an uncertain economic future.

Recovery. While some agricultural sectors remained hard-pressed and the outlook on the Iron Range was increasingly bleak, economic conditions brightened overall. Seasonally adjusted unemployment in July was 7.5% statewide and 6.5% in the Twin Cities, compared with 8.0% and 6.7%, respectively, in July 1982. August housing starts were twice those of a year earlier, and retail sales rose steadily through the year.

Iron Range. The shutdown in taconite operations was extended indefinitely in reaction to the slump in the iron and steel industries. In Lake County, site of the largest taconite operation, unemployment exceeded 30%, while emergency task forces were helping families weather the siege of unemployment and attempting to create new jobs.

Agriculture. On the farms there was good news and bad news. Crop farmers, less affected by the drought than in other states, enjoyed good yields while the payment-in-kind (PIK) program, by requiring crop reductions, was causing prices to rise. Meanwhile livestock producers were suffering the pinch of higher feed prices resulting from the PIK program. Overall farm income was stronger in 1983, mainly because of the PIK program, but farmers still faced high interest rates and large operating costs, and they cautiously awaited federal actions to come after the end of PIK.

State Finance. Recovery from the economic recession eased the state's critical revenue problem in 1983. A substantial balance was forecast for the end of the biennium, July 1, 1985, offering the prospect of an early end to the special 10% income-tax surcharge. The legislature made the 6% sales tax permanent and

---

MINNESOTA • Information Highlights

Area: 84,402 sq mi (218 601 km²).
Population (1982 est.): 4,133,000.
Chief Cities (1980 census): St. Paul, the capital, 270,230; Minneapolis, 370,951; Duluth, 92,811.
Government (1983): *Chief Officers*—governor, Rudy Perpich (DFL); lt. gov., Marlene Johnson (DFL). *Legislature*—Senate, 67 members; House of Representatives, 134 members.
State Finances (fiscal year 1982): *Revenues,* $7,060,000,000; *expenditures,* $6,925,000,000.
Personal Income (1982): $46,184,000,000; per capita, $11,175.
Labor Force (July 1983): *Nonagricultural wage and salary earners,* 1,699,800; *unemployed,* 164,900 (7.5% of total force).
Education: *Enrollment* (fall 1981)—public elementary schools, 480,008; public secondary, 253,733; colleges and universities (1982), 214,133. *Public school expenditures* (1981–82), $2,321,765,000.

---

raised the tax on gasoline. During the year aggressive campaigns were launched to attract and hold high-tech industries.

Environment. The Minnesota Waste Management Board encountered local resistance in its final selection of sites for hazardous waste disposal. A new conflict was brewing with Gov. Rudy Perpich's determined effort to make the state's peat deposits (the largest in the nation) a primary energy source. State leaders intensified their efforts to get the federal government and other states to respond to Minnesota's growing concern over the damage to its waters and forests from acid rain.

Politics. Six Democratic-Farmer-Laborites maneuvered for the party's nomination to oppose U.S. Republican Sen. Rudy Boschwitz in 1984. Meanwhile, politicians were viewing the 1984 election with special interest as they observed native son Walter Mondale's strong bid for the Democratic presidential nomination.

ARTHUR NAFTALIN, *University of Minnesota*

MISSISSIPPI

For Mississippians, 1983 was a year marked by continued economic distress, multiple sessions of the legislature, and quadrennial state elections.

The Economy. Mississippi's troubled economy consistently lagged behind that of both the South and the nation. Unemployment climbed to a record 13.8% in June, and the state unfailingly remained among the nation's leaders insofar as jobless statistics were concerned. Tax collections were persistent in their failure to meet Budget Commission estimates, and for the third year in succession Gov. William Winter was forced to order budget cutbacks for state agencies. Despite year-end indications of economic improvement, the mood of the state remained cautious at best.

Legislative Sessions. At its regular annual session, which began January 6 and was extended two weeks beyond its normal 90-day period, an election-year legislature approved a "compromise package" aimed at funding penitentiary construction and covering a projected budget deficit through transfers of funds, a "crime tax" on both misdemeanor and felony convictions, and a temporary increase in the wholesale sales tax. Other major legislative actions included pay raises for teachers and state employees, reform of public-utility laws, and strengthening of drunk-driving statutes.

Lawmakers were called into special session on June 24 to correct a regular-session oversight that threatened the existence of the Textbook Procurement Commission, and beginning November 16 a lame-duck session met to bring revenues in line with expenditures.

Quadrennial Elections. A rather lackluster governor's race changed character less than

William ("Bill") Allain easily won the Mississippi governorship despite campaign accusations of sexual misconduct.

two weeks before the November 8 general election when a group of supporters of Republican landowner Leon Bramlett of Clarksdale publicly accused Democratic nominee Attorney General William ("Bill") Allain of sexual misconduct. Despite the accusations, Allain, 55, who earlier had overtaken former Lt. Gov. Evelyn Gandy in her second bid to become the Democratic candidate, captured 55% of the more than 735,000 ballots cast and carried 74 of the state's 82 counties. Bramlett received 39% of the vote. Charles Evers, a black Independent and former mayor of Fayette, realized 4%, while the remainder was split between two other Independents.

In other contests, Democrats maintained their traditional hold on statewide offices and continued to dominate legislative and local posts. The number of Republicans in the legislature declined from 9 to 7, blacks increased

---

MISSISSIPPI • Information Highlights

Area: 47,689 sq mi (123 515 km²).
Population (1982 est.): 2,536,000.
Chief Cities (1980 census): Jackson, the capital, 202,895; Biloxi, 49,311; Meridian, 46,577.
Government (1982): *Chief Officers*—governor, William F. Winter (D); lt. gov., Brad Dye (D). *Legislature*—Senate, 52 members; House of Representatives, 122 members.
State Finances (fiscal year 1982): *Revenues,* $3,230,000,000; *expenditures,* $3,039,000,000.
Personal Income (1982): $19,840,000,000; per capita, $7,778.
Labor Force (July 1983): *Nonagricultural wage and salary earners,* 783,000; *unemployed,* 144,000 (13.4% of total force).
Education: *Enrollment* (fall 1982)—public elementary schools, 328,016; public secondary, 143,599; colleges and universities (1981–82), 105,974 students. *Public school expenditures* (1981–82), $787,100,000.

---

from 15 to 18, and women remained constant at 3. The number of blacks gaining local offices exceeded that of four years earlier.

The Weather. Above-average rainfall delayed spring planting and produced major floods along the Pearl River. Then, a summer drought resulted in much of the state being declared an agricultural disaster area.

Miscellaneous. Other items of interest in 1983 included county redistricting, funding approval for completing the Tennessee-Tombigbee Waterway, continued controversy over the possible storage of high-level nuclear waste, and a Mississippi Supreme Court decision forbidding legislators from serving on executive boards.

DANA B. BRAMMER
The University of Mississippi

MISSOURI

The state's fiscal balance continued to ride a roller coaster from temporarily large surpluses to amounts dangerously close to a level that would be unable to meet expenses. Poor crops and low farm returns, following a severe drought, clearly presaged a drop in state income.

Since Missouri's taxes are among the lowest in the nation, one obvious remedy would be an increase. But Gov. Christopher S. Bond (R) remained adamantly opposed until late summer, when he summoned the General Assembly to a special session beginning October 19 to consider means of raising additional revenue.

Desegregation. A factor in the governor's reversal was the order by U.S. District Judge William L. Hungate for the state to pay one half of the expenses ($79–109 million) entailed in the desegregation of St. Louis schools.

Meanwhile the desegregation plan for St. Louis appeared to be working well. After 11 years of court battles, an agreement reached early in 1983 and approved by Judge Hungate in July called for the transfer of 3,000 black students from city to county schools. Six hundred white students from the county would enroll in city magnet programs, and about 50 black teachers and administrators from the St. Louis district would be hired by county school districts.

Because the plan was voluntary, the transfers proceeded smoothly as schools opened in September, but the state's attorney general, John D. Ashcroft (R), asked the Eighth U.S. Circuit Court of Appeals to thow out the plan on the ground that it interfered with school district autonomy—the traditional argument for segregation overturned by the Supreme Court in 1954—and that it was unconstitutional for a judge to "raise taxes." On September 30 the court froze further transfers from city schools until after the November 18 hearing.

MISSOURI · Information Highlights

Area: 69,697 sq mi (180 515 km²).
Population (1982 est.): 4,951,000.
Chief Cities (1980 census): Jefferson City, 33,619; St. Louis, 453,085; Kansas City, 448,159; Springfield, 133,116; Independence, 111,806.
Government (1983): *Chief Officers*—governor, Christopher S. Bond (R); lt. gov., Kenneth J. Rothman (D). *General Assembly*—Senate, 34 members; House of Representatives, 163 members.
State Finances (fiscal year 1981): *Revenues,* $4,435,000,000; *expenditures,* $4,422,000,000.
Personal Income (1982): $50,346,000,000; per capita, $10,170.
Labor Force (July 1983): *Nonagricultural wage and salary earners,* 1,905,200; unemployed, 222,000 (9.4% of total force).
Education: *Enrollment* (fall 1981)—public elementary schools, 553,012; public secondary, 265,693; colleges and universities (1981–82), 243,672. *Public school expenditures* (1980–81), $1,759,104,000 ($2,079 per pupil).

Dioxin. State and federal environmental agencies had known about widespread areas of contamination by the chemical dioxin for a decade, but only at the end of 1982 did public outcry force action. Officials blamed a chemical plant in Verona, MO, which manufactured hexachlorophene with dioxin as a byproduct. The company, in an effort to rid itself of the waste, buried it in drums on farms, mixed it with waste oil to be sprayed on horse arenas, and sold it as filler material to go under houses and roads. As people fell mysteriously ill, and large numbers of animals died, officials began to measure the levels of dioxin in the state. They found it so high in some places, such as Times Beach, that residents were warned to evacuate immediately. The General Assembly appropriated $3.5 million as the state's share of a federal plan to buy the property of Times Beach inhabitants. (*See also* ENVIRONMENT.)

RUTH W. TOWNE
Northeast Missouri State University

MONTANA

The year 1983 was highlighted by legislative action, important judicial decisions, the end of an era in the state's metals industry, and electric-power development.

Legislature. In accord with Gov. Ted Schwinden's Build Montana Program, the legislature pushed economic development. The program provided for implementation of Initiative 95, which requires that one fourth of coal-tax trust-fund revenues be invested within the state. Legislators established a program of low-interest loans for beginning farmers and increased taxes on cigarettes, gasoline, and diesel fuel to construct public works and rebuild and maintain the state's highways. However, they rejected the governor's request for authorization to sell state water for slurry lines. Sale of bonds to underwrite a vast water development program was tied up in the state Supreme Court. Authorized by the past two legislatures, the program includes repair of unsafe dams, rehabilitation of municipal water and sewer systems, and irrigation and hydroelectric projects.

Montana became the first state to limit campaign spending by political action committees for legislative candidates as well as the first to prohibit insurance companies from discriminating on the basis of sex in setting rates and benefits. In response to 1982's prison riot, the legislature appropriated money for expansion of the prison. It provided stiffer penalties for driving under the influence of alcohol and created a wildlife research and education program for nongame animals.

Judicial Decisions. A federal court upheld the reapportionment plan of the Reapportionment Commission. The U.S. Supreme Court broadened the power of state courts to resolve disputes over water rights involving Indian tribes, making it possible to proceed with a water right adjudication plan established by the 1979 legislature. A state district court, backed by the Montana Supreme Court, decided that laws of 1921 and 1927 give veterans and the handicapped an absolute preference in hiring by public agencies. This decision has had an enormous impact on state hiring. Law suits were brought by veterans and the handicapped whose applications were previously rejected.

Economic News. After repeated cutbacks in recent years, Anaconda Minerals Company officials on June 30 ceased all mining operations in Butte, with the loss of about 700 jobs. This ended all mining on the once richest hill on earth.

Montana Power Company dedicated coal-fired generating units 3 and 4. Cost overruns, which nearly quadrupled original estimates of construction costs, and a decline in electricity use forced the company to request the largest utility rate increases in its history.

RICHARD B. ROEDER
Montana State University

MONTANA · Information Highlights

Area: 147,046 sq mi (380 849 km²).
Population (1982 est.): 801,000.
Chief Cities (1980 census): Helena, the capital, 23,938; Billings, 66,842; Great Falls, 56,725.
Government (1983): *Chief Officers*—governor, Ted Schwinden (D); lt. gov., George Turman (D). *Legislature*—Senate, 50 members; House of Representatives, 100 members.
State Finances (fiscal year 1982): *Revenues,* $1,331,000,000; *expenditures,* $1,135,000,000.
Personal Income (1982): $7,673,000,000; per capita, $9,580.
Labor Force (July 1983): *Nonagricultural wage and salary earners,* 266,600; *unemployed,* 32,200 (8.3% of total force).
Education: *Enrollment* (fall 1981)—public elementary schools, 106,235; public secondary 47,200; colleges and universities (fall 1982), 36,811 students. *Public school expenditures* (1981–82), $488,553,000.

King Hassan II of Morocco continued to maintain friendly relations with the United States.

MOROCCO

The continuing war against the Polisario Front in the Western Sahara was a serious drain on Morocco's dwindling economic resources, but the almost total agreement within the country that the war was justified appeared to be the main source of King Hassan II's political strength. This situation partially explained some of the conflicting and confusing signals which emerged from Rabat during 1983.

Foreign Relations. The admission of the Polisario government, the Saharan Arab Democratic Republic (SADR), to the Organization of African Unity (OAU) had caused Morocco and its allies to boycott and effectively cancel the 1982 OAU summit. In 1983, Morocco again threatened to walk out of the meeting in Addis Ababa, Ethiopia. The SADR, in the interest of preserving the summit, withdrew at the last minute, and the summit proceeded. During the June meeting, Morocco agreed to a resolution calling for a referendum on self-determination for the people of Western Sahara.

King Hassan later retreated from the position, saying that in the unlikely event of the SADR winning a referendum, nothing would oblige Morocco to "offer our Sahara on a plate to a group of mercenaries." Hassan saw a clear distinction between the Saharawi people and the Polisario, whom he considered to be foreign-backed mercenaries. Later in the year, at a meeting of the OAU Implementation Committee on the Western Sahara referendum resolution, Morocco refused to sit at the same table with Polisario representatives. Still, Hassan claimed that Morocco would be bound by the results of the referendum, saying that there was no need to talk with the Polisario before a referendum is held. Taken together, these statements indicated that Hassan would be willing to accept the results of the referendum so long as he is the winner. The Polisario responded to Hassan's remarks by attacking Moroccan positions in Western Sahara.

During 1983, Hassan met with Algeria's President Chadli Benjedid and Libya's leader,

Col. Muammar el-Qaddafi. Both Chadli and Qaddafi were supporting the Polisario in the war against Morocco, and the meetings raised some hope that a settlement could be found. Hassan also discussed the issue during a September meeting in Rabat with U.S. Vice-President George Bush. U.S. and Moroccan forces took part in earlier joint military exercises.

Economy. The declining price of phosphates, Morocco's largest export, was one of the factors that forced the government to institute draconian austerity measures. Among them were a 13% cut in public expenditure; a substantial tax increase, including a special "solidarity tax" to help finance the war; a reduction in food subsidies; a creeping devaluation of the currency; and a hiring freeze on civil-service jobs. Moroccan officials proceeded cautiously, bearing in mind that similar measures imposed in 1981 led to bloody riots. But there were no signs of civil unrest during 1983, and Hassan appeared to be more in control than ever.

Morocco also asked Western banks and governments to reschedule its $10 billion (U.S.) debt. That request came as the International Monetary Fund was approving a $315 million loan. Morocco's account deficit ran to $1.3 billion, and payments on debt due amounted to $1.7 billion, bringing the country's debt service to 40% of the value of its exports and payments.

MICHAEL MAREN, *"Africa Report"*

MOROCCO • Information Highlights

Official Name: Kingdom of Morocco.
Location: Northwest Africa.
Area: 157,992 sq mi (409 200 km²).
Population (July 1983): 22,889,000.
Government: *Head of state,* Hassan II, king (acceded 1961). *Head of government,* Maati Bouabid, prime minister (took office March 1979).
Monetary Unit: Dirham (6.8 dirhams equal U.S.$1, June 1983).
Gross National Product (1982 U.S.$): $14,900,-000,000.
Foreign Trade (1982 U.S.$): Imports, $4,315,000,000; exports, $2,062,000,000.

MOTION PICTURES

By its very nature the motion-picture industry is generally in a state of flux, but some periods bring more dramatic changes than others. Developments in 1983, both on and off the screen, were striking. The success of numerous new films brought attention to a contingent of rising stars capable of competing with and perhaps ultimately replacing in popularity some of the contemporary favorites.

Another basic shift could be discerned in the balance of power involved in the making of films. The trend toward viewing cassettes on television sets in the privacy of a living room brought intense competition for that market, and there was a similar scramble in the cable-television field for the movie market.

Actors. For years the standard list of so-called bankable actors—those whose names are considered collateral for borrowing money with which to produce films—has included such stalwarts as Robert Redford, Clint Eastwood, Dustin Hoffman, Robert De Niro, Al Pacino, Paul Newman, and several others in the charmed circle. Although they still were at the top, certain newcomers were being regarded in a stronger light.

Perhaps the most charismatic of the new actors was Ed Harris, who in *The Right Stuff,* a rousing film based on Tom Wolfe's book about America's pioneering astronauts, had the highly publicized role of the young John Glenn. With Glenn a 1984 presidential candidate, the focus was on Harris to see whether his characterization would help or hurt Glenn. Although Glenn was portrayed as stuffy in some scenes, his heroism was also accented, and the handsome, blue-eyed Harris's screen appeal could only help the candidate.

Among other rising stars, Timothy Hutton, very good in *Ordinary People* (1980), further proved his range in the emotionally charged film *Daniel,* in which he played a son struggling to learn the truth about the controversial case of his parents, executed on a conspiracy-to-commit-espionage charge. Mandy Patinkin, an actor already noted for his portrayal of the film director in *Ragtime* (1981) and also seen in *Yentl,* was outstanding as the father in *Daniel,* which was based on E. L. Doctorow's novel *The Book of Daniel,* which in turn was based on the still-disputed case of Julius and Ethel Rosenberg. Eric Roberts, who had shown promise in *King of the Gypsies* (1978), gave one of the best performances of the year in *Star 80* as Paul Snider, who murdered *Playboy* magazine model Dorothy Stratten, then killed himself. Tall, gangling Jeff Goldblum, who has a talent for comedy, was outstanding as the *People* magazine reporter in *The Big Chill,* which also served as a vehicle for the continued development of Kevin Kline into a major star.

© 1983 Ladd Company
Ed Harris (left) is John Glenn in "The Right Stuff," adapted from Tom Wolfe's tale of the original astronauts.

Between *Betrayal* and 1982's *Gandhi,* British actor Ben Kingsley became known to a wide American public as an actor capable of handling vastly different roles.

Some actors made headway as a result of appearing in films popular with the young, an age group that producers try to attract. When *WarGames* became a hit of the summer, it brought to the attention of its fans the appealing young actor Matthew Broderick, one of the most sought after among the newcomers. If you asked a member of an older generation who Tom Cruise was, the response might be a shrug. But the box-office clout of *Risky Business,* a light comedy that spoofs success when its hero demonstrates business acumen by turning his home into a brothel while his parents are away, made Cruise a favorite of young moviegoers across the United States. The same could be said for Michael Keaton's turn in *Mr. Mom,* another unexpected financial bonanza.

Certainly one of the most original comic talents to arrive in many years was Eddie Murphy, who first gained attention as a member of the *Saturday Night Live* television troupe, then

From the United Artists release "WarGames" © 1983 United Artists Corporation

Newcomers Matthew Broderick and Ally Sheedy shine in "WarGames," a tale of computer break-ins.

made a brilliant transition to the movies in *48 Hours* (1982) and *Trading Places*. Paramount quickly signed him to a lucrative contract. The Matt Dillon bandwagon, which had begun in 1982, accelerated with *The Outsiders* and *Rumble Fish*, and Sean Penn, effective in *Bad Boys*, was living up to predictions that he would be a big star.

Actresses. Female stars with box-office draw have been limited to a few, including Barbra Streisand and Jane Fonda, and to some extent Meryl Streep, Jill Clayburgh, and Diane Keaton. Here, too, there was movement toward the establishment of potential successors. One of the year's major surprises was the effectiveness of Mariel Hemingway as the murdered *Playboy* model Dorothy Stratten in *Star 80*, directed by Bob Fosse. The granddaughter of the renowned novelist Ernest Hemingway had won a best supporting actress Oscar nomination for her role as Woody Allen's young girlfriend in *Manhattan* (1979), but nothing she had done previously suggested the mature performance that she delivered as Stratten. Cher left behind her Sonny and Cher television image when she began acting seriously in *Come Back to the 5 and Dime Jimmy Dean, Jimmy Dean* (1982) and also in *Silkwood*, in which she proved that she could be both touching and funny. Other actresses who finally seemed to be getting their due in films included JoBeth Williams and Mary Kay Place, both in *The Big Chill*, and, in

the same film, newcomer Meg Tilly made an impact. Just as *WarGames* did wonders for Matthew Broderick, his young costar Ally Sheedy also gained by virtue of her sympathetic performance as his colleague in computer break-ins. Another actress on the rise was Kathleen Turner, first noticed for her sex appeal in *Body Heat* (1981), who demonstrated an outstanding talent for comedy opposite Steve Martin in the otherwise forgettable *The Man With Two Brains*. Newcomer Sandra Bernhard staked out her claim with the offbeat dimension she brought to the autograph hound in *The King of Comedy*.

Competition. A major commercial development was the entry into the movie production business of Time Inc.'s Home Box Office (HBO), which decided it would be more profitable to make films specifically for showing over its cable outlets than to rely solely on acquisition of product from other movie companies. HBO further cemented its power base by pursuing a plan with Columbia Pictures and CBS, Inc. under the banner of Tri-Star, to make movies for theatrical distribution. With HBO becoming the new giant in the field, there was inevitably a heightened competition with the existing studios, which were drafting plans of their own to cash in on the cable market. The solid financial position of HBO made it possible to compete for the services of top stars, as evidenced by HBO's initial films that included

Elizabeth Taylor and Carol Burnett in *Between Friends*.

An estimated seven million American homes had video recorders, and the public interest was reflected in the rush to buy or rent film cassettes, with some 10,000 stores providing the service. A growing number of movie fans were finding it less expensive to watch films at home. Earnings on films in the cassette market were projected as totaling $240 million by the end of 1983. Filmmakers were fighting in the U.S. Supreme Court to establish the principle of a levy on video recorders as a form of guaranteeing profit. The move was based on the reasoning that the manufacturers of video equipment were enabling buyers to ignore copyrights and simply record films at home and play them as often as they liked. The outcome regarding the issue was pending as arguments continued in the fall session of the court. Two kinds of piracy were also troubling filmmakers. Prints were frequently stolen and copied on cassettes for illegal worldwide sales, and satellite broadcasts of films for television were intercepted in various countries and rebroadcast without contracts or payment of fees. *See also* feature article, pages 55–63.

Censorship. One attraction of cable television was the possibility of enjoying an alternative to network programming. Since movies coming in on cable were not using the airwaves, they were not subject to federal restrictions. As might be expected, cable channels began showing adult movies replete with explicit, though not quite pornographic, sex. No longer a novelty, cable is available in some 35% of U.S. households that have television, a figure approaching 85 million. In many communities there developed a backlash to the kind of films on view, and the predictable consequences were moves to ban them. Thus a civil liberties issue developed, and just as efforts to censor have been fought with regard to the theaters, a new battleground was staked out for the home.

Movies and the Box Office. One indicator of the box-office health of the motion-picture industry is how well films fare during the summer. Generally, the public is given a heavy helping of escapism, and 1983 was no exception. The biggest hit was the *Star Wars* spin-off *Return of the Jedi,* which earned some $232 million. *Flashdance,* which caught on with young audiences, garnered $87 million, and *Trading Places,* $80 million. *WarGames* reached $68 million, *Octopussy,* $63 million, and *Superman III,* $62 million. The movie industry was elated at the record total of $1.5 billion for the summer months.

The fall lineup of movies was more of a gamble, with inclusion of the kind of topical, controversial films that generally cause industry nervousness. *Daniel,* directed by Sidney Lumet, was one case in point, with the mixed reviews seemingly reflecting attitudes about the Rosenberg case itself. *Under Fire,* starring Nick Nolte, Gene Hackman, and Joanna Cassidy and set in Nicaragua at the time of Somoza's fall, questioned journalistic responsibility. *Silkwood,* with Meryl Streep in the title role and Mike Nichols directing, was an indictment of unsafe conditions in a nuclear plant, and despite a disclaimer at the end, leaned sharply in its dramatic presentation toward the view that the real life Karen Silkwood's mysterious death as she fought to expose those conditions was not an accident. Director Costa-Gavras, who had tackled controversial subjects attempted to deal with Arab-Israeli relations in *Hanna K,* starring Jill Clayburgh.

Rescue Mission. When 20th Century-Fox first tested *Heart Like a Wheel,* it flopped decisively. Director Jonathan Kaplan blames the failure in part on an advertising campaign that misrepresented what the film was really about and was aimed at the wrong audiences. After a change of personnel at the studio, a new executive became a fan of the film and arranged for it to have a second chance. Based on the true story of woman hot-rod racer Shirley Muldowney, who broke racing barriers against women, *Heart Like a Wheel* was showcased by the New York Film Festival and enthusiastically received by critics. The deeply moving, true-to-life performance by Bonnie Bedelia as Muldowney gave the actress's career a new boost. The new life given the film was something unusual in bottomline Hollywood economics.

See OBITUARIES; PRIZES AND AWARDS.
WILLIAM WOLF, *"New York Magazine"*

"Flashdance," featuring Jennifer Beals and Michael Nouri, did better at the box office than it did with the critics.

"The Big Chill," about 1960s students reunited at the funeral of one of their group, featured fine ensemble acting.

MOTION PICTURES | 1983

ALL THE RIGHT MOVES. Director, Michael Chapman; screenplay by Michael Kane. With Tom Cruise.

ANGELO MY LOVE. Written and directed by Robert Duvall. With Angelo Evans.

BABY IT'S YOU. Written and directed by John Sayles. With Rosanna Arquette, Vincent Spano.

BAD BOYS. Director, Richard Rosenthal; screenplay by Richard Di Lello. With Sean Penn.

BERLIN ALEXANDERPLATZ. Written and directed by Rainer Werner Fassbinder. With Gunter Lamprecht, Hanna Schygulla, Gottfried John.

BETRAYAL. Director, David Jones; screenplay by Harold Pinter. With Jeremy Irons, Ben Kingsley, Patricia Hodge.

THE BIG CHILL. Director, Lawrence Kasdan; screenplay by Mr. Kasdan, Barbara Benedek. With Tom Berenger, Glenn Close, Jeff Goldblum, William Hurt, Kevin Kline, Mary Kay Place, Meg Tilly, JoBeth Williams.

THE BLACK STALLION RETURNS. Director, Robert Dalva; screenplay by Richard Kletter, Jerome Kass. With Kelly Reno, Teri Garr, Vincent Spano.

BLUE THUNDER. Director, John Badham; screenplay by Dan O'Bannon, Don Jakoby. With Roy Scheider.

BRAINSTORM. Director, Douglas Trumbull; screenplay by Robert Stitzel, Philip Frank Messina. With Christopher Walken, Natalie Wood, Cliff Robertson.

BREATHLESS. Director, Jim McBride; screenplay by Mr. McBride, L. M. Kit Carson. With Richard Gere.

BRITANNIA HOSPITAL. Director, Lindsay Anderson; screenplay by David Sherwin. With Malcolm McDowell.

CAN SHE BAKE A CHERRY PIE? Written and directed by Henry Jaglom. With Karen Black, Michael Emil.

CROSS CREEK. Director, Martin Ritt; screenplay by Dalene Young, based on Marjorie Kinnan Rawlings' memoirs. With Mary Steenburgen, Rip Torn.

DANIEL. Director, Sidney Lumet; screenplay by E. L. Doctorow. With Timothy Hutton.

THE DEAD ZONE. Director, David Cronenberg; screenplay by Jeffrey Boam. With Christopher Walken.

THE DRESSER. Director, Peter Yates; screenplay by Ronald Harwood. With Albert Finney, Tom Courtenay.

EDUCATING RITA. Director, Lewis Gilbert; screenplay by Willy Russell. With Michael Caine, Julie Walters.

EXPOSED. Written and directed by James Toback. With Nastassia Kinski, Rudolf Nureyev, Harvey Keitel.

FANNY AND ALEXANDER. Written and directed by Ingmar Bergman. With Bertil Guve, Pernilla Allwin.

THE FINAL OPTION. Director, Ian Sharp; screenplay by Reginald Rose. With Lewis Collins, Judy Davis.

FLASHDANCE. Director, Adrian Lyne; screenplay by Tom Hedley, Joe Eszterhas. With Jennifer Beals.

THE FLIGHT OF THE EAGLE. Director, Jan Troell; screenplay by George Oddner, Ian Rakoff, Klaus Rifbjerg, Jan Troell. With Max von Sydow.

GORKY PARK. Director, Michael Apted; screenplay by Dennis Potter. With William Hurt, Lee Marvin, Joanna Pacula, Brian Dennehy.

THE GREY FOX. Director, Phillip Borsos; screenplay by John Hunter. With Richard Farnsworth.

HANNA K. Director, Costa-Gavras; screenplay by Franco Solinas from an original screenplay by Solinas and Costa-Gavras. With Jill Clayburgh.

HEART LIKE A WHEEL. Director, Jonathan Kaplan; screenplay by Ken Friedman. With Bonnie Bedelia, Beau Bridges.

HEAT AND DUST. Director, James Ivory; novel and screenplay by Ruth Prawer Jhabvala. With Greta Scacchi, Julie Christie.

THE HUNGER. Director, Tony Scott; screenplay by Ivan Davis, Michael Thomas. With Catherine Deneuve, David Bowie, Susan Sarandon.

THE KING OF COMEDY. Director, Martin Scorsese; screenplay by Paul D. Zimmerman. With Robert De Niro, Jerry Lewis.

LIQUID SKY. Director, Slava Tsukerman; screenplay by Mr. Tsukerman, Anne Carlisle, Nina V. Kerova. With Anne Carlisle.

THE LORDS OF DISCIPLINE. Director, Franc Roddam; screenplay by Thomas Pope, Lloyd Fonvielle. With David Keith.

LOVESICK. Written and directed by Marshall Brickman. With Dudley Moore, Elizabeth McGovern.

LA NUIT DE VARENNES. Director, Ettore Scola; screenplay by Mr. Scola, Sergio Amidei. With Marcello Mastroianni, Jean-Louis Barrault, Hanna Schygulla.

LA TRAVIATA. Written and directed by Franco Zeffirelli. With Teresa Stratas, Placido Domingo.

THE MAN WHO LOVED WOMEN. Director, Blake Edwards; screenplay by Blake and Geoffrey Edwards, based on a film by François Truffaut. With Julie Andrews, Burt Reynolds.

THE MAN WITH TWO BRAINS. Director, Carl Reiner; screenplay by Mr. Reiner, Steve Martin, George Gipe. With Steve Martin, Kathleen Turner.

MAX DUGAN RETURNS. Director, Herbert Ross; screenplay by Neil Simon. With Marsha Mason, Jason Robards, Donald Sutherland, Matthew Broderick.

MERRY CHRISTMAS MR. LAWRENCE. Director, Nagisa Oshima; screenplay by Mr. Oshima, Paul Mayersberg. With David Bowie, Tom Conti.

MR. MOM. Director, Stan Dragoti; screenplay by John Hughes. With Michael Keaton, Teri Garr.

MONTY PYTHON'S THE MEANING OF LIFE. Director, Terry Jones; screenplay by Graham Chapman, John Cleese, Terry Gilliam, Eric Idle, Terry Jones, Michael Palin.

THE MOON IN THE GUTTER. Written and directed by Jean-Jacques Beineix. With Gérard Depardieu.

NATIONAL LAMPOON'S VACATION. Director, Harold Ramis; screenplay by John Hughes. With Chevy Chase.

NEVER CRY WOLF. Director, Carroll Ballard; screenplay by Curtis Hanson, Sam Hamm, Richard Kietter. With Charles Martin Smith.

NEVER SAY NEVER AGAIN. Director, Irvin Kershner; screenplay by Lorenzo Semple, Jr. With Sean Connery.

OCTOPUSSY. Director, John Glen; screenplay by George MacDonald Fraser, Richard Maibaum, Michael G. Wilson. With Roger Moore, Maud Adams.

THE OUTSIDERS. Director, Francis Coppola; screenplay by Kathleen Knutsen Rowell. With Matt Dillon.

PAULINE AT THE BEACH. Director, Eric Rohmer; screenplay by Mr. Rohmer. With Amanda Langlet, Arielle Dombasle, Pascal Greggory, Feodor Atkine, Simon De La Brosse, Rosette.

THE PIRATES OF PENZANCE. Director, Wilford Leach; screenplay by Mr. Leach. With Kevin Kline, Angela Lansbury, Linda Ronstadt, George Rose, Rex Smith.

PSYCHO II. Director, Richard Franklin; screenplay by Tom Holland. With Anthony Perkins, Vera Miles.

RETURN OF THE JEDI. Director, Richard Marquand; screenplay by Lawrence Kasdan, George Lucas. With Mark Hamill, Harrison Ford, Carrie Fisher.

THE RETURN OF MARTIN GUERRE. Director, Daniel Vigne; screenplay by Mr. Vigne, Jean-Claude Carrière. With Gérard Depardieu.

THE RIGHT STUFF. Written and directed by Philip Kaufman. With Sam Shepard, Scott Glenn, Ed Harris, Dennis Quaid.

RISKY BUSINESS. Written and directed by Paul Brickman. With Tom Cruise.

ROMANTIC COMEDY. Director, Arthur Hiller; screenplay by Bernard Slade, based on his stage play. With Dudley Moore, Mary Steenburgen.

SCARFACE. Director, Brian De Palma; screenplay by Oliver Stone. With Al Pacino.

SILKWOOD. Director, Mike Nichols; screenplay by Nora Ephron, Alice Arlen. With Meryl Streep, Kurt Russell, Cher.

THE STAR CHAMBER. Director, Peter Hyams; screenplay by Mr. Hyams, Roderick Taylor. With Michael Douglas.

STAR 80. Written and directed by Bob Fosse. With Mariel Hemingway, Eric Roberts.

STAYING ALIVE. Director, Sylvester Stallone; screenplay by Mr. Stallone, Norman Wexler. With John Travolta.

STREAMERS. Director, Robert Altman; screenplay by David Rabe from his play. With Matthew Modine, Michael Wright, Mitchell Lichtenstein, David Alan Grier.

SUPERMAN III. Director, Richard Lester; screenplay by David and Leslie Newman. With Christopher Reeve, Richard Pryor, Robert Vaughn, Margot Kidder.

TENDER MERCIES. Director, Bruce Beresford; screenplay by Horton Foote. With Robert Duvall.

TERMS OF ENDEARMENT. Written and directed by James L. Brooks. With Debra Winger, Shirley MacLaine, Jack Nicholson.

TESTAMENT. Director, Lynne Littman; screenplay by John Sacret Young. With Jane Alexander, William Devane.

TO BE OR NOT TO BE. Director, Alan Johnson; screenplay by Thomas Meehan, Ronny Graham. With Mel Brooks, Anne Bancroft.

TRADING PLACES. Director, John Landis; screenplay by Timothy Harris, Herschel Weingrod. With Dan Aykroyd, Eddie Murphy.

TWILIGHT ZONE—THE MOVIE. Segments directed by John Landis, Steven Spielberg, Joe Dante, George Miller; screenplays by Landis, George Clayton Johnson, Richard Matheson, Josh Rogan. With Dan Aykroyd, Albert Brooks, Vic Morrow, Kathleen Quinlan, Kevin McCarthy, John Lithgow.

UNDER FIRE. Director, Roger Spottiswoode; screenplay by Ron Shelton, Clayton Frohman. With Nick Nolte, Ed Harris, Gene Hackman, Joanna Cassidy.

WARGAMES. Director, John Badham; screenplay by Lawrence Lasker, Walter F. Parkes. With Matthew Broderick, Dabney Coleman, Ally Sheedy.

WAYS IN THE NIGHT. Director, Krzysztof Zanussi; screenplay by Mr. Zanussi. With Mathieu Carriere.

THE WHITE ROSE. Director, Michael Verhoeven; screenplay by Mr. Verhoeven, Mario Krebs. With Lena Stolze, Wulf Kessler.

THE YEAR OF LIVING DANGEROUSLY. Director, Peter Weir; screenplay by Mr. Weir, David Williamson, C. J. Koch. With Mel Gibson, Sigourney Weaver.

YENTL. Director, Barbra Streisand; screenplay by Miss Streisand, Jack Rosenthal. With Barbra Streisand, Mandy Patinkin, Amy Irving.

ZELIG. Written and directed by Woody Allen. With Woody Allen, Mia Farrow.

"The Return of the Jedi," the concluding feature of the *"Star Wars"* trilogy, was the blockbuster movie of 1983.

MUSIC

Each in its own way, the major music forms looked to the past in 1983. The opera world remembered 100 years at the Met. Jazz musicians returned to older, established forms. And the pop scene reflected trends of the late 1950s and early 1960s.

Classical

Opera. The Metropolitan Opera in New York City both made history and celebrated it as it began its centennial season. On the actual anniversary of its first performance, October 22, the Met produced a marathon gala of unprecedented scope. Televised live over the Public Broadcasting System, the event was given in two four-hour sections, afternoon and evening. Nearly 100 singers, many of them international stars, performed solos and ensembles from 46 operas. Seven conductors, including Leonard Bernstein and the Met's artistic director-designate, James Levine, presided in the pit. Soloists included Placido Domingo, Luciano Pavarotti, Joan Sutherland, Kiri Te Kanawa, Marilyn Horne, Birgit Nilsson, and Montserrat Caballe.

The gala was staged in front of a variety of opera sets, and at a climax of the second part the curtains opened to reveal an honored stage audience of former Met stars, including Zinka Milanov, Marian Anderson, Ramon Vinay, and Ferruccio Tagliavini.

The centenary was in continual celebration throughout New York City. Special exhibits were devoted to aspects of the Met's history in eight museums and in window displays in 25 stores. Other museum exhibits were set up in Washington (DC), Atlanta, Dallas, and Cleveland.

The Met offered no new works for its 1983–84 centennial season but featured stellar casts starting with the opening production of Berlioz' epic *Les Troyens*. The complete, five-hour work was presented, and the production was musically outstanding. Jessye Norman made a long-awaited and historic Met debut as Cassandra, giving a searing and beautiful performance. As planned, later in the fall she assumed the opera's other heroic role, Dido, which Tatiana Troyanos had sung vibrantly at the opening. The conducting, by James Levine, was splendid. Levine's promotion from music director to artistic director, effective in 1986, had been announced ten days before. He also conducted another successful Met event, its new production of Verdi's *Ernani* with Leona Mitchell and Luciano Pavarotti.

The San Francisco Opera introduced its new Wagner *Ring* cycle, to unfold over a three-year period in its summer seasons. *Das Rhein-gold* and *Die Walküre* premiered on May 27 and 28, produced by Nikolaus Lehnhoff and designed by John Conklin. The productions turned away from both the dark, symbolic approach and the stark, modern approach in favor of the romantic era's way of evoking a mythic past through painterly visions of classical antiquity and a wild, craggy nature. Edo de Waart conducted excellently, and *Die Walküre* flourished with a superior cast that included Leonie Rysanek, Jeanine Altmeyer, Peter Hofmann, and Thomas Stewart.

The San Francisco Opera had an unintentionally dramatic season opening when the tenor Carlo Cossutta became ill on the morning of the opening night of *Otello*. Placido Domingo flew cross-country from New York in a private jet, and the audience waited bemusedly for his arrival. The curtain finally rose three hours late.

On October 15, the San Francisco Opera presented the American premiere of Sir Michael Tippett's *The Midsummer Marriage* (1955). While the music did not develop or sustain tension or wide-ranging contrasts, the production by John Copley, with fanciful settings by Robin Donn, conveyed Tippett's ambiguous allegory with a certain measure of delight.

The Finnish National Opera, which had produced 15 new Finnish operas in the previous ten years, visited New York to perform two of them in the Metropolitan Opera House. Joonas Kokkonen's *The Last Temptations* (1975), an inwardly turned opera about a 19th-century revivalist preacher, was stirring, its music distinctive and fresh. Aulis Sallinen's *The Red Line* (1978), about the impact of revolutionary politics on peasant villagers in 1907, was dramatically strong. The performances by the Finnish company were excellent.

Leonard Bernstein's one-act opera, *A Quiet Place*, two hours in length, received its premiere by the Houston Opera on June 17 and drew severely critical notices. A sequel to Bernstein's *Trouble in Tahiti* (1952), *A Quiet Place* resumes the story of a suburban couple's failed marriage and uses a mixture of styles.

Hans Werner Henze's *Pollicino, or The New Adventures of Tom Thumb* (1980), a children's opera with a modern and socialist twist, was well-received in its American premiere on August 18, at the Cabrillo Music Festival, Aptos, CA, Dennis Russell Davis conducting.

Resurrection, by Franco Alfano, was revived by the Cincinnati Opera on June 23. The performance, in an English translation by Andrew Porter, revealed the individuality of Alfano, who is best remembered for his completion of Puccini's *Turandot* after that composer's death in 1924.

Other important revivals included a May 24 production of Rameau's *Zoroastre,* in the tercentenary year of the composer's birth, by the Boston Early Music Festival, Martin Pearlman

Photos J. Heffernan

The New York Metropolitan Opera celebrated its 100th birthday on Oct. 22, 1983, with an eight-hour, two-part extravaganza that was televised live. Opera stars from the past 40
years participated and concluded the evening with a "Happy
Birthday," above. Two current favorites, Leontyne Price and
Luciano Pavarotti, left, sang a duet from Verdi's "The
Masked Ball." The voice of Enrico Caruso, below, who made
his Met debut at the original house in 1903 and who has
been called the company's "most legendary singer," was a
great memory for many buffs.

conducting; and Rimsky-Korsakov's *The Legend of the Invisible City of Kitezh,* performed on April 17 by the Opera Company of Boston.

The first of two major world premieres in Europe was Philip Boesmans' *La Passion de Gilles,* on October 18, by the Belgian National Opera in Brussels. It was a violent, expressionistic dream fantasy around the life of a 15th-century monster, the man who actually led Joan of Arc's army. The advanced and demanding score was described as a descendant of Strauss' *Elektra.* On November 29 the Paris Opera introduced *St. Francis of Assisi,* a work it had commissioned of Olivier Messiaen.

A 54-day strike by the New York City Opera's orchestra delayed the opening of the company's season from July 7 until September 21. The NYC Opera's introduction of "supratitles," the projection of English paraphrases of the sung text onto a screen above the stage, was widely praised. The San Francisco Opera later tried the innovation for its student matinee performances. "Supratitles" was originally devised by the Canadian National Opera.

New Music. With its extensive festival, Horizon '83, held June 1–15, the New York Philharmonic made a notable contribution to music of the current era. Under the theme "Since 1968, a New Romanticism?", the orchestra presented seven programs covering a wide range of music by 25 living composers, mostly American. Zubin Mehta and five others conducted, and four guest ensembles participated. Jacob Druckman, the Philharmonic's composer-in-residence, selected the works.

Nostalgic and retrospective approaches were conveyed in David del Tredici's *All in the Golden Afternoon,* Luciano Berio's *Sinfonia,* and George Rochberg's *Imago Mundi,* with outright romantic expression affirmed in John Harbison's Violin Concerto. Works in the manner of the new impressionism included Toru Takemitsu's *Far Calls, Coming Far!,* Joseph Schwantner's *Sparrows,* and Druckman's *Aureole.* Other more highly structured, advanced, and complex works included Leonard Rosenman's *Foci I* and Fred Lerdahl's *Chords.*

The Horizon '83 concerts and four symposia stimulated discussions of aesthetics and attitudes and of the pendulum swing between the classical and the romantic ideals. A consensus emerged that, musically, the age is characterized by individualism, a more subjective approach, renewed acoustic sensuality, visionary attitudes, nostalgia, and an interest in simpler, more accessible styles.

Witold Lutoslawski's Symphony No. 3, the Polish composer's only major work in the past five years, was outstanding for individuality and craft. Sir Georg Solti conducted the September 29 premiere with the Chicago Symphony, which had commissioned it. Krzystof Penderecki's 50th birthday was celebrated by the National Symphony, Washington, DC, conducted by Mstislav Rostropovich, with a concert introducing nine movements of his incomplete "Polish" Requiem. It was written in his dramatic, romantic manner combined with elements of his earlier avant-garde style and was acclaimed as "electrifying." On the same program, Penderecki's new Cello Concerto also was well received, with Rostropovich as soloist and the composer conducting. Other premieres included the German composer Manfred Trohahn's *Sea Pictures* by the New York Philharmonic, February 24, and Mario Davidovsky's *Romancero* by Speculum Musicae in New York, May 18.

Elliott Carter and Elie Siegmeister, both celebrating their 75th birthdays, were the subjects of special performances, while the 150th anniversary of Johannes Brahms' birth was observed with even more attention in orchestra programming than customary.

The fifth annual New Music American Festival was held in Washington, DC, October 7–17. Performances were given in the capital's major museums, with emphasis on performance art and sound-installation sculptures. The Contemporary Music Festival at the California Institute for the Arts in Valencia, March 3–6, offered a more evenly balanced presentation of styles than in past seasons, with music by Milton Babbitt, Witold Lutoslawski, and Iannis Xenakis as well as works by minimalist and avant-garde composers.

Symphony Orchestras. Carlo Maria Giulini announced that he would relinquish the music directorship of the Los Angeles Philharmonic by September 1984 for reasons of health. Edo de Waart announced his decision to give up the music directorship of the San Francisco Symphony in June 1985 to become music director and conductor of the Netherlands Opera.

New symphony music directors appointed included Joseph Silverstein, the Utah Symphony; Kenneth Schermerhorn, Nashville Symphony; Lawrence Leighton Smith, Louisville Orchestra; Richard Buckley, Oakland Symphony; and David Zinman, Baltimore Symphony. Sergiu Commissiona, artistic adviser of the Houston Symphony, was appointed its next music director beginning with the 1984–85 season.

Awards. Elmar Oliveira, violinist, on April 20 won the Avery Fischer Award of $10,000, a solo recital, and a recording. Peter Serkin, pianist, won the second annual Premio Accademia Musicale Chigiana in Siena, on August 18, and received a prize of 10 million lire and a silver sculpture. The Rumanian Mihaela Martinu won the first Quadrennial International Violin Competition in Indianapolis, IN, and was awarded a gold medal and $10,000. The fourth annual Arthur Rubinstein International Piano Competition in Israel was won by Jeffrey Kahane.

ROBERT COMMANDAY
Music Critic, "San Francisco Chronicle"

Jazz

The jazz scene during 1983 was characterized by the lack of any new style, trend, or sound establishing itself as a major new vehicle, and on the continuing downtrend in top jobs in the recording and television industries. Many of the top studio players were playing Broadway shows, touring with name jazz artists and singers, teaching at universities, or forming their own bands and combos. These instrumentalists, like trumpeter Jon Faddis who toured Europe during the summer with Dizzy Gillespie, were devoting most of their time and talents to jazz as an art form.

With the absence of any important new thrust, free-jazz advocates started to use older, established formats for their compositions, improvisations, and programming. Everything from Gospel music to early New Orleans jazz songs were utilized by Jack DeJohnett's Special Edition, Ornett Coleman's Prime Time, and groups led by Henry Threadgill, Lester Bowie, Oliver Lake, and Ronald Shannon Jackson.

Festivals. The 1983 Newport Jazz Festivals were, compared with previous years, much more conservative in content and scope, presenting such commercially successful artists as Stan Getz, Dave Brubeck, and Gerry Mulligan, as well as pop-jazz personages Dave Grusin and Chuck Mangione. The New York Festival also reflected a growing phenomenon—the piano bar or lounge, where a solo piano, duo, or trio make an important jazz statement. Besides featuring solo piano performances by Michael Petrucciani, Oscar Peterson, Dick Hyman, and Don Pullen, the New York Festival also presented a tribute to Bill Evans, which featured George Shearing, Teddy Wilson, John Lewis, and others. Other festival highlights included tributes to Coleman Hawkins, featuring Illinois Jacquet and Zoot Sims, to Kai Winding, featuring J. J. Johnson, and to Slide Hampton, as well as salutes to Gil Evans and the Big Band Era.

Among the new U.S. jazz festivals founded in 1983 were the Dick Grove All-Star Music Festival in Los Angeles, The American Jazz Festival in Lexington, KY, and The Mary Lou Williams Festival at Duke University. The year also saw the debut of The Hoagy Carmichael Jazz Society in Bloomington, IN, and The Alaska Jazz Society, as well as the 25th anniversary of the Collegiate Jazz Festival at Notre Dame University.

Vocal Jazz. In 1983 the vocal jazz movement gained maturity and recognition in all areas of the music scene. High schools and colleges were experiencing a fast-growing interest and participation in vocal jazz improvisation and jazz ensemble singing. The movement is personified in the record and concert success of the vocal group Manhattan Transfer, which

© Gary Gershoff/Retna Ltd.

Trumpeter Wynton Marsalis, cited by the International Critics Poll, released a jazz album and classical album.

mixes pop-rock with be-bop scat (jazz singing with nonsense syllables) in their concert format. Here was seen for the first time a jazz trend that came from the high schools and colleges to the professional jazz scene, rather than from the professionals to the schools. The success of vocal jazz can be seen and heard in the growth of high school and college programs and performing groups, festivals, recordings, and publications.

Accomplishments and Awards. One of the year's most important accomplishments must be attributed to trumpeter Wynton Marsalis, whose new record releases included a jazz disk, *Think of One,* and a classical album containing works by Haydn, Hummel, and Leopold Mozart. Both recordings received rave reviews.

The year's most impressive and important new group was likely Steps Ahead, with Michael Brecker, Elaine Elias, Peter Erskine, Eddie Gomez, and Mike Mainieri.

Winners in the 31st annual International Critics Poll included: Albert Ayler—Hall of Fame; Muhal Richard Abrams, *Blues Forever* —record of the year; Wynton Marsalis—trumpet; Jimmy Knepper—trombone; Phil Woods —alto sax; Pepper Adams—baritone sax; Gary Burton—vibes; Cecil Taylor—acoustic piano; Jim Hall—guitar; Charlie Haden—acoustic bass; Mac Roach—drums; Joe Williams—male singer; Sarah Vaughan—female singer; Manhattan Transfer—vocal group; Ray Charles— soul/R&B artist.

DOMINIC SPERA, *Indiana University*

© De Wildenberg/Sygma

Diana Ross' free concert in New York's Central Park was cut short by rain. She was back on stage the next night.

Popular

Despite the modern trappings of synthesizers, video technology, sophisticated production methods, and lyrics that spoke of the sexual, social, and political concerns of the 1980s, the pop-music scene of 1983 in many ways reflected trends of the late 1950s and early 1960s. The pop and rock charts were again alive with new young bands, just as they had been 20–30 years before. As then, many groups faded after a hit or two, although the Police grew ever more popular and remained undisputed leaders of the New Wave.

Almost all of these groups were swept under the heading of "New Music," a broad category which embraced sounds as diverse as the synthesizer-laden rock (called synth pop or techno pop) of Thomas Dolby, the Eurythmics, Culture Club, and teen heartthrobs Duran Duran, the Fifties-inspired rockabilly of the Stray Cats, the horn-heavy r&b of Trouble Funk, and the stark clamor of the Dead Kennedys.

The fresh and exciting sounds of New Music were credited with the commercial recovery of the pop-music industry after four years of hard times. This mini-boom echoed the prosperity of earlier days. An astonishing 3,000 people attended the Fourth Annual New Music Seminar, the music industry's largest event of the year.

The 1983 equivalent of the Sixties' British Invasion was an Australian Invasion, spearheaded by the hugely successful Men At Work. The U.S. music scene was much more open to international influences, readily accepting Ireland's U_2 and Dexy's Midnight Runners, Germany's Falco, and Africa's King Sunny Adé and Juluka. On the pop side, Julio Iglesias, one of the best known singers in the world, finally made inroads into the U.S. market.

Among the new names topping the charts were several stalwart superstars. Michael Jackson dominated the air waves and video screens throughout the year with his enormously successful album *Thriller*. He became the first artist in history to place five singles from one album in the Top Ten. When Motown Records, the Detroit-based record company that first introduced black artists into the pop mainstream, celebrated its 25th anniversary with a star-studded TV special, Jackson stole the show.

Another Motown figure, Diana Ross, gave a much-publicized free concert in New York's Central Park. The show was expected to draw one million people, the largest audience ever for a solo pop performance, but the occasion was marred by bad weather and crowd violence.

David Bowie proved to be an artist of impressive versatility and longevity. His "Serious Moonlight" world tour, supporting his hot album *Let's Dance,* outdrew the Rolling

Linda Ronstadt tried her hand at Big Band vocals; David Bowie took on the dandy look for his smash world tour.

Stones' record-breaking 1982 tour. He was profiled in depth in both *Time* and *Newsweek* magazines; not since Bruce Springsteen had the general press deemed a rock star so important.

The music of the past echoed not only in the rockabilly style of new bands like the Stray Cats, but in nostalgic new releases by such established stars as Billy Joel and Neil Young. Recognizing the tenor of the times, rock monoliths of the past reappeared. Reuniting in 1983 after many years of separation were the Everly Brothers, the Animals, the Hollies, and Simon & Garfunkle.

The recovering pop industry provided audiences for many different styles, old and new. Heavy metal entered a strong upswing, with new bands like Def Leppard and Iron Maiden finding major audiences. Bowing to demand, the second annual US Festival incorporated a heavy metal day. Journey headed the arena rock scene and became the top-grossing concert act of the year. Psychedelic rock returned with such bands as the Psychedelic Furs and the Dream Syndicate. Rocker Linda Ronstadt, teaming with eminent band leader and arranger Nelson Riddle, came out with an album of popular standards.

Radio, the traditional disseminator of pop music, firmly opted for a Top Forty-type format reminiscent of the 1950s and early 1960s. The new Contemporary Hits category strung together individual hit songs in a variety of pop styles. Music video channels, still dominated by the powerfully influential MTV, had led the way in this type of programming. In 1983 it became clear that promotional video recordings were essential to a pop artist's commercial success.

Black artists still had difficulty breaking the video color barrier. Notable exceptions were Prince, whose overtly sexy funk sound attracted a rock audience on MTV, as did the reggae-influenced rock of Eddy Grant. Enormous energy arose from black and Hispanic street culture. Grand Master Flash and the Furious Five blended social protest and rapping, a combination unique to the 1980s. Syncopated "hip-hop" dance music and the "break" dancing that went with it came up from the streets, capturing the larger culture's attention in the film *Flashdance*.

Country artists also recognized the influence of the video media; cable TV's new Nashville Network gave country artists greater exposure than such limited network programs as PBS' *Austin City Limits*. As in the rock/pop field, country music contained different movements, all attesting to renewed vitality. More and more country artists became familiar to pop audiences as they filled the Middle of the Road and Contemporary formats vacated by pop performers adopting harder rocking or electronic sounds.

PAULETTE WEISS, *"Stereo Review"*

NEBRASKA

Agriculture, legislative concerns, and football dominated state news in 1983.

Agriculture and the Economy. Excessive spring rains and mountain snowmelt caused rivers to flood. Extremely hot and dry summer weather, particularly in eastern Nebraska, and the federal payment-in-kind (PIK) program, together reduced grain production. Estimated production in millions of bushels was: corn 475.3 (38% below 1982); wheat 98.9 (3% below 1982); grain sorghum 63.7 (48% below 1982); and soybeans 60.9 (25% below 1982).

As 1983 began unemployment was at 7%, with job losses especially heavy in meatpacking; several plants closed.

The Legislature and State Government. Budget and tax problems dominated legislative attention as the new governor, Bob Kerrey, warned in January that Nebraska faced "pending bankruptcy." An austere general fund budget of $746 million—allowing less than a 4% increase—was adopted. State employees received no pay raise; the homestead exemption was repealed; state takeover of Medicaid payments was extended over four years; allocations to various agencies were cut; and an attempt to freeze corporate income taxes failed. The State Board of Equalization and Assessment, moreover, raised the individual income tax rate from 18% to 20% of federal liability, the sales tax temporarily from 3½% to 4%, and the gasoline tax from 13.7 to 15.3 cents per gallon. All of these rates were the highest on record.

The legislature repealed the sales tax on groceries and, beginning in 1984, will replace the board of equalization as determiner of income and sales-tax rates. Two water laws permitted transfer of water to other areas of use and recognized underground water as an economic benefit for which user fees will be charged. Multibank holding companies were legalized and the interest-rate ceiling on credit cards was eliminated. State employees received improved health insurance and an economic development act was passed. Autos may use studded tires, children must be restrained in autos, and increased auto-liability insurance was required.

Miscellaneous. A possible statewide lottery aroused great interest. Although the legislature failed to approve it, at least 11 cities, including Omaha, approved local lotteries.

The U.S. Supreme Court, in a case brought by state Sen. Ernest Chambers, ruled constitutional the opening of state legislative sessions with prayer and the payment of a chaplain.

Football was a top attention-getter in Nebraska. The University of Nebraska team had an undefeated season and an invitation to the Orange Bowl.

ORVILLE H. ZABEL
Midland Lutheran College

NETHERLANDS

Public life in the Netherlands during 1983 continued to be dominated by the effects of economic recession and by deeply split opinion about the role of the country in world affairs.

Economy and Business. Faced with one of the most costly social welfare systems in Europe, the center-conservative government of the Christian Democratic (CDA) and Liberal (VVD) coalition, headed by Prime Minister Rudolph (Ruud) F. M. Lubbers, attempted to reduce government spending in every category but defense. Public employees were cut in number and salary. Subsidies to welfare and cultural organizations also were reduced.

Business grappled with competitive difficulties arising from high costs and declining foreign demand, a factor of special importance for a country as heavily dependent on foreign trade as the Netherlands. Business failures continued to increase; among them were the ship- and machine-building conglomerate Rijn-Schelde-Verolme, which closed down many of its enterprises after bankruptcy and reorganization. The department store chain De Bijenkorf also was compelled to reorganize to escape bankruptcy. Dutch agriculture, one of the most efficient and productive in the world, labored under the restrictions imposed by the European Community (EC), where more politically powerful countries such as France exacted measures favorable to their own farmers.

The response of the labor unions, which comprise a majority of the working force in private industry and government, was angry but restrained. Short protest strikes were much more common against the government than against employers in the private sector. Attempts to expand part-time employment, usually in combination with welfare payments, were undertaken. Early-retirement programs on a similar basis also were encouraged.

NEBRASKA • Information Highlights

Area: 77,355 sq mi (200 349 km²).
Population (1982 est.): 1,586,000.
Chief Cities (1980 census): Lincoln, the capital, 171,932; Omaha, 314,255; Grand Island, 33,180.
Government (1983): *Chief Officers*—governor, Bob Kerrey (D); lt. gov., Donald McGinley (D). *Legislature* (unicameral)—49 members (nonpartisan).
State Finances (fiscal year 1981): *Revenues,* $1,583,000,000; *expenditures,* $1,558,000,000.
Personal Income (1982): $16,939,000,000; per capita, $10,683.
Labor Force (July 1983): *Nonagricultural wage and salary earners,* 592,300; *unemployed,* 43,700 (5.4% of total force).
Education: *Enrollment* (fall 1981)—public elementary schools, 186,755; public secondary, 86,585; colleges and universities (1981–82), 93,507 students. *Public school expenditures* (1980–81), $583,426,000 ($2,105 per pupil).

Queen Beatrix (center) and other royal family members are hosts at a reception for Vice-President and Mrs. Bush.

Politics and Domestic Affairs. Political responses to the troubled economic situation were varied. Among the major groups, the Liberal (conservative) Party held most firmly to a deflationary position, while the Christian Democrats tended to be more divided, with their government ministers following harder policies than some of their supporters in and out of the States General (parliament) found to their liking. The Labor Party (PvdA), although the strongest single party, remained in opposition and was confined to bitter protests. The democratic parties of all hues were disturbed by the election of a local councilman belonging to the new right-wing extremist Center Party in Almere. Whether this development portended new strains on the Dutch democratic system or was a temporary aberration was uncertain.

NETHERLANDS · Information Highlights

Official Name: Kingdom of the Netherlands.
Location: Northwestern Europe.
Area: 13,100 sq mi (33 929 km²).
Population (July 1983 est.): 14,374,000.
Chief Cities (Jan. 1982 est.): Amsterdam, the capital, 700,759; Rotterdam, 568,167; The Hague, the seat of government, 454,300.
Government: *Head of state,* Beatrix, queen (acceded April 30, 1980). *Head of government,* Rudolph F. M. Lubbers, prime minister (took office Nov. 1982). *Legislature*—States General: First Chamber and Second Chamber.
Monetary Unit: Guilder (3.021 guilders equal U.S.$1, Nov. 25, 1983).
Gross Domestic Product (1982 U.S.$): $137,031,-000,000.
Economic Indexes (1982): *Consumer Prices,* all items (1975 = 100), 151.3; food, 138.6. *Industrial Production* (1975 = 100), 110.
Foreign Trade (1982 U.S.$): *Imports,* $62,583,-000,000; *exports,* $66,322,000,000.

Foreign Affairs. The principal foreign policy issue remained the place of the Netherlands in the North Atlantic Treaty Organization (NATO). The government, although often critical of U.S. policies, adhered to plans to locate cruise missiles at Dutch bases despite wide public opposition. Relations with China were very strained because of Dutch insistence on maintaining and extending relations with Taiwan. Particularly painful was the situation in the former colony of Surinam, where the violent deaths of opponents of the Daysi Bouterse regime in December 1982 led to a suspension of Dutch economic aid projects. Charges that the former Dutch intelligence chief in Surinam had been involved in the coup that brought Bouterse to power in February 1982 caused embarrassment.

Troubling in a different way to the Dutch people were scandals in the business community. The large Slavenburg's Bank was found to have been involved in fraud, and it was reorganized as an affiliate of the French bank Crédit Lyonnais. The Algemeen Burgerlijk Pensioenfonds, the huge pension fund for government employees, was revealed to have been involved in fraudulent real-estate transactions.

During the year a new constitution was adopted and put into effect. It did not change the political system in any significant way, but it brought the provisions of fundamental law, some of which had become antiquated, into conformity with modern practice. The royal family continued to play its symbolic and representational role despite the withdrawal from public appearances for most of the year of Prince Claus, the husband of Queen Beatrix.

HERBERT H. ROWEN, *Rutgers University*

NEVADA

Taxation and modest economic recovery were Nevada's principal news items in 1983.

Legislative Session. Democratic Gov. Richard Bryan inherited a depleted state treasury. However, his proposals to enable the state to meet its January payroll were approved by the legislature, and the state ended the fiscal year with a small surplus. Most of Bryan's legislative proposals were approved, but the property-tax increase voted by the legislature fell short of the amount the governor wanted to help education, and only one part of his campaign reform package was enacted. His proposals to increase state expenditures for tourism promotion and economic development were approved, as was his status quo budget that carried no salary increases for state employees for the 1983–85 biennium.

Bryan-Cashell Split. During the legislative session, there was little contact between Bryan and Democratic Lt. Gov. Robert Cashell, who had indicated during the 1982 campaign that he had his eye on the governor's chair. Cashell actually worked against some of Bryan's proposals, including the property-tax increase. Following the legislative session, Cashell met with state Republican leaders and in August changed his party registration, thus setting the stage for a race against Bryan in 1986.

Economy. Nevada's tourist-based economy showed improvement in the late spring of 1983. However, the large annual increases in profits experienced by the gambling industry in the 1970s were generally considered to be a thing of the past because of competition from Atlantic City and the possibility that other states might legalize casino gambling.

Gambling-tax revenues increased by only 3.6%, and sales-tax revenues suffered a decline of 4.8% in 1982–83 over the previous fiscal year. However, the revenues from both taxes increased beginning in May 1983.

FBI Sting. The main target of an FBI "sting" operation in 1981 was longtime State Sen. Floyd Lamb, the senior member of the Nevada legislature who chaired the powerful Senate finance committee for more than 20 years. Lamb was convicted by a federal jury on extortion and conspiracy charges in September 1983; he resigned from the Senate shortly afterward.

Mob Influence. Indictments handed down by a federal grand jury in Kansas City on Sept. 30, 1983, accused 15 mob figures of having hidden interests in four Las Vegas casinos and of participating in a skimming operation that funneled illegal gambling profits into mob activities in Chicago, Kansas City, and Milwaukee. The casinos had been investigated by Nevada gaming officials, who did not have access to the wiretap evidence used by the FBI.

DON W. DRIGGS
University of Nevada, Reno

NEW BRUNSWICK

The growing importance of mining to New Brunswick's economy was underlined by developments in 1983.

Mining and Energy. In February, plans were announced for a $280 million potash mining project near Sussex, in southern New Brunswick. Denison Mines of Toronto, in partnership with Potash Co. of Canada Ltd., owned by French and German interests, expected to begin extracting operations in 1985. Natural Resources Minister Gerald Merrithew predicted in September that mining will be a billion-dollar-a-year business in New Brunswick by 1990.

New Brunswick's first nuclear-power plant was opened on June 25 at Point Lepreau. Four months earlier, Atomic Energy of Canada Ltd. and the New Brunswick Electric Power Commission signed an understanding aimed at early construction of a second 630-megawatt station at Point Lepreau. Much of Lepreau II's output, like that of Lepreau I, will be exported to New England.

The Media. In August the Canadian Radio-Television and Telecommunications Commission (CRTC) rendered a controversial decision renewing the license of TV station CHSJ in Saint John for three years. CHSJ is owned by the Irving family, which also owns all four of New Brunswick's English-language daily newspapers, two in Saint John. In 1982, the federal government asked the CRTC to refuse renewal of broadcast licenses to stations whose owners controlled newspapers in the same market. But the commission was allowed to make exceptions.

The provincial government stepped in to ensure that New Brunswick's 250,000 French-speaking citizens will have a daily newspaper available in their own language. It announced in July that it would establish a $4 million endowment for such a newspaper, to be published in Moncton. Moncton's French-language daily *L'Evangeline* ceased publication in 1982.

Defense. The federal government was under continuous attack by political opponents for its decision to discontinue basing a squadron of fighter aircraft at Chatham. Up to 3,200 people could be out of work.

JOHN BEST, *"Canada World News"*

NEWFOUNDLAND

The year in Newfoundland was characterized by conflicts with the federal government. At issue were the fishing industry, offshore oil development, and power rights on the Churchill River in Labrador. The world recession affected production in the newsprint and iron ore industries. In February the Supreme Court of Newfoundland ruled that the province does not have jurisdiction over resources on the continental shelf. A Quebec court later ruled that the province does not have the right to recall water rights leased to the Newfoundland Hydro Corp.

In March provincial authorities ordered offshore drilling rigs to shut down and move away from the ice pack. Federal authorities ordered drilling resumed. Two weeks later Mobil Oil made an "operational" decision to recall two rigs. At issue was which level of government had the right to regulate offshore activities.

Control of undersea resources remained unresolved, awaiting the Supreme Court of Canada. A tentative agreement was announced Jan. 13, 1983, but talks broke off.

The most serious intergovernmental conflict was over federal proposals to restructure the bankrupt fishing industry. The province would not agree to three plant shutdowns, and the two sides were stalemated until October. Then, in a matter of ten days, negotiation recommenced, and officials signed a bilateral agreement.

Government-labor relations were characterized by lockouts (teachers), strikes (civil

Wayne Sturge/Government of Newfoundland

Sir Humphrey Gilbert's landing in St. John's was reenacted as Newfoundland marked the 400th anniversary of its establishment as England's first overseas possession.

servants), and staff cutbacks (hospitals), as the province tried to cope with rising expenditures and falling revenues. The March provincial budget held the line on taxes, reduced spending, and added C$28.4 million to what was the highest per capita debt in Canada.

Helping relieve the gloom was a visit in June by Britain's Prince Charles and Princess Diana, who joined in celebrations of the 400th anniversary of the founding in Newfoundland of the first of the British overseas possessions.

SUSAN MCCORQUODALE
Memorial University of Newfoundland

NEWFOUNDLAND • Information Highlights

Area: 156,185 sq mi (404 520 km²).
Population (July 1983): 578,600.
Chief Cities (1981 census): St. John's, the capital, 83,770; Corner Brook, 24,339.
Government (1982): *Chief Officers*—lt. gov., Anthony J. Paddon; premier, A. Brian Peckford (Progressive Conservative); min. of jus., Gerald R. Ottenheimer. *Legislature*—Legislative Assembly, 52 members.
Education (1982–83): *Enrollment*—elementary and secondary schools, 142,800; postsecondary, 9,790.
Public Finance (1983 fiscal year, est.): *Revenues,* $1,886,400,000; *expenditures,* $1,999,600,000.
Personal Income (average weekly salary, March 1983): $380.80.
Unemployment Rate (Aug. 1983, seasonally adjusted): 16.5%.
(All monetary figures are in Canadian dollars.)

NEW HAMPSHIRE

The year commenced on a sad note as the state mourned Gov. Hugh J. Gallen (D), who died on Dec. 24, 1982, eight days before the end of his term.

Finances and Economy. Governor Gallen's death was one of several bleak features of the winter of 1982–83. The economy was injured by a lack of snow in ski country, while the state government faced its usual biennial problem of raising revenue to fund an acceptable state budget. The budgetary effort was made more difficult because of the existing $41 million deficit. Conservative Gov. John Sununu (R) sought successfully to avoid any broad-based tax and to keep a tight fiscal rein on state programs. His take-charge style resulted in an increase of 4% for a biennial budget of slightly less than $2 billion.

Late spring and summer brought an assist to the economy as splendid weather attracted a record influx of tourists to the state. By August, unemployment statewide declined to 4.1%, with Nashua having the lowest level of any metropolitan area in the nation.

Environment. Environmental issues dominated the news throughout the year. During the legislative session, advocates of returnable bottles endeavored to bring the state into conformity with its neighbors, but once more opponents defeated the legislation. The issue of acid rain prompted a resolution, endorsed at a majority of town meetings, urging a 50% reduction in Midwestern sulfur dioxide emissions.

Energy. Probably the most contentious and beleaguered matter of the year was the fate of the second nuclear reactor under construction in Seabrook. In the news almost continually since the mid-1970s, the Public Service Company of New Hampshire's project has had cost projections rise from less than $1 billion to more than $5 billion. Several out-of-state utility shareholders, under pressure from their state regulatory commissions, persuaded Public Service to cease construction on Seabrook II, which many now believe will never be completed. The decision does not affect Seabrook I, scheduled to be completed in mid-1985.

Miscellaneous. Two long-pending matters reached resolution in 1983. Since 1980, when a devastating fire left Rockingham Park in ruins, the owners have sought various ways to get the horse-racing track back in operation. In August a syndicate, Rockingham Venture, purchased the facility, promising to resume racing by late spring 1984. This was welcome news for the state because of the significant tax revenue generated by the track.

On June 30, Guilford Transportation Company formally acquired the Boston & Maine Railroad, giving Guilford some 2,400 mi (3860 km) of track and promising a stronger, better integrated rail system for much of the region.

WILLIAM L. TAYLOR
Plymouth State College

NEW JERSEY

Financial problems, conflict-of-interest cases, toxic wastes, and the Meadowlands Sports Complex were among the major topics of interest in New Jersey in 1983.

Financial Problems. Republican Gov. Thomas H. Kean and the Democratic-controlled legislature continued to battle over attempts to reduce the cost of government. Faced with possible public-service cutbacks, the legislature at the end of December 1982 increased the income tax to 3% on incomes over $50,000 and raised the sales tax to 6%. The governor proposed an "austerity budget" of $6.8 billion without new taxes or elimination of existing programs. The governor's plea for bipartisanship was unheard by a legislature of which all 120 members would be up for reelection in November. Meanwhile there was a threat of a reduction in federal funds for New Jersey, from $44.3 million to $13.8 million.

Conflicts of Interest. State Sen. John T. Gregorio, also mayor of Linden, was placed on probation and fined $10,000 in February for concealing his interests in two go-go bars in Linden. He was forced to resign, reducing the Democratic membership in the Senate to 20, one below the number needed for passage of legislation, until the party's majority was restored by a special election in Gregorio's district.

Reese Palley, chairman of the New Jersey Lottery Commission, was indicted on charges of falsifying documents describing his involvement with two companies supplying video lotteries to the state. He pleaded innocent but was suspended by the governor.

Toxic Wastes. A continuing problem in New Jersey was the locating and cleaning up of toxic waste sites resulting from the earlier dumping of poisonous industrial wastes. Early in September the Environmental Protection Agency announced that New Jersey had 85 of the nation's 546 most toxic sites. The $21 million already allocated for cleaning up the sites was only the beginning. Ultimately the cost of cleaning up the 85 sites was estimated at $500 million. Meanwhile a bill requiring companies to reveal toxic materials used in making their products was signed by Governor Kean on August 29.

Meadowlands Sports Complex. In September the New York Jets announced that, starting in 1984, they would play their home football games at Giants Stadium in the Meadowlands complex. Early in the year the New Jersey Generals of the newly formed United States Football League announced that they were making their home in the Meadowlands.

A government worker uses a special high-powered vacuum to pick up Dioxin-tainted dirt in the Newark area.

© George Ott/Gamma-Liaison

NEW JERSEY · Information Highlights

Area: 7,787 sq mi (20 168 km²).
Population (1982 est.): 7,438,000.
Chief Cities (1980 census): Trenton, the capital, 92,124; Newark, 329,248; Jersey City, 223,532; Paterson, 137,970; Elizabeth, 106,201; Camden, 84,910.
Government (1983): *Chief Officer*—governor, Thomas H. Kean (R). *Legislature*—Senate, 40 members; General Assembly, 80 members.
State Finances (fiscal year 1982): *Revenues,* $11,341,000,000; *expenditures,* $11,152,000,000.
Personal Income (1982): $97,361,000,000; per capita, $13,089.
Labor Force (July 1983): *Nonagricultural wage and salary earners,* 3,134,300; *unemployed,* 309,300 (8.3% of total force).
Education: *Enrollment* (fall 1981)—public elementary schools, 787,700; public secondary, 411,300; colleges and universities (1981–82), 322,797 students. *Public school expenditures* (1980–81), $3,655,487,000 ($2,791 per pupil).

Reapportionment. The state's 1982 congressional reapportionment plan, designed to reduce New Jersey's seats in the House of Representatives from 15 to 14, as based on the results of the 1980 census, was disapproved by the U.S. Supreme Court on June 22.

Tourism. In April a $1.7 million campaign was launched to attract tourists and business to the state. It features the slogan "New Jersey and You: Perfect Together."

Miscellaneous. Following the shooting down of Korean Airlines flight 007 by a Soviet military plane near Sakhalin Island on September 1, the governors of New Jersey and New York denied Soviet Foreign Minister Andrei Gromyko access to commercial airports in the New York metropolitan area for his attendance at the UN General Assembly. Gromyko was given permission to land at McGuire Air Force Base, but he declined to attend the General Assembly session.

In October, the state's law requiring public schools to begin the day with a minute of silence for "quiet and private contemplation or introspection" was declared unconstitutional by a federal district court judge in Newark.

HERMANN K. PLATT
St. Peter's College

NEW MEXICO

In 1983, New Mexico faced some unusual health problems and withstood the ravages of floods in early fall. While the effects of high water were not so widespread as in neighboring Arizona, they still did $12 million worth of damage to homes, crops, and public works in four southwestern counties.

The annual International Balloon Fiesta in Albuquerque, the first week of October, was dedicated to the memory of native son and famous balloonist, Maxie Anderson, killed during a June 1982 flying accident in Germany.

Politics. On January 1, Toney Anaya (D) was inaugurated as New Mexico's 25th governor. He was the first former state attorney general to win the governorship and was at the time the only Hispanic governor in the nation. During his first months in office he traveled and spoke widely around the country, leading some observers to suggest that he was attempting to build a national constituency. At home, he worked toward improving educational opportunities, economic growth, and social justice.

Health. A serious outbreak of bubonic plague grabbed national headlines during the summer months. A total of 27 cases were registered, including two fatalities. That was the highest number since 1975, when 16 cases were reported. Half of the victims were Indians living in remote rural areas. They are more susceptible than the urban population because the disease is transmitted by fleas found on wild rodents. The state Health and Environment Department worked closely with tribal governments and the Indian Health Service to take preventive steps.

Sixteen persons in northern New Mexico were stricken by an unknown disease in September. Two died of the illness, which was produced by a rare virus. It was traced to *queso blanco* (white cheese) marketed by a small dairy near Española and was found to be caused by use of unpasteurized milk.

Economy. New Mexico's extractive mining industry, suffering from a recession that had idled hundreds of workers in the past two years, staged a slow recovery. In May, Phelps-Dodge called back 450 workers to its Tyrone copper mine near Silver City, but that represented only 70% of the work force.

Several other branches of the industry showed little sign of a rebound. Potash, uranium, and coal remained severely depressed. The Questa molybdenum mine in Colfax County also slowed production because of inactivity in the steel mills, its only customers.

NEW MEXICO • Information Highlights

Area: 121,592 sq mi (314 923 km²).
Population (1982 est.): 1,359,000.
Chief Cities (1980 census): Santa Fe, the capital, 48,899; Albuquerque, 331,767; Las Cruces, 45,086.
Government (1983): *Chief Officers*—governor, Toney Anaya (D); lt. gov., Mike Runnels (D). *Legislature*—Senate, 42 members; House of Representatives, 70 members.
State Finances (1982): *Revenues,* $3,020,000,000; *expenditures,* $2,392,000,000.
Personal Income (1982): $12,492,000,000; per capita, $9,190.
Labor Force (July 1983): *Nonagricultural wage and salary earners,* 481,200; *unemployed,* 64,400 (10.6% of total force).
Education: *Enrollment* (fall 1981)—public elementary schools, 187,192; public secondary, 80,899; colleges and universities (1981–82), 60,413 students. *Public school expenditures* (1980–81), $704,814,000 ($2,219 per pupil).

Environment. The Department of Energy released a report at midyear in support of the $2.1 billion Waste Isolation Pilot Project near Carlsbad. Designed to serve as a low-level nuclear waste repository, the facility has drawn sharp criticism from environmentalists and some state officials. A network of tunnels stretching 100 mi (161 km) through underground salt beds is proposed. Miners worked around the clock, extracting 900 tons of salt a day.

MARC SIMMONS, *Author*
"Albuquerque, A Narrative History"

NEW YORK

On New Year's Day 1983, Mario M. Cuomo (D) took the oath of office as New York State's 52d governor and pledged to shape the Empire State into a family "feeling one another's pain, sharing one another's blessings, reasonably, equitably, fairly, honestly."

Recession had left more than enough pain to go around. Along western New York's economically stricken Niagara Frontier, Bethlehem Steel began closing its Lackawanna steel mills, an economic linchpin of the area. In New York City the ranks of the homeless swelled as fast as new shelters could open up.

Criminal Justice. Eight days after the new governor took office, attention turned to the state's troubled criminal justice system, as inmates at the Ossining Correctional Facility (Sing Sing) seized 17 guards in a spontaneous uprising. After 53 hours of negotiation, the hostages were released unharmed and prison officials agreed to address the conditions caused by overcrowding—filth, vermin, and few recreational or other programs.

Still, the problem caused by a prison system packed to 117% of capacity did not evaporate. In September inmates at Attica Correctional Facility refused to leave their cells for a week; the demonstration started just days after the 12th anniversary of the bloody uprising that had made Attica a synonym for prison insurrection. The prisoners were locked in their cells for more than another week before tensions were defused.

In response to the overcrowding, the 206th session of the Legislature authorized a $380 million construction program to add 8,424 new cells. It also established a commission to revamp the state's sentencing system.

In April, Lemuel Smith, a convicted murderer already serving several life sentences, was found guilty of the 1981 slaying of a corrections officer. Smith was sentenced to death in the electric chair, setting the stage for a court test of the one section of New York's capital punishment statute not struck down by the State Court of Appeals in 1977—the part applying to murder by a prisoner already sentenced to life. Governor Cuomo, meanwhile, followed

Joe Traver/Gamma-Liaison

In his inaugural, Mario Cuomo asked New Yorkers to feel "one another's pain" and share "one another's blessings."

the lead of predecessor Hugh L. Carey by vetoing a new death penalty bill.

Nuclear Safety. The debate over nuclear-power safety also came to dominate the year. In February officials of Suffolk County in eastern Long Island refused to draw up an emergency evacuation plan for the nearly completed $3.4 billion Shoreham nuclear-power plant. They argued that Long Island's geography made evacuation impossible and that the plant should be abandoned. A special commission set up by Governor Cuomo reported in December that the county's refusal to draw up an evacuation plan was not capricious; that the state should not overrule it; that LILCO, which owns the plant, is not equipped to operate it; and that electricity from Shoreham would not be needed in the next decade.

The issue arose again when the federal Nuclear Regulatory Commission threatened to shut down two operating reactors at Indian Point, 35 mi (56 km) north of New York City, unless an adequate emergency plan were established. This time the governor deputized state and utility workers to stand in for Rockland County, which refused to participate in evacuation exercises. The plants remained open.

Legislation. Cuomo and the Legislature reached accord on a new state budget in unusually timely fashion, closing the projected deficit through program cuts and close to $1 billion in new user fees and taxes. In other major action, the Legislature and governor raised unemployment benefits and approved a partial state takeover of local Medicaid costs. In September the state's bottle deposit law took effect.

Politics. In June, Nassau County GOP Chairman Joseph Margiotta, who had wielded iron control of one of the nation's most power-ful political organizations, went to federal prison for mail fraud and extortion in connection with municipal insurance fee-splitting.

Albany Mayor Erastus Corning II, 73, the nation's longest-tenured mayor and one of the last big-city Democratic bosses, died of an apparent heart attack.

Baby Jane Doe. A baby born October 11 became the subject of a drawn-out court battle. The parents rejected life-prolonging surgery, and the New York State Court of Appeals ruled that they had the right to do so. The U.S. Justice Department intervened, however, requesting the complete medical records. In mid-November, a federal judge denied the request; the Justice Department said it would appeal.

ALISON MITCHELL
Chief, Albany News Bureau, "Newsday"

NEW YORK • Information Highlights

Area: 49,108 sq mi (127 190 km²).
Population (1982 est.): 17,659,000.
Chief Cities (1980 census): Albany, the capital, 101,727; New York, 7,071,030; Buffalo, 357,870; Rochester, 241,741; Yonkers, 195,351; Syracuse, 170,105.
Government (1983): *Chief Officers—governor,* Mario M. Cuomo (D); lt. gov., Alfred B. Del Bello (D). *Legislature*—Senate, 60 members; Assembly, 150 members.
State Finances (fiscal year 1982): *Revenues,* $33,396,000,000; *expenditures,* $30,160,000,000.
Personal Income (1982): $217,457,000,000; per capita, $12,314.
Labor Force (July 1983): *Nonagricultural wage and salary earners,* 7,201,100; *unemployed,* 731,900 (8.7% of total force).
Education: *Enrollment* (fall 1981)—public elementary schools, 1,778,207; public secondary, 982,567; colleges and universities (1982–83), 1,012,421. *Public school expenditures* (1981–82), $9,982,204,000.

NEW YORK CITY

A deteriorating infrastructure, some controversial appointments, and several newsworthy celebrations highlighted 1983 in New York City.

The Infrastructure. On the morning of August 10, one of the century-old water pipes running under Manhattan ruptured, and it was as if the urban infrastructure suffered a stroke. Water flooded into a basement substation of Consolidated Edison Company, causing an electrical fire. The substation crashed, and a 12-block area in the busy garment center was blacked out. Losses were estimated at $150–$300 million. The three-day blackout also affected the subway system, knocking out service on one major line and causing delays and rerouting on others.

The subway system was already suffering. Because of the city's continuing financial squeeze, routine maintenance was deferred, and the trains were plagued by derailments. Trainmen along the 710 track-miles (1 143 km) had to operate at reduced speeds, raising the frustration level of daily commuters.

Meanwhile, major structural defects were also cited on the Williamsburg Bridge, spanning the East River. The State Transportation Department found that one of the four main support cables had rusted through because of air pollution. It was not clear whether the bridge would be renovated, at an estimated minimal cost of $3 billion, or whether it would be cheaper in the long run to build a new one.

Appointments. In the wake of these problems came a wave of resignations by high officials, including Richard Ravitch, chairman of the Metropolitan Transportation Authority. He was replaced by Robert R. Kiley, a 48-year-old Bostonian. Blacks and other minority groups objected to the appointment, claiming that the $150,000-a-year post should have gone to "a qualified minority candidate."

This came on the heels of another struggle for power by city minorities. When the post of chancellor of the Board of Education became vacant, Mayor Edward I. Koch nominated Robert F. Wagner, Jr., a deputy mayor. But the City Council refused to confirm the appointment, and Wagner's name was withdrawn in favor of Anthony Alvarado, an Hispanic with long experience in the school system.

Celebrations. Renovation did begin on the fabled Brooklyn Bridge, which on May 24 celebrated its centennial. There were parades, fireworks, and an outpouring of appreciation.

Not all of the city's celebrations went off so smoothly. On March 17, St. Patrick's Day, the annual parade down Fifth Avenue was marred by controversy. Michael Flannery, an outspoken sympathizer with the provisional wing of the Irish Republican Army, was chosen as the grand marshall. Among those who refused to participate were New York's senior U.S. senator, Daniel Patrick Moynihan, and the government of Northern Ireland. Terence Cardinal Cooke (who died of cancer in October) declined his customary greeting of the grand marshall.

On October 22, New York also celebrated the 100th anniversary of its Metropolitan Opera.

Phase 1 of a rejuvenated South Street Seaport, a re-creation of the old East River waterfront near Fulton Street, opened in late July. When completed, the project is to cost an estimated $351 million and will involve more than 25 buildings, a pier, and other attractions.

KENNETH GROSS, *"Newsday"*

Fulton Market is the centerpiece of New York City's newest tourist attraction, the restored South Street Seaport.

NEW ZEALAND

In the midterm year of the national administration of Prime Minister Robert Muldoon, economic matters clearly dominated popular concern.

The Economy. A freeze on wages and prices imposed in June 1982 achieved a significant reduction in the rate of inflation. By mid-1983 the rate had dropped to 8.3%, the lowest in a decade, and there were signs that it would drop as low as 5%. To restrain incipient pressure, the freeze was extended until February 1984, and government interest rates were severely slashed. However, a mounting price was paid in the number of unemployed. The July figure of 115,723 (including those on special work schemes) represented some 8.7% of the work force. In October 1983 public opinion polls, unemployment exceeded all other matters combined as the single most important problem facing New Zealand.

A month before the presentation of the budget in late July, a 72-page report on the state of the economy by the Organization for Economic Cooperation and Development (OECD) urged that a decade of stop-and-go policies be replaced by pursuit of a steady path toward economic recovery. However, the budget itself featured a 79% rise in the internal deficit to N.Z. $3 billion. Some relief was given to low-income taxpayers, modest funds were earmarked for job creation, and tax-deductible job expenses were adjusted. In the context of the freeze and a 13% jump in government spending, Muldoon, also the minister of finance, had left little room in which to maneuver.

Foreign Affairs. Prime Minister Muldoon made several overseas visits during 1983. In January he attended a symposium on international finance in Davos, Switzerland; at the UN Conference on Trade and Development in Yugoslavia he repeated his call for a new Bretton-Woods type conference; he visited Australia twice, the second time in late August for the

UPI

Rod Dixon of New Zealand, 1972 Olympic bronze medalist in the 1,500 meters, won the 1983 New York City Marathon in 2:08:59. It was only the second marathon of his career.

14th South Pacific Forum; and prior to attending the Commonwealth finance ministers conference in Trinidad, Muldoon met U.S. Secretary of State George Shultz to discuss security and trade. Among the visitors to New Zealand was Zhao Ziyang, the first leader of China ever to come.

Politics. Party politics in New Zealand during 1983 was exceptionally volatile. Two Labour parliamentarians, one of them the son of former Prime Minister Norman Kirk, became independents. In February the Labour Party elected Deputy David Lange, a 40-year-old lawyer, as its leader, succeeding Bill Rowling; Lange's post was filled by Geoffrey Palmer. A new right-wing body, the New Zealand Party, was unveiled in August. Emphasizing free enterprise and individual rights, the party chose as its spokesman Bob Jones, a real estate millionaire. Meanwhile, popular support for the various parties fluctuated wildly. For most of the year Labour was comfortably ahead, but it suffered from publicity about internal wrangling. The October poll gave National 45%, La-

---

NEW ZEALAND • Information Highlights

Official Name: New Zealand.
Location: Southwest Pacific Ocean.
Area: 110,531 sq mi (268 276 km²).
Population (July 1983): 3,142,000.
Chief Cities (1981 census): Wellington, the capital, 342,504; Auckland, 825,707; Christchurch, 321,-373.
Government: *Head of state,* Elizabeth II, queen, represented by David Beattie, governor-general (took office Nov. 1980). *Head of government,* Robert Muldoon, prime minister (took office Dec. 1975). *Legislature* (unicameral)—House of Representatives.
Monetary Unit: New Zealand dollar (1.514 N.Z. dollars equal U.S.$1, Oct. 14, 1983).
Gross National Product (1981 U.S.$): $21,190,-000,000.
Economic Index (1982): *Consumer Prices* (1970 = 100), all items, 434.9; food, 447.1.
Foreign Trade (1982 U.S.$): *Imports,* $5,752,000,000; *exports,* $5,524,000,000.

bour 37%, Social Credit 11%, and the New Zealand Party 6%. In the triennial local-body elections, the mayoralty of Auckland City was won by Cath Tizard.

Other. In July, Lorraine Downes, a 19-year-old Auckland model, was crowned Miss Universe in St. Louis, MO. The visit of the nuclear cruiser *USS Texas* brought on major peace protests in August. And the government introduced a bill to outlaw compulsory unionism.

GRAHAM BUSH, *University of Auckland*

NIGERIA

The second general election in Nigeria since the return of civilian rule in 1979 was held in August 1983. Despite continued economic problems, President Alhaji Shehu Shagari was returned to office. The year ended, however, with the military returning to power. Maj. Gen. Mohammed Buhari, a former oil minister, led a coup against Shagari "to save the nation from imminent collapse." The new leaders said that economic difficulties and political corruption led to their action. A curfew was imposed, the four-year-old constitution was suspended, and political parties were banned.

Politics and Government. The Federal Elections Commission (FEDECO) had begun preparations for the elections in early 1982, ultimately registering more than 65 million voters. There were five separate elections, beginning with the one for president on August 6. Then, at one week intervals, balloting was held for governors, senators, and members of the House and state assemblies. Six political parties contested the elections; the most important were the NPN, the Nigerian People's Party (NPP), and the Unity Party of Nigeria (UPN). In the presidential race, President Shagari was challenged by two old foes, Nnamdi Azikiwe (NPP) and Obafemi Awolowo (UPN). President Shagari increased his winning margin of 1979 by gaining 47% of the 25.5 million votes cast. The subsequent elections confirmed the dominance of the president's party. The NPN gained 14 of the 19 governorships with an even more impressive 56% of the vote, and showed its strength also in the balloting for the Senate and House. There were, however, some instances of violence, coercion, and corruption and many appeals to FEDECO.

The president and all parties agreed to consider seriously an increase in the number of states comprising the federation. A plebiscite was to determine the final decision.

Economy. Nigeria's worsening economic position was shown by a number of indicators. The rate of growth of the gross domestic product was −5.2% for 1981 and −2.4% for 1982. Further evidence was the decline of imports and exports for the first half of 1983 to N1,054 million from N1,180 million for the same period

---

NIGERIA • Information Highlights

Official Name: Federal Republic of Nigeria.
Location: West Africa.
Area: 356,999 sq mi (924 630 km^2).
Population (July 1983): 85,219,000.
Chief Cities (1976 est.): Lagos, the capital, 1,100,000; Ibadan, 850,000; Ogbomosho, 435,000.
Government: Head of state and government, Maj. Gen. Mohammed Buhari, leader, federal military government, (took office Jan. 1, 1984). *Legislature*—Senate and House of Representatives.
Monetary Unit: Naira (1.33 naira equals U.S.$1, June 1983).
Gross Domestic Product (1982 U.S.$): $64,765,-000,000.
Economic Index (1981): *Consumer Prices* (1971 = 100), all items, 235.8; food, 235.
Foreign Trade (1980 U.S.$): *Imports*, $14,644,-000,000; *exports*, $21,345,000,000.

---

in 1982. Despite government efforts to halt devaluation, the Naira continued to fall. The official rate in June was N1.33 per U.S.$1.00, yet black market exchanges in Lagos reached N3.50 per $1.00. The continued downturn in Nigeria's once booming economy was tied directly to the world petroleum surplus and attempts by the Organization of Petroleum Exporting Countries (OPEC) to provide stability. The reference price of $29 per barrel was $5 lower than the price one year earlier. Nigeria's petroleum production averaged 1.42 million barrels per day through June, slightly above the 1.3 million barrel quota assigned by OPEC; this represented only two thirds of the daily production achieved in the late 1970s. Perhaps the most telling evidence of Nigeria's economic woes was its application for a $2 billion loan from the International Monetary Fund (IMF) with the knowledge that the IMF would impose stringent controls on the economy and a possible currency devaluation.

Foreign Affairs. The decision in January 1983 to force two million aliens to leave Nigeria was the most serious foreign policy decision of the Shagari government. Caused largely by the ailing economy, the enforcement of the decree resulted in a flood of non-Nigerians pouring into even poorer neighboring countries.

President Shagari continued to oppose Libyan expansionism in northern Africa and to favor modification of South Africa's government, with the immediate corollary of independence for Namibia. Nigeria continued to oppose the admission of the Saharan Arab Democratic Republic (SADR) to the Organization of African Unity (OAU) and the Economic Community of West Africa (ECOWAS). Shagari pressed for a negotiated settlement of the civil war in Chad, and, despite border clashes with the Habré regime, allowed northern Nigeria to be used to funnel relief supplies to Chad.

See also AFRICA; BIOGRAPHY—Shagari.

HARRY A. GAILEY
San Jose State University

NORTH CAROLINA

The weather and the indictment of several public officials vied for top billing in North Carolina in 1983.

Weather. On August 21, the temperature reached 110°F (43°C) in Fayetteville, an all-time official record for the state. On the same day, local records were broken at five of the state's six weather stations. Although rainfall was above average for the first six months, a prolonged siege of high temperature and low precipitation beginning in July resulted in severe damage to crops and in water restrictions in some areas.

Indictments. The boast "Good Government Is a Habit in North Carolina" was tarnished by a flurry of indictments of public officials. The sheriff of Brunswick County and the police chief of Banner Elk were convicted of drug-related offenses; the sheriff of Clay County was charged with vote fraud; and a superior court judge at Greensboro resigned from the bench after being accused of sexual improprieties. An FBI undercover operation called Colcor ("Columbus County corruption") led to indictments against an assortment of citizens, including a legislator, county commissioner, district judge, and police chief. State Sen. R. C. Soles, though exonerated from charges including perjury and vote-buying, faced investigation by the state board of elections. Lt. Gov. James C. Green, Jr., an unofficial candidate for governor, was acquitted late in the year of charges of receiving a bribe and consenting to receive bribes.

Legislature. Faced with a slower growth in revenues, the General Assembly raised a number of taxes and adopted a tight budget. Teachers and state employees were given an average pay hike of 5%, the first in two years. The executive branch periodically froze agency positions as they became vacant. The legislature then abolished the frozen positions. The minimum drinking age was raised to 19, and a tough law was passed against driving while intoxi-

NOAA

The coral-encrusted anchor of the Monitor, *ironclad gunboat of the Civil War, was raised near Cape Hatteras, NC.*

NORTH CAROLINA • Information Highlights

Area: 52,669 sq mi (136 413 km²).

Population (1982 est.): 6,019,000.

Chief Cities (1980 census): Raleigh, the capital, 149,771; Charlotte, 314,447; Greensboro, 155,642; Winston-Salem, 131,885; Durham, 100,538.

Government (1983): *Chief Officers*—governor, James B. Hunt, Jr. (D); lt. gov., James C. Green (D). *General Assembly*—Senate, 50 members; House of Representatives, 120 members.

State Finances (fiscal year 1982): *Revenues,* $7,128,000,000; *expenditures,* $6,851,000,000.

Personal Income (1982): $54,431,000,000; per capita, $9,044.

Labor Force (July 1983): *Nonagricultural wage and salary earners,* 2,320,400; *unemployed,* 254,900 (8.6% of total force).

Education: *Enrollment* (fall 1981)—public elementary schools, 772,876; public secondary, 336,084; colleges and universities (1982), 300,910. *Public school expenditures* (1981–82), $2,313,259,000.

---

cated. Included was a controversial "dram shop" provision, which made sellers of alcoholic beverages liable in certain cases for accidents caused by drunken drivers. Hurried passage of an act exposing the names of confidential informants to defense attorneys led to a special session to provide better protection of such informants.

Politics. Tar Heels prepared for an epic contest in 1984 between Sen. Jesse Helms (R) and Gov. James B. Hunt, Jr., (D) for the seat held a dozen years by Helms, a leader of conservative causes at the national level. Both remained highly visible, and Hunt gained national attention as chairman of the National Task Force on Education for Economic Growth, a group of 41 governors and corporate executives.

Culture. The first of several planned portions of the North Carolina Museum of Art was finally opened in Raleigh, and a $22 million central library was completed at the University of North Carolina at Chapel Hill. The *Elizabeth II*, a representation of a 16th century sailing vessel, was built at Roanoke Island for the quadricentennial of English America.

Names in the News. Deneen Z. Graham became the first black woman to be crowned Miss North Carolina. Astronaut William E. Thornton received a hero's welcome in Faison, where he delivered newspapers as a child, after his September flight aboard the space shuttle *Columbia*. Secretary of State Thad Eure, the dean of American elected officials, announced plans to run for his 13th four-year term in 1984.

H. G. JONES
University of North Carolina at Chapel Hill

NORTH DAKOTA

State lawmakers held their biennial legislative session in 1983, tackling some of the worst financial problems in North Dakota history. Also during the year, gun play—and a subsequent manhunt and court trial—captured the attention of North Dakotans.

Legislature. Slumping oil-tax collections and the stagnant farm economy cut the state's general-fund budget surplus from $174 million to $43 million by the close of the 1981–83 biennium in mid-1983.

Lawmakers, meeting in their biennial session, were forced to cut many areas of spending and increase taxes on income, alcohol, cigarettes, retail sales, gasoline, and electricity to provide a balanced budget for 1983–85. They deliberated 75 days, the state's longest-ever regular session, in fashioning a two-year package to increase revenues nearly $338 million.

A tough law against driving under the influence of alcohol was enacted. It mandated license suspensions, fines, and addiction evaluations for first convictions and jail terms for repeat offenders.

Lawmakers also approved a measure changing the name of Minot Sate College to Dakota Northwestern University, but opponents petitioned to have the potentially divisive question put to a public vote in 1984.

Crime. Two U.S. marshals were killed and three officers were wounded in a February gun battle when authorities tried to arrest federal tax protester Gordon Kahl, wanted for parole violation, at a highway roadblock near rural Medina, ND. Kahl escaped, touching off a nationwide manhunt that culminated in June in a second shootout in Arkansas that left Kahl and another law officer dead. Kahl's son, Yorie, and Scott Faul received life sentences for the Medina murders. Two others were convicted of lesser crimes.

Agriculture. The state's farmers led the nation in signing up for the federal government's payment-in-kind (PIK) wheat program. They idled nearly 4.7 million acres (1.9 million ha) of cropland and received 73.4 million bushels of government-owned or mortgaged wheat for not growing their own. The state's wheat harvest still totaled an estimated 195 million bushels.

Nine North Dakota farmers filed suit to force the Farmers Home Administration to change its loan foreclosure policies. They claimed federal law requires FHA to provide 30 days written notice to allow for possible loan deferrals before beginning a foreclosure action. Farmers won every round of the battle in 1983. U.S. District Judge Bruce Van Sickle granted statewide class action status for the suit and ordered a temporary injunction that effectively halted FHA foreclosures in the state. Before year's end, Van Sickle certified a national class action status and extended the temporary injunction to cover 230,000 FHA borrowers in 44 states.

Politics. The year 1983 was not a good one for some North Dakota elected and appointed officials. Superintendent of Public Instruction Joseph Crawford, up for reelection in 1984, was convicted of driving while intoxicated and underwent treatment for alcohol dependency. Robert Melland, director of the Office of Management and Budget and Governor Olson's chief budget adviser, resigned. Melland left in the wake of reports that the Internal Revenue Service had placed liens totaling nearly $95,000 against his personal property and family-owned business. The dispute involved income-tax deductions Melland had claimed and employee withholding and Social Security taxes the IRS said the firm had failed to file. Another of Olson's top appointees, state Human Services director Dale Moug, resigned after he was convicted in December of shoplifting.

JIM NEUMANN
"The Forum," Fargo

NORTH DAKOTA • Information Highlights

Area: 70,702 sq mi (183 118 km²).
Population (1982 est.): 670,000.
Chief Cities (1980 census): Bismarck, the capital, 44,485; Fargo, 61,308; Grand Forks, 43,765; Minot, 32,843.
Government (1983): *Chief Officers*—governor, Allen I. Olson (R); lt. gov., Ernest Sands (R). *Legislative Assembly*—Senate, 53 members; House of Representatives, 106 members.
State Finances (fiscal year 1982): *Revenues,* $1,286,000,000; *expenditures,* $1,191,000,000.
Personal Income (1982): $7,287,000,000; per capita, $10,876.
Labor Force (July 1983): *Nonagricultural wage and salary earners,* 254,200, *unemployed,* 14,300 (4.3% of total force).
Education: *Enrollment* (fall 1981)—public elementary schools, 79,579; public secondary, 38,129; colleges and universities (1982), 36,224. *Public school expenditures* (1981–82), $274,126,000.

NORTHWEST TERRITORIES

The year 1983 was an active one politically in the Northwest Territories (NWT).

Legislative Assembly. An election was held on November 21 for the 24 member Legislative Assembly of the Northwest Territories. There was an increase of two seats over the previous assembly whose four-year term ended in 1983. Those elected reflected the ethnic diversity of the NWT, with 14 members being of native origin (Inuit, Indian, or Metis). Interest in the election was very high with a 70% voter turnout. It was announced that one additional elected member would sit on the executive council or cabinet and the position of deputy commissioner would be abolished. The executive council now consists of eight elected members and the commissioner of the NWT.

Aboriginal Rights. The Northwest Territories had considerable input into the first ministers' conference on aboriginal rights and the Constitution held in Ottawa in March. The government of the NWT was represented by the leader of the elected executive and the minister of aboriginal rights and constitutional development, and NWT native leaders were part of the delegations of the Inuit committee on national issues and the assembly of first nations. The conference, which included participation by the prime minister of Canada and the ten provincial premiers, approved a resolution directed at amending the Canadian Constitution to require further constitutional conferences on aboriginal rights, guaranteeing aboriginal and treaty rights equally to men and women, and protecting rights that may be acquired in future land claims agreements.

Economy. The economy suffered due to low mineral prices and depressed prices and markets for fur and arts and crafts products. The largest mine in the NWT, Cominco's Pine Point Mine, was shut down for six months due to low world prices for lead and zinc. Cantung Mining Corporation's operation at Tungsten halted production for much of the year. Adverse publicity and a ban on importation of Canadian seal skins by some European countries led to a decline in seal-skin harvesting by the Inuit.

ROSS M. HARVEY

NORTHWEST TERRITORIES ·
Information Highlights

Area: 1,304,903 sq mi (3 379 700 km²).
Population (July 1983 est.): 48,400.
Chief City (1981 census): Yellowknife, the capital, 9,483.
Government (1983): Chief officers—commissioner, John H. Parker. Legislature—Legislative Assembly, 24 elected members.
Education (1983–84): Enrollment—public and secondary schools, 12,690 pupils. Public school expenditures (1982–83), C$86,675,000.
Public Finance (1982–83 fiscal year): Revenues, C$462,084,000; expenditures, C$475,996,000.

NORWAY

Satisfaction with an improvement in Norway's balance of trade in 1983 was more than offset by public concern over a rising unemployment rate, which led to a change in the party composition of the government. By the end of August, unemployment had reached 4.1% of the labor force. This compared with 2.7% in August 1982 and 1.7% in August 1981.

Governmental Changes. The labor market crisis and the growing social problems it was creating came as a shock to a society accustomed to regard full employment as the norm. It led to increasing dissatisfaction in the Storting (parliament) with the policies of the minority Conservative government.

In June, two small nonsocialist parties that had hitherto backed the government in most Storting votes decided the time had come to join it in a coalition. As their price for joining, the two parties—the Christian Democrats and the Center (farmers') Party—demanded changes in economic policy aimed at stimulating the economy, in particular a reduction of interest rates. After tough bargaining, the two parties were given portfolios in a coalition that held 79 seats in the 155-member Storting.

The new government's makeup reflected the relative parliamentary strengths of the three parties. The Conservative Party, with 53 seats, was the dominant partner. Conservative Prime Minister Kåre Willoch remained in office, as did his Conservative cabinet colleagues in the ministries of foreign affairs, finance, and defense. Christian Democrats were given the ministries of oil and energy, trade, education, and foreign aid, a newly created department that was an offshoot of the foreign ministry. Center Party representatives took over the ministries of communications, agriculture, and the environment.

The coalition government proceeded to cut interest rates, as the Conservatives' new partners had demanded. It was assumed that the Conservatives would also acquiesce in their partners' wish not to cut public spending.

Local Elections. During the campaigning for the September local elections, unemployment was a major issue. Conservative politicians blamed it on the mistakes made by the earlier Labor government, coupled with international trends over which Norway had no control. This somewhat negative line proved to be without political value. The Conservative Party lost votes to both the left and the right, whereas its coalition partners more or less held their ground. While the Conservative share of the vote dropped to 26.1% (against 31.6% in 1981 and 29.7% in 1979), the outstanding victors were the opposition Labor Party and the small, far-right Progress Party. The former secured 39.3% of the vote (against 37.3% in 1981) and the latter 6.3% (compared with 4.5% in 1981).

NORWAY · Information Highlights

Official Name: Kingdom of Norway.
Location: Northern Europe.
Area: 124,999 sq mi (323 750 km²).
Population (July 1983 est.): 4,131,000.
Chief Cities (Jan. 1981): Oslo, the capital, 452,023; Bergen, 207,799; Trondheim, 134,976.
Government: *Head of state,* Olav V. king (acceded Sept. 1957). *Head of government,* Kåre Willoch, prime minister (took office October 1981). *Legislature*—Storting; Lagting and Odelsting.
Monetary Unit: Krone (7.7775 kroner equal U.S.$1, Dec. 14, 1983).
Gross Domestic Product (1981 U.S.$): $56,434,000,000.
Economic Indexes (1982): *Consumer Prices* (1970 = 100), all items, 289.9; food 288.0. *Industrial Production* (1975 = 100), 131.
Foreign Trade (1982 U.S.$): *Imports,* $15,476,000,000; *exports,* $17,595,000,000.

Labor and other, smaller socialist parties maintained that public spending was too low to halt the recession. Their leaders argued that it would be better to spend more on creating jobs than to pay people unemployment benefits for doing nothing. The Progress Party scored with right-wing voters because it claimed that the Conservatives had not been conservative enough. They had not kept their promises to slash government spending and make really substantial cuts in high taxation levels.

The Budget. The budget, tabled on October 5, showed a deficit and clearly gave priority to stimulating the economy. It proposed continued high spending on job creation schemes and no curbs on expenditure in sectors that could affect domestic demand. Business and industry were given tax concessions designed to improve competitiveness and encourage investment. Some modest cuts in personal-income-tax rates were included—just enough to match the expected 6% inflation rate in 1984.

THØR GJESTER, *"Økonomisk Revy,"* Oslo

NOVA SCOTIA

The year 1983 opened with Nova Scotia moving deeper into economic recession. Inflation had crumbled, but not without leaving in its wake high unemployment, skyrocketing interest rates, general restraint on government spending, and a ceiling of 6% on annual wage increases for public-sector employees. However, later in the year there was general economic optimism due to anticipated development of offshore oil and gas reserves.

The Economy. During the third quarter of 1983 the Nova Scotian economy was spurred by the belief that Mobil Oil Canada Limited would begin construction early in 1984 on the C$3 billion Venture offshore natural gas field. This optimism was reinforced by a high level of exploration activity, causing Industrial Estates Limited to speed up development of an $8 million, 200-acre (81-ha) site in Dartmouth.

Construction activity received additional stimulus from the announced federal and provincial grants given to first-time home buyers. In urban areas, housing starts were up, as were retail sales, notably of furniture and cars. These trends caused unemployment to register a marginal decline. In the meantime, farm income improved and the value of fish landings increased. Real wages tended to move up as the rate of inflation declined to 6%.

Government and Legislation. The provincial legislature enacted 101 bills, covering education, health, housing, economic development, social welfare, and collective bargaining in the public sector to the schooner *Bluenose* in the private sector. Laws were enacted to regulate the activities of degree-granting institutions, to prevent unwed teenage mothers from claiming welfare payments if alternate sources of aid can be identified, and to develop the schooner *Bluenose* Foundation to ensure its existence as one of the world's tall ships.

The government also appointed the Royal Commission on Education for streamlining the structure of post-secondary education, appointed a commission of inquiry to review the status of rent control in Nova Scotia, organized one of the world's largest expositions on Canadian offshore resources, and canceled the Moscow Circus' visit to protest the Soviet downing of a Korean Air Lines plane.

Energy. Although a 30% increase in electric-power rates during the year caused Nova Scotians' electric bills to escalate, the province continued to advance in the exploitation of its gas and oil reserves. Plans were under way to transport newly recovered offshore natural gas to provincial export markets. In addition an $11.3 million exploratory oil and gas drilling program was announced. Feasibility studies were under way to develop a coal-liquefaction plant in Cape Breton, while an 18-million-watt pilot project for harnessing tidal power in the Annapolis Basin came on line during the year.

R. P. SETH
Mount Saint Vincent University

NOVA SCOTIA · Information Highlights

Area: 21,425 sq mi (55 490 km²).
Population (July 1983): 860,100.
Chief Cities (1981 census): Halifax, the capital, 114,594; Dartmouth, 62,277; Sydney, 29,444.
Government (1983): *Chief Officers*—lt. gov., John E. Shaffner; premier, John Buchanan (Progressive Conservative); Att. Gen., Henry W. How; Legislative Assembly, 52 members.
Education (prelim., 1983–84): *Enrollment*—elementary and secondary schools, 178,111; secondary schools, 22,062.
Public Finance (1984 fiscal year budget): *Revenues,* $2,141,842,800; *expenditures,* $2,390,355,700.
Personal Income (average weekly salary, March 1983): $340.13.
Unemployment Rate (September 1983, seasonally adjusted): 12.6%.
(All monetary figures are in Canadian dollars.)

OBITUARIES[1]

BRYANT, Paul William (Bear)

American football coach: b. Moro Bottom, AR, Sept. 11, 1913; d. Tuscaloosa, AL, Jan. 26, 1983.

In 38 years as football coach at four universities, Paul (Bear) Bryant won more games than any other college coach in history. His 323 victories (along with 85 defeats and 17 ties) broke the record of 314 set by Amos Alonzo Stagg. Only 37 days after retiring as Alabama coach, Bryant died of a heart attack.

He was a taskmaster, a disciplinarian, and a motivator. He also was a familiar figure on the sidelines with his craggy face and black and white houndstooth hat. Bryant supervised Alabama practices from a tower overlooking two fields. Said one of his quarterbacks, "There's something about him up in that tower that makes you want to run through a wall."

In his years as a head coach, his teams played in 29 bowl games, including 24 consecutive ones (1960–83), both records. Six of his Alabama teams were named national champions by wire-service polls. His quarterbacks included Joe Namath, George Blanda, Vito (Babe) Parilli, Ken Stabler, Richard Todd, and Steve Sloan. More than 40 of his players, including Ray Perkins, his successor at Alabama, became college or professional head coaches. For years, he earned $99,999.99 a year because he did not think a football coach should make as much as the university president, who was paid $100,000.

Background. Paul William Bryant grew up in poverty on an Arkansas farm. During his high-school years, while picking cotton in the summer for 50 cents a day, he accepted a dare to wrestle a carnival bear for $1 a minute. But when he went to collect his money, the bear and its owner were gone, and he was left only with a bitten ear and a nickname.

At Alabama, he played end opposite the celebrated Don Hutson. After graduation, he became an assistant coach for four years (at $1,250 a year) at Alabama and two years at Vanderbilt. He then served in the Navy during World War II. After that, he was head coach for one year (1945) at Maryland, eight (1946–53) at Kentucky, four (1954–57) at Texas A&M, and 25 (1958–82) at Alabama. There was success and controversy everywhere, no controversy greater than a *Saturday Evening Post* article that accused Bryant and Wally Butts, the Georgia coach, of conspiring to fix the 1962 Alabama-Georgia game. Both sued the magazine for libel. Butts won his suit, and Bryant's resulted in a large settlement.

FRANK LITSKY

BLAKE, Eubie

American pianist/composer: b. Baltimore, MD, Feb. 7, 1883; d. Brooklyn, NY, Feb. 12, 1983.

Five days after his 100th birthday, an event celebrated by a 24-hour marathon of music by numerous jazz performers at New York's St. Peter's Lutheran Church and a second concert at the Shubert Theater, Eubie Blake succumbed to pneumonia. Too ill to attend the ceremonies, the jazz-ragtime musician nonetheless was able to hear the music and receive tributes through a special telephone hookup.

In terms of longevity, Mr. Blake's career matched his life. His career spanned from the dawning of the ragtime era of the late 19th century to the contemporary Broadway theater. His life reached back even further to a link with the era of American slavery through parents who had been born slaves, a fact not hidden by Eubie. He had said, "I'm proud of my heritage. I want everyone to know that I came from slavery and went to the top of my profession."

Background. Born James Hubert Blake, the youngest of 11 children of John and Emily Blake, he was the only one of the children to live past infancy. At the age of 15 he got a job as a pianist in a bordello for $3.00 a week plus tips. Although his mother disapproved of "ungodly music," Eubie soon was playing saloons and clubs and in 1899 composed his first piano rag which was published some years later as *Charleston Rag*. In 1915 he met Noble Sissle, a singer from Indianapolis, with whom he formed a partnership. The pair worked as composers, performers, and as co-leaders of an orchestra. In 1921 they collaborated on the first black musical on Broadway, *Shuffle Along*. Its score included *I'm Just Wild about Harry*, a tune that became a pop standard, and *Love Will Find a Way*. The team eventually broke up, and Blake went on to compose with others.

He retired at age 63 and began studying the Schillinger method of composition at New York University. For the next 23 years he composed or transcribed in this method songs that he had memorized but had never written down. In 1969 he found himself in demand after the release of a retrospective record album *The 86 Years of Eubie Blake*. In 1972 he started his own record company.

An adaptation of *Shuffle Along* was presented off Broadway in 1978, and an expanded version entitled *Eubie* opened later that year on Broadway. Blake did not appear in the show, but it enhanced his fame. In 1981 he was awarded the Presidential Medal of Freedom.

SAUNDRA FRANCE

[1]Arranged chronologically by death date

WILLIAMS, Tennessee

American writer: b. Columbus, MS, March 26, 1911; d. New York, NY, Feb. 25, 1983.

Tennessee Williams, the leading American dramatist of his time, second only to Eugene O'Neill among all U.S. dramatists, established his true stature with his first two Broadway plays, *The Glass Menagerie* and *A Streetcar Named Desire*. Subsequent plays of great interest, including *Summer and Smoke, Cat on a Hot Tin Roof,* and *Sweet Bird of Youth,* added to his fame, but nothing that came later matched the two modern classics which astonishingly inaugurated his career. Williams broke new ground with his frankness, passion, violence, occasional poetry, and especially his living portraits of outsiders, loners, and eccentrics.

No doubt his warm defense of harried loners was in some measure fueled by his own experiences as a homosexual, and both the persecuted ladies and the virile male upstarts in his plays are, after a fashion, self-portraits. Speculation on this issue became public during and after the 1960s, when homosexuality became less of a taboo subject. Williams' sexual preferences were revealed publicly in 1970 and were, in effect, proclaimed in his *Memoirs* of 1975. He had created a particularly rich gallery of women characters, insisting that they were not really men gotten up as women as some have claimed. On that point he surely has been proved right in view of the unceasing interest that ambitious actresses exhibit in his creations.

It is possible that the increasing liberalism of the times caused him to feel less embattled and contributed to his decline as a dramatist. In the 1960s he became increasingly dependent on drink and drugs and was committed briefly to a hospital in 1969. Even so, he kept writing and rewriting plays to the end of his life, although his last works found few admirers. In addition to plays, he wrote the novel *The Roman Spring of Mrs. Stone* (1950) and collections of short stories and poetry.

Background. Born Thomas Lanier Williams, he moved from his birthplace to St. Louis in 1918. His mother, a genteel southerner, the daughter of a clergyman, struggled for survival in this strange urban environment. His father, a traveling salesman, thought young Tom a sissy. Williams studied at the University of Missouri, Washington University, and the University of Iowa (A.B., 1938), worked in a shoe factory, wrote poetry and fiction, and first had a play produced in 1935. His *Battle of Angels,* scheduled for Broadway, closed in Boston in 1940. *The Glass Menagerie* reached Broadway in 1945. Its main characters—an aging southern belle, a young girl incapable of coping with the real world, and a would-be poet

© 1983 Martha Swope

sidetracked in a shoe factory—closely resembled his mother, his sister, and himself. It was followed in 1947 by *A Streetcar Named Desire,* which graphically exposed the fateful encounter between Blanche, a decadent daughter of the Old South, and her brother-in-law Stanley Kowalski, who symbolized a vital embodiment of the new America. *Summer and Smoke,* a commercial failure of 1948, made history in 1952 when its revival was a signal event in the birth of Off Broadway.

Williams' prolificacy continued during the 1950s with *The Rose Tattoo;* the unconventional *Camino Real,* which exhibited such exemplary rebels as Casanova, Camille, and Don Quixote; and *Cat on a Hot Tin Roof,* which introduced a memorable older figure, the vigorous Big Daddy. *Baby Doll,* a controversial 1956 film by Williams, was based on two of his one-act plays. In 1957 Williams, an indefatigable rewriter, redid *Battle of Angels* as *Orpheus Descending,* a characteristic portrait of sexual passion besieged by sick envy. *Suddenly Last Summer* was first presented along with *Something Unspoken* in the 1958 Off-Broadway double bill *Garden District.* The tragicomedy *Sweet Bird of Youth* in 1959 again put a Williams play on Broadway. It was followed by the comedy *Period of Adjustment* and the playwright's last Broadway success, *The Night of the Iguana* (1961).

The last 22 years of his life saw a decline in his creative powers. Such later works as *The Milk Train Doesn't Stop Here Anymore, Small Craft Warning,* and *A Lovely Sunday at Creve Coeur* drew attention, but none won the large audiences or substantial critical acclaim of his earlier work.

HENRY POPKIN

GODFREY, Arthur

American radio and television personality: b. New York, NY, Aug. 31, 1903; d. New York, NY, March 16, 1983.

A homespun manner, an infectious grin, and a ukulele as a trademark, helped make Arthur Godfrey one of the best-loved radio and TV personalities of all time. At the height of his popularity, from 1945 to 1959, he was on the air roughly ten hours a week and brought CBS as much as 12% of its total revenues.

The self-styled "ole redhead" regularly tossed out scripts and prepared commercials, spoofing his sponsors and ad-libbing in what the late Fred Allen once described as a "barefoot" voice. At the same time, however, Godfrey's popularity brought him star-making powers. He became an influential and somewhat feared figure in broadcasting. In addition to a half-hour radio show which began in 1945, he was host of television's *Arthur Godrey's Talent Scouts* (1948–58), *Arthur Godfrey and His Friends* (1949–56), and *Arthur Godfrey Time* (1952–59). His cast included the McGuire Sisters, Julius La Rosa, and Marion Marlowe.

Background. The son of a newspaper writer and a former concert singer, he was brought up in Hasbrouck Heights, NJ, and left school at 15 to help support his family. Eventually he joined the Navy; after his discharge he worked in various jobs before enlisting in the Coast Guard. It was in the Coast Guard that he gained his first on-the-air experience, as an amateur banjo player on a Baltimore radio station.

Hours of listening to the radio in a hospital room following an auto accident in 1931 convinced him that, as he put it, "there is no radio audience, just one guy or one girl in a room." Soon after, he went to work for NBC in Washington, DC, and in 1941 he moved to New York, where he joined CBS.

ELAINE P. SEDITO

BALANCHINE, George

Russian-American choreographer and ballet director: b. St. Petersburg, Russia, Jan. 22 (Jan. 9, Old Style), 1904; d. New York City, April 30, 1983.

Widely considered one of the greatest choreographers in ballet history, George Balanchine also guided his own company, the New York City Ballet, to international eminence. The foremost master of plotless ballet, he rejected ballet's traditional emphasis on storytelling and spectacle. Balanchine concentrated on movement and on the close relationship he saw between dancing and music. Balanchine expanded the ballet vocabulary—a result visible in the more than 200 works he choreographed during six decades. Most were created for the New York City Ballet, where he was artistic director after founding the company with the American dance scholar, Lincoln Kirstein. Among Balanchine's best-known ballets were *Serenade, Agon, Concerto Barocco*, and his highly popular version of *The Nutcracker*.

Background. The son of Meliton Balanchivadze, a well-known Georgian composer, and a Russian mother, the young Georgi Balanchivadze became a boarder at the ballet school of the Maryinsky Theater in St. Petersburg (now Leningrad) in 1914. The academic ballet idiom in which he was trained was later consciously used by Balanchine to expand dancers' capacities in 20th-century terms. His insistence that movement was interesting in itself caused his best-known ballets to be called "abstract." He himself rejected the term and said "the controlling image for me comes from the music." Praised for his musicianship by collaborators, including Igor Stravinsky, Balanchine also had studied for three years at the Petrograd State Conservatory before graduating from the ballet school in 1921.

After showing his first choreography in 1923, he left for a summer tour of Germany with other dancers in 1924. Balanchine remained in the West with his wife, Tamara Geva, and Alexandra Danilova, the ballerina who became his companion after Miss Geva went on to America. Serge Diaghilev, director of the famed Ballets Russes, simplified Balanchine's original surname and had him choreograph ten ballets for his company. Among these was the 1928 *Apollo* in which Balanchine first showed the neoclassical style with which he became identified.

After Diaghilev's death in 1929, Balanchine worked for English revue producers, the Royal Danish Ballet, the new Ballets Russes de Monte Carlo, and his own short-lived troupe, Les Ballets 1933. An American admirer, Lincoln Kirstein, invited him to the United States and both men founded the School of American Ballet in New York in 1934.

Their first company, the American Ballet, was the precursor to other companies—American Ballet Caravan and Ballet Society, which became the New York City Ballet in 1948. Balanchine also choreographed for more than 19 Broadway shows and for four films. In 1936, Miss Geva and Ray Bolger danced his celebrated "Slaughter on Tenth Avenue" ballet in the musical *On Your Toes*.

After his divorce from Miss Geva, Balanchine married three other dancers, Vera Zorina, Maria Tallchief and Tanaquil LeClercq. He and Miss LeClercq were divorced in 1969.

After a Russian Orthodox funeral service, Balanchine was buried in Sag Harbor, NY.

ANNA KISSELGOFF

FULLER, R(ichard) Buckminster

American futurist inventor: b. Milton, MA, July 12, 1895; d. Los Angeles, July 1, 1983.

Believing that through technology "man can do anything he needs to do," R. Buckminster Fuller considered himself "an engineer, inventor, mathematician, architect, cartographer, philosopher, poet, cosmogonist, comprehensive designer, and choreographer." He held more than 2,000 patents, received 39 honorary degrees, and was elected to the exclusive American Academy and Institute of Arts and Letters. Yet in 1947 his geodesic dome blueprints had to be signed by an associate because Fuller lacked architectural credentials.

Fuller's first design was the Dymaxion House in 1928. With glass walls, this prefabricated house was hung from a central mast and could rotate. He offered the patent to the American Institute of Architects, but the Institute refused it and passed a resolution against all prefabricated houses.

Background. Richard Buckminster Fuller was born in 1895 into a merchant's family. At Milton Academy he did well in math and science but poorly in English and Latin. Entering Harvard where his forebears had attended, he cut classes and was dismissed. After working in a Canadian machine factory, he returned to Harvard but again was put out. Eventually he joined the Navy, received science training at the U.S. Naval Academy, and was discharged in 1919. Having married Anne Hewlett in 1917, he held assorted jobs but soon formed a building block construction firm with his father-in-law. Devastated by his small daughter's death in 1922, Fuller drank heavily and considered suicide after his dismissal from the family firm that had been purchased by outside interests. In 1927 he stopped drinking, determined to discover the design principles at work in the universe and to use the results to benefit society.

In 1933–35 he experimented with a three-wheel car, but adverse publicity following a fatal accident kept it from production. In 1943 he designed the Dymaxion Airocean World Map, showing the earth's surface in a single flat view with no distortions. In 1944 he hoped to mass produce the Wichita House, a new version of the Dymaxion House, but the building industry was not interested. The geodesic dome, source of Fuller's fame and fortune, was used on the Ford Motor Co. Rotunda Building in Dearborn, MI, 1952; the American Exhibit in Moscow, 1959; and the U.S. Pavilion at Expo 67 in Montreal.

Fuller, an iconoclastic inventor and visionary futurist, spoke boldly of mile-high floating cities free of noise and pollution. He envisioned a 3-mi (4.8-km) dome over mid-Manhattan. A popular lecturer, Fuller wrote 25 books.

FRANKLIN PARKER

JACKSON, Henry Martin

U.S. politician: b. Everett, WA, May 31, 1912; d. Everett, WA, Sept. 1, 1983.

Shortly after holding a news conference to denounce the downing of a South Korean commercial airliner by the USSR, Henry M. Jackson, the senior U.S. senator from the state of Washington, died in his hometown of Everett. The ranking minority member of the Senate Armed Services Committee, the Democrat was considered one of the nation's leading authorities on military affairs. Jackson had been a member of Congress for more than 40 years—a representative from 1941 until 1953 and a senator since 1953. His vote total reached 55% or more in 11 of his 12 Congressional races.

A candidate for the presidency in 1972 and 1976 and chairman of the Democratic National Committee (1960–61), the senator was a "Jackson Democrat"—usually a liberal on domestic matters and a conservative on issues involving defense and foreign affairs. Jackson's liberalism went back to the days when he worked in a local campaign for Franklin D. Roosevelt and continued, with some deviation, during succeeding administrations. As a freshman senator, he opposed Sen. Joseph R. McCarthy during the Army-McCarthy hearings.

In addition to national defense, Jackson's chief domestic preoccupations were energy and the environment. Prior to the 1980 elections, he had chaired the Senate Energy and Natural Resources Committee. He worked hard to place hydroelectric dams along the Columbia River, was a proponent of nuclear energy, and backed the 1969 National Environmental Policy Act.

Throughout his career, Henry Jackson sought to warn the nation of the threat posed by the Soviet Union. His distrust of the Soviets led him to be a critic of both strategic arms limitation treaties. At the same time he was unrelenting in his support of Israel. In 1974 he fought for the Jackson-Vanik amendment, prohibiting most-favored-nation trade status to nations that restrict emigration. (The action was aimed at the Soviets and their policy of barring the emigration of Jews.)

Background. The son of Norwegian immigrants, Peter and Marine Anderson, Henry Martin Jackson played basketball and was a member of the debating team in high school. After earning a law degree from the University of Washington and being admitted to the Washington bar in 1935, the future legislator practiced law and served as prosecuting attorney.

Senator Jackson married Helen Eugenia Hardin on Dec. 16, 1961. He is survived also by their daughter and son. As a child, Jackson's sister called him "Scoop," because he reminded her of a cartoon strip character. The nickname remained throughout his life.

JAMES E. CHURCHILL, JR.

MIRÓ, Joan

Spanish artist: b. Barcelona, Spain, April 20, 1893; d. Palma, Majorca, Dec. 25, 1983.

A painter, sculptor, printmaker, designer, and muralist, Joan Miró was a seminal figure in the art and imaginative life of the 20th century. At once mythic and childlike, playful and archetypal, his works are bright-colored fantasies that celebrate the sensual pleasures of everyday experience. His best-known canvases—such as *The Hunter* (*Catalan Landscape,* 1923–24), *The Harlequin's Carnival* (1924–25), *Dog Barking at the Moon* (1926), *Dutch Interior* (1928), *Composition* (1933), and the ceramic mural *Wall of the Sun* (1955–58, at the UNESCO building in Paris)—are filled with geometric or amoeba-like ideograms of musicians, women, cats, dogs, chickens, plants, birds, and astral bodies. "I find all my themes in the fields and on the beaches," Miró once said. His sculptures and ceramics, many of them collaborations with his friend José Lloréns Artigas, are typified by the incongruous assemblage of familiar objects.

Y. Coatsaliou/Sygma

Ever whimsical and a touch mischievous, Miró's style brings together primary human experience and irrational fantasy. As such, it put him at the center of the surrealist movement that included Max Ernst, René Magritte, Salvador Dali, and Jean Arp in the 1920s and 1930s. According to critics and art historians, his influence was nowhere greater than in the United States, where such artists as Arshile Gorky, Robert Motherwell, Jackson Pollock, and Alexander Calder drew on his style.

Background. The son of a watchmaker, Joan Miró began taking drawing lessons at the age of ten and later studied at the Barcelona School of Art and Academy Galí. His parents tried to steer him toward a business career, but Joan resisted. When he was 17, his family moved to a farm at Montroig, between Barcelona and Tarragona, whose landscape and blanched buildings would become an important creative inspiration, reflected in such notable early paintings as *Montroig* (*The Olive Grove,* 1919) and *The Farm* (1921–22).

At the age of 26, Miró moved to Paris, where he joined with Picasso and others in exploding many of the conventions of artistic form and composition. At the same time, however, he remained attached to the world of nature, spending summers in Montroig. It was during the 1920s and 1930s that Miró emerged as a fully modernist innovator, with a reputation for a universal but highly unique imagery.

Settling in Palma, Miró elaborated his style on canvas and in other artistic media—sculptures, lithographs, etchings, and even stage designs. He first visited the United States in 1947, and the impact was mutually powerful. For Miró the subsequent decades—with several more trips to America—brought a gradual shift toward a more abstract expressionism. As his fame increased, he was exhibited extensively and in great demand for large-scale murals and sculptures. Among the latter are the 55-ft (17-m) *Personage and Birds* in Houston and the 72-ft (22-m) *Woman and Bird* in Barcelona.

JEFF HACKER

The following is a selected list of prominent persons who died during 1983. Articles on major figures appear in the preceding pages.

Abboud, Ibrahim (82), leader of Sudan (1958–64). Gen. Abboud seized power in 1958 and resigned under civilian pressure in 1964: d. Khartoum, Sudan, Sept. 8.

Abernathy, William (50), Harvard Business School professor; his work was instrumental in getting companies to focus more closely on production and technology. Along with colleague Robert Hayes he wrote a controversial article "Managing Our Way to Economic Decline," blaming industrial decline on corporate management itself: d. Lexington, MA, Dec. 29.

Adair, Edwin Ross (75), U.S. representative (R-IN, 1951–71): d. Fort Wayne, IN, May 7.

Adam, Claus (65), composer and cellist, played with the Juilliard String Quartet (1955–74). He was a founding member of the New Music Quartet (1948–55). As a composer he produced chamber scores and concertos: d. New York City, July 4.

Aiken, Frank (85), Irish political figure; was the Irish Republic Army chief of staff (1923–25) and a member of the Irish parliament for 50 years, following his election in 1923. He served as deputy prime minister and foreign minister from 1951 until 1969, when he retired. For many years he led the Irish delegation at the United Nations. He was a cofounder, along with Eamon de Valera, of Fianna Fail, Ireland's largest political party: d. Dublin, May 18.

Albion, Robert G. (86), maritime historian; former professor at Princeton and Harvard universities. He wrote several books on naval history, and his *Naval and Maritime History,* written in 1972, remains the standard bibliography. From 1943 to 1950 he was Historian of Naval Administration: d. Groton, CT, August 9.

Albright, Ivan (86), American painter; identified with the 1930s style "magic realism" and known for his images of decaying human flesh: d. Woodstock, VT, Nov. 18.

Aldrich, Robert (65), motion-picture director; known for such films as *Vera Cruz*, *What Ever Happened to Baby Jane?* *Hush, Hush, Sweet Charlotte*, *The Dirty Dozen*, *Ulzana's Raid*, and *The Longest Yard*: d. Los Angeles, Dec. 5.

Alemán, Miguel (79?), president of Mexico (1946–52); was an advocate of industrialization and agriculture improvements. In the 1960s he became president of a national tourist council, a position he retained until his death: d. Mexico City, May 14.

Andrzejewski, Jerzy (73), Polish writer and political dissident; wrote eight novels including *Ashes and Diamonds*, a bestseller in 1961, later made into a movie. He was a former delegate to Poland's parliament but turned back his membership in the Communist Party in 1957: d. Warsaw, April 20.

Aron, Raymond (78), French conservative political thinker; was a historian, sociologist, teacher, and political writer. Following World War II, Mr. Aron went into journalism, working first on the paper *Combat*, on *Le Figaro* (1947–77), and then writing a weekly column for the news magazine *L'Express*. He taught at the Sorbonne between 1955 and 1968 and became professor of sociology at the College de France in 1970. His important writings include *Peace and War Between Nations* and a two-volume study of Carl Clausewitz, the German strategic thinker: d. Paris, Oct. 17.

Aspinall, Wayne N. (87), U.S. representative (D-CO, 1949–73): d. Palisade, CO, Oct. 9.

Averill, Earl (81), baseball outfielder, played primarily with the Cleveland Indians and was often remembered as the batter whose hitting helped end the career of pitcher Dizzy Dean. He was voted to the baseball Hall of Fame in 1975: d. Everett, WA, August 16.

Bailey, Thomas A. (80), historian and professor emeritus at Stanford University; was a writer on foreign policy. Dr. Bailey wrote at least 17 books, and two—*The American Pageant* (1956) and *The Diplomatic History of the American People* (1940)—went through several editions: d. Menlo Park, CA, July 26.

Bakaric, Vladimir (70), vice-president of Yugoslavia and the senior member of the Communist Politburo: d. Zagreb, Yugoslavia, Jan. 16.

Balderston, William (86), president (1948–54) and chairman (1954–57) of the Philco Corporation, was a leader in the development and promotion of the car radio: d. Abington, PA, July 25.

Bane, Frank B. (89), first administrator of the Social Security System (1935–38); was an author of the legislation that created the system: d. Alexandria, VA, Jan. 23.

Bee, Clair (87), basketball coach; pioneered the 1-3-1 zone defense and in his college coaching career at Rider College and Long Island University compiled the highest winning percentage (87.7) of any major college coach. He later coached the National Basketball Association's Baltimore Bullets (1952–54) and wrote more than 40 books: d. Cleveland, OH, May 20.

Berberian, Cathy (54), mezzo-soprano; best known for her performances of contemporary music. She was an important figure in the international avant-garde for more than 25 years: d. Rome, March 6.

Bergamin Gutiérrez, José (87), Spanish novelist and poet: d. San Sebastian, Spain, August 28.

Bidault, Georges (83), former prime minister of France. A Resistance fighter during World War II, Mr. Bidault was head of the underground movement in Nazi-occupied France. At the end of the war he served as foreign minister in the government set up by the president and prime minister of France, Gen.

Charles de Gaulle. In the late 1940s and early 1950s, besides his service as foreign minister, he served as prime minister and deputy prime minister. From 1945 to 1962 he was a member of Parliament. His political downfall came during the Algerian fight for independence. Mr. Bidault resisted the Algerian struggle for independence. Because of his activities, he eventually lost his parliamentary immunity from arrest. He fled the country in 1962, remaining in exile for six years: d. Cambo-les-Bains, France, Jan. 27.

Bishop, Maurice (39), prime minister of Grenada (1979–83): d. Grenada, Oct. 19.

Black, William (80), founder and chairman of the Chock Full o'Nuts Corporation: d. New York City, March 7.

Bloch, Felix (77), Swiss-born physicist; professor emeritus of physics at Stanford University and winner of the Nobel Prize for Physics (shared with Edward Mills Purcell in 1952): d. Zurich, Switzerland, Sept. 10.

Blunt, Anthony (75), British art curator and member of a Soviet spy ring. He was curator of Queen Elizabeth II's art collection. In 1964 he secretly confessed to the British government to spying for the Soviet Union, acknowledging that he recruited spies for the Soviet Union from among radical students at Cambridge. His role as a member of a four-man Soviet spying ring was revealed by Prime Minister Margaret Thatcher in 1979. He was stripped of his knighthood in 1979, long after the British government knew of his activities. Mr. Blunt resigned from the British Academy, but he was never directly punished by the government as he had been granted immunity: d. London, March 26.

Bocca, Geoffrey (59), British novelist and historian: d. London, July 7.

Bok, Bart J. (77), Dutch-born astronomer; director of the Steward Observatory of the University of Arizona (1966–70), he was professor of astronomy at Harvard (1933–57), the Australian National University (1957–66), and the University of Arizona (1966–74). He served as president of the American Astronomical Society. His classic work is *The Milky Way* (1941), written jointly with his wife Priscilla: d. Tucson, AZ, Aug. 5.

Boscone, Reva (88), U.S. congresswoman (D-UT, 1949–53): d. Vienna, Utah, July 21.

Boult, Sir Adrian (93), British music conductor; was conductor of the BBC Symphony Orchestra and the London Philharmonic Orchestra. In his 60 years of conducting he was associated with most of the major musical institutions of England. He wrote two handbooks on conducting and an autobiography. He was knighted in 1937: d. Kent, England, Feb. 23.

Boyd, William C. (79), biochemist; his early work in blood sciences led to modern immunology. He wrote textbooks in immunology and anthropology and works of a technical nature as well as science fiction; he was also a mushroom collector and linguist. In 1945 he discovered that chemicals in the lima bean reacted to blood type A. His report on the chemicals, which he named lectins, helped lead to the discovery of thousands of plants containing substances that reacted to particular blood types. Dr. Boyd wrote one of the first anthropological textbooks, *Genetics and the Races of Man* (1950): d. Falmouth, MA, Feb. 19.

Bradley, Jenny (97), Belgium-born, internationally known literary agent; she assisted the author James Joyce and other literary luminaries: d. Cap d'Antibes, France, June 3.

Brandt, William (Bill) (79), British photographer; known for his pictures of British social life, landscapes, portraits, and stylized female nudes. He worked as a photo-journalist for British and French newspapers and magazines and later for American publications. His early photos were collected in two volumes, *The English at Home* (1936) and *A Night in London* (1938). His other books include *Camera in London, Literary Britain*, and *Nudes 1945–80*: d. London, Dec. 20.

Brewin, Andrew (76), member of Canadian Parliament (1962–79) and a founder of the New Democratic Party: d. Victoria, British Columbia, Sept. 21.

Buckmaster, Henrietta (born Henrietta Henkle) (74), novelist, historian, and editor; best known for her novel about the underground railroad and the abolition movement, *Let My People Go*: d. Chestnut Hill, MA, April 26.

Buñuel, Luis (83), Spanish-born filmmaker; regarded by critics as one of the world's greatest. On his first film, *An Andalusian Dog* (1928), Buñuel collaborated with the artist Salvador Dali. Other films included the controversial *Golden Age* (1930), the documentary *Land Without Bread* (1932), *Milky Way* (1969), *Belle de jour* (1966), *Tristana* (1970), *The Discreet Charm of the Bourgeoisie* (1972), *The Phantom of Liberty* (1974), and *That Obscure Object of Desire* (1977): d. Mexico City, July 29.

Burke, James A. (73), U.S. congressman (D-MA, 1959–79): d. Boston, MA, Oct. 13.

Burton, Phillip (56), U.S. congressman (D-CA, 1964–83); a longtime Liberal Democrat, he was considered an expert on welfare legislation: d. San Francisco, April 10.

Canova, Judy (66), comedian, singer, and actress; most often played the role of the country bumpkin: d. Los Angeles, CA, August 5.

Raymond Aron

Laurent Maous/Gamma-Liaison

Sir Adrian Boult

UPI

Bonnie Schiffman/Gamma-Liaison

Karen Carpenter

Richard Kalvar/Magnum

Lillian Carter

UPI

Kenneth Clark

National Catholic News Service

Terence Cardinal Cooke

Carpenter, Karen (32), pop singer; along with her brother Richard, she sold more than 30 million records. The two were a major pop team of the early 1970s, winning three Grammy awards: d. Downey, CA, Feb. 4.

Carroll, John A. (82), U.S. representative (D-CO, 1947–51) and U.S. senator (D-CO, 1957–63): d. Denver, CO, August 31.

Carter, Lillian (85), mother of former President Jimmy Carter. She had been a nurse, Peace Corps volunteer, unofficial ambassador, and a supporter of civil rights and women's causes: d. Americus, GA, Oct. 30.

Casariego, Mario Cardinal (74), Roman Catholic archbishop of Guatemala and was the first clergyman elevated to Cardinal in Central America. Ordained in 1936, he became an archbishop in 1963 and a cardinal in 1969: d. Guatemala City, June 15.

Catledge, Turner (82), journalist; associated with *The New York Times* from 1929 until his retirement in 1970, except for a 19-month stint at *The Chicago Sun* beginning in 1941. He wrote, with journalist Joseph Alsop, *The 168 Days*, about President Franklin Roosevelt's attempt to "pack" the U.S. Supreme Court: d. New Orleans, LA, April 27.

Chang Da-Chien (84), Chinese painter; noted for his blending of modern and ancient art forms: d. Taipei, Taiwan, April 2.

Prince Charles (79), Prince of Belgium; served as the Belgian regent from 1944 to 1950 while his brother King Leopold III was in exile. He is credited with saving the monarchy there: d. Ostend, Belgium, June 1.

Clark, Barney (62), first recipient of a permanent artificial heart: d. Salt Lake City, UT, March 23.

Clark, Kenneth Mackenzie (79), British art historian, museum director, and author/narrator of the television series *Civilisation*. Educated at Winchester School and Trinity College, Oxford, he was director of the National Gallery in London (1934–45) and was appointed Surveyor of the King's Pictures, with responsibility for the thousands of paintings and drawings at the various royal establishments. From 1939 to 1941 he worked in the Ministry of Information and between 1949 and 1950 was Slade Professor of Fine Art at Oxford. Clark was knighted in 1938 and was made a life peer in 1969. Among his important books are *Piero della Francesca* (1951), *The Nude* (1955), *Rembrandt and the Italian Renaissance* (1966), and *The Drawings of Botticelli for Dante's Divine Comedy* (1976). In 1939 he edited the English art critic Roger Fry's *Last Lectures*. As the writer and narrator of the books and television series *Civilisation* and *The Romantic Rebellion*, he became internationally known: d. Hythe, England, May 21.

Claude, Albert (84), Belgium-born cell biochemist; was awarded a Nobel Prize for Medicine in 1974 for his research on the structure and function of cells. He did much of his work at what is now Rockefeller University in New York. Dr. Claude never graduated from high school, but because of his World War I service, the Belgium government allowed him to start university studies in 1922: d. Brussels, Belgium, May 22.

Cohen, Benjamin (88), attorney; one of the architects of Franklin Roosevelt's New Deal, he was part of the famous brain trust and framed much of the social legislation passed during the Depression era of the 1930s. He also served under Presidents Harry Truman and John Kennedy: d. Washington, DC, August 15.

Conrad, Michael (58), actor; best known as Sgt. Philip Esterhaus on the television series *Hill Street Blues*: d. Los Angeles, CA, Nov. 22.

Cooke, Terence Cardinal (62), Roman Catholic cardinal (1969–83); was the head of the archdiocese of New York (1968–83) and was the Military Vicar of the United States: d. New York City, Oct. 6.

Corning, Erastus 2d (73), mayor of Albany, NY (1942–83). A Democrat, he served as mayor of a major American city longer than anyone else: d. Boston, May 28.

Cowles, John, Sr. (84), newspaper publisher; led *The Minneapolis Star* and *The Minneapolis Tribune* from the 1940s through the 1960s. In 1973 he retired as chairman of his newspaper company in favor of his son: d. Minneapolis, MN, Feb. 25.

Crabbe, Buster (Clarence Linden) (75), Olympic swimmer and film actor. During his career as a swimmer he took 16 world and 35 national records and a gold medal in the 1932 Olympics. He made 180 films for movies and television: d. Scottsdale, AZ, April 23.

Cukor, George (83), motion-picture director; made more than 50 movies and was sometimes labeled a "woman's director" for his seemingly intuitive understanding of actresses. His major discovery was Katharine Hepburn, whom he first directed in *A Bill of Divorcement;* he continued to work with her throughout his life. Under his direction James Stewart, Ronald Colman, and Rex Harrison won Oscars. Mr. Cukor himself won one for *My Fair Lady*. In his early years he worked in the theater, and he also occasionally worked in television, winning an Emmy in 1975 for *Love Among the Ruins:* d. Los Ángeles, Jan. 24.

Dalio, Marcel (born Israel Mosche Blauschild) (83), French-born actor, found success in both America and in France in such films as *Pepe Le Moko, Le Grand Illusion, To Have and Have Not, Casablanca, The Snows of Kilimanjaro, Gentlemen Prefer Blondes,* and *Sabrina:* d. Paris, Nov. 20.

Dana, Leora (60), stage and film actress; appeared on stage in *The Madwoman of Chaillot, Sabrina Fair, The Best Man, Beekman Place,* and *Mourning Pictures*. Her screen performances included those in *Kings Go Forth, Some Came Running, Shoot the Moon,* and *Baby It's You:* d. New York City, Dec. 13.

Debus, Kurt Heinrich (74), German-born engineer, a pioneer of modern rocketry. In the 1950s he worked on the Redstone Ballistic program and in 1952 became director of operations at what was to become Kennedy Space Center. He directed the launch of the first American earth satellite and presided over the first American landing on the moon, retiring from the space program in 1974: d. Cocoa, FL, Oct. 10.

de Funes, Louis (born Louis de Funes de Galarza) (68), French film comedian; portrayed the average Frenchman and became one of the biggest box-office draws in that country: d. Nantes, France, Jan. 27.

de la Guardia, Ernesto (79), president of Panama (1956–60): d. Panama City, May 2.

de la Renta, Françoise (62), leader in the international fashion and social world; she was the wife of fashion designer Oscar de la Renta. She worked for several years as a contributing editor to *Vogue* magazine: d. New Yərk City, June 17.

Del Rio, Delores (born Lolita Dolores Martinez Asunsdo Lopez Negrette) (77), Mexican-born actress. In 1933 she introduced the two-piece swimsuit in *Flying Down to Rio*. She returned to Mexico in 1943 where she enjoyed a career on screen and stage and helped establish the Mexican film industry. In the 1960s she returned to Hollywood: d. Newport Beach, CA, April 11.

Demarest, William (91), actor; beginning in vaudeville, he entered a film career in 1927, appearing in more than 100 movies including *The Jazz Singer, The Lady Eve, Mr. Smith Goes to Washington,* and several Preston Sturges comedies. He also appeared on Broadway but was best known for the role of Uncle Charley in the television series *My Three Sons:* d. Palm Springs, CA, Dec. 28.

Demaret, Jimmy (73), golfer, was the first to win three Masters tournaments, in 1940, 1947, and 1950. He was named to the PGA (Professional Golfer Association) Hall of Fame in 1960 and the World Golf Hall of Fame in May 1983: d. Houston, Dec. 28.

Dempsey, Jack (William Harrison) (87), U.S. boxer; was the heavyweight boxing champion from 1919 to 1926. Known as the "Manassa Mauler," he won the heavyweight title in 1919 when he knocked out Jess Willard. He lost his title in 1926 to Gene Tunney in a ten-round decision. He also lost a rematch the following year in a fight characterized by a long count. That fight ended Dempsey's active ring career although he did stage a series of exhibitions from 1931 to 1942. Dempsey drew boxing's first million-dollar gate in fighting Georges Carpentier. Dempsey also appeared on Broadway, made a movie, and ran a New York restaurant: d. New York City, May 31.

Denby, Edwin (80), poet and dance critic; he began his career as a critic with *Modern Music* magazine (1936–42) and from there went to *The New York Herald Tribune* (1942–45). Thereafter he devoted himself to free-lance writing. He wrote two books of dance criticism and several volumes of poetry: d. Searsport, ME, July 12.

Denham, Reginald (89), British-born director, actor, and playwright; directed *Dial M for Murder* on Broadway as well as seven British films. He also wrote several plays and 100 television scripts: d. Englewood, NJ, Feb. 4.

Dietz, Howard (86), songwriter; wrote the words to such popular standards as *Dancing in the Dark, That's Entertainment,* and *You and the Night and the Music.* Over the years Dietz collaborated with such composers as Jerome Kern, George Gershwin, and Vernon Duke. After 1929, however, he wrote mostly with Arthur Schwartz: d. New York City, July 30.

Dobbs, Farrell (76), pioneer union leader of the Teamsters. He left the Teamsters in 1939 to become national labor secretary of the Socialist Workers Party. He sought the U.S. presidency four times: d. Pinole, CA, Oct. 31.

Docking, Robert (57), Democratic governor of Kansas (1967–75): d. Arkansas City, KS, Oct. 8.

Dodson, Owen (68), poet, novelist, playwright, and teacher; was for 20 years professor of drama at Howard University and was an influential figure in black drama: d. New York City, June 21.

Dorticos Torrado, Osvaldo (64), Cuban president under Fidel Castro (1959–76); had been minister of justice since 1980: d. Havana, June 23.

Drummond, Roscoe (81), reporter, editor, and syndicated columnist for more than 50 years. In his career he wrote for *The Christian Science Monitor, The New York Herald Tribune,* and *The Los Angeles Times* Syndicate. His column was titled "State of the Nation": d. Princeton, NJ, Sept. 30.

Egk, Werner (82), German composer; among his better-known operas were *Die Zaubergeige, Peer Gynt, Der Revisor,* and *Die Verlobung in San Domingo.* He conducted at the Berlin State Opera (1938–41) and served as head of the German Union of Composers (1941–45): d. Inning, West Germany, July 10.

Ehrlich, Simcha (67), deputy prime minister of Israel and leader of the Liberal Party. Ehrlich was Prime Minister Begin's minister of finance (1977–79) and as such steered Israel's economy to private enterprise after 30 years of socialism. In 1979 he became deputy prime minister, and in 1981 the minister of agriculture. He was also chairman of the government's settlement committee: d. Jerusalem, June 19.

Emerson, Faye (65), actress; was one of television's first late-night television interviewers: d. Deya, Majorca (Spain), March 9.

Everest, Frank F. (78), U.S. Air Force general; commanded the Fifth Air Force during the Korean War and later was commander of the air forces in Europe. He retired in 1961: d. Myrtle Beach, SC, Oct. 10.

Princess Faika (55), sister of King Farouk of Egypt: d. Cairo, Jan. 7.

Fante, John (74), novelist and screen writer. His novels are often set in California during the Great Depression: d. Woodland Hills, CA, May 8.

Feinsinger, Nathan (81), emeritus professor of law, University of Wisconsin; one of the leading U.S. labor mediators: d. Glenwood Springs, CO, Nov. 2.

Fellner, William J. (77), Hungarian-born Sterling Professor emeritus of Economics at Yale University. Known for his conservative views on inflation and monetary policy, he served as an economic adviser to Presidents Nixon and Ford: d. Washington, DC, Sept. 15.

Fénelon, Fania (74), Jewish survivor of the Holocaust; wrote the memoir *Playing for Time,* which described her experiences singing in the inmate orchestra at Auschwitz. The memoir was later made into a television movie: d. Paris, Dec. 20.

Fielding, Temple Hornaday (69), author of travel books; particularly well known for his travel books of Europe. He is credited as a pioneer of modern travel guidebooks: d. Palma, Majorca, May 18.

Fisher, Adrian (69), U.S. arms-control negotiator; was the first deputy director of the U.S. Arms Control and Disarmament Agency (1961–69). During his tenure with the agency he helped negotiate the 1963 Limited Test Ban Treaty and the 1968 Treaty for the Nonproliferation of Nuclear Weapons. In 1977 he was appointed a member of the U.S. Mission to the United Nations. A former dean of the Georgetown University

Pictorial Parade   UPI
Lynn Fontanne   *Ira Gershwin*

Law Center, he was a law professor at George Mason University (1979–82): d. Washington, DC, March 18.

Fontanne, Lynn (95), British-born stage actress; along with her husband Alfred Lunt (1892–1977) created one of the greatest husband and wife acting teams. They worked together in 27 productions, appearing in three Noel Coward plays—*Design for Living, Point Vaiaine,* and *Serena in Quadrille.* Actress Laurette Taylor brought Miss Fontanne to the United States where she made her debut in 1916 in *The Harp of Life.* She married Mr. Lunt after a three-year courtship on May 22, 1922. Their biggest hit was *O Mistress Mine,* which opened in New York in 1946 and ran for 451 performances. She later was seen appearing in *The Magnificent Yankee* and *Anastasia:* d. Genesee Depot, WI, July 30.

Ford, Aaron (80), U.S. representative (D-MS, 1935–43): d. Mississippi, July 8.

Foy, Eddie, Jr. (78), vaudeville and film actor, toured with his father and siblings in an act called Eddie Foy and the Seven Little Foys: d. Woodland Hills, CA, July 15.

Friendly, Alfred (71), managing editor of *The Washington Post* (1955–65): d. Washington, DC, Nov. 7.

Gates, Thomas S., Jr. (76), served as the secretary of the Navy (1957–59) and secretary of defense (1959–61): d. Philadelphia, March 25.

Gershwin, Ira (86), lyricist; collaborated with his brother George on numerous Broadway musicals, including *Lady Be Good, Porgy and Bess,* and the Pulitzer Prize winning *Of Thee I Sing.* He also provided the lyrics for Kurt Weill's songs for *Lady in the Dark,* Harold Arlen's compositions for the remake of *A Star Is Born,* and Jerome Kern's songs for the movie *Cover Girl. My One and Only,* the hit musical that opened on Broadway in 1983, had a score of George and Ira Gershwin songs taken from other theatrical works: d. Beverly Hills, CA, August 17.

Ginastera, Alberto (67), Argentine composer; his operas *Bomarzo* and *Beatrix Cenci* received wide attention for segments considered vocal and sexually explicit. He also composed concertos, vocal and chamber music, and film scores: d. Geneva, June 25.

Godowsky, Leopold, 2d (82), inventor, with his friend Leopold Mannes, of the Kodachrome color photography process: d. New York City, Feb. 18.

Goyen, William (68), novelist and short-story writer; his books include *The House of Breath, Ghost and Flesh, In a Farther Country, The Faces of Blood Kindred, The Fair Sisters,* and *Come the Restorer:* d. Los Angeles, August 30.

Gramm, Donald (56), American bass-baritone. His work was divided between opera and concert appearances; he sang regularly with the Metropolitan and New York City Operas and with opera companies, symphony orchestras, and chamber series throughout the United States: d. New York City, June 2.

Grimm, Charles John (85), first baseman and baseball manager; he played 20 years in the major leagues, mostly with the Pittsburgh Pirates and the Chicago Cubs. As a manager he led the Chicago Cubs to National League pennants (1932, 1935, and 1945): d. Scottsdale, AZ, Nov. 15.

Gruenther, Alfred M. (84), U.S. Army general; was supreme military commander of the North Atlantic Treaty Organization (NATO) (1953–56). He became a four-star general at the age of 53, the youngest in Army history. During World War II he was the deputy chief of staff under Gen. Dwight Eisenhower, chief of staff of the Fifth Army under Gen. Mark W. Clark, and deputy commanding general of the U.S. forces in Austria. After the war he was deputy commandant of the National War College, director of the staff of the Joint Chiefs of Staff, and the Army's deputy chief of staff for plans and operations. He became chief of staff at NATO headquarters in 1951: d. Washington, DC, May 30.

Guthrie, Marjorie (65), wife of folksinger Woody Guthrie; she devoted the last 15 years of her life to creating an awareness of Huntington's chorea, a hereditary disease: d. New York City, March 13.

Hackett, Joan (49), actress; well known for her supporting role in the film *Only When I Laugh,* for which she won an Oscar nomination. She also appeared in several New York stage productions: d. Encino, CA, Oct. 8.

Halas, George Stanley (88), owner of the Chicago Bears of the National Football League. He was one of the pioneers of professional football and was the last survivor of a group of 12 men who founded modern professional football at a Canton, OH, automobile agency in 1920. He coached 40 seasons for the Bears, winning six championships before retiring in 1968. In 1970 he was elected president of the NFL's National Conference: d. Chicago, Oct. 31.

Hanks, Nancy (55), chairman of the U.S. National Endowment for the Arts and the National Council on the Arts (1969–77): d. New York City, Jan. 7.

Hartline, H. Keffer (79), professor of biophysics at Rockefeller University (1953–74); he shared the 1967 Nobel Prize for Physiology: d. Fallston, MD, March 17.

Heaton, Leonard (80), surgeon general of the Army (1959–1969); Heaton had been the personal physician of President Dwight Eisenhower: d. Washington, DC, Sept. 10.

Hildebrand, Joel (101), chemist; faculty member at the University of California from 1913 until 1952, when he was forced by age restrictions to take emeritus status. He continued to teach graduate students, to conduct research projects, and to write until a few months prior to his death. His last published paper was in 1981. On his 100th birthday, the Joel Hildebrand chair of chemistry was established: d. Kensington, CA, April 30.

Hines, Earl (Fatha) (77), jazz pianist; known as the father of modern jazz piano. He worked with Louis Armstrong in the late 1920s, virtually redefining jazz piano. In the 1930s and 1940s he led a Chicago big band: d. Oakland, CA, April 22.

Hoffer, Eric (80), author/philosopher and dock worker; his first book, *The True Believer,* was published in 1951. Despite success as a writer he remained a dock worker until his retirement in 1967. During his working years he wrote between work assignments. For a time he also lectured at the University of California at Berkeley and wrote a column for *The San Francisco Examiner.* Other Hoffer books include *The Passionate State of Mind* (1955), *The Ordeal of Change* (1963), *Temper of Our Time* (1967), *Working and Thinking on the Waterfront* (1967), *First Things, Last Things* (1970), *Reflections on the Human Condition* (1972), *In Our Time* (1976), and *Before the Sabbath* (1979): d. San Francisco, May 21.

Hoffman, Julius J. (87), U.S. federal district judge; presided over the Chicago Seven conspiracy trial of 1969–70, where five of the defendants were found guilty, but none were ever sent to jail. Black Panther leader Bobby Seale was one of the eight original defendants. But after he called Hoffman a "pig" and a "fascist" and subsequently was bound and gagged in the courtroom, his case was separated from the other seven, and he was never tried: d. Chicago, July 1.

Holyoake, Sir Keith (79), New Zealand politician; he served as prime minister for 11 weeks in 1957 and from 1960 until 1972. Sir Keith was governor-general of New Zealand (1977–80): d. New Zealand, Dec. 8.

Hovde, Frederick (75), president of Purdue University (1946–71): d. Lafayette, IN, March 1.

King Idris I (93), king of Libya (1951–69): d. Cairo, May 25.

Illia, Arturo (82), president of Argentina (1963–66): d. Córdoba, Argentina, Jan. 18.

Ingersoll, Stuart (84), U.S. Navy admiral. During his career he was a commander of the U.S. Sixth and Seventh Fleets, superintendent of the U.S. Naval Academy, and head of the Naval War College. Gerald Ford and Jimmy Carter served under his command: d. Newport, RI, Jan. 29.

Jacobs, Paul (53), pianist (1962–83) and harpsichordist (1974–83) of the New York Philharmonic Orchestra: d. New York City, Sept. 25.

James, Harry (67), band leader and trumpet player; a major figure of the swing era, he played with Benny Goodman in the late 1930s before forming his own band in 1939. He was married to the actress Betty Grable for a number of years: d. Las Vegas, NV, July 5.

Johnson, Gen. Harold (71), Army chief of staff under President Lyndon Johnson (1964–68): d. Washington, DC, Sept. 24.

Jones, Carolyn (50), actress; best known for her role as Morticia in the television series *The Addams Family.* Among her several movies are *Marjorie Morningstar, The Road to Bali, The Man Who Knew Too Much, The Seven Year Itch, The Tender Trap,* and *Ice Palace:* d. Los Angeles, CA, August 3.

Jones, Willie (58), baseball player; third baseman for the Philadelphia Phillies team that won the 1950 National League pennant. He began his major-league career in 1947, retiring in 1961: d. Cincinnati, OH, Oct. 18.

Jordan, Len B. (84), Idaho Republican politician; was governor of the state (1951–55) and in 1962 was appointed to the U.S. Senate, and thereafter elected, serving until 1973: d. Boise, ID, June 30.

Kahn, Herman (61), futurist and nuclear strategist; founded the Hudson Institute in 1961 after rising to prominence with the publication of his first book *On Thermonuclear War* (1960). In the 1940s he had begun his career as a physicist and mathematician for aviation companies and the Rand Corporation: d. Chappaqua, NY, July 7.

Kaplan, Mordecai M. (102), Lithuanian-born Jewish rabbi; founder of the Jewish Reconstructionist movement and emeritus professor at the Jewish Theological Seminary of America, where he taught from 1909 to 1963. Rabbi Kaplan is credited with creating the ceremony of the bat mitzvah for Jewish girls: d. New York City, Nov. 8.

Keats, Ezra J. (67), award-winning illustrator and writer of children's books. He illustrated 33 books, 22 of which he also wrote: d. New York City, May 6.

Kline, Nathan S. (66), psychiatrist; pioneered the use of tranquilizers and antidepressants in the treatment of mental illness. He won the Lasker Award for medicine in 1956 and 1964: d. Orangeburg, NY, Feb. 11.

Knox, James Cardinal (69), archbishop of Melbourne (1967–74), was the first Australian to serve in the Vatican's administrative body: d. Rome, June 26.

Koestler, Arthur (77), Hungarian-born writer; perhaps best known for his novel *Darkness at Noon* (1941), which examined revolutionary politics. Mr. Koestler, a Zionist as a young man, was a Communist for a time (1932–38), but he later disavowed that ideology because of its totalitarianism. As a correspondent for *The London News Chronicle,* he covered the Spanish Civil War. He wrote at first in Hungarian and German but switched to English in 1940. In 1945 he became a British subject. He wrote some 30 books, including six novels and four volumes of autobiography, as well as a brief memoir in a 1949 anthology *The God That Failed.* In recent years he had belonged to a British organization dedicated to "the right to die with dignity." Mr. Koestler, along with his wife Cynthia, apparently committed suicide: d. London, March 3.

Kotar, Douglas Allan (32), New York Giant football running back (1974–81): d. Pittsburgh, PA, Dec. 16.

Kullman, Charles (80), opera tenor; sang at New York's Metropolitan Opera (1935–60): d. New Haven, CT, Feb. 8.

La Follette, Suzanne (89), conservative writer and editor; was the founding editor of several magazines including *The National Review.* An early feminist, she was also the author of the books *Concerning Women* (1926) and *Art in America* (1929). She ran unsuccessfully for the U.S. House of Representatives on the Conservative Party ticket in 1964: d. Palo Alto, CA, April 23.

H. Keffer Hartline	*Eric Hoffer*	*Harry James*	*Herman Kahn*
UPI	UPI	UPI	UPI

UPI   UPI   UPI   UPI

Mary Livingstone   *Lloyd McBride*   *Raymond Massey*   *William E. Miller*

Lansky, Meyer (born Maier Suchowljansky) (80), reputed financial expert of organized crime; he was, according to law-enforcement officials, once director of Murder Inc. and for decades a leader in organized crime. He went to jail only once —for two months on a gambling charge: d. Miami Beach, FL, Jan. 15.

Ledbetter, Bob (49), National Football League backfield coach of the New York Jets (1977–83) and Giants, which he had joined earlier in the year: d. Smithtown, NY, Oct. 7.

Leonard, Emil John (Dutch) (74), major league baseball pitcher who played 21 seasons for the Washington Senators before retiring in 1953: d. Springfield, IL, April 17.

Leopold III (81), king of Belgium (1934–51); he abdicated the throne in 1951 in favor of his son Prince Baudouin because his surrender to invading Nazi forces during World War II prompted suspicions that he might be a Nazi sympathizer: d. Brussels, Sept. 25.

LeSourd, Catherine Marshall (68), author; was the widow of Peter Marshall, a Presbyterian minister who served as chaplain to the U.S. Senate (1947–49). She wrote the best-selling biography *A Man Called Peter* (1951): d. Boynton Beach, FL, March 18.

Lewis, Oren R. (80), federal district judge in Alexandria, VA; wrote a school desegregation opinion that was the basis of the Supreme Court's landmark ruling in *Brown v. Board of Education*: d. Arlington, VA, June 12.

Lewis, Robert A. (65), copilot of the Enola Gay, the B-29 that dropped the atomic bomb on Hiroshima, Japan: d. Newport News, VA, June 18.

Liao Chengzhi (75), a political leader of Communist China; he was the Communist Party's expert on Taiwan and the chief negotiator in talks with Britain on the future of Hong Kong: d. Peking, June 10.

Liberace, George (71), bandleader and violinist; was a performer with his brother, the pianist Liberace, for some years: d. Las Vegas, NV, Oct. 16.

Livingstone, Mary (77), radio and television personality; the wife of the late comedian Jack Benny: d. Holmby Hills, CA, June 30.

Llewellyn, Richard (76), Welsh-born novelist and playwright; his first novel, *How Green Was My Valley* (1939), became an international best-seller: d. Dublin, Ireland, Nov. 30.

Lofts, Nora (79), British writer of about 50 historical novels: d. Bury St. Edmunds, England, Sept. 10.

McBride, Lloyd (67), president of United Steelworkers of America (1977–83): d. Whitehall, PA, Nov. 6.

McCall, Tom (69), governor of Oregon (1967–75), A Republican, he was known for his strong stand in protecting Oregon's environment: d. Portland, OR, Jan. 8.

McDonald, Lawrence Patton (48), conservative U.S. congressman (D-GA, 1975–83): d. aboard the Korean airliner shot down by the Soviets, Aug. 31 (U.S. time).

Macdonald, Ross (born Kenneth Millar) (67), famous for his detective novels featuring the private eye Lew Archer: d. Santa Barbara, CA, July 11.

Maclean, Donald (69), British-born Soviet spy; was recruited by the Soviets while at Cambridge University in the 1930s. He entered the British Foreign Service in 1935 and passed information to the Soviets. In 1944 he was assigned to Washington. He betrayed U.S. atomic secrets to the Soviets and in 1951 defected to the USSR: d. Moscow, March 6.

Markevitch, Igor (70), Russian-born conductor and composer. He conducted the Stockholm Philharmonic, Montreal Symphony, the Paris Lamoureux, and the Boston Symphony orchestras and the Spanish Radio-Television Orchestra. His compositions include ballets, an oratorio, piano concerto, and a cantata: d. Antibes, France, March 7.

Martin, Freddy (76), tenor saxophonist and band leader for more than 50 years; he helped establish the "sweet" sound in jazz.

His career took off in 1941 when his band recorded *Tonight We Love:* d. Newport Beach, CA, Sept. 30.

Massey, Raymond (86), Canadian-born actor; had a long career in the theater, motion pictures, and television and was probably best known for his stage and movie performances of Lincoln in *Abe Lincoln in Illinois*. He also played the role of Dr. Gillespie in the successful television series *Dr. Kildare*. Among other stage performances of importance were those in *Ethan Frome, Pygmalion, J.B., Julius Caesar, The Father,* and a dramatic reading of *John Brown's Body*. Born into a prominent Canadian family, his family controlled the Massey-Ferguson implement company where he was employed briefly. His numerous films include *The Fountainhead, The Scarlet Pimpernel, The Prisoner of Zenda, Mourning Becomes Electra, Arsenic and Old Lace, East of Eden,* and *Seven Angry Men:* d. Los Angeles, CA, July 29.

Masters, John (68), writer; born in India, he made use of his knowledge of India in his writings, which include *Bhowani Junction, Nightrunners of Bengal,* and *Coromandel*. He became an American citizen in 1954: d. Albuquerque, NM, May 6.

Medeiros, Humberto Cardinal (67), Portuguese-born Roman Catholic archbishop of Boston (1970–83); he had been a cardinal since 1973: d. Boston, Sept. 17.

Meem, John Gaw (88), architect; was a leading exponent of the "Santa Fe style" of architecture that uses traditional Spanish pueblo lines and building styles: d. Santa Fe, NM, August 4.

Mennin, Peter (60), American composer and president of the Juilliard School of Music (1962–83). He established the Juilliard Theater Center in 1968 and the American Opera Center in 1970. As a composer, Mennin wrote nine symphonies, instrumental concertos, music for chorus and orchestra, as well as chamber and other choral music: d. New York City, June 17.

Micombero, Michel (43), president of Burundi (1966–76): d. Mogadishu, Somalia, July 16.

Miller, William E. (69), U.S. congressman (R-NY, 1951–65); was chairman of the Republican National Committee (1961–64) and Barry Goldwater's vice-presidential running mate in 1964: d. Buffalo, NY, June 24.

Model, Lisette (76), photographer and teacher; she was a proponent of strong realism in her photography: d. New York City, March 30.

Monroe, Marion (85), child psychologist, who along with Dr. William Gray authored the "Dick and Jane" series of school reading books: d. Long Beach, CA, June 25.

Moorehead, Alan (73), Australian-born writer; was a distinguished World War II correspondent for *The Daily Express* of London and later was a popular author of works of history, biography, and reportage. He contributed about 40 articles to *The New Yorker* magazine, and his books include *Gallipoli, The White Nile, The Blue Nile, Cooper's Creek,* and *The Fatal Impact:* d. London, Sept. 29.

Moross, Jerome (69), composer who wrote symphonic works and scores for Broadway shows and motion pictures. For the dance he wrote the ballet *American Patterns* (1937), and dancer Ruth Page gave the premiere of his *Frankie and Johnnie* in 1938. In 1943 his *First Symphony* premiered: d. Miami, FL, July 25.

Nakagawa, Ichiro (57), Japanese politician. A conservative, he had served in the government of Prime Minister Zenko Suzuki and previously was minister of agriculture. He had made a bid for the presidency of his party, the governing Liberal Democratic Party, two months prior to his death: d. Hokkaido, Japan, Jan. 9.

Nearing, Scott (100), U.S. environmentalist, pacifist, and radical; Dr. Nearing was a leader of the "back to the land" movement in the years since World War II. His antiwar book during World War II, *The Great Madness*, got him charged with sedition, but

Movie Still Archives

David Niven

Movie Still Archives

Pat O'Brien

UPI

Nikolai Podgorny

UPI

Frank Reynolds

he was acquitted. His other books include his autobiography *The Making of a Radical* (1972) and *Living The Good Life* (1954): d. Harborside, ME, August 24.

Nicholson, John Robert (81), Canadian political figure; served as lieutenant-governor of British Columbia (1968–73). Nicholson served in Parliament and held several cabinet posts in Lester Pearson's government (1963–68): d. Vancouver, British Columbia, Oct. 8.

Niven, David (73), British-born actor, known for his debonair charm and urbane wit. He was a popular actor who first rose to prominence in the 1930s with such films as *Dodsworth* (1936), *Dawn Patrol* (1938), and *Wuthering Heights* (1939). Other important performances were those of *Stairway to Heaven* (1946), *The Bishop's Wife* (1947), *Enchantment* (1948), *The Moon Is Blue* (1953), and his Academy Award winning performance in *Separate Tables* (1958). In television, Niven served as host of *The David Niven Show* (1959–64) and starred in *The Rogues* (1964–65). Late in his life, he was a successful author: d. Château-d'Oex, Switzerland, July 29.

Noble, Alfred Houston (88), four-star Marine Corps general, he retired in 1956 after 40 years of service: d. LaJolla, CA, Sept. 27.

Notte, John A., Jr. (73), Democratic governor of Rhode Island (1961–63): d. Providence, RI, March 6.

O'Brien, Pat (born William Joseph) (83), motion-picture actor; in a movie career that began in the 1920s he appeared in more than 100 films. The better-known are *The Front Page, Knute Rockne*, and *Ragtime*: d. Santa Monica, CA, Oct. 15.

Payne, Robert (71), author; had written more than 100 books. Beginning as a novelist and poet, he later turned to writing biography. His subjects included Hitler, Stalin, Lenin, Trotsky, Gandhi, Charlie Chaplin, Greta Garbo, Shakespeare, Alexander the Great, and Sun Yat-sen: d. Bermuda, Feb. 18.

Pearlroth, Norbert (89), sole researcher for the *Ripley's Believe It or Not* newspaper feature for 52 years, beginning in 1923: d. Brooklyn, NY, April 14.

Pelshe, Arvid Y. (84), member of the Politburo of the USSR. A former party chief of Latvia, he had been on the Politburo since 1966 and was the only present leader to have participated in the 1917 revolution: d. Moscow, May 29.

Perlman, Alfred E. (80), railroad industrialist; was president of the New York Central Railroad (1954–68) and head of Penn Central until its demise in 1970. Then he became president and later chairman of Western Pacific: d. San Francisco, April 30.

Pevsner, Sir Nikolaus (81), German-born architectural critic and historian; he went to England in 1933, a refugee from Nazi Germany, after working as an assistant keeper in the Dresden Art Gallery (1924–28). His early publications were *The Baroque Architecture of Leipzig* (1928) and *Italian Painting from the End of the Renaissance to the End of the Rococo* (1927–30). Later he took a position at Birkbeck College in the University of London (1944–69). Sir Nikolaus was the author of such classic studies as *Pioneers of the Modern Movement: From William Morris to Walter Gropius, An Outline of European Architecture, The Englishness of English Art*, and *A History of Building Types*. He also was the originator and chief contributor to the 46-volume survey *The Buildings of England* and editor and coordinator of the multivolumed *Pelican History of Art*. In addition he was a Slade Professor of Fine Arts at Cambridge (1949–55) and held a Slade professorship at Oxford (1968–69): d. London, August 18.

Pickens, Slim (born Louis Bert Lindley, Jr.) (64), cowboy movie actor; was a rodeo performer before he got into movies. He appeared in countless Westerns and in television before appearing as the B-52 bombardier in the film *Dr. Strangelove:* d. Modesto, CA, Dec. 8.

Plimpton, Francis T. P. (82), diplomat and lawyer; founded one of New York City's largest law firms. He served as deputy U.S.

representative to the United Nations in the 1960s and president of the American Bar Association (1968–70): d. Huntington, NY, July 30.

Podgorny, Nikolai (79), president of the USSR (1965–77): d. USSR, Jan. 12 (announced).

Preston, Maurice A. (70), U.S. military general; was a World War II bomber pilot who led the 1943 "Black Thursday" raid on a German ball-bearing works in Bavaria that resulted in the loss of 600 U.S. officers and men and 65 U.S. planes. He was a commander of the U.S. Air Force in Europe and in Japan during the 1960s: d. Bethesda, MD, Jan. 25.

Pridi Phanomyong (82), former prime minister of Siam (now Thailand); he served briefly in 1946 after leading the "Free Thai" underground group that aided the Allies in World War II. He was one of the leaders of the 1932 revolution that transformed the absolute monarchy in Siam to a constitutional one: d. Paris, May 2.

Qiao Guanhua (70), foreign minister of China (1974–76): d. Peking, Sept. 22.

Raphaelson, Samson (87), playwright; wrote more than a dozen plays, including *The Jazz Singer*. He also wrote the screenplays *Heaven Can Wait, The Merry Widow*, and *Trouble in Paradise:* d. New York City, July 16.

Renault, Mary (born Mary Challans) (78), novelist, based her books on the history and legends of Greece. Her many best-selling novels included *The King Must Die, The Bull From the Sea*, and *The Last of the Wine*. A nurse turned novelist, she wrote most recently *Funeral Games* (1981), which completed a trilogy on Alexander the Great begun in 1970: d. Cape Town, South Africa, Dec. 13.

Rey, Jean (80), one of the founders of the European Economic Community; was a member of the European Commission beginning in 1958 and served as president (1967–70): d. Liège, Belgium, May 19.

Reynolds, Frank (59), news anchorman; he had appeared on ABC's *World News Tonight* since 1978. Reynolds began his career in Chicago. In 1965 he became an ABC network correspondent in Washington and in 1968 became a co-anchor on ABC's *Evening News*. He was replaced soon by Harry Reasoner and spent the next several years covering major news stories for the network: d. Washington, DC, July 20.

Richardson, Sir Ralph (80), British actor; his theatrical reputation was among the best in British theater. He was well known for his portrayal of Falstaff in *Henry IV*. For years critics considered him as an actor who could represent the ordinary man. In addition to outstanding work on the stage (most recently in *Inner Voices*), he worked in several films, including *The Fallen Idol, Anna Karenina*, and *Long Day's Journey Into Night*, and sometimes in television, including the 1982 television version of *Witness for the Prosecution:* d. London, Oct. 10.

Robinson, Joan (79), English economist; was a collaborator of John Maynard Keynes. She began lecturing at Cambridge University in the early 1930s and was made a professor of economics in 1965. She retired in 1971. She questioned the direction of professional economics, writing *Economics of Imperfect Competition* (1933): d. Cambridge, England, Aug. 5.

Robinson, John A. T. (64), Anglican theologian; wrote the controversial *Honest to God* (1962): d. Yorkshire, England, Dec. 5.

Rochet, Waldeck (77), French Communist Party leader (1964–72): d. Paris, Feb. 15.

Rosenthal, Benjamin (59), U.S. congressman (D-NY, 1962–83): d. Washington, DC, Jan. 4.

St. George, Katharine (86), U.S. congresswoman (R-NY, 1947–65): d. Tuxedo Park, NY, May 2.

Samore, Antonio Cardinal (77), Italian churchman, leading Vatican diplomat and expert on Latin America; he became a cardinal in 1967: d. Rome, Feb. 3.

Savitch, Jessica (35), reporter for the NBC television network (1977–83); she was killed when the car in which she was riding fell into the Delaware Canal: d. near New Hope, PA, Oct. 23.

Schanze, Edwin Stansbury (79), U.S. Naval rear admiral; served aboard the battleship *Washington* during World War II and survived 53 kamikaze attacks: d. New York City, Dec. 25.

Schnitzler, William F. (79), American labor leader; was the secretary-treasurer of the American Federation of Labor and the Congress of Industrial Organizations (1955–69) after having been made secretary-treasurer of the AFL in 1952 prior to its merger with the CIO: d. Lewes, DE, June 17.

Seghers, Anna (born Netti Reiling) (82) German author, wrote the novel *The Seventh Cross* (1942). She became a member of the Communist Party in 1928 and fled Nazi Germany in 1933 for France and later Mexico. She returned to the Soviet sector of Berlin in 1947. In 1951 she received the Stalin Peace Prize for *The Dead Stay Young:* d. East Berlin, June 1.

Sert, José (80), Spanish-born architect; was dean of the Harvard University School of Design (1953–69). A follower of the architect Le Corbusier, he merged elements of Le Corbusier with his more Mediterranean background. Committed to the modernist movement in architecture, he served as president of the International Congresses for Modern Architecture which lasted until 1956. He was awarded the Gold Medal of the American Institute of Architects in 1980: d. Barcelona, Spain, March 15.

Shearer, Norma (80), actress; was one of the Hollywood stars of the 1920s and 1930s and won an Academy Award in 1930 for her role in *The Divorcee:* d. Woodland Hills, CA, June 12.

Shoup, David M. (78), commandant of the U.S. Marine Corps and a World War II hero; he retired in 1963. He was an early and outspoken critic of the Vietnam war: d. Alexandria, VA, Jan. 13.

Skolsky, Sidney (78), Broadway and Hollywood reporter, wrote a column "Tintypes," which appeared in various newspapers for more than 50 years: d. Los Angeles, CA, May 3.

Slezak, Walter (80), Austrian-born character actor; was a matinee idol in Germany in the 1920s, and in the 1930s appeared in Broadway musicals. He made a number of films, including Alfred Hitchcock's *Lifeboat* (1944). In 1954 he appeared in the Broadway musical *Fanny*, for which he won a Tony Award, and in 1957 sang in the operetta *Gypsy Baron* at New York's Metropolitan Opera: d. Flower Hill, NY, April 22.

Spiegelman, Sol (68), microbiologist and Columbia University professor; internationally known for his research on genetics, virology, and the molecular basis of cancer: d. New York City, Jan. 21.

Stankiewicz, Richard (60), American sculptor; created whimsical scrap-iron constructions that made him one of the pioneers of "junk art": d. Worthington, MA, March 27.

Stapleton, Ruth Carter (54), Baptist evangelist and spiritual healer; she was the sister of former U.S. President Jimmy Carter: d. Fayetteville, NC, Sept. 26.

Stead, Christina (80), Australian novelist; best known for her book *The Man Who Loved Children* (1940). She lived in Europe and the United States before returning to Australia in 1974: d. Sydney, Australia, March 31.

Steed, Thomas J. (79), U.S. congressman (D-OK, 1949–79): d. Shawnee, OK, June 8.

Stevens, Robert (83), secretary of the army (1953–55); was a major figure in the 1954 Army-Joseph McCarthy Senate hearings: d. Edison, NJ, Jan. 30.

Struble, Arthur D. (88), U.S. Navy commander; known as one of the Navy's foremost experts on minesweeping operations and amphibious landings. d. Chevy Chase, MD, May 1.

Strudwick, Shepperd (75), character actor; appeared in more than 200 roles in films, television, and on the stage in a career spanning 50 years: d. New York City, Jan. 15.

Sun Yefang (75), Chinese economist; was imprisoned at the beginning of the Cultural Revolution in 1966. His ideas later were accepted officially and helped to make up the basis of Deng Xiaoping's economic modernization program: d. Peking, Feb. 22.

Swanson, Gloria (born Gloria Svensson) (84), actress; best known for her performance in *Sunset Boulevard* (1950). Miss Swanson began her career as an extra at the age of 14. She played in Mack Sennett comedies and reached stardom in Cecil B. DeMille melodramas. Through the 1920s she was Hollywood's top box-office draw and reportedly earned $8 million between 1918 and 1929. After filming *Sunset Boulevard* she appeared on Broadway in *Twentieth Century* and again in 1971 in *Butterflies Are Free:* d. New York City, April 4.

Taft, Charles P. (85), mayor of Cincinnati (1955–57) and son of former U.S. President William Howard Taft: d. Cincinnati, OH, June 24.

Tailleferre, Germaine (91), French composer; last surviving member of the group known as Les Six: d. Paris, Nov. 7.

Tan Zhenlin (81), Chinese political leader; was most recently the deputy chairman of the Communist Party's Central Advisory Commission. He was among the prominent figures purged in the Cultural Revolution of 1966–76: d. Peking, Sept. 30.

Tarsis, Valery (76), Soviet author; wrote the novel *Ward Seven*, based on his experiences in a Soviet asylum: d. Bern, Switzerland, March 3.

Tate, James H. J. (73), Democratic mayor of Philadelphia (1962–72): d. Somers Point, NJ, May 27.

Terayama, Shuji (47), avant-garde Japanese poet, playwright, and filmmaker. In 1975 his play *Knock* had caused such a stir in Tokyo that members of the cast were arrested: d. Tokyo, May 4.

Troisgros, Jean (56), French chef. One of the top chefs in France, he and his brother Pierre ran their restaurant Les Frères Troisgros in Roanne. Theirs is one of only 18 restaurants in France to merit three Michelin stars: d. Vittel, France, August 8.

Tuck, William Munford (86), conservative Democratic governor of Virginia (1946–50); he served as U.S. congressman from 1953 until his retirement in 1969: d. South Boston, VA, June 9.

Tunner, William H. (76), lieutenant general in the U.S. Air Force; regarded in his time as the Air Force's foremost authority on airlifts, he directed the Berlin airlift of 1948–49: d. Gloucester, VA, April 6.

Umberto II (78), king of Italy (May–June 1946). His father, Victor Emmanuel III, was associated with Mussolini; in 1944 in an attempt to save the monarchy, Victor transferred "royal prerogatives" to his son, making Umberto the de facto sovereign until his father's formal abdication. In 1946, Italy voted to become a republic, and under the republican constitution, Umberto, his queen, and their male descendants were barred from entering Italy again: d. Geneva, Switzerland, March 18.

Van Brocklin, Norm (57), professional football player and coach; as a quarterback Van Brocklin led the Los Angeles Rams and the Philadelphia Eagles to championships. He later coached the Minnesota Vikings and the Atlanta Falcons: d. Atlanta, GA, May 2.

Van Der Zee, James (96), photographer; first gained public acclaim at age 82 when a Metropolitan Museum of Art exhibition, "Harlem on My Mind," featured his work. He had begun working in Harlem around 1915 and recorded Harlem events for 60 years: d. Washington, DC, May 15.

Vargas, Alberto (87), Peruvian-born artist; famous for his "Vargas girls" pinups that appeared in *Esquire* and *Playboy* magazines: d. Los Angeles, CA, Dec. 30, 1982, announced Feb. 11, 1983.

Vinogradov, Ivan M. (92), Soviet mathematician; one of the foremost experts on number theory. Since 1932 he had directed the Soviet Institute of Mathematics: d. Moscow, March 20.

Jessica Savitch

UPI

Walter Slezak

UPI

Sol Spiegelman

UPI

Gloria Swanson

Jim Pozarik/Gamma-Liaison

UPI	Wide World	Movie Still Archives	UPI
John Vorster	*Sir William Walton*	*Muddy Waters*	*Vic Wertz*

Von Euler, Ulf (78), Swedish biochemist; won the 1970 Nobel Prize for Medicine: d. Stockholm, March 10.

Vorster, John (Balthazar Johannes) (67), South African prime minister (1966–78); president (1978–79). A symbol of apartheid in South Africa, he became a member of the Nationalist Party with some difficulty because of his World War II affiliation with a group that espoused Fascism; he was elected to Parliament in 1953 and in 1961 became minister of justice. One of his more drastic measures while in that position was the Sabotage Act of 1962, whereby suspected subversives could be detained for up to 180 days without trial and stripped of their civil rights. As prime minister he made some overtures to leaders of neighboring black countries and black South Africans. He later served as the nation's president but resigned the office because of a scandal centering on a plan to use millions of dollars of government money without proper authorization to promote South Africa's image: d. Cape Town, Sept. 10.

Wallenstein, Alfred (84), music conductor; began his career as a cellist, occupying first-chair positions with the Chicago Symphony and the New York Philharmonic, and was a classical music pioneer on radio. In 1943 he was appointed music director of the Los Angeles Philharmonic, a position he held until 1956. Thereafter he was music director of the Caramoor Festival (1958–61), a guest conductor of major U.S. and European orchestras, and a member of the faculty at the Juilliard School: d. New York City, Feb. 8.

Walton, Sir William (80), British composer; best known for *Façade*, first performed in 1923. He lived for 15 years with Sacheverell (whom he had met at Oxford) and Edith and Osbert Sitwell, a famous British literary family, during which time he became a sort of unofficial composer-in-residence. He later worked at the home of society hostess Alice Wimborne. When she died she left him a small house and about $40,000. His works include *Belshazzar's Feast;* two symphonies; viola, violin, and cello concertos; and the opera *Troilus and Cressida*. He was knighted in 1951: d. on the island of Ischia, Italy, March 8.

Ward, Theodore (80), playwright; his major works include *Big White Fog* and *Our Lan':* d. Chicago, May 8.

Waterfield, Bob (62), football quarterback; in eight seasons with the Cleveland (later Los Angeles) Rams, he earned all-pro honors three times. He was inducted into the Pro Football Hall of Fame and coached the Rams from 1960–62: d. Burbank, CA, March 25.

Waters, Muddy (born McKinley Morganfield) (68), guitarist and singer; played a key role in the development of electric blues and rock 'n' roll. Known as a great singer of vernacular music as well as an innovative guitarist, he was widely imitated. In the 1970s, he received six Grammy awards: d. Downers Grove, IL, April 30.

Weiss, Louise (90), French feminist and oldest member of the European Parliament. Known as the Susan B. Anthony of France, she was an author, journalist, and pacifist. She led the women's suffrage movement in France, where women received the right to vote in 1944. The founder and editor of *L'Europe Nouvelle* from 1918 to 1943, she had been active in the French Resistance during World War II: d. Paris, May 26.

Wertz, Victor W. (Vic) (58), professional baseball player (1949–63); at his peak he regularly hit 20 home runs per year, and in 1956, one year after his recovery from polio, he hit 32 home runs: d. Detroit, MI, July 7.

West, Dame Rebecca (born Cicely Isabel Fairfield) (90), British writer; worked as a reporter and wrote political commentary, essays, history, and novels. She published her first book in 1916 and continued writing book reviews into the 1980s. Among her best-known journalistic writings are her accounts of the Nuremberg war-crimes trials. Her book about Yugoslavia, *Black Lamb and Grey Falcon*, is generally regarded as her masterpiece. Dame Rebecca began her literary career in 1911, writing for *The Freewoman*, a radical feminist journal. She remained a feminist all her life, calling the women's liberation movement "more fundamental than suffragism." She also wrote several novels. After a ten-year affair with H. G. Wells, by whom she had her only child, she married a Scottish banker: d. London, March 15.

Wibberley, Leonard (68), a journalist and author of more than 100 books, including *The Mouse That Roared* (1955): d. Santa Monica, CA, Nov. 22.

Widnall, William B. (77), U.S. representative (R-NJ, 1950–75): d. Ridgewood, NJ, Dec. 28.

Williams, John Bell (64), U.S. politician; was governor of Mississippi (1968–72) and a member of the U.S. House of Representatives (1947–67). He was known as a staunch segregationist. A Democrat, he was stripped of his seniority in the House in 1965 for supporting Republican Barry Goldwater in the 1964 presidential election: d. Brandon, MS, March 26.

Wilson, Dennis (39), drummer for the Beach Boys, a pop music group that specialized in the "surfing sound" of the 1960s. Some of the group's best known songs include *Slip on Through, Got to Know the Woman,* and *Cuddle Up:* d. Marina del Rey harbor, Dec. 28.

Winding Kai (I. Kai Chresten) (60), Danish-born American jazz trombonist; played with the Stan Kenton and Benny Goodman bands and in the 1950s developed a two-trombone sound when he teamed with J. J. Johnson: d. Yonkers, NY, May 6.

Yang Yong (70), Chinese military official; had served in the Chinese-Japanese War of 1937–45 and in the civil war against the Nationalists. He was a Red Army commander who led units of so-called Chinese volunteers in the final stages of the Korean War, and he commanded Chinese troops until they withdrew from North Korea in 1958. Purged at the start of the Cultural Revolution, he reappeared five years later: d. Peking, Jan. 6.

Young, Claude (Buddy) (57), college and professional football player; was an all-American running back at the University of Illinois. He turned pro in 1947 and played with the New York Yankees and Dallas Texans of the old American Football League and with the Baltimore Colts: d. near Terrell, TX, Sept. 4.

Young, Milton R. (85), U.S. senator (R-ND, 1945–81): d. Sun City, AZ, May 31.

Zablocki, Clement J. (71), U.S. representative (D-WI, 1949–83); served as chairman of the House Committee on Foreign Affairs: d. Washington, DC, Dec. 3.

Dame Rebecca West

Clement J. Zablocki

UPI

UPI

OCEANOGRAPHY

In the North Atlantic, a program for Subtropical Atlantic Climate Studies (STACS) has been set up to identify those processes that contribute most to the transport of heat and to obtain data for numerical modeling. In 1983 attention was directed toward the Florida Current near Miami, FL, since it is known that the largest poleward heat transport occurs between 20°N and 30°N and is more pronounced in the Atlantic than in the Pacific Ocean. Several techniques were being tested for long-term monitoring of the Florida Current.

A multidisciplinary program in the Atlantic Ocean also was studying the warm core rings formed when a meander separates to the north of the Gulf Stream, using satellite infrared images to follow their movement and interaction with the Gulf Stream and the slope water. Such rings are the major variable in the offshore waters of the East Coast of the United States. Typically, two or three separate rings exist at any given time, usually migrating at a rate of 3 to 5 km (2 to 3 mi) per day in a south-westerly direction between the Gulf Stream and the continental shelf. Cold core rings are generated from meanders into the Sargasso sea and have been studied previously. All such rings can have complex life cycles that may involve repeated interaction with the Gulf Stream. The warm core rings have been found to be biologically rich, but they show rapid changes and large chemical fluxes as cold water organisms invade the isolated eddies.

El Niño. A major disruption of oceanic circulation in the southeast Pacific Ocean, known as El Niño, was experienced in 1982–83. During the upset, westward wind flow ceases or even reverses, and the normal upwelling of cold, nutrient-rich water along Ecuador and Peru ceases, with a marked decline of the fisheries. The latest event has also had disastrous effects on weather patterns worldwide. It became the strongest warming of the equatorial Pacific in the 20th century. Heavy rains in coastal Peru and drought in northern Australia and Indonesia resulted. Even the pattern of the jet stream in the upper atmosphere of the northern hemisphere changed because of the 5°C to 7°C (9°F to 13°F) increase above normal in the average surface water temperatures near the equator. This warming brought heavy winter storms to the West Coast of the United States, heavy snows in the Rockies, and a mild winter in the East. Other associated weather anomalies were felt in Europe and North Africa. So vast have been the natural, human, and economic effects over most of the globe that a multinational study, the Tropical Ocean Global Atmospheric Experiment (TOGA), will begin in 1984.

By August 1983 researchers were optimistic about El Niño's departure because both the ocean and the atmosphere seemed to be returning to normal. The tongue of unseasonable warm water that had stretched 13 000 km (8,000 mi) along the equator from the South American coast to the archipelagoes of the western Pacific had shrunk 5 000 km (3,100 mi) back toward the coast. The maximum warming had then dropped from 5°C to 1°C (9°F to 2°F) above normal sea surface temperature in the central Pacific; near the coast the anomaly had fallen from 7°C to 5°C. The atmospheric system, the Southern Oscillation, had reached a record extreme in late 1982 as the trade winds reversed in direction in some areas; but by May the trades were blowing normally again.

The 1982–83 El Niño-Southern Oscillation (ENSO) event broke all the rules based on earlier observations and triggered new suggestions about the interrelated ocean-atmosphere system and the weather that results from it. Intensive monitoring which began with this event will be continued over a ten-year period to make such ENSO events more predictable in the future. Already, moored current meter, sea level, hydrographic, and surface-drifter measurements are available that indicate that sea level rose 22 cm (8.6 inches) at the Galapagos Islands and the thermocline (depth of warmed surface water) was displaced downward by 50 to 70 m (164 to 230 ft) along the equator and the South American coast at the event's height.

The Deep Sea Drilling Project (DSDP). In recent cruises the DSDP has investigated the mechanics of subduction and the deformation that results from it where the Pacific Ocean crust thrusts beneath Japan. Also studied was evidence of intense submarine volcanic activity in the western Pacific Ocean. An unmanned, computer-controlled earthquake monitoring station was placed in a borehole drilled into the basaltic lavas of the deep Pacific sea floor 1,000 mi (1 600 km) southwest of Tahiti. The installation will provide information for an area far away from land-based seismic stations. The instrument package was planted 500 ft (152 m) into the oceanic crust some 18,000 feet (5 km) below the sea surface. During five days of testing, more than 60 earthquakes were recorded.

In November the *Glomar Challenger*, which had carried out the DSDP program for many years, was retired and replaced by an oil-industry exploration drilling ship capable of utilizing a drill string 9 144 m (5 mi) long.

Deep Sea Vents. The presence of hydrothermal vents in the Marianas Trough, as first identified from DSDP-drill data, has been verified on the basis of excessive quantities of methane in solution. Biologically and geologically, the setting for vents in the Marianas Trough, located in the western Pacific above a subduction zone, is in contrast to that for the vents previously found in the East Pacific Rise.

DAVID A. MCGILL
U.S. Coast Guard Academy

OHIO

As employment conditions improved slightly, Ohioans turned in 1983 to worrying about the increase in their state tax burden.

Politics and the Election. U.S. Sen. John H. Glenn, America's first astronaut to orbit the earth, opened his official campaign for the Democratic presidential nomination on April 21 in his home town, New Concord. In a change that might have some advantage for Glenn's candidacy, the Ohio legislature advanced the state's primary date to the first Tuesday after the first Monday in May. Politicians had held that the effect of Ohio's voting choices had been dimmed because the traditional early June primary came after many major states had made their choices.

Statewide voting in the November 8 election passed judgment on three constitutional amendment proposals. One proposal would have required 60% of both houses of the legislature to approve revenue-raising bills, rather than a simple majority; it was defeated by a wide margin. A second proposal would have canceled (as of June 30, 1984) tax laws that had been enacted after Jan. 1, 1983—in effect reducing the state income tax by about half; this, too, was rejected by the voters. A third proposal, to raise from 19 to 21 the legal age for buying or consuming intoxicating liquor, also was defeated.

In city elections, Toledo elected its first woman mayor, Mrs. Donna Owens (R). Thomas C. Sawyer in Akron and Sam D. Purses in Canton unseated Republican incumbents. The loser in Canton, Stanley A. Cmich, had been mayor for 20 years. Former Cleveland Mayor Carl B. Stokes, the first black to hold the office of mayor in a major U.S. city, rallied to win a Cleveland municipal judgeship.

Taxes and the Budget. Proponents of the proposed constitutional amendments to require a three-fifths vote of both houses of the legislature for passage of future tax increases, and to cancel 1983 tax legislation, acted after the legislature, at the behest of Gov. Richard F. Celeste (D), had increased tax rates so that some individuals' state income taxes soared by 90%. The general fund budget for July 1, 1983–June 30, 1985, totaled $16.9 billion, of which $8.1 billion in the biennium's first half represented an increase of 15.7% over that of the previous fiscal year. With federal and miscellaneous fund additions, biennium receipts were estimated at $27.6 billion. The top recipients of state money would be educational and welfare agencies.

The Water Belt. Governors and other officials from Ohio, Indiana, Illinois, Michigan, Wisconsin, and Minnesota met in Cleveland in May for a "Great Lakes Economic Summit." They generally agreed to present a united front on common interests and to oppose preferential treatment in the granting of federal funds to other areas, including the Sunbelt. Pledges were made to protect the Great Lakes' Water Belt environment and to prevent diversion of the lake's water.

Business. The Republic Steel Corp., with about 7,000 employees in its Cleveland plants and headquarters, and the Pittsburgh-based Jones & Laughlin Steel Co., with 3,600 employees at its Cleveland operations, in September proposed a merger. Agreement that the merger would not violate antitrust laws would be needed, as would the approval of the shareholders concerned.

The Honda Motor Co. of Japan officially dedicated its $250 million plant at Marysville, near Columbus, in April. Employment was expected to increase from 1,600 to about 2,000 by 1985. Honda's nearby motorcycle factory, opened in 1979, might be expanded for motorcycle engine production.

The expectation that construction costs of the Zimmer nuclear power plant, 30 mi (48 km) east of Cincinnati, might rise to $3.5 billion (from a 1969 estimate of $240 million) could cause the Cincinnati Gas and Electric Co. to abandon the project, according to its president. Two other Ohio utility companies are partners in the project. As allegations of mismanagement were made, the Nuclear Regulatory Commission had halted safety-related construction.

Other Events. Prospective homeowners in May lined up days in advance for mortgage and home-improvement loans at lowered interest rates (about 10%) through the state's issuance of $400 million in tax-exempt bonds.

In Cleveland, construction was completed on an elegant new theater for the city's famous Play House.

FBI figures showed a significant decrease in the incidence of felonies in major Ohio cities from 1981 to 1982.

JOHN F. HUTH, JR., Former Reporter
"The Plain Dealer," Cleveland

OHIO • Information Highlights

Area: 41,330 sq mi (107 045 km²).
Population (1982 est.): 10,791,000.
Chief Cities (1980 census): Columbus, the capital, 565,032; Cleveland, 573,822; Cincinnati, 385,457; Toledo, 354,635; Akron, 237,177; Dayton, 193,444.
Government (1983): *Chief Officers*—governor, Richard F. Celeste (D); lt. gov., Myrl H. Shoemaker (D). *General Assembly*—Senate, 33 members; House of Representatives, 99 members.
State Finances (fiscal year 1982): *Revenues,* $15,308,000,000; *expenditures,* $13,742,000,000.
Personal Income (1982): $115,217,000,000; per capita, $10,677.
Labor Force (July 1983): *Nonagricultural wage and salary earners,* 4,089,200; *unemployed,* 578,700 (10.9% of total force).
Education: *Enrollment* (fall 1981)—public elementary schools, 1,292,831; public secondary, 615,723; colleges and universities (1982), 532,361. *Public school expenditures* (1981–82), $4,591,000,000.

OKLAHOMA

The Oklahoma Legislature faced a revenue shortfall when it convened in January 1983. State revenues had decreased starting in November 1982 because of a decline in the oil boom, and increased unemployment related to the recession. Thus, gross production and state sales-tax revenue decreased sharply. State agencies suffered five months of allocation cutbacks beginning in fall 1982, and they were further reduced by $90 million or 5.3% on a selective basis in the new budget. General revenue expenditures fell to $1.689 billion, to create a standstill budget. Basic support for higher education, common schools, and vocational education was maintained. Funding for the Department of Human Services was reduced. The Department of Transportation received less in appropriated funds but would benefit from a $43.9 million increase in state-dedicated revenues and federal funds. The Corrections Department received a $13.9 million increase in order to fund inmate education and work-release programs, and to expand facilities. New funds for water-development programs were reduced drastically. State employees, including school teachers, received no salary increases.

Gov. George Nigh held to his campaign promises of no general tax increases over the opposition of some legislative leaders. The legislators agreed to his request to use almost $200 million in several reserve funds to forestall further budget cuts and made available a $37 million sinking bond fund for the next session. Estimates included a $90 million shortfall for the 1983 fiscal year and a $250 million reduction in 1984.

The Legislature acted to permit branch banking and to raise the age to 21 for consumption of 3.2 beer. A new state law requires children under age four to be restrained for safety when riding in automobiles. A bill was signed to authorize cities and counties to establish enterprise zones to create jobs. A commission was established to govern pari-mutuel horse racing.

Special Session. Governor Nigh convened a special legislative session on September 19.

The five-day session met to consider special funding requests to rebuild prison facilities destroyed during a riot at Conner Correctional Center, Hominy, on August 29. Lesser incidents occurred at Lexington and McAlester near the tenth anniversary of the 1973 McAlester State Penitentiary riots. The Legislature rejected Governor Nigh's plan to tap a reserve fund; instead it approved $2.5 million from funds appropriated to the Corrections Department for repair to the Hominy prison.

House Speaker. The special session saw Jim L. Barker, Muskogee Democrat, elected to replace Dan Draper as House speaker. Draper and Majority Leader Joe Fitzgibbon were suspended from the House after conviction on vote fraud charges.

Appointees. Dan Fick was appointed as director of the Horse Racing Commission. Robert Fulton was named director of the Department of Human Services.

The Economy. Governor Nigh remained optimistic about an upturn in the state's economy, though it was lagging behind the national recovery. Unemployment decreased. The housing construction industries improved. Heavy manufacturing and oil and gas production showed little change. Retail trade was better.

JOHN W. WOOD, *University of Oklahoma*

Order is restored at the Conner Correctional Center, Hominy, after an August 29 riot. Damage exceeded $3 million.

"The Hominy News-Progress"

ONTARIO

Despite pressure from the federal government, Premier William Davis made it quite clear in 1983 that Ontario was not going to become officially a bilingual province. He preferred to continue the current policy of giving Franco-Ontarians access to government services in French as a matter of fact without enshrining it in law as a right. In keeping with this policy, Intergovernment Affairs Minister Thomas Wells indicated that Franco-Ontarians would be guaranteed primary and secondary schooling in French.

In January the financial community was shaken when the province seized three trust companies—Crown Trust, Seaway Trust, and Greymac Trust—citing doubts about their lending practices and beginning an investigation into $152 million advanced by them in third mortgages. These mortgages were part of a deal in which apartments originally purchased for $270 million were eventually sold to mysterious numbered companies for $500 million.

Ontario Hydro came under heavy attack during the year from politicians and environmentalists for its plans to add 12 more nuclear reactors to its existing ten. With 50% excess generating capacity, several plants have already been mothballed. Hydro's debt stood at C$16 billion, and fears of rising costs and environmental risks have led to demands that further work on the Darlington nuclear-power plant be stopped. Added embarrassment was caused by heavy-water leaks at Bruce and Douglas Point, and at Pickering, where leaking pressure tubes have been a major problem and four out of five reactors had to be shut down. Some 60% of Ontario's electricity is generated by nuclear power.

To speed the rate of economic recovery, the May budget of Treasurer Frank Miller was slanted toward helping business. Business received $358 million in tax cuts and incentives,

while individual taxpayers picked up the tab with a 5% surcharge on the provincial income tax, disguised as a "social services" tax. Health insurance premiums went up 5%, and liquor and cigarette taxes were raised. To create jobs, $82 million was to be spent on roads and construction projects and $36 million on youth employment schemes. Government spending was cut by $300 million, largely in grants to municipalities and education. An unemployment rate of 11.7% was anticipated, along with a deficit of $2.7 billion and anticipated real growth of 1.9%.

Ontario's universities felt the full weight of government curbs on spending. Funded well below the inflation rate for the last few years and encountering increasing enrollment pressure in September, they had to curtail admission to many programs. Education Minister Bette Stephenson was forced to admit that a university place could no longer be guaranteed to every qualified student in the province, abandoning a guarantee given 25 years earlier by John Robarts.

Plans to celebrate the province's bicentennial in 1984, the 200th anniversary of the arrival of Loyalist settlers from the United States after the American Revolution, proved unexpectedly divisive. Many saw the planned celebration as an insult to Franco-Ontarians and the province's ethnic groups and as a ploy to generate a spirit of well-being in an election year.

PETER J. KING
Carleton University

OREGON

In 1983 the citizens of Oregon were concerned with economics. There were insufficient funds to operate some of the state's schools, despite high property and state income taxes and a legislature working to generate more revenues. In addition the timber industry continued depressed.

Legislature. The state legislature failed in regular session to pass any form of property-tax relief. Oregon property-tax and income-tax rates are among the nation's highest. The Oregon constitution prohibits a sales tax.

Called into special session by Gov. Victor Atiyeh, the legislature referred to the people a constitutional amendment removing the sales-tax prohibition and initiating a 4% sales tax. However, it imposed as a prerequisite that the initiative first be approved by a majority of the state's property-taxing jurisdictions.

In other action the legislature imposed stiffer drunk-driving penalties, lowered the legal definition of intoxication, and passed a $14 million appropriation to convert Eastern Oregon State Hospital in Pendleton to a 350-bed medium-security prison. Taxes were increased on cigarettes, gasoline, drivers' licenses, and auto

---

ONTARIO • Information Highlights

Area: 412,582 sq mi (1 068 587 km²).

Population (July 1983 est.): 8,822,000.

Chief Cities (1981 census): Toronto, the provincial capital, 599,217; Ottawa, the federal capital, 295,163; North York, 559,521; Mississauga, 315,056; Hamilton, 306,434; London, 254,280.

Government (1983): *Chief Officers*—lt. gov., John Black Aird; premier, William G. Davis (Progressive Conservative); atty. gen., Roy McMurtry. *Legislature*—Legislative Assembly, 125 members.

Education (1982–83): Enrollment—elementary and secondary schools, 1,847,400 pupils; postsecondary, 246,200 students.

Public Finance (1983 fiscal year, est.): *Revenues,* $21,369,200,000; *expenditures,* $23,232,100,000.

Personal Income (average weekly salary, March 1983): $402.70

Unemployment Rate (August 1983, seasonally adjusted): 10.1%.

(All monetary figures are in Canadian dollars.)

OREGON • Information Highlights

Area: 97,073 sq mi (251 419 km²).
Population (1982 est.): 2,649,000.
Chief Cities (1980 census): Salem, the capital, 89,233; Portland, 366,383; Eugene, 105,624.
Government (1983): *Chief Officers—*governor, Victor Atiyeh (R); secretary of state, Norma Paulus (R). *Legislative Assembly—*Senate, 30 members; House of Representatives, 60 members.
State Finances (fiscal year 1982): *Revenues,* $4,382,000,000; *expenditures,* $4,210,000,000.
Personal Income (1982): $27,373,000,000; per capita, $10,335.
Labor Force (July 1983): *Nonagricultural wage and salary earners,* 942,200; *unemployed,* 127,800 (9.5% of total force).
Education: *Enrollment* (fall 1981)—public elementary schools, 315,388; public secondary, 141,777; colleges and universities (fall 1982), 141,312 students. *Public school expenditures* (1981–82), $1,608,595,000.

registration. An 8% income-tax surcharge was enacted, and the $1,000 personal income-tax exemption was withdrawn.

Education. High property taxes prompted widespread resistance to local school district levies. Schools were closed in several districts, although on September 20, Oregon residents approved tax rates for 50 of 56 districts, and Lincoln County schools were reopened. Junction City schools remained closed until Nov. 8, 1983. About 40% of the state's elementary and secondary students began school in September without any guarantee that their districts could operate the entire school year. Faculty layoffs continued in state higher institutions.

Followers of the Bagwan Shree Rajneesh, a guru from India, have become the majority in Antelope, OR, and have secured control of the Antelope school board. It has been alleged that the tenets of the cult are being taught in the Antelope public school and that the faculty, entirely cult members, is not state certified. State Superintendent Vern Duncan, after an investigation, freed state basic school support monies for use in the Antelope district. The intrusion of the cult and the development of a new city, Rajneesh Puram, came under fire as well.

Economy. Though the market for some timber products showed signs of improvement, Oregon's timber and wood-products industry continued to suffer from depression. Plywood-mill closures and consolidation continued apace, and Boise Cascade's large paper mill in Salem was closed permanently. Prolonged strikes idled workers in several plants that had been reopened during the year. Many timber operators called for recision or other relief from timber contracts with the federal government that were bid some years ago at extremely high prices.

The first trees were harvested in an area that was largely destroyed by the "Tillamook Burn" forest fire some 50 years earlier.

L. Carl Brandhorst
Western Oregon State College, Monmouth

OTTAWA

In Ottawa, 1983 was a relatively prosperous year. The C$250 million Rideau Centre shopping-convention-hotel complex opened. A tight housing supply—with an apartment vacancy rate of about 1% and escalating house prices—made Ottawa one of the strongest housing markets in Canada. In the first six months housing starts were 77% above the same period in 1982, and single-family-dwelling starts were up by 500%. The federal government began a series of construction projects. The airport terminal was receiving a $50 million facelift. Architects were selected to begin on a new National Art Gallery and a new National Museum building, one at each end of the Interprovincial Bridge. Plans also were announced for a new Public Archives building in nearby Hull, Quebec, across the Ottawa River.

Transportation was much on Ottawans' minds during the year. Facing deficits of $11.3 million and federal plans to eliminate a subsidy of $1.6 million, the Ottawa and Outaouais bus systems may have to drop the single-fare service enjoyed by commuters. The city's motorists suffered frustration as well. Traffic on the Queensway, the East-West freeway, was disrupted badly by construction of intersections for the new Transitway. The start of a project to reconstruct and widen the freeway threatened reduced traffic flows for up to seven years.

The University of Ottawa and the Civic Hospital opened a new Heart Institute. The 118-bed, $13.5 million facility features unique preventive and rehabilitation centers.

After the September Korean airliner accident, the Ottawa City Council helped abort the tour of the Moscow Circus.

Peter J. King, *Carleton University*

Ottawa's Rideau Centre complex opened during 1983.

Robert Moon

Pakistan took in up to 3 million Afghan refugees. Above, children attend "school" at a refugee camp in Peshawar.

PAKISTAN

Gen. Mohammed Zia ul-Haq completed his sixth year of martial law rule on July 5, 1983; he has held power longer than any previous Pakistani ruler except President Mohammed Ayub Khan (1958–69). On August 12, Zia announced a phased 18-month program for return to a civilian order. The 1973 constitution, suspended at the time of the 1977 military coup, was to be restored, but with several modifications. The powers of the president were to be strengthened, those of the prime minister correspondingly weakened, and a National Security Council established to ensure a continuing military role in government. Local elections, held in September on a nonpartisan basis, were to be followed in 1984 with polls at the provincial level, and in 1985 with parliamentary elections. Whether political parties, still officially banned but openly active, would be permitted to contest provincial or national elections was still uncertain. Zia once again made clear that his top priority was "to carry forward the process of Islamization and to consolidate the measures already taken in this behalf to a degree that no future government can reverse."

Far from assuaging demands for an end to military rule, Zia's announcements served instead as a prelude to increased public protest. The eight-party Movement for the Restoration of Democracy (MRD) began its antigovernment campaign as scheduled on August 14, Pakistan's 36th anniversary of independence. Although MRD leaders attempted to keep the demonstrations peaceful, violence erupted, particularly in the rural areas of Sind Province.

Outbreaks earlier in the year included sectarian clashes between Sunnis and Shias in Karachi and protests by women against changes in the law of evidence. Based on scriptural interpretation, the new law equates the testimony of two women with that of one man.

Economy. Pakistan's economy continued to show improvement. The midyear Economic Survey showed the GNP to have risen 6.5% in fiscal 1983, up from 5.4% the previous year. Exports were estimated to have increased 13% and remittances by overseas workers 28%; imports declined, apparently in response to Pakistan's more flexible foreign-exchange policies. Thus, the country expected a balance-of-payments surplus for the first time in ten years. Despite price increases in oil and gas, inflation was held to 5%.

External assistance was increased. The Aid-Pakistan Consortium pledged $1.406 billion (U.S.), a 30% increase from the previous year. The effect of such aid, however, was mitigated by heavy debt-service requirements. One estimate indicated that 93% of Consortium aid in fiscal 1982 was used to repay old debts and interest charges. The government continued to encourage private foreign enterprise, hosting prospective investors from the United States and the Gulf region. Pakistan embarked on its sixth five-year plan, with priority on such "human needs" as literacy, health, clean drinking water, and village electrification.

Foreign Affairs. Relations with India improved throughout most of the year. The India-

---

PAKISTAN • Information Highlights

Official Name: Islamic Republic of Pakistan.
Location: South Asia.
Area: 310,402 sq mi (803 943 km²).
Population (July 1983 est.): 96,874,000.
Government: *Head of state and government,* Mohammed Zia ul-Haq, president (took power July 5, 1977). *Legislature*—Parliament: Senate and National Assembly (dissolved July 1977); Majlis-i-Shura (Federal Advisory Council, formed Dec. 1981).
Monetary Unit: Rupee (13.24 rupees equal U.S.$1, Nov. 18, 1983).
Gross National Product (1982 U.S.$): $25,800,-000,000.
Economic Indexes (1982): *Consumer Prices* (1971 = 100), all items, 372.9; food, 378.6. *Manufacturing Production* (1981, 1975 = 100), 169.
Foreign Trade (1982 U.S.$): *Imports,* $5,298,000,000; *exports,* $2,381,000,000.

Pakistan Joint Commission met in June to carry on the process of normalization in cultural, trade, and other spheres. President Zia attended the Nonaligned Summit in March, and Foreign Minister Sahabzada Yaqub Khan participated in the inaugural meeting of the South Asia Regional Cooperation Organization in August. The improvement in Indo-Pakistani relations suffered a setback in late August, however, when remarks by Indian leaders concerning Pakistan's internal political situation drew strong protests from Islamabad.

On the Afghan front as well, there appeared to be progress toward negotiated settlement during the first half of the year but deterioration of the situation later, when Afghan and Soviet planes bombed Pakistani border areas. UN-sponsored negotiations over the Afghan conflict continued in Geneva. Visits to Pakistan by U.S. Cabinet members George Shultz in July and Caspar Weinberger in October brought encouragement to Afghan refugees and promises of further military support to Pakistan.

WILLIAM L. RICHTER
Kansas State University

PARAGUAY

On Aug. 25, 1983, Gen. Alfredo Stroessner was sworn in for his seventh consecutive term as president of Paraguay. In the February elections he had won 90% of the popular vote, with the remaining portion roughly split between Enzo Doldán of the Radical Liberal Party (PLR) and Fulvio Hugo Celauro of the Liberal Party (PL). Other parties boycotted the elections. Eight exiled politicians, who attempted to return on election day, were turned back by airport authorities. By gaining a majority of the popular vote, the official Colorado Party automatically won two thirds of the seats in both the 60-member lower chamber of congress and the 30-member senate.

Suppression of Dissent. During the interval between general elections and the inauguration, a wave of repression swept the country. In April the government impeded the distribution of ABC, the Asunción daily newspaper with the largest circulation, and its editor was imprisoned in July. A popular radio station was silenced in July, and an affiliated weekly news magazine was denied permission to publish. Arrests of 30 persons in May were attributed to the government's curbing of opposition activity, as well as divisions within the Colorado Party prior to internal elections within the party in July. Among those detained—and in some cases tortured—were employees of the Banco Paraguayo de Datos, an independent organization reporting on economic and social conditions in the nation; university students; and trade unionists. Dissident members of the Colorado Party had led some industrial strikes.

Economy. A sharp economic downturn that had been evident in 1982 deepened in 1983, because of the worldwide recession, an over-evaluation of the guaraní, and a decline in construction. Demand for Paraguayan exports fell, except for soybeans and cotton. The trade deficit at the end of April reached $90 million. In July, the guaraní fell to a rate of 330 to the dollar on the black market. An official rate of 126 guaranies remained for the public debt, with rates of Gs143 and Gs160 for essential imports and exports. Inflation was set at 30% in July, with midyear price increases on diesel oil and gasohol already in place. In May, private banks accepted a proposal made by industry for a 36-month debt moratorium. At that time 60 companies were on the verge of bankruptcy, and business sources claimed that 80% of productive capacity was idle. In July unemployment was placed at 15% and worsening. As neighboring Brazil and Argentina devalued their currencies and sought more realistic exchange rates, as well as export policies, Paraguayan exports became less competitive.

With the Itaipú dam inaugurated and the first of its hydroelectric power generators in operation, Paraguay pressed for a start-up of civil works, valued at $1.5 billion (U.S.), on the Yacyretá hydroelectric project. Yacyretá, to be produced jointly with Argentina, will be one of the biggest dams in the world upon completion in 1990–91. In September, Argentina remained dissatisfied with the exchange rate for the guaraní and Paraguay's demand for a 25% share of the civil works for its own companies.

Foreign Relations. On January 12 the foreign ministry submitted the name of Mario López Escobar, its current representative before the Organization of American States (OAS), as the Paraguayan candidate for the post of OAS secretary-general. An election will be held in November 1984 for a replacement of incumbent Alejandro Orfila, who is not eligible for reelection.

LARRY L. PIPPIN, *University of the Pacific*

PARAGUAY • Information Highlights

Official Name: Republic of Paraguay.
Location: Central South America.
Area: 157,000 sq mi (406 630 km²).
Population (July 1983 est.): 3,526,000.
Chief Cities (1982 census): Asunción, the capital, 455,517; San Lorenzo, 74,632; Fernando de la Mora, 66,810; Lambaré, 61,722.
Government: *Head of state and government,* Gen. Alfredo Stroessner, president (took office Aug. 1954). *Legislature*—Congress: Senate and Chamber of Deputies.
Monetary Unit: Guarani (126 guaranies equal U.S.$1, July 1983).
Gross Domestic Product (1981 U.S.$): $4,600,-000,000.
Economic Index (1982): *Consumer Prices* (1970 = 100), all items, 407.1; food, 411.9.
Foreign Trade (1982 U.S.$): *Imports,* $586,000,000; *exports,* $378,000,000.

PENNSYLVANIA

The year began joyfully as the Penn State football team won the national championship on New Year's Day. The rest of the year was less euphoric as a weak economy brought hard times to many and difficult decisions to the state's political leaders.

The Economy. Although the national recession officially ended in November 1982, according to the index of coincidental indicators in Pennsylvania the recovery began in March 1983. By August unemployment was still 11.5% in the state and double that figure in many localities. Steel continued to decline in spite of mergers, tax incentives, and wage concessions. Agriculture, the largest single industry, suffered a serious drought, which reduced yields.

Budgets and Taxes. The poor economy, along with cutbacks in federal aid, presented a large deficit for the fiscal year ending in June. Republican Gov. Dick Thornburgh proposed a lean budget of $7.9 billion. Democratic Majority Leader James Manderino responded with PennPRIDE, the Pennsylvania Program for Recovery, Investment, Development and Education. To be funded by an emergency surtax of 1% on incomes, the proposal was designed to reduce unemployment. After months of wrangling, the Democratic-controlled House and the Republican-controlled Senate passed a budget slightly higher than Thornburgh's proposal with an income tax increase from 2.2% to 2.45%. Few of the PennPRIDE elements were included.

Unemployment Compensation. A second deficit problem was a debt to the federal government of $2.7 billion in the state's unemployment compensation fund. The state faced a September cutoff of federal contributions if it could not agree on a plan to bring the fund into balance. After Governor Thornburgh's plan met with little enthusiasm, the state AFL-CIO and Chamber of Commerce worked together to fashion a compromise. The legislature quickly enacted the agreement into law.

Other Legislation. In perhaps the most controversial piece of legislation, the legislators increased their own salaries from $25,000 to $35,000, their first pay increase since 1979.

Another controversial issue, restrictions on abortions, briefly returned. Republican Rep. Stephen Freind introduced a bill that would have denied funding to any organization that provided abortion counseling or referrals. With the changed composition of the legislature from 1982 and the focus on economic issues, the bill died quietly. Court challenges kept restrictive abortion legislation passed in 1982 from implementation. With the U.S. Supreme Court ruling similar provisions in laws from other states unconstitutional, several provisions of the 1982 act were expected to be overturned.

Administration. The effects of acts passed in 1982 were evident in 1983. Act 75, the welfare reform act, removed 68,000 "transitionally needy" clients from the welfare rolls. These single, able-bodied poor people between the ages of 18 and 45 were to receive job placement priority in a public "workfare" program that would lead to permanent employment. Under 10% obtained "workfare" jobs, and an even smaller percentage advanced to permanent positions. Protesters camped out in the Capitol for two weeks in the fall in a futile call for repeal of Act 75. Also in the fall, state prison guards protested that legislation mandating prison terms had so overtaxed the prison system that overcrowding had become dangerous.

Items of great controversy in the past received little attention. The undamaged nuclear reactor at Three Mile Island remained dormant as court fights continued, while federal funds supported the cleanup of the damaged reactor.

ROBERT E. O'CONNOR
The Pennsylvania State University

PENNSYLVANIA • Information Highlights

Area: 45,308 sq mi (117 348 km²).
Population (1982 est.): 11,865,000.
Chief Cities (1980 census): Harrisburg, the capital, 53,264; Philadelphia, 1,688,210; Pittsburgh, 423,959; Erie, 119,123; Allentown, 103,758; Scranton, 88,117.
Government (1983): *Chief Officers*—governor, Dick Thornburgh (R); lt. gov., William W. Scranton III (R). *General Assembly*—Senate, 50 members; House of Representatives, 203 members.
State Finances (fiscal year 1982): *Revenues,* $16,290,000,000; *expenditures,* $15,328,000,000.
Personal Income (1982): $129,985,000,000; per capita, $10,955.
Labor Force (July 1983): *Nonagricultural wage and salary earners,* 4,468,100; *unemployed,* 616,800 (10.9% of total force).
Education: *Enrollment* (fall 1981)—public elementary schools, 1,839,015; public secondary, 652,194; colleges and universities (fall 1982), 529,341. *Public school expenditures* (1981–82), $5,692,000,000.

PERU

An increasingly violent war with leftist guerrillas, torrential rains in the north and a drought in the south that caused $900 million in damage, and a July agreement with foreign banks restructuring the foreign debt were significant events for Peru in 1983.

Martial Law. Fernando Belaúnde Terry, one of Latin America's few democratically elected presidents, renewed a state of emergency August 19 that suspended most civil rights in seven provinces in the highland departments of Ayacucho, Apurimac, and Huancavelica. Guerrillas belonging to the group called *Sendero Luminoso* (Shining Path) dynamited factories, police stations, and other public facilities in Lima and northern cities. Their attacks had been stepped up in December 1982, when Belaúnde Terry ordered soldiers into the central highlands to eliminate the group.

In the bloodiest incident in the capital to date, *Sendero Luminoso* terrorists attacked the national headquarters of Belaúnde's Popular Action Party (AP) with dynamite and machine guns on July 11. Two party activists and 32 others were wounded.

Floods and Drought. Torrential downpours between late January and April devastated much of northern and central Peru. The rain was said to be caused by shifts in Pacific coastal currents and winds brought about by the movement of warm water from the South Pacific, a pattern known as El Niño. Ocean temperatures, which rose to 30°C (86°F) in June, began dropping in October.

On April 11, Agriculture Minister Mirko Cuculiza estimated that $137 million in potatoes, sugar, cotton, and other crops on 277,500 acres (111 000 ha) had been totally destroyed. Another 665,000 acres (266 000 ha) suffered damage estimated at $46 million. It was also said that Peru would have to import 130,000 metric tons of rice and 90,000 tons of sugar.

PETROPERU, the national oil corporation, estimated April 15 that floods and landslides caused $100 million damage to oil wells, oil and water pipelines, roads, and pumping stations. Oil production on the northern coast dropped from 74,200 barrels per day (bpd) in September 1982 to 52,100 bpd in March 1983. More rain in the next two months raised petroleum production losses to $200 million.

To combat leftist guerrillas, a state of emergency and national security plan were put into effect.

J. C. Criton/Sygma

PERU • Information Highlights

Official Name: Republic of Peru.
Location: West Coast of South America.
Area: 496,000 sq mi (1 284 640 km²).
Population (July 1983 est.): 19,161,000.
Government: *Head of state,* Fernando Belaúnde Terry, president (took office July 1980). *Head of government,* Fernando Schwalb Lopez Aldana, prime minister (took office Jan. 3, 1983). *Legislature*—Congress: Senate and Chamber of Deputies.
Monetary Unit: Sol (2,101 soles equal U.S.$1, Oct. 31, 1983).
Gross National Product (1981 U.S.$): $19,500,-000,000.
Economic Index (1982): *Consumer Prices* (1970= 100), all items, 4,063.7; food, 4,415.5.
Foreign Trade (1981 U.S.$): *Imports,* $3,803,000,000; *exports,* $3,255,000,000.

Economy. In early June the Central Bank expanded the money supply in an effort to improve the economy, which faced a 9.8% drop in gross domestic product and an expected inflation rate of 150%—easily the worst combination of figures in Peruvian economic history. In a further effort to "tranquilize" the economy, the bank said it would not increase interest rates and announced periodic declines, averaging 3.8%, in the value of the *sol.* By the end of October, the official rate for the *sol* was 2,101 per U.S.$1.

A July agreement with representatives of 275 foreign banks and the International Monetary Fund refinanced $2.38 billion (U.S.) in private commercial loans, provided $450 million in capital, and extended over an eight-year period interest and principal payments on another $1 billion of Peru's $11.6 billion foreign debt.

The government agreed to a drastic austerity program in an effort to control the deficit and repay the foreign loans. It was embarrassed in May by the discovery by an IMF team of $137 million for the purchase of 26 French Mirage 2000 fighter planes and $263 million in other military orders.

Exports were expected to reach $3.03 billion, nearly $500 million less than original 1983 estimates. Imports were expected to reach $2.79 billion, or 26% less than in 1982. The expected modest surplus would probably be wiped out by other military purchases.

One bright spot was an expected 14% increase in mineral exports.

Foreign Policy. In addition to upgrading its Air Force, Peru signed contracts with Dutch firms, worth $116 million, to install modern electronic equipment in the *Almirante Grau* battle cruiser and several Freisland-class destroyers purchased in the 1970s.

In a July 22 speech in Caracas, Venezuela, on the 200th anniversary of the birth of Simón Bolívar, Belaúnde Terry revived an old South American dream by calling for a common passport, a common Andean peso, and projects to connect the Amazon and Orinoco river basins.

NEALE J. PEARSON, *Texas Tech University*

PHILADELPHIA

W. Wilson Goode became the first black mayor of the City of Brotherly Love in 1983.

The Primary. May 17 marked the failure of former Mayor Frank L. Rizzo to regain the office he held from 1972 to 1980. Known then for his tough talk on crime and sometimes divisive remarks on race, Rizzo in 1983 ran a campaign of mostly gentle rhetoric in which he stressed his record in city hall. The authenticity of the "new" Rizzo, however, was called into question by some strident, old-style statements. If Goode were elected, he said on several occasions, he would move to Italy. Moreover, Rizzo's slate included more longtime supporters than new faces.

W. Wilson Goode, 44, had been a member of the state Public Utilities Commission before serving as managing director of the city under outgoing Mayor William Green, Jr. New to electoral politics, Goode stressed his administrative experience and competence. Nationally recognized black leaders such as the Rev. Jesse Jackson visited Philadelphia to help in fundraising and voter registration, but Goode downplayed their involvement in his campaign. He also kept his distance from the more flamboyant local black leaders, such as State Sen. T. Milton Street. In a large voter turnout, Goode won the Democratic primary, 53% to 46%.

The greatly outnumbered Republicans, meanwhile, gave their nomination to John J. Egan, Jr., the wealthy 39-year-old chairman of the Philadelphia Stock Exchange. Egan, who had only recently changed parties, defeated former city controller (and basketball star) Thomas J. Gola and former U.S. Rep. Charles F. Dougherty.

General Election. Unlike Harold Washington in Chicago who campaigned against the regular Democratic organization, W. Wilson Goode sought to unite all elements of the party behind his candidacy. Joseph F. Smith, the party chairman and a Rizzo supporter, endorsed Goode the day after the primary. Rizzo himself later endorsed Goode, who continued to stress his administrative skills, as well as his family values and moral rectitude. His appeal was that of a personally honest, competent technocrat—a nonthreatening image to the white majority. Egan, meanwhile, contended that his business experience would bring new jobs to the city. A third candidate, former Democrat and city controller Thomas A. Leonard, ran as an independent.

On November 8, Philadelphians gave Goode a smashing victory: 55% of the vote, to 37% for Egan and 8% for Leonard. In an electorate that was 39% black, Goode won 98% of the black vote and about one fourth of the white vote.

ROBERT E. O'CONNOR
The Pennsylvania State University

PHILANTHROPY

Despite a multitude of economic problems, Americans contributed a record $60.3 billion to a cross section of more than 300,000 charitable organizations in 1982. This represented an increase of 11.7% from the amount given in 1981. Contributions were boosted substantially by a single bequest to a museum in California by the late J. Paul Getty. With inflation running at an annual rate of 3.0%, the real growth in charitable giving came to 7.8%; it was the second consecutive year in which philanthropic growth outpaced inflation.

Donors. Living individuals, traditionally the largest donor segment, gave an estimated $48.69 billion in 1982, an increase of 9.2%. Including bequests, individual giving accounted for 89.8% of all contributions in 1982; gifts from living individuals equaled 80.7%. Settlement of the Getty estate boosted bequests to their highest total ever and accounted for the overall double-digit increase. Totaling $5.45 billion and registering an increase of 56.1%, bequests accounted for an unusually high portion of all giving in 1982—9.0% as against the usual 6%.

Giving by foundations reached a record $3.15 billion in 1982, an increase of 3%; foundations accounted for 5.2% of the total philanthropic contribution. Corporations, meanwhile, increased their giving by 6.9% to a record $3.1 billion; that represented 5.1% of all contributions.

Donees. As every year, the largest share of the money went to religious organizations. In 1982 they received $28.06 billion, or 46.5% of the total and an increase of 12.9%. Much of this money was used for social services—such as food, day care, and aid for the less fortunate—at the local church level.

Contributions to education, social services, and health care also increased at double-digit rates. The educational community received $8.59 billion, or 14.2% of all contributions in 1982, an increase of 13.2%. Total giving to hospitals and health-related activities rose by 13.9% to $8.41 billion, or 13.9% of all charitable contributions. And social services—everything from scouting to care for the homeless—increased by 16.8% to a record $6.33 billion, or 10.5% of the total.

Giving to the arts and humanities reached a record $4.96 billion. Not including the Getty bequest, however, the total reflected an increase of only 6% from 1981—a considerable slowing. Gifts to civic organizations were up 5.6% to $1.67 billion, or 2.8% of the total. And giving to the "other" category—including international aid organizations—totaled $2.37 billion; this represented a 36% decline, primarily because of the vast sums collected in 1981 for earthquake victims in southern Italy.

FRED SCHNAUE, *American Association of Fund-Raising Counsel*

PHILIPPINES

The August 21 murder of opposition leader Benigno Aquino, Jr., plunged the Philippines into a political and civil unrest rooted in the struggle to succeed President Ferdinand E. Marcos, 65 and said to be ailing.

Politics. Former Senator Aquino, a longtime rival of Marcos, had been in self-imposed exile for three years in the United States. He was shot to death at Manila International Airport immediately upon his return to the Philippines. The political opposition quickly blamed the government, and protesters took to the streets. President Marcos countered the charge and condemned the assassination ''in the strongest possible terms.'' He accused his foes of ''an orchestrated attempt to spread panic,'' and he denied rumors that he was seriously ill and that he had declared martial law.

An estimated one million Filipinos lined Aquino's funeral procession in Manila on August 3. The most violent protests since Marcos came to power in 1965 occurred September 17, when 11 persons were killed. By mid-October a total of more than 50 had died in demonstrations throughout the country. Militant labor unionists and Marxist student leaders joined with moderate politicians in organizing the protests, but no political figure or organization emerged as an effective alternative likely to succeed Marcos.

President Marcos contended that the slaying had been carried out by a gunman hired by the Communists, and he appointed a five-member investigation panel. When the commission members (four retired Supreme Court justices and an assemblyman) resigned October 10 citing public doubts about their impartiality, Marcos announced that he would create a new panel composed of private citizens.

With rumors about the president's ill health persisting, political maneuvering among Marcos loyalists appeared to intensify. First Lady Imelda Marcos and military Chief of Staff Gen. Fabian C. Ver represented the dominant faction within the government. Gen. Fidel Ramos and Defense Minister Juan Ponce Enrile appeared to be losing influence. The paramilitary Philippine Constabulary earlier was moved from General Ramos' command to General Ver's. On October 31, attempting to clear up ''doubts about the issue of presidential succession,'' Marcos announced that if he were unable to govern, the prime minister (César E. Virata) would assume his responsibilities.

Economy. The political crisis provoked by Aquino's slaying intensified mounting economic difficulties. The peso had been devalued 7.3% in June and was devalued another 21.4% after the Aquino incident in October. Valued at 9.1 to the U.S. dollar at the end of 1982, the peso had a rate of 14 to the dollar after the October devaluation. To cushion the shock, prices were frozen and an increase in the minimum wage was postponed.

Suffering a shortage of dollars with which to repay foreign loans, the Philippines experienced a balance-of-payments deficit of $800 million in the quarter ending September 30. With a foreign debt of $17.5 billion ($6.5 billion short-term), the government faced the additional burden of a capital outflow of $200-500 million in the two months after Aquino's murder. Filipino businessmen began converting pesos into black-market dollars, while new foreign loans and investments slowed.

Insurgencies. The Muslim uprising in the southern Philippines, in which 10,000 insurgents had participated in the mid-1970s, had shrunk to a few hundred rebels by 1983.

Meanwhile, however, the Communist New People's Army appeared to have expanded dramatically, particularly in Muslim Mindanao but also in Samar and northern Luzon. Communist rebels numbered between 7,000 and 10,000, with an estimated 100,000 nonarmed sympathizers. In February the government mounted its biggest anti-Communist offensive in years.

Foreign Affairs. A new accord governing U.S. military bases in the Philippines was signed June 1. Clark Air Force Base, Subic Bay Naval Base, and three smaller communications stations were leased for another five years. The pact increased U.S. economic and military aid by $400 million—to $900 million—over the period. Prior to the Aquino incident, Marcos had told visiting U.S. legislators that the Philippines would seek an accommodation with the Soviet Union if Congress did not appropriate the funds promised in the bases pact. The Aquino murder intensified U.S. congressional criticism of Marcos.

U.S. President Ronald Reagan had planned to visit the Philippines during his November Asian tour, but the stopover was postponed.

RICHARD BUTWELL
The University of South Dakota

PHILIPPINES • Information Highlights

Official Name: Republic of the Philippines.
Location: Southeast Asia.
Area: 115,984 sq mi (300 400 km²).
Population (July 1983 est.): 53,162,000.
Chief Cities (1980 census): Manila, the capital, 1,630,485; Quezon City, 1,165,865; Davao, 610,375; Cebu, 490, 281.
Government: *Head of state*, Ferdinand E. Marcos, president (took office Dec. 30, 1965). *Head of government*, César Virata, premier (appointed April 8, 1981). *Legislature* (unicameral)—National Assembly.
Monetary Unit: Peso (14.002 pesos equal U.S.$1, floating rate, Nov. 4, 1983).
Gross National Product (1982 U.S.$): $39,000,-000,000.
Economic Index (1982): *Consumer Prices,* (1978 = 100), all items, 173.2; food, 162.5. *Industrial Production* (1980, 1975 = 100), 129.
Foreign Trade (1981 U.S.$): *Imports,* $7,946,000,000; *exports,* $5,722,000,000.

PHOTOGRAPHY

Despite the effects of the economic recession on the photography art world in 1983—the demise of galleries, a stagnant marketplace, and reduction of grant support—the medium was alive and well in exhibition halls and publishing, and more popular than ever in the hands of both the committed practitioner and average picture-taker. In 1983 more than ten million units of Kodak's truly pocket-size, fully automatic Disc camera, introduced in 1982, were in the marketplace; and 35mm cameras had achieved almost total automation. Simultaneously, a revolution in color film emulsion technology was occurring, as Kodak, Fuji, and 3M Company introduced a new generation of 35mm film that promised well-exposed pictures with better sharpness, brighter color, extraordinary skin tones, very fine grain, and in some instances film speeds 2½ times faster than any ISO emulsion previously available. What all this meant to the photographer was that quality previously obtainable only with larger-format cameras was now possible with 35mm equipment.

Cameras and Film. Refinements in the former, a revolution in the latter tell the new product story for 1983. At the annual Photographic Manufacturers' Association (PMA) show, the already-advanced automation of 35mm single-lens reflex cameras continued in both exposure and focusing. The Pentax Super Program camera offered six different exposure options, including a programmed mode, while Olympus' OM-3 and OM-4 offered multispot metering, the reading and computer-averaging of eight separate spots in the picture area. Nikon's flagship F3, an interchangeable-lens, pro-quality SLR, made news because of the availability of its autofocusing version, the F3AF, and two brand-new autofocusing telephoto lenses—an 80mm f/2.8 and 200mm f/3.5. A slew of non-SLR 35mm cameras, many with the popular "clamshell" design, were introduced for the candid street-shooter, while cherrywood-and-brass view cameras from de Golden Busch, in 8 × 10 to 20 × 24-inch formats, appealed to the growing ranks of larger-format camera fans.

The promised Nikon FE2 finally appeared, with its titanium shutter capable of a top speed of 1/4000 second and flash synchronization at 1/250; these fast shutters are considered the wave of the future, especially with the arrival of new super-high-speed films.

In color film, the "available-darkness" race was on, as 3M introduced its ISO 1,000 Color Slide film and Kodak its Kodacolor VR 1,000 color-print emulsion, both the world's fastest (needing less light) in their respective categories. The VR 1,000 is part of a new line of color-negative films from Kodak—including VR 100, 200, 400—made possible by its new silver-halide development-inhibitor-release

This 1931 photo of a Texas cotton-picking family (photographer unknown) was featured at "The American Image" show.

(DIR) chemistry. Competitor Fuji also introduced color-print films—HR 100 and HR 400—that utilize another new technology—double structure grain (DSG). Fuji became the second to enter the disc film market created by Kodak in 1982, with its ISO 200 cartridge, also with 15 tiny 8 × 10mm negatives.

Polaroid's Autoprocess 35mm slides, with lightweight processor and slide mounter, were due in 1983; built around a series of color and black-and-white films, they may be used in *any* 35mm camera (a Polaroid first) then developed instantly after the entire roll is shot, without a darkroom, washing, or temperature control.

To improve exposure and final print quality and further to automate and simplify photography, Kodak initiated its DX (digital indexing) system: four electronically readable codes were added to the edges of its VR films and will appear on all popular Kodak 35mm film by 1984. A camera designed to read these codes will be capable of automatic film advance, count-down exposures, and automatic rewind, expected to hasten the redesign of some cameras—especially compact non-SLR 35s.

And on the still-camera video front, Kodak introduced a prototype video display unit to view Disc photos on a home TV screen (camera and viewer, no more than $300) in answer to Sony's Mavica ($640), the first 35mm video SLR, and its TV viewer ($220), both due in 1983.

In enlarging papers, there were two more firsts: Agfachrome-Speed's processing system that results in one-step color prints from color slides in 90 seconds using a single solution and hardly any time or temperature control; and Ilford's black-and-white Ilfospeed multigrade II, a developer-incorporated, resin-coated paper with exceptionally long contrast range that can be used in activation processors or in trays with a conventional developer.

Exhibitions. American history—its highlights and daily life—was the focus of many shows in 1983. At the Brooklyn (NY) Museum and in several galleries, photographs helped celebrate the 100th anniversary of the Brooklyn Bridge; "The American Image: Photographs from the National Archives," at the International Center of Photography, provided a U.S. family album from 1860 to 1960; and "Color Work from the Farm Security Administration," at the newly reopened Light Gallery, captured farm life between the Depression and World War II.

The contributions of two exceptionally important photographers on the American scene were recognized: "Alfred Stieglitz," at the National Gallery in Washington, DC, Metropolitan Museum in New York, and Art Institute of Chicago, was the first retrospective in almost 50 years for the early 20th-century photographer; and "Carleton E. Watkins: Photographs of the American West," at the Museum of Fine Arts in Boston—including his 1861 views of Yosemite that persuaded the U.S. Congress to make it a national park—paid tribute to the accomplishments of the 19th-century landscapist.

Several retrospectives honored some of the medium's masters—August Sander's portrait of Germany from 1904–59, at the National Gallery; Yousuf Karsh's 50 years of celebrity portraits, in New York; and, on the occasion of his 80th birthday, Aaron Siskind's abstractions. Younger notables also were represented on New York gallery walls and in publication: Robert Mapplethorpe's color flower portfolio, and lady body builder in black-and-white (*Lady: Lisa Lyon*); Cindy Sherman's large-scale color in which she is the model, and a ten-year retrospective book; and photojournalist Annie Leibovitz's portraits of rock-'n'-roll stars and other "glitterati."

The recent tendency to treat the print's size and physical presence as consciously considered formal elements was apparent in the Museum of Modern Art's show, "Big Pictures by Contemporary Photographers"; and the revival of interest in the calotype (paper negative) process was evident in three major shows and the book *The Art of the French Calotype, With a Critical Dictionary of Photographers, 1840–1870,* by Eugenia Parry Janis and Andre Jammes.

Obituaries. Lisette Model, at age 76: photographer of the wealthy in Cannes ("Promenade des Anglais," 1937), she was best known in recent years as a teacher; the late photographer Diane Arbus was her pupil. James Van Der Zee, at 97: he acquired his first studio in Harlem in 1916 and for more than 50 years did portraits and photographed that community's rituals; he was the single largest contributor to the Metropolitan Museum's 1969 exhibit, "Harlem on My Mind." Jacob Deschin, at 83: this editor and writer joined *The New York Times* in 1941 and wrote its "Camera View" column until 1970, wrote for *Popular Photography* magazine for more than 30 years, ran "Discovery" gallery in a New York custom lab, and wrote many books.

BARBARA LOBRON
Writer, Editor, Photographer

Courtesy, Museum of Fine Arts, Boston

An 1885 photo of Cypress Point, Monterey, CA, was on view during the Carleton E. Watkins retrospective at the Museum of Fine Arts, Boston, during the summer.

PHYSICS

In 1983 the intermediate vector boson was discovered, efforts were under way to measure the lifetime of the proton, and science-education policy was debated.

Discovery of the W and Z Particles. In early 1983, at the European Center for Nuclear Research (CERN) in Switzerland, the long-sought intermediate vector boson was observed. In recent years physicists have made significant progress toward the theoretical unification of the forces of nature. The "electroweak theory" combines the weak nuclear force and the electromagnetic force. All interactions have particles which transfer the force. For electromagnetism the particle is the quantum of light —the photon. For the weak interaction there are predicted to be three such particles, two with charge W^+ and W^-, and one neutral Z°. These intermediate vector bosons are predicted to be 100 times as massive as the ordinary protons and neutrons that make up nuclei. Detecting these new particles requires exceptionally high energies and special equipment. The Super Proton Synchrotron was converted into a colliding beams accelerator in which 270 GeV proton and antiproton beams collide. The quarks and antiquarks in the nucleons combine to produce the W and Z particles.

Identifying the new particles was a major task. A group consisting of more than 100 U.S. and European physicists worked with a huge detection system which recorded approximately one billion (U.S.) events. Initial restrictions reduced this number to some 140,000 events, which were analyzed after completion of the experiment. Stringent requirements finally reduced to five the number of events that have all the right properties for the formation of a W particle. The mass of the W was measured at 81 GeV/c^2, in close agreement with the predicted value. Later experiments by the same group also confirmed the existence of Z°.

Elementary Particle Physics. With the observation of the intermediate vector boson, the theory of quantum chromodynamics is very well established. In this theory, such particles as nucleons and mesons consist of quarks. The quarks have angular momentum, fractional charge, and come in several types (flavors). There are thought to be six quarks: up, down, strange, charmed, bottom, and top. The first four were observed by the early 1970s. In the late 1970s the bottom quark was observed indirectly. In 1983 a group of physicists at the Cornell (NY) electron-positron accelerator found the clearest evidence yet for the bottom quark. Recent results from the Electron-Synchrotron Laboratory (DESY) at Hamburg, West Germany, found no top quarks at the highest energy presently available (near 37 GeV). Observation of the top quark probably will await the construction of a much higher-energy electron-positron system. With the success of the electroweak theory, physicists would like to push unification even further.

"Grand unification" combines the electromagnetic and weak nuclear forces with the strong nuclear force, and predicts that the proton should be unstable. A number of experiments are in progress to measure the proton's lifetime, which is expected to be at least 10^{31} years. Preliminary evidence indicates that the proton lasts longer than predicted by some grand unification theories.

Controlled Thermonuclear Fusion. Fusion continues to be an attractive long-term possibility as an energy source. Major advantages include unlimited fuel and no nuclear proliferation. The process, however, is far from the power-plant stage. The primary technical problem is the ultra-high temperature (10–100 million degrees) required to initiate fusion. To contain the ionized gas (plasma), one of two indirect methods is used: magnetic confinement or inertial confinement.

In the former, a doughnut-shaped magnetic field usually is employed; the most common configuration is called Tokamak. Four new Tokamaks are at various stages of development. The Tokamak Fusion Test Reactor (TFTR) at Princeton (NJ) has achieved its first plasma. Scientific break-even (as much energy produced as input) is expected with the TFTR in 1986. The Joint European Tokamak in England was almost ready to start operation in 1983.

The other major approach to confinement is implosion, either with particle beams or with lasers. Major laser fusion projects are under way at Los Alamos (NM) and Livermore (CA) national laboratories. The Novette laser system at Livermore is a two-beam system capable of up to 30 terawatts of power. Novette is the first step toward the Nova laser, which will consist of ten novette arms. For various applications, such as defense research, laser fusion is quite successful, while for commercial reactors magnetic confinement seems superior.

Science Policy, Manpower, and Education. The 1984 U.S. federal budget reflects an increased concern for basic scientific research. Presidential Science Adviser George Keyworth has described the funding increases as an "overriding national priority." Finding the required scientists and technologists, however, may be as difficult as raising the research money. In 1983 concern was raised over science education at all levels, especially secondary. The shortage of qualified math and science teachers is closely related to low enrollments and test scores in these subjects. The number of new science and math teachers has dropped by two thirds in the past ten years. In physics the percentage of foreign first-year graduate students rose to 40% in 1982.

GARY MITCHELL
North Carolina State University

Chip Hires/Gamma/Liaison

Gerard Rancinan/Sygma

Solidarity supporters, left, defied the regime by holding protests August 31, the third anniversary of the Gdansk Accords. On the May 1 labor holiday, another occasion for protest, the government organized its own parade in Warsaw.

POLAND

The events of 1983 in Poland were dominated by conflict between supporters of Solidarity and the Communist regime.

Underground Solidarity. Although the union had been outlawed the previous October, much of Solidarity's leadership and some of its rank and file continued its clandestine opposition to the regime of Gen. Wojciech Jaruzelski. The government, in turn, cracked down even harder on Solidarity and its sympathizers.

The year began with the trial of union leader Zbigniew Romaszewski and his wife, Irena, as well as seven unidentified associates, for operating illegal Radio Solidarity installations. They were charged with "broadcasting false information on Poland's social and political situation which could have led to public disquiet and riots." All were found guilty; sentences ranged from seven months to four and a half years. Meanwhile, other Solidarity leaders were being arrested and jailed throughout Poland.

The regime announced in January that more than 5,000 Polish citizens had applied for permission to emigrate for "political reasons" since March 1982. About 4,500 were said to have been issued emigration permits, but only 1,070 were actually allowed to leave.

In late January the underground leadership of Solidarity called for the preparation of a general strike against the regime, declaring such an action "imminent." The call was issued by Bogdan Lis, Zbigniew Bujak, Wladyslaw Har-

dek, Jerzy Pinior, and Eugeniusz Szumiejko— all operating out of hideouts since the imposition of martial law in December 1981.

In early March, Lech Walesa, speaking to Western television reporters, urged his followers to organize protests and strikes, including hunger strikes, to force the regime to restore the status of Solidarity as a legal, independent union federation. He asserted that the regime had been completely unresponsive to all private and public appeals. He protested against the trials of former Solidarity leaders and called for popular demonstrations against government mistreatment of Solidarity sympathizers. Underground leaders called for popular demonstrations on May 1 in defiance of martial law. The regime threatened police retaliation.

Arrests of Solidarity underground leaders continued in mid-April. Radio transmitters and printing presses were reported seized in Warsaw. Walesa and his wife, Danuta, were detained and interrogated in Gdansk on April 13. Despite the arrest, Walesa insisted to Western reporters that he would continue to meet with underground leaders on issues of national policy. The official media threatened cancellation of the papal visit planned for June if Solidarity persisted in its support of street disturbances during the May 1–3 holidays. In mid-April the government announced the arrest of Solidarity leader Janusz Onyszkiewicz, one of the alleged organizers of antigovernment demonstrations.

Ghetto Uprising Anniversary. Official observances of the 40th anniversary of the Warsaw Ghetto uprising on April 14–21 were marked by controversy and Solidarity demonstrations. The Palestine Liberation Organization (PLO) representative in Warsaw insisted on laying a wreath at the monument to the Jews who perished in Warsaw in 1943. He also referred to Israelis as the new Nazis of the world. Jewish survivors in Poland expressed outrage at what they regarded as desecration. Dr. Marek Edelman, a Solidarity supporter who had fought in the Ghetto resistance, called for an international boycott of the ceremonies.

Police broke up crowds of Solidarity followers who had gathered in Warsaw for independent observances of the anniversary. Solidarity spokesmen drew parallels between the persecution of Jews by the Nazis and the persecution of their own members by the Communist regime.

Open Protests. As Solidarity leaders had urged, an estimated 40,000 people took part in protests, marches, and meetings throughout the country in the first days of May. As the regime had warned, police used violence to break up demonstrations in Gdansk, Warsaw, Krakow, and Nowa Huta on May 1—the official Labor Day holiday—and May 3—the anniversary of Poland's constitution of 1791.

Also in early May, Walesa met with several leaders of the banned union to draft a letter of protest to the Polish parliament over the persecution of Solidarity. In response, the Communist authorities seized Walesa and several of his aides. He was subjected to de facto house arrest and various forms of harassment.

The death of 19-year-old Warsaw youth Grzegorz Przemek, beaten to death by police, spurred great popular resentment. His funeral May 19 was attended by some 20,000 people. The youth's mother, Barbara Sadowska, was a well-known poet who worked for a church-sponsored committee aiding families of jailed Solidarity members.

Role of the Church. In January, Pope John II elevated Archbishop Jozef Glemp to the rank of cardinal. Glemp had succeeded the late Stefan Cardinal Wyszynski as primate of the Polish Catholic Church in 1981.

Cardinal Glemp, the pope, and other spokesmen of the Church were highly vocal during the first part of the year in appealing for a lifting of martial law, a general amnesty for political prisoners, and a dialogue between the government and the opposition.

Between June 16 and June 23, Pope John Paul II visited his native land, with major stops in Warsaw, Poznan, Krakow, Wroclaw, Czestochowa, and Katowice. In a meeting with General Jaruzelski and in speeches around the country, the pontiff supported the right of Solidarity to formal recognition and the powers accorded to it under the August 1980 worker-government agreement. The renewal of Solidarity was "indispensable as a way out of Poland's internal crisis," he declared in Warsaw on June 17. Several million people—probably between 15 and 20% of the country's total population—saw and heard the pontiff face-to-face.

The high point of the pope's visit was a service held in Czestochowa at the shrine of the Black Madonna on Sunday, June 19. With Solidarity banners and slogans prominently displayed, the pope celebrated mass for approximately one million persons. To tumultuous acclaim (and despite regime warnings against political-nationalist appeals), the pope declared: "I am a son of this nation and that is why I deeply feel all its yearnings, its wish to live in truth, in freedom, in justice and social solidarity."

On the last day of his visit to Poland, Pope John Paul II granted an audience to Lech Walesa. After the meeting, Walesa told Western news media that his resolve to continue the struggle for the rights of Solidarity was strengthened. But the papal visit was followed by reports in Poland and abroad that the pope had negotiated some sort of "new solution" with the Polish regime. According to some versions, Walesa had been persuaded to give up his personal political role in exchange for key government concessions, including the lifting of martial law, amnesty for political prisoners, and more freedom for the Church and workers. The allegations were denied by the Vatican, although Josef Cardinal Glemp, who visited Rome a week after the papal trip to Poland, said on July 1 that Walesa's future role was "still not settled."

In early July, talks between leaders of the Church and the government led to an apparent agreement in principle on "joint" financial aid for farmers. The Church was to obtain multi-million-dollar funds from private individuals and charitable foundations in the West and funnel these to needy Polish farmers—with government cooperation and approval. In August, however, Cardinal Glemp called off further talks with General Jaruzelski on the aid program. He blamed the regime's disrespect of human rights and failure to make the abolition of martial law a genuinely meaningful action.

Party Developments. The ruling Polish United Workers' Party (PZPR) held its first Central Committee meeting in eight months in Warsaw on May 31. General Jaruzelski told members that "the enemies of socialism have been weakened but still have not given up." Jaruzelski's own dominant role in the party apparently was reaffirmed. In November the Sejm (parliament) elected Jaruzelski chairman of the National Defense Council, with wide-ranging powers including the right to declare martial law. Jaruzelski's deputy, Gen. Florian Sawicki, took over as defense minister. And Politburo member Zbigniew Messner became deputy premier in charge of economic policy.

The 40th anniversary of the Warsaw Ghetto uprising, a Jewish resistance against the Nazis, was observed in April.

Lifting of Martial Law. On July 21, 1983, in conjunction with the anniversary of the founding of the Communist regime in Poland in 1944, General Jaruzelski announced the lifting of martial law throughout the country. Jaruzelski's declaration, delivered before the Polish parliament (Sejm), was coupled with measures that made the change more semantic than real.

Illustrative of the new regulations was a measure calling for up to five years in jail for "spreading false information broadcast by a foreign radio station." Belonging to an illegal organization could bring up to three years' imprisonment. In fact the regulations contained so many restrictions on workers, students, scholars, and media that Lech Walesa declared the change meaningless. Solidarity remained outlawed. Censorship was continued. Severe controls were maintained on the rights of association, expression, and assembly—now all under "ordinary law." Nevertheless, between

On July 21 the parliament passed an amnesty bill, and General Jaruzelski (bottom, right) lifted martial law.

600 and 800 political prisoners were released from jail in several installments. Undergound Solidarity leaders were promised freedom from criminal prosecution if they gave themselves up and refrained from further "unlawful activities." The amnesty offer was to end October 31, and all those not surrendering before then would be subject to imprisonment. The offer did not extend to the arrested members of the Committee for Worker Self-Defense (KOR) and its leader, Jacek Kuron, all of whom remained in jail. As many as 200 political prisoners were believed to be unaffected by the original amnesty; many more were arrested. A few persons were "temporarily" released from jail at Christmastime.

Continuing Opposition. A large part of the underground Solidarity movement did not accept the largely cosmetic end of martial law. Many leaders remained in hiding and focused their efforts on protest actions. Through much of August, police attacked sporadic demonstrations in the Gdansk area, and there were reports of work stoppages in various parts of Poland. Solidarity's underground leadership called for a boycott of public transportation and protest marches on August 31, the anniversary of the 1980 Gdansk Accord (between Solidarity and the government). Demonstrations by Solidarity supporters on the anniversary erupted in several cities, including Gdansk, Nowa Huta, Wroclaw, and Warsaw. Police units resorted to their customary methods to control the crowds, using tear gas, water cannons, and clubs. There were more demonstrations in several large cities on November 11, the traditional independence-day holiday. Demonstrations called for by the Solidarity underground to mark the December 13 anniversary of martial law, however, drew relatively few participants but a massive police response.

Lech Walesa. Government media attacks on Lech Walesa persisted throughout the year, as the regime attempted to discredit him in the eyes of the Polish public. Walesa was variously charged with treasonable and subversive activities, as well as personal financial corruption. In May the government newspaper *Rzeczposolita* charged Walesa with a "twisted line of conduct" and said that he had "allied himself with the Solidarity underground which is busy inciting street riots and which does not conceal its long-term political ambitions."

In late April, Walesa returned to his $300-per-month job as an electrician at the Gdansk shipyards, a job he had last held in 1980 when the Solidarity movement began. While Walesa was being reinstated at work, he was simultaneously accused in the party press of having embezzled union funds.

On August 28 the government media published a speech by Walesa disclaiming any "subversive aims" by Solidarity and appealing for a dialogue between government and the opposition. This rare action, perhaps intended to defuse popular unrest, was followed by a televised debate between Walesa and one of the party leaders, Mieczyslaw Rakowski. In late September, however, Polish television showed a half-hour documentary alleging that Lech Walesa had amassed a million-dollar personal fortune that he had deposited at the Vatican bank in Rome. Accusations of "slandering People's Poland" were also being leveled against Walesa's personal priest and friend.

Beginning in September, Walesa began to reformulate his position. Apparently discouraged by the prospects of Solidarity in its struggle against the regime, he sought a new "vehicle." He now advocated not only the abandonment of Solidarity but the surrender of its underground leaders under the terms of the amnesty law. Walesa called for a new organizational structure and a new leadership to carry on the struggle for union rights. In December, Walesa advocated the lifting of Western sanctions against Poland, although with some guarantees on just how Poland would use the resources.

On October 5, Lech Walesa was awarded the 1983 Nobel Peace Prize. The Norwegian Nobel Committee cited Walesa's efforts "as an exponent of the active longing for peace and freedom which exists, in spite of unequal conditions, unconquered in all the peoples of the world." The news of the award apparently dismayed the Polish Communist regime, which officially called it "politically motivated," but it also appeared to give a great psychological lift to millions of Poles who had identified with Walesa as the champion of freedom and justice.

Economic Developments. In mid-June the government announced that Poland could repay its staggering $26 billion (U.S.) debt to Western banks but only if the latter would extend more favorable credit terms. The government also demanded an eight-year moratorium on any interest payments to Western creditors. It claimed that the output of goods and services was increasing slowly in relation to 1982.

Official statements of the Polish government indicated that basic food rationing would be continued until perhaps 1985 and that prices were likely to rise between 25–40%.

In October the government announced sweeping food price increases, including a 44% boost in the price of bread, with more to follow in 1984. The new officially sanctioned trade unions had attracted fewer than 3 million members, according to government sources, as compared with the 9.5 million that had been enrolled in Solidarity before it was outlawed.

Foreign Relations. In early June, Poland announced that it would boycott the annual conference of the UN's International Labor Organization (ILO), claiming that the body had interfered in Polish domestic affairs. The regime threatened a permanent break with the ILO if such "interference" persisted.

As an act of reprisal against the United States, the Polish government ordered the United Press International (UPI) office in Poland closed until the Polish Press Agency (PAP) would be allowed to reopen its operations in the United States. In diplomatic exchanges early in July, the U.S. government promised Poland an easing of trade restrictions in return for a substantial political amnesty and "meaningful, liberalizing measures." In November, the United States indicated its willingness to negotiate the question of Polish debts and to allow Poland a resumption of fishing rights in American waters. Poland demanded compensation for economic damages inflicted by U.S. sanctions since December 1981.

In mid-August, Polish leaders welcomed East German leader Erich Honecker, apparently for a discussion of strains that had developed between the two regimes. Jaruzelski was reported to have held talks on undisclosed subjects with Soviet leaders at midyear.

ALEXANDER J. GROTH
University of California, Davis

POLAND • Information Highlights

Official Name: Polish People's Republic.
Location: Eastern Europe.
Area: 120,600 sq mi (312 354 km²).
Population (July 1983 est.): 36,556,000.
Chief Cities (Dec. 1981): Warsaw, the capital, 1,611,600; Lodz, 843,000; Cracow, 722,900.
Government: *Head of state,* Henryk Jablonski, president of the Council of State (took office 1972). *Head of government,* Gen. Wojciech Jaruzelski, chairman of the Council of Ministers (Feb. 1981) and first secretary of the Polish United Workers' Party (Oct. 1981). *Legislature* (unicameral)—Sejm.
Monetary Unit: Zloty (88.00 zlotys equal U.S.$1, April 1983).
Gross National Product (1981 U.S.$): $88,100,-000,000–$133,800,000,000.
Foreign Trade (1982 U.S.$): *Imports,* $10,248,-000,000; *exports,* $11,208,000,000.

POLAR RESEARCH

Antarctic. The National Science Foundation (NSF) sponsored 88 Antarctic research projects in the earth sciences, biology, ocean sciences, glaciology, and atmospheric sciences during 1982–83. Some 270 U.S. scientists conducted these projects at four all-year stations, from small remote camps, and aboard NSF's research ship and two Coast Guard icebreakers.

Researchers working near the Allan Hills (140 mi, or 225 km, from McMurdo Station) in January 1983 found a 1-ounce (31-gram) light green meteorite. Subsequent testing by more than 20 groups of scientists revealed that the meteorite was probably a moon rock. They compared their data with data analyses of lunar samples brought back to earth by the U.S. Apollo and Soviet Luna missions. The comparison showed that the likely origin of the meteorite was the lunar highlands.

Near McMurdo Station, biologists with special computer monitoring equipment observed how Weddell seals slow their heart rates during deep dives. The seals dive to depths of more than 1,600 ft (490 m) and remain submerged for almost an hour. Heart rate and depth were recorded every 30 seconds. For one seal the longest dive was 52 minutes, and its deepest dive was 1,594 ft (485 m). With each dive a slowed heart rate was recorded. These observations support laboratory experiments in which similar phenomena have been recorded.

Geophysicists found that on Oct. 8, 1982, some 700 small earthquakes (measuring about 2 on the Richter scale) occurred near Mt. Erebus, a 12,000-ft (3 650-m) active volcano on Ross Island about 45 mi (72 km) from the Antarctic coast. Previously an average of 20 to 80 small tremors were recorded daily. Because the center of these earthquakes was about 6 mi (10 km) from the summit of Mt. Erebus, the geophysicists believe that the magma producing the tremors did not come from the main magma chamber but that it is a new batch of magma that formed an armlike dike below the surface near the volcano.

Between January and March 1983 the U.S. Coast Guard icebreaker *Polar Star* circumnavigated Antarctica. This was the first circumnavigation of the continent by a U.S. ship, although the *Glacier* almost completed a similar trip in 1955. The icebreaker carried Department of State observers who inspected 14 foreign stations in compliance with the Antarctic Treaty of 1959. Scientists on this unique trip recorded distributions of marine mammals and birds, performed chemical oceanography and microbial studies, and collected daily air samples for analysis of carbon dioxide levels.

Arctic. Data analysis from a seven-year study in the southeastern Bering Sea was completed in 1983. The Bering Sea, the world's third-largest sea, has an area of more than 880,000 sq mi (2 300 000 km²). Although primary production is not exceptionally high there, the area contributes about 4% of the world fishery catch. Scientists from nine institutions focused on the Alaskan pollock, a major fishery. One of their findings was that the size of the fishery is related to the number of fish surviving on the middle continental shelf. On the outer shelf, prey are more concentrated, and fish survival rates do not vary greatly. The results of this investigation provide an ecological basis for managing resources of the Bering Sea.

President Reagan affirmed that the United States has unique and critical interests in the Arctic, particularly relating to national defense, resource and energy development, scientific research, and environmental protection. The president requested that the interagency policy group determine how U.S. Arctic programs should be coordinated with activities of other countries bordering on the Arctic Ocean, and what services the U.S. government should provide in the Arctic over the next decade.

WINIFRED REUNING
National Science Foundation

PORTUGAL

Socialist Mario Soares, who emerged as prime minister following spring 1983 parliamentary elections, moved decisively to implement "100 measures in 100 days" to revive Portugal's ailing economy.

Government and Politics. On February 4, President Antonio Ramahlo Eanes responded to the resignation of Premier Franciscó Pinto Balsemão, a Social Democrat, by dissolving parliament and calling for elections designed to "clarify" the political picture and produce a new government capable of coping with the critical economic problems besetting the nation.

The Socialists emerged from the April 25 voting as the dominant party, winning 101 seats compared with 75 seats for the centrist Social Democrats, 44 for the Moscow-oriented Communists, and 30 for the moderate Center Christian Democrats. These results gave rise to a coalition cabinet—Portugal's 15th government since the restoration of democracy in 1974—headed by Soares. Social Democratic leader Carlos Mota Pinto was to serve as deputy premier and defense minister. The 17-member cabinet consists of 9 Socialists, 7 Social Democrats, and 1 independent (Finance Minister Ernani Lopes).

The coalition boasts support from the army, the middle class, broad segments of the business community, and President Eanes, a Socialist. Still, the Communists, angered at their exclusion from the cabinet, voiced opposition to a "social contract" proposed by Soares to guarantee labor peace. In June, Communist-led unions launched a series of strikes and work stoppages to protest belt-tightening measures adopted by the new government.

Economy. Upon being sworn in, Soares pledged to present a National Emergency Plan because "Portugal has been paralyzed for months; the economy is out of control; major companies, both state and private, are on the edge of collapse; capital is being illegally drained from the country; inflation [exceeding 20%] is eroding our standard of life; corruption is a serious blight on the country. . . ."

On June 24, parliament by a 161–67 vote approved a package of austerity measures requested by Soares. This program, fashioned to secure credits from the International Monetary Fund (IMF), raised interest rates to approximately 30%, imposed new taxes, slashed state spending, and reduced subsidies on bread, milk, sugar, cooking oils, and other foodstuffs. Enactment of the plan followed a 12% devaluation of the escudo against other currencies.

The Socialist premier also opened to private investment the state-controlled beer, insurance, cement, and banking industries. At the same time, he attacked drug smuggling, tax evasion, and waste.

This no-nonsense program persuaded the IMF to grant a $738 million loan to Portugal, just more than one third of which was earmarked to offset an anticipated fall in export earnings. The IMF emphasized that the external debt, $13.6 billion (U.S.) when Soares took office, could not exceed $14.6 billion in 1983 and $16 billion in 1984. Further, the current account deficit, $3.2 billion in mid-1983, would have to drop to $2 billion by year's end and to $1.25 billion in 1984. Officials believed that the stabilization plan combined with the IMF credits would make it easier to obtain foreign loans. In late September, a London-based bank was seeking participants for a $400 million syndicated loan for Portugal.

Foreign Affairs. The Soares government pressed the European Community to act promptly on the nation's application for membership, which was submitted in 1976. Soares warned that continued delay would lead Portugal to "find other alternatives."

The premier reaffirmed his country's commitment to the North Atlantic Treaty Organization (NATO), although economic hardship may prevent its paying dues to the organization. During a mid-September visit to Washington, Eanes met with President Reagan to discuss mutual interests, including continued U.S. use of an airbase in the Azores. Soares cultivated good relations with former Portuguese territories in Africa, especially Mozambique. He also held meetings with leaders of southern Europe's other Socialist governments.

GEORGE W. GRAYSON
College of William and Mary

Mario Soares, 48, casts his ballot in April 25 elections. Later the victorious Socialist formed a coalition government.

Joao Da Silva/Sygma

PORTUGAL • Information Highlights

Official Name: Republic of Portugal.
Location: Southwestern Europe.
Area: 36,399 sq mi (94 276 km²).
Population (July 1983): 10,008,000.
Chief Cities: (1981 census): Lisbon, the capital, 2,061,627; Oporto, 1,550,806; Braga, 700,728.
Government: *Head of state,* António Romalho Eanes, president (took office July 1976). *Head of government,* Mario Soares, prime minister (took office June 9, 1983). *Legislature* (unicameral)— Assembly of the Republic.
Monetary Unit: Escudo (126.8 escudos equal U.S.$1, Nov. 4, 1983).
Gross National Product (1981 U.S.$): $23,600,-000,000.
Economic Indexes (Oct. 1982): *Consumer Prices* (1976 = 100), all items, 343.2; food, 350.6. *Industrial Production* (1975 = 100), 154.
Foreign Trade (1982 U.S.$): *Imports,* $9,521,000,000; *exports,* $4,167,000,000.

POSTAL SERVICE

For the second year in a row the U.S. Postal Service (USPS) ended in the black. The final tally for fiscal year (FY) 1982, ending Sept. 30, 1982, showed a surplus of $802 million compared with an earlier estimate of $600 million. In FY 1983, revenues of more than $23 billion exceeded expenditures by an estimated $500 million. The USPS was accused of "hiding" another $400 million in a reserve to pay workmen's compensation claims, which have been declining. The service may have been overcautious in its accounting, but only time will tell whether any of this fund can be transferred to surplus.

Finance and Rates. As the USPS received no general subsidy in FY 1983, it can be said to have had a true surplus for the first time. However, the USPS did receive from Congress a "revenue foregone subsidy" of $789 million for services it must provide free or under cost (for example, to libraries, the blind, and nonprofit organizations).

This good fiscal performance stems only in part from the general rate increases of late 1981. The continually rising volume of mail, increasing productivity, decreasing fuel costs, declining workmen's compensation claims, and, especially, the rapidly lessening inflation greatly helped. At one point the USPS found itself committed to a mere one cent cost-of-living pay raise instead of the 26 cents anticipated when the union contracts were negotiated in 1981.

Earlier general subsidies plus recent surpluses have enabled the USPS to avoid borrowing for the last seven years. Nevertheless, the prospect for FY 1984 was unclear for several reasons, including continuing inflation, escalating health care insurance costs, and further pay increase commitments. Postmaster General William F. Bolger stated that the latter two factors alone could raise expenses by as much as $1 billion in FY 1984. Robert Hardesty, chairman of the USPS Board of Governors, said there could be a deficit for FY 1984 of up to $1.3 billion.

On November 1 a closely divided (5-4) USPS Board of Governors announced that it was requesting the Postal Rate Commission to approve a general rate increase. If approved, first-class letters could cost 23 cents.

Volume. In light of the great expansion of electronic communications, the continued rise in the volume of regular mail was surprising. The postmaster general estimated the volume for FY 1983 at 119 billion pieces (an increase of 40 billion since 1971) and predicted a rise to 135 billion by 1988.

Adding to the volume was a modestly expanding market for E-COM (Electronic Computer-Originated Mail) services. That volume, a great disappointment at first, grew from about 100,000 pieces a week in late 1982 to 350,000 by late 1983. Though encouraging, this was still below early projections. Competitors charged that the E-COM rates are unfairly below cost, and the USPS requested the Postal Rate Commission to approve increased rates from 26 to 31 cents for one sheet and from 31 to 40 cents for two. The USPS is also working to improve its marketing approach.

The Future. While the USPS is still optimistic about E-COM, it appears to have pinned its greatest hopes for reducing costs to a heavy emphasis on automation everywhere, continued marketing innovations, and expansion of its new voluntary 9-digit (ZIP + 4) code system. This went into operation on Oct. 1, 1983. Bolger predicted that, when the 9-digit code is fully on line in five or six years, an additional 60,000 jobs, mainly clerical, will be eliminated. Productivity, up 47% since 1971, continued to climb.

The service's traditional approach to the future has been criticized, but Congress may not permit the agency to play any greater electronics role. Moreover, critics have steadily underestimated mail volume and the capacity of the USPS to innovate. A series of congressional hearings in the fall of 1983 illustrated by conflicting testimony that the future of communications is very difficult to predict.

Meanwhile, a Roper poll in the summer listed the USPS as the most popular government agency and the best in "value for dollar."

Other Events. In January 1983 the USPS issued "Official Mail" stamps for government agencies and officials to replace the familiar "frank" (official signature) for the first time since 1873. A few months later the Supreme Court upheld the service against an attack on certain of its rate-determination procedures. In Houston, TX, 15 letter carriers were fired in September for an alleged wildcat strike. A month later the USPS was given the President's Occupational Health and Safety Award for 1982. Since 1977, lost-time injuries have been nearly halved. The postal unions are in some disarray, and the 1984 contract bargaining is expected to turn less on pay than other issues.

Canada. For the new Canada Post Corporation, formed in 1981, balancing the books is an eventual goal but not a firm requirement. Large rate increases in early 1982 (e.g., from 17 to 30 cents Canadian for domestic first class) helped reduce the deficit of $660 million for FY 1982, ending March 31, to an estimated $300 million for FY 1983. Small increases in early 1983 (e.g., from 30 to 32 cents for domestic first class) should help further. Several union contracts ran out in December 1983, setting the scene for a round of hard bargaining, expected some time in 1984. Total volume for FY 1983 declined slightly to an estimated 6.4 billion.

PAUL P. VAN RIPER, *Texas A&M University*

PRINCE EDWARD ISLAND

The impact of leaner economic times and government efforts to come to grips with them dominated affairs in 1983. The new Liberal Opposition leader, Joe Ghiz, made his presence felt in the legislature.

The Budget. Finance Minister Lloyd MacPhail presented a mildly austere budget to the House on April 14. He projected expenditures of C$415.4 million and a deficit of $18.2 million. The tax on cigarettes was increased by 12.5 cents for a pack of 25, while highway spending was cut by $11 million. A small number of public-sector employees were to be laid off; job sharing and part-time work with the government increased.

Legislature. The legislature adjourned June 23 after a 14-week sitting marked by labor dissatisfaction with wage restraints and repercussions from an alleged highways scandal. It ended on a friendly note when opposition leader Ghiz thanked Speaker Marion Reid for her "patience." This indicated the healing of a rift that occurred May 31 when Ghiz led his Liberals out of the House to protest Reid's ruling disallowing questions about the scandal because it was under RCMP investigation.

Ghiz was on the attack on another front two months after the adjournment, charging at a press conference that Conservative Premier Jim Lee had violated Islanders' trust by promising a 20% cut in electricity rates just before the Sept. 27, 1982 election.

Wage Freeze. Premier Lee, at the end of March, backed down on his threat to freeze the wages of provincial government employees. He had threatened to cancel the 10% increases provided in collective agreements scheduled to take effect April 1, 1983. Explaining his reversal, Lee said he had revised his timetable for eliminating the provincial deficit, and planned to do it in three years instead of two.

Solutions Scarce. In briefs to the federal royal commission on the Canadian economy in September, P.E.I. organizations said they were tired of the province's dependence on government support. But few solutions were offered. David Hooley, president of the Charlottetown Chamber of Commerce, said Islanders were not asking governments to stop their handouts "but to rechannel and refocus."

Medicare. The Council of Maritime Premiers, meeting at Cavendish, P.E.I., in July, denounced federal Health Minister Monique Bégin's proposal to penalize provinces that permit extra charges against patients under Medicare. The Medicare scheme is financed in roughly equal proportions by the federal and provincial governments. Charges beyond those authorized under the scheme are levied in some provinces by hospitals and doctors.

JOHN BEST, *"Canada World News"*

PRISONS

Prison conditions continued to deteriorate across the United States in 1983, as the number of inmates increased at all levels. Shifts in public attitudes toward the death penalty became evident, while support for long-range programs failed to emerge.

Overcrowding. The number of imprisoned Americans again climbed to record heights, and overcrowding continued as the major problem facing "keepers" as well as the "kept" throughout the country. Official figures, released in April, listed a total of 412,303 persons incarcerated in state and federal prisons in 1982, an increase of 11.6% over the previous year and well over the designed capacity for the majority of institutions. The increase in sentenced inmates again surpassed by far increases in the number of crimes committed. Authorities attributed the rise to longer mandatory sentencing policies adopted by almost 40 states. The increases were expected to continue into the foreseeable future, bringing with them greater turmoil and tensions, already on the rise for the past decade.

Federal and state courts have begun acting to rectify prison conditions described in some instances as barbaric, but court orders seldom were sufficient to stem the growing tide. Particular cases may take years to clear the courts and seldom result in noticeable improvements. In January, a federal court issued a settlement in a ten-year-old case involving the Alabama prison system. But the arrangement held out little promise for change. It included the establishment of a panel to oversee the state system but did not impose penalties on state officials who refuse to implement specific recommendations for the improvement of conditions.

In January, prisoners at New York State's Ossining Correctional Facility, formerly known as Sing Sing, seized 19 guards as hostages and took control of an area holding more

Fred R. Conrad/NYT Pictures

The Manhattan (NY) House of Detention, known as the Tombs, was reopened after a complete interior reconstruction.

than 600 inmates. The hostages were released only after intense negotiations, directed by Gov. Mario Cuomo, succeeded in ending the 53-hour takeover without loss of life or physical injury. A report issued in September suggested that the uprising had been sparked by irregular disciplinary actions taken by the sergeant in charge of the cell block. It went on to note, however, that problems at the facility were and remained "endemic" to the entire system, which has been operating at more than 110% of capacity for several years.

In the United States today, there are more than 6,500 penal institutions, jails, detention centers, and prisons of all security levels for juveniles and adults. Because they vary greatly in the quality of conditions it is difficult to obtain a valid picture for the entire system. By all indications, however, there are growing tensions and few prospects for improvement.

In September a jury in Houston found the sheriff of San Jacinto County and two of his deputies guilty of violating the rights of prisoners by forcing them to undergo a water torture. The prosecution cited incidents over a four-year period in which prisoners were handcuffed to tables while their heads were tightly wrapped in towels. When water was poured over the towel, threatening suffocation, many of the prisoners agreed to talk about alleged crimes and internal prison plotting. Volatile conditions heightened the authorities' need to know, but the jury was not convinced by defense arguments that the victims, many of whom had long criminal records and whom the prosecution conceded were not "model citizens," had testified in order to gain parole or probation.

Death Penalty. The number of prisoners awaiting execution also reached a new high, more than 1,200. For some, execution will be stayed through a successful appeals judgment, but a sharp rise in the number of executions across the country, especially in the south, appeared more and more likely as prospects for appeal diminished. Public opinion polls showed a shift in attitude toward capital punishment. A decade earlier, those supporting the death penalty were a minority, while recent studies showed almost three fourths of Americans in favor. In May, U.S. Supreme Court Justice Lewis F. Powell, Jr., urged that states either speed up the appeals process or abolish capital punishment. Powell argued that present practices were abusing the judicial processes, undermining public confidence in sentencing procedures, and "unfair to the hundreds of persons confined anxiously on death row." Thirty-eight states had death penalty laws on the books in 1983. Florida had 189 prisoners awaiting execution, Texas had 153, and Georgia and California had 118 each. *See* CRIME.

Cuban Refugees. In 1980, U.S. authorities arrested more than 1,000 recently arrived Cuban immigrants, many for crimes committed in Cuba, and held them in U.S. prisons. In July 1983, a federal court in Atlanta ruled that the confined immigrants were entitled to certain basic constitutional rights, including due-process, the right to cross-examine witnesses, and to petition for release. It appeared that long discussions between U.S. and Cuban officials would have to take place before the fate of the imprisoned Cubans would be decided. Meanwhile, in June, a number of U.S. prisoners held in the federal penitentiary in Atlanta, claiming they were outnumbered by the Cubans four to one, filed a suit protesting their confinement.

DONALD GOODMAN
John Jay College of Criminal Justice

PRIZES AND AWARDS

NOBEL PRIZES[1]

Chemistry: Henry Taube, Stanford University, for "his work in the mechanisms of electron transfer reactions, especially in metal complexes."

Economics: Gerard Debreu, French-born American professor of mathematics and economics, University of California at Berkeley, cited for his work on the problem of how prices operate to balance supply and demand.

Literature: William Golding, British novelist. (*See* page 331.)

Peace Prize: Lech Walesa, Polish founder of the Solidarity labor union, cited for his "contribution, made with considerable personal sacrifice, to ensure the workers' right to establish their own organizations." (*See also* pages 78–79.)

Physics: Subrahmanyan Chandrasekhar, University of Chicago; William A. Fowler, California Institute of Technology, cited for "their explorations of what happens as stars age, consume their nuclear fuel, form new elements, and finally collapse."

Physiology or Medicine: Barbara McClintock, Cold Spring Harbor (NY) Laboratory, "for her discovery that genes can move from one spot to another on the chromosomes of a plant and change the future generations of plants" produced.

[1] about $190,000 each category.

ART

American Academy and Institute of Arts and Letters Awards

Academy-Institute Awards ($5,000 ea.): art—Carl Andre, Jennifer Bartlett, Susan Rothenberg, Angelo Savelli, Michael C. Spafford; music—William Thomas McKinley, Bernard Rands, Bruce Saylor, Joan Tower

Arnold W. Brunner Memorial Prize in Architecture ($1,000): Frank O. Gehry

Charles Ives Fellowship ($10,000): Richard Danielpour

Charles Ives Scholarship ($5,000 ea.): Robert Convery, David Froom, Daron Aric Hagen, Michael H. Kurek, Steven Mackey, John Sackett

Distinguished Service to the Arts: Sidney Yates, U.S. representative (D-Il)

Goddard Lieberson Fellowship ($10,000 ea.): John H. Thow, Walter Keith Winslow

Gold Medal in Sculpture: Louise Nevelson

Marjorie Peabody Waite Award ($1,500): Giorgio Cavallon (in art)

Richard and Hinda Rosenthal Foundation Award ($3,000): Joanne Lowenthal (in art)

American Institute of Architects Gold Medal Award: Nathaniel Owings

Avery Fisher Prize ($10,000): Elmar Oliveira

Capezio Award for lifetime achievement in dance ($5,000): Harvey Lichtenstein, Brooklyn Academy of Music

Dance Magazine Awards: Jeannot Cerrone, John Neumeier, Michael Smuin, Martine van Hamel

Edward MacDowell Medal: Elliott Carter

John F. Kennedy Center Honors for career achievement in the performing arts: Katherine Dunham, Elia Kazan, Frank Sinatra, James Stewart, Virgil Thomson

National Academy of Recording Arts and Sciences Grammy Awards for excellence in phonograph records

Album of the year: *Toto IV,* Toto

Classical album: *Bach: The Goldberg Variations,* Glenn Gould (artist and producer), Samuel Carter (producer)

Country music song: *Always on My Mind,* Johnny Christopher, Mark James, Wayne Carson, songwriters

Jazz vocal performance, female: Sarah Vaughan, *Gershwin Live!*

Jazz vocal performance, male: Mel Tormé, *An Evening with George Shearing and Mel Tormé*

New artist: Men At Work

Record of the year: *Rosanna,* Toto

Song of the year: *Always on My Mind,* Johnny Christopher, Mark James, Wayne Carson, songwriters

Pritzker Architecture Prize ($100,000): I. M. Pei

Pulitzer Prize for Music: Ellen T. Zwilich, *Three Movements for Orchestra*

Samuel H. Scripps/American Dance Festival Award ($25,000): Paul Taylor

JOURNALISM

George Polk Memorial Awards

Criticism: Stanley Kauffmann, *The New Republic*

Financial reporting: Philip L. Zweig, *The American Banker*

Foreign reporting: Thomas L. Friedman, David K. Shipler, *The New York Times*

Local reporting: David Johnston, Joel Sappell, *Los Angeles Times*

Magazine reporting: Roger Rosenblatt, *Time*

Metropolitan reporting: Doug Cummings, *The (Providence, RI) Journal-Bulletin*

National reporting: Richard Halloran, *The New York Times*

News photography: Robby Castro, The Associated Press

Regional reporting: Jim Henderson, *The Dallas Times Herald*

Television documentary: Andrew Stern, Public Broadcasting Service for *Much Is Enough: Decision Making in the Nuclear Age*

Television reporting—local: Dick Gelfman, Theresa Crawford, John Surrick, WBAL-TV, Baltimore

Television reporting—network: CBS News, *CBS Reports*

Special award: Rod Nordland, *The Philadelphia Inquirer*

Maria Moors Cabot Prizes ($1,000 ea.): Emilio Filippi, *Hoy* magazine (Chile); Everett Martin, *The Wall Street Journal*. Special citations to Jack Fendell; the publishing company Editora Abril Ltda., São Paulo, Brazil; Marcel Niedergang

National Magazine Awards

Design: *New York*

Essays and criticism: *The American Lawyer*

Fiction: *The North American Review*

General excellence awards: *Life, Science '82, Harpers, Louisiana Life*

Public service: *Foreign Affairs*

Reporting: *Institutional Investor*

Single-topic issue: *IEEE Spectrum*

Overseas Press Club Awards

Book on foreign affairs: Fox Butterfield, *China: Alive in the Bitter Sea*

Business news reporting from abroad: Larry Gurwin, *Institutional Investor*

Cartoon on foreign affairs: Richard Locher, *The Chicago Tribune*

Daily newspaper or wire service interpretation of foreign affairs: Joseph Kingsbury Smith, Hearst Newspapers

Daily newspaper or wire service reporting from abroad: Walter Wisniewski, Jack Redden, UPI

Magazine story on foreign affairs: *Time,* "After Brezhnev"

Magazine reporting from abroad: *Newsweek,* Mideast Coverage

Photographic reporting from abroad (magazine and books)—Bill Pierce, *Time;* (newspapers and wire services)—Eli Reed, *San Francisco Examiner*

Radio interpretation of foreign affairs: ABC News Radio

Radio spot news from abroad: Walter Wisniewski, UPI Audio

Television interpretation or documentary on foreign affairs: Anthony Potter, Marvin Kalb, NBC-TV, *White Paper*—"The Man Who Shot the Pope: A Study in Terrorism"

Television spot news reporting from abroad: *CBS Evening News with Dan Rather,* Middle East Coverage

Robert Capa Gold Medal: Harry Mattison, *Time*

Madeline Dane Ross Award: Walt Bogdanich, Joe Frolik, Christopher Jensen, *The Plain Dealer*, Cleveland, OH

Pulitzer Prizes

Commentary: Claude Sitton, *The News and Observer*, Raleigh, NC

Criticism: Manuela Hoelterhoff, *The Wall Street Journal*

Editorial cartooning: Richard Locher, *The Chicago Tribune*

Editorial writing: editorial board of *The Miami Herald*

Feature photography: James B. Dickman, *The Dallas Times Herald*

Feature writing: Nan Robertson, *The New York Times*

General local reporting: *The News-Sentinel*, Ft. Wayne, IN

International reporting: Thomas L. Friedman, *The New York Times*

National reporting: *The Boston Globe* for a special section "War and Peace in the Nuclear Age"

Public service: *The Clarion-Ledger*, Jackson, MS

Special local reporting: Loretta Tofani, *The Washington Post*

Spot news photography: Bill Foley, The Associated Press

LITERATURE

Alfred and Ellen Knowles Harcourt Awards ($10,000 ea.)

Alfred Harcourt Award in biography and memoirs: Elisabeth Young-Bruehl, Hannah Arendt: *For Love of the World*

Ellen Knowles Harcourt Award in biography and memoirs: Sharon N. White for her dissertation *Mabel Loomis Todd: Gender, Language, and Power in Victorian America*

American Academy and Institute of Arts and Letters Awards

Academy-Institute Awards ($5,000 ea.): Alfred Corn, Stephen Dixon, Robert Mezey, Mary Oliver, David Plante, George Starbuck, Leo Steinberg, Edmund White

The American Academy in Rome Fellowship in Literature: Gjertrud Schnackenberg

Award of Merit Medal for the Short Story ($5,000): Elizabeth Spencer

Gold Medal in Fiction: Bernard Malamud

Harold D. Vursell Memorial Award ($5,000): Jonathan D. Spence

Loines Award in Poetry ($2,500): Geoffrey Hill

Medal for Spoken Language: Alistair Cooke

The Mildred and Harold Strauss Livings ($35,000 ea. annually for five years): Raymond Carver, Cynthia Ozick

Richard and Hinda Rosenthal Foundation Award ($3,000): A. G. Mojtabai

Sue Kaufman Prize for First Fiction ($1,000): Susanna Moore

Witter Bynner Prize for Poetry ($1,500): Douglas Crase

American Book Awards

Hardcover ($1,000 ea.)—

Autobiography/Biography: Judith Thurman, *Isak Dinesen: The Life of a Storyteller*

Children's fiction: Jean Fritz, *Homesick: My Own Story*

Children's nonfiction: James Cross Giblin, *Chimney Sweeps*

Children's picture books (cowinners): Barbara Cooney, *Miss Rumphius;* William Steig, *Doctor De Soto*

Fiction: Alice Walker, *The Color Purple*

First novel: Gloria Naylor, *The Women of Brewster Place*

General nonfiction: Fox Butterfield, *China: Alive in the Bitter Sea*

History: Alan Brinkley, *Voices of Protest: Huey Long, Father Coughlin and the Great Depression*

Poetry: (cowinners)—Galway Kinnell, *Selected Poems;* Charles Wright, *Country Music*

Science: Abraham Pais, *'Subtle Is the Lord . . .' The Science and Life of Albert Einstein*

Translation: Richard Howard, Charles Baudelaire's *Les Fleurs du Mal*

Paperback ($1,000)—

Autobiography/Biography: James R. Mellow, *Nathaniel Hawthorne in His Times*

Children's fiction: (cowinners)—Paula Fox, *A Place Apart;* Joyce Carol Thomas, *Marked by Fire*

Children's picture books: Mary Ann Hoberman, *A House Is a House for Me*

Fiction: *The Collected Stories of Eudora Welty*

History: Frank E. Manuel, Fritzie P. Manuel, *Utopian Thought in the Western World*

Nonfiction: James Fallows, *National Defense*

Original paperback: Lisa Goldstein, *The Red Magician*

Science: Philip J. Davis, Reuben Hersh, *The Mathematical Experience*

Graphic—

Design—Cover (mass market paperback): (*Key Exchange* by Kevin Wade) Martha Sedgwick, designer; Matt Tepper, art director

Design—Cover (trade paperback): (*Bogmail* by Patrick McGinley) Doris Ettlinger, illustrator; Neil Stuart, designer/art director

Design—Jacket: (*Soul on Fire* by Elie Wiesel) Fred Marcellino, designer; Frank Metz, art director

Design—Pictorial: (*Alice's Adventures in Wonderland* by Lewis Carroll) Barry Moser, designer/illustrator; Steve Renick, art director

Design—Typographical: (*A Constructed Roman Alphabet* by David Lance Goines) David Lance Goines, designer/illustrator; William F. Luckey, art director

Illustration—collected art: (*John Singer Sargent* by Carter Ratcliff) Howard Morris, designer; Nancy Grubb, editor; Dana Cole, production manager

Illustration—original art: (*Porcupine Stew* by Beverly Major) Erick Ingraham, illustrator; Cynthia Basil, designer/art director

Illustration—photographs: (*Alfred Stieglitz: Photographs and Writings* by Sarah Greenough and Juan Hamilton) Eleanor Morris Caponigro, designer

Bancroft Prizes ($4,000 ea.): John P. Demos, *Entertaining Satan: Witchcraft and the Culture of Early New England;* Nick Salvatore, *Eugene V. Debs: Citizen and Socialist*

Canada's Governor-General's Literary Awards ($5,000 ea.)

English drama: John Gray, *Billy Bishop Goes to War*

French drama: Rejean Ducharme, *Ha ha!*

English fiction: Guy Vanderhaeghe, *Man Descending*

French fiction: Roger Fournier, *Le cercle de arenes*

English nonfiction: Christopher Moore, *Louisburg Portraits: Life in an Eighteenth Century Garrison Town*

French nonfiction: Maurice Lagueux, *Le marxisme des annes soixante*

English poetry: Phyllis Webb, *The Vision Tree*

French poetry: Michel Savard, *Forages*

PEN/Faulkner Award for Fiction ($5,000): Toby Olson, *Seaview*

Pulitzer Prizes

Biography: Russell Baker, *Growing Up*

Fiction: Alice Walker, *The Color Purple*

General nonfiction: Susan Sheehan, *Is There No Place on Earth for Me?*

History: Rhys L. Isaac, *The Transformation of Virginia, 1740–1790*

Poetry: Galway Kinnell, *Selected Poems*

Robert F. Kennedy Book Award ($2,500): Stephen B. Oates, *Let the Trumpet Sound: The Life of Martin Luther King, Jr.*

(See also LIBRARIES.)

MOTION PICTURES

Academy of Motion Picture Arts and Sciences ("Oscar") Awards
Actor—leading role: Ben Kingsley, *Gandhi*
Actor—supporting role: Louis Gossett, Jr., *An Officer and a Gentleman*
Actress—leading role: Meryl Streep, *Sophie's Choice*
Actress—supporting role: Jessica Lange, *Tootsie*
Cinematography: Billy Williams and Ronnie Taylor, *Gandhi*
Costume design: John Mollo and Bhanu Athaiya, *Gandhi*
Director: Sir Richard Attenborough, *Gandhi*
Film: *Gandhi*
Foreign-language film: *Volver a Empezar* (To Begin Again) (Spain)
Music—original score: John Williams, *E.T. The Extra-Terrestrial*
Music—adapted score: Henry Mancini and Leslie Bricusse, *Victor/Victoria*
Music—song: Jack Neitzsche, Buffy Sainte-Marie, Will Jennings, *Up Where We Belong* from *An Officer and a Gentleman*
Screenplay—original: John Briley, *Gandhi*
Screenplay—adaptation: Costa-Gavras and Donald Stewart, *Missing*
Gordon E. Sawyer Award: John O. Aalberg
Jean Hersholt Humanitarian Award: Walter Mirisch
Honorary Award: Mickey Rooney
Special Award: August Arnold and Erich Kaestner
American Film Institute's Life Achievement Award: John Huston
Cannes Film Festival Award
Best actor: Gian Maria Volonte, *Death of Mario Ricci*
Best actress: Hanna Schygulla, *Story of Pierra*
Best artistic contribution: *Carmen* (Spanish)
Creative cinema prize: (shared)—Robert Bresson, *Money;* Andrei Tarkovsky, *Nostalgia*
Golden Palm award: *The Ballad of Narayama* (Japan)
Jury prize: *The Case Is Closed,* Mrinal Sen
Special grand prize: *The Meaning of Life*

PUBLIC SERVICE

Alexander Onassis Foundation Prize ($100,000): Andrzej Wajda
American Institute for Public Service Jefferson Awards
Local public service awards ($1,000 ea.): Dean Crisp, Darlene Handley, Robert Kustra, Candy Lightner, Tony Messineo
National public service awards ($5,000 ea.): Kirk Douglas, Helen Hayes, Paul A. Volcker, Jan Scruggs
Four Freedoms Foundation Awards: W. Averell Harriman, Joseph L. Rauh, Jr., Coretta Scott King, Robert S. McNamara, Jacob K. Javits
Harry S. Truman Public Service Award: Coretta Scott King (and the late Martin Luther King, Jr.)
Templeton Prize for progress in religion ($170,000): Aleksandr I. Solzhenitsyn
U.S. Presidential Medal of Freedom (presented by President Ronald Reagan on Feb. 23): George Balanchine, Paul W. (Bear) Bryant (posthumously), James Burnham, James Cheek, R. Buckminster Fuller, Billy Graham, Eric Hoffer, Clare Booth Luce, Dumas Malone, Mabel Mercer, Simon Ramo, Jacob K. Javits

SCIENCE

Albert Lasker Awards
Basic research ($15,000 shared): Eric R. Kandel, Columbia University; Vernon B. Mountcastle, Jr., Johns Hopkins University
Clinical research ($15,000): F. Mason Sones, Jr., Cleveland Clinic Foundation
Public service award ($15,000 shared): Saul Krugman, New York University; Maurice R. Hilleman, Merck Sharp and Dohme Research Laboratories

Wide World

Soviet writer Aleksandr Solzhenitsyn accepted the 1983 Templeton Prize for progress in religion in London in May.

Bristol-Myers Award ($50,000): Leo Sachs, Weizmann Institute of Science, Rehovot, Israel
General Motors Cancer Research Foundation Awards ($130,000 ea.): Bruce N. Ames; Raymond L. Erikson; and (shared) Emil Frei 3d and Emil J. Freireich
Lita Annenberg Hazen Award for excellence in clinical research ($100,000): Robert J. Lefkowitz
Louisa Gross Horwitz Prize for research in biology or biochemistry ($22,000): (shared)—Viktor Hamburger, Rita Levi-Montalcini, Washington University; Stanley Cohen, Vanderbilt University
National Inventor Hall of Fame Inventor of the Year Award: Robert Jarvik, artificial heart developer
National Medal of Science Awards (presented by President Ronald Reagan on May 24): Philip W. Anderson, Seymour Benzer, Glen W. Burton, Mildred Cohn, F. Albert Cotton, Edward F. Heinemann, Donald L. Katz, Yoichiro Nambu, Gilbert Stork, Edward Teller, Charles H. Townes, Marshall Stone
U.S. Energy Department Enrico Fermi Award ($25,000 ea.): Herbert Anderson, Seth Neddermeyer
U.S. National Science Board Vannevar Bush Award: Frederick Seitz

TELEVISION AND RADIO

Academy of Television Arts and Sciences ("Emmy") Awards
Actor—comedy series: Judd Hirsch, *Taxi* (NBC)
Actor—drama series: Ed Flanders, *St. Elsewhere* (NBC)
Actor—limited series: Tommy Lee Jones, *The Executioner's Song* (NBC)
Actress—comedy series: Shelley Long, *Cheers* (NBC)
Actress—drama series: Tyne Daly, *Cagney and Lacey* (CBS)
Actress—limited series: Barbara Stanwyck, *The Thorn Birds* (ABC)
Children's Program: *Big Bird in China* (NBC)
Classical program in the performing arts: *Pavarotti in Philadelphia: La Bohème* (PBS)
Comedy series: *Cheers* (NBC)
Drama series: *Hill Street Blues* (NBC)
Informational series: *The Barbara Walters Specials* (ABC)
Informational special: *The Body Human: The Living Code* (CBS)
Limited series: *Nicholas Nickleby* (syndicated)
Special drama: *Special Bulletin* (NBC)
Supporting actor—comedy series: Christopher Lloyd, *Taxi* (NBC)

Supporting actor—drama series: James Coco, *St. Elsewhere* (NBC)

Supporting actor—limited series or special: Richard Kiley, *The Thorn Birds* (ABC)

Supporting actress—comedy series: Carol Kane, *Taxi* (NBC)

Supporting actress—drama series: Doris Roberts, *St. Elsewhere* (NBC)

Supporting actress—limited series or special: Jean Simmons, *The Thorn Birds* (ABC)

Variety, music, or comedy program: *Motown 25: Yesterday, Today, Forever*

Governors Award: Sylvester L. "Pat" Weaver, Jr., former president of NBC

George Foster Peabody Awards

Radio: CBC Radio for *Morningside/1905;* The Mutual Broadcasting System, *The Larry King Show;* National Public Radio for *The Sunday Show* and for *Taylor Made Piano: A Jazz History;* NBC Radio News for *Banks on the Brink;* The Radio Foundation, New York, for *The Bob and Ray Public Radio Show;* WMAL, Washington, DC, for *They Served with Honor.*

Television: ABC News for *ABC News Closeup,* "Vietnam Requiem"; BBC, Paramount Television, and Operation Prime Time for *Smiley's People;* CBS News for *The CBS News Special,* "Juilliard and Beyond: A Life of Music"; CBS Entertainment and Cinetex International for *The Wall;* Daniel Wilson Productions and Taurus Film for *Blood and Honor: Youth Under Hitler;* KGMB-TV, Honolulu, and Lee Productions, Inc. for *Beyond the Great Wall: Journey to the End of China;* KQED-TV, San Francisco, for *Current Affairs/The Case of Dashiell Hammett;* KOCO-TV, Oklahoma City, for *Oklahoma Shame;* KYW-TV, Philadelphia, for *Sweet Nothing;* NBC and Highgate Pictures for *The Electric Grandmother;* NBC News for *NBC White Paper* "The Man Who Shot the Pope: A Study in Terrorism"; NBC-TV, Margie-Lee Enterprises, Inc., and The Blue Marble Company, Inc., in association with ITC Productions, Inc., for *Skeezer;* the Television Corporation of America for *784 Days that Changed America—from Watergate to Resignation;* Texaco, Inc., The Texaco Foundation, and the Metropolitan Opera Association for "their commitment to both radio and television presentations of great opera"; WAGA-TV, Atlanta, for *Paradise Saved;* Warner Amex Satellite Entertainment Company for overall programming for children and young people on the Nickelodeon channel; WBBM-TV, Chicago, for *Killing Crime: A Police Cop-Out;* WCVB-TV, Boston, for *Ground Zero: Victory Road;* WQED, Pittsburgh, for Stravinsky's *Firebird* by the Dance Theatre of Harlem; WTSP-TV, St. Petersburg, FL, for *Prisoners of the Harvest;* WWL-TV, New Orleans, for *The Search for Alexander*

Individual award: Alistair Cooke

Humanitas Awards

Long-form category ($25,000): Marshall Herskovitz (original story by Herskovitz and Edward Zwick), *Special Bulletin*

One-hour category ($15,000): David Milch, *Hill Street Blues* episode

One-half-hour category ($10,000): David Pollock, Elias Davis, *M*A*S*H*

THEATER

Antoinette Perry ("Tony") Awards

Actor-drama: Harvey Fierstein, *Torch Song Trilogy*

Actor—musical: Tommy Tune, *My One and Only*

Actress—drama: Jessica Tandy, *Foxfire*

Actress—musical: Natalia Makarova, *On Your Toes*

Choreography: Tommy Tune, Thommie Walsh, *My One and Only*

Costume design: John Napier, *Cats*

Director—drama: Gene Saks, *Brighton Beach Memoirs*

Director—musical: Trevor Nunn, *Cats*

Featured actor—drama: Matthew Broderick, *Brighton Beach Memoirs*

Featured actor—musical: Charles "Honi" Coles, *My One and Only*

Featured actress—drama: Judith Ivey, *Steaming*

Featured actress—musical: Betty Buckley, *Cats*

Lighting design: David Hersey, *Cats*

Musical: *Cats*

Musical—book: T. S. Eliot (posthumously), *Cats*

Musical—score: T. S. Eliot, Andrew Lloyd Webber, *Cats*

Play: *Torch Song Trilogy* by Harvey Fierstein

Reproduction of a play or musical: *On Your Toes*

Scenic design: Ming Cho Lee, *K2*

Special awards: The Oregon Shakespeare Festival Association, The Theater Collection of the Museum of the City of New York

New York Drama Critics Circle Theater Awards

Best new play: *Brighton Beach Memoirs,* Neil Simon

Best foreign play: *Plenty,* David Hare

Best musical: *Little Shop of Horrors*

Pulitzer Prize for Drama: Marsha Norman, *Night, Mother*

Susan Smith Blackburn Prize ($2,000): Marsha Norman, *Night, Mother*

In 1983, Tony Award winners included (left to right): Tommy Tune, Natalia Makarova, Jessica Tandy, Harvey Fierstein.

UPI

PUBLISHING

In 1982, Americans spent an estimated $727 per household on media products, an increase of 52% since 1978. According to a study by Knowledge Industry Publications, Inc., $210 went for newspapers, magazines, and books; $294 for television, radio, and other electronic products; and $223 for subscription TV, video games, recorders and home computers. The conventional print media are expected to remain healthy in the next five years, the report said, but the "new electronic media" will account for an increasing percentage of the total.

Media leaders, optimistic about the future, still eyed the economy, inflation, and interest rates with uneasiness. Specialist Robert Koen predicted that advertising spending would climb 11% in 1983 to $73 billion (U.S.), and 12.2% in 1984 to $82.8 billion; magazines would receive $4.1 billion and newspapers $2.6 billion.

President Ronald Reagan and the press remained at odds. Upset over leaks, Reagan told the American Newspaper Publishers Association he thought "the press is free to print those things that should be printed," adding that politicians and publishers "have a lot in common. We both see articles in the papers that make us very angry, but there's nothing we can do about them." In an effort to control the leaking of classified information, the president proposed that all government officials with access to such information submit their writings for government review. The American Society of Newspaper Editors called the proposal "peacetime censorship."

New magazines arrived. Chicago and Houston newspapers were up for sale, but there were no immediate buyers. *USA TODAY* expanded its national circulation and prompted other dailies to improve their graphics.

Magazine and newspaper circulations held steady. More money was spent on books.

Books. Sales were up 10% early in 1983, after 1982 ended on a "disappointing note." Bookstore owners continued to report narrow profits. Sales in 1983 were expected to top $8.7 billion, up $800 million over 1982. John Dessauer, in *Trends Update,* was optimistic, basing his outlook on the "growing cultural maturation" of the people, the increased role of books in "vocation, avocational, and leisure time pursuits," more outlets for book buyers, and improved distribution methods.

However, many potential buyers were turned back by prices that averaged about $27 for hardback books and nearly $10 for trade paperbacks. Those who did buy preferred biographies, histories, and reference books, according to a Gallup survey in *Publishers Weekly.* Rapidly developing technology challenged publishers to adopt new techniques. Some feared rising labor and paper costs.

Extensive interest was displayed in books about computers, with some 100 new titles in the first half of 1983 alone. *Publishers Weekly* reported there were 2,700 books and 225 magazines in print about computers.

Romance books continued to sell by the millions. The Harlequin series, with sales of more than 200 million yearly, was challenged by Silhouette Books and other series. *Newsweek* reported that ten romance titles each sold in excess of one million copies in 1982. A bibliography covering the last 15 years by Mary June Kay listed 19,000 titles, 3,700 authors, and 750 pen names. About 130 new titles reach the market each month. Plots were becoming more modern, reflecting changes in modern society.

"Business is hotter than sex," reported the *Wall Street Journal.* Despite an average price of $25, business titles were selling extremely well. Peter Drucker, who finally succeeded in having his *Concept of the Corporation* published in 1946, now has 15 business titles with total hardback sales of more than 1.2 million. Television and movie personalities continued to publish books and pushed them on TV talk shows; prominent among them were Linda Evans and her *Beauty and Exercise Book.* *Publishers Weekly* reported that prejudices toward rock 'n' roll books were being shed by publishers; more than 50 Elvis Presley and 35 Beatles volumes already were on the market. And, despite at least 130 novels based on Vietnam, more were expected.

Publishers Weekly's study of the longest running best-sellers in 1982 included Robert Ludlum's *The Parsifal Mosaic* for 38 weeks on the hardcover-fiction list, followed by John Jakes' *North and South,* 32 weeks. In nonfiction, *Jane Fonda's Workout Book* appeared for 48 weeks. Television commentator Andy Rooney expanded his audience with *A Few Minutes With Andy Rooney,* on the list for 43 weeks. *When Bad Things Happen to Good People,* by Harold Kushner, was on 41 weeks. The paperback market was dominated by Andrew M. Greeley's *The Cardinal Sins* and Martin Cruz Smith's *Gorky Park,* both 22 weeks.

Jim Davis' "Garfield" books continued as bestsellers.

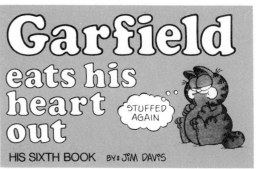

GARFIELD: © 1978 United Feature Syndicate, Inc.

Carole Jackson's *Color Me Beautiful* and five of Jim Davis' *Garfield* collections were trade leaders.

Rooney continued to sell well in 1983, especially his *And More of Andy Rooney*. Leo Buscaglia's television shows hiked sales of his *Living, Loving and Learning*. *Garfield* continued to appear, as did Stephen King with *Different Seasons* and *Christine*. Danielle Steel's *Remembrance* and *Thurston House* sold well. James A. Michener's *Space* and Arthur C. Clarke's *2010: Odyssey Two* were early 1983 bestsellers. Later, John le Carré's *The Little Drummer Girl* and Barbara Taylor Bradford's *Voice of the Heart* joined the list, along with Umberto Eco's *The Name of the Rose* and Lawrence Sanders' *The Seduction of Peter S*. John Naisbitt's *Megatrends: Ten New Directions Transforming Our Lives*, sold more than 600,000 hardback copies. Other best-sellers were Kenneth Blanchard and Spencer Johnson's *The One-Minute Manager* and *In Search of Excellence* by Thomas J. Peters and Robert Waterman, Jr.

George Orwell's *1984* gained new interest as that year approached; since the book appeared in 1948, more than 10 million copies have been sold. Seymour Hersh's book on Henry Kissinger, *The Price of Power* was a "summer newsmaker"; the book received extensive media coverage and was debated heatedly.

In 1983, John Wiley & Sons celebrated the firm's 175th year, the University of California Press marked its 90th, and Viking's Junior Books reached 50.

Magazines. With advertising revenues up more than 10% and circulation up 1.5% for the first half of 1983, magazine-industry leaders predicted further gains for 1984, providing the economy continued upward. Competition held down printing costs. Salaries edged upward slightly. More emphasis was placed on newsstand sales.

Playboy and *Penthouse* lost circulation and advertising; *Playboy*'s guarantee dropped from 4.4 to 4.1 million, and *Penthouse*'s from 4 to 3.4 million. *Hustler* publisher Larry Flynt lost a Supreme Court ruling in his suit against Eastman Kodak.

Circulation leaders remained about the same. *Reader's Digest* edged *TV Guide*, 18,299,091 to 17,275,471, according to Audit Bureau of Circulation figures for mid-1983. *National Geographic* reported 10,357,853; *Modern Maturity* 8,822,161, and *Better Homes & Gardens*, 8,022,794. *Family Circle* with 7,303,488, and *Woman's Day* with 6,949,344, continued their rivalry. *McCall's* with 6,277,293, *Good Housekeeping* with 5,420,830, and *Ladies' Home Journal* with 5,200,705, demonstrated the staying power of these women's periodicals. The tabloid *National Enquirer* had 5,075,123 weekly circulation.

In a year of anniversaries, *Automotive News* reached 75; *Esquire, Newsweek,* and *U.S. News & World Report* their 50th; *Time,* 60 years old, maintained its leadership among

Courtesy, "Newsweek"

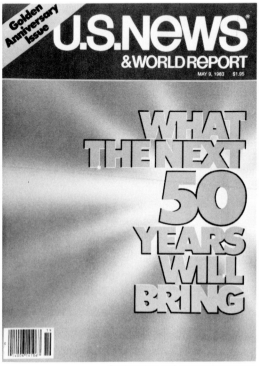

the news weeklies with 4,719,343 circulation to *Newsweek*'s 3,022,727, and *U.S. News*' 2,112,057.

TV Guide's 30th anniversary reminded readers of its first cover, which featured Lucille Ball and her baby, Desi Arnez, Jr. In 1983 *TV Guide* spent $200 million in content and production changes, adding cable coverage and other editorial segments. Its potential competitor, Time Inc.'s *TV-Cable News*, folded in September.

Oldtimers underwent changes. *Woman's Day* was redesigned, and *Family Circle* sought a younger audience. *Business Week* adopted a "radically different" format with a faster production schedule. *Inside Sports* hoped to resume publication, and *Saturday Review* found a new home in Missouri. *Nation* lost a copyright suit over its early publication of excerpts of President Gerald Ford's memoirs. *Vanity Fair* made a rocky return. *Advertising Age* began a German-language edition and *Discover* a Chinese-language version.

Researchers reported greater interest in food, automobile, shelter, science, travel, and business periodicals. Magazines for the intellect slipped; *People* readers increased.

Time edged *TV Guide* for the 1982 advertising revenue lead, $256,409,613 to $241,472,723. Other periodicals with $100 million or more included *Newsweek, Sports Illustrated, People, Business Week, Good Housekeeping, Family Circle, Reader's Digest,* and *Better Homes & Gardens.* During the first quarter of 1983, *TV Guide* regained the lead.

In total ad pages, *Business Week* led *BYTE,* followed by *The New Yorker, TV Guide, People, Forbes, Newsweek, Vogue, Fortune,* and *Sports Illustrated.* The business press reported its first page loss since 1975. Page leaders were *Computerworld, Electronic Design, Oil & Gas Journal,* and *Medical Economics. Folio* magazine reported that the fastest-growing business magazines in ad revenues included *Computer Decisions, Mini-Micro Systems, Institutional Investor,* and *The Blood Horse.*

Newspapers. U.S. daily newspapers spent $805 million in 1982 for new equipment and facilities and planned similar expenditures for 1983. The Associated Press, observing its 135th birthday, budgeted a record $185 million and planned additional satellite facilities.

Gannett President Al Neuharth predicted an era of unprecedented growth, Newspaper executives continued to cut costs by greater use of computers. A standard ad-size based on column inches was another goal. The expansion of community shoppers, however, drew advertising revenues from the dailies.

The *New York Daily News'* circulation of 2,004,835 led all Sunday papers in mid-1983, followed by the *New York Times, Chicago Tribune, Philadelphia Inquirer,* and *Washington Post,* each with more than a million. The *Wall Street Journal* led dailies with 2,036,789 circulation. Only the *New York Daily News* (1,513,941) and the *Los Angeles Times* (1,060,588) had more than one million. The *Daily News* moved from a $14 million deficit in 1982 to a profit in 1983, aided in part by union concessions.

Editor & Publisher International Yearbook reported a total U.S. circulation of 33,150,291 for 433 morning papers; 29,287,783 for 1,711 afternoon and 34 all-day papers; and 56,152,405 for 768 Sunday editions. The 7,626 weeklies had a total of 44 million circulation. Gannett remained the largest newspaper group with 87 dailies and 57 Sunday editions, for a combined circulation of 4,239,158. Other group leaders were Knight-Ridder, Newhouse, and The New York Times Co.

In 1983, Robert C. Maynard acquired the *Oakland Tribune* from Gannett for $22 million, becoming the first black owner of a general circulation metro daily. Rupert Murdoch bought the *Boston Herald American* and *Chicago Sun-Times. Grit,* the century-old feature weekly, was sold to Stauffer Communications. And in Peoria, IL, the *Journal Star* became employee-owned, a rarity in the United States. Employment of minorities showed slight gains. Women accounted for 39% of the newspaper work force. Most dailies cost 25¢, with Sunday issues 50¢. Newsprint consumption, down in 1982, edged upward in early 1983.

The long-debated merger of the International Typographical Union (ITU) and The Newspaper Guild was vetoed by the ITU. In New York, Boston, Buffalo, and other cities across the nation, unions made concessions in attempts to save ailing publishers.

The National News Council, under its new leader, former CBS News chief Richard S. Salant, campaigned for funds to probe the press. One topic for its study was the relationship between George Will and Ronald Reagan during the Carter-Reagan debates. At least eight newspapers dropped the columnist because of his assistance to Reagan.

Editors, publishers, and journalism professors responded to a Media Research Institute questionnaire and listed their top 15 papers as follows: *New York Times, Wall Street Journal, Washington Post, Los Angeles Times, Chicago Tribune, Christian Science Monitor, Philadelphia Inquirer, Boston Globe, Miami Herald, St. Petersburg Times, Newsday, Atlanta Constitution, Louisville Courier-Journal, Milwaukee Journal,* and *St. Louis Post-Dispatch.*

Editor & Publisher will celebrate its 100th birthday in 1984. The *Christian Science Monitor* was 75 in 1983. *Parade,* a Sunday magazine supplement, added the *New York Daily News* to its 132 other papers and reached a record 24.2 million circulation.

WILLIAM H. TAFT
University of Missouri-Columbia

PUERTO RICO

A new political party, the Puerto Rican Renewal Party (PRP), was organized in August 1983 under the leadership of San Juan Mayor Hernán Padilla. The purpose of the party, according to Padilla, is to suspend indefinitely debate on the problem of Puerto Rico's political status.

Traditionally, Puerto Rican political parties have supported one of three status alternatives —statehood, autonomy, or independence. Padilla, formerly a member of the pro-statehood New Progressive Party (PNP), said the PRP wants to "liberate the people from that ideological prison." The PRP collected 90,000 signatures on its registration petition, 10,000 more than required, in its first two months of existence.

The decision of Gov. Carlos Romero Barceló, head of the PNP, to seek a third term in 1984 triggered the split in the PNP and led to the founding of the PRP. Observers said the rift strengthens the electoral chances of the Popular Democratic Party (PPD), which supports autonomy for Puerto Rico and seeks to improve the island's status as a self-governing commonwealth with the United States. Former Gov. Rafael Hernández Colón was expected to be the PPD gubernatorial candidate in 1984.

The status issue was also raised in the U.S. Congress, where Rep. Bill Richardson (D-NM) introduced a resolution to create a select committee on Puerto Rico's political relationship with the United States. The measure was opposed by Baltazar Corrada del Rio, the resident commissioner for Puerto Rico in the House, who called it an "ambush" of the island.

Cerro Maravilla. Insular legislative hearings were held in a four-year-old case in which two independence supporters were shot to death by police as they allegedly tried to blow up an important communications tower atop a hill named Cerro Maravilla. It was charged at the time that the two were "set up" by police. The hearings probed additional charges that the insular government had covered up its complicity in the killings.

PUERTO RICO · Information Highlights

Area: 3,421 sq mi (8 860 km²).
Population (1982 est.): 3,300,000.
Chief Cities (1980 census): San Juan, the capital, 434,849; Bayamón, 196,206; Ponce, 189,046.
Government (1983): *Chief Officers*—governor, Carlos Romero Barceló (New Progressive Party); secretary of state, Samuel R. Quirós. *Legislature*—Senate, 27 members; House of Representatives, 51 members.

Economy. The tourism and construction industries continued to feel the effects of the U.S. recession. Arrival of passengers by air in the second quarter of the year fell by 100,000 from the second quarter of 1982. In construction, new building permits, cement consumption, and sales of construction materials declined.

Other economic sectors performed better than expected, however, with manufacturing leading the way, particularly during the second half of fiscal 1983. Average manufacturing employment rose from 698,000 in January to 723,000 in August, on a seasonally adjusted basis. Personal income increased 1.4% in the April-June quarter, following a 0.5% rise during the previous three-month period. The Consumer Price Index increased by only 0.6%, compared with 7.3% the previous year.

There was considerable controversy over the potential impact of the Caribbean Basin Initiative (CBI—*see* CARIBBEAN) on Puerto Rico. Commonwealth officials lost their battle to exclude rum and tuna, two products important to the island's economy, from duty-free entry into the United States. But some economists said Puerto Rico stood to benefit from a "twin plant" scheme under which items would undergo primary processing in a CBI beneficiary country and would be finished in Puerto Rico.

Puerto Rico's cash-benefit Program for Aid to Nutrition (PAN), which replaced the food stamp program in 1982, was ordered terminated by the federal government on October 1. Congress extended the program through Jan. 1, 1984, and legislation to make the extension permanent was introduced in late October.

RICHARD C. SCHROEDER, *"Visión" Magazine*

UPI

Gov. Carlos Romero Barceló (left) and opposition leaders Rafael Hernández Colón (center) and Ruben Barrios Martínez held a panel discussion on the political status of Puerto Rico at Harvard in April. Romero favored statehood, Hernández supported continuation of commonwealth status, and Barrios called for full independence.

QUEBEC

The perennial question of Quebec's place in the Confederation, and issues related to it, occupied center stage in 1983. Premier René Lévesque found himself in a complex position as he pondered future strategy for maintaining his hold on power and making Quebec an independent state. The year's continuing slow economic recovery did not help him.

Politics. Robert Bourassa recaptured the leadership of the Quebec Liberal Party on October 15. He easily defeated two other candidates, Daniel Johnson and Pierre Paradis, on the first ballot. In his victory speech, Bourassa took a firmly pro-federalist position, proclaiming his intention to "fight for Canada."

Bourassa was premier from 1970 to 1976, when the Separatist Parti Québécois (PQ) came to power. Opinion polls taken in 1983 indicated that he has an excellent chance of regaining his old job. However, a provincial election could be delayed until 1986, by which time the PQ could regain its lost popularity.

Progressive Conservatives (PCs). The return to the political scene of Bourassa, a proven vote-getter in the past, was one of several developments that could indicate future trouble for Lévesque and his Parti Québécois. Another was the selection of M. Brian Mulroney, a native Quebecer, to lead the federal Conservative Party. Mulroney's win on June 11 meant that, for a time at least, Quebec men were at the helm of Canada's two major federal political parties. (Prime Minister Pierre Trudeau was still the Liberal leader.) This undoubtedly served in subtle ways to blunt the PQ's pro-independence appeal. The PQ lost a referendum on independence in 1980 but remains committed to the goal. Somewhat bizarrely, the PQ's first response to Mulroney's nomination was to establish a federal offshoot, the Parti Nationaliste, to contest the next federal election. Lévesque gave the venture only dubious and reluctant support, however.

Scandals. Two highly publicized scandals compounded PQ misfortunes. A cofounder of the party with Lévesque, Gilles Gregoire, was convicted on seven morals charges involving young girls and was sentenced to two years in jail. Disowned by his party, he became an independent and continued to hold his National Assembly seat for Frontenac riding.

Earlier, Claude Charron, the government House leader, was convicted of shoplifting from an Eaton's department store. He resigned both his cabinet position and his legislature seat. Charron's Montreal seat subsequently was won by the opposition Liberals in a by-election, one of three by-elections the Liberals won June 20.

Constitution. The PQ also had its troubles in the constitutional and judicial arenas. Lévesque's furious opposition to Canada's new Constitution led him to launch a case before the Quebec Appeal Court that ended with the unwelcome finding—for him—that Quebec has no right of veto over constitutional development in Canada.

In another major ruling, June 9, the Appeal Court upheld a lower court finding that the new Canadian Bill of Rights takes precedence over Quebec's controversial Bill 101 in determining whether a child may attend an English-language school. The court unanimously confirmed that Canadians educated in English anywhere in Canada have the right to send their children to English schools. Bill 101 restricts such schooling to children of parents educated in English in Quebec.

Lévesque to Paris. Premier Lévesque's visit to Paris in June culminated in a letter of intent from a French government-owned corporation to construct a C$1.5 billion aluminum smelter near Trois-Rivières on the St. Lawrence River. However, the premier was unable to mobilize French support for Quebec independence from Canada, "our ally and long-time friend," as Prime Minister Mauroy called it. All in all, the French government showed less interest in promoting Quebec sovereignty than any French administration since the time of President Charles de Gaulle in the 1960s.

Labor Difficulties. In late January and early February a wave of public-sector strikes swept the province, called to protest pay cuts and curbs on collective-bargaining rights. At one point about 200,000 workers were off the job. Most of the walkouts fizzled in the face of tough reprisals by the government, but about 85,000 teachers stayed out for nearly four weeks and had to be legislated back to work.

Economic. Quebec continued to suffer the lingering effects of the recession, with unemployment constantly in the 14–15% range, about three points higher than the national average. The dismal economic picture provoked demonstrations in October at Grande-Vallée.

JOHN BEST, *"Canada World News"*

QUEBEC • Information Highlights

Area: 594,860 sq mi (1 540 687 km²).
Population (July 1983): 6,524,700.
Chief Cities (1981 census): Quebec, the capital, 166,474; Montreal, 980,354; Laval, 268,335; Longueil, 124,320.
Government (1983): *Chief Officers*—lt. gov., Jean-Pierre Coté; premier, René Lévesque (Parti Québécois). *Legislature*—Legislative Assembly, 122 members.
Education (1982–83): Enrollment—elementary and secondary schools, 1,160,640 pupils; postsecondary, 221,800 students.
Public Finance (1983 fiscal year, est.): *Revenues,* $23,473,000,000; *expenditures,* $25,239,000,000.
Personal Income (average weekly salary, March 1983): $402.70.
Unemployment Rate (August 1983, seasonally adjusted): 14.0%.
(All monetary figures are in Canadian dollars.)

RECORDINGS

After a devastating four-year slump, the recording industry was on the road to recovery in 1983. From $4.13 billion (U.S.) in 1978, its peak year, business dropped to a low of $3.59 billion in 1982, then began to rise once again in 1983. Factors stimulating this "miniboom" were the new video and digital recording technologies, the "New Music" influx from Europe and Australia, the popularity of the cassette format, the production of less expensive recording formats, and the proliferation of reduced-price cassettes and discs.

Classical. For several years classical producers had been releasing digital recordings as ordinary long-playing (LP) discs. When the digital Compact Disc (CD) playback system was introduced in 1983, a stockpile of classical music was ready for the new format. Included were impressive performances by such classical superstars as conductors James Levine, Neville Marriner, Lorin Maazel, George Solti, and Herbert von Karajan, pianists Alfred Brendel and the late Glenn Gould, and singers Luciano Pavarotti, Joan Sutherland, and Kiri Te Kanawa.

To celebrate the 150th anniversary of the birth of Johannes Brahms, Deutsche Grammophone released a set of recordings of all his works. Called the "Brahms Edition," it ran to eight volumes containing 62 discs. In the year when the 100th anniversary of the death of Richard Wagner also was commemorated, new recordings of his operas included a *Parsifal,* conducted by Armin Jordan on RCA/Erato; a *Tristan and Isolde,* conducted by Carlos Kleiber on DG; and another *Tristan,* conducted by Leonard Bernstein on Philips. Seraphim released "Wagner on Record," a seven-disc set of opera excerpts recorded during a golden age of Wagnerian singing between 1926 and 1942.

Popular. The pop segment of the industry became hit oriented. The new hits, many from neophyte "New Music" artists (60% of the artists receiving awards at the 25th annual Grammy Awards presentation were first-time recipients), broke long-standing statistical records. Michael Jackson's *Thriller* sold 14 million copies worldwide, becoming CBS's largest-selling album ever. It became the first album in recording history to place five consecutive singles in the Top Ten. It went platinum in 14 countries, gold or silver in four more, and was the Number 1 LP in eight countries.

Britain's Culture Club became the first group in 20 years to place three singles from a debut album in the Top Ten. Men At Work was the first group to chart two albums in the Top Ten since the Rolling Stones did so in 1975.

In the heavy metal arena, Def Leppard's *Pyromania* was the biggest non-soundtrack album in PolyGram history, and Quiet Riot was the first heavy metal group to crack the Top Ten since Led Zeppelin 14 years earlier. *Flashdance* was the runaway best-seller in movie soundtracks, and RCA's original cast recording of *La Cage Aux Folles* became the fastest-selling Broadway show album since *Hair* in the 1960s; it also was the first original Broadway cast album ever to appear as a Compact Disc.

The popularity of "New Music" drew many foreign releases to the United States. Besides a heavy British and Australian showing, Dutch, Irish, and German discs found their way across the ocean. Jem contracted to distribute the WEA International label in the United States, and RCA International debuted Latin products there. CBS's Julio Igelsias sold an unprecedented 100 million records worldwide.

The vinyl analog disc lost its ascendancy. For the first time, prerecorded cassettes pulled ahead of discs in sales, especially for hard rock and country material.

Although the new Compact Disc format developed jointly by Sony, PolyGram, and Philips

The Compact Disc (CD) format, whose digitally recorded, laser-read sound is superior to that of conventional records, appeared to be on the brink of a mass market.

Sony

Marvin Schwartz (cover design)/Angel Records

Epic Records

Marking the 100th anniversary of the composer's death, Seraphim released a seven-record anthology of great Wagner performances. On the pop charts, Michael Jackson's "Thriller" sold 14 million copies, the most ever for a CBS LP.

had not yet reached the mass-consumer level, feverish preparations were under way for the eventual domination of the industry by this medium, whose digitally produced, laser-read sound was superior to standard analog recordings. There was controversy over the rate of supply of CD hardware and software. The 50,000 CD machines sold in the United States in 1983 fell short of the projected 75,000. Only 500 software titles were available, all cataloged by the Compact Disc Group, an organization of 29 active CD manufacturers. These titles were in short supply. Most were classical; original digital recordings were rare in the pop sector, though many titles were digitally mastered.

At this critical juncture in the marketing of CD technology, a catch-22 developed. Manufacturers hesitated to produce more software until more machines were sold, and the public would not buy machines until more software appeared. Still, manufacturers vied to produce less expensive hardware. In Japan the lowest-priced machine retailed for $400. In the United States, manufacturers predicted availability of a $500 machine by year's end.

Some recording companies feared the CD's misuse as a home taping device. Two bills in Congress to combat the $1 billion profit drain on the recording industry from home taping and record rentals, the Home Recording Act and the Record Rental Amendment, were held up pending a decision (in 1984) on the Sony v. Universal "Betamax" case posing similar legal questions for home video taping.

Audiophile labels continued to manufacture direct-to-disc and half-speed recordings, though many began to produce CDs as well. Mobile Fidelity Sound Labs put out a 16-disc, half-speed remastered set of Frank Sinatra.

Promotional video became essential to a pop recording artist's commercial success. Cable's MTV, the most influential avenue of exposure for a pop artist, reaching 15 million subscribers, employed videos produced by record companies. These usually cost up to $150,000 to produce, though Michael Jackson's *Thriller* cost $500,000.

For home consumption, Sony developed the Video 45, consisting of about two cuts of an album; at $15 it was priced well below a full-length video. The popular Duran Duran took advantage of the new medium by sending its video album on tour in place of the group itself.

Along with the boost that video gave to album sales, record companies sought to maximize their profits by pushing less expensive formats and reducing prices on catalog items. Twelve-inch and mini-albums or EPs (Extended Plays) costing from $3.49 to $6.98 became big sellers and offered name pop artists as well as modern dance music. Warner Communications, the largest U.S. distributor of records and tapes, reduced 1,100 catalog items from $8.98 to $6.98, its lowest price in five years.

Reissues of 1950s and 1960s jazz recordings for $5.98 were both popular and profitable. PolyGram Classics imported Japanese reissues of vintage Verve, EMarcy, and Limelight recordings, while Fantasy reissued the classic Riverside and Prestige labels.

Independent labels succumbed to the onslaught of these successful retail maneuvers by the major labels. Indie Arista contracted with RCA for distribution, while Chrysalis went with CBS and Motown with MCA. The largest companies grew even larger.

PAULETTE WEISS, *"Stereo Review"*

RECORDINGS | 1983

CLASSICAL

BARTÓK: String Quartets Nos. 1–6; Juilliard Quartet (CBS).

BEETHOVEN: Sonatas Nos. 4 and 11 for Piano; Murray Perahia (CBS).

BEETHOVEN: The Late String Quartets: Amadeus Quartet (Philips).

BEETHOVEN: Symphony No. 9 "Choral"; M. Price, Horn, Vickers, Salminen, Mehta, New York Philharmonic (RCA).

BERLIOZ: Symphonie fantastique; Varujan Kojian, Utah Symphony Orchestra (Reference Recordings).

BIZET: Carmen; Baltsa, Carreras, Van Dam, Von Karajan, Berlin Philharmonic (Deutsche Grammophon).

BRAHMS: Quintet in f for Piano and Strings, Op. 34; Maurizio Pollini, Quartetto Italiano (Philips).

LISZT: Piano Concerto No. 1; **SAINT-SAËNS:** Piano Concerto No. 2; Cécile Ousset, Simon Rattle, City of Birmingham Orchestra (Angel).

MOZART: Piano Concertos Nos. 15 and 21; Alfred Brendel, Neville Marriner, Academy of St. Martin-in-the-Fields (Philips).

RACHMANINOFF: Symphony No. 2; Ashkenazy, Amsterdam Concertgebouw Orchestra (London).

RAMEAU: Anacréon; Schirrer, Mellon, Christie, Les Arts Florissants (Harmonia Mundi).

ROSSINI: Il barbiere di Siviglia; Allen, Baltsa, Araiza, Lloyd, Marriner, Academy of St. Martin-in-the-Fields (Philips).

SCHUBERT: An die Musik and Other Songs; Elly Ameling, Dalton Baldwin (Philips).

SHOSTAKOVICH: Symphony No. 5; Bernard Haitink, Amsterdam Concertgebouw Orchestra (London).

R. STRAUSS: Four Last Songs; Death and Transfiguration; Lucia Popp, Klaus Tennstedt, London Philharmonic Orchestra (Angel).

VERDI: Falstaff; Bruson, Ricciarelli, Nucci, Guilini, Los Angeles Philharmonic (Deutsche Grammophon).

VERDI: Nabucco; Cappuccilli, Domingo, Nesterenko, Dimitrova, Valentini-Terrani, Sinopoli, Deutsche Oper Orchestra and Chorus (Deutsche Grammophon).

JAZZ

ERNESTINE ANDERSON: Big City (Concord Jazz).

JAKI BYARD: To Them—To Us (Soul Note).

JACKIE CAIN & ROY KRAL: A Stephen Sondheim Collection (Finesse).

GIL EVANS: Priestess (Antilles).

DAVE FRISHBERG: The Dave Frishberg Songbook Vol. II (Omnisound).

GRIFFITH PARK COLLECTION 2: In Concert (Elektra/Musician).

WYNTON MARSALIS: Think of One (Columbia).

SUSANNAH McCORKLE: The People That You Never Get to Love (Inner City).

DAVID MURRAY: Murray's Steps (Black Saint).

MAL WALDRON: One Entrance, Many Exits (Palo Alto).

BOB WILDER & THE BECHET LEGACY: On the Road (Bodeswell).

THE YOUNG LIONS: (Elektra/Musician).

DENNY ZEITLIN, CHARLIE HADEN: Time Remembers One Time Once (ECM).

MUSICALS, MOVIES

THE BIG CHILL: soundtrack (Motown).
FLASHDANCE: soundtrack (Casablanca).
LA CAGE AUX FOLLES: original cast (RCA).
ON YOUR TOES: 1983 Broadway cast (Polydor).
STAYING ALIVE: soundtrack (RSO).
YENTL: soundtrack (Columbia).

POPULAR

ALABAMA: The Closer You Get (RCA).
JOHN ANDERSON: All the People Are Talkin' (Warner Bros.).
THE ANIMALS: Ark (International Record Syndicate).
ASHFORD & SIMPSON: High Rise (Capitol).
PAT BENATAR: Live from Earth (Chrysalis).

GEORGE BENSON: In Your Eyes (Warner Bros.).
BIG COUNTRY: The Crossing (Mercury).
ANGELA BOFILL: Too Tough (Arista).
DAVID BOWIE: Let's Dance (EMI/America).
JACKSON BROWNE: Lawyers in Love (Asylum).
PEABO BRYSON, ROBERTA FLACK: Born to Love (Capitol).
PHIL COLLINS: Hello I Must Be Going (Atlantic).
ELVIS COSTELLO: Punch the Clock (Columbia).
CULTURE CLUB: Colour by Numbers (Virgin/Epic).
DEF LEPPARD: Pyromania (Mercury).
THE DOORS: Alive, She Cried (Elektra).
DURAN DURAN: Seven & the Ragged Tiger (Capitol).
BOB DYLAN: Infidels (Columbia).
EARTH, WIND, & FIRE: Electric Universe (Columbia).
SHEENA EASTON: Best Kept Secret (EMI/America).
EURYTHMICS: Sweet Dreams (Are Made of This) (RCA).
THE FIXX: Reach the Beach (MCA).
ARETHA FRANKLIN: Get It Right (Arista).
GENESIS: Genesis (Atlantic).
EDDY GRANT: Killer on the Rampage (Portrait).
MERLE HAGGARD: That's the Way Love Goes (Epic).
DARYL HALL & JOHN OATES: Rock 'n Soul Part I (RCA).
HERBIE HANCOCK: Future Shock (Columbia).
EMMYLOU HARRIS: White Shoes (Warner Bros.).
JENNIFER HOLLIDAY: Feel My Soul (Geffen).
JULIO IGLESIAS: Julio (Columbia).
MICHAEL JACKSON: Thriller (Epic).
RICK JAMES: Cold Blooded (Gordy).
AL JARREAU: Jarreau (Warner Bros.).
WAYLON JENNINGS: Waylon & Company (RCA).
BILLY JOEL: An Innocent Man (Columbia).
GEORGE JONES: Jones Country (Epic).
JOURNEY: Frontiers (Columbia).
KOOL & THE GANG: In the Heart (De-Lite).
HUEY LEWIS AND THE NEWS: Sports (Chrysalis).
PAUL McCARTNEY: Pipes of Peace (Columbia).
JOHN COUGAR MELLANCAMP: Uh-Huh (Riva/Mercury).
MEN AT WORK: Cargo (Columbia).
RONNIE MILSAP: Keyed Up (RCA).
MOODY BLUES: The Present (Threshold).
THE MOTELS: Little Robbers (Capitol).
ANNE MURRAY: A Little Good News (Capitol).
WILLIE NELSON, WAYLON JENNINGS: Take It to the Limit (Columbia).
STEVIE NICKS: The Wild Heart (Modern/Atlantic).
THE OAK RIDGE BOYS: Deliver (MCA).
DOLLY PARTON: Burlap & Satin (RCA).
PINK FLOYD: The Final Cut (Columbia).
ROBERT PLANT: The Principle of Moments (Swan Song).
THE POLICE: Synchronicity (A&M).
PRINCE: 1999 (Warner Bros.).
LIONEL RICHIE: Can't Slow Down (Motown).
MARTY ROBBINS: A Lifetime of Song (Columbia).
SMOKEY ROBINSON: Blame It on Love and All the Great Hits (Tamia).
KENNY ROGERS: Eyes That See in the Dark (RCA).
ROLLING STONES: Undercover (Rolling Stones).
LINDA RONSTADT: What's New (Asylum).
RUFUS & CHAKA KHAN: Live: Stompin' at the Savoy (Warner Bros.).
BOB SEGER: The Distance (Capitol).
CARLY SIMON: Hello Big Man (Warner Bros.).
PAUL SIMON: Hearts & Bones (Warner Bros.).
RICKY SKAGGS: Don't Cheat in Our Hometown (Sugar Hill/Epic).
RICK SPRINGFIELD: Living in Oz (RCA).
STRAY CATS: Rant and Rave with the Stray Cats (EMI/America).
DONNA SUMMER: She Works Hard for the Money (Mercury).
TALKING HEADS: Speaking in Tongues (Sire).
38 SPECIAL: Tour de Force (A&M).
CONWAY TWITTY: Lost in the Feeling (Warner Bros.).
U2: War (Island).
LUTHER VANDROSS: Forever, for Always, for Love (Epic).
STEVIE RAY VAUGHAN & DOUBLE TROUBLE: Texas Flood (Epic).
WAS (NOT WAS): Born to Laugh at Tornadoes (Geffen).
HANK WILLIAMS, JR.: Man of Steel (Curb).
YES: 90125 (Atco).

REFUGEES AND IMMIGRATION

In 1983, once again, the U.S. Congress struggled with the problem of illegal immigration and found itself unable to resolve the issue. Legislation to make sweeping changes in U.S. immigration law was introduced in the 98th Congress in February and passed by the Senate, 76–18, in May. But the bill bogged down in the House, where it faced strong opposition from Hispanic groups, organized labor, and civil libertarians. With the nation moving into the early stages of congressional and presidential campaigns, Speaker of the House Thomas ("Tip") O'Neill (D-MA) announced in October that he would not bring the bill to the floor for a vote in 1983.

The Simpson-Mazzoli bill, named for its principal sponsors, Sen. Alan Simpson (R-WY) and Rep. Romano L. Mazzoli (D-KY), was virtually identical to legislation that failed in the 97th Congress. It formulated a three-pronged attack on the problem of illegal immigration. The most important part of the bill provided for a series of fines, up to $1,000 per case, for employers who knowingly hire illegal aliens. It authorized the development of a nationwide identification system and provided for speeded-up legal procedures to deport illegal aliens and to consider requests for asylum. The second part of the bill set a quota of 425,000 legal immigrants and persons granted asylum each year. It authorized a guest worker program for migrants who cross the border for seasonal jobs, principally in agriculture. The third section of the bill would have granted legal residence to illegal aliens already in the country. It would have tightened rules on foreign students in the United States. Parenthetically, the bill approved by the Senate declared as the "sense of the Senate" that English is the official language of the United States, a statement never before written into law.

The employer sanctions generated the strongest political controversy. Groups supporting them included the Reagan administration, NAACP, AFL-CIO, and National Association of Manufacturers. Opposing them were the U.S. Chamber of Commerce, American Bar Association, Mexican-American Legal Defense and Educational Fund, and American Civil Liberties Union.

Immigration Increase. The United States has faced mounting refugee and immigration problems for several years. The Simpson-Mazzoli bill was the product of seven years of work by a select national commission, a presidential task force, and half a dozen congressional committees. Violence and poverty in many parts of the world have generated a steady rise in the number of aliens seeking to enter the United States, raising numerous new social problems.

In two years, the U.S. border patrol expanded its force by 20%, to a total of 2,800 officers. In fiscal 1983 (ended September 30), border guards apprehended more than 1 million illegal aliens, a 40% rise over fiscal 1982.

In testimony before the Senate Judiciary Committee in September, Sen. Mark Hatfield (R-OR) said that 1.1 million individuals entered the United States in fiscal 1983. About 5%, or 60,000 were refugees; 420,000 were legal immigrants; and at least 600,000 were illegal immigrants. According to other estimates, more than 1 million illegals slip into the United States each year. According to the Federation for American Immigration Reform (FAIR), a private group seeking to tighten immigraton laws, nearly 50% of U.S. population growth is due to legal and illegal immigration. FAIR says that 1 of 12 people in the Washington, DC, area is a recent immigrant, or some 250,000 aliens in all.

In 1983, Mexico, Central America, and the Caribbean islands were the principal sources of illegal immigration into the United States. A deep recession in Mexico, internecine strife in El Salvador, and endemic poverty in such Caribbean countries as Haiti induce more and more people from these areas to try to enter the United States. An esimated 500,000 Salvadorans, more than 10% of that country's population of 4.5 million, have emigrated to the United States. The Census Bureau says that 7.69 million Mexicans live in the United States.

International Problems. Worldwide the number of refugees increased from 10 million in 1982 to 10.6 million in 1983, according to the U.S. Committee for Refugees. More important than the increase in numbers of refugees, said that private, nonprofit organization, is the deterioration in the quality of their treatment.

Africa remains the world's most refugee-impacted region. The Office of the UN High Commissioner for Refugees stated that approximately 5 million Africans are homeless. In addition to longstanding refugee problems in Chad, Uganda, and Ethiopia, Nigeria expelled 400,000 illegal immigrants, mostly citizens of Ghana, in 1983. Angola reported that nearly 100,000 Namibians, Zairians, and South Africans were within its borders.

In February, rioting factions murdered more than 4,000 illegal Bengali immigrants in the Indian state of Assam. The three-and-a-half-year "holy war" of Afghan guerrillas against occupying Soviet troops continued in 1983, bringing to 3 million the number of Afghan refugees in neighboring Pakistan. In the Middle East, fighting in Lebanon created an estimated 150,000 new refugees. In the Western Hemisphere, 40,000 Guatemalans entered the southern Mexican state of Chiapas, fleeing battles between guerrillas and army troops in northern Guatemala. As in so many other countries, the refugees in Mexico have no legal status and receive minimum care and protection.

RICHARD C. SCHROEDER, *"Visión" Magazine*

RELIGION

Survey

Famed Soviet expatriate Aleksandr Solzhenitsyn received the 1983 Templeton Foundation Prize for Progress in Religion ($170,000). He was cited as a "pioneer in the renaissance of religion in atheist nations."

A schism in American Presbyterianism, which developed in the late 1800s over slavery and the Civil War, was mended in June. . . . Issues of peace and the possibilities of nuclear war remained a focus of religious attention. . . . The reactionary Islamic government of Iran extended its persecution of members of the Baha'i faith.

Luther Anniversary. The 500th anniversary of the birth of Martin Luther was commemorated. Pilgrimages were conducted to important places in Luther's life. Italian Protestants planned a series of television programs, and the Waldensian Theological Seminary in Rome scheduled 12 public lectures. In May the German Democratic Republic hosted a festival service at Wartburg Castle where Luther spent 300 days in 1521, during which time he translated the New Testament into German. The East German government also sponsored a sixth International Congress for Luther Research in Wartburg and an ecumenical meeting in Leipzig. Washington, DC, was the site of a national celebration during Martin Luther Jubilee week, Nov. 6–12, 1983.

Born in Eisleben on Nov. 10, 1483, Martin Luther was the son of a peasant father and a more socially prominent mother. Destined to become one of the most important figures in Western history, he began the study of law at Erfurt and later entered the Augustinian order. He was a man of the people. A bit coarse, enthusiastic, and impatient, he became the most colorful of the charismatic leaders of the 16th century Reformation of Western Christianity.

His dramatic actions and provocative ideas created a revolution in religion. Historians may point to many forces that led to and influenced the Reformation, but it was Martin Luther whose life and thought changed the patterns of religion. He also was a prime mover in man's cultural and intellectual history.

One of the most persistent themes in the development of modern history is the problem of authority, and Martin Luther was a very significant participant in the development of that issue. As he observed the reforming forces in the Catholic Church of the 16th century, he remarked: "Others have attacked the life. I attack the doctrine." He was not concerned primarily with the abuses of medieval Catholicism, but with the understanding of the Christian Gospel advocated by the magisterial teaching of the Church. As a youth, Luther had been asking himself a set of questions that agitated his soul well into his mature years. He wanted to know: What is the essential nature of God? How does man relate to this God? What is the *source* of man's knowledge of such things? These are questions that demonstrate a growing awareness of the crisis of authority. Authority is a matter of source (authorship), of what one relies upon as the ultimately dependable basis of thought and action.

In a rather cohesive and traditional society such as the Christendom of the Middle Ages, authority tended to center itself in the common assumptions that were hierarchically supported by the sacerdotal and political orders. Luther's questions and his attempts to answer them undermined the medieval structure of authority and produced a crisis that has marked modernity.

In theological terms, Luther came to the conclusion that the righteousness of God is understood primarily as mercy and forgiving love; that the only means of receiving that righteousness is by a recognition of one's absolute dependence upon it. He also concluded that the ultimate authority of human existence is God's

Theologians met at Wartburg Castle, East Germany, for ceremonies marking the 500th birthday of Martin Luther.

grace; the authority that incarnates that truth is Jesus Christ; and the authority that transmits it to man is the Holy Scriptures. According to Luther, authority resides in God's saving love and in the revealed record of that love; neither the individual nor any institution, tradition, or church leader can usurp that authority. This is the heritage of Martin Luther and it is present in many secularized forms today.

RICHARD E. WENTZ
Department of Religious Studies
Arizona State University

Far Eastern

To the outsider, the sectarian struggles within Islam seem puzzling and unjustifiable. However, they reflect more than the pervasiveness of evil and the persistence of ethnic jealousies. In Karachi, Pakistan, clashes between Shiite and Sunni Muslims required the imposition of curfews. The Sunni Muslims believe that the community of scholars always can arrive at consensus interpretations of the Sunna (one of the forms of Muslim law) which are in keeping with the Koran and the words and actions of Muhammad. The Shiites reject the principle of consensus and invest authority in the hands of an imam, who is in the divine succession of Ali, adopted cousin of Muhammad. Such emphases have tended to promote different ways of viewing the world and its meaning. Conflict often is inevitable.

Sikhism is an Indian tradition combining aspects of Vaishnava Hinduism with Muslim theism. Militant Sikhs have been campaigning for increased autonomy for the northern state of Punjab, where most of India's 12 million Sikhs live. Riots have accounted for many deaths and injuries. In an attempt to control the increasing violence, the Indian government assumed direct control of the state in October.

A visitor to Buddhist temples in Japan may witness an interesting development in popular religion. Rows of infant statues called *jizos* may be seen, many with special offering-adornments of candy, toys, or flowers. Some of the stone figures wear caps, bibs, or pinwheels. For 25 years or more there has been an increase in services and ritual acts attempting to atone for abortions. These practices have been gaining the attention of sociologists, theologians, and government officials.

RICHARD E. WENTZ

Islam

In several countries during 1983, Muslims found it necessary to counter moves which threatened the cohesiveness or, in some cases, the very survival of their communities. Fundamentalist groups continued to press other Muslims to conform to their conservative interpretations of Islam and to agitate against governments that they felt deviated from Islamic traditions.

The early months of the year saw serious clashes between Muslims and Hindus in the Indian province of Assam which may have claimed as many as 3,000 lives. The troubles began during an election campaign in February when Assamese students demanded the expulsion or disenfranchisement of many of the province's Muslims, who constitute about 20% of its population. The protests were sparked by the recent influx of large numbers of Muslims from neighboring Bangladesh, many of whom were without resources. The fighting, however, involved the entire Muslim community, including some persons who had come to Assam from East Pakistan (now Bangladesh) in the 1950s. Later in the year, the provincial government announced plans to halt movement across the border, and thus ease communal tensions, by erecting a fence along the Bangladesh frontier. Although the violence erupted along religious lines, it was economic and political issues—the competition for limited resources and political influence—that aroused antipathy toward the immigrants and, by extension, their coreligionists who represented earlier waves of immigration.

Similarly in Lebanon, militias affiliated with various religious communities fought bitterly. The people of Lebanon traditionally have organized themselves along religious lines, with little mingling among the sects. Since the 1940s, each sect has shared political power in proportion to its numbers. It is because the once-minority Muslim community has become a majority, but has not received a commensurate measure of political power, that it has taken arms against the Christian-dominated government. Here, as in Assam, what may appear as a religious war is, in fact, a political struggle.

Afghanistan provides another example of political activity closely linked with religious concerns. Guerrillas resisting the Soviet occupation of that country continued to find during 1983 that the call to protect the country's Islamic traditions was the most effective means of rallying popular support. It also was virtually the only way to create a united front linking many factions that opposed the Soviets for a variety of reasons but agreed on little else.

Several Middle Eastern governments conducted active campaigns against Muslim fundamentalists whom they accused of seeking to overthrow existing regimes and replace them with others more committed to conservative interpretations of Islam and its role in the state. Major trials of militants took place in Turkey and Egypt, while fundamentalist groups caused concern for the status quo in Tunisia, Algeria, Syria, Iraq, and parts of the Gulf.

Ceremonies were held in September marking the laying of the cornerstone of the first Jewish Chapel at the U.S. Military Academy, West Point, NY. Architect Max Abramovitz, a former cadet, designed the building (drawing above).

A much different instance of activism against threats to Islamic customs and values occurred in Great Britain. Some of the one million Muslims living there have begun to work for the creation of state-aided schools for Muslim students similar to those for Catholics and Jews. Muslim parents expressed concern that the regular school system does not provide a proper Islamic environment for their children.

The year 1983 marked the 1,000th anniversary of the teaching of Islamic subjects at Cairo's al-Azhar Mosque, an institution respected throughout the Muslim world as a major seat of religious instruction. During the year, however, Saudi Arabia's King Fahd asked Muslim religious officials attending a meeting of the Organization of the Islamic Conference in the holy city of Mecca to review the teachings of the faith in light of the demands of modernity. The king, who has in the past supported rather strict interpretations of Muslim law but who was, nonetheless, criticized by fundamentalists for his own Westernized life-style and that of many of the Saudi princes, was by no means suggesting major substantive changes in Islamic law. In fact, the review process which he advocated has occurred informally throughout Islamic history.

KENNETH J. PERKINS
University of South Carolina

Judaism

In 1983 world Jewry experienced a reversal of attitudes on several levels. The Israeli war in Lebanon continued to have an impact: world condemnation of Israel was replaced by a "reevaluation of facts" on the part of some groups and by sympathy and understanding on the part of others. Overt expressions of anti-Semitism were fewer in number, while manifestations of empathy with Judaism and Israel markedly increased. The unprecedented scope of public Holocaust commemorations and the arrest of a notorious Nazi leader added to the mood of empathy. Among Jews themselves, controversies were precipitated by Israel's refusal to recognize the Conservative and Reform branches, a redefinition of Jewish identity by U.S. Reform rabbis, and an ultra-Orthodox charge of desecration of graves by Israeli archaeologists.

Changed attitudes toward Israeli and world Jewry were expressed on one level by increases in political and financial support for Israel and by an upswing of tourism, immigration, and volunteerism in Israel, and on another level by an upsurge of Christian-Jewish dialogue. The 7th National Conference of Christian-Jewish Relations in Boston drew an unprecedented number of participants. The Rev. Edward Flannery of the National Council of Catholic Bishops declared that in Christian-Jewish relations "the debt is entirely on the Christian side." At a conference in Stockholm, world religious leaders adopted a Lutheran declaration rejecting Martin Luther's anti-Semitic teachings. Meeting in Hanover, the leadership of the United Lutheran Church of Germany issued a strong indictment of anti-Semitism. A London *Times* editorial entitled "Jesus Was a Jew" declared anti-Semitism a rejection of Christianity. Led by the Christian Embassy in Jerusalem, Protestant fundamentalists stepped up their activities on behalf of Jews, spreading their message that the Old and

New Testaments are one and that God's covenant with the Jews extended to all mankind.

For the first time since it occurred 40 years before, the Polish government commemorated the anniversary of the Warsaw ghetto uprising in mid-April. More than 1,000 Jewish leaders from around the world were invited to the 13-day observance, held in Warsaw, Auschwitz, Treblinka, and Majdanek. Also in mid-April, the "Days of Remembrance of Victims of the Holocaust" brought some 15,000 survivors and their families to Washington, DC. The four-day reunion was the largest of its kind ever held.

The most poignant reminder of the Holocaust was the apprehension of Klaus Barbie, known as the "Butcher of Lyons," who as Gestapo chief had ordered the execution of more than 4,000 Resistance fighters and the deportation to death camps of 7,500 French Jews. U.S. Jews were shocked at disclosures that in the years following World War II the government had shielded Barbie from French authorities and employed him as an intelligence source.

According to a U.S. State Department report released in February, "alone among the recognized religious groups in the USSR, Soviet Jews have no functioning seminary for the training of clergy, no authorized religious publications, no national organization, and no approved ties with coreligionists abroad." Although an estimated 300,000 Soviet Jews held letters of invitation, a prerequisite for exit, Jewish emigration plummeted to 100 per month, compared with 4,000 per month in 1970.

In Israel the Knesset rejected a proposal for official recognition of the Conservative and Reform movements, barring them from performing religious ceremonies. In the United States, the convention of Reform rabbis adopted a resolution stating that "the child of one Jewish parent is under the assumption of Jewish descent," rejecting the traditional law that the religion of the mother determines the religion of the child. Conservative, Orthodox, and Israeli Reform leaders opposed the move.

Religious controversy erupted in violence when ultra-Orthodox demonstrators attempted to halt the City of David excavation in Jerusalem. The detention of several demonstrators set off a world outcry by the ultra-Orthodox.

The election of a new Chief Rabbinate of Israel raised hopes for a rabbinic leadership that will narrow factional gaps among Jews.

Livia E. Bitton Jackson
Herbert H. Lehman College, CUNY

Orthodox Eastern

Representatives of Orthodox churches had the opportunity of meeting with each other during the 6th General Assembly of the World Council of Churches (WCC), of which all are members, in Vancouver, B.C., in 1983.

While differing among themselves on social and political questions, and generally taking exception to the domination of such issues in WCC activities, the more than 200 Orthodox delegates, from among a total of 900, played a more active and articulate part in the assembly than previously. This was because of their maturing experience in the ecumenical movement. The Orthodox showed a particular interest in the consensus statement on "Baptism, Eucharist and Ministry" produced by the WCC Faith and Order Commission in Lima, Peru, in 1982. The Orthodox support not only what they take to be the document's "orthodox" contents and spirit, but also its centrality as an issue in the movement for Christian unity. Response to this document would be a priority item in Orthodox circles in 1984, as attested by the fact that it was chosen as the theme for the August meeting of the Orthodox Theological Society in America.

The movement for greater unity and cooperation within world Orthodox progressed little in 1983. At the last major meeting in Switzerland in September 1982, only such secondary issues as the church calendar, fasting regulations, and marriage discipline were discussed. Nothing was done to improve the situation of Orthodox Christians living in separate national church jurisdictions in Western Europe, Australia, and the Americas. In his "Sunday of Orthodoxy" sermon in Paris in March, Bishop Kallistos (Ware) of Great Britain, the only non-Greek bishop of the Ecumenical Patriarchate of Constantinople in Europe and the foremost Orthodox theologian in the West, said that action on the issue was needed urgently.

Steps for greater administrative unity among the national Orthodox dioceses were taken by the Orthodox Church in America, the former Russian Orthodox missionary archdiocese which became a self-governing church in 1970, and the Antiochian Orthodox Christian Archdiocese of America, which is part of the Patriarchate of Antioch centered in Damascus, Syria. Representatives of these bodies continued to meet to plan cooperative programs intended to lead to their complete unification.

Ignatius IV, patriarch of Antioch, who intends to visit North America in 1984, visited Western Europe in May. In Rome he conferred with Pope John Paul II and blessed the congregation at the papal mass on the feast of the Ascension. The patriarch's message was a plea for peace in the Middle East and a call for unity and cooperation among Christians and people of good will. The Orthodox in the Middle East have struggled to remain politically neutral.

The Moscow Patriarchate received permission from the Soviet government to open the Daniel Monastery in Moscow, closed in the 1920s, as a church headquarters.

Thomas Hopko
St. Vladimir's Orthodox Seminary

Protestantism

U.S. Protestant bodies took a number of significant steps in 1983 toward the long-term goal of Christian unity.

Ecumenism. In June two major Presbyterian denominations—the 2.4-million-member United Presbyterian Church and the largely southern 850,000-member Presbyterian Church in the U.S.—ended a 122-year separation, reuniting to form the Presbyterian Church (U.S.A.). The Presbyterians had split in 1861 over the slavery issue.

The black Methodist denominations, the African Methodist Episcopal Zion Church (AMEZ) with 1.1 million members and the Christian Methodist Episcopal Church (CME) with 786,000 members, set 1985 as a target date for drafting a plan of union. The two denominations were founded by blacks who withdrew from white Methodist churches in response to racial discrimination in the 19th century.

Lutherans figured prominently in three ecumenical developments. Lutheran and Catholic theologians wound up a five-year dialogue and issued a joint statement summing up points of agreement on Martin Luther's key doctrine of justification by faith. A two-year dialogue involving Lutheran and Reformed-tradition theologians culminated in the recommendation to the participating church bodies that they celebrate communion together, exchange pulpits,

The Rev. Jay Randolph Taylor of Charlotte, NC, was selected as moderator of the new Presbyterian Church (U.S.A.).

Presbyterian News Service

and initiate common mission projects. Four Lutheran bodies took part, though the Lutheran Church-Missouri Synod issued its own minority report disagreeing with the proposal for eucharistic sharing. Reformed bodies participating were the Presbyterian Church (U.S.A.), the United Church of Christ, the Reformed Church in America, and the Cumberland Presbyterian Church. Lutheran and Episcopal churches began celebrating joint communion services in 1983 in accordance with approval issued by their denominations in 1982. Theologians of the two traditions turned their attention to the questions of ministry and the nature of the office of bishop.

World Council of Churches (WCC). For the first time since 1954, a WCC Assembly convened in North America. The meeting in Vancouver, B.C., of some 900 delegates, representing 300 churches in 100 countries, focused attention on a major ecumenical development that had previously received little exposure in the United States—the document issued by Protestant, Orthodox, and Catholic theologians at a 1982 meeting in Lima, Peru, titled *Baptism, Eucharist and Ministry (BEM)* and expressing theological "convergences" on those three topics. The Lima text was the culmination of 55 years of ecumenical dialogue. A communion celebration attended by almost 4,000, using the "Lima Liturgy," a rite based on the *BEM* convergences, was regarded widely as a high point of the Assembly. Churches were asked to submit official responses to *BEM* by the end of 1985; a world Faith and Order Conference to consider the responses will be held in 1987 or 1988.

Ecumenical controversy was another pervasive theme in 1983. The WCC Assembly's stances on international issues drew sharp criticism. A resolution strongly condemning U.S. policy in Central America stood in marked contrast to a much milder statement criticizing Soviet involvement in Afghanistan, whose wording was influenced by Russian Orthodox delegates. A Middle East resolution in support of Palestinian rights was thought by some to show a lack of concern about Christian-Jewish relations.

National Council of Churches (NCC). Earlier in the year, U.S. supporters of the WCC and the NCC went on the defensive in reaction to media attacks on the ecumenical bodies by *Reader's Digest* and CBS-TV's *60 Minutes*. On the TV investigative news program, reporter Morley Safer alleged that the WCC and NCC were supporting violent leftist political movements in many parts of the world. Ecumenical and denominational leaders accused CBS of inaccurate, unbalanced reporting, and produced materials to refute the charges.

The NCC also was engaged in a quiet internal process of self-criticism as a "Presidential Panel" headed by Church of the Brethren

Archbishop Ted Scott (left), the primate of the Anglican Church in Canada, Philip Potter, general secretary of the World Council of Churches, and British Methodist Pauline Webb came together for the WCC's Sixth Assembly.

leader Robert Neff developed proposals for revamping the council, whose current decentralized structure and funding patterns are regarded by many as counterproductive to its mission.

Still unsettled was a final decision on the application for NCC membership submitted by the Universal Fellowship of Metropolitan Community Churches, a denomination with a largely homosexual membership. Some member bodies had threatened to withdraw from a council if a "gay church" was admitted.

In October the NCC's Divison of Education and Ministry introduced its controversial "Inclusive Language Lectionary," a collection of Scripture readings for public worship in which the language of the Revised Standard Version Bible is altered to eliminate "sexism" and "male domination." All references to a solely masculine deity are eliminated, with, for example, the phrase "your heavenly Father" becoming "(*God*) your heavenly Father (*and Mother*)." Critics, including some within the NCC, accused the revisers of "rewriting history" and of "making the Bible into a manifesto for feminism."

The Supreme Court ruled against two fundamentalist schools, Bob Jones University and Goldsboro Academy, in their fight to recover federal tax-exempt status. The Internal Revenue Service had lifted the schools' exemptions because of racial discrimination. The schools claimed to discriminate for reasons of religious conviction, based on Scripture; they argued that the IRS ruling denied them religious freedoms guaranteed in the Constitution. The high court ruled that the government has a clear secular interest in combating racial discrimination, as it "contravenes public policy."

Other. The Crystal Cathedral, in Garden Grove, CA, whose pastor is the noted TV preacher Robert Schuller, fought the loss of its state property-tax exemption, revoked when a tax investigator deemed that church facilities were being used for nonreligious, commercial purposes, including a series of profit-making secular concerts with big-name performers.

Some 50 local churches in the United States, mostly Protestant, were giving sanctuary to illegal refugees from El Salvador and Guatemala, who were said to risk death if forced to return to their politically unstable countries. The act of harboring illegal aliens in violation of federal law could subject participating churches and their leaders to penalties of up to $2,500 and five years in prison.

A.D. magazine, an 11-year-old joint monthly publication of the United Church of Christ and the United Presbyterian Church published in two editions, was discontinued by a unilateral decision of a Presbyterian agency. The fiscally ailing Religious News Service was taken over by the Texas-based *United Methodist Reporter* newspaper chain.

JEAN CAFFEY LYLES
"The Christian Century"

Roman Catholicism

Pleas for peace, disarmament, religious freedom, and alleviation of world hunger dominated the Roman Catholic Church's social agenda in 1983. A highlight was the U.S. bishop's controversial pastoral letter on peace.

On the ecumenical level, there was a major breakthrough in the Lutheran-Catholic dialogue on justification, which had been considered a major obstacle to unity. A new series of talks in the Anglican-Catholic dialogue was launched.

The Pope. Church leaders, led by Pope John Paul II, sought to reestablish stronger control over the doctrinal and spiritual aspects of church life, confronting head-on dissent and deviation from traditional norms of church conduct and operation.

The pope, while joining the American bishops and other churchmen in making impassioned appeals for an end to the arms race and a growing incidence of social injustice worldwide, called even greater media attention to his demands on behalf of maintaining priestly celibacy, his opposition to women priests, and his pleas for renewal of religious orders, seminaries, and liturgical experience, particularly in the United States. In March the pope instituted an unprecedented Holy Year, calling the world's Catholics to rededicate themselves, through prayer and special devotions, to a personal spiritual renewal that focuses on "the riches of salvation."

In late September, the pope called together a world Synod of Bishops to confront the decline in the practice of confession within the Church and to study the role of reconciliation

Pope John Paul II greets the Rev. Peter-Hans Kolvenbach, the new superior general of the Society of Jesus (Jesuits).

Gamma-Liaison

and penance in the mission of the Church. During the four-week Synod, a list of 63 propositions was drawn for papal consideration.

The pope also approved the issuance of a new code of canon law, which became effective in November; made trips to Central America, Poland, Lourdes in France, and Austria; and installed 18 new cardinals, including Joseph Cardinal Bernardin of Chicago, who engineered the U.S. bishops' peace pastoral; Joseph Cardinal Glemp, the Primate of Poland; and the Rev. Henri de Lubac, a Jesuit theologian.

Confrontation. The year saw several confrontations between Church leaders and governments. In January the Canadian bishops criticized their government's economic policies, especially in failing to assist the poor and powerless. Bishops' conferences in El Salvador, Nicaragua, Honduras, Chile, and Guatemala condemned policies of their respective governments which they claimed violated human rights. The U.S. bishops' long-awaited pastoral opposed many U.S. policies on the production, deployment, and use of nuclear weapons. The U.S. Catholic community showed signs of serious division over the bishops' peace pastoral. Dissent came on such issues as nuclear deterrence and retaliation, conscientious objection, pacifism, and the nuclear freeze movement.

Several Episcopal priests, sometimes with their congregation, joined the Catholic Church, thus introducing more married clergy into the Church.

Church and State. Catholics joined efforts by President Ronald Reagan to furnish tax credits to tuition-paying parents of parochial school children.

The refusal of Sister of Mercy Agnes Mary Mansour to follow the order of the archbishop of Detroit to resign as director of Michigan's Department of Social Services brought national attention and Vatican intervention. Church spokesmen said her job was inappropriate for a religious because it dealt with funding abortions. She was released from her vows and remained in the job.

The people of the Irish Republic, in response to pleas from their bishops, passed a constitutional amendment prohibiting abortion.

Transition. During a September meeting in Rome, the world's Jesuit leaders elected a new superior general, the Rev. Peter-Hans Kolvenbach. The 54-year-old Dutch linguist had spent much of his priestly life in the Middle East and had recently headed the Pontifical Oriental Institute in Rome. The archdioceses of Boston and New York were to undergo leadership changes following the deaths of Boston's Humberto Cardinal Medeiros on September 17 and New York's Terence Cardinal Cooke on October 6.

ROBERT L. JOHNSTON, *"The Catholic Review"*

Food retail chains expanded their outlets into "super-stores," featuring a new variety of specialty counters.

© Juneburg Clark/The Kroger Co.

RETAILING

Retailing in the United States in 1983 was almost everything that retailing in 1982 was not. Sales volume rose to double-digit gains over the prior year. Profits were up sharply. Sales productivity enjoyed a healthy rise either in the same or reduced space. And in a touch of irony, as millions of Americans unloosed their purse strings to buy clothes, furniture, appliances, home electronics, and personal computers, the tight expense controls which retailers had installed in the disappointing 1982 helped to translate the improved sales rate into higher profit dollars. The industry's euphoria began early, prompting a Wall Street banking house, Paine Webber Mitchell Hutchins Inc., to remark that merchants were singing, "Happy Days Are Here Again."

All the economic indicators that could turn reluctant shoppers into buyers improved. Inflation, interest rates, the unemployment level, and federal income taxes were reduced, while personal income and housing starts rose. Although the sum of all these indicators may not have fully reversed the recession, it produced enough improvement in family finances to improve store sales sharply. Greater consumer confidence did the rest.

Discounting. Among retailers, irrespective of size or specialty, the primary efforts centered on capitalizing on the business boom, by improving sales output, expanding market share, intensifying customer service, and building store traffic. But the proliferating "off-price" trend in nationally-branded apparel, a euphemism for discounting, increased. It not only led to more growth by such off-pricers as Marshalls, T. J. Maxx, Hit or Miss, Syms Inc., and Loehmann's but to many new entrants and the launching of complete off-price malls. It also compelled conventional retailers to match the price lure.

Although only about 5% of the nation's $100-billion retail apparel sales could be attributed to off-price, proponents insisted that the movement was growing by at least 20% annually. By 1990, they claimed, it would reach some 20% of all apparel sales. But the real proof of the trend's vitality was the public's growing purchases.

Whether the most famous national brands and designer products should be sold to the new wave of discounters became the year's most controversial issue. In June in New York, 600 retailers and producers gathered at an all-day, off-price seminar sponsored by the Institute of Retail Management of New York University and the Retail Research Society. Several major retail chains, including Federated Department Stores, and several manufacturers, including the Arrow Shirt Company, threatened to cut off any suppliers or trade customers who dealt with discounters. The proceedings were subpoenaed later by the Federal Trade Commission (FTC) to study any possible, planned violations of the antitrust statutes. Although fair trade or price-maintenance laws largely had been voided in 1975, the fear was that any "collective" moves to curtail distribution to discounters would restrain trade.

Company News. The year also was marked by a number of major company actions. The J. C. Penney Company, the third-largest general merchandiser, dropped most of its household durables operations and all of its automotive centers in order to expand its fashion business. Associated Dry Goods Corporation, which already owned the Caldor discount chain, acquired Loehmann's, the pioneer fashion discounter. The Dayton Hudson Corporation launched its own upscale, off-price chain, Plum's. And Federated Department Stores said it would open a popular-priced apparel chain with an initial 8 to 10 stores in Chicago.

The F. W. Woolworth Company, after discontinuing its domestic Woolco discount stores in 1982 because of Woolco's protracted losses, bought the California-based Holtzman's Little Folks Shops. This move, two years after Federated's acquisition of The Children's Place, a major juvenile-wear chain, signaled retailing's revived interest in the potential of children's wear merchandising.

Despite 1982's interruption in its dramatic economic boom, the Sunbelt continued to draw retailers from the North and West. Bloomingdale's, the trendy New York department store, opened its first Texas store in Dallas in October. Macy's New York indicated it hoped to join the Dallas invasion in 1985. Saks Fifth Avenue, Lord & Taylor, and Marshall Field, which also had come to Texas, said they planned more units there. Gump's of San Francisco and Fred Joaillier of Beverly Hills also had opened in Dallas in 1982.

Store-Label Products. Many conventional department stores expanded their use of "private" or store-label goods. The objective was to obtain more exclusivity, a better markup and less identical competition. Richard C. Marcus, chief executive of Neiman-Marcus, the Texas fashion chain, epitomized the philosophy: "Customers tell us they want something from us that they can't get elsewhere." Neiman-Marcus has boosted its own-label goods sales by 50% in both 1982 and 1983. Its "Red River" label, initiated years ago with only a Western hat, has been expanded to include jeans, gift merchandise, and food—including a Neiman-Marcus peanut butter.

However, a by-product of the store-label trend was a record number of apparel imports which flowed to American stores in 1983, arousing protests of domestic branded producers, the domestic textile industry, and unions. The latter staged protest demonstrations on the import tide, occasionally picketing retailers.

Store News. Closed stores in both urban and suburban markets were recycled. Sites of former Woolco, Fedmart, Korvettes, and Two Guys stores were leased by more successful discounters, supermarkets, and flea markets. This created a trend-within-a-trend in which large, shuttered retail stores were transformed into vertical shopping centers, with small retailers taking ministores or booths.

Computer stores grew in number. Large chains opened new computer divisions or set aside main-aisle locations for computer departments. Consumer interest appeared to coincide with reduced interest in home-video games. But home-computer sales, too, ran into a bit of a slump caused by excessive promotion of low-priced, basic models.

Industry interest mounted over financial services, led by the example of Sears Roebuck, which opened a chain of financial service stores. Sears had jumped massively into the field via two 1982 acquisitions of major companies.

The big food-retail chains expanded further into super-stores to allow a larger component of the more profitable nonfoods. Combined food-drug stores were launched, too, and the concept of the European-style hypermarkets, combining food and general merchandise, was revived tentatively in the Midwest. The goal of all these actions was to prop up the low operating margin of food retailing.

In all, it was a stimulating year for American retailers, although not without hints of a looming shakeout coming from the battle for market share. This was portended particularly for the off-price retailer, the general discounter, and the secondary and tertiary urban department stores.

ISADORE BARMASH, *Business Writer*
"The New York Times"

In the age of computers and two-career families, the Phone In—Drive Thru Market has found success in Los Angeles. Choosing from a catalog, the customer calls in an order, which is processed by computer and sent on to a packer; the groceries are ready for pickup in three hours. Seventeen more stores are expected to be built in California.

Ed Fortson/Gamma-Liaison

RHODE ISLAND

The America's Cup yacht races, an improved economy, and the redistricting of the state Senate were highlights of the year 1983 in Rhode Island.

America's Cup. In the spring and summer, reports of winners and losers in the trials off Newport alternated with charges and countercharges over *Australia II*'s mysterious and innovative new keel. When the September races were finally sailed, suspense was high and precedents were shattered. Never in 132 years had a challenger managed to deadlock the series at three each for the United States and the challenger, or to win the seventh race (this time by 41 seconds) to take the cup. Newport will miss the excitement, the massive tourist influx, and the resulting economic boost as the scene shifts to Perth, Australia, in 1987.

The Economy. The Strategic Development Commission, appointed by Gov. J. Joseph Garrahy in September 1982, spent much of 1983 gathering and analyzing economic data about Rhode Island. Its volunteer staff, directed by international business consultant Ira C. Magaziner, probably did the most massive and comprehensive study of a state's economy that has ever been attempted. The commission's report and recommendations were issued in October.

During the year the state's economic condition improved steadily. The seasonally adjusted unemployment rate was 10.7% in February and by October had dropped to 7.6%. Home sales and construction climbed.

Redistricting. The year saw a precedent-shattering finish to the long battle over redistricting of the state Senate, which began during the 1982 General Assembly session. The ensuing court tests forced postponement of Senate elections from November 1982 to June 21, 1983. A limited turnout of voters, apparently angry at Democratic handling of redistricting, raised the Republican share of the 50 Senate seats from 7 to 21.

RHODE ISLAND • Information Highlights

Area: 1,212 sq mi (3 139 km²).
Population (1982 est.): 958,000.
Chief Cities (1980 census): Providence, the capital, 156,805; Warwick, 87,123; Cranston, 71,992.
Government (1983): *Chief Officers*—governor, J. Joseph Garrahy (D); lt. gov., Thomas R. DiLuglio (D). *Assembly*—Senate, 50 members; House of Representatives, 100 members.
State Finances (fiscal year 1982): *Revenues,* $1,686,000,000; *expenditures,* $1,628,000,000.
Personal Income (1982): $10,728,000,000; per capita, $10,723.
Labor Force (July 1983): *Nonagricultural wage and salary earners,* 388,300; *unemployed,* 44,500 (9.3% of total force).
Education: *Enrollment* (fall 1981)—public elementary schools, 91,642; public secondary, 51,173; colleges and universities (1982), 68,351 students. *Public school expenditures* (1981–82): $395,139,000.

This blow to the Democratic Party, on top of its 1982 success in retaining half of the state's congressional delegation and capturing the secretary of state's office, brought major repercussions. Rocco A. Quattrocchi, Senate majority leader and Democratic state chairman, stepped down and was replaced by John C. Revens, Jr., in the Senate and by former Attorney General Julius C. Michaelson as state party head.

Politics. The 1983 General Assembly session focused largely on state finances. Temporary taxes were imposed early in the year to avert a deficit. A confrontation between the governor and the Assembly leaders forced a $25 million reduction in 1983–84 spending plans and held the overall budget increase to 4.2%.

In September, four-term Governor Garrahy announced that he would not seek reelection, thereby averting a bitter 1984 primary with Mayor Joseph W. Walsh of Warwick, who is allied with the Assembly leaders. Rep. Claudine Schneider (R) felt pressure to run against Sen. Claiborne Pell (D).

In January, Vincent A. Cianci, Jr., was sworn in for his third term as mayor of Providence, and the city's new home rule charter took effect. In the spring, Cianci was indicted for kidnapping and other felonies. His trial was pending at the end of the year.

ELMER E. CORNWELL, JR., *Brown University*

RUMANIA

The repressive Stalinist regime of President and Rumanian Communist Party chief Nicolae Ceauşescu faced continuing economic shortages and growing political opposition.

Economy. In February the official Rumanian news agency reported that national income had increased by only 2% in 1982, industrial production 3.3%, and agricultural production 7.6%. In March, responding to Rumania's worst food shortage since the late 1940s, Ceauşescu called for harsh steps against inefficiency and profiteering in the distribution of farm products and announced a program of bonuses to stimulate animal production. A proposal submitted to the Political Executive Committee of the Rumanian Communist Party for draining the Danube Delta and using the fertile soil for food production and cash crops was denounced by Rumanian ecologists.

At the end of 1982, Rumania's debts to Western banks and governments alone amounted to more than $11 billion (U.S.). In December 1982, a consortium of 14 major banks signed an agreement rescheduling 80% of Rumania's commercial debt for 1981 and 1982 over six and a half years, with the remaining 20% to be paid in 1983. On Jan. 3, 1983, Rumania announced that it would withhold repayment of the principal due on its commercial debt in 1983 pending a rescheduling agreement. The agreement was signed in June. Canada subsequently reopened a $680 million loan, halted in 1982, to finance a nuclear reactor project in the city of Cernavodă.

Rumania's economic position was further complicated by a new decree published in November 1982, requiring Rumanian citizens under retirement age who wish to immigrate to the West to surrender part of their property and repay to the state the costs of their education beyond the required ten years. Reaction was sharp in West Germany and the United States. On March 4, President Reagan announced that, as a result, Rumania's most-favored-nation status, granted in 1975, would be revoked on July 1. Although Ceauşescu denounced this U.S. "interference in Rumania's internal affairs," Rumania announced in May that it was dropping the "emigration tax."

Popular Discontent. Although Ceauşescu's 65th birthday in January was celebrated with the usual lavish adulation, it was evident that his 18-year-long reign was faced with serious challenges. Rumors circulated in the West that a number of Rumanian army officers had been executed in late January after the failure of a military coup involving the attempted assassination of Ceauşescu himself. The rumor was officially denied. Among the government's new restrictive measures was an April decree requiring the registration of all typewriters and prohibiting anyone with a criminal record or "posing a danger to public order or state security" from owning a typewriter. Defections from the country multiplied.

Foreign Affairs. Rumania remained highly visible and independent in its foreign relations and was particularly active in the Third World. Ceauşescu, together with Prime Minister Constantin Dascalescu, Foreign Minister Stefan Andrei, and the minister of defense, Major Gen. Constantin Olteanu, attended the summit meeting of the Warsaw Pact in Prague in January. Disagreements with the Soviets were reported; Rumania said it would freeze its defense expenditures at 1982 levels for three years.

In July 1983, Ceauşescu paid a two-day visit to Ethiopia, the first by a Rumanian head of state, then continued on to Zimbabwe, Mozambique, and Zambia. Official foreign visitors to Rumania in 1983 included Chinese Communist Party Secretary Hu Yaobang in May and in June PLO leader Yasir Arafat, who sought support against a rebellious faction in the Al-Fatah organization.

JOSEPH F. ZACEK
State University of New York at Albany

SAINT CHRISTOPHER AND NEVIS

The islands of Saint Christopher and Nevis (area: 101 sq mi; 262 km²), located in the northern Leeward Islands in the eastern Caribbean, were granted full independence on Sept. 19, 1983. The new nation of 45,000 (1983 est.) became the 48th member of the British Commonwealth. At the independence ceremonies in the capital, Basseterre (1980 pop., 14,725), Princess Margaret represented Queen Elizabeth II. The prime minister, Dr. Kennedy Simmonds, indicated that the nation would maintain good relations with the West. On September 23, it was admitted to the UN.

Originally inhabited by the Carib Indians, St. Christopher was discovered by Christopher

The two-starred flag of the new nation of St. Christopher and Nevis made its debut at the United Nations in September.

UPI

RUMANIA • Information Highlights

Official Name: Socialist Republic of Rumania.
Location: Southeastern Europe.
Area: 91,700 sq mi (237 503 km²).
Population (July 1983): 22,649,000.
Chief Cities (July 1, 1981): Bucharest, the capital, 2,165,997; Braşov, 320,168; Cluj-Napoca, 289,808.
Government: *Head of state,* Nicolae Ceauşescu, president (took office 1967) and secretary-general of the Communist Party (1965). *Head of government,* Constantin Dascalescu, premier (took office May 1982). *Legislature* (unicameral)— Grand National Assembly.
Monetary Unit: Leu (16.5 lei equal U.S.$1, May 1983).
Gross National Product (1981 est. U.S.$): $94,700,000,000.
Foreign Trade (1981 U.S.$): *Imports,* $12,458,000,000; *exports,* $12,610,000,000.

Columbus in 1493. The first British settlers, who dubbed the island St. Kitts, arrived in 1623, and in the early 19th century St. Kitts and neighboring Nevis, as well as Anguilla and the Virgin Islands, became a single British colony. In 1967, St. Kitts-Nevis-Anguilla was granted internal autonomy as an associated state, from which Anguilla withdrew in 1971, separating formally in 1980.

The new nation has a parliamentary government. G. W. Bullard is the governor-general. Economically underdeveloped, its industries are sugar, cotton, light manufacturing, and tourism.

SAUNDRA FRANCE

SAN FRANCISCO

The downtown high-rise commercial construction boom continued in San Francisco at an annual $1 billion rate, and more than $300 million was spent on urban renewal in 1983. But the construction encountered serious opposition both because it tended to concentrate on high-cost shops and offices and not facilities for those of modest income, and also because high-rise buildings will obscure the famous view of the city's bay and steep hills. In November an initiative was narrowly defeated that would have limited growth, controlled the size of skyscrapers, and forced developers to set aside funds to create new jobs and build residential housing.

San Francisco has a small land area. A 1983 study indicated that the downtown rental cost per square foot is exceeded in the nation only in New York's Manhattan. Even as building continued, there has been a steady movement of corporations to the suburbs and further afield. Thousands of jobs were transferred out of the city in 1983 or are scheduled for removal in the next two years. About 100 companies of all sizes plan to relocate, at least in part, along with 18,000 mostly white-collar jobs. Grave parking and transportation problems remained, but the Golden Gate Bridge and the entire cable-car system are being renovated.

In April, Mayor Dianne Feinstein faced a recall election forced by a small left-wing group objecting to her support of gun control. The vote was 81% in her favor and projected her into the national political limelight. Feinstein was reelected to a second term in November over token opposition. She is a moderate in a city with a broad political spectrum and gains support with her effective downplaying of the city's reputation as a haven for eccentrics. A healthy local economy and a $49.5 million city budget surplus placated conservatives.

On June 3 the mayor signed a law requiring smoking and nonsmoking areas to be established in private workplaces. It is the first such ordinance in the state.

CHARLES R. ADRIAN

SASKATCHEWAN

While the government sought to hold down inflation and cut expenses, the province looked forward to good harvests and improved mineral output in 1983.

Government. The Progressive Conservative government of Premier Grant Devine emphasized job-creation programs and technical training in its 1983 budget. Through tax incentives, the government hoped to create 4,000 new jobs in the private sector. In an effort to combat inflation, an "inflation-minus-one" restraint program was introduced, guaranteeing that public-sector wages would not fall more than 1% below the average consumer price index.

Faced with an increasing deficit of $317 million, the government continued to reorganize its departments and redistribute or eliminate public-sector jobs. Despite promises of less government, the premier created a cabinet of 25, the largest in the province's history. Premier Devine continued to travel abroad to promote the province's resources.

The Conservatives won a by-election in February and increased their ranks in the Legislative Assembly to 56, as compared with the New Democratic Party (NDP) opposition's 8.

The Economy. As in 1982, agricultural production was expected to cushion the economic recession as the province anticipated only modest growth. The Conference Board of Canada predicted a growth rate for Saskatchewan of 1.5% in real terms. Even though the unemployment rate rose to 7% in 1983, Saskatchewan continued to be one of the few provinces with an unemployment rate below 10%. The inflation rate reached 8%, as compared with 10.8% nationwide. There was optimism in the housing industry as federal and provincial housing grants and lower mortgage rates pushed housing starts up 54% over those of 1982.

Agriculture. Saskatchewan expected in 1983 to harvest the second-largest grain crop on rec-

---

SASKATCHEWAN • Information Highlights

Area: 251,700 sq mi (651 900 km²).
Population (July 1983 est.): 994,000.
Chief Cities (1981 census): Regina, the capital, 162,613; Saskatoon, 154,210; Moose Jaw, 33,941.
Government (1983): Chief Officers—lt. gov., C. Irwin McIntosh; premier, Grant Devine (Progressive Conservative); atty. gen., J. G. Lane. Legislature —Legislative Assembly, 64 members.
Education (1982–83): Enrollment—elementary and secondary schools, 208,600 pupils; postsecondary, 17,320 students.
Public Finance (1983 fiscal year, est.): Revenues, $3,208,300,000; expenditures, $3,365,500,000.
Personal Income (average weekly salary, March 1983): $390.20.
Unemployment Rate (September 1983, seasonally adjusted): 7.5%.
(All monetary figures are in Canadian dollars.)

ord with a projected yield of 21.2 million metric tons. Total production for the Prairie Provinces was forecast at 42.3 million metric tons. However, bumper crops over the past two years have not increased farm incomes, which fell 19% as cash receipts declined and producer costs rose. Farmers wanting to purchase land were encouraged to do so by government interest rate subsidies, which rebated land mortgages down to 8% and 12%, regardless of interest rates.

Debate over proposed changes in the Crow's Nest Pass freight rate—the subsidized statutory charge for shipping grain to export terminals—dominated the agricultural scene.

Resources. The government's energy-recovery program, which included the elimination of royalties and taxes for new drilling operations, helped to revive oil production and drilling activity in 1983. The sale of oil and gas exploration rights to oil companies reached record highs. Plans were under way to develop a heavy-oil upgrading operation that will enable the province to take full advantage of its oil resources.

Potash, still the province's number-one mineral resource, was plagued by weak demand and slumping prices. However, shipments were up marginally over the previous year and producers were hopeful that the market was improving. Sales of coal, uranium, and sodium sulfate improved, and the Conference Board of Canada expected mining to grow.

JEANNETTE PYRCH and MARY LOCHHEAD
Regina Public Library

SAUDI ARABIA

Saudi Arabia in 1983 managed to adjust to drastic cuts in government revenue from the sale of oil as it struggled to maintain existing economic development.

Oil and Finance. Saudi Arabia cut its oil production in 1982 to about two thirds of the 1981 total in order to match decreased world demand. As production fell, so did the surplus in the balance of trade—from $83 billion (U.S.) in 1981 to $38 billion in 1982.

To avoid cuts in the price of oil, Saudi Arabia arranged at the December 1982 meeting of the Organization of Petroleum Exporting Countries (OPEC) for a compromise whereby production level would be increased slightly in an effort to induce Iran, Libya, and Nigeria to stop giving special discounts on their oil. This plan did not succeed, however, because world demand continued to decline and non-OPEC countries expanded their production. By February 1983, Saudi Arabia was pumping only about 3.6 million barrels per day, as compared with a 9.8 million average for 1981.

On March 14, OPEC (under Saudi leadership) reduced the price of oil from $34 to $29 per barrel and assigned production quotas to all member countries except Saudi Arabia. The Saudis were expected to vary their own production so as to keep total OPEC production in line with the new targets. Saudi Oil Minister Ahmed Zaki Yamani said this arrangement would put OPEC back in "the driver's seat" of world energy.

As oil income went down, government revenue fell by one third in the fiscal year 1982–83, necessitating the slashing in spending. The 1983–84 budget predicted expenditures of $76 billion, which was at least $10 billion more than income. This deficit, the first since 1973, was to be met from accumulated foreign and domestic reserves. Revenues began to increase in the summer of 1983 as Saudi oil production rose to more than 5 million barrels per day.

Despite its financial problems, Saudi Arabia completed a major crude-oil pipeline and a number of other petrochemical projects in 1983. More than half of the 1983–84 government expenditures were committed to economic development. The budgetary crunch was felt especially by the construction industry as spending for new buildings fell sharply. Foreign contractors were required in February to subcontract at least 30% of all public-sector jobs to Saudi companies.

Government. When King Fahd announced the new budget on April 13, he emphasized that the Saudi government would continue despite the drop in oil revenue. Several seats in the cabinet were given to new ministers. In May the king moved Ibrahim al-Anqari, the minister for labor, to the ministry for municipal and rural affairs. Al-Anqari was replaced in the labor ministry by a newcomer to the cabinet, Ali al-Faiz. The ministry of health was being supervised by the minister for industry, Ghazi al-Gosaibi.

King Fahd undertook measures to consolidate his support among the ulema by more strictly enforcing the segregation of women from men in public places, encouraging the observance of prayers, and forbidding proselytizing by Christians. In early June, while presiding over the 43-nation Islamic Conference at Mecca, Fahd called for a reinterpreta-

---

SAUDI ARABIA • Information Highlights

Official Name: Kingdom of Saudi Arabia.
Location: Arabian peninsula in southwest Asia.
Area: 899,614 sq mi (2 331 000 km²).
Population (July 1983 est.): 10,443,000.
Government: *Head of state and government,* Fahd ibn Abd al-Aziz, king and prime minister (acceded June 1982).
Monetary Unit: Riyal (3.4805 riyals equal U.S.$1, Nov. 25, 1983).
Gross National Product (1981–82 U.S.$): $152,207,000,000.
Foreign Trade (1982 U.S.$): *Imports,* $40,654,000,000; *exports,* $79,123,000,000.

tion by the ulema of Islamic holy law so that it could more comprehensively deal with modern conditions.

Foreign Affairs. The three-year-old war between Iran and Iraq finally had a direct impact on Saudi Arabia. A massive oil slick in the Persian Gulf, resulting from an Iraqi bombing of an Iranian oil installation on March 2, forced the Saudis to build floating booms and earth barriers to protect desalinization plants. Fishing was banned in some areas in May, and damage to marine life was considerable. The Gulf Cooperation Council presented a peace plan in May to Iran and Iraq, but since it was ultimately rejected by Iran, the Saudis continued lending money to Iraq to help finance the war.

The United States sought Saudi help in mediating the Lebanese civil war in May and July, but the Saudis were unable to persuade Syria and the Lebanese factions to agree. Saudi Arabia claimed that this failure was due largely to the inability of the United States to pressure Israel to withdraw from southern Lebanon. In October the new Saudi ambassador to the United States, Prince Bandar, helped secure a cease-fire and the promise of Lebanese groups to conduct talks aimed at national reconciliation.

Saudi Foreign Minister Prince Saud became the first Saudi official since 1932 to visit Moscow, when in December 1982 he took part in a delegation that explained to Soviet officials the Arab plan to end the Arab-Israeli dispute. However, formal Saudi-Soviet diplomatic relations were not established as a result.

WILLIAM OCHSENWALD
Virginia Polytechnic Institute

SINGAPORE

The number of potential heirs to political power continued to diminish, and Prime Minister Lee Kuan Yew indicated that he may remain in power longer than expected.

Politics. The secretary-general of the National Trades Union Congress (NTUC), Lim Chee Onn, was dismissed by the prime minister in April following complaints that Lim had lost contact with the member unions. He later was relieved of his cabinet position as well.

The minister of labor and communications, Ong Teng Cheong, was named the new NTUC secretary-general. Ong, like Lim, was one of seven younger members of the People's Action Party (PAP) chosen in the late 1970s to be given increasing responsibilities and tested as a successor generation. Five remained, but only the three who are Chinese, Ong among them, could be considered realistic possibilities for the top in predominantly Chinese Singapore. In August two junior ministers, Yeo Ning Hong and S. Jayakumar, were made acting ministers to replenish the ranks of younger leaders.

SINGAPORE • Information Highlights

Official Name: Republic of Singapore.
Location: Southeast Asia.
Area: 239 sq mi (618 km^2).
Population (July 1983 est.): 2,503,000.
Government: *Head of state,* C. V. Devan Nair, president (took office October 1981). *Head of government,* Lee Kuan Yew, prime minister (took office 1959). *Legislature* (unicameral)—Parliament.
Monetary Unit: Singapore dollar (2.1335 S. dollars equal U.S.$1, Nov. 25, 1983).
Gross Domestic Product (1981–82 U.S.$): $15,125,000,000.
Economic Index (1982): *Consumer Prices* (1976 = 100), all items, 126.9; food 127.3.
Foreign Trade (1982 U.S.$): *Imports,* $28,167,000,000; *exports,* $20,788,000,000.

Prime Minister Lee's 60th birthday in September was a public occasion for the first time in ten years. In his speech, he hinted that he would like "to sit back if only for the day" on his 70th birthday. In introducing the possible successors in 1980, he had indicated that he expected them to assume power in the late 1980s.

A June correction turned to near panic as the stock market index fell hundreds of points in July amid rumors that Lee was ill or dead. The market came back as the rumors proved false, but the incident demonstrated that business shared the prime minister's worries about the capabilities of possible successors.

In August speeches, Lee caused public furor as he urged educated, professional women to have more children to improve the pool of local talent. He expressed concern that the next generation in the small nation would be largely the children of the less well educated. Critics were alarmed at what they saw as championing nature over nurture. Lee suggested the possibility of financial incentives to encourage the educated to have more children (in contrast to the highly successful family-planning program). Matchmaking became popular as Deputy Prime Minister Goh Keng Swee indicated that the government was exploring computer software from Japan to match promising young people, and the university introduced programs to educate male students in proper behavior and courtship.

Economy. While weak by Singapore's standards, the real domestic product grew 5.6% in the first half of 1983. Manufacturing output was down 7.8%, but construction, finance and business services, and transport and communication offset the drop. A return to the double-digit growth of the past decade would depend on the course of the recoveries of the United States and international markets.

In July the Monetary Authority of Singapore closed the local Overseas Union Finance for granting unsecured loans and loans to directors.

K. MULLINER, *Ohio University*

SOCIAL WELFARE

Global economic recovery was too slow to reduce unemployment significantly in most industrial nations, or to lighten debts of developing nations that reached a crisis level and reduced welfare spending. Military action in the Middle East, Central America, Africa, and Southeast Asia kept the number of homeless refugees high. In Pakistan, those who had fled from Afghanistan had passed the three-million mark by year's end. Natural disasters, particularly droughts, threatened many more, especially in sub-Saharan Africa. Officials of the UN Food and Agricultural Organization (FAO) warned in February that a famine on the disastrous scale of 1973–74 might be repeated on that continent; by midsummer the London-based Save the Children fund confirmed that in Ethiopia alone more than 2 million people needed emergency aid then and over the next year due to famine and the flight from guerrilla wars in Tigre and Eritrea. By November, FAO Secretary-General Édouard Saouma called for immediate help for 150 million people in 22 African countries threatened by starvation from the Sachel to Botswana. A World Food Day, sponsored by various church and private organizations in the United States, sought in the meantime to "raise the consciousness" of people to the problem of hunger both at home

As the number of homeless Americans increases, the need for shelters, such as the one below in Denver, grows.

© Anthony Suau/Picture Group

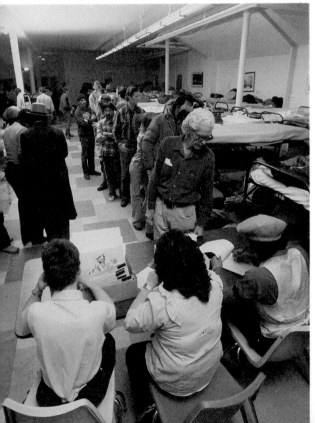

and abroad. The problem may have been worst on the borders of Nigeria, where about 2 million foreign workers and their families were deported on short notice in the wake of the oil-boom collapse. A World Bank study blamed Africa's plight and bleak prospects in food production on poor distribution of aid and bad government policies and urged a long-sought coordination of aid and better production incentives. Parts of West Central Africa did much better, and Gabon became the first nation south of the Sahara to extend a social security system and welfare scheme to all of its resident native population.

Welfare problems also mounted in Latin American countries staggering under growing external debts, due to poor exports and high interest rates. A sharp increase in Mexico's crime rate was attributed to high unemployment, while the burden of higher levels of air pollution, inadequate housing, and poor water and sewage facilities made Mexico City, growing at a rate that will give it from 30 to 35 million inhabitants by century's end, an object warning about skewed urban growth. Perhaps the worst of the Western Hemisphere's urban problems, linked to unabated population growth, was the estimated 40 million abandoned youngsters; researchers found that of the 2 million homeless children in Rio de Janeiro, Brazil, only 20,000 received government aid. In São Paulo, Brazil, the numbers were 50,000 out of 2.5 million. By September, poor adults squeezed by inflation in food staples running at 200% went on nightly rampages, looting food stores. Similar pressures in Chile brought mass demonstrations and the seizure of plots of land by groups of homeless citizens.

The welfare problems of several major developing nations—including Mexico, Brazil, Argentina, Poland, the Philippines, and Chile—were intensified by the efforts of the International Monetary Fund (IMF), their chief source of external fiscal support since private banks stopped new loans, to impose a regimen of austerity on all borrowing nations to help them renegotiate debts that have risen to a world total of more than $600 billion (U.S.). (*See* special report page 277.)

Fiscal affairs were not the only concern. Several leading authorities bitterly assailed the granting in September of the 1983 UN Population Award jointly to Qian Xinzhong, minister of China's State Family Planning Commission, and to Prime Minister Indira Gandhi of India. Critics of the 1983 award charged that China's birth-control policy was responsible for an "appallingly high rate of female infanticide" and that Mrs. Gandhi was responsible for a "cruel mandated sterilization program."

The European Scene. Declining inflation rates and a slight economic growth rate began to help European nations cope with a multitude of problems by autumn. In Great Britain, persistent unemployment and fiscal problems forced further reductions in health care and pension levels, and a questioning of the universality of access to such basic programs. Throughout Western Europe, welfare costs had risen at an alarming rate, from an average of 19.3% of gross national product (GNP) going into social programs in 1970 to about 33% for 1983. Rapid increases in "moonlighting" and in the "underground economy" hampered revenue collections while entitlements grew. Unemployment ranged from 10 to 12% in the region; one estimate claimed that the jobless number exceeded 12 million and would continue to rise, especially among younger workers. In France, the socialist government of François Mitterrand was forced in April to adopt an austerity program that raised social security taxes, utility and transport costs, and income taxes, though lowering the retirement age for workers from 65 to 60 years. Socialist regimes in both Spain and Portugal also sought to impose austerity in welfare as part of their programs. Even relatively prosperous West Germany, with the world's highest rate of social security taxes and spending, began confronting short-term problems and the serious long-term need for adjustment that declining birth rates and longer life spans will bring. Commissions in several countries were at work suggesting some basic changes. Luxembourg shifted more costs of hospital and medical care to patients; Belgium lowered the retirement age to create jobs but also reduced medical benefits while hiking taxes; Poland's beleaguered government improved pension laws and extended their coverage to women and farmers. In nonfiscal issues, Greece promoted the status of women by abolishing dowries, making divorce legal, and raising minimum marriage age for females from 14 to 18 years; in Spain the rightwing opposition challenged a liberalized abortion law in the courts amid widespread debate. Reports on the Soviet Union indicated serious decline in life expectancy, fertility, and hospital treatment, with increased infant mortality, all the result of poor health-care delivery relative to need. By many estimates, the shortage of housing in Soviet cities has worsened, in spite of an urgent program that puts up more than 2 million new apartments annually.

Social Security. Difficulties with the immediate or long-term financing of social security systems in Western Europe and Japan—due largely to continued inflation distorting indexing provisions—led to major changes in contribution rates and ceilings, modifications of indexes, capping of annual increases in pensions, and changes in the index review period. In Britain, where the basic pension for the average worker was about $53 per week, the newly reelected Thatcher government cut more than $3 billion from the social security budget, affecting not only pensioners but the unem-

David Hume Kennerly/Gamma-Liaison

On April 20—"a happy day for Americans"—President Reagan signed the 1983 Social Security reform bill.

ployed and disabled. In Japan, the average worker was eligible for monthly pensions of $547 at 60, though many larger companies also provided lump-sum payments at retirement. Yet the nation's high life-expectancy rate—and high cost of living—kept more than 45% of workers over 65 on the job, and the national savings rate at 19.4% of personal disposable income—highest of any industrial nation—also reflected the continued fear of penury in old age.

A Parliamentary Special Committee held public hearings throughout Canada on proposals released in December 1982 for an overhaul of the Social Security and pension systems, but there was no public consensus by year's end that would obtain the necessary approval of the provincial governments. Meanwhile, the issue of restructuring Canada's national health service was being pressed by the Trudeau government in an effort to regain popular support.

Revisions of social security laws and federally paid health care were the major welfare concerns in the United States, too. The bipar-

453

tisan National Commission on Social Security Reform submitted its recommendations to President Reagan and Congress on January 20, and the resulting bill, which provided only slight changes in the recommendations, passed more quickly than expected. On April 20, President Reagan signed the bill with praise for both the commission and the Congress in reaching appropriate compromises. The act delayed the annual cost-of-living adjustments in benefits from July to January, made up to one half of the benefits received by higher-income beneficiaries subject to income taxes, gradually raised the retirement age early in the next century, called for earlier implementation of scheduled payroll-tax increases, and put new federal employees under the Social Security program. It also established a new system of prospective payment for hospital services under Medicare to keep costs down and extended supplementary benefits for the unemployed that otherwise would have expired. Attending the signing was the new Secretary of Health and Human Services, Margaret M. Heckler (*See* BIOGRAPHY).

There was considerable criticism of welfare policies and administration as the high tide of unemployment receded slowly over the year. By midsummer it was clear that the Medicare fund that pays hospital bills for the elderly and aged was running a deficit at a rapidly increasing rate, and a reform similar to the basic one would be needed very soon for this part of the system. Administration efforts to give states new power to restrict eligibility, reduce benefits, and increase payments by recipients ran into considerable opposition, although the cost of medical and health care continued to rise to a point where roughly 10% of the national income was going to pay for those services. The system's trustees warned that "either disbursements will have to be reduced by 30% or financing will have to be increased by 43%" to prevent exhaustion of the Hospital Insurance Trust Fund by 1996. More pessimistic predictions put the date at 1986. The need for basic change was clear for a system serving 26 million elderly and 3 million disabled Americans, even as hospitals grew fearful about the impact of fixed-rate policies for services. Meanwhile, resentments continued to mount over the enforcement of more stringent reviews of disability payments under Social Security, some of which were nullified by federal judges in Minnesota and California. That kind of conflict reached its most bizarre form in late September, when a Hawaiian federal district judge ordered the arrest and imprisonment of the state's director of Social Services and Housing for refusing to obey a court order to increase benefits to 2,000 recipients under Aid to Families with Dependent Children. By November, a 13-member panel chaired by former Indiana Gov. O. R. Bowen had formulated a set of recommendations to meet the crisis in Medicare, including raising the age of eligibility to 67, raising the premium $100 a year, raising excise taxes on tobacco and alcohol products, and reducing the payment rate to hospitals. As a new debate swirled around such proposals, and the general soundness in the long run of the entire Social Security system, less attention was paid to the greater accessibility the new law provided and to tougher efforts to end fraud.

The U.S. Scene. An economic recovery more rapid than experts predicted helped ameliorate the more immediate and urgent welfare problems connected with high unemployment. In January the jobless rate stood at 10.2%. In March the administration acceded to congressional pressure by endorsing a supplement to the Job Training Partnership Act of 1982, about to take the place of the CETA program. By the end of the year, the jobless rate was dropping below 9%, though critics claimed the figures did not take into account those who had stopped seeking employment. There was no doubt that the number of homeless Americans rose dramatically by summer, with considerable strain on the resources of New York, Philadelphia, and other cities to provide beds and meals for the indigent. The situation gained political coloration with revelations by the Census Bureau in midsummer that 2.6 million people had been added to the numbers below the poverty line in 1982, and that the officially defined poor had risen to 15% of the national population, the highest figure since 1965. The disparity between incomes of black and white Americans was as high as it had been in 1960, and 1 of every 2 black children lived in poverty; among Hispanic-Americans it was 1 in 3. Census data also showed that the "femininization of poverty" was continuing, with almost 6 million families headed by women, who still earned about two thirds of the wages of males in equivalent work. Efforts to make further reductions in the food-stamp program aroused such an outcry, and evidence of hunger and malnutrition was so prevalent, that President Reagan appointed a task force to investigate the causes and extent of hunger in the nation.

Another delayed effect of the economic slump was the pressure it exerted on pensions covering about 40% of those working for private businesses. The federal Pension Benefit Guaranty Corporation, established in 1974, faced insolvency after having covered $220 million in fiscal 1982 (its worst losses ever) and projected losses of $600 million over the next five years. As winter drew near, the struggle over a new budget involved differences over the federal role in extending again health insurance for the unemployed and their families, and providing additional help for the young in view of exceptionally bleak job prospects in Midwestern and Eastern cities.

MORTON ROTHSTEIN, *University of Wisconsin*

SOUTH AFRICA

Patterns of black-white confrontation and of social and political upheaval and change continued to characterize events in South Africa in 1983. The African National Congress (ANC) intensified its struggle by increasing its urban guerrilla activities, while the white South African government proposed a revision of the constitution for the first time since the Union of South Africa came into being in 1910.

Urban Guerrilla Activities. A car-bomb explosion outside the headquarters of South Africa's Air Force Command in Pretoria, the country's administrative capital, on May 20 killed 18 persons and wounded 217. This was the worst sabotage incident in South Africa's history. The banned ANC for the first time took direct responsibility for this act of guerrilla warfare. On February 18 a smaller bomb had exploded at a government employment office in Bloemfontein, killing one man and wounding 76.

On May 23 the government retaliated for the May 20 bombing in Pretoria with a raid on ANC bases in Maputo, the capital of Mozambique. The Mozambique government claimed that South Africans had bombed civilian targets, killing at least five people and wounding more than 20.

On May 26 a car bomb exploded, also in Bloemfontein, near a labor office that provides permits for Africans to work in urban areas. It caused extensive damage but no casualties. Thus urban guerrilla activities, followed by reprisals and retaliations, seem to be a new phase in black-white relations in South Africa.

The Constitutional Referendum. On May 5, South Africa's new constitution was formally introduced in parliament. It provided for a new Coloured House of Representatives with 85 members, and an Asian House with 45 members. The House of Assembly for whites would continue to have 178 members. This plan, referred to by Prime Minister P. W. Botha as "healthy power sharing" but rejected by both the Progressive Federal and the Conservative parties, went before the electorate in a referendum on November 2. The Progressives were opposed to the constitution because Africans, who make up 70% of the population, are given no form of representation. The government's position is that they have political rights in one or another of the nine homelands. The Conservatives opposed the constitution because they felt it would cause a major dilution in the policy of apartheid.

Because of fears that lack of willingness to participate by Coloureds or Asians could destroy the effectiveness of the new constitution, the key part of the new bill has a provision that makes it possible for parliament to continue to operate if either of these groups withdraws. In addition, if disputes occur among the various

Severe drought intensified in South Africa during 1983.

chambers over legislation of general interest, the president will have the power to refer the issue to the President's Council. This council will have 20 white, 10 Coloured, and 5 Asian members, all elected by the respective chambers, and 25 members appointed by the president. The president will be elected by a college dominated by whites. The office of prime minister will be abolished, and all powers will be transferred to the new president.

Of the 2.7 million eligible voters, 76% participated in the November 2 referendum, and

66% of them voted "yes." Prime Minister Botha indicated that the new constitution would probably be implemented in the second half of 1984.

Battle of the Bergs. In a parliamentary debate in February 1983, the minister of labor, Stephanus (Fanie) P. Botha (not related to the prime minister), became involved in a confrontation with the leader of the Conservative Party, Andries P. Treurnicht. Botha challenged Treurnicht, a former cabinet minister and an extreme conservative, to resign his seat in parliament. Treurnicht had broken away from the National Party in 1982 because he felt the party was not adhering to the basic premises of apartheid. In return, Botha offered to resign and seek reelection in a by-election.

Treurnicht accepted the challenge, and what became known as the "Battle of the Bergs" began. Treurnicht's constituency is Waterburg, and Botha's is Soutpansburg, both in the northern Transvaal. Treurnicht was reelected in the Soutpansburg constituency, substantially defeating the National Party candidate, and Botha retained his seat by only 621 votes out of the 11,579 cast. The results indicated a solid, but not necessarily substantial, support for the right-wing conservatives. It also indicated a trend to the right by rural voters and a concern by them over constitutional changes by the National Party.

Mkhize Incident. Saul Mkhize was an accountant who had fought to save Driefontein's 5,000 African residents from being removed from an area that they had farmed since 1912 when they had purchased 300 plots of land, one year before implementation of the Natives Land Act that created the reserves. Driefontein, in the southeastern Transvaal 200 miles (320 km) from Johannesburg, was one of the last remaining "black spots" in the white areas, and it was the government's intention to move its inhabitants to one of the homelands.

On April 2, Mkhize was shot in the chest in a scuffle with South African police, who had declared the protest meeting at which he was speaking illegal, and who had tried to drag him away. They said that they had to shoot him in self-defense, but Africans at the meeting insisted that tear gas canisters fired into the crowd had caused the problem, and that the policeman had fired at Mkhize from a distance.

Drought. The worst drought in nearly 100 years intensified in 1983. It severely affected southern Africa, and in particular the black rural farmers, who have suffered from starvation and other hardships. In South Africa many reservoirs were less than half full, and many rivers dried up completely. The loss to South Africa in reduced crop exports was estimated at $822 million in 1983.

Black Urban Residents. At the end of May the five judges of the Appeals Court unanimously ruled that migrant workers who had had jobs in South Africa for ten consecutive years were entitled to permanent residence with their families in the black townships. The court ruled that an African engineering worker, Tom Mehlolo, could continue to live in a black township, even though under the "influx control" policy he was required to return to his homeland each year to renew his contract. The court thus removed one of the major restrictions on black families living in South Africa's urban areas. The ruling affects workers who now are classified as temporary employees.

At first the government proposed to institute new legislation to counteract the Appeals Court ruling. However, in June, after pressure from the United States and other governments, the minister for cooperation and development, Pieter G. Koornhof, stated that the government would abide by the court's decision, with the proviso that it would pass new legislation requiring black workers to have official certification that adequate housing was available in the urban areas for their wives and children.

Gold. Fluctuations in the international price of gold has caused severe problems for South Africa. The national budget at the end of March reflected this fluctuation, since gold in 1982 had represented 40% of the country's export earnings. South Africa's gross domestic product (GDP) was expected to fall again in 1983. The 1982 drop in the GDP was the first since World War II. Because of the severe drought, it was estimated that farm output would also drop even more than the 1982 decline of 7.5%.

Death of John Vorster. John (Balthazar Johannes) Vorster, who had been prime minister for 12 years (1966–78), died on September 10. In 1978 he had accepted the largely ceremonial position of president but left the presidency after eight months as a result of a government investigation that involved him in a cover-up in which more than $70 million was illegally spent by the Department of Information.

PATRICK O'MEARA, *Indiana University*

SOUTH AFRICA • Information Highlights

Official Name: Republic of South Africa.
Location: Southern tip of Africa.
Area: 472,000 sq mi (1 222 480 km²).
Population (July 1983 est.): 30,938,000.
Chief Cities (1980 census): Pretoria, the administrative capital, 528,407; Cape Town, the legislative capital, 213,830; Johannesburg, 1,536,457; Durban, 505,963.
Government: *Head of state,* Marais Viljoen, president (took office June 1979). *Head of government,* P. W. Botha, prime minister (took office Sept. 1978). *Legislature*—Parliament: President Council and House of Assembly.
Monetary Unit: Rand (1.1983 rands equal U.S.$1, Nov. 18, 1983.)
Gross Domestic Product (1982 U.S.$): $71,668,-000,000.
Economic Index (1981): *Consumer Prices* (1970 = 100), all items, 319.0; food, 384.1.
Foreign Trade (1980 U.S.$): *Imports,* $18,553,-000,000; *exports,* $12,502,000,000.

UPI

Spoleto Festival U.S.A., which opened its seventh season May 20, brings in an estimated $40 million in business.

SOUTH CAROLINA

Under a tight budget ($2.1 billion), Gov. Richard W. Riley campaigned for improvement in the quality of public education and other services. The narrow defeat of his sales-tax proposal served as a catalyst for developing new strategies and obtaining additional resources.

Government. Spending had to be reduced early in the budget year, but state revenues increased enough to prevent the firing of employees and to leave a slight surplus. An intermediate court of appeals was created to reduce the four-year backlog in the state Supreme Court. The release of nonviolent criminals reduced the extreme overcrowding in state prisons, but lack of resources continued to plague the correctional system. The General Assembly liberalized the state's blue laws, stiffened punishment for drunk driving, tightened regulations for granting utility rate increases, required restraining seats in cars for children under the age of four, mandated the licensing of hospice programs and approved a single member district plan for the state Senate. The fight between the Supreme Court and the legislature for control of rule-making power in the court system continued, resulting in a proposed constitutional amendment. New tax proposals were defeated.

For the first time in 95 years, a black was elected to the state Senate to fill a vacancy.

Education. The state department of education proposed a 41-point program for improving the quality of education in the public schools, tying in with the governor's own objectives. Pilot programs were created to demonstrate effective school programs. Still the lowest in the nation, SAT scores statewide did show improvement; indeed, testing performance at many grade levels increased. A nationally accredited center for evaluating prospective school principals and administrators was established. Under federal mandate, blacks were added to the trustees of major institutions of higher learning. The two state medical schools resolved some of their competition for support and student quotas.

Industry and Agriculture. Industrial expansion slowed, particularly in capital investment. The number of plants, however, increased by 25% over the previous year. Unemployment slightly exceeded the national average. The state government created several programs to aid in acquiring capital and developing small industries, especially in rural areas. Exporting was stressed, and efforts to attract foreign cap-

457

ital and expand imports were coordinated. Agriculture and fishing, especially of crayfish and shrimp, were developing in the coastal region.

Freezes in the winter and record-breaking heat and drought in the summer seriously reduced agricultural production. The peach crop was one fourth the normal size, early vegetable crops were killed, and soybean yields were reduced. Much of the state qualified for emergency federal assistance. The 69,000 acres (27 600 ha) planted in cotton was the lowest in history. Tobacco yields were normal, however, and tobacco continued as the state's leading cash crop. The food processing industry continued to develop, albeit slowly.

Social and Cultural. Institutional care continued to be decentralized and community resources for nonresidential services expanded. Indigent medical care, especially in highly technical areas, became a problem. Reduction in infant mortality, elimination of child abuse, and prison overcrowding received special attention.

A state symphony orchestra was being formed, community theaters and folk festivals were on the rise, a performing arts center was opened at Camden, and a major state museum was begun in downtown Columbia. The Spoleto Festival in Charleston enjoyed another successful year.

ROBERT H. STOUDEMIRE
University of South Carolina

SOUTH DAKOTA

The South Dakota legislature passed several statutes of importance during 1983. Economic conditions hurt many farmers but were satisfactory for most other residents. Bankers found favorable new opportunities. And the U.S. Interior Department's "Operation Eagle" was a source of controversy among Sioux Indians.

Legislation. An inordinate number of significant new laws were passed during the state legislative session. One tightened state control over religious schools by applying more stringent attendance regulations. Another sought to limit drug abuse by controlling the sale and distribution of drug paraphernalia. Others prohibited local governments from restricting the possession of firearms and threatened underage persons with the loss of their driver's license for attempting to purchase alcoholic beverages.

The 1983–84 appropriations bill allocated a total of $709,621,699 in state, federal, and other resources. The largest amounts went to higher education ($165 million) and human services ($133 million).

Economy. Ranchers and farmers reaped the benefits of steady prices and curbs on inflation but suffered gravely from bad weather conditions. Crops were nearly drowned out by heavy rains in the spring and early summer, then were parched by drought through harvest. Some small operators went bankrupt despite receiving federal aid.

Other residents enjoyed more favorable conditions. Non-Indians had an unemployment rate of only 6.2% and tax rates that were the second lowest in the nation. Retail sales and tourism grew slightly. Many who had grown accustomed to entitlement assistance, however, disappeared from public rolls. One reason was the reduction of federal assistance to the state by some 27%; the other reason was a "workfare" requirement in most counties of the state which required able-bodied recipients to repay benefits with public service.

Banking and Insurance. With the national economic recovery already boosting Citicorp's giant credit card operation in Sioux Falls, the South Dakota legislature and Gov. William Janklow (R) attracted additional outside banking investment by allowing bank holding companies to own state banks, which in turn were allowed to own insurance companies. Citicorp quickly purchased a 53% interest in American State Bank of Rapid City and awaited approval from federal regulators. Other outside banking interests stood ready to make similar purchases in order to gain access to profits from the sale of insurance.

Native Americans. In June, then U.S. Secretary of the Interior James Watt staged a press conference in Sioux Falls to initiate "Operation Eagle," an undercover sting operation against Sioux traditionalists accused of selling parts of eagles and other birds on the endangered species list. Victims of the sting accused Watt of courting environmentalists with a display of concern for wildlife, while Watt charged the Indians with wanton destruction of the national symbol. Trials in federal district court in Sioux Falls brought convictions for most of the accused.

HERBERT T. HOOVER
University of South Dakota

SOUTH DAKOTA • Information Highlights

Area: 77,116 sq mi (199 730 km²).
Population (1982 est.): 691,000.
Chief Cities (1980 census): Pierre, the capital, 11,973; Sioux Falls, 81,343; Rapid City, 46,492.
Government (1983): *Chief Officers*—governor, William J. Janklow (R); lt. gov., Lowell C. Hansen II (R). *Legislature*—Senate, 35 members; House of Representatives, 70 members.
State Finances (fiscal year 1982): *Revenues,* $873,000,000; *expenditures,* $829,000,000.
Personal Income (1982): $6,675,000,000; per capita, $9,666.
Labor Force (July 1983): *Nonagricultural wage and salary earners,* 234,400; *unemployed,* 16,400 (4.8% of total force).
Education: *Enrollment* (fall 1981)—public elementary schools, 85,887; public secondary, 39,770; colleges and universities (fall 1982), 35,874 students. *Public school expenditures* (1981–82), $270,252,000.

SPACE EXPLORATION

Jan. 31, 1983, marked the 25th anniversary of the launch of the first U.S. satellite, the 31-lb (14 kg) Explorer I. During 1983 the 215,000-lb (97 524-kg) *Challenger* joined *Columbia* as part of the U.S. space-shuttle fleet, and four successful shuttle missions were flown; the last of them featured the debut of Spacelab, a unique orbital laboratory carried in the shuttle's cargo bay. Soviet cosmonauts Vladimir Lyakhov and Aleksandr Aleksandrov reactivated and occupied the Salyut space station for 150 days. In interplanetary space exploration, the USSR launched two spacecraft into orbit around Venus. The U.S. Voyager 2, now beyond the orbit of Saturn, continued on its course toward encounters with Uranus and Neptune. Pioneer 10 crossed the orbit of Neptune and became the first man-made object to leave the solar system. In exploration of the distant universe, the Infrared Astronomy Satellite provided the first direct evidence of another solar system.

Manned Space Flight. Four U.S. space-shuttle missions were conducted in 1983 as the shuttle continued the transition from an experimental test vehicle to an operational space transportation and experiment carrier. *Challenger,* the second of four planned orbiters, joined *Columbia* as part of the fleet. *Challenger*'s first flight, designated Space Transportation System Mission 6 (STS 6), began on April 4 with a launch from the Kennedy Space Center, FL, and ended five days later with a perfect landing at Edwards Air Force Base, CA. Paul J. Weitz was the mission commander; the crew included pilot Karol J. Bobko and mission specialists Donald H. Peterson and Story F. Musgrave. The highlight of the mission was a spacewalk by Peterson and Musgrave, the first U.S. extravehicular activity (EVA) since Skylab 4 in 1972. The Tracking and Data Relay Satellite (TDRS 1) was also successfully deployed from the orbiter, but a malfunction in the Inertial Upper Stage left the satellite several thousand miles from its desired orbit; by firing the spacecraft's six small thrusters periodically over an eleven-week period, the satellite was slowly moved to the desired geosynchronous orbit. STS 6 also carried three small self-contained payloads, called Getaway Specials: a Japanese artificial snow crystal experiment, fruit and vegetable seeds to determine how seeds should be packaged to withstand spaceflight, and a group of metallurgical and microbiological experiments.

The six-day STS 7 mission, the second flight of *Challenger,* began on June 18 with launch from the Kennedy Space Center and was commanded by Robert L. Crippen, who had been aboard the first mission of *Columbia* (STS 1) in 1981; Frederick H. Hauck was the pilot, and the mission specialists were John M.

Tass from Sovfoto

Cosmonauts Vladimir Lyakhov (left) and Aleksandr Aleksandrov reactivated the Salyut 7 space station for 150 days.

Fabian, Norman E. Thagard, and Sally K. Ride —the first U.S. woman to go into space. Two international communication satellites, Canada's Anik C-2 and Indonesia's Palapa B-1, were deployed from *Challenger*'s cargo bay and boosted to geosynchronous orbit by Payload Assist Modules (PAM-Ds). The highlight of the mission was the deployment and retrieval of the West German Shuttle Pallet Satellite (SPAS) using *Challenger*'s Remote Manipulator System. While outside the orbiter, SPAS had been used to acquire scientific data and take photographs of earth and *Challenger.* The STS 7 mission was completed June 24 with a successful landing at Edwards.

The first night launch and night landing of a space shuttle were accomplished by the six-day STS 8 mission. The launch took place August 30 at the Kennedy Space Center, and the landing was made September 5 at Edwards Air Force Base. *Challenger*'s commander was Richard H. Truly, a veteran of the STS 2 test flight; the pilot was Daniel C. Brandensten; and mission specialists were Dale A. Gardner, William E. Thornton, and Guion S. Bluford—the first black American to go into space. The principal payload was the Indian weather and communications satellite INSAT IB, deployed from the shuttle's cargo bay and boosted to orbit by a PAM-D upper stage.

The ten-day STS 9/Spacelab 1 mission, launched November 28 from the Kennedy Space Center, marked the return to service of *Columbia* and was the most ambitious and complex space-shuttle mission to date. The mission featured the debut of Spacelab, a spe-

Guion S. Bluford, the first black American to travel in space, was a mission specialist on STS 8, a six-day flight of the space shuttle Challenger launched August 30.

cial laboratory developed by the European Space Agency. The Spacelab 1 system consisted of a cylindrical-shaped pressurized module 14 ft (4.3 m) in diameter and 23 ft (7 m) long and a platform in the cargo bay for those instruments requiring direct exposure to space. A tunnel connected the Spacelab module with the orbiter cabin. A six-man crew was carried on the mission—commander John W. Young, who had flown on five previous space missions; pilot Brewster H. Shaw; mission specialists Owen K. Garriott, who had flown on the Skylab 3 mission, and Robert A. Parker; and payload specialists (scientists) Ulf Merbold of West Germany and Byron K. Lichtenberg. Some 38 different scientific instruments located both inside and outside the habitable module were used to perform a wide variety of investigations in astronomy and astrophysics, solar physics, space plasma physics, materials science, life science, and earth observations.

On June 28 the Salyut 7/Cosmos 1443 space-station complex was occupied and reactivated by mission commander Vladimir Lyakhov and flight engineer Aleksandr Aleksandrov, who had been launched in Soyuz T-9 the previous day. The station had been unoccupied since Dec. 10, 1982, following the 211-day manned space-endurance record established by Anatoly Berezovoy and Valentin Lebedev. During the 150 days that they occupied the space complex, Lyakhov and Aleksandrov performed a series of scientific-technical experiments, including materials processing, earth observations, and medical and biological studies. The cosmonauts were resupplied with more than 4,400 lbs (1 996 kg) of fuel and cargo by an unmanned Progress logistic spacecraft on August 17. Six days later, some 700 lbs (318 kg) of exposed film, materials-processing samples, and spent hardware were returned to earth by the unmanned Cosmos 1443.

A major anomaly occurred on September 9, when a propellant line on Salyut 7 ruptured, venting toxic nitrogen tetroxide into space. The emergency forced Lyakhov and Aleksandrov to don spacesuits and enter the safety of the Soyuz descent craft until the hazard abated. On November 1 and again on November 3, both cosmonauts exited the space station for three-hour spacewalks to install extra solar panels for additional electrical power. On November 23, after 150 days in space, Lyakhov and Aleksandrov returned to earth in Soyuz T-9.

A previous attempt to reoccupy Salyut 7, on April 21 by Soyuz T-8 cosmonauts, had been unsuccessful when the spacecraft could not rendezvous with the station and the mission had to be aborted. The Soyuz T-8 crew—mission commander Lt. Col. Vladimir Titov, researcher Aleksandr Serebrov, and flight engineer Gennady Strekalov—then flew a nominal reentry and landed on April 22.

During the summer the Soviets again prepared for a launch of Titov and Strekalov to replace the crew aboard the Salyut 7 space station. On September 27, however, as the cosmonauts sat in their Soyuz T-10 spacecraft preparing for a night launch, the SL-4 booster rocket exploded. Fortunately, emergency escape tower rockets had pulled the spacecraft to safety just seconds before the explosion. Neither cosmonaut was injured seriously, but the launchpad was damaged heavily.

Soviet development of a reusable space plane continued with two orbital flights of an unmanned, small-scale model on the Cosmos 1445 and 1517 missions. After the orbits, parachute landings were made in the Indian Ocean and Black Sea.

Planetary Probes. The U.S. Voyagers 1 and 2, Pioneer Venus Orbiter, and Pioneers 10 and 11 all continued operations in the extended mission mode. On June 13, Pioneer 10, after a flight of 2.8 billion mi (4.5 billion km), crossed the orbit of Neptune, currently the outermost planet, and became the first man-made object to leave the solar system. Communications with Pioneer 10 will be possible until it is about 5 billion mi (8 billion km) from earth, in about ten years. Voyager 2 continued toward its planned encounter with Uranus in 1986 and Neptune in 1989, while Voyager 1, on a widely divergent flight path, continued outward toward the heliospheric boundary.

The Soviet Union, meanwhile, continued to focus its planetary exploration program on Venus. Following up on its two successful probe landings in 1982, the USSR launched two spacecraft carrying radar imaging systems to orbit Venus. Venera 15 and Venera 16 arrived at Venus on October 10 and October 14, respectively, and began high-resolution radar mapping of the Venusian surface.

Application Satellites. U.S. weather satellites in geosynchronous and low-altitude polar orbit, which provide data for national and international weather prediction and warning, were restored to full operational utility with the launch of GOES 6 and NOAA 8 in 1983. GOES 6, launched April 28, and GOES 5 comprise a geosynchronous weather system which provides hourly observations over the Atlantic and Pacific. NOAA 8, launched March 28 to replace the older NOAA 6, and NOAA 7 comprise a low earth-orbital system which provides weather observations of the entire planet four times each day. NOAA 8 also carries an instrument provided by Canada and France called SARSAT, which joins the Soviet Union's COSPAS 1 to form a two-satellite network for detecting aircraft and ships in distress.

The Landsat 4 remote sensing satellite continued to provide data on changing conditions on the earth's surface. Landsat 4 is able to view the entire cloud-free land surface of the earth every 16 days and acquire data for a variety of scientific studies and applications in botany, hydrology, geology, geography, agriculture, and forestry.

On April 17, India launched a remote sensing satellite from its Sriharikota launch facility. The satellite is designed to help India develop technology to survey the earth from space.

The Soviet Union continued to emphasize earth remote sensing with the launch of an electronic imaging satellite, Cosmos 1484, on July 24. The satellite provides natural-resources data via radio transmissions. The Soviets also continued to launch film-return satellites on a periodic basis. An ocean remote-sensing research satellite, Cosmos 1500, was launched September 28 to provide data on sea and ice conditions in the Arctic Ocean.

Scientific Satellites. The first direct evidence that a second solar system may exist was provided by the Infrared Astronomical Satellite (IRAS), which discovered that solid objects of substantial size surround Vega, the third-brightest star. Vega, also known as Alpha Lyrae, is located in the Milky Way Galaxy 26 light years from earth. The objects, which may range in size from 1 mm to tens of kilometers, extend out from the star about 7.5 billion mi (12 billion km). They are probably left over from Vega's formation and may resemble objects in our own solar system, such as asteroids or meteorites.

IRAS is a joint undertaking by the United States, the Netherlands, and the United Kingdom. In performing the first infrared survey of the entire sky, IRAS also discovered five new comets, two regions in our galaxy where stars like the sun are being born, several very young stars that are just now coalescing out of dust and gas clouds, and two intersecting galaxies that are being torn apart by each other's gravity.

The European X-ray Observatory Satellite (Exosat) was launched May 26 to perform a detailed study of known X-ray sources, to map diffuse extended sources such as supernova remnants, and to probe emission patterns from pulsars, active galaxies, binary star systems, and burster stars in the process of disintegration.

Prognoz 9, a Soviet astrophysical mission that includes several French scientific instruments, was launched July 1 to conduct magnetospheric research and observe solar X-ray and gamma-ray emissions.

Communication Satellites. In 1983, 18 communication satellites were launched to augment the approximately 45 operating civilian communication satellites already in geosynchronous orbit. Of these, the United States launched seven, the USSR four, France two, Japan two, and one each for Canada, India, and Indonesia. U.S. Delta vehicles were used to launch two communication satellites for the Radio Corporation of America (RCA), two for Hughes Communications, Inc., and one for American Telephone & Telegraph (AT&T). A U.S. Atlas-Centaur and a French Ariane were used to launch Intelsat V-Fs for the International Telecommunications Satellite Organization (Intelsat); a French Ariane also launched an ECS-1 communications satellite for the European Telecommunications Satellite Organization. Japanese N-2 boosters were used to launch two Japanese communications satellites.

The four civilian communication satellites placed in geosynchronous orbit in 1983 by the USSR included two Radugas, one Gorizont, and one Ekran (Stratsionar T-2). In addition, the USSR placed one communication satellite —Molniya 3—into a low earth orbit.

WILLIAM L. PIOTROWSKI

SPAIN

The Socialist Workers' Party (PSOE) of Prime Minister Felipe González registered advances in spring municipal elections, as Spain's first left-of-center government in nearly half a century took steps to reform the military and shore up a sagging economy.

Government and Politics. González, the popular, boyishly handsome leader who took office in December 1982, campaigned vigorously in behalf of candidates in the May municipal contests. His efforts helped the Socialists capture 46% of the popular vote, compared with 26% for the right-wing Popular Alliance and 8% for the Communists. The United Center Party, which along with the Communists suffered devastating losses in the October 1982 congressional contests, formally dissolved itself in February but received 2% of the vote in the May balloting.

The Socialists emerged victorious in 26 of Spain's 52 major cities, including the ten largest; the discredited and politically bankrupt Communists retained control of Córdoba; the Popular Alliance won majorities in the others.

González moved discreetly to reduce the role of the military, whose officer corps still included many loyalists to the late Generalissimo Francisco Franco. Defense Minister Narcis Serra unveiled a plan to reduce the size of the army from 250,000 to 160,000 men and cut the number of officers by 25%. Modernization efforts also focused on the navy and air force.

On August 10, Spain's constitutional court rejected key articles in a 1982 law regulating the powers of regional governments. Among the articles voided was a provision that legislation approved by the parliament in Madrid took precedence over statutes adopted by regional governments. Basque and Catalan nationalists had attacked the law as a veiled effort to deprive their regions of the autonomy granted under the 1978 constitution. The ETA, the largest Basque terrorist organization, continued its activities in 1983. The government tried to dry up ETA's funding by outlawing the payment of ransom or extortion money to guerrillas.

Economy. The Popular Alliance and other right-wing opponents of González attacked the government's nationalization of Rumasa, a conglomerate with activities ranging from agriculture and wine exports to shipping and real estate. The shock over the takeover on February 24 was accentuated as the Economics Ministry revealed widespread fraud, mismanagement, and tax evasion practiced by the Rumasa group, which generated 1.8% of Spain's gross domestic product in 1982 but many of whose companies teetered on the brink of bankruptcy. Critics claimed that the nationalization discouraged private investment and created a climate of economic uncertainty that would make it difficult to "put Spain back to work" as González promised in the 1982 campaign. Unemployment was at 17% in the fall.

In June and July, steelworkers from Sagunto, near Valencia, launched protests against the government's proposed reorganization of the steel industry, a plan that would eliminate more than 9,000 jobs. Industry Minister Carlos Solchaga pledged to take steps to cushion the impact on Sagunto.

Foreign Affairs. Leaders of the United States and Spain approved a protocol in February designed to assure ratification of a treaty permitting the United States to maintain military bases in Spain. The treaty had been signed by both governments in 1982 and ratified by the U.S. Senate, but it had not been approved by the Spanish parliament. The parliament, after 1982, was controlled by Socialists who objected to references in the treaty to Spain's entry into NATO. The protocol annulled the parts of the treaty that specifically presupposed Spain's membership in the alliance.

In April the Spanish government expressed "concern and displeasure" over a visit by British warships to Gibraltar, a British colony claimed by Spain. The Spanish protest stated a "desire to resolve the Gibraltar question through negotiations, in accordance with United Nations resolutions in order to assure Spanish territorial integrity." The visit rankled because Spain believed that its partial opening of its land border with Gibraltar in 1982 was a gesture that Britain should reciprocate.

Agriculture ministers of the European Community (EC) agreed in October to new rules for marketing Mediterranean farm products. This long-delayed action gave impulse to talks on the crucial agricultural aspects of Spain's entry into the EC, expected in 1986.

During a U.S. visit, Prime Minister González urged President Reagan to back the Central American peace effort of the Contadora Group.

GEORGE W. GRAYSON
College of William and Mary

SPAIN · Information Highlights

Official Name: Spanish State.
Location: Iberian Peninsula in southwestern Europe.
Area: 195,000 sq mi (505,050 km²).
Population (July 1983 est.): 38,234,000.
Chief Cities (1982 est.): Madrid, the capital, 3,271,834; Barcelona, 1,720,998; Valencia, 770,277.
Government: *Head of state,* Juan Carlos I, king (took office Nov. 1975). *Head of government,* Felipe González Márquez, prime minister (took office Dec. 1982). *Legislature*—Cortés: Senate and Chamber of Deputies.
Monetary Unit: Peseta (151.75 pesetas equal U.S.$1, Oct. 31, 1983).
Gross Domestic Product (1982 est. U.S.$): $177,499,000,000.
Economic Indexes (1982): *Consumer Prices* (1970 = 100), all items, 543.2; food, 487.2. *Industrial Production* (1982, 1975 = 100), 113.
Foreign Trade (1982 U.S.$): *Imports,* $31,535,000,000; *exports,* $20,522,000,000.

SPORTS

Ira Wyman/Sygma

The Year in Sports

If followers of sport in 1983 had a sense of turning tides and shifting fortunes, it was not without reason. Major competition saw case after case of the come-from-behind victory, late-in-the-game surge, or breaking away from the pack with a burst of speed and skill. While success was familiar to a few, some perennial second-placers finally emerged as champions. There was a promising new football league, a disturbing new wave of drug abuse, and the end of the Bowie Kuhn era in baseball. It was, above all, a year of dramatic moments.

For starters, the longest winning streak in sports—132 years—came to an end in the waters off Newport, RI. In the seventh and deciding race of America's Cup yachting, *Australia II* (photo, previous page) blew past the defending U.S. entry, *Liberty,* on the fifth of six legs.

In similar fashion, Tom Sneva won his first Indianapolis 500 by roaring past three-time winner Al Unser with only nine laps to go; Martina Navratilova got the "monkey off her back" with her first U.S. Open women's tennis title, whipping six-time champion Chris Evert Lloyd; the Philadelphia '76ers dispatched their own monkey—and the defending champion L.A. Lakers—in the NBA finals; and underdog North Carolina State took the NCAA basketball crown with a last-second dunk against Houston.

Other surges: In golf's Masters Tournament, Seve Ballesteros shot four-under-par on the first four holes of the final round to take the lead and then win the green jacket. In men's singles of U.S. Open tennis, Jimmy Connors fought back from set-point in the pivotal third set and then poured it on over Ivan Lendl. In the World Series, Baltimore lost Game 1 to Philadelphia and fell behind 1–0 in Game 2; they stormed back with 3 runs the next inning and took the series 4 games to 1. In hockey, the New York Islanders waited until the playoffs to get it all together and then won their fourth straight Stanley Cup.

JEFF HACKER

Auto Racing

The popular Tom Sneva, three times a runner-up, won the Indianapolis 500 on his tenth try and earned $385,886 from a record purse of $2,411,450. Al Unser, Sr., one of American auto racing's all-time greats, captured the Championship Auto Racing Teams (CART) national title. Of the 13 championship races in 1983, however, there were eight different winners, and several new faces appeared in racing headlines during the year. There was also a move from oval to road racing, as 6 of the 13 CART events were held on winding courses.

AUTO RACING
Major Race Winners

Indianapolis 500: Tom Sneva, U.S.
Michigan 500: John Paul, Jr., U.S.
Pocono: Teo Fabi, Italy
Daytona 500: Cale Yarborough, U.S.

1983 Champions

World Championship: Nelson Piquet, Brazil
CART: Al Unser, Sr., U.S.
Can-Am: Jacques Villeneuve, Canada
NASCAR: Bobby Allison, U.S.

Grand Prix for Formula One Cars, 1982

Brazil: Nelson Piquet, Brazil
Long Beach: John Watson, Great Britain
France: Alain Prost, France
San Marino: Patrick Tambay, France
Monaco: Keke Rosberg, Finland
Belgium: Alain Prost
Detroit: Michele Alboreto, Italy
Canada: Rene Arnoux, France
Britain: Alain Prost
Germany: Rene Arnoux
Austria: Alain Prost
Netherlands: Rene Arnoux
Italy: Nelson Piquet
Europe: Nelson Piquet
South Africa: Riccardo Patrese, Italy

Rookie Teo Fabi of Italy made a sensational U.S. debut, smashing the qualifying records at Indianapolis with speeds of 208.049 mph (334.81 km/h) for one lap and 207.395 mph (333.76 km/h) for four. Al Unser, Jr., and Mike Andretti (son of Mario) brought attention to a second generation of drivers. Young Al was consistently competitive throughout the season, finishing seventh in the final point standings. Mike Andretti joined the touring troupe for the final four races.

Nelson Piquet of Brazil slipped past Alain Prost of France to win the World Driving title by two points. Piquet finished third in the South African Grand Prix, the final race of the season, while Prost was forced to drop out with turbocharger problems. It was Piquet's second Formula One championship in three seasons.

Cale Yarborough won the major race of the National Association for Stock Cars (NASCAR) season—the Daytona 500—for the third time. However, the great Bobby Allison took the overall NASCAR title.

BOB COLLINS, *"The Indianapolis Star"*

Baseball

Although the commissioner resigned, several superstars retired, and a rules controversy held up completion of a game for three weeks, the 1983 season was a good one for baseball. A record 45,530,856 fans, one million more than in 1982, attended major-league games, and 17.6 million visited minor-league ballparks. Ten major-league teams drew at least two million fans, while the American Association franchise in Louisville became the first minor-league club to exceed one million. Baseball kept its grip on the fans through exciting pennant races. For the second year in a row, each league had new winners in both divisions.

Play-Offs and World Series. The Chicago White Sox, rebounding from a 16–24 start, won 99 games, the most in the majors, to finish 20 games ahead of the second-place team in the American League (AL) West. The six also-rans in that division became known as the "Sorry Six" for their inability to win more than they lost. Five teams topped .500 in the AL East, but the superior pitching of the Baltimore Orioles returned the divisional title to Maryland for the first time since 1979.

In the American League Championship Series, White Sox sluggers succumbed to the strong-armed Oriole pitchers. Chicago won the opener, 2–1, but then lost, 4–0, 11–1, and 3–0 as the Orioles advanced to the World Series. Rookie right-hander Mike Boddicker, who tied a play-off record with 14 strikeouts in the second game, was named Most Valuable Player (MVP) in the series.

A hitter was the hero in the National League (NL) Championship Series. Gary Matthews hammered three home runs, tying Hank Aaron's 1969 play-off mark, to power the Philadelphia Phillies to victory over the Los Angeles Dodgers (who had beaten the Phils 11 out of 12 times during the regular season). Philadelphia took the opener, 1–0, and then lost, 4–1, before winning the final two games at home by identical 7–2 scores.

The Phillies took momentum into the play-offs; the team had won 11 straight during the September stretch drive to top the Eastern Division by six games over second-place Pittsburgh. Los Angeles won the West, but only after a mid-August ankle fracture sidelined Atlanta slugger Bob Horner, short-circuiting the robust Braves' offense and sending the team from six-and-a-half games ahead of the Dodgers to three games behind.

In the World Series, Philadelphia took an early lead, riding John Denny's pitching to a 2–1 triumph in the opener at Baltimore. Oriole pitching prevailed in the remaining games, however. The Orioles won, 4–1, behind Boddicker's three-hitter in Game 2 and took all three games in Philadelphia's Veterans Stadium, 3–2, 5–4, and 5–0, to win the World Series. Baltimore bullpen ace Tippy Martinez saved wins for Jim Palmer and Storm Davis in the third and fourth games, before Scott McGregor threw a five-hit shutout to clinch the World Championship in Game 5; Eddie Murray homered twice for Baltimore in the finale.

World Series MVP honors went to Baltimore catcher Rick Dempsey, a .231 hitter who turned slugger in the Series. Dempsey's five extra-base hits—a record for a five-game World Series—included four doubles and a home run.

Regular Season. Though Joe Altobelli was the winning manager in the World Series and

Focus on Sports

Baltimore's Cal Ripken, Jr., made his father (the third base coach) proud in 1983. Playing every inning of every game, the smooth-fielding shortstop batted .318 with 27 homers and 102 RBIs. His season was capped by victory in the World Series and selection as the American League's MVP.

Philadelphia's John Denny won 19 games in the regular season, one in the World Series, and the NL Cy Young Award.

Paul Owens (a midseason replacement for Pat Corrales) was his opponent, The Associated Press gave its 1983 Manager of the Year awards to play-off losers Tony LaRussa of the White Sox and Tom Lasorda of the Los Angeles Dodgers. (Altobelli did win a similar award from United Press International.) LaRussa and Lasorda also were honored by the Baseball Writers' Association of America.

Bill Madlock of Pittsburgh hit .323 to win his fourth NL batting title, and Boston's Wade Boggs hit .361 to win his first in the AL. The most impressive batting performance of the season, however, was produced by Dale Murphy of the Atlanta Braves. Murphy hit .302 with 36 home runs, 121 runs batted in, 131 runs scored, 30 stolen bases, a .393 on-base percentage, and a .540 slugging average. He ranked first in RBIs and slugging, second in runs scored and home runs, third (tied) in on-base percentage, fourth (tied) in game-winning hits, and fifth in base hits. He also became the sixth player to join the "30-30 Club" (at least 30 home runs and 30 stolen bases in one season). Murphy was a runaway winner in the voting for MVP in the National League, winning the award for the second straight year. The American League MVP was Baltimore's durable

shortstop Cal Ripken, Jr. In only his second major-league season, Ripken hit .318 with 27 homers and 102 RBIs while playing in every inning of the 162-game schedule.

Milwaukee's Cecil Cooper and Boston's Jim Rice shared the major-league RBI lead with 126, while Rice won AL home run honors with 39. Mike Schmidt of the Phillies led the majors with 40 round-trippers.

Sluggers Ron Kittle and Darryl Strawberry were named rookies of the year in the AL and NL, respectively. Kittle slammed 35 home runs for the White Sox and played in the All-Star Game. Strawberry hit 26 homers, knocked in 74 runs, and stole 19 bases in 122 games after being called up to the New York Mets in May. On June 26, Strawberry's teammate Rusty Staub cracked his eighth consecutive pinch hit, tying the single-season record. Staub tied another record with 25 RBIs as a pinch hitter—an achievement made possible by a record 81 at-bats in a pinch-hitting role. Another veteran star, Steve Garvey, established a National League record for consecutive games played on April 16, when he appeared in his 1,118th straight contest (breaking Billy Williams' mark). The streak ended at 1,207, however, when the San Diego first baseman, in his first full season with the Padres, dislocated his thumb while sliding on July 29.

There were also outstanding pitching performances. LaMarr Hoyt won the American League's Cy Young Award after leading the majors with 24 victories. Teammate Rich Dotson, along with Detroit's Jack Morris and New York's Ron Guidry, also won 20 games in the American League. National League Cy Young Award winner John Denny led his league with 19 wins. Denny's Philadelphia teammate, Steve Carlton, slipped from his usual form to a 15–16 record but won the 300th game of his career on September 23. Carlton also became the career strikeout leader after staging a seesaw battle with Houston's Nolan Ryan. Both men surpassed Walter Johnson's career total of 3,508 during the 1983 campaign; Carlton ended with 3,709. (*See* BIOGRAPHY.)

Yet another Philadelphia pitcher, lefty reliever Al Holland, saved a club-record 25 games to share NL Fireman of the Year honors with Chicago's Lee Smith, but neither could duplicate the effort of AL winner Dan Quisenberry. The sidearming Kansas City right-hander saved a record 45 games. The National League leader in earned run average (ERA) was southpaw Atlee Hammaker (2.25) of the San Francisco Giants. Another lefty, Rick Honeycutt, led the American League with a 2.42 ERA before the Texas Rangers waived him out of the league in a late-summer transaction with the Dodgers.

Dave Righetti of the New York Yankees pitched a July 4 no-hitter against the Boston Red Sox, Bob Forsch pitched his second career

BASEBALL

Professional—Major Leagues
Final Standings, 1983

AMERICAN LEAGUE

Eastern Division	W.	L.	Pct.	Western Division	W.	L.	Pct.
Baltimore	98	64	.605	Chicago	99	63	.611
Detroit	92	70	.568	Kansas City	79	83	.488
New York	91	71	.562	Texas	77	85	.475
Toronto	89	73	.549	Oakland	74	88	.457
Milwaukee	87	75	.537	California	70	92	.432
Boston	78	84	.481	Minnesota	70	92	.432
Cleveland	70	92	.432	Seattle	60	102	.370

NATIONAL LEAGUE

Eastern Division	W.	L.	Pct.	Western Division	W.	L.	Pct.
Philadelphia	90	72	.556	Los Angeles	91	71	.562
Pittsburgh	84	78	.519	Atlanta	88	74	.543
Montreal	82	80	.506	Houston	85	77	.525
St. Louis	79	83	.488	San Diego	81	81	.500
Chicago	71	91	.438	San Francisco	79	83	.488
New York	68	94	.420	Cincinnati	74	88	.457

Play-offs—American League: Baltimore defeated Chicago, 3 games to 1; National League: Philadelphia defeated Los Angeles, 3 games to 1.

World Series—Baltimore defeated Philadelphia, 4 games to 1. First Game (Memorial Stadium, Baltimore, Oct. 11, attendance 52,204): Philadelphia 2, Baltimore 1; Second Game (Memorial Stadium, Oct. 12, attendance 52,132): Baltimore 4, Philadelphia 1; Third Game (Veterans Stadium, Philadelphia, Oct. 14, attendance 65,792): Baltimore 3, Philadelphia 2; Fourth Game (Veterans Stadium, Oct. 15, attendance 66,947): Baltimore 5, Philadelphia 4; Fifth Game (Veterans Stadium, Oct. 16, attendance 67,064): Baltimore 5, Philadelphia 0.

All-Star Game (Comiskey Park, Chicago, July 6, attendance 43,801): American League 13, National League 3.

Most Valuable Players—American League: Cal Ripken, Jr., Baltimore; National League: Dale Murphy, Atlanta.

Cy Young Memorial Awards (outstanding pitchers)—American League: LaMarr Hoyt, Chicago; National League: John Denny, Philadelphia.

Managers of the Year—American League: Tony LaRussa, Chicago (AP) and Joe Altobelli, Baltimore (UPI); National League: Tom Lasorda, Los Angeles (AP and UPI).

Rookies of the Year—American League: Ron Kittle, Chicago; National League: Darryl Strawberry, New York.

Leading Hitters—(Percentage) American League: Wade Boggs, Boston, .361; National League: Bill Madlock, Pittsburgh, .323. (Runs Batted In) American League: Cecil Cooper, Milwaukee, and Jim Rice, Boston (tied), 126; National League: Murphy, 121. (Home Runs) American League: Rice, 39; National League: Mike Schmidt, Philadelphia, 40. (Hits) American League: Ripken, 211; National League: André Dawson, Montreal, and José Cruz, Houston (tied), 189. (Runs) American League: Ripken, 121; National League: Tim Raines, Montreal, 133.

Leading Pitchers—(Earned Run Average) American League: Rick Honeycutt, Texas, 2.42; National League: Atlee Hammaker, San Francisco, 2.25. (Victories) American League: LaMarr Hoyt, 24; National League: Denny, 19. (Strikeouts) American League: Jack Morris, Detroit, 232; National League: Steve Carlton, Philadelphia, 277. (Shutouts) American League: Mike Boddicker, Baltimore, 5; National League: Steve Rogers, Montreal, 5. (Saves) American League: Dan Quisenberry, Kansas City, 45; National League: Lee Smith, Chicago, 29.

Stolen Bases—American League: Rickey Henderson, Oakland, 108; National League: Raines, 90.

Professional—Minor Leagues, Class AAA

American Association: Denver	Pacific Coast League: Portland
International League: Tidewater	Triple-A World Series: Tidewater

Amateur

NCAA: University of Texas
Little League World Series: Marietta, GA

no-hitter against the Montreal Expos on September 26, and Oakland rookie Mike Warren held the White Sox hitless on September 29.

Two days after Righetti's no-hitter, the 50th Anniversary All-Star Game was played at Chi-cago's Comiskey Park, site of the original game. The American League erupted for 13 runs, an All-Star Game record, and got the first grand slam in All-Star history (from California's Fred Lynn) to rout the Nationals, 13–3, ending an 11-year losing streak.

Certainly the most controversial play of the season took place July 24 at Yankee Stadium. With two out in the top of the ninth and his team behind 4–3, Kansas City's George Brett hit a two-run homer, apparently giving the Royals a 5–4 lead. But Yankee manager Billy Martin asked the umpires to examine Brett's bat, and the umpires called Brett out, nullifying the home run. The reason? Pine tar, a sticky substance used for a better grip, extended more than 18 inches from Brett's bat handle, in violation of the rules. League President Lee MacPhail subsequently upheld the Royals' protest, however, and the game was resumed on August 18 with the Royals leading, 5–4, and two outs in the ninth. The game ended quietly, but the controversy continued.

Another controversy surrounded the possible reappointment of Baseball Commissioner Bowie K. Kuhn, who had been ticketed for replacement by a vocal minority of major-league club owners. When no successor could be found, a proposal was drawn up to allow Kuhn to stay on indefinitely while the search continued. On August 3, however, Kuhn announced that he would retire.

Carl Yastrzemski of the Boston Red Sox and Johnny Bench of the Cincinnati Reds retired when the season closed, ending careers that seemed certain to lead to Cooperstown.

On August 1, pitcher Juan Marichal, third basemen Brooks Robinson and George Kell, and manager Walter Alston were enshrined in the Hall of Fame.

Drug Abuse. A sad footnote to the season was the revelation that several well-known players were involved in drug abuse. Dodger relief pitcher Steve Howe, previously treated for chemical dependency, suffered an apparent relapse, was fined $54,000 (one month's pay), and was suspended several times—including during the play-offs. Outfielder Lonnie Smith of the Cardinals underwent voluntary drug rehabilitation during the season but was able to return to action and perform well.

The major scandal, however, did not break until after the season, when two current and one former member of the Kansas City Royals were charged with attempting to purchase cocaine. Outfielder Willie Wilson, the 1982 batting champion, and first baseman Willie Aikens received $5,000 fines and three-month jail terms; former outfielder Jerry Martin was fined $2,500 and also sentenced to three months in prison. Commissioner Kuhn suspended Howe, Wilson, and Aikens for a season.

DAN SCHLOSSBERG
"World of Sport" Magazine

Focus on Sports

Moses Malone, Philadephia's multimillion-dollar MVP center, powered the '76ers to a long-awaited NBA title.

Basketball

Only one thing could have stopped the Philadelphia 76ers during the 1982–83 season, and that problem went by the wayside when National Basketball Association (NBA) players and management beat an April 2 strike deadline to arrive at a new collective bargaining agreement. Once a full season was guaranteed, the powerful 76ers, led by Player of the Year Moses Malone (*see also* BIOGRAPHY), went on to whip the defending champion Los Angeles Lakers in four straight games to clinch the league title. It marked the 14th straight time an NBA champion had failed to defend successfully its crown.

On the college level, North Carolina State completed a Cinderella season by winning its second National Collegiate Athletic Association (NCAA) championship. Southern California claimed the second annual NCAA women's title.

The Professional Season

Although the Philadelphia 76ers had appeared in the NBA play-off finals three times (1977, 1980, and 1982) in six years (1977–82), the home fans were impatient for a championship. The 76ers knew *1982–83* had to be *the* year and, before the season even started, management made a player move that sought to guarantee the title. The Sixers handed out the largest contract in team-sport history—a reported $13.2 million over six years—to free agent Moses Malone, the Houston Rockets' superstar center. The 76ers had to unload the large contracts of some of their veterans—including centers Caldwell Jones and Darryl Dawkins, guard Lionel Hollins, and forward Steve Mix—to afford Malone but, in the end, the personnel strategy paid off handsomely.

The strengths of the 76ers were many. No player dominated the game as Malone did during the regular season. He averaged 24.5 points per game, while collecting his third straight league rebound championship with a 15.3 average. He teamed with all-stars Julius Erving (21.4 average) and Andrew Toney (19.7), playmaker Maurice Cheeks, and defensive wizard Bobby Jones, to produce an NBA-best 65–17 record. Still, many believed that the Sixers would have a battle on their hands in the play-offs and that they would come up short, just as they had in previous seasons. Ultimately, nothing could have been further from the truth.

The Play-offs. The surging New York Knicks, who had survived seven straight losses at the opening of the season and overcame nine new players in coach Hubie Brown's first season, fell first before the Sixers. The Knicks were wiped out in four straight play-off games. Then came Central Division champion Milwaukee, which would be playing without its own heralded newcomer—Dave Cowens, the former Boston star who injured a knee near the end of the regular season. Still, the Bucks had enough firepower behind all-stars Sidney Moncrief and Marques Johnson to blank the perennially powerful Celtics in Eastern Conference semifinal play. Yet they, too, failed to handle the 76ers, who won in five games.

Their opponent for the second straight season was Los Angeles, which had won another Pacific Division crown behind the strength of its neon-light superstars, Magic Johnson and Kareem Abdul-Jabbar. The Lakers had a tough time of it in the Western finals against San Antonio—which had beefed up its front line for 1983 with the acquisition of the former Chicago center, 7'2" (2.18 m) Artis Gilmore. The Lakers, however, still managed to reach the league's championship series for the third time in four years. They were no match, however, for Philadelphia. Admittedly, the Lakers were playing without all their guns—rookie forward James Worthy suffered a broken leg in mid-

PROFESSIONAL BASKETBALL

National Basketball Association
(Final Standings, 1982–83)

Eastern Conference

Atlantic Division	W	L	Pct.
*Philadelphia	65	17	.793
*Boston	56	26	.683
*New Jersey	49	33	.598
*New York	44	38	.537
Washington	42	40	.512
Central Division			
*Milwaukee	51	31	.622
*Atlanta	43	39	.524
Detroit	37	45	.451
Chicago	28	54	.341
Cleveland	23	59	.280
Indiana	20	62	.244

Western Conference

Midwest Division	W	L	Pct.
*San Antonio	53	29	.646
*Denver	45	37	.549
Kansas City	45	37	.549
Dallas	38	44	.463
Utah	30	52	.366
Houston	14	68	.171
Pacific Division			
*Los Angeles	58	24	.707
*Phoenix	53	29	.646
*Seattle	48	34	.585
*Portland	46	36	.561
Golden State	30	52	.366
San Diego	25	57	.305

*Made play-offs

Play-Offs
Eastern Conference

First Round	Boston	2 games	Atlanta	1
	New York	2 games	New Jersey	0
Semifinals	Milwaukee	4 games	Boston	0
	Philadelphia	4 games	New York	0
Finals	Philadelphia	4 games	Milwaukee	1

Western Conference

First Round	Denver	2 games	Phoenix	1
	Portland	2 games	Seattle	0
Semifinals	Los Angeles	4 games	Portland	1
	San Antonio	4 games	Denver	1
Finals	Los Angeles	4 games	San Antonio	2
Championship	Philadelphia	4 games	Los Angeles	0
All-Star Game	East 132, West 123			

Individual Honors

Most Valuable Player: Moses Malone, Philadelphia
Most Valuable Player (play-offs): Moses Malone
Most Valuable Player (all-star game): Julius Erving, Philadelphia
Rookie of the Year: Terry Cummings, San Diego
Coach of the Year: Don Nelson, Milwaukee
Leading Scorer: Alex English, Denver, 28.4 points per game
Leader in Assists: Earvin Johnson, Los Angeles, 10.5 per game
Leading Rebounder: Moses Malone, 15.3 per game

April and guard Norm Nixon and reserve forward Bob McAdoo were hurt during the play-offs—but, as they said later, it would not have mattered. Philadelphia was that good, especially in the second half of each game. They trailed at all four intermissions, yet outscored the Lakers by a total of 54 points in the final two quarters of play to create the awesome sweep of the defending champs. Malone led the way with averages of 25 points and 18 rebounds in head-to-head play against Abdul-Jabbar, while Erving, the legendary "Doctor J," who earned his first NBA championship ring.

While Malone was adding a third Player of the Year award to his collection, Milwaukee's

Don Nelson took home NBA Coach of the Year honors. The Bucks had only two of their players healthy enough to appear in even 80 of their 82 regular season games, but Nelson held them together en route to a fourth straight division championship. San Diego forward Terry Cummings, with a 23.7 scoring average, was Rookie of the Year. On the scoring front, Denver forward Alex English led the way with a 28.4 average, while teammate Kiki Vandeweghe was second with 26.7 per game. It was only the second time in NBA history that teammates had finished 1–2 in the scoring race.

The College Season

The attention of the college basketball world continually came back to the mighty Atlantic Coast Conference. Initially, there was Virginia, which featured reigning Player of the Year Ralph Sampson, the 7'4" (2.23 m) center who would go on to be selected first in the annual NBA draft. In December, the Cavaliers won their Made-for-TV Game of the Decade (68–63 against Georgetown and Patrick Ewing, 7'1", 2.16 m) and then lost the Upset of the Century (77–72 to tiny Chaminade College). Later, there was defending national champion North Carolina vaulting to the top of the national polls. The Tar Heels replaced departed playmaker Jimmy Black with Jim Braddock, and All-American frontcourter James Worthy with freshman Brad Daugherty, and ran off 18 straight midseason victories after stumbling with a 1–2 record. In the end, though, it would be the unlikely upstarts from North Carolina State who would take the NCAA title.

COLLEGE BASKETBALL

Conference Champions*

Atlantic Coast: North Carolina State
Atlantic 10: West Virginia
Big East: St. John's
Big Eight: Oklahoma State
Big Sky: Weber State
Big Ten: Indiana
East Coast: La Salle
Ivy League: Princeton
Metro: Louisville
Mid-American: Ohio University
Midwestern City: Xavier (0)
Missouri Valley: Illinois State
Ohio Valley: Morehead State
Pacific Coast Athletic: Nevada-LasVegas
Pacific 10: UCLA
Southeastern: Georgia
Southern: Tennessee-Chattanooga
Southland: Lamar
Southwest: Houston
Southwestern Athletic: Alcorn State
Sun Belt: Alabama-Birmingham
West Coast Athletic: Pepperdine
Western Athletic: Brigham Young, Texas-El Paso, Utah
*Based on postseason conference tournaments, where applicable.

Tournaments

NCAA: North Carolina State
NIT: Fresno State
NCAA Div. II: Wright State
NCAA Div. III: Scranton
NAIA: College of Charleston
NCAA (women's): Southern California

North Carolina State's Lorenzo Charles slams home a last-second shot to upset Houston, 54-52, in the NCAA finals.

Going into the NCAA's annual postseason tournament, eyes were focused on numerous contenders, including Virginia and North Carolina; Houston, which ended the season ranked Number 1 nationally on the strength of such All-American talent as forward Clyde Drexler and center Akeem Abdul Olajuwon; Missouri who lost the Big Eight tournament to Oklahoma State; Big East titlist St. John's; Big Ten champ Indiana, which had won the NCAA crown two seasons earlier; UCLA, which returned to the Pacific-10 penthouse after an absence of three years; and Louisville, which would use an 80–68 overtime rout of Kentucky —the in-state team which had steadfastly refused to schedule the Cardinals for a regular-season meeting—in the Mideast Regional finals as a springboard to its third NCAA Final Four berth in four years.

For good reason, N.C. State was not considered in this elite group. In fact, at midyear, it was all but given up for dead, when guard Dereck Whittenburg broke his foot and took the heart of the Wolfpack offense with him. At that point, coach Jim Valvano gave up hopes of an NCAA tourney bid for his team. Whittenburg, one of three senior starters on the team, bounced back faster than doctors predicted, however. He was available for the stretch drive, and N.C. State gained momentum quickly, surprising Virginia in the ACC tournament finals, 81–78. Still NCAA selection officials were unimpressed, and banished State all the way to the West Regional, where it was given only a Number 6 seed.

NCAA Tournament. Pepperdine was quickly dispatched by the Wolfpack. Then State dropped highly regarded UN Las Vegas, Utah, and Virginia in a rematch, making it to Albuquerque and the Final Four, which was rounded out by Georgia, Louisville, and Houston.

After Georgia tumbled in the national semifinals, 67–60, it was simply a matter of another game, another upset for the Pack. Thanks to Lorenzo Charles' stunning dunk shot at the buzzer, N.C. State nipped Houston, 54–52, completing one of the most surprising championship drives in college basketball history. Despite the loss, Houston's Olajuwon earned the tournament's outstanding-player vote following his 20-point, 18-rebound, 7-blocks performance in the championship game. Earlier, he had scored 21 points, with 22 rebounds, in a 94–81 semifinal rout of Louisville.

Other Postseason Play. Cheryl Miller's 27 points led Southern Cal past defending champ Louisiana Tech, 69–67, for the NCAA women's crown. Bernard Thompson scored 22 points as Fresno State topped DePaul, 69–60, in the NIT finals.

MARK ENGEL, *"Basketball Weekly"*

Boxing

Boxing in 1983 came under the scrutiny of the U.S. Congress, which was seeking ways to standardize safety. In the ring, one version of the world heavyweight championship changed hands, while the other remained monotonously secure. The lighter weight divisions were dominated by a handful of fighters.

Heavyweights. The World Boxing Association (WBA) version of the heavyweight title changed hands on September 23 at Richfield, OH, where Gerrie Coetzee of South Africa, a 5–1 underdog, knocked out previously unbeaten Michael Dokes at 2:58 of the 10th round. The 28-year-old Coetzee became the first South African to win any version of the heavyweight crown. Dokes had taken the title on Dec. 10, 1982, when he stopped Mike Weaver in 63 seconds of the first round. In a rematch May 20, the 24-year-old Dokes retained the title but had to struggle through 15 rounds before gaining a draw.

In the other version of the title, sanctioned by the World Boxing Council (WBC), Larry Holmes defended four times, three officially, during the year against nondescript opponents. In March he won a unanimous 12-round decision over Lucien Rodriquez in Scranton, PA. On May 20 in Las Vegas, headlining the card that also offered the Dokes-Weaver rematch, Holmes fought 25-year-old Tim Witherspoon, an 11–2 underdog. Witherspoon embarrassed the champion before losing a 12-round split decision. On September 10 in Atlantic City, Holmes stopped Scott Frank in the fifth round. The champ's last fight of the year came on November 25 against Marvis Frazier, son of former heavyweight champion Joe Frazier. Although the WBC had withdrawn title recog-

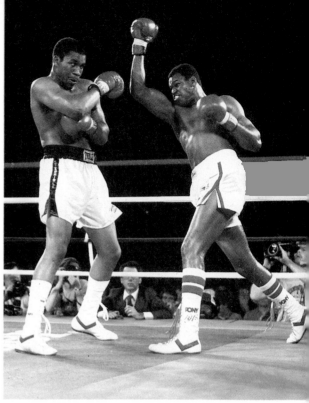

Focus on Sports

Larry Holmes (right) defended his WBC heavyweight title four times, including a split decision over Tim Witherspoon.

nition from the bout, Holmes knocked out Frazier in the first round. Later Holmes gave up the crown to promote his own fights.

Other Divisions. Aaron Pryor, Marvelous Marvin Hagler, and Roberto Duran were the headliners in the lighter weight classes. Pryor distinguished himself by retaining his WBA junior welterweight title in a return bout with Alexis Arguello in September. Their 1982 bout would have been hard to repeat for excitement. Indeed, the return bout fell short, but the outcome was the same: Pryor again stopped Arguello, in the 10th round. Shortly afterward, Pryor announced that he would retire.

Hagler continued to display awesome power. He knocked out Tony Sibson and Wilford Scypion early in the year, then went into training to defend his middleweight title against Duran on November 10. Duran had made a tremendous comeback by knocking out Davey Moore for the WBA junior middleweight crown in June. Duran fought well against Hagler but lost a unanimous decision.

The light-heavyweight title was unified in March, when Michael Spinks, the WBA champion, won a 15-round decision over Dwight Braxton, the WBC titleholder. Milton McCrory won the WBC title that had been vacated by the retirement of Sugar Ray Leonard with a split decision over Colin Jones in August.

GEORGE DE GREGORIO
"The New York Times"

BOXING

World Champions*

Junior Flyweight—Lupe Madera, Mexico (1983), World Boxing Association (WBA); Chang Chong Ku, South Korea (1983), World Boxing Council (WBC).

Flyweight—Santos Laciar, Argentina (1982), WBA; Frank Cedeño, Philippines (1983), WBC.

Junior Bantamweight—Jiro Watanabe, Japan (1982), WBA; Rafael Orono, Venezuela (1982), WBC.

Bantamweight—Jeff Chandler, Philadelphia (1980), WBA; Alberto Davila, Pomona, CA (1983), WBC.

Junior Featherweight—Leo Cruz, Dominican Republic (1982), WBA; Jaime Garza, Los Angeles (1983), WBC.

Featherweight—Eusebio Pedroza, Panama (1978), WBA; Juan LaPorte, Puerto Rico (1982), WBC.

Junior Lightweight—Ray Mayweather, Las Vegas (1983), WBA; Hector Camacho, Puerto Rico (1983), WBC.

Lightweight—Ray Mancini, Youngstown, OH (1982), WBA; Edwin Rosario, Puerto Rico (1983), WBC.

Junior Welterweight—Aaron Pryor, Cincinnati (1980), WBA; Bruce Curry, Fort Worth, TX (1983), WBC.

Welterweight—Donald Curry, Fort Worth, TX (1983), WBA; Milton McCrory, Detroit (1983), WBC.

Junior Middleweight—Roberto Duran, Panama (1983), WBA; Thomas Hearns, Detroit (1982), WBC.

Middleweight—Marvelous Marvin Hagler, Brockton, MA (1980).

Light-Heavyweight—Michael Spinks, St. Louis (1981).

Cruiserweight—Ossie Ocasio, Puerto Rico (1982), WBA; Carlos De Leon, Puerto Rico (1983), WBC.

Heavyweight—Gerrie Coetzee, South Africa (1983), WBA.

*Year of achieving title in parentheses

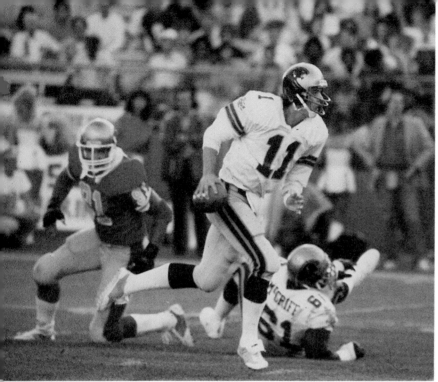

At Denver's Mile High Stadium, Bob Hebert (11) leads the Michigan Panthers to victory over the Philadelphia Stars in the first USFL championship game. The Panthers' quarterback completed 20 of 39 passes and was named the game's most valuable player.

Focus on Sports

Football

On Sunday, Jan. 22, 1984, the favored Washington Redskins missed the opportunity of becoming only the fourth team to win two consecutive Super Bowls. Before 72,920 fans at Tampa Stadium, the Redskins were completely outclassed by the Los Angeles Raiders, 38–9. The score was the widest margin of victory in Super Bowl history, and the Raiders' 38 points was the most ever scored by a Super Bowl team.

The Raiders dominated from the start as tight end Derrick Jensen recovered a blocked punt in the end zone for the game's first points. Just before halftime, the Raiders' Jack Squirek picked off a Joe Theismann screen pass deep in Redskins territory and took it in for a 21–3 lead. Marcus Allen of the Raiders scored two second-half touchdowns, including the longest TD run in Super Bowl history; established a Super Bowl rushing record of 191 yards; and was named the game's most valuable player. The Raiders' defense was outstanding, limiting Washington's star fullback John Riggins to 64 yards.

The 1983 football year also saw the birth of the United States Football League (USFL) and the pro debut of the league's prime attraction, Heisman Trophy winner Herschel Walker. The new USFL did more to raise the National Football League (NFL) players' salaries than the 57-day strike in 1982. This was especially true for the first-round draft choices, for whom million-dollar packages were almost commonplace. The top draft picks were estimated, on the average, to receive about two thirds more in bonuses and pay than their 1982 counter-

parts. Salaries also jumped for the veterans, and a number were able to renegotiate their current contracts. Rookie and veteran players were able to hold the threat of going to the USFL over the heads of the NFL owners. The bidding war for talent between the two leagues promised to become even more hectic. (*See* page 473.)

The Toronto Argonauts captured the 1983 Grey Cup by shading the British Columbia Lions, 18–17. The 71st title game of the Canadian Football League was played indoors at Vancouver's domed British Columbia Place Stadium and saw the end of the five-year reign of the Edmonton Eskimos as champions.

On the college level the Nebraska Cornhuskers failed to cap a perfect season, losing to Miami of Florida in the Orange Bowl and in the final polls.

The National Football League

During the NFL season, the Redskins dominated the league offensively, scoring 541 points, a record for a 16-game schedule. They lost only to the Dallas Cowboys, 31–30, in the opener and to the Packers, 48–47, en route to the NFL best mark of 14–2. The point-making elements were familiar: Joe Theismann on the pass and John Riggins on the run. Behind the huge but quick line nicknamed the Hogs, Riggins usually carried out of coach Joe Gibb's one-back formation. The durable 12-year pro bulled his way for 1,347 yards and 24 touchdowns to surpass the mark of 23 set by O. J. Simpson with the Buffalo Bills in 1973.

Theismann, well protected by the Hogs, was sacked only 35 times as he passed for 3,714

SPORTS / SPECIAL REPORT

The New USFL

Before the 12-team United States Football League (USFL)—which played its first 18-week season March 6–July 3, 1983—was formed officially, prospective team owners employed a top marketing research firm to determine if there was sufficient fan interest in spring-summer pro football. The surveys not only showed that such interest existed but also that spring-summer pro football could compete against baseball and other warm-weather sports on the television screen. As a result, the new league's owners quickly obtained a two-year, $22-million contract with ABC-TV that gave the league necessary financial support and national exposure. Not so coincidentally, Chester R. (Chet) Simmons, a longtime TV executive, was selected as the USFL's first commissioner.

The owners also lined up large, adequate stadiums for all but one franchise. (The home of the Boston Breakers, Boston University's Nickerson Field, seats only 20,535.) They also corraled several prominent coaches, including George Allen (Chicago Blitz), Robert (Red) Miller (Denver Gold), John Ralston (Oakland Invaders), and Chuck Fairbanks (New Jersey Generals). But the biggest coup was the signing of Herschel Walker by the Generals.

In three seasons at the University of Georgia, Walker had run for 5,259 yards, a total bettered in collegiate history only by Tony Dorsett of Pittsburgh and Charley White of USC in four years. From his freshman year on, Walker, the powerful halfback with sprinter-speed, was an all-American. In his junior year, he was awarded the Heisman Trophy. The USFL, like the National Football League (NFL), had adopted a rule prohibiting the drafting and signing of a player until his college class graduates. However, the opportunity to get Walker proved too irresistible; without a blush the USFL ignored its rule because of "special circumstances." The celebrated collegian was rewarded with the most lucrative contract to that time: $4 million over three years.

The opening games drew 235,023, an impressive average of 39,171, and the TV ratings were high. Then the bubble burst. The Generals had provided their star with an inept supporting cast. Unfamiliar with pro systems and short on practice time, Walker gained only 65 yards as New Jersey lost its first game to the Los Angeles Express, 20–15. Equally unimpressive were the other games. Too many were low-scoring affairs, and offenses were dull and unimaginative. The owners had erred in on-the-field preparations. Training camps were only five weeks long, and no exhibition games were played. Of the 600 players in the USFL, more than 80% were rookies or one-year pros.

That the caliber of play was below NFL standards could be forgiven; the boring games could not. Attendance and TV ratings fell sharply the next week, but both gradually improved as the season progressed and the teams performed better.

In the fifth game, Walker achieved his first 100-yard-plus effort, and duplicated that for the next four contests. While the Generals stumbled to a 6–12 record, he finished with a league-high rushing total of 1,812 yards. But the Number 1 General, surehanded at Georgia, also had fumbled away the ball eight, often costly, times. Walker was paying the price of back-to-back seasons. The 20-year-old had played through a 12-game Georgia campaign just before embarking on an 18-game stint as a professional.

The Philadelphia Stars, thanks to the running of Kelvin Bryant, a rookie back from North Carolina, quickly became the top team in the regular season. Bryant and quarterback Chuck Fusina, the former Penn Stater who spent three years on the Tampa Bay Buccaneer bench, led the Stars to the league's best record —15–3—while winning the Atlantic Division. Bryant rushed for 1,442 yards, second to Walker, but his spectacular efforts gave him the league's MVP honors. The Michigan Panthers, after a horrendous 1–4 start, solidified their offensive line and took the Central Division at 12–6 behind the league's top-rated passer, Bob Hebert.

In the play-offs the Stars beat the Blitz in overtime, 44–38, and the Panthers routed the Invaders, 37–21. For the first title game, before 50,905 fans at Denver's Mile High Stadium, the Panthers edged the Stars, 24–22. Anthony Carter, the fleet all-American at Michigan, caught the winning 48-yard touchdown pass.

Outlook. Only Denver and the Tampa Bay Bandits were believed to have ended the season in the black, and New Jersey may have broken even. The others lost between $1 million and $3 million.

The USFL averaged nearly 25,000 fans per game. More importantly, Simmons said TV ratings were slightly higher than expected. ABC reportedly made a profit and will be able to raise its rates for commercials in 1984. Another positive sign is that six new franchises have been awarded at $6 million each, and the league will reach more TV markets with the expansion clubs.

LUD DUROSKA

UPI

Mark Moseley kicks a last-minute field goal to give the Red-skins a 24–21 win over the 49ers and a trip to Super Bowl.

yards and 29 TDs. The former Notre Damer was intercepted a mere seven times.

In the play-offs, the Redskins overwhelmed the Los Angeles Rams, 51–7, but then had a battle subduing the San Francisco 49ers, 24–21, for the National Conference (NFC) crown. Mark Moseley, whose reliable foot so often had made the difference in 1982, kicked the deciding 25-yard field goal after missing four earlier attempts. Washington seemed to have matters well in hand with a 21–0 lead through three quarters, but the 49ers exploded for three TDs on Joe Montana's passes in the first eight minutes of the final period to make it a new ball game at 21–21. Washington's march for the clincher was aided immeasurably by two controversial pass-interference calls against the 49ers.

The noteworthy feature of the Los Angeles Raiders' fourth trip to the Super Bowl was the changing of quarterbacks twice during the season. Jim Plunkett, the most valuable player in the Raiders' Super Bowl win in January 1981, was benched by Coach Tom Flores after the seventh game in favor of Marc Wilson. But three weeks later Wilson was injured against the Kansas City Chiefs. Plunkett directed two late-scoring drives for a 28–20 triumph and then led Los Angeles to the Western Division title with a career-high completion percentage of 60.7.

Interestingly, when the Redskins and Raiders met early in the season, Plunkett exploited the Washington secondary for 372 yards in a losing 37–35 effort.

To reach the Super Bowl, the Raiders had to get by the upstart Seattle Seahawks in the American Conference (AFC) finale. They had lost twice to Seattle, 38–36 and 34–21, as a two-game total of 13 turnovers proved to be their undoing. But Los Angeles turned the tables in the title match by intercepting five passes in fashioning a 30–14 victory. The Raiders received top performances from Plunkett and Marcus Allen, who rushed for 154 yards.

In contrast to the ease with which the Redskins became an NFC finalist, the 49ers barely managed to edge the Detroit Lions, 24–23. Eddie Murray of the Lions failed on a field-goal try with 5 seconds left. Montana had taken San Francisco on a 70-yard drive in the closing minutes, tossing to Freddie Solomon in the end zone for the winning TD. The 49ers, with the conference's second-best defense (293 points), intercepted five passes by Gary Danielson, the Detroit quarterback making his first start of the season in place of the injured Eric Hipple.

The Cowboys, the perennial play-off qualifier, kept even with the Redskins at 12–2 until their key rematch in the 15th game. Then they slumped. Dallas was trounced, 31–10, by Washington and then by the 49ers, 42–17. The Rams dispatched the Cowboys in the wild-card game, 24–17. It was, however, the Cowboys' 17th play-off appearance in 18 years.

The Seahawks, who qualified for the play-offs for the first time in their eight seasons, had advanced to the AFC finals by defeating the Miami Dolphins, 27–20. Curt Warner, Seattle's rookie from Penn State, rushed for 113 yards and two touchdowns. He had already topped AFC backs for the season with 1,449 yards, only the second rookie to win the AFC rushing title. Earl Campbell of the Houston Oilers was the first in 1978.

Regular Season. The Dolphins also boasted an oustanding first-year star in Dan Marino. Taking over for David Woodley in the fifth game, Marino paced Miami to a 12–4 record and Eastern Division honors. He threw for 2,210 yards and 20 touchdowns. Coach Don Shula's latest protégé also earned the distinction of becoming the first rookie quarterback to gain the passing efficiency title in either conference.

Another rookie standout was Eric Dickerson, the slashing back for the Rams. He finished with 1,808 yards, tops in the league. He also broke the rookie rushing mark of 1,674

PROFESSIONAL FOOTBALL

National Football League

Final Standings

NATIONAL CONFERENCE

Eastern Division

	W	L	T	Pct.	Points For	Against
Washington	14	2	0	.875	541	332
Dallas	12	4	0	.750	479	360
St. Louis	8	7	1	.531	374	428
Philadelphia	5	11	0	.313	233	322
N.Y. Giants	3	12	1	.219	267	347

Central Division

	W	L	T	Pct.	For	Against
Detroit	9	7	0	.563	347	286
Chicago	8	8	0	.500	311	301
Green Bay	8	8	0	.500	429	439
Minnesota	8	8	0	.500	316	348
Tampa Bay	2	14	0	.125	241	380

Western Division

	W	L	T	Pct.	For	Against
San Francisco	10	6	0	.625	432	293
L.A. Rams	9	7	0	.563	361	344
New Orleans	8	8	0	.500	319	337
Atlanta	7	9	0	.438	370	389

PLAY-OFFS

L.A. Rams 24, Dallas 17
San Francisco 24, Detroit 23
Washington 51, L.A. Rams 7
Washington 24, San Francisco 21

AMERICAN CONFERENCE

Eastern Division

	W	L	T	Pct.	Points For	Against
Miami	12	4	0	.750	389	250
Buffalo	8	8	0	.500	283	351
New England	8	8	0	.500	274	289
N.Y. Jets	7	9	0	.438	313	331
Baltimore	7	9	0	.438	264	354

Central Division

	W	L	T	Pct.	For	Against
Pittsburgh	10	6	0	.625	355	303
Cleveland	9	7	0	.563	356	342
Cincinnati	7	9	0	.438	346	302
Houston	2	14	0	.125	288	460

Western Division

	W	L	T	Pct.	For	Against
L.A. Raiders	12	4	0	.750	442	338
Seattle	9	7	0	.563	403	397
Denver	9	7	0	.563	302	327
Kansas City	6	10	0	.375	386	367
San Diego	6	10	0	.375	358	462

PLAY-OFFS

Seattle 31, Denver 7
Seattle 27, Miami 20
L.A. Raiders 38, Pittsburgh 10
L.A. Raiders 30, Seattle 14

SUPER BOWL XVIII: L.A. Raiders 38, Washington 9

United States Football League

Final Standings

Atlantic Division

	W	L	T	Pct.	Points For	Against
Philadelphia	15	3	0	.833	379	204
Boston	11	7	0	.611	399	334
New Jersey	6	12	0	.333	314	437
Washington	4	14	0	.222	297	442

Central Division

	W	L	T	Pct.	For	Against
Michigan	12	6	0	.667	451	337
Chicago	12	6	0	.667	456	271
Tampa Bay	11	7	0	.611	363	378
Birmingham	9	9	0	.500	343	346

Pacific Division

	W	L	T	Pct.	For	Against
Oakland	9	9	0	.500	319	317
Los Angeles	8	10	0	.444	296	370
Denver	7	11	0	.389	284	304
Arizona	4	14	0	.222	261	442

PLAY-OFFS

Philadelphia 44, Chicago 38
Michigan 37, Oakland 21

CHAMPIONSHIP GAME: Michigan 24, Philadelphia 22

yards established by George Rogers of the New Orleans Saints two years ago.

The highly touted John Elway, who signed the sport's most lucrative contract ($5 million for five years) with the Denver Broncos, had a sensational preseason debut but faltered early on, troubled by Coach Dan Reeves' complex offensive formations. The former Stanford quarterback, after posting a 2–3 mark, went to the bench. After Steve DeBerg was hurt, Elway returned and helped pilot the Broncos to a 9–7 record and a wild-card play-off berth.

Besides the Seahawks, the New Orleans Saints had a surprising season, attaining the .500 level for only the second time since their formation in 1967. The turnaround began in 1981 with the arrival of O. A. (Bum) Phillips, the former Oilers' coach. The Saints had gone through seven coaches and were 1–15 the year before. The team obtained the crafty veteran quarterback Ken Stabler, from Houston, and also strengthened the defense. Among Phillips' key acquisitions was Dennis Winston, the Steelers' linebacker.

With ailing Terry Bradshaw playing only 15 minutes of the season, the Pittsburgh Steelers nose-dived after a 9–2 start, losing 5 of their last 6 games, with Cliff Stoudt at quarterback. The Raiders eliminated the Steelers in the play-offs, 38–10.

The New York Jets, who announced that they would move to the New Jersey Meadowlands in 1984, were beset by offensive problems and were not the factor that many had expected in the preseason ratings. Freeman McNeil, the Jets all-pro back, was lost through injury to Joe Walton, the new head coach, for much of the season.

The second Bart Starr era ended in Green Bay when he was dismissed as head coach after nine frustrating seasons. He was unable to carry over the magic of the Packers' glory years when he quarterbacked to NFL and Super Bowl crowns in the 1960s. Starr's replacement was Forrest Gregg, another hero of the Coach Vince Lombardi teams. Gregg had relinquished his post with the Cincinnati Bengals.

Reflecting the league's growing concern with the illegal-drug problem, commissioner Pete Rozelle, in his most severe action, suspended Tony Peters, the Redskins' defensive back, for two years after his arrest for attempting to sell cocaine. Four other players were suspended without pay for the preseason and the first four games of the season for drug involvement. Players were put on notice to report for treatment for any usage of an illegal drug.

Rozelle also suspended Art Schlichter, the Baltimore Colt quarterback, indefinitely for betting on NFL games in 1982. Schlichter admitted his compulsive gambling had cost him $389,000.

The College Season

Nebraska's Cornhuskers started the season like a runaway prairie fire. In their August 29 opener, the first Kickoff Classic at Giants Stadium, New Jersey, they routed Penn State, the reigning national champion, 44–6. Then it was Wyoming by 56–20, Minnesota by 84–13, UCLA by 42–10, and Syracuse by 63–7. The composite score for Nebraska's first five games was 289 to 56.

A talented trio paced Coach Tom Osborne's high-powered offense: Mike Rozier, who went on to win the Heisman Trophy, at tailback; Turner Gill at quarterback; and Irv Fryar at wingback. The key blocker was Dean Steinkuhler, a 270-lb (122-kg) guard who was on his way to capturing the Outland and the Lombardi trophies as the outstanding interior lineman in the nation.

Unlike most recent years, in which the Number 1 rung in the weekly ratings often proved slippery, the Cornhuskers were season-long occupants as they racked up 12 consecutive victories. Only two games were close: Oklahoma State (14–10) and Oklahoma (28–24), in which Nebraska needed a late goal-line stand to prevail. Averaging 52 points per contest, the Cornhuskers were the first college team to score more than 600 points (624) in one season. Only the 1944 Army squad with Glenn Davis and Doc Blanchard—playing against wartime competition—set a better pace with a 56-point average.

And so unbeaten Nebraska headed for the 50th Orange Bowl with its third straight Big Eight crown, and as a heavy favorite to defeat Miami of Florida and clinch the national championship. Miami and its own highly successful coach, Howard Schnellenberger, however, had other ideas. The Hurricanes had suffered through eight losing seasons in ten years before Schnellenberger came to the rescue in 1979; in a five-year span, the calm, pipe-smoking former Miami Dolphins assistant compiled a 40–16 record, and his teams had won 24 of 26 contests on their home gridiron, the Orange Bowl. Indeed, Miami also went into the game against Nebraska on a winning streak. After an opening 28–3 loss to Florida at Gainesville, the Hurricanes reeled off ten triumphs in a row. They were led by Bernie Kosar, a freshman quarterback, and Ken Sisk and Jay Brophy, linebackers in a defense that was fourth best in the country.

The game proved to be most memorable. The Hurricanes shocked Nebraska in the first period, buildling a 17–0 lead, as Kosar passed for two touchdowns. Nebraska rallied to tie at 17–17. Two third-quarter touchdowns put Miami ahead, 31–17, but the Cornhuskers stormed back. They closed to within 31–30 on a 24-yard run by Jeff Smith, who had replaced the injured Rozier, in the final 48 seconds. Then came the fateful decision for Osborne: should Nebraska go for the tie or try to win with a two-point conversion? A tie probably would have saved the national championship for the unbeaten Cornhuskers, but Osborne wanted to win. The gamble failed, as Gill's pass was tipped away. Miami had a 31–30 upset.

Nebraska's loss ended the longest winning streak in the nation (22 games) and cost it the

Mike Rozier (30) leads Nebraska to victory over Oklahoma. Only an Orange Bowl defeat spoiled the Cornhuskers' season.

title. Miami was voted the champion in both major polls; Nebraska placed second.

In another surprising outcome, Texas, which had gone into the Cotton Bowl with an unblemished (11–0) record and a Number 2 ranking, was foiled by Georgia, 10–9. Texas had boasted the top defense in the nation and had yielded an average of only 9.5 points per game. In the final moments of the Cotton Bowl, however, the Longhorns fumbled away a punt, and Bulldog quarterback John Lastinger ran 17 yards for the winning touchdown. Georgia finished the season with a 10–1–1 mark despite the absence of 1982 Heisman winner Herschel Walker.

In a defensive struggle, Auburn edged Michigan, 9–7, in the Sugar Bowl on Al Del Greco's third field goal with only 23 seconds remaining. With an 11–1 record, Coach Pat Dyke felt the Tigers deserved the national title because they had played the most rugged schedule, but the selectors gave Auburn third place.

In its first trip to the Rose Bowl in 20 years Illinois (10–1) was trounced by UCLA, 45–9. A Big Ten team has not triumphed in Pasadena since Ohio State in 1974. UCLA (6–4–1), which had lost decisively to Nebraska and Georgia, became the Pacific Ten representative only after Washington had been upset by Washington State, 17–6, in the season finale.

Rozier ran away with the Heisman voting by rushing for 2,148 yards and tying an NCAA record with 29 touchdowns. He became the 49th winner of the prestigious award, receiving 1,801 points to 1,172 for Steve Young, Brigham Young's sterling passer. It was the 12th straight year that a running back had won, a streak started by another Nebraska star, Johnny Rogers, in 1972. Rozier's teammates, Gill and Fryar, were also among the leading vote-getters, Gill placing fourth. Young, ironically, in his last big play for BYU, was on the receiving end of a pass in the closing seconds of the Holiday Bowl, to down Missouri, 21–17.

Despite the nation's Number 2-rated defense and a 10–1 mark, Southern Methodist was ignored by the major bowl committees and went to the Sun Bowl, only to be upset by Alabama, 28–7. The defeat was only the third in 35 games for the Mustangs. The win over SMU capped an 8–4 season for Ray Perkins, the former New York Giants' coach, in his first year at the helm in Alabama. Perkins had taken over for the legendary Paul (Bear) Bryant, who retired with a record 323 victories in a 38-year career. Bryant died of a heart attack a month later.

Notre Dame again had a disappointing season, its third under Coach Gerry Faust. A 19–18 squeaker over Boston College in the Liberty Bowl gave Notre Dame a 7–5 mark and put Faust's three-year record at 18–15–1; the vocal Irish alumni were up in arms.

COLLEGE FOOTBALL

Conference Champions	Atlantic Coast—Maryland
	Big Eight—Nebraska
	Big Ten—Illinois
	Pacific Coast—Fullerton State
	Pacific Ten—UCLA
	Southeastern—Auburn
	Southwest—Texas
	Western Athletic—Brigham Young
NCAA Champions	Division I–AA—Southern Illinois
	Divison II—North Dakota State
	Division III—Augustana
NAIA Champions	Divison I—Carson-Newman
	Division II—Northwestern (IA)
Individual Honors	Heisman Trophy—Mike Rozier, Nebraska
	Lombardi Trophy—Dean Steinkuhler, Nebraska
	Outland Trophy—Dean Steinkuhler

Major Bowl Games

Independence Bowl (Shreveport, LA, Dec. 10)—Air Force 9, Mississippi 3
California Bowl (Fresno, CA, Dec. 17)—Northern Illinois 20, Fullerton State 13
Florida Citrus Bowl (Orlando, FL, Dec. 17)—Tennessee 30, Maryland 23
Hall of Fame Bowl (Birmingham, AL, Dec. 22)—West Virginia 20, Kentucky 16
Holiday Bowl (San Diego, CA, Dec. 23)—Brigham Young 21, Missouri 17
Sun Bowl (El Paso, TX, Dec. 24)—Alabama 28, Southern Methodist 7
Aloha Bowl (Honolulu, HI, Dec. 26)—Penn State 13, Washington 10
Liberty Bowl (Memphis, TN, Dec. 29)—Notre Dame 19, Boston College 18
Peach Bowl (Atlanta, GA, Dec. 30)—Florida State 28, North Carolina 3
Gator Bowl (Jacksonville, FL, Dec. 30)—Florida 14, Iowa 6
Bluebonnet Bowl (Houston, TX, Dec. 31)—Oklahoma State 24, Baylor 14
Fiesta Bowl (Tempe, AZ, Jan. 2)—Ohio State 28, Pittsburgh 23
Cotton Bowl (Dallas, TX, Jan. 2)—Georgia 10, Texas 9
Rose Bowl (Pasadena, CA, Jan. 2)—UCLA 45, Illinois 9
Sugar Bowl (New Orleans, LA, Jan. 2)—Auburn 9, Michigan 7
Orange Bowl (Miami, FL, Jan. 2)—Miami 31, Nebraska 30

Final College Rankings

	AP Writers	UPI Coaches
1	Miami	Miami
2	Nebraska	Nebraska
3	Auburn	Auburn
4	Georgia	Georgia
5	Texas	Texas
6	Florida	Florida
7	Brigham Young	Brigham Young
8	Michigan	Ohio State
9	Ohio State	Michigan
10	Illinois	Illinois

In the most puzzling incident of the season, Marcus Dupree, Oklahoma's star sophomore tailback—considered to be the next Herschel Walker—suddenly quit the team and the university after the fifth game. As a freshman, Dupree had set a Sooner record by rushing for 905 yards. Friction between the talented sophomore and Coach Barry Switzer was thought to be the primary reason for his leaving; Switzer felt Dupree was not in condition. Dupree also wanted to be closer to his home in Philadelphia, MS, and he subsequently enrolled at Southern Mississippi. He becomes eligible to play again on Oct. 20, 1984.

Just as it won the first one in 1875, Harvard defeated Yale in their 100th meeting, 16–7, enabling the Crimson to share the Ivy League title with Penn.

LUD DUROSKA, *"The New York Times"*

Focus on Sports

Severiano Ballesteros of Spain shot an eight-under-par 280 to win his second Masters tournament by four strokes.

Golf

Two players at opposite ends of the age spectrum survived dogfights to win honors on the U.S. professional golf tours in 1983, but one veteran stood alone among the amateurs.

Hal Sutton, a 25-year-old in his second year on the Professional Golf Association (PGA) tour, won the Tournament Players Championship and the PGA title, finished as the leading money-winner with $426,668, and was named Player of the Year by the PGA and Golf Writers Association of America (GWAA).

JoAnne Carner, 44 and in her 14th year on the Ladies PGA Tour, won two tournaments, led in money for the second straight year with $291,404, was awarded the Vare Trophy for low stroke average for the third year in a row, and repeated as GWAA Player of the Year.

Meanwhile, Jay Sigel, a 39-year-old Philadelphia insurance executive, easily earned the No. 1 amateur ranking by winning the U.S. Amateur for the second straight year and the Mid-Amateur; he was the first man since Bobby Jones to win two United States Golf Association titles in the same year.

Nobody won more than twice on the PGA tour, and only eight players did that. One of them was Fuzzy Zoeller, who was second on the money list with $417,597. Zoeller was almost $100,000 ahead of third-place Lanny Wadkins, who beat out Gil Morgan for *Golf Digest*'s Byron Nelson Award for most tour-

PGA 1983 Tournament Winners

Joe Garagiola-Tucson Open: Gil Morgan (271)
Glen Campbell Los Angeles Open: Gil Morgan (270)
Bob Hope Desert Classic: Keith Fergus (335)
Phoenix Open: Bob Gilder (271)
Bing Crosby National Pro-Am: Tom Kite (276)
Hawaiian Open: Isao Aoki (268)
Isuzu-Andy Williams San Diego Open: Gary Hallberg (271)
Doral-Eastern Open: Gary Koch (271)
Honda Inverrary Classic: Johnny Miller (278)
Bay Hill Classic: Mike Nicolette (283)
USF&G Classic: Bill Rogers (274)
Tournament Players Championship: Hal Sutton (283)
Greater Greensboro Open: Lanny Wadkins (275)
Masters: Seve Ballesteros (280)
Sea Pines Heritage Classic: Fuzzy Zoeller (275)
Mony Tournament of Champions: Lanny Wadkins (280)
Byron Nelson Golf Classic: Ben Crenshaw (273)
Houston Open: David Graham (275)
Colonial National Invitation: Jim Colbert (278)
Georgia-Pacific Atlanta Golf Classic: Calvin Peete (206)
Memorial Tournament: Hale Irwin (281)
Kemper Open: Fred Couples (287)
Manufacturers Hanover Westchester Classic: Seve Ballesteros (276)
U.S. Open: Larry Nelson (280)
Danny Thomas Memphis Classic: Larry Mize (274)
Western Open: Mark McCumber (284)
Greater Milwaukee Open: Morris Hatalsky (275)
Quad Cities Open: Danny Edwards (266)
Anheuser-Busch Golf Classic: Calvin Peete (276)
Canadian Open: John Cook (277)
PGA Championship: Hal Sutton (274)
Buick Open: Wayne Levi (272)
Sammy Davis, Jr.-Greater Hartford Open: Curtis Strange (268)
World Series of Golf: Nick Price (270)
B.C. Open: Pat Lindsey (268)
Bank of Boston Classic: Mark Lye (273)
Las Vegas Pro-Celebrity Classic: Fuzzy Zoeller (340)
LaJet Coors Classic: Rex Caldwell (282)
Texas Open: Jim Colbert (261)
Southern Open: Ronnie Black (271)
Walt Disney World Golf Classic: Payne Stewart (269)
Pensacola Open: Mark McCumber (266)

LPGA 1983 Tournament Winners

Mazda Classic of Deer Creek: Pat Bradley (272)
Elizabeth Arden Classic: Nancy Lopez (285)
Sarasota Classic: Donna H. White (284)
Tucson Conquistadores LPGA Open: Jan Stephenson (207)
Samaritan Turquoise Classic: Anne-Marie Palli (205)
Women's Kemper Open: Kathy Whitworth (288)
Nabisco Dinah Shore Invitational: Amy Alcott (282)
J&B Scotch Pro-Am: Nancy Lopez (283)
Combanks Orlando Classic: Lynn Adams (208)
S&H Golf Classic: Hollis Stacy (277)
CPC International: Hollis Stacy (285)
Lady Michelob: Janet Coles (206)
United Virginia Bank Classic: Lenore Muraoka (212)
Chrysler Plymouth Charity Classic: Pat Bradley (212)
LPGA Corning Classic: Patty Sheehan (272)
West Virginia LPGA Classic: Alice Miller (216)
LPGA Championship: Patty Sheehan (279)
Lady Keystone Open: Jan Stephenson (205)
Rochester International: Ayako Okamoto (282)
Peter Jackson Classic: Hollis Stacy (277)
McDonald's Kids Classic: Beth Daniel (286)
Mayflower Classic: Lauren Howe (280)
U.S. Women's Open: Jan Stephenson (290)
Boston Five Classic: Patti Rizzo (277)
Henredon Classic: Patty Sheehan (272)
Chevrolet World Championship of Women's Golf: JoAnne Carner (282)
Columbia Savings Classic: Pat Bradley (277)
Rail Charity Classic: Lauri Peterson (210)
Portland Ping Championship: JoAnne Carner (212)
Safeco Classic: Juli Inkster (283)
Inamori Classic: Patty Sheehan (209)
San Jose Classic: Kathy Postlewait (213)
Mazda Japan Classic: Pat Bradley (206)

Other Tournaments

British Open: Tom Watson (275)
U.S. Men's Amateur: Jay Sigel
U.S. Women's Amateur: Joanne Pacillo
U.S. Men's Public Links: Billy Tuten
U.S. Women's Public Links: Kelli Antolock
U.S. Senior Open: Billy Casper
U.S. Men's Mid-Amateur: Jay Sigel
U.S. Senior Men's Amateur: Bill Hyndman
U.S. Senior Women's Amateur: Dorothy Porter
U.S. Boy's Junior: Tim Straub
U.S. Girl's Junior: Kim Saiki
Ryder Cup: U.S. 14½, Great Britain-Europe 13½
Walker Cup: U.S. 13½, Great Britain-Ireland 10½

nament victories (two, as well as two seconds, a third, and a tie for fourth).

Tom Watson, who failed to win for the first time in seven years on the PGA tour, earned his fifth British Open title and won the Jack Nicklaus Performance Average Award given by *Golf Digest*. Quiet Larry Nelson outgunned Watson for the U.S. Open crown. Seve Ballesteros, the brilliant young Spaniard, won the Masters, one other tournament (Westchester Classic), and $210,933 in only eight starts.

Back on the women's side, Patty Sheehan captured the LPGA Championship and three other tournaments and was second in money-winnings with $248,161. Pat Bradley won four times and was third in money with $240,207. Three-time winners included Jan Stephenson, who held on to capture the U.S. Open, and Hollis Stacy, whose victories included the major Peter Jackson Classic. Amy Alcott won the other designated major title on the LPGA tour, the Nabisco Dinah Shore Classic.

In the biennial Ryder Cup competition between pros from the United States and Great Britain-Europe, an 18th-hole birdie by Lanny Wadkins gave the United States a victory.

On the PGA Senior tour, Don January won six tournaments, but four-time winner Miller Barber was the overall leading money-winner.

LARRY DENNIS, *"Golf Digest"*

HORSE RACING

Major U.S. Thoroughbred Races

American Handicap: John Henry, $164,600 (value of race)
Beldame: Dance Number, $222,000
Belmont Stakes: Caveat, $358,500
Budweiser Million: Tolomeo, $1,000,000
Champagne: Devil's Bag, $237,000
Hollywood Futurity: Fali Time, $999,725
Hollywood Gold Cup: Island Whirl, $500,000
Hollywood Invitational: Erins Isle, $300,000
Hollywood Starlet: Althea, $500,000
Hollywood Turf Cup: John Henry, $500,000
Jockey Club Gold Cup: Slew o' Gold, $570,000
Kentucky Derby: Sunny's Halo, $531,000
Man o' War Stakes: Majesty's Prince, $294,500
Marlboro Cup: Highland Blade, $400,000
Meadowlands Cup: Slewpy, $400,000
Oak Tree Invitational: Zalataia, $400,000
Preakness: Deputed Testamony, $346,200
Rothmans International: All Along, $520,350
San Juan Capistrano: Erins Isle, $300,000
Santa Anita Handicap: Bates Motel, $542,350
Suburban Handicap: Winter's Tale, $281,000
Travers: Play Fellow, $225,000
Turf Classic: All Along, $585,700
Washington, D.C., International: All Along, $250,000
Woodward: Slew o'Gold, $231,500

Major U.S. Harness Races

Blue Bonnets Challenge: Cam Fella, $75,000
Cane Pace: Ralph Hanover, $559,230
Hambletonian: Duenna, $1,080,000
Kentucky Futurity: Power Seat, $150,000
Little Brown Jug: Ralph Hanover, $358,800
Meadowlands Pace: Ralph Hanover, $1,251,000
Messenger: Ralph Hanover, $379,004
Roosevelt International: Idéal du Gazeau, $250,000
Woodrow Wilson Pace: Carls Bird, $1,700,000
Yonkers Trot: Joie De Vie, $489,150

Horse Racing

All Along, Devil's Bag, and Slew o' Gold were the stars of American thoroughbred racing in 1983.

All Along, a four-year-old French-bred filly owned by Parisian art dealer Daniel Wildenstein and trained by Patrick-Louis Biancone, put together a brilliant winning streak in the fall. She won the Prix de l'Arc de Triomphe on October 2 in France and then went to North America to sweep three races—the Rothmans International on October 16, the Turf Classic on October 29, and the Washington, DC, International on November 12. In winning those four major races on two different continents in a period of less than six weeks, All Along pulled off one of the greatest feats in racing history. Besides the purse money, she picked up an additional $1 million for winning the fall turf triple (Rothmans, Turf Classic, and Washington International).

Devil's Bag, a two-year-old colt sired by Halo, was unbeaten in five starts, including the Cowdin, Champagne, and Laurel Futurity. Devil's Bag won the five races by a total of 27 lengths and set a stakes record of 1:34⅕ in the Champagne.

Slew o' Gold, from the first crop of 1977 Triple Crown champion Seattle Slew, won the Woodward and Jockey Club Gold Cup and ran second in the Marlboro Cup.

Play Fellow, a three-year-old colt trained by Harvey Vanier, also achieved an outstanding record in 1983. The son of On the Sly won the Travers, Blue Grass, Arlington Classic, and American Derby.

For the second straight year, no horse ran in all three Triple Crown races. Sunny's Halo took the Kentucky Derby, Deputed Testamony won the Preakness, and Caveat outran the field in the Belmont Stakes.

Eddie Delahoussaye, who had ridden 1982 Derby winner Gato Del Sol, came back to make it two in a row, guiding Sunny's Halo to a two-length victory in the Churchill Downs classic. Sunny's Halo, a Canadian-bred son of Halo, became the first winner of the Arkansas Derby to triumph in the Kentucky Derby.

Hall of Fame trainer W. C. "Woody" Stephens had another highly successful year, conditioning such standouts as Devil's Bag, Caveat, Swale, Miss Oceana, Number, and Vision.

Sales. A son of Northern Dancer sold for a world-record $10.2 million at Keeneland's July Selected Yearling Sale.

Harness Racing. Cam Fella was named Harness Horse of the Year for the second season in a row. Ralph Hanover became the seventh three-year-old to win the Pacing Triple Crown —Cane Pace, Little Brown Jug, and Messenger Stakes.

JIM BOLUS
"The Louisville Times"

© Jerry Wachter/Focus on Sports

Goalie Bill Smith anchored a stingy defense for the New York Islanders, who won a fourth straight Stanley Cup.

Ice Hockey

The 1982–83 National Hockey League season may be best remembered as the year in which the 21 teams truly took offense at one another. Never in the 66-year history of the league had so many clubs scored so many goals at such an astonishing rate. Never had electrifying goal-scorers sprouted in such abundance and never had defenses seemed so weak and vulnerable. Yet, it was the team with the best defense that won the Stanley Cup, as the New York Islanders became only the second franchise in history, along with Montreal, to win the championship for a fourth straight season.

NHL. Although Edmonton Oiler center Wayne Gretzky easily led the league in scoring for the third straight season, he was joined by the most dangerous platoon of scorers in years. With 71 goals and a record 125 assists, Gretzky captured a record fourth straight Hart Trophy as most valuable player (MVP), but there were ten other players who also topped 100 points. Three of them—Mark Messier, Glenn Anderson, and Jari Kurri were teammates of Gretzky. With Paul Coffey, another Oiler, ranking high (96 points), Edmonton had 5 of the league's 15 top point-scorers. So it was no surprise that the team finished the season with 424 goals, the most ever scored in a single season. Other teams boasted superior offensive players as well. Los Angeles center Marcel Dionne became the first player to score at least 100 points

in seven consecutive seasons. New York Islander Mike Bossy became the first player to score at least 60 goals in three straight years, and he was not even the highest scoring right wing during the season.

That honor belonged to veteran Lanny McDonald of Calgary, whose 66 goals were the third highest ever for a player at his position. Gretzky continued his dominance in the playoffs, setting a postseason record of 38 points, but even he could not prevent the Islanders from rallying to another championship. They tied the Montreal dynasty of 1976–79 for the second-longest title string and drew within one of the record five straight Stanley Cups won by the Canadiens in 1956–60.

The season did not start out so effortlessly for the Islanders. Overall point leaders during the two previous regular seasons, they slumped to second place in their own division behind the Philadelphia Flyers and lagged in a sixth-place tie in points, the poorest finish ever for a Stanley Cup champion. But when the play-offs began, the Flyers were ousted in the first round by the New York Rangers, while the Islanders defeated Washington. Philadelphia's loss was one of two major surprises in play-offs that lacked the many shocking upsets of previous seasons. The other surprise victim was Montreal, which owns a record 22 championships but failed to survive the first play-off round for the third straight season.

The Islanders outlasted the rival Rangers in six games to win the Patrick Division final, earning the right to meet Boston in the Prince of Wales Conference championship. The Bruins, who led the league with 110 points during the regular season, defeated Quebec and Buffalo to win the Adams Division final. The Campbell Conference championship pitted Chicago, winner of the Norris Division final, against Edmonton, which clinched the Smythe Division final. The Islanders won their series against Boston in six games, while the Oilers completed a stunning four-game sweep of Chicago.

That paired the Islanders and Edmonton, teams drastically different in both style and substance. The Islanders, wise and experienced, allowed only 226 goals during the season, the fewest number of any team. Edmonton, young and brash, staked its success on swift skating and sharp shooting. In an eagerly awaited confrontation, the teams met in Northlands Coliseum in Edmonton for the first two games of the best-of-seven series with Game 1 proving to be especially dramatic.

An early goal by Islander Duane Sutter was the only score for more than two periods until teammate Ken Morrow scored late into an empty net as the Islanders won, 2–0, becoming the first team to shut out the vaunted Oiler offense in two years. It was only the sixth time all season that Gretzky failed to score a point,

ICE HOCKEY

National Hockey League
(Final Standings, 1982–83)

Wales Conference

Patrick Division	W	L	T	Pts	Goals For	Goals Against
*Philadelphia	49	23	8	106	326	240
*N.Y. Islanders	42	26	12	96	302	226
*Washington	39	25	16	94	306	283
*N.Y. Rangers	35	35	10	80	306	287
New Jersey	17	49	14	48	230	338
Pittsburgh	18	53	9	45	257	394
Adams Division						
*Boston	50	20	10	110	327	228
*Montreal	42	24	14	98	350	286
*Buffalo	38	29	13	89	318	285
*Quebec	34	34	12	80	343	336
Hartford	19	54	7	45	261	403

Campbell Conference

Norris Division	W	L	T	Pts	Goals For	Goals Against
*Chicago	47	23	10	104	338	268
*Minnesota	40	24	16	96	321	290
*Toronto	28	40	12	68	293	330
*St. Louis	25	40	15	65	285	316
Detroit	21	44	15	57	263	344
Smythe Division						
*Edmonton	47	21	12	106	424	315
*Calgary	32	34	14	78	321	317
*Vancouver	30	35	15	75	303	309
*Winnipeg	33	39	8	74	311	333
Los Angeles	27	41	12	66	308	365

*Made play-offs

Stanley Cup Play-offs
Wales Conference

Boston	3 games	Quebec	1
Buffalo	3 games	Montreal	0
N.Y. Islanders	3 games	Washington	1
N.Y. Rangers	3 games	Philadelphia	0
Boston	4 games	Buffalo	3
N.Y. Islanders	4 games	N.Y. Rangers	2
N.Y. Islanders	4 games	Boston	2

Campbell Conference

Calgary	3 games	Vancouver	1
Chicago	3 games	St. Louis	1
Edmonton	3 games	Winnipeg	0
Minnesota	3 games	Toronto	1
Chicago	4 games	Minnesota	1
Edmonton	4 games	Calgary	1
Edmonton	4 games	Chicago	0
Championship N.Y. Islanders	4 games	Edmonton	0

Individual Honors

Hart Trophy (most valuable player): Wayne Gretzky, Edmonton Oilers
Ross Trophy (leading scorer): Wayne Gretzky
Vezina Trophy (top goaltender): Pete Peeters, Boston
Norris Trophy (best defenseman): Rod Langway, Washington
Selke Award (best defense forward): Bobby Clark, Philadelphia
Calder Trophy (rookie of the year):Steve Larmer, Chicago
Lady Byng Trophy (sportsmanship): Mike Bossy, N.Y. Islanders
Conn Smythe Trophy (most valuable in play-offs): Billy Smith, N.Y. Islanders
Coach of the Year: Orval Tessier, Chicago

All-Star Game

Campbell Conference 9, Wales Conference 3

NCAA: Wisconsin

and his disappointment lingered. The Islanders held him to only two assists in Game 2, while recording a 6–3 victory.

Behind more spectacular goaltending by Bill Smith, the Islanders won Game 3 at Nassau Coliseum, 5–1, with Gretzky managing only an assist. He added just one more assist when the Islanders completed a four-game

sweep with a 4–2 victory. In four games, the Oilers scored just six goals. Gretzky, the greatest scorer in history, was limited to no goals and four assists. For his part in the impenetrable Islander defense, Smith was awarded the Conn Smythe Trophy as play-off MVP, becoming the fourth consecutive Islander to win the award. It was the Islanders' second straight sweep in the finals, following one over Vancouver the year before, and gave them an astonishing four-year record in the final series of 16–3.

There were big losers as well as big winners. Montreal general manager Irving Grundman was fired and replaced by Serge Savard, one of the team's former defensemen. Hartford general manager Larry Pleau was replaced by Emile Francis, who left his position with the St. Louis Blues just as an attempt to sell the financially troubled Blues to a group in Saskatoon, Saskatchewan, was turned down by the league. The team was saved from extinction when it was later sold to Beverly Hills businessman Harry Ornest.

Other. The Soviet Union won its 15th straight world championship in Düsseldorf, West Germany, defeating Czechoslovakia for the title. Canada finished third. The United States won the ''B'' pool title of the world championship in Tokyo. The University of Wisconsin defeated Harvard, 6–2, to capture the NCAA's Division I crown.

PAT CALABRIA, *"Newsday"*

Ice Skating

Scott Hamilton, the 24-year-old, 5'3" (1.6 m) athlete from Denver, CO, was the standout figure skater of 1983. He won his third consecutive world and United States championships.

World Figure Championships. In March at Helsinki, Finland, Hamilton beat a field of 21 skaters from 14 countries and became the first man since Ondrej Nepela of Czechoslovakia (1971–73) to win three straight world titles. The last previous American to win three titles in a row was David Jenkins (1957–59).

The 110-lb (50 kg) Hamilton brought an athletic quality to his artistic repertory and displayed an all-around ability that has made him unique in the sport. His use of flawless jumps, loops, and swirls dazzled the judges, who awarded him frequent 5.9s (out of 6.0).

The world championships proved exciting, but were disappointing for Elaine Zayak, the 1982 champion from Paramus, NJ, who was forced to withdraw with a fractured ankle. This opened the way for 18-year-old Rosalynn Sumners of Edmonds, WA, to use her best techniques and take the title from a field of 15 finalists. She, too, dazzled the judges with three difficult triple jumps and 11 doubles. Claudia Leistner of West Germany was the runner-up.

In the pairs competition, Yelena Valova and Oleg Vasiliev of the Soviet Union dethroned the East German pair of Sabine Baess and Tassilo Thierbach. The British dance team of Jayne Torvill and Christopher Dean retained their title, scoring 6.0s in the free-dancing portion for artistry.

U.S. Figure Championships. At Pittsburgh in the nationals in February, Hamilton excited the spectators by capturing his third straight crown. All nine judges gave him 5.9s for his composition and style. His program included seven triple jumps, double jumps, cartwheels, and standing spins. "I'm excited about my skating," he said, "everything has come into place." He won all three phases—compulsory figures, short program, and free skating—and received 26 of 27 possible first-place points.

Miss Sumners retained the national title against 14 finalists with a combination of delicate glides and physical power. Miss Sumners outmaneuvered Miss Zayak, the runner-up, who had taken the title in 1981.

The national pairs went to the defending champions, Peter and Caitlin Carruthers of Wilmington, DE, and the dance crown was retained by Judy Blumberg of Tarzana, CA, and Michael Seibert of Washington, PA.

Speed Skating. Rolf Falk-Larssen of Norway won the world championship, with 166.637 points by taking the 500-, 1,500-, and 5,000-meter races. The 10,000 was won by Tomas Gustafson of Sweden. Andrea Schoene of East Germany won the 1,500-, 3,000-, and 5,000-meters races and the women's title, with 178.983 points. Natalya Glebova of the Soviet Union won the 500-meter race.

Michael Ralston of Streamwood, IL, and Janet Hainstock of Alpena, MI, each won the national and North American championships.

GEORGE DE GREGORIO

Pan American Games

Two drug scandals—one real and one implied—overshadowed the actual competition in the IX Pan American Games, held August 14–28 in Caracas, Venezuela.

The quadrennial Western Hemisphere sports festival attracted 4,000 athletes from 35 nations in 25 sports. Between 700 and 800 athletes—medal-winners and others chosen at random—underwent urine tests to detect the presence of any of the 91 generic drugs banned by the International Olympic Committee. Positive results were reported for 16 athletes from 10 nations in 5 sports, the largest such finding in international sports history. In 12 of the 16 cases, the drug was anabolic steroids. These artificial male hormones help athletes build muscles and train more heavily. They had been banned because of such possible side effects as arteriosclerosis, liver damage, and sterility. In

Steve Kelley/"The San Diego Union"

all but one minor case, the athletes who tested positively were disqualified from the Games, and those who won medals had to return them. The only U.S. athlete who tested positively was Jeff Michels of Chicago, winner of three gold medals in weight lifting.

Only hours after the first positive findings were announced, 12 U.S. male track and field athletes flew home before they had competed. Though one had become a father the day before and others spoke of injuries and personal problems, the inference remained that most feared drug testing. One of the 12, Mike Tully of Los Angeles, returned to Caracas, won the pole vault, and passed the drug test.

Competition. Led by its swimmers and divers, the United States set Pan Am Game records with 137 gold and 285 total medals. Cuba was next with 79 gold and 175 total medals, followed by Canada with 18 and 109.

U.S. swimmers won 25 of 29 events. Among the men, freestyler Rowdy Gaines won four gold medals; backstroker Rick Carey, breaststroker Steve Lundquist, and butterflyer Matt Gribble won three each. Among the women, medleyist Tracy Caulkins and freestyler Tiffany Cohen took two titles each. In addition, Greg Louganis won both men's diving competitions, while Kelly McCormick and Wendy Wyland won on the women's side.

In track and field, U.S. athletes won 13 events, relatively low by traditional standards. Among the successes, however, were all four relay races. The only individual double-winners in track and field were Cuba's Luis Delis, in the shot put and discus, and Brazil's Agberto Guimares in the 800 and 1500 m. Still, it was in boxing that the Cubans made their best showing, winning in 8 of the 12 weight divisions. In basketball the United States won the men's and women's tournaments, but in baseball it finished third behind Cuba and Nicaragua.

FRANK LITSKY
"The New York Times"

© David Lissy/Focus on Sports

Tamara McKinney of Olympic Valley, CA, became the first U.S. woman to win the overall World Cup championship.

Skiing

The United States established itself as a dominant force on the 1983 international skiing scene, sweeping both the men's and women's overall World Cup championships.

World Cup. Tamara McKinney of Olympic Valley, CA, became the first American to win the women's overall title, and Phil Mahre of Yakima, WA, took the overall crown for the third year in a row. The American sweep marked the third time in the World Cup's 17-year history that one country captured both overall divisions. Karl Schranz and Gertrud Gabl of Austria did it in 1969 and Andreas and Hanni Wenzel of Liechtenstein won in 1980.

The 20-year-old Miss McKinney ended European domination of the title with a late-season surge. She took an early lead at the start of the season, but from late January to early March she began to falter. In the standings she dropped to third, and critics began to ask whether the pressure of going for a World Cup title was too much for her. "I was trying too hard," she said, "but I learned to relax and not worry about the title." She made a dramatic comeback and early in March she won three consecutive giant slaloms in the United States. She clinched the giant slalom title for the second time with a victory at Waterville, NH, on March 10. She had won the giant slalom in 1981.

Mahre clinched the overall title as early as March 7, at Aspen, CO. He also won the giant slalom with a thrilling victory in the last race of the season at Furano, Japan. He was third behind Ingemar Stenmark of Sweden and Max Julen of Switzerland before the race. He beat Julen by one-hundredth of a second. Stenmark was seven-hundredths of a second behind Mahre, in third. Stenmark, who had won overall titles in 1976, 1977, and 1978, finished second to Mahre overall and in the giant slalom. He won the slalom, with Mahre sixth. Mahre repeated as combined champion.

The women's 1982 overall champion, Erica Hess of Switzerland, who underwent minor surgery on her knee during the season, finished third. Hanni Wenzel was runner-up to Miss McKinney and also captured the combined title. Miss Hess won the slalom and was third in combined.

Franz Klammer of Austria and Doris de Agostini of Switzerland won the downhill crowns.

Tom Kelly, coach of the U.S. team, was generally pleased with the team's showing, indicating that the key to success at the 1984 Winter Olympics in Sarajevo, Yugoslavia, would be keeping athletes "patient and cohesive." The Mahre brothers, Phil and Steve, have been with the team eight years. McKinney was in her fourth season in 1983. Steve Mahre, who was third overall in 1982, was 12th in 1983. He was fourth in the slalom. Cindy Nelson of Vail, CO, and Christin Cooper of Sun Valley, ID, were seventh and 12th overall, the next best to McKinney among Americans.

U.S. Alpine. In the U.S. championships, Phil Mahre won the slalom and Miss McKinney took the slalom and giant slalom. Bill Johnson of Van Nuys, CA, and Pam Fletcher of Hayward, MA, won the downhill, and Tiger Shaw of Stowe, VT, captured the giant slalom.

Nordic. The overall cross-country championship went to Aleksandr Zavialov of the Soviet Union, with Bill Koch of Guilford, VT, the 1982 champion, third. Matti Nykaenen of Finland won the jumping.

GEORGE DE GREGORIO

Soccer

The year 1983 was one of surprises and disappointments for professional soccer in the United States.

The biggest story concerned the rejection by FIFA (Federation of International Football Associations, the world governing body of soccer) of a U.S. bid to host the 1986 World Cup. Mexico was awarded soccer's most prestigious event after FIFA turned down an invitation to visit the United States. Discrepancies in the U.S. bid was the reason given by FIFA for its rejection of the visit, and not even last-minute pleas by former U.S. Secretary of State Henry Kissinger and retired soccer great Pelé could keep Mexico from being named the host. Canada had also made an attempt to land the Cup.

Elsewhere on the international scene, the U.S. National Youth and Pan American teams were eliminated in the first round of major championships. The National Youth team beat the Ivory Coast, 1–0, in the Youth World Cup at Mexico, but then lost 3–2 to Uruguay and 2–0 to Poland and was ousted. The U.S. Pan Am squad, which beat Canada in a home-and-home series to earn a berth at the Games in Caracas, Venezuela, fell by the wayside after tying Cuba, 0–0, and losing to Guatemala, 3–0, and Chile, 2–1.

NASL. In the North American Soccer League, the season began with 12 teams, two less than the previous year. Jacksonville, Edmonton, and Portland all dropped out, while Team America was added.

Team America was the U.S. National Team in-training and was headquartered in Washington, DC. The purpose of the team was to bring together the best U.S. players under the direction of newly-hired U.S. National Team Coach Alkis Panagoulias, and to play in the NASL in order to prepare for the 1986 World Cup tournament. The squad also looked forward to the 1984 Summer Olympic Games in Los Angeles, hoping that professional players would be allowed to compete; that issue had not been settled by late 1983. But not all of the best U.S. players accepted invitations to join Team America, and this proved to be the team's undoing. After winning 8 of its first 13 games, Team America lost 15 of its last 17 matches and wound up with the lowest point total in the NASL. Principal owner Robert K. Lifton, citing losses in excess of $1 million, said after the season that certain conditions would have to exist before Team America could return to the NASL in 1984.

While Team America struggled on the field, the defending champion New York Cosmos won their sixth straight regular-season point title and was favored to win Soccer Bowl-83 in Vancouver. But New York was upset in the first round of the play-offs by Montreal, which had earned the eighth and final play-off berth on only the last day of the regular season.

Second-seeded Vancouver also lost in the first round, bowing to Toronto, the seventh qualifier. Toronto went on to oust Golden Bay in the semifinals, while Montreal lost to Tulsa. Tulsa, which had won 15 of its last 20 regular-season matches after a 2–8 start, then won its first league title by defeating Toronto, 2–0, in

SOCCER

NORTH AMERICAN SOCCER LEAGUE
(Final Standings, 1983)

Eastern Division

	W	L	G.F.	G.A.	Pts.
*New York	22	8	87	49	194
*Chicago	15	15	66	73	147
*Toronto	16	14	51	48	135
*Montreal	12	18	58	71	124

Southern Division

	W	L	G.F.	G.A.	Pts.
*Tulsa	17	13	56	49	145
*Ft. Lau'dale	14	16	60	63	136
Tampa Bay	7	23	48	87	83
Team America	10	20	33	54	79

Western Division

	W	L	G.F.	G.A.	Pts.
*Vancouver	24	6	63	34	187
*Golden Bay	20	10	71	54	169
Seattle	12	18	62	61	119
San Diego	11	19	53	65	106

* Made play-offs

NASL Champion: Tulsa Roughnecks
NASL MVP: Roberto Cabañas, New York Cosmos
NASL Indoor Champion: Tampa Bay Rowdies

ASL Champion: Jacksonville Tea Men
MISL Champion: San Diego Sockers
European Cup: Hamburg
NCAA Champion: Indiana University

front of 53,623 fans at B.C. Place Stadium in Vancouver.

Award winners in the NASL included Cosmos standout Roberto Cabañas, who won the scoring title (25 goals, 16 assists) and earned the Most Valuable Player (MVP) award; Tampa Bay's Gregg Thompson, the Rookie of the Year; and Golden Bay Coach Dan Popovic, who took Coach of the Year honors.

After the season, the NASL lost Soccer Bowl-82 finalist Seattle, which folded; all-time league scoring leader Giorgio Chinaglia of the Cosmos, who retired to join his old Italian team, Lazio; and Soccer Bowl itself, which would become a best-of-three championship series in 1984.

Indoor. In the Major Indoor Soccer League (MISL), three NASL clubs crossed over, and one of them—the San Diego Sockers—won the 1982–83 league title, beating the Baltimore Blast in a five-game finale.

San Diego, Chicago, and Golden Bay, the latter led by MISL regular-season MVP Steve Zungul, were the three NASL/MISL clubs, and all three announced that they would stay in the NASL and play in the league's new indoor program in 1983–84. Seven teams were set to play a 32-game schedule. The MISL, meanwhile, began its 1983–84 schedule with 12 teams, including the expansion Tacoma Stars.

ASL. Another crossover team, Jacksonville, joined the American Soccer League from the NASL and won the title by beating the Pennsylvania Stoners. Goalkeeper Peter Simonini of Jacksonville was MVP.

JIM HENDERSON
V.P., Public Relations, Team America

UPI

A new face on the scene: 20-year-old backstroker Rick Carey churned out new world records in the 100 and 200 meters.

Swimming

Fourteen new world swimming records were set in 1983. American men accounted for five of them, three at the Pan American Games in Caracas, Venezuela.

A new face on the scene was Rick Carey, a 20-year-old sophomore at the University of Texas, who took two Pan Am titles and set two world records in the backstroke. Carey surpassed the two oldest swimming records, both set at the 1976 Olympics by John Nabers. Carey's 1:58.93 for 200 meters at the U.S. Long Course Nationals in Fresno, CA, on August 3 broke Nabers' 1:59.19. Three days later, in a preliminary heat of the 100-m competition, Carey did 55.44 to better Nabers' 55.49; in the final later that day he won the title with 55.38. Then at Caracas later in the month, Carey lowered the record again to 55.19.

Steve Lundquist, who set the world 100-m breaststroke record (1:02.53) in 1982, lowered the mark twice in 1983. He swam 1:02.28 in the Pan Am Games after lowering the standard to 1:02.34 only 11 days earlier in Fresno. Matt Gribble, 21, from the University of Miami, shattered the 100-m butterfly record with a 53.44 clocking, erasing the 1981 mark of 53.81 set by William Paulus. Carey, Lundquist, and Gribble were joined by Rowdy Gaines in setting a new standard for the 400-m medley, 3:40.42, at Caracas.

The other new world records in 1983 were set by East German, West German, and Soviet swimmers. Michael Gross of West Germany excelled at the European championships at Rome in August, establishing two world marks. In June at Hanover, West Germany, he had broken Gaines' 1982 clocking of 1:48.93 in the 200 freestyle with a time of 1:48.28. Then in Rome he lowered that to 1:47.87 and also smashed Craig Beardsley's two-year-old 200 butterfly mark (1:58.01) with a time of 1:57.05. Vladimir Salnikov of the Soviet Union, holder of the 400-, 800-, and 1,500-m freestyle records, continued to improve his times during 1983. In February at Moscow he clipped 1.25 seconds off the 400 mark with a timing of 3:48.32. A week later he swam 14:54.76 for the 1,500 to reduce his old mark by 1.59 seconds. In July at Los Angeles, Salnikov was clocked in 7:52.33 for 800 m, breaking the record he had set in 1982 by .50 seconds. The West German men's 800-m freestyle relay team set a mark of 7:20.40 on August 23, breaking by .42 seconds the 1978 record posted by a U.S. team.

East Germans accounted for all three of the world records registered by women. Ute Geweniger broke her two-year-old 100-m breaststroke record with a time of 1:08.51 at Rome; the 800-m freestyle relay team turned in a record 8:02.27; and the 400-m medley relay squad notched a record 4:05.79, bettering the 1982 mark of another East German team.

GEORGE DE GREGORIO

Tennis

Open tennis marked its 15th anniversary in 1983, and while it continued to earn generally high grades from players, promoters, the press, and the public, confusion and controversy elicited many a grin or grimace, or both.

Men's professional tennis was dominated by the not-always-so-holy trinity of John McEnroe, Ivan Lendl, and Jimmy Connors. McEnroe won Wimbledon with ease, Connors surprisingly defended his title at the U.S. Open, and Ivan Lendl was a surprise mainly because he again failed to win a Grand Slam championship yet continued to win so much elsewhere that he topped the prize-money list for the third straight year and finished as the world's second-ranked player. McEnroe was number one, and Connors was number three.

The women's tour was virtually a solo performance by Martina Navratilova, who lost one match the entire year (to Kathy Horvath at the French Open). After that Martina won both Wimbledon and the U.S. Open without the loss of even a set. She so overwhelmed her opponents that the only obstacle seeming to threaten her winning in perpetuity was old age or retirement.

Tennis again proved that it not only could survive scandal, lawsuits, and the retirement of Björn Borg, but that it could thrive. Borg, in truth, retired only from the pressure and frenzy of major tournaments. He continued to play in exhibitions and small events, earning as much as $2 million a year as one of the game's leading celebrities.

If there seemed to be more on- and off-court misconduct in 1983, it was because discipline was becoming more effective and more publicized than in previous years. For instance, John McEnroe was suspended for three weeks and Ilie Nastase for three months for an accumulation of misdeeds. And Yannick Noah, who captured his countrymen's hearts forever by winning the French Open, was sidelined by authorities for three weeks for failing to appear at a televised Nations Cup match in Germany.

The most debated case of all was the formal accusation by the Pro Council that Guillermo Vilas had accepted an illegal $60,000 guarantee at the Rotterdam Grand Prix. The action stirred emotions and legal questions to equal levels of

Martina Navratilova "got the monkey off her back" by winning her first U.S. Open. She lost only one match all year.

Focus on Sports

TENNIS

Major Team Competitions

Davis Cup: Australia
Federation Cup: Czechoslovakia
Wightman Cup: United States

Major Tournaments

U.S. Open—men's singles: Jimmy Connors; men's doubles: Peter Fleming and John McEnroe; women's singles: Martina Navratilova; women's doubles: Navratilova and Pam Shriver; mixed doubles: Elizabeth Savers and John Fitzgerald; men's 35 singles: Georges Goven (France); junior men's singles: Stefan Edberg (Sweden); women's 35 singles: Louise Feingold.
U.S. Clay Court Championships—men's singles: Jimmy Arias; men's doubles: Mark Edmondson (Australia) and Sherwood Stewart; women's singles: Andrea Temesvari (Hungary); women's doubles: Kathleen Horvath and Virginia Ruzici (Rumania).
U.S. National Indoor—men's singles: Jimmy Connors; men's doubles: Peter McNamara (Australia) and Paul McNamee (Australia).
National Men's 35 Clay Court Championships—men's singles: Armistead Neely; men's doubles: Neely and Z. Mincek.
USTA Women's Clay Court Championships—35 singles: Astrid Suurbeek; 35 doubles: Wendy Overton and Suurbeek; 40 singles: Judy Alvaraz; 40 doubles: Alvaraz and Cathie Anderson; 45 singles: Nancy Reed; 45 doubles: Jane Crofford and Olga Palafox; 50 singles: Reed; 50 doubles: Charleen Grafton and Palafox; 55 singles: Betty Pratt; 55 doubles: Betty Brink and Mariann Hanley; 60 singles: Dodo Cheney; 60 doubles: Cheney and Sheila Evans; 65 singles: Cheney; 65 doubles: Marga Lee Mahony and Libby Kelly; 70 singles: Lui Shang-Ku and Ann Hoffman.
National Girls 18's Singles—Caroline Kuhlman.
Volvo Grand Prix Masters—men's singles: Ivan Lendl (Czechoslovakia); men's doubles: Peter Fleming and John McEnroe.

Other U.S. Championships

NCAA (Division 1)—singles: Greg Holmes; doubles: Ola Malmquist and Allen Miller (Georgia).

Professional Championships

U.S. Pro Indoor Championships—men's singles: John McEnroe; men's doubles: Kevin Curren (South Africa) and Steve Denton.
World Championship Tennis Tour—men's singles: John McEnroe.
Virginia Slims—women's singles: Martina Navratilova.

Other Countries

Wimbledon—men's singles: John McEnroe; men's doubles: Peter Fleming and John McEnroe; women's singles: Martina Navratilova; women's doubles: Navratilova and Pam Shriver; mixed doubles: John Lloyd (England) and Wendy Turnbull (Australia).
Australian Open—men's singles: Mats Wilander (Sweden); men's doubles: Mark Edmondson (Australia) and Paul McNamee (Australia); women's singles: Martina Navratilova.
French Open—men's singles: Yannick Noah (France); men's doubles: Anders Jarryd (Sweden) and Hans Simonsson (Sweden); women's singles: Chris Evert Lloyd; women's doubles: Rosalyn Fairbank (South Africa) and Candy Reynolds; mixed doubles: Kathy Jordan and Elliott Teltscher.
Italian Open—men's singles: Jimmy Arias; men's doubles: Francisco Gonzalez (Paraguay) and Victor Pecci (Paraguay); women's singles: Andrea Temesvari (Hungary); women's doubles: Virginia Wade (England) and Virginia Ruzici (Rumania).
Canadian Open—men's singles: Ivan Lendl (Czechoslovakia); men's doubles: Sandy Mayer and Ferdi Taygan; women's singles: Martina Navratilova; women's doubles: Andrea Jaeger and Anne Hobbs.

N.B. All players are from the United States, unless otherwise noted.

Leading Money Winners

(As of Jan. 9, 1984)		(As of Jan. 7, 1984)	
Ivan Lendl	$1,687,128	M. Navratilova	$1,456,003
John McEnroe	1,089,844	Chris Evert Lloyd	430,436
Mats Vilander	1,089,650	Pam Shriver	312,216
Guillermo Vilas	677,035	Andrea Jaeger	261,954
Jimmy Connors	568,047	Kathy Jordan	211,786
Tomas Smid	434,886	Jo Durie	211,342
Yannick Noah	368,394	Wendy Turnbull	206,391
Brian Teacher	332,948	Andrea Temesvari	168,301
Jimmy Arias	330,033	Sylvia Hanika	154,950
Kevin Curran	306,852	Hana Mandlikova	151,762

frustration. Defenders of Vilas, one of the sport's most intelligent and sensitive stars, asked "Why Vilas?" when tournament guarantees are known to be common on the tour.

The controversy with the most far-reaching impact, however, was the lawsuit by one of the game's leading promoters, Lamar Hunt, who claimed that his World Championship Tennis (WCT) company was being prevented from participating in the professional tennis world by the ATP (players' union), ITF (International Tennis Federation), and Pro Council.

Three new names brightened the upper horizons of the men's Top Ten: Mats Wilander, Yannick Noah, and Jimmy Arias, ranked four, five, and six, respectively. Another youngster, 16-year-old Aaron Krickstein, became the youngest U.S.Open quarterfinalist ever and the youngest to win a Grand Prix title (Israel). Add to the list Eric Korita and a handful of little-known Swedes—Henrik Sundstrom, Anders Jarryd, Stefan Simmonson, and Joachim Nystrom—plus a brilliant teenage French left-hander, Henri Laconte, and the trend toward youth and speed is clearly evident.

The teen trend in the women's ranks, meanwhile, had been a truism for a decade or more. Andrea Jaeger, Tracy Austin, Kathy Horvath, and Kathy Rinaldi may have seemed like veterans, but not one of them was yet 20 years old. Two newcomers, Andrea Temesvari and Carling Bassett, appeared in the Top 20 for the first time, and yes, both were teenagers.

Mid- and over-sized rackets prevail in equipment sales; manufacturers continue to compete for elusive shares of a fragmented tennis market.

EUGENE L. SCOTT
"Tennis Week" Magazine

© Paul J. Sutton/Duomo

At the World Track and Field Championships, Carl Lewis took golds in the long jump, 100-m dash, and 400-m relay.

Track and Field

The first World Track and Field Championships, held August 7–14 in Helsinki, Finland, drew virtually all of the top world-class performers and produced exciting competition in almost all events. The United States sent one of its strongest contingents, led by Carl Lewis, Mary Decker, and Edwin Moses, who together accounted for six gold medals. All told, the U.S. squad took 24 medals (8 gold, 9 silver, and 7 bronze), one more than the Soviet Union and two more than East Germany.

Lewis, 22, accomplished a rare "triple," winning the 100-m dash (10.07 seconds) and the long jump (28'¾"; 8.55 m) and anchoring the 400-m relay team, which set a world record of 37.86 seconds. Decker, who in February was named the best amateur athlete in the United States for 1982, won the 1,500 m (4:00.90) and the 3,000 m (8:34.62), capping another fine season. Moses won the 400-m hurdles (47.50), despite an untied shoelace; two weeks later at Koblenz, West Germany, Moses celebrated his 28th birthday by winning his 87th race in a row and lowering his world mark to 47.02. Other Americans to take gold medals in Helsinki were Calvin Smith in the 200-m dash (20.14) and Greg Foster in the 110 hurdles (13.42).

In women's world-class competition, Jarmila Kratochvilova of Czechoslovakia was the season's standout performer. She set two world records, in the 400 m (47.99) at the world championships on August 10, and in the 800 m (1:53.28) at Munich on July 26. She also captured the 800 in the Helsinki meet, considered a gauge for the 1984 Olympics, with a time of 1:54.68. No woman has ever won the 400–800 double in the Olympics, and only Alberto Juantorena of Cuba has done it among men (1976).

The men's 1,500-m mark changed hands twice during 1983. Sydney Maree of the United States broke the three-year-old record of Britain's Steve Ovett (3:31.36) by .12 seconds at Cologne, West Germany, on August 28. On

September 4, Ovett reclaimed the record with a clocking of 3:30.77 at Rieti, Italy. On July 3 at Colorado Springs, Calvin Smith erased the standard for the 100-m dash set by Jim Hines in the 1968 Olympics; Smith's 9.93 seconds clipped .02 seconds from Hines' mark. On the same day, Evelyn Ashford lowered the women's 100-m record by .02 seconds to 10.79. In June, Marlies Gohr of East Germany, who had set the standard (10.88) six years earlier, reduced the time to 10.81.

In the men's high jump, Zhu Jianhua of China leaped 7'9¼" (2.37 m) at Shanghai in June to break the record, and on September 22 he raised the standard even higher, to 7'9¾" (2.38 m). Udo Beyer of East Germany broke his five-year-old record in the shot put with a toss of 72' 10¾" (22.22 m) on June 25 in Los Angeles.

The pole vault was also a busy event. Pierre Quinon of France cleared 19' 1" (5.82 m) in late August at Cologne. Five days later, Thierry Vigneron, another Frenchman, improved on Quinon's effort with 19'1½" (5.83 m) at a meet in Rome. Other new men's records were set by Yuri Dumchev of the USSR in the discus throw, 235' 9" (71.86 m); Sergei Litvinov of the USSR in the hammer throw, 276'0" (84.14 m); Tom Petranoff of the United States in the javelin throw, 327'2" (99.72 m); and Jurgen Hingsen of West Germany in the decathlon, 8,777 points.

Other new women's records were set by Raisa Sadretdinova of the USSR in the 10,000 m, 31:27.57; Joan Benoit of the United States in the marathon (Boston), 2 h, 22 min, and 42 sec; Anna Ambrosene of the Soviet Union in the 400-m hurdles, 54.02; East Germany in the 400-m relay, 41.53; Tamara Bykova of the USSR in the high jump, 6'8¼" (2.04 m); Anisoara Cusmir of Rumania in the long jump, 24'4½" (7.43 m); Galina Savinkova of the USSR in the discus, 240'4" (73.26 m); Tiina Lillak of Finland in the javelin, 245'3" (74.76 m); and Ramona Beubert of East Germany in the heptathlon, 6,836 points.

The Pan American Games at Caracas, Venezuela, in mid-August did not produce any world records, but 12 U.S. track and field athletes withdrew rather than undergo testing for banned drugs. Earlier, 15 male athletes in other sports had been disqualified for the use of steroids and other prohibited substances.

GEORGE DE GREGORIO

Yachting

For 132 years the United States had held a 132-oz (3.74 kg) ornate silver trophy known as the America's Cup, the most celebrated prize in the sport of yachting. *Australia II,* a revolutionary sloop from "Down Under," ended that reign in 1983.

Australia II was the fourth yacht built by Alan Bond, an Australian businessman, solely to challenge for this trophy. His 12-year, $16 million investment paid off when John Bertrand skippered *Australia II* to victory over the U.S. defender *Liberty,* 4 races to 3, in the finals off Newport, RI, September 14–26.

Of the seven original challengers, three from Australia, *Australia II* clearly was the best. She won 48 races and lost only six in the challengers' trials from June to September. In separate competitions, *Liberty* defeated two other U.S. boats for the right to defend the cup. Even before the trials had ended, however, a bitter argument erupted.

At the center of the controversy was *Australia II*'s unique keel, with two 2-ft- (.61-m-) long, swept-back wings, or fins. When the yacht was hauled out of the water, the wings were shrouded in a security skirt of plywood and green plastic. The New York Yacht Club, however, in whose possession the cup was being held, had seen enough and protested that the wings were illegal.

The yachts raced in America's Cup competition are of the 12-meter class, a designation that refers not to the boat's length but to a formula based on length, width, sail area, and other factors. The New York Yacht Club contended that when *Australia II* heeled (tipped to one side when wind filled her sails), the wings made her measure more than 12 m. Thus, the club argued, she could not compete with the winged keel. International officials ruled that the fins were legal, and the races continued.

Australia II seemed the faster yacht and quicker to turn, but Dennis Conner of San Diego, CA, *Liberty*'s skipper, outsailed the challenger in taking a 3–1 lead in the finals. *Australia II* won the last three races over the 24.3-mi (39.1 km) course by 1 minute and 47 seconds, by 3 minutes and 25 seconds, and by 41 seconds. In the decisive race, trailing after four of the six legs, *Australia II* took the lead with the wind at her back and never surrendered it.

This was the 25th challenge for the trophy, won in 1851 by the schooner *America* off the Isle of Wight. In previous defenses the United States had won 77 of 85 races. Only once before had a challenger won even two races.

In other yachting competition, West Germany won the Admiral's Cup, the unofficial world championship for Grand Prix craft; *Scarlett O'Hara,* a 42-ft (12.8-m) sloop owned by Monroe Wingate of Piedmont, CA, captured the Southern Ocean Racing Conference's six-race series for the unofficial U.S. championship; and Philippe Jeantot of France won the first-ever round-the-world solo sailing race, covering the 27,550-mi (44 336-km), four-legged course in a total sailing time of 159 days, 2 hours, and 26 minutes.

FRANK LITSKY

SPORTS SUMMARIES[1]

ARCHERY—World Champions: men's singles: Rich McKinney, Glendale, AZ; team: United States; women's singles: Jin Ho Kim, South Korea; team: South Korea.

BADMINTON—U.S. Champions: men's singles: Rodney Barton, Tempe, AZ; women's singles: Cheryl Carton, San Diego, CA.

BIATHLON—World Champions: men's 10 km: Erik Kvalfoss, Norway; 20 km: Frank Ullrich, E. Germany; world cup: Peter Angerer, W. Germany.

BILLIARDS—World Champions: men's pocket: Steve Mizerak, Fords, NJ; women's pocket: Jean Balukas, Brooklyn, NY; world three-cushion: Ray Ceulemans, Belgium.

BOBSLEDDING—World Champions: two-man: Ralph Pichler and Urs Levthold, Switzerland; four-man: Ekkehard Fasser (driver), Switzerland.

BOWLING—Professional Bowling Association: national champion: Earl Anthony, Dublin, CA; men's world cup: Yu-Tien Chu, Taiwan; women's world cup: Jeannette Baker, Australia. **American Bowling Congress:** singles: Rickey Kendrick, Springfield, IL; doubles: Rick McCardy and Tony Loiacano, Detroit, MI; all-events: Tony Cariello, Chicago, IL; masters: Mike Lastowski, Havre de Grace, MD; team: Doug Hime's Niagara Frontier Bowling Supply, Niagara Falls, NY. **Women's International Bowling Congress:** open division, singles: Aleta Rzepecki, Detroit; doubles: Jeanne Maiden, Solon, OH, and Sue Robb, Euclid, OH; all-events: Virginia Norton, South Gate, CA; team: Telectronic Systems, Inc.

CANOEING—U.S. Champions (flatwater): kayak: men's 500 m: Terry White, Peru, VT; 1,000 m: Terry White; 10,000 m: Greg Barton, Homer, MI; women's 500 m: Cathy Marino-Gregory, Huntington Beach, CA; canoe: men's 500 m: Rob Plankenhorn, Roselle, IL; 1,000 m: Rob Plankenhorn; 10,000 m: Rob Plankenhorn.

CRICKET—World Champion: India.

CROSS COUNTRY—World Champions: men: Bekele Debele, Ethiopia; women: Grete Waitz, Norway. **NCAA:** men: Zakaria Barie, Texas-El Paso; women: Betty Springs, North Carolina State.

CURLING—World Champions: men: Ed Werenich, Canada; women: Penny LaRocque, Canada.

CYCLING—Tour de France: Laurent Fignon, France. **World Pro Champions:** sprint: Koichi Nakano, Japan; pursuit: Steele Bishop, Australia; road: Greg LeMond, New York City. **U.S. Amateur Road Racing Champions:** men: Ron Keifel, Denver, CO; women: Rebecca Twigg, Colorado Springs, CO.

DOG SHOWS—Westminster (New York): best: Ch. Kabik's The Challenger, Afghan owned by Chris and Marguerite Terrell, Anacortes, WA. **International** (Chicago): best: Ch. Seaward's Blackbeard, Newfoundland owned by Seaward Kennels, Manchester Center, VT.

FENCING—U.S. Champions: men's foil: Mark Smith, Philadelphia, PA; epée: Paul Presthy, New York City; saber: Peter Westbrook, New York City; women's foil: Debra Waples, Portland, OR. **NCAA:** men's team: Wayne State; women's team: Penn State.

FIELD HOCKEY—NCAA (women): Old Dominion.

GYMNASTICS—World Champions: men's all-around: Dmitri Belozertchev, USSR; team: China; women's all-around: Natalia Yurtchenko, USSR; team: USSR. **U.S. Gymnastics Federation Champions:** men's all-around: Mitch Gaylord, Van Nuys, CA; women's all-around: Dianne Durham, Gary, IN. **NCAA:** men's team: Nebraska; women's team: Utah.

HANDBALL—U.S. Handball Association Champions (4-wall): men's singles: Naty Alvarado, Hesperia, CA; women's singles: Diane Harmon, Long Beach, CA; collegiate team: Lake Forest (IL).

HORSESHOE PITCHING—World Champions: men: Dale Lipovsky, Bloomington, MN; women: Phyllis Negaard, St. Joseph, MN.

HORSE SHOWS—World Cup: Norman Dello Joio, Bedford, NY, on I Love You. **U.S. Equestrian Team Champions:** three-day event: Bruce Davidson, Chesterton, PA, on J. J. Babu and Pilot Kid; show jumping: Michael Matz, Collegeville, PA, on Chef; dressage: Robert Dover, Alexandria, VA, on Romantico.

JAI ALAI—World Champions: front court: Jesus (Ondarres) Ariola, Spain; back court: Ricardo (Lasa) Sotil, Trumbull, CT.

JUDO—U.S. Champions: men's 132-lb class: Edward Liddie, Union City, GA; 143: Craig Agena, Colorado Springs; 156: Mike Swain, Middletown, NY; 172: Kenny Patteson, Los Angeles; 189: Robert Berland, Wilmette, IL; under 209: Leo White, U.S. Army; over 209: Miguel Tudela, Los Angeles; open: Dewey Mitchell, Seven Springs, FL. Women's 106-lb class: Darlene Anaya, Albuquerque, NM; 114: Robin Takemori, Alexandria, VA; 123: Ann-Marie Burns, Spring Valley, CA; 134: Robin Chapman, Rahway, NJ; 145: Christine Penick, San Jose, CA; 158: Tina Stump, Baltimore, MD; over 158: Margaret Castro, New York City; open: Heidi Baversachs, New York City.

LACROSSE—NCAA: men's Div. I: Syracuse; Div. III: Hobart; women: Delaware. **Club Champion:** Maryland Lacrosse.

LUGE—World Champions: men's singles: Miroslav Zajonc, Canada; doubles: Jorg Hoffman and Jochen Pietzsch, E. Germany; women's singles: Steffi Martin, E. Germany.

MODERN PENTATHLON—World Champions: men: Anatoly Starostin, USSR; women: Lynn Chorobrywy, Canada. **U.S. Champions:** men: Dean Glenesk, Santa Maria, CA; women: Ruth Hayes, Medina, CA.

PADDLEBALL—U.S. Champions (4-wall): men: Steve Wilson, Flint, MI; women: Carla Teare, Clarkston, MI.

POLO—World Cup: Anadariya. **Gold Cup:** White Birch. **America Cup:** Aloha, Hawaii. **North America Cup:** San Antonio. **U.S. Open:** Fort Lauderdale.

RACQUETBALL—U.S. Champions: men's amateur open: Dan Ferris, St. Cloud, MN; women's open: Cindy Baxter, Lewistown, PA; men's pro: Mike Yellen, Southfield, MI; women's pro: Lynn Adams, Costa Mesa, CA.

RODEO—Professional Rodeo Cowboy Association: all-around: Roy Cooper, Durant, OK.

ROWING—International Rowing Federation Lightweight Champions: single sculls: Denmark; doubles: Italy; straight 4: Spain; eight: Spain. **U.S. Collegiate Champions:** pair with coxswain: Navy; pair without coxswain: MIT, Massachusetts; four with coxswain: Wisconsin; four without coxswain: Wisconsin; eight: Brown. **National Women's Rowing Association Champions:** single sculls: Virginia Gilder, Boston, R.C.; pair with coxswain: Virginia Gilder and Ann Strayer, Boston, R.C.; pair without coxswain: Abigail Peck and Sue Proctor, Boston, R.C.; four with coxswain: College Boat Club, PA; four without coxswain: Canadian National Team; eight: Boston, R.C.

RUGBY—U.S. Champions: club: Old Blues, Berkeley, CA; collegiate: University of California, Berkeley. **Test Matches:** Australia 49, United States 3; Canada 15, United States 9.

SHOOTING—U.S. National Rifle and Pistol Champions: men's pistol: Roger Willis, Fort Benning, GA; small-bore rifle, 3-positions: Lones Wigger, Fort Benning, GA; small-bore rifle, prone: David Weaver, Oil City, PA; high-power rifle, Patrick McCann, Staunton, IL. Women's pistol: Ruby Fox, Parker, AZ; small-bore rifle, 3 positions: Kirsten Pasch, Hibbing, MN; small-bore rifle, prone: Carolynn Millard, Tullahoma, TN; high-power rifle: Nona McCollough, Newhall, CA.

SOFTBALL—U.S. Amateur Softball Association Champions: men's major fast pitch: Franklin Cardinals, West Haven, CT; class-A fast pitch: Holiday Market, Chico, CA; major slow pitch: Number One Electric, Gastonia, NC; class-A slow pitch: Lawson Auto Parts, Altamonte Springs, FL; women's major fast pitch: Raybestos Brakettes, Stratford, CT; class-A fast pitch: Bettencourt Plumbing, Hayward, CA; major slow pitch: The Spooks, Anoka, MN; class-A slow pitch: Somerset, Sacramento, CA.

SQUASH—World Champion: Janhangir Khan, Pakistan; **U.S.Champion:** Mark Talbott, Kudjoe Keys, FL.

TABLE TENNIS—U.S. Champion: men: Eric Boggan, Merrick, NY.

VOLLEYBALL—U.S. Champions: men: Nautilus Pacifica, Long Beach, CA; women: Syntex, Stockton, CA; **NCAA (men):** UCLA.

WATER POLO—World Cup: USSR. **U.S. Champions:** men's outdoor: Newport Beach, CA; women's outdoor: Seal Beach, CA. **NCAA:** University of California, Berkeley.

WEIGHTLIFTING—U.S. Weightlifting Federation Champions: men's 114-lb class: Dirk Yasko, Great Bend, KS; 123: Ron Crawley, Washington, DC; 132: Brian Miyamoto, Los Angeles; 148: Michael Jacques, Atlanta; 165: Cal Schake, Butler, PA; 181: Curt White, Colorado Springs; 198: Michael Cohen, Savannah, GA; 220: Ken Clark, Pacifica, CA; 242: Jeff Michaels, Chicago; over 242: Mario Martinez, Salinas, CA. Women's 97-lb class: Miriam Hoffer, S. Euclid, OH; 105: Karen Derwin, Snoqualmie, WA; 114: Kathy Regan, St. Charles, IL; 123: Mary Beth Cervenak, Colorado Springs; 132: Jane Camp, Smyrna, GA; 148: Judy Glenney, Farmington, NM; 165: Lisa Long, Auburn, WA; 181: Karyn Tarter, New Rochelle, NY; over 181: Lorna Griffin, Huntington Beach, CA.

WRESTLING—World Champion (freestyle): team: USSR. **AAU Freestyle:** 105.5-lb class: Bobby Weaver, Lehigh, PA; 114.5: Joe Gonzalez, Bakersfield, CA; 125.5: Barry Davis, Iowa City; 136.5: Lee Roy Smith, Stillwater, OK; 149.5: Nate Carr, Ames, IA; 163: Dave Schultz, Palo Alto, CA; 180.5: Mark Schultz, Palo Alto; 198: Ed Banach, Iowa City; 220: Greg Gibson, U.S. Marines; heavyweight: Bruce Baumgartner, Stillwater. **AAU Greco-Roman:** 105.5: Mark Fuller, Little C A.C.; 114.5: Jeff Clark, Voorheesville, NY; 125.5: Rob Hermann, Navy; 136.5: Abdurrahim Kuzu, Lincoln, NE; 149.5: Jim Martinez, Minneapolis, MN; 163: Jim Andre, Minneapolis; 180.5: Dan Chandler, Minneapolis; 198: Mike Hauck, Robbinsdale, MN; 220: Dennis Koslowski, St. Paul, MN; heavyweight: Pete Lee, Grand Rapids, MI. **NCAA:** 118: Adam Cuestas, California State, Bakersfield; 126: Barry Davis, Iowa; 134: Clark Anderson, Oklahoma State; 142: Darryl Burley, Lehigh; 150: Nate Carr, Iowa State; 158: Lenny Zalesky, Iowa; 167: Mike Sheets, Oklahoma State; 177: Mark Schultz, Oklahoma; 190: Ed Banach, Iowa; heavyweight: Lou Banach, Iowa; team: Iowa.

---

[1] Sports not covered separately in pages 464–488.

SRI LANKA

The government, headed by President Junius R. Jayewardene, continued to strengthen its political position in 1983. It also adopted austerity measures to deal with a shaky economy and took strong action to counter the worst outbreak of violence since independence.

Political Events. The Sri Lankan Parliament, elected in 1977, was due to expire in 1983, but a national referendum on Dec. 22, 1982, overwhelmingly approved a six-year extension. On Feb. 4, 1983, Jayewardene began his second term as president. A few days later his dynamic finance minister, Ronnie de Mel, together with several deputy ministers and members of the ruling United National Party (UNP) in the Parliament, resigned under pressure. This seemed to strengthen rather than weaken the position of the UNP, which before parliamentary by-elections on May 18 had 125 of the 168 seats in the Parliament. In the by-elections the UNP won 14 of the 18 parliamentary seats and control of 9 of 12 municipal councils and 25 of 34 urban councils.

The elections were preceded by a major wave of terrorism and violence. On April 29 three prominent members of the UNP were killed in the northern city of Jaffna, the center of the Tamil population. The murders were generally attributed to an outlawed guerrilla group known as the "Liberation Tigers" and were strongly disavowed by the Tamil United Liberation Front, the leading opposition party.

The state of emergency imposed in October 1982 had been allowed to lapse on Jan. 20, 1983, but it was reimposed after the May elections. In late July a second and even more serious wave of violence erupted, involving the two major communal groups in the country, the dominant Buddhist Sinhalese and the Hindu Tamils. The violence escalated rapidly after 13 soldiers were killed in an ambush in Jaffna on July 25. According to government figures (generally regarded as far too low) the communal violence resulted in 179 deaths between July 25 and July 29. Hundreds of Tamils were rounded up and confined in prisons or refugee camps. Arson attacks destroyed the homes of several thousand Tamils. On August 3 the government proscribed three leftist parties and arrested many of their leaders.

The Economy. In its annual report, released on April 29, the Central Bank of Sri Lanka stressed the adverse impact of the international economic climate on primary producers like Sri Lanka. It also emphasized the country's disappointing agricultural performance, due in part to drought. The bank reported a general slowing down in the economy and a deterioration in the terms of trade for the fourth successive year. On the positive side it noted that the per capita income had increased 3.5%. The national budget, presented to Parliament on February 9, envisioned a deficit of $1.3 billion (U.S.) and a continuing rise in the external debt. The budget included a series of austerity measures. It also reflected a continuing reliance on export markets and on external aid.

Foreign Affairs. President Jayewardene participated in the nonaligned summit conference in New Delhi in March and in the Commonwealth summit in New Delhi and Goa in November. In August he made a state visit to Britain. Meanwhile, in April and May, Prime Minister Ranasinghe Premadasa visited five countries, including the United States. A ten-member Chinese delegation made a goodwill visit to Sri Lanka in March.

NORMAN D. PALMER,
University of Pennsylvania

STAMPS AND STAMP COLLECTING

After a decade of the wildest speculative buying of glamour stamps in philatelic history, the market finally declined to more realistic levels. Prices dropped dramatically to affordable levels, and collectors again were able to obtain needed items for their albums.

The decreased prices hurt some who had invested during the boom. The worst monetary beating was taken by a financier, who in 1977 had been convinced by a self-styled "philatelic investment adviser" to buy a block of four 1918 airmail stamps with inverted plane. Ignorant of true stamp values, he had paid $500,000 for the block which was once owned by Princeton University. When the block was offered at auction on Dec. 13, 1982, only one dealer advanced the opening bid and got it for $175,000.

In Washington, the Postal Service so intensified its production of stamps and pseudo-philatelic novelties that stamp collectors vociferously charged that their avocation was being

Selected U.S. Commemorative Stamps, 1983

Subject	Denomination	Date
Science	20¢	Jan. 19
Nonprofit	5.2¢	March 21
Sweden	20¢	March 24
Handcar	3¢ coil	March 25
Ballooning	4x20¢ block	March 31
Civilian Conservation Corps	20¢	April 5
Olympics	4x40¢ air-mails	April 8
Joseph Priestly	20¢	April 13
Volunteers	20¢	April 20
German Immigrants	20¢	April 29
Physical Fitness	20¢	May 14
Brooklyn Bridge	20¢	May 17
TVA	20¢	May 18
Carl Schurz	4¢	June 3
Medal of Honor	20¢	June 7
Scott Joplin	20¢	June 9
Thomas H. Gallaudet	20¢	June 10
Olympics	4x28¢ air-mails	June 17
Pearl Buck	5¢	June 25
Babe Ruth	20¢	July 6
Nathaniel Hawthorne	20¢	July 8
Henry Clay	3¢	July 13
Olympics	4x13¢	July 28
Omnibus	1¢	Aug. 19
Treaty of Paris	20¢	Sept. 2
Civil Service	20¢	Sept. 9
Metropolitan Opera	20¢	Sept. 14
Inventors	4x20¢	Sept. 21
Dorothea Dix	1¢	Sept. 23
Streetcars	4x20¢	Oct. 8
Motorcycles	5¢ coil	Oct. 10
Christmas	2x20¢	Oct. 28
Olympics	4x35¢ air-mails	Nov. 4
Martin Luther	20¢	Nov. 11
Booklet	$4	Nov. 17
Olympics	28¢ air-mail	Dec. 29

exploited to lessen postal deficits. Particularly criticized were the large number of stamps and blocks to publicize the 1984 Olympics and a $9.35 stamp to prepay basic charges on Express Mail. The latter has the highest face value of any domestic stamp made for public use.

In addition to processing 77,858 first-day covers for collectors and the trade, the Postal Service affixed one of these to each of 260,000 envelopes carried by the *Challenger* space shuttle mission. When the shuttle returned, the covers were inserted in a folder and sold for $15.35, with a limit of one, later increased to two per order. To assuage protests by collectors and the International Stamp Dealers Federation, the Postal Service announced that $500,000 of the premium would help finance a 1986 stamp show in Chicago.

United Nations stamps began to lose some of their appeal. Collectors felt that unduly large numbers had been produced for sale at the New York headquarters and for the Geneva and Vienna offices. A philatelic writer discovered that 1982's printing orders had been cut by 200,000 specimens of new issues.

Major international stamp exhibitions were held in Brazil, Great Britain, Italy, Switzerland, and Thailand.

As 1983 ended, the Society of Philatelic Americans, the second-largest U.S. collectors group, announced that it was bankrupt and would end its 90-year existence.

ERNEST A. KEHR
Director, Stamp News Bureau

STOCKS AND BONDS

The U.S. stock market rose sharply in record trading for the second consecutive year in 1983, as the economy began a vigorous recovery from a long recession.

Riding the momentum of a historic rally that began in August 1982, the Dow Jones average of 30 industrials—the oldest and best-known yardstick of stock-price trends—repeatedly set new highs, reaching a peak of 1,287.29 on November 29. It closed out the year at 1,258.64, for a net gain of 212.10 points, or 20.3%, after having risen 19.6% in 1982.

Volume on the New York Stock Exchange (NYSE) totaled 21.59 billion shares, far surpassing the previous high of 16.46 billion in 1982. Figures from other leading markets told a similar story. In the National Association of Securities Dealers' Automated Quotes (NASDAQ) system, a computerized network of dealers in over-the-counter stocks, an unprecedented total of more than 15 billion shares was traded.

Corporations large and small capitalized on the revived popularity of stocks by selling new shares in record amounts. In the first nine months of the year, 598 companies "went public" by selling stock on the open market for the first time. These offerings alone raised almost $9.5 billion (U.S.) in capital.

The thriving markets also prompted a proliferation of new ways to play the ups and downs of stock prices—e.g., futures and options contracts on various market indexes or on specific industry groups. While these brought new sources of revenue to Wall Street, some industry leaders voiced concern that their rapid growth could foster excessive speculation.

With the continuing deregulation of the financial-services industry, many businesses sought new ways to tap the public's appetite for stocks and other investments. Banks expanded their securities services, testing the limits of decades-old laws separating their roles from those of brokerage firms. Some retailing and supermarket chains experimented with financial-services departments.

All the participants in this scramble got plenty of encouragement from the domestic economy, which was putting on its best performance in years. Experts calculated that the nation's worst recession since the 1930s reached bottom in November 1982. By the second quarter of 1983, government figures showed the gross national product growing at a 9.7% annual rate, after adjustment for inflation. In the third quarter, the pace was almost as rapid, at an estimated 7.7%. Unemployment remained a stubborn problem, but the jobless rate was falling steadily, to 8.2% by November from 10.8% at the end of 1982. Inflation, meanwhile, appeared to remain dormant as the economy heated up. As of November, the

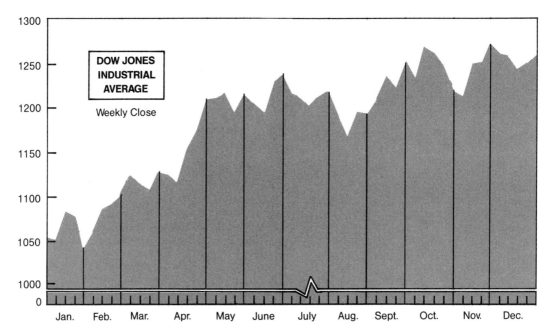

Consumer Price Index stood just 2.9% above its level of 12 months earlier.

But the bond market, which had enjoyed a banner year in 1982, lost a lot of its zip as 1983 passed and interest rates remained high. In the waning weeks of the year, the bank prime lending rate stood at 11%. Some experts laid the blame for the high cost of credit at the door of the Federal Reserve, whose chairman, Paul Volcker, declared his intention of keeping inflation under control by limiting the growth of the money supply. Others, including Volcker, said the real culprit was the federal-budget deficit, running at about $200 billion annually. The gap between the government's income and outlay meant that the treasury had to borrow heavily and often in the credit markets.

There were some other developments to dampen investors' spirits as the year passed. For one thing, "high technology," a phrase almost synonymous with glamour in the early stages of the bull market, proved to have its pitfalls. Makers of video games and small computers announced one disappointing financial result after another, sometimes with dramatic results in the stock market. In October, for example, when Digital Equipment Corp. said it expected a big drop in earnings, the shares of the maker of minicomputers fell $21 in a day.

Stocks of leading publicly owned Wall Street houses also fell in the summer and early fall, after a dramatic rise in late 1982 and the first half of 1983. The firms were doing a brisk business, but it became clear that their costs had also mounted rapidly as they added staff, offices, and equipment to handle the increased load. At the NYSE, facilities were being expanded to handle a trading volume of as much as 250 million shares per day.

Amid its problems, however, there were also some historic high points for Wall Street during the year. In late November, the Big Board conducted its largest single-day introduction of new stock ever—more than 1.5 billion shares of the eight companies created by the breakup of the nation's largest company, American Telephone & Telegraph. Though the "children of Ma Bell" were not scheduled to become separate entities until 1984, under an agreement that settled an old antitrust case brought by the government, their stocks began trading early on a "when-issued" basis to allow the markets to begin setting a value on each piece. The new stocks did a combined volume of more than 30 million shares in the first four days of trading.

U.S. institutions and individuals, of course, were the main participants in such stock-market dramas. But foreign investors also played a significant and growing role. A strong dollar in the foreign-exchange markets helped to heighten the allure of U.S. stocks for international investors. At midyear, according to the Securities Industry Association, foreign investors owned more than 10% of the total market value of stocks listed on American exchanges.

Wall Street's strong showing during the year was mirrored in the gains posted by most markets in other leading industrialized countries. In late November a world index of nine markets, calculated by Capital International S.A. of Geneva, was up 16.7% from the end of 1982. The Australian market led the pack, up more than 51%; followed by France, up 50%; Germany, up 33%; Canada, up 26%; Britain, up 20%; Switzerland, up 17%; Japan, up 13%; and Hong Kong, up 4%.

CHET CURRIER, *The Associated Press*

SUDAN

For the government of President Jaafar al-Nemery, beleaguered by opposition for most of his 14 years in office, 1983 was another trying year. By late 1983, kidnapping of foreign nationals was increasing, unrest in the southern regions was growing, and resistance from Islamic fundamentalist groups in the north also was rising.

Foreign Relations. The world's attention was focused on Sudan in February, when Libya was accused of plotting to invade Sudan and overthrow Nemery. Egyptian intelligence charged that the plan involved lightning-fast assaults across the border, the assassination of Nemery, and the capture of Khartoum airport by Libyan troops, who would then install Sudanese dissidents in power. U.S. President Ronald Reagan dispatched four Airborne Warning and Control System (AWACS) planes, as tension built on the Sudan-Libya border. Many observers were skeptical as to whether the Libyan threat ever was real, but that passed quickly after several arrests were made and Sudan found itself with $60 million in U.S. aid instead of the $25 million originally slated. In September, Nemery again accused Libya, along with Iran, Ethiopia, and the USSR of plotting to overthrow his regime.

Domestic Politics and Internal Security. At the same time, there was a resurgence of resistance in Sudan's Christian South against domination from the Arab-Muslim North. A group calling itself Anya Nya II, after the group which waged war against the Khartoum government for 17 years until 1972, claimed responsibility for a number of attacks on northerners in the South. In May army garrisons composed of southerners mutinied, but the rebellion was rapidly quelled by loyalist troops flown in from the North; the captured soldiers were executed. In June a previously unknown group calling itself the Southern Sudan Liberation Front (SSLF) captured 11 foreign missionaries and aid workers and held them for ransom. The Sudanese army rescued the hostages unharmed. Libyan involvement was charged in all of these incidents.

Southern Sudan, which was granted partial autonomy as part of the 1972 truce with the North, lost that autonomy in the midst of the violence. The region was divided into three provinces, Bahr Al Ghazal, Equatoria, and Upper Nile. The move was aimed at dividing southern opposition to the government.

Meanwhile, Nemery was also facing opposition in the North from Islamic fundamentalist groups. In part to head off fundamentalist attacks on his regime, Nemery announced in September that Sudan would adopt the code of the *sharia,* Islamic law. Days later he arrested members of the Muslim Ansar movement, including their leader, former Prime Minister Sadiq al-Mahdi, who had been campaigning for the adoption of the *sharia* as well as agitating against Nemery. The new code prohibits consumption of alcohol and punishes the crime of theft by amputation of a hand. Sudan's jails were then emptied of all prisoners because they had not been sentenced under the *sharia*. President Nemery also offered amnesty to southern rebels still at large.

Economy. Early in the year, Sudan reached agreement on the rescheduling of its $3 billion debt. The deal included price hikes and a devaluation. Sudan's oil fields began producing more, and agreements were completed for the construction of a 900-mi (1 448-km) pipeline to carry the oil to Port Sudan.

MICHAEL MAREN
Assistant Editor, "Africa Report"

SWEDEN

A generally improving economic picture, despite a record unemployment rate exceeding 4% in August, and continued friction with the Soviet Union over the suspected presence of Soviet submarines in Swedish waters were among the highlights of the year 1983 in Sweden.

The Economy. The production rate of Swedish industry moved upward in 1983, owing mainly to an increase in exports amounting to 50% of all industrial output. The 16% devaluation of the krona announced by the new Social-Democratic government that took office in the late fall of 1982 aided the export trade (exports to the United States alone had increased by 17.4% by the fall of 1983) and made businessmen optimistic. Business was concerned, however, about the government's proposal to introduce "wage earners' funds," described by the four main employers' associations as "a form of socialization that has not been tried anywhere else in the world" and as representing "a radical change at a time when Sweden's economy is in crisis."

The funds—which would comprise voting stock rather than cash—were authored by economist Rudolf Meidner of the Swedish trade union confederation (LO) and proposed by the LO for more than eight years. They have

---

SUDAN • Information Highlights

Official Name: Democratic Republic of Sudan.
Location: Northeast Africa.
Area: 966,988 sq mi (2 504 503 km²).
Population (July 1983 est.): 20,585,000.
Government: *Head of state,* Gen. Jaafar Mohammed al-Nemery, president. *Legislature* (unicameral)— National People's Assembly.
Monetary Unit: Pound (1.300 pounds equals U.S.$1, June 1983).
Foreign Trade (1982 U.S.$): *Imports,* $1,285,000,000; *exports,* $499,000,000.

Svenskt Pressefoto/Pictorial Parade

European Royalty: King Carl XVI Gustaf of Sweden welcomed Britain's Queen Elizabeth II in Stockholm in May.

been reduced in number since their original proposal from 24 to 5, and a variety of contributions to them has been reduced to "cash based on real profits." As proposed in Parliament, a tax of up to 20% of company profits would be levied to raise money for the funds. Adjustments would be made for inflation. The funds would be used to buy shares in the companies on behalf of employees. By 1990, it was estimated, the purchased shares would represent 7% of all Swedish industry. The funds might thus be considered an extra pension fund based on profit sharing.

In August 1983, Datatronic, Sweden's leading manufacturer of computer programs, announced that it would be moving its main operations to the United States, starting with the software division. Other companies were expected to follow Datatronic's example and to cause an exodus of venture capital if the government should set up such union-controlled investment funds at the expense of privately owned companies. On October 4, some 75,000 business leaders and white-collar workers held a march in Stockholm to protest the proposed wage earners' funds program.

The Ericsson Company, specializing in telecommunications, made stock offers in the United States in 1980 and 1983. Anaconda-Ericsson, the U.S. company involved, had about 15% of Ericsson's capital in American hands in the form of depository receipts representing rights to the Swedish shares, traded over the counter.

Foreign Policy. On April 26, Sweden recalled its ambassador to the Soviet Union and issued a strong protest, accusing the USSR of sending six submarines on spying missions into Swedish waters, one of them near a top-secret Swedish naval base, in the fall of 1982. In 1983, at least one, and possibly four, incursions by Soviet submarines into Swedish waters were suspected.

On March 24, Sweden and the Vatican renewed diplomatic relations after a break of about 450 years. Diplomatic relations between the two states were broken in the 16th century when Sweden, Denmark, and Norway established an independent Lutheran church.

Defense. The submarine incursions prompted an improvement in and expansion of Sweden's antisubmarine capability. Aware of a possible Soviet threat to northern Sweden, the government relocated a squadron of interceptor aircraft to Lulea in the north as a defense against incursion by land or air. Included in this program was $136 million for improvement and expansion of the helicopter segment of the armed forces.

Sweden planned to develop a new air-to-air missile for its existing JA-37 interceptor planes. The government has placed a contract for the first 30 of a planned 140 JAS-39 multipurpose combat aircraft, and has planned a new low-level surveillance radar system. An increased defense budget for 1983–84 called for modernization of defense control centers.

MAC LINDAHL, *Free-Lance Writer*

SWEDEN • Information Highlights

Official Name: Kingdom of Sweden.
Location: Northern Europe.
Area: 161,753 sq mi (448 070 km²).
Population (July 1983 est.): 8,331,000.
Chief Cities (Dec. 31, 1980): Stockholm, the capital, 647,214; Göteborg, 431,273; Malmö, 233,803; Uppsala, 146,192.
Government: *Head of state,* Carl XVI Gustaf, King (acceded Sept. 1973). *Head of government,* Olof Palme, prime minister (took office Oct. 7, 1982). *Legislature* (unicameral)—Riksdag.
Monetary Unit: Krona (7.779 kronor equal U.S. $1 Oct. 20, 1983).
Gross Domestic Product (1982 U.S.$): $98,795,-000,000.
Economic Indexes (1982): *Consumer Prices* (1970 = 100), all items, 294.0; food, 321.6. *Industrial production* (1975 = 100), 96.
Foreign Trade (1982 U.S.$): *Imports,* $27,573,-000,000; *exports,* $26,822,000,000.

SWITZERLAND

Economic issues, plus deteriorating Soviet-Swiss relations, marked Swiss affairs in 1983.

Soviet-Swiss Tensions. On April 29 the Swiss government expelled the chief correspondent of *Soviet Novosti*, the Russian news agency in Switzerland, and closed its Bern office. Allegations of Russian attempts to use Swiss employees of the agency to infiltrate antinuclear and dissident youth movements were only the latest in a series of espionage charges resulting in the expulsion of Soviet diplomatic officials on January 7 and February 27.

Dioxin Scandal. Between April and June, Swiss attention was riveted on an international hunt for 41 missing cans of dioxin-impregnated earth, produced by a 1976 explosion at the Seveso, Italy, subsidiary of the Swiss firm of Hoffmann-LaRoche. Finally located in France on May 19, the material was trucked to Basel and incinerated. On September 24, five former Hoffmann-LaRoche executives were found guilty of charges stemming from the explosion.

International Fiscal Affairs. In January the inner circle "Group of Ten" of the 146-member International Monetary Fund agreed to admit Switzerland as a full member, even though it does not formally belong to the IMF. This "Group of Eleven" constitutes those nations who contribute heavily to the IMF and therefore control its use.

The American Express Co. announced plans on January 18 to purchase Trade Developing Bank Holding SA., which would make American Express' International Banking Corporation one of the five largest Swiss banks.

A major confrontation with the United States occurred on August 12 when the Swiss government seized records and files of the Swiss commodities trading firm, Marc Rich and Co. AG. The firm had agreed reluctantly to provide documents to an American grand jury that was investigating possible income-tax evasion by Marc Rich's American subsidiary.

Swiss officials indicated on September 21 that the documents would not be released until the U.S. government ensured that Swiss laws would not be compromised.

Economic Concerns. In light of increasingly severe competition from Hong Kong and Japan, Switzerland's two largest watchmakers announced plans to merge on May 15. The makers of Longines and Omega watches hoped that resulting efficiencies would allow the industry to regain the 30% of the world market it had lost in the past decade.

In a related matter, the union representing 300,000 workers in the watch industry agreed on July 9 to a pact reducing the workweek in stages from 42 to 40 hours by 1988. This agreement not only preserved the national record of strike-free labor-management relations since 1937 but also promised to ease problems of unemployment.

On August 24 the Swiss government announced its decision to purchase 420 West German Leopold II tanks during the next 15 years. This order, the largest Swiss military contract ever placed with a foreign country, was won by West Germany because it agreed to allow 70% of the tanks to be assembled in Switzerland, thus providing employment.

PAUL C. HELMREICH, *Wheaton College (MA)*

SYRIA

In 1983, Syria regained the preeminent position in Arab politics it had lost following its woeful military performance against Israel in Lebanon in 1982. President Hafez al-Assad, rearmed by massive shipments of Soviet weaponry, used his army's strong positions in the Bekaa Valley to dictate events in Lebanon and used his ability to manipulate Palestine Liberation Organization (PLO) factions not only to scuttle a major U.S. peace initiative but also to curb, if not destroy, PLO Chairman Yasir Arafat's independence.

Role in Lebanon. Syria's occupation of nearly half of Lebanon allowed Assad to play a power broker's role while Lebanese President Amin Gemayel attempted to consolidate his government's authority, rebuild his army, and negotiate the withdrawal of Syrian, PLO, and Israeli forces. By refusing to negotiate with the Israelis, Assad greatly influenced internal events and the U.S.-mediated Israeli-Lebanese talks. All parties realized that whatever was negotiated would require Assad's approval if Lebanon were to be free of foreign forces.

While Assad had maintained that Syria would withdraw only after Israel had done so, two days after U.S. Secretary of State George Shultz's May 7 meeting with Assad in Damascus, the Syrian Information Ministry announced that Assad would consider a simultaneous withdrawal. When a final Leba-

---

SWITZERLAND • Information Highlights

Official Name: Swiss Confederation.
Location: Central Europe.
Area: 15,998.9 sq mi (41 440 km²).
Population (July 1983): 6,463,000.
Chief Cities (1980): Bern, the capital, 145,254; Zurich, 369,522; Basel, 182,143.
Government: *Head of state*, Pierre Aubert, president, (took office Jan. 1983). *Legislature*—Federal Assembly: Council of States and National Council.
Monetary Unit: Franc (2.2135 francs equal U.S.$1, Dec. 16, 1983).
Gross Domestic Product (1982 U.S.$): $196,100,000,000.
Economic Index (1982): *Consumer Prices* (1970 = 100), all items, 182.8; food, 192.0. *Industrial Production* (1975 = 100), 109.
Foreign Trade (1982 U.S.$): *Imports*, $28,670,000,000; *exports*, $26,024,000,000.

nese-Israeli agreement was reached on May 17, however, Syria rejected the plan out of hand and refused to withdraw. In early June, Assad increased his troop strength in Lebanon from 30,000 to 50,000.

By rejecting the pact (because it came too close to "normalizing" relations with Israel), Assad positioned himself perfectly to determine the outcome of Gemayel's long-delayed attempt to bring Lebanon's warring factions into a national reconciliation dialogue. In fact, Assad dictated the composition of the government's delegation, the site, and the agenda of the meeting by manipulating events during a September outbreak of fighting in Lebanon's Chouf Mountains. By sustaining the Muslim opposition's ability to fight government troops and their Christian militia allies to a standstill (thus delaying the start of reconciliation talks), Assad brokered the conditions of the September 26 cease-fire with the threat of unleashing the opposition again if he became displeased with political developments.

Syria's primary goals at the reconciliation talks, which began October 31 in Geneva, Switzerland, were clear: abrogation of the May 17 pact, Israeli withdrawal, and the installation of a decidedly pro-Arab government in Lebanon. The insistence of Syrian Foreign Minister Abdel Halim al-Khaddam, an official observer, that the conferees immediately address the Israeli agreement forced a temporary adjournment after only four days and a desperation trip by Gemayel to the United States and Arab capitals to seek a way out of the impasse.

U.S. Peace Plan and the PLO. Assad was just as ruthless in his handling of developments surrounding an American proposal calling for Israeli-Jordanian negotiations over the future of the occupied West Bank. Assad previously had rejected the September 1982 initiative because it did not address Syria's right to reclaim the strategic Golan Heights, annexed by Israel in December 1981.

More importantly, PLO Chairman Arafat, who had enraged Assad by publicly scorning Syria's military showing the previous summer, appeared willing to sell out his former benefactor by bargaining with Jordan's King Hussein for a role in the U.S. scheme. Accordingly, Assad used his control over the PLO's most radical elements to induce them to reject the U.S proposal, in February. By April he had caused a breakdown of the Arafat-Hussein negotiations with a threat to split the PLO by supporting a rival, Damascus-based group to represent Palestinians in Syria and Lebanon.

By late May, Assad was able to incite a full-scale rebellion within the PLO ranks. Arafat was expelled from Damascus on June 24 and denied access to his followers in Syrian-occupied Lebanon. When Arafat secretly reentered Lebanon in September, rebellious PLO troops supported by the Syrian army drove Arafat loyalists out of the Bekaa Valley, forcing them to retreat to refugee camps in northern Lebanon, outside Tripoli. By early November, Arafat and the last remnants of his Fatah power base were surrounded. On November 23 the Arafat faction and the Syrian-backed PLO rebels agreed to a cease-fire arrangement promoted by Saudi Arabia. On December 20, Arafat and 4,000 of his supporters were evacuated from Tripoli in five Greek transport ships.

Power and Prestige. Syria's standing in the Arab world—and the stakes of its involvement in Lebanon—were raised even further on December 4, when it downed two U.S. carrier jets, killing one flier and capturing another; heavy artillery fire the same day killed eight more U.S. Marines. The U.S. air raids, against Syrian antiaircraft positions east of Beirut, were said to be a response to ground attacks against unarmed reconnaissance planes and a warning against Assad's efforts to undermine the Gemayel government and force the Americans and Israelis out of Lebanon. But, even as the U.S. Sixth Fleet opened fire with heavy guns on the hills overlooking Beirut, there were signs of increasing restlessness in the United States and other MNF countries—at least among their respective legislatures and general publics—over the "peacekeeping" role. Moreover, the loss of the two planes at the hands of Syria came only a few days after a new U.S.-Israeli strategic accord that had rankled leaders throughout the Arab world.

Thus, possessing both strong Soviet and Arab support, Assad clearly was the key to future developments in the Middle East. Late in the year there were rumors of serious illness, perhaps even a heart attack, but the 53-year-old Syrian president was photographed back at work in December. Barring death or incapacitation, Assad apparently was in a position to take advantage of his new-found power and prestige. Because a military solution to the Lebanese dilemma was improbable, all diplomatic avenues seemed to end in Damascus.

See also LEBANON; MIDDLE EAST.

F. NICHOLAS WILLARD

SYRIA · Information Highlights

Official Name: Syrian Arab Republic.
Location: Southwest Asia.
Area: 72,000 sq mi (186 480 km²).
Population (July 1983 est.): 9,739,000.
Government: *Head of state*, Lt. Gen. Hafez al-Assad, president (took office officially March 1971). *Head of government*, Abdel Raouf al-Kassem, prime minister (took office Jan. 1980). *Legislature* (unicameral)—People's Council.
Monetary Unit: Pound (3.925 pounds equal U.S.$1, July 1983).
Gross Domestic Product (1981 U.S.$): $16,200,-000,000.
Economic Index (1981): *Consumer Prices* (1970 = 100), all items, 386; food, 425.
Foreign Trade (1982 U.S.$): *Imports*, $4,028,000,000; *exports*, $2,026,000,000.

TAIWAN (Republic of China)

The year 1983 saw continued political stability in Taiwan. More people took part in politics as the government widened the channels of participation. The ruling Kuomingtang captured 62 of the 71 seats contested in December elections. Taiwan's lagging economy showed signs of recovery in the second quarter. The Nationalists were much distressed by Washington's efforts to strengthen relations with Peking.

Anticommunism. Taiwan continued to stand resolute against Communist China. In January, when Deng Xiaoping again called for negotiations on peaceful reunification, Taiwan branded his proposal as more Peking double-talk to communize Taiwan. "We had held several peace talks with the Chinese Communists and learned a bitter lesson," said President Chiang Ching-kuo. "Therefore, since 1949, we have made up our minds not to talk with them again."

Peking had never publicly renounced the use of force against Taiwan. The Nationalist government reported progress on a number of projects to develop advanced weapons in case of any possible invasion. But though capable of making nuclear weapons, Taipei said that it would never develop them for use against Chinese on the mainland. The Nationalist government emphatically denied that it had cooperated with South Africa to develop nuclear bombs. And it stated that it had no contact with France or Israel in regard to military supplies.

The Economy. Taiwan's strong economic performance during the second quarter of 1983 gave signs that the downward trend in the previous two years would be reversed. With the growth rate estimated at 6.3% for the second quarter, the rate for the year was expected to exceed 6.5%.

To improve the investment climate, Taiwan took steps to relax foreign-exchange regulations. Money supply was increased to facilitate business financing, and import duties were reduced on machines. By capitalizing on its pool

Armand Borlant/Gamma-Liaison

The late Chiang Kai-shek remains an inspiration, as Taiwan maintains its anticommunism, and seeks new investment.

of highly trained, well-educated labor, Taiwan hoped to attract foreign investment in technology-intensive enterprises.

In the industrial sector, Taiwan's attention was directed to such industries as automobiles, computers, electronics, communication equipment, and precision machinery. Considering automobiles still the most important transportation means for the coming decades, Taiwan planned to produce cars that could compete in the world market. Toyota, Japan's leading automaker, agreed in July on a joint venture of automobile production in Taiwan. The plan called for manufacturing 300,000 cars annually in the early 1990s, at an eventual cost of $582 million. The Japanese were to invest no more than 49%.

In agriculture, emphasis was on enlargement of family farms, development of food processing, and better water conservation and flood control. Taiwan's price-support program for farmers, adopted in 1974 to ensure a sufficient supply of rice and to raise farmers' incomes, had led to overproduction. The rice output in 1983 was expected to reach 2.4 million metric tons, exceeding the government's target by 300,000 tons. The oversupply forced Taiwan to lower prices for rice exports.

Taiwan's foreign trade for the first eight months of 1983 totaled $28.9 billion (U.S.), an increase of 4.1% over the corresponding period of the preceding year. Exports to the United States for the first nine months were $8.1 billion against American-produced imports valued

---

TAIWAN (Republic of China) • Information Highlights

Official Name: Republic of China
Location: Island off the southeastern coast of mainland China.
Area: 13,885 sq mi (35 962 km²).
Population (mid-1983 est.): 18,900,000.
Chief Cities (Dec. 31, 1981): Taipei, the capital, 2,270,983; Kaohsiung, 1,227,454; Taichung, 607,238.
Government: *Head of state,* Chiang Ching-kuo, president (installed May 1978). *Head of government,* Sun Yunsuan, premier (took office May 1978). *Legislature* (unicameral)—Legislative Yüan.
Monetary Unit: New Taiwan dollar (38 NT dollars equal U.S.$1, Nov. 1983).
Gross National Product (1981–82 est. U.S.$): $46,000,000,000.

at $3.3 billion, for a surplus of $4.8 billion. Concerned about pressure in the United States for protectionist actions, Taiwan decided to buy more American products.

Foreign Affairs. Taiwan considers the United States its trusted friend and "natural ally" against international communism.

Taipei was unhappy about Washington's numerous efforts to placate the Chinese Communists. But it felt reassured when the United States continued to sell it advanced weapons while increasing "unofficial contacts" with Taiwan. The Nationalists were gratified at the American rejection of Peking's demand that Washington discontinue issuing visas to persons in Taiwan and prevent Americans from traveling to Taiwan.

Relations between Taiwan and South Korea were ruffled by the outcome of a hijacking incident. Six Chinese from the mainland forced a Communist Chinese plane to land at a U.S. military base near Seoul. Taipei asked that the six "freedom seekers" be allowed to go to Taiwan, but Seoul declared that they must be tried according to Korean law. Taiwan's displeasure was the more acute because of South Korea's attempts to establish relations with Communist China. Although these gestures were spurned by Peking, the six hijackers were convicted and given prison terms of four to six years. Taipei felt better when in August a Communist Chinese air force defector, Sun Dianjin, flew a MiG-21 jet fighter to South Korea and was allowed to accept political asylum in Taiwan.

See also CHINA, PEOPLE'S REPUBLIC OF.

CHESTER C. TAN, *New York University*

TANZANIA

A small but ominous army mutiny and a continued collapse of the economy were the main developments in Tanzania in 1983.

Army Mutiny. On New Year's Day 1983, a small army mutiny occurred at Bukoba barracks on Lake Victoria. Though easily suppressed, the event was a sign that even the great prestige and respect for President Julius K. Nyerere were no longer enough to keep Tanzania calm in the face of worsening economic conditions. Twenty-eight soldiers, including two lieutenant generals, were arrested for their role in the mutiny, and several civilians, including a university professor and several businessmen, also were seized for being sympathetic to the plot. Nyerere moved quickly to defuse the situation and ensure the loyalty of the army, arresting more than 300 for "sabotage" and granting the army such rare luxuries as free beer, cigarettes, and soft drinks.

Economic Decline. Tanzania was among the poorest and most depressed nations in Africa. Two consecutive years of drought caused some

---

TANZANIA · Information Highlights

Official Name: United Republic of Tanzania
Location: East coast of Africa.
Area: 362,800 sq mi (939 652 km²).
Population (July 1983): 20,524,000.
Government: *Head of state,* Julius K. Nyerere, president (took office Jan. 1964); Aboud Mwinyi Jumbe, vice-president and president of Zanzibar (elected Nov. 1980); *Head of government,* Edward Sokoine, prime minister (took office Feb. 1983). *Legislature* (unicameral)—National Assembly, 239 members.
Monetary Unit: Tanzanian shilling (12.2 shillings equal U.S.$1, June 1983).
Gross National Product Per Capita (1983 est. U.S.$): $208.
Economic Index (1981): *Consumer Prices* (1970 = 100), all items, 464.2; food, 525.2.
Foreign Trade (1981 U.S.$): *Imports,* $1,140,000,000; *exports,* $566,000,000.

---

deaths and widespread hunger, but the root of the nation's economic misery appeared to be Nyerere's insistence on hewing to a purely socialist economic course in the face of clear evidence that egalitarian, state-directed development was not working.

By 1983, Tanzania's factories were working at about 30% of capacity; fuel and spare parts were hard to obtain due to lack of foreign exchange. The country's external debt was $2.1 billion (U.S.), and the gross national product was declining by 3.6% per year. Inflation was running 34% a year, and even Nyerere, who normally spurns foreign interference or even criticism of domestic affairs, acceded to International Monetary Fund pressure and devalued the Tanzanian shilling by 20%. Imports, exports, and general economic activity all fell sharply, though actual figures are misleading since a flourishing "parallel economy," which the government was trying to suppress, was providing most of the everyday necessities.

For the average Tanzanian, the economic disintegration has caused severe hardship, illustrated by the price of $2.50 for a bottle of beer and new taxes on tobacco, cement, sugar, and other consumer goods. Nyerere, however, continued his socialistic program, pushing toward completion of his "Ujaama Village" plan and beginning the move of the capital from coastal, outward-looking Dar to the inland town of Dodoma. The move, both costly and inward-looking, is part of Nyerere's plan to further insulate Tanzania from outside, capitalist influence.

Politics. The nation was politically stifled, as agents of the state and ruling party supervised all daily activities. Cool relations with the United States led to a drop in aid from $28 million to $14 million for fiscal 1984. Lack of aid and foreign exchange led to the physical and fiscal collapse of the Tazara railway, and the virtual disappearance of such items as soap from stores.

ROBERT GARFIELD, *DePaul University*

TAXATION

Although general economic performance improved and the rate of inflation slowed somewhat in most countries, governments generally were still struggling to hold growing deficits in check without adverse effects on the economy. Tax-policy changes were designed to provide more government revenue, either through raising taxes or providing incentives to stimulate economic growth that in turn would produce greater revenues from existing tax systems.

United States

Congressional Action. In the Social Security Amendments of 1983, signed into law by President Ronald Reagan on April 20, Congress included several significant tax provisions designed to help restore the solvency of the social-security system. In subjecting to income tax a portion of the social-security benefits of some taxpayers, the law represented a significant departure from previous policy. Starting Jan. 1, 1984, up to one half of social-security benefits would be included in taxable income for taxpayers whose incomes exceed certain base amounts—$25,000 for single taxpayers, $32,000 for married taxpayers filing jointly, and zero for married taxpayers filing separately.

Another feature of the law that attracted wide attention was the inclusion of tax-exempt interest income in the formula for determining the taxable income base for social-security recipients. The formula is intended to provide similar treatment of benefits for individuals whose total income consists of different mixes of taxable and nontaxable income, as well as to limit opportunities for manipulation of tax liability on benefits. For purposes of figuring the base amounts, income includes adjusted gross income under prior law plus nontaxable interest income and one half of social-security benefits. The amount of benefits included in taxable income will be the lesser of one half of benefits or one half of the excess of the taxpayer's combined income over the base amounts.

The amendments also advanced the dates on which social-security tax increases had been scheduled to take effect. For employers and employees the previously scheduled tax increase (from 6.7% to 7%) for 1985 was shifted to 1984; part of the increase slated for 1990 was advanced to 1988. Tax rates for the self-employed were revised to equal the combined employer-employee rate; previously they had been lower. To cushion the effects of the tax increases, Congress provided a credit for employees against their social-security tax of 0.3% of their covered wages in 1984 only, and a credit for the self-employed for the years 1984–1989. The credits are to be financed from general revenues, rather than through the social-security trust funds.

In another revenue move, Congress repealed the 10% withholding tax on dividends and interest that had been scheduled to take effect on July 1. The new law, the Interest and Dividend Tax Compliance Act of 1983, was signed by the president on August 5. It retained the withholding requirement only in cases in which taxpayers fail to meet reporting and compliance rules.

Supreme Court. An unusually heavy agenda of tax cases was presented to the U.S. Supreme Court, which handed down 19 decisions that touched upon a broad range of tax issues.

In *Container Corporation of America v. Franchise Tax Board* the court ruled for the first time that a state may tax the worldwide income of a U.S. corporation with foreign subsidiaries if a unitary relationship exists between the companies. In several previous cases the court had dealt only with the question of whether a unitary relationship existed among the companies and did not address the issue of a state's rights to tax such income.

Container Corporation, a paperboard packaging manufacturer, is a Delaware company headquartered in Illinois, doing business in California and elsewhere, with a number of overseas subsidiaries. In calculating the portion of its net taxable income in California, the company omitted all of its subsidiaries' payroll, property, and sales. The California Franchise Tax Board issued notices of additional taxes due, asserting that the company should have treated its overseas subsidiaries as part of its unitary business rather than as a passive investment. The company challenged the tax in California state courts, which upheld the additional assessment. Container Corp. appealed the case to the U.S. Supreme Court, arguing that California's tax scheme violated the Due Process and Commerce clauses of the Constitution.

Pointing out that it generally defers to the judgment of state courts in deciding what constitutes a unitary business, the court reasoned that its task was to determine whether the state court had applied the correct standards to the case and, if so, whether its judgment was within the realm of a "permissible judgment." The court decided that the California court had analyzed the case under the correct legal standard. Moreover, the justices held, such factors as the company's assistance to its subsidiaries in obtaining equipment, in filling personnel needs that could not be met locally, in lending funds to the subsidiaries, and other factors—taken together—demonstrated that the California court reached a conclusion within the realm of permissible judgment.

The court's decision was met by immediate outcries from several foreign governments, which threatened retaliatory action. President Reagan appointed a special commission to consider issues raised by the court's decision and to recommend solutions. In taxing multinational corporations, 12 states use the worldwide income approach, estimated to generate between $600 million and $900 million annually in state revenues.

In *U.S. v. Ptasynski* the court removed the uncertainty over the government's budgetary process that had resulted from a district court's decision that the crude-oil windfall-profits tax was unconstitutional. In overturning the decision, the Supreme Court ruled that the exemption of certain Alaskan oil did not violate the Uniformity Clause of the Constitution.

The amount of revenue at stake in *Ptasynski* surpassed that of any other federal-tax case ever presented to the court. The government had collected a net $53 billion between April 1980, when the tax became effective, and the end of December 1982, and it expected billions of additional receipts from the tax over the next five years. Enacted as part of the decontrol of domestic oil pricing, the tax at issue is an excise tax on the production of domestic crude oil. Because of the difficulties of producing oil on the North Slope of Alaska—the remote location, hazardous environment, and extreme climate—Congress had exempted certain Alaskan oil from the tax. In 1982 a U.S. district judge declared the law unconstitutional on the ground that it violated the Uniformity Clause, which states that excise taxes must be uniform throughout the nation. He also struck down the whole statute, holding that the Alaskan oil exemption was unseverable from the rest of the law. The government filed an appeal to the Supreme Court.

In reaching its decision, the court cited the *Head Money Cases* (1884), in which it was held that a "tax is uniform when it operates with the same force and effect in every place where the subject is found." In *Ptasynski* the court noted that the Uniformity Clause "does not require Congress to devise a tax that falls equally or proportionately on each state nor does the clause prevent Congress from defining the subject of a tax by drawing distinctions between similar classes." The justices also asserted that neither the Uniformity Clause nor the court's previous decisions prohibit all geographically defined classifications. Congress has wide latitude in deciding what to tax, the court said, and the exemption of the Alaskan oil reflected its judgment that "unique climatic and geographic conditions" justified the exemption from the windfall-profits tax.

In a case involving an Alabama oil and gas severance tax, the court ruled that a law increasing the tax by 2% was valid insofar as it deals with intrastate sales of gas; insofar as the law applies to sales of gas in interstate commerce, however, a provision prohibiting the producer from passing the tax on to others was preempted by federal law and therefore invalid (*Exxon Corp. et al. v. Edgerton et al.*).

In another case the court's decision ended more than 35 years of unsettled jurisprudence resulting from a footnote in a 1947 decision. In *Commissioner of Internal Revenue v. Tufts* the court ruled that tax-shelter investors who had used the device of a nonrecourse loan were required to include the outstanding amount of obligation in computing the amount realized on the sale of property, even though that amount exceeds the fair market value of the property. As a result of the decision, tax-shelter investors using the nonrecourse loan device will realize a taxable gain, instead of a loss, when the venture fails and is sold.

In cases involving state taxes on banks, the court struck down laws in Texas and Tennessee. In *American Bank and Trust Company et al. v. Dallas County et al.* the court ruled that a law permitting local governments to tax the value of commercial-bank stocks without deduction for tax-exempt U.S. obligations was in violation of a 1959 federal law that prohibits a tax "that would require consideration of federal obligations in computing the tax." The ruling was of wide interest because similar lawsuits were pending in major Texas cities and also because it called into question similar taxes in Louisiana, Nevada, Ohio, Pennsylvania, and West Virginia.

In *Memphis Bank & Trust v. Garner* the court invalidated a Tennessee tax on bank earnings, ruling that the tax was illegal because it taxed income from obligations of the United States and all other states except Tennessee. Federal law exempts U.S. obligations from state taxation, except where the taxes are "nondiscriminatory" franchise or nonproperty taxes. The Tennessee tax was held to be discriminatory and thus did not qualify for the exemption.

The court consolidated two similar cases, involving the tax-exempt status of fundamentalist and segregationist private schools, and held that in both instances the policies violated the antidiscrimination thrust of a federal law that denies tax-exempt status to discriminatory social clubs. Bob Jones University and Goldboro Christian Schools claimed that the Internal Revenue Service had exceeded its authority and violated their First Amendment rights by denying them tax-exempt status. Their segregationist policies, they claimed, were biblically dictated.

Another case involving schools had implications for the administration's proposal for a tuition tax credit against federal income taxes. In *Mueller et al. v. Allen et al.* the court upheld a 1955 Minnesota law that allows parents of school children an income-tax deduction for certain educational expenses, even though parochial schools receive the greatest benefit. Two Minnesota taxpayers challenged the deduction as a violation of the Establishment Clause of the Constitution. The most important

UPI

The U.S. flag was at half-staff at Bob Jones University as the Supreme Court ruled against its tax-exempt status.

sonal-income-tax increases, enacted in 12 states, were the largest component of the total, with estimated additional yields of $2.9 billion annually. General-sales-tax boosts occurred in 14 states, for an aggregate of $1.9 billion in new revenue. Motor-fuel taxes were increased in 15 states, corporate-income taxes in 12, cigarette taxes in 15, and alcoholic-beverage levies in 6.

International

Canada. An indexed security investment plan went into effect in Canada on Oct. 1, 1983. The plan provides tax exemption for the inflationary portion of capital gains on publicly traded common shares in Canadian companies. The tax exemption for bonds issued by provinces and municipalities to nonresidents was extended to bonds issued in 1983.

Europe. In May, debate was stopped on Britain's first finance bill, presented in March, as Parliament was dissolved because of the announcement of a general election on June 9. Proposals by the new chancellor of the exchequer, Nigel Lawson, were enacted in July. The changes included an increase in income-tax thresholds and rate brackets to an extent more than necessary to compensate for inflation, and reductions in the corporate tax for small companies. A bill, dealing with tax relief for oil companies, was published in the autumn.

The French government introduced strong austerity measures, effective April 1, that included higher taxes on income, liquor, tobacco, and gasoline, as well as mandatory loans to the government for most taxpayers. An additional 1% tax was levied on all taxable income to help finance the social-security system. The forced loans, equal to 10% of tax assessments, are required for income taxpayers whose 1981 tax exceeded 5,000 francs and for net-worth taxpayers who are subject to income tax. The 1984 budget, presented in September, calls for a new progressive surtax ranging from 5% to 8% on income tax assessments above 20,000 francs.

The West German government approved measures reducing the net-worth tax for businesses, liberalizing depreciation allowances on business investment, and allowing full deductibility of the costs of issuing new shares for corporate-income-tax purposes.

A decree-law in Italy, published Dec. 30, 1982, called for sharp increases in the assumed income from real property for income-tax purposes, a higher tax on government concessions, and a 16% consumption tax on radio and TV sets, cameras, and similar products.

Japan. Taxes in Japan were raised on both foreign and domestic cigarettes by the equivalent of about eight cents per pack, effective May 1. At the same time, the tariff on imported cigarettes was reduced to narrow the differential between prices of domestic and foreign cigarettes from 46 cents to 34 cents per pack.

ELSIE M. WATTERS, *Tax Foundation, Inc.*

characteristic of the law arguing for the validity of the tax, the court indicated, was that the deduction is available for all parents, including those with children in public schools and in sectarian and nonsectarian private schools.

State and Local Taxes. In fiscal 1983, U.S. state and local governments collected $283.766 billion in tax revenues, an increase of $16.802 billion—or 6.3%—over the previous year. The percentage increase was the lowest in many years, comparing with 9.8% in fiscal 1982.

Because of the lingering effects of national economic recession, state legislatures in 1983 continued their efforts to increase revenues for the third straight year in order to avoid budget deficits. Legislatures in 31 states enacted measures designed to increase taxes by close to $7.7 billion annually. The 1983 increase compared with about $4 billion in 1982 and was the largest dollar amount legislated since 1971. Per-

TELEVISION
AND
RADIO

Two blockbuster miniseries were highlights of the television year. Richard Chamberlain (right) and Rachael Ward starred in the adaptation of Colleen McCullough's "The Thorn Birds." Robert Mitchum, (below center), Ali MacGraw, and Jan-Michael Vincent were featured in Herman Wouk's "The Winds of War."

Photos © 1983 American Broadcasting Companies, Inc./Jim Globus

Just as the national economy was pulling out of a recession, the American television industry was discovering that it had overreached itself. In the 1982–83 season, according to a page one article in *The New York Times* of Nov. 25, 1983, the number of national cable television channels declined for the first time, from 42 to 37, and only a "handful" of the channels were profitable even though the number of cable subscribers had grown to 33 million, or 39% of all homes with television.

The *Times* story cited the demise of such projects as The Entertainment Channel, the joint venture of RCA and Rockefeller Center that collapsed in February after losses of $34 million, as an omen for many of the channels

that "narrowcast" a specific type of program for a limited, upscale audience. The article said that cable would need to move toward "mass broadcasting," like network television, in order to continue the phenomenal growth rate of the late 1970s and early 1980s.

Another type of programming that discovered its limits was network news, which had rapidly expanded in recent years as a response to the 24-hour Cable News Network (CNN). The National Broadcasting Company's late-night newscast, *NBC News Overnight,* was canceled in November 1983 after 16 months on the air, because of low advertising revenue. The Columbia Broadcasting System (CBS) counterpart, *Nightwatch,* reduced its live programming from four hours to two hours per night and moved its headquarters from New York to Washington to cut costs. The first and most successful of the late-night news shows, the American Broadcasting Company's (ABC's) *Nightline*, experimented with a one-hour format but was expected to return to a cheaper half-hour in 1984.

Although a study sponsored by the National Association of Broadcasters showed that only 57% of viewers were satisfied with the quality of television programming generally, there were signs in 1983 that television may have reached a new stage of maturity, addressing national issues with more force and insight than many of its critics had given it credit for. On the Public Broadcasting Service (PBS), a 13-part documentary called *Vietnam: A Television History* was hailed as one of the most complete treatments of the Vietnam War anywhere, one that drew its emotional power purely from dispassionate reportage.

And the November 20 airing of ABC's *The Day After*, a harrowing dramatization of the effects of a nuclear war on a Kansas town, was an important news event in itself, one that "was not only on the nation's agenda, but helped to set it," in one critic's words. The graphic, controversial program with Jason Robards was watched by 100 million Americans; only the final episode of the long-running CBS series *M*A*S*H**, in March, was a higher-rated dramatic program, with 125 million viewers.

Network Programming. For the fourth straight year, CBS dominated the ratings race. For the 29-week season from Sept. 27, 1982, through April 17, 1983, CBS had an average of 18.2 points, while ABC had 17.1 and NBC 15.1. (One ratings point equals 1% of all U.S. households with a television turned on.) CBS won 19 of the 29 weeks, while four of ABC's seven winning weeks were due to blockbuster miniseries based on best-selling books—*The Thorn Birds* with Richard Chamberlain and *The Winds of War* with Robert Mitchum—and all three of NBC's weeks were attributable to coverage of major sports events, the World Series and the Super Bowl.

60 Minutes, the CBS News magazine, was the top-rated series for the second time in its 15-year career, and CBS placed seven programs in the top ten. *The A Team*, the police/adventure series that made the muscular "Mr. T" into a minor cult hero, was NBC's only program in the top ten. However, NBC generally appealed most to critics, introducing sophisticated series like *Cheers*, a comedy about the denizens of a Boston bar, and *St. Elsewhere*, a hard-hitting hospital drama. Led by *Cheers* and the hit series *Hill Street Blues*, NBC dominated the 1983 Emmys with 21 awards. The gap between critical opinion and mass appeal was seen most clearly perhaps in

the fact that Judd Hirsch won the best actor award for his performance in NBC's *Taxi*, a series that had already been canceled because of low ratings.

The first half of the 1983–84 season provided no major surprises in new network entertainment. CBS parlayed the immense popularity of *M*A*S*H* into a surprisingly successful sequel, *Aftermash*, featuring some of the original characters after they had returned home from the Korean War to resume their civilian lives. There was a new ABC vehicle for film star Madeline Kahn, *Oh, Madeline*, and the continuing popularity of racy serials, or "nighttime soaps," engendered ABC's hit *Hotel* and CBS's flop *Emerald Point, N.A.S.*

Sports programming continued to expand and diversify, particularly on the weekend anthology programs. Football, however, the traditional king of sports programming, showed its first major ratings slippage in many years during the early part of the 1983–84 season. Partly as a result of the 1982 football strike, which disrupted viewer habits, ABC's *Monday Night Football* fell 4 ratings points through the end of November, and CBS and NBC football also suffered a loss of audience.

News Programming. The death of longtime ABC anchorman Frank Reynolds and the entrenchment of CBS's Dan Rather as the most-watched anchor set off a shuffle of personnel in the network newsrooms. On September 5, ABC scuttled its three-city evening news format to make Peter Jennings the sole anchor, and NBC dropped Roger Mudd as Washington co-anchor to consolidate its New York newscast around Tom Brokaw.

A shakeup was also predicted at NBC's *Today* program, which had slipped steadily in the ratings in the year since Bryant Gumbel took over for Brokaw as co-anchor with Jane Pauley. *Today* had fallen behind ABC's *Good Morning America* in 1979, and in May 1983 the two-year-old *CBS Morning News* also caught up with the long-running *Today*. Gumbel's firing was predicted in many quarters, but in late 1983 he was still in the anchor chair.

Cable News Network, which continued to grow rapidly—reaching more than 20 million subscribers by year's end—was assured further domination in cable news when, in what one analyst called a "a tremendous coup," owner Ted Turner bought out his only major competitor, Satellite News Channel, which had lost $40 million in its one year of operation.

60 Minutes created almost as much news as it reported. In a highly publicized trial, correspondent Dan Rather was found innocent in a $30 million slander suit filed by a California physician whom Rather had linked to medical insurance fraud. In another case an appeals court overruled a federal judge's order to black-out, in Dallas, a *60 Minutes* segment about alleged New Orleans police brutality. At-

The new comedy series "Cheers" with Ted Danson (extreme right), Shelley Long, Rhea Perlman, and Nicholas Colasanto, took five Emmy Awards. After a slow start in the ratings, the show picked up during the fall.

Herb Ball/NBC

torneys had argued that the broadcast would hamper the policemen's trial in Dallas. And in yet another legal tangle, Gen. William C. Westmoreland pursued his $120 million libel suit against *60 Minutes* by getting a court order for the news magazine to hand over an internal report on the preparation of a controversial 1982 segment on the general's role in the Vietnam War. The suit was regarded as an important test of how much of their internal affairs television journalists are obligated to make public under the First Amendment.

Cable Programming. With the falling survival rate for new cable channels, programmers were under more pressure than ever to develop original and profitable products. New entries in the market ranged from the The Disney Channel to The Playboy Channel, spin-offs of entertainment empires based on rather different values.

But no channel seemed to embody the new video age as well as MTV, the slick new network centered around rock music. Thanks to MTV, a new term entered the lexicon: A "video" is not really a complete story recorded on videotape, but rather a visual stream of consciousness, a set of impressionistic and sometimes startling images designed to capture the mood of a rock song. The new Nashville Network, meanwhile, was built around country music and stuck to more conventional video techniques.

The two largest cable programmers, Home Box Office (HBO) and Showtime, entered a stage of more intense bidding for prestigious properties and big entertainment names. HBO began making its own films with budgets of up to $2 million; *Between Friends,* a vehicle for Elizabeth Taylor and Carol Burnett, was a prime example. HBO also explored the comedy series area with a hip, mock news show, *Not Necessarily the News,* and the HBO spin-off network, Cinemax, picked up the award-winning satire series *SCTV* from NBC, where it had failed to attract a big enough audience for commercial network television.

With the demise of CBS Cable in 1982 and The Entertainment Channel in 1983, Show-time's *Broadway on Showtime* series remained almost the only outlet on cable for legitimate theater; among its respectable 1983 offerings was a studio production of the Lanford Wilson drama, *The Fifth of July,* with Richard Thomas and Swoozie Kurtz. Showtime also got extensive media coverage for a novel project called *Faerie Tale Theater,* produced by actress Shelly Duvall and featuring such film stars as Bernadette Peters and Christopher Reeve.

Syndication. Many regulations were relaxed or repealed by the Federal Communications Commission (FCC) under the conservative chairmanship of Mark Fowler. The most controversial FCC rulings concerned the distribution of profits from the sale of syndicated programs, an $800 million market. Though the issue was not resolved by year's end, it was understood that the independent producers had temporarily set back the networks' attempt to win the syndication rights. As a result, ABC announced a freeze on programming costs for 1984.

Radio. National Public Radio (NPR), known for its serious news and commentary, raised and lightened its image with the growing success of *A Prairie Home Companion,* a Saturday evening anthology of wry humor and folk music broadcast live from St. Paul, MN. But in mid-1983 NPR was close to bankruptcy, and it was only a last-minute government loan of $7 million that kept the network on the air.

The new technologies transforming TV continued to be adapted for radio. Several stations across the country were experimenting with a system called "pay radio." For example, listeners of WEEI-FM in Boston could pay $50 a month for a special receiver that would pick up the *Dow Jones Alert* business report on a special closed frequency.

There also appeared to be a shift in the album-oriented rock (AOR) format. Partly because of their growing exposure on the MTV cable network, such rock acts as Men at Work, Culture Club, and Stray Cats were crossing over from more specialized "New Wave" stations of the mainstream rock format.

See also THE NEW HOME VIDEO, page 55.
DAN HULBERT, *"The Dallas Times Herald"*

TELEVISION | 1983

Some Sample Programs

ABC News Special—JFK—A critique of the administration of John F. Kennedy. With Peter Jennings. ABC, Nov. 11.

Adam—A 1983 TV-movie based on the real-life story of a couple whose son was kidnapped and later found dead. With Daniel J. Travanti. NBC, Oct. 10.

American Journey—Journalist Richard Reeves traveled across the United States, making a journey similar to that of Alexis de Tocqueville. PBS, March 30.

Blood Feud—Drama based on the battle of wills between Jimmy Hoffa and Bobby Kennedy. With Robert Blake, Jose Ferrer, Ernest Borgnine. Independent, April 25.

Callas: An International Celebration—A musical salute to the late Maria Callas, featuring rare film footage of the star. With Kiri Te Kanawa, Placido Domingo, Jessye Norman, James McCracken. PBS, Dec. 12.

Chiefs—A three-part miniseries about a string of murders in a small southern town that links three generations of police chiefs. With Charleton Heston, Wayne Rogers, Keith Carradine. CBS, Nov. 13.

Choices of the Heart—A 1983 TV-movie based on the life of Jean Donovan, an American lay missionary murdered in El Salvador. With Melissa Gilbert, Martin Sheen. NBC, Dec. 5.

The Citadel—A ten-part adaptation of the A. J. Cronin novel. With Ben Cross. PBS, Nov. 20.

The Cocaine Cartel—An *ABC News Closeup* documentary about the smuggling of drugs into the United States. ABC, August 20.

The Day After—The 1983 TV-movie about a nuclear holocaust in America. With Jason Robards, John Lithgow, JoBeth Williams. ABC, Nov. 20.

Dempsey—A three-hour drama special on the life of boxer Jack Dempsey. With Treat Williams. CBS, Sept. 28.

Ellington: The Music Lives On—A salute to Duke Ellington; with hostess Cicely Tyson. PBS, March 7.

Fifth of July—Television dramatization of the Lanford Wilson stage play. With Richard Thomas, Swoozie Kurtz. PBS, May 10.

The Good Soldier—A television adaptation of the Ford Madox Ford novel. PBS, Jan. 9.

Happy Birthday, Bob—Bob Hope celebrates his 80th birthday with a star-studded special. NBC, May 23.

Heart of Steel—TV-movie about an unemployed steelworker. With Peter Strauss. ABC, Dec. 4.

Idomeneo—Mozart's 1781 opera, with Luciano Pavarotti and the Metropolitan Opera orchestra. PBS, Jan. 26.

I, Leonardo—Biographical film of Leonardo da Vinci. With Frank Langella. CBS, April 26.

Jacobo Timerman: Prisoner Without a Name, Cell Without a Number—A 1983 TV-movie based on the experiences of Jacobo Timerman, a former newspaper publisher jailed in Argentina. With Roy Scheider, Liv Ullmann. NBC, May 22.

Jazz in America—The first of four jazz shows from New York's Avery Fisher Hall. PBS, Sept. 8.

Kennedy—Three-part dramatization of the White House years of President John F. Kennedy. With Martin Sheen, Blair Brown, E. G. Marshall, John Shea, Geraldine Fitzgerald. NBC, Nov. 20.

The Life and Adventures of Nicholas Nickleby—A television production of the Royal Shakespeare Company's adaptation of the Charles Dickens' novel. Independent, Jan. 10.

The Life of Verdi—Six-part dramatization of the composer's life. With Ronald Pickup. PBS, Oct. 24.

Live from Lincoln Center—Beethoven's Ninth Symphony was performed by the New York Philharmonic under the direction of Zubin Mehta. PBS, Feb. 2.

Live from the Met—A Centennial Celebration—A televised celebration marked the New York Metropolitan Opera's 100th anniversary. PBS, Oct. 22.

King Penguin: Stranded Beyond the Falklands—A study of the king penguin colony of South Georgia Island. CBS, June 22.

The Magic Flute—A New York City Ballet performance choreographed by Peter Martins. PBS, April 25.

Mario Lanza: The American Caruso—A documentary on the life of Mario Lanza. PBS, March 11.

M*A*S*H—"Goodbye, Farewell, and Amen"—The final episode of the series *M*A*S*H* was lengthened to 2½ hours. CBS, Feb. 28.

Medea—The Euripedes tragedy, with Zoe Caldwell, Mitchell Ryan, Judith Anderson. PBS, April 20.

National Geographic Special: "Australia's Animal Mysteries"—PBS, Feb. 9.

Princess Daisy—Two-part dramatization of Judith Krantz's book. With Stacy Keach, Claudia Cardinale, Lindsay Wagner. NBC, Nov. 6.

Princess Grace Remembered—A National Symphony Concert in tribute to the late Princess Grace of Monaco who was to have narrated *The Carnival of the Animals* as part of this concert; the narration was performed by Nancy Reagan. PBS, Sept. 26.

The Ring of the Nibelung (Das Rheingold, Die Walkure, Siegfried, and Gotterdammerung)—Richard Wagner's operatic tetralogy was presented. PBS, Jan. 24, Feb. 21–28, April 11–18, June 6–13.

Roosevelt Reminiscences—A special commemorating the inauguration on March 4, 1933, of Franklin D. Roosevelt as U.S. president. PBS, March 4.

Sadat—Two-part dramatization of the life and career of the late Egyptian President Anwar Sadat. With Louis Gossett, Jr. Independent, Oct. 31.

The Scarlet and the Black—A 1983 TV-movie based on the true life World War II experiences of Msgr. Hugh O'Flaherty. With Gregory Peck, Christopher Plummer. CBS, Feb. 2.

Shakespeare Plays—1983's offerings included *Richard III*, with Ron Cook; and *Macbeth*, with Nicol Williamson. PBS, May 2, Oct. 17.

The Skin of Our Teeth—The *American Playhouse* series presented Thornton Wilder's play live. With Harold Gould, Sada Thompson, Blair Brown. PBS, Jan. 18.

Solti Conducts Rossini—The overtures to five operas by Gioacchino Rossini, performed by the Chicago Symphony. PBS, June 20.

Sons and Lovers—A *Masterpiece Theatre* telecast of the D. H. Lawrence novel. With Eileen Atkins, Tom Bell, Karl Johnson. PBS, May 15.

Special Bulletin—A 1983 TV-movie about terrorists in control of an A-bomb. NBC, March 20.

Still the Beaver—A 1983 TV-movie with the characters, now grown up, from the old television series *Leave It to Beaver*. With Jerry Mathers, Tony Dow, Barbara Billingsley. CBS, March 19.

Svengali—A dramatization of the "Trilby" story. With Peter O'Toole, Jodie Foster. CBS, March 9.

The Thorn Birds—A four-part miniseries based on the Colleen McCullough novel. With Richard Chamberlain, Rachel Ward, Barbara Stanwyck, Jean Simmons, Richard Kiley, Piper Laurie, Earl Holliman, Christopher Plummer. ABC, March 27.

Vietnam: A Television History—A 13-part documentary series. PBS, Oct. 4.

Who Will Love My Children?—A 1983 TV-movie based on a true story of a woman dying of cancer who found homes for her ten children. With Ann-Margret. ABC, Feb. 14.

Will There Really Be a Morning?—A TV-movie biography based on the life of actress Frances Farmer. With Susan Blakely, Lee Grant, John Heard. CBS, Feb. 22.

The Winds of War—A seven-part adaptation of Herman Wouk's bestselling novel. With Robert Mitchum, Ali MacGraw, Polly Bergen, Jan-Michael Vincent, Victoria Tennant, David Dukes. ABC, Feb. 6.

Wings—An *American Playhouse* adaptation of the Broadway play which portrayed the recovery of a stroke victim. With Constance Cummings. PBS, April 26.

Winston Churchill: The Wilderness Years—Eight-part dramatization of Winston Churchill's life from 1929 to 1939. With Robert Hardy, Sian Phillips. PBS, Jan. 16.

The Winter of Our Discontent—A dramatization of the John Steinbeck novel. With Donald Sutherland, Teri Garr. CBS, Dec. 6.

World of James Joyce—Documentary of the Irish writer. PBS, June 15.

TENNESSEE

Bank and crop failures and legislative activity were major happenings in Tennessee in 1983.

Banks. The third-largest bank failure in U.S. history shocked the financial world in February when the United American Bank of Knoxville collapsed due to "large and unusual loan losses." Jake Butcher, financier, Democratic politician, twice gubernatorial candidate, and organizer of the 1982 World's Fair in Knoxville, had headed a banking empire that included the United American and that stretched from Memphis to Bristol and into the surrounding states of Virginia, Georgia, West Virginia, and Kentucky. By midyear he had gone into involuntary bankruptcy. More than a dozen lawsuits filed on behalf of bank stockholders revealed the tangled nature of the Butcher empire. Butcher moved to Florida and pledged to "do all we can to try to satisfy those debts." Meanwhile the United American was purchased and reopened by the First Tennessee Bank of Memphis.

Larry Hamilton, an ordained minister, and wife Deborah resisted chemotherapy for their cancer-stricken, 12-year-old daughter, Pamela, on religious grounds. In September, Tennessee state courts ordered immediate treatment.

UPI

Agriculture and Drought. Continued cold and wet weather during the spring curtailed planting. Then, by mid-August, one of the worst droughts in Tennessee's history threatened to cut crop production by at least one third. Production of soybeans, for years the state's largest cash crop, declined by about 40%, and corn production was the lowest since 1952. Weather records revealed that Tennesseans had endured the hottest August in more than 100 years as temperatures exceeded 90 degrees on 25 days, as compared with only four days in 1982. Water supplies reached a critical stage in some areas.

The Legislature. The legislature postponed some major issues until 1984, including Gov. Lamar Alexander's Master Teacher program, designed to upgrade the quality of instruction, and a one-half-cent sales tax to fund it. Other measures enacted into law included the repeal of the May presidential primary, a requirement of one minute of silence in public schools at the beginning of each school day, a 24% maximum effective interest rate on loans of more than $100, the merger of in-state banks across county lines, and a tax on video games.

Unemployment. Unemployment continued to decline after March, and by late fall the rate was below 9%. Davidson county's (Nashville) unemployment rate, at 6%, was the lowest in the state. The number of employed workers at midyear had increased by more than 15,000. The number of industrial plants also continued to increase, and in June the Nissan Motor Company, which during the past two years injected more than $660 million into the state's economy with the construction of a plant at Smyrna, rolled its first truck off the assembly line. The number of Tennesseans drawing unemployment benefits was the lowest since 1981.

People in the News. Murfreesboro businessman Hubert McCullough and Gallatin Circuit Judge Ernest Pelligrin joined the governor's cabinet. McCullough has the powerful administrative position of finance commissioner. One of Judge Pelligrin's duties will be to find ways of relieving overcrowded prisons.

Imprisonment of former Democratic House Majority Leader Thomas Burnett, convicted of failure to file timely income tax returns, was postponed until 1984 after serious illness developed in the legislator's family.

Former Gov. Ray Blanton had been convicted in June 1981 of extortion, conspiracy, and mail fraud in the issuance of liquor licenses. His conviction was subsequently overturned by a three-judge appellate panel, but it was upheld on September 28 by the U.S. Court of Appeals for the Sixth Circuit in Cincinnati.

ROBERT E. CORLEW
Middle Tennessee State University

TEXAS

The Economy. For the first time since the 1930s, economic growth in Texas was stalled. Declining prices for oil and natural gas were principally responsible for the severity of the recession in the state. While the national unemployment rate dropped, that for Texas went up. Bankruptcies increased in the construction and drilling industries. Houston was particularly hard hit, and many who had come from the Northeast and Middle West seeking employment in the Sunbelt returned home jobless.

Politics. The most significant political development was the unexpected announcement that John Tower would not seek reelection to the U.S. Senate in 1984. A force in Congress since the early 1960s—particularly on defense and military matters—Tower's decision caught many of his colleagues by surprise. Robert Kreuger, who lost to Tower in 1978, and liberal state Representative Lloyd Doggett will contend for the Democratic nomination. On the Republican side, Congressmen Phil Gramm and Ron Paul, both conservative supporters of President Reagan, announced their intention to run.

Newspaper polls indicated that most Texans endorsed the policies of Gov. Mark White and favored a second term for him. Although he failed to deliver on a campaign promise to dramatically raise teacher's salaries, his record was generally successful.

Education. A blue-ribbon committee, chaired by controversial millionaire Ross Perot, was created by the state legislature to make recommendations concerning public education in Texas. A number of hearings were held and much dissatisfaction was expressed with educational standards, particularly at the precollege level. The committee was expected to recommend a "back to basics" approach and substantially increased state spending for education.

Enrollment at the University of Texas at Austin, Texas A & M University, and the University of Houston remained high, while private colleges such as Rice, Baylor, and Southern Methodist University also maintained stable enrollments. Budgetary restrictions in other parts of the country have led to "raiding" of Nobel laureates from Harvard and the University of Illinois by the University of Texas and Texas A & M University.

Weather. Hurricane Alicia struck the Texas Gulf Coast and particularly the cities of Galveston and Houston with devastating force in August. The worst storm to hit the Lone Star state since Carla in 1963, Alicia wrought an all-time high amount of damage. In downtown Houston many office buildings and hotels suffered property damage, and in Galveston and Houston, police were ordered into the streets to prevent looting. In the wake of the storm, the state attorney general's office procured a number of indictments against tree-removal and glass-repair firms for price gouging.

While the Texas Gulf Coast sustained hurricane damage, the Panhandle area of West Texas suffered through the worst drought in memory. Excessive heat and lack of rainfall combined to strike a double blow at cotton production and cattle raising. Some emergency aid was forthcoming from the federal government, but many farmers were forced into bankruptcy.

Sports. The hopes of Dallas Cowboy football fans were dashed when "America's team" lost to the Washington Redskins in the National Conference championship in January 1983. The Cowboys rebounded, however, by getting off to a fine start in the fall. Perhaps even more frustrating was the defeat suffered by the University of Houston in the NCAA basketball tournament finals. The Cougars lost to North Carolina State by two points.

STANLEY E. SIEGEL
University of Houston

TEXAS · Information Highlights

Area: 226,807 sq mi (691 030 km²).
Population (1982 est.): 15,280,000.
Chief Cities (1980 census): Austin, the capital, 345,496; Houston, 1,594,086; Dallas, 904,078; San Antonio, 786,023; El Paso, 425,259; Fort Worth, 385,141.
Government (1983): *Chief Officers*—governor, Mark White (D); lt. gov., William P. Hobby (D). *Legislature*—Senate, 31 members; House of Representatives, 150 members.
State Finances (fiscal year 1982): *Revenues,* $16,365,000,000; *expenditures,* $14,152,000,000.
Personal Income (1982): $174,493,000,000; per capita, $11,419.
Labor Force (July 1983): *Nonagricultural wage and salary earners,* 6,164,900; unemployed, 637,100 (8.3% of total force).
Education: *Enrollment* (fall 1981)—public elementary schools, 2,098,126; public secondary, 837,421; colleges and universities (1981–82), 716,297. *Public school expenditures* (1980–81), $6,140,941,000 ($1,955 per pupil).

THAILAND

Through a combination of good luck and good management, Thai leaders steered their country through dangerous political and economic currents in 1983. Bangkok experienced some of the worst flooding in nearly 40 years.

Political Events. The main developments were the parliamentary election in April and the promotion of Gen. Arthit Kamlang-ek to a position of undisputed control of the Royal Thai Army. Both events confirmed the army's dominant political role, a position it has held for more than 50 years.

The election followed a pattern by which the army periodically allows civilian politicians and parties a larger share of political power. This is done for a variety of reasons: to take advantage of civilian expertise; to gain public support for higher taxes and other forms of sacrifice; and to reassure the Thai people and foreign observers that Thailand is "moving toward democracy." Certain temporary provisions of the constitution were allowed to lapse in April 1983, and now active-duty military officers as well as civilian political appointees are barred from holding cabinet-level positions. This limits the army's power.

The monarchy remained extremely popular and a powerful force for national unity. King Bhumibol Adulyadej continued to exercise quiet political influence on the side of moderation. For example, he is believed to have persuaded Gen. Prem Tinsulanonda to remain as prime minister after the election because of Prem's skill at finding broadly acceptable answers to difficult problems. The king also may have helped to persuade General Arthit to involve himself less in political affairs and concentrate more on the military.

The king's health improved in 1983, to the relief of his subjects, but the future of the monarchy may depend on whether the king is eventually succeeded by his very popular daughter or by his less popular son.

The Economy. Thailand maintained an acceptable rate of growth in 1983, despite the

© P. Chauvel/Sygma

After April elections, Gen. Prem Tinsulanonda decided not to retire and accepted a second term as prime minister.

slow economic recovery of many countries that buy its exports. Thailand's success in exporting primary products (rice, tin, rubber) and manufactured goods (furniture, textiles, electronic components) resulted in one of the lowest trade deficits in years. The reasons for Thailand's success included relatively favorable weather conditions, a lack of major strikes or other internal unrest, reasonably strong prices for many chief exports, and some skillful adaptations to changing world-market conditions by Thai economic managers.

Foreign Affairs. Thai Foreign Minister Sitthi Sawetsila won a seat in the parliamentary election and continued to play a leading role in the Association of Southeast Asian Nations (ASEAN). Since the 1975 Communist victories in Indochina, ASEAN has sought to contain the influence of Vietnam. In 1983 the ASEAN states continued to take the lead—at the United Nations and elsewhere—in organizing worldwide political opposition to Vietnam's control of Cambodia. Along with several neighboring nations, Thailand supported the Cambodian resistance, which harassed the Vietnamese army in Cambodia.

Despite the postponement of U.S. President Ronald Reagan's visit to Southeast Asia, Thailand and the United States continued to have excellent relations. Two-way trade increased, as did U.S. economic and military aid to Thailand. Thousands of Thai students were studying in the United States, and tourism and cultural exchanges reached an all-time high.

PETER A. POOLE

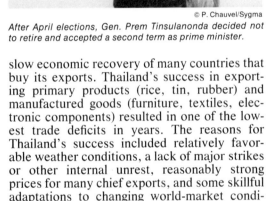

THAILAND • Information Highlights

Official Name: Kingdom of Thailand.
Location: Southeast Asia.
Area: 198,772 sq mi (514 820 km²).
Population (July 1983 est.): 50,731,000.
Chief City (1982 est.): Bangkok, the capital, 5,396,997.
Government: *Head of state,* Bhumibol Adulyadej, king (acceded June 1946). *Head of government,* Gen. Prem Tinsulanonda, prime minister (took office March 1980).
Monetary Unit: Baht (23.00 baht equal U.S.$1, July 1983).
Gross National Product (1982 U.S.$): $38,400,000,000.
Economic Index (1982): *Consumer Prices* (1970 = 100), all items, 297.4; food, 310.1.
Foreign Trade (1982 U.S.$): *Imports,* $8,573,000,000; *exports,* $6,882,000,000.

THEATER

The Broadway theater has continued to be dominated by musicals. Although there have been about an equal number of musical/straight-play offerings, musicals—when they succeed—do so more spectacularly. They not only earn more money and run longer, but they quickly become part of American culture. The musical *La Cage aux Folles* is by now a household word, and it has been credited with changing public attitudes toward homosexuals. The straight play *'night, Mother,* while running longer, has had modest success in comparison, with little fame outside New York, and it is not likely to have influenced attitudes toward would-be suicides.

Broadway Musicals. In 1983, the year in which *A Chorus Line* succeeded *Grease* as the longest-running Broadway show in history (a distinction once held by nonmusical plays like *Tobacco Road* and *Life with Father*), the most spectacular hit was *La Cage aux Folles,* which began as a straight play in France and then became an internationally popular French film. The play celebrates the homosexual marriage of the couple in charge of the nightclub that gives the show its name. One is an ostentatious transvestite; the other, who has fathered a son, must keep his transvestite mate out of the way (until the right theatrical moment, of course) in order to persuade his son's stuffy in-laws-to-be

that he is really respectable. The show provides both a high-minded liberal sermonette on the right to be different and an audacious, imaginatively staged homosexual extravaganza, with George Hearn, as the transvestite, getting the lion's share of attention.

If any other show could claim to have earned a special prestige that set it off from the rest, it was Peter Brook's adaptation of Georges Bizet's classic opera *La Tragédie de Carmen,* which reopened the Vivian Beaumont Theater at Lincoln Center. The theater had been closed while the Beaumont management battled the Lincoln Center management for the right to make extensive, expensive alterations. Predictably, the success of *Carmen* has been urged as a reason against making the alterations, but the controversy continued. Brook's *Carmen,* first performed in Paris, is an intense 80-minute condensation of Bizet's original, with some material added from the story by Prosper Mérimée on which the opera is based. Performed by five rotating casts of singers, it is neither the opera nor the story but a remarkable distillation of some high moments of music and drama. This *Carmen* seems not to be about hostile attitudes enchantingly expressed by opera singers but about the earthy, passionate encounters of a Gypsy girl, a soldier, and a toreador.

Many of the other musicals were revivals or were, like *Cage* and *Carmen,* based on revived material. A bright exception was *Baby,* which

Broadway's dramatic hit, " 'night, Mother" offered fine performances by Kathy Bates (right) and Anne Pitoniak.

Richard Feldman

deals engagingly with three couples of different ages as they approach parenthood. Their diversity is presented in an intelligent and friendly fashion in a cheerful little musical that has, for once, no intention of overpowering its audience. *Doonesbury* was also new, but it is based on a comic strip whose idiosyncratic characters —many of them college students (the strip originated at Yale)—are used as vehicles of liberal satire. Evidently those who did not know the strip were bewildered, although the characters do make sense, but true believers were delighted to see their old friends in song and action on the stage.

My One and Only was, in a way, new, but its score, which was its original raison d'être, consists of great old songs by George Gershwin. The book, set in the 1920s, has to do with an enterprising American aviator (the boy) and an English swimmer (the girl); it was much doctored on the road—and on the basis of that experience one national magazine prophesied disaster—but the book kept its one main virtue: it unites the dancing and singing talents of Tommy Tune and Twiggy. He mainly dances, she mainly sings, and they sing and dance Gershwin. That seems a sufficient formula for success.

Among the revivals, only *On Your Toes* and *Zorba* seemed destined for long runs. The first was a 1936 musical that presented the clash between jazz and ballet, culminating in a memorable jazz ballet. The songs of Richard Rodgers and Lorenz Hart are as irresistible as ever, and the Russian-born ballerina Natalia Makarova made an astonishing musical comedy debut in the role of a Russian ballerina. *Zorba* got a needed lift from the presence of the star of the original movie, the grizzled but ageless Anthony Quinn, supported by Lila Kedrova, who was also in the film. It was, in effect, a revival more authentic than the original production.

Splendid scores justified the briefer revivals of *Porgy and Bess* and *Show Boat*. This *Porgy* was, essentially, the 1976 version of the Houston Grand Opera, and so it did more justice to Gershwin's score than its early predecessors. Without being as authoritative, *Show Boat* made its audiences grateful for the songs of Jerome Kern and Oscar Hammerstein.

There seemed to be less reason for reviving *Mame*, despite the presence of the ageless Angela Lansbury, or to turn two old plays into musicals—James Baldwin's memoir of life among black revivalists, *The Amen Corner*, retitled *Amen Corner*, and Robert Sherwood's urbane comedy drama of European politics, ineffectively brought up to date as *Dance a Little Closer*.

Other efforts included *Marilyn: An American Fable*, which erratically invoked the memory of Marilyn Monroe. Peggy Lee invoked her own memories by singing her songs in her autobiographical one-woman show, *Peg*. *Five-*

Six-Seven-Eight . . . Dance! was a dance revue enlivened by the presence of Sandy Duncan, but performed (as with *Porgy and Bess*) in Radio City Music Hall, which seems too large for such enterprises. *The Flying Karamazov Brothers* was a more adventurous and quite funny revue, based primarily on juggling acts. *Merlin* was a book musical that would have been better off as a revue, since its main virtue consisted of the magic act of its star, Doug Henning.

Broadway Plays. Among the plays, Neil Simon contributed *Brighton Beach Memoirs,* a patently autobiographical play about the problems of adolescence and family life in a Jewish family in the 1930s. More serious than most of Simon's writing, it was occasionally moving and benefited from some good acting, notably that of Matthew Broderick in the lead. Playwright Marsha Norman made her Broadway debut and won a Pulitzer Prize with *'night, Mother,* in which a daughter explains to her mother her reasons for contemplating suicide. Its effect owed much to the expert performances of Kathy Bates and Anne Pitoniak. In Patrick Meyers' *K2,* two men were observed in the act of climbing a mountain. Some interesting personal clashes developed, although it was never fully explained why two men with so little in common were engaged in this joint effort. The real attraction, however, was the mountain, designed by Ming Cho Lee. Special credit must be given, however, to Jeffrey De Munn, who actually did some climbing. These plays represented the best offerings of original American writing on Broadway in 1983.

Among the other new plays was Edward Albee's *The Man Who Had Three Arms,* which is nearly a monologue by a man whose deformity once made him a celebrity; some took it to be a spiritual autobiography. Two other plays, *Brothers* and *The Guys in the Truck,* owed their productions to stars who had made their names in other media—Carroll O'Connor, the television star of *All in the Family,* and film star Elliott Gould. In fact, the latter play lost its star before it opened.

Foreign plays on Broadway were in all cases British. Michael Frayn's late-year hit, *Noises Off,* was a farce in which English actors are performing or trying to perform a terrible comedy probably headed for enormous popularity. Peter Nichols' *Passion* (known in England as *Passion Play*) dealt with marriage and infidelity and had the sole novelty of providing two additional actors to portray the private selves of the husband and wife in question. *Edmund Kean,* a one-man play about the English actor, won credit for Ben Kingsley, even if Kingsley did not give a full portrait of the 19th-century English tragedian. *Teaneck Tanzi: The Venus Flytrap,* adapted from *Trafford Tanzi,* was originally a lively feminist tract about a wronged wife who becomes a wrestler and conquers her husband; transferred to a New Jersey setting, it lost most of its snap.

Revivals abounded. Al Pacino with all of his old fervor again played the lead in David Mamet's *American Buffalo*. Jessica Tandy, in the role of the mother, gave distinction to Tennessee Williams' *The Glass Menagerie*. George Kaufman and Moss Hart's *You Can't Take It with You* and Arthur Miller's *A View from the Bridge* drew favorable attention in their latest versions. A new and short-lived producing company, headed by Elizabeth Taylor and Zev Bufman, produced *Private Lives,* in which the misinterpretations of the performers Richard Burton and Miss Taylor disappointed those who came with any expectation of seeing Noel Coward's comedy. A second venture, *The Corn Is Green*, with Cicely Tyson oddly cast in the lead, was less grossly misconceived. The Circle in the Square, on the other hand, maintained a high level of workmanlike effort, offering Molière's *The Misanthrope* with Brian Bedford, Herman Wouk's *The Caine Mutiny Court-Martial* with John Rubinstein and Michael Moriarty as the fiery antagonists, and George Bernard Shaw's *Heartbreak House* in a production of English origin, with Rex Harrison in the lead.

Broadway had its share of Shakespeare in *All's Well That Ends Well,* a respectable but not brilliant Royal Shakespeare version.

Theater in Central Park. The 1983 Shakespeare offering of the summer theater was *Richard III*, with Kevin Kline in the title role adding to his laurels. The rewriting and gagging up of Donizetti's opera *Don Pasquale* was less successful.

Off Broadway. Off Broadway and Off-Off-Broadway provided much of the serious drama in 1983. Samuel Beckett was represented by a triple bill. His *Ohio Impromptu* and *What Where* are additional exercises in the examination of old age and the repetitiousness of life, but *Catastrophe* presented a new political element in its study of the humiliation of an artist, inspired by the fate of the Czech dramatist Vaclav Havel. Sam Shepard contributed *Fool for Love*, a wild comedy about two young lovers who cannot live with or without each other. Directed by the author for the San Francisco Magic Theater before coming to New York, the play starred Ed Harris, who later rocketed to fame by acting along with Shepard in the film *The Right Stuff*. Shepard was represented also by two more modest plays in a double bill, *Superstitions* and *The Sad Lament of Pecos Bill on the Eve of Killing His Wife*.

Plays dealing with various aspects of family life were in evidence. Christopher Durang wrote a savagely satirical comedy, *The Baby with the Bathwater*, about the lunatic upbringing of a child who ultimately survives his early environment. Tina Howe's *Painting Churches* presented a sympathetic portrait of an aging, absent-minded poet and his family. A. R. Gurney, Jr., provided two more gently comic portraits of life among the Wasps—*The Middle Ages* and *What I Did Last Summer*. In *Isn't It Romantic?*, Wendy Wasserstein tellingly observed the problems of a nice Jewish girl and incidentally brought Betty Comden back to the stage in the role of her mother; Meryl Streep was present as a distraught voice on the telephone. Dana Coen, in *Sympathy,* looked in on another nice Jewish girl, recently widowed. Ronald Tavel, often an experimental dramatist, wrote a conventionally naturalistic play involving two brothers with *Success and Succession*. Vaughn McBride's *Elba* interpreted the problems of an aging married couple, with James Whitmore playing the husband. Thomas Babe exhibited a theatrical confrontation between mother and daughter in *Home Again Kathleen*.

In *Buck,* Ronald Ribman made a brutal frontal attack on pornography mongers in cable television. Lee Kalcheim, in *Breakfast with Les and Bess*, more gently satirized the family talk shows of yesterday.

Richard Nixon and Watergate drew the notice of three plays—*Dick Deterred*, in which a British dramatist, David Edgar, furnished parallels from *Richard III; Secret Honor*, by Donald Freed and Arnold M. Stone, a one-man play that won more sympathy than might have been considered possible for the former president; and a coarser view of the subject, Erik Brogger's *Basement Tapes*. Another celebrity of our recent past, Maria Callas, was the subject of Charles Ludlam's extravaganza, *Galas*.

Except for the Beckett plays and *Dick Deterred,* virtually all of the Off-Broadway plays mentioned were relatively straightforward examples of realism, sometimes a bit stylized. Richard Foreman's boldly antinaturalistic *Egyptology* and Len Jenkin's rambling *My Uncle Sam* provided relatively isolated examples of theatrical experimentation.

Black dramatists were heard, but they seemed less intent upon black issues. Gus Edwards' *Manhattan Made Me* had as much to do with whites as blacks; Samm-Art Williams' *Friends* was a farce that made minimal use of its characters' blackness, and Pearl Cleage's *Puppetplay* touched upon a universal issue, the increasingly mechanical quality of contemporary life.

Pride of place among foreign plays, in addition to Beckett's program, went to Caryl Churchill's *Fen*, about a depressed area in England, acted by a British cast as part of the Public Theater's exchange program; Vaclav Havel's *Private View*, three one-acts on the plight of this harried Czech dramatist; and Simon Gray's *Quartermaine's Terms*, a comedy of faculty life at a school in England.

See also Prizes and Awards.

Henry Popkin
State University of New York at Buffalo

BROADWAY OPENINGS | 1983

MUSICALS

Amen Corner, book by Philip Rose and Peter Udell, based on a James Baldwin play, music by Garry Sherman, lyrics by Mr. Udell; directed by Mr. Rose; with Rhetta Hughes; Nov. 10–Dec. 4.

Baby, book by Sybille Pearson, music by David Shire, lyrics by Richard Maltby, Jr., based on a story developed with Susan Yankowitz; directed by Mr. Maltby; with Liz Callaway, Todd Graff, Beth Fowler, James Congdon, Martin Vidnovic, Catherine Cox; Dec. 4–

Dance a Little Closer, book and lyrics by Alan Jay Lerner, based on *Idiot's Delight* by Robert E. Sherwood, music by Charles Strouse; directed by Mr. Lerner; with Len Cariou, Liz Robertson, George Rose; May 11.

Doonesbury, book and lyrics by Garry Trudeau; music by Elizabeth Swados, based on *Doonesbury* by Mr. Trudeau; with Laura Dean, Ralph Bruneau; Nov. 21–

La Cage Aux Folles, book by Harvey Fierstein, based on the play by Jean Poiret, music and lyrics by Jerry Herman; directed by Arthur Laurents; with Gene Barry, George Hearn; Aug. 21–

La Tragedie de Carmen, adapted from George Bizet's opera by Marius Constant, Jean-Claude Carrière, and Peter Brook; musical director, Mr. Constant; with Patricia Schuman, Laurence Dale; Nov. 17–

Mame, book by Jerome Lawrence and Robert E. Lee, music and lyrics by Jerry Herman, based on the book *Auntie Mame* by Patrick Dennis and the play by Lawrence and Lee; directed by John Bowab; with Angela Lansbury, Vera Charles, Jane Connell, Sab Shimono, Roshi Handwerger, Byron Nease; July 24–Aug. 28.

Marilyn: An American Fable, libretto by Patricia Michaels, music and lyrics by Jeanne Napoli, Doug Frank, Gary Portnoy, Beth Lawrence, Norman Thalheimer, and others; directed by Kenny Ortega; with Alyson Reed; Nov. 20–Dec. 3.

Merlin, book by Richard Levinson and William Link, songs and incidental music by Elmer Bernstein, lyrics by Don Black; directed by Ivan Reitman; magic illusions created by Doug Henning; with Doug Henning; Feb. 13–Aug. 7.

My One and Only, book by Peter Stone and Timothy S. Mayer, music by George Gershwin, lyrics by Ira Gershwin; staged and choreographed by Thommie Walsh and Tommy Tune; with Tommy Tune, Twiggy; May 1–

On Your Toes, book by Richard Rodgers, Lorenz Hart, George Abbott, music and lyrics by Rodgers and Hart; directed by George Abbott; original choreography by George Balanchine; with Natalia Makarova, Dina Merrill, George S. Irving; March 6–

Porgy and Bess, Libretto by DuBose Heyward, music by George Gershwin, lyrics by Mr. Heyward and Ira Gershwin; directed by Jack O'Brien; with Michael V. Smartt, Robert Mosley, Jr., Priscilla Baskerville, Naomi Moody, Larry Marshall; April 7–May 15.

Show Boat, book and lyrics by Oscar Hammerstein 2d, based on the novel by Edna Ferber, music by Jerome Kern; directed by Michael Kahn; with Donald O'Connor, Lonette McKee, Bruce Hubbard, Sheryl Woods, Karla Burns; April 24–June 26.

The Tap Dance Kid, book by Charles Blackwell, music by Henry Krieger, lyrics by Robert Lorick, based on the novel *Nobody's Family Is Going to Change* by Louise Fitzhugh; directed by Vivian Matalon; with Alfonso Ribeiro, Hinton Battle, Samuel E. Wright; Dec. 21–

Zorba, book by Joseph Stein, based on the novel by Nikos Kazantzakis, music by John Kander, lyrics by Fred Ebb; directed by Michael Cacoyannis; with Anthony Quinn, Lila Kedrova; Oct. 16–

PLAYS

All's Well That Ends Well, by William Shakespeare; directed by Trevor Nunn; with Harriet Walter, Philip Franks, Stephen Moore; April 13–May 15.

American Buffalo, by David Mamet; directed by Arvin Brown; with Al Pacino, James Hayden, J. J. Johnston; Oct. 27–

Angels Fall, by Lanford Wilson; directed by Marshall W. Mason; with Bernard Hughes, Fritz Weaver; Jan. 22–March 13.

Brighton Beach Memoirs, by Neil Simon; directed by Gene Saks; with Matthew Broderick, Joyce Van Patten, Elizabeth Franz, Peter Michael Goetz, Zeljko Ivanek; March 27–

Brothers, by George Sibbald; directed by Carroll O'Connor; with Dennis Christopher, Carroll O'Connor; Nov. 9.

The Caine Mutiny Court-Martial, by Herman Wouk; directed by Arthur Sherman; with John Rubinstein, Michael Moriarty; May 5–Nov. 6.

The Corn Is Green, by Emlyn Williams; directed by Vivian Matalon; with Cicely Tyson, Peter Gallagher; Aug. 22–Sept. 18.

Edmund Kean, by Raymund FitzSimons; directed by Alison Sutcliffe; with Ben Kingsley; Sept. 27–Oct. 30.

The Glass Menagerie, by Tennessee Williams; directed by John Dexter; with Jessica Tandy, Bruce Davidson, Amanda Plummer, John Heard; Dec. 1–

The Guys in the Truck, by Howard Reifsnyder; directed by David Black; with Harris Laskawy; June 19.

Heartbreak House, by George Bernard Shaw; directed by Anthony Page; with Rex Harrison, Rosemary Harris, Jan Miner, Amy Irving; Philip Bosco; Dec. 7–

K2, by Patrick Meyers; directed by Terry Schreiber; with Jeffrey De Munn, Jay Patterson; March 30–June 11.

The Man Who Had Three Arms, written and directed by Edward Albee; with William Prince, Patricia Kilgarriff, Robert Drivas; April 5–17.

Moose Murders, by Arthur Bicknell; directed by John Roach; Feb. 22.

The Misanthrope, by Molière (English translation by Richard Wilbur); directed by Stephen Porter; with Brian Bedford, Mary Beth Hurt, Stephen D. Newman, Carole Shelley; Jan. 27–March 27.

Night, Mother, by Marsha Norman; directed by Tom Moore; with Anne Pitoniak, Kathy Bates; March 31–

Noises Off, by Michael Frayn; directed by Michael Blakemore; with Dorothy Loudon, Brian Murray; Dec. 11–

Passion, by Peter Nichols; directed by Marshall W. Mason; with Frank Langella, Bob Gunton, E. Katherine Kerr, Cathryn Damon, Roxanne Hart; May 15–Aug. 8.

Private Lives, by Noel Coward; directed by Milton Katselas; with Richard Burton, Elizabeth Taylor; May 8–July 17.

Slab Boys, by John Byrne; directed by Robert Allan Ackerman; with Sean Penn, Kevin Bacon; March 7–Apr. 17.

Teaneck Tanzi: The Venus Flytrap, by Claire Luckham; directed by Chris Bond; with Deborah Harry, Andy Kaufman; April 20.

Total Abandon, by Larry Atlas; directed by Jack Hofsiss; with Richard Dreyfuss, John Heard, George N. Martin, Clifton James; April 28.

A View from the Bridge, by Arthur Miller; directed by Arvin Brown; with Tony Lo Bianco, Saundra Santiago, James Hayden; and Rose Gregorio; Feb. 3–June 12.

You Can't Take It with You, by Moss Hart and George S. Kaufman; directed by Ellis Rabb; with Elizabeth Wilson, Jason Robards, Colleen Dewhurst, Jack Dodson, Bill McCutcheon, Maureen Anderman, Nicholas Surovy, Rosetta Le Noire, Arthur French, James Coco; April 4–Dec. 31.

OTHER ENTERTAINMENT

Dance Theatre of Harlem; Jan. 25–Feb. 27.

Five Six Seven Eight . . . Dance! Dance and music revue; directed and choreographed by Ron Field; with Sandy Duncan; June 15–Sept. 5.

The Flying Karamozov Brothers; setting and costumes by Robert Fletcher; with Paul David Magid, Randy Nelson, Timothy Daniel Furst, Sam Williams, Howard Jay Patterson; May 10–June 12.

Marcel Marceau on Broadway; March 9–Apr. 17.

Peg, a story and new lyrics by Peggy Lee; musical direction by Larry Fallon; with Peggy Lee; Dec. 14–17.

The theater season was sparked in 1983 by the award-winning offerings, "Brighton Beach Memoirs," below, an autobiographical memory play that provided a return to Broadway by playwright Neil Simon, and "My One and Only," top right, featuring a pastiche of George and Ira Gershwin songs, the introduction of former model Twiggy to Broadway, and inspired dancing by Tommy Tune. "La Cage aux Folles," top left, adapted from the Jean Poiret play and the French film of the same name, arrived in August and was suddenly the must-see musical for many theatergoers.

THIRD WORLD

Efforts to alleviate the economic problems of the Third World continued in 1983. These efforts sometimes were marred, however, by political conflicts between the Third World states and the rich industrial democracies.

Debt. The debt of Third World developing countries was estimated to have risen to more than $700 billion. Default by certain heavily indebted states could have tremendous ramifications, including the possibility of a world depression. This was one of the reasons the United States and other Western creditor nations sought to use the International Monetary Fund (IMF) as a channel of aid to the debt-burdened states. Paradoxically, this aid effort often strained relations between the rich and poor. (*See* special report, page 277.)

The Rich. The rich states, and above all the United States, demanded greater fiscal and economic responsibility from the debtor countries. Within the United States there was opposition to the Reagan administration's support of the IMF aid program. This opposition was based in part on the belief that increasing IMF resources to aid the poor states would only bail out the big Western banks that had lent huge sums to Third World states; it was argued by some that the American taxpayer to a great extent would be footing the cost of the IMF program. Thus the Reagan administration had to tread a narrow line between backing increased aid and emphasizing that such aid was in the U.S. interest. Washington asserted that defaults in the Third World would hurt U.S. exports and lead to higher domestic unemployment. Fears also were expressed that unless the IMF program were implemented, shock waves would reverberate through the U.S. banking system, affecting the economy as a whole. Visions of the Great Depression of the 1930s were conjured up to defend increased U.S. financial support of the IMF and the debtor countries.

The Poor. Aid through the IMF was conditioned on the debtor countries taking belt-tightening austerity measures. But most debt-ridden countries already had enormous economic problems, including massive poverty. Austerity measures threatened social unrest. In Brazil, for example, there was rioting over IMF requirements that the government take austerity measures in order to receive IMF aid.

Excuses and Explanations. Much of the debt problem was blamed on the large oil-price increases of the 1970s, and this was partly true. But there were other reasons, as evidenced by the fact that among the debtors were such major oil-producers as Mexico, Venezuela, Nigeria, and Indonesia. The scars of colonialism —illiteracy, primitive industrial facilities, lack of farm machinery, and others—remain, but this also is only partly to blame.

While Mexico, Nigeria, and other Third World governments were complaining of economic plight, billions of dollars of private money from those countries were flowing into the United States. The Third World blamed high U.S. interest rates, but the fact remained that money too often was being invested in the United States instead of trusted to Third World governments. Also, certain Third World countries with corrupt governments and ruling elites lost huge sums to embezzlement, bribery, and other illicit activity.

Adding to these problems were enormous expenditures on some unrealistic economic projects and, perhaps more important, huge sums for the purchase of armaments. India has developed the atomic bomb, and Pakistan reportedly is trying to do likewise; Iran and Iraq continued their war; and Libya meddled in the Chad conflict. Third World trouble spots were made worse by the policy of the Soviet Union to exploit these situations, particularly in Central America and Africa.

Nonalignment. The Nonaligned Movement, which serves as the political arm of the Third World, held its seventh summit in New Delhi, March 7–12, 1983. Under the chairmanship of India's Prime Minister Indira Gandhi, the 1983 summit was not so rabidly anti-U.S. as the previous conference in 1979, which was held in Havana under the chairmanship of Fidel Castro. Nevertheless, the United States was often the target of criticism for much that was wrong in the world, including the international recession, southern Africa, Latin America, and the Middle East. Four states—Bahamas, Barbados, Colombia, and Vanuatu—were admitted to the Nonaligned Movement, bringing the total membership to 101.

In September, U.S. President Ronald Reagan used his address to the General Assembly of the United Nations to tell the Third World that true nonalignment must be based on freedom and justice. Reagan also warned the Third World states to beware of Soviet puppets who pose as nonaligned while trying to steer the Movement in the direction of Soviet goals.

Ironically, the Soviet Union gives little aid to the Third World, except to such ardent pro-Soviet governments as those in Afghanistan, Vietnam, and Cuba. In attacking the United States at New Delhi and elsewhere, many Third World states were in fact lashing out at the one country that was doing more to help them than any other.

If 1983 proved anything, it was nothing new: Some sort of political consensus is sorely needed between the rich Western states and the poorer countries of the Third World. Unfortunately, no such consensus was anywhere visible on the horizon.

See also articles on individual countries; NATIONS OF THE WORLD, page 571.

AARON R. EINFRANK, *Free-Lance Writer*

© Herman Kokojan/Black Star

In hard times for U.S. airlines, Continental sought protection from union demands by filing under Chapter 11.

TRANSPORTATION

The transportation industries benefited in 1983 from economic recovery which proceeded more rapidly than anticipated in the United States and at a more modest rate in a number of other industrialized countries. By late September cumulative railroad ton-miles had slightly surpassed those of the prior year, but were running more than 18% above the declining loadings of the same period in 1982. TOFC/COFC (trailer-on-flatcar and container-on-flatcar) traffic was showing surprising strength, with cumulative loadings approximately 18% above 1982. Truck traffic, as reflected in the index of the American Trucking Associations, was only moderately higher than in 1982, but the index has become less representative as new carriers have entered the business in the aftermath of regulatory reform. Domestic air cargo ton-miles were up significantly, though international traffic was down slightly. The increase in air passenger traffic, on the other hand, was less than hoped for. Meanwhile the capacity offered by the scheduled lines grew more rapidly than the demand for passenger service.

Increased housing starts, higher automobile sales, and an improved rate of operation in the iron and steel industries all contributed to the rise in freight movement. Nearly all categories of freight traffic had, by late in the year, surpassed 1982 volumes. Coal production and movement, especially for export, were disappointing, and grain movement was depressed until late in the year. The severe drought which sharply reduced corn and soybean crops was overcome by the repositioning of old grain in order to meet government commitments under the payment-in-kind (PIK) program. By September railroads were cross-hauling grains to fulfill those requirements, and scattered shortages of grain hopper cars developed. Barge traffic had been severely depressed earlier in the year, but record grain loadings on the upper Mississippi were reported by September. Rail earnings showed significant improvement. Air and motor carrier earnings, however, remained depressed in the face of limited traffic gains and continued rate discounting and fare cutting. Those larger motor carriers with broad route patterns and predominately less-than-truckload traffic fared well.

Legislation and Regulation. Though much legislation affecting transportation was pending in the U.S. Congress, little emerged. Maritime legislation again failed despite active committee work. The quest for eminent domain for the building of coal slurry pipelines suffered a resounding defeat in the House of Representatives. A combination of railroad, agricultural, and environmental opposition proved to be unexpectedly effective. Fear of diverting scarce water resources in western coal-producing states was a major factor.

Administration of the 1978, 1980, and 1982 regulatory reform acts continued, however, in the direction of greater deregulation. The Interstate Commerce Commission (ICC) approved major new exemptions for railroad traffic. On initial petition by Conrail, all traffic moving in boxcars was exempted, despite the opposition of many other railroads. Export coal traffic, too, was granted an exemption from the ICC's jurisdiction. Hence a very large portion of rail traffic was entirely freed of regulation, and great uncertainties were faced concerning the terms on which cars would be interchanged and compensated for in these classes of traffic. A rule designed to relieve railroads of the "special circumstances" test when they seek to buy a motor carrier, combined with a 1981 ruling which removed the test for extensions of existing rail-owned truck operations, would enable railroads to move freely in the trucking industry from which they had been barred since 1936 (except for services auxiliary or supplemental to rail service). Court challenges could reverse these rulings, however.

Throughout the year contrasting views continued to develop among shippers with regard to the revised regulation of motor and rail carriers. Since, in the view of the organized truckers as well as shippers, the ICC was not enforcing the Motor Carrier Act of 1980 either with respect to rates or entry, sentiment was growing for complete deregulation of trucking. Associations of shippers in particular sought early removal of all antitrust exemption for group rate-making activities on the part of motor carriers. In intrastate regulation there was a parting of the ways on this issue. Some states had completely deregulated trucking; others had revised their laws to require group rate-making and to prescribe minimum rates.

Shippers obliged to use railroads because of the nature of some of their traffic were more inclined to insist upon administration of the Staggers Rail Act of 1980 in accord with congressional intent. Displeasure with ICC performance was evident also in Congress, and the threat of legislation to provide greater protection for rail shippers was growing. Criticism focused on coal rates, the box car and export coal exemptions, the reduction of competition among railroads caused by merger, the closure of through-routes with other lines, and the widespread cancellation of reciprocal switching in terminals served by more than one railroad.

The ICC adopted standards, including geographic and product competition, for judging market dominance by railroads. The exemption of export coal was justified, in part, by the proposition that foreign purchasers were buying in a world market which afforded them alternative sources of coal, e.g., Australia and South Africa. U.S. mines, however, which seek to participate in the export market, very rarely have the service of more than one railroad at origin. While the rails argue that coal rates, when adjusted for inflation, have declined slightly since 1971, the incidence of the freight rate has grown sharply since 1975, i.e. the freight rate has increased more rapidly than the mine price of coal. Thus the average rail rate was 21.4% of the destination-value of coal in 1975, but had grown to 30.5% in 1982. Shippers of "captive" rail traffic also expressed concern at the ICC's unwillingness to consider the Long-Cannon amendment to the Staggers Act, which requires examination of the progress made by railroads in eliminating below-cost rates as a condition for raising rates on market-dominant traffic. Even railroad pricing officers believed that there was undue price-cutting on some of the exempt traffic. Captive shippers viewed this activity as an inequitable and unlawful tax upon their business.

Railroads. As economic recovery continued, it was apparent that the railroads had survived the 1981–82 recession in better shape than any other segment of the U.S. transport industry. What had appeared to be a sick industry a decade earlier was now highly regarded in the financial markets, enjoyed the prospect of rapid earnings recovery, and had a physical plant in good condition. The merger of Union Pacific, Missouri Pacific, and Western Pacific had been consummated, and Western Pacific's track was being rapidly upgraded. Chicago & North Western had won its battle with the Soo Line for control of the former Rock Island route between Minnesota's "Twin Cities" and Kansas City. Indeed, most of the defunct Rock Island's more important lines were back in operation under other auspices. North Western was in competition with Grand Trunk for control of Milwaukee. Sante Fe and Southern Pacific commenced new merger plans which, if carried out, would create the third largest rail system in the country and precipitate a move on the part of smaller western railroads to seek homes in large systems.

Conrail continued to demonstrate modest profitability and enjoyed increasing freight traffic late in the year. Hence it was eligible for disposition to private parties. Its employees enjoyed priority of consideration for any plan to purchase the property, and the unions did develop a proposal. Prior to its renewed involvement with Southern Pacific, Santa Fe indicated some interest in acquiring Conrail. Both the Department of Transportation (DOT), which must decide the issue, and Conrail's chief executive officer were concerned by the fact that no new money would be put up under the union plan and that the position of management was not made clear. The unions, however, regarded the continuance of wage and other concessions made in order to restore Conrail to profitability as their contribution to the purchase price. Such concessions were not expected to be continued if another party or parties purchased the system.

North Western's joint ownership of 100 mi (161 km) of railroad built by Burlington Northern (BN) to better serve the coal mines in the Powder River Basin of Wyoming was confirmed. North Western was rebuilding some connecting line of its own and constructing a 54-mi (87-km) extension to the Union Pacific in order to create a competitive route for Wyoming coal. Its contract with Arkansas Power & Light (AP&L) for the long-term delivery of coal struck a powerful blow at the most active of the slurry pipeline proposals. BN immediately increased its coal rates to AP&L pending completion of North Western's construction.

Some railroads moved forcefully to diversify further. Thus, Burlington Northern, already involved in numerous nonrail operations, won a battle to control El Paso Natural Gas. CSX, the Chessie System-Seaboard parent, acquired Texas Gas. The latter acquisition posed an unusual problem since Texas Gas owned American Commercial Bargelines, the largest operator in the river barge industry. The Panama Canal Act prohibits railroad control of a barge line without ICC approval, but that body accepted a trustee arrangement for the stock proposed by CSX and then launched an investigation to determine the lawfulness of railroad control. An appelate court refused to upset these arrangements. Meanwhile, both Southern New England Telephone and MCI were reaching contract arrangements with CSX, Amtrak, and others to lay fiber-optic cable for long-distance communications on railroad rights of way. Ordinarily, railroads would have use of a part of the installed capacity for their own communications requirements and would receive lease payments.

The weather dealt unkindly with some railroads in the western United States. Flooding and washouts produced by heavy rains in California closed both the coastal and Tehachapi routes of Southern Pacific for short periods and required major rebuilding. More spectacular was the landslide in the Wasatch Range which blocked the Spanish Fork River and, with heavy runoff from melting snow, created a lake 200 ft (61 m) above the railroad grade of the Rio Grande's main line and drowned the railroad town of Thistle. The line ceased operation on April 14. By July 4 a new line high on the mountainside with a 3,015-ft (919-m) tunnel enabled restoration of operations. A diversion tunnel held further growth of the lake in check. Since this was the only route for the movement of most of Utah's westbound coal, the state's economy was adversely affected.

Motor Carriers. Despite some improvement in freight traffic volume, the rate of failure remained high, capacity was still in excess, and rate discounting continued. Some carriers bargained successfully with Teamsters Union locals for wage concessions, sometimes in exchange for a profit-sharing plan. Transcon, however, secured a 12% reduction in wages in return for distribution of 49% of the stock among employees. Teamsters Union officials took the initiative in reopening the Master Freight Agreement with a view to concede substantially reduced rates for nonemployed teamsters who returned to work and for new hires. The membership resoundingly defeated the agreement reached with carriers, an event regarded as a serious blow to Jackie Presser, president of the union. New entrants continued to appear in the industry, increasing the pressure on unionized carriers.

The larger and more profitable carriers of less-than-truckload freight continued their territorial expansion and the opening of new terminals. At the same time they lost truckload business to carriers specializing in that type of freight, many of which have obtained nationwide authority. The number of owner operators was thought to have continued to decline, although a number had secured authority to carry certain regulated commodities for hire and the leasing rules had been relaxed to permit private carriers to use such operators.

All elements of the trucking industry were concerned by the tax increases called for in the Surface Transportation Assistance Act of 1982.

(*See* special report, page 519.) The 12% sales tax on vehicles over 10,000 lbs and the heavy-duty vehicle use-tax which, effective July 1, 1984, would increase from $210 per vehicle to $3,900. This is a fixed tax regardless of mileage made by the taxed vehicle. The General Accounting Office anticipated that some 35% of owner/operators will be forced out of business if the tax becomes effective. Hence strenuous efforts were underway to secure its replacement by a variable tax designed to raise equivalent revenue.

The same legislation imposed uniform weight limits and provided increased size limits for heavy truck rigs, including authorization of twin 28-ft trailers, on a DOT-designated national highway system. States were to ensure access between carrier terminals, servicing and repair facilities, and the designated routes. A system of 162,000 mi (206 707 km) of interstate and primary highways was tentatively designated, but a number of states challenged the authority of Congress to impose such regulations. Most carriers were deferring purchase of larger equipment pending resolution of the controversy, but some improvement in motor-carrier productivity is anticipated when the designation comes into force.

Air Transportation. The U.S. airline industry as a whole continued to experience severe losses. Summer passenger traffic was less than anticipated, and the carriers faced a bleak winter. While many of the nonunion carriers which had entered the industry since deregulation became profitable and expanded, 6 of the 11 major trunk carriers were in perilous financial condition and were seeking additional concessions from their unions in order to bring labor costs down to a more nearly competitive level. Fare wars continued and threatened to spread into all major markets, where overscheduling also tended to persist. Efforts failed to reduce the commission rates paid to travel agents.

Continental, fifth largest of the trunks, survived a strike by its machinists, only to seek protection under Chapter 11 of the federal bankruptcy law. The object was to avoid its union contracts and resume operations on a reduced scale with wages and working conditions dictated by the company. Eastern Air Lines threatened similar action, or a shutdown, unless workers accepted a further 15% cut in pay. Frontier sought to establish a nonunion affiliate. Transworld Corp. considered a spin-off of its unprofitable and shrinking airline. Stronger carriers proposed to move quickly into any voids created and to match the sharp fare reductions proposed by the "new" Continental. The unions were preparing to press Congress for remedial regulation to bring a halt to below-cost rate making.

The investigations and oversight subcommittee of the House Committee on Public Works and Transportation issued the results of

The first section of Dade County's METRORAIL system in Miami was readied for opening late in the year.

a two-year inquiry in a report highly critical of the Civil Aeronautics Board and the departments of State and Transportation. The report found efforts to export the domestic open-skies policy highly damaging to the position of U.S.-flag airlines in international commerce. Numerous discriminatory situations were pointed to, and hard bargaining in bilateral negotiations was advocated. The report also recommended a return to active participation by U.S. carriers in the International Air Transport Association, from whose rate-making activities they had been compelled to withdraw.

Ocean Transportation. Little improvement was expected over the performance of 1982, which was generally regarded as the industry's worst year since World War II. Despite heavy scrapping, particularly of tankers, surplus tonnage grew in the face of declining world trade. Charter rates for bulk ships were forced below break-even rates in many trades. Recovery was expected to be slow for the major bulk commodities: petroleum, iron ore, coal, and grain. Nevertheless a substantial tonnage of new ships was on order. The liner trades were in somewhat better condition, and their general cargo volume could be expected to respond more quickly to economic recovery than would the major bulk commodities.

The Code of Conduct for Liner Conferences of the United Nations Conference on Trade and Development (UNCTAD) came into force on October 6, six months after countries controlling the necessary 25% of world liner tonnage had acceded to the agreement. The United States would not and did not intend to ratify the code, which was sponsored by the developing countries. Japan was expected to accede, subject to the reservations which the Western European signatories incorporated with respect to trade among industrialized nations. The most controversial feature of the code was ambiguous, but was generally interpreted to imply that 40% of liner cargo moving between two trading partners belongs to each, leaving only 20% of the business to cross traders, i.e. ships flying the flags of third countries. When combined with the closed conference provisions of the code, there was a good possibility that service on affected trade routes would be reduced and cargo rates increased. Whether developing countries will reap any benefit from the code remains to be seen.

Urban Transit. On Jan. 1, 1983, various commuter operations formerly operated by Conrail passed into the control of a variety of public agencies. The largest such operation is Metro-North, a unit of the New York State Metropolitan Transportation Authority. The transfer was not accomplished without incident; most of the commuter lines were struck for various periods pending negotiation of new labor agreements. In Metro-North's case the strike lasted six weeks and, despite its normal volume of 170,000 riders per day, commuters seemed to have only moderate difficulty in making alternate arrangements. Significant modernization programs were underway on many of those lines.

Baltimore's 8-mi (13-km) metro system, begun in 1976, opened late in the year. The first 11 mi (18 km) of Dade County's system in Miami was expected to open in December. Congress appropriated $4.2 billion for the Urban Transit Administration, nearly half a billion more than the administration recommended, and preserved the level of operating assistance despite administration opposition. With some $400 million appropriated for new rail starts, the controversial Los Angeles system received initial funding of $117 million. Houston found its proposals rejected in a local referendum, and proposed major federal funding was dropped.

ERNEST W. WILLIAMS, JR.,
Columbia University

TRANSPORTATION / SPECIAL REPORT

The Highways—An Update

In recent years many U.S. highways have experienced accelerated deterioration. Some of these highways have reached the end of their design life, and traffic volumes continue to increase dramatically each year, adding wear and tear to pavement surfaces. In 1981, for example, there were more than 158 million motor vehicles registered in the United States, accounting for an estimated 1.5 trillion travel mi (2.4 trillion km).

As a cornerstone of a bold commitment to revitalize the nation's highways and bridges, Congress passed and President Reagan signed on Jan. 6, 1983, the Surface Transportation Assistance Act of 1982. The centerpiece of this omnibus legislation is a five-cents-per-gallon increase in federal motor-fuel taxes. This was the first time in 23 years that Congress had increased the federal tax on motor fuels. Motorists and commercial users of highways now pay a total of nine cents into the Highway Trust Fund for every gallon of gasoline or diesel fuel they purchase.

As a result of the passage of the 1982 act, an additional $4.4 billion (U.S.) a year in federal highway-user fees will be collected. The extra money will be added to the existing Highway Trust Fund and will allow a significant increase in the level of federal assistance to the states for highway-building and rehabilitation programs. In fiscal year (FY) 1983, for example, the Federal Highway Administration (FHWA) apportioned slightly more than $11 billion to the states for highway programs. This was a 44% increase from the $7.7 billion level for FY 1982. Federal-aid highway apportionments for FY 1984 are expected to exceed $13 billion.

The states, in their turn, are putting the increased federal funds to rapid use. In FY 1983, the departments of transportation of the states were obligating about $1 billion a month for highway-building and improvement projects.

This trend is expected to continue in the years ahead as the Federal-Aid Highway Program continues to address the highway-transportation needs of the nation. Clearly, these substantial increases in funds are necessary to combat further deterioration of U.S. federal-aid highways and bridges. If left unchecked, such continued deterioration would negatively affect the daily lives of all Americans.

In the United States, the FHWA estimates that $456 billion will be needed to maintain adequately all of the highway systems and bridges, including the completion and care of the Interstate Highway System, through the year 2000. Under the Federal-Aid Highway Program, federal funds are dispersed to the states to help construct and repair those highways and bridges that are eligible for federal funds.

The vast majority (some 93%) of the nearly 4 million mi (6.4 million km) of roads and streets in the United States are under the jurisdiction of state and local governments. Most of these roads also are financed entirely by state and local authorities. (The federal government owns outright only about 6% of the total U.S. roadways, mainly in national parks and forests and other government-owned lands.)

About 21.5% of the total mileage in the United States is eligible to receive federal funding under the Federal-Aid Highway Program. While the Interstate System and other federal-aid highways account for only 21.5% of the U.S. route mileage, they carry nearly 80% of the country's vehicular travel.

The most significant changes occurring on the nation's highways have been on the interstate-highway network. Interstate-highway construction began in 1956 under the authorization of the Federal-Aid Highway Act. Since that time, $87 billion has been invested to build the Interstate System. Today 95.9%—40,752 mi (65 582 km)—of the U.S. interstate network is open to traffic. Construction is underway on 566 new mi (911 km) of interstate, and engineering or right-of-way acquisition prior to construction is in progress on an additional 912 mi (1 468 km).

A recent inventory of bridges has revealed that more than 40% of the nation's 564,499 highway bridges are classified as structurally deficient or functionally obsolete. While these bridges pose no safety hazards to the motoring public, it is clear that they must be rehabilitated to carry the modern, larger truck sizes and traffic volumes more efficiently.

With the additional revenues generated by the Surface Transportation Assistance Act, it will be possible to complete the Interstate System in the early 1990s and provide assistance to states in meeting their interstate needs.

International Highways. The road systems of other countries range from the extensive Japanese network of 694,717 mi (1 118 008 km) to the less intricate 23 mi (37 km) road system in the Falkland Islands. Such countries as Austria, Denmark, Malta, Monaco, and the Netherlands have road systems in which 100% of the roadways are paved. Canada has 594,476 mi (884 272 km) of roadway. In 1982 alone, Canada spent more than C$4 billion on highway, road, and street construction.

R. A. BARNHART

A record number of Americans flocked to Paris, above, and other European cities throughout 1983.

TRAVEL

With improvement in the U.S. economy and the U.S. dollar exchanging with other currencies at record levels, Americans traveled in 1983 as if they had been locked in their homes for a decade. When all the figures are in, 1983 may be seen as a signal year in travel, certainly the best since the beginning of worldwide recession.

By July passport offices were being beleaguered by applicants to the extent that the situation made headlines in *The New York Times* and other publications. At one point the New York passport office was struggling with 3,000 applications a day, and similar scenes were taking place elsewhere. Most passport offices had telephone numbers with recorded instructions on how to file an application, and usually a second number for other information, but in this situation not even a recording answered the second number.

By the end of the year, it was estimated that more than four million Americans had visited Europe alone, a record. In addition, the Orient, Pacific islands, Australia, New Zealand, and Mexico reported an increase in American visitors.

It almost goes without saying that some parts of the turbulent world were avoided by travelers—most of Central America, for example, and several areas of the Middle East, all of which formerly were quite dependent on tourism for hard currency. Israel, however, reported a late resurgence of visitors. As for "reverse tourism," the number of visitors to the United States dwindled in proportion to the strength of the dollar against their currencies. For example, Mexicans stayed home because of their country's financial problems, and the French did likewise because of their government's restrictions on the amount of money they could take out of the country.

After initial euphoria, tourism officials, restaurateurs, shopkeepers, and their colleagues began to notice a difference in this decade's American travelers: They were not spending money as freely as their predecessors. After several seasons of at-home belt-tightening, Americans stayed in hotels with moderate rates; ate in bistros, trattorias, and the like; window-shopped but did not buy; and were observed actually checking their bills.

Though airlines continued to experience financial difficulties, Pacific carriers, including Pan American and Northwest Orient, reported a sizable increase in passenger traffic. Most continued to offer special packages and promotional fares, of which cost-conscious travelers took advantage. In the process of shopping around, Americans also revived the charter business, which as late as 1979 had been pronounced dead.

Also, taking up where bankrupt Laker Airways left off, PEOPLExpress began in May offering one-way flights between Newark, NJ,

It was standby only as PEOPLExpress introduced a $149 one-way flight between Newark (NJ) and London.

and London at a no-frills (box lunch), virtually standby basis for $149. It was booked to overflowing late in the year.

Because of the activity, some officials and airline executives worried that within a few years many airports, including these recently built, would be badly overcrowded or even obsolete. However, construction and improvements are constantly under way.

Sales of Eurailpasses for train travel increased significantly, and the regenerated Orient Express from London or Paris to Venice was selling out well into fall. In the United States, Amtrak reported passenger business holding its own, and even a slight increase, mainly attributable to promotional fares.

Cruises. Cruises remained popular to the extent that a record number of passengers were carried, but competition became such that, with the incentives offered—free airfares to points of departure, low or no charge for children in same cabin, discounts on certain reser-

vations—revenues remained about the same as in 1982. Nonetheless, Holland America launched the liner *Nieuw Amsterdam* with a sail to the West Coast, where it is making its home port in San Francisco for cruises to Alaska and Mexico. Reportedly, five more new ships were being planned by other companies.

Having created a buyers' market and a crush in the Caribbean, cruise owners were switching more ships to the Pacific Coast, looking for new ports and itineraries, planning different "theme" cruises, and introducing innovations aboard. Cunard's *QE2,* for instance, installed a computer center complete with instructors for its passengers.

Trends. Paradoxically, throughout the recession, companies that catered to first-class travel experienced few losses. First class and business class on many airlines were well patronized. Tour operators who offered unusual trips at premium rates (balloon-soaring over France, expeditions to the North Pole or Falklands, mountain climbing in Nepal, river rafting in Yugoslavia) felt little pain. An advertisement in a major magazine sought to tempt the affluent in search of new experiences. Registered in Norway, ships of Sea Goddess Cruises will offer Mediterranean and Caribbean adventures at "stylish resorts" to the "one in ten thousand people" who can afford the rates.

Across the United States, particularly on the East and West Coasts, there has been a proliferation of small hostelries or bed-and-breakfast inns. The rates at these establishments, particularly in popular vacation areas, are considerably higher than the name suggests to those familiar with English accommodations known as B&Bs, and their facilities usually cannot match those of a good motel.

CAROLYN STULL, *Free-lance Travel Writer*

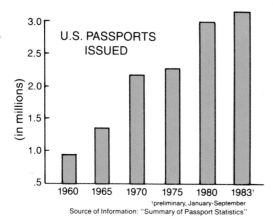

U.S. PASSPORTS ISSUED

(in millions)

3.0 — 2.5 — 2.0 — 1.5 — 1.0 — .5

1960 1965 1970 1975 1980 1983[1]

[1]preliminary, January-September
Source of Information: "Summary of Passport Statistics"

TUNISIA

As President Habib Bourguiba completed his 25th year in power in Tunisia, the country's stability was threatened by undercurrents of Islamic fundamentalism and unrest based on declining economic fortunes. The best news for Tunisia in 1983 was the rapprochement with Algeria.

Foreign Relations. The opening of relations with Algeria may provide Tunisia with a ready market for its goods, and Algerian tourists were expected to begin spending their money on the popular Tunisian coast. But so far, the most direct benefit from the opening of relations between the two countries comes from the pipeline between Algeria and Italy that passes through Tunisia. Under a trilateral agreement, Tunisia has the right to 5.25% of the gas that travels through the line.

The transfer of the headquarters of the Palestine Liberation Organization to Tunis as a result of the Israeli invasion of Lebanon thrust Tunisia into the Middle East spotlight. The conservative Gulf oil states, fearing the possibility of destabilization in Tunisia, sent unprecedented amounts of economic assistance.

The Reagan administration, which sees Tunisia as an American ally, requested $140 million in military aid for Tunisia in 1983, but Congress reduced the figure to $95 million.

Thirty members of the international fundamentalist Islamic Liberation Party were arrested and convicted in August. The 19 soldiers and 11 civilians were tried before a military court on charges of treason. Tunisian officials suspected that a foreign power was behind attempts to destabilize the government.

Economy. Tunisia's economy in 1983 fell short of goals set by the sixth development plan. A positive note was that inflation was reduced to 9.5% from 13.7% in 1982, but gross national product (GNP) growth was only 4.5% compared with the 6% forecast by the plan. Some 42,000 new jobs were created in Tunisia in 1983, but this was 6,000 short of the plan's goal. A state of emergency was enforced as 1984 began after an increase in the price of cereals and bread led to a wave of riots.

The Central Bank's economic report, released in August, said that the economic picture was bleak, and it warned that Tunisia's foreign-exchange shortage was critical. The report cautioned against the unnecessary importation of consumer goods at the expense of the industrial sector's ability to import capital equipment. The bank also said that the balance-of-trade deficit grew by 10% in the first half of 1983.

Volkswagen, the German auto manufacturer, signed an agreement to build a $19 million plant and to begin producing cars in Tunisia by 1985. General Motors is teaming up with the Japanese firm Isuzu to start building small trucks, and Peugeot, which is already operating in Tunisia, made plans to double its production with the Tunisian government as a 60% partner in an auto-component factory.

Mansour Moalla lost his position as minister of finance and planning. Moalla was known to be friendly with Western banks and financial institutions, and he readily imposed austerity measures recommended by the World Bank. The finance ministry was then divided into several departments, enabling Prime Minister Mohamed Mzali to exert more control over the economy.

MICHAEL MAREN, *"Africa Report"*

TURKEY

For Turkey, 1983 witnessed the first national parliamentary elections since the military took over the government three years before.

The Military Government. The Turkish military government, which had been in power since a coup on Sept. 12, 1980, faced criticism that it was authoritarian. Gen. Kenan Evren, chief architect of the 1980 coup, remained the leader of the country. In November 1982, Evren had become president of the republic for a seven-year term under the provisions of a new, military-sponsored constitution that had taken effect that same month upon the holding of a national referendum. His closest associates were five general officers of the National Security Council. The prime minister, who had been in office since September 1980, was former admiral Bülent Ulusu.

President Evren and his associates defended the record of their government, emphasizing that they had brought internal security and much more economic stability to a country that previously had been beset by unrest.

In April 1983, Evren announced that elections would be held on November 6 for a 400-member Grand National Assembly to serve for

---

TUNISIA • Information Highlights

Official Name: Republic of Tunisia.
Location: North Africa.
Area: 63,399 sq mi (164 206 km²).
Population (July 1983 est.): 7,020,000.
Chief City (1975 census): Tunis, the capital, 550,404.
Government: *Head of state,* Habib Bourguiba, president-for-life (took office 1957). *Chief minister,* Mohamed Mzali, prime minister (took office April 1980). *Legislature* (unicameral)—National Assembly.
Monetary Units: Dinar (.681 dinar equals U.S.$1, June 1983).
Gross Domestic Product (1981 U.S.$): $8,100,000,000.
Economic Indexes (1982): *Consumer Prices* (1970 = 100), all items, 154.6; food, 162.8. *Industrial Production* (1982, 1975 = 100), 153.
Foreign Trade (1982 U.S.$): *Imports,* $3,287,000,000; *exports,* $1,959,000,000.

The conservative Motherland Party of Turgut Ozal, left, won a clear majority in parliamentary elections November 6. The week before, an earthquake in eastern mountain regions left thousands dead or homeless in freezing temperatures.

five years, as provided by the new constitution. That same constitution, however, placed a ban on any political party that had existed before the 1980 coup and specifically prohibited many important politicians from taking any role in politics for ten years. Among them were former prime ministers Bülent Ecevit and Süleyman Demirel, whom the military deemed chiefly responsible for Turkey's pre-September 1980 political and economic difficulties. As for the 1983 assembly vote, the government allowed only three parties to bring forth candidates. They were the Nationalist Democracy Party (NDP), headed by Turgut Sunalp, a retired general who obviously enjoyed Evren's support; the Motherland Party of an economist, Turgut Ozal, who had resigned his post as deputy prime minister in July 1982 over a dispute with the military; and the populist Social Democratic Party of Necdet Calp, a former governor. Prime Minister Ulusu ran as an independent on the ticket

of the Nationalist Democracy Party, and individual candidates for each of the three parties had to be approved by the National Security Council.

In the November 6 elections, the Motherland Party of Ozal won a major victory, the electorate obviously voting against the military's favorite, the Nationalist Democracy Party. The Motherland Party received 211 seats in the Grand National Assembly; the populist party, 117; and the Nationalist Democracy Party only 71. One seat went unfilled because the government barred the candidate.

The Grand National Assembly convened on November 24, and on the same day Ulusu submitted his resignation to Evren, who asked him to remain with a caretaker ministry until a new cabinet took office. In early December the National Security Council formally dissolved itself, and Turgut Ozal formed a civilian government. Martial law, however, was not to be lifted immediately, and President Evren, with his seven-year term, retained vast powers.

Economics. Despite the fact that inflation had been reduced enormously since the military took power, Turkey's economy and vast military system, which includes a 400,000-man army, still needed considerable outside assistance. In November 1983 the U.S. Congress passed and President Ronald Reagan signed a $1 billion (U.S.) aid bill. That same month President Evren announced that in 1984, Turkey would begin to build three nuclear-power plants rather than only one as had previously been planned. Contracts for the three were granted to American, West German, and Canadian companies.

Anti-Turkish Acts. A Turkish diplomat, Dursun Aksoy, was assassinated in Brussels on July 14. The next day a bomb exploded at the

---

TURKEY • Information Highlights

Official Name: Republic of Turkey.
Location: Southeastern Europe and southwestern Asia.
Area: 296,000 sq mi (766 640 km²).
Population (July 1983 est.): 49,155,000.
Chief Cities: (1980 census): Ankara, the capital, 2,585,293; Istanbul, 3,904,588; Izmir, 1,673,966.
Government: *Head of state,* Gen. Kenan Evren, president (took office Nov. 10, 1982). *Head of government,* Turgut Ozal, prime minister (took office Dec. 13, 1983). *Legislature*—Grand National Assembly.
Monetary Unit: Lira (268.85 liras equal U.S.$1, Dec. 8, 1983).
Gross Domestic Product (1982 U.S.$): $52,771,-000,000.
Economic Index (1982): *Consumer Prices* (1970 = 100), all items, 2,831.1; food, 2,974.1.
Foreign Trade (1982 U.S.$): *Imports,* $8,753,000,000; *exports,* $5,701,000,000.

Turkish Airlines counter at France's Orly Airport, killing 7 persons and injuring 55. Twelve days later, on July 27, five men invaded the Turkish embassy compound in Lisbon, Portugal. One was killed by a guard, and the other four took the wife of the Turkish chargé d'affaires and her 17-year-old son hostage. The four then blew up the ambassador's residence, killing themselves, the wife of the chargé, and a policeman.

Responsibility for these and similar acts against Turkish officials and interests in the last decade was claimed by secret, revolutionary Armenian groups. These groups sought to avenge the killing of Armenians in the old Turkish Ottoman Empire and to protest the lack of an independent Armenian state. The Turkish government categorically refused to issue any condemnations of past regimes.

Natural Disaster. Turkey suffered a catastrophic earthquake in its two eastern provinces on October 30. More than 1,300 people were killed, and about 30,000 left homeless.

Turkish-Greek Relations and Cyprus. Relations with Turkey's NATO partner Greece remained cool in 1983. Part of this stemmed from matters such as airspace and other rights concerning the Greek Aegean islands. A significant cause of friction was Cyprus, where since 1974, Turkey had maintained an estimated 20,000-man army. The Turkish government reiterated that the force was needed to protect the Turkish Cypriots. (*See also* CYPRUS.) When the Turkish Cypriots under Rauf Denktaş unilaterally declared their independence on Nov. 15, 1983, the Turkish government immediately recognized the act and criticized those, including the UN Security Council, who condemned it.

GEORGE J. MARCOPOULOS, *Tufts University*

UGANDA

An improving economy, refugee problems, and violence were news in Uganda in 1983.

The Economy. With the partial return of peace and stability to Uganda, the nation's economy continued in 1983 to recover from the ravages of the Idi Amin years. Manufacturing rose from 15% to 25% of capacity in one year, and export earnings of both coffee and cotton were strong, as reflected in the $51 million trade surplus. Necessities were less scarce than in past years, although imported products were still expensive and hard to obtain, owing to the government's strict foreign-exchange regulations. Further financial help came in the form of a $30 million debt rescheduling by the United States, France, Italy, and Britain, and by a hoped-for final division of some $1.2 million of East African Community assets. Fuel remained the commodity in shortest supply.

Politics. The government of President Milton Obote maintained control of Uganda in

---

UGANDA • Information Highlights
Official Name: Republic of Uganda.
Location: Interior of East Africa.
Area: 91,000 sq mi (235 690 km²).
Population (July 1983): 13,819,000.
Chief City (1980 census): Kampala, the capital, 458,423.
Government: *Head of state,* Milton Obote, president (elected Dec. 1980). *Head of government,* Otema Alimadi, prime minister (appointed Dec. 1980). *Legislature* (unicameral)—Parliament, 126 members.
Monetary Unit: Uganda shilling (124.5 shillings equal U.S.$1, April 1983).
Gross Domestic Product (1981 U.S.$1): $765.

1983, as continuing raids by rebel groups and random personal violence posed less of a threat than in the past. There were reports of massacres in refugees' camps, with government and opposition blaming each other for the deaths, which numbered more than 500. Buses also were a target, and two raids in early 1983 resulted in more than 30 dead.

Nevertheless the government seemed to be increasingly successful in restoring order in the country. Most rebel groups had been pushed far back from the capital, and most deaths now appeared to be from lack of food and medicine rather than from outright killing. The government also was successful in bringing pressure on the main political opposition groups in Parliament, notably the Democratic Party. Some DP members were arrested, and some in Parliament joined Obote's Uganda People's Congress. Vice-President Paulo Muwanga appeared to be the main force behind the political undermining of the opposition.

Some of the Uganda army's successes can be attributed to North Korean instructors, who directed the retraining of the army and police, and to the flight of many potential opponents from the country. It was estimated that as many as 175,000 Ugandan refugees were in camps in the Sudan and nearby countries.

Refugee Problems. In an attempt to end an old injustice, President Obote invited back to Uganda all Asians who had been expelled by Idi Amin and allowed them to reclaim their confiscated property or receive compensation for it. Some 45,000 Uganda Asians were affected, as were 3,500 businesses worth more than $400 million. Assets not retaken by former owners were sold to Ugandans, with the Asians getting cash. By late 1983, only a few Asians had returned or filed property claims.

Another refugee problem was created when 60,000 Rwandans, many of whom had lived in southern Uganda for generations, were expelled in November 1982. The Rwandans were resented for their generally higher level of education and employment. Obote promised to allow those who could prove Ugandan citizenship to return to Uganda.

ROBERT GARFIELD, *DePaul University*

USSR

In the Soviet Union, 1983 was the year of Yuri Vladimirovich Andropov, who assumed the Kremlin leadership on the death of President Leonid Brezhnev in late 1982. And it was a year in which the Soviet Union's three-year economic recession was reversed, at least temporarily, while relations with the industrialized West, especially the United States, badly soured. The atmosphere of relations with China continued to thaw, although there was no progress on resolving the issues of substance that divide the neighboring Communist giants. Soviet troops pursued their war against opponents of the client Afghan regime of Babrak Karmal, not in any danger of losing the conflict but not visibly close to winning it either.

By year's end the Soviets and the United States were without any agreed forum for bilateral arms-control talks. Moscow, angered by the deployment of new U.S. missiles in Europe, pointedly refrained from setting a date for resuming talks after their regular late-year recess. Briefly during the summer, there were signs that both superpowers were anxious to start undoing the chill in relations that began at the end of the 1970s and greatly intensified after President Ronald Reagan moved into the White House in 1981. But this process promptly ran into crisis over the Kremlin's downing of a Korean Air Lines civilian jet that had strayed near sensitive military installations in the Soviet Far East. Amid a storm of Western criticism, Moscow initially said very little about the incident beyond charging that the Boeing jumbo had been on a U.S. spy mission. Six days after the fact the Soviet chief of staff publicly acknowledged that the plane had been shot down.

Also by the end of 1983, the physical health of the 69-year-old Andropov—who had not appeared publicly for more than four months because of what Soviet spokesmen insisted was a bad cold—began unavoidably to cloud an otherwise impressively smooth Kremlin transition from the 18-year reign of Mr. Brezhnev.

Domestic Affairs

Economy. Andropov, chief of the KGB security police for some 15 years before becoming Communist Party chief in November 1982, oversaw in 1983 a shift in policy priorities from foreign to domestic affairs. Arms control, relations with the United States, and other key international issues were still very much on the Kremlin agenda. This was inescapably so, if only due to the publicly announced Western intention to deploy new U.S. missiles in Europe by year's end. But as one senior official put it privately at midyear, 1983 was a time for a long-overdue look at the home front, particularly a stagnant economy.

On balance, the year's results were reason for cheer in the Kremlin and among consumers, who were treated to an end of serious shortages of meat, dairy products, and other food items. With the man at the top old and visibly frail, all aspects of political and economic activity seemed to stagnate. The econ-

An ailing Yuri Andropov missed November anniversary observances of the Bolshevik revolution, but his presence was felt.

Wide World

More than 30 Soviet tankers and freighters were trapped in an early October ice pack off northeastern Siberia. One sank and nearly all the others suffered some damage. Nuclear-powered ice breakers freed the vessels by the end of the month.

omy was hampered by abysmal farming weather, as well as by labor shortages, low worker productivity, and general inefficiencies and corruption. But a report made in the name of Andropov (who was absent) at a December 1983 Communist Party Central Committee session trumpeted industrial growth of some 4% for the year, up sharply from a dismal 2.8% in 1982. No figure was yet given for the year's grain crop, but it was sure to be the best in four very lean years—marked by record imports— if still below the wildly optimistic annual target (230 million metric tons) set for the present five-year plan. And the crucially important harvest of animal feed grain also began looking up in the winter of 1982–83. Since the Soviets had avoided distress slaughter of herds during the lean 1979–1981 period, the improvement led to relatively rapid increases of meat and dairy products on state store counters in 1983.

Implementation began of a national food program announced shortly before Brezhnev's death and designed to afford better coordination of the stages in agriculture and food marketing and to give regional and local officials more say. A network of district agro-industrial associations (known as their Russian acronym, RAPO, and an intended linchpin in the food program) was set up in 1983. Officials hailed this step but lamented a reluctance among some RAPOs to use their new authority.

Worker productivity—which the Kremlin acknowledged as the key to economic growth in the 1980s—also rebounded markedly after several years in the doldrums. Energy production, crucial to hard-currency export earnings, also did well. Oil output rose slightly, defying a U.S. Central Intelligence Agency (CIA) prediction in the late 1970s that oil figures would begin to decline before too long. And extraction of natural gas, which the Kremlin hopes will compensate for an end to the oil boom of previous decades, continued to expand.

These improvements were due in part to Andropov's early emphasis on discipline throughout the economy and, in the case of farming, to widened incentives introduced along with the food program. But key obstacles to a sustained improvement in on-the-job discipline—alcoholism, lack of worker initiative, inefficient planning, and corruption—survived the discipline campaign. Productivity's major spurt occurred at the start of 1983, wavering somewhat thereafter. In what appeared to be an official acknowledgment that there is no early cure for widespread drinking, vodka prices were lowered in the autumn, a reversal of a steady upward trend. On the farm the major catalyst for the year's upward swing came in the form of markedly better weather.

Aware of major systemic roadblocks to economic expansion, Andropov's team began a cautious search for reform of the economic mechanism—Moscow shorthand for measures to give local managers greater autonomy and to make wider use of incentives for workers who work well. Despite talk by Western pundits of rapid, wholesale shifts in the way the Soviet economy is run, officials made clear that the Andropov regime intended the changes to be gradual. An experiment in reform was announced, to begin at the start of 1984, for the heavy machinery and electro-technical industries and for various individual factories outside Moscow.

Andropov did hint publicly at what could be one major economic change: bringing the nation's centrally set, and subsidized, prices more closely into line with market forces of supply and demand. But by year's end there had been no follow-up on his remarks.

Politics. The Brezhnev-Andropov transition was the most carefully prepared and smoothest in Soviet history. For several years before Brezhnev died in November 1982, Moscow's top officials had been as aware as the rest of the world that a change in leadership could not be far off. There also had been widespread recognition of the inevitable policy priorities of the post-Brezhnev era. Indeed, Brezhnev's own public utterances during his last few years in power foreshadowed Andropov's early empha-

Visiting West German Chancellor Helmut Kohl (far left) *discussed arms control with Yuri Andropov* (far right) *in July.*

sis on discipline and economic efficiency and on generally combating a laxness that had come to pervade all facets of Soviet society and politics (with the exception of the dissident movement). Having beaten out longtime Brezhnev protégé and fellow Politburo member Konstantin Chernenko for the top party spot, Andropov in 1983 set about consolidating a consensus for putting the Soviets' own economic house in order. Chernenko, by the start of the year, had relinquished his powerful parallel duties as head of the General Department of the party's inner Secretariat, which along with the Politburo rules the country. The General Department, among other things, handles all policy reports and other documents drawn up for the Politburo and Secretariat. But Chernenko did retain his dual, full membership on the Politburo and Secretariat—a distinction shared only by Andropov and two other senior colleagues —and was given the traditionally important Secretariat portfolio for ideology and foreign affairs.

Three younger men received important Kremlin promotions during the year. Grigory Romanov, the Leningrad party chief who shares Andropov's preoccupation with discipline and cautious reform but is reputed to have strong leadership ambitions of his own, added a spot on the Secretariat to his Politburo chair and moved to Moscow. He handles heavy-industry issues in the Secretariat. At the end of the year, two Andropov protégés—Vitaly Vorotnikov and Yegor Ligachov—also were promoted. Vorotnikov was named to full Politburo membership, and Ligachov to a seat on the Secretariat. The moves, though boosts for Andropov within the ruling bodies, were in effect automatic results of promotions made earlier in the year. Vorotnikov had become prime minister for the Russian Republic, the largest and most important of the Soviet Union's 15 constituent republics. Ligachov had been handed the directorship of one of the key

policy-specific departments attached to the Secretariat, dealing with organizational and personnel issues. Andropov himself added the ceremonial post of Soviet president to his position as general secretary of the ruling Communist Party in 1983. He was only the second Soviet leader to hold both posts simultaneously; Brezhnev had been the first.

Yet one key to implementing any major policy changes—a turnover of political and economic personnel at regional and local levels— progressed slowly. Andropov and his team worked vigorously toward this end, with local party elections set for early in 1984. Still, some Western diplomats in Moscow wondered whether Andropov's health problems might limit his ability to place his own stamp on the outcome.

Dissidence and Reform. Any doubt of Kremlin determination to crack down hard on organized dissidence was erased in 1980, with the internal exile to the city of Gorky of Nobel Prize-winning physicist Andrei Sakharov, the linchpin in a dissident movement already shrunk by the detention or exile of other major figures. Since then the authorities have carried their campaign to its logical conclusion with a series of trials, imprisonments, or other sanctions against lesser dissident figures. The process continued without interruption as Yuri Andropov shifted from KGB head to the party leadership. In 1983, amid worsening relations with the United States, Jewish emigration from the USSR also dropped to its lowest annual level—about 1,300—since the Soviets first allowed large numbers of Jews to leave in the 1970s.

Within the confines of the party establishment and in the official media, meanwhile, a widening Kremlin consensus on the need to examine alternatives for economic reform did yield a livelier brand of discussion, even debate, than in recent years. There were also cautious moves, owing partly to the events next-door in Poland, to sanction widened polling, research, and analysis of public opinion.

Armed Forces. The Soviet military received high political priority in 1983, amid the Kremlin's publicly expressed determination to safeguard the nation's defense in light of worsening relations with the United States and the deadlock in arms-control talks. The USSR maintained more than 4 million men in uniform, including an estimated 100,000 in combat conditions in Afghanistan.

On the nuclear-arms front the Soviets tested at least one new ballistic missile, with some U.S. officials alleging that a second had been tested in defiance of the still-unratified SALT II agreement of 1979. The Soviets also moved energetically toward development of a radar-elusive cruise missile along the lines of the U.S. cruise, having unsuccessfully called on the Reagan administration to agree to a moratorium on such weapons. With no agreement in Geneva negotiations on the larger issue of limiting medium-range nuclear arms in Europe, the Kremlin also announced it would base new nuclear rockets in Czechoslovakia and East Germany. Moscow also vowed to site new nuclear arms within short striking distance of U.S. territory in reply to the West's Euromissile deployment—and hinted this could mean sea-basing of the new Soviet cruise missile.

Moscow meanwhile sent long-range conventional antiaircraft missiles—SAM-5s—to Syria as part of a major rearmament program. An estimated 7,000 Soviet military advisers and other personnel were said to be manning the missiles and helping operate new, more so-

At the Madrid Conference on Security and Cooperation in Europe, September 7, Soviet Foreign Minister Andrei Gromyko defended the downing of Korean Air Lines Flight 007.

Thierry Campion/Gamma-Liaison

phisticated radar and command-control apparatus also provided by Moscow. But despite attacks on Syrian-held areas of Lebanon by both Israeli and U.S. forces, none of the new Soviet weaponry within Syria proper had come into play by year's end. Both private and public evidence in Moscow suggested that the Soviets were leery of encouraging Syria into action that might risk a major showdown with the United States.

At home, top Soviet military figures took an unprecedentedly high public profile in enunciating Kremlin arms policy—a development seen by many Western diplomats as a reflection of an expanded military role in Kremlin decision making. Chief of Staff Marshal Nikolai Ogarkov and his deputy both gave Moscow news conferences—although Ogarkov's debut was prompted by the need to explain the Soviet's position on the downing of the Korean Air Lines jumbo jet, an embarrassing episode that seemed, at least briefly, to cause strain between Moscow's civilian and military officials.

Civilian and military spokesmen, meanwhile, stepped up warnings that the deployment of new U.S.rockets in Western Europe could force the Kremlin formally to shift to a policy of launch-on-warning, whereby the first electronic signal of an enemy launch could, without civilian intervention, trigger a major counterstrike.

Space. Soviet space officials, amid the rapid expansion of the U.S. shuttle program, focused their own efforts on assembly of a large, permanently manned orbital complex. The project involves adding, in building-block fashion, independently powered space modules to the Salyut-series orbital station. The seventh and latest in the Salyut series was launched in 1982; and in 1983, cosmonauts worked for the first time aboard a prototype complex consisting of Salyut-7 plus a single additional module. The module later uncoupled from Salyut and was sent toward earth, where, apparently according to plan, it burned up upon reentry.

But the Soviets did suffer at least two space setbacks during the year. One occurred when the first crew sent aloft to dock with the expanded Salyut was unable to do so, apparently because of problems with their capsule's guidance system; such hitches had occurred in previous Soviet missions. The second setback involved the launch-pad explosion of a rocket that was to have sent a new crew to Salyut. Fail-safe mechanisms propelled the capsule free of the explosion, and the crew parachuted back to earth.

By year's end the Soviet's were gradually softening their contention that Moscow had no need for a reusable space vehicle and hinted that a Soviet shuttle craft might be in the works. Also in 1983, the Soviets charged repeatedly that the U.S. shuttle program represented a bid to militarize outer space. The

After a 23-year struggle, a total of 31 Siberian Pentecostals were granted exit visas. Several of them had been residing in the basement of the U.S. embassy since 1978.

Soviets denied a U.S. charge that they have been testing a hunter-killer satellite designed to destroy rival orbital vehicles either by hurling debris in their path or crashing into them. Moscow formally proposed banning the militarization of outer space. But the proposal, seen by U.S. officials as largely aimed at curbing the shuttle program and a separate U.S. move to test an antisatellite weapon, triggered no visible interest in Washington.

Trade. Official figures pointed to a relative increase in the share of Eastern bloc and Third World countries in Soviet foreign commerce, but trade with the West continued in large, slightly increased volume. In an effort to compensate for a drop in world oil prices, the USSR—the world's top producer—skillfully timed price adjustments and spot-market sales. The Soviets also signed a new grain import pact with the United States that included a 50% increase in the annual minimum volume.

Foreign Affairs

Soviet foreign policy was dominated in 1983 by the issue of relations with the United States and other Western states. Moscow concentrated on efforts to keep Washington and its NATO allies from going ahead with plans to deploy new, medium-range nuclear missiles near Soviet territory. Ultimately, the Kremlin efforts failed, as the new U.S. missiles began arriving in Europe near the end of the year. The Soviets, as threatened, broke off talks in Geneva on a negotiated limit for such weapons. Other priority areas were China and the Mideast and, to a lesser extent, Latin America.

United States/Arms Control. Even before Yuri Andropov assumed the Soviet party leadership, Moscow had been engaged in a spiraling war of invective with the administration of President Reagan. And on the key substantive issue between the superpowers—nuclear-arms control—the Soviets rejected administration

approaches on both European nuclear arms and, at the separate START talks, on longer-range strategic weapons. On strategic arms, the Soviets continued to bridle at Reagan's contention that an agreement must above all limit large-yield land ballistic missiles. These, officials in Moscow noted, form a far larger proportion of the Soviet nuclear force than of the U.S. one, which relies more heavily on submarine-launched missiles. Near year's end there was some hint of progress in START, as the United States signaled readiness to include in the talks such other arms as cruise missiles and nuclear-capable bombers. As it happened, however, any potential progress in START was quickly overshadowed by the superpower stalemate on shorter-range European weapons. After all, the Geneva talks on this issue were working against the deadline of NATO's intention to deploy new U.S. missiles by the end of 1983 if there were no palatable compromise at the negotiating table.

Andropov's major arms proposals during the year focused on the Euromissile issue. They involved a softening of some elements of Moscow's initial negotiating stand, but they did not get at the main bone of contention in the talks. The West argued that Moscow enjoyed a monopoly on such arms, in the form of more than 300 mobile, triple-warhead SS-20 rockets deployed since the late 1970s and capable of hitting all of Western Europe with devastating accuracy. The West said that NATO would cancel deployment of the new U.S. rockets only if all SS-20s were scrapped. The Soviets said the counting was unfair, that Britain and France possessed 162 nuclear missiles of their own and Moscow needed SS-20s to balance them. Moreover, it contended, Britain had begun adding warheads to its missiles and France had similar modernization plans. The United States argued that the British and French forces could not be counted for two reasons: first, they are independently controlled, outside NATO, and not intended for the defense of other European states like West Germany; and second, the weapons are less powerful and accurate than the SS-20s. Gradually, Andropov ceded on some points. He abandoned Moscow's opening position that all SS-20s, rather than just an equivalent force for the British and French missiles, must stay. Then he abandoned an initial contention that SS-20s targeted on Europe might be moved into Soviet Asia, rather than scrapped, as part of an accord. And finally he offered to count warheads, rather than just SS-20 launchers. He did insist that British and French arms must be counted and that at least 150 SS-20s must stay in the European USSR in order to balance the warheads on British and French weapons.

And so NATO deployment began. The Euromissile talks in Geneva were broken off. And, amid a chorus of public Soviet statements presenting an unprecedented bleak post-Cold War view of superpower relations, Moscow at least temporarily suspended other arms talks. These included the START negotiations and the decade-old talks in Vienna on reducing conventional forces in Europe. Both negotiations recessed as scheduled, but without Moscow's agreement on when they would resume.

Europe. A leitmotiv of the Soviet's Euromissile strategy in 1983 was a continued bid to encourage strains between key West European nations and the United States—particularly on issues of trade, where the Europeans have a far greater stake in détente than the United States. The efforts met with some success. Partly under pressure from Western allies, for instance, President Reagan canceled an embargo on U.S.-made equipment for a huge gas-export pipeline from Siberia to Western Europe. But electoral triumphs by conservative leaders in Britain and West Germany—and the rule of a socialist government in France less friendly toward Moscow than its predecessor under Valéry Giscard D'Estaing—contributed to an overall souring of Soviet relations with Western Europe as well. NATO's start on deploying U.S. missiles exacerbated the situation.

China. The Soviets pursued a bid, begun at the tail end of the Brezhnev era, to end their 20-year split with China. A third round of normalization talks between the Communist superpowers was held in the fall. A new trade pact in 1983 envisaged a substantial increase in Sino-Soviet turnover, though the volume was still nowhere near that of Sino-U.S. trade. Atmospherically, relations between Moscow and Peking brightened with revived cultural, scientific, and sports exchanges. But there was no visible progress on three major bones of contention—the Sino-Soviet frontier issue, the Soviet presence in Afghanistan, and Moscow's backing of the Vietnamese military presence in Cambodia.

Middle East. The Soviets rearmed Syria on a major scale in the aftermath of the beating that Syrian forces took during Israel's 1982 invasion of Lebanon. Soviet officials left little doubt that Moscow would side firmly with Syria, its major Arab ally, in the case of a major Israeli-Syrian conflict or a direct threat to Syrian territory. But the Soviets and Syrians both appeared reluctant to encourage such a showdown over the crisis in Lebanon. Moscow sharply criticized the U.S. role in Lebanon, particularly the presence of American Marines. But on that issue, too, the Kremlin seemed, at least for the time being, more interested in savoring the Americans' vulnerability to Lebanese unrest than in courting a showdown.

Soviet ties with Iran continued to wilt. The Iranian authorities cracked down on the country's pro-Soviet Communist party in May 1983 and immediately thereafter expelled 18 Soviet diplomats. Moscow's media took a more hostile tone toward Tehran and also gradually abandoned their carefully even-handed treatment of the war between Iran and Iraq.

In neighboring Afghanistan, Soviet troops pressed their war with antigovernment guerrillas. Moscow let it be known that a political settlement to the conflict would be welcome but made it equally clear that this must involve peace with honor, notably the survival of a regime in Kabul basically friendly to Moscow.

Latin America. The Soviets continued publicly to back Cuba and Nicaragua, as well as antigovernment rebels in El Salvador. Western officials reported continued conventional arms transfers from the USSR to Nicaragua. But despite U.S. charges of ambitious Soviet designs in the region, Moscow seemed intent in 1983 on steering clear of a superpower test of strength there. When U.S. forces invaded Grenada the Soviets limited themselves to virulent public criticism. One emphasis of Soviet policy in Latin America remained to consolidate trade relationships with Brazil and Argentina.

NED TEMKO
"The Christian Science Monitor"

USSR • Information Highlights

Official Name: Union of Soviet Socialist Republics.
Location: Eastern Europe and northern Asia.
Area: 8,649,498 sq mi (22,402,200 km²).
Population (July 1983 est.): 272,308,000.
Chief Cities (Jan. 1, 1982 est.): Moscow, the capital, 8,301,000; Leningrad, 4,719,000; Kiev, 2,297,000.
Government: *Head of state,* Yuri V. Andropov, president (took office June 16, 1983). *Head of government,* Nikolai A. Tikhonov, premier (took office Oct. 1980). Secretary-general of the Communist Party, Yuri V. Andropov (took office Nov. 1982). *Legislature*—Supreme Soviet: Soviet of the Union Soviet of Nationalities.
Monetary Unit: Ruble (0.763 ruble equals U.S. $1, September 1983—noncommercial rate).
Economic Index (1982): *Industrial Production,* 1975 = 100), 132.
Foreign Trade: *Imports,* $77,793,000,000; *exports,* $86,949,000,000.

UNITED NATIONS

The atmosphere of escalating confrontation between the United States and Soviet Union cast its pall over the United Nations throughout much of 1983. It dominated the meetings of virtually every UN organ and, combined with the chronic political limitations of the institution, curtailed its ability to achieve progress on many issues facing it. A drive launched by Secretary-General Javier Pérez de Cuellar to reinvigorate the UN as a forum for negotiation and settlement of disputes bogged down after several months, and officials blamed the Cold War atmosphere. The actions of both superpowers appeared to be out of the mainstream of international opinion—in particular the destruction of a civilian airliner by Soviet warplanes on September 1 and the American-led intervention in Grenada the following month, as UN debates demonstrated. The widening gulf between Washington and Moscow on arms control was criticized in many resolutions.

It was during the debate on the destruction of Korean Air Lines Flight 007 that the representative of Nigeria—one of the swing countries in the Third World—articulated the prime concern of many nations. Nigeria's O. O. Fafowora took a strong stand against the Soviet action but added: "This incident is a symptom of a much deeper malaise. The superpowers appear to have embarked on confrontation and on a collision path, thereby posing a grave danger to the very existence and safety of ordinary men, women, and children throughout the world who simply want to live in peace. It is a totally deplorable situation and one which calls for a deliberate and sustained effort by the superpowers to seek accommodation."

Instead, the dispute over the airliner led to a situation that threatened the functioning of the UN itself. The governors of New York and New Jersey, angered by the deaths of the 269 people on the plane, barred landing rights to local airports for Soviet Foreign Minister Andrei Gromyko, who was due in for his annual visit to the General Assembly and a meeting with Secretary of State George Shultz. The Soviets rejected a U.S. offer to let Gromyko land at a nearby military base, canceled his UN visit, and charged at a UN committee meeting that the United States was not a fit host for the United Nations. U.S. delegate Charles Lichenstein replied that if the Soviets and others want to move UN headquarters out of New York, "we will put no impediment in your way" and in fact "will be down at dockside waving you a fond farewell as you sail into the sunset." His attack on the UN won the blessing of President Reagan and helped spur an overwhelming Senate vote to cut U.S. contributions to the UN budget.

The furor died down after Reagan, in a speech to the General Assembly on September

UPI

Jorge Illueca of Panama, president of the General Assembly, addresses the world body after his election September 20.

26, restated U.S. support for the UN. A House-Senate conference committee quietly restored the budget cut, though it did require that U.S. payments not rise above 1983 levels. The incident served as a reminder of the UN's shaky status in the eyes of the American public.

General Assembly. In addition to its regular 38th session, which opened September 20 and was suspended December 20, the Assembly's 37th session reconvened briefly in May to adopt a resolution calling for the withdrawal of Turkish troops from Cyprus. The Turkish Cypriots, objecting to the move, refused to participate in the intercommunal talks with the Greek Cypriots that had been scheduled to resume.

Jorge Illueca, the vice-president of Panama, was elected president of the 38th Assembly by a vote of 83 to 70 over Davidson Hepburn of the Bahamas. St. Christopher-Nevis was admitted as the UN's 158th member.

In addition to President Reagan, a number of world leaders attended the annual general debate at the start of the Assembly, including the presidents of France, Egypt, Yugoslavia, Finland, Colombia, Tanzania, and Nicaragua and the prime ministers of Britain, Canada, Sweden, India, and Austria. At the invitation of India's Prime Minister Indira Gandhi, chair of the Nonaligned Movement, a number of leaders from the East, West, and Third World attended two informal gatherings in the UN basement, at which a range of world problems was discussed. But the absence of Soviet and U.S. officials limited the meetings' impact on world tensions.

ORGANIZATION OF THE UNITED NATIONS

THE SECRETARIAT

Secretary-General: Javier Pérez de Cuellar (until Dec. 31, 1986)

THE GENERAL ASSEMBLY (1983)

President: Jorge E. Illueca/Panama
The 158 member nations were as follows:

Afghanistan	Central African	German Demo-	Laos	Papua New	Surinam
Albania	Republic	cratic Republic	Lebanon	Guinea	Swaziland
Algeria	Chad	Germany, Federal	Lesotho	Paraguay	Sweden
Angola	Chile	Republic of	Liberia	Peru	Syria
Antigua and	China, People's	Ghana	Libya	Philippines	Tanzania
Barbuda	Republic of	Greece	Luxembourg	Poland	Thailand
Argentina	Colombia	Grenada	Madagascar	Portugal	Togo
Australia	Comoros	Guatemala	Malawi	Qatar	Trinidad and Tobago
Austria	Congo	Guinea	Malaysia	Rumania	Tunisia
Bahamas	Costa Rica	Guinea-Bissau	Maldives	Rwanda	Turkey
Bahrain	Cuba	Guyana	Mali	Saint Christopher	Uganda
Bangladesh	Cyprus	Haiti	Malta	and Nevis	Ukrainian SSR
Barbados	Czechoslovakia	Honduras	Mauritania	Saint Lucia	USSR
Belgium	Denmark	Hungary	Mauritius	Saint Vincent and	United Arab Emirates
Belize	Djibouti	Iceland	Mexico	the Grenadines	United Kingdom
Belorussian SSR	Dominica	India	Mongolia	São Tomé and	United States
Benin	Dominican	Indonesia	Morocco	Principe	Upper Volta
Bhutan	Republic	Iran	Mozambique	Saudi Arabia	Uruguay
Bolivia	Ecuador	Iraq	Nepal	Senegal	Vanuatu
Botswana	Egypt	Ireland	Netherlands	Seychelles	Venezuela
Brazil	El Salvador	Israel	New Zealand	Sierra Leone	Vietnam
Bulgaria	Equatorial Guinea	Italy	Nicaragua	Singapore	Western Samoa
Burma	Ethiopia	Ivory Coast	Niger	Solomon Islands	Yemen
Burundi	Fiji	Jamaica	Nigeria	Somalia	Yemen, Democratic
Cambodia	Finland	Japan	Norway	South Africa	Yugoslavia
Cameroon	France	Jordan	Oman	Spain	Zaire
Canada	Gabon	Kenya	Pakistan	Sri Lanka	Zambia
Cape Verde	Gambia	Kuwait	Panama	Sudan	Zimbabwe

COMMITTEES

General. Composed of 29 members as follows: The General Assembly president; the 21 General Assembly vice presidents (heads of delegations or their deputies of Algeria, Belgium, Bhutan, Burundi, Canada, China, Czechoslovakia, France, Guyana, Lebanon, Liberia, Nepal, Pakistan, Sierra Leone, Singapore, Sudan, Swaziland, USSR, United Kingdom, United States, Venezuela); and the chairmen of the following main committees, which are composed of all 158 member countries.

First (Political and Security): Tom Eric Vraalsen (Norway)
Special Political: Ernesto Rodriguez Medina (Colombia)
Second (Economic and Financial): Peter Dietze (German Democratic Republic)
Third (Social, Humanitarian and Cultural): Saroj Chavanaviraj (Thailand)
Fourth (Decolonization): Ali Treiki (Libya)
Fifth (Administrative and Budgetary): Sumihiro Kuyama (Japan)
Sixth (Legal): Eliès Gastli (Tunisia)

THE TRUSTEESHIP COUNCIL

President: John W. D. Margetson (United Kingdom)

China[2]   France[2]   USSR[2]   United Kingdom[2]   United States[1]

[1] Administers Trust Territory. [2] Permanent member of Security Council not administering Trust Territory.

THE SECURITY COUNCIL

Membership ends on December 31 of the year noted; asterisks indicate permanent membership.

China*	Netherlands (1984)	USSR*
Egypt (1985)	Nicaragua (1984)	United Kingdom*
France*	Pakistan (1984)	United States*
India (1985)	Peru (1985)	Upper Volta (1985)
Malta (1984)	Ukrainian SSR (1985)	Zimbabwe (1984)

THE INTERNATIONAL COURT OF JUSTICE

Membership ends on February 5 of the year noted.

President: Taslim O. Elias (Nigeria, 1985)
Vice President: José Sette Camara (Brazil, 1988)

Roberto Ago (Italy, 1988)
Mohammed Bedjaoui (Algeria, 1988)
Guy Ladreit De Lacharrière (France, 1991)
Abdallah Fikri El-Khani (Syria, 1985)
Robert Y. Jennings (United Kingdom, 1991)
Manfred Lachs (Poland, 1985)

Kéba Mbaye (Senegal, 1991)
Platon D. Morozov (USSR, 1988)
Hermann Mosler (Fed. Rep. of Germany, 1985)
Shigeru Oda (Japan, 1985)
José María Ruda (Argentina, 1991)
Stephen Schwebel (United States, 1988)
Nagendra Singh (India, 1991)

THE ECONOMIC AND SOCIAL COUNCIL

President: S. Correa da Costa (Brazil)
Membership ends on December 31 of the year noted.

Algeria (1985)	Greece (1984)	St. Lucia (1984)
Argentina (1986)	Indonesia (1986)	Saudi Arabia (1985)
Austria (1984)	Japan (1984)	Sierra Leone (1985)
Benin (1984)	Lebanon (1985)	Somalia (1986)
Botswana (1985)	Liberia (1984)	Sri Lanka (1986)
Brazil (1984)	Luxembourg (1985)	Surinam (1985)
Bulgaria (1985)	Malaysia (1985)	Swaziland (1984)
Canada (1986)	Mali (1984)	Sweden (1986)
China (1986)	Mexico (1985)	Thailand (1985)
Colombia (1984)	Netherlands (1985)	Tunisia (1984)
Congo (1985)	New Zealand (1985)	Uganda (1986)
Djibouti (1985)	Pakistan (1984)	USSR (1986)
Ecuador (1985)	Papua New Guinea (1986)	United Kingdom (1986)
Finland (1986)	Poland (1986)	United States (1985)
France (1984)	Portugal (1984)	Venezuela (1984)
German Democratic Republic (1985)	Qatar (1984)	Yugoslavia (1986)
Germany, Federal Republic of (1984)	Rumania (1984)	Zaire (1986)
	Rwanda (1986)	

INTERGOVERNMENTAL AGENCIES

Food and Agricultural Organization (FAO); General Agreement on Tariffs and Trade (GATT); International Atomic Energy Agency (IAEA); International Bank for Reconstruction and Development (World Bank); International Civil Aviation Organization (ICAO); International Fund for Agricultural Development (IFAD); International Labor Organization (ILO); International Maritime Organization (IMO); International Monetary Fund (IMF); International Telecommunication Union (ITU); United Nations Educational, Scientific and Cultural Organization (UNESCO); Universal Postal Union (UPU); World Health Organization (WHO); World Intellectual Property Organization (WIPO); World Meteorological Organization (WMO).

The Security Council heard a tape of the Soviet fighter pilot who shot down KAL Flight 007: "The target is destroyed."

The most serious U.S. setback in the Assembly was the adoption of a resolution on November 2 that "deeply deplored" the armed intervention in Grenada and called for the immediate withdrawal of foreign troops. The vote was 108 to 9, with 27 abstentions, leaving the United States isolated from virtually all its allies. Only Israel and El Salvador joined the United States and the six Caribbean nations that participated in the operation in voting against the draft. By comparison, the vote was 116 to 20, with 17 abstentions, on a resolution calling on the USSR to end its occupation of Afghanistan.

There were several challenges to delegations' credentials. For the second straight year, Iran moved for the ouster of the Israeli delegation, and the United States warned that if the effort succeeded, Washington would walk out of the Assembly and cut off all UN funds. A showdown was averted by a Norwegian motion, adopted by a 79–43 vote, with 19 abstentions, to pigeonhole Iran's proposal; the Iranians vowed to try again in 1984. A number of resolutions critical of Israel were adopted, but few broke new ground.

The United States challenged the credentials of Grenada's delegation, which had been appointed by Prime Minister Maurice Bishop, whose assassination triggered the takeover of the island. Grenada's Governor-General Sir Paul Scoon also sought to oust the delegates, but both sides agreed to defer any action.

The Assembly, without a vote, seated the Cambodian coalition regime headed by Prince Norodom Sihanouk rather than the government backed by Vietnam. In a separate resolution, the Assembly called for the withdrawal of Vietnamese troops from Cambodia, by a 105–23 vote, with 19 abstentions.

At the request of Nicaragua, the Assembly took up the crisis in Central America for the first time. The outcome was a resolution adopted by consensus that condemned all acts of aggression in the region and supported the establishment of democracy. The outcome was seen as a U.S. victory and a setback for Nicaragua's attempt to single out Washington for blame. The resolution endorsed mediation efforts by the "Contadora Group," composed of Mexico, Panama, Venezuela, and Colombia. The United States did suffer a setback on Latin American policy when the Assembly, over the intense protest of U.S. Ambassador Jeane Kirkpatrick, adopted resolutions condemning human-rights violations by Guatemala, El Salvador, and Chile. Many allies split with Washington on these texts, which called for an end to U.S. military aid and a political role for the Salvadoran rebels.

During the Assembly's annual debate on terrorism, 43 delegations singled out the October 9 bombing in Burma that killed 17 visiting South Korean officials. Almost half the delegations concurred with the conclusion of Burmese investigators that the North Korean regime was behind the attack.

There was one political issue on which the United States and Soviet Union saw eye to eye. Both were reluctant to let the UN explore the present treaty system on Antarctica, under which 16 countries with territorial claims or scientific interests in the continent define the rules governing its use. The 16 feared that if all nations were to participate and assert a common claim on the continent's potential oil and mineral wealth, the 24-year-old treaty setting aside national claims to parts of Antarctica—and its vital disarmament provisions—would be jeopardized. The Assembly compromise was to ask for a study of the issue.

Security Council. The Council dealt with a wide range of crisis situations in 1983 but was unable to take effective action on any, either because no resolution could be passed or because the resolutions were ignored.

On September 6 the United States played to the hushed Council chamber a recording of the Soviet pilot who shot down the Korean airliner reporting that "the target is destroyed." More than 35 nations spoke out against the Soviet action, but a resolution deploring it won just a bare majority of Council members and was vetoed by the Soviet Union. A similar resolution was passed by the International Civil Aviation Organization, a UN agency, which conducted an investigation and reported in December the likelihood that the crew had set its navigation system incorrectly and that Soviet jets never established contact before firing.

It was a U.S. vote that prevented the adoption of a resolution October 28 deploring the occupation of Grenada. During the debate, Prime Minister Eugenia Charles of Dominica revealed that Grenada's governor-general had asked his neighbors to intervene to return the island to "normalcy."

In February and again in November all five big powers joined in calls for an end to the war between Iraq and Iran and for free navigation in the Persian Gulf. Iran rejected the resolutions—and the Council—as biased.

On November 18, after the Turkish community on Cyprus declared an independent state on its sector of the island, the Council declared the secession "legally invalid." The Turkish Cypriots offered to resume talks with the Greek Cypriot government, but only on an equal footing. The danger of a military confrontation eased when, in December, the Council unanimously renewed the mandate of the UN peace force that has been on Cyprus since 1964.

There were several meetings on the crisis in Central America, featuring bitter exchanges between the United States and Nicaragua. One resolution was adopted urging a regional dialogue. The Council also debated, without practical result, the Middle East, independence for Namibia, and the Libyan intervention in Chad.

Secretariat. As part of his drive to restore the UN as a focal point for the settlement of disputes, the secretary-general tried throughout the year to maintain his capacity—independent from the Council or Assembly—to act as a mediator of crises, including those in the Persian Gulf, Central America, Namibia, Cyprus, and Afghanistan. Within the Secretariat he set up an "early warning system" of information gathering to alert him of disputes before they reach the crisis stage. But he remained frustrated by the inability to establish a record of successful mediation.

Pérez de Cuellar made proposals in June to bridge the gaps between the two communities on Cyprus, but they were rejected by the Turkish Cypriots in October. His representative, Diego Cordovez, had three rounds of negotiations with Pakistan, Iran, and the USSR on an agreement to end the Soviet occupation of Afghanistan and at one point announced that a package deal was 95% complete. But the main issues—a timetable for Soviet withdrawal and guarantees against outside support for the Afghan rebels—remained unresolved.

The secretary-general won concessions from South Africa on procedures for Namibia's transition to independence. But again the main obstacle remained unmoved, in this case South African insistence on linking independence for the territory with the withdrawal of Cuban troops from neighboring Angola. The UN rejected any such linkage. As the year ended, South Africa offered a military "disengagement" starting Jan. 31, 1984, on condition that Angolan and Cuban troops, and guerrillas of the Namibian liberation movement, SWAPO, reciprocate.

Pérez de Cuellar also maintained his welcome as interlocutor in Central America and in disputes between Iran and Iraq, and Guyana and Venezuela. But there were no tangible negotiations on these issues.

The secretary-general also faced strong pressure from major contributors, including the United States and Soviet Union, over UN budget growth. In September he proposed a budget for 1984–85 totaling $1.6 billion (U.S.), an increase of 9% but just 0.7% in real growth (after inflation). The Soviets voted against the budget, and the United States, noting the effort at frugality, abstained. A more serious dispute developed between Washington and the UN Educational, Scientific and Cultural Organization (UNESCO). The United States served notice that it will withdraw from UNESCO at the end of 1984 because of its failure to exercise budgetary restraint and because its political stands were seen as a threat to press freedom.

Human Rights. The UN Human Rights Commission, meeting in Geneva in February and March, adopted resolutions critical of rights violations in South Africa, Israel, Chile, Poland, Iran, El Salvador, and Guatemala. It also took action on generic types of rights violations, such as summary executions, mass exoduses, torture, and "disappeared" persons.

MICHAEL J. BERLIN
"The Washington Post"

UNITED STATES

"Yes, we still have problems. . . ," President Ronald Reagan declared early in 1983. "But it is just plain wrong . . . to let those problems stand in the way of the most important truth of all: America is on the mend."

This hopeful note sounded by the president in his State of the Union Address on January 25 was borne out so far as the recession, the nation's number-one domestic problem, was concerned. After suffering through its deepest slump since World War II, the economy staged a strong recovery, gaining ground even faster than the administration's own forecasters had expected.

But other problems remained, particularly the budget deficit, which cast a shadow over the economy's future. The Republican president and the Democratic congressional leaders could not agree on an approach to significantly reduce the huge margin of debt.

Moreover, with the Democrats strengthened by the 1982 election returns, and with both political parties conscious of the approach of the 1984 presidential election, partisan skirmishing intruded in a number of other domestic problem areas, notably civil rights and the environment.

It also was a year in which U.S. military forces saw combat action for the first time since the mid-1970s and one in which the possibility of nuclear war became a greater concern for many Americans.

Diana Walker/Gamma-Liaison

As 1983 ended, a key question was whether Ronald Reagan would seek and win another four years in the White House.

Domestic Affairs

Administration. In his first major appointments of the year, the president nominated two women to cabinet posts. They were Elizabeth Dole, 46, White House assistant for public liaison and wife of Kansas Sen. Robert Dole, who was named January 5 to replace Drew Lewis as secretary of transportation; and former Republican Congresswoman Margaret Heckler of Massachusetts, who was named January 12 to succeed Richard Schweiker as secretary of health and human services. Both men resigned to take posts in private industry. Both women easily won confirmation. (*See also* BIOGRAPHY.)

But another presidential appointment, in the national security field, stirred more opposition. This was the selection, announced January 12, of Kenneth L. Adelman, deputy representative to the United Nations, to replace Eugene V. Rostow as director of the Arms Control and Disarmament Agency. Rostow was dismissed because of disagreement with other administration officials about U.S. strategy in arms-control negotiations with the Soviet Union.

Adelman came under fire in the Senate from critics who charged that he lacked experience in the field and was not strongly committed to arms control. The Senate Foreign Relations Committee voted 9 to 8 against confirmation, but at the same time the committee decided to submit the nomination to the full Senate for its consideration. Criticism of Adelman mounted with the release of several memorandums that his foes contended indicated he had misled the Foreign Relations Committee when he testified that he had given "no thought" to making personnel changes in the Arms Control Agency. Nevertheless, the president continued to support the nomination, and after vigorous lobbying by the White House, Adelman was confirmed on April 14 by a 57 to 42 Senate vote.

More difficult for the administration to handle was the continuing controversy over the management of the Environmental Protection Agency (EPA). This dispute had been touched off in 1982 by allegations that EPA's administration of the federal government's toxic-waste program had been influenced by political factors and by the attempts to give private industry special treatment. The controversy flared anew with the firing on February 7 of EPA assistant administrator Rita M. Lavelle, who was in charge of the toxic-waste program. With House committees pressing investigations into the affair, President Reagan announced February 16 that he had ordered a Justice Department probe into all the charges made against the agency and promised that he would not invoke executive privilege "to cover up wrong doing."

On March 1, Rep. John Dingell (D-MI), chairman of the House Energy and Commerce Committee's investigations subcommittee, claimed that his panel had received evidence supporting allegations of political manipulation and indicating possible perjury by Rita Lavelle. And in the face of increasing demands for the resignation of Anne McGill Gorsuch Burford, the head of EPA, she announced on March 9 she was quitting. The White House then agreed to turn over documents sought by the House committees in connection with their inquiries. Burford had refused to submit this material, contending she was under orders from the president not to do so.

Attempting to ward off criticism of the agency, Reagan on March 21 named William D. Ruckelshaus to succeed Burford. Ruckelshaus, who as EPA's first administrator in the early 1970s had won the respect of environmentalists, pledged to bring "an iron integrity" to EPA and was confirmed by a 97 to 0 Senate vote on May 17.

On May 27, Rita Lavelle was cited for contempt of Congress for failure to testify before a House subcommittee looking into the hazardous-waste program. She was acquitted by a federal court jury in the District of Columbia on July 22 after she testified she was ill at the time of the hearings. But on August 4 she was indicted for perjury in connection with the federal investigation into the program. In December a federal jury found her guilty of the charges.

Another administration official, Interior Secretary James G. Watt, who was a frequent target of environmentalists because of his actions on land use and development, came under fire for alleged bigotry. In a public appearance in Washington, Watt described the membership of an advisory commission on coal policy as comprised of "every kind of a mix you can have. I have a black, a woman, two Jews, and a cripple." Though Watt apologized for his comments, a number of prominent Republican senators called for his dismissal and introduced a resolution condemning him. On October 9, Watt resigned, and in a surprise move the president named his national security adviser, William P. Clark, to replace him. Clark was confirmed by the Senate by a 71 to 18 vote. Robert C. McFarlane (*see* BIOGRAPHY) replaced Clark in the national security post.

President Reagan created a furor in another area where his administration had drawn fire by announcing on May 25 that he intended to replace three Democratic members of the Civil Rights Commission who had criticized him for not being rigorous enough in enforcing civil-rights laws with three other Democrats. Leaders of civil-rights groups and their supporters charged that the president was trying to muzzle the commission and rob it of its independence.

Kenneth L. Adelman took the oath of office as director of the U.S. Arms Control and Disarmament Agency on April 22.

UPI

Martin Luther King III went to the Capitol to lobby for legislation establishing a national holiday in memory of his late father. Congress passed such a bill, and the president signed it in a Rose Garden ceremony on November 2.

© David Hathcox

The Senate refused to confirm the president's three nominees—Morris Abram, John Bunzel, and Robert Destro—who were designated to replace commissioners Mary Francis Berry, Blandina Cardenas Ramirez, and Rabbi Murray Saltzman. And the president's foes blocked appropriations to continue funding the agency. After a long stalemate that threatened the continued life of the agency, the Senate on November 14 adopted a compromise reconstituting the commission as an eight-member panel, instead of six, with four members to be appointed by the president and four by Congress. The compromise also stipulated that commissioners could be removed only for cause and that the president's appointees did not require Senate confirmation. Later President Reagan nominated Esther Gonzales-Arroyo Buckley, a high-school science teacher; Morris Abram; and John Bunzel to the new commission. He also appointed Clarence M. Pendleton, Jr., to remain committee chairman.

The administration also ran into trouble from an unexpected quarter, the 1980 presidential election campaign, when it was disclosed in June that aides who had helped Reagan get ready for his televised debate with then President Jimmy Carter had possession of briefing material that had been prepared for Carter's own use. James Baker, White House chief of staff, and David Stockman, director of the Office of Management and the Budget, confirmed the report, which came to light in a book about Reagan called *Gambling With History,* by *Time* magazine correspondent Laurence Barrett. Baker had been in overall charge of debate preparations for the Reagan campaign organization, and Stockman had impersonated President Carter during debate rehearsals with Reagan. Baker said that the Carter briefing papers had been turned over to him by William Casey, director of the Central Intelligence Agency, who had been Reagan's campaign manager. But Casey denied this, claiming that any such action on his part would have been "incredible."

With the press and many Democrats demanding an inquiry, the president announced he was turning the matter over to the Justice Department, which launched a formal investigation. A subcommittee of the House Post Office and Civil Service Committee, headed by Rep. Don Albosta (D-MI), also mounted an inquiry. An agreement was reached July 29 under which the subcommittee could obtain material it wanted after it had been screened by the General Accounting Office. After twice postponing public hearings, Albosta announced they would commence early in 1984.

Congress. Probably the most significant accomplishment of Congress in 1983 was one for which the president also could claim some credit. This was the adoption on March 25 of a social security reform package based on recommendations made by a bipartisan commission the president had appointed in 1982. In its final report to the president on January 20, the commission had recommended that Congress should not change either "the fundamental structure" or "fundamental principles" of the program that had been established during the New Deal. Nevertheless, the commission did reach agreement on a number of changes designed to deal with the program's financial problems, and these proposals served as the framework for the legislation approved by Congress and signed into law by the president.

537

Though interest rates remained high, consumer confidence was burgeoning. Demand for new cars, for example, climbed back toward the record levels of the late 1970s. As both a consequence and cause of economic recovery, U.S. automobile production rebounded 10.1% from the 25-year low of the 1982-model run.

The major component of the reform package, which advocates expected would protect the system from financial difficulty for as long as 75 years, was a combination of revenue increases and reductions in growth of benefits totaling $164.3 billion during the 1980s. These included an acceleration of already scheduled payroll-tax increases, higher taxes for the self-employed, a six-month delay in payment of cost-of-living increases, and raising the age of retirement from 65 to 66 by the year 2009 and to 67 by 2027. Coverage was also extended to federal employees and to employees of nonprofit institutions. The bill passed the House 243 to 102 and the Senate 58 to 14.

Much of Congress' time was spent in a vain effort to reduce the federal deficit, which the president had projected at $188.8 billion for fiscal 1984 in the budget that he submitted on January 31. Reagan's spending proposals totaled $848.5 billion, based on a freeze in most domestic programs and an increase of 10% above the inflation rate for defense. On June 23, after the House had adopted a Democratic-sponsored budget program and the Republican-controlled Senate also had rejected the president's plan, both houses adopted a compromise plan that called for $73 billion in additional taxes and $12 billion in spending reductions, thus reducing the deficit by $85 billion. But after weeks of hassling, the lawmakers were unable to reach specific agreement on even modest increases in taxes or reductions in spending. Instead, before adjourning on November 18, Congress merely acted to raise the ceiling on the national debt to $1.490 trillion, thus allowing the Treasury to continue to issue bonds and borrow money.

Some congressional leaders were critical of their colleagues for failing to act to stem the tide of red ink facing the government as their budget resolution had called for. But others also criticized the president for failing to take the lead, and thus the public responsibility, in pushing for unpopular measures needed to curb the debt.

Not only did Congress fail to enact new taxes, it also on July 28 repealed a revenue measure already on the books. This was the provision that would have required banks and brokerage houses to withhold for payment of income taxes 10% of the dividend and interest income due investors. The Treasury had estimated that this law, adopted in 1982 to go into effect in 1983, would have yielded an additional $13.4 billion in taxes otherwise lost to the government as a result of taxpayer evasion. The repeal measure included provisions for strengthened enforcement of tax collection expected to produce about $2.4 billion. Repeal had been spurred by an intensive lobbying campaign spearheaded by the banking industry, which regarded the withholding plan as an expensive inconvenience, and supported by individual taxpayers who complained it was an intrusion on their rights. Though President Reagan originally had threatened to veto the legislation, he signed the measure in part because it included an amendment granting trade concessions to 28 Caribbean and Central American countries under the President's Caribbean Basin Initiative plan.

One of the biggest spending measures Congress enacted was a $249.8 billion appropriation for the Defense Department, representing an increase of 4% in defense spending over inflation. This compared with the 10% increase sought by the president. At the last minute Congress also rejected an administration request for $124.4 million for production of a new type of nerve gas weapon after a 14-year moratorium on production of such weapons. But the administration did get its way on two other controversial weapons systems. Congress appropriated $5.6 billion for production of 10 B-1 bombers and $2.1 billion for production of 21 MX missiles. In April a report issued by the President's Commission on Strategic Forces, headed by Brent Scowcroft, had recommended deployment of 100 MXs to be based in existing minuteman silos in Wyoming and Nebraska. The commission also called for developing a small single-war-head ICBM, dubbed "Midgetman." President Reagan's assurances that development of the weapon would aid him in adopting a more flexible approach to arms negotiations with the Soviet Union helped to win congressional backing for the MX.

The administration scored another victory in the national security area when the Senate Foreign Relations Committee voted September 20 to reject a resolution calling for the United States and the Soviets to negotiate a mutual verifiable freeze on production, testing, and deployment of nuclear weapons. The resolution was then shelved by the Senate. A freeze resolution had passed the House by a 278 to 149 vote on May 4, after it had been amended to provide that the freeze would terminate if arms reductions were not achieved "within a reasonable, specified period of time."

Early in the year, before the economic recovery hit full stride, Congress voted $4.65 billion to provide jobs and emergency relief to victims of the recession. The bill, signed by President Reagan on March 24, was expected to create 300,000 to 400,000 jobs. Congress also acted to spend $15.6 billion to revamp federal

UPI

With presidential elections a year away, Democratic hopefuls were hard on the campaign trail. Former Vice-President Walter Mondale, *extreme left, is joined by AFL-CIO President Lane Kirkland after receiving the union's endorsement at its October convention in Hollywood, FL. On the GOP side, President Reagan had yet to throw his hat in the ring, but on October 17 he signed a letter to the Federal Election Commission authorizing Sen. Paul Laxalt (R-NV) to form a reelection committee.*

Michael Evans/The White House

housing and community development programs and to establish new housing for low- and moderate-income families. The administration had opposed additional spending for housing but agreed to the congressional proposal because it was tied to a measure increasing by $8.4 billion American support for the International Monetary Fund.

In dealing with its internal problems, the House of Representatives on July 20 voted to censure Reps. Daniel B. Crane (R-IL) and Gerry E. Studds (D-MA) for having sexual relations with Congressional pages. This was a harsher penalty than the reprimand that had been recommended for both by the House Ethics Committee. Crane, who had been involved with a 17-year-old female page, asked "God's forgiveness" for his actions. By contrast, Studds, who had a relationship with a 17-year-old male page, did not apologize. Only three other members of the House had been censured in the 20th century.

Other noteworthy Congressional action included establishing a national holiday, on the third Monday in January, honoring slain civil-rights leader Dr. Martin Luther King, Jr., to be observed beginning in 1986; revising Medicare payments to hospitals, so that hospitals that could treat patients for less than the government payment could keep the difference, while denying additional funds to hospitals charging more; and cutting off additional funding for development of the Clinch River breeder reactor in Oak Ridge, TN.

The Economy. Just as the economy had been a dark cloud on the 1982 domestic landscape, it was a bright star on the 1983 scene. In January civilian unemployment dropped to 10.4% from 10.8% in December 1982. This was the first drop since July 1981, and it marked the beginning of steady progress on the job front. In July the civilian jobless rate fell .5% to 9.5%, the biggest decline in the index since December 1959. And in October the rate declined to 8.8%, a level that the White House had not expected to reach until December 1984.

And the good news on the job front was only part of a broad picture of recovery. According to Commerce Department figures, the economy grew at a real rate of 2.6% in the first quarter, 9.7% in the second quarter, and 7.7% in the third quarter. The inflation rate was running at just below 4%, roughly the same as in 1982 when the economy was in the grip of the recession. Corporate profits climbed at a rate of 17.6% in the second quarter and 11.6% in the third quarter.

Some analysts believed that one factor contributing to the surprisingly good showing was President Reagan's decision to reappoint Paul A. Volcker to a second term as chairman of the Federal Reserve Board. Although Volcker's policy of keeping a tight rein on the money supply was blamed by some for causing the 1982 recession, he was respected widely for his determination to curb inflation.

Politics. The 1984 presidential race swung into high gear early in 1983 as Democratic presidential contenders sought to prepare for a compressed schedule of primaries and caucuses in 1984 by rallying public support, raising funds, and building organizations in key states. By the year's end, eight Democrats had declared their candidacy for the party's nomination. Former Vice-President Walter F. Mondale and Ohio Sen. John Glenn dominated

Events in Lebanon and Grenada brought a surge of enlistments to the U.S. Marine Corps.

As the arms race accelerated, and as negotiations between East and West yielded increasingly harsh rhetoric, U.S. public concern over nuclear weapons rose to unprecedented heights.

Scrawls/"Atlanta Constitution"

the field. The six considered to be long shots were former Florida Gov. Reubin Askew, California Sen. Alan Cranston, Colorado Sen. Gary Hart, South Carolina Sen. Ernest F. Hollings, civil-rights leader Jesse Jackson, and 1972 party nominee George McGovern.

A good deal of public attention focused on a series of straw polls on presidential preference conducted at state party conventions. Although the results of these polls had no direct bearing on the makeup of delegations to the 1984 national convention, some candidates regarded these competitions as opportunities to build their prestige and test their organizations. Of the seriously contested polls, Mondale won in Massachusetts in April and in Maine in October, while Cranston scored a surprising victory in Wisconsin in June.

Mondale's candidacy was also buoyed by his high standing in public opinion surveys, by his success in raising funds, and by endorsements from the AFL-CIO, the National Education Association, the National Organization for Women, and a number of key party leaders.

Glenn ran second in most polls and in financial contributions.

On the Republican side, Reagan's renomination was taken for granted if, as generally expected, he decided to seek another term in the White House. The president withheld announcing his decision until 1984, but a campaign committee began fund raising and organizing on his behalf. Meanwhile, as the president's rating in the polls rose along with the economic indexes, Republicans were optimistic.

Republicans also took heart from the victory of Sen. Daniel J. Evans (R) of Washington, in the year's only Senate contest. Evans, a former governor of the state, had been appointed to fill the vacancy created by the death of Sen. Henry M. Jackson (D).

Local elections in 1983 were notable for advances made by blacks and women. Democratic Rep. Harold Washington became the first black mayor of Chicago, the nation's second-largest city, and Democrat W. Wilson Goode the first black mayor of Philadelphia. Harvey Gantt was the first black to be elected mayor of Charlotte, NC, and James A. Sharp, Jr., the first black to win the mayoralty of Flint, MI.

Martha Layne Collins (D) became the first woman governor of Kentucky; Donna Owens (R) won the mayor's chair in Toledo, OH; and Democratic Mayors Dianne Feinstein of San Francisco and Kathy Whitmire of Houston won reelection. In the year's only two other governor's races, Democratic Attorney General Bill Allain won in Mississippi, while another Democrat, former Gov. Edwin W. Edwards, won in Louisiana.

ROBERT SHOGAN, "Los Angeles Times"

UNITED STATES • Information Highlights

Official Name: United States of America.
Location: Central North America.
Area: 3,618,770 sq mi (9 372 614 km²).
Population (July 1983 est.): 234,193,000.
Chief Cities (1980 census): Washington, DC, the capital, 638,432; New York, 7,071,639; Chicago, 3,005,072; Los Angeles, 2,966,850; Philadelphia, 1,688,210.
Government: *Head of state and government,* Ronald Reagan, president (took office Jan. 20, 1981). *Legislature*—Congress: Senate and House of Representatives.
Monetary Unit: Dollar

The New Deal Through 50 Years

March 1983 marked the 50th anniversary of the beginning of the New Deal, a series of measures instituted by President Franklin Roosevelt to combat the Great Depression. Looking back, one can only conclude that the New Deal has had a major impact on the economic and social policies of modern America. Roosevelt established important new directions with which every subsequent president has had to contend. A variety of federal agencies created during the 1930s are still in operation today, and the economic "revolution" begun by the New Deal has been notably expanded and transformed.

Relief and Reform. Roosevelt's first task was to halt the nation's economic decline. Neither a socialist nor a totalitarian, he waged the battle with means intended to restore Americans' faith in capitalism and democracy. He believed that the old laissez-faire ideology was inadequate for dealing with the new reality, and from 1933 to 1938 groped for an effective policy. Full recovery was attained only with the advent of World War II, but moderate improvement was seen before then. The Gross National Product (GNP), which had fallen from $103 billion (U.S.) in 1929 to $56 billion in 1933, rose to $110 billion before a recession in fall 1937. Unemployment, which had risen from 3.2% in 1929 to 24.1% in 1932, fell to 14.3% in 1937.

In response to the recession of 1937–38, the New Dealers devised a new liberalism—a coordinated scheme of fiscal and monetary measures to influence the level of economic activity without altering the structure of the economy or involving the government in business decisions. This Keynesian approach (based on the writings of John Maynard Keynes) contrasted with the old liberalism of institutional reform on which FDR had relied since 1933.

Policies and Legacies. The lasting impact of the New Deal is as tangible as the Grand Coulee Dam (built under the New Deal's Public Works Administration—PWA) and as controversial as welfare. Although the 32nd president had an aversion to "systems," his later New Deal represented an approach to economic stabilization that has endured to the present.

From the spring of 1938 on—except during World War II; the Korean War; and the years 1971–73, when President Nixon adopted wage-and-price controls—Democratic and Republican administrations alike formulated economic policies within the boundaries of the Keynesian "trade-off" between unemployment and inflation. Until the early 1970s the trade-off worked—that is, manipulation of one side of the equation yielded the desired effect on the other side, with movement on both sides within tolerable limits. From 1948 to 1970, there were five recessions but no depressions, as the "built-in" stabilizers of the New Deal acted as a brake and a cushion in economic downturns and were supplemented by ad hoc antirecession action, including public-jobs and public-works programs reminiscent of the PWA and Works Progress Administration (WPA).

A number of New Deal measures pertaining to securities exchange, banking, and housing, as well as Federal Reserve Board credit policies, prevented the kind of house-of-cards structure that had developed in the 1920s. A second group of New Deal stabilizers related to purchasing power: unemployment compensation, farm price supports, and Social Security retirement benefits. In 1983 these stabilizers were still operative. Indeed, welfare had moved well beyond the New Deal idea of temporary aid to the unemployed. Congress had added Medicare, Medicaid, and a free school-lunch program and had greatly expanded the Food Stamp Plan and the Aid to Families with Dependent Children Program. Another development aimed at bolstering purchasing power was labor's right to organize and bargain collectively, obtained under the National Institute Recovery Act (NIRA) of 1933 and the Wagner Act of 1935.

President Nixon's announcement in August 1971 of wage-and-price controls amounted to recognition that the Keynesian trade-off no longer was working. As the nation suffered both high unemployment and high inflation through the 1970s, however, policymakers still were trading off unemployment and inflation. Under the Carter and Reagan administrations, the Federal Reserve Board attacked inflation with a tight money policy. During the Reagan years, there has been a substantial decline in inflation, but there has been little sign, even with the recovery of 1983, of a significant decrease in unemployment or, despite tax reductions based on "supply-side" economics, of a notable interest in capital investment.

It took Roosevelt five years to initiate an economic policy that worked for his times. Since President Nixon proclaimed the inadequacy of the old trade-off ideology in 1971, no chief executive has introduced an equally effective program. That the New Deal had even a moderately positive effect ranks Roosevelt as one of the top U.S. presidents. Today, government leaders must emulate him by coming up with new policies suitable for a new age.

BERNARD STERNSHER

The Economy

Almost everyone conceded the point: the performance of the U.S. economy in 1983 was a bit of a surprise, and, for a change, a pleasant one. Most of the surprises over the previous few years had been decidedly bad.

As the year began, expectations were modest in the White House and in the homes of most Americans, because they had just come through what, by some criteria, was the worst recession since the Great Depression of the 1930s. The mood seemed to suit the gray January weather. To recover swiftly and strongly from such a debilitating economic experience was too much to expect, especially in view of the crippled condition of so much heavy industry, the existence of nearly 11.5 million unemployed workers, continued high interest rates, huge federal budget deficits, the worrisome financial condition of some states and municipalities, and the shaky economic condition of many less-developed nations.

Even Martin S. Feldstein, chairman of President Ronald Reagan's Council of Economic Advisers, was concerned. He cautioned that the administration's forecast of a 4.4% rise in Gross National Product (GNP) was too high. More likely, said the former Harvard economist, it would be just 3–3.5%.

He was wrong. At Christmastime, great crowds of shoppers on most main streets of the nation testified to the robust economic performance. Those who study consumer sentiment measured it at record highs, and merchants proclaimed the holiday selling period one of the best in history. "The consumer is basically tired of holding back," said a retail analyst at the investment firm of Bear, Stearns & Co.

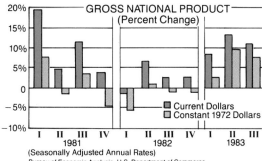

GROSS NATIONAL PRODUCT (Percent Change)

☐ Current Dollars
☐ Constant 1972 Dollars

I   II   III   IV   I   II   III   IV   I   II   III
     1981   1982   1983
(Seasonally Adjusted Annual Rates)
Bureau of Economic Analysis, U.S. Department of Commerce.

By late 1983, Martin Feldstein was calling for spending cuts and tax increases to overcome the budget deficit.

UPI

Evidence of that assessment seemed to abound. At R. H. Macy & Co., hot sellers included 4,250 boxes of Godiva chocolates at $19 a pound, 12,000 tins of Bavarian pretzels at $14.95 a can, and thousands of video tape recorders ranging in price from $399 to $699. Millions of youngsters ordered from Santa Claus electronic computers ranging from $100—and sometimes less—to thousands of dollars. The consensus of economists was that when everything was tallied, the GNP would show a rise of 6.5% for the year, about double what Feldstein had forecast.

The Indicators. Viewing the evidence, Walter D. Fackler, University of Chicago economist, commented: "We are in the midst of a whacking good economic upswing." The economy, he told 2,000 people gathered at the school's annual forecast luncheon, "has outrun all expectations voiced a year ago—including my own." Most estimates of GNP put it at $3.3 trillion, compared with $3.07 trillion a year earlier, and other statistics, subject to official confirmation in 1984, were equally impressive: disposable personal income, inflation wrung out, up 3.3%; corporate profits after taxes, up 14.5% to $131.7 billion; housing starts, up more than 60% to 1.7 million units; employment up at least 1.3 million to 100.8 million; the jobless rate down to 8.2% in December; retail automobile sales, up to 9.1 million units; and the average prime interest rate for the year, down to 10.8% from 14.9% in 1982.

Outstanding as these performances were, three others stood out even more. The Consumer Price Index, which Americans were accustomed to seeing on the rise, advanced only 3.9% for the year, compared with 6.2% in 1982 and an average of 11% a year for the years 1979 through 1981. But the other two measurements looked bad. One showed that the federal government budget deficit had risen to more than $195 billion, a record high. The other showed the country running a mammoth trade deficit, which meant in effect that it was borrowing heavily from abroad to sustain the expansion.

If Reaganomics was to be given credit for the dynamic economy, some people thought it

U.S. CONSUMER PRICES (Percent Change)

(All Items Seasonally Adjusted)

Bureau of Labor Statistics, U.S. Department of Labor.

should also accept the verdict of "failure" in regard to the budget deficit. It represented an embarrassing irony, too, because the administration was committed philosophically and politically to spending cuts. But costly interest expenditures on the deficit and a dedication to defense spending more than offset what savings were made in social, cultural, and so-called entitlements areas. The Heritage Foundation, a conservative think tank, chided the president, observing that federal spending as a percentage of GNP rose to more than 25% in 1983 from 22.4% in 1982. That is, government involvement in the economy had risen for the year rather than declined as the president had hoped and promised.

The trade deficit seemed almost beyond control and would total $40 billion or more when the final figures were in. Moreover, the imbalance was worsening. In the third quarter alone it reached $11.98 billion, as Americans expressed a taste for imported goods ranging from French wines to Japanese machine tools. Two big factors helped to swell the imports. First, the dollar's value in relation to other currencies grew almost by the day, a consequence in part of the desire by foreigners to invest where interest rates were high and politics stable. The dollar's high value made imported goods relatively inexpensive and therefore desirable. Second, most foreign economies had not yet achieved the U.S. level of expansion. Non-Americans were less able to buy U.S. goods, especially since the dollar's value made American goods relatively more expensive.

While these factors created doubts, it was difficult to prove they interfered with growth. To the dismay of forecasters, many of whom revised their estimates at midyear, the economy surged in the second quarter, relaxed some in the third, and perked up again as the year ended. It defied bad news.

Causes for Expansion. What had brought about the expansion remained the subject of debate, but a few things seemed certain. Primed by a tax cut, Americans late in 1982 began regaining confidence, a process strengthened by the policy of the Federal Reserve Board, led by chairman Paul Volcker, that permitted interest rates, although high, to fall several points. As buying interest picked up, job creation intensified and the stock market rose, adding to the assets of individuals. Conditions were now in place for people to take on more credit, and they did. The pace of buying compelled retailers to rebuild inventories, and as retailers' orders were received by manufacturers, they in turn made plans to expand and rehire.

Nowhere was the improvement greeted with more thanks than in the Midwest, the industrial heartland of the United States that had become devastated by the decline of orders for cars, steel, farm equipment, and industrial machinery—the very products that once symbolized America's might. Soup kitchens had become common throughout the area, and on many front lawns the "For Sale" sign stood side by side with the mailbox. Unemployment was pervasive. Reports abounded that the dev-

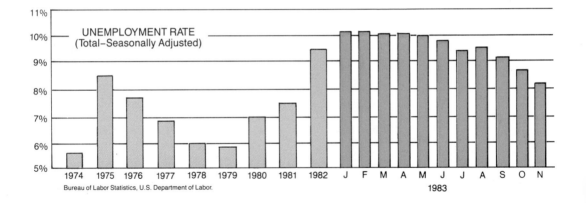

Bureau of Labor Statistics, U.S. Department of Labor.

astation was to some degree permanent. The United States, it was said, had entered a post-industrial age whose hardware would be the electronic computer and whose products would be services such as the assembly and transfer of information.

There was some truth to the assertions. Business never had been better in some of the high-technology belts in the Silicon Valley south of San Francisco and Route 128 near Boston. While unemployment ranged close to 20% in parts of Michigan, for example, in Massachusetts it was falling through the single numbers, and new companies were being established every day. But the Midwest was not dead, merely wounded, and while things never would be the same, there would be a recovery. The automotive industry had retooled and, with the help of an agreement to limit Japanese imports, began reopening plants to serve the quickening interest at dealer's showrooms. Retail automobile sales, which had fallen to an annual rate of 7.8 million units in the third quarter of 1982, rebounded to 9.3 million in the same quarter of 1983, and to an estimated 9.6 million units in the year's final three months. Of these, more than 7 million units were made in the United States, compared with a rate of only 5.6 million American-made units in the third quarter of 1982.

Another big change, this one legislated, created problems and opportunities in other areas of the economy, too. It was deregulation, and it especially affected financial institutions and companies in the transportation industry. The continued deregulation of financial institutions tended to throw savings organizations, commercial banks, brokers, and others into the same vast market, whereas once they had been beneficiaries of protected segments of it. Restrictions also continued to be lifted on their ability to compete with each other by offering the highest return, considered by some to be a mixed benefit. The freedom of banks to raise the level of interest offered to depositors, for example, also restricted their ability to offer lower rates to borrowers. But competition did result, and the so-called financial supermarket that could sell you a house, insurance, stocks, bonds, and money management emerged.

In transportation the result in some instances was to leave towns and cities on the least profitable routes without train, bus, or airline service and to encourage more competitors on lucrative routes. Braniff Airways, among others, sought the protection of the bankruptcy laws. And some companies, such as Eastern Air Lines and Greyhound, found the new conditions such a strain that, as steel and automotive companies had done before them, they sought and won wage and benefit concessions from workers.

Competition came via the Justice Department, too, with the scheduled divestiture of 22

Ed Stein/Reprinted Courtesy, "Rocky Mountain News"

operating companies by Amercan Telephone & Telegraph Co. and its Bell System. Eight regional operating companies, newly independent, would emerge in 1984, the better, the courts said, to promote competition and serve users. The coming apart of AT&T left it with long distance services—and competitors for that service—but freed it from regulations that before had stymied its efforts to compete in the electronic computer field with the likes of International Business Machines. Some saw the decision as the drawing and quartering of an efficient giant. Others insisted that it freed the giant from the shackles that prevented it from exploiting market opportunities.

Accustomed to big happenings, the stock market took the news calmly. In fact, it had been relatively calm throughout the second half of the year after a roaring start. From a low of 1027.04 points, the Dow Jones industrial average reached a high for the year of 1287.29 in November, and the forecasts at year's end were mildly bullish. The economy, which the market is said to anticipate in its pricing, was expected to be solid and unexciting in 1984.

The Outlook. Said Fackler: "The present strength of the recovery . . . makes 1984 an easy year to forecast." In 1984, he said, the "momentum of the recovery will continue albeit at a declining rate." A sense of security and anticipation had been reestablished.

True as that was, some people still wondered if the country was foresaking caution. They observed that people had begun "buying up" again—in cars, houses, and vacations. They wondered if the economy might race away from its controls, throwing the country back into a battle with inflation. Some people wanted taxes to be raised, and President Reagan suggested he might consider such a move, but only if spending cuts were enacted first.

JOHN CUNNIFF, *The Associated Press*

Foreign Affairs

The year 1983 brought dramatic shifts in the foreign policy of the Reagan administration. President Reagan dismissed or transferred several key foreign-policy advisers, delegated policy authority for arms control and Central America to independent commissions, and committed U.S. troops to foreign combat for the first time since the administration of Gerald Ford.

Foreign-Policy Management. When the Reagan administration assumed office in January 1981, U.S.-Soviet arms-control negotiations, the perennial crisis in the Middle East, and the pressure for revolutionary change in Central America were the most pressing foreign-policy issues facing the nation. In 1983 there were important changes in the personnel dealing with all three areas.

On January 12 the president dismissed Eugene Rostow as director of the Arms Control and Disarmament Agency and named Kenneth Adelman, former deputy permanent representative of the U.S. Mission to the United Nations, to assume that position. Only nine days earlier the president had appointed a bipartisan, 11-member panel to recommend new deployment options for the MX (missile experimental). Selected as chairman was Brent Scowcroft, a retired Air Force general who had served as national security adviser during the Ford administration and who had been critical of the administration's proposal to cluster the MX in hardened silos in the "dense-pack" basing system. In appointing the commission, Reagan effectively delegated a major share of authority for U.S. policy in the defense and arms-control field to a body not under the control of the administration.

A similar pattern emerged in the field of Central America. On May 27, Secretary of State George Shultz announced that Langhorne Anthony Motley, the U.S. ambassador to Brazil, was to replace Thomas O. Enders as assistant secretary of state for inter-American affairs and that Thomas R. Pickering, the U.S. ambassador to Nigeria, would replace Deane R. Hinton as U.S. ambassador to El Salvador. On July 18 the president announced the appointment of a bipartisan commission, headed by former Secretary of State Henry Kissinger, to make long-term recommendations concerning U.S. policy toward Central America.

In the Middle East, the administration changed its chief negotiator for the Arab-Israel dispute twice and also appointed a new assistant secretary of state for Near Eastern affairs. On November 3, Donald Rumsfeld, former secretary of defense in the Ford administration, was named the chief negotiator for the Middle East.

Potentially the most important personnel change took place on October 9 with the transfer of Judge William Clark from the position of national security adviser to secretary of the interior. Replacing him was Robert C. McFarlane, Clark's deputy on the National Security Council.

The overall impact of these personnel changes was difficult to assess by the end of the year. Most commentators interpreted the changes in the Latin American field as a sign that the administration intended to pursue a tougher line toward Central America. But the Kissinger Commission was not scheduled to report until early 1984, and its judgments were expected to have a major impact on the direction of U.S. policy in Latin America. The Scowcroft Commission's report was generally judged to have moved the administration toward a more centrist position. Many observers

On Air Force 1, President Reagan, Secretary Shultz (left), and Robert McFarlane review the latest news from Lebanon.

Bill Fitz-Patrick/The White House

saw the appointment of McFarlane as a sign of increased foreign-policy professionalism in the senior ranks of the administration. It was noteworthy that although the initial appointments of the Reagan administration—reflecting the bitter primary fight between President Ford and Ronald Reagan in 1976—had excluded most prominent foreign-policy figures from the Ford administration, Kissinger, McFarlane, Rumsfeld, and Scowcroft all had important positions under President Ford. The 1983 appointments therefore brought together the two major wings of the Republican Party for the first time since President Reagan's election.

Use of Force. The year 1983 also marked a sharp rise in the resort to force by the U.S. government in its conduct of foreign relations. The United States financed and armed a resistance movement in Nicaragua whose objective was the overthrow of the legitimate government there; sent airborne warning and control system aircraft (AWACs) to the Sudan in response to civil strife in Chad; used naval firepower to defend the Lebanese army from defeat by Druse militia in the civil war in Lebanon; and invaded the Caribbean island of Grenada. The record seemed to signal an end to the political and psychological restraints that, following the U.S. withdrawal from Vietnam, had dissuaded administrations during the 1970s from the use of force for diplomatic ends. One result of this repeated resort to military power was to reopen a national debate over the War Powers Resolution of 1973. (*See* special report, page 549).

Arms Control and Defense Policy. For most of the post-World War II period, arms control negotiations between the United States and the Soviet Union have been characterized more by efforts at onus-shifting than by serious negotiations. Talks in 1983 fit that pattern. Each government maneuvered to ensure that if the negotiations failed the other side would receive the bulk of the blame.

Yet the result was prospectively some significant shifts in the policy of each side if negotiations were successful in building on some of the proposals advanced. To gain congressional support for the MX missile, the Reagan administration had to convince its congressional critics that the United States was making a serious effort to gain an arms-control agreement with the USSR. It therefore accepted on April 19 the recommendation of the Scowcroft Commission that the United States attempt to persuade the Soviet Union that both superpowers should attempt to move away from multiple-warhead missiles like the MX toward single-warhead missiles that do not invite preemptive attack (because one or two incoming warheads could destroy a single missile with several warheads on it). On October 4 the White House accepted a version of the congressional build-down proposal, which called for the destruction of more than one warhead for each new warhead deployed. Finally, on October 27, NATO agreed to withdraw over a five-year period 1,400 of the 6,000 tactical nuclear weapons that the United States had been stockpiling in Europe.

The Soviets, who in March 1977 categorically rejected the concept of deep cuts in nuclear weapons when proposed by the Carter administration, now ·proposed a three-stage 25% reduction in the SALT II limits and sublimits. At the intermediate-range nuclear forces (INF) talks in Geneva, they accepted the principle of destruction of SS-20 missiles above the number negotiated. If an agreement were ever reached for the actual destruction of SS-20s, it would represent the first time that a superpower had agreed to scrap first-line, modern weapons for which it had just expended considerable sums of money.

Nevertheless, at year's end the positions of the two sides remained far apart. Moreover, on September 1, Korean Air Lines flight 007 penetrated Soviet airspace, and the Soviet air force shot it down, killing all 269 persons aboard, including 61 Americans. The superpower relationship reached levels of tension not seen since the 1962 Cuban missile crisis, and the prospects for an arms-control agreement dropped accordingly.

Of special note was President Reagan's March 23 speech calling for long-term development of military technology capable of destroying Soviet missiles before they could reach their targets. Experts differed on whether such a system was feasible or desirable. The Soviet Union contended that the development of such a system would violate the 1972 Anti-Ballistic Missile Treaty between the United States and the Soviet Union.

Central America. Throughout 1983 the United States continued to increase its political, economic, and military presence in Central America. On March 3 the government announced an increase in the number of U.S. military advisers in El Salvador from 35 to 55, and the White House pressed for major increases in U.S. military assistance to El Salvador. The administration entered into a major battle with Congress over the legality of U.S. financial and arms support for resistance movements attempting to overthrow the Sandinista government in Nicaragua.

On May 25 the United States suffered its first military death in El Salvador; on July 19 it announced military maneuvers lasting four to five months to be conducted with Honduran troops near the border of Nicaragua; and on October 25, after a bloody coup on Grenada, which resulted in the execution of Prime Minister Maurice Bishop, President Reagan sent 6,000 U.S. troops to occupy the island as part of a multinational force "to restore order and democracy."

The rising U.S. presence in Central America caused concern among Latin American states, which feared the outbreak of a regional war. In January 1983 the foreign ministers of Colombia, Mexico, Panama, and Venezuela met on the Panamanian island of Contadora and issued an appeal for the settlement of the security problems of Central America apart from the East-West context in which they had been placed. By July both President Reagan and Cuban President Fidel Castro had endorsed the Contadora effort. And on July 19, the Nicaraguan government announced that it was prepared to participate in international talks aimed at finding a peaceful solution. Previously it had insisted on bilateral talks with Honduras and with the United States.

Notwithstanding the efforts of the Contadora Group, progress toward a negotiated settlement was negligible. The U.S. invasion of Grenada added a new complication. In El Salvador the government announced on August 19 that it was postponing until 1984 the elections previously scheduled to take place in December. The rebels refused to participate in the elections without a negotiated settlement beforehand, and the government in turn rejected any power-sharing except as a consequence of the elections.

Middle East. The U.S. position in the Middle East suffered several setbacks in 1983. Suicide car-bombings demolished the American Embassy in Beirut on April 18 and the Marine headquarters on October 23. The attacks seemed designed to end U.S. participation in the multinational force that had been sent to Lebanon to facilitate the withdrawal of all foreign troops and to protect Palestinian refugees in the Beirut area. President Reagan's response to these attacks was to declare that stability in Lebanon was "central to [U.S.] credibility on a global scale."

In April, King Hussein of Jordan failed to convince the leaders of the Palestinian Liberation Organization (PLO) that they should agree to participate in talks with Israel concerning the future of the Israeli-occupied West Bank and Gaza. This development ended all momentum behind the September 1982 Middle East peace initiative of President Reagan, who had declared that the United States supported "self-government by the Palestinians of the West Bank and Gaza in association with Jordan."

The Iran-Iraq war posed the danger of another commitment of U.S. troops. France's agreement to sell sophisticated fighter planes to Iraq led Baghdad on July 20 to threaten to escalate its attacks on Iranian oil centers once the aircraft were delivered. Iran replied with a threat to block all oil shipments through the Persian Gulf. On July 26 the United States stated that it would use force if necessary to maintain the flow of oil. In mid-October, amid

Wide World

Donald Rumsfeld, defense secretary under Gerald Ford, joined the Reagan team as special Middle East envoy.

reports that five French planes had been delivered to Iraq, U.S. ships were dispatched to the Arabian Sea.

The effect of these developments was to enhance the roles of the Soviet Union and Syria in the Middle East. With thousands of Soviet military advisers on its territory, Syria backed Iran in its war with Iraq; used military pressure against the PLO to limit severely the ability of Yasir Arafat to lead his organization in a direction not approved by Damascus; refused to withdraw its troops from Lebanon; and was a major presence in Geneva in November when the leaders of the major Lebanese political factions tried to reach a political compromise.

Other Areas. Other areas of importance to the United States were scarcely more tranquil. The August 21 assassination of Benigno Aquino, leader of the opposition to President Ferdinand Marcos of the Philippines, roiled the politics of that country. President Reagan decided to drop a long-planned visit to Manila from his November trip to the Far East. Earlier in the year, the two countries renewed their pact on U.S. bases in the Philippines, vital to the American naval presence in the Far East.

Another flashpoint was South Korea, where 39,000 U.S. troops were stationed. On October 9, terrorists in Rangoon, Burma, detonated a bomb that killed five South Korean cabinet ministers on an official visit. The Burmese investigators concluded that North Korean agents were responsible for the attack. President Reagan visited South Korea in November.

Within the United Nations system, U.S. discontent with the direction of several agencies again surfaced. Although President Reagan warned on September 29 that congressional failure to appropriate $8.4 billion (U.S.) for the International Monetary Fund would result in "a major disruption of the entire world trading and financial system," Congress' reluctant approval raised fears that new money would be hard to obtain.

CHARLES WILLIAM MAYNES
Editor, "Foreign Policy"

The War Powers Resolution

Barling in "The Christian Science Monitor" © 1983 TCSPS

The use of military force by the U.S. government during 1983 in the Middle East and the Caribbean triggered the first major debate in a decade over the respective powers of the president and the Congress in the field of foreign policy. At issue was whether the War Powers Resolution of 1973 had succeeded in establishing that the Congress under the Constitution is entitled to share with the president the power to commit U.S. military forces to combat abroad.

Background. According to Article I, Section 8, of the U.S. Constitution, the Congress is empowered to declare war and to provide the military forces to fight it. Nevertheless, in the 174 years prior to the passage of the War Powers Resolution, U.S. troops had been sent into military engagements 199 times without a declaration of war; 103 took place outside the Western Hemisphere.

In the age of nuclear terror and Cold War, the case for congressional involvement in decisions involving military force seemed to be weaker than at any time in U.S. history. A decision to respond to nuclear attack would have to be taken too quickly for Congress to be consulted. Or the means needed to participate in the Cold War might have to be so covert that congressional participation and debate would prove awkward. Presidents Harry Truman, Dwight Eisenhower, and Lyndon Johnson thus sent American troops into Korea, Lebanon, and the Dominican Republic, respectively, without seeking or obtaining the authorization of Congress.

Vietnam marked a watershed. In 1964 the Congress, in response to an alleged attack on U.S. naval vessels in the Gulf of Tonkin, passed the Tonkin Gulf Resolution, which authorized the president to take all necessary measures "including the use of armed force" to help South Vietnam defend its freedom. As the level of the conflict mounted, so did congressional discontent with the implications of the Tonkin Gulf Resolution. By the early 1970s both houses began to debate bills limiting the president's war-making power.

In July 1973 both houses passed draft legislation. A joint resolution was worked out and passed by the Senate on October 10 and by the House two days later. President Nixon vetoed the measure on October 24, but there was enough support on the congressional side to override the veto.

Stipulations. The purpose of the War Powers Resolution is stated in Section 2(a):

> to fulfill the intent of the framers of the Constitution of the United States and insure that the collective judgment of both the Congress and the President will apply to the introduction of United States armed forces into hostilities, or into situations where imminent involvement in hostilities is clearly indicated by the circumstances, and to the continued use of such forces in hostilities or in such situations.

The resolution requires the president to keep Congress informed both before and during any involvement by U.S. forces in hostilities. Under Section 4(a), the president is required to report to Congress within 48 hours when U.S. troops are introduced:

> *(1) into hostilities or into situations where imminent involvement in hostilities is clearly indicated by the circumstances;*
> *(2) into the territory, airspace or waters of a foreign nation, while equipped for combat, except for deployments which relate solely to supply, replacement, repair, or training of such forces; or*
> *(3) in numbers which substantially enlarge United States armed forces equipped for combat already located in a foreign nation.*

A written report must be submitted to the speaker of the House of Representatives and the president pro tempore of the Senate setting forth:

> *a—the circumstances necessitating the introduction of the United States armed forces;*
> *b—the constitutional and legislative authority under which such introduction took place; and*
> *c—the estimated scope and duration of the hostilities or involvement*

Only in the first circumstance (U.S. forces likely to be engaged in combat) is the length of the commitment limited by the resolution. In that event, Section 5(b) of the resolution requires the president to withdraw U.S. troops within 60 to 90 days unless the Congress authorizes their continued presence. The resolution also contains a provision, 5(c), permitting Congress, by concurrent resolution without approval by the president, to order the withdrawal of U.S. troops from hostilities abroad.

Since passage of the act, all U.S. presidents have sought ways to avoid the trigger mechanism in Section 5(b). Presidents Ford, Carter, and Reagan have all reported to the Congress under the act's provisions but often without citing which precise provision in the act applied to their deployment of forces. In this way they have been able to avoid the 60- to 90-day clock. As a result, the role of Congress in the deployment of U.S. troops abroad has not been any greater after the enactment of War Powers than before.

Further weakening the role of Congress under the War Powers Resolution was the June 1983 *Chadha* decision of the Supreme Court, which held the legislative veto to be an unconstitutional infringement of the separation of powers under the Constitution. Some scholars hold that this decision invalidates the legislative veto in Section 5(c) of the War Powers Resolution.

Lebanon. In August 1982, President Reagan ordered a contingent of Marines to Lebanon to participate in a multinational force. Although he reported to the Congress under the War Powers Resolution, he did not refer to any specific provision of the resolution, and the administration resisted any effort to report to the Congress under Section 4(a)(1), which would have started the legislative clock.

For a year the Congress accepted this position. But the first deaths of U.S. soldiers serving in Lebanon on Aug. 29, 1983, opened a major legal battle between the executive and legislative branches over the applicability of the War Powers Resolution. The result was a compromise measure signed by President Reagan on October 12, in which the president appeared to win more than did his congressional opponents. Under the compromise, the president won the right to keep the Marines in Lebanon for another 18 months or beyond the next presidential election and to use "such protective measures as may be necessary to ensure the safety" of the troops. The legislation declared that the War Powers Resolution applies to the conflict in Lebanon, requiring the president to notify Congress when U.S. troops face hostilities and to bring the troops home within 90 days unless Congress permits them to stay. But the president upon signing the legislation disputed whether "the initiation of isolated or infrequent acts of violence against United States armed forces" necessarily constitutes actual or imminent involvement in hostilities. In addition, the president refused to acknowledge the constitutionality of Section 5(b), which establishes the time limit.

At the same time, the legislation required the president to report to the Congress on the status of the Lebanese civil war by the end of November 1983 and every 30 days after that. Particularly after the October 29 car-bombing attack on Marine headquarters, which caused 241 deaths, if new fighting were to break out, these reports would make it increasingly difficult for the president to avoid stating whether or not U.S. troops were involved in hostilities and thus setting in motion the provisions of the War Powers Resolution.

Grenada. Congressional sensitivity over the War Powers Resolution was also in evidence during the Grenada crisis. When the administration failed to report to the Congress under Section 4(1)(a), the House of Representatives on November 1 voted 403–23 to declare that the 1973 War Powers Resolution "became operative" when U.S. troops were introduced into Grenada. Although the Senate delayed action on a similar measure, the administration announced in mid-November that all U.S. combat troops would be withdrawn from Grenada before Christmas or in time to avoid a conflict with the Congress over the applicability of the War Powers Resolution. Except for some 300 noncombat personnel, the last U.S. troops left Grenada on December 15.

CHARLES WILLIAM MAYNES

URUGUAY

Political maneuvering in preparation for the 1984 elections and stressful economic problems overshadowed other matters of public interest in 1983.

Political Developments. Political activity centered on whether, and under what conditions, the military dictatorship would turn control over to an elected civilian regime. At the end of January the three parties legalized in 1982—the Blancos, Colorados, and the Civic Union—held national conventions to choose new leaderships and prepare the ground for negotiations with the military.

However, consultations between the three parties and the Armed Forces Political Affairs Committee (COMASPO) were ultimately broken off. Between May and July, seven sessions were held before the parties withdrew from them. Civilian leaders claimed that the military had been unwilling to budge from their insistence that a new constitution contain all those provisions for the participation of the armed forces in politics that had been defeated in a popular referendum two years before.

At various times the military threatened to cancel the tentative plan to hold elections late in 1984. However, at the end of October, Gen. Julio Rapela, head of COMASPO, stated that "The military, even without the parties' agreement, will submit to the population a draft constitutional reform and will call elections."

The military government permitted a May Day demonstration for the first time in a decade. Organized by the unions, the meeting was attended by 100,000 workers. Speakers demanded among other things a general political amnesty.

It had been reported in February that the regime was still holding 1,500 political prisoners. In June there was a new police roundup of opponents of the government, and on several occasions during the year periodicals were suspended for criticizing the regime.

Economy. The economic situation worsened during the year. The gross domestic product during the first quarter was 9.1% below that of the same period in 1982. Construction was particularly badly hit, falling by 32.3%. The unemployment rate was 15.7% in June.

The Uruguayan peso was allowed to float at the beginning of the year. Whereas in November 1982 the rate had been 13.7 to the U.S. dollar, it reached 40 to the dollar in January and finally stabilized at about 30 to the dollar.

Foreign trade remained sluggish. Although trade missions from Austria, Taiwan, and Czechoslovakia visited the country early in the year, sales of the principal export, wool, remained virtually unchanged.

Uruguay's foreign debts amounted to about $3 billion (U.S.). In March the government requested a 90-day moratorium on repayments of principal on the $570 million currently maturing. Negotiations on rescheduling continued.

Foreign Visitors. In February, U.S. Assistant Secretary of State Thomas Enders visited Montevideo, where he talked with members of the government. In that same month, Elliott Abrams, U.S. assistant secretary for human rights, praised the Uruguayan regime's "move toward democracy." But in April, Uruguay's political leaders lamented that there had been a decline in U.S. official contact with them.

In May, Spain's King Juan Carlos and Queen Sofia made a two-day visit during which the king conferred not only with government officials but also with opposition leaders.

ROBERT J. ALEXANDER, *Rutgers University*

UTAH

Natural disasters, efforts to control child kidnapping and abuse, and the death of Barney Clark were among the prominent developments in Utah during 1983.

Natural Disasters. Near-record snowfall followed by early warm weather affected nearly the entire state during the spring. As temperatures soared, cities and towns were inundated by floodwaters and mudslides. In downtown Salt Lake City, major streets became veritable rivers—up to 7 ft (2.1 m) deep—as drainage systems overflowed. Thousands of volunteers used sandbags to transform streets into canals to save businesses and residences. In mid-April, a mudslide in Spanish Fork Canyon in central Utah completely buried the town of Thistle, blocked a canyon stream—creating a lake more than 100 ft (30 m) deep—and covered a major highway and railroad line. In late May, mudslides from the hills in Davis County inundated the communities of Bountiful and Farmington; more than 60 homes were damaged, displacing some 1,400 residents. Much of the area was declared a federal disaster area, thus providing funds for individual victims and clean-up efforts.

In an unusually hot July, brush fires destroyed hundreds of thousands of acres of

---

URUGUAY · Information Highlights

Official Name: Oriental Republic of Uruguay.
Location: Southeastern coast of South America.
Area: 72,200 sq mi (186 998 km²).
Population (July 1983 est.): 2,916,000.
Government: *Head of state,* Gregorio Alvarez, president (took office Sept. 1981). *Legislature*—Council of state.
Monetary Unit: Peso (37.5 pesos equal U.S.$1, Nov. 9, 1983).
Gross Domestic Product (1981 U.S.$): $11,000,-000,000.
Economic Index (1982): *Consumer Prices* (1970 = 100), all items, 20,747; food, 19,112.
Foreign Trade (1982 U.S.$): *Imports,* $1,041,000,000; *exports,* $1,027,000,000.

woodland. Then in August, violent storms brought new flooding.

Crime. A rash of kidnappings in recent years was solved in part during 1983. Arthur Gary Bishop, 38, was bound over on 11 felony counts, including capital homicide and aggravated kidnapping, in connection with the murders of five youths, ages 6 to 13, who had disappeared between 1979 and 1982. As a consequence of these incidents, the Utah legislature unanimously approved what was considered the toughest child kidnapping and molestation law in the United States.

Medicine. On Dec. 2, 1983, Barney B. Clark, a 61-year-old former dentist from the Seattle area, became the first human patient to receive a permanent artificial heart. The transplant was performed at the University of Utah Medical Center in Salt Lake City by a team of surgeons led by Dr. William DeVries. On March 23, 1983, after 112 days on the device, Clark died at the center of circulatory collapse secondary to multiorgan system failure.

Land Title. The federal government in August presented Gov. Scott Matheson with title to 93,803 acres (37 521 ha) that had been promised to Utah when it became a state in 1896. Much of the land, in 11 blocks over 8 counties, is in rural areas with mineral resources.

LORENZO K. KIMBALL, *University of Utah*

UTAH • Information Highlights
Area: 84,899 sq mi (219 888 km²).
Population (1982 est.): 1,554,000.
Chief Cities (1980 census): Salt Lake City, the capital, 163,697; Provo, 73,907; Ogden, 64,407.
Government (1983): *Chief Officers*—governor, Scott M. Matheson (D); lt. gov., David S. Monson (R). *Legislature*—Senate, 29 members; House of Representatives, 75 members.
State Finances (fiscal year 1982): *Revenues,* $2,324,000,000; *expenditures,* $1,994,000,000.
Personal Income (1982): $13,788,000,000; per capita, $8,875.
Labor Force (July 1983): *Nonagricultural wage and salary earners,* 558,800; *unemployed,* 58,000 (8.7% of total force).
Education: *Enrollment* (fall 1981)—public elementary schools, 261,722; public secondary, 93,832; colleges and universities (1982), 99,481. *Public school expenditures* (1981–82), $836,038,000.

VENEZUELA

Presidential elections, staggering foreign debts, and the Pan American Athletic Games marked the year 1983 in Venezuela.

General Elections. Jaime Lusinchi, the 59-year-old candidate of the left-of-center Democratic Action Party, won the December 4 election over Christian Democrat Rafael Caldera, who held the post from 1969 to 1974. AD also won control of the legislature. Lusinchi was committed to an increase in public expenditures, wage increases to meet inflation, and greater power for the trade union movement. Caldera, candidate of the incumbent government headed by Luís Herrera Campíns, was more sympathetic to the austerity program demanded by the International Monetary Fund (IMF) and by foreign creditors. The latter were asked in July to reschedule $13.7 billion (U.S.) of an estimated $34 billion foreign debt.

In other political developments, police claimed to have broken up the last of the left-wing *Bandera Roja* guerrilla group. Among 24 persons arrested on June 7 was Juan Pablo Miranda, a Chilean who had been deported previously in 1974 but returned clandestinely.

Three-Tier Exchange System Set. After foreign-exchange transactions were suspended for a week, Venezuela announced on February 28 a three-tier exchange rate system and froze prices for 60 days. The new system established a preferential rate of 4.3 bolivars to the U.S. dollar for essential imports, official expenditures overseas, and study abroad; an intermediate rate of 6 bolivars for nonessential imports; and a floating rate of 8 bolivars for luxury imports, travel abroad, and cash transactions.

While the free rate sank to 10–1 in May and 12.4–1 in early November, the Venezuelan government resisted IMF recommendations in March of a single rate of 14 bolivars to the dollar. Venezuela had set no foreign-exchange controls or price controls since the 1960s, al-

Makeshift wooden bridges enabled pedestrians to cross Salt Lake City's State Street during heavy spring flooding.

UPI

At the UN, former President Rafael Caldera marked the bicentennial of the birth of Simon Bolivar (painting right).

though the government had imposed price controls on a few items in 1982.

Economy. Venezuela expected to have a trade surplus in 1983 of $2.5 billion based on $14.5 billion of exports and $12 billion of imports. However, the nation's current deficit was expected to be worse than the 1982 deficit of $2.2 billion due to continued capital flight. The government hoped to hold inflation at 10% in 1983, compared with 8.3% in 1982, through a budget that was 5% lower than 1982 and 12% lower than the 1981 budget. Nevertheless, there were signs in July that the continued devaluation of the bolivar and the inability to resist demands for inflationary wage settlements in an election year would see inflation rise to 25%. Unemployment—8% in August 1982—rose to 15% in June 1983.

Oil production in 1983 averaged 1.7 million barrels per day (bpd), compared with the 1.78 million bpd of 1982 but substantially less than the 2.1 million bpd on which the 1983 budget was based.

Venezuela and Mexico announced on July 17 that they were reducing oil subsidies to ten Central American and Caribbean nations.

Under new terms, the two nations raised the interest rate on unpaid balances from 4% to 8% —or 6% if the balance was used for development projects.

On May 24, LAGOVEN, a subsidiary of the government-owned oil company PDVSA, confirmed reports that it had dropped plans to produce 140,000 bpd of heavy crude oil from the Eastern Orinoco Tar Belt. PDVSA also announced it was scrapping two major refinery projects costing $1.5 billion.

Venezuela also suspended payment of nearly $5 billion due on the estimated $34 billion foreign debt. Finance Minister Arturo Sosa announced he would seek to refinance $14 billion of interest and payments on principal, due in late 1983 and 1984.

Foreign Policy. While Venezuela previously supported a negotiated settlement of the four-year-old Salvadoran civil war, the Herrera Campíns government was mildly embarrassed by January 21 revelations by the United States that the Venezuelan government had trained two battalions of Salvadoran soldiers and had stationed military advisers in El Salvador.

Bolívar Bicentennial. Representatives of more than 50 nations celebrated in Caracas the 200th anniversary of the birth of Simon Bolívar, who led forces from five nations to their independence from Spain, 1810–24.

Problems at Pan American Games. The IX Pan American Games were held in Caracas August 14–28. Government officials admitted on August 19 that not all of the dormitories housing 4,000 participants were finished. Athletic achievements and a financial deficit of $30 million were overshadowed by a scandal involving the apparent use of anabolic steroids by athletes from at least nine nations. (*See also* SPORTS—Pan American Games.)

NEALE J. PEARSON, *Texas Tech University*

VENEZUELA • Information Highlights

Official Name: Republic of Venezuela.
Location: Northern coast of South America.
Area: 352,000 sq mi (911 680 km²).
Population (July 1983 est.): 17,993,000.
Government: *Head of state and government,* Luís Herrera Campíns, president (took office March 1979). *Legislature*—Congress: Senate and Chamber of Deputies.
Gross National Product (1982 U.S.$): $71,000,-000,000.
Economic Index (1982): *Consumer Prices* (1970 = 100), all items, 285.9; food, 407.3.
Foreign Trade (1981 U.S.$): *Imports,* $11,807,-000,000; *exports,* $20,125,000,000.

VERMONT

In the March local elections, Socialist Bernard Sanders won reelection as mayor of Burlington, Vermont's largest city, over Democratic and Republican opponents with 52% of the vote. Democrat Judith Stepheny, minority leader in the State House of Representatives, resigned her seat in order to run against Sanders but placed only second with 32% of the vote. Elsewhere in the state at least five towns voted in favor of proposals regulating the transportation of nuclear waste; about 20 towns rejected participating in the federal crisis relocation plan; and a handful called for ending military aid to El Salvador.

The regular legislative session was marked by bitter controversy over health-care cost controls. A "maxicap" bill to put a ceiling on all hospital budgets was watered down by setting up instead a hospital data council to make public the budgets of Vermont's hospitals. Other legislative highlights included placing the burden of a criminal insanity defense on the defendant; the banning of child pornography; and the creation of a modest "Vermont Futures" job program for the unemployed.

Vermont faced revenue shortfalls due to the recession and to federal income tax cuts, which had the effect of lowering revenue because the Vermont tax is calculated as a percentage of the federal tax. As a result, the General Assembly was forced to raise the state income and gasoline taxes. At the same time it cut the governor's recommended 1983–84 appropriation by roughly 2%. Nevertheless a projected deficit of nearly $40 million, or 10% of the budget, at the end of the 1982–83 fiscal year compelled Gov. Richard Snelling to convene a special session of the legislature in July. After a week of controversy, the legislature voted a second temporary raise in the state income tax from 25% to 26% of the federal liability, a permanent boost in the cigarette tax, and a 3.5% cut in state programs for 1983–84.

VERMONT • Information Highlights

Area: 9,614 sq mi (24 900 km²).
Population (1982 est.): 516,000.
Chief Cities (1980 census): Montpelier, the capital, 8,241; Burlington, 37,712; Rutland, 18,436.
Government (1983): *Chief Officers*—governor, Richard A. Snelling (R); lt. gov., Peter Smith (R). *General Assembly*—Senate, 30 members; House of Representatives, 150 members.
State Finances (fiscal year 1982): *Revenues,* $832,000,000; *expenditures,* $888,000,000.
Personal Income (1982): $4,907,000,000; per capita, $9,507.
Labor Force (July 1983): *Nonagricultural wage and salary earners,* 204,300; *unemployed,* 16,900 (6.3% of total force).
Education: *Enrollment* (fall 1981)—public elementary schools, 64,988; public secondary, 28,195; colleges and universities (1982), 30,648. *Public school expenditures* (1982), $240,823,000.

Despite its tax shortfalls, Vermont suffered less from the 1981–83 recession than the nation as a whole, though recovery came later and unemployment peaked at 6.3% in mid-1983. The state's economy, heavily dependent on tourism and recreation, was further depressed by the lack of snow until comparatively late in the 1982–83 skiing season. The biggest ski-industry news was the takeover of Sugarbush Valley's parent company by ARA Services, the nation's largest food-service conglomerate.

In the field of education, a University of Vermont honorary doctorate awarded to Dr. Alex Novikoff of the Albert Einstein College of Medicine attracted national attention. Dr. Novikoff, who had done groundbreaking research in biochemistry, was dismissed from the University of Vermont in 1953 for refusing to cooperate with a Senate Internal Security Committee investigating subversive influences in education. The degree was in recognition of Novikoff's scientific achievements, but many also viewed it as a gesture of atonement.

SAMUEL B. HAND and ROBERT V. DANIELS
University of Vermont

VIETNAM

Vietnam's aged leadership made only minor adjustments in its internal and external policies during 1983. The leaders had little room to maneuver because of the country's economic weakness and dependence on the Soviet Union.

Internal Developments. The main policy decisions were clearly aimed at achieving political and ideological aims—at the expense of the economy and the welfare of the people. Thus, in north Vietnam, the government sought to limit and gradually reverse the trend toward free-market incentives. In the south, it tried to speed up the process of building a Communist society. These moves risked canceling out the modest economic gains that the market incentives had produced.

Meanwhile, because of its occupation of Cambodia, Vietnam continued to suffer an economic boycott by most Western and Third World nations. The boycott has prevented Vietnam from obtaining the capital and trade it needs to solve its economic problems. Ironically, the boycott also has made Vietnam more dependent than ever on the Soviets.

In 1983 the rice harvest was better than in previous years, partly because of favorable weather and partly because the people had received economic incentives to produce. Even so, the country was far from self-sufficient in food. Malnutrition was reported to be common, especially among children.

The Soviet Union and East European countries continued to provide the means by which Vietnam was able to import rice and oil and

In early June the Vietnamese government returned the remains of eight U.S. servicemen killed during the Vietnam War. At a meeting with ASEAN foreign ministers later in the month, U.S. Secretary of State George Shultz charged that the remains of several hundred more MIAs were being withheld.

UPI

spare parts for machinery. A few Western countries, including Sweden and France, also provided aid. But the World Bank announced that Vietnam was one of the few countries that had achieved almost no economic growth in the previous 40 years. A black market was reported to be flourishing in Vietnam.

Large-scale unemployment apparently made it possible to recruit workers for low-paying factory jobs in East European countries, as a way of paying part of Vietnam's debt to those states. Meanwhile, large numbers of city dwellers, including many members of the Chinese minority, were forced to move to "new economic zones" in underdeveloped areas of Vietnam, where living conditions are poor.

In public statements, Soviet and Vietnamese leaders vented their frustrations over an economic and security relationship that costs Moscow billions each year and has brought no development to Vietnam. However, the alliance permits the Soviets access to Vietnamese bases, and it enables Vietnam to survive if not to grow economically.

Foreign Relations. In 1983, Vietnam still sought international recognition of its occupation of Cambodia. But Hanoi showed no willingness to restore Cambodia's independence or to adopt a more independent attitude toward Moscow. Vietnamese forces in Cambodia attacked and destroyed several Cambodian resistance and refugee camps on the Thai border.

Leaders of the Cambodian resistance groups accused the Vietnamese of wantonly killing hundreds of Cambodians and of settling large numbers of Vietnamese (perhaps 500,000) in Cambodia. Thailand supported the charges; Vietnam denied them. But Hanoi officials told visiting Western scholars that about 30,000 Vietnamese who lived in Cambodia before their flight in 1970 had recently returned there.

Vietnamese leaders expressed distrust of the Soviets, who were engaged in talks with Vietnam's chief enemy, China. But the Soviets apparently did not press Vietnam to accept a Chinese proposal for settling the regional conflict. China offered to negotiate a settlement of its differences with Vietnam if Vietnam would first pull its troops out of Cambodia. The Vietnamese rejected the proposal—perhaps because they felt that withdrawal from Cambodia would leave them without any leverage in dealing with China.

The Vietnamese made it very clear that they would not allow Cambodia to come under the control of the resistance groups, particularly the Democratic Kampuchea (DK) group, which was armed and supported by China. According to the Vietnamese, if they allowed the DK back into Cambodia, they would be at the mercy of China. It was far better, from their point of view, to push the DK as far west as possible.

In April 1983 the Thai foreign minister offered to visit Hanoi to discuss the Cambodian problem if the Vietnamese would withdraw their forces 30 km (19 mi) from the Thai border. Vietnam was not willing to make this concession. In October, Vietnam lost two major votes on the issue of Cambodian representation at the United Nations.

PETER A. POOLE

VIETNAM · Information Highlights

Official Name: Socialist Republic of Vietnam.
Location: Southeast Asia.
Area: 127,300 sq mi (329 707 km²).
Population (July 1983 est.): 57,036,000.
Chief Cities (1979 census): Hanoi, the capital, 2,570,905; Ho Chi Minh City, 3,419,067; Haiphong, 1,279,067.
Government (1982): Communist party secretary, Le Duan; State Council chairman, Truong Chinh; Council of Ministers, chairman, Pham Van Dong.
Monetary Unit: Dong (9.757 dongs equal U.S.$1, May 1983).
Gross National Product (1981–82 U.S.$): est. $6,000,000,000 to $16,000,000,000.

VIRGINIA

The 1983 General Assembly wrestled with amendments to the state's $13.9 billion budget, but the most heated debates were over other issues, such as raising the drinking age and establishing a new court. The legislators agreed to increase the legal age for buying beer from 18 to 19 but refused to go along with proposals to raise the age to 21. They also established a nine-member intermediate court of appeals, to begin its work in January 1985, to relieve the Virginia Supreme Court of its case overload.

In other major actions, the General Assembly agreed to spend $200,000 to study suggestions that a coal-slurry pipeline be built across the state; extended for one year the state's moratorium on uranium mining; and stiffened the state's conflict of interest laws.

Gov. Charles S. Robb stepped up efforts to attract new business and industry—especially hi-tech industry—to Virginia. He endorsed a proposal by a state advisory committee to build a $30 million research center for innovative technology. State officials hailed the Department of Energy's decision to locate a $100 million National Electron Accelerator Laboratory in Newport News.

Concerned about the quality of education in public schools, the State Board of Education approved tougher graduation standards that go into effect for students entering the ninth grade in 1984–85. Those pupils must have 20 credits

to graduate instead of the previous 18, and they must take two additional courses in mathematics and science.

U.S. District Judge Jackson L. Kiser ruled August 1 that the Bristol public schools' Bible classes were unconstitutional. But Kiser said the classes would be acceptable if certain conditions were met, such as shifting control of the courses from a private group to the school board and requiring that teachers be certified.

Civil Rights. Feeling that blacks were not exercising their political power, Virginia's branch of the NAACP started a campaign in 1983 not only to push voter registration but also to have 11 cities change their at-large local election systems to ward systems. The NAACP said the at-large systems discriminated against black voters. Blacks scored a major step forward during the year when the governor named John Charles Thomas, a 32-year-old Richmond lawyer, to the Virginia Supreme Court. Thomas became the first black ever appointed to the state's highest court.

Redevelopment. Richmond's downtown revitalization and the state's cultural renaissance got a boost when the Virginia Center for the Performing Arts opened in May. The center is in the former Loew's Theater, built in 1928 as an "atmospheric theater" modeled after a Spanish courtyard. Altered through the years, it was meticulously restored in a two-year, $6 million effort. Meanwhile, the Virginia Museum of Fine Arts in Richmond was working toward completion of a major expansion.

Other. Virginia made headlines in late May, when seven heads of state and the leader of the European Community met in Williamsburg. Other news included a June 21 explosion at Clinchfield Coal Co.'s McClure #1 mine in Dickenson County. The explosion, apparently caused by methane gas, killed seven miners.

VIRGINIA MUNSCH
"Richmond Times-Dispatch"

The Virginia Center for the Performing Arts opened in Richmond, after a $6 million restoration of the old Loew's Theater.

Virginia Center for the Performing Arts

VIRGIN ISLANDS

The tourism-oriented economy of the U.S. Virgin Islands continued a four-year slump in 1983, prolonging the territory's deep recession and creating mounting fiscal problems.

Tourism. The tourist industry accounts for 22.2% of the Virgin Islands' gross territorial product and for nearly 30% of total employment. But the number of visitors, declining since 1980, fell by more than 10% in 1982. Visitor air arrivals dropped by 1.1% in 1982, and by 3.7% in the first half of 1983. Hotel occupancy rates for the three islands of St. Thomas, St. John, and St. Croix fell from 75% in 1979 to 58% in 1982. Eleven hotels were closed in 1982, four permanently, with a loss of 710 jobs. In September, American Airlines temporarily cut its New York-Virgin Islands schedule from two flights to one flight per day. But at the same time, Air Florida announced it would resume its Virgin Islands service, discontinued since January 1980, starting November 15.

Government Budget. With tourism revenues down, the territorial Senate was forced to appropriate a supplemental budget of $19 million to fund government operations in the last quarter of fiscal year 1983. Excise taxes on cigarettes and alcoholic beverages were raised in August. Proposals by Gov. Juan Luis for a four-day workweek for government employees and for elimination of pay for six legal holidays were rejected, but summer sessions of public schools were canceled to save costs.

The proposed budget for fiscal year 1984 contained $34 million in new income taxes and taxes on gross receipts, along with a built-in $48 million deficit. Government department heads said they expected a 7 to 9% reduction in operations. About 75% of the government budget is spent on salaries.

Legislative Change. The political balance of the unicameral Virgin Islands legislature (Senate) changed in July when two members of the coalition United People's Majority switched to the Democratic Party, giving the Democrats a 9–6 edge in the 15-seat body. Issues under debate during the year included proposals to legalize casino gambling to stimulate tourism, and to create a commission to recommend changes in the status of the Virgin Islands. Governor Luis vetoed a bill that would have eliminated Lincoln's Birthday, February 12, as a legal holiday and substituted August 7, the birthday of former Gov. Melvin H. Evans.

Disasters. On September 26 an American Airlines flight from New York to the Virgin Islands was hijacked to Cuba, with 105 passengers and seven crew members aboard. On April 17–18 a tropical storm dumped 18 inches (46 cm) of rain on St. Thomas and St. John in 12 hours, producing extensive flooding and property damage and causing one death.

RICHARD C. SCHROEDER, *"Vision"*

WASHINGTON

Sen. Henry M. Jackson, Democrat, Washington's senior senator who was serving his sixth term, died suddenly of a heart attack on September 1 at the age of 71. Approximately half the members of the Senate and several members of Congress attended his funeral in his hometown, Everett, Washington. (*See also* OBITUARIES.)

Senatorial Election. Senator Jackson's unexpected death posed a succession problem for Gov. John Spellman, a Republican. State succession statutes are ambiguous regarding the manner of succession (whether by appointment or election) when there is a short time before the next general election. The state's attorney general ruled that the vacancy would be filled at the next general election, and a special primary was scheduled. Governor Spellman appointed former Gov. Daniel J. Evans, Republican, senator for the interim. By the primary filing deadline, 34 people had filed candidacy, including 20 Democrats, 13 Republicans, and 1 Socialist Workers Party member. Senator Evans won the Republican nomination by nearly a 2–1 margin over his closest opponent, Lloyd Cooney, a former television executive, and Rep. Mike Lowry won the Democratic nomination by about the same margin over Seattle Mayor Charles Royer. Evans was the victor in the general election November 8.

WPPSS Default. In a conclusion that had been expected for months, but was stalled by legal maneuvers, the Washington Public Power Supply System (WPPSS) on July 25 was declared in default of payment against bonds issued to construct 2 of 5 WPPSS nuclear plants. Work on the two plants had been halted 18 months earlier when the WPPSS had been unable to sell additional bonds to finish construction. The 88 sponsoring northwest utilities then claimed that the WPPSS had misrepresented its

---

WASHINGTON • Information Highlights

Area: 68,139 sq mi (176 480 km²).
Population (1982 est.): 4,245,000.
Chief Cities (1980 census): Olympia, the capital, 27,447; Seattle, 493,846; Spokane, 171,300; Tacoma, 158,501; Bellevue, 73,903; Everett, 54,413.
Government (1983): *Chief Officers*—governor, John Spellman (R); lt. gov., John A. Cherberg (D). *Legislature*—Senate, 49 members; House of Representatives, 98 members.
State Finances (fiscal year 1982): *Revenues,* $7,446,000,000; *expenditures,* $7,256,000,000.
Personal Income (1982): $49,074,000,000; per capita, $11,652.
Labor Force (July 1983): *Nonagricultural wage and salary earners,* 1,578,700; *unemployed,* 213,100 (10.5% of total force).
Education: *Enrollment* (fall 1981)—public elementary schools, 513,018; public secondary, 237,170; colleges and universities (1982): 227,812. *Public school expenditures* (1981–82): $2,473,466,000 ($2,653 per pupil).

Wide World

Daniel J. Evans (R), former Washington governor, assumed the Senate seat vacated by the death of Henry M. Jackson.

ability to finance and build the two plants and further claimed that the utilities had no authority to enter into sponsorship contracts. The state Supreme Court concurred. At default, Chemical Bank of New York, trustee for $2.25 billion of bonds for the two plants, initiated suits seeking recovery of the $2.25 billion plus interest and other costs, which could reach $7 billion. These efforts placed in jeopardy the supply system's three other plants.

Wage Discrimination. A landmark wage-discrimination decision on September 16 was certain to have national impact. U.S. District Judge Jack Tanner ruled that Washington State had been guilty of discriminating against women because it pays them less than men for comparable work. The case was significant because it focused on the theory of comparable worth rather than the concept of equal pay for men and women in the same job. The remedy phase of the case was scheduled for later in the year. State officials planned to await the results of that phase before deciding how to provide the compensation money, which was estimated to be in excess of $500 million.

Mass Murder. On February 19 three men entered the Wah Mee high-stakes gambling club in Seattle's International District and, in the state's worst mass homicide, gunned down the 14 people in the club after tying and robbing them. One victim survived, and his testimony helped convict two of the gunmen.

WARREN W. ETCHESON
University of Washington

WASHINGTON, D.C.

Mayor Marion Barry (D) was sworn in to his second term of office on January 2, along with newly elected City Council Chairperson David A. Clarke (D), and six other council seat winners.

March. The March on Washington II on August 27 commemorated the 20th anniversary of the historical civil rights demonstration led by the late Martin Luther King, Jr., in 1963. Participants arrived from many regions of the nation to mark the event and develop the march's "Jobs, Peace and Freedom" theme.

Bomb. A time bomb exploded outside the Senate Chamber in the Capitol on the night of November 7 but caused no injuries. A group calling itself the Armed Resistance Unit claimed responsibility. The incident lent urgency to the adoption of new security measures, which were proposed after an October bomb threat and approved November 8.

Statehood. The proposed constitution for statehood was submitted by Mayor Barry to Congress in September. Progress was made by the end of the year, when the draft constitution was referred to the House Subcommittee on DC Fiscal Affairs and Health.

Amendment. Maine, West Virginia, and Rhode Island legislatures ratified the proposed U.S. constitutional amendment giving DC residents the right to elect two senators and two representatives to Congress. This raised the number of states ratifying the amendment to 13 of 38 needed by 1985.

No-Fault Insurance. A new mandatory no-fault automobile insurance law took effect October 1. DC drivers must carry insurance to cover personal injuries and property damage and to protect them in accidents caused by an uninsured driver. The no-fault feature provides that payments are made by the injured person's insurance company whether the person caused the accident or was the victim. Persons may sue an offending motorist in certain cases.

New Attractions. The Washington Convention Center, on New York Avenue, housed its first show on January 5. The $98.7 million, 800,000-sq ft (72 000-m²) facility was initiated by congressional authorization in 1978.

The Pavilion at the Old Post Office opened as another step in the downtown area redevelopment drive, to complete the $38 million renovation of the towering Romanesque structure in the Federal Triangle area near the Mall. Three floors of shops and restaurants, along with eight floors of federal offices, surround a spectacular courtyard roofed by a skylight.

Metro. The new Yellow Line subway opened in two segments to link downtown DC to Fairfax County, VA, crossing the Potomac River on its own bridge. The new line adds five stations and 8.47 mi (13.8 km) to the system.

MORRIS J. LEVITT, *Howard University*

WEST VIRGINIA

West Virginia's rate of unemployment—12.5% as measured by the state and 15.1% according to federal statistics for September—led the nation for most of 1983. Although the rate was lower than it had been earlier in the year, the fact that it did not fall further reflected the continuing decline of the coal industry.

Mining Unemployment. More than 60,000 West Virginia miners were employed in October 1981. The figure had shrunk to 44,000 by the end of 1982 and stood at just 32,000 in October 1983, a 28% drop in 12 months. Overall unemployment exceeded the 100,000 level at times during 1983 and declined to 92,000 by the end of the third quarter. The percentage of unemployed rose well beyond 25% in the leading coal-producing counties, although production stayed relatively steady. This apparent anomaly was credited to technical advances in mining and processing coal, advances that economists predict may eventually have as great an effect on the industry—and on employment figures—as did the first great wave of mechanization in the 1950s.

Legislative Session. The regular session produced a near-record $92 million tax hike, including higher personal income taxes for individuals making more than $12,000, and a 12% surcharge on those higher rates. Similar surtaxes were levied on industry, although tax credits were extended to employers making special efforts to aid the jobless.

In a session that critics again charged produced far more heat than light, legislators also enacted tougher laws concerning drunk driving and raised the drinking age from 18 to 19 and to 21 for out-of-state residents. A controversial cost-containment law for hospitals passed in the final hours of the session, a statute that still was generating widespread debate and argument at year's end.

Spending Cuts and Wages. Gov. John D. (Jay) Rockefeller IV, who had imposed major cutbacks in spending over the past two years,

---

WEST VIRGINIA • Information Highlights

Area: 24,231 sq mi (62 758 km²).
Population (1982 est.): 1,948,000.
Chief Cities (1980 census): Charleston, the capital, 63,968; Huntington, 63,684; Wheeling, 43,070.
Government (1983): *Chief Officers*—governor, John D. Rockefeller IV (D); secy. of state, A. James Manchin (D). *Legislature*—Senate, 34 members; House of Delegates, 100 members.
State Finances (fiscal year 1982): *Revenues,* $3,100,000,000; *expenditures,* $2,842,000,000.
Personal Income (1982): $17,078,000,000; per capita, $8,769.
Labor Force (July 1983): *Nonagricultural wage and salary earners,* 590,400; *unemployed,* 133,500 (17.4% of total force).
Education: *Enrollment* (fall 1981)—public elementary schools, 266,944; public secondary, 110,828; colleges and universities (fall 1982), 82,891. *Public school expenditures* (1981–82), $861,397,000.

---

decreed another of 3% when the new fiscal year was but hours old in July, despite a year-end surplus that was slightly higher than expected. This surplus was used in part to pay off claims against the state employees' insurance program. Many of the claims had gone unpaid in the last months of the fiscal year.

Nor were these unpaid claims the public employees' only cause for complaint. As another legislative session neared, those employees, including teachers, were making certain that both the public and the legislators knew they had received virtually no increases for three years and had not profited from the additional tax revenues, despite the fact that a modest increase for the employees had been one of the major arguing points of those backing the tax increase.

In September, employees of National Steel's giant Weirton plant—once the state's largest single employer—approved a plan allowing them to purchase and operate the plant themselves rather than face a permanent shutdown.

DONOVAN H. BOND
West Virginia University

WINE

The winds of change were blowing across the vineyards of Europe and the United States as the worldwide recession began to taper off. Fortunately for America's wine drinkers and winemakers, not all of the change was bad.

California wine production and sales grew in 1981, while import wines continued to capture a larger part of the growing U.S. wine market. White-wine sales rose about 14% in 1980–81, but red-wine sales began to erode, dropping off by 4.3% in 1981–82.

Sparkling-wine sales, however, have shown improvement, partly because of the growing demand for white wines, but also because of the increased interest shown in California vineyards by European vintners. As the American economy began to pull out of the recession and the European economy weakened, French and Spanish sparkling-wine producers looked to California as a safe investment haven. Beginning in 1982, the French began to move into California, following an earlier lead by Moët-Hennessy. Piper Heidsieck opened Piper Sonoma; Laurent-Perrier launched an arrangement with Almadén; and Louis Roederer purchased vineyard land in Mendocino, and Deutz in San Luis Obispo. Spain's two leading sparkling-wine producers, Codorníu and Freixenet, also bought land in California.

But in 1982 the wind began to shift for California table wine sales. An abundant harvest in 1981 was followed by another big one in 1982. New vineyards came into production, creating a surplus of wine grapes. At the same time, wine sales grew by only 2.6%, as compared with 6.7% in 1980–81. By the end of 1982 it was estimated that winemakers had 135 billion gallons of unsold wine.

Per capita wine consumption in 1982 showed only a marginal increase to 2.7 gallons (10.2 l), of which 1.4 gallons (5.2 l) were white wine. Although California and New York account for one third of all wine sales, Texas and Florida showed the greatest gain in 1981 and 1982.

During the same period, European vintners began to close the gap in import-wine sales in the United States, especially in moderately priced proprietary wines. Italy's Principato went from 33d to 16th place on the import list. Simultaneously, French vintners sought to take some of Italy's 60% share of the U.S. import market. French Rabbit, a new wine sold under a brand name, moved in fast on the sales of such favorites as Mouton Cadet and Partager. Adding to the French gain was the 1982 vintage —a great one in quantity and quality. The Germans, long content to sell their wines at home or nearby, created a new class of wine called *Landwein,* similar to the *vin de table* of France. Of the top ten imported wines, Italy produced seven, Germany two, and Portugal one.

The outlook for the U.S. wine industry in 1983 brightened. Legislation was drafted to help break barriers against American wine sales abroad. California wine shipments were up and prices were going down.

GERALD D. BOYD
Editor, "Wine & Spirits Buying Guide"

WISCONSIN

State administration policies toward business seemed to dominate much of 1983 news in Wisconsin.

Business Climate. In his first year in office, Gov. Anthony Earl was faced with increasing demands that Wisconsin do something to improve the climate for business, or at least to change the image that it was an antibusiness state. The state had had this reputation for years, although there had been few hard facts to back it up and no mass exodus of business.

In May, however, the Kimberly-Clark Corp., the state's biggest company, announced that it would move its corporate headquarters out of Neenah unless the business climate improved. The company, whose products include Kleenex and Kotex, soon became a symbol of business dissatisfaction. Later, the head of the Fort Howard Paper Co. of Green Bay complained about a "relentless antagonism" toward business, and the Kohler Co. announced that it would build a new faucet factory in Tennessee or Arkansas.

Governor Earl, citing Wisconsin's population growth, improved air and water quality, and the lowering of capital gains and top-bracket income taxes, pleaded with business to look at the state's strengths. He reluctantly called a special session of the legislature to deal with business incentives. The October session resulted in measures to promote agricultural products, create a state trade office, and give a tax break to the printing industry.

State Finances. The confrontation with business took place in a year when the Democratic governor, elected by a wide margin in 1982, was attempting to hold the line on finances. The state, he said, was in the midst of hard times, brought on in part by policies of his predecessor, Republican Lee S. Dreyfus. Governor Earl proposed heavy income-tax increases and spending constraints. The Democratic legislature responded with a $16 billion budget calling for a 10% income-tax surcharge.

Faculty Pay. One item in the budget that received much attention was a freeze on the pay of University of Wisconsin faculty members in 1983 and only a 3.8% increase in 1984. The move brought an outcry, and even demonstrations, from faculty, who said it would erode quality. By year's end, a task force named by the governor and the university president was studying the issue.

Reapportionment. Refusing to accept a court-ordered legislative reapportionment plan, drawn up after the legislature could not agree on one in 1982, Democrats in the new session proposed a new one. Republicans denounced the plan as a gerrymander to help Democrats, but they were outnumbered and it passed.

Economy. With an economy dependent on the production of durable goods, the state had a high unemployment rate in the first half of the year. But this dipped below the national average in the second half. Farm income rebounded; the state was less seriously affected by the drought than others, and it had the highest per-acre corn yield of all states.

PAUL SALSINI, *"The Milwaukee Journal"*

WISCONSIN • Information Highlights

Area: 56,153 sq mi (145 436 km²).
Population (1982 est.): 4,765,000.
Chief Cities (1980 census): Madison, the capital, 170,616; Milwaukee, 636,236; Green Bay, 87,899.
Government (1983): *Chief Officers*—governor, Anthony S. Earl (D); lt. gov., James T. Flynn (D). *Legislature*—Senate, 33 members; Assembly, 99 members.
State Finances (fiscal year 1982): *Revenues,* $7,533,000,000; *expenditures,* $6,895,000,000.
Personal Income (1982): $51,341,000,000; per capita, $10,774.
Labor Force (July 1983): *Nonagricultural wage and salary earners,* 1,858,200; *unemployed,* 228,200 (9.4% of total force).
Education: *Enrollment* (fall 1981)—public elementary schools, 512,831; public secondary, 291,431; colleges and universities (fall 1982), 276,176 students. *Public school expenditures* (1981–82), $2,304,456,000.

WOMEN

The "gender gap" and its implications for the 1984 presidential and congressional elections dominated the list of women's concerns in 1983. The phrase refers to the results of various surveys showing that women are a majority of the electorate and that they are more likely than men to vote for Democratic candidates for public office.

Political and Economic Issues. The Reagan administration spent much of the year trying to close the gap, but with mixed results. Women's groups applauded when Reagan named two women to his cabinet—Elizabeth Hanford Dole as secretary of transportation and Margaret Heckler as secretary of health and human services—but they criticized his record in appointing women to federal judgeships. (*See also* BIOGRAPHY.) A November *New York Times* poll indicated that only 38% of all women felt Reagan deserved reelection as compared with 53% of all men.

In a speech before the Republican Women's Leadership Forum in San Diego August 26, the president enumerated steps his administration had taken to help women, including strengthening the federal child-support enforcement system, extending the program providing flexible work hours for federal employees, and increasing the maximum child-care tax credit.

Reagan also promised to speed up his administration's review of sex discrimination in federal law. Earlier in August the Justice Department official in charge of the review, Barbara Honegger, resigned, saying the project was a "sham." In September, Reagan announced that he would support changes in 112 federal laws containing sex-based distinctions. But even the Justice Department acknowledged that the changes were "cosmetic" and "not substantial."

Throughout the year Reagan stressed how women had benefited from his economic policies, particularly his success in bringing inflation under control. Despite such emphasis, there were signs that many women were unhappy with the president's economic policies. According to a September *Washington Post-ABC* poll, only 40% of the women respondents approved of the way Reagan was handling the economy while 54% disapproved. For men, 57% approved while 39% disapproved.

Women's concerns about the economy were not surprising. The U.S. Commission on Civil Rights released a report in April that showed that a "disproportionate number of America's poor in the early 1980s [were] women." The report, entitled *A Growing Crisis: Disadvantaged Women and Their Children,* found that between 1960 and 1981, the number of poor families headed by women rose 54% while the number of poor families headed by white men dropped by 51%.

There were other signs in 1983 that economic issues were among women's top priorities. For example, while women's groups had continued to lobby for passage of the Equal Rights Amendment (ERA), which was reintroduced in Congress in January and defeated by the House in November, their top legislative priority in 1983 was the Economic Equity Act, a package of legislation aimed at improving the economic status of women.

There was movement in 1983 on selected elements of the package, which included mea-

In an August speech, President Reagan stressed that "it's economic recovery that will move women forward the fastest."

Mary Anne Fackelman/The White House

In October, Katherine Davalos Ortega, near right, 49-year-old former banker of Hispanic background, became U.S. treasurer. In November, former California feminist Ginny Foat was acquitted of the 1965 murder of an Argentine businessman. The chief witness against her was her husband. Mrs. Foat called her acquittal a victory for women generally.

sures to strengthen child-support enforcement laws, make it easier for homemakers to open individual retirement accounts (IRAs), reform insurance laws, revise the tax code to make dependent care more available, and reform pension laws. On pension reform, for example, the Senate on November 18 approved a bill that would permit employed individuals to take maternity or paternity leave without losing time built up for participation or vesting in a company pension plan. The measure also broadens spouses' rights to a pension if a worker dies before retirement age.

In another pension-related matter, the U.S. Supreme Court ruled July 6 that employer-sponsored pension plans cannot give men and women unequal benefits. The fact that women as a group live longer than men is not a permissible basis for paying them different monthly retirement benefits, the court said. The ruling had sweeping implications for the insurance industry, which had traditionally used sex-based actuarial tables.

On June 15 the Supreme Court upheld its 1973 ruling that women have a constitutional right to have an abortion when it overturned a number of state laws that put a variety of restrictions on women seeking abortions. Under the ruling, states may no longer require that all abortions after the first trimester be performed in hospitals, for example, or require minors to obtain parental or judicial consent for an abortion.

In another setback for the antiabortion movement, the Senate in June rejected a proposed constitutional amendment that would have permitted state legislatures to ban the procedure. The Senate did, however, go along with the House in approving a stopgap appropriations measure that included a provision prohibiting federal workers from using their government health insurance benefits to pay for abortions, unless the mother's life was in danger.

Women in the News. A number of individual women made headlines in 1983. In June astronaut Sally K. Ride became the first American woman to fly on a space mission. Botanist Barbara McClintock won the 1983 Nobel Prize for Physiology or Medicine. (*See also* BIOGRAPHY.)

A federal judge in Kansas City on October 31 ordered a new trial for former television anchorwoman Christine Craft. In August a jury's advisory verdict had awarded Craft $500,000 in her sex-discrimination suit against a television station whose executives demoted her, she claimed, for being "too old, too unattractive and not deferential to men."

Elections. Women did well in the 1983 elections. Mayors Dianne Feinstein of San Francisco and Kathy Whitmire of Houston were reelected, while Martha Layne Collins, a Democrat, was elected Kentucky's first woman governor. Sonia Johnson, who gained national attention when she was excommunicated from the Mormon Church in 1979 for her activities on behalf of the ERA, announced in October that she was seeking the Citizens Party nomination for president.

While few were taking Johnson's candidacy seriously, there was much speculation during the year about the possibility of a woman being named as a vice-presidential candidate by either the Republican or Democratic Party. Appearing before the annual convention of the National Organization for Women, six of the Democratic presidential contenders—Alan Cranston, John Glenn, Gary Hart, Ernest Hollings, George McGovern, and Walter Mondale—indicated that they would be willing to consider naming a female running mate. Jesse Jackson (D) said that if he gets the nomination he will name a woman to the second spot.

SANDRA STENCEL, *"Congressional Quarterly"*

WYOMING

In 1983 the state experienced the crunch and consequences of economic recession; began planning for the MX missile system, which will be deployed in the Cheyenne area by 1986; and suffered the loss of passenger rail service, a development that marked the passing of an era.

The Economy. As markets for Wyoming coal, gas, and oil softened in response to the national recession, mineral exploration and production in the state leveled off or dropped. So did severance- and sales-tax revenues and mineral royalty payments to the state. The uncertainties of nuclear power left the uranium industry in decline, and the state's production of that mineral dropped to a 16-year low. In August, U.S. Steel closed its Atlantic City iron ore operation near Lander, leaving some 500 workers jobless. For the first time in 20 years the state's unemployment rate reached double-digit figures—11.2% in March. This dropped to 8.7% by midsummer but remained well above 5.8%, the state's average for all of 1982. An unprecedented drain on Wyoming's unemployment-benefits trust fund forced a two-day special session of the legislature, which kept the fund solvent through a mix of internal and federal loans. On August 15, Gov. Ed Herschler, announcing that state revenues were down by some 10%, directed state agencies to cut current spending by 4%. He predicted that the next biennial budget would be a no-growth document. His austerity program echoed a note set by the legislature in its regular session earlier in the year. The lawmakers passed a school finance bill leveling out disparities between rich and poor districts, debated water development projects but left them largely unfunded, and limited state pay increases to 2%. Killed by the legislature were bills to set up a wildlife trust fund, establish in-stream flow minimums, and extend state jurisdiction over hazardous wastes.

The MX. Plans to deploy 100 MX missiles in existing launch silos near Cheyenne proceeded with informational meetings and impact studies preliminary to actual construction work. A regional anti-MX coalition continued to oppose the mammoth defense project, but Wyoming's congressional delegation and some state officials favored it. Proponents pointed to the promise of some 3,000 new jobs for the area and the prospect of more than $1 million in immediate construction funds.

Rail Service. Amtrak discontinued passenger trains through Wyoming, rerouting them through Colorado. Effective in July, the change came from economic projections that made the Colorado route seem more promising. But it left Wyoming without passenger service for the first time in 115 years, setting off a round of public protest. Then, nostalgic good-bye parties were held in such former railroad towns as Rawlins, Evanston, and Laramie.

H. R. DIETERICH, *University of Wyoming*

WYOMING • Information Highlights

Area: 97,809 sq mi (253 325 km²).
Population (1982 est.): 502,000.
Chief Cities (1980 census): Cheyenne, the capital, 47,283; Casper, 51,016; Laramie, 24,410.
Government (1983): *Chief Officer*—governor, Ed Herschler (D). *Legislature*—Senate, 30 members; House of Representatives, 64 members.
State Finances (fiscal year 1982): *Revenues,* $1,559,000,000; *expenditures,* $1,123,000,000.
Personal Income (1982): $6,207,000,000; per capita, $12,372.
Labor Force (July 1983): *Nonagricultural wage and salary earners,* 214,400; *unemployed,* 23,400 (8.7% of total force).
Education: *Enrollment* (fall 1981)—public elementary schools, 71,842; public secondary, 27,699; colleges and universities (1981–82), 21,235. *Public school expenditures* (1981–82), $368,774,000.

YUGOSLAVIA

The country's domestic crisis intensified in 1983, but the collective leaderships at both the state (Socialist Federal Republic of Yugoslavia, SFRY) and the ruling-party (League of Communists of Yugoslavia, LCY) levels maintained overall control.

Domestic Affairs. On May 13 and June 30, Mika Špiljak and Dragoslav Marković were elected to one-year terms as president of the SFRY presidency and president of the LCY central committee presidium, respectively. The system of rotating short-term leadership, however, came under increasing criticism, as did other elements of Tito's legacy.

The most intractable domestic problem continued to be the devolution of economic and political authority (following the 1974 constitution) upon Yugoslavia's six republics and two autonomous provinces, limiting the federal government's role in economic policy making. Weakening of central authority and increased regionalism have split the country's unified market and intra-republican solidarity.

Among Yugoslavia's other domestic troubles, the multiform conflict in the autonomous province of Kosovo remained unresolved. Despite arrests and punitive measures, the authorities failed to eradicate the militancy of ethnic Albanians who persisted in fighting the constitutional status quo. Sporadic violence against the Serbian minority and the forced exodus of some members fueled Serbian nationalism elsewhere. The spread of Pan-Islamism in Bosnia-Herzegovina, by which the province would be made purely Muslim, led by the end of the summer to trials and heavy sentences.

Church-state relations continued to be delicate. The elevation to cardinal of the outspoken archbishop of Zagreb, Franjo Kuharić, encouraged the nationalist and anti-Communist elements among the Croatian Catholic clergy and faithful. The hierarchy of the Serbian Orthodox Church protested to state organs the acts of vandalism perpetrated against churches and monasteries in Kosovo. It also resisted the regime's pressure to recognize the independence of the Macedonian Orthodox Church.

Hoping to quell dissidence, the regime banned numerous books, newspapers, periodicals, and other materials. Articles focusing on the nation's economic shortcomings and critical student publications were the main targets of the censorship. Conversely, in widely diffused *samizdat* pamphlets, the dissidents bombarded the regime with protests over the suppression of constitutional and civil rights. Unable to coalesce into a formal political opposition, some of the best-known and most gifted writers, intellectuals, and professors joined the nonviolent protest movement.

Amid these problems, a highly emotional meeting of the LCY central committee in October testified to the degree of disorientation and disagreement among party leaders. Internal and external LCY enemies were denounced, and hints about the necessity of new purges were in the air. The dominant faction won the upper hand, insisting on the launching of ideological orthodoxy, the teaching of Marx-

In Yugoslavia's system of rotating leadership, Mika Špiljak was elected to a one-year term as formal head of state.

UPI

ism in schools, and the rejection of a pluralistic reform of the LCY organizational structure.

Economy. With some exceptions, the performance of the Yugoslav economy in 1983 was dismal. The two key problems were a $20 billion (U.S.) external debt and the illiquidity of the domestic economy and banks. By year's end the rate of inflation was 60%; industrial and labor production both were declining. Of some 915,000 unemployed, 50% were specialists, 76% were under age 30, and 57% were women. Unemployment was highest in the least-developed regions, such as Kosovo.

The Yugoslav people also suffered shortages of many essential commodities and blackouts of electricity. Cooking oil, sugar, coffee, milk, meat, and drugs were in short supply, leading to hoarding of stock, an outbreak of looting in early March, and a flourishing black market. The electricity blackouts, introduced late in the year to conserve energy, were held several times a week in major cities.

Bright spots in the economy were a bumper wheat harvest, a satisfactory tourist season, and some improvement in the foreign-trade balance. Exports to the hard-currency convertible zone rose; the perennial trade deficit was cut.

A Western financial program to restore Yugoslavia's solvency included an intitial package of $4.5 billion put together by the International Monetary Fund (IMF) and involving the World Bank, 15 governments, the Bank of International Settlements, and 600 commercial banks. Intricate financial arrangements would reschedule payments of debts and interest and offer the country new loans, mainly to stimulate exports. The basic condition of the rescue operation was the introduction of an economic austerity program, accepted by the Yugoslav government and the Chamber of Republics and Provinces on July 3. In view of internal politics, however, it remains uncertain whether the austerity program, designed to encourage private enterprise and the functioning of a market economy, will bring positive results.

Foreign Relations. Yugoslav foreign policy continued to be guided by four precepts established during the Tito era: nonalignment; the worker self-management system as Yugoslavia's special contribution to contemporary Marxism; rejection of a single socialist model as mandatory to all Communist-led countries; and belief that the duty of the LCY leadership is to "always be at the helm of the struggle for socialism in the world."

Yugoslav representatives acted in the spirit of these principles at three major conferences: the seventh summit of the nonaligned nations in New Delhi, March 7–12; the sixth meeting of the UN Conference on Trade and Development (UNCTAD), hosted in Belgrade, June 6–July 3; and the Conference on Security and Cooperation in Europe, which ended its 1983 deliberations September 7–9 in Madrid.

YUGOSLAVIA • Information Highlights

Official Name: Socialist Federal Republic of Yugoslavia.
Location: Southwestern Europe.
Area: 98,800 sq mi (255 892 km²).
Population (July 1983 est.): 22,826,000.
Chief Cities (1981 census): Belgrade, the capital, 1,209,360 (1971); Zagreb, 763,426; Skopje, 503,449.
Government: *Head of state,* collective state presidency, Mika Špiljak, president (took office May 1983). *Head of government,* Mika Planinc, prime minister (took office May 1982). *Legislature—* Federal Assembly: Federal Chamber and Chamber of Republics and Provinces.
Monetary Unit: New Dinar (2.486 dinars equal U.S.$1, August 1983).
Gross National Product (1981 U.S.$): $51,800,-000,000.
Economic Indexes (1982): *Consumer Prices* (1970 = 100), all items, 1,040; food (1981), 853.3. *Industrial Production* (1975 = 100), 144.
Foreign Trade (1982 U.S.$): *Imports,* $14,057,-000,000; *exports,* $10,713,000,000.

In efforts to maintain fruitful relations with the superpowers, Yugoslav leaders received top Soviet, U.S., and Chinese dignitaries. Soviet Premier Nikolai Tikhonov paid an official visit March 21–24, at the time that the USSR had become Yugoslavia's principal trade partner. Increased deliveries of Soviet oil were promised, and an extensive program of economic, scientific, and technical cooperation was signed for the period ending in 1990. A joint communiqué declared that the two countries held identical views on war, peace, and disarmament, and that existing differences were of secondary importance.

Belgrade was pleased by the U.S. reaction to the systematic post-Titoist wooing by the Soviet Union. During a visit September 16–18, U.S. Vice-President George Bush met with the highest Yugoslav officials. He stated in a speech that U.S.-Yugoslav relations "today are excellent" and, alluding to the Soviet Union, complimented his audience: "You are prepared resolutely to resist any attempt to limit your independence and sovereignty. By your courage and determination, you have gained the respect of the whole world."

In May, Hu Yaobang, secretary of the Chinese Communist Party, was the guest of the LCY; closer party relations were planned. Earlier in the year, Vidoje Žarković, vice-president of the SFRY presidency, toured North Korea and China; he reported about the blossoming of Chinese-Yugoslav relations.

Other travels by Yugoslav diplomats were for the purpose of economic benefits or political visibility. The most intensive economic contacts were maintained with the European Economic Community (EC), Libya, and countries of the Middle East. Nothing of real importance developed with Yugoslavia's neighbors.

MILORAD M. DRACHKOVITCH
The Hoover Institution, Stanford University

YUKON

With the resignation of Joe Clark as national leader of the Progressive Conservative (PC) Party of Canada, Yukon Member of Parliament Erik Nielsen was appointed acting party leader in the House of Commons. Following the election in June 1983 of Brian Mulroney as PC leader, Nielsen was named deputy national leader for the opposition.

An agreement-in-principle on Yukon Indian land claims between the federal and Yukon governments and the Council for Yukon Indians neared completion. The agreement will provide for monetary and land settlements with Yukon's 6,000 to 8,000 Indians, along with certain political guarantees and involvement in the territory's resource management.

Economy. Yukon's mining industry continued to slump throughout 1983, despite aid from the federal and Yukon governments. Economic troubles were compounded with the closing of the White Pass railway, which provided the only rail link with tidewater for Yukon's raw minerals. The railway closing also had a negative impact on the territory's tourism industry.

Gold placer mining operations remained strong, but the industry expressed fears that strict new environmental regulations proposed by the federal government could severely restrict the continued viability of the industry. A public review process on the new guidelines was conducted during the fall. The collapse of Yukon's hard-rock mining industry translated into a population decline of between 15 and 20% and a substantial drop in resource-related revenues.

Two major development proposals on Yukon's north coast were considered, including a deep-sea port to service offshore oil and gas exploration activities in the Beaufort Sea, and a major sandstone quarrying operation. The federal government denied both applications, fearing that development might jeopardize land claims negotiations.

During the fall the Yukon government announced a $10 million economic stimulation program to ease the high unemployment throughout the territory. Unemployment peaked in the fall at about 25%.

ANDREW HUME
Free-lance Writer, Yukon

YUKON • Information Highlights

Area: 207,076 sq mi (536 327 km²).
Population (July 1983 est.): 22,200.
Chief City (1981 census): Whitehorse, the capital, 14,814.
Government (1983): *Chief Officers—*commissioner, Douglas Bell; government leader, Christopher Pearson. *Legislature—*16-member legislative assembly.
Education (1982–83): Enrollment—elementary and secondary schools, 4,800 pupils.
Public Finance (1983 fiscal year): *Revenues,* $169,500,000; *expenditures,* $167,300,000.

ZAIRE

Zaire's economy remained precarious in 1983 amid cabinet reshuffles, charges of political repression, aid to Chad, and strained relations with Belgium.

Economy and Mining. Zaire's total external debt was more than $5 billion (U.S.), and how much would be repaid to foreign creditors remained uncertain. Just as in recent years, Zaire was unable to service even the total interest due on its debt.

The increased export revenues from more favorable copper and cobalt sales were encouraging. Zaire ended its experiment in selling its industrial diamonds outside the monopoly of the South African firm, DeBeers. By returning to DeBeers' marketing, Zaire hoped to share in the expected recovery of the international diamond market in the future. Although modest, oil production rose, allowing for a cut of about 50% in oil imports.

In September the zaire was devalued by nearly 80% as part of a program of economic reforms stipulated by the International Monetary Fund in exchange for a $350 million loan.

Domestic Affairs. In March and November, President Mobutu Sese Seko once again reshuffled his cabinet. With the president's blessing, Prime Minister Kengo Wa Dondo launched an anticorruption campaign aimed at businessmen who evaded taxes and engaged in fraud and at heads of state enterprises who violated regulations. Reports cited the arrest of several dozen officials and businessmen, some of whom were heavily fined.

The opposition, titularly headed by former Prime Minister Nguza Karl-I-Bond, continued to criticize the Mobutu regime for its corruption. From exile, Karl-I-Bond claimed that his Brussels-based Congolese Front for the Restoration of Democracy "include[d] all forces for change," but it lacked unity. The Front had at its core two divergent groups: the middle-of-the-road Union for Democracy and the radical Marxist People's Revolutionary Party. The Front also needed the full support of the Committee for the Liberation of Congo-Kinshasa and the National Congolese Movement, led by François Lumumba, son of the mercurial Patrice Lumumba.

Foreign Affairs. Mobutu's newly forged diplomatic and military links with Israel brought his government criticism from Moscow, which claimed the existence of an Israel-South Africa-Zaire military axis. Reliance on Israeli military support became important after Belgian socialists advocated a reassessment of Brussel's military training assistance and economic support for Zaire and of Belgian dependence on Zaire's raw materials. At the same time, they pushed for Kinshasa to implement "democratic reforms." Mobutu reacted by announcing a halt in Belgium's exclusive refining of Shaba copper.

Amnesty International criticized Zaire for holding without trial hundreds of political detainees and subjecting them to torture and starvation. But the report in March noted fewer killings by police and troops in the last two years. Mobutu visited Washington in August to discuss Zaire's troubled economy and the conflict in Chad. He earlier had sent military aid for Hissène Habré's beleaguered government.

THOMAS H. HENRIKSEN, *Hoover Institution*

ZIMBABWE

Zimbabwe, which became independent in 1980, continued to face problems of ethnic reconciliation and national development in 1983.

On February 19, Joshua Nkomo, the leader of the Zimbabwe African People's Union (ZAPU), tried to leave Zimbabwe to attend a conference in Czechoslovakia, but he was stopped at Harare airport and his passport was confiscated. Early in March, Nkomo fled into exile, first to Botswana and later to Britain. Robert Mugabe and Joshua Nkomo had formed an uneasy alliance immediately before independence in 1980. In 1982, Prime Minister Mugabe dropped Nkomo from the cabinet after the discovery of extensive hidden arms caches in different parts of the country, and on Saturday, March 5, 1983, Fifth Brigade soldiers raided Nkomo's house in Bulawayo. Nkomo was not at home at the time, but his driver was killed.

Unrest in Matabeleland. In January, the Zimbabwean government used the army's North Korean-trained and predominantly Shona Fifth Brigade against what it termed "dissidents" in the country's western province of Matabeleland. This area is the stronghold of Joshua Nkomo and the home of the Ndebele tribe, who constitute approximately 20% of the population. The campaign of the 5,000-strong Fifth Brigade was aimed primarily against former Zimbabwe People's Republic Army (ZIPRA) guerrillas who had deserted from the integrated national army. For about a year,

Joshua Nkomo, leader of the opposition Zimbabwe African People's Union arrived in London on March 13 for a period of voluntary exile. He returned home in August.

Keith Butler/Spooner/Gamma Liaison

these former guerrillas had been involved in sporadic activities in Matabeleland, including attacks on white farmers and the 1982 abduction of six foreign tourists. In response, the Fifth Brigade is alleged to have killed between 2,000 and 3,000 civilians. The Zimbabwean government claimed the total was exaggerated, but church leaders and relief agencies maintained that it was accurate and called for an independent investigation. Shona-Ndebele conflict goes back to the 19th century and continued through the liberation period, despite efforts to reconcile the Zimbabwe African National Union (ZANU) of Mugabe and the Zimbabwe African People's Union (ZAPU) of Nkomo. By August 1983, when Joshua Nkomo returned to Zimbabwe from exile, the situation in Matabeleland was calmer and the Fifth Brigade had been withdrawn. The government was also more conciliatory in its approach to Nkomo and withdrew its motion to expel him from the Zimbabwean Parliament.

By late 1983, Nkomo faced the important task of attempting to rally his badly divided party and to develop an approach to the one-party state proposed by Mugabe and the ruling ZANU establishment. While Nkomo remained an important symbol for the Ndebele, he faced serious problems. Several senior members of ZAPU and four cabinet ministers continued to work closely with Mugabe within the ZAPU-ZANU coalition, but at the same time, military deserters and younger militant Ndebele, apparently without Nkomo's approval, were operating underground in Matabeleland. Furthermore, because of continuing harassment, the ZAPU party organization was in disarray. There was an ongoing fear that the party might be banned, and several of the party's branch offices in Matabeleland were ordered shut at the time of the unrest.

Bishop Muzorewa. On Monday, October 31, Abel Muzorewa, a bishop of the United Methodist Church who had been prime minister of the 1979 transitional government of Rhodesia-Zimbabwe, was arrested. He was accused of collaborating with South African authorities against Zimbabwe and of criticizing the Zimbabwe government while on a trip to Israel. South Africa had given substantial backing to the Bishop's United African National Council (UANC) in the election immediately before independence that Mugabe's ZANU sweepingly won, and in which UANC only won three seats. In addition, when arrested, the bishop was said to have 5,000 members of his party undergoing military training in South Africa. The underlying cause for the bishop's arrest appeared to be part of an effort by the government to neutralize opposition groups, especially with the prospect of the establishment of a one-party state. It also must be seen as an attempt to contain criticism of the government by opposition leaders.

Trial of the Air Force Officers. On August 31, six white Zimbabwean air force officers were found not guilty in the High Court. They were accused of helping South Africans blow up 13 air force jet airplanes, about a quarter of the country's air force, at the Thornhill air base near Gweru in July 1982. Immediately after the verdict had been delivered by Judge Enoch Dumbutshena, the men were discharged, but they were then issued with a detention order signed by Home Affairs Minister Herbert Ushewokunze. The Zimbabwean government had based its case on signed confessions by the accused, in which they had admitted their involvement. Judge Dumbutshena, however, ruled that the confessions were inadmissible as evidence because they were obtained under electric-shock torture. Diplomats from the United States and Britain lodged protests at the redetention of the officers and began concerted efforts to free them. On September 7, Robert Mugabe left Zimbabwe on an official visit to Europe and the United States without resolving the question of the release of the airmen. Later in the month, three of the officers—Air Vice Marshall Hugh Slatter, Air Commodore Philip Pile, and Wing Commander Peter Briscoe—were released, but the three others remained under detention. There had been four previous incidents in which accused had been acquitted of charges and then immediately redetained. These included six supporters of Joshua Nkomo who were redetained on April 27, after being acquitted of treason charges.

The Press. On July 31, the southern African nations of Angola, Botswana, Mozambique, Tanzania, Zambia, and Zimbabwe signed a declaration in Kadoma, Zimbabwe, to exclude entry to foreign correspondents based in South Africa. While the other five signatories of the Kadoma declaration interpreted the agreement very loosely, the Zimbabwean government stringently enforced it. In addition, five days after the declaration was signed, the government made it a criminal offense for journalists to publish "any act of terrorism or sabotage or any action by security forces to combat terrorism in any area designated by the government." Ironically, the Zimbabwean government based this decree on the emergency powers act that was used by the white Rhodesian government of Ian Smith.

The Budget and the Economy. The budget presented to Parliament on July 28 by Bernard Chidzero, the minister of finance, economic planning and development, indicated that in 1983 there were problems with foreign-exchange shortages, inflation, drought, limited demands for local products, as well as weak commodity prices because of world market problems. It was estimated that Zimbabwe would have a 3% negative growth rate for 1983. Previous Zimbabwean budgets had been ones of expansion. The 1983 budget included cuts in spending as well as tax increases. A controversial item in the budget made more than 500,000 eligible for tax payments, by the imposition of a 2% tax on all worker earnings above $98 a month. Defense spending was increased by 11% compared with 1982–83 and now represents about 19% of the total budget. Education was given a 4.4% increase, but most other programs were cut. At independence there were 600,000 African students in primary and secondary schools, and there now are more than 3 million. The budget for the Housing Ministry was cut by 67%, and land resettlement and rural development was cut to $31.3 million, half

---

ZIMBABWE · Information Highlights

Official Name: Zimbabwe.
Location: Southern Africa.
Area: 151,000 sq mi (391 090 km²).
Population (July 1983 est.): 8,376,000.
Chief Cities (provisional census, Aug. 1983): Harare (formerly Salisbury), the capital, 656,000; Bulawayo, 413,800.
Government: *Head of state,* Canaan Banana, president (took office April 1980). *Head of government,* Robert Mugabe, prime minister (took office March 1980). *Legislature*—Parliament: Senate and House of Assembly.
Monetary Unit: Zimbabwe dollar (1.016 Z. dollar equals U.S.$1, July 1983).
Gross Domestic Product (1981–82 U.S.$): $6,238,-000,000.
Economic Indexes (1982): *Consumer Prices* (1970 = 100), all items, 258.5; food, 244.7. *Industrial Production* (1975 = 100), 109.
Foreign Trade (1982 U.S.$): *Imports,* $1,430,000,000; *exports,* $1,250,000,000.

---

of the 1982–83 estimate. By late 1983, Zimbabwe's public debt was close to $980 million, and the government had to allocate $490 million to cover interest and loan payments.

The government did double funds available for its export incentive scheme and also continued support for industries, especially mining, in search of commercial loans.

There was a 5% increase on the surcharge on company tax, bringing it to 20%. Sales and import taxes were increased to 19% from 16% on general goods and from 19% to 23% on luxury items. Cutbacks on social programs, tax increases, and the new tax program for low income groups were an indication of the seriousness of its economic predicament.

Since independence there has only been one major foreign investment, by the food-processing firm H.J. Heinz and Co., but this venture has not opened the way for expansion of foreign investment. The 5,000 white commercial farmers remain critical to the agricultural sector, and their tobacco crops earn more than half of Zimbabwe's foreign exchange.

A 1983 report by the Chamber of Mines estimated that since independence, labor costs have increased by 64%. In 1983, food prices increased substantially; maize, which is the staple food for Africans, increased by 43%, and meat and milk prices increased by 50%. Inflation was estimated at between 17–20%. This serious economic situation will further deteriorate if the United States cuts its $65 million aid appropriation by as much as 50%, because of Zimbabwe's abstention on the United Nations vote deploring the Soviet Union's shooting down of a South Korean airliner in September, and because of its cosponsorship of the Nicaraguan motion in the UN that condemned the United States for invading Grenada.

Since 1981, Zimbabwe has suffered through a major drought, which has had a severe effect on its food production and its economy.

PATRICK O'MEARA, *Indiana University*

ZOOS AND ZOOLOGY

Zoos and aquariums in the United States were singled out for special attention in 1983, when President Ronald Reagan proclaimed June as "Zoo and Aquarium Month." It was the second time that the nation's zoos and aquariums have been honored by the president for their contributions to education, research, recreation, and conservation. The presidential proclamation cited the role of zoos and aquariums in preserving threatened species and in providing education and enjoyment for the more than 125 million people who visit them annually. More people in the United States visit zoos and aquariums than go to all professional football and baseball games combined.

Reintroduction. A major wildlife conservation landmark occurred July 15, when three female Arabian oryx, straight-horned antelopes, were shipped from the San Diego Wild Animal Park to their native homeland in the desert sultanate of Oman. They joined nine other oryx—six males and three females—which also had been zoo-bred and reintroduced in the Arabian Desert. The species had been hunted to extinction in its native habitat but was saved by captive breeding at the San Diego Park, the Phoenix Zoo, and the Los Angeles Zoo. In Oman the oryx inhabit a vast plateau called the Jiddat Al Harasis and are protected from poachers by the Harasis tribe. The reintroduction program is under the supervision of the nation's conservation and environmental agency.

Breeding. One of the most successful programs for the breeding of rare species in captivity has been the elephant propagation effort by The Washington Park Zoo in Portland, OR. On April 1, 1983, the zoo announced the birth of a male Asian elephant, named Rama; it was the 23rd of the species to be born there. The mother of the calf arrived at the zoo from Thailand in 1953. Rama was her sixth infant, a record number for an Asian elephant in captivity.

Former home of the extinct dodo, the island of Mauritius is also the native land of the exceedingly rare pink pigeon. Until 1983 the only zoos to have bred pink pigeons were the Rio Grande Zoological Park in Albuquerque, NM, and the Jersey Wildlife Preservation Trust in the Channel Islands. In January 1983, however, and again in July, a pink pigeon hatched at the Bronx Zoo in New York City. Captured on Mauritius in 1982, the parents of the chicks were brought back to the Bronx Zoo for a propagation program. It is hoped that birds obtained through this program eventually can be released on their native island, where possibly fewer than a dozen pink pigeon survive.

Rescues. Besides captive breeding of rare animals, zoos and aquariums carried on myriad other conservation programs during the year. The Mystic Marinelife Aquarium in Mystic,

UPI
Two condor chicks, the first ever born in captivity, were hatched at the San Diego Zoo in a government breeding program to save the endangered species.

CT, put its stranded cetacean rescue team in the field during March to save a 10,000-lb (4 536-kg), 30-ft (9-m) humpback whale entangled in lobster trap lines off Narragansett, RI. Members of the team donned wet suits and SCUBA, plunged into the chill ocean, dodged the whale's flailing flippers and flukes, and cut the creature loose. The rescue unit is one of several operated by aquariums around the United States in cooperation with the National Marine Fisheries Service.

Education. The New England Aquarium in Boston, together with the World Wildlife Fund, sponsored an April symposium on whales and seabirds. It featured internationally known experts on marine life and was open to the public. The focus of the panel was on how the world's consumers can use marine resources and at the same time preserve the marine ecosystem.

A major environmental education program was launched in 1983 by the Bronx Zoo, Philadelphia Zoo, Riverside Zoo in Columbia, SC, and Topeka (KS) Zoo. Aimed at sixth- and seventh-grade students and conceived by the New York Zoological Society, Project WISE (Wildlife Inquiry through Zoo Education) provides such classroom resource materials as animal teeth, bones, and other objects, along with reading and visual material on wildlife ecology and conservation. Funded by the National Science Foundation, the program combines classroom lessons with zoo visits for some 2,000 students.

Exhibits. The primary attractions of zoos and aquariums are, of course, their exhibits of wildlife. One of the most ambitious exhibits

A new exhibit at Sea World in San Diego houses 400 penguins, of six species, in simulated Antarctic conditions.

built by any zoo or aquarium in many years was opened Memorial Day weekend at Sea World in San Diego. Costing $7.5 million, the exhibit houses 400 penguins of six different species. It is contained in a 5,000-sq-ft (454–m²) building on the aquarium grounds. The penguins live in a glass-front enclosure, with the temperature behind the glass at 24° to 27°F (−4.4° to −2.8°C) to simulate conditions on the edges of Antarctica. Between 10,000 and 12,000 lbs (4 536 and 5 443 kg) of real ice is used every day. Visitors move past the front of the exhibit on a traveling sidewalk. The structure also has an upper level from which the birds can be viewed. It is also equipped with 16 television monitors showing scenes related to penguins, their behavior, and their environment. Among the televised presentations for the public are the hatching of a penguin and the exploration of Antarctica.

Formally opened in late 1982, the Joseph Regenstein Large Mammal Habitat at Chicago's Lincoln Park Zoo began full operation in spring 1983. Landscaping was completed on the $11.5 million, four-acre (1.6-ha) complex, and several groups of new animals were introduced. Among them are Baringo giraffes, timber wolves, a young elephant, and a pair of rare maned wolves from South America.

Zoological Research. A scientist from Burma, I Toke Gale, discovered in 1983 that working Asian elephants live longer if they are allowed some leisure time. According to the World Wildlife Fund, the research demonstrated that the lifespan of the elephants, normally about 150 years, drops to 70 when the animals are in captivity. Working less, said the Burmese zoologist, improves the elephants' longevity, especially if the workday does not exceed eight hours.

A major program aimed at studying the sea turtle and cetacean populations in the North Atlantic ended in February 1983. The $4 million program, headed by Professor Howard Winn of the University of Rhode Island Graduate School of Oceanography and financed by the federal Bureau of Land Management, involved five years of observations on the distribution and abundance of whales, dolphins, and turtles off the northeastern coast of the United States. The scientists logged more than 11,000 cetacean and 2,800 turtle sightings. Twenty-six species of cetaceans were seen. The results of the study, when analyzed, will help in planning offshore oil and gas development so that it will not be harmful to the marine creatures.

EDWARD R. RICCIUTI
Free-lance Environment and Wildlife Writer

Statistical and Tabular Data

Subject		Page(s)
Table of Contents		
Nations of the World	A Profile and a Synopsis	571–76
	Population	577
	Agricultural Production	578
	Industrial Production	579
	World Mineral and Metal Production	580–81
United States	Major Legislation Enacted During First Session of 98th Congress	582
	The Government	583
	Congress	584–85
Societies and Organizations		586–88
Contributors		589–92

NATIONS OF THE WORLD

A Profile and Synopsis of Major 1983 Developments

Nation, Region	Population in millions	Capital	Area Sq mi (km²)	Head of State/Government
Angola, S.W. Africa	7.6	Luanda	481,000 (1 245 790)	José Eduardo dos Santos, president

Angola and China agreed to establish diplomatic relations in January. Angola was represented at a Lesotho meeting that condemned South Africa's economic domination of the area. Interior Minister Manuel Alexandre Rodrigues discussed Namibia with U.S. leaders in Washington in April. Alexandre do Nascimento of Lubango, Angola, was appointed a cardinal of the Roman Catholic Church. (See also AFRICA.) Gross Domestic Product (GDP) Per Capita (1981 U.S.$): $790.

Nation, Region	Population in millions	Capital	Area Sq mi (km²)	Head of State/Government
Antigua and Barbuda, Caribbean	0.08	St. John's	170 (440)	Sir Wilfred E. Jacobs, governor-general; Vere C. Bird, prime minister

Antigua participated in a multinational effort "to restore order and democracy" in Grenada. GDP (1981 U.S.$): $124.5 million.

Nation, Region	Population in millions	Capital	Area Sq mi (km²)	Head of State/Government
Bahamas, Caribbean	0.2	Nassau	5,382 (13 939)	Sir Gerald C. Cash, governor-general; Lynden O. Pindling, prime minister

In September, Bahamian politicians were angered by charges made by a U.S. news program that U.S. fugitive financier Robert Vesco operated a drug ring in the Bahamas. In a letter to President Ronald Reagan, Prime Minister Pindling noted that Vesco had been deported from the Bahamas in 1981. Gross National Product (GNP, 1981 U.S.$): $1.4 billion. Foreign Trade (1981; nonoil): Imports, $783 million; exports, $176 million.

Nation, Region	Population in millions	Capital	Area Sq mi (km²)	Head of State/Government
Bahrain, W. Asia	0.4	Manama	258 (668)	Isa ibn Salman, emir

A huge oil spill, caused by Iraqi air attacks on an Iranian offshore oil rig, reached Bahrain's coast in late May. The oil, flowing at an estimated 10,000 barrels a day, threatened to permanently damage the aquatic life of the Persian Gulf. GDP (1982 U.S.$): $4 billion. Foreign Trade (1982): Imports, $3.7 billion; exports, $3.8 billion.

Barbados, Caribbean	0.25	Bridgetown	166 (430)	Sir Deighton Ward, governor-general John M. G. Adams, prime minister

Barbados was admitted to the movement of nonaligned nations on March 7. Barbadian troops were part of the force that invaded Grenada in late October. GDP (1981 U.S.$): $909 million. Foreign Trade (1982): Imports, $550 million; exports, $257 million.

Benin, W. Africa	3.75	Porto Novo	43,484 (112 624)	Mathieu Kerekou, president

In January, Benin opened its borders to hundreds of thousands of Ghanaians expelled from neighboring Nigeria. The Ghanaians, who had been residing illegally in Nigeria, had to pass through Benin and Togo to return to Ghana. GNP (1981 U.S.$): $1.2 billion. Foreign Trade (1981): Imports, $662.4 million; exports, $368.4 million.

Bhutan, S. Asia	1.4	Thimphu	18,000 (46 620)	Jigme Singye Wangchuk, king

GNP (1982 fiscal year U.S.$): $131 million. Foreign Trade (1982 fiscal): Imports, $50.8 million; exports, $20.9 million.

Botswana, S. Africa	1.0	Gaborone	224,711 (582 000)	Quett Masire, president

In January representatives from Botswana and eight other southern African nations met in Lesotho to discuss ways of reducing their economic dependence on South Africa. Botswanan Finance Minister Peter Mmusi condemned South Africa for acts of economic destabilization against its neighbors in southern Africa. GNP (fiscal year 1980–81 U.S.$): $949 million. Foreign Trade (1981): Imports, $798.6 million; exports, $399.7 million.

Brunei, S.E. Asia	.2	Bandar Seri Begawan	2,230 (5 766)	Sir Muda Hassanal Bolkiah, sultan and prime minister

Brunei, a tiny Islamic sultanate on Borneo's northern coast, gained complete independence from Great Britain as 1984 began. Oil and natural gas resources make the new nation one of the world's wealthiest. The estimated per capita income is $20,000.

Burundi, E. Africa	4.56	Bujumbura	10,747 (27 835)	Jean-Baptiste Bagaza, president

Michel Micombero, president of Burundi (1966–76), died in Somalia on July 16. GDP (1981 U.S.$): $1.1 billion. Foreign Trade: Imports (1982), $214 million; exports (1981), $88 million.

Cameroon, Cen. Africa	9.2	Yaoundé	183,569 (475 444)	Paul Biya, president Luc Ayang, interim prime minister

In legislative elections on May 29, Cameroonians elected 120 representatives to the National Assembly. The only candidates permitted to run were those from the Union nationale camerounaise (UNC), the country's sole political party. In August, President Biya announced that a plot against the state had been foiled. He also announced the dismissal of Prime Minister Bella Bouba and the appointment of Luc Ayang as interim prime minister. GDP (1981 U.S.$): $7 billion. Foreign Trade (1982): Imports, $1.2 billion; exports, $1 billion.

Cape Verde, W. Africa	0.3	Praia	1,557 (4 033)	Aristides Maria Pereira, president Pedro Pires, prime minister

GDP (1981 U.S.$): $100 million. Foreign Trade (1980): Imports, $68 million; exports, $4 million.

Central African Republic, Cen. Africa	2.5	Bangui	240,535 (622 986)	André Kolingba, president of the military committee

In August, Gen. André Kolingba announced a reorganization of the ruling Military Committee for National Recovery. On April 22, two leaders of the banned Oubanguien Patriotic Front-Party of Labor were sentenced to five years in jail and ten years' loss of civil rights. The two had been arrested in August 1982 and charged with subversive revolutionary activities. GDP (1981 U.S.$): $565 million. Foreign Trade (1980): Imports, $180 million; exports, $140 million.

Comoros, E. Africa	0.4	Moroni	838 (2 170)	Ahmed Abdallah, president Ali Mroudjae, prime minister

On July 25 the Australian government announced its intention to prosecute six men on charges of plotting to overthrow the government of Comoros. The alleged mercenaries were accused of planning to sail from Australia to Reunion Island to pick up weapons and troops, and thence to Grande Comore to initiate a coup. GNP (1981 U.S.$): $90 million. Foreign Trade (1981): Imports, $33 million; exports, $17 million.

Congo, Cen. Africa	1.7	Brazzaville	132,047 (342 000)	Denis Sassou-Nguesso, president Louis-Sylvain Goma, prime minister

Chinese Premier Zhao Ziyang visited the Congo in January, meeting with President Sassou-Nguesso in Brazzaville. GDP (1981 U.S.$): $1.6 billion. Foreign Trade (1981): Imports, $650 million; exports, $995 million.

Djibouti, E. Africa	0.3	Djibouti	8,494 (22 000)	Hassan Gouled Aptidon, president Barkat Gourad Hamadou, prime minister

In February, Ethiopia and Djibouti reached an agreement for the voluntary repatriation of some 3,000 Ethiopian refugees living in Djibouti. The resolution was initiated by the office of the UN High Commissioner for Refugees. GNP (1981 U.S.$): $357 million. Foreign Trade (1981): Imports, $152 million; exports, $66 million.

Dominica, Caribbean	0.07	Roseau	289 (749)	Aurelius Marie, president Mary Eugenia Charles, prime minister

Dominica fully supported U.S. actions against the Marxist government in Grenada. Prime Minister Mary Eugenia Charles, chairman of the Organization of Eastern Caribbean States (OECS), was present at the White House when President Ronald Reagan announced that military forces were being sent to Grenada. GNP (1981 U.S.$): $65 million. Foreign Trade (1981): Imports, $50.7 million; exports, $18.9 million.

Nation, Region	Population in millions	Capital	Area Sq mi (km²)	Head of State/Government
Dominican Republic, Caribbean	6.2	Santo Domingo	18,818 (48 739)	Salvador Jorge Blanco, *president*

In January the Dominican Republic agreed to impose austerity measures in order to qualify for a $455 million loan package from the International Monetary Fund. (See also CARIBBEAN.) GNP (1981 U.S.$): $7.6 billion. Foreign Trade (1982): Imports, $1.25 billion; exports, $768 million.

Equatorial Guinea, Cen. Africa	0.27	Malabo	10,831 (28 052)	Teodoro Obiang Mbasogo, *president* Cristino Seriche Bioko, *prime minister*

The government reported on May 24 that it had arrested 80 members of the military for involvement in a coup attempt against President Mbasogo. On August 28, the country held its first parliamentary elections in more than ten years, electing 41 members of a new National Assembly. The Assembly was created in accordance with the 1982 constitution, but all candidates were selected by President Mbasogo. GNP (1981 U.S.$): $140 million. Foreign Trade (1980): Imports, $37.1 million; exports, $13.3 million.

Fiji, Oceania	0.67	Suva	7,055 (18 272)	Ratu Sir Penaia Ganilau, *governor-general* Ratu Sir Kamisese Mara, *prime minister*

In February, Deputy Prime Minister Ratu Sir Penaia Ganilau left the Cabinet to become governor-general. On March 15, a commission of inquiry began to conduct investigations of alleged irregularities in the 1982 election campaign. GDP (1980 U.S.$): $1.2 billion. Foreign Trade (1982): Imports, $515 million; exports, $285 million.

Gabon, Cen. Africa	0.9	Libreville	103,346 (267 666)	Omar Bongo, *president* Léon Mébiame, *prime minister*

Chinese Premier Zhao Ziyang visited Gabon in January as part of a ten-nation tour of Africa. French President François Mitterrand also visited Gabon in January, taking part in the inauguration ceremony for the trans-Gabon railway. GDP (1981 U.S.$): $3.3 billion. Foreign Trade (1981): Imports, $1 billion; exports, $2.3 billion.

Gambia, W. Africa	0.6	Banjul	4,361 (11 295)	Sir Dawda K. Jawara, *president*

A state of emergency was extended for 1983. Fifty-one persons held without trial since an attempted coup in July 1981 were released in August. A new weekly newspaper, The Senegambia Sun, was introduced. GNP (1981 U.S.$): $100 million. Foreign Trade (1982): Imports, $97 million; exports, $44 million.

Guinea, W. Africa	5.4	Conakry	94,926 (245 858)	Ahmed Sékou Touré, *president* Louis Lansana Beavogui, *prime minister*

President Touré attended the tenth French-American summit on October 3–4 in Vittel, France. The conference focused on finding ways to settle the civil war in Chad. GNP (1981 U.S.$): $1.1 billion. Foreign Trade (1981): Imports, $375 million; exports, $385 million.

Guinea-Bissau, W. Africa	0.8	Bissau	13,948 (36 125)	Joao Bernardo Vieira, *president of the Council of the Revolution* Victor Saude Maria, *prime minister*

The Council of the Revolution established a commission for the revision of the constitution and the electoral law. M. Fidelis Cabral Almada succeeded M. Samba Lemine Mane as foreign minister. A further reshuffling of the government occurred in August. GDP (1981 U.S.$): $235 million. Foreign Trade (1982): Imports, $50 million; exports, $12 million.

Haiti, Caribbean	5.66	Port-au-Prince	10,714 (27 750)	Jean-Claude Duvalier, *president*

Haiti held its first free municipal elections in more than 25 years in April and May. French and U.S. observers affirmed that the voting was conducted properly, but the government invalidated the results in two towns. (See also CARIBBEAN.) GNP (1981 U.S.$): $1.9 billion. Foreign Trade (1981): Imports, $358 million; exports, $151 million.

Ivory Coast, W. Africa	8.9	Abidjan	124,503 (322 463)	Felix Houphouet-Boigny, *president*

President Houphouet-Boigny visited the United States in June in an attempt to attract American investment. Contacts with Ghana were reestablished in December, when Ghanaian leader Jerry Rawlings visited Ivory Coast. Also in December, President Houphouet-Boigny expelled Bokassa I, former leader of the Central African Republic, who had been exiled in Ivory Coast since his government was overthrown in 1979. GDP (1981 U.S.$): $9 billion. Foreign Trade (1982): Imports, $2.2 billion; exports, $2.3 billion.

Jamaica, Caribbean	2.3	Kingston	4,410 (11 422)	Florizel Glasspole, *governor-general* Edward Seaga, *prime minister*

As a member of OECS, Jamaica sent forces into Grenada in October. Prime Minister Seaga announced that the Jamaican dollar would be devalued as part of an agreement for a new IMF loan. Seaga's Jamaica Labor Party won the six seats contested in December elections. The left-wing opposition, the People's National Party, boycotted the voting. Queen Elizabeth II visited the island in February.

Kiribati, Oceania	0.06	Tarawa	331 (857)	Reginald Wallace, *governor-general* Ieremia Tabai, *president*

In March, Kiribati purchased all the land on the islands of Teraina and Tabuaeran in the Northern Line Group from an Australian firm that had operated copra plantations on the islands. GDP (1979 U.S.$): $36 million. Foreign Trade (1979): Imports, $15 million; exports, $20 million.

Kuwait, W. Asia	1.65	Kuwait	6,880 (17 819)	Jabir al-Ahmad al-Sabah, *emir* Saad al-Abdullah al-Sabah, *prime minister*

In August the national assembly approved a government plan to compensate investors for losses incurred when Kuwait's unofficial stock market collapsed in September 1982. The reimbursements were expected to cut potential bankruptcies from 1,700 to 500. GDP (1981–82 U.S.$): $20.2 billion. Foreign Trade (1981): Imports, $6.9 billion; exports, $16.3 billion.

Nation, Region	Population in millions	Capital	Area Sq mi (km²)	Head of State/Government
Lesotho, S. Africa	1.4	Maseru	11,720 (30 355)	Moshoeshoe II, *king* Leabua Jonathan, *prime minister*

In April, Prime Minister Leabua Jonathan announced to the national assembly that Lesotho was in a virtual state of war with South Africa. He accused South Africa of armed attacks and economic sabotage against Lesotho. South Africa denied the accusation. On April 30, the two countries discussed the revival of a 20-year joint water project. GNP (1979–80 U.S.$): $473.6 million. Foreign Trade (1981): Imports, $532.6 million; exports, $51.1 million.

Liberia, W. Africa	2.1	Monrovia	43,000 (111 370)	Samuel K. Doe, *chairman, People's Redemption Council*

In August, Liberia resumed diplomatic relations with Israel. On a visit to Israel, August 22–26, President Doe signed an agreement with Israeli Prime Minister Menaham Begin providing for Israeli aid to Liberia. On August 24, Doe accused Libya of conducting widespread subversive activity in Africa, including support of a failed 1981 coup attempt in Liberia. GDP (1981 U.S.$): $1.13 billion. Foreign Trade (1981): Imports, $450 million; exports, $485 million.

Liechtenstein, Cen. Europe	0.03	Vaduz	62 (161)	Franz Joseph II, *prince* Hans Brunhart, *prime minister*
Luxembourg, W. Europe	0.37	Luxembourg	998 (2 586)	Jean, *grand duke* Pierre Werner, *prime minister*

In March the Luxembourg franc was valued upward by 1.5% in economic realignments made by the European Monetary System. GDP (1982 U.S.$): $3.4 billion. Foreign Trade (1982, Belgium-Luxembourg Economic Union): Imports, $58 billion; exports, $52.4 billion.

Madagascar, E. Africa	9.4	Antananarivo	226,657 (587 039)	Didier Ratsiraka, *president* Desire Rakotoarijaona, *prime minister*

President Ratsiraka's Avant-garde of the Malagasy Revolution (Arema) remained the nation's strongest political party following a series of 1983 elections. The government ministry was reshuffled in July due to an economic crisis. GDP (1981 U.S.$): $2.7 billion. Foreign Trade (1981): Imports, $486 million; exports, $305 million.

Malawi, E. Africa	6.6	Lilongwe	45,747 (118 485)	Hastings Kamuzu Banda, *president*

The deaths of four prominent Malawian political leaders were reported on May 22. Malawian exiles in Zambia charged that the four had been murdered on the orders of President Banda after a failed coup attempt. Two of the slain men had planned to run in a June 29–30 election called by Banda. The elections, the nation's second since independence in 1964, resulted in an enlarged parliament of 101 members. All candidates belonged to Malawi's sole legal political party, the Congress Party. GDP (1981 U.S.$): $1 billion. Foreign Trade (1982): Imports, $314 million; exports, $259 million.

Maldives, S. Asia	0.17	Malé	115 (298)	Maumoon Abdul Gayoom, *president and prime minister*

GNP (1981 U.S.$): $67 million. Foreign Trade (1981): Imports, $41.4 million; exports, $10.3 million.

Mali, W. Africa	7.4	Bamako	478,776 (1 204 021)	Moussa Traore, *president*

Mali was part of a seven-nation committee of the Organization of African Unity (OAU) members assigned to implement an OAU resolution designed to end the conflict in the Western Sahara. The resolution called for direct negotiations between Morocco and the Polisario preparatory to a cease-fire. GDP (1981 U.S.$): $1 billion. Foreign Trade (1981): Imports, $269 million; exports, $154.2 million.

Malta, S. Europe	0.36	Valletta	122 (316)	Agatha Barbara, *president* Dominic Mintoff, *prime minister*

In January, Prime Minister Mintoff banned contacts between foreign embassies and members of the opposition Nationalist Party. The ban was the latest in a series of moves that appeared designed to eliminate Mintoff's political opposition. GNP (1982 U.S.$): $1.2 billion. Foreign Trade (1982): Imports, $790 million; exports, $421 million.

Mauritania, W. Africa	1.6	Nouakchott	397,950 (1 030 691)	Mohammed Khouna Ould Haidala, *president* Maaouya Ould Sidi Taya, *prime minister*

Mauritania was among the first nations to assign an ambassador to Cambodia's government in exile, on April 30. GNP (1982 est. U.S.$): $800 million. Foreign Trade (1982): Imports, $273 million; exports, $179 million.

Mauritius, W. Africa	1.0	Port Louis	790 (2 046)	Sir Dayendranath Burrenchobay, *governor-general* Aneerood Jugnauth, *prime minister*

In elections held on August 21, a three-party coalition headed by Prime Minister Aneerood Jugnauth won 41 of 62 seats in parliament. The primary goal of the new government was to fulfill terms of loans from the IMF and the World Bank. GNP (1980 U.S.$): $890 million. Foreign Trade (1982): Imports, $463 million; exports, $362 million.

Monaco, S. Europe	0.03	Monaco-Ville	0.7 (1.81)	Rainier III, *prince*

Princess Caroline, daughter of Prince Rainier and the late Princess Grace, married Stefano Casiraghi, the son of an Italian industrialist, on December 29. Her earlier marriage to Philippe Junot ended in divorce.

Mongolia, E. Asia	1.8	Ulan Bator	604,251 (1 565 000)	Yumjaagiyn Tsedenbal, *president* Jambyn Batmonh, *prime minister*

According to reports in May, Mongolia began to expel thousands of Chinese nationals who had lived in Ulan Bator for years. The action by Mongolia, which has close ties with the Soviet Union, was believed to be a reflection of strained USSR-China relations.

Mozambique, E. Africa	13.0	Maputo	302,330 (783 035)	Samora Machel, *president*

On January 12, Mozambique, suffering the effects of a severe drought, appealed to the international community for aid. On May 23, South African fighter planes attacked a suburb of Maputo in retaliation for a May 20 car-bomb attack on South African air force headquarters by the African National Congress (ANC). South Africa claimed to have bombed ANC guerrilla camps in the reprisal raid, but Mozambique reported that private homes and civilians were the subjects of the attack. GNP (1981 U.S.$): $2.9 billion.

Nauru, Oceania	0.008	Nauru	8 (21)	Hammer DeRoburt, *president*

GNP (1981 U.S.$): $155 million. Foreign Trade (1979): Imports, $11 million; exports, $75 million.

Nation, Region	Population in millions	Capital	Area Sq mi (km²)	Head of State/Government
Nepal, S. Asia	16.2	Katmandu	54,600 (141 400)	Birendra Bir Bikram, *king* Lokendra B. Chand, *prime minister*

King Birendra and Queen Aishwarya visited the United States in December to discuss Nepal's economic development. With much of its land already developed, the nation planned to harness its enormous potential hydroelectric power. Lokendra B. Chand replaced Surya Bahadur Thapa as prime minister on July 12, after Thapa received a no-confidence vote in the national assembly. GDP (fiscal year 1981–82 U.S.$): $2.5 billion. Foreign Trade (1981–82 est.): Imports, $379.5 million; exports, $123.9 million.

Niger, W. Africa	6.1	Niamey	489,191 (1 267 005)	Seyni Kountché, *president* Oumarou Mamane, *prime minister*

On October 6, Niger's army prevented a coup attempted by three military aides while President Kountché was away at a summit meeting in France. Libyan leader Muammar el-Qaddafi was suspected by some of involvement in the attempted overthrow. GDP (1981 U.S.$): $2.1 billion. Foreign Trade (1980): Imports, $801 million; exports, $558 million.

Oman, W. Asia	1.0	Muscat	89,029 (230 585)	Qabus ibn Said, *sultan*

Joint U.S.-Oman military maneuvers took place in Oman during August. GNP (1981 U.S.$): $6.2 billion. Foreign Trade (1981): Imports, $2.7 billion; exports, $4.7 billion.

Papua New Guinea, Oceania	3.3	Port Moresby	178,704 (462 843)	Sir Tore Lokoloko, *governor-general* Michael Somare, *prime minister*

Australian Prime Minister Robert Hawke visited Papua New Guinea in June. After his election in March, Hawke had promised to increase Australia's aid to Papua New Guinea by an additional A$10 million. GDP (1981 U.S.$): $2.5 billion. Foreign Trade (1982): Imports, $1 billion; exports, $753 million.

Qatar, W. Asia	0.3	Doha	4,402 (11 400)	Khalifa ibn Hamad al-Thani, *emir*

Qatar's coast was damaged severely by a massive oil spill caused by Iraqi air attacks on an Iranian offshore oil rig. GDP (1981 U.S.$): $6.8 billion. Foreign Trade (1981): Imports, $1.5 billion; exports, $5.8 billion.

Rwanda, E. Africa	5.6	Kigali	10,169 (26 338)	Juvenal Habyarimana, *president*

The fourth ordinary national congress of the National Revolutionary Movement for Development ended in Kigali on June 29. Gen. Juvenal Habyarimana was unanimously reelected the party's leader. GDP (1981 U.S.$): $1.4 billion. Foreign Trade (1981): Imports, $188 million; exports, $115 million.

Saint Lucia, Caribbean	0.1	Castries	238 (616)	Sir Allen Lewis, *governor-general* John Compton, *prime minister*

Both St. Lucia and St. Vincent are members of the OECS and were part of the multinational effort in Grenada. GDP (1981 U.S.$): $131 million. Foreign Trade (1981): Imports, $138 million; exports, $40.4 million.

Saint Vincent and the Grenadines, Caribbean	0.13	Kingstown	150 (389)	Sir Sydney Gun-Munro, *governor-general* Robert Milton Cato, *prime minister*

GNP (1980 U.S.$): $59 million. Foreign Trade (1981): Imports, $58.5 million; exports, $24.4 million.

San Marino, S. Europe	0.022	San Marino	24 (62)	Co-regents appointed semiannually

In May elections, a left-wing coalition retained its majority in the Great and General Council, overcoming a challenge by the Christian Democratic Party.

São Tome and Príncipe, W. Africa	0.09	São Tome	372 (964)	Manuel Pinto da Costa, *president*

São Tome was represented at the nonaligned nations meeting in New Delhi, India, and at the OAU summit in Addis Ababa, Ethiopia. GNP Per Capita (1981 U.S.$): $382.

Senegal, W. Africa	6.3	Dakar	75,955 (196 723)	Abdou Diouf, *president* Moustapha Niasse, *interim prime minister*

In August, President Diouf met with U.S. President Ronald Reagan in Washington, DC, to discuss Libyan air attacks on Chad. The two leaders agreed to continue to pursue peace and international security in the region. President Diouf and the ruling Socialist Party were returned to power in elections held on February 27. On April 3, President Diouf announced changes in the government, including a proposal to abolish the post of prime minister. Habib Thiam was removed from the office, and Moustapha Niasse was made interim prime minister pending approval of a constitutional reform abolishing the position. GDP (1981 U.S.$): $2.3 billion. Foreign Trade (1981): Imports, $900 million; exports, $434.6 million.

Seychelles, E. Africa	0.065	Victoria	119 (308)	France-Albert René, *president*

On August 7, in the first national elections since 1982, Seychelles voters elected 23 delegates to Parliament. All candidates were members of the Marxist Seychelles People's Progressive Front, the country's only political party. GDP (1982 U.S.$): $128 million. Foreign Trade (1981): Imports, $87 million; exports, $7.2 million.

Sierra Leone, W. Africa	3.7	Freetown	27,699 (71 740)	Siaka P. Stevens, *president*

In late May the government strongly denied reports of unrest in Pujehun District. Two new newspapers were introduced. The Académie Française named former President Léopold Senghor to its ranks. GDP (1981 U.S.$): $800 million. Foreign Trade (1981): Imports, $278.3 million; exports, $152.1 million.

Solomon Islands, Oceania	0.256	Honiara	10,983 (28 446)	Baddeley Devesi, *governor-general* Solomon Mamaloni, *prime minister*

In June it was announced that Guangdong Province, China, would invest in a forestry project in the Solomon Islands. Foreign Trade (1981): Imports, $76 million; exports, $66 million.

Somalia, E. Africa	6.25	Mogadishu	246,201 (637 661)	Mohammed Siad Barre, *president*

(See AFRICA.) GDP (1981 U.S.$): $1.75 billion. Foreign Trade (1981): Imports, $260 million; exports, $146 million.

Nation, Region	Population in millions	Capital	Area Sq mi (km²)	Head of State/Government
Surinam, S. America	0.35	Paramaribo	63,067 (163 266)	Col. Desi Bouterse, *head of National Military Council* Errol Alibux, *prime minister*

The killings of 15 prominent citizens on government orders in December 1982 shocked observers in Surinam and abroad. The 15 had been accused by Colonel Bouterse of plotting a coup, and during 1983 two more alleged coup attempts resulted in further arrests by the government. In February, Bouterse installed a new 12-member cabinet and named Errol Alibux prime minister. In October, after the United States discovered Cuban arms in Grenada, Bouterse expelled the Cuban ambassador, fearing a Cuban-backed insurrection against his regime. Foreign Trade (1981 U.S.$): Imports, $568 million; exports, $474 million.

Swaziland, S. Africa	0.6	Mbabane	6,704 (17 363)	Prince Bhekimpi Dlamini, *prime minister*

In March, Prince Mabandla Dlamini was dismissed from his position as prime minister and replaced by Prince Bhekimpi Dlamini. In August, Queen Regent Dzeliwe, who had ruled since the death of King Sobhuza in 1982, was deposed by a conservative faction in the royal family. At the same time, Sobhuza's successor as king was announced to be one of his sons, Makhosetive. Makhosetive's mother, LaDwhala, was to rule as regent until her son reached adulthood. GNP Per Capita (1981 U.S.$): $844.

Togo, W. Africa	2.8	Lomé	21,622 (56 000)	Gnassingbe Eyadema, *president*

An alleged attempt to assassinate President Eyadema was reported in January. The plot was thought to have been financed by opposition groups in Togo and organized by a Canadian arms dealer. GNP (U.S.$ 1981): $900 million. Foreign Trade (1981): Imports, $323.5 million; exports, $235.2 million.

Tonga, Oceania	0.1	Nuku'alofa	289 (749)	Taufa'ahau Tupou IV, *king* Prince Fatafehi Tu'ipelehake, *prime minister*

Foreign Trade (1981 U.S.$): Imports, $40 million; exports, $7 million.

Trinidad and Tobago, Caribbean	1.2	Port-of-Spain	1,980 (5 128)	Ellis Clarke, *president* George Chambers, *prime minister*

GNP (1981 U.S.$): $6.8 billion. Foreign Trade (1982): Imports, $3.7 billion; exports, $3 billion.

Tuvalu, Oceania	0.008	Funafuti	10 (26)	Fiatau Penitala Teo, *governor-general* Tomasi Puapua, *prime minister*

United Arab Emirates, W. Asia	1.4	Abu Dhabi	32,278 (83 600)	Zaid ibn Sultan al-Nuhayan, *president* Rashid ibn Said al-Maktum, *vice-president, prime minister*

The government announced in April that it intended to trim budget expenditures by 40% and lay off 10% of government employees in response to declining oil revenues. GNP (1982 est. U.S.$): $36 billion. Foreign Trade (1981): Imports, $8.6 billion; exports, $21.8 billion.

Upper Volta, W. Africa	6.56	Ouagadougou	105,870 (274 203)	Thomas Sankara, *head of state*

In a purge of the government in May, President Jean-Baptiste Ouedraogo ousted Prime Minister Thomas Sankara. On August 5, Sankara overthrew the government and imprisoned Ouedraogo, whom he had helped put in power in a November 1982 coup. A national revolutionary council was formed to govern the nation. Libya was suspected of backing the coup, Upper Volta's third in three years. GNP (1981 U.S.$): $1.3 billion. Foreign Trade (1981): Imports, $281.3 million; exports, $126.8 million.

Vanuatu, Oceania	0.13	Port-Vila	5,700 (14 763)	Ati George Sokomanu, *president* Walter Lini, *prime minister*

Vanuatu's ruling party, led by Prime Minister Walter Lini, retained power in November elections, but with a reduced majority in Parliament. Foreign Trade (1981 U.S.$): Imports, $58 million; exports, $33 million.

Vatican City, S. Europe	0.001	Vatican City	0.17 (0.44)	John Paul II, *pope*

Western Samoa, Oceania	0.16	Apia	1,095 (2 836)	Malietoa Tanumafili II, *head of state* Taisi Tupuola Tofilau Eti, *prime minister*

The tala was devalued by 10% in February and by an additional 6% in March to reduce the level of nonessential imports. In May, Vaovasamanaia Filipo was appointed chief justice of Western Samoa; he was the first Samoan to hold the position. Foreign Trade (1981 U.S.$): Imports, $67 million; exports, $11 million.

Yemen, North, S. Asia	5.7	San'a	75,000 (194 250)	Ali Abdullah Saleh, *president* Abdel Karim al-Iryani, *prime minister*

Col. Muammar el-Qaddafi of Libya and Palestinian leader Yasir Arafat both visited North Yemen in June. Each leader met separately with President Saleh, and each vowed to improve their relations. President Saleh was unanimously reelected to another four-year term by the People's Assembly, it was reported in May. GDP (1982 U.S.$): $2.8 billion. Foreign Trade (1981): Imports, $1.7 billion; exports, $11 million.

Yemen, South, S. Asia	2.1	Aden	112,000 (290 080)	Ali Nasser Mohammed al-Hasani, *chairman, Council of Ministers*

GDP (1981 U.S.$): $1 billion.

Zambia, E. Africa	6.3	Lusaka	290,585 (752 615)	Kenneth D. Kaunda, *president* Nalumino Mundia, *prime minister*

President Kaunda visited the United States on March 31 to discuss the situation in Namibia with U.S. President Reagan. Kaunda urged the United States to persuade South Africa to remove its troops from Namibia and Angola. The same day, the United States announced that it would extend duty-free status to certain types of Zambian copper. In August the Vatican announced the resignation of the archbishop of Lusaka, Emmanuel Milingo, who had long been accused of faith healing and other practices inconsistent with the Roman Catholic faith. GNP (1981 U.S.$): $3.5 billion. Foreign Trade (1982): Imports, $831 million; exports, $1.06 billion.

POPULATION
Vital Statistics of Selected Countries

	Estimated population mid-1983 (millions)	Birthrate per 1,000 population[1]	Death rate per 1,000 population[1]	Infant mortality[2]	Life expectancy at birth	Urban population (%)
World	4,677.0	29	11	84	62	39
Afghanistan	14.2	48	23	205	40	15
Albania	2.9	27	7	47	69	34
Algeria	20.7	46	14	116	56	52
Angola	7.6	47	22	153	42	21
Argentina	29.1	24	9	41	70	82
Australia	15.3	16	7	10	73	86
Austria	7.6	13	12	12.6	72	54
Bangladesh	96.5	49	18	135	47	10
Belgium	9.9	13	11	11.7	72	95
Bolivia	5.9	43	16	130	50	42
Brazil	131.3	31	8	76	63	68
Burma	37.9	38	14	99	54	29
Cambodia	6.0	38	19	201	37	15
Cameroon	9.1	44	18	108	47	35
Canada	24.9	15	7	10.4	74	76
Cen. Afr. Republic	2.5	45	20	147	43	41
Chile	11.5	22	7	33	66	81
China	1,023.3	23	8	44	69	21
Colombia	27.7	28	8	56	63	60
Cuba	9.8	14	6	18.5	72	65
Cyprus	0.7	20	9	18	72	48
Czechoslovakia	15.4	16	12	16.8	70	67
Denmark	5.1	10	11	8	74	84
Ecuador	8.8	41	10	81	61	45
Egypt	45.9	43	12	102	56	44
El Salvador	4.7	36	10	53	64	41
Ethiopia	31.3	48	23	146	40	14
Finland	4.8	13	9	7.6	73	62
France	54.6	15	10	9.6	74	78
Germany, East	16.7	14	14	12.3	72	76
Germany, West	61.5	10	12	11.6	72	85
Ghana	13.9	48	16	102	50	36
Greece	9.9	15	9	17.9	73	65
Guatemala	7.9	42	10	65.9	59	37
Haiti	5.7	41	14	113	52	27
Hungary	10.7	13	14	20.6	70	53
India	730.0	36	15	122	50	22
Indonesia	155.6	32	15	92	49	21
Iran	42.5	43	13	106	55	50
Iraq	14.5	46	12	77	56	72
Ireland	3.5	21	9	11.2	73	58
Israel	4.1	24	7	14.6	72	89
Italy	56.3	11	10	14.1	73	69
Japan	119.2	13	6	7.1	76	78
Jordan	3.6	47	11	68	61	60
Kenya	18.6	54	13	86	55	13
Korea, North	19.2	32	8	34	64	33
Korea, South	41.3	25	8	34	64	57
Laos	3.6	44	20	128	45	15
Lebanon	2.6	30	9	41	66	78
Liberia	2.1	47	15	153	54	33
Libya	3.3	47	13	99	57	52
Malaysia	15.0	31	7	31	64	30
Mexico	75.7	32	6	55	66	67
Morocco	22.9	44	13	106	57	41
Netherlands	14.4	13	8	8.2	74	88
New Zealand	3.2	16	8	11.7	73	83
Niger	6.1	51	22	145	43	13
Nigeria	84.2	50	17	134	49	20
Norway	4.1	13	10	8.1	75	44
Pakistan	95.7	43	15	124	51	29
Panama	2.1	29	6	34	70	51
Paraguay	3.5	35	8	46	65	40
Peru	19.2	37	11	87	58	67
Philippines	52.8	34	8	54	62	39
Poland	36.6	19	9	20.6	71	58
Portugal	9.9	16	10	26.0	71	31
Rumania	22.7	18	10	29.3	71	49
Saudi Arabia	10.4	44	13	112	54	70
South Africa	30.2	36	10	95	61	50
Spain	38.4	14	8	10.3	73	64
Sweden	8.3	11	11	7.0	75	83
Syria	9.7	46	8	61	65	48
Taiwan	18.9	23	5	9.1	72	66
Tanzania	20.5	46	14	102	52	13
Thailand	50.8	26	7	54	61	17
Tunisia	6.8	35	10	98	59	52
Turkey	49.2	31	10	121	62	45
Uganda	13.8	46	15	96	54	7
USSR	272	19	10	33	70	62
United Kingdom	56.0	13	12	12.1	73	77
United States	234.2	16	9	11.4	74	74
Uruguay	3.0	18	10	34.1	70	84
Venezuela	18.0	33	5	41	67	76
Vietnam	57.0	37	9	99	54	19
Yugoslavia	22.8	17	9	30.6	70	39
Zaire	31.3	46	18	111	47	30
Zambia	6.2	48	16	105	50	43
Zimbabwe	8.4	47	13	73	53	20

[1] More Developed Countries—1980–81 data
Less Developed Countries—Late 1970s data

[2] Deaths under age one per 1,000 live births

Source: 1983 World Population Data Sheet, Population Reference Bureau, Inc., Washington, DC

AGRICULTURAL PRODUCTION: SELECTED COUNTRIES
(in thousand metric tons)

	Barley	Corn	Eggs (million pieces)	Milk	Rice[1]	Soybeans	Sugar[2]	Wheat
Afghanistan	365	770	—	—	460	—	10	2 860
Albania	10	250	—	—		—	20	410
Algeria	480	1	—	—	1	—	11	980
Angola	—	325	—	—	31	—	45	11
Argentina	161	8 600	3 150	5 700	262	3 570	1 617	14 500
Australia	1 858	95	3 460	5 650	522	39	3 545	8 818
Austria	1 436	1 551	1 745	3 554	—	—	547	1 237
Bangladesh	10	—	—	—	21 593	—	194	1 094
Belgium[3]	814	52	3 200	4 080	—	—	1 200	1 063
Bolivia	61	338	—	—	86	52	277	66
Brazil	98	19 500	10 300	10 700	7 800	14 750	9 300	1 849
Bulgaria	1 426	3 415	2 350	—	70	116	210	4 902
Burma	—	95	—	—	14 420	19	130	70
Canada	14 074	6 513	6 050	8 100	—	857	129	26 790
Chile	118	470	—	930	131	1	231	590
China	8 200	60 300	—	—	161 240	9 030	3 850	68 420
Colombia	34	867	—	—	2 071	127	1 343	74
Costa Rica	—	52	—	—	114	—	200	—
Cuba	—	25	—	—	497	—	7 200	—
Czechoslovakia	3 649	939	5 308	6 130	—	6	885	4 613
Denmark	6 388	—	1 380	5 370	—	—	584	1 234
Dominican Republic	—	50	—	—	331	—	1 200	—
Ecuador	32	162	—	—	378	37	254	21
Egypt	121	3 347	2 250	—	2 441	166	770	2 017
El Salvador	—	408	—	—	35	—	229	—
Ethiopia	700	720	—	—	—	—	170	400
Finland	1 599	—	1 395	3 261	—	—	116	435
France	10 277	10 400	15 200	28 042	26	16	4 822	25 206
Germany, E.	4 100	3	5 600	8 000	—	—	974	2 850
Germany, W.	9 460	1 054	12 900	26 300	—	—	3 587	8 632
Ghana	—	360	—	—	45	—	20	—
Greece	853	1 449	2 535	685	83	—	323	2 983
Guatemala	—	1 017	—	—	44	2	555	40
Guyana	—	5	—	—	276	—	290	—
Haiti	—	170	—	—	100	—	44	—
Honduras	—	476	—	—	68	—	210	—
Hungary	885	7 800	4 400	2 750	48	52	587	5 770
India	2 012	5 900	—	15 200	68 769	450	9 580	37 833
Indonesia	—	3 207	—	—	34 104	590	1 569	—
Iran	1 100	60	—	—	1 350	80	300	5 600
Iraq	800	100	—	—	220	—	25	1 300
Ireland	1 570	—	590	5 270	—	—	242	350
Israel	20	2	1 800	—	—	—	—	200
Italy	1 060	6 847	11 650	10 950	991	9	1 295	8 903
Japan	390	3	34 900	7 000	12 838	226	912	742
Kenya	85	2 350	—	—	42	—	346	220
Korea, N.	—	1 900	—	—	4 200	330	—	350
Korea, S.	815	117	—	—	7 307	233	—	66
Lebanon	5	2	—	—	—	—	6	15
Madagascar	—	113	—	—	1 995	—	88	—
Malaysia	—	20	—	—	1 844	—	70	—
Mexico	320	7 000	9 800	6 500	510	550	3 078	4 200
Morocco	2 334	247	—	—	5	—	407	2 183
Mozambique	—	250	—	—	30	—	126	3
Nepal	25	600	—	—	1 874	—	17	660
Netherlands	247	1	11 200	13 200	—	—	1 210	967
New Zealand	348	163	—	6 800	—	—	—	312
Nicaragua	—	182	—	—	131	—	255	—
Nigeria	—	1 785	—	—	1 376	65	65	30
Norway	635	—	—	2 017	—	—	—	60
Pakistan	157	950	—	—	5 060	—	1 285	11 473
Panama	—	68	—	—	169	—	200	—
Paraguay	—	600	—	—	65	500	80	80
Peru	155	625	—	550	696	10	614	100
Philippines	—	3 180	—	—	7 805	8	2 521	—
Poland	3 647	69	7 500	15 920	—	—	2 011	4 476
Portugal	58	413	1 223	798	140	—	6	445
Rumania	3 100	12 600	7 600	—	50	352	675	6 465
Saudi Arabia	28	30	—	—	3	—	—	400
South Africa	110	3 915	2 844	2 530	—	23	1 538	2 296
Spain	5 280	2 332	12 400	6 000	409	9	1 247	4 368
Sri Lanka	—	—	—	—	2 176	—	30	—
Sudan	—	—	—	—	4	—	285	150
Sweden	2 378	—	—	3 766	—	—	396	1 490
Switzerland	236	170	760	3 666	—	—	120	406
Syria	630	50	—	—	—	—	81	1 500
Taiwan	—	110	—	—	3 160	12	658	3
Tanzania	—	1 000	—	—	110	—	105	75
Thailand	—	3 450	—	—	16 750	110	2 070	—
Tunisia	339	—	—	—	—	—	12	916
Turkey	6 400	1 360	—	—	323	40	1 700	13 800
USSR	41 000	13 500	74 200	95 000	2 400	490	7 392	86 000
United Kingdom	10 884	—	13 400	18 150	—	—	1 543	10 260
United States	11 374	213 302	68 119	62 418	6 995	60 677	5 305	76 441
Uruguay	47	80	—	—	313	15	100	316
Venezuela	—	501	3 112	1 472	670	—	360	1
Vietnam	—	475	—	—	13 900	—	45	—
Yugoslavia	669	11 130	4 750	4 550	43	198	697	5 217
Zaire	—	520	—	—	246	—	60	3
Zambia	—	900	—	—	12	—	105	12
Zimbabwe	33	1 045	—	—	—	96	405	213

Source: U.S. Department of Agriculture.   [1] Rough rice   [2] Centrifugal sugar   [3] Includes Luxembourg
Crop production represents 1982–83 crop year. Animal product production represents 1983.

INDUSTRIAL PRODUCTION: SELECTED COUNTRIES (1981)
(in thousand metric tons)

	Cotton yarn	Cement	Gas, manufactured (terajoules)	Gasoline	Newsprint	Rubber, synthetic	Steel, crude
Argentina	57.6	6 912	——	5 257	109.2	30.2	2 196
Australia	21.6	5 736	418 884	10 932	214.8	43.0	7 956
Austria	18.0	5 280	12 768	1 824	177.6	——	5 076
Bangladesh	46.8	360		45	31.2	——	
Belgium	40.8	6 684	10 944	4 771	102.0	108.0	12 288
Bolivia	——	——	——	392	——	——	——
Brazil	——	26 052	——	10 179	105.6	222.8	13 104
Bulgaria	85.2	5 448	——	——	——	——	2 484
Burma	15.6	312	——	246	——	——	——
Canada	——	10 152	48 000	27 413	8 946.0	263.3	14 808
Chile	——	1 860	——	1 057	129.6	——	52
China	2 203.2	——	——		——	95.0	——
Colombia	——	4 500	——	2 506	——	——	264
Cuba	26.4	3 288	2 556	——	——	——	——
Czechoslovakia	136.8	10 644	140 148	1 518	76.8	63.2	15 264
Denmark	——	1 608	5 112	1 159	——	——	612
Ecuador		——	——	118	——	——	
Egypt	244.8	3 432	——	2 055	——	——	
Ethiopia	7.2	——	360	80	——	——	
Finland	8.4	1 788	360	2 008	1 556.4	6.0	2 424
France	217.2	28 224	——	17 284	246.0	487.4	21 264
Germany, E.	134.4	12 204	87 036	3 442	105.6	155.0	7 464
Germany, W.	146.4	31 500	226 068	15 021	669.6	415.4	42 156
Ghana	——	——	——	210	——	——	——
Greece	110.4	13 260	132	1 811	——	——	——
Haiti	——	228	——	——	——	——	——
Hungary	58.8	4 632	9 000	1 391	——	——	3 648
India	1 015.2	20 772	——	1 629	57.6	28.8	10 632
Indonesia		5 604	——	2 985	——	——	——
Iran	——	——	——	2 500	——	——	——
Iraq	——	——	——	1 300	——	——	——
Ireland	——	1 944	3 396	——	——	——	——
Israel	——	2 304	——	——	7.2	——	——
Italy	13.4	42 096	67 188	14 903	234.0	235.0	24 780
Japan	38.0	84 828	797 460	25 856	2 575.2	1 020.2	101 676
Jordan	——	960	——	310	——	——	——
Korea, S.	20.4	15 612	——	727	236.4	82.1	5 892
Lebanon	——	——	——	450	——	——	——
Libya	——	——	——	550	——	——	——
Malaysia	14.4	2 832	——	——	——	——	——
Mexico	——	17 844	——	15 130	68.4	105.0	7 452
Morocco	——	3 612	——	450	——	——	——
Netherlands	12.0	3 324	18 996	6 672	182.4	211.0	5 472
New Zealand		756	780	1 263	——	——	228
Nigeria	——	1 800	——	2 500	——	——	——
Norway	1.2	1 776	216	1 133	696.0	——	852
Pakistan	388.8	3 660	——	485	——	——	——
Panama	——	——	12	——	——	——	——
Philippines	——	4 008	324	1 340	——	——	——
Poland	195.6	14 232	——	3 025	81.6	111.6	15 720
Portugal	112.8	6 036	2 388	1 085	——	——	348
Rumania	189.6	14 748	——	3 600	103.2	145.7	13 020
Saudi Arabia	——	——	——	3 520	——	——	——
South Africa	5.4	8 100	——	——	225.6	36.5	8 940
Spain	——	28 752	28 488	5 037	108.0	60.0	13 176
Sri Lanka	——	708	——	99	——	——	——
Sweden	4.8	2 328	——	2 379	1 604.4	——	3 768
Syria	26.4	2 316	——	170	——	——	——
Thailand	——	6 264	——	——	——	——	——
Tunisia	——	2 004	480	163	——	——	168
Turkey	42.0	15 036	——	2 113	126.0	20.0	1 272
USSR	1 645.2	126 996	612 240	——	1 532.4	——	149 004
Un. Kingdom	84.0	12 732	64 248	17 198	112.8	189.8	15 576
United States	990.0	64 920	369 864	276 282	4 788.0	2 248.0	108 876
Uruguay				186			
Venezuela	——	——	——	7 049	——	——	——
Yugoslavia	117.6	10 080	3 024	2 367	51.6	——	2 436
Zimbabwe	——	300	——	——	——	——	——

Source: *Monthly Bulletin of Statistics,* United Nations, October 1983.

WORLD MINERAL AND METAL PRODUCTION

ALUMINUM, primary smelter (thousand metric tons)

	1981	1982
United States	4,489	3,274
USSR[e]	1,800	1,875
Canada	1,116	1,070
West Germany	729	723
Norway	633	645
Australia	379	381
France	436	390
China[e]	360	370
Spain	397	367
Japan	771	351
Brazil	256	300[e]
Netherlands	262	248
Venezuela	314	244
United Kingdom	339	241
Other countries[a]	2,789	2,808
Total	15,070	13,287

ANTIMONY, mine[b] (metric tons)

	1981	1982
Bolivia	15,301	13,978
China[e]	10,000	10,000
South Africa	9,750	9,134
USSR[e]	8,600	9,000
Mexico	1,800	1,565
Yugoslavia	1,455	1,517
Turkey	838	1,237
Australia	901	1,203
Thailand	1,199	970
Morocco	1,140	845
Canada	1,415	—
Other countries[a]	5,077	4,730
Total	57,476	54,179

ASBESTOS[c] (thousand metric tons)

	1981	1982
USSR[e]	2,105	2,180
Canada	1,122	822
China[e]	250	250
Zimbabwe	248	240[e]
South Africa	236	212
Other countries[a]	519	607
Total	4,480	4,311

BARITE[c] (thousand metric tons)

	1981	1982
United States	2,584	1,674
China[e]	800	900
USSR[e]	510	520
Morocco	465	418
Peru	409	365[e]
India	354	326
Mexico	318	324
Thailand	307	318
Chile	259	240[e]
Other countries[a]	2,210	2,070
Total	8,216	7,155

BAUXITE[d] (thousand metric tons)

	1981	1982
Australia	25,541	23,621
Guinea	11,112	11,827
Jamaica	11,682	8,334
USSR[de]	6,380	6,380
Brazil	5,770	4,187
Yugoslavia	3,249	3,668
Surinam	4,100	3,276
Greece	3,216	2,853
Hungary	2,914	2,627
India	1,923	1,854
France	1,827	1,671
Guyana	1,681	953
United States	1,510	732
Indonesia	1,203	704
Other countries[a]	4,946	4,449
Total	87,054	77,136

CEMENT[c] (thousand metric tons)

	1981	1982
USSR	127,169	124,000
China	84,000	94,000
Japan	84,832	79,212
United States	66,163	59,014
Italy	41,553	40,900[e]
West Germany	33,000	32,000
France	28,229	26,200
Spain	28,571	29,000[e]
Brazil	26,052	24,660
India	20,760	22,500
Mexico	18,066	19,420[e]
Poland	14,225	16,035
Rumania	14,750	15,000[e]
Other countries	301,839	305,035
Total	889,209	886,976

COAL, anthracite and bituminous[c] (million metric tons)

	1981	1982
United States	700	756
China	620	630[e]
USSR	540	560[e]
Poland	163	189
South Africa	130	140[e]
United Kingdom	126	125
India	125	125[e]
Australia	112	109[e]
West Germany	88	89
North Korea[e]	45	45
Canada	37	36
Other countries[a]	163	170

COAL, Anthracite and bituminous[c] (cont'd.) (million metric tons)

	1981	1982
Total	2,849	2,974

COAL, lignite[cf] (million metric tons)

	1981	1982
East Germany	267	280[e]
USSR	164	165[e]
West Germany	131	127
Czechoslovakia	96	99[e]
Yugoslavia	52	53[e]
United States	47	50[e]
Poland	36	38
Australia	33	38[e]
Other countries[a]	172	177
Total	998	1,027

COPPER, mine[b] (thousand metric tons)

	1981	1982
Chile	1,081	1,241
United States	1,538	1,140
USSR[e]	950	1,000
Canada	691	606
Zambia	588	530
Zaire	505	495
Peru	342	369
Poland	315	338
Philippines	302	280
Australia	226	245
Mexico	231	239
China[e]	200	200
South Africa	209	189
Papua New Guinea	165	170
Other countries[a]	832	922
Total	8,175	7,964

COPPER, refined, primary, and secondary (thousand metric tons)

	1981	1982
United States	2,038	1,686
USSR[e]	1,060	1,120
Japan	1,050	1,075
Chile	776	852
Zambia	560	585
Belgium	428	480
West Germany	387	394
Poland	327	348
Canada	477	298
China[e]	280	280
Peru	209	225
Australia	192	183
Zaire	152	175
Spain	152	167
South Africa	144	143
Other countries[a]	1,087	1,108
Total	9,319	9,119

DIAMOND (thousand carats)

	1981	1982
USSR[e]	10,600	10,600
South Africa	9,526	9,154
Zaire[e]	9,000	9,000
Botswana	4,961	7,769
China[e]	1,900	2,000
Brazil	1,089	1,150[e]
Other countries[a]	5,481	5,493
Total	42,557	45,166

FLUORSPAR[g] (thousand metric tons)

	1981	1982
Mexico	1,116	725[e]
Mongolia[e]	595	660
USSR[e]	530	540
China[e]	480	480
South Africa	497	331
Spain	313	260[e]
Thailand	212	260[e]
France	256	250[e]
Italy	164	160[e]
United Kingdom	150	160[e]
Other countries[a]	738	713
Total	5,051	4,539

GAS, natural[h] (billion cubic ft)

	1981	1982
United States	20,241	18,619
USSR	16,421	17,680[e]
Canada	3,006	3,094
Netherlands	3,240	2,773
Mexico	1,214	2,245[e]
United Kingdom	1,321	1,393[e]
Rumania[e]	1,200	1,300
Norway	920	938
Algeria	900	910
Other countries[a]	8,168	8,250
Total	56,631	57,202

GOLD, mine[b] (thousand troy ozs)

	1981	1982
South Africa	21,121	21,355
USSR[e]	8,425	8,550
Canada	1,673	2,008
United States	1,378	1,447
Brazil[e]	1,200	1,450
Australia	568	881
Philippines	753	778[e]

GOLD, mine[b] (cont'd.) (thousand troy ozs)

	1981	1982
Papua New Guinea	540	564
Chile	400	547
Other countries[e]	5,167	5,136
Total	41,225	42,716

GRAPHITE[c] (thousand metric tons)

	1981	1982
China[e]	160	160
USSR[e]	105	105
Czechoslovakia[e]	45	45
India	56	44[e]
South Korea	35	36[e]
Mexico	42	34[e]
North Korea[e]	25	25
Other countries[e]	106	101
Total	574	550

GYPSUM[c] (thousand metric tons)

	1981	1982
United States	10,430	9,560
Japan	6,137	6,350[e]
France	6,204	6,170[e]
Canada	7,025	5,726
USSR[e]	5,400	5,400
Spain	5,288	5,260
Iran[e]	6,000	5,000
China[e]	3,400	3,500
United Kingdom	2,984	2,700[e]
West Germany	2,250	2,270[e]
Italy	1,544	1,630[e]
Mexico	1,883	1,500[e]
Other countries[e]	17,727	18,068
Total	76,272	73,134

IRON ORE[e] (thousand metric tons)

	1981	1982
USSR	242,417	244,000
Brazil	97,860	110,000[e]
Australia	84,661	87,789
China	70,107	70,000[e]
India	41,354	40,902
United States	74,348	35,907
Canada	49,551	34,496
South Africa	28,319	24,554
France	21,598	19,392
Liberia	19,704	18,165
Sweden	23,225	16,138
Venezuela	15,531	12,367
Other countries[a]	88,062	81,490
Total	856,737	795,200

IRON, steel ingots (thousand metric tons)

	1981	1982
USSR	148,445	147,800
Japan	101,676	99,548
United States	109,613	66,137
China	35,600	37,160
West Germany	41,610	35,900
Italy	24,777	23,981
France	21,258	18,416
Czechoslovakia	15,270	14,992
Poland	15,719	14,500
United Kingdom	15,576	13,700
Spain	12,912	13,160
Rumania	13,025	13,000
Brazil	13,230	12,999
Canada	14,811	12,600
South Korea	10,754	11,753
India	10,780	10,715
Belgium	12,286	9,900
South Africa	9,004	8,271
Australia	7,635	6,370
Other countries[a]	71,235	70,109
Total	705,216	641,011

LEAD, mine[b] (thousand metric tons)

	1981	1982
USSR[e]	570	575
United States	445	512
Australia	389	465
Canada	332	341
Peru	192	205
China[e]	155	155
Mexico	157	146
Yugoslavia	119	115
Morocco	116	110[e]
Other countries[a]	881	840
Total	3,356	3,464

LEAD, refined, primary, and secondary[i] (thousand metric tons)

	1981	1982
United States	1,136	1,032
USSR[e]	645	650
West Germany	348	351
France	321	309
United Kingdom	333	306
Japan	317	302
Australia	239	247
Canada	238	242
China[e]	170	170
Mexico	200	153
Italy	130	134
Spain	117	132

	1981	1982
LEAD, refined, primary, and secondary (cont'd.)		
(thousand metric tons)		
Bulgaria[e]	119	119
Other countries[a]	1,012	981
Total	5,325	5,128
MAGNESIUM, primary		
(thousand metric tons)		
United States	130	90[e]
USSR[e]	78	81
Norway	48	35
France	7	10
Canada	9	8[e]
Italy	8	8
China[e]	7	7
Other countries[a]	9	9
Total	297	248
MANGANESE ORE[c]		
(thousand metric tons)		
USSR	9,153	9,200
South Africa	5,039	5,216
China[e]	1,600	1,600
Gabon	1,488	1,512
India	1,526	1,448
Brazil	2,042	1,300[e]
Australia	1,449	1,132
Other countries[a]	1,250	1,033
Total	23,547	22,441
MERCURY[b]		
(76-lb flasks)		
USSR	63,000	64,000
Spain	45,253	45,000[e]
United States	27,904	25,760
Algeria[e]	25,000	20,000
China[e]	20,000	20,000
Other countries[a]	32,813	29,249
Total	213,970	204,009
MOLYBDENUM, mine[b]		
(metric tons)		
United States	63,458	34,496
Chile	15,360	20,000[e]
Canada	14,134	16,461
USSR[e]	10,700	11,000
Peru	2,488	2,565
China[e]	2,000	2,000
Other countries[a]	1,270	1,220
Total	109,410	87,742
NATURAL GAS LIQUIDS		
(million barrels)		
United States	577	548
Saudi Arabia[e]	140	150
USSR[e]	134	145
Canada	119	113
Mexico	88	100[e]
Algeria	68	70[e]
Other countries[a]	171	168
Total	1,297	1,294
NICKEL, mine[b]		
(thousand metric tons)		
USSR[e]	158	170
Canada	160	89
Australia	74	82
New Caledonia	78	59
Cuba	39	36
Indonesia	31	29[e]
South Africa	26	22[e]
Philippines	31	20[e]
Other countries[a]	115	101
Total	712	608
NITROGEN, content of ammonia[j]		
(thousand metric tons)		
USSR	12,900	13,100
United States	14,169	11,560
China	9,860	10,257
India	3,193	3,650
Canada	2,181	2,509
Rumania	2,200	2,150
France[e]	2,000	2,000
West Germany	1,961	2,000[e]
Mexico	1,725	1,980
Norway	1,814	1,900[e]
Other countries[a]	21,999	21,980
Total	74,002	73,086
PETROLEUM, crude		
(million barrels)		
USSR	4,476	4,506

	1981	1982
PETROLEUM, crude (cont'd.)		
(million barrels)		
United States	3,129	3,165
Saudi Arabia	3,580	2,362
Mexico	844	1,096
China	739	745
Iran	490	723
Venezuela	768	691
United Kingdom	651	607
Indonesia	586	489
Nigeria	525	472
Canada	469	447
United Arab Emirates	548	444
Libya	408	415
Iraq	326	349
Other countries[a]	4,098	3,858
Total	21,637	20,369
PHOSPHATE ROCK[c]		
(thousand metric tons)		
United States	53,627	37,414
USSR	25,600	26,100
Morocco	18,562	17,754
China	11,500	12,500
Jordan	4,244	4,431
Tunisia	4,596	4,196
South Africa	2,618	3,173
Brazil	2,764	2,732
Israel	1,919	2,300
Togo	2,215	2,128
Other countries[a]	9,879	9,905
Total	137,524	122,633
POTASH, K2O equivalent basis		
(thousand metric tons)		
USSR	8,449	9,000[e]
Canada	6,549	5,196
East Germany	3,490	3,500[e]
West Germany	2,591	2,600[e]
France	1,831	1,823
United States	2,156	1,784
Other countries[a]	1,980	2,827
Total	27,046	26,730
SALT[c]		
(thousand metric tons)		
United States	35,303	34,333
China	18,320	16,000[e]
USSR[e]	15,200	15,500
West Germany	12,541	11,500[e]
India	8,925	10,004[e]
Canada	7,240	8,076
Mexico	7,953	8,000[e]
United Kingdom	6,720	6,900[e]
France	6,636	6,700[e]
Rumania	5,000	5,000[e]
Italy	4,564	4,500[e]
Poland	4,271	4,300
Other countries[a]	37,679	37,983
Total	170,352	168,796
SILVER, mine[b]		
(thousand troy ozs)		
Peru	46,940	53,639
Mexico	53,204	49,841
USSR[e]	46,500	46,900
United States	40,683	40,239
Canada	36,298	38,709
Australia	23,896	29,196
Poland	20,576	21,058
Chile	11,610	11,799
Japan	9,010	9,831
South Africa	7,568	6,943
Sweden	5,337	5,626
Bolivia	6,394	5,472
Other countries[a]	54,292	53,275
Total	362,308	372,528
SULFUR, all forms[k]		
(thousand metric tons)		
USSR[e]	9,790	9,990
United States	12,145	9,787
Canada	6,799	6,264
Poland	5,123	5,270
Japan	2,573	2,476
China[e]	2,300	2,300
France	2,042	2,101
Mexico	2,178	1,916
West Germany	1,742	1,785
Spain	1,268	1,238
Other countries[a]	7,603	7,533
Total	53,563	50,660

	1981	1982
TIN, mine[b]		
(thousand metric tons)		
Malaysia	60	52
USSR[e]	36	37
Indonesia	35	37[e]
Bolivia	30	27
Thailand	31	26[e]
China[e]	15	15
Other countries[a]	46	47
Total	253	241
TITANIUM MATERIALS[cl]		
(thousand metric tons)		
Ilmenite		
Australia	1,337	1,178
Norway	658	552
USSR	425	430
United States	462	207
India	189	190[e]
Finland	162	160[e]
Other countries[a]	403	341
Total	3,636	3,058
Rutile		
Australia	239	221
Other countries[a]	133	126
Total	372	347
Titaniferous slag		
Canada	759	680
South Africa	370	381
Total	1,129	1,061
TUNGSTEN, mine[b]		
(metric tons)		
China[e]	13,500	12,500
USSR[e]	8,800	9,000
Canada	1,993	2,947
Australia	3,517	2,588
Bolivia	2,779	2,534
South Korea	2,642	2,233
North Korea[e]	2,200	2,200
United States	3,605	1,521
Austria	1,450	1,400[e]
Portugal	1,394	1,360[e]
Thailand	1,210	856
Other countries[a]	6,116	5,733
Total	49,206	44,872
URANIUM OXIDE (U3O8)[bm]		
(metric tons)		
United States	17,454	12,247
Canada	8,853	9,657
South Africa	7,220	6,863
Australia	3,446	5,251
Niger	5,136	5,039
Namibia	4,681	4,536
Other countries[a]	4,925	5,545
Total	51,715	49,138
ZINC, mine[b]		
(thousand metric tons)		
Canada	911	1,033
USSR[e]	790	795
Australia	518	665
Peru	499	541
United States	312	300
Japan	242	250
Mexico	212	232
Sweden	181	185
Ireland	117	167
Spain	182	167[e]
China[e]	160	160
Poland	147	145[e]
Other countries[a]	1,386	1,407
Total	5,657	6,047
ZINC, smelter, primary, and secondary		
(thousand metric tons)		
USSR[e]	870	875
Japan	720	708
Canada	619	505
West Germany	367	335
United States	393	302
Australia	300	295
Belgium	257	260[e]
France	257	244
Spain	180	187
Netherlands	177	180[e]
Poland	167	165
China[e]	160	160
Italy	181	159
Finland	140	144
Other countries[a]	1,324	1,362
Total	6,112	5,881

[a] Estimated in part. [b] Content of concentrates. [c] Gross weight. [d] Includes calculated bauxite equivalent of estimated output of aluminum ores other than bauxite (nepheline concentrate and alunite ore). [e] Estimate. [f] Includes coal classified in some countries as brown coal. [g] Marketable gross weight. [h] Marketed production (includes gas sold or used by producers, excludes gas reinjected to reservoirs for pressure maintenance and that flared or vented to the atmosphere, which is not used as fuel or industrial raw material, and which thus has no economic value). [i] Excludes bullion produced for refining elsewhere. [j] Series changed from that in previous editions to make it more complete, and to place data on a calendar year basis. [k] Includes (1) Frasch process sulfur, (2) elemental sulfur mined by conventional methods, (3) by-product recovered elemental sulfur, and (4) elemental sulfur equivalent obtained from purite and other materials. [l] Excludes output (if any) by China. [m] Excludes output (if any) by Albania, Bulgaria, China, Czechoslovakia, East Germany, Hungary, North Korea, Mongolia, Poland, Rumania, and Vietnam.

Compiled by Charles L. Kimbell, U.S. Bureau of Mines

UNITED STATES: Major Legislation Enacted During First Session of the 98th Congress

SUBJECT	PURPOSE
Social Security	Increases the Social Security payroll taxes for employees and employers, delays for six months the cost-of-living increases for recipients, and raises the age of retirement from 65 to 67 by the year 2027. Signed April 20, 1983. Public Law 98-21.
Saccharin	Extends for two years the authorization for research on saccharin and the requirement for health-warning labels on saccharin-sweetened products. Signed April 22, 1983. Public Law 98-22.
Harry S. Truman	Establishes the Harry S. Truman National Historic Site in the state of Missouri. Signed May 23, 1983. Public Law 98-32.
Senate Salaries	Increases the annual salaries of U.S. senators from $60,662 to $69,800. Signed July 30, 1983. Public Law 98-63.
Caribbean Economic Development	Establishes the Caribbean Basin Initiative under which certain Caribbean exports may enter the United States duty free and allows U.S. businessmen tax deductions for attending conventions in the Caribbean region. (The bill also repeals the 10% withholding of taxes on interest and dividend income.) Signed Aug. 5, 1983. Public Law 98-67.
Korean Air Lines Resolution	Condemns the USSR's September 1 destruction of the Korean Air Lines passenger plane with 269 aboard. Signed Sept. 28, 1983. Public Law 98-98.
U.S. Constitution Bicentennial	Gives the president the authority to name a commission to plan and coordinate observances in honor of the 200th anniversary (Sept. 17, 1787) of the drafting of the U.S. Constitution. Signed Sept. 29, 1983. Public Law 98-101.
Radio Cuba	Approves Radio Marti, a new U.S. government radio station to broadcast to Cuba. Signed Oct. 4, 1983. Public Law 98-111.
War Powers Resolution	See page 549. Signed Oct. 12, 1983. Public Law 98-119.
Trade Adjustment Assistance	Extends for two years the trade adjustment assistance program, which provides benefits to workers from industries affected by import competition. Signed Oct. 12, 1983. Public Law 98-120.
Product Tampering	Permits federal fines and prison terms for persons convicted of tampering with over-the-counter drugs, food, cosmetics, and other household products. Signed Oct. 13, 1983. Public Law 98-127.
Unemployment Compensation	Extends federal supplemental unemployment compensation through March 31, 1985. Persons who have used their state and federal jobless aid are provided a minimum of eight and a maximum of 14 additional weeks of benefits. Signed Oct. 24, 1983. Public Law 98-135.
King Holiday	Establishes, beginning in 1986, the third Monday of January as a federal holiday in honor of the late civil-rights leader the Rev. Martin Luther King, Jr. Signed Nov. 2, 1983. Public Law 98-144.
Government Ethics	Extends for another five years the Office of Government Ethics. Signed Nov. 11, 1983. Public Law 98-150.
Veterans Job Training	Authorizes a $300 million emergency job training program for veterans of the Korean and Vietnam wars. Signed Nov. 14, 1983. Public Law 98-151.
Vietnam Veterans	Extends for four additional years counseling centers for Vietnam veterans. Signed Nov. 21, 1983. Public Law 98-160.
Public Debt	Increases the U.S. public debt by $101 billion to $1,490 billion. Signed Nov. 21, 1983. Public Law 98-161.
Eleanor Roosevelt	Approves the commemoration of the centennial of Eleanor Roosevelt's birth. Signed Nov. 21, 1983. Public Law 98-162.
Danny Thomas	Awards a special gold medal to Danny Thomas in recognition of his humanitarian services. Signed Nov. 29, 1983. Public Law 98-172.
Dairy Products	Reduces excess dairy production through a combination of payments to farmers for cuts in production, and repeated reductions in the federal support if certain production goals are not met. Signed Nov. 29, 1983. Public Law 98-180.
Housing/IMF	Authorizes $15.6 billion for housing and community development programs and a U.S. contribution of $8.4 billion for the International Monetary Fund (IMF). Signed Nov. 30, 1983. Public Law 98-181.
Civil Rights	Reconstitutes the U.S. Civil Rights Commission. The president and the Congress each are to appoint four members to the panel. Signed Nov. 30, 1983. Public Law 98-183.
Revenue Sharing	Continues the federal revenue sharing program for three years. Signed Nov. 30, 1983. Public Law 98-185.

THE UNITED STATES GOVERNMENT

(selected listing, as of Dec. 31, 1983)

President: Ronald Reagan   **Vice-President:** George Bush

Executive Office of the President
The White House

Counsellor to the President: Edwin Meese III

Chief of Staff and Assistant to the President: James A. Baker III

Deputy Chief of Staff and Assistant to the President: Micheal K. Deaver

Assistant to the President for National Security Affairs: Robert C. McFarlane

Assistant to the President for Policy Development: John Svahn

Assistant to the President and Press Secretary: James S. Brady

Assistant to the President for Public Liaison: Faith Ryan Whittlesey

Counsel to the President: Fred R. Fielding

Assistant to the President for Legislative Affairs: M. B. Oglesby, Jr.

Deputy Counsellor to the President: James Jenkins

Assistant to the President for Presidential Personnel: John S. Herrington

Assistant to the President for Political Affairs: Edward J. Rollins, Jr.

Assistant to the President for Intergovernmental Affairs: Lee Verstandig

Assistant to the President and Principal Deputy Press Secretary: Larry Speakes

Office of Management and Budget, Director: David A. Stockman

Council of Economic Advisers, Chairman: Martin S. Feldstein

Office of United States Trade Representative, U.S. Trade Representative: William E. Brock

Council on Environmental Quality, Chairman: A. Alan Hill

Office of Science and Technology Policy, Director: George A. Keyworth II

Office of Administration, Director: John F. W. Rogers II

The Cabinet

Secretary of Agriculture: John R. Block

Secretary of Commerce: Malcolm Baldrige

Secretary of Defense: Caspar W. Weinberger
- Joint Chiefs of Staff, Chairman: Gen. John W. Vessey, Jr. USA
- Secretary of the Air Force: Verne Orr
- Secretary of the Army: John O. Marsh, Jr.
- Secretary of the Navy: John F. Lehman, Jr.

Secretary of Education: Terrel H. Bell

Secretary of Energy: Donald P. Hodel

Secretary of Health and Human Services: Margaret M. Heckler
- National Institutes of Health, Director: James B. Wyngaarden
- Surgeon General: C. Everett Koop
- Commissioner of Food and Drugs: Arthur Hull Hayes, Jr.

Commissioner of Social Security: Martha McSteen

Secretary of Housing and Urban Development: Samuel R. Pierce, Jr.

Secretary of the Interior: William P. Clark

Department of Justice, Attorney General: William French Smith
- Federal Bureau of Investigation, Director: William H. Webster

Secretary of Labor: Raymond J. Donovan
- Women's Bureau, Director: Lenora Cole-Alexander
- Commissioner of Labor Statistics: Janet L. Norwood

Secretary of State: George P. Shultz

Secretary of Transportation: Elizabeth H. Dole

Secretary of the Treasury: Donald T. Regan
- Internal Revenue Service, Commissioner: Roscoe L. Egger, Jr.

Independent Agencies

ACTION, Director: Thomas W. Pauken

Central Intelligence Agency, Director: William J. Casey

Civil Aeronautics Board, Chairman: Dan McKinnon

Commission on Civil Rights, Chairman: Clarence M. Pendleton, Jr.

Commission of Fine Arts, Chairman: J. Carter Brown

Consumer Product Safety Commission, Chairman: Nancy H. Steorts

Environmental Protection Agency, Administrator: William D. Ruckelshaus

Equal Employment Opportunity Commission, Chairman: Clarence Thomas

Export-Import Bank, President and Chairman: William H. Draper III

Federal Communications Commission, Chairman: Mark S. Fowler

Federal Deposit Insurance Corporation, Chairman: William M. Isaac

Federal Election Commission, Chairman: Danny L. McDonald

Federal Emergency Management Agency, Director: Louis O. Giuffrida

Federal Farm Credit Board, Chairman: John D. Naill

Federal Home Loan Bank Board, Chairman: Edwin J. Gray

Federal Labor Relations Authority, Chairman: Barbara J. Mahone

Federal Maritime Commission, Chairman: Alan Green, Jr.

Federal Reserve System, Chairman: Paul A. Volcker

Federal Trade Commission, Chairman: James C. Miller III

General Services Administrator: Gerald P. Carmen

Interstate Commerce Commission, Chairman: Reese H. Taylor, Jr.

National Aeronautics and Space Administration, Administrator: James M. Beggs

National Foundation on the Arts and Humanities
- National Endowment for the Arts, Chairman: Francis S. M. Hodsoll; National Endowment for the Humanities, Chairman: William J. Bennett

National Labor Relations Board, Chairman: Donald L. Dotson

National Science Foundation, Director: Edward A. Knapp

National Transportation Safety Board, Chairman: James E. Burnett

Nuclear Regulatory Commission, Chairman: Nunzio J. Palladino

Peace Corps, Director: Loret M. Ruppe

Postal Rate Commission, Chairman: Janet D. Steiger

Securities and Exchange Commission, Chairman: John S. R. Shad

Selective Service System, Director: Thomas K. Turnage

Small Business Administrator: James C. Sanders

Tennessee Valley Authority, Chairman: Charles H. Dean, Jr.

U.S. Arms Control and Disarmament Agency, Director: Kenneth L. Adelman

U.S. Information Agency, Director: Charles Z. Wick

U.S. International Trade Commission, Chairman: Alfred Eckes

U.S. Postmaster General: William F. Bolger

Veterans Administrator: Harry N. Walters

The Supreme Court
Chief Justice, Warren E. Burger

William J. Brennan, Jr.	Byron R. White	Thurgood Marshall	Harry A. Blackmun
Lewis F. Powell, Jr.	William H. Rehnquist	John Paul Stevens	Sandra Day O'Connor

UNITED STATES: 98th CONGRESS
Second Session

SENATE MEMBERSHIP

Alabama
* H. Heflin, D
** J. Denton, R

Alaska
* T. Stevens, R
** F. H. Murkowski, R

Arizona
** B. Goldwater, R
*** D. DeConcini, D

Arkansas
** D. Bumpers, D
* D. Pryor, D

California
** A. Cranston, D
*** P. Wilson, R

Colorado
** G. Hart, D
* W. Armstrong, R

Connecticut
*** L. P. Weicker, Jr., R
** C. J. Dodd, D

Delaware
*** W. V. Roth, Jr., R
* J. R. Biden, Jr., D

Florida
*** L. M. Chiles, Jr., D
** P. Hawkins, R

Georgia
* S. Nunn, D
** M. Mattingly, R

Hawaii
** D. K. Inouye, D
*** S. M. Matsunaga, D

Idaho
* J. A. McClure, R
** S. D. Symms, R

Illinois
* C. H. Percy, R
** A. J. Dixon, D

Indiana
*** R. G. Lugar, R
** D. Quayle, R

Iowa
* R. Jepsen, R
** C. E. Grassley, R

Kansas
* R. J. Dole, R
* N. Kassebaum, R

Kentucky
* W. Huddleston, D
** W. H. Ford, D

Louisiana
** R. B. Long, D
* J. B. Johnston, D

Maine
* W. Cohen, R
*** G. Mitchell, D

Maryland
** C. M. Mathias, Jr., R
*** P. S. Sarbanes, D

Massachusetts
*** E. M. Kennedy, D
* P. E. Tsongas, D

Michigan
*** D. W. Riegle, Jr., D
* C. Levin, D

Minnesota
*** D. Durenberger, R
* R. Boschwitz, R

Mississippi
*** J. C. Stennis, D
* T. Cochran, R

Missouri
** T. F. Eagleton, D
*** J. C. Danforth, R

Montana
*** J. Melcher, D
* M. Baucus, D

Nebraska
*** E. Zorinsky, D
* J. Exon, D

Nevada
** P. Laxalt, R
*** C. Hecht, R

New Hampshire
* G. Humphrey, R
** W. Rudman, R

New Jersey
* B. Bradley, D
*** F. R. Lautenberg, D

New Mexico
* P. V. Domenici, R
*** J. Bingaman, D

New York
*** D. P. Moynihan, D
** A. D'Amato, R

North Carolina
* J. Helms, R
** J. P. East, R

North Dakota
*** Q. N. Burdick, D
** M. Andrews, R

Ohio
** J. H. Glenn, Jr., D
*** H. M. Metzenbaum, D

Oklahoma
* D. Boren, D
* D. Nickles, R

Oregon
* M. O. Hatfield, R
** B. Packwood, R

Pennsylvania
*** J. Heinz, R
** A. Specter, R

Rhode Island
* C. Pell, D
*** J. H. Chafee, R

South Carolina
* S. Thurmond, R
** E. F. Hollings, D

South Dakota
* L. Pressler, R
** J. Abdnor, R

Tennessee
* H. H. Baker, Jr., R
*** J. Sasser, D

Texas
* J. G. Tower, R
*** L. M. Bentsen, D

Utah
** E. J. Garn, R
*** O. Hatch, R

Vermont
*** R. T. Stafford, R
** P. J. Leahy, D

Virginia
* J. Warner, R
*** P. S. Trible, Jr., R

Washington
*** D. J. Evans, R [1]
** S. Gorton, R

West Virginia
* J. Randolph, D
*** R. C. Byrd, D

Wisconsin
*** W. Proxmire, D
** R. W. Kasten, Jr., R

Wyoming
*** M. Wallop, R
* A. Simpson, R

HOUSE MEMBERSHIP

Alabama
1. J. Edwards, R
2. W. L. Dickinson, R
3. W. Nichols, D
4. T. Bevill, D
5. R. Flippo, D
6. B. Erdreich, D
7. R. Shelby, D

Alaska
At-L. D. Young, R

Arizona
1. J. McCain, III, R
2. M. K. Udall, D
3. B. Stump, R
4. E. Rudd, R
5. J. McNulty, Jr., D

Arkansas
1. W. V. Alexander, Jr., D
2. E. Bethune, Jr., R
3. J. P. Hammerschmidt, R
4. B. Anthony, Jr., D

California
1. D. H. Bosco, D
2. E. A. Chappie, R
3. R. Matsui, D
4. V. Fazio, D
5. *S. Burton, D
6. B. Boxer, D
7. G. Miller, D
8. R. V. Dellums, D
9. F. H. Stark, Jr., D
10. D. Edwards, D
11. T. Lantos, D
12. E. Zschau, R
13. N. Y. Mineta, D
14. N. Shumway, R
15. T. Coelho, D
16. L. E. Panetta, D
17. C. Pashayan, Jr., R
18. R. Lehman, D
19. R. J. Lagomarsino, R
20. W. M. Thomas, R
21. B. Fiedler, R
22. C. J. Moorhead, R
23. A. C. Beilenson, D
24. H. A. Waxman, D
25. E. R. Roybal, D
26. H. L. Berman, D
27. M. Levine, D
28. J. Dixon, D
29. A. F. Hawkins, D
30. M. G. Martinez, D
31. M. Dymally, D
32. G. M. Anderson, D
33. D. Dreier, R
34. E. Torres, D
35. J. Lewis, R
36. G. E. Brown, Jr., D
37. A. McCandless, R
38. J. M. Patterson, D
39. W. Dannemeyer, R
40. R. E. Badham, R
41. W. D. Lowery, R
42. D. Lungren, R
43. R. Packard, R
44. J. Bates, D
45. D. L. Hunter, R

Colorado
1. P. Schroeder, D
2. T. E. Wirth, D
3. R. Kogovsek, D
4. H. Brown, R
5. K. Kramer, R
6. *D. Schaefer, R

Connecticut
1. B. Kennelly, D
2. S. Gejdenson, D
3. B. Morrison, D
4. S. B. McKinney, R
5. W. Ratchford, D
6. N. L. Johnson, R

Delaware
At-L. T. R. Carper, D

Florida
1. E. Hutto, D
2. D. Fuqua, D
3. C. E. Bennett, D
4. W. V. Chappell, Jr., D
5. B. McCollum, Jr., R
6. K. H. MacKay, D
7. S. M. Gibbons, D
8. C. W. Young, R
9. M. Bilirakis, R
10. A. Ireland, D
11. B. Nelson, D
12. T. Lewis, R
13. C. Mack, R
14. D. A. Mica, D
15. E. C. Shaw, Jr., R
16. L. Smith, D
17. W. Lehman, D
18. C. Pepper, D
19. D. B. Fascell, D

Georgia
1. R. L. Thomas, D
2. C. Hatcher, D
3. R. Ray, D
4. E. H. Levitas, D
5. W. Fowler, Jr., D
6. N. Gingrich, R
7. *G. Darden, D
8. J. R. Rowland, Jr., D
9. E. L. Jenkins, D
10. D. D. Barnard, Jr., D

Hawaii
1. C. Heftel, D
2. D. K. Akaka, D

Idaho
1. L. Craig, R
2. G. V. Hansen, R

Illinois
1. *C. Haynes, D
2. G. Savage, D
3. M. A. Russo, D
4. G. M. O'Brien, R
5. W. O. Lipinski, D
6. H. J. Hyde, R
7. C. Collins, D
8. D. Rostenkowski, D
9. S. R. Yates, D
10. J. Porter, R
11. F. Annunzio, D
12. P. M. Crane, R
13. J. N. Erlenborn, R
14. T. Corcoran, R
15. E. R. Madigan, R
16. L. Martin, R
17. L. Evans, D

18. R. H. Michel, R
19. D. B. Crane, R
20. R. J. Durbin, D
21. M. Price, D
22. P. Simon, D

Indiana
1. K. Hall, D
2. P. R. Sharp, D
3. J. Hiler, R
4. D. Coats, R
5. E. H. Hillis, R
6. D. Burton, R
7. J. T. Myers, R
8. F. X. McCloskey, D
9. L. H. Hamilton, D
10. A. Jacobs, Jr., D

Iowa
1. J. A. S. Leach, R
2. T. Tauke, R
3. C. Evans, R
4. N. Smith, D
5. T. R. Harkin, D
6. B. W. Bedell, D

Kansas
1. P. Roberts, R
2. J. Slattery, D
3. L. Winn, Jr., R
4. D. Glickman, D
5. B. Whittaker, R

Kentucky
1. C. Hubbard, Jr., D
2. W. H. Natcher, D
3. R. L. Mazzoli, D
4. G. Snyder, R
5. H. Rogers, R
6. L. Hopkins, R
7. C. D. Perkins, D

Louisiana
1. R. L. Livingston, Jr., R
2. L. Boggs, D
3. W. J. Tauzin, D
4. B. Roemer, D
5. J. Huckaby, D
6. W. H. Moore, R
7. J. B. Breaux, D
8. G. W. Long, D

Maine
1. J. R. McKernan, Jr., R
2. O. Snowe, R

Maryland
1. R. Dyson, D
2. C. D. Long, D
3. B. A. Mikulski, D
4. M. S. Holt, R
5. S. Hoyer, D
6. B. Byron, D
7. P. J. Mitchell, D
8. M. Barnes, D

Massachusetts
1. S. O. Conte, R
2. E. P. Boland, D
3. J. D. Early, D
4. B. Frank, D
5. J. Shannon, D
6. N. Mavroules, D
7. E. J. Markey, D
8. T. P. O'Neill, Jr., D
9. J. J. Moakley, D
10. G. E. Studds, D
11. B. Donnelly, D

Michigan
1. J. Conyers, Jr., D
2. C. D. Pursell, R
3. H. Wolpe, D
4. M. Siljander, R
5. H. S. Sawyer, R
6. B. Carr, D
7. D. E. Kildee, D
8. B. Traxler, D
9. G. A. Vander Jagt, R
10. D. Albosta, D
11. R. Davis, R
12. D. E. Bonior, D
13. G. Crockett, Jr., D
14. D. Hertel, D
15. W. D. Ford, D
16. J. D. Dingell, D
17. S. Levin, D
18. W. S. Broomfield, R

Minnesota
1. T. J. Penny, D
2. V. Weber, R
3. B. Frenzel, R

4. B. F. Vento, D
5. M. Sabo, D
6. G. Sikorski, D
7. A. Stangeland, R
8. J. L. Oberstar, D

Mississippi
1. J. L. Whitten, D
2. W. Franklin, R
3. G. V. Montgomery, D
4. W. Dowdy, D
5. T. Lott, R

Missouri
1. W. L. Clay, D
2. R. A. Young, D
3. R. A. Gephardt, D
4. I. Skelton, D
5. A. Wheat, D
6. E. T. Coleman, R
7. G. Taylor, R
8. B. Emerson, R
9. H. L. Volkmer, D

Montana
1. P. Williams, D
2. R. Marlenee, R

Nebraska
1. D. Bereuter, R
2. H. Daub, R
3. V. Smith, R

Nevada
1. H. Reid, D
2. B. Vucanovich, R

New Hampshire
1. N. E. D'Amours, D
2. J. Gregg, R

New Jersey
1. J. J. Florio, D
2. W. J. Hughes, D
3. J. J. Howard, D
4. C. Smith, R
5. M. Roukema, R
6. B. J. Dwyer, D
7. M. J. Rinaldo, R
8. R. A. Roe, D
9. R. G. Torricelli, D
10. P. W. Rodino, Jr., D
11. J. G. Minish, D
12. J. Courter, R
13. E. B. Forsythe, R
14. F. Guarini, D

New Mexico
1. M. Lujan, Jr., R
2. J. Skeen, R
3. B. Richardson, D

New York
1. W. Carney, R
2. T. J. Downey, D
3. R. J. Mrazek, D
4. N. F. Lent, R
5. R. McGrath, R
6. J. P. Addabbo, D
7. *G. L. Ackerman, D
8. J. H. Scheuer, D
9. G. Ferraro, D
10. C. E. Schumer, D
11. E. Towns, D
12. M. R. Owens, D
13. S. J. Solarz, D
14. G. V. Molinari, R
15. B. Green, R
16. C. B. Rangel, D
17. T. Weiss, D
18. R. Garcia, D
19. M. Biaggi, D
20. R. L. Ottinger, D
21. H. Fish, Jr., R
22. B. A. Gilman, R
23. S. S. Stratton, D
24. G. B. H. Solomon, R
25. S. L. Boehlert, R
26. D. Martin, R
27. G. C. Wortley, R
28. M. F. McHugh, D
29. F. Horton, R
30. B. B. Conable, Jr., R
31. J. F. Kemp, R
32. J. J. LaFalce, D
33. H. J. Nowak, D
34. S. N. Lundine, D

North Carolina
1. W. B. Jones, D
2. I. T. Valentine, Jr., D

3. C. O. Whitley, Sr., D
4. I. F. Andrews, D
5. S. L. Neal, D
6. R. Britt, D
7. C. Rose, D
8. W. G. Hefner, D
9. J. G. Martin, R
10. J. T. Broyhill, R
11. J. M. Clarke, D

North Dakota
At-L. B. Dorgan, D

Ohio
1. T. A. Luken, D
2. W. D. Gradison, Jr., R
3. T. Hall, D
4. M. Oxley, R
5. D. L. Latta, R
6. B. McEwen, R
7. M. DeWine, R
8. T. N. Kindness, R
9. M. Kaptur, D
10. C. E. Miller, R
11. D. E. Eckart, D
12. J. R. Kasich, R
13. D. J. Pease, D
14. J. F. Seiberling, D
15. C. P. Wylie, R
16. R. Regula, R
17. L. Williams, R
18. D. Applegate, D
19. E. F. Feighan, D
20. M. R. Oakar, D
21. L. Stokes, D

Oklahoma
1. J. R. Jones, D
2. M. Synar, D
3. W. W. Watkins, D
4. D. McCurdy, D
5. M. Edwards, R
6. G. English, D

Oregon
1. L. AuCoin, D
2. R. F. Smith, R
3. R. Wyden, D
4. J. Weaver, D
5. D. Smith, R

Pennsylvania
1. T. Foglietta, D
2. W. Gray, III, D
3. R. A. Borski, Jr., D
4. J. P. Kolter, D
5. R. T. Schulze, R
6. G. Yatron, D
7. R. W. Edgar, D
8. P. H. Kostmayer, D
9. B. Shuster, R
10. J. M. McDade, R
11. F. Harrison, D
12. J. P. Murtha, D
13. L. Coughlin, R
14. W. Coyne, D
15. D. Ritter, R
16. R. S. Walker, R
17. G. W. Gekas, R
18. D. Walgren, D
19. W. F. Goodling, R
20. J. M. Gaydos, D
21. T. J. Ridge, R
22. A. J. Murphy, D
23. W. Clinger, Jr., R

Rhode Island
1. F. J. St Germain, D
2. C. Schneider, R

South Carolina
1. T. Hartnett, R
2. F. D. Spence, R
3. B. C. Derrick, Jr., D
4. C. Campbell, Jr., R
5. J. Spratt, Jr., D
6. R. M. Tallon, Jr., D

South Dakota
At-L. T. Daschle, D

Tennessee
1. J. H. Quillen, R
2. J. J. Duncan, R
3. M. Lloyd, D
4. J. Cooper, D
5. W. H. Boner, D
6. A. Gore, Jr., D
7. D. Sundquist, R
8. E. Jones, D
9. H. E. Ford, D

Texas
1. S. B. Hall, Jr., D
2. C. Wilson, D
3. S. Bartlett, R
4. R. Hall, D
5. J. Bryant, D
6. *W. P. Gramm, R
7. B. Archer, R
8. J. Fields, R
9. J. Brooks, D
10. J. J. Pickle, D
11. J. M. Leath, D
12. J. C. Wright, Jr., D
13. J. E. Hightower, D
14. W. Patman, D
15. E. de la Garza, D
16. R. Coleman, D
17. C. Stenholm, D
18. G. T. Leland, D
19. K. Hance, D
20. H. B. Gonzalez, D
21. T. Loeffler, R
22. R. Paul, R
23. A. Kazen, Jr., D
24. M. Frost, D
25. M. Andrews, D
26. T. Vandergriff, D
27. S. P. Ortiz, D

Utah
1. J. Hansen, R
2. D. D. Marriott, R
3. H. C. Nielson, R

Vermont
At-L. J. M. Jeffords, R

Virginia
1. H. H. Bateman, R
2. G. W. Whitehurst, R
3. T. Bliley, Jr., R
4. N. Sisisky, D
5. D. Daniel, D
6. J. R. Olin, D
7. J. K. Robinson, R
8. S. Parris, R
9. F. C. Boucher, D
10. F. Wolf, R

Washington
1. J. M. Pritchard, R
2. A. Swift, D
3. D. L. Bonker, D
4. S. Morrison, R
5. T. S. Foley, D
6. N. D. Dicks, D
7. M. Lowry, D
8. R. Chandler, R

West Virginia
1. A. B. Mollohan, D
2. H. O. Staggers, Jr., D
3. R. E. Wise, Jr., D
4. N. J. Rahall, II, D

Wisconsin
1. L. Aspin, D
2. R. W. Kastenmeier, D
3. S. Gunderson, R
4. vacant
5. J. Moody, D
6. T. E. Petri, R
7. D. R. Obey, D
8. T. Roth, R
9. F. J. Sensenbrenner, Jr., R

Wyoming
At-L. R. Cheney, R

AMERICAN SAMOA
Delegate, Fofó Sunia, D

DISTRICT OF COLUMBIA
Delegate, W. E. Fauntroy, D

GUAM
Delegate, Antonio Borja Won Pat, D

PUERTO RICO
Resident Commissioner
B. Corrada, D

VIRGIN ISLANDS
Delegate, Ron de Lugo, D

SOCIETIES AND ORGANIZATIONS

This article lists some of the most noteworthy associations, societies, foundations, and trusts of the United States and Canada. The information has been verified by the organization concerned.

Academy of Motion Picture Arts & Sciences. Membership: 4,500. Executive director, James M. Roberts. Headquarters: 8949 Wilshire Blvd., Beverly Hills, CA 90211.

Alcoholics Anonymous (The General Service Board of A.A., Inc.). Membership: more than 1,000,000 in more than 40,000 affiliated groups. Chairman, Gordon Patrick. Headquarters: 468 Park Ave. S., New York, NY. Mailing address: Box 459, Grand Central Station, New York, NY 10163.

American Academy and Institute of Arts and Letters. Membership: 250. Executive director, Margaret M. Mills. Headquarters: 633 W. 155th St., New York, NY 10032.

American Academy of Political and Social Science. Membership: 10,500, including 5,500 libraries. President, Marvin E. Wolfgang. Headquarters: 3937 Chestnut St., Philadelphia, PA 19104.

American Anthropological Association. Membership: 10,268. Executive director, Edward J. Lehman. Headquarters: 1703 New Hampshire Ave. NW, Washington, DC 20009.

American Association for the Advancement of Science. Membership: 140,000 and 285 affiliated groups. Meeting: New York City, May 24–29, 1984. President, Anna J. Harrison; executive officer, William D. Carey. Headquarters: 1515 Massachusetts Ave. NW, Washington, DC 20005.

American Association of Museums. Membership: 7,500. Meeting: Washington, DC, June 1984. Director, Lawrence L. Reger. Headquarters: 1055 Thomas Jefferson St., Suite 428, Washington, DC 20007.

American Association of Retired Persons. Membership: 14,500,000. Convention: St. Louis, MO, April 24–27, 1984. Executive director, Cyril F. Brickfield. Headquarters: 1909 K St. NW, Washington, DC 20049.

American Association of University Professors. Membership: approximately 65,000. President, Victor J. Stone. Headquarters: One Dupont Circle, #500, Washington, DC 20036.

American Association of University Women. Membership: 193,000. President, Mary Purcell. Headquarters: 2401 Virginia Ave. NW, Washington, DC 20037.

American Astronomical Society. Membership: 3,900. Meetings: Las Vegas, NV, Jan. 8–11, 1984; Baltimore, MD, June 10–13, 1984. Executive officer, Peter B. Boyce. Headquarters: 1816 Jefferson Place NW, Washington, DC 20036.

American Automobile Association. Membership: 23,200,000 in 169 affiliated clubs. President, James B. Creal. Headquarters: 8111 Gatehouse Rd., Falls Church, VA 22047.

American Bankers Association (ABA). Membership: nearly 13,000. President, William H. Kennedy, Jr. Headquarters: 1120 Connecticut Ave. NW, Washington, DC 20036.

American Bar Association. Membership: 284,670. Annual meeting: Chicago, Aug. 2–9, 1984; Midyear meeting: Las Vegas, Feb. 8–15, 1984. President, Morris Harrell; president-elect, Wallace D. Riley. Headquarters: 1155 E. 60th St., Chicago, IL 60637.

American Bible Society. Distribution: 124,362,426 copies. Annual meeting: New York City, May 10, 1984. President, Edmund F. Wagner. Headquarters: 1865 Broadway, New York, NY 10023.

American Booksellers Association, Inc. Membership: 5,935. Convention: Washington, DC, May 26–29, 1984. President, Donald Laing. Headquarters: 122 E. 42nd St., New York, NY 10168.

American Cancer Society, Inc. Membership: 119 voting members; 58 chartered divisions. Executive vice-president, Lane W. Adams. Headquarters: 777 Third Ave., New York, NY 10017.

American Chemical Society. Membership: 127,000. National meetings, 1984: St. Louis, MO, April 8–13; Philadelphia, PA, August 26–31; Honolulu, HI. President, Warren D. Niederhauser. Headquarters: 1155 Sixteenth St. NW, Washington, DC 20036.

American Civil Liberties Union. Membership: 200,000. Chairman, Norman Dorsen. Headquarters: 132 W. 43rd St., New York, NY 10036.

American Correctional Association. Membership: 12,000. Executive director, Anthony P. Travisono. Headquarters: 4321 Hartwick Rd., College Park, MD 20740.

American Council of Learned Societies. Membership: 43 professional societies concerned with the humanities and the humanistic aspects of the social sciences. President, John William Ward. Headquarters: 228 East 45th St., New York, NY 10017.

American Council on Education. Membership: 1,366 institutional members, 117 associated organizations, 56 constituent organizations, 83 affiliates, and 22 international affiliates. Annual meeting: Denver, CO, Nov. 12–14, 1984. President, Jack W. Peltason. Headquarters: One Dupont Circle NW, Washington, DC 20036.

American Dental Association. Membership: 140,000. Annual Session: Atlanta, GA, Oct. 20–25, 1984. President, Donald E. Bentley, D.D.S.; executive director, John M. Coady, D.D.S. Headquarters: 211 East Chicago Ave., Chicago, IL 60611.

American Economic Association. Membership: 20,000 and 6,000 subscribers. President, W. Arthur Lewis. Headquarters: 1313 21st Ave. S., Nashville, TN 37212.

American Electroplaters' Society, Inc. (AES). Membership: 10,000. Meeting: New York City, July 16–19, 1984. President, Herbert Tilton, CEF; executive director, J. Howard Schumacher, Jr. Headquarters: 1201 Louisiana Ave., Winter Park, FL 32789.

American Farm Bureau Federation. Membership: 3,261,352 families. President, Robert B. Delano. Headquarters: 225 Touhy Ave., Park Ridge, IL 60068.

American Geographical Society. Fellows and subscribers: 5,500. President, John E. Gould; director, Mary Lynne Bird. Headquarters: 25 West 39th Street, Suite 1501, New York, NY 10018.

American Geophysical Union. Membership: about 16,000 individuals. Meetings, 1984: Cincinnati, OH, May 14–18; San Francisco, CA, December. President, James A. Van Allen. Headquarters: 2000 Florida Ave. NW, Washington, DC 20009.

American Heart Association. Membership: 140,000 in 55 affiliates, 125 chapters, and approximately 1,000 local subdivisions. President, Antonio M. Gotto, M.D. Headquarters: 7320 Greenville Ave., Dallas, TX 75231.

American Historical Association. Membership: 13,000. Annual meeting: Chicago, IL, Dec. 27–30, 1984. President, Arthur Link; executive director, Samuel Gammon. Headquarters: 400 A St. SE, Washington, DC 20003.

American Horticultural Society. Membership: 35,000 individuals. Symposium: Southern Florida, March 1984. National congress: San Antonio, TX, fall 1984. President, Edward N. Dane. Headquarters: Box 0105, Mount Vernon, VA 22121.

American Hospital Association. Membership: 36,948 persons; 6,128 institutions. Annual meeting: Washington, DC, Jan. 29–Feb. 1, 1984; convention: Denver, CO, Aug. 13–15, 1984. Chairman of the board, Thomas R. Matherlee. Headquarters: 840 North Lake Shore Drive, Chicago, IL 60611.

American Hotel & Motel Association. Membership: 8,200. Annual convention: Chicago, IL, May 7–11, 1984. Executive vice-president, Robert L. Richards. Headquarters: 888 Seventh Ave., New York, NY 10019.

American Institute of Aeronautics and Astronautics. Membership: 27,315 plus 6,800 student members. Annual meeting: Washington, DC, May 1–4, 1984. Executive director, James J. Harford. Headquarters: 1633 Broadway, New York, NY 10019.

American Institute of Architects. Membership: 42,000. Convention 1984: Phoenix, AZ. President, George M. Notter, Jr., FAIA. Headquarters: 1735 New York Ave. NW, Washington, DC 20006.

American Institute of Biological Sciences. Membership: 8,000 with 40 member societies and 7 affiliate organizations. Annual meeting: Colorado State University, Fort Collins, Aug. 5–9, 1984. President, Kendric C. Smith. Headquarters: 1401 Wilson Blvd., Arlington, VA 22209.

American Institute of Certified Public Accountants. Membership: 200,000. Annual meeting: Atlanta, GA, Oct. 14–16, 1984. Chairman, B. Z. Lee. Headquarters: 1211 Avenue of the Americas, New York, NY 10036.

American Institute of Chemical Engineers. Membership: 60,000. President, J. H. Sanders. Headquarters: 345 E. 47th St., New York, NY 10017.

American Institute of Graphic Arts. Membership: 2,200. President, David Brown; executive director, Caroline Hightower. Headquarters: 1059 Third Ave., New York, NY 10021.

American Institute of Mining, Metallurgical and Petroleum Engineers, Inc. Membership: More than 90,000. Annual meeting: Los Angeles, CA, Feb. 26–March 2, 1984. President, Edward E. Runyan. Headquarters: 345 E 47th St., New York, NY 10017.

American Institute of Nutrition. Membership: 2,000. Annual meeting: St. Louis, April 1–6, 1984. Executive officer, M. Milner. Headquarters: 9650 Rockville Pike, Bethesda, MD 20814.

American Legion, The. Membership: 2,500,000. National Executive Committee is governing body. National Convention: Salt Lake City, UT, Aug. 31–Sept. 6, 1984. Headquarters: 700 N. Pennsylvania St., Indianapolis, IN 46204.

American Library Association. Membership: 38,000. Meetings 1984: Midwinter, Washington, DC, Jan. 7–12; annual conference, Dallas, TX, June 23–28. Executive director, Robert Wedgeworth. Headquarters: 50 E. Huron, Chicago, IL 60611.

American Lung Association. Membership: 175 affiliated groups. Annual meeting: Miami Beach, FL, May 1984. President, Edward M. Sewell, M.D. Headquarters: 1740 Broadway, New York, NY 10019.

American Management Associations. Membership: 84,000. Chairman of the board, James L. Hayes; president and chief executive officer, Thomas R. Horton. Headquarters: 135 W. 50th St., New York, NY 10020.

American Mathematical Society. Membership: 19,994. President, Julia B. Robinson; secretary, Everett Pitcher. Headquarters: P.O. Box 6248, Providence, RI 02940.

American Medical Association. Membership: 250,000. President, Frank J. Jirka, Jr. MD. Headquarters: 535 N. Dearborn St., Chicago, IL 60610.

American Meteorological Society. Membership: 10,000 including 128 corporate members. President, Earl G. Droessler. Headquarters: 45 Beacon St., Boston, MA 02108.

American Newspaper Publishers Association. Membership: 1,390. Annual convention: Montreal, April 30–May 2, 1984. Chairman and president, William C. Marcil. Executive Offices: The Newspaper Center, 11600 Sunrise Valley Dr., Reston, VA 22091. Mailing Address: The Newspaper Center, Box 17407, Dulles International Airport, Washington, DC 20041.

American Nurses' Association. Membership: 165,000 in 53 state and territorial associations. National convention: New Orleans, LA, June 22–28, 1984. President, Eunice Cole. Headquarters: 2420 Pershing Road, Kansas City, MO 64108.

American Physical Society. Membership: 33,641 American and foreign. Annual meeting: San Antonio, Jan. 30–Feb. 2, 1984. President, Mildred Dresselhaus; executive secretary, W. W. Havens, Jr. Headquarters: 335 E. 45th St., New York, NY 10017.

American Psychiatric Association. Membership: 27,000; 75 district branches. Annual meeting: Los Angeles, CA, May 5–11, 1984. President, George Tarjan, M.D. Headquarters: 1400 K St. NW, Washington, DC 20005.

American Psychological Association. Membership: 58,000. Annual meeting: Toronto, Canada, Aug. 24–28, 1984; Los Angeles, CA, Aug. 23–27, 1985. President, Max Siegel. Headquarters: 1200 17th St. NW, Washington, DC 20036.

American Red Cross. Chapters: 2,963. National convention: San Antonio, TX, May 13–16, 1984. Chairman, Jerome H. Holland; president, Richard F. Schubert. Headquarters: 17th and D Sts. NW, Washington, DC 20006.

American Society of Civil Engineers. Membership: 90,000. Executive director, Louis L. Meier. Headquarters: 345 E. 47th St., New York, NY 10017-2398.

American Society of Composers, Authors, and Publishers. Membership: 27,394 composers and authors; 9,667 publishers. President, Hal David; secretary, Morton Gould. Headquarters: One Lincoln Plaza, New York, NY 10023.

American Society of Mechanical Engineers. Membership: 107,000. President, Frank M. Scott. Headquarters: 345 E. 47th St., New York, NY 10017.

American Society of Newspaper Editors. Membership: 875. National convention: Washington, May 1984. President, Creed C. Black. Headquarters: Box 17004, Washington, DC 20041.

American Sociological Association. Membership: 14,000. Meeting: San Antonio, TX, Aug. 27–31, 1984. President, James F. Short, Jr. Executive Office: 1722 N. Street NW, Washington, DC 20036.

American Statistical Association. Membership: 14,200. President, I. Richard Savage. Philadelphia, PA, Aug. 13–16, 1984. Headquarters: 806 15th St. NW, Suite 640, Washington, DC 20005.

American Youth Hostels, Inc. Membership: 100,000; 31 councils in the United States. Executive director, Robert Johnson. Headquarters: 1332 I St. NW, Suite 800, Washington, DC 20005.

Archaeological Institute of America. Membership: 8,000; subscribers, 50,000. President, Machteld J. Mellink; executive director, Raymond A. Liddell. Headquarters: 808 Commonwealth Ave., Boston, MA 02215.

Arthritis Foundation. Membership: 71 chapters. Annual scientific meeting: Minneapolis, MN, June 4–9, 1984. Chairman, Edward J. Malone; president, Clifford M. Clarke. Headquarters: 1314 Spring St., Atlanta, GA 30309.

Association of American Publishers. Membership: approximately 350. Annual meeting, March 1984. Chairman of the board, Brooks Thomas; president, Townsend W. Hoopes; vice-president, Richard Kleeman. Addresses: One Park Ave., New York, NY 10016 and 2005 Massachusetts Ave. NW, Washington, DC 20036.

Association of Junior Leagues, Inc. Membership: 252 member leagues in U.S., Canada, and Mexico. Annual conference: Philadelphia, PA, May 6–9, 1984. President, Anne B. Hoover. Headquarters: 825 Third Ave., New York, NY 10022.

Association of Operating Room Nurses, Inc. Membership: 30,518 with 317 local chapters. Convention: March 4–9, 1984. President, Joan S. Koehler; executive director, Clifford H. Jordan. Headquarters: 10170 E. Mississippi Ave., Denver, CO 80231.

Benevolent and Protective Order of Elks. Membership: 1,621,356 in 2,271 lodges. 1984 Convention: Houston, TX, July 15–19. Grand exalted ruler, Marvin Lewis; grand secretary, S. F. Kocur. Headquarters: 2750 Lake View Ave., Chicago, IL 60614.

Bide-A-Wee Home Association. Executive director, Richard F. L. Carlson. Headquarters: 410 E. 38th St., New York, NY 10016.

Big Brothers/Big Sisters of America. Membership: 400+ local affiliated agencies. National conference: Memphis, TN, June 19–23, 1984. Executive vice-president, David W. Bahlmann. Headquarters: 117 South 17th St., Suite 1200, Philadelphia, PA 19103.

B'nai B'rith. Membership: 500,000 in approximately 3,000 men's, women's, and youth lodges, chapters, and units. President, Gerald Kraft; executive vice president, Daniel Thursz. Headquarters: 1640 Rhode Island Ave. NW, Washington, DC 20036.

Boat Owners Association of the United States. Membership: 125,000. Executive director, Richard Schwartz. Headquarters: 880 S. Pickett St., Alexandria, VA 22304.

Boys Clubs of America. Youth served: 1,200,000 in 1,100 affiliated clubs. National conference: Kansas City, MO, April 6–10, 1984. Chairman, John L. Burns; national director, William R. Bricker. Headquarters: 771 First Ave., New York, NY 10017.

Boy Scouts of America. Membership: total youth members and leaders—4,542,533 in 413 local councils. Biennial meeting: Salt Lake City, UT, May 25, 1984. President, Edward C. Joullian III; chief scout executive, J. L. Tarr. National office: 1325 Walnut Hill Lane, Irving, TX 75062-1296.

Camp Fire, Inc. Membership: 500,000 boys and girls in more than 35,000 communities. President, Evelyn deGhetaldi (Evelyn Ballard, M.D.). Headquarters: 4601 Madison Ave., Kansas City, MO 64112.

Canadian Library Association. Membership: 4,050 personal, 1000 institutional, 5,050 total. 1984 Annual conference: Toronto, Ont. Executive director, Paul Kitchen. Headquarters: 151 Sparks St., Ottawa, Ont. K1P 5E3.

Canadian Medical Assocation. Membership: 37,000. Annual meeting: Edmonton, Alberta, Aug. 20–24, 1984. Secretary General, B.E. Freamo. Address: 1867 Alta Vista Drive, Ottawa, Ontario K1G 0G8, Canada.

Chamber of Commerce of the United States of America. Membership: approximately 4,000 trade associations and local and state chambers, approximately 212,000 business members. Convention: Washington, DC, April 29–May 3, 1984. President, Richard Lesher; chairman of the board, Edwin Dodd. Headquarters: 1615 H St. NW, Washington, DC 20062.

Common Cause. Membership: 250,000. Chairman, Archibald Cox. Headquarters: 2030 M St. NW, Washington, DC 20036.

Consumers Union of United States, Inc. Executive director, Rhoda H. Karpatkin. Headquarters: 256 Washington St., Mount Vernon, NY 10550.

Council of Better Business Bureaus. Membership: 1,000. Headquarters: 1515 Wilson Blvd., Suite 300, Arlington, VA 22209.

Council on Foreign Relations, Inc. Membership: 2,195. Annual meeting: New York City, fall 1984. President, Winston Lord. Headquarters: 58 E. 68th St., New York, NY 10021.

Daughters of the American Revolution (National Society). Membership: 210,000 in 3,150 chapters. Continental Congress: Washington, DC, April 16–20, 1984. President general, Mrs. Walter Hughey King. Headquarters: 1776 D St. NW, Washington, DC 20006.

Esperanto League for North America. Membership: 750. President, Thomas A. Goldman. Headquarters: P.O. Box 1129, El Cerrito, CA 94530.

Foreign Policy Association. President, William E. Schaufele, Jr. Headquarters: 205 Lexington Ave., New York, NY 10016.

Freemasonry, Ancient Accepted Scottish Rite of (Northern Masonic Jurisdiction): Supreme Council, 33°. Membership: 487, 273 in 113 valleys. Sovereign grand commander, Stanley F. Maxwell. Headquarters: 33 Marrett Rd., Lexington, MA 02173.

Freemasonry, Ancient and Accepted Scottish Rite of (Southern Jurisdiction): Supreme Council, 33°. Membership: 660,000 in 219 affiliated groups. Sovereign grand commander, Henry C. Clausen. Headquarters: 1733 16th St. NW, Washington, DC 20009.

Future Farmers of America. Membership: 465,000 in 50 state associations. National FFA Convention: Kansas City, MO, Nov. 8–10, 1984. Executive secretary, Coleman Harris. Headquarters: Box 15160, Alexandria, VA 22309.

Gamblers Anonymous. Membership: 6,500. National executive secretary, James J. Zeysing. Headquarters: 2703A W. Eighth St., Los Angeles, CA 90005.

Garden Club of America, The. Membership: 15,000 in 185 clubs. Annual meeting: Nashville, TN, April 25–28, 1984. President, Mrs. Niels W. Johnsen. Headquarters: 598 Madison Ave., New York, NY 10022.

General Federation of Women's Clubs. Membership: 500,000 in 11,000 U.S. clubs and 10,000,000 worldwide. President, Juanita M. Bryant. Headquarters: 1734 N St. NW, Washington, DC 20036.

Geological Society of America. Membership: 14,500. President, Paul A. Bailly; executive director, F. Michael Wahl. Headquarters: 3300 Penrose Place, P.O. Box 9140, Boulder, CO 80301.

Girl Scouts of the U.S.A. Membership: 2,819,000. National president, Mrs. Orville L. Freeman; national executive director, Frances R. Hesselbein. Headquarters: 830 Third Ave., New York, NY 10022.

Humane Society of the United States. Membership: approximately 200,000. Annual convention: San Diego, CA, October 1984. President, John A. Hoyt. Headquarters: 2100 L St., NW, Washington, DC 20037.

Institute of Electrical and Electronics Engineers, Inc. Membership: 234,000. President, Richard J. Gowen. Headquarters: 345 E. 47 Street, New York, NY 10017.

Jewish War Veterans of the U.S.A. Membership: 100,000 in 750 units. 89th Annual national convention: Arlington, VA, Aug. 25–Sept. 3, 1984. National commander, Stanley Zwaik; national executive director, Harris B. Stone. Headquarters: 1712 New Hampshire Ave. NW, Washington, DC 20009.

Kiwanis International. Membership: 300,000 in 8,000 clubs in U.S. and abroad. President, Aubrey E. Irby. Headquarters: 3636 Woodview Trace, Indianapolis, IN 46268.

Knights of Columbus. Membership: 1,374,460. Supreme knight, Virgil C. Dechant. Headquarters: Columbus Plaza, New Haven, CT 06507.

Knights of Pythias, Supreme Lodge. Membership: 106,965 in 1,165 subordinate lodges. Supreme chancellor, Joseph Kalish. Office: 47 N. Grant St., Stockton, CA 95202.

League of Women Voters of the U.S. Membership: 111,200. President, Dorothy S. Ridings. Headquarters: 1730 M St. NW, Washington, DC 20036.

Lions Clubs International. Membership: 1,350,000 in 36,300 clubs in 157 countries and areas. Annual convention: San Francisco, CA, July 4–7, 1984. President, James M. Fowler. Headquarters: 300 22nd St., Oak Brook, IL 60570.

March of Dimes Birth Defects Foundation. Membership: 763 chapters. President, Charles L. Massey. Headquarters: 1275 Mamaroneck Ave., White Plains, NY 10605.

Mental Health Association. Membership: 800 state and local organizations. Headquarters: 1800 N. Kent St., Arlington, VA 22209.

Modern Language Association of America. Membership: 26,000. Annual convention: Washington, DC, Dec. 27–30, 1984. President, Carolyn G. Heilbrun. Headquarters: 62 Fifth Ave., New York, NY 10011.

National Academy of Sciences. Membership: approximately 1,344. Annual meeting: Washington, DC, Apr. 29–May 2, 1984. President, Frank Press. Headquarters: 2101 Constitution Ave. NW, Washington, DC 20418.

National Association for the Advancement of Colored People. Membership: 400,000 in 1,700 branches and 500 units. National convention: Kansas City, MO, July 1984. President, James Kemp; board chairman, Margaret Bush Wilson; executive director, Benjamin L. Hooks. Headquarters: 186 Remsen St., Brooklyn Heights, NY 11201.

National Association of Manufacturers. Membership: 13,200. President, Alexander B. Trowbridge. Headquarters: 1776 F St. NW, Washington, DC 20006.

National Audubon Society. Membership: 500,000. President, R.W. Peterson. Headquarters: 950 Third Ave., New York, NY 10022.

National Committee for the Prevention of Child Abuse. Executive director, Anne H. Cohn. Headquarters: 332 S. Michigan Ave., Suite 1250, Chicago, IL 60604.

National Conference of Christians and Jews, Inc. Membership: 82 regional offices. President, Jacqueline G. Wexler. Headquarters: 43 W. 57th St., New York, NY 10019.

National Council of the Churches of Christ in the U.S.A. Membership: 31 Protestant, Anglican, and Orthodox denominations. General secretary, Claire Randall. Headquarters: 475 Riverside Dr., New York, NY 10115.

National Council on the Aging, Inc. Membership: 5,000. Executive director, Jack Ossofsky. Headquarters: 600 Maryland Ave. SW, West Wing 100, Washington, DC 20024.

National Easter Seal Society, Inc. Annual conference: Denver, CO, mid-Nov. 1984. President, Michael Smith. Headquarters: 2023 West Ogden Ave., Chicago, IL 60612.

National Education Association of the U.S. Membership: 1,687,697, with units in every state, and 12,389 local affiliates. Annual convention: Minneapolis, MN, July 1984. President, Mary Hatwood Futrell. Headquarters: 1201 16th St. NW, Washington, DC 20036.

National Federation of Business and Professional Women's Clubs, Inc. Membership: 160,000 in 3,700 clubs. President, Polly Madenwald. Headquarters: 2012 Massachusetts Ave. NW, Washington, DC 20036.

National Federation of Independent Business, Inc. Membership: 560,000. President, Wilson S. Johnson. Headquarters: 150 W. 20th

Ave., San Mateo, CA 94403. Washington Office: 600 Maryland Ave. SW, Suite 695, Washington, DC 20024.

National Federation of Music Clubs. Membership: 500,000 in 4,300 clubs and 12 national affiliates. President, Mrs. Dwight D. Robinson. Headquarters: 1336 North Delaware St., Indianapolis, IN 46202.

National Fire Protection Association. Membership: 32,000. Annual meeting: New Orleans, May 21–24, 1984; fall meeting: San Diego, Nov. 12–14, 1984. President, Robert W. Grant. Headquarters: Batterymarch Park, Quincy, MA 02269.

National Organization for Women. Membership: 250,000 in 800 local groups. President, Judy Goldsmith. Headquarters: 425 13th St NW, Suite 723, Washington, DC 20004.

National PTA (National Parent-Teacher Association). Membership: 5,300,000 in 25,000 local units. National convention: Las Vegas, NV, June 17–20, 1984. President, Elaine Stienkemeyer. Headquarters: 700 N. Rush St., Chicago, IL 60611.

National Safety Council. Membership: 12,500. Executive vice-president and acting president, T. C. Gilchrest. Headquarters: 444 N. Michigan Ave., Chicago, IL 60611.

National Urban League, Inc. President, John E. Jacob. Headquarters: 500 E. 62nd St., New York, NY 10021.

National Woman's Christian Temperance Union. Membership: approximately 250,000 in 6,000 local unions. National convention: Little Rock, AR, August 1984. President, Mrs. Kermit S. Edgar. Headquarters: 1730 Chicago Ave., Evanston, IL 60201.

Parents Without Partners. Membership: 215,000. International convention: New Orleans, LA, July 3–8, 1984. Executive director, Conrad Scheetz. International Office: 7910 Woodmont Ave., Suite 1000, Bethesda, MD 20814.

Phi Beta Kappa. Membership: 380,000. Secretary, Kenneth M. Greene. Headquarters: 1811 Q St. NW, Washington, DC 20009.

Photographic Society of America. Membership: 16,200. President, Henry W. Greenhood. Headquarters: 2005 Walnut St., Philadelphia, PA 19103.

Planned Parenthood Federation of America, Inc. (Planned Parenthood—World Population). Membership: 188 U.S. affiliates. President, Faye Wattleton; chairperson of the Federation, Jean Mahoney. Headquarters: 810 Seventh Ave., New York, NY 10019.

Rotary International. Membership: 919,500 in 20,171 clubs functioning in 157 countries and geographical regions. International convention: Birmingham, West Midlands, England, June 3–7, 1984. General secretary, Herbert A. Pigman. Headquarters: 1600 Ridge Ave., Evanston, IL 60201.

Salvation Army, The. Membership: 414,999. National commander, Norman Marshall. National headquarters: 799 Bloomfield Ave., Verona, NJ 07044.

Special Libraries Association. Membership: 11,500. Annual conference: New York, NY, 1984. President, Pat Molholt. Headquarters: 235 Park Ave. S., New York, NY 10003.

United Dairy Industry Association (including American Dairy Association, Dairy Research Inc., National Dairy Council). Annual convention: San Antonio, TX, March 28–31, 1984. Chief executive officer, John W. Sliter. Headquarters: Dairy Center, 6300 N. River Rd., Rosemont, IL 60018.

United States Jaycees. Membership: 275,000 in 7,000 affiliated chapters. Annual meeting: Atlanta, GA, June 18–21, 1984. President, Thomas F. Bussa of Ladd, IL. Headquarters: P.O. Box 7, Tulsa, OK 74121.

United Way of America. Service organization for more than 2,200 autonomous local United Way organizations. 1984 Volunteer leaders conference: New York, NY, Apr. 29–May 1, 1984. Chairman of the board of governors, Robert A. Beck. Headquarters: United Way Plaza, Alexandria, VA 22314.

U.S. Metric Association. Membership: 3,500. President, Valerie Antoine. Headquarters: 10245 Andasol Ave., Northridge, CA 91325.

Veterans of Foreign Wars of the United States. Membership: V.F.W. and Auxiliary 2,650,000. Commander-in-chief, Clifford G. Olson, Jr. Headquarters: V.F.W. Building, Broadway at 34th St., Kansas City, MO 64111.

World Council of Churches (U.S. Conference). Membership: 27 churches or denominations in U.S. Moderator, Cynthia Wedel. Headquarters: 150, route de Ferney, 1211 Geneva 20, Switzerland. New York Office: 475 Riverside Dr., Room 1062, New York, NY 10115.

YMCA of the USA. Membership: 10,926,761 in 1,855 associations. Board chairman, L. Stanton Williams. Headquarters: 101 North Wacker Dr., Chicago, IL 60606.

YWCA of the USA. Members and participants: approximately 2,500,000. President, Jewel Freeman Graham. Headquarters: 135 W. 50th St., New York, NY 10020.

Zionist Organization of America. Membership: 130,000 in 600 districts. President, Alleck A. Resnick; executive vice-president, Paul Flacks. Headquarters: ZOA House, 4 E. 34th St., New York, NY 10016.

Contributors

ABRAM, MORRIS B., Chairman, President's Commission for the Study of Ethical Problems in Medicine and Biomedical and Behavioral Research (1979–83): ETHICS AND MODERN MEDICINE

ADRIAN, CHARLES R., Professor of Political Science, University of California, Riverside; Coauthor, *Governing Urban America:* BIOGRAPHY—*George Deukmejian;* CALIFORNIA; LOS ANGELES; SAN FRANCISCO

ALEXANDER, ROBERT J., Professor of Economics and Political Science, Rutgers University: BOLIVIA; ECUADOR; GUYANA; URUGUAY

AMBRE, AGO, Economist, Bureau of Economic Analysis, U.S. Department of Commerce: INDUSTRIAL REVIEW

BARMASH, ISADORE, Business Writer, *The New York Times;* Author, *More Than They Bargained For—The Rise and Fall of Korvettes* and *The Chief Executives:* RETAILING

BARNHART, R. A., Administrator, U.S. Federal Highway Administration: TRANSPORTATION—*The Highway—An Update*

BATRA, PREM P., Professor of Biochemistry, Wright State University: BIOCHEMISTRY

BAUM, LAWRENCE, Associate Professor of Political Science, Ohio State University; Author, *The Supreme Court:* LAW—*The Overburdened U.S. Supreme Court*

BECK, KAY, School of Urban Life, Georgia State University: GEORGIA

BERGEN, DANIEL P., Professor, Graduate Library School, University of Rhode Island, Kingston, RI: LIBRARIES

BERLIN, MICHAEL J., United Nations Correspondent, *New York Post* and *The Washington Post:* UNITED NATIONS

BEST, JOHN, Chief, *Canada World News,* Ottawa: NEW BRUNSWICK; PRINCE EDWARD ISLAND; QUEBEC

BITTON-JACKSON, LIVIA E., Professor of Judaic and Hebraic Studies, Herbert H. Lehman College, City University of New York; Author, *Elli: Coming of Age in the Holocaust:* ISRAEL; RELIGION—*Judaism*

BÖDVARSSON, HAUKUR, Free-lance Journalist, Reykjavik, Iceland: ICELAND

BOLUS, JIM, Sports Department, *The Louisville Times;* Author, *Run for the Roses:* SPORTS—*Horse Racing*

BOND, DONOVAN H., Professor Emeritus of Journalism, West Virginia University: WEST VIRGINIA

BOULAY, HARVEY, Senior Administrator, Rogerson House; Author, *The Twilight Cities:* BOSTON; MASSACHUSETTS

BOYD, GERALD J., Wine Writer and Critic; Author, American wine section, *Harvey's Pocket Guide to Wine:* WINE

BRAMMER, DANA B., Associate Director, Bureau of Governmental Research, University of Mississippi: MISSISSIPPI

BRANDHORST, L. CARL, Associate Professor of Geography, Western Oregon State College, Monmouth, OR: OREGON

BURKS, ARDATH W., Professor Emeritus of Asian Studies, Rutgers University; Author, *Japan: Profile of a Post-industrial Power:* BIOGRAPHY—*Yasuhiro Nakasone;* JAPAN

BUSH, GRAHAM W. A., Associate Professor of Political Studies, University of Auckland, New Zealand; Author, *Local Government & Politics in New Zealand:* NEW ZEALAND

BUTWELL, RICHARD, Vice President for Academic Affairs and Professor of Political Science, University of South Dakota, Vermillion, SD; Author, *Southeast Asia, a Political Introduction, Southeast Asia Today and Tomorrow, U Nu of Burma,* and *Foreign Policy and the Developing State:* ASIA; BURMA; LAOS; PHILIPPINES

CALABRIA, PAT, Sports Department, *Newsday,* Long Island, NY: SPORTS—*Ice Hockey*

CARLYLE-GORDGE, PETER, Free-lance Writer and Broadcaster, Winnipeg, Manitoba: MANITOBA

CHALMERS, JOHN W., Concordia College, Edmonton, Alberta; Editor, *Alberta Diamond Jubilee Anthology:* ALBERTA

CLARKE, JAMES W., Professor of Political Science, University of Arizona: ARIZONA

COHEN, SIDNEY, Clinical Professor of Psychiatry, UCLA School of Medicine; Author, *The Alcohol Abuse Problems, The Beyond Within: The LSD Story, The Drug Dilemma,* and *The Substance Abuse Problems:* DRUGS AND DRUG ABUSE

COLE, GORDON H., Senior Staff Associate, George Meany Center for Labor Studies: LABOR

COLE, JOHN N., Contributing Editor, *Maine Times;* Author, *From the Ground Up, Countryside/Cityside,* and *In Maine:* MAINE

COLLINS, BOB, Sports Editor, *The Indianapolis Star:* SPORTS—*Auto Racing*

COMMANDAY, ROBERT, Music Critic, *San Francisco Chronicle:* MUSIC—*Classical*

CONRADT, DAVID P., Professor of Political Science, University of Florida; Author, *Germany at the Polls, The German Polity,* and *The West German Party System:* GERMANY

CORLEW, ROBERT E., Dean, School of Liberal Arts, Middle Tennessee State University: TENNESSEE

CORNWELL, ELMER E., JR., Professor of Political Science, Brown University: RHODE ISLAND

CUNNIFF, JOHN, Business News Analyst, The Associated Press; Author, *How to Stretch Your Dollar:* HOUSING; UNITED STATES—*The Economy*

CUNNINGHAM, PEGGY, Staff Reporter, *Baltimore News American:* MARYLAND

CURRIER, CHET, Financial Writer, The Associated Press: STOCKS AND BONDS

CURTIS, L. PERRY, JR., Professor of History, Brown University: IRELAND

DANIELS, ROBERT V., Professor of History, University of Vermont: VERMONT

DARBY, JOSEPH W., III, Reporter, *The Times-Picayune/States-Item:* LOUISIANA

DE GREGORIO, GEORGE, Sports Department, *The New York Times;* Author, *Joe DiMaggio, An Informal Biography:* SPORTS—*Boxing, Ice Skating, Skiing, Swimming, Track and Field*

DELZELL, CHARLES F., Professor of History, Vanderbilt University; Author, *Italy in the Twentieth Century:* BIOGRAPHY—*Benedetto Craxi;* ITALY

DENNIS, LARRY, Senior Editor, *Golf Digest;* Coauthor, *How to Become a Complete Golfer:* SPORTS—*Golf*

DIETERICH, H. R., Professor, History/American Studies, University of Wyoming, Laramie: WYOMING

DRACHKOVITCH, MILORAD M., Senior Fellow, The Hoover Institution on War, Revolution and Peace, Stanford University; Author, *U.S. Aid to Yugoslavia and Poland:* YUGOSLAVIA

DRIGGS, DON W., Professor of Political Science, University of Nevada; Coauthor, *The Nevada Constitution: Its Origin and Growth:* NEVADA

DUFF, ERNEST A., Professor of Political Science, Randolph-Macon Women's College; Author, *Agrarian Reform in Colombia:* COLOMBIA

DURNIAK, ANTHONY, Data Processing Editor, *Business Week:* COMPUTERS

DUROSKA, LUD, *The New York Times;* Author/editor, *Football Rules in Pictures, Great Pro Quarterbacks,* and *Great Pro Running Backs:* SPORTS—*Football, The New USFL*

DURRENCE, J. LARRY, Department of History and Political Science, Florida Southern College; Mayor of Lakeland, FL: FLORIDA

EINFRANK, AARON R., Free-lance Foreign Correspondent, Specialist in the Middle East, Third World, and Soviet Affairs: ENERGY—*OPEC: A New Appraisal;* IRAN; IRAQ; THIRD WORLD

ELKINS, ANN M., Fashion Director, *Good Housekeeping Magazine:* FASHION

ENGEL, MARK, Managing Editor, *Basketball Weekly:* SPORTS—*Basketball*

ENSTAD, ROBERT H., Writer, *Chicago Tribune:* BIOGRAPHY—*Harold Washington;* CHICAGO; ILLINOIS

ETCHESON, WARREN W., Graduate School of Business Administration, University of Washington: WASHINGTON

EWEGEN, BOB, Editorial Writer, *The Denver Post:* COLORADO

FAGEN, M. D., Bell Telephone Laboratories (retired); Editor, *A History of Engineering and Science in the Bell System,* Vols. I and II: COMMUNICATION TECHNOLOGY; COMMUNICATION TECHNOLOGY—*New Telephone Equipment and Services*

FRANCIS, DAVID R., Business Editor, *The Christian Science Monitor:* INTERNATIONAL TRADE AND FINANCE; INTERNATIONAL TRADE AND FINANCE—*The World Debt*

FRIIS, ERIK J., Editor-Publisher, *The Scandinavian-American Bulletin;* Author, *The American-Scandinavian Foundation 1910–1960: A Brief History:* DENMARK; FINLAND

GAILEY, HARRY A., Professor of History and Coordinator of African Studies, San Jose State University, California: BIOGRAPHY—*Alhaji Shehu Shagari;* CHAD; GHANA; NIGERIA

GARFIELD, ROBERT, Associate Professor of History, Co-Director, Afro-American Studies Program, De Paul University, Chicago, IL; Editor, *Readings in World Civilizations:* KENYA; TANZANIA; UGANDA

GEIS, GILBERT, Professor, Program in Social Ecology, University of California, Irvine; Author, *Man, Crime and Society:* CRIME; CRIME—*The Crackdown on Drunk Driving*

GJESTER, THØR, Editor, *Økonomisk Revy,* Oslo: NORWAY

GOODMAN, DONALD, Associate Professor of Sociology, John Jay College of Criminal Justice, City University of New York: PRISONS

GORDON, MAYNARD M., Editor, *Motor News Analysis:* AUTOMOBILES

GRAYSON, GEORGE W., Professor of Government, College of William and Mary: BRAZIL; PORTUGAL; SPAIN

GREEN, MAUREEN, British Author and Journalist: GREAT BRITAIN—*The Arts;* LONDON

GREGORY, BARBARA J., Associate Editor, *The Numismatist:* COINS AND COIN COLLECTING

GROSS, KENNETH, Columnist, New York City Bureau, *Newsday:* NEW YORK CITY

GROTH, ALEXANDER J., Professor of Political Science, University of California, Davis; Author, *People's Poland: Government and Politics:* POLAND

GRUBERG, MARTIN, Professor of Political Science, University of Wisconsin, Oshkosh: LAW

HAKKARINEN, IDA, Research Meteorologist, Severe Storms Research Program, Support Group GSFC, General Software Corporation: METEOROLOGY—*The Weather Year*

HAND, SAMUEL B., Professor of History, University of Vermont: VERMONT

HARVEY, ROSS M., Assistant Director of Information, Government of the Northwest Territories: NORTHWEST TERRITORIES

HATHORN, RAMON, Associate Professor of French, University of Guelph, Guelph, Ontario: LITERATURE—*Canadian Literature: French*

HAYES, KIRBY M., Professor of Food Science and Nutrition, University of Massachusetts: FOOD

HEADY, EARL O., Distinguished Professor of Agricultural Economics, Iowa State University; Author, *Economics of Agricultural Production and Resource* and *Agricultural Policies Under Economic Development:* AGRICULTURE

HECHINGER, FRED M., President, The New York Times Company Foundation, Inc.; Educational Columnist, *The New York Times:* PUBLIC EDUCATION IN AMERICA—*Calls for Reform*

HELMREICH, E. C., Thomas B. Reed Professor of History and Political Science, Bowdoin College, Bowdoin, ME; Author, *The German Churches Under Hitler: Background, Struggle, and Epilogue:* AUSTRIA

HELMREICH, PAUL C., William C. H. and Elsie D. Prentice Professor of History, Wheaton College, Norton, MA: SWITZERLAND

HENBERG, MARVIN, Department of Philosophy, University of Idaho: IDAHO

HENDERSON, JIM, Vice President, Public Relations, Team America; Former Publisher, *Annual Soccer Guide:* SPORTS—*Soccer*

HENRIKSEN, THOMAS H., Research Fellow, The Hoover Institution on War, Revolution and Peace, Stanford, CA; Author, *Mozambique: A History:* ZAIRE

HOGGART, SIMON, Political Writer, *The Observer,* London: GREAT BRITAIN

HOOVER, HERBERT T., Professor of History, University of South Dakota: SOUTH DAKOTA

HOPKO, THE REV. THOMAS, Assistant Professor, St. Vladimir's Orthodox Theological Seminary, Crestwood, NY: RELIGION—*Orthodox Eastern*

HOYT, CHARLES K., Associate Editor, *Architectural Record;* Author, *More Places for People:* THE NEW TALL BUILDINGS; ARCHITECTURE

HULBERT, DAN, *The Dallas Times-Herald:* TELEVISION AND RADIO

HULL, RICHARD W., Associate Professor of African History, New York University; Author, *Southern Africa: Civilization in Turmoil, Modern Africa: Change and Continuity,* and *African Cities and Towns Before the European Conquest:* AFRICA

HUME, ANDREW, Free-lance Writer/Photographer; Former Reporter, *The Whitehorse (Yukon) Star;* Author, *The Yukon:* YUKON

HUTH, JOHN F., JR., Free-lance Writer; Former Reporter, *The Plain Dealer,* Cleveland: OHIO

JAFFE, HERMAN J., Department of Anthropology and Archaeology, Brooklyn College, City University of New York: ANTHROPOLOGY

JENNINGS, PETER, Anchor and Senior Editor, ABC's "World News Tonight": THE YEAR IN REVIEW

JEWELL, MALCOLM E., Professor of Political Science, University of Kentucky; Coauthor, *Kentucky Politics:* KENTUCKY

JOHNSTON, ROBERT L., Editor, *The Catholic Review,* Baltimore, MD: BIOGRAPHY—*Joseph Cardinal Bernardin;* RELIGION—*Roman Catholicism*

JOHNSTONE, J. K., Professor of English, University of Saskatchewan; Fellow of the Royal Society of Literature; Author, *The Bloomsbury Group:* LITERATURE—*English*

JONES, H. G., Curator, North Carolina Collection, University of North Carolina Library: NORTH CAROLINA

JOSEPH, LOU, Senior Science Writer, Hill and Knowlton: MEDICINE AND HEALTH—*Dentistry*

KARNES, THOMAS L., History Professor, Arizona State University; Author, *Latin American Policy of the United States* and *Failure of Union: Central America 1824–1960:* BIOGRAPHY—*Richard B. Stone;* CENTRAL AMERICA

KASH, DON E., George Lynn Cross Research Professor of Political Science, University of Oklahoma; Coauthor, *Our Energy Future* and *Energy Under the Oceans:* ENERGY

KEHR, ERNEST A., Stamp News Bureau; Author, *The Romance of Stamp Collecting:* STAMPS AND STAMP COLLECTING

KIMBALL, LORENZO K., Professor of Political Science, University of Utah: UTAH

KIMBELL, CHARLES L., Senior Foreign Mineral Specialist, United States Bureau of Mines: STATISTICAL AND TABULAR DATA—*World Mineral and Metal Production*

KING, PETER J., Associate Professor of History; Carleton University, Ottawa: ONTARIO; OTTAWA

KIRKPATRICK, LYMAN B., JR., Professor Emeritus, Brown University; Author, *The U.S. Intelligence Community:* ESPIONAGE

KISSELGOFF, ANNA, Chief Dance Critic, *The New York Times:* DANCE; OBITUARIES—*George Balanchine*

LAI, CHUEN-YAN DAVID, Associate Professor of Geography, University of Victoria, B.C.: HONG KONG

LAURENT, PIERRE-HENRI, Professor of History, Tufts University; Adjunct Professor of Diplomatic History, Fletcher School of Law and Diplomacy: BELGIUM

LAWRENCE, ROBERT M., Professor of Political Science, Colorado State University; Coauthor, *Arms Control and Disarmament: Promise and Practice* and *Nuclear Proliferation: Phase II:* ARMS CONTROL; MILITARY AFFAIRS

LEE, STEWART M., Chairman, Department of Economics and Business Administration, Geneva College, Beaver Falls, PA; Coauthor, *Economics for Consumers;* Editor, *Newsletter,* American Council on Consumer Interests: BUSINESS AND CORPORATE AFFAIRS; CONSUMER AFFAIRS

LEVINE, LOUIS, Department of Biology, City College of New York; Author, *Biology for a Modern Society* and *Biology of the Gene:* GENETICS; MICROBIOLOGY

LEVITAN, SAR A., Research Professor of Economics and Director of the Center for Social Policy Studies, The George Washington University; Author, *Second Thoughts on Work:* LABOR—*Job Search and Retraining*

LEVITT, MORRIS J., Professor, Department of Political Science, Howard University; Coauthor, *Of, By and For the People: State and Local Government and Politics:* WASHINGTON, DC

LEWIS, JEROME R., Director for Public Administration, College of Urban Affairs and Public Policy, University of Delaware: DELAWARE

LIDDLE, R. WILLIAM, Professor of Political Science, The Ohio State University; Author, *Political Participation in Modern Indonesia:* INDONESIA

LINDAHL, MAC, Free-lance Writer and Translator: SWEDEN

LITSKY, FRANK, Sportswriter, *The New York Times;* Author, *New York Times Official Sports Record Book (1965–1969)* and *Superstars:* OBITUARIES: *Paul (Bear) Bryant;* SPORTS—*Pan American Games, Yachting*

LOBRON, BARBARA, Writer, Editor, Photographer; Former Copy Editor, *Camera Arts:* PHOTOGRAPHY

LOCHHEAD, MARY, Regina Public Library, Regina, Saskatchewan: SASKATCHEWAN

LYLES, JEAN CAFFEY, Associate Editor, *The Christian Century;* Author, *A Practical Vision of Christian Unity:* RELIGION—*Protestantism*

MABRY, DONALD J., Professor of History, Mississippi State University; Coauthor, *Neighbors—Mexico and the United States:* MEXICO

McALOON, THOMAS P., III, Managing Editor, *Iron and Steelmaker* magazine: INDUSTRIAL REVIEW—*The Stagnant U.S. Steel Industry*

McCORQUODALE, SUSAN, Associate Professor of Political Science, Memorial University of Newfoundland: NEWFOUNDLAND

McGILL, DAVID A., Professor of Marine Science, U.S. Coast Guard Academy, New London, CT: OCEANOGRAPHY

MADIER, MONIQUE, Free-lance Writer and Editor, Paris, France: FRANCE

MARCOPOULOS, GEORGE J., Associate Professor of History, Tufts University, Medford, MA: CYPRUS; GREECE; TURKEY

MAREN, MICHAEL, Assistant Editor, *Africa Report,* The African-American Institute: ALGERIA; MOROCCO; SUDAN; TUNISIA

MASOTTI, LOUIS H., Professor of Political Science, Urban Affairs and Policy Research, Northwestern University, Evanston, IL; Author, *The New Urban Politics* and *The City in Comparative Perspective:* CITIES AND URBAN AFFAIRS; INDUSTRIAL REVIEW—*High-Tech Industry*

MAYNES, CHARLES W., Editor, *Foreign Policy* magazine: UNITED STATES—*Foreign Affairs;* UNITED STATES—*The War Powers Resolution*

MEYER, EDWARD H., President and Chairman of the Board, Grey Advertising Inc.: ADVERTISING

MICHAELIS, PATRICIA A., Curator of Manuscripts, Kansas State Historical Society: KANSAS

MIRE, JOSEPH, Former Executive Director, National Institute for Labor Education: LABOR

MITCHELL, ALISON, Chief, Albany Bureau, *Newsday:* BIOGRAPHY—*Mario Cuomo;* NEW YORK STATE

MITCHELL, GARY, Professor of Physics, North Carolina State University, Raleigh: PHYSICS

MORTON, DESMOND, Professor of History, University of Toronto; Author, *A Peculiar Kind of Politics, Canada and War,* and *Working People: An Illustrated History of Canadian Labour:* BIOGRAPHY—*Brian Mulroney;* CANADA

MULLINER, K., Assistant to the Director of Libraries, Ohio University; Coeditor, *Southeast Asia, An Emerging Center of World Influence?* and *Malaysian Studies:* MALAYSIA; SINGAPORE

MUNSCH, VIRGINIA, Reporter and Assistant Editor, *The Richmond Times-Dispatch,* Richmond, VA: VIRGINIA

MURPHY, ROBERT F., *The Hartford Courant:* CONNECTICUT

MURRAY, JAMES R., Policy Research Corporation: INDUSTRIAL REVIEW—*High-Tech Industry*

NADLER, PAUL S., Professor of Finance, Rutgers University; Author, *Commercial Banking in the Economy* and *Paul Nadler Writes About Banking:* BANKING

NAFTALIN, ARTHUR, Professor of Public Affairs, Hubert H. Humphrey Institute of Public Affairs, University of Minnesota: MINNESOTA

NEUMANN, JAMES, *The Forum,* Fargo, ND: NORTH DAKOTA

NOLAN, WILLIAM C., Professor of Political Science, Southern Arkansas University: ARKANSAS

OCHSENWALD, WILLIAM L., Associate Professor of History, Virginia Polytechnic Institute, Blacksburg, VA; Author, *The Hijaz Railroad;* Coeditor, *Nationalism in a Non-National State: The Dissolution of the Ottoman Empire:* SAUDI ARABIA

O'CONNOR, ROBERT E., Associate Professor of Political Science, Pennsylvania State University: PENNSYLVANIA; PHILADELPHIA

O'MEARA, PATRICK, Director, African Studies Program, Indiana University, Bloomington, IN; Coeditor, *Southern Africa: The Continuing Crisis* and *International Politics in Southern Africa:* SOUTH AFRICA; ZIMBABWE

PALMER, NORMAN D., Emeritus Professor of Political Science and South Asian Studies, University of Pennsylvania; Author, *Elections and Political Development: The South Asian Experience:* INDIA; SRI LANKA

PANO, NICHOLAS C., Professor of History, Western Illinois University; Author, *The People's Republic of Albania:* ALBANIA

PARDES, HERBERT, Director, National Institute of Mental Health: MEDICINE AND HEALTH—*Mental Health*

PARKER, FRANKLIN, Benedum Professor of Education, West Virginia University; Author, *Battle of the Books, British Schools and Ours,* and *U.S. Higher Education: A Guide to Education Sources;* Coauthor, *Crucial Issues in Education:* EDUCATION; OBITUARIES—*Richard Buckminster Fuller*

PEARSON, NEALE J., Professor of Political Science, Texas Tech University, Lubbock, TX: CHILE; PERU; VENEZUELA

PERKINS, KENNETH J., Assistant Professor of History, University of South Carolina: LIBYA; RELIGION—*Islam*

PIOTROWSKI, WILLIAM, National Aeronautics and Space Administration: SPACE EXPLORATION (article written independently of NASA)

PIPPIN, LARRY L., Professor of Political Science, Elbert Covell College, University of the Pacific; Author, *The Remón Era:* ARGENTINA; GREAT BRITAIN—*The Falkland Islands: One Year After War;* PARAGUAY

PLATT, HERMANN K., Professor of History, Saint Peter's College, Jersey City: NEW JERSEY

POOLE, PETER A., Author, *ASEAN in the Pacific Community, Eight Presidents and Indochina,* and *The Vietnamese in Thailand:* CAMBODIA; KOREA; THAILAND; VIETNAM

POPKIN, HENRY, Professor of English, State University of New York at Buffalo: OBITUARIES—*Tennessee Williams;* THEATER

POULLADA, LEON B., Professor of Political Science, Northern Arizona University; Author, *Reform and Rebellion in Afghanistan:* AFGHANISTAN

PYRCH, JEANNETTE, Regina Public Library, Regina, Saskatchewan: SASKATCHEWAN

QUIRK, WILLIAM H., Construction Consultant; Former North American Editor, *Construction Industry International* magazine: ENGINEERING, CIVIL

RAGUSA, ISA, Research Art Historian, Department of Art and Archaeology, Princeton University: ART

REUNING, WINIFRED, Writer, Polar Programs, National Science Foundation: POLAR RESEARCH

RICCIUTI, EDWARD R., Free-lance Writer; Author, *Audubon Society Book of Wild Animals* and *The Beachwalker's Guide:* ENVIRONMENT; ZOOS AND ZOOLOGY

RICHTER, WILLIAM L., Director, South Asia Center, Kansas State University: BANGLADESH; PAKISTAN

RIGGAN, WILLIAM, Associate Editor, *World Literature Today,* University of Oklahoma; Author, *Picaros, Madmen, Naifs, and Clowns: The Unreliable First-Person Narrator* and *Comparative Literature and Literary Theory:* LITERATURE—*World*

ROBINSON, LEIF J., Editor, *Sky & Telescope:* ASTRONOMY

ROEDER, RICHARD B., Professor of History, Montana State University: MONTANA

ROSS, RUSSELL M., Professor of Political Science, University of Iowa; Author, *Iowa Government & Administration:* IOWA

ROTHSTEIN, MORTON, Professor of History, University of Wisconsin, Madison: SOCIAL WELFARE

ROWEN, HERBERT H., Professor of History, Rutgers University; Editor, *The Low Countries in Early Modern Times: A Documentary History:* THE NETHERLANDS

ROWLETT, RALPH M., Professor of Anthropology, University of Missouri, Columbia: ARCHAEOLOGY

RUFF, NORMAN J., Assistant Professor, University of Victoria; Coauthor, *Reins of Power: Governing British Columbia:* BRITISH COLUMBIA

SALSINI, PAUL, State Editor, *The Milwaukee Journal:* WISCONSIN

SAVAGE, DAVID, Course Supervisor, Continuing Studies Department, Simon Fraser University: CANADA—*The Arts;* LITERATURE—*Canadian Literature: English*

SCHLOSSBERG, DAN, Baseball Writer; Author, *The Baseball Catalog, The Baseball Book of Why,* and *Hammerin' Hank: The Henry Aaron Story:* SPORTS—*Baseball*

SCHNAUE, FRED, Vice-President, American Association of Fund-Raising Counsel: PHILANTHROPY

SCHROEDER, RICHARD C., Washington Bureau Chief, *Vision;* Syndicated Writer, U.S. Newspapers: GRENADA—*Flash Point in the Caribbean;* CARIBBEAN; LATIN AMERICA; PUERTO RICO; REFUGEES AND IMMIGRATION; VIRGIN ISLANDS, U.S.

SCHWAB, PETER, Professor, Political Science, State University of New York at Purchase; Author, *Decision Making in Ethiopia* and *Haile Selassie I:* ETHIOPIA

SCOTT, EUGENE L., Publisher and Founder, *Tennis Week;* Author, *Bjorn Börg: My Life & Game, Tennis: Game of Motion,* and *The Tennis Experience:* SPORTS—*Tennis*

SEDITO, ELAINE, Free-lance Writer and Editor: BIOGRAPHY—*Richard Attenborough, Stephen King, Jessica Lange, Dudley Moore, Jessica Tandy;* CHILDREN; OBITUARIES—*Arthur Godfrey*

SETH, R. P., Professor of Economics, Mount Saint Vincent University, Halifax: CANADA: *The Economy;* NOVA SCOTIA

SEYBOLD, PAUL G., Professor of Chemistry and Biological Chemistry, Wright State University, Dayton, OH: CHEMISTRY

SHEPRO, CARL, Department of Political Science, University of Alaska, Fairbanks: ALASKA

SHOGAN, ROBERT, National Political Correspondent, Washington Bureau, *Los Angeles Times;* Author, *A Question of Judgment* and *Promises to Keep:* UNITED STATES—*Domestic Affairs*

SIEGEL, STANLEY E., Professor of History, University of Houston; Author, *A Political History of the Texas Republic, 1836–1845:* TEXAS

SIMMONS, MARC, Author, *Albuquerque: A Narrative History* and *New Mexico, A Bicentennial History:* NEW MEXICO

SNODSMITH, R. L., Ornamental Horticulturist: GARDENING AND HORTICULTURE

SPERA, DOMINIC, Associate Professor of Music, Indiana University; Author, *The Prestige Series—16 Original Compositions for Jazz Band:* MUSIC—*Jazz*

STENCEL, SANDRA, Director of Market Research, Congressional Quarterly: WOMEN

STERN, JEROME H., Associate Professor of English, Florida State University: LITERATURE—*American*

STERNSHER, BERNARD, Bowling Green State University; Author, *Rexford Tugwell and the New Deal:* UNITED STATES—*The New Deal Through 50 Years*

STEWART, WILLIAM H., JR., Associate Professor of Political Science, The University of Alabama; Author, *The Alabama Constitutional Commission:* ALABAMA

STOKES, WILLIAM LEE, Professor, Department of Geology and Geophysics, University of Utah; Author, *Essentials of Earth History* and *Introduction to Geology:* GEOLOGY; GEOLOGY—*Earthquake Prediction*

STOUDEMIRE, ROBERT H., Professor of Government Emeritus, University of South Carolina: SOUTH CAROLINA

STULL, CAROLYN, Free-lance Travel Writer: TRAVEL

SYLVESTER, LORNA LUTES, Associate Editor, *Indiana Magazine of History,* Indiana University, Bloomington; Editor, *No Cheap Padding: Seventy-Five Years of the Indiana Magazine of History:* INDIANA

TABORSKY, EDWARD, Professor of Government, University of Texas, Austin; Author, *Communism in Czechoslovakia, 1948–1960* and *Communist Penetration of the Third World:* CZECHOSLOVAKIA

TAFT, WILLIAM HOWARD, Professor Emeritus of Journalism, University of Missouri; Author, *American Journalism History, American Magazines for the 1980s:* PUBLISHING

TAN, CHESTER C., Department of History, New York University; Author, *The Boxer Catastrophe* and *Chinese Political Thought in the 20th Century:* CHINA; TAIWAN

TAYLOR, WILLIAM L., Professor of History, Plymouth State College, Plymouth, NH: NEW HAMPSHIRE

TEMKO, NED, Foreign Correspondent, formerly Moscow Bureau, *The Christian Science Monitor:* USSR

TESAR, JENNY, Science Writer: BIOGRAPHY—*Barbara McClintock;* MEDICINE AND HEALTH

THEISEN, CHARLES W., Assistant News Editor, *The Detroit News:* MICHIGAN

THOMPSON, O. E., Associate Professor, University of Maryland: METEOROLOGY

TOWNE, RUTH W., Professor of History, Northeast Missouri State University: MISSOURI

TURNER, ARTHUR CAMPBELL, Professor of Political Science, University of California, Riverside; Author, *Tension Areas in World Affairs;* Coauthor, *Control of Foreign Relations:* BIOGRAPHY—*Yitzhak Shamir;* EGYPT; MIDDLE EAST

TURNER, CHARLES H., Staff Writer, *The Honolulu Advertiser:* HAWAII

VAN RIPER, PAUL P., Professor and Head (retired), Department of Political Science, Texas A&M University: POSTAL SERVICE

VOLSKY, GEORGE, Center for Advanced International Studies, University of Miami: CUBA

WATTERS, ELSIE M., Director of Research, Tax Foundation, Inc.: TAXATION

WEEKS, JEANNE G., Member, American Society of Interior Designers; Coauthor, *Fabrics for Interiors:* INTERIOR DESIGN

WEISS, PAULETTE, Popular Music Editor, *Stereo Review:* MUSIC—*Popular;* RECORDINGS

WENTZ, RICHARD E., Professor of Religious Studies, Arizona State University; Author, *Saga of the American Soul:* RELIGION—*Survey, Far Eastern*

WILLARD, F. NICHOLAS, Professor, Washington, DC: JORDAN; LEBANON; SYRIA

WILLIAMS, DENNIS A., General Editor, *Newsweek:* BIOGRAPHY—*Jesse Jackson;* ETHNIC GROUPS

WILLIAMS, ERNEST W., JR., Professor of Transportation, Graduate School of Business, Columbia University; Coauthor, *Transportation and Logistics* and *Shipping Conferences in the Container Age:* TRANSPORTATION

WILLIS, F. ROY, Professor of History, University of California, Davis; Author, *Italy Chooses Europe* and *France, Germany, and the New Europe:* EUROPE

WOLF, WILLIAM, Contributing Editor, *New York* magazine; Author, *The Marx Brothers* and *The Landmark Films: The Cinema and Our Century:* MOTION PICTURES

WOOD, JOHN, Professor of Political Science, University of Oklahoma: OKLAHOMA

WOODS, GEORGE A., Children's Book Editor, *The New York Times;* Author, *Vibrations* and *Catch a Killer:* LITERATURE—*Children's*

YOUNGER, R. M., Author, *Australia and the Australians, Australia's Great River,* and *Australia! Australia! March to Nationhood:* AUSTRALIA; BIOGRAPHY—*Robert Hawke*

ZABEL, ORVILLE H., Midland Lutheran College, Fremont, NE; Professor Emeritus, Creighton University, Omaha: NEBRASKA

ZACEK, JOSEPH FREDERICK, Professor of History, State University of New York at Albany: BULGARIA; HUNGARY; RUMANIA

Index

Main article headings appear in this index as bold-faced capitals; subjects within articles appear as lower-case entries. Both the general references and the subentries should be consulted for maximum usefulness of this index. Illustrations are indexed herein. Cross references are to the entries in this index.

A

ABC: *see* American Broadcasting Company
Abortion 73, 160, 286, 312, 314, 409, 562
Abrams, Elliott 551
Abu Dhabi 80
Academy Awards (films) 161, 427
ACCIDENTS AND DISASTERS 80, 345 fol.
Acid Rain 159, 217, 243, 244, 345
Acquired Immune Deficiency Syndrome (AIDS) 340, 344
Adelman, Kenneth L. 111, 535, 546
Illus. 536
ADVERTISING 81, 429, 431
AFGHANISTAN 82, 119, 578
Espionage 51
Pakistan 408
Refugees 437, 452
Religion 439
United Nations 534
AFL-CIO: *see* American Federation of Labor-Congress of Industrial Organizations
AFRICA 85
Agriculture 94
China 178
Conservation 213
Famine 452
Refugees 437
Weather 346
See also specific countries
African National Congress (ANC) 90, 455
Agca, Mehmet Ali 151, 292
Agee, William M. 153
Agency for International Development (AID) 147, 163
AGRICULTURE 92, 228, 578
Archaeology 101
Gardening and Horticulture 234
Ahidjo, Ahmadou 88
AIDS: *see* Acquired Immune Deficiency Syndrome
Aid to Families with Dependent Children 454
Aircraft Production 268
Air Florida 557
Air Illinois 261
Airlines 152, 153, 545
Air Pollution 244, 345
Air Transportation 515, 517, 520, 521
Accidents 80, 261
Hijackings of Airplanes 193, 498, 557
History of 37, 38
See also Korean Airliner Incident
Aksyonov, Vasily 331
ALA: *see* American Library Association
ALABAMA 95, 188, 423, 500
School Prayer Law 314
ALASKA 96, 188, 215, 216, 346
ALBANIA 97, 578
ALBERTA 98
Alcohol Abuse 342
Alaska 96
See also Drinking Age; Drunk Driving
Aleksandrov, Aleksandr 459, 460
Alexander, Lamar 44, 506
Alfonsín, Raúl 205
Illus. 106
ALGERIA 98, 578, 580, 581
Morocco 362
Tunisia 522
Alia, Ramiz 97

Alicia, Hurricane 80, 347, 507
Allain, William 360
Aluminum 580
Alvarado, Anthony J. 45, 382
Alzheimer's Disease 341, 344
American Academy and Institute of Arts and Letters Awards 425, 426
American Airlines 557
American Ballet Theatre 195, 196
American Bar Association (ABA) 315
American Book Awards 327, 426
American Broadcasting Company (ABC) 503
American Civil Liberties Union (ACLU) 314
American Dance Festival, Durham, NC 196
American Express Company 495
American Federation of Labor-Congress of Industrial Organizations (AFL-CIO) 304, 306, 307, 541
American Federation of Teachers (AFT) 201
American Indians: *see* Indians, American
American Institute of Architects (AIA) Awards 103, 104
American Library Association (ALA) 321, 327
American Literature 323
King, Stephen 139
American Motors 126 fol.
American Newspaper Publishers Association 34
American Telephone & Telegraph (AT&T) 153, 183, 184, 306, 461, 492, 545
Illus. 21, 67
America's Cup Yacht Races 124, 447, 464, 488
Amtrak 521, 563
Anabolic Steroids (drugs) 482
Anaconda Minerals Company 361
Anaya, Toney 220, 380
Anderson, Maxie 379
Andreotti, Giulio 291, 292
Andropov, Yuri 83, 221, 358, 526
Illus. 244
Anemia 132
Angola 571, 89, 90, 578
Airplane Crash 80
Cuba 192
Refugees 437
Animals: *see* Zoos and Zoology
Antarctica 120, 316, 420
Meteorite 238
United Nations 533, 534
ANTHROPOLOGY 100
Anti-Ballistic Missile Treaty (1972) 547
Antigua and Barbuda 571
Antimony 580
Antinuclear Movement: *see* Peace Movement
Antisatellite Weapon System (ASAT) 111
Anti-Semitism 440
Antonov, Sergei 151, 292
ANZUS Council 124
Applebaum-Hébert Report: *see* Federal Cultural Policy Review Committee
Aquariums 569
Aquino, Benigno, Jr. 118, 412
Arab-Israeli Conflict 287
United States 546
West Bank Controversy 297
Arafat, Yasir 204, 297, 298, 319, 322, 448, 496
ARCHAEOLOGY 100
Archery 489

ARCHITECTURE 103, 114
Fuller, R. Buckminster 392
Interior Design 274
Prizes and Awards 425
Skyscrapers 64
Arctic 420
Arens, Moshe 287, 12
ARGENTINA 105, 311, 578, 579
Agriculture 94
Chile 174
Cuba 192
Falkland Islands 251
Foreign Debt 278, 279
Great Britain 249
Libya 322
Literature 331
Motor Vehicles 127
Nuclear Technology 54
Paraguay 408
Venezuela 553
Argonne National Laboratories, IL 103
Ariyoshi, George 256
ARIZONA 107, 80, 210
ARKANSAS 108
Armed Forces: *see* Military Affairs
Armenian Terrorists 232, 524
ARMS CONTROL 109, 221, 247, 356, 529, 547
Arms Control and Disarmament Agency (ACDA) 111, 535, 546
Arms Sales 289, 358
ART 112
Canada 162
Great Britain 254
Philanthropy 411
Photography 414
Prehistoric Indian Art 102
Prizes and Awards 425
Arthit Kamlang-ek 508
Artificial Heart 68, 69, 340, 552
Artificial Sweeteners 229, 344
Art Institute of Chicago, IL 414
Asbestos 580
ASEAN: *see* Association of Southeast Asian Nations
ASIA 118
Agriculture 94
Conservation 214
Drug Abuse 199
Religion 439
See also specific countries
Aspartame 229
Assad, Hafez al- 317, 495, 496
Assam, state, India 262, 437
Illus. 263
Associated Press 431
Association of Southeast Asian Nations (ASEAN) 119, 155, 296, 508
Associations: *see* Societies and Organizations
Asthma 341
ASTRONOMY 120, 461
Asylum (law) 437
AT&T: *see* American Telephone & Telegraph
Atiyeh, Victor 405
Atlanta, GA 239
Atlantic Ocean 402
Atmospheric Research 345
El Niño, Effects of 402
Atrazine (herbicide) 235
ATTENBOROUGH, Sir Richard 133
Attica Correctional Facility, NY 380
Austin, Hudson 28, 33
Illus. 33
AUSTRALIA 122, 578 fol.
Agriculture 94, 228
Archaeology 101
Fires 80
Geology 238
Hawke, Robert 137
Motor Vehicles 127
Stocks and Bonds 492
Weather 346
Australia II (yacht) 124, 447, 464, 488

AUSTRIA 125, 578, 579, 581
Literature 333
Motor Vehicles 127
AUTOMOBILES 126, 152, 268, 350, 522, 543, 545
Canada 160
Drunk Driving, 191
Iacocca, Lee 138
Japanese Exports 296
Labor 306
Safety 187, 314
Taiwan 497
Tennessee 506
Illus. 538
Auto Racing 464
Autry, James 189
Axworthy, Lloyd 159

B

B-1 Bombers 109, 538
Babbitt, Bruce E. 107
Babrak, Karmal 83, 119
Bacteria 351
Badminton 489
Bahamas 571
Bahrain 572
Baker, James 537
BALANCHINE, George 391, 195, 196
Bald Eagles 217
Baldrige, Malcolm 99, 119, 177
Ballesteros, Seve 478
Ballet: *see* Dance
Balloons 35 fol., 379
Baltimore, MD 179, 180, 338, 518
Baltimore Orioles (baseball team) 465 fol.
Banco Ambrosiano Scandal (It.) 291
BANGLADESH 129, 578, 579
Accidents and Disasters 80
Canal 211
Espionage 51
Bank for International Settlements (BIS) 106, 174, 279, 564
BANKING 129, 186, 197, 458, 506
Bloomfield IA, 281
Deregulation 545
Foreign Loans 277 fol.
Securities Services 491
Taxation 500
Bankruptcies 152, 153, 307, 314
Butcher, Jake 506
Barbados 572
Barbie, Klaus 147, 233, 441
Barite 580
Barley 578
Barnebey, Malcolm R. 165
Barnett, David H. 53
Barre, Mohammed Siad 89
Barry, Marion 558
Baryshnikov, Mikhail 195
Baseball 464, 482
Carlton, Steve 134
Basketball 468, 482
Malone, Moses 141
Basques (Eur. people) 222, 462
Baudouin, King (Belg.) 131
Bauxite 580
Beach Boys:
Illus. 76
Beagle Channel, S. Amer. 174
Beatrix, Queen (Neth.) 375
Beef 92, 229
Begin, Menahem 218, 287, 317
Bégin, Monique 158
Begun, Yosef 289
Behavior 235, 344
Beirut, Leb. 318, 319, 548
Illus. 15
Belaúnde Terry, Fernando 409, 410

Belgian National Opera 370
BELGIUM 131, 578 fol.
  Industrial Production 270
  Military Affairs 357
  Motor Vehicles 127
  Social Welfare 453
  Turkish Diplomat,
    Assassination of 523
  Zaire 566
Belize 164, 166
Bell, Terrel H. 39
  Illus. 40
Bell Laboratories 184
Bench, Johnny 467
Benin 572
Bennett, William R. 150
Bering Sea 420
Berlin, West: see West Berlin
Berlinguer, Enrico 292
BERNARDIN, Joseph Louis
  Cardinal 133, 444
Bernstein, Leonard 368
Berton, Pierre 328
Betancur Cuartas, Belisario
  181, 182
Beta Phi Mu Award 320
Bhumibol Adulyadej, King
  (Thai.) 508
Bhutan 572
Biaschina Viaduct, Switz. 210
Biathlon 489
Bible 443
BIEBER, Owen Frederick 134,
  306
  Illus. 307
Big Chill, The (film) 363, 364,
  366
Bignone, Reynaldo 105, 106
Big Pine II (mil. operation) 168,
  169
Billiards 489
Biltmore Hotel, New York, NY
  104
BIOCHEMISTRY 132
BIOGRAPHY 133
BIOMEDICAL ETHICS 68
Biotechnology 272
Birth Control 340, 452
Bishop, Arthur Gary 552
Bishop, Maurice 28, 34, 192
  Illus. 30
Biya, Paul 88
Black Americans 219, 315, 454
  Elections 179, 541
  Jackson, Jesse 139
  Maynard, Robert C. 154
  Music 373
  Virginia 556
  Illus.: Alabama March 95
  See also School
    Desegregation
Black Holes (astron.) 121
Black South Africans 90, 456
Bladder Cancer 132
BLAKE, Eubie 389
Blanchard, James J. 350
Blanton, Ray 507
Blizzards 80, 346, 347
Block, John R. 229
  Illus. 228
Bloomington Baby 71
Bluenose (schooner) 388
BLUFORD, Gulon Stewart, Jr.
  134, 459
  Illus. 460
Bob Jones University, SC 202,
  220, 312, 443, 500
  Illus. 501
Bobko, Karol J. 459
Bobsledding 489
Boddicker, Mike 465
Bolger, William F. 422
Bolívar, Simón 553
Bolivar (Venez. currency) 552
BOLIVIA 147, 80, 578 fol.
  France 233
Bond, Christopher S. 360
  Illus. 190
Bonds: see Stocks and Bonds.
Books: see Literature; Prizes
  and Awards; Publishing
Borg, Björn 486

BOSTON, MA 147, 179, 220, 339
  Election Districts 314
  Photography 414
Boston & Maine Railroad 378
Boston Early Music Festival
  368
Botha, P. W. 455, 456
Botswana 572
  Minerals 580
Bourassa, Robert 433
Bourguiba, Habib 522
Bowie, David 372
  Illus. 373
Bowling 489
Boxing (sport) 471, 482
Boyer, Ernest L. 41
Bradley, Thomas 334
Brain Death 69, 70
Brandensten, Daniel C. 459
Brandstad, Terry 281
Braniff Airways 545
Brandt, Willy 240
  Illus. 241
BRAZIL 148, 311, 578 fol.
  Accidents and Disasters 80
  Agriculture 94
  Foreign Debt 278, 279
  Gold Nugget 238
  Libya 322
  Motor Vehicles 127
  Social Welfare 452
Brennan, Joseph 336
Brennan, William 314
Bridges 210, 519
  Collapse, Connecticut 186
Bristol, VA 556
BRITISH COLUMBIA 150, 158
  fol.
Brizola, Leonel 148
Broadbent, Ed 158
Brock, William 296
Brodsky, Joseph 331
Bronx Zoo, New York, NY 569
Brooklyn Academy, New York,
  NY 196
Brooklyn Bridge, New York, NY
  382
  Illus. 74
Brooklyn Museum, New York,
  NY 414
Brown, John Y. 299
Brown, Marcia 327
Brunei 572
Bryan, Richard 376
BRYANT, Paul William (Bear)
  389
Bubonic Plague 380
Buddhism 439
Budget, U.S. 538 fol.
  Deficit 276, 492, 538, 543
  Education 201
  Food Programs 229
  Highways 519
  Libraries 320
  Military Spending 109
  Occupational Training 305
  Social Welfare 454
Building and Construction 103,
  152, 257, 268
  Ottawa 406
  San Francisco 449
  Saudia Arabia 450
  Skyscrapers 64
BULGARIA 150, 578, 579, 581
  Agriculture 94
  Italy 292
  Military Affairs 357
Bullard, G. W. 449
Buñuel, Luis 365
Burford, Anne Gorsuch 213,
  216, 536
  Illus. 215
Burger, Warren E. 313
Burger King 81
Burglaries 188
Burlington Northern Railroad
  516
BURMA 151, 578, 579
  Korea, North 302, 303
  Korean Officials, Killing of
    118, 301, 302
  United Nations 533

Burnham, Forbes 255
Burundi 572
Busbee, George 239
Bush, George 197
  Algeria 99
  Argentina 105
  Austria 125
  Italy 292
  Morocco 362
  Yugoslavia 565
  Illus. 375
BUSINESS AND CORPORATE
  AFFAIRS 152, 540, 543 fol.
  Advertising 81
  Industrial Espionage 47, 54
  Retailing 445
  Retraining of Workers 305
  Stocks and Bonds 491
  Taxation 499
Butcher, Jake 506
Byrne, Jane M. 172

C

CAB: see Civil Aeronautics
  Board
Cabañas, Roberto 484
Cabbage Patch Doll:
  Illus. 270
Cabinet (U.S.) 583
Cable Television 57 fol., 61, 63,
  365, 502, 504
Cabrillo Music Festival, Aptos,
  CA 368
Caldecott Medal 320, 327
Calder, Alexander 180
Caldera, Rafael 552
  Illus. 553
CALIFORNIA 154, 80, 236 fol.,
  346
  Capital Punishment 424
  Deukmejian, George 136
  Draft Registration 314
  Los Angeles 334
  Nuclear Power Moratorium
    315
  San Francisco 449
  Taxation 499
  Wine 559, 560
  Illus. 10, 347
Callaghan, Morley 329
Calvi, Roberto 291
CAMBODIA 155, 119, 533
  China 178
  Vietnam 554, 555
Cameroon 572, 88, 333
CANADA 156
  Advertising 82
  Agriculture 94, 578
  Archaeology 102
  Banking 130
  Caribbean 163
  Dance 196
  Economy 276
  Espionage 51
  Fishing Zones 316
  Highways 519
  Industrial Production 270,
    579
  Labor 307, 308
  Literature 328, 329
  Military Affairs 357
  Minerals 580, 581
  Ministry 159
  Motor Vehicles 127
  Mulroney, Brian 142
  Newspapers 431
  Pan American Games 482
  Postal Service 422
  Rumania 448
  Social Security 453
  Space Exploration 459, 461
  Stocks and Bonds 492
  Taxation 501
Canadian Broadcasting
  Corporation (CBC) 161
Canals 210
Cancer 132, 235, 340, 342

Cannon, Billy 335
Canoeing 489
Cape Verde 572
Capital Punishment 188, 252,
  312, 380, 424
Capitol, Washington, D.C. 558
Caramanlis, Constantine 254
Carey, Rick 485
CARIBBEAN 163, 214
Caribbean Basin Initiative
  (CBI) 34, 163 fol., 311, 432
Caribbean Common Market
  (CARICOM) 163
Carl XVI, King (Swed.):
  Illus. 494
Carlin, John 298
CARLTON, Steven Norman
  134, 466
Carner, JoAnne 478
Carter, Jimmy 239
  Briefing Papers Controversy
    537
Casey, William J. 537
  Illus. 50
Castro, Fidel 192, 548
  Illus. 265
Catalans (Eur. people) 222
Caterpillar Tractor
  Corporation 306
Catholicism 444
  Bernardine, Joseph 133
  Czechoslovakia 194
  Latin America 311
  Lutheran-Catholic Dialogue
    442
  Mansour, Sister Agnes Mary
    350
  Poland 417
  Yugoslavia 563
CBC: see Canadian
  Broadcasting Corporation
CBI: see Caribbean Basin
  Initiative
CBS: see Columbia
  Broadcasting System
Ceauşescu, Nicolae 447, 448
Cement 268, 579, 580
Censorship:
  Cable Television 365
  Government Employees 429
  Paraguay 408
  Yugoslavia 564
Central African Republic 572
CENTRAL AMERICA 164, 309,
  310
  Refugees 437
  Stone, Richard B. 144
  United Nations 533, 534
  United States 546 fol.
  See also specific countries
Central American Defense
  Council (CONDECA) 169,
  310
Central Arizona Project 107,
  210
Central Intelligence Agency
  (CIA) 169
CERN: see European Center
  for Nuclear Research
Cerro Maravilla Incident, PR
  432
Certificates of Deposit 130
Césaire, Aimé 333
Ceylon: see Sri Lanka
CHAD 170, 89
  France 233
  Libya 321, 322
  Nigeria 384
  United States 547
  Zaire 566
  Illus. 91
Chadli Benjedid 98
Chagos Archipelago, Indian
  Ocean 265
Challenger (space shuttle) 36,
  234, 459, 491
Chamoun, Camille 318
Champion Plaza Building,
  Stamford, CT 103
Charity: see Philanthropy
Charles, Prince of Wales 101,
  252, 377, 128

Charles, Eugenia 29, 534
Charles, Lorenzo 470
Charron, Claude 433
Cheers (TV program) 503
  Illus. 504
Cheese 93, 351
Chemical Industry 269
Chemical Warfare 83
CHEMISTRY 171
  Prizes and Awards 425
Chesapeake Bay, VA-MD 338
Chiang Ching-kuo 497, 498
CHICAGO, IL 172, 179, 180,
  219, 315
  Photography 414
  School Desegregation 202
  Washington, Harold 146
  Illus. 65, 66
Chicago & North Western
  Railroad 516
Chicago Symphony 370
Chichon, El, volc., Mex. 345
CHILDREN 173, 72, 454
  Abandoned 452
  Child Abuse 173
  Drug Use 190, 199
  Wildlife, Attitudes toward 217
  See also Drinking Age
Children's Literature 327
CHILE 174, 578 fol.
  Social Welfare 452
  United Nations 533
CHINA, People's Republic of
  175, 119, 578 fol.
  Accidents and Disasters 80
  Afghanistan 83
  Agriculture 94, 228
  Albania 97
  Arms Sales 358
  Birth-Control Policy 452
  Brazil 149
  Cambodia 155
  Hong Kong 257
  India 265
  Japan 296
  Korea, North 303
  Literature 332
  Nuclear Technology 54
  Railway Bonds Liability
    Ruling 314
  Taiwan 497
  Vietnam 555
  Yugoslavia 565
  Illus. 77, 103, 189
China, Republic of: *see* Taiwan
Chirac, Jacques 230, 231
Chitman, Leo 108
Chitov, Vasily I. 49
Chouf Mountains, Leb. 318
Christian Democratic Party
  (CDU) (Ger.) 222, 240, 241,
  245
Christian Democratic Party
  (It.) 222, 290, 291
Christo:
  Illus.: Surrounded Islands 74
CHRONOLOGY 10
Chrysler Corporation 126, 128,
  306, 350
  Iacocca, Lee 138
Chun Doo Hwan 118, 301, 303
Church and State 374, 444
Cianci, Vincent A., Jr. 447
Cincinnati Opera 368
CITIES AND URBAN AFFAIRS
  179
  Homeless Persons 454
  Skyscrapers 64
  Transportation 518
Civil Aeronautics Board (CAB)
  518
Civil Engineering: *see*
  Engineering, Civil
Civil Rights: *see* Human Rights
Civil Rights Commission (U.S.)
  220, 536, 537
Clark, Barney 68, 69, 340, 552
  Illus. 71
Clark, Joe 156 fol.
Clark, William P. 34, 207, 215,
  310, 358, 536, 546
  Illus. 25

Clausen, A. W. 276
Clinch River Nuclear Reactor,
  TN 207, 540
Clinton, Bill 108
Clothes: *see* Fashion
Coal 207, 268, 270, 580
  British Columbia 150
  Transportation 515, 516
  West Virginia 559
Coalinga, CA 154, 236
Coal Slurry Pipelines 515
Coard, Bernard 28, 33
Cocaine 199
Cocos Island, Indian O. 124
Coetzee, Gerrie 471
Coetzee, J.M. 330
COINS AND COIN
  COLLECTING 180
Coleman, William T., Jr. 220
Colleges and Universities:
  High-Tech Research 272, 273
  Occupational Training 305
  Student Loans 202, 314
  Taxation of Racially
    Discriminatory Schools
    202, 220, 312, 443, 500
Collins, Martha Layne 299, 562
COLOMBIA 181, 578, 579
  Accidents and Disasters 80,
    346
  Drug Traffic 199
  Tunnel 212
COLORADO 182
Colorado River, U.S. 107
Columbia (space shuttle) 459
Columbia Broadcasting
  System (CBS) 153, 502, 503
Columbia University, New
  York, NY 116
COMECON: *see* Council for
  Mutual Economic
  Assistance
Comets 121
Commerce: *see* International
  Trade and Finance
Common Markets: *see*
  Caribbean Common
  Market; European
  Community
Communications Satellites 57,
  59, 183, 459, 461
COMMUNICATION
  TECHNOLOGY 183, 153
Communications Workers 306
Communist Parties:
  Afghanistan 84
  Cyprus 193
  France 230, 233
  India 262
  Italy 290 fol.
  Japan 293
  Poland 417
  Portugal 420, 421
  Rumania 447
  Spain 462
  USSR 527
  Yugoslavia 563, 564
Comoros 572
Compact Disc (CD) (recording)
  434, 435
COMPUTERS 185, 153, 269,
  272, 492
  Books 429
  Espionage 54
  Retailing 446
  Weather Forecasting 345
Concrete 268
Condor (bird):
  Illus. 569
Congo 572, 333
Congress, U.S. 314, 535 fol.
  Caribbean Basin Initiative
    163
  Civil Rights 220
  Coins 180
  Immigration Law 437
  Jordan 298
  Legislative Veto 187
  Membership 584
  Taxation 499
  War Powers Resolution 358,
    549

CONNECTICUT 186, 191
Connors, Jimmy 485, 486
Conrail 516, 518
Conservation 213, 569
Conservative Party (Can.): *see*
  Progressive Conservative
  Party
Conservative Party (Gt. Brit.)
  247, 248
Constantine II, King (Gr.) 255
CONSUMER AFFAIRS 187
Consumer Price Index (CPI)
  306, 543
  Canada 161
Contadora Group 164, 169,
  182, 310, 349, 533, 548
Container Corporation 499
Contemporary Music Festival,
  Valencia, CA 370
Continental Airlines 152, 153,
  517
Contraceptives 340
  Mail Advertisements 314
  Minors 314
Cooke, Christopher M. 53
Cooke, Terence Cardinal 395,
  382
Cooney, Barbara 327
Copper 107, 174, 580
Coptic Christians 204
Copyright Law 63, 320, 321,
  365
Corn 92, 93, 101, 228, 229, 578
  Herbicides 235
  Illinois 261
  Iowa 281
  Kansas 298
  Kentucky 299
  Nebraska 374
  Tennessee 506
  Wisconsin 560
Coronary Bypass Surgery 341
Corporate Affairs: *see*
  Business and Corporate
  Affairs
Corsica, isl., Fr. 222, 232
Corticosteroids (drugs) 341
Cosmology 121
Costa Rica 51, 165, 166, 578
Cotton 92 fol., 458, 579
Council for Mutual Economic
  Assistance (COMECON)
  244
Craft, Christine 315, 562
Crane, Daniel B. 540
Cranston, Alan 541
CRAXI, Benedetto (Bettino)
  135, 222, 290, 292
Cricket (sport) 489
CRIME 188, 252, 312, 314
  China 176
  Cuban Refugees 424
  Juvenile Delinquency, Japan
    294
  Kidnapping 173
  Pact Allowing Foreign
    Convicts to Serve Prison
    Sentences at Home 125
  Wells Fargo Robbery 186
Crime Victims, Rights of 190
Crippen, Robert L. 459
Crosbie, John 157
Cross Country (sport) 489
Crowsnest Pass Freight Rate
  (Can.) 156, 462
Cruise Missiles 109, 110, 159,
  160
Cruzeiro (Braz. currency) 149
Crystal Cathedral, Garden
  Grove, CA 443
CUBA 192, 578, 579, 581
  Central America 168, 169
  Grenada 29, 30, 33, 34
  Pan American Games 482
Cuban Refugees 192, 193, 424
Cunningham, Mary 153
CUOMO, Mario Matthew 135,
  380, 424
Curling (sport) 489
Currituck National Wildlife
  Refuge, NC 215
Cycling 489

Cyclosporin-A (drug) 351
CYPRUS 193, 524, 531, 534
CZECHOSLOVAKIA 194, 578
  Military Affairs 357
  Motor Vehicles 127

D

Dairy Commodities 93
Daley, Richard M. 172
Dali, Salvador 116
Dallas, TX 180
Dam, Kenneth 34
Dams 211, 408
DANCE 195
  Balanchine, George 391
  Great Britain 254
  Prizes and Awards 425
Daniel (film) 363, 365
Dario Paredes del Rio, Rubén
  169
Datatronic (Swed. mfr.) 494
Davis, William 405
Day After, The (TV program)
  109, 503
Day Care 173
Death, Ethical Issues of 69 fol.
Death of a Salesman, play
  (Miller):
  Illus. 77
Death Penalty: *see* Capital
  Punishment
Decker, Mary 487
Defense Department, U.S. 538
Degas, Edgar 112
Dekker, Henry:
  Illus. 75
de Kooning, Willem 112
  Illus. 113
Delahoussaye, Eddie 479
de la Madrid Hurtado, Miguel
  348
DELAWARE 197
Delaware, University of 197
Democratic Party (U.S.) 219,
  220, 541, 561
  Jackson, Henry M. 392
  Jackson, Jesse 139
Dempsey, Rick 465
Deng Xiaoping 175 fol., 358,
  497
DENMARK 198, 101, 222, 578,
  579
  Fishing Disputes 316
  Military Affairs 357
Denny, John 465, 466
Dentistry 343
Denver, CO 182, 220
Department Stores 152, 445,
  446
Deregulation 187, 545
  Banking 129
  Telephone Service 184
  Transportation 515, 516
Deschin, Jacob 414
Desegregation of Schools: *see*
  School Desegregation
Detroit, MI 350
DEUKMEJIAN, George 136, 154
Devaluation of Currencies:
  see Revaluation of
  Currencies
Developing Countries: *see*
  Third World
Diamonds 566, 580
Diana, Princess of Wales 252,
  377
  Illus. 123
Diet Pills 199
Diouf, Abdou 87
Dioxin 216, 298, 361, 495
  Illus. 379
Direct Mail Advertising 82
Disability Payments 454
Disarmament: *see* Arms
  Control
Disneyland, Toyko, Jap.:
  Illus. 77

Divestitures 153
  Telecommunications
    Industry 184
Dividends, Taxation of 499,
  538
Dixon, Rod:
  Illus. 383
Djibouti 572
Docking, Robert B. 298
Dog Shows 489
DOLE, Elizabeth Hanford 137,
  535
  Illus. 11
Dollar (Austr. currency) 122
Dollar (Hong Kong currency)
  257
Dollar (U.S. currency) 222, 277,
  280, 492, 544
Dominica 572
Dominican Republic 573, 163,
  578
Downes, Lorraine 384
Doyle, Sir Arthur Conan 100
Draft Registration 202, 314
Drinking Age 191
  Alaska 96
  Connecticut 186
  Oklahoma 404
  Virginia 556
  West Virginia 559
Droughts 92, 228, 229, 345 fol.,
  402
  Africa 85, 89
  Latin America 311
Drugs (med.) 132, 187, 341, 344,
  351
DRUGS AND DRUG ABUSE
  199, 190
  AIDS 340
  Baseball Players 467
  Colombia 181
  Pan American Games 482
Drug Stores 152
Drunk Driving 191
  Alaska 96
  Georgia 239
  Indiana 266
  North Dakota 386
Druze 318, 319
Dukakis, Michael S. 339
duPont, Pierre 197
Durrell, Lawrence 330
Duvalier, Jean Claude 163
Duwamish Waterway
  Crossing, Seattle, WA 210

E

Eagles 216, 458
Eakins, Thomas 113
Eanes, Antonio Ramalho 420
Earl, Anthony 560
Earthquakes 80, 236 fol.
  Antarctica 420
  California 154
  Colombia 182; *Illus.* 181
  Japan 295
  Oceans 402
  Turkey 524; *Illus.* 523
Eastern Air Lines 517, 545
East Germany: *see* German
  Democratic Republic
Eastman Kodak 153
EC: *see* European Community
Economic and Social Council
  (UN) 532
Economic Community of West
  African States (ECOWAS)
  87, 88
Economic Equity Act 561
Economics, Nobel Prize in 425
Economic Summit Meeting,
  Williamsburg, VA 280
  Colombia 182
  France 233
  Italy 292
  Japan 293
  Illus. 17

ECUADOR 200, 80, 346, 578,
  579
Ecumenism 440 fol.
Edinburgh Festival, Scot. 253
EDUCATION 39, 201
  Environment 569
  Florida's RAISE program 227
  Philanthropy 411
  Retraining of Workers 305
  Science and Math 415
  Taxation Decisions 220, 312,
    443, 500
  See also School
    Desegregation; Teachers;
    Information Highlights
    section in articles on
    provinces of Canada and
    states of the U.S.
Edwards, Edwin W. 335
Eggs 92, 578
EGYPT 203, 578, 579
  Accidents and Disasters 80
  Israel 289
  Libya 321
  Literature 332
  Sudan 88
Elections, U.S. 179, 541
Electric Utilities 345
Electronic Mail 422
Electronic Road Pricing
  System (Hong Kong) 257
Elephants 569, 570
Elizabeth II, Queen (Gt. Brit.)
  98, 252, 494
  Illus. 75, 160
El Salvador 164, 166, 309, 311
  Agriculture 578
  Emigration 437
  United Nations 533
  United States 547, 548
  Venezuela 553
Elway, John 182
Emigration: *see* Refugees and
  Immigration
Emmy Awards 427, 503
Employment: *see* Labor; and
  articles on countries,
  provinces of Canada; and
  states of the U.S.
Endangered Species 213
Enders, Thomas O. 164, 310,
  546, 551
ENERGY 205
ENGINEERING, CIVIL 210
England: *see* Great Britain
English Literature 330
Enterprise (space shuttle):
  Illus. 36
ENVIRONMENT 213
  Acid Rain 345
  Canada 159
  Chesapeake Bay 338
  EDB Ban 256
  Germany, East 244, 245
  Germany, West 243
  Persian Gulf Oil Slick 451
  Zoology 569
Environmental Protection
  Agency (EPA) 213, 216,
  535, 536
Episcopal Churches 442
Equal Rights Amendment
  (ERA) 561
Equatorial Guinea 573
ERA: *see* Equal Rights
  Amendment
Eritrea, reg., Eth. 218
Ershad, Hossein Mohammed
  129
Erving, Julius 468, 469
Escudo (Port. currency) 421
ESPIONAGE 47, 495
ETHIOPIA 218, 89, 578, 579
  Cuba 192
  Famine 452
ETHNIC GROUPS 219
  India 262, 264
  Lebanon 318, 319
  Northwest Territories 387
  South Africa 455
  Sri Lanka 490
  Yugoslavia 563

  See also specific ethnic
    groups
Ethylene Dibromide (EDB) 256
Etna, Mount, It. 238
  Illus. 236
Eugenics 73
Eurailpasses 521
Eure, Thad 386
Euromarket 280
EUROPE 221
  Agriculture 228
  Weather 346, 347
  See also Missile Deployment
    Controversy; and specific
    countries
European Center for Nuclear
  Research (CERN) 415
European Community (EC) 222
  Africa 88
  Agriculture 94
  Caribbean Marine Protection
    214
  Greece 254
  Spain 462
Evans, Daniel J. 541, 557
  Illus. 558
Evans, John 260
Evans, John Louis, III 95, 188
Evren, Kenan 522, 523
Exclusive Economic Zone
  (EEZ) 316
Exclusionary Rule 312
Explosions 80
  Virginia Coal Mine 556
Extraterrestrial Intelligence
  120

F

Fabi, Teo 464
Fabian, John M. 459
Fahd, King (Saudi Ar.) 440, 450
Falkland Islands 107, 246, 251
  Highways 519
Famine 452
  Africa 85, 89, 218
Fanfani, Amintore 290, 292
FAO: *see* Food and Agriculture
  Organization
Farm Equipment 269
Farmers Home Administration
  (FHA) 386
Farming: *see* Agriculture
FASHION 223
  Retailing, 445, 446
FBI: *see* Federal Bureau of
  Investigation
FCC: *see* Federal
  Communications
  Commission
FDA: *see* Food and Drug
  Administration
Federal Bureau of
  Investigation (FBI) 315
Federal Communications
  Commission (FCC) 59, 184
Federal Cultural Policy
  Review Committee (Can.)
  161
Federal Highway
  Administration (FHWA)
  519
Federal Housing
  Administration (FHA) 257
Federal Lands: *see* Public
  Lands
Federal Reserve Board 130,
  492, 540, 542
Federal Trade Commission
  (FTC) 81, 187, 445
Feinstein, Dianne 449, 562
Feldstein, Martin S. 276 fol.,
  543
Fencing (sport) 489
FHA: *see* Farmers Home
  Administration; Federal
  Housing Administration
Field Hockey 489

Fierstein, Harvey:
  Illus. 428
Figueiredo, João Baptista 148,
  149
Fiji 573
Finance, International: *see*
  International Trade and
  Finance
Financial-Services Industry
  446, 491, 545
FINLAND 226, 578, 579, 581
  Korea, North 303
  World Track and Field
    Championships 487
Finnish National Opera 226,
  368
Fires 80
Fish and Wildlife Service, U.S.
  217
Fisheries 402
  Arctic 420
  Canada 159
  Denmark and Greenland 198
  Fishing Zones 316
  Iceland 260
  Newfoundland 377
FitzGerald, Garret 286
Flashdance (film) 365, 366, 373,
  434
FLIGHT, History of 35
Floods 80, 236, 346, 347
  Arizona 107
  California 154
  Latin America 200, 311, 410
  Louisiana 335
  New Mexico 379
  Railroads 517
  Utah 551
  Virgin Islands 557
FLORIDA 227, 80, 102, 201, 424
  Illus.: Surrounded Islands 74
Fluorspar 580
Flynn, Raymond 147, 148, 179
Flynt, Larry 430
Foat, Ginny 335
  Illus. 562
FOOD 228, 269, 452
  Africa 85, 89
  Ghana 245
  Retailing 446
  Wine 559
Food and Agriculture
  Organization (FAO) 213,
  452
Food and Drug Administration
  (FDA) 229, 340
Food Stamps 229, 454
Foot, Michael 247, 248
Football 472
  Bryant, Paul 389
  Television 503
Ford Motor Company 126 fol.,
  306, 350
Foreign Aid 452, 514
  Africa 88, 89
  Caribbean 163
  Central America 164 fol.
  See also International
    Monetary Fund; World
    Bank; and articles on
    specific countries
Foreign Debt 130, 277
  Africa 85, 87
  Central America 165
  Europe 222
  Latin America 311
  Third World Countries 514
  See also articles on countries
Fournier, Roger 329
Franc (Fr. currency) 230
FRANCE 230, 222, 578 fol.
  Art 114, 116
  Balloons 35, 36
  Chad 89, 170
  Chile 174
  China 178
  Dance 196
  Economy 276
  Espionage 47, 49, 51, 54
  Germany, West 244
  India 265
  Industrial Production 270

France (con't.)
  Labor 308
  Lebanon 318
  Literature 333
  Military Affairs 357
  Motor Vehicles 127
  Orly Airport Bombing 524
  Social Welfare 453
  Space Exploration 461
  Stocks and Bonds 492
  Taxation 501
  Wine 560
  Illus. 91
Franjieh, Sulieman 318
Fraser, Douglas A. 306
  Illus. 307
Fraser, Malcolm 122, 123
Free Democratic Party (FDP)
  (Ger. pol.) 222, 240, 245
Freeman, Derek 100
Freight 515, 516
  Canada 156, 450
French Canadians 329, 405
Frost, Robert 180
Frye, Northrop 328
FTC: *see* Federal Trade
  Commission
Fuel Economy, Automobile
  127
Fukuda, Takeo 293
FULLER, R(ichard)
  Buckminster 392
Furniture 113, 268, 270
Futrell, Mary Hatwood 306

G

Gabon 573, 452, 581
Gairy, Sir Eric 34
Gallen, Hugh J. 378
Galleries: *see* Museums and
  Galleries
Gallstones 342
Galtieri, Leopoldo 251
Galveston, TX 507
Gambia 573
Gandhi, Indira 262 fol., 452,
  514
Garcia Meza, Luis 147
GARDENING AND
  HORTICULTURE 234
Gardner, Dale A. 459
Gardner, David P. 39
Garfield, books (Davis) 430
  Illus. 429
Garrahy, J. Joseph 447
Garriott, Owen K. 460
Gas: *see* Manufactured Gas;
  Natural Gas
Gasoline 205, 519, 579
Gaza, area, Middle East 548
Gemayel, Amin 317 fol., 495,
  496
General Assembly (UN) 531,
  532
General Motors (GM) 126 fol.,
  296, 350, 522
GENETICS 235, 132
  Biomedical Ethics 73
  McClintock, Barbara 140
Geneva Disarmament Talks
  110
GEOLOGY 236
  Polar Research 420
GEORGIA 239, 424
Gerena, Victor M. 186
GERMAN DEMOCRATIC
  REPUBLIC (East
  Germany; DDR) 244, 240,
  578 fol.
  Literature 333
  Luther Anniversary 438
  Military Affairs 357
  Motor Vehicles 127
GERMANY, Federal Republic
  of (West Germany) 240,
  221, 222, 578 fol.
  Archaeology 101

Arms Control 110
Burma 151
Espionage 51
Floods 346
Industrial Production 270
Labor 308
Literature 333
Military Affairs 357
Motor Vehicles 127
Social Welfare 453
Space Exploration 459, 460
Stocks and Bonds 492
Switzerland 495
Taxation 501
Wine 560
GHANA 245, 87, 88, 578, 579
  Refugees 384
Ghiz, Joe 423
Gibraltar 462
Ginzburg, Natalia 333
Giulini, Carlo Maria 370
Glass and Glass Products 268,
  270
Glemp, Jozef 417
Glenn, John 201, 541
Glomar Challenger (ship) 402
GM: *see* General Motors
GNP: *see* Gross National
  Product
GODFREY, Arthur 391
Golan Heights, Isr. 496
Gold 580
  Brazil 238
  South Africa 456
Gold Coins 180
Golding, William 331
Goldsboro Christian Schools,
  NC 202, 220, 443, 500
Golf 478
González, Felipe 222, 462
  Illus. 233
Gonzalez, Julio 116
Goode, Wilson 179, 220, 411
Goodlad, John I. 46
Good Samaritans Laws 190
Gorbanevskaya, Natalia 331
Gore, Albert 109
Governor-General's Awards
  (Can. lit.) 329, 426
Graham, Bob 227
Graham, Deneen Z. 386
Graham, Martha 195, 197
Grains 92 fol., 228, 229
  Czechoslovakia 194
  Saskatchewan 449
  Transportation 515
Grammy Awards 425, 434
Graphite 580
Graves, Michael 103, 274
Gray, Jimmy Lee 188
GREAT BRITAIN 246, 578 fol.
  Archaeology 101
  Arms Control 110
  Capital Punishment 189
  China 178
  Cyprus 194
  Drug Abuse 199
  Espionage 49, 51
  Falkland Islands 107
  Fishing Disputes 316
  Hong Kong 119, 257
  Ireland 286
  Labor 308
  Literature 330
  London 334
  Malaysia 337
  Military Affairs 357
  Motor Vehicles 127
  Muslims 440
  Social Welfare 452, 453
  Space Exploration 461
  Spain 462
  Stocks and Bonds 492
  Sweden 494
  Taxation 501
GREECE 254, 578 fol.
  Albania 97
  Military Affairs 357
  Social Welfare 453
  Turkey 524
Green, Julien 333
Greenhouse Effect 217

Greenland 102, 198
Greens (Fin. pol.) 226
Greens (Ger. pol.) 221, 241, 243
Gregoire, Gilles 433
GRENADA 28, 163, 309, 311
  Cuba 192
  Great Britain 249
  Italy 292
  Nicaragua 164, 169
  United Nations 533, 534
  United States 547, 548
  War Powers Resolution 550
Gretzky, Wayne 480, 481
Greyhound Lines, Inc. 306, 545
  Illus.: Strike 26
Gritz, Bo 309
Grolier Foundation Award 320
Gromyko, Andrei 379, 531
Gross National Product (GNP)
  152, 276, 491, 543
  See also articles on countries
Growth Hormone 132
Guaraní (Para. currency) 408
Guatemala 165 fol., 309, 311,
  578
  Refugees 437
  United Nations 533
Guerrilla and Terrorist
  Activities 88 fol., 118, 119,
  166, 222
  Afghanistan 82, 84, 437, 439
  Anti-Turkish Acts 523, 524
  Burma 301, 302, 533
  Colombia 181
  Ethiopia 218
  France 232
  Great Britain 246
  Greece 97
  India 262, 264, 437, 439
  Indonesia 267
  Israel 289
  Italy 291
  Lebanon 233, 287, 318, 319,
  548
  Northern Ireland 250
  Peru 409, 410
  South Africa 455
  Spain 462
  Sri Lanka 490
  Sudan 493
  Uganda 524
  Venezuela 552
  Washington, D.C. 558
  Zimbabwe 566, 567
Guggenheim Museum, New
  York, NY 116
Guilford Transportation
  Company 378
Guinea 573, 580
Guinea-Bissau 573
Gum Disease 343
Gurrier, Patrick 54
GUYANA 255, 578, 580
Gymnastics 489
Gypsum 580

H

Habré, Hissène 89, 170
  Illus. 91
Haiti 573, 163, 578, 579
  Emigration 437
Hailey's Comet 121
Hamburg, David 43
Hamilton, Larry and Deborah:
  Illus. 506
Hamilton, Scott 481, 482
Handball 489
Handke, Peter 333
Hansen, George 261
Harness Racing 479
Harper, James Durward, Jr. 53
  Illus. 49
Harris, Ed 363
Harris, Joe Frank 239
Harrison, Rex 253
Harrods Department Store,
  London, Eng. 250

Hart, Gary 201
Hassan II, King (Mor.) 98, 322,
  362
Hatch, Orrin 201
Hatfield, Mark 437
Hauck, Frederick H. 459
HAWAII 256, 238, 454
HAWKE, Robert James Lee
  137, 122 fol.
Hazardous Wastes: *see* Toxic
  Wastes
HBO: *see* Home Box Office
Health: *see* Medicine and
  Health
Heart Disease 340
Heart Institute, Ottawa, Ont.
  Can. 406
Heart Like a Wheel (film) 365,
  366
Heat Waves 80, 346, 347
Hebron, Isr. 289
HECKLER, Margaret Mary 138,
  344, 454, 535
  Illus. 11
Helms, Jesse 385
Helprin, Mark 323
Hemingway, Mariel 364
Hemoglobin (biochem.) 132
Herbicides 235
Herculaneum, It. 101
Heritage Foundation 544
Hernández Colón, Rafael 432
Heroin 199
Herrera Campíns, Luis 553
Hershler, Ed 563
Herzog, Chaim 287
High Technology 272, 492, 545
  Japan 296
Highways 191, 519
  Electronic Road Pricing
  System, Hongkong 257
  Weight Limits 108, 517
Hijackings of Airplanes 193,
  498, 557
Hinduism 439
Hinton, Deane R. 310, 546
Hirohito:
  Illus. 294
Hispanic Americans 179, 220,
  454
Hitachi (Jap. mfr.) 47
Hitler Diaries Hoax 252
  Illus. 16
Hoban, Russell 323
Hockey: *see* Field Hockey; Ice
  Hockey
Hodel, Donald:
  Illus. 205
Hogs 92, 93
Hollings, Ernest F. 201
Holmes, Larry 471
Holocaust, The 441
Home Box Office (HBO) 58,
  364, 504
Homeless Persons 452, 454
HOME VIDEO 55, 365, 435
Homicides 188
  Great Britain 252
  Seattle, WA 558
  Utah 552
Homosexuality 340, 443
Honduras 166, 168, 309, 578
  Illus. 20
Honecker, Erich 240, 244, 245,
  419
Honegger, Barbara 561
HONG KONG 257, 119, 178, 492
Hope, Bob 76
Horizon '83 (mus. festival) 370
Horse Racing 479
Horseshoe Pitching 489
Horse Shows 489
Horticulture: *see* Gardening
  and Horticulture
Hospitals 454, 540
House of Representatives,
  U.S. 536 fol.
  Abortions 562
  Arms Control 109
  Grenada 30
  Libraries 320
  Membership 584

HOUSING 257, 152, 180, 406, 543
Houston, TX 422, 507, 518
Houston Opera 368
Hoxha, Enver 97
Hoyt, LaMarr 466
Hughes, Ted 330
Hughes Communications, Inc. 461
Human Research Subjects 69, 70
Human Rights 220, 312, 315
  Argentina 105, 106
  Central America 166 fol.
  Chile 174
  Germany, West 242
  Health Care, Access to 70
  Latin America 311
  March on Washington 558
  Paraguay 408
  Poland 416
  Political Asylum 314
  Prisoners 424
  School Desegregation 172, 202, 360
  United Nations 533, 534
  Uruguay 551
  Yugoslavia 564
  Zaire 566
  Zimbabwe 567, 568
Hu Na 177, 314
HUNGARY 259, 578 fol.
  Agriculture 94
  Literature 332
  Military Affairs 357
  Mine Explosion 80
  Motor Vehicles 127
Hunger 452, 454
Hunt, James B., Jr. 40, 43, 385
Hunting 215
Hurricanes 80, 345, 347, 507
Hurtado Larrea, Osvaldo 200
Hussein, King (Jor.) 297, 298, 496, 548
  Illus. 131
Hussein, Saddam 285
Hutton, Timothy 363
Hu Yaobang 448, 565
Hypermarkets (superstores) 446

I

IACOCCA, Lee Anthony 138
  Illus. 126
Ice Hockey 480
ICELAND 260
Ice Skating 481
IDAHO 260
Ideal Weight Tables 343
Idris, King (Lib.) 322
Iglesias, Julio 434
Ignatius IV (patriarch of Antioch) 441
Illegal Aliens 220, 437, 443
ILLINOIS 261
  Chicago 172
Illueca, Jorge 531
  Illus. 531
IMF: see International Monetary Fund
Immigration: see Refugees and Immigration
Income: see Wages and Salaries
INDIA 262, 119, 578 fol.
  Accidents and Disasters 80
  Bangladesh 129
  Bengali Immigrants 437
  Birth Control 452
  Canal 211
  Literature 332
  Motor Vehicles 127
  Nuclear Technology 54
  Pakistan 407, 408
  Religion 439
  Space Exploration 461
  Weather 346

INDIANA 266
Indianapolis 500 Auto Race 464
Indians, American:
  Alaska 96
  Central America 168
  Montana 361
  Northwest Territories 387
  Prehistoric Art 102
  South Dakota 458
  Yukon 565
INDONESIA 266, 119, 578 fol.
  Espionage 52
  Space Exploration 459, 461
  Volcanoes 238
  Weather 346
INDUSTRIAL REVIEW 268, 152, 544, 579
  Advertising 81
  Auto Industry 126, 350
  Computers 185
  Fashion 223
  Food Industry 229
  Gardening 234
  High-Tech Industry 272
  Home Video 55
  Housing 257
  Mineral and Metal Production 580
  Publishing 429
  Recording Industry 434
  Steel Industry 271
  Telecommunications Industry 184
  Transportation 515
  Travel 520
Infant Formula 229
Inflation 187, 276, 491, 492, 540, 542
  Central America 165
  Europe 222
  Medical Costs 71
  See also articles on countries
Information, Freedom of 320
Infrared Astronomical Satellite (IRAS) 121, 459
Intelligence Operations: see Espionage
Intelsat: see International Telecommunications Satellite Organization
Interactive Cable Television 61
Inter-American Development Bank (IDB) 200, 310
Inter-American Satellite Television 59
Interest Income, Taxation of 499, 538
Interest Rates 130, 152, 257, 276 fol., 492, 543 fol.
Interior Department, U.S. 207, 214, 215
INTERIOR DESIGN 274
Intermediate-Range Nuclear Forces (INF) 110, 547
Internal Revenue Service (IRS) 202, 220, 443, 500
International Balloon Fiesta, NM 379
International Bank for Reconstruction and Development: see World Bank
International Business Machines (IBM) 153, 185
  Illus.: Center, New York 67
International Center of Photography, New York, NY 414
International Civil Aviation Organization (ICAO) 534
International Court of Justice (UN) 532
International Debt: see Foreign Debt
International Development Association (IDA) 279, 280
International Energy Agency (IEA) 207
International Labor Organization (ILO) 419

International Law 316
  Pact Allowing Foreign Convicts to Serve Prison Sentences at Home 125
International Monetary Fund (IMF) 276, 278, 279, 452, 514, 548
  Africa 87, 89
  Argentina 106
  Brazil 149
  Central America 165, 168
  Chile 174
  Dominican Republic 163
  Ecuador 200
  Kenya 300
  Latin America 311
  Morocco 362
  Nigeria 384
  Peru 410
  Portugal 421
  Switzerland 495
  Yugoslavia 564
  Zaire 566
International Telecommunications Satellite Organization (Intelsat) 461
International Telephone and Telegraph (ITT) 184
INTERNATIONAL TRADE AND FINANCE 276, 492
  Agricultural Products 92, 94
  Apparel 446
  Automobiles 128
  Caribbean Basin Initiative 163
  China 177
  Food 228
  Japanese Surplus 296
  Latin America 311
  Third World 514
  United States Trade Deficit 544
  See also Information Highlights section in articles on countries
Interstate Commerce Commission (ICC) 515
IOWA 281
IRA: see Irish Republican Army
IRAN 282, 578 fol.
  Refugees 82
  United Nations 533
Iran-Iraq War 282, 284, 354
  France 233
  Saudi Arabia 451
  United Nations 534
  United States 548
  Illus. 283
IRAQ 284, 578, 579, 581
  Egypt 204
  France 233
  United States 548
IRAS: see Infrared Astronomical Satellite
IRAS-Araki-Alcock (comet) 121
IRELAND 286, 578, 579, 581
Irish Americans:
  New York City 382
Irish Republican Army (IRA) 222, 250
Iron 359, 580
IRS: see Internal Revenue Service
Islam 439
  Afghanistan 84
  France 232
  Iran 282
  Iraq 285
  Lebanon 318, 319
  Philippines 412
  Sudan 88, 493
  Tunisia 522
  Yugoslavia 563
Islamic Conference, Mecca, Saudi Ar. 450
Islamic Foreign Ministers Conference 129
Islamic Law 88, 451, 493
ISRAEL 287, 352, 440, 441, 578, 579, 581
  Archaeology 101

Egypt 204
Espionage 52
Ethiopia 218
Jordan 297, 298
Lebanon 317 fol.
Libya 322
Literature 332
Nuclear Technology 54
Pakistan 407
Shamir, Yitzhak 144
Syria 495, 496
Tourism 520
United Nations 533
Zaire 566
ITALY 290, 221, 222, 578 fol.
  Archaeology 100
  Art 117
  Bulgaria 150, 151
  Conservation 213
  Craxi, Bettino 135
  Economy 276
  Espionage 52
  Fire 80
  Industrial Production 270
  Labor 308
  Literature 333
  Military Affairs 357
  Motor Vehicles 127
  Mount Etna 238
  Taxation 501
  Wine 560
ITT: see International Telephone and Telegraph
Ivory Coast 573, 88

J

JACKSON, Henry Martin 392, 557
JACKSON, The Rev. Jesse Louis 139, 219, 562
Jackson, Michael 372, 434, 435
Jai Alai 489
Jakes, John 429
Jamaica 573, 163, 580
Janklow, William 458
JAPAN 293, 119, 578 fol.
  Accidents and Disasters 80, 236, 238, 347
  Agriculture 94
  Archaeology 101
  Automobiles 128
  Burma 151
  China 178
  Espionage 52
  Fashion 223
  Fishing Zones 316
  Highways 519
  Industrial Production 270
  Korea, North 302, 303
  Korea, South 302, 303
  Labor 308
  Literature 332
  Motor Vehicles 127
  Nakasone, Yasuhiro 143
  Religion 439
  Social Security 453
  Space Exploration 461
  Stocks and Bonds 492
  Taxation 501
  Tunnel 212
  Videocassette Recorders 60
  Illus.: Tokyo Disneyland 77
Jaruzelski, Wojciech 222, 416 fol.
Jaycees, U.S. 315
Jayewardene, Junius 119, 490
Jeantot, Philippe 488
Jenkins, Roy 248
Jerusalem, Isr. 441
Jesuits (rel. ord.) 444
Jewish Affairs: see Judaism
Job Training Partnership Act 305, 454
Joffrey Ballet 195
John Paul II, Pope 444
  Assassination Attempt (1981) 151

John Paul II, Pope (con't.)
Austria 125
Central America 164, 166,
167, 169
Poland 94, 417
Illus. 18, 168
Johnson, Sonia 562
Johnson, Uwe 333
JORDAN 297, 204, 579, 581
Jorge Blanco, Salvador 163
Journalism:
Prizes and Awards 425
Television 502, 503
See also Newspapers; Press,
Freedom of the
J. Paul Getty Museum, Malibu,
CA 112, 114
Juan Carlos, King (Sp.) 551
Judaism 289, 440
Judo 489
Jumblatt, Walid 318, 319
Justice Department, U.S. 184,
187

K

Kádár, János 259
Kahl, Gordon 386
Kampuchea: *see* Cambodia
KANSAS 298
Karami, Rashid 318
Karens (people) 151
Karinthy, Ferenc 332
Karl-I-Bond, Nguza 566
Kaysone Phomvihane 309
Kean, Thomas H. 378, 379
**Kenai National Wildlife
Refuge,** AK 216
Kennedy, William 323
KENTUCKY 299
Kentucky Derby 479
KENYA 300, 89, 578
Kerrey, Bob 374
Keyworth, George 415
Khomeini, Ayatollah Ruhollah
282, 283
Illus. 283
Kibaki, Mwaii 300
Kidnapping 173, 552
Kidney Stone 342
Kilauea, volc., HI 238
Kiley, Robert R. 382
Kim, Duk Koo 70
Kimberly-Clark Corporation
560
Kim Il Sung 303
**King, Martin Luther, Jr.,
Holiday** 540
King, Martin Luther, III:
Illus. 537
King, Melvin H. 220
KING, Stephen Edwin 139
Kingsley, Ben 363
Kinnock, Neil 248, 249
Kip (Laotian currency) 309
Kiribati 573
Kirkland, Lane 306, 307
Illus. 539
Kirkpatrick, Jeane 533
Kirstein, Lincoln 195
Kissinger, Henry 164, 169, 310,
546, 547
Illus. 24
Kittle, Ron 466
Kohl, Helmut 222, 240 fol.
Illus. 13
Kohler Company 560
Koivisto, Mauno 226
Kolvenbach, Peter-Hans 444
**KOREA, Democratic People's
Republic of (North Korea)**
303, 118, 302, 578, 580, 581
Grenada 33
Uganda 524
United Nations 533
Zimbabwe 566
**KOREA, Republic of (South
Korea)** 301, 119, 578 fol.

Dam 212
Explosion, Burma 118
Fire 80
Japan 296
Korea, North 303
Literature 332
Motor Vehicles 127
Taiwan 498
United States 548
See also Korean Airliner
Incident
Korean Airliner Incident 118,
301, 316, 547
Canada 160
Japan 296
United Nations 531, 534
Illus. 23, 533
Kratochvilova, Jarmila 487
Kreisky, Bruno 125
Krona (Swed. currency) 493
Kudelka, James 196
Kuhn, Bowie K. 467
Kurile Islands 296
Kuwait 573
Kyprianou, Spyros 193, 194

L

Labor 304, 222, 270, 312
Auto Industry 126
Bieber, Owen F. 134
Central America 165
High-Tech Industry 273
Illegal Aliens 437
Illinois Public Employees 261
Jobs Bill 539
New Deal 542
Newspapers 431
Postal Service 422
Steel Industry 271
Transportation Workers 517,
518
Unemployment 152, 280, 453,
454, 540, 543 fol.
See also Strikes; articles on
countries, provinces of
Canada, and states of the
U.S.
Labor Party (Austr.) 122 fol.
Labour Party (Gt. Brit.) 246 fol.,
308
Lacrosse (sport) 489
Lalonde, Marc 158
Lamb, Floyd 376
Lamm, Richard D. 182
Landslides 80
LANGE, Jessica 140
**Language Controversy,
Canadian** 158, 160, 405,
433
Lanham Act 81, 82
LAOS 309
Lao She 332
Lapointe, Gatien 329
Larcenies 188
Larosière, Jacques de 276,
280
Lasers 183
Nuclear Fusion 415
Videodiscs 61
Weapons 111, 357
Las Vegas, NV 376
LATIN AMERICA 309
Literature 331
Social Welfare 452
United States 546
Weather 346
See also specific countries
Lavelle, Rita 216, 536
LAW 312
Advertising 81
Banking 129
Bankruptcy 152
Biomedical Ethics 68
Consumer Affairs 187
Drunk Driving 191
Immigration 437
Legislative Veto 187

Missing Children's Act 173
Sex Discrimination 561, 562
Taxation 499
Law of the Sea Treaty (LOST)
316
Lead 580
Lead Poisoning 101, 102
LEBANON 317, 352, 439, 578,
579
Blizzard 80
France 233
Israel 287
Italy 292
Palestinian Massacre (1982)
287
Reconciliation Talks, Geneva
318, 496; *Illus.* 319
Saudi Arabia 451
Syria 495
United States 547, 548, 550
Illus. 15
le Carré, John 330
Lee, James 423
Lee Kuan Lee 451
Legal Ethics 315
Legislative Veto 187, 312, 550
Lehman Brothers Kuhn Loeb
153
Illus. 152
Lemon Laws 187
Lendl, Ivan 485
Leopards 213
Leopold III, King (Belg.) 131
Lesotho 574
Lessing, Doris 330
Lever House, New York, NY
104
Lévesque, René 433
Levine, James 368
Lewis, Carl 487
**Liberal-Democratic Party
(LDP)** (Jap.) 293, 294
Liberal Party (Can.) 156
Liberal Party (Gt. Brit.) 246,
248
Liberia 574, 289, 580
Liberty (yacht) 488
LIBRARIES 320
LIBYA 321, 89, 579, 581
Brazil 149
Chad 170
Morocco 362
Sudan 493
Lichenstein, Charles 531
Lichtenberg, Byron K. 460
Liechtenstein 574
**Life-Sustaining Medical
Intervention** 69 fol.
Lightning 345
**Lightwave Communication
System** 183
Lincoln Park Zoo, Chicago, IL
570
Liner Cargo 518
**Liner Conferences, Code of
Conduct for** 518
Liquidity Crisis 278
Lisa Computer 185
Lisbon, Port. 114
LITERATURE 323
China 177
Prizes 198, 425, 426
Publishing 429
Little Rock, AR 108
Liuzzo, Viola 315
Li Xiannian 175
Lockheed Scandal (Jap.) 293
LONDON, Eng. 334, 246, 250,
252
Art 116
Sotheby Parke Bernet 112
LOS ANGELES, CA 334
Art 114
Transportation 518
Illus. 446
Los Angeles County Museum,
CA 114
Los Angeles Lakers
(basketball team) 468, 469
Los Angeles Philharmonic 370
Los Angeles Raiders (football
team) 472, 474

LOUISIANA 335, 236, 315
Louisville, KY 299
Illus. 347
Lubbers, Rudolph F. M. 374
LUCAS, George 140
Lucy (fossil) 100
Ludlum, Robert 429
Lugano, Switz. 114
Luis, Juan 557
Lumber 268, 270, 406
Lusinchi, Jaime 552
Luther, Martin 438
Lutheranism 440, 442
Luxembourg 574, 357, 453
Lyakov, Vladimir 459, 460

M

M-19 Movement (Colom.) 181
McBride, Lloyd 306
McCLINTOCK, Barbara 140
McEnroe, John 485, 486
McFARLANE, Robert Carl 141,
310, 358, 536, 546, 547
McGee Creek Dam, OK 211
Machinery Production 269
McIntyre, Alister 30
McKinney, Tamara 483
Madagascar 574, 214, 578
Madrid, Sp. 116
**Madrid Conference on
Security and Cooperation
in Europe** 221, 564
Magaña, Alvaro 166, 167
Magazines 429, 430
Advertising 82
Prizes and Awards 425
Magnesium 581
Magritte, René 116
Mahathir Mohammad 337
Mahre, Phil 483
Mailer, Norman 323
MAINE 336
Makarova, Natalia:
Illus. 428
Malawi 574
MALAYSIA 336, 578, 579, 581
Maldives 574
Mali 574, 88
Malibu, CA 346
Illus. 10
Malik, Adam 266
MALONE, Moses 141, 468, 469
Malta 574
Manet, Edouard 114
Illus. 116
Manganese 581
MANITOBA 337, 158, 160
Mansour, Agnes Mary 350, 444
Manufactured Gas 579
Manufacturing: *see* Industrial
Review
Manville Corporation 152
Marc Rich and Company 495
March on Washington II 558
Illus. 22
Marcos, Ferdinand E. 412
Margaret, Princess (Gt. Brit.)
448
Marianas Trough, Pac. O. 402
Marijuana 199
Marković, Dragoslav 563
Maronite Christians 318, 319
Marsalis, Wynton 371
Martens, Wilfried 131
Martinique, Fr. isl., W.I. 333
Martins, Peter 195, 196
MARYLAND 338
Mary Rose (ship) 101
Illus. 102
MAS (Colom. terrorists) 181
Masonic Lodge Scandal (It.)
291
MASSACHUSETTS 339, 545
Boston 147
Massood, Ahmad Shah 84
Matheson, Scott 552
Mauritania 574

Mauritius 574, 569
Mauroy, Pierre 36, 230
Maynard, Robert C. 154, 431
MCC: see Microelectronics and Computer Technology Corporation
MCI: see Microwave Communications, Inc.
Mead, Margaret 100
Meadowlands Sports Complex, NJ 379
Meat 92 fol., 229
Medeiros, Humberto Cardinal 339
Medicare 454, 540
Alberta 98
MEDICINE AND HEALTH 340, 132, 453, 454
Ethical Standards 68
Food 229
Microbiology 351
Prizes and Awards 425
Mejía Victores, Oscar Humberto 167
Mellon, Paul 117
Melvil Dewey Award 320
Mengistu Haile Mariam 87, 218
Mental Health 344
Merbold, Ulf 460
Mercury 581
Merit Pay for Teachers 44, 201, 227
Metals 268, 270, 580
Meteorites 120, 238, 420
METEOROLOGY 345, 236
El Niño, Effects of 402
Latin America 311
Weather Satellites 461
Methodist Churches 442
Metropolitan Museum, New York, NY 113 fol., 414
Metropolitan Opera, New York, NY 368
Illus. 369
MEXICO 348, 311, 578 fol.
Accidents and Disasters 80, 347
Agriculture 94
Brazil 149
Emigration 437
Foreign Debt 278, 279
Literature 331
Motor Vehicles 127
Refugees 437
Social Welfare 452
Mexico City, Mex. 452
MIA: see Missing in Action
Miami, FL 179, 180, 518
Mianus River Bridge Collapse, CT 186
MICHIGAN 350, 545
Michigan, University of 103
MICROBIOLOGY 351
Microelectronics 183
Microelectronics and Computer Technology Corporation (MCC) 273
Microwave Communications, Inc. (MCI) 183, 184
MIDDLE EAST 352
Refugees 437
United States 546, 548
Midgetman Missiles 111, 357, 539
MILITARY AFFAIRS 356, 538, 539, 547, 549
Arms Control 109
Japan 296
Illus.: U.S.-Honduran Maneuvers 20
Milk 93, 578
Miller, Cheryl 470
Miłosz, Czesław 331
Mining 268, 270
Accidents 80, 556
Bolivia 147
Canada 159, 376, 387, 565
Montana 361
New Mexico 380
West Virginia 559
World Production 580
Wyoming 563

MINNESOTA 359, 190, 315, 346
Tax Deduction for School Expenses 202, 312, 500
Minnesota, University of 321
Minorities: see Ethnic Groups
MIRO, Joan 393
Miss America:
Illus. 75
Missile Deployment Controversy 109, 110, 221, 358
Belgium 131
Denmark 198
France 233
Germany, West 241, 243
Italy 290
Netherlands 375
Missiles 109 fol., 356 fol., 538, 539, 547
Testing in Canada 159, 160
USSR 528
Wyoming 563
Missing Children 173
Missing in Action (MIA) 309
Illus. 555
MISSISSIPPI 359, 188
Mississippi River 236
MISSOURI 360
Miss Universe 384
Mitterrand, François 222, 230 fol.
Chad 170
China 178
Illus. 242
Mkhize, Saul 456
MNF: see Multinational Peacekeeping Forces
Mobile Homes 269
Mobil Oil 322, 377, 388
Mobutu Sese Seko 170, 566
Model, Lisette 414
Modern Pentathlon 489
Moi, Daniel arap 89, 300
Molybdenum 581
Monaco 574
Mondale, Walter F. 201, 541
Labor 304
Illus. 539
Monge, Luis Alberto 165, 166
Mongolia 574, 580
Monitor (gunboat):
Illus. 385
Mono-Inyo Craters, CA 238
Monopoly Game 82
MONTANA 361
Montgolfier, Joseph and Jacques-Étienne 35
Moore, Brian 329
Moore, Charles 103
MOORE, Dudley Stuart John 142
Moore, Henry 116
Moose 336
Morante, Elsa 333
Morgenthaler, Henry 160
MOROCCO 362, 87, 578 fol.
Algeria 98, 99
Libya 322
Mortgages 152, 257
Moses, Edwin 487
Mosquito Control 351
MOTION PICTURES 363
Attenborough, Sir Richard 133
Canada 160, 161
Great Britain 254
Home Video 58, 60, 63
Lange, Jessica 140
Lucas, George 140
Moore, Dudley 142
Prizes and Awards 427
Motley, Langhorne A. 310, 546
Motor Carriers 515 fol.
See also Automobiles; Trucks
Motorcycles 296
Mozambique 574, 90, 455, 578
MTV 435, 504
Mubarak, Hosni 203, 204
Mudslides 80, 236
Colombia 182
Utah 551

Mugabe, Robert 90, 566 fol.
Hungary 259
Muldoon, Robert 383
MULRONEY, M. Brian 142, 157, 158, 160, 433
Multinational Peacekeeping Forces (MNF) (Leb.) 317, 318
'Murdani, Benny 266
Murders: see Homicides
Murdoch, Iris 330
Murdoch, Rupert 59, 431
Murphy, Eddie 363
Museum of Contemporary Art, Los Angeles, CA 114
Museum of Fine Arts, Boston, MA 414
Museum of Modern Art, New York, NY 117, 414
Museums and Galleries 112 fol.
Air and Space Museum 36
Canada 162
Photography 414
Illus.: High Museum, Atlanta 239
Musgrave, Story F. 459
MUSIC 368
Blake, Eubie 389
Great Britain 253
Prizes and Awards 425
Recordings 434
Television 504
Musical American Festival, Washington, DC 370
Mussolini, Benito 291
Mutations 132
Muzorewa, Abel 567
MX Missiles 109, 356, 357, 538, 539, 547, 563
Mystic Marinelife Aquarium, CT 569

N

Naira (Nig. currency) 384
Nairobi University, Kenya 300
NAKASONE, Yasuhiro 143, 119, 293 fol., 501
Illus. 17
Namibia (South-West Africa) 90, 384, 534, 581
Narayan, R. K. 332
National Aeronautics and Space Administration (NASA) 120
National Air and Space Museum, Washington, D.C. 36
Illus. 35
National Association of Broadcasters (NAB) 81
National Bipartisan Commission on Central America 164, 169
Illus. 24
National Broadcasting Company (NBC) 502, 503
National Conference of Christian-Jewish Relations 440
National Council of Churches (NCC) 442
National Education Association (NEA) 201, 306, 541
National Endowment for the Arts 195
National Film Board (NFB) (Can.) 161
National Gallery, Washington, D.C. 117, 414
National Highway Traffic Safety Administration (NHTSA) 187
National Medal of Freedom Awards 427
National News Council 431

National Oceanic and Atmospheric Administration (NOAA) 345
National Organization for Women (NOW) 541
National Parks 214, 215
National Salvation Front (Leb.) 318
National Science Foundation (NSF) 237, 238, 420, 569
National Symphony, Washington, DC 370
Native Americans: see Indians, American
NATO: see North Atlantic Treaty Organization
Natural Gas 205, 268, 270, 388, 580
Alberta Blowout 98
Taxation 500
Nauru 574
Nautilus (submarine) 186
Navratilova, Martina 486
NBC: see National Broadcasting Company
Ndebele (people) 566, 567
NEA: see National Education Association
NEBRASKA 374
Nebraska, University of 374, 476
Nemery, Jaafar al- 88, 493
Egypt 204
Libya 321
Nepal 575, 578
Nerve Gas Weapons 538
NETHERLANDS 374, 578 fol.
Conservation 214
Industrial Production 270
Military Affairs 357
Motor Vehicles 127
Space Exploration 461
NEVADA 376, 102
Newbery Medal 320, 327
NEW BRUNSWICK 376
New Caledonia 581
New Deal (U.S. econ. policy) 542
New Democratic Party (NDP) (Can.) 150, 156, 160
New England Aquarium, Boston, MA 569
NEWFOUNDLAND 377, 159
NEW HAMPSHIRE 378
Ne Win 151
NEW JERSEY 378, 314
Fingerprinting of Children 173
New Jersey (ship):
Illus. 358
New Jewel Movement (Grenada) 30, 34
NEW MEXICO 379
New Orleans, LA 315, 335
New People's Army (Philipp.) 412
Newport Jazz Festival 371
New Rockford Canal, ND 211
New South Wales, state, Austr. 122
Newspapers 429, 431
Advertising 82
Great Britain 252
New Brunswick 377
Paraguay 408
Prizes and Awards 425
Newsprint 579
NEW YORK, state 380
Cuomo, Mario 135
Drinking Age 191
Prisons 423
NEW YORK CITY 382, 180
Architecture 104
Art 113 fol.
Dance 195
Interior Design 274
Music 368, 370, 371
Photography 414
Water Tunnel 212
Illus. 67, 74, 369, 424
New York City Ballet 195, 254

New York City Marathon:
　Illus. 383
New York City Opera 370
New York Daily News 431
New York Islanders (hockey
　team) 480, 481
New York Philharmonic 370
New York University 321
NEW ZEALAND 383, 94, 578,
　579
Nicaragua 164, 166, 168, 169,
　309
　Agriculture 578
　Bulgaria 151
　Libya 322
　United Nations 533, 534
　United States 547, 548
Nickel 581
Niger 575, 581
NIGERIA 384, 87, 578, 579, 581
　Airplane Crash 80
　Chad 170
　Expulsion of Aliens 437, 452
　Literature 333
　Shagari, Alhaji Shehu 144
　United Nations 531
　Illus. 86, 88
Nigh, George 404
1984, book (Orwell) 430
Niño, El (oceanog.) 345, 346,
　402
Nissan Auto Company 128,
　308, 506
Nitrogen 581
　Ocean Organisms 351
Nitze, Paul 111
　Illus. 110
Nixon, Richard M. 542
　Presidential Library and
　　Museum 321
Njonjo, Charles 89, 300
Nkomo, Joshua 90, 566, 567
NMR: *see* Nuclear Magnetic
　Resonance
Noah, Yannick 486, 487
Nobel Prizes 425
**Nonaligned Nations Summit
　Meeting,** New Delhi, India
　119, 264, 265, 514
　Afghanistan 83
　Bangladesh 129
　Burma 151
　Cambodia 155
　Colombia 182
　Sri Lanka 490
　Yugoslavia 564
Nordic Council 198
Nordic Literary Prize 198
Norman, Jessye 368
**North Atlantic Treaty
　Organization (NATO)** 221,
　357, 547
　Greece 255
　Italy 292
　Netherlands 375
　Portugal 421
　See also Missile Deployment
　　Controversy
NORTH CAROLINA 385, 215
**North Carolina State
　University** 468 fol.
NORTH DAKOTA 386, 211
Northern Ireland 222, 250, 286
　Bridge 210
　Literature 330
　See also Great Britain
NORTHWEST TERRITORIES
　387
North Yemen: *see* Yemen,
　North
NORWAY 387, 578 fol.
　Espionage 52
　Hydroelectric Project 211
　Literature 333
NOVA SCOTIA 388, 158, 159
Novikoff, Alex 554
NOW: *see* National
　Organization for Women
Nuclear Energy 207, 315
　China 178
　Espionage 54
　India 265

New Brunswick 376
New Hampshire 378
Ontario 405
Nuclear Freeze Movement:
　see Peace Movement
**Nuclear Magnetic Resonance
　(NMR)** 342
Nuclear Weapons 356 fol., 547
Numismatics: *see* Coins and
　Coin Collecting
Nuremberg Code 69
Nut, Bernard 54
Nutrition 229
Nyerere, Julius 89, 498

O

Oakland Tribune (news.) 154
OAU: *see* Organization of
　African Unity
OBITUARIES 389
Obote, Milton 89, 524
Occupational Training 305
OCEANOGRAPHY 402, 238
　Law of the Sea Treaty 316
　Nitrogen in Ocean Organisms
　　351
　Polar Research 420
Ocean Transportation 80, 518,
　521
O'Connor, Sandra 312 fol.
Odessa, TX 188
Odinga, Oginga 300
Ohio Wesleyan University 120
Oil: *see* Petroleum
OKLAHOMA 404, 108, 211
Olajuwon, Akeem Abdul 470
Older Population:
　Alzheimer's Disease 341, 344
　Social Security 453, 454
　Women 562
Olympic Coin Act 180
Olympic Games 334
　Ueberroth, Peter V. 146
Oman 575, 569
Oncogenes (biol.) 132, 235
O'Neill, Thomas P. (Tip) 220,
　437
Onley, Toni 162
ONTARIO 405
OPEC: *see* Organization of
　Petroleum Exporting
　Countries
Opera 253, 368
Operation Eagle 458
Operation Solidarity (Can.) 150
Oral Contraceptives 340
OREGON 405
**Organization of African Unity
　(OAU)** 87, 218, 362
**Organization of American
　States (OAS)** 165, 166, 310,
　311
　Grenada, U.S. Invasion of 33
　St. Christopher and Nevis 163
**Organization of Petroleum
　Exporting Countries
　(OPEC)** 205, 208, 222, 276,
　278
　Nigeria 384
　Saudi Arabia 450
Organizations: *see* Societies
　and Organizations
Organ Transplants (surg.) 351
Orly Airport Bombing, Paris,
　Fr. 524
Orr, Robert D. 266
Ortega, Daniel 168
Ortega, Katherine Davalos:
　Illus. 562
Orthodox Eastern Churches
　441
　Yugoslavia 564
**Osborne Computer
　Corporation** 153, 185
Oscars: *see* Academy Awards
Ossining Correctional Facility,
　NY 380, 423

Osteoarthritis 343
OTTAWA, Ont., Can. 406
Oueddei, Goukouni 89, 170
　Illus. 91
Ouedraogo Jean-Baptiste 88
Owen, David 248
**Owens-Corning Fiberglas
　Energy-Conservation
　Awards** 104
Owings, Nathaniel 104
Ozal, Turgut 523

P

Pacific Ocean 402
Paddleball 489
Padilla, Hernán 432
Painting: *see* Art
PAKISTAN 407, 578, 579
　Agriculture 94
　Cyprus 194
　Espionage 49
　India 265
　Refugees 82, 437, 452
　Religion 439
**Palestine Liberation
　Organization (PLO)** 297,
　298, 548
　Lebanon 317, 319
　Libya 322
　Poland 417
　Syria 496
**Pan-African News Agency
　(PANA)** 87
Panama 166, 169, 578, 579
Pan American Games 482,
　485, 488, 553
Papandreou, Andreas 254, 255
Paper and Paper-Products 269
Papua New Guinea 575, 332,
　580
PARAGUAY 408, 578
Paraquat (herbicide) 199
Paris, Fr. 230, 231
　Art 114, 116
Paris Opera 370
Parker, Robert A. 460
Parker Brothers 82
Particle-Beam Weapons 357
Parti Nationaliste (Can.) 158
Pastora Gómez, Edén 169
Pavarotti, Luciano:
　Illus. 369
Pawley, Howard 337
Payment-in-Kind (PIK) 92, 93,
　229, 281, 298, 386
Pay Television 58, 63
　Canada 162
PC: *see* Progressive
　Conservative Party
Peace Corps 34
Peace Movement 109
　Czechoslovakia 194
　Germany, East 244
　Germany, West 241
　Great Britain 250
　Hungary 259
　Nuclear Freeze Resolution,
　　U.S. Congress 539
　Roman Catholic Bishops 444
　Illus. 243
Peace Prize, Nobel 419, 425
Peaches 458
Peacock, Andrew 123
Peat 359
Pei, I. M. 103
Pelli, Cesar 64
PEMEX (Mex. oil co.) 348
Peña, Federico 182, 220
Penguins 570
Penney, J. C., Company 223,
　445
PENNSYLVANIA 409, 271
　Philadelphia 411
**Pension Benefit Guaranty
　Corporation** 454
Pensions: *see* Retirement
　Benefits

PEOPLE Express (airline) 520,
　521
Pérez de Cuellar, Javier 83,
　531, 534
Periodontal Disease 343
Perlmutter Case 71
Peronists (Arg. pol.) 105
Perpich, Rudy 359
Pershing Missiles 109, 110,
　243, 358
　Illus. 356
Persian Gulf Oil Slick 451
Pertini, Sandro 290
PERU 409, 578, 580, 581
　Accidents and Disasters 80,
　　346
　Archaeology 101
　Drug Abuse 199
　Literature 331
Peso (Mex. currency) 278
Peso (Philipp. currency) 412
Peso (Uru. currency) 551
Peterson, Donald H. 459
Petroleum 205 fol., 268 fol., 581
　Alaska 96
　Algeria 99
　Brazil 149
　Colorado 182
　Denmark 198
　Ecuador 200
　Libya 322
　Mexico 348, 349
　Newfoundland 377
　Nigeria 87, 384
　Peru 410
　Prices 276, 277
　Profits 152
　Saskatchewan 450
　Saudi Arabia 450
　Sudan 493
　Taxation 500
　Venezuela 553
　Zaire 566
Phalangists (Leb.) 318
Phelps Dodge 107, 380
PHILADELPHIA, PA 411, 179,
　220
Philadelphia Phillies (baseball
　team) 465 fol.
Philadelphia 76ers (basketball
　team) 468, 469
PHILANTHROPY 411
Philately: *see* Stamps and
　Stamp Collecting
Philip, Prince (Gt. Brit.) 494
　Illus. 75
PHILIPPINES 412, 118, 578 fol.
　Accidents and Disasters 80
　Earthquake 238
　United States 548
　Weather 346
Phosphates 581
　Morocco 362
PHOTOGRAPHY 413
　Espionage 50
　Prizes and Awards 425
PHYSICS 415
　Prizes and Awards 425
**Physiology or Medicine, Nobel
　Prize in** 425
Pickering, Thomas R. 546
PIK: *see* Payment-in-Kind
Piltdown Fossil Hoax 100
Pine-Tar Game (baseball) 467
Pinochet Ugarte, Augusto 174
Pioneer (spacecraft) 459, 461
Pipelines:
　Algeria-Italy 99, 522
　Coal Slurry 515
　Natural Gas 205
Piquet, Nelson 464
Piracy:
　Home Video 63
　Motion Pictures 365
Pirates of Penzance, The (film)
　58, 367
　Illus. 59
Pittsburg, PA:
　Illus. 268
Plain Language Laws 187
Plankton 351
Plastics 269

Platelet-Derived Growth Factor (PDGF) 132, 235
Plays: see Theater
POLAND 416, 222, 578 fol.
  Agriculture 94
  Foreign Debt 278
  Military Affairs 357
  Motor Vehicles 127
  Religion 441
  Social Welfare 453
  Illus.: Pope John Paul II 18
POLAR RESEARCH 420
Polavchak, Walter 314
Police 315
  Los Angeles 334
  Mexico 348
  Puerto Rico 432
Polisario Front (Western Sahara) 98, 322, 362
Political Asylum 314
Political Prisoners:
  Korea, South 301
  Poland 418
  Sudan 88
  Uruguay 551
Polo 489
Population 577, 213, 228, 452
  Children 173
  See also Information Highlights section in articles on countries, provinces of Canada, and states of the U.S.
Pork 92
Portland Building, OR 103, 274
  Illus. 66
Portland Museum of Art, ME 114
PORTUGAL 420, 222, 578, 579, 581
  Art 114
  Espionage 52
  Literature 331
  Motor Vehicles 127
  Social Welfare 453
  Turkish Embassy Incident 524
POSTAL SERVICE 422, 490, 491
Post-Modernism (arch.) 67, 103
Potash 581
  New Brunswick 376
  Saskatchewan 450
Potter, Philip 443
Poultry 92, 93
Pound Sterling (Brit. currency) 246
Poverty 454
  Children 173
  Women 561
Powell, Anthony 330
Powell, Lewis F., Jr. 313, 424
Powers, Hiram 113
Pregnancy 340 fol.
Pregnancy Discrimination Act 312
Premature Birth 340
Prem Tinsulanonda 508
Presbyterian Churches 442
Presidential Medal of Freedom 427
Press, Freedom of the:
  Africa 87
  Grenada, U.S. Invasion of 33
  Uruguay 551
  Yugoslavia 564
  Zimbabwe 568
Presser, Jackie 306, 517
Price, George 165
Prices 187, 276
  Agricultural Products 92, 94
  Automobiles 127
  Books 429
  Computers 185
  Energy 205
  Fashion 223
  Food 229
  Freight Rates 516
  Health Care Costs 71, 454
  Houses 258
  Petroleum 384, 450

Postal Rates 422
  Stamps 490
  Stocks and Bonds 491
  Telephone Service 184
  Welfare Costs 453
Prime, Geoffrey A. 51
Primrose Weapons Testing Range, Can. 159
PRINCE EDWARD ISLAND 423
PRISONS 423
  Arizona 107
  California 154
  Cuban Refugees 193
  Hawaii 256
  New York 380
  Oklahoma 404
  Pact Allowing Foreign Convicts to Serve Prison Sentences at Home 125
  Sudan 88
PRIZES AND AWARDS 425
  Architecture 103, 104
  Canadian Films 161
  Dance 197
  Library Awards 320
  Literature 323, 327, 329, 330
  Motion Pictures 365
  Music 370, 371
  Nordic Literary Prize 198
  Recordings 434
  Sports: see Specific sports
  Television 503
Product Safety 187
Profits 152, 153, 540, 543
  Transportation 516
Prognoz 9 (spacecraft) 461
Program for Aid to Nutrition (PAN) 432
Progressive Conservative (PC) Party (Can.) 156, 157, 160, 433, 449
Pronin, Viktor 54
Protestantism 440, 442
  Germany, East 244
  Latin America 311
Prototype Regional Observing and Forecasting Service (PROFS) 345
Proxmire, William 120
Public Health Service, U.S. 69
Public Lands:
  Leasing of Energy Resources 207, 215
Public Service Awards 427
PUBLISHING 429, 323
PUERTO RICO 432
Pulitzer Prizes 426
Punjab, state, India 264, 439
Pym, Francis 249, 251

Q

Qaddafi, Muammer el- 170, 321, 322
Qatar 575
Quasars (astron.) 121
QUBE Cable Television System 62
  Illus. 56, 61
QUEBEC 433, 157, 158
Quinlan, Karen Ann 70

R

Racquetball 489
Radio: see Television and Radio
Radio Corporation of America (RCA) 461
Radio Shack 185
Radon Gas 342
Railroads 153, 268, 515 fol.
  Accidents 80
  Alaska Railroad 96

  Canada 156
  Guilford Transportation Company 378
  Passenger Business 521
  Wyoming 563
  Yukon 565
Rain 80, 345 fol., 402
Rajneesh, Bagwan Shree 406
Ranch, art work (Wood) 162
Rangoon, Burma 151
Rape 188
Raphael 117
Rather, Dan 503
Rawlings, Jerry 245
RCA: see Radio Corporation of America
RCMP: see Royal Canadian Mounted Police
Reader's Digest 430, 442
Reagan, Ronald 535 fol.
  Arctic 420
  Arms Control 109 fol.
  Austria 125
  Bicentennial of Air and Space Flight 35, 36
  Caribbean Basin Initiative 163
  Central America 164, 168, 310
  Chad 170
  China 177
  Crime 189
  Education 201, 202
  Energy 205, 207
  Ethnic Groups 220
  Food Programs 229
  Grain Exports to USSR 92
  Grenada 28, 30, 33, 34
  Housing 257
  India 265
  International Finance 279
  Japan 295, 296
  Jordan 297, 298
  Korea, South 301, 302
  Korean Airliner Incident 118
  Mexico 349
  Military Affairs 356 fol.
  Philippines 412
  Press, The 429
  School Desegregation 172
  Social Welfare 454
  Star Wars Speech 357
  Third World 514
  United Nations 531
  War Powers Resolution 550
  Women 561
  Zoos 569
  Illus. 17, 40, 362, 453, 539, 546
Real Interest Rates 277
Reapportionment and Redistricting 314
  Alabama 95
  Louisiana 335
  Montana 361
  New Jersey 379
  Rhode Island 447
  Wisconsin 560
Reclamation, U.S. Bureau of 210, 211
Recombinant-DNA 235
Reconnaissance Aircraft 50
RECORDINGS 434, 425
Red Brigades (It. terrorists) 291
Redistricting: see Reapportionment and Redistricting
REFUGEES AND IMMIGRATION 437, 452
  Afghan 82, 84
  Aliens Expelled from Nigeria 384
  Cambodia 155
  Central America 166
  Cuban 192, 193, 424
  Foreign Residents in Germany 242
  France 232
  Hong Kong 257
  Laos 309
  Poland 416
  Sanctuary in Churches 443

  Uganda 524
  Vietnamese Workers in Bulgaria 150
  Illus. 407
RELIGION 438
  Legislative Chaplains 374
  Philanthropy 411
Religious News Service 443
Republican Party (U.S.) 541
Republic Steel Corporation 153
Research, Ethical Issues in 69, 70
RETAILING 445, 152, 153, 543 fol.
  Automobiles 126
  Books 429
  Wine 559
Retirement Age 454
Retirement Benefits 312, 562
Return of the Jedi (film) 365, 367
Revaluation of Currencies:
  Australia 122
  Brazil 149
  Ecuador 200
  Finland 226
  France 230, 231
  Iceland 260
  Indonesia 267
  Israel 288
  Kenya 300
  Laos 309
  Philippines 412
  Portugal 421
  Sweden 493
  Tanzania 498
  Zaire 566
Rhinoceros Horn 214
RHODE ISLAND 447
Rice 94, 101, 228, 578
  Laos 309
  Taiwan 497
  Vietnam 554
Richmond, VA 556
RIDE, Sally Kristen 143, 459
  Illus. 19
Rideau Centre, Ottawa, Ont., Can. 406
Right Stuff, The (film) 363, 367
Riley, Richard W. 457
Rio de Janeiro, Braz. 452
Ríos Montt, Efraín 165, 167, 168, 311
Ripken, Cal, Jr. 466
  Illus. 465
Rizzo, Frank L. 411
Roads: see Highways
Robb, Charles S. 556
Robberies 186, 190
Robbins, Jerome 195, 196
Robots 308
  Illus. 273
Rockefeller, John D., IV 559
Rock Island Railroad 516
Rodeo 489
Roman Catholic Church: see Catholicism
Rome, It. 117
Romero Barceló, Carlos 432
Ronstadt, Linda 373
Rooney, Andy 429, 430
Roosevelt, Franklin D. 542
Ross, Diana 372
Rostow, Eugene V. 111, 535, 546
Rowe, Gary Thomas 315
Rowing 489
Roy, Gabrielle 329
Royal Canadian Mounted Police (RCMP) 156
Royal Commission on the Economic Union and Development Prospects for Canada 158
Royal Shakespeare Company (Gt. Brit.) 253
Rubber 152, 269
Rubber, Synthetic 579
Ruckelshaus, William D. 216, 536
  Illus. 14

Rugby 489
RUMANIA 447, 119, 578 fol.
  Agriculture 94
  Military Affairs 357
  Motor Vehicles 127
Rumasa (Sp. conglomerate) 462
Rumsfeld, Donald 546, 547
  Illus. 548
Rupiah (Indon. currency) 267
Rwanda 575

S

Sadat, Esmat 203
Saharan Arab Democratic Republic (SADR) 87, 362, 384
SAINT CHRISTOPHER AND NEVIS 448, 163
Saint John, N.B., Can 377
Saint Louis, MO 360
Saint Lucia 575
Saint Vincent and the Grenadines 575
Salaries: *see* Wages and Salaries
Sales:
  Houses 258
  See also Retailing
SALT: *see* Strategic Arms Limitation Talks
Salt (min.) 380, 581
Salt Lake City, UT 346, 551
  Illus. 552
Salyut Space Station 459, 460
Sampson, Ralph 469
Sanders, Bernard 554
San Diego, CA 346
Sandinistas (Nicar.) 169
SAN FRANCISCO, CA 449, 180
San Francisco Ballet:
  Illus. 196
San Francisco Opera 368
San Francisco Symphony 370
Sankara, Thomas 88
San Marino 575
Santa Fe Industries 153
San Yu 151
São Paulo, Braz. 452
São Tome and Principe 575
Sarraute, Nathalie 333
Sartre, Jean-Paul 333
SASKATCHEWAN 449
Satellites, Artificial 50, 57, 59, 183, 345, 459, 561
Saud, Prince (Saudi Ar.) 451
SAUDI ARABIA 450, 279, 578 fol.
  West Bank Negotiations 297
Savimbi, Jonas 90
Schaefer, William Donald 179, 338
Schaufelberger, Albert A. 166
Schizophrenia 344
School Desegregation:
  Chicago 172, 202
  St. Louis 360
School Enrollment 202
School Prayer 201, 314, 379
School Violence:
  Japan 294
Schlüter, Poul 198
Schuller, Robert 443
Scotland: *see* Great Britain
Schwinden, Ted 361
Scoon, Sir Paul 30, 533
Scott, Ted:
  Illus. 443
Sculpture: *see* Art
Schweiker, Richard S.:
  Illus. 11
Science Prizes and Awards 425, 427
Seabrook Nuclear Reactor, NH 378
Seals (zool.) 387, 420
Sears Roebuck & Co. 446

Seattle, WA 210, 558
Sea World, San Diego, CA 570
Securities: *see* Stocks and Bonds
Security Council (UN) 532, 534
Seeberg, Peter 198
Semiconductor Research Corporation (SRC) 273
Semper Enterprises Inc. 153
Senate, U.S. 535 fol.
  Abortions 562
  Arms Control 109
  Jackson, Henry M. 392
  Membership 584
Senegal 575, 87, 214
Serebrov, Aleksandr 460
Severance Tax 500
Sex Discrimination 561, 562
  Court Rulings 312, 315
  Libraries 320, 321
  Washington Wage Discrimination Case 558
Seychelles 575
SHAGARI, Alhaji Shehu 144, 87, 384
  Illus. 86
Shale Oil 182
SHAMIR, Yitzhak 144, 288, 289
Shanker, Albert 45, 202
Sharia: *see* Islamic Law
Sharon, Ariel 287
Shaw, Brewster H. 460
Shaw Festival, Ont., Can. 162
Sheehan, Patty 478
Sheeler, Charles 112
Sheffield, William 96
Shekel (Isr. currency) 288
Shenouda III 204
Shergar (horse) 286
Shiite Muslims 84, 318, 319, 439
Shilling (Kenyan currency) 300
Shilling (Tanz. currency) 498
Shining Path Movement (Peru) 409, 410
Ships 80, 268, 518, 521
Shona (people) 566, 567
Shooting (sport) 489
Showtime (cable TV) 504
Shroud of Turin 291
Shultz, George 119, 546
  Afghanistan 83
  China 177
  India 265
  Japan 295
  Lebanon 317
  New Zealand 383
  Pakistan 408
  Syria 495
Sickle-Cell Anemia 132
Sierra Leone 575
Sigel, Jay 478
Sikhs 264, 439
Siles Suazo, Hernan 147
Silkwood (film) 365
Sillitoe, Alan 330
Silver 581
Simmonds, Kennedy 448
Simpson-Mazzoli Bill 437
SINGAPORE 451, 52
Singer, Isaac Bashevis 332
Single-Parent Families 173
Sinhalese (people) 490
Sinowatz, Fred 125
Sioux Indians 458
60 Minutes (TV program) 442, 503
Sizer, Theodore R. 46
Skidmore Owings & Merrill 104
Skiing 483
SKYSCRAPERS 64
Smith, Bill 481
  Illus. 480
Smith, Lemuel 380
Smith, William French 188
Smithsonian Institution, Washington, D.C. 36
  Illus. 35
Smoking 342 fol., 449
Snelling, Richard 554
Sneva, Tom 464
Snowcroft, Brent 356, 546, 547

Snowcroft Commission 356, 357, 539, 546
Snowstorms 346, 347, 402
Soares, Mario 222, 420, 421
Soccer 483
Social Credit Party (Can.) 150, 158
Social Democratic Party (Fin. pol.) 226
Social Democratic Party (SPD) (Ger. pol.) 240, 241, 243, 245
Social Democratic Party (Gt. Brit.) 246 fol.
Socialist Parties 222
  France 230, 233
  Greece 254
  Italy 290, 291
  Japan 293, 294
  Portugal 420
  Spain 462
Social Security 453, 537, 538
  Taxation of Benefits 499
SOCIAL WELFARE 452
  Children 173
  New Deal 542
  Nutrition Aid, Puerto Rico 432
  Pennsylvania 409
SOCIETIES AND ORGANIZATIONS 586
Softball 489
Soft Drinks 229
  Illus. 269
Solar Eclipse:
  Illus. 120
Solidarity (Pol. union) 416 fol.
Solidarity Day (U.S. labor) 307
Sollers, Philippe 333
Solomon Islands 575
Solzhenitsyn, Aleksandr 438
  Illus. 427
Somalia 575, 89, 218
Sony Betamax Videocassette Recorder 60, 63, 435
Sorsa, Kalevi 226
Sotheby Parke Bernet 112, 113
SOUTH AFRICA 455, 87, 90, 578 fol.
  Bridges 210
  Mine Explosion 80
  Nuclear Technology 54
  United Nations 534
  Zimbabwe 567
SOUTH CAROLINA 457
SOUTH DAKOTA 458
Southern Pacific Company 153
South Korea: *see* Korea, Republic of
South Street Seaport, New York, NY:
  Illus. 382
South West Africa People's Organization (SWAPO) 90
South Yemen: *see* Yemen, South
Soviet Union: *see* Union of Soviet Socialist Republics
Soyaven (infant formula) 229
Soybeans 92, 228, 229, 578
  Iowa 281
  Nebraska 374
  Tennessee 506
Soyuz Spacecraft 460
Space-Based Defense System 357, 358
SPACE EXPLORATION 459, 121
  Bluford, Guion S. 134
  History of 38
  Meteorology 345
  Nuclear-Powered Spacecraft 316
  Ride, Sally 143
Spacelab 459, 460
Space Operations Center, CO 182
SPAIN 462, 222, 578 fol.
  Accidents and Disasters 80
  Art 116
  Chile 174
  Espionage 53

Literature 331
Motor Vehicles 127
Social Welfare 453
Uruguay 551
Spellman, John 557
Špiljak, Mika 563
  Illus. 564
Spoleto Festival U.S.A., Charleston, SC 458
  Illus. 457
Sponge, Contraceptive 340
SPORTS 463
  Television 503
Spratly Islands, South China Sea 337
Spying: *see* Espionage
Squash (sport) 489
SRC: *see* Semiconductor Research Corporation
SRI LANKA 490, 119, 578, 579
SS-20 Missiles 110, 358, 529, 547
STAMPS AND STAMP COLLECTING 490
Star 80 (film) 363, 364, 367
Stars 121, 461
START: *see* Strategic Arms Reduction Talks
State Government:
  Consumer Affairs 187
  Highways 519
  Taxation 501
STATISTICAL AND TABULAR DATA 571
Steel, David 248
Steel 152, 153, 268, 271, 380, 462, 579, 580
Steelworkers Union 306
Steig, William 327
Stern, Robert 274
Stevens, John Paul 313
Stevens, J. P., and Company 306
Stieglitz, Alfred 414
Stockman, David 93, 537
STOCKS AND BONDS 491, 545
  Municipal Bonds 179
  Prices 276
STONE, Richard B. 144, 164
Storms 80, 236, 345 fol., 402
  California 154
  Japan 295
Strategic Arms Limitation Talks (SALT) 111, 547
Strategic Arms Reduction Talks (START) 110, 111, 221
Stratford Festival, Can. 162
Strauss, Franz Josef 240
Strawberry, Daryl 466
Strekalov, Gennady 460
Strikes 306
  Argentina 106
  Belgium 131
  Brazil 149
  Central America 165
  Chicago Teachers 172
  Commuter Railroads 518
  Copper Workers 107
  Ecuador 200
  Great Britain 308
  Guyana 255
  Israeli Doctors 288
  New York City Opera 370
  Portugal 421
  Quebec 433
  Teachers 202
  Illus. 26, 41
Stroessner, Alfredo 408
Studds, Gerry E. 540
  Illus. 339
Student Loans 202, 314
STV: *see* Subscription Television
Suazo Córdova, Roberto 168
Submarine Sightings:
  Swedish Waters 494
Subscription Television (STV) 58
Subtropical Atlantic Climate Studies (STACS) 402
Subways 382, 558

Sucre (Ecua. currency) 200
SUDAN 493, 88
  Agriculture 578
  Egypt 204
  Libya 321
  United States 547
Sugar 192, 578
Sugar Substitutes 229, 344
Suharto 266, 267
Sulfur 581
Sumners, Rosalynn 481, 482
Sunar Showroom, New York
  City 274
  Illus. 275
Sunni Muslims 318, 319, 439
Sununu, John 378
Supreme Court, U.S. 313, 312,
  315, 583
  Abortions 562
  Automobile Safety 187
  Civil Rights 220
  Legislative Chaplains 374
  Legislative Veto 187
  Religion, Rulings on 443
  Sex Discrimination 562
  Student Loans 202
  Taxation Cases 202, 499
**Surface Transportation
  Assistance Act** 519
Surinam 576, 375, 580
Surrounded Islands, art
  (Christo):
  Illus. 74
Suslov, Ilya 331
Sutton, Hal 478
SWAPO: *see* South West Africa
  People's Organization
Swaziland 576
SWEDEN 493, 578 fol.
  Chile 174
  Denmark 198
  Espionage 53
  Labor 308
  Literature 333
  Motor Vehicles 127
Swimming 485, 482
SWITZERLAND 495
  Agriculture 578
  Art 114
  Bridge 210
  Espionage 53
  Motor Vehicles 127
  Stocks and Bonds 492
SYRIA 495, 352, 548, 578, 579
  Lebanon 317 fol.
  West Bank Negotiations 297

T

Table Tennis 489
TAIWAN (Republic of China)
  497, 578
Tamils (people) 490
Tampa, Fl:
  Illus. 227
Tanaka, Kakuei 293
Tandy, Jessica 145
  Illus. 428
TANZANIA 498, 80, 89, 578
Tasmania, state, Austr. 122
Taubman, Alfred 112
TAXATION 499, 538
  Gasoline 519
  Racially Discriminatory
    Schools 202, 220, 312, 443
  Sex Discrimination Case 562
  Social Security 454
  Supreme Court Rulings 312
  Trucking Industry 517
  Tuition Tax-Credit 202
Taylor, Jay Randolph:
  Illus. 442
Taylor, Paul 195, 197
Teachers 40 fol.
  Merit Pay 201, 227
  Number of 202
  Quebec Strike 433
  Strikes 172, 200, 202; *Illus.* 41

Team America (soccer) 484
Teamsters Union 306, 517
Teeth: *see* Dentistry
**Telecommunication
  Equipment** 183
Telephones 183, 184
Telescopes 120
TELEVISION AND RADIO 502,
  269
  Advertising 82
  Canada 162
  Godfrey, Arthur 391
  Great Britain 254
  Home Video 55
  Music 373
  New Brunswick 377
  Prizes and Awards 425, 427,
    428
  Sex Discrimination Case 315
Templeton Foundation Prize
  438
TENNESSEE 506, 102, 315, 500
Tennis 485
  Hu Na 177
Territorial Waters 316
  Submarine Sightings,
    Sweden 494
Terrorism: *see* Guerrilla and
  Terrorist Activities
TEXAS 507, 347, 424, 500
Texas A&M University 238
Texas Instruments 153
Textile Industry 152, 269
  Chinese Exports 177
Thagard, Norman E. 459
THAILAND 508, 578 fol.
  Vietnam 555
Tharp, Twyla 196
Thatcher, Margaret 221, 222,
  246 fol., 286
  Falkland Islands 251
  Grenada, U.S. Invasion of 33
  London 334
  Illus. 18
THEATER 509
  Canada 162
  Great Britain 253
  Prizes and Awards 428
  Tandy, Jessica 145
  Williams, Tenessee 390
  Illus.: China 77
Thefts 190
  Irish Horse 286
Thériault, Yves 329
Thermonuclear Fusion 415
THIRD WORLD 514, 276 fol.
Thomas, John Charles 556
Thompson, James R. 261
Thorn Birds, The (TV program)
  503, 505
  Illus. 502
Thornburgh, Dick 409
Thornton, William E. 386, 459
Thoroddsen, Gunnar 260
Tico, Hurricane 347
Tidal Power:
  Nova Scotia 388
Tikhonov, Nikolai A. 255, 565
Timber: *see* Lumber
Times Beach, MO 216, 361
Timor, prov., Indon. 267
Tin 581
Tin Oo 151
Titanium 581
Titov, Vladimir 460
Tobacco 269, 299, 458, 568
Togo 576, 88, 581
Tokamak (phys.) 415
Tomasson, Helgi 196
Tonga 576
Tony Awards 428
Tornadoes 80, 345, 347
Tourism: *see* Travel
Tower, John 507
Toxic-Shock Syndrome 351
Toxic Wastes 216
  Kansas 298
  Minnesota 359
  Missouri 361
  New Jersey 378
  New Mexico 380
  Illus. 213, 379

Track and Field 487, 482
Trade: *see* International Trade
  and Finance
Trains: *see* Railroads
TRANSPORTATION 515, 268
  Cities 180
  Deregulation 545
**Transportation, U.S.
  Department of** 516
  Dole, Elizabeth 137
Trans World Airlines (TWA)
  153
TRAVEL 520
  Air 517
  Florida 227
  Hawaii 256
  Maine 336
  Puerto Rico 432
  Virgin Islands 557
Treen, David C. 335
Trevor, William 330
Trinidad and Tobago 576
Tripoli, Leb. 319
Trucking Industry 515 fol.
Trucks 126, 268
  Weight Limits 108
Trudeau, Pierre Elliott 156,
  159, 160, 163
Truly, Richard H. 459
Trump Tower, New York, NY:
  Illus. 67
Trusteeship Council (UN) 532
Tsongas, Paul 43
Tuition Tax-Credit 201, 202,
  500
Tulsa Roughnecks (soccer
  team) 484
Tune, Tommy:
  Illus. 428
Tungsten 581
TUNISIA 522, 578, 579, 581
  Algeria 98
Tunnels 212
TURKEY 522, 578 fol.
  Accidents and Disasters 80
  Cyprus 193, 194
  Greece 255
  Literature 332
  United Nations 531
**Turkish Republic of Northern
  Cyprus** 194
Tuvalu 576
TV Guide 430
TWA: *see* Trans World Airlines
Twentieth Century Fund 40, 45
Two Women, painting (de
  Kooning) 112
  Illus. 113
**Typewriter Registration
  Decree** (Rum.) 448
Typhoons 80, 295, 347
Tyre, Leb. 319

U

UAW: *see* United Auto Workers
UEBERROTH, Peter V. 146
UGANDA 524, 89
Ulusu, Bülent 522, 523
Umberto II, King (It.) 291
UNCTAD: *see* United Nations
  Conference on Trade and
  Development
Unemployment: *see* Labor
UNESCO: *see* United Nations
  Educational, Scientific and
  Cultural Organization
**Uniform Definition of Death
  Act** 70
Union of Concerned Scientists
  111
**UNION OF SOVIET SOCIALIST
  REPUBLICS (USSR)** 525,
  221
  Accidents and Disasters 80
  Afghanistan 82 fol., 119
  Agriculture 93, 578
  Archaeology 100

  Arms Control 110, 111
  Cambodia 155
  Canada 160
  Capital Punishment 189
  China 119, 178
  Cuba 192
  Egypt 204
  Espionage 47 fol.
  Finland 226
  Fishing Zones 316
  France 233
  Germany, East 244, 245
  Germany, West 243
  Grain Imports 92, 94, 228
  Greece 255
  Grenada 33, 34
  Hungary 259
  Industrial Production 270,
    579
  Israel 289
  Italy 292
  Japan 296
  Korean Airliner Incident 118,
    316
  Laos 309
  Libya 321
  Literature 331
  Military Affairs 356 fol.
  Minerals 580, 581
  Motor Vehicles 127
  Religion 441
  Rumania 448
  Saudi Arabia 451
  Social Welfare 453
  Space Exploration 459 fol.
  Sweden 493
  Switzerland 495
  Third World 514
  United Nations 531, 533, 534
  United States 547
  Uranium-Powered Satellite
    316
  Vietnam 554, 555
  Yugoslavia 565
Union Pacific Railroad 516
Unions, Labor: *see* Labor
United American Bank 506
United Arab Emirates 576, 581
United Auto Workers (UAW)
  134, 306
**United Kingdom of Great
  Britain and Northern
  Ireland:** *see* Great Britain
UNITED NATIONS 531
  Afghanistan 83
  Cambodia 155
  Cyprus 193, 194
  Falkland Islands 107
  Grenada, U.S. Invasion of 33
  Stamps 491
  United States 548
**United Nations Conference on
  Trade and Development
  (UNCTAD)** 265, 280, 518,
  564
**United Nations Educational,
  Scientific, and Cultural
  Organization (UNESCO)**
  213, 534
**United Nations Environment
  Programme** 213
**United Nations High
  Commissioner for
  Refugees** 437
UNITED STATES 535
  Afghanistan 83
  Algeria 99
  Austria 125
  Brazil 149
  Canada 159, 160
  Caribbean 163
  Central America 164 fol.
  Chad 89, 170
  China 119, 177, 358
  Colombia 181
  Cuba 192
  Cyprus 194
  Egypt 203, 204
  Ethiopia 218
  Europe 221
  France 233
  Germany, West 243

UNITED STATES (con't.)
Government 583
Great Britain 249, 250
Greece 254, 255
Grenada 28 fol.
Guyana 255
India 265
Israel 289
Italy 292
Japan 293, 295
Jordan 297, 298
Laos 309
Latin America 309 fol.
Lebanon 318, 319
Libya 321
Mexico 349
Morocco 362
Philippines 412
Poland 419
Rumania 448
Saudi Arabia 451
Spain 462
Sudan 88, 493
Switzerland 495
Syria 496
Taiwan 497, 498
Tanzania 498
Thailand 508
Third World 514
USSR 92, 94, 228, 529
United Nations 531, 533, 534
Uruguay 551
Yugoslavia 565
Zimbabwe 568
United States Military Academy, NY:
Illus.: Jewish Chapel 440
United States Steel Corporation 153, 563
Universal Fellowship of Metropolitan Community Churches 443
Unser, Al, Sr. 464
Upper Volta 576, 88, 322
Uranium Oxide 581
Urban Affairs: *see* Cities and Urban Affairs
Urban Transit 180, 518
Urea Formaldehyde Insulation 187
URUGUAY 551, 578, 579
USDA: *see* Agriculture, U.S. Department of
USSR: *see* Union of Soviet Socialist Republics
UTAH 551, 80, 236
Utilities 268, 345

V

Vancouver Art Gallery, B.C., Can. 162
Van Der Zee, James 414
Vanuatu 576
Variety Stores 152
Vatican Art Show 113
Illus. 115
Vatican City 576
Sweden 494
Veal 229
Venera (spacecraft) 461
VENEZUELA 552, 578 fol.
Dam 211
Guyana 255
Venturi, Robert 274
VERMONT 554
Vesuvius, Mount, volc., It. 101
Victoria Hall, Cobourg, Ont., Can. 162
Video Games 492
Video Recording Equipment 56, 59 fol., 365, 435
Videotext 62

Vienna, Aus. 125
VIETNAM 554, 119
Agriculture 578
Cambodia 155
China 178
Indentured Workers in Bulgaria 150
Laos 309
Refugees 257
Spratly Islands 337
Thailand 508
Typhoons 80
United Nations 533
Vilas, Guillermo 486, 487
Violence: *see* Crime; Guerrilla and Terrorist Activities; School Violence
Viral Diseases 351
VIRGIN ISLANDS 557
VIRGINIA 556, 102
Voigt, Cynthia 327
Volcanoes 80, 238, 345, 420
Illus.: Hawaii 256
Volcker, Paul 492, 540, 541
Illus. 130
Volleyball 489
Volpe, John 191
von Damm, Helene 125
Vorster, John 456
Voyager (spacecraft) 459, 461
Vrdolyak, Edward R. 172

W

Waart, Edo de 370
Wage-Earner Funds (Swed.) 308, 493, 494
Wages and Salaries 276, 306, 543
Canada 158
Teachers 40, 44, 45
Washington Sex Discrimination Case 558
See also Information Highlights section in articles on provinces of Canada and states of the U.S.
Wagner, Richard 434
Illus. 435
Waiting, pastel (Degas) 112
Walesa, Lech 79, 151, 416 fol.
Illus. 78
Walker, Herschel 473
Wallace, George C. 95
Wall Street Journal 33
WarGames (film) 363 fol., 367
War Powers Resolution (U.S.) 358
Warsaw Ghetto Uprising (Pol. 1943) 417, 441
Illus. 418
Warsaw Pact Countries 357
Summit Meeting, Prague 151, 259, 448
WASHINGTON, Harold 146, 172, 179, 219, 315
Illus. 15
WASHINGTON, state 557, 210
WASHINGTON, D.C. 558
Art 117
Music 370
Photography 414
Illus. 22
Washington Convention Center, D.C. 558
Washington Park Zoo, Portland, OR 569
Washington Post 33
Washington Public Power Supply System (WPPSS) 207, 315, 557
Illus. 206

Washington Redskins (football team) 472, 474
Wastes, Toxic: *see* Toxic Wastes
Watch Industry 495
Water Pollution:
Chesapeake Bay 338
Hawaii 256
Persian Gulf Oil Slick 451
Water Polo 489
Watkins, Carleton E. 414
Watson, Tom 478
Watt, James 207, 213 fol., 458, 536
Weather: *see* Meteorology
Weather Satellites 345, 459, 461
Webb, Pauline:
Illus. 443
Weight, Body 343
Weightlifting 489
Weinberger, Caspar 119, 358
China 177, 178
Japan 295, 296
Pakistan 408
Weitz, Paul J. 459
Weizsäcker, Richard von 245
Welfare: *see* Social Welfare
Wells Fargo Armored Services Corporation 186, 190
West Bank, area, Middle East 297, 548
West Berlin, Ger. 245
Western Electric Company 184
Western Pacific Railroad 516
Western Sahara 87, 98, 322, 362
See also Saharan Arab Democratic Republic
Western Samoa 576
Western Union 184
Westmoreland, William C. 503
WEST VIRGINIA 559
West Germany: *see* Germany, Federal Republic of
Whales 213, 316, 569, 570
Wheat 92 fol., 228, 229, 578
Kansas 298
Manitoba 338
Nebraska 374
North Dakota 386
White, Byron 189
White, Mark 507
Whitmire, Kathy 562
Wiesel, Elie 332
Wildlife Conservation 215, 569
Will, George 431
Williams, Robert Wayne 335
WILLIAMS, Tennessee 390
Williams, Vanessa 75
Williamsburg Summit Meeting: *see* Economic Summit Meeting
Willoch, Kåre 387
Wilmington, DE 197
Wilson, Angus 330
Windfall-Profits Tax 500
Winds of War, The (TV program) 503, 505
Illus. 502
WINE 559
Winter, William 359
Wirahadikusumah, Umar 266
WISCONSIN 560
WOMEN 561
Court Rulings 312, 315
Dole, Elizabeth 137
Elections 299, 541
Heckler, Margaret 138
Ride, Sally K. 143
Social Welfare 454
Washington Wage Discrimination Case 558
Wood, Allan 162
Wood Products 268, 270, 406
Woolworth, F.W., Company 445

World Assembly for Peace and Life and Against Nuclear War, Prague, Czech. 194
World Bank (International Bank for Reconstruction and Development) 276, 279, 280
Brazil 149
India 264
Lebanon 319
Yugoslavia 564
World Congress of the International Confederation of Free Trade Unions (ICFTU), Oslo, Nor. 307
World Council of Churches (WCC) 441, 442
World Food Day 452
World Series (baseball) 465, 467
World Track and Field Championships, Helsinki, Finland 226, 487
World University Games, Edmonton, Alta., Can. 98
World Wildlife Fund 213
WPPSS: *see* Washington Public Power Supply System
Wrestling 489
Wright, Frank Lloyd 114
WYOMING 563, 346

X

Xylitol (sugar substitute) 344

Y

Yachting 488
Yarborough, Cale 464
Yastrzemski, Carl 339, 467
Yemen, North 576, 214
Yemen, South 576
Yevtushenko, Yevgeny 331
Young, John W. 460
Youth Corps (MI) 350
YUGOSLAVIA 563, 578 fol.
Albania 97
Mine Explosion 80
Motor Vehicles 127
YUKON 565
Yukon Delta National Wildlife Refuge, AK 216

Z

Zahir Shah, Mohammed 83
ZAIRE 566, 85, 578, 580
Chad 170
China 178
Zaire (Zairian currency) 566
Zambia 576, 578, 580
Zhao Ziyang 175, 178
Zhivkov, Todor 150, 151
Zia ul-Haq, Mohammed 83, 407, 408
ZIMBABWE 566, 87, 90, 578 fol.
Zinc 581
Zircon 238
Zoeller, Fuzzy 478
ZOOS AND ZOOLOGY 569
Polar Research 420